图书馆学家文库
Library of Library Scientists

李华伟文集
Collected Works of Hwa-Wei Lee

李华伟 著

中山大学出版社
·广州·
Sun Yat-Sen University Press
·Guangzhou·

版权所有　翻印必究

图书在版编目（CIP）数据

李华伟文集：全2册/李华伟著．广州：中山大学出版社，2011.10
（图书馆学家文库/谭祥金主编）

ISBN 978-7-306-04052-7

Ⅰ.李… Ⅱ.李… Ⅲ.图书馆学—文集 Ⅳ.G250-53

中国版本图书馆CIP数据核字（2011）第208566号

出 版 人：祁　军
责任编辑：王俊辉
封面设计：林绵华
责任校对：程　杰
责任技编：黄少伟
出版发行：中山大学出版社
电　　话：编辑部（020）84111996，84113349
　　　　　发行部（020）84111998，84111981，84111160
地　　址：广州市新港西路135号
邮　　编：510275　传　真：（020）84036565
网　　址：http://www.zsup.com.cn　E-mail：zdcbs@mail.sysu.edu.cn
印　刷　者：惠州市海天印刷有限公司
电　　话：（020）37217189，37217733
规　　格：787mm×1092mm　1/16　103.5印张　2600千字
版次印次：2011年10月第1版　2011年10月第1次印刷
定　　价：460.00元（上、下卷）

如发现本书因印装质量影响阅读，请与出版社发行部联系调换

《图书馆学家文库》
Library of Library Scientists

顾　问：周和平（中国图书馆学会名誉理事长，国家图书馆馆长）
主　编：谭祥金
副主编：程焕文　吴　晞（常务）
编辑委员会委员：（按姓氏拼音顺序排列）
　　　　　　　程焕文　杜秦生　李国新　刘洪辉　倪晓建　邱冠华
　　　　　　　谭祥金　吴建中　吴　晞　谢灼华　赵燕群
编辑部
主　任：杜秦生
副主任：赵燕群（常务）　肖容梅

李华伟博士肖像
A Portrait of Dr. Hwa-Wei Lee

总 目
Contents

《图书馆学家文序》总序 ·· 周和平（Ⅰ）
Preface by Zhou Heping

自序 ·· 李华伟（Ⅱ）
Preface by Hwa-Wei Lee

图说李华伟博士 ·· （1）
Selected Photographs of Dr. Hwa-Wei Lee

上卷 学术著作
Volume I Works

1. 图书馆学的世界观 ··· （1）
   Librarianship in World Perspective

2. 现代化图书馆管理 ··· （193）
   On Modern Library Management

3. 20 世纪 90 年代图书馆募款所面对的挑战 实用指南：从新手到专家 ············· （326）
   Fundraising for the 1990s: The Challenge Ahead A practical Guide for Library Fundraising: From Novice to Expert

4. 巴布亚新几内亚高等院校间的图书馆发展、资源共享和联网 ························· （446）
   Library Development, Resource Sharing, and Networking among Higher Education Institutions in Papua New Guinea

5. OCLC 联机与光盘编目概论（节选） ··· （477）
   OCLC Compact Disk and Online Cataloging (extract)

6. 知识管理的理论与实践（节选） ·· （486）
   The Theory and Practice of Knowledge Management (extract)

7. 亚太地区图书馆发展的合作领域（节选） ··· （501）
   Areas of Cooperation in Library Development in Asia and Pacific Regions (extract)

8. 台湾的教育发展（1945—1962） ··· （507）
   Educational Development in Taiwan, China (1945 – 1962)

下卷 学术论文
Volume II Articles

1. 图书馆建设与管理 ······(647)
   Library Development and Management

2. 图书馆交流与合作 ······(848)
   Library Exchange and Cooperation

3. 图书馆数字化与网络化 ······(952)
   Library Digitization and Networking

4. 亚洲研究与区域研究资源 ······(1156)
   Resources for Asian Study and Area Study

5. 序言与书评 ······(1317)
   Preface and Review

附录1 李华伟著述系年 ······(1336)
Appendix I: A Chronicle of Hwa-Wei Lee's Writing

附录2 李华伟研究资料 ······(1351)
Appendix II: Research Materials about Hwa-Wei Lee

后记 ······ 程焕文(1561)
Epilogue by Cheng Huanwen

《图书馆学家文库》总序

图书馆是社会文明进步的标志，为传承历史、延续文明、开拓未来提供着信息与知识保障；是建设学习型社会的重要阵地，承担着提高公民学习能力与创新能力，滋养公民文明素质的重要责任；是通向知识之门，为构建国家知识创新体系提供着知识与智力支撑；是公共文化服务体系的重要组成部分，对于弥合数字鸿沟、保障人民群众的基本文化权益发挥着重要作用。

新中国成立以来，尤其是改革开放以来，在党和政府的高度重视下，在广大图书馆理论与实践者的共同努力下，我国图书馆事业得到了长足的发展。在这个发展历程中，一代又一代图书馆学家做出了卓越贡献。

图书馆学，图书馆工作，是学术性和实践性都很突出的一个领域。何为图书馆学家？我以为，既要有深厚的专业学术造诣，还要有勇于实践、善于探索的精神。对于图书馆的学科发展和事业发展，更要有理论和实践的双重推动，两者犹如双翼：理论研究要总结实际工作、带动实际工作；实际工作要注重正确理论的指引，还要不断给学术研究带来新的活力和突破。

由深圳公共图书馆研究院编撰、中山大学出版社出版的《图书馆学家文库》（以下简称《文库》），旨在荟萃一批优秀图书馆专业工作者在长期的图书馆学理论研究与工作实践中积累的成果，将为我们展现出一幅图书馆学研究和图书馆事业发展的绚丽画卷，这些成果对于当今图书馆事业发展仍然具有指导和借鉴意义。

《文库》首批结集出版的是业界老一辈学人的成果。他们或身居学术研究前沿，或奋斗于事业发展一线，或身居海外关注中国图书馆事业，他们当中的很多人都是在极其艰苦的条件下，孜孜以求，不懈努力，取得了丰硕的成果，为图书馆学和图书馆事业做出了不可磨灭的贡献，他们对事业的热爱在中国图书馆事业发展史上留下了令人感动的篇章。

公共图书馆研究院是 2009 年在深圳成立，是国内第一家以公共图书馆为研究对象的专业研究团体。公共图书馆研究院是一家非政府机构，由文化部社会文化司、中国图书馆学会和深圳市文体旅游局出任指导单位，深圳图书馆、深圳图书情报学会主办，汇聚了中国大陆、台港澳及海外众多的专业学者和图书馆管理者，为公共图书馆事业发展提供了一个新的学术研究和交流平台。研究院自成立以来，取得了多项有影响的成果，这次编撰《文库》又展现了其眼光和实力，值得赞许。

最后，还要感谢中山大学出版社。正是他们的远见卓识和鼎力支持，才使《文库》得以面世。

周和平

中国国家图书馆馆长
中国图书馆学会名誉理事长
2011 年春于北京

自　序

　　能够将我近五十年来的拙作汇集成册，由中山大学出版社出版，作为《图书馆学家文库》的一集，至感荣幸。我的这些作品涵盖面虽然广，品质也参差不齐，但也真实地反映了近半世纪来我在学习及工作中的心得和体验。希望能借此机会向读者们请教，并起到抛砖引玉的作用。

　　我的祖籍是福建省福州市，1931年1月25日生于广州，当时父亲李干军是广东省四会县的县长。两年后，因为父亲工作的调动，全家迁往南京。抗日战争前半段在广西桂林度过，这期间还随母亲去越南住了一年，等到小妹出生以后再迁回桂林。抗日战争后期在重庆度过。当时我以流亡学生身份进入国立第二华侨中学，读初一和初二。胜利后，父亲因为是李宗仁将军的参军，全家迁往北京住进中南海。我则由政府分发到南京市立一中读初三。1947年，因内战关系，全家又迁到桂林，我则进入国立汉民中学，读高一和高二。1949年，国民党迁台，全家迁往台湾台中，父亲应聘任教于当时的省立台中农学院，我则进入省立台中一中，读高三。毕业后，考进当时的省立台湾师范学院教育系，1954年毕业。受完一年预备军官训练之后，分配到台北师专附小担任训导主任。一年后由已升格的省立台湾师范大学聘为助教，派到训导处课外活动组，指导学生社团活动。我之所以能得到这份工作，一方面是得到我的恩师——师院刘真院长的提拔，另一方面是因为我做学生时，喜欢参与课外活动，学习到很多做人处事的道理，被认为是学生领袖之一。

　　1957年，我获得匹兹堡大学免学费奖学金，赴美留学，进入该校教育研究所就读，因为生活上的需要，在1958年有幸能在匹兹堡大学图书馆以学生助理的身份，半工全读，开始了我的图书馆生涯。从基层工作做起，一直做到馆长，一晃就是半个多世纪。亲身经历了图书馆的巨大变革和发展，体会甚深。在20世纪50年代以前，图书馆的发展是比较平稳，缺少大波大浪。但是到了60年代，几乎每5年一小变，每10年一大变；从"纸张"图书馆，到"自动化"图书馆，到"网络化"图书馆，到"数字化"图书馆，到"虚拟"图书馆……可以说是变化无穷。我能身临其境，随波起伏，增加见识，同时也参与兴风作浪，颇感荣幸及机会难得。

　　就在这个年代，中国经历了巨大的政治动乱，图书馆的发展可以说是完全停顿，百废待举。从20世纪80年代开始，我有幸能经常回国讲学，认识了一批老一辈的图书馆员，看到他们奋斗、敬业、苦干，看到他们重整图书馆的精神和决心，令我十分感动。当时我认为培训新一代的图书馆员十分重要。因此除了在中国各地讲学之外，也在我当时工作的俄亥俄大学建立了一个国际图书馆员培训项目，从1983年开始，每年培训了大约四五位中国选派来的图书馆员，其中有来自国家图书馆、北京大学、清华大学、北京师范大学、北京邮电大学、武汉大学、浙江大学、南开大学、中山大学、中国科学院、中国科技情报所、深圳图书馆等。为了要加强中美两国图书馆界的合作，加快中国图书馆的发展，我曾经与中国图书馆界的朋友们合作，先后举办了五届中美图书馆合作会议，影响深远。身为海外华人，我也尽力为收集保存海外华人资料，在俄大图书馆设立了"邵友保海外华人文献研究中心",还举办了四届海外华人研究与收藏机构国际合作会议。在国会图书馆工作期间,我也首次建立了一个亚太裔的专藏。

回顾我在美国图书馆五十年的经历,我必须感谢匹兹堡大学我最初给的机会,让我能与图书馆结缘。匹兹堡大学图书馆不仅雇用和训练了我,还资助我在工作之余去念了一个图书馆学的硕士学位。三年后我虽然被在匹兹堡的杜肯大学(Duquesne University)图书馆挖角,从采购部助理馆员的职位升任到采购及编目部主任的职位,匹兹堡大学图书馆馆长不仅不责怪我,而且鼓励我去,并且表示这个升迁是个好机会。1965年,当我从匹兹堡大学教育学院获得博士学位后,我的指导教授强生博士推荐我去宾州的爱丁堡州立学院担任图书馆副馆长,次年升为馆长。1968年6月,在一个偶然的场合里,认识了美国国际发展总署一位官员,他希望能借调我去曼谷一年,为当时新成立的亚洲理工学院建立该院的图书馆。在得到爱丁堡州立学院院长同意之后,我的全家七口就在两个月后由宾州搬到地球另一边的泰国,开始接受一项新的挑战。没想到一去就是七年,一直到这个美援项目圆满结束。1975年回到美国后,先到科罗拉多州立大学担任副馆长三年,重新熟悉了美国大学图书馆的情况,然后在1978年8月很幸运地被俄亥俄大学聘为图书馆馆长,一直做了21年,到1999年9月第一次退休。

在1982年初,当我在俄亥俄大学担任图书馆馆长时,接到加拿大国际发展研究中心(IDRC — International Development Research Centre)的邀请要我参加加拿大一个图书馆学及信息学的专家团,前往中国的昆明,办一个为期两周的"情报中心管理"的培训班(1982年12月6日~18日)。这个班是由中国科技情报所和加拿大国际发展研究中心合办。这个团有六位专家,其中两位是美籍华人,我是其中的一位。参加培训的包括了中央部委、各省及专业情报中心的主管。在培训班结束后,我应中国科技情报所之邀前往北京及老家福州参观。除了参观中国科技情报所及福建省科技情报中心之外,我也借此机会参观了一些大学图书馆,因而对当时中国图书馆的发展有所了解,并开始与中国图书馆界建立了长久的友谊关系。

自从1982年破冰之旅后,我几乎每一年都会应邀回国一次进行讲学或参加学术会议,有时一年还不止一次。我曾经多次在国家图书馆、上海图书馆、中科院图书馆、北京大学、清华大学、北京师范大学、南开大学、武汉大学、中山大学、四川大学等大学图书馆讲学。在世界银行贷款项目的支持下,中国的教育部也经常邀请我前往师范院校图书馆讲学及指导。教育部条件装备司图书馆处董哲潜处长在他任内曾多次亲自陪同。

在北大图书馆前馆长庄守经的大力支持下,北大图书馆先后派遣了好几批馆员到俄亥俄大学接受培训,他们培训的重点是学习图书馆的自动化系统。北京邮电大学图书馆前任馆长马自卫也以访问学者的身份到俄亥俄大学进行图书馆自动化的研究,开始起草他的《图书情报自动化》一书[1]。华东师范大学刁维汉教授在俄亥俄大学做访问学者时编著了《OCLC联机与光盘编目概论》[2]。清华大学图书馆资深馆员孙平也是访问学者之一。她回国后编写了一本极为重要的图书馆工具书——《英汉图书馆情报学词汇》[3]。

深圳图书馆、中科院武汉图书馆也和俄亥俄大学图书馆建立了兄弟馆的关系,进行馆员交换。这种交流有助于深圳图书馆对于ILAS图书馆自动化集成系统的开发。在2009年

---

[1] 马自卫编著,李华伟审. 图书情报自动化. 北京邮电学院出版社,1993
[2] 刁维汉,王行仁,李华伟. OCLC联机与光盘编目概论. 上海:华东师范大学出版社,1999
[3] 孙平编,李华伟审. 英汉图书馆情报学词汇. 北京:清华大学出版社,2006

"ILAS 二十周年技术研讨会"上,文化部文化科技司于平司长指出,"ILAS 二十年,是我国图书馆自动化取得长足进步的二十年。在这二十年中,ILAS 伴随着我国图书馆自动化事业的发展而不断成长,从文化部的一个重点科技项目成为全球拥有 4000 多用户的图书馆自动化产品。"①

1996 年正是在中国加入国际互联网之后积极筹划中国教育科研网的建设时期。当时我认为:"面对 21 世纪的信息时代,发展现代化的图书信息事业是每一个发展中国家当务之急。中国要加速科技、经济、政治、教育、文化及社会的发展,必须加速现代化图书馆及信息工作的发展。因为有了这个教育科研网,中国的高等学府才能与国际上的互联网衔接交流,吸取世界上最先进的知识。"②

为了要引进世界上一些最重要的信息源,我曾协助清华大学图书馆的刘桂林馆长与美国最大的信息机构 OCLC 联网计算机图书馆中心签订了长期互惠合作的协定。1996 年 8 月在清华大学举行的协定签字仪式上,我曾经被称为是 OCLC 与清华大学联姻的"红娘",并被当时海南大学图书馆徐国定馆长赞誉为"中国图书馆界和信息界全面走向网络化的牵线人之一。是中美乃至全世界信息相通、心心相连的桥梁。"

徐国定馆长还特别送给我他亲笔写的横联"经纬枢纽,美华桥梁"。后来还在《书与人》杂志上著文介绍说:"多年来,他奔走于海峡两岸,教学、演讲及参加各有关会议,宣扬图书馆经营的新理念。可以说,他是当今外籍华人中在这方面所作的贡献最大的一个。"③

2003 年,我退而复出,担任美国国会图书馆亚洲部主任时,曾应前中国国家图书馆詹福瑞馆长之请,从 2006 年开始,每年在国会图书馆办一个为期一个月的高级培训班,由国家图书馆每年选派十位馆员参加。曾经受过培训的馆员,都是国家图书馆的精英,其中有一位魏大卫主任已经升任为副馆长。这个项目大大促进了中美两国两个国家图书馆间的交流与合作。

在 2007 年,我曾参与中美两国政府高层次的文化交流活动的规划。当时美国总统的艺术人文委员会(U. S. President's Committee on the Arts and the Humanities)应中国文化部之邀请正在准备前往中国访问。因为美国没有文化部的设置,因此总统的艺术人文委员会被当作对口单位。这个委员会的成员包括了美国的国家人文基金会主席、国家艺术基金会主席、国会图书馆馆长、史密森学会(Smithsonian Institution)主席、国务卿、内政部部长、教育部部长、财政部部长、博物馆与图书馆服务署署长等重要人物。由国会图书馆馆长詹姆斯·毕林顿博士(Dr. James H. Billington)领队。我则代表毕林顿馆长,担任部分联络及准备工作,包括后来中国文化部的回访。因为这次成功的交流,中美两国政府(中国文化部与美国博物馆与图书馆服务署 Institute of Museum and Library Services)在 2008 年 11 月正式签订了《加强中美图书馆合作协议》。当时我已从国会图书馆退休,被协议项目执行单位伊利诺伊大学聘为该合作项目的美方评审专家。

此协议名为"放眼全球,行诸全球",旨在建立中美图书馆专业人员之间的合作与文化交流。伊利诺伊大学厄尔巴拉—香槟校区下属的亚洲图书馆以及摩藤森国际图书馆项目中心与美国华人图书馆员协会和中国图书馆学会展开合作,以期完成这个两年期的试点项

---

① ILAS20 回顾与展望. 见: 公共图书馆. 2009 (2): 9.
② 徐国定. 经纬枢纽 美华桥梁——李华伟博士印象. 见: 书与人. 1997 (5): 155.
③ 徐国定. 经纬枢纽 美华桥梁——李华伟博士印象. 见: 书与人. 1997 (5): 152-155.

目。① 在 2009—2010 两年的时间里，美方先后选派了六批共 36 人的专家团队前往中国，在 13 个省市举办了 13 个图书馆员培训班。将近有 2200 人参加了培训。中国方面也先后选派了三批共 32 人的高级代表团前往美国参观、学习及交流。对促进中美图书馆界双方的合作和交流，起了明显的推动作用。

为了庆贺我的 80 寿诞，国内图书馆界的朋友，在中山大学图书馆馆长程焕文教授及深圳图书馆吴晞馆长的发起下，要出版我的文集及传记。中山大学资讯管理学院前院长谭祥金教授，中山大学图书馆前馆长赵燕群教授，他们两位是中国图书馆界著有名望的模范夫妇，在他们退休后还要费神来编辑我的文集。在中国中央电视台主持节目编导的俄大毕业校友杨阳特别在百忙之中抽出时间来写我的传记，对他们以及其他为此出力的朋友，我要特别表示衷心的感谢。

当程馆长提出要出版我的文集时，我的第一个反应是一种诚惶诚恐的感觉。因为我自己知道我的大多数写作都是报告性和建议性的，是根据我的实际工作经验提出来与同行共享与探讨的，学术性不够强，而且很多是在繁忙的工作压力下赶出来的。即使是我的几本专著，也是在这种情况之下完成的。可是程馆长认为我的著作可以反映出中美图书馆半个世纪以来发展的历程，具有参考价值，因此我就大胆地答应他了。其中很多不完美的地方，要请读者原谅。

在这本文集中，除了我的博士论文是关于教育之外，其他的写作都与图书馆相关，包括图书馆行政与管理、新技术的使用、馆藏发展、国际合作、馆员培训、图书馆联盟、资源共享、募款、海外华人文献、美国国会图书馆的亚洲馆藏、知识管理等，范围相当广，反映了我图书馆工作的层面、兴趣和关注点。

讲到知识管理，我觉得很遗憾的是在我退休之前，没有机会把它实际推动起来。我个人始终认为图书馆员应该把自己看成是知识管理者。信息是静态的。知识是动态的。只有把静态的信息转变成动态的知识，才能创造智慧，才能提高图书馆的功能。在我写的几篇关于知识管理的文章中，曾经比较信息管理与知识管理的主要不同点，并强调知识管理的重要性。我很希望我的观点能引起国内图书馆界朋友进一步的探讨，加强对知识管理这个概念的认识。

另外，承蒙程馆长的建议，把一部分有关我生平的照片和一些有关我的文章也包括在这部文集中。在有关我的文章中有六篇是"美华"名作家吕红（笔名弘晓）写的。吕红是美国华文文艺界协会副会长，美国《红杉林》杂志总编，中国侨联文协海外顾问。著有长篇小说、散文集、小说集等多种。她的文笔与才华，无与伦比，特此向她致谢。

最后，我万分感谢深圳公共图书馆研究院、中山大学出版社以及《图书馆学家文库》编委会各位委员为了出版我的文集所作的努力。希望我的文集能起到抛砖引玉的作用，与国内图书馆同行相互切磋，共同为促进中国图书馆的发展及中美图书馆的合作而继续努力。近几年来，中国图书馆界随着经济的快速发展和社会的进步，得到各级政府的大力支助，正在进行划时代的巨大变革；希望能借此良机，百尺竿头，更进一步，创造一个具有中国特色的图书馆新纪元。

李华伟

2011 年 7 月 26 日

---

① http://www.library.illinois.edu/china/chinese/index.html

图说李华伟博士
Selected Photographs of Dr. Hwa-Wei Lee

李华伟博士（右一）与父亲李干军、长兄李华星（李暋）、姐姐李华宇于1932年在南京合影。
Dr. Lee with his father, elder brother and sister in Nanjing in 1932.

李华伟博士与母亲王晓晖于1932年在南京留影。
Dr. Lee with his mother in Nanjing in 1932.

李华伟博士1935年于南京。
Dr. Lee in Nanjing in 1935.

李华伟博士的父亲李干军和母亲王晓晖1935年摄于南京。
Dr. Lee's father and mother in Nanjing in 1935.

李华伟博士兄弟姐妹1936年于南京合影（左起：三弟华明，大哥华星，姐华宇，华伟，四弟华宁）。
From left to right, brothers Hwa-Min, Hwa-Xin, sister Hwa-Yu, Dr. Lee, and brother Hwa-Nin in 1936 in Nanjing.

李华伟博士兄弟姐妹1936年于南京合影（左起：大哥华星，姐华宇，华伟，三弟华明，四弟华宁）。
From left to right, brother Hwa-Xin, sister Hwa-Yu, Dr. Lee, brothers Hwa-Min and Hwa-Nin in 1936 in Nanjing.

李华伟博士的长兄李华星（李暋）结婚照。
The wedding photo of brother Lee Hwa-Xin (Lee Min).

李华伟博士（前排右二）1947—1949年在桂林汉民中学念高一和高二。
Sophomore and junior years at the National Han-Min High School in Guilin, 1947—1949.

李华伟博士（前排左三）课余喜欢打篮球。
Dr.Lee's favorite sport in school was basketball.

李华伟博士在高三时参加校外流动教育活动。
Taking part in the extra-curricular activity—
the mobile education services of Taichung City.

李华伟博士（左一）1949年进入台湾省立台中第一中学高三年级。
Dr.Lee's senior year at the Taiwan Provincial Taichung First High School in 1949.

1，2. 李华伟博士于1950年进入台湾省立师范学院教育系（1954改名为台湾师范大学）。
Dr.Lee entered the Department of Education of Taiwan Provincial Teachers College in 1950(The name of the college was changed to Taiwan Normal University in 1954, Taipei).

3. 李华伟博士（前排右一）与师院教育系班友1952 于台北合影。
Dr.Lee with classmates in Taipei,1952.

4，5. 李华伟博士在师院时代表教育系参加校运会。
Dr.Lee represented the Department of Education at the annual college game.

李华伟博士（后排右五）还参加了师范学院的很多课外活动。
Dr.Lee also participated in many extra-curricular activities.

李华伟博士（三排左四）参加师院的服务团。
Dr.Lee participated in the student service team.

李华伟博士（二排右二）师范学院毕业照。
Graduation photo of the Department of Education.

1, 2. 李华伟博士（下图二排右五）师院毕业，受完预备军官训练后，分配到台北师专附小担任训导主任（1955—1956）。
After one year of ROTC training, Dr. Lee was assigned to work as the Dean of Students at the Affiliated Elementary School of the Taipei Junior Teachers College(1955—1956).

1，2. 李华伟博士1957年9月赴美国进入匹兹堡大学教育学院攻读教育硕士学位。
In September of 1957, Dr. Lee went to the U.S. for graduate studies in Education at the University of Pittsburgh.

3. 匹兹堡大学36层的主楼，名为"学习殿堂"。
The main building of the University of Pittsburgh is 36 floors high and is called "The Cathedral of Learning".

1	2	3
4	5	6
7		

1-6. 在匹兹堡大学求学期间，李华伟博士认识同班同学Mary Kratochvil。
Dr. Lee met his classmate—Mary Kratochvil during his study in the University of Pittsburgh.

7. 李华伟博士与Mary Kratochvil的父母合影。
Photo with Mary's parents.

李华伟博士参加匹兹堡大学学生活动。
Dr.Lee participated in student activities at the University of Pittsburgh.

李华伟博士的姨妈王肖珠和Rev.Paul Offenhiser（匹兹堡大学指导国际学生的教会牧师）是促成李华伟博士留学美国的两位恩人。
His aunt, Phyllis Chiu-chu Wang, and the student minister for foreign students of the University of Pittsburgh, Rev.Paul Offenhiser, were instrumental in making it possible for him to come to the U.S. for graduate study.

1, 2. 李华伟博士1959年1月与Mary Kratochvil同时获得匹兹堡大学教育学硕士学位。
Dr.Lee and Mary Kratochvil received their Master of Education degrees from the University of Pittsburgh at the same time in January, 1959.

1-3. 李华伟博士1959年3月14日与 Mary Kratochvil在她家乡的教堂结婚。
Dr.Lee and Mary Kratochvil got married on March 14,1959 at Mary's home church in Jeannette, Pennsylvania.

李华伟博士1965年6月在匹兹堡大学获得主修教育副修图书馆学的哲学博士学位。
In June 1965, Dr. Lee Hwa-Wei completed his Ph.D. degree from the University of Pittsburgh.

李华伟博士参加毕业典礼后与夫人Mary Kratochvil合照。
Graduation photo with Mary Kratochvil.

李华伟博士一家与王肖珠女士合影。
Dr.Lee's family pictured with Aunt phyllis Xiao-Chu Wang.

1966年李华伟博士在宾州爱丁堡州立学院担任图书馆馆长时与特别从台湾来美团聚的父母亲合影（李华伟博士的姨妈王肖珠，三弟华明，五弟华俊，小妹华宙都赶来参加）。

When Dr. Lee served as the Head Librarian at Edinboro State College of Pennsylvania in 1966, his parents travelled from Taiwan to have a family reunion. Aunt Phyllis, brothers Hwa-Min, Hwa-Tsun and sister Hwa-Chou all joined together.

李华伟博士的父母亲与李华伟博士的大女儿Shirley合照。
Hwa-Wei's parents had a photo together with their granddaughter Shirley.

李华伟博士的父亲与玛丽的父亲合照。
Mary's father and Hwa-Wei's father had a photo together.

1957年8月李华伟博士由美国国际发展总署借调，全家迁往泰国曼谷，担任新设立的亚洲理工学院图书馆及信息中心主任。
In August 1957, Dr.Lee was recruited by the U.S. Agency for International Development to go to Bangkok,Thailand,serving as the Director of the Library and Information Center at the newly established Asian Institute of Technology.

2001年李华伟博士担任美国福尔白莱资深专家前往泰国清迈大学讲学时,在皇宫受到泰国公主诗琳通接见,感谢李博士对泰国的贡献。
In 2001, Dr. Lee was a Fulbright Senior Specialist at Chiangmai University. He was honored by having a private audience with her Royal Highness Princess Maha Chakri Sirindhorn of Thailand in the Royal Palace.

李华伟博士全家游览曼谷的阿伦寺。
Toured the Arun Royal Temple in Bangkok.

每天临睡前李华伟博士的夫人Mary Kratochvil都会给孩子们念书及讲故事。
Mary Kratochvil read books and told stories to her children each night before bedtime.

李华伟博士全家游览曼谷。
Sightseeing in Bangkok.

 1, 2. 游览曼谷。
Other places in Bangkok.

在泰国7年，李华伟博士一家有机会游览世界各地。这是在伦敦唐宁街10号英国首相官邸前的合影。

During the seven years in Thailand, the whole family had many opportunities to travel around the world. This picture shows No.10 Downing Street, the office of the British Prime Minister, in London.

李华伟博士与夫人在雅典的卫城遗址。
The Acropolis in Athens.

李华伟博士的儿女参观台湾历史馆。
The Museum of History in Taipei.

李华伟博士的夫人和小孩在印度孟买的街头。
A street corner in Mumbai, India.

李华伟博士和夫人在香港的小寺庙。
A small temple in Hong Kong.

李华伟博士的夫人和小孩在台湾的日月潭。
Sun-Moon Lake in Taiwan.

李华伟博士与孩子们在伦敦塔桥。
The Tower Bridge in London.

李华伟博士的夫人和孩子在夏威夷。
Tour of Hawaii.

李华伟博士夫妇和五个孩子（玉骅Shirley，书怡James，书芬Pamela，书千Edward和书真Charles）在泰国合照。
Their five children: Shirley, James, Pamela, Edward, and Charles, in Thailand.

李华伟博士的孩子们与李华伟博士的姨妈王肖珠在匹兹堡合照。王肖珠女士在1948年以前曾任广州岭南大学图书馆馆长。
Dr. Lee's children pictured with Grand-aunt Phyllis Xiao-Chu Wang in Pittsburgh. Miss Wang was the Library Director of Lingnan University in Guangzhou before 1948.

李华伟博士的父亲1973年70大寿时与李华伟博士的母亲在台湾合照。
Dr. Lee's parents in Taiwan for his father's 70th birthday.

Christmas Greetings from Thailand

1974年圣诞节在泰国。
Christmas in Thailand in 1974.

1975年李华伟博士应美国科罗拉多州立大学之聘回美国工作，担任该校图书馆副馆长.全家离开泰国前合照（六子书泰Robert出生在泰国）。

In 1975, Dr. Lee and his family returned to the U.S. where Dr. Lee accepted the position of Associate Director of Libraries at the Colorado State University in Fort Collins, Colorado. Their 6th child, Robert, was born in Bangkok.

1975年李华伟博士应美国科罗拉多州立大学之聘回美国工作，担任该校图书馆副馆长。全家离开泰国前合照（六子书泰Robert出生在泰国）。
In 1975, Dr. Lee and his family returned to the U.S. where Dr. Lee accepted the position of Associate Director of Libraries at the Colorado State University in Fort Collins, Colorado. Their 6th child, Robert, was born in Bangkok.

1975年的冬天在科罗拉多州立大学度过。
In the winter of 1975 in Fort Collins, Corolodo.

Mary Kratochvil的父母亲在1980年的合照。
Photo of Mary's parents taken in 1980.

李华伟博士与Mary Kratochvil的父母、兄弟及家人在宾州团聚。
Gathering with Mary's parents, brothers, and their families in Pennsylvania.

图说李华伟博士　Selected Photographs of Dr. Hwa-Wei Lee

1. 1978年8月李华伟博士应俄亥俄大学之聘前往该校担任图书馆馆长兼教育学院教授。全家迁往俄亥俄州的雅典城。
In August 1978, Dr. Lee was appointed Director of Libraries and Adjunct Professor of Education by Ohio University in Athens, Ohio. The whole family moved from Colorado to Ohio.
2. 俄亥俄大学图书馆外景。
The Vernon Alden Library of Ohio University.
3. 俄亥俄大学图书馆二楼的一部分。
A view of the second floor of the Library.

李华伟博士在雅典城住了24年的家。
This was Dr.Lee's home in Athens for 24 years.

俄亥俄大学成了中国图书馆员、留学生及访问学者之家。近170位图书馆员曾以访问学者身份在俄亥俄大学图书馆学习过。
Ohio University became the home of Chinese librarians, students,and visiting scholars. About 170 Chinese librarians studied at the library as visiting scholars.

海南大学图书馆徐国定馆长亲赠李华伟博士的题字。
Director Yu Guoding of Hainan University Library presented his writing praising Dr. Lee's work.

李华伟博士欢迎程焕文馆长、燕今伟馆长等一行前来访问。
Welcoming the visit of Director Cheng Huanwen, Director Yan Jingwei, and others from China.

1,2. 李华伟博士的家成了留学生及访问学者之家。
The home of Dr.Lee became the home of Chinese students and visiting scholars.

1. 1982年，李华伟博士应中国科技情报所及加拿大国际研究发展中心之邀，前往昆明科技情报中心管理培训班授课。这是李华伟博士在1949年离开中国大陆后第一次回国。
In 1982, Dr.Lee was invited by the Institute of Scientific and Technical Information of China and the International Research Development Center of Canada to be one of the lecturers at the Seminar on the Management of Scientific and Technical Information Centers in China. This was the first time that Dr.Lee returned to China after he left Mainland China in 1949.

2，3. 1988年南开大学聘请李华伟博士担任客座教授。
In 1988, Dr.Lee was appointed Guest Professor by Nankai University.

1991年李华伟博士（三排左一）被选为俄亥俄州代表之一，参加美国图书馆和信息服务的白宫会议。
In 1991 Dr.Lee was elected as one of the delegates from Ohio to participate in the White House Conference on Library and Information Services.

1991年天津高校图书馆馆长来新夏一行来美访问，李华伟博士（左一）陪同前往华盛顿特区参观美国国会图书馆。
During their visit to Ohio in 1991, the university library directors from Tianjin were accompanied by Dr. Lee in their visit to the Library of Congress in Washington, D.C.

1991年天津高校图书馆馆长来美访问俄亥俄大学时，李华伟博士的夫人在家里热情接待。
During the visit of university library directors from Tianjin, they were warmly welcomed by Mrs.Lee at home.

1993年俄亥俄大学图书馆与深圳图书馆签署馆际合作协议。
Ohio University Libraries and Shenzhen Library signed agreement for inter-library cooperation.

1. 1996年李华伟博士作为主要策划者之一在北京参加第一届中美图书馆合作会议。
As one of the chief organizers, Dr. Lee attended the First China-U.S. Library Cooperation Conference held in Beijing in 1996.

2, 3. 1997年北京大学聘请李华伟博士担任客座教授。
In 1997, Dr. Lee was appointed Guest Professor by Peking University.

1. 李华伟博士被选为俄亥俄州1987年最杰出图书馆员及俄亥俄大学1987年荣誉校友。
Dr. Lee was selected as the 1987 Ohio Librarian of the Year and an Honorary Alumnus of Ohio University the same year.

2. 1999年9月，李华伟博士在俄亥俄大学退休时，大学的董事会特别把一座新建的图书馆分馆命名为李华伟图书馆分馆。
When Dr. Lee retired from Ohio University in September 1999, the Board of Trustees of Ohio University named a new library building as the Hwa-Wei Lee Library Annex.

3. 俄亥俄大学董事会董事长亲临颁发董事会证书。
The Chair of the Board of Trustees of Ohio University presented the official resolution of the Board for naming the Hwa-Wei Lee Library Annex.

俄亥俄大学校长及两位前任校长，董事会正副董事长，亲临剪彩。
The current president and two previous presidents of Ohio University, and the Chair and Deputy Chair of the Board of Trustees were presented in ribbon cutting.

李华伟博士的家人很高兴地参加了这个盛典。
Dr.Lee's family members participated in the special event.

李华伟图书馆门前特别安置了一对从中国购买的汉白玉石狮子。
In front of the Library Annex is a pair of white marble lions especially purchased from China.

中国国家图书馆的贵宾参观李华伟博士退休后的办公室。
Visitors from the National Library of China visited Dr. Lee at his office in the Library Annex.

李华伟博士接待来自中国高校图书馆的贵宾。
Visitors from university libraries in China.

李华伟博士接待来自中国教育部及北大图书馆的贵宾。
Visitors from the Ministry of Education and Peking University Library.

李华伟博士接待来自广州图书馆和深圳图书馆的贵宾。
Visitors from Guangzhou Library and Shenzhen Library.

俄亥俄大学图书馆还特别将总馆第一层命名为李华伟国际藏书中心。
Ohio University Libraries named the first floor of the Vernon Alden Library as the Hwa-Wei Lee Center for International Collections.

李华伟博士与夫人Mary在俄亥俄大学校园内合照。
Dr.Lee & Mrs.Lee on campus of Ohio University.

1. 李华伟博士从俄亥俄大学退休后，应闻名全球的OCLC联机图书馆中心之聘，担任该中心的杰出访问学者，国内很多图书馆专家前来访问。图为北大前馆长庄守经、中科院武汉图书馆钟永恒馆长、华南理工大学楼宏青馆长等来访时合影。

Right after his retirement from Ohio University, Dr.Lee was invited by the world-renown OCLC Online Computer Library Center as a visiting distinguished scholar. He helped to welcome many librarians from China who visited OCLC.

2, 3. 2003年2月，李华伟博士应美国国会图书馆之聘前往该馆担任亚洲部主任。

In February 2003, Dr.Lee accepted the appointment from the Library of Congress to serve as the Chief of the Asian Division.

国会图书馆的杰弗逊大楼,也是该馆亚洲部的所在地。
The Jefferson Building of the Library of Congress where the Asian Division is located.

杰弗逊大楼的背景。
A rare scene of the Jefferson Building.

华丽堂皇的内景。
The magnificent interior of the Library.

总阅览室。
The Main Reading Room.

1. 亚洲部的阅览室。
Asian Division Reading Room.
2, 3, 4. 亚洲部经常举办各种学术活动。
Asian Division organized many scholarly programs.

李华伟博士建立亚洲部之友会，创始董事会成员包括陈香梅女士。
Dr.Lee established the Asian Division Friends Society. Madam Anna Chennault was one of the founding Board Directors.

亚洲部之友会活动之一。
One of the activities of the Asian Division Friends Society.

李华伟博士退休会一景。
The retirement party.

2008年李华伟博士从国会图书馆退休，馆长James Billington亲临祝贺及表扬。
At his retirement party, Dr. James Billington, Librarian of the Congress, expressed his appreciation to Dr. Lee for his outstanding accomplishments.

To Dr. Hwa-Wei Lee
With best wishes,

Elaine L. Chao
Secretary of Labor

1，2. 美国联邦政府劳工部赵小兰部长亲临参加李华伟博士退休餐会。
Secretary of Labor, Honorable Elaine L.Chao, also participated in the dinner party.

3. 2009年是李华伟博士和Mary结婚50周年纪念。
Dr.Lee and Mary celebrated the 50th Anniversary of their wedding in 2009.

> *Your international librarianship and professionalism have been exceptional since your arrival at the Library of Congress on February 10, 2003. During your tenure, you worked tirelessly to build our collections and to ensure that our referece service and outreach activities served the nation in the best possible ways.*

> *You should feel enormously gratified in knowing that you have made a huge difference in this institution, and you have touched the lives of a great number of LC staff, librarians around the world, and international scholars.*

THE LIBRARY OF CONGRESS
LIBRARY SERVICES
WASHINGTON, D.C. 20540-4900

Collections & Services Directorate

February 1, 2008

Dear Hwa-Wei:

    It has been my honor and pleasure to work with you as Director of the Collections and Services Directorate for the past two years, and as a fellow division chief before that during your first three years at the Library of Congress. Your enthusiasm and support of the Asian Division, as well as your professional acumen and scholarly integrity have been an inspiration to your staff and to those you served as Chief of the Asian Division of the Library of Congress. Your generosity in establishing the Asian Pacific American Collection Fund and your support of the Friends of the Asian Division have inspired the goodwill of others which will ensure the good work of both for many years to come. I add my congratulations and best wishes to the chorus of your Library colleagues as you leave us for your next adventure outside the halls of the Library of Congress, and send my personal thanks for your wise counsel and friendship.

Sincerely,

> *Your enthusiasm and support of the Asian Division, as well as your professional acumen and scholarly integrity have been an inspiration to your staff and to those you served as Chief of the Asian Division of the Library of Congress.*

THE LIBRARY OF CONGRESS
101 INDEPENDENCE AVENUE, S.E.
WASHINGTON, D.C. 20540-4860

DIRECTOR OF SCHOLARLY PROGRAMS
AND THE JOHN W. KLUGE CENTER

February 6, 2008

Dear Hwa-Wei:

    When you came to the Library, you promised me that you would stay for five years. We are all reluctant to see that five years come to an end, but what an astonishing five years you have given to the Asian Division. When you arrived, the Asian Division was a sleepy backwater, and as you leave it is one of the most dynamic divisions of the Library. One of my 3 or 4 greatest successes in my 16-plus years at the Library of Congress was hiring you as chief of the Asian Division, or more accurately, having somehow created the atmosphere and the psychological space that facilitated your wanting to come to lead the Division.

    I don't recall the earliest details of the attempt Peter Young and I made to recruit you as acting chief. I do recall that you begged off for health reasons and helped persuade Karl Lo to come, which was a wonderful contribution in itself. When we began searching for a permanent chief, you offered your services in searching for potential candidates. What is most dramatic in my memory was the moment during which I read the email in which you detailed why each potential chief candidate on your list, and there were about 8 of them, had expressed unwillingness to apply for the position. At the very end, with your characteristic modesty, you asked what I might think if you were to submit an application yourself.

> *Your tenure as chief has been a triumph and demonstration of what is possible with a leader of vision and experience, one who long ago discarded the encumbrances of ego and who has led with deep appreciation for the gifts of others, with great humility, and with a rare wisdom.*

2010年6月，李华伟博士全家在爱荷华团聚（侄儿书超夫妇，侄女鸿敏都赶来参加）。
Family reunion in Iowa, June 2010.

李华伟博士的11位孙子女一起参加全家聚会。
Eleven grand children also attended.

2009年起，李华伟博士开始参加中美两国政府间所共同主持的中美图书馆员专业交流项目，担任该项目的美方评审员。
In 2009, Dr. Lee began to take part in the China—U.S. Librarian Collaboration Project and serves as the U.S. Project Evaluator.

2009年9月李华伟博士参加在兰州及西安举行的图书馆系统高级研修班。
Dr.Lee participated in the Advanced Library Seminars held in Lanzhou and Xi'an in September 2009.

2009年9月李华伟博士参加在合肥举行的国际图书馆计算机管理系统发展趋势报告会。
Dr.Lee participated in the International Seminar on Library Computer Management Trends held in Hefei in September 2009.

2010年3月李华伟博士参加在成都、重庆及广州举行的图书馆馆长高级研修班。
Dr.Lee participated in the Advanced Library Seminars held in Chengdu, Chongqing, and Guangzhou in March 2010.

2010年5月李华伟博士参加在天津、烟台及上海举行的图书馆馆长高级研讨班。
Dr. Lee participated in the Advanced Library Seminars held in Tianjin, Yantai, and Shanghai in May 2010.

2009年5月李华伟博士代表俄亥俄大学图书馆参加在广州暨南大学举行的第四届海外华人研究与文献收藏机构国际会议。
Dr. Lee represented Ohio University Libraries at the Fourth International Conference of Institute & Libraries for Chinese Overseas Studies held in Guangzhou Jinan University, May 2009.

1, 2. 2009年11月李华伟博士参加在深圳举行的公共图书馆国际高峰论坛和公共图书馆研究院成立大会。
In November 2009, Dr. Lee participated in the International Summit on Public Libraries and the inauguration ceremony of the Public Library Institute organized by Shenzhen Library in Shenzhen.

3. 2010年6月李华伟博士参加由上海财经大学图书馆主办的大学图书馆馆长论坛。
In June 2010, Dr. Lee participated in the Academic Library Directors' Forum organized by the Library of Shanghai University of Finance and Economics.

2010年9月，美华图书馆员学会代表们向国家图书馆周和平馆长赠送感谢状，感谢他多年来为加强中美图书馆合作所做的贡献。

In September 2010, officials of the Chinese American Librarians Association presented a plaque to Director Zhou Heping of the National Library of China in appreciation of his contributions in strengthening the cooperation between Chinese and American libraries in recent years.

2010年11月，李华伟博士参加在台北举行的第八次中文文献资源共建共享国际会议。

Dr. Lee participated in the 8th International Conference on Cooperative Development and Sharing of Chinese Resources and Digital Collections held in Taipei in November 2010.

2011年5月，李华伟博士参加在长沙及福州举行的图书馆馆长高级研讨班。
Dr.Lee participated in the Advanced Library Seminars held in Changsha and Fuzhou in May 2011.

李华伟博士的姨妈王肖珠曾长期任职于前岭南大学图书馆并在1945至1948年担任该校图书馆馆长，在"二战"后为图书馆重建有卓越贡献。李博士为此特别在中山大学信息管理系设立王肖珠纪念奖学金以资纪念。

Aunt Phyllis Chiu-Chu Wang held key positions at the former Lingnan University from 1945 to 1948 and was the library director there from 1945 to 1948. She made significant contributions in the re-building of the Lingnan University Library after the Second World War. In her memory, Dr.Lee established a memorial scholarship in her name at the College of Information Management, Sun Yat-sen University.

王肖珠照片。
Photos of Miss Phyllis Chiu-Chu Wang (Wang Xiaozhu).

王肖珠与李华伟博士夫妇合照。
Picture of Ms.Wang with Dr.Lee & Mrs.Lee.

王肖珠与李华伟博士夫妇及其家人合照。
Picture of Ms.Wang with Dr.Lee and Mrs.Lee and other family members.

李华伟博士肖像。
A portrait of Dr. Hwa-Wei Lee.

李华伟博士的夫人Mary Kratochvil肖像。
A portrait of Mrs. Lee Mary Kratochvil.

· 上卷 ·

学术著作

上卷目录
Table of Contents of Volume I

1. **图书馆学的世界观** ··· (1)
   Librarianship in World Perspective

   前言 ·· (1)
   Foreword

   第一部分　地区研究的馆藏 ··· (3)
   Section I　Area Studies Collections

   第二部分　目录控制 ··· (32)
   Section II　Bibliographic Control

   第三部分　国际合作 ··· (49)
   Section III　International Cooperation

   第四部分　国际交换与馆员培训 ··· (69)
   Section IV　International Exchanges and Internships

   第五部分　图书馆及资讯服务 ··· (78)
   Section V　Library and Information Services

   第六部分　图书馆自动化 ··· (115)
   Section VI　Library Automation

   第七部分　图书馆发展 ··· (148)
   Section VII　Library Development

   第八部分　图书馆联网 ··· (167)
   Section VIII　Library Networking

   参考书目 ··· (189)
   Bibliography

2. **现代化图书馆管理** ·· (193)
   On Modern Library Management

编者的话 ……………………………………………………………… (193)
Editor's Comments

周　序 …………………………………………………………………… (195)
Preface by Zhou Ning shen

王　序 …………………………………………………………………… (196)
Preface by Wang Zheng-gu

自　序 …………………………………………………………………… (198)
Author's Preface

第一章　绪言 ………………………………………………………… (199)
Chapter 1　Introduction

第二章　20 世纪西方管理学的发展 ……………………………… (210)
Chapter 2　The Development of Management Science in the West in the Twentieth Century

第三章　图书馆的规划 ……………………………………………… (218)
Chapter 3　Library Planning

第四章　图书馆的组织 ……………………………………………… (231)
Chapter 4　Library Organization

第五章　图书馆人力资源管理 ……………………………………… (249)
Chapter 5　Management of Human Resources in Libraries

第六章　图书馆的领导和作业 ……………………………………… (280)
Chapter 6　Leadership and Operations in Libraries

第七章　图书馆的控制与评估 ……………………………………… (299)
Chapter 7　Control and Assessment in Libraries

第八章　跨世纪的图书馆发展 ……………………………………… (316)
Chapter 8　Library Developments into the Next Century

3. 20 世纪 90 年代图书馆募款所面对的挑战　实用指南：从新手到专家 …………… (326)
Fundraising for the 1990s：The Challenge Ahead A Practical Guide for Library Fundraising：From Novice to Expert

前　言 …………………………………………………………………… (326)
Forword

第一章　绪论 ·· (327)
Chapter 1　Introduction

第二章　募款规划 ·· (331)
Chapter 2　Planning for Fundraising

第三章　捐款的来源:公共部门 ·· (342)
Chapter 3　Sources of Funds：The Public Sector

第四章　捐款的来源:私人来源 ·· (348)
Chapter 4　Sources of Funds：The Private Sector

第五章　为募款成功所建立的组织 ·· (366)
Chapter 5　Organizing for Success

第六章　两个募款成功的计划 ··· (376)
Chapter 6　Two Successful Fundraising Programs

第七章　对捐款者负责及对捐款的管理 ·· (390)
Chapter 7　Donor Stewardship

第八章　结论 ·· (409)
Chapter 8　Conclusion

附录1:主管发展副院长的工作描述 ··· (414)
Appendix I：Job Description of an Assistant Dean for Development

附录2:俄亥俄大学图书馆之友章程 ··· (416)
Appendix II：By-Laws of the Friends of the Library of Ohio University

附录3:俄亥俄大学三百周年庆典捐赠协议 ··· (420)
Appendix III：The Ohio University Third Century Campaign Gift Agreement

附录4:参加俄亥俄大学三百周年庆典活动报名表 ·· (421)
Appendix IV：The Ohio University Third Century Campaign Prospect Entry Form

附录5:俄亥俄大学三百周年庆典认捐表 ··· (422)
Appendix V：The Ohio University Third Century Campaign Cultivation/Solicitation Plan

附录6:俄亥俄大学三百周年庆典活动联系报告 ··· (423)
Appendix VI：The Ohio University Third Century Campaign Contact Report

附录7:专业募款机构 ··· (424)
Appendix VII：Professional Fundraising Organizations

附录 8：政府资助相关信息 ……………………………………………………（426）
Appendix VIII：Sources of Information on Government Grants

附录 9：基金会相关信息 ………………………………………………………（428）
Appendix IX：Sources of Information on Foundations

附录 10：募捐社团相关信息 …………………………………………………（430）
Appendix X：Sources of Information on Corporate Prospects

附录 11：募捐个人相关信息 …………………………………………………（432）
Appendix XI：Sources of Information on Individual Prospects

附录 12：募捐软件产品 ………………………………………………………（433）
Appendix XII：Fundraising Software Products

附录 13：俄亥俄大学图书馆：馆内政策与程序 ……………………………（436）
Appendix XIII：Ohio University Libraries：Internal Policy & Procedure

引用资料及建议阅读书目 ……………………………………………………（437）
Sources and Suggested Reading

4. 巴布亚新几内亚高等院校间的图书馆发展、资源共享和联网 ……………（446）
Library Development, Resource Sharing, and Networking among Higher Education Institutions in Papua New Guinea

执行摘要 ………………………………………………………………………（446）
Executive Summary

主要建议 ………………………………………………………………………（447）
Key Recommendations

报告 ……………………………………………………………………………（452）
Report

附录 1：咨询和面谈的人士 …………………………………………………（467）
Appendix 1：Individuals Consulted/Interviewed

附录 2：巴布亚新几内亚的国家图书馆服务 ………………………………（471）
Appendix 2：National Library Service of Papua New Guinea

附录 3：六所主要图书馆的图书资讯资源 …………………………………（472）
Appendix 3：Library and Information Resources in the Six Major Libraries

附录 4：师范学院图书馆的图书资讯资源 …………………………………………（473）
Appendix 4： Library and Information Resources in the Teachers College Libraries

附录 5：其他院校的图书资讯资源 …………………………………………………（474）
Appendix 5： Library and Information Resources in Other College Libraries

附录 6：参考文献 ……………………………………………………………………（475）
Appendix 6： References

5. OCLC 联机与光盘编目概论（节选）………………………………………………（477）
   OCLC Compact Disk and Online Cataloging（extract）

   第二章　图书馆编目的自动化 ……………………………………………………（477）
   Chapter 2　Automated Cataloging in Libraries

6. 知识管理的理论与实践（节选）……………………………………………………（486）
   The Theory and Practice of Knowledge Management（extract）

   第十四章　知识管理与图书馆在 21 世纪所扮演的角色 ………………………（486）
   Chapter 14　Knowledge Management and the Role of Libraries in the 21st Century

7. 亚太地区图书馆发展的合作领域（节选）…………………………………………（501）
   Areas of Cooperation in Library Development in Asia and Pacific Regions（extract）

   合作的新途径：图书馆员培训 ……………………………………………………（501）
   Library Internships： A New Approach to Cooperation

8. 台湾的教育发展（1945—1962）……………………………………………………（507）
   Educational Development in Taiwan，China（1945 – 1962）

   前言 …………………………………………………………………………………（507）
   Foreword

   绪论 …………………………………………………………………………………（507）
   I. Introduction

   台湾教育的历史背景 ………………………………………………………………（513）
   II. Historical Background of Taiwan's Education

   战后教育项目的复原（1945—1949）………………………………………………（528）
   III. Postwar Rehabilitation of the Educational Program（1945 – 1949）

国民党的教育项目(1949—1962) ……………………………………（536）
IV. Educational Program of the KuoMingtang (1949 – 1962)

初等教育的发展 ……………………………………………………（553）
V. The Development of Primary Education

中等教育的发展 ……………………………………………………（569）
VI. The Development of Secondary Education

高等教育的发展 ……………………………………………………（588）
VII. The Development of Higher Education

师范教育的发展 ……………………………………………………（604）
VIII. The Development of Teacher Education

社会教育的发展 ……………………………………………………（616）
IX. The Development of Social Education

摘要和结论 …………………………………………………………（631）
X. Summary and Conclusion

1. 图书馆学的世界观
Librarianship in World Perspective[①]

前 言

Foreword

During my thirty-one year library career—beginning at the University of Pittsburgh in 1959, including seven years in Bangkok, Thailand, 1968 to 1975, under the sponsorship of the United States Agency for International Development, and through the present directorship of the Ohio University Libraries since 1978, I have been fortunate to have many opportunities to write for professional journals and to present papers at conferences. Additionally, I have served on several editorial boards for library journals, written many book reviews, and co-edited two conference proceedings. Despite my heavy administrative responsibilities, the writings and accompanying research have enriched my professional knowledge and served to broaden my understanding in many areas of librarianship. I can well remember the many evenings, weekends, holidays, and vacations spent, instead of with my family or friends, in my study reading, researching, thinking, and writing. These have become my prime hobbies.

Because of my Chinese origin and years of library work in the United States and Asia, I long have been interested in international librarianship and have had opportunities to cultivate a world perspective in my professional outlook. This is reflected in my writings. I fortuitously have been privileged to be involved in or be witness to the development of library and information services in the many Asian countries with which I have had the honor to be associated.

At the suggestion of many friends and associates—and especially with the encouragement of the Library Association of China in Taiwan which is publishing this collection of my professional writings—I have selected twenty eight papers published between 1963 to 1989 as representative of my professional interests and concerns. These papers are grouped under eight topics: Area Studies Collections, Bibliographic Control, International Cooperation, International Exchanges and Internships, Library and Information Services, Library Automation, Library Development, and Library Networking. Two are written in Chinese and the remainder in English. Within each group, papers are arranged in chronological order. The British spelling in some of the papers published in journals using that form has been preserved.

Throughout my years of writing, I have been indebted to many former and current colleagues and friends with whom I have collaborated in writing. Each is acknowledged in the Table of Contents and in the Bibliography. I am especially grateful to Kent Mulliner, my close colleague at Ohio University, for his most valuable assistance in preparing this final form for publication.

In reviewing the papers, I realize that many tend more to reportage than scholarly work; nevertheless, they fairly represent my feelings and thoughts on issues confronting librarianship around the world. Some earlier papers now are dated but serve as records of the past, providing a historical perspective on more recent developments.

This collection of my writings could not have been published without the encouragements and

---

① This is a Selected Writings from 1963 to 1989. Published by Student Book Company, Taipei, 1991.

sponsorship of the Library Association of China. Ms. Teresa, Y. Wang Chang, Professor Margaret Chang Fung, Mr. Karl Min Ku, Professor Lucy Te-Chu Lee, Professor Harris B. H. Seng, and Professor Chen-Ku Wang, among others, all deserve special and heartfelt thanks for making this publication possible. I sincerely and humbly invite the comments and advice of all readers and will accept all criticisms and responsibility for any shortcomings of this book.

Finally, I must single out my wife, Mary, for my profound gratitude for her continuing support, tolerance and understanding of my "workaholic" life style. In many of my writings, she was the very first reader and constructive critic. To my late parents, I would like to dedicate this book as a memorial to their love.

Hwa-Wei Lee
Ohio University Libraries
Athens, Ohio 45701
U. S. A.
December 1990

第一部分 地区研究的馆藏

Section I Area Studies Collections

Africana — A Special Collection at Duquesne University

The rapidly expanding African Collection at Duquesne was first inspired by the work of the Holy Ghost Fathers who were the founders of Duquesne. Their missionary zeal has for many years penetrated deep into the African Continent. The interest they have always held in the civilization and Christianization of Africa[①] was the prime source of inspiration for the establishment of an African Collection at Duquesne.

History

In the early years, the book budget of the collection was far from sufficient and the importance of such a collection still far from being properly recognized. Pioneer efforts sought to enlist the help of missionaries stationed in Africa. It was not surprising that many warm responses were received. From knowledgeable persons such as the Reverends Constantine Conan, Stephen J. Lasko and Anton Morgenroth, all of whom have had long careers as devoted missionary workers in Africa, many valuable materials and suggestions were obtained. Father Morgenroth later joined the faculty of the Institute of African Affairs at Duquesne where he now also serves as Consultant for the African Collection.

The founding of the Institute of African Affairs in 1956 made Duquesne the fifth university in this country and the first Catholic university to offer an organized African program of studies.[②] Under the directorship of Dr. Geza Grosschmid, the Institute has acquired nation-wide recognition. This is evident from the annual grant begun in 1960 from the United States Office of Education to establish within the Institute an "African Language and Area Center." The Federal Government has thus provided part of the much needed book funds for the collection. Since then the collection has been growing steadily. As of July 1963, the total volume of book materials and periodicals almost trebled the 1960 figures.

Scope

At present there are nearly 4,500 volumes in the collection. The number of periodicals in the stacks amounts to 217 titles, more than two thirds of which are current subscriptions. Pamphlets number nearly 1,000. There are also 74 reels of microfilms, most of which are made from the archives of the Missionaries de la congregation du Saint-Esprit et du Saint-Coeur de Marie in Paris, 18 records of linguistics and music, 19 reels of tapes recording the complete lessons of language instruction in Swahili and Gio. The former was made under the direction of Father A. Loogman assisted by Mr. Peter Kyara; the latter was made by Kenneth E. Griffes and William E. Welmers to accompany their language text. The collection also includes a small number of manuscripts including scripts such as the *English-Idoma Dictionary* by Rev. *John M. Schreier, Nomen und Verbum in Afrikanischen Sprachen; Eine Strukturstudie* by Robert Laessig, etc., and some 200 photographs on North Africa, especially Algeria, collected by Mrs. L. E. Hubbell.

---

  ① Henry J. Koren, *The Spiritans; A History of the Congregation of the Holy Ghost* (Pittsburgh: Duquesne University, 1958) p. 440.
  ② Thomas Patrick Melady, "A Suggestion for the Establishment of the Institute of African Affairs at Duquesne University." (Pittsburgh: Duquesne University, 1955?) p. 2. (Mimeographed)

Staff

The collection is housed in a well equipped room separate from the general collection of the University Library. A professional librarian from the Reference Department spends half of his time in the collection and has the assistance of a half-time secretary who is proficient in German and French, a part-time cataloger, and two graduate assistants assigned to work for the collection by the Institute of African Affairs. Both the assistants have had extensive training in Swahili and possess a general knowledge of African matters.

Specialization

The collection originally had its special concentrations. Geographically, its interest was mainly on East Africa. Topically, its emphasis was centered on linguistics, history, anthropology, sociology, economics and missionary works. During recent years as more funds were made available, it no longer limited itself to the above areas. A broadened acquisition program was adopted to include the whole continent and works of various subject areas.

The expansion of the African program in the Institute of African Affairs has been responsible for the expansion of the African library collection. In addition to the teaching of the Swahili Language, a lingua franca in central Africa spoken by nearly 13 million people, Classical Arabic and Hausa are to be added this fall. The latter is also widely spoken by more than 9 million people in northern Nigeria and the Sudan. ①

For interested scholars and African specialists, the following specialties of the collection are worth noting.

Linguistic works

There are some 96 African languages represented in the collection. About 20 of these are spoken by more than one million people—Arabic, Swahili, Hausa, Amharic, Fula, Ibo, Malagasy, Yoruba, Luba, Somali, Sotho, Zulu, Kanuri, Moundu, Shona, Xhosa, Fang-Bulu, Ganda, Kongo and Nyamwesi-Sukuma. Most of the books in these languages are grammars, bilingual dictionaries, readers and religious teachings.

Studies on the Former Belgian Congo

The collection possesses an almost complete set of the publications (nearly 400 titles) by the Academie Royale des Sciences d'Outre-mer in Brussels. It includes the *Biographie Coloniale Beige*, *Bulletin des Seances*, and the *Memoires* which are in three classes: The *sciences morales et politiquesl*; the *sciences naturelles et medicales*; and *sciences techniques*. Many of these *Memoires* begin with Tome I, fasc. 1 which were published as early as 1930 and present a most thorough study of that region.

Bibliographies and Catalogs

To assist scholarly research, various bibliographical works are indispensable. The collection has a good collection of bibliographies and catalogs. The notable ones include those on official publications of various countries or regions by the Library of Congress and the *Catalog of African Government Documents and African Area Index* by Boston University. For national bibliographies, there are *Nigerian Publications*, *Bibliographie du Congo Beige et du Ruanda-Urundi*, and *South Africa Bibliography*, etc. The International African Institute's *Africa Bibliography Series* provides good bibliographic information on ethnography, sociology and linguistics. In the missionary field,

---

① C. F. and F. M. Voegelin, ed., "Languages Now Spoken By Over a Million Speakers", *Anthropological Linguistics*, III, no. 8 (Nov. 1961), pp. 15–18.

there are two important bibliographies: the *Bibliotheca Missionum* by Robert Streit and the *Bibliografia Missionaria*. Perhaps the most up-to-date bibliography indexing books and periodical articles of social and economic interest is the *Fiches Bibliographiques* of the Centre de Documentation Economique et Sociale at Brussels. It is arranged on 3 "x 5" cards. Some 1,500 items are indexed each year with full bibliographic information.

The published Catalogs of the African Collections of both Northwestern University Library and Howard University Library are also sources of information to supplement the National Union Catalog for locating rare items in Africana.

There are also a few periodicals in the collection which regularly feature book reviews and abstracts. They include: *Africa*, *African Abstracts*, *African Affairs*, *African Studies*, *African Ecclesiastical Review*, *Africana Nova*, *Bibliographie Courante*, *Current Bibliography on African Affairs*, *Bulletin of the Institute Francais d'Afrique Noire*, *Journal of African History*, *Journal of Modern African Studies*, *Bulletin of the School of Oriental and African Studies of London University* and *The Rhodes-Livingstone Journal*.

Publications

In addition to contributing regularly to the *Joint Acquisitions List of Africana* compiled by the African Department of the Northwestern University Library, the collection also publishes a monthly acquisitions list of its own which is distributed free upon request. Publication of a printed catalog of the collection is being considered and it is hoped that it will provide needed bibliographic assistance to scholars and specialists who are interested in such information.

International Information Exchange and Southeast Asia Collections: A View from the U. S. ①

Historical Summary

Southeast Asia as a focus of academic concentration is a relatively recent arrival on the American academic scene. Even Cornell University's internationally acclaimed Echols (formerly part of Wason) Collection dates only after World War II. In the 1960s, interest in Southeast Asia Studies (and supporting library holdings) as a legitimate academic endeavor increased (probably as much from the efforts of graduates of the existing centers [Yale and Hawaii as well as Cornell] as from increasing military involvement in Indochina. But even with expansion, there are fewer than ten major collections focusing on Southeast Asia—although a number of additional libraries afford access to significant materials on the region, especially with regard to the Philippines as a former colony. Today these include (in alphabetical order to avoid offense) California at Berkeley, Cornell, Hawaii, Michigan, Northern Illinois, Ohio, Wisconsin, and Yale as well as the Library of Congress.

Such a small number of collections, in comparison even to major collections on other parts of Asia (37 on East Asia and 20 on South Asia),② has contributed to cooperation among the collections. This is best reflected in the Committee on Research Materials on Southeast Asia (CORMOSEA); a committee of the Southeast Asia Council of the Association of Asian Studies). Founded in 1967, this committee—with a membership of scholars and librarians—has provided focus for information exchange both within and outside the United States. By obtaining financial assistance, it was able to commission the publication of a large number of reference aids on the area at minimal cost. ③ Most recently, it has successfully sponsored (under the direction of Shiro Saito of Hawaii, financially supported by the National Endowment for the Humanities, NEH) a survey of existing and needed research tools on each Southeast Asian nation and the region as a whole. ④ Having identified existing weaknesses and needs, it is currently seeking financial support for production of these bibliographies, directories, dictionaries, etc. ⑤

CORMOSEA's other apparent accomplishment has been the publication of the *CORMOSEA Bulletin* (formerly *Newsletter*) which has featured articles on important sources of information, reviews, reprints, news, and announcements relevant to scholars and librarians with Southeast Asian interests. Despite lapses in its frequency of issue, its past editors have provided a valuable reference tool and an important medium for disseminating and sharing information on the region

---

① Co-authors: K. Mulliner and Lian The-Mulliner. This joint paper was presented by Hwa-Wei Lee at the Meeting of the International Association of Orientalist Librarians, August 19, 1980; held concurrently with the 46th General Conference of IFLA in Manila, August 18 – 23, 1980.

② Extracted from Lee Ash, *Subject Collections: A Guide to Special Book Collections And Subject Emphases* (5th ed.; New York: Bowker, 1978).

③ A list of projects supported and a summary of the most recent report on efforts at publication of the projects can be found in the *CORMOSEA Bulletin*, Vol. 9, No. 3 (Nov. 1977), p. 9 – 13.

④ Three surveys, identified collectively as Southeast Asia Paper No. 16 – *Southeast Asian Research Tools* (Honolulu: Southeast Asia Studies, University of Hawaii, 1979), were issued separately as: Part I, *Summary and Needs* by Shiro Saito; Part II, *Indonesia* by Lan Hiang Char; Part III, *Burma* by Michael Aung Thwin; Part IV, *Malaysia* by William R. Roff; Part V, *The Philippines* by Edita Baradi; Part VI, *Thailand* by Charles F. Keyes; and Part IX, *Vietnam* by Michael G. Cotter. The final part, covering Southeast Asia as a region by Pat Lim Pui Huen will be published by the Institute of Southeast Asian Studies in Singapore.

⑤ A report on this new effort will appear in a forthcoming issue of *CORMOSEA Bulletin*. Editor's note, 1991: That effort proved unsuccessful.

internationally. [1]

CORMOSEA, which meets at least annually, serves as a forum in which inter-institutional competition can give way to exchanges of information, sharing of experiences, and cooperation in projects of import to the international research community.

One major obstacle to international information exchange has been the absence of agreed upon standards of bibliographic reference. International efforts, such as the ISBD and the ISDS, have provided overall guidance in addressing this problem, but inconsistencies in orthography, forms of reference, and local usages (not to mention personal preferences) can only be addressed by those concerned. In this regard, CORMOSEA has served as an umbrella organization for dedicated librarians from the United States who have worked with librarians within the nations concerned and in Europe in an attempt to alleviate this situation. [2]

The other national medium of exchange of import has been the Library of Congress, particularly through the Southeast Asia Field Office of its Cooperative Acquisitions Program (CAP), headquartered in Jakarta, Indonesia. This program has provided materials and preliminary descriptive cataloging for publications from Brunei, Indonesia, Malaysia, and Singapore to participating collections. While the primary beneficiaries have been the cooperating libraries in the United States, the program has dramatically increased the accessibility of information produced in Southeast Asia for users in the United States and abroad. [3]

While national efforts have yielded the most dramatic results, the major burden in information exchange has been carried by individual institutions and, more correctly, by active and concerned Southeast Asian Studies librarians within those institutions (most of whom comprise the librarian membership of CORMOSEA). Of greatest importance have been the exchange programs which have provided Southeast Asian institutions with materials of interest published in the United States in return, in most cases, for materials from Southeast Asia. In addition to increasing resources in the United States, these programs have helped overcome the complaints of academic exploitation in which researchers have availed themselves of hospitality—yet have neglected to share their research with the scholars and libraries of the host nation.

Appropriately for the Asian context, much of the international exchange of information in the past has been through personal contacts and consultations. [4] These have included exchanges of visits and conference attendance by American and Southeast Asian librarians, attendance at American universities and library schools by would-be librarians from the region, and secondment through AID, Fulbright, Peace Corps, and other agencies of practicing American librarians to work for periods of a few months to several years in Southeast Asian libraries and with the librarians serving those bodies.

Because of the topic of this paper, the foregoing discussion has omitted the significant role of individual scholars and librarians in the U. S. outside the major research centers in contributing to international information exchange. Even more importantly, it has not touched upon the substantial efforts of librarians in Southeast Asia in intra-and extra-regional cooperation and the development

---

[1] A brief summary of the *Bulletin's* publishing history is provided by the current editor, Joyce Wright, in Vol. 9, No. 3 (Nov. 1977), p. 34. Beginning with Vol. 11 (late 1980/early 1981, *Insya Allah*, two of the authors of this paper, Lian The-Mulliner and K. Mulliner, have been named as editors).

[2] Noteworthy examples include the efforts of Abdul Kohar Rony, J. N. B. Tairas, and others in the Library of Congress meeting with Indonesian librarians to standardize entry elements and forms of entry for personal and corporate Indonesian authors, described in J. N. B. Tairas, "Some Aspects of Descriptive Cataloguing standardization in Indonesia," in International Congress of Orientalists, 1971 *International Co-operation in Orientalist Librarianship* (Canberra: National Library of Australia for the Library Seminars Planning Committee, 1972), pp. 58 – 82, and Lian Tie Kho, with regard to Burmese, described most recently in *CORMOSEA Bulletin*, Vol. 10, No. 1 (Dec. 1979), pp. 21 – 23.

[3] Recently the descriptive cataloging, if not the Cooperative Acquisitions Program has been expanded to include materials from Burma and Thailand. [By 1990, The Philippines has also been added and a Cooperative Acquisitions Program has been established for Thailand with the intent to expand it to other countries in mainland Southeast Asia.] These can be found in the Library of Congress, Accessions List, *Southeast Asia*.

[4] The early efforts of Cecil Hobbs of the Library of Congress are noteworthy in this regard. See his *An Account of an Acquisition Trip in the Countries of Southeast Asia* (Ithaca, NY: Southeast Asia Program, Cornell University); reports on subsequent trips appeared in Cornell's Southeast Asia Data Paper Series Nos. 11, 40, 67, and 85.

and production of needed research aids. ① The increasingly dominant role of Southeast Asians, scholars and institutions, in facilitating exchange of information about the region in the past decade has been a welcome development. It should also be noted that omission of British, Canadian, European, Australian, and Japanese contributions to information exchange does not indicate a lack of appreciation of the substantive gains provided by their efforts.

Current Assessment

This short historical sketch was intended to provide a basis for assessment of the current role of Southeast Asia Collections in the United States in international information exchanges as a prelude to projecting future possibilities.

Having highlighted cooperative efforts among collections in the United States, it is appropriate to note one at least temporarily divisive element accompanying automated library systems and networks. These have been well-developed and widely accepted in U. S. libraries. The overall result has been the effective emergence of a national online union catalog among the networks serving 2,000 libraries nationally as part of the OCLC system. ② In 1979 this was augmented by an online interlibrary loan subsystem which enhanced the value of the online union catalog. Since that point, OCLC's monopoly has been challenged by the RLIN system which serves many of the major research libraries. ③ The intricacies of the current situation lie beyond our scope and interest here, but it is important to note that the division into two major information utilities has split the Southeast Asia Collections which effectively reduces accessibility and understanding regarding each other's holdings. ④ With efforts currently underway to interface the two major systems as well as the Library of Congress system, it is hoped that the gap can at least be bridged. With such a small number of important collections, intra-national communication is vital and a necessary prelude to future trends in facilitating international information exchange. ⑤

Individual and collective efforts in such projects as exchanges and research tools have been successful in the past and should continue. There is a need for greater efforts in this direction and, hopefully, greater cooperation between Southeast Asian Institutions and those outside the region, as exemplified in CORMOSEA's Research Tools Project (see Endnote 4). In this regard, there should be an important role for organizations such as this [International Association of Orientalist

---

① Some of the important efforts in this direction were featured in Hwa-Wei Lee, "Co-operative Regional Bibliographic Projects in South-East Asia," *UNESCO Bulletin for Libraries*, Vol. 31, No. 6 (Nov. – Dec. 1977), pp. 344 – 351 & 370. Particularly noteworthy since that summation has been the appearance through the efforts of the Southeast Asia Branch of the International Council on Archives (SARBICA) and the Congress of Southeast Asian Librarians (CONSAL), under the editorship of the late Winardi Partaningrat, of *Masterlist of Southeast Asia Microforms* (Singapore: Singapore University Press, 1978). The UNESCO-supported project originally known as the "UNESCO Study of Malay Culture" and now the "Study of South East Asian Cultures" is another potentially important effort which has, however, suffered from funding problems. See P. Lim Pui Huen, "Bibliography on Malay Culture (UNESCO Study of Malay Culture)" *CORMOSEA Bulletin*, Vol. 10, No. 1 (Dec. 1979), p. 10, and addendum on p. 12.

② The growth and refinement of OCLC as a national library utility has been well documented in Susan K. Martin, *Library Networks* (White Plains, NY: Knowledge Industry Publications, Inc., 1978), esp. pp. 35 – 42, but the entire volume is of interest to consideration of online systems development.

③ RLIN also cooperates with the WLN (Washington [State] Library Network), CLASS (California Library Authority for Systems and Services), and the Library of Congress in projects. Its vision of its role and relation to OCLC is well presented in Richard DeGennaro, "Research Libraries Enter the Information Age", *Library Journal*, Vol. 104, No. 20 (Nov. 1979), pp. 2405 – 2410.

④ The University of Hawaii, Northern Illinois University, Ohio University, and the University of Wisconsin are served by OCLC while the University of California at Berkeley, Cornell University, the University of Michigan, and Yale University are participants in RLIN.

⑤ The impact of this division extends far beyond the Southeast Asia Collections, and its alleviation has been recognized as an important task. The Council on Library Resources, Inc. (One Dupont Circle, N. W., Suite 620, Washington, D. C. 20036) is just now (mid-August 1980) receiving a study from Battelle Columbus Laboratories on interfacing these systems. This paper will probably be published by the Council in September 1980 and hopefully will provide ways of overcoming the current impasse. The findings and recommendations should be of interest internationally in terms of interfacing as well as of national importance in the U. S. [1990: This was the basis of the Linked Systems Project (LSP) which is still underway.]

Librarians] and other librarians' organizations to encourage greater international cooperation. Although exchanges have been mutually beneficial in the past, there is still considerable need for extending these efforts, particularly to include the younger universities in Southeast Asia as well as the major research institutions in each nation. Intra-national and intra-regional cooperation can address some of this need, but it is important for Southeast Asia Collections and Programs in the United States and the rest of the world to recognize the explosion in higher education in Southeast Asia as these nations strive to meet their internal technological and manpower needs.

Accompanying the expansion of higher education in Southeast Asia has been the growth and maturation of academic libraries and library schools in the region to meet internal informational needs. While this growth may continue to require international personnel (of whom many will be those with a Southeast Asia focus or at least interest) to contribute to libraries and library instruction, there is an increasing body of trained personnel with most of the nations which can respond to these needs. This will require some reassessment of the role of American and other international institutions in meeting the technical requirements of Southeast Asia as well as the personal and professional preferences of those librarians who in the past have welcomed an opportunity to live and work in the region.

In this regard, the Ohio University Library has recently been pioneering an internship program for librarians from Southeast Asia. The goal is to offer hands-on experience working with the technological tools and systems which are transforming our profession. Southeast Asia Collections are in a unique position to offer such experience for, in addition to the technological facilities, they are able to offer an intern an opportunity to work with the same types of materials (and languages) with which they will have to deal in their home institutions. Although still in its nascent phase (initially, participants have come only from Chulalongkorn University), the program has been discussed with UNESCO, which has indicated an interest in exploring such an offering library school faculty members from the region to enhance their abilities to serve as cadre in preparing Southeast Asian libraries for technological innovation. A complementary program is also being initiated to more-senior library administrators (initial participants are from Taiwan).

While this approach is only a small beginning, we do think that it affords an indication of the types of programs that will be needed in the future, especially if some of the developments which will be discussed in the following section are realized. Special note should be made that this is not a simple donor-done program, but, in affording interns an opportunity to work with Southeast Asian materials, the internees are also providing the host library and Southeast Asia Collection with language as well as other professional skills which are in rather short supply in the U. S. — and which are likely to remain so, if institutions seek to avoid contributing to the brain drain from the Southeast Asian nations.

The Future: Some Projections

Despite identification of favorable activities by American Southeast Asia Collections and libraries in Southeast Asia, one must concur with the 1969 assessment by a member of the Library of Congress staff that the international transfer of information "is still in a relatively primitive state of development."[①] That progress is being made is evidenced in the preceding, but real international information exchange is yet to be realized.

In this section we will attempt some crystal ball gazing to identify what appear to be likely developments and the role of Southeast Asia Collections in facilitating and perhaps cushioning these developments.

Underlying this analysis is the belief that information is the property of no individual, institution, or nation and that its accession and dissemination is the goal of librarianship. Yet we must also recognize that political, economic, ideological, and belief systems are often major

---

① John G. Lorentz, "International Transfer of Information" *Annual Review of Information Science and Technology*, 1969 (White Plains, NY: Knowledge Industry Publications, Inc., 1969), p. 398.

obstacles in disseminating information. The following projections are primarily directed toward the member-nations of the Association of Southeast Asian Nations (ASEAN), not because of any desire to discriminate against the other nations of the region but simply because those nations presently have the most developed information systems on which to base projections.

It seems likely that the most dramatic changes in international information exchange for the region will be technologically driven. In part, these will probably follow the trends in other parts of the world where networking and automation are rapidly transforming our profession. ① The seeds of cooperation and online systems are evident in the area of bibliographic searches. ②

Probably more important than the automation systems—which will have the greatest impact on the internal operation of libraries and the domestic services provided within each nation—are the potentialities offered by satellite communications. Previously, many of the innovations in information technology have been inappropriate to Southeast Asia because of the distances separating the research facilities in the many nations, a problem compounded by sometimes unreliable telephone line communications and the costs associated with such systems.

But satellite systems virtually eliminate geographical distance as a factor. In considering this development we are not so naive as to believe that research libraries much less Southeast Asia Collections will be in the vanguard of this process. A recent article in *Asiaweek* focusing on the online business office in Southeast Asia is one indication of the direction from which major innovations are likely to come. ③ In her seminal article on telelibraries, Rosa Liu, Librarian for INTELSAT indicated that the special libraries associated with corporate communications systems are likely to derive the earliest benefits arising from advances in transmission and transcription technology. ④ And, based on current developments in Europe and North America, other early applications of the system will be for technical and medical information. Because at least some this data is so time-sensitive, one can hardly fault such a development.

But this technology should also offer new opportunities to area studies collections (Southeast Asia in this case) and to the libraries in Southeast Asia. For example, our library is currently linked by landline to the OCLC database in Columbus, Ohio (a distance of 75 miles). Yet if satellite transmission were used, the difference in contacting Malaysia rather than Columbus would be negligible (at least theoretically, depending on usage charges). Particularly encouraging are the cost possibilities. The trend (as well as the increasing sophistication) is well demonstrated in the appended charts from Ms. Liu's paper.

While the declining cost of a unit of service is documented, equally exciting are the developments which will determine just what such a unit includes. A recent library test of facsimile transmission systems sponsored by the U. S. Department of Health, Education, and Welfare compared two major types of systems as well as slowscan television (which was considered generally unacceptable). One was a system requiring six minutes per page and the other 35 seconds (90 seconds for very high resolution work). ⑤ Even as this paper was being written, we learned of a new system which will reduce this to under one second. ⑥ The combination on non-real time satellite transmission of facsimiles greatly expands the possibilities for meaningful international exchange of information.

---

① These have been well summarized in John J. Eyre, "The Impact of Automation on Libraries — A Review", *Journal of Library and Information Science*, Vol. 5, No. 1 (Apr. 1979), pp. 1 – 15.

② An excellent discussion of prospects and proposals can be found in Lim Huck Tee, "The Southeast Asia University Library Network (SAULNET): A Proposal and a Model for Resource Sharing in ASEAN Countries," in IFLAAJNESCO Pre-session Seminar for Libraries from Developing Countries, *Resource Sharing of Libraries in Developing Countries* (IFLA Publications 14; Munchen: K. G. Saur, 1979), pp. 217 – 233. A very elaborate model can be found in the work prepared for the UNESCO/ UNISIST Programme by Bo Karlander and Sverre Sem-Sandberg, *Information Networks for Online Bibliographic Retrieval* (Paris: UNESCO, 1977).

③ *Asia week*, 20 June 1980, pp. 52 – 54.

④ Rosa Liu, "Telelibrary, Library Services Via Satellite", *Special Libraries*, Vol. 70, No. 9 (Sept. 1979), pp. 363 – 372.

⑤ *Telefax Library Information Network* (*TALINET*). Final Report (New Grant 032A – 7804 – P4041; Denver: Graduate School of Librarianship and Information Management, University of Denver, 1979).

⑥ Satellite Business Systems and AM International Demonstrate World's First Communicating Copier, "joint press release", May 14, 1980.

While we are hardly prepared to deal with the technical intricacies of these developments (and it is disappointing how few librarians are), it is clear that the information explosion will soon be taking on megaton dimensions for librarians. It is in meeting this exponential challenge that area collection librarians can provide major services. If the innovators in this new information barrage are the businesses, the sciences, engineering and medicine, it is likely that much of this information will be in non-Southeast Asian languages. It will fall to the librarians in Southeast Asia and those concerned with Southeast Asia in other countries to assure that information-handling systems are compatible with Southeast Asian languages and that Southeast Asian materials are available in machine-readable format and are in an accessible form.

Essentially these exciting developments should provide additional emphasis on the role of the area collections, in conjunction with librarians in the region as mediators between the technology and the region. Their combination of professional skills, language competence, experience, and cultural sensitivity, if augmented by awareness of technological developments and implications, will qualify them to recommend gates and parameters which must be considered in preparing systems for international exchange. Complementary to this is the potential role of area collections in providing the practical exposure to the new technology for Southeast Asia librarians in a context familiar to the librarians. Our university's efforts in this direction were indicated in the earlier section.

Stimulating as it is to consider the benefits arising from overnight, if not instantaneous, transmission of information between America (for example) and Southeast Asia libraries, no one can believe that the contact through a terminal can compare with the opportunity to meet socially and professionally with one's counterparts in the other parts of the world. Area collections are likely to remain potential homes away from home for visiting professionals from Southeast Asia and, similarly, the area bibliographers will continue to treasure the opportunities to visit their colleagues in Southeast Asia. For this we can be grateful, especially for an opportunity such as afforded by this conference to meet jointly with colleagues with shared interests from throughout the world.

Acknowledgements

Special thanks for assistance in preparing this final section are due to Rosa Liu (INTELSAT Library, Washington, D. C.), Mary Diebler (Public Service Satellite Consortium, Denver, Colorado), and John J. Welsh and Joan Maier (U. S. National Oceanic and Atmospheric Administration Library, Boulder, Colorado), all of whom were most generous in sharing their knowledge and resources which they had available. Thanks also to Dennis Rose (Satellite Business Systems, Washington, D. C./McLean, Virginia) for timely assistance.

Appendix A

Five Generations of INTELSAT Satellites Showing Increased Circuit Capacity and Decreased Cost

Intelsat Satellites

	I	II	III	IV	IVA	V
Year of First Launch	1965	1967	1966	1971	1975	1979
Dimensions Diameter (m)	0.72	1.42	1.42	2.38	2.38	2.0
Height (m)	0.60	0 673	1.04	5.28	5.90	15.7
In-Orbin Mass (kg)	38	67.3	152	700	790	967
Launch Vehicle	— Thor-Delta—			—Atlas-Centaur—		Atlas-Centaur or Shuttle
Primary Power (watts))	40	75	120	400	500	1200

(Continuing)

	I	II	III	IV	IVA	V
Number of Transponders	2	1	2	12	20	27
Total Usable Bandwidth (MHz)	50	130	500	500	800	2300
eirp/Beam (dBW)	11.5	15.5	23	22.5 global 32.7 spot beam	22 global 29 HEMI	22.29 at 4GHz 44 at 11 GHz
Two-Way Telephone Circuits	240	240	1200	4000	6000	12,500
Design Lifetime (years)	15	3	5	7	7	7
Cost/Circuit Year ($K)	30	10	2	1	1	0.7

Appendix B

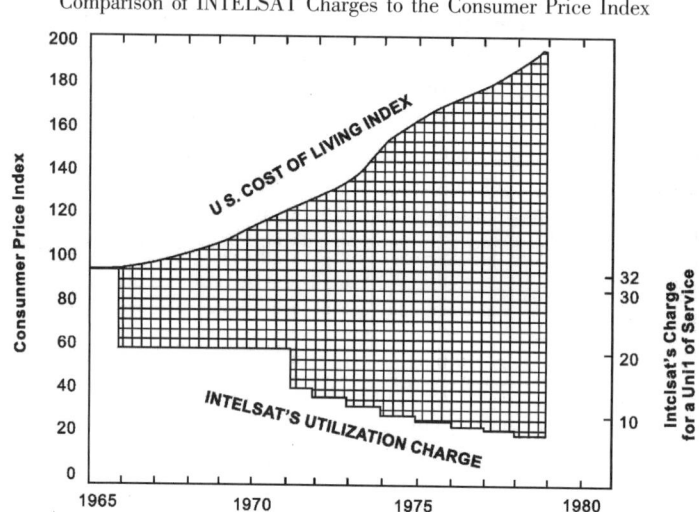

Comparison of INTELSAT Charges to the Consumer Price Index

Library Acquisitions from the Third World: An Introduction[①]

Before discussing the contents of this issue, consideration must be given to the title and scope of the contents. As a first defense, the editors aver that the title was inherited rather than chosen by them. This comment is necessary as a number of contributors questioned the validity or content of the term "Third World". Yet the experience of compiling and editing this issue has forced the recognition that this term, whatever its limitations, is among if not the most appropriate to identify those countries other than the OECD member nations (the Organization for Economic Cooperation and Development, which includes the nations of Western Europe as well as the United States, Canada, and Japan) or the Soviet Union and its allies in Eastern Europe.

As becomes evident in the following articles, the term is most easily defined by what it is not rather than what it is. To refer to many of the same countries, the Library of Congress uses "developing nations," a not altogether pleasing alternative to the pejorative "underdeveloped." Those interested in rationales for grouping the nations included should consult the Library of Congress Acquisitions Policy Statement no. 30, summarized by Mulliner in this issue.[②] The case is further elaborated in the Samore article[③] which follows it.

With the acknowledgement that there are criteria for grouping these nations, the editors are sympathetic with observers such as Maureen Patterson (South Asian Bibliographer, University of Chicago Library) who felt that the industrial capacity as well as the level of literacy and enormous book trade in a country such as India preclude meaningful comparisons with some of the poorer nations of the world. This argument is further amplified when applied to a nation such as Singapore where the per capital GNP is expected to surpass that of Great Britain next year. Unlike some OPEC states, this wealth is based on a diverse industrial and trading base. Additionally, Singapore would fail to qualify under virtually any of the criteria established by the Library of Congress.

The editors have become doubly aware of the problems involved in the term as they have been asked by the British Library (engaged in the preparation of an article to appear in a supplementary issue) to specify countries to be included or excluded. Thus, while denying any claims to scientific rigor, the editors have used the term Third World to refer to the nations covered by the exclusionary definition given at the end of the opening paragraph.

The term is further justified by its currency in library literature. Based on a conference of the Ligue des Bibliotheque Europeennes de Recherche (LIBER) at the University of Sussex in 1973 on the same theme as this special issue, the proceedings were reported under the title, *Acquisitions from the Third Worlds*.[④] This conference and its proceedings represented a marked departure from two efforts which immediately preceded it. In 1971 the Institute on the Acquisition of Foreign Materials at the University of Wisconsin—Milwaukee presented a 2-week program on acquiring foreign materials.[⑤] Demonstrating the synchronicity which often characterizes important intellectual

---

[①] Co-Author: K. Mulliner. This article introduced a special thematic issue (Vol. 6, Number 2, 1982) of the *Library Acquisitions: Practice and Theory*, on acquisitions from Third World Countries. Subsequent references in this article refer to this issue, identified as *LAPT*, unless noted otherwise. So many excellent articles were received that a number of articles were carried over to Vol. 6, No. 4.

[②] K. Mulliner, "Library of Congress Acquisitions Policies: Synopsis Covering Developing Countries", *LAPT*, pp. 103 – 106.

[③] Theodore Samore, "Acquisitions of Materials from Third World Countries for U. S. Libraries", *LAPT*, pp. 107 – 112.

[④] D. A. Clarke, ed. *Acquisitions from the Third World*, Papers of Ligue des Bibliotheque Europeennes de Recherche seminar, 17 – 19 September 1973 (London. Mansell, 1975).

[⑤] Theodore Samore, ed. *Acquisitions of Foreign Materials for U. S. Libraries*, 2nd rev. ed. (Metuchen, N. J. : The Scarecrow Press, Inc. , 1983).

concerns (as well as the importance of the issue for librarians and scholars), the Librarian of the School of Oriental and African Studies, B. C. Bloomfield, was also organizing a session on the same theme for the University, College and Research Section for the Annual Conference of the Library Association. ① Both of these efforts shared the characteristic of addressing the problem from a particular nation perspective (the U. S., for the Institute and the United Kingdom for Bloomfield) and the problem of attempting to treat acquisitions from the rest of the world. Before returning to the LIBER Conference, mention should also be made of the 1965 conference of the Graduate Library School at the University of Chicago② which addressed much the same theme and which Bloomfield credited with inspiring the Library Association program. ③

In several regards, the LIBER conference was able to go beyond the earlier efforts because of its narrower focus (the Third World) and because of the larger number of nations represented by participants (including France, West Germany, Nigeria, Finland, and Australia in addition to the U. S. and the U. K.). The resulting publication has guided the editors in attempting to develop the articles which follow (and those which will be included in a supplement). There is one major distinction. The articles in this special issue were solicited especially for this publication rather than growing out of a conference. This has permitted a (minimal) degree of editorial guidance but has precluded the cross-fertilization and exchanges possible in a conference. It has further necessitated considerable international correspondence and accompanying mail delays (including a postal strike in Australia).

In citing the illustrious forebears, one additional note on content is in order. Specifically missing from this issue are historical discussions of Third World acquisitions. These are certainly important to understanding the field (and the fact that *plus ca change, plus c'est la meme chose*) but the above volumes and citations therein provide sufficient background as to make additional treatment redundant. Thus the articles herein focus largely on the present and the future.

Since the LIBER Conference, much of the collective effort at addressing problems of Third World acquisitions has focused on specific geographical/cultural regions. ④ Articles in this issue refer to several of these, such as the Seminar on the Acquisition of Latin American Library Materials, and others which operate in cooperation with or as part of library professional or area studies organizations. Additionally, cooperative efforts have been increasing (primarily as the magnitude of materials published in the Third World and the costs of obtaining them have soared) both at national and international levels (as reflected in the introduction of international participation in Library of Congress programs and in the international membership of some of the microform programs of the Center for Research Libraries).

Concern with acquisitions particularly in Third World nations has also received the attention of international organizations and related bodies. As a result, there has been a burgeoning of the literature on books and publishing in the Third World. ⑤ Even while preparing this introduction the editors chanced across two recent major works on the book industry in Africa, one from UNESCO

---

① B. C. Bloomfield, *Acquisition and Provision of Foreign Books by National and University Libraries in the University Libraries in the United Kingdom: Papers of the Morecambe Conference, 16 April 1972* (London: Mansell, 1972).

② Tsuen-hsuin Tsien and Howard Winger, eds. *Area Studies and the Library*, Proceedings of the 30th annual conference of the University of Chicago Graduate Library School, May 20 – 22, 1965 (Chicago: University of Chicago, 1966).

③ Bloomfield, *Acquisition and Provision*, p. ix.

④ One notable exception to this trend was the 1977 Library of Congress workshop on "Acquisitions and the Third World," which included presentations on the Middle East (by George Atiyeh), Africa (by Hans Panofsky), and Latin America (by John Hebert) as well as a presentation on U. S. Government Documents (by Merwin C. Phelps). The proceedings and discussion were summarized and edited by Janice Carroll and James Thompson, "Workshop on Acquisitions from the Third World: Proceedings." In: *Library Acquisitions: Practice and Theory*, 1 (2), pp. 117 – 133. The inclusion of U. S. Documents, justified because "problems in acquiring [them] present many of the same difficulties, and do so for (in many ways) analogous reasons" (p. 117), certainly extended the definition of Third World well beyond that used in this issue.

⑤ These are discussed and identified in Philip G. Altbach and Eva-Maria Rathgeber, *Publishing in the Third World: Trend Report and Bibliography* (New York: Praeger, 1980).

and one from a monographic series at the editors' home institution. ① An additional factor of relevance to the discussion is the growing concern within the Third World of access to materials published within each of the nations and, increasingly, from nearby nations and other regions. As evidenced by the UNESCO discussions on a new world information order, Third World nations are increasingly unwilling to learn about each other through the media of non-Third World sources. ② Without digressing to that issue, it must be recognized that citizens, scholars, and librarians of Third World nations usually share the same difficulties as described by the contributors here, even within their own nations. ③

Further contributing to expanded concern regarding acquisitions of Third World materials has been the international spread of information and bibliographic databases. ④ A number of these offer document delivery533 as well as bibliographic entries, but even in these cases the acquisition of one article or document frequently leads to the identification of a further dozen titles of relevance. As a result, questions regarding access to Third World publications are becoming as important to Third World institutions as they have been to research libraries elsewhere. Cooperation both in acquisitions and in sharing materials from the Third World is now significant not only for the traditional research centers, which have had to face a Malthusian dilemma in which the growth in published materials has far outpaced funding for acquisitions, but also for universities and agencies in the Third World which have recognized that many of the problems of development are not unique to each individual nation. ⑤ This is an important issue for achieving IFLA's medium-term programme for Universal Availability of Publications (UAP). ⑥

Turning then to the contents of this special issue, contributions are divided into three: those discussing cross-regional patterns, those focusing on collection materials from a specific region, and those focusing on cooperative efforts. Before considering these, be advised that the articles are only a partial reporting. Because of the press schedule for this volume, a number of anticipated articles have had to be deferred to a subsequent issue. This is most important for consideration of the role and practices of British institutions (specifically the British Library⑦ and the Library of the School of Oriental and African Studies⑧) in acquisitions from the Third World. Their omission represents only a deferral of their contributions, not a slight of their pioneering efforts and substantial contributions.

The emergence of the Library of Congress as a major force in Third World acquisitions is a

---

① S. I. A. Kotei, *The Book Today in Africa* (Paris: UNESCO, 1981). *Mazungumzo: Interviews with East African Writers, Publishers, Editors and Scholars*, edited and compiled by Bernth Lindfors. Papers in International Studies, Africa Series No. 41 (Athens: Ohio University Center for International Studies, 1980).

② International Commission for the Study of Communication Problems. *Many Voices One World: Towards a New More Just and More Efficient World Information and Communication Order* (London/New York: Kogan Page/Unipub, 1980).

③ In a recent bibliographic compilation, a librarian with the Malaysian National University [University Kebangsaan Malaysia] Library succinctly presented the problems encountered "by libraries in Malaysia" in collecting Malaysiana. Ding Choo Ming, *A Bibliographies of Bibliographies on Malaysia* (Petaling Jaya, Malaysia: Hexagon Elite Publications, 1981) pp. vii-ix. These remarks, which parallel comments found in the Acquisition from Regions section of this issue, were initially aired as the first section of a paper by the same author, "Problems in Acquiring Malaysiana Materials and Prospects for Resource Sharing in the 1980s" presented to the International Association of Orientalist Librarians meeting in Manila, August 19, 1980.

④ An excellent but not exhaustive summary of these can be found in *International Cooperative Information Systems*. Proceedings of a seminar held in Vienna, Austria, 9 - 13 July 1979 (Ottawa: International Development Research Centre, 1980).

⑤ H. D. L. Vervliet, *Resource Sharing of Libraries in Developing Countries*, Proceedings of the 1977 IFLAAJNESCO Pre-Session Seminar for Librarians from Developing Countries, Antwerp University, August 30 - September 4, 1977. IFLA Publications 14 (Munich et al.; K. G. Saur, 1979).

⑥ Approaches to UAP for the Third World are discussed in M. B. Line. "Universal Availability of Publications and developing countries," *Ibid.*, pp. 162 - 169. Although much pf the emphases in UAP is on interlibrary loan, loans depend on availability. The importance of acquisitions, and retention, to an effective interlibrary loan system is made in M. B. Line et al., *National Interlending Systems: A Comparative Study of Existing Systems and Possible Models* (Paris: UNESCO General Information Programme, 1978), p. ix; cf. ERIC ED 188611.

⑦ Diana Grimwood-Jones, "British Library Acquisition of Material from the Third World", *LAPT*, VII, 1 (1983), pp. 71 - 80.

⑧ Rosemary Stevens, "Acquisition of Serials from Asia and Africa at the Schooi of Oriental and African Studies (SOAS) Library", *LAPT*, VII, 1 (1983), pp. 59 - 70.

post-World War II phenomenon; in fact, that this year marks the twentieth anniversary of its field office in New Delhi attests to its recency. Today, it not only provides information to the libraries of the world on what is available through its regional Accessions Lists but also oversees the actual acquisition of a significant quantity of materials, through its PL 480 and CAP (Cooperative Acquisitions) programs, for libraries in the United States. In discussing the Overseas Operations Division (of which she is Assistant to the Chief), Alice Kniskern describes the current plans for international participation in these acquisitions programs① (in Egypt initially) as well as provides details on the related microfilming programs which, through the Photoduplication Service of LC, now provide relatively inexpensive copies to libraries anywhere in the world of materials which previously would have existed in only one or two institutions.

In contrast to this sprawling effort which serves a multitude of institutions as well as governmental users is the activity of a special agency library, such as that of the International Labor Organization described by Aileen Ng②. At this level, the need for information is practical, directly related programs and policies. The acquisitions problems are the same as those faced by LC, but with only a fraction of the staff. Yet both LC and the ILO Library find that reliable information on what is available and acquisition thereof depends on having a knowledgeable and dedicated person present in the region—even if, in the case of the ILO, this may be someone not specifically responsible for acquisitions. Akin to the mission of the ILO Library in providing useful information when needed are the programs of the International Development Research Centre (IDRC) to identify and deliver, through international cooperation and databases, information to meet the needs of government agencies and others involved in development. Maureen Sly outlines the growth of the service. Allowing that "the medium is the message," the IDRC deserves special recognition for its introduction of online searching and databases (with software such as MINISIS which is adaptable to a number of library functions) to many Third World nations. The information and document delivery services of SALUS and DEVSIS are valuable sources but are probably outweighed by the significance of the introduction of automation to Third World librarians and information specialists.

The Acquisitions from Regions section addressees the specific acquisitions problems for each of the major Third World areas. Contrasting experiences are offered as acquisitions problems not only vary from region to region but also considerably within a region and frequently depend as much on the acquiring institution as on the supplier. In considering African materials, the articles by Panofsky and Rathgeber③ cite many of the same source materials but with distinct evaluations of the contributions of each. In this instance there is the added benefit of comparing the perspectives of the doyen in the field and of an active and published post-doctoral fellow. On Asia, the article from the Australian National University④ cites materials from Taiwan as presenting problems while for the People's Republic of China today it is more a question of selectivity in avoiding duplication. In contrast, William Wong (Assistant Director for Technical Services [for the Asian Library], University of Illinois) in an article that will appear in the supplement⑤ concentrates on the PRC since there are few problems in acquiring Taiwan materials. Disparities within a region are apparent in the article by Laura Gutierrez-Witt and Donald L. Gibbs⑥compared with that of

---

① Alice Kniskern, "Library of Congress Overseas Offices: Acquistion Programs in the Third World", *LAPT*, pp. 87 – 102.
② Aileen W. K. Ng, "Coping with Collection Building of Third World Material in an International Organization Library", *LAPT*, pp. 113 – 116.
③ Hans E. Panofsky, "Acquisitions of Africana", *LAPT*, pp. 123 – 128; Eva-Maria Rathgeber, "Africana Acquisitions Problems: The View from Both Sides", *LAPT*, pp. 137 – 148.
④ Enid Bishop, Y. S. Chan, and W. G. Miller, "Recent Australian Experience with China and Southeast Asia", *LAPT*, pp. 149 – 160.
⑤ William Sheh Wong, "Acquiring Library Materials from the People's Republic of China", *LAPT*, VII, 1 (1983), pp. 47 – 58.
⑥ Laura Guutiérrez-Witt and Donald L. Gibbs, "Acquiring Latin American Books", *LAPT*, pp. 167 – 176.

Salvador Miranda.① An issue not considered here, since it has become largely academic, is the very definition of a region. In many cases, geographic proximity offers little indication of linguistic, economic, or cultural affinities, but, even for the Middle East, which shares a common religion in Islam and a common basic language in Arabic (not to neglect Persian-speaking peoples), political strife is perhaps an even greater problem for acquisitions efforts than in more heterogeneous regions.

The two contributions by Directors of LC Field Offices, Gene Smith② and Michael Albin,③ deserve special comment. A theme explicit or implicit in most of the articles is the value of the field acquisitions trip to identify available materials, suppliers, and ways of surmounting difficulties. The Field Office Directors are talented individuals on extended or semi-permanent acquisitions trips. They are intimately involved in the regions for which they are responsible and daily must cope not only with the vagaries of dealers and government agencies but also with the insatiable demands of researchers and libraries as well as the LC Washington staff, all of whom want everything that has never been published on a topic and want it yesterday. The articles by the two Directors are valuable in themselves but their inclusion here should also be considered a salute to the services provided by all of the Field Office Directors. One testament to the value of these services was the creation of similar offices in Indonesia by the Dutch and the Australians. Gene Smith's article is additionally important as, on its twentieth anniversary, the New Delhi office must devise a dollar-based cooperative program for the first time, Michael Albin affords insights into an area seldom trod by Field Office Directors, and excluded from LC acquisitions for the most part, conference proceedings. His article documents the immensity of the task of attempting to acquire proceedings,④ but also whets the appetite of the researcher for these largely inaccessible "publications." Note should be made that efforts such as those of the IDRC index are beginning to bridge the inaccessibility chasm—presumably to the chagrin of catalogers using different systems.

Despite the contrasts, an overriding impression from this section is that the problems are largely similar, while the languages, cultural, and economic practices may vary from region to region (and within a region), many of the difficulties transcend national and regional delineations (giving credence to the consideration of Third World acquisitions as a theme). This results in a certain repetitiveness but a repetition which should encourage the individual concerned with a particular region to consider what is being attempted and achieved in other regions. One constant in Third World acquisition is that solutions are seldom transplantable. What works in one cultural-economic milieu is likely to remain fruitless in another. But an idea or an approach translated to meet socio-political realities can afford new avenues for exploring possibilities. Robert Theobald has cogently phrased the choice: a situation can be approached as a problem or as a possibility.⑤

Evidence of the possibilities of cross-fertilization can be found in the section on cooperation. Waxing publishing industries in Third World nations, static acquisitions budgets elsewhere, and inflation everywhere are combining to greatly reduce the number of institutions attempting, or even claiming to attempt, comprehensive collecting for one or more Third World region. While the less well off are likely to take satisfaction in seeing the mighty humbled, no one can celebrate the demise or even the decline of a major collection on the Third World. As on occasion in the past, cooperation is an obvious alternative. Perhaps now economic realities have caught up with

---

① Salvador Miranda, "Library Materials from Latin American and the Caribbean: Problems and Approaches in Acquisitions", *LAPT*, pp. 177 – 184.
② E. Gene Smith, "The New Delhi Office of the Library of Congress at Twenty: Changing Acquisition Parameters", *LAPT*, pp. 161 – 166.
③ Michael W. Albin, "Acquisition of Conference Proceedings from the Arab World", *LAPT*, pp. 201 – 211.
④ This point is reinforced by the forthcoming publication of the estimated 12,550 listings in the *Africana Conference Paper Index*, prepared by the Melville J. Herskovits Library of African Studies, Northwestern University (Boston: G. K. Hall, November 1982).
⑤ Robert Theobald, *Teg's 1994*; *An Anticipation of the Near Future* (Chicago: Swallow Press, 1972).

idealistic platitudes.

One working example in the U. S. for cooperation can be found in the area microform programs administered by the Center for Research Libraries (CRL). While these are hardly of the magnitude required to meet more than a very selective need, they do present an approach to the acquisition and retention of valuable research materials which would otherwise be largely unavailable. Additionally, as described by Boylan and Shores[①], the program for each region has maintained a distinct operational character. One of the characteristics of area or Third World studies is that the participants, scholars and librarians alike, assume many of the patterns of interpersonal and organizational interaction found among the peoples and nations which they study. In part this is commendable and in part quaint. But it is a reality which must be considered in cooperative undertakings. Many of the same sensitivities that are required in Third World areas are needed in organizing even mutually beneficial efforts. If meaningful cooperation is achieved, it is unlikely to resemble Western concepts of organizational structure. Nor, as cited by Boylan and Shore, are the decisions likely to be arrived at in uniform fashion. One additional characteristic of these programs is some provision for international participation, a theme which is echoed in the opening of LC CAP programs to participating institutions outside the United States.

Lessons there are in the CRL experience but—with its concentration on centralized holdings—the microform projects are not the seeds of future amplified cooperation. Libraries in the U. S., at least, are unlikely to commit substantial financing for an area collection which will be stored 1,000 miles away. Thus, the reports by Cason et al.[②] and by Lesnik[③] indicate a more likely avenue of distributed acquisitions foci (shades of the Farmington Plan). The two articles also afford a view of the two approaches to cooperation found in the U. S.: through professional area studies organizations and through professional library organizations. The paper by Cason, Easterbrook, and Scheven was originally three papers presented to the annual meeting of the African Studies Association. While such an organization assures a vitally concerned constituency, it also is a constituency with a limited voice in library decisions. The Research Libraries Group (RLG) is the parent body of the Research Libraries Information Network (RLIN) utility. Within this group, the problem of Third World Collections is reversed. Decisions are likely to have greater impact on policies in participating institutions but the support for Third World collections is greatly diluted and the priority which they receive reduced accordingly. Completing this bleak picture for the U. S. are the federal budget cuts anticipated for area studies and Title II-C (Strengthening Research Library Resources Program) of the Higher Education Act, both of which have provided substantial funding for Third World collections.

Despite these problems, the approaches described and proposed in the papers of Cason et al. and Lesnick are a glimmer of hope. Realistically, their papers do not propose a comprehensive solution to the need for cooperation. But they do describe current steps toward increasing cooperation. Unfortunately (from the editors' perspective), both approaches are located within RLG and will rely on RLIN for sharing. While meaningful cooperation is to be applauded, sitting such activities within RLIN excludes the larger number of libraries in the United States which participate in OCLC. During preparation of this issue, the research library organization in OCLC was queried as to possible plans for cooperation or even study groups of Third World collections held by participants. The response was negative and the indication was that no need was seen for such. Given this atmosphere, librarians and scholars in the U. S. must support the cooperative undertakings described for RLG and hope that the example set will stimulate greater consideration of additional avenues for other libraries and other Third World areas.

---

① Ray Boylan and Cecelia L. Shores, "Collecting Retrospective Materials from Developing Nations: A Cooperative Approach Through Microforms", *LAPT*, pp. 211 – 220.

② Maidel Cason, David L. Easterbrook, and Yvette Scheven, "Cooperative Acquisitions of Africana: Past Performance And Future Directions", *LAPT*, pp. 211 – 232.

③ Pauline Tina Lesnik, "The Research Libraries Group's Cooperative Acquisitions Program for South Asia", *LAPT*, pp. 233 – 238.

One of the goals prompting this issue was the wish to reestablish and enlarge the international approach to Third World acquisitions provided by the LIBER conference. Yet it has concluded with a discussion on cooperation in the U.S. No justification is given beyond the necessity to place one's own house in order before asking the neighborhood to improve. The article from the Australian National University provides information on cooperative efforts there. What is missing in all of this, and what is needed, is a concentrated consideration of international cooperation to address the difficulties described in the articles of this issue. Particular attention must be given to increasing concern for the question among Third World nations and for increasing understanding among Third World peoples through access to the intellectual and cultural products of each society, rather than just news stories—whether of the great accomplishment or the great failure type.

International bodies such as UNESCO and IFLA have substantially contributed to increasing awareness of the value of information among Third World nations. IDRC and some other national aid agencies have provided practical assistance in information sharing and in modern information technology. But, too often, questions such as technology transfer focus on the flow of information to the Third World. What needs to be considered, and what is the vital question of this issue, is the flow of information from the Third World. To this should be added the flow of information among Third World countries. Some indications of the problems and approaches have been given here. Whether these will continue for another decade, as has been the case since the LIBER conference, will depend on international concern and, of course, funding.

Funding for the Southeast Asia Collection And Research Resources at Ohio University[①]

As our topic requires a historical background, it is appropriate that we offer a historical prologue regarding the panel. Of the Southeast Asia Collections and study programs in the United States, that at Ohio University is the youngest, looking forward to its 20th anniversary next year. It is particularly appropriate that Professor Varner, our fellow contributor, and Dr. Provencher, the Chair, are from Northern Illinois University, also one of the younger Southeast Asia programs in the U. S. In tracing the genealogy of Southeast Asian Studies at Ohio University, the common ancestor is Cornell University but the immediate parentage is from Northern Illinois University.

When Ohio University's activist president, Vernon R. Alden, decided that, if Ohio University was going to be active in Southeast Asia (operating a model high school in Vietnam for U. S. AID), it was appropriate to learn and teach more about the area, a search for staff was begun in 1967. The leader selected to build the program was one of the founders of Northern Illinois University's Southeast Asia Program, Professor J Norman Parmer (now a professor of History at Trinity University), who was hired as Assistant Dean of Arts and Sciences for International Studies. Professor Parmer asked one of his colleagues at N. I. U., Professor Paul W. van der Veur, to join him as the Director of Southeast Asian Studies. To add just one more, of many, connections, in that year Northern Illinois University was seeking a librarian for its Southeast Asia Collection to replace Donald Clay Johnson, who had accepted a position at Yale University. One of the candidates that was interviewed was an Indonesia-born cataloger at Cornell University, Ms. Lian The (now Lian The-Mulliner). Following her interview in DeKalb, she was interviewed in Chicago by Professors Parmer and van der Veur. The upshot was that she accepted the position at Ohio University and has overseen the development of one of the major research collections on Southeast Asia in the U. S.

Others, particularly in history, have given attention to the development of Southeast Asian Studies in the U. S.[②] (although with less attention to genealogy). Our purpose is not to add to that effort but to focus on a micro study of a specific institution. Before that, however, it is perhaps appropriate to observe one significant similarity between Ohio University and Northern Illinois University, that is the stature of Southeast Asian Studies within the institution. At both universities, Southeast Asian Studies has emerged as the major area studies program and the Southeast Asian library collection at each is the major research collection in the university library. To this I would add that the University Presidents have also demonstrated a commitment to each university's involvement in the region. While we are loath to comment on other institutions, I believe that many of you can envy the primacy which Southeast Asia studies and research enjoy within the two institutions.

Southeast Asia Studies at Ohio University—Historical Highlights

To turn our gaze from descent to ascent, we return to Ohio University and the establishment of Southeast Asian Studies in the fall of 1967. Although now Distinguished Professor Emeritus John Cady had taught at Ohio University for several years and other faculty occasionally offered courses

---

[①] Co-Author: K. Mulliner
[②] The 1981 Annual Meeting of the American Historical Association in Los Angeles had a program on "Southeast Asia History R. I. P. ?" with papers presented by William Frederick (Ohio University) and Craig Lockard (University of Wisconsin—Green Bay) and comments by Bruce Cruikshank and Bob van Niel. A decade earlier, the late Jay Maryanov provided a broad assessment: Gerald S. Maiyanov, *The Condition of Southeast Asian Studies in the United States*: 1972 (Occasional Papers No. 3; DeKalb: Center for Southeast Asian Studies, 1974).

treating the region, there was nothing resembling a program of study and the library resources were hardly adequate to support even that relative neglect. While Professor van der Veur has since indicated that he regrets not having asked the University for greater assured funding for Southeast Asian materials, it is demonstrative of the development of Southeast Asian Studies at Ohio University that the Librarian was hired at the same time as the leadership of the program.

One other important trend which has shaped the direction of Southeast Asian Studies at Ohio University also dates from this early period. This has come to be known on campus as "the Malaysia Connection."① In 1968, six Malaysian students enrolled at Ohio University under a tripartite agreement among the Mara Institute of Technology (ITM), the Asia Foundation, and Ohio University. These were the first of thousands of Malaysians who have studied at Ohio University since, under a variety of sponsorships, and Ohio University offers its degrees in selected programs on the ITM campus. In recent years, students from ASEAN countries account for about 1/3 of the University's international student population (which comprises about 10% of the student body).

During this period, Ms. The was responsible for building an appropriate collection almost from scratch, but she also divided her time between work within the library and work in the Center for International Studies, establishing the close ties between the Southeast Asia Studies program and the library which continue to this day. She was also able to demonstrate the interrelationship between the library and research in the major works which she compiled jointly with the Director of Southeast Asia Studies.②

The next significant developments were in the 1970s. Emerging from its infancy, the Ohio University Library was able to join the Library of Congress administered Cooperative Acquisitions Program (CAP) in 1970, just as that program was expanding to cover materials from Malaysia and Singapore as well as Indonesia. Ohio University was partially able to capitalize on its relatively late membership as a result of Indiana University transferring uncataloged materials which it had received during participation in the 1960s (giving us a backlog almost from the beginning). Ohio University also took over Indiana's slot on the priority list.

It is difficult to overemphasize how important the CAP program has been to the growth of the Southeast Asia Collection at Ohio University but a review of our records also reveals how demanding it was in terms of budget. The history of the programs of the Jakarta Field Office is deserving of a separate treatment in the history of Southeast Asian Studies in the U. S. Suffice it to say that the doubling in cost of even partial participation in the program after only one year was traumatic for the then library administration. Unfortunately, that trauma has only slightly abated.

Offsetting the influx of materials (and bills) from CAP was the success of the Southeast Asia Program in gaining federal support from a grant under the National Defense Education Act (NDEA). The importance of that grant support, which continued for about 8 years, cannot be over-stated. Indeed, without that federal support, Southeast Asian Studies likely would have withered at Ohio University, especially as those years of support fell during a time that the University and the Library faced sharp enrollment drops accompanied by slashed budgets. The present stature of our Southeast Asia Collection owes much to that funding but even more so to the concern of the faculty associated with Southeast Asian Studies at Ohio University who were perceptive enough to recognize that of all of the things for which the grants might be used that library resources would yield the greatest benefits over the longest period. That this awareness was not unique to Ohio University was evident in a study of NDEA Centers for 1978 – 1979 which found that Southeast Asia Centers expended 21.7% of their budgets on library acquisitions

---

① Felix Gagliano, "The Malaysian Connection: Ohio University's Link to the World's Other Side is a Decade Old", *The Ohio University Alumnus Magazine*, March 1977, pp. 8 – 13.

② Lian The and Paul W. van der Veur, *Treasures and Trivia: Doctoral Dissertations Accepted by Universities in the United States* (Papers in International Studies, Southeast Asia Series No. 1; Athens: Ohio University Center for International Studies, 1968) and Lian The with Paul W. van der Veur, *The Verhandelingen van het Bataviaasch Genootschap: An Annotated Content Analysis* (Papers in International Studies, Southeast Asia Series No. 26; Athens: Ohio University Center for International Studies, 1973).

compared to an average of 11.1% for all Centers. ①

While this funding was crucial, we would also emphasize an additional consideration, one which was occasionally the subject of criticism in grant competitions: the decision to focus efforts on those parts of Southeast Asia most consistent with the foci of the Southeast Asia Program and the University, rather than inadequately attempt to blanket the region. This is not to ignore particular countries in Southeast Asia or to claim that some are more important than others. Rather it was and is a recognition that comprehensive collecting on the ten countries of the region is prohibitively expensive for any institution. Further it recognizes that researchers nationally are better served by the availability of research collections concentrating on specific countries, particularly if some coordinated distribution of collection development could be implemented, than by a number of collections ranging from moderate to mediocre. ②

While there have been various attempts at distributed collection development among the fewer than ten collections in the U.S. that focus on Southeast Asia, these remain in the exploratory phase. This is in rather marked contrast to the success achieved with SEASSI (Southeast Asian Studies Summer Institute) in cooperative summer language programs. In the meantime, each collection, depending on its budgetary resources, has been forced to emphasize some materials and areas and to neglect others. Lacking central coordination, Ohio University assayed the strengths of various collections in the U.S. and identified the countries of Brunei, Malaysia, and Singapore as unserved by a comprehensive research collection. Having identified this niche, the basis for a rational collection development policy was laid. Beyond seeking comprehensive coverage on these three countries, materials on Indonesia, the Philippines, and Thailand are collected (forming the core of an ASEAN focus) in decreasing priority and on the rest of Southeast Asia, with increasingly largely western language materials.

The budgetary rationale is obvious, but this concentration also facilitates the cultivation of relationships with librarians, scholars, and others concerned with the area and greater familiarity with research needs and interests. It has also evolved into the compilation of a bibliography of new materials on and from Brunei, Singapore, and Malaysia which appears regularly in *Berita*, the newsletter of the national Malaysia/Singapore/Brunei Studies Group.

The discussion of this collection development policy, which evolved over a number of years, marks an appropriate transition from history to the subject at hand, funding at Ohio University for the Southeast Asia Collection and research programs. Funding such as from federal grants is commonly referred to as "soft money", in contrast to regular operating allocations which are called "hard money". One of the lessons learned at Ohio University, during the budget and enrollment crises of the mid-1970s, alluded to above, was just how "soft" that hard money could be. In fact during one year the library, but not the Southeast Asia Collection which enjoyed grant support, was forced to forego the purchase of monographs. When revisions for the regulations covering NDEA centers resulted in the loss of federal funding, that source of support also disappeared. It is relevant to note that, just as the library identified a niche to serve national scholarship and research, the Southeast Asia Studies Program had similarly emphasized its unique capacities to provide well prepared students with masters degrees to other institutions, to provide strong background at the masters level for those seeking to work in Southeast Asia, and to stimulating awareness of Southeast Asia outside the centers (what is commonly termed outreach). While Southeast Asian foci were available in a few doctoral areas, there seemed no overwhelming demand for additional doctoral programs. Unfortunately for the university, the new federal

---

① Ann I. Schneider, "NDEA Centers: How They Use Their Federal Money", in *President's Commission on Foreign Language and International Studies: Background Papers and Studies* (Washington, D.C.: U.S. Department of Health, Education, and Welfare, 1979), p.174.

② The importance of distributed collection development is cited from a number of sources in William E. Carter," International Studies and Research Library Needs, *President's Commission on Foreign Language and Area Studies: Background Papers and Studies* (Washington, D.C.: Department of Health, Education and Welfare, 1979), pp.177-178. While the citations are concentrated on East Asian collections, they are equally applicable to Southeast Asia.

regulations indicated that doctoral programs were to be the basis in identifying centers.

Having been spared much of the crisis of the mid-1970s that shook the rest of the university, failure to continue federal funding shocked the Southeast Asia Studies program and the library. While care had been taken, as far as possible, to transfer positions from soft funding to regular university positions, it was recognized among the faculty that the greatest threat was to the library. If the Collection, which had emerged as a major resource under federal funding, were not to be severely crippled, alternative funding would be needed. This was especially true for continued meaningful participation in CAP where reducing or halting acquisitions for a year can result in the loss of irreplaceable resources.

Ohio University Responses

It was at this point that the strong support of the President and senior administrators, alluded to in our opening, and became crucial. Interim emergency funding was approved to cover the cost of CAP participation and for retention of a Southeast Asia Cataloging position through a competitive internal program of project grants.

It was also at this time that the pioneering "Tun Abdul Razak Chair in Southeast Asian Studies" was created. Through matching funding from the Malaysian Government and American corporations doing business in Malaysia, earnings provide for the presence of a distinguished Malaysian professor on our campus each year. This year we have been very pleased that the Tun Razak Chair holder is Professor Zainal Abidin bin Abdul Wahid of the History Department of the National University of Malaysia. In addition to the usual provisions in an endowed Chair, this also provides a special allocation each year for library acquisitions.

Challenges & Responses

With this historical introduction, we now will expand our view while retaining a local focus consonant with our theme. Our rationale is that, with so few collections offering any depth on Southeast Asia, each of the collections is de facto a national resource center. Moreover, to continue to grow, each must consider the national community of users to justify such growth.

In describing funding, we will focus on funding for libraries as the basis for most research activity. This reflects our area of greatest experience but it also, we believe, targets the area of greatest neglect.[①] While funding for research from various sources (SSRC, ACLS, Fulbright, etc.), the major continuing external source of funding for library collections in the U.S. has been for National Centers under Title VI of the Higher Education Act. We will return to this point later.

Before discussing approaches to funding for library collections, two points should be emphasized. The first is that in discussing funding, we do not necessarily mean money, that is, gifts in kind can be an important means of building and maintaining collections. Depending on the nature of such gifts, they can contribute to the growth of the collection with little or minimal acquisitions cost to the collection and thus free money for other purposes.

The second point, partially the antithesis of the first, is that the cost of acquiring materials is of secondary importance to collection growth. It is a rule of thumb in libraries that acquisitions budgets account for 30 to 35% of a library budget. To be of use to researchers the materials must be made available, preferably easily accessible via national bibliographic utilities such as RLIN or OCLC. Even more striking in this regard, a single title acquired under CAP may cost $4 or $5 but the processing costs will be many times that figure ($100 per title was the figure given for the

---

[①] An indication of the neglect is evident in the study by Robert A. McCaughey, *International Studies and Academic Enterprise: A Chapter in the Enclosure of American Learning* (New York: Columbia University Press, 1984) which concentrates on international expertise and the production of graduates with Ph. D. s but ignores the resources on which research, Ph. D. or otherwise depend. There is no entry for libraries in the detailed index to the volume. This may partially explain why the Head of Ohio University's Southeast Asia Collection entitled her bibliography of dissertations on Southeast Asia *Treasures and Trivia* (see fn. 3 above), to the chagrin of some reviewers.

Library of Congress a few years ago). In addressing funding, consideration must be given to processing and servicing the materials as well as simply acquiring them. Discussions among Southeast Asia collection curators and librarians at the eight universities with identified collections indicate that significant cataloging and processing backlogs, especially of vernacular materials, are the rule rather than the exception. The result, for the research community, is that the materials may be no more accessible than if they had not been acquired. [1]

1. Local Support. Although funding will be addressed from a number of perspectives, the local situation is the most critical. Without the support of the library and the university administration as well as the faculty, the other approaches to funding which we will discuss will be unlikely. At the same time, it is at the local university level that a collection is likely to be most directly challenged. To the extent that it depends on operating funds and even undesignated non-operating funds, it is in competition with most other academic areas and programs. Without regard to the size of a particular institution's budget, an area collection, in this case a Southeast Asia Collection, must be able to justify its slice of that particular pie. Moreover, with considerable institutional variation, there will be ongoing challenges to the size of that slice, no matter how great or small.

Translating this discussion to Ohio University, we have prepared graphs, focusing on the current acquisitions budget, which indicates how that budget is spent (Figure 1) and how it is financed (Figure 2). We have mentioned our collection development foci (Brunei, Singapore, and Malaysia) and as a result acquisitions through the Southeast Asia Cooperative Acquisitions Program in Jakarta (referred to simply as CAP in this paper, although we recognize that there are many other CAP programs). Within that program, the acquisitions money divides 2:1 for Brunei, Singapore, and Malaysia materials compared to Indonesian materials. Yet Indonesia is the next most important area of focus. That so many Indonesian materials are now microfiched in New Delhi, subscription to the Library of Congress Photoduplication offering of Southeast Asia microfiche is a significant adjunct to our CAP participation. And the Southeast Asia Microform project (SEAM) is important in obtaining and preserving rare research materials but also in supporting doctoral research. As was evident in the historical discussion, the remainder of the money is spent for current western language materials on the area (many of these materials are acquired also from the disciplinary allocations but identifying a specific amount was not possible) and for some retrospective buying and research collections in microformat as well as newspapers (a not insignificant expense) and other materials from other countries in the region. Also, these graphs reflect expenditures and not the value of gifts in kind.

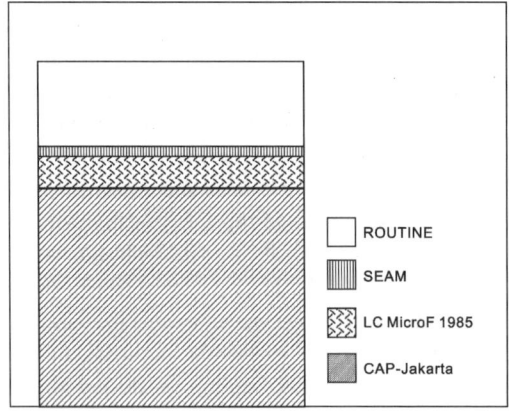

Figure 1　Ohio University Southeast Asia Collection 1985 – 1986 Acquisitions Budget

---

[1]　The most recent assessment of area studies collections is the chapter, "Library And Information Resources" in Richard D. Lambert et al. *Beyond Growth: The Next Stage in Language and Area Studies* (Washington, D. C.: Association of American Universities, 1984), pp. 232 – 259. Pages 244 – 247 specifically address staffing and cataloging backlogs.

Dollar figures for the expenditures are omitted as these change substantially from year to year (generally upward, with the exception of SEAM) but the proportions are illustrative. Implicit in the graph is that the first three expenses (are basically fixed costs) while expansions and contractions in budgets mostly affect the "routine" portion, increasing or decreasing the ability to buy retrospective materials and vernacular materials from other areas.

As Figure 2 evidences, meeting the cost of the expenditures in Figure 1 requires a blending of funding sources. The routine allocation is the share of operating funding for acquisitions identified for the Southeast Asia Collection (about 1.1%), The special allocation is also from the operating budget (about 1% of the 1985/86 budget) to assure continuation in the CAP programs. The funding from Razak Chair is based on endowment earnings. As it is subject to variation, it is shown at its minimum level. Depending on other needs of the Tun Razak Professor, it can increase 50% or more from that illustrated. These funds are used to intensify our efforts at comprehensive collecting on Malaysia and to support special research efforts of the Tun Razak Professor. The endowment earnings reflect our current fund raising campaign (discussed below). The proportion reflects the current year allocation but actually would be over twice the level shown when the endowment has been invested for the full earning period. The small "other" reflects private gifts to support the collection.

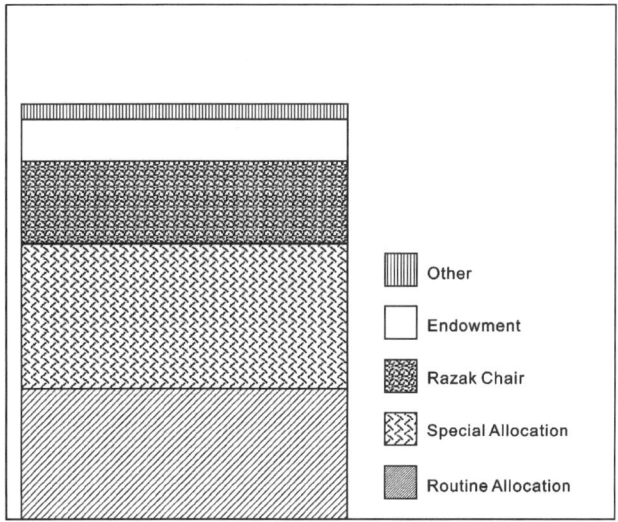

Figure 2   Ohio University Southeast Asia Collection Funding for 1985 – 1986 Acquisitions

to assure continuation in the CAP programs. The funding from Razak Chair is based on endowment earnings. As it is subject to variation, it is shown at its minimum level. Depending on other needs of the Tun Razak Professor, it can increase 50% or more from that illustrated. These funds are used to intensity our efforts of the Tun Razak Professor. The endowment earnings reflects the current fund raising campaign (discussed below). The proportion reflects the currant year allocation but actually would be over twice the level shown when the endowment has been invested for the full earning period. The small "other" reflect private gifts to support the collection.

As noted, other operating funds are used to acquire Southeast Asian materials from disciplinary allocations,[1] library-wide endowment funding for special collections, and one-time money for research collections.

Without dwelling on these graphs, which are simply selective snapshots of a single year, it should be clear that local funding can require considerable imagination. It is also obvious that what we are

---

[1]   Ohio University's approach to allocating acquisitions funds in general is described in K. Mulliner, "The Acquisitions Allocation Formula at Ohio University," *Library Acquisitions: Practice and Theory*, Vol. X, 4 (1986), pp. 315 – 327.

calling local funding is not entirely local funding. This affords a transition to other funding areas.

2. Private, Corporate, and Foundation Support. Having experienced how "soft" both grant and operating funding can be, the Library and the University are currently engaged in a campaign to raise a substantial endowment for the Southeast Asia Collection, the earnings from which will provide for the acquisition and processing of materials. It would be premature to report in detail on this effort at this time. As was evident in the last graph on local funding, earnings from this campaign have begun to be available to support the acquisitions effort, but the goal of the campaign is to generate sufficient earnings to contribute to the cost of processing and bringing researchers and research materials together as well.

Figure 2 also indicates the role of the endowment for the Tun Abdul Razak Chair for Southeast Asian Studies in supporting the Collection. While the Malaysian Government played a key role in developing and supporting the Chair, American corporations doing business in Malaysia provided two-thirds of the funding. We continue to be appreciative of their contributions which continue to support the activities of the Chair and the Collection in perpetuity (see acknowledgement of donors in Appendix A).

In concluding the brief discussion of this source of funding, we would be remiss if we did not caution that considerable time and travel by senior University administrators were required to achieve the goal. While the donors indicated varying degrees of support, both in their efforts and the amounts given, a significant factor in the success of the campaign was the demonstrated commitment by the University at the highest levels, not to neglect the manifest support of the Malaysian Government, which convinced donors of the importance of the Tun Razak Chair.

It is also important to note that the beneficiaries of these donations have been scholars and researchers throughout the nation, the thousands of Malaysian students studying in North America, and the members of the Ohio University community who have had the opportunity to consult with the distinguished Malaysian professors who have been named to the Chair to date or have used the materials acquired by the Southeast Asia Collection (at Ohio University) through interlibrary loan, or, as not infrequently occurs, through urgent telephone requests to the Collection for information.

3. Southeast Asia. The Malaysian Government was particularly farsighted in its support for the Tun Razak Chair. But this is not the only example of how governments, organizations, and individuals can support Southeast Asia Collections. In recent years the Malaysian Government has also recognized that it is important to provide the thousands of students which it sends to North America with authoritative information on what is happening in Malaysia. As American newspapers (even the best) are most likely to provide regular reports on Southeast Asia only when there is a particular crisis—and that in a manner aimed at the American reader, Malaysia has provided for regular air mail subscriptions to Malaysian newspapers for universities with sufficient Malaysian students enrolled. This, of course, provides the students with a basis to interpret the crisis news which they receive in American newspapers and to help the students remain in touch. From a library perspective, in which air-mailed newspapers can be a substantial expense, even through CAP, the newspapers are a valuable addition. The Indonesian Government, through the Embassy, has also provided special gifts to Southeast Asia Collections of special series on Indonesian and local language literature.

These are but examples of the potential for mutually beneficial cooperation between Southeast Asian individuals, groups and governments. An even more important effort may be the creation last May of the Malaysian Resource Center at Ohio University, which was dedicated by Minister of Education Abdullah Ahmad Badawi. The Resource Center represents a further stage of cooperation between the Collection and Malaysian agencies and organizations. The goal, approved at several levels but difficult to implement (librarians will appreciate that government officials and diplomats do not always understand the needs of a library, especially for continuity), is to have Ohio University as a depository in the U. S. for government publications. News of the Center has also attracted deposits from a number of nongovernmental organizations. Of particular note was the deposit of a number of historic films from the Malaysian Embassy which otherwise would have been discarded. These have since been transferred to videotape. In moving to assure accessibility of Southeast Asian resources in the U. S., we think this is a fertile field for exploration.

Having identified some of the possibilities, we would be remiss if we did not also mention an important hazard. Despite some concerns expressed at the time of its establishment by informed scholars, the Tun Razak Chair has provided benefits to Malaysia and to Ohio University without compromising the integrity of either (see description in Appendix B). Similarly, the Malaysian Resource Center receives valuable support in kind from the Malaysian Government but it is not a governmental information agency but a research and media resource of and about the people and nation of Malaysia. While we have not been troubled by financing or associations which would compromise Ohio University, the library or the Southeast Asia Collection, it is always a concern.

4. International. We use this term to refer to non-Southeast Asia funding and to international agencies. We have little to say about it beyond noting that Southeast Asia nations are not the only nations that rely on the U. S. to educate their scholars and researchers. It remains to be seen whether the governments, organizations, and corporations in these other nations will realize that investing in the research resources that these students and researchers use in the U. S. is an investment in their future. At the international level, UNESCO was instrumental in helping Ohio University to develop and refine a pioneering internship program[①] for library science faculty from Southeast Asia which continues to serve professional librarians from the region and other parts of Asia as well as to provide contacts and expertise in processing and handling Southeast Asia materials. Such funding is no longer available but it remains an area that cannot be ignored.

5. Federal. At a time when Gramm-Rudman-Hollings has precipitated virtual panic, we are contrarians in discussing the present and potential federal support of Southeast Asian resources and research. In the first place, we unlikely would be here today were it not for past federal support as an NDEA/FLAS center, as apparent in the history section of this paper. Also, we are presently in the midst of a cataloging project supported under Title II-C of the Higher Education Act which will both greatly alleviate our backlog and will provide the basis for national online access to the wealth of information in the Southeast Asia microfiche produced in New Delhi. Our project focuses on the pre-AACR2 fiche[②] and was intended to provide access to the fiche that Delhi could not. Whether scholars will receive access to the remainder (those produced since 1982) is reportedly threatened by present and pending forced budget reductions.

Without entering into partisan issues, one of the international areas reportedly least threatened is the Caribbean Initiative, yet when this thrust was announced it was likened to creating Singapore in Central America. That, of course, was before the present economic slump in Singapore. The allusion was evidence of a lack of understanding of Southeast Asia in general and Singapore in particular. Without belaboring it, the previous identification of international programs as "National Defense Education" was not entirely inappropriate. We share the contention of many of the papers presented to the Presidents Commission on Foreign Language and Area Studies that this country needs people and research familiar with different world areas and those people and that research depends upon access to comprehensive and timely information from and about the areas.

As Dr. Senese has discussed the role of Title II-C, we would only emphasize the importance of

---

① Described in Hwa-Wei Lee and K. Mulliner, "International Exchange of Librarians and the Ohio University Internship Program," *College & Research Libraries News*, Vol. X (November 1982), pp. 345 – 348; and Hwa-Wei Lee, "International Library Internships: An Effective Approach to Co-operation," *International Library Review*, Vol. XVII (1985), pp. 17 – 25, which is also available as "Library Internships: A New Approach to Cooperation," in *Areas of Cooperation in Library Development in Asian and Pacific Regions*, (Athens, Ohio: Chinese-American Librarians Association, 1985), pp. 21 – 27.

② About one-half of the activity in Ohio University's present HEA Title II-C Grant is aimed at providing full AACR2 cataloging in machine readable form for Southeast Asia microfidie produced in New Delhi prior to the implementation of AACR2 by the Library of Congress. This is being done as a Major Microform Project through OCLC, which permits other institutions with the fiche to add holdings at a fraction of the cost of separate cataloging. It also provides a tape which can be loaded into RLIN for institutions using that utility. "AACR2" stand for the Second Edition of the Anglo American Cataloging Rules, which made substantial changes in the way information is entered in machine-readable format. With machine-readable records, consistency in entries is essential to assure fullest retrieval of information sought.

the two grants which we have received under that Title to increase the availability of our Collection nationally.

We focus instead on Title VI, which is specifically intended to strengthen international and area awareness. In the history section, we indicated that support for libraries under Title VI was significant as a proportion of the grants which represented a permanent investment in the research resources of the nation (21.7% of the grants to Southeast Asia Centers in 1978/79) and for our Collection in particular. Unfortunately, this has not necessarily been the case. Of the eight universities supporting Southeast Asia Collections, three have been designated as National Centers. As a generalization, a Department of Education paper has documented that for all Title VI Centers, library expenditures as a proportion of the federal grants fell from 21.2% in 1973/74 to 15.9% in 1981/82. Combining Southeast Asia and the Pacific Islands, it noted that an average of only 4.5% of the Title VI funds went for library expenditures (least of any of the world areas) but these accounted for an average of 15.2% of library expenditures for the area collection (highest of any world area). ①A more recent compilation, by Dr. Ann Schneider of the Department of Education, reports that Title VI Southeast Asia Centers spent an average of 16.9% of the grants for library acquisitions (back to highest among the regions) and 10.4% for library staff. ②

Our purpose is not to criticize centers but to emphasize the lesson learned at Ohio University, when a Federal grant disappears, the one major legacy is the library collection. Moreover, such collections, built with Federal funds, should be truly National Centers, serving researchers spread throughout the nation. To address this Bill Frederick, a member of the Ohio University faculty, two years ago suggested a rethinking of the "Center Concept" as it applies to Southeast Asia. He emphasized that with only eight centers and programs concentrating on Southeast Asia that "all centers should be treated as national repositories and receive basic support for, in particular, library and other materials."③ At the same conference, Shiro Saito called for "the formation of a consortium of Southeast Asia collections" to engage in "a nationally coordinated collection plan to acquire systematically Southeast Asian research materials". ④ While we find the suggested levels of funding ($3,000 – $5,000) and matching ($800 – $1,500) impossibly low, the concept has merit and would be a natural continuation of current discussions within the Collection Development Sub-Committee of the Committee on Research Materials on Southeast Asia (CORMOSEA).

Finally, considering Federal programs, the role of the Library of Congress and its Jakarta Field Office cannot be neglected. Cutbacks in the funding for the Jakarta office, just as a new director has come on board, would be a severe blow to CAP participants for Southeast Asia. The program is significant for both acquisitions and cataloging. If anything greater attention should be given to opportunities afforded by microcomputers to increase productivity and for Jakarta to provide machine readable records to LC which can be added to national online databases such as RLIN and OCLC.

6. Access. Previous mention has been made of the importance of access to materials. In citing access as a challenge, we are concerned that researchers can identify materials, can afford to borrow or otherwise use them, and have as full access as possible internationally as well as nationally. In identifying materials, the problem is both the backlogs in cataloging and processing and the problems for institutions in RLIN or OCLC to share records with those in the other utility.

---

① Ann I. Schneider, "Libraries of Title VI Centers: Some Impressions and Questions", unpublished paper provided by U. S. Department of Education, April 13, 1982.

② Ann I. Schneider, "Center Budgets — Analysis of 1983 – 1984 Data," Memo to Directors of Title VI Centers and Fellowships Programs, U. S. Department of Education, Center for International Education, June 24, 1985.

③ William H. Frederick, "Adapting the Area Study Center Concept to New Needs", in Ronald A. Morse, ed. *Southeast Asian Studies: Options for the Future* (Papers presented at a conference held at the Woodrow Wilson International Center for Scholars, March 26, 1984; Lanham, Md.: University Press of America, 1984), p. 92. Emphasis in original.

④ Shiro Saito, "Progress and Needs for Research Tools and Resources in Southeast Asia Studies", in *Ibid.*, p. 154. Emphasis in original.

For users outside the eight academic Southeast Asia Centers, the problem is even greater. We would hope that the Linked Systems Project might eventually bridge this chasm on a national (and possibly international) basis, but at present print sources seem the only solution. ① Beyond identifying materials, users need to be able to obtain them. This is particularly critical for graduate students, the next generation of researchers, who are severely pressed to meet the interlibrary lending charges imposed by institutions housing some of the Southeast Asia Collections. There is no easy solution in sight, particularly as the collections at some of the larger institutions, apparently are following an institutional policy in which they have a small voice. In our own institution, we strive to maintain the principle of free access to information by not charging other than for photocopy charges or in reciprocity to those institutions that impose a charge on our institution.

The question of international cooperation remains wide open. Various approaches have been made from the U. S. , Australia, and Southeast Asia, but little concrete has been accomplished to date. New initiatives are obviously needed.

7. New and Special Collecting Problems. Time and technology are also bringing new challenges to Southeast Asia Collections. In the history of Southeast Asian studies in this country, we are at a point where many of the pioneering researchers have retired or are nearing retirement. This seems an area deserving special attention if potentially valuable ephemeral materials and field notes are not to be lost to future scholars. Obviously those associated with a particular collection or institution may wish to leave their work with that institution but there are many more across the U. S. whose lifework deserves preservation. We have made small steps in this direction, but it deserves national consideration in conjunction with distributed collection development.

Technology is also providing a proliferation of formats in which materials need to be collected: beyond the traditional audio-visual media are data tapes, recordings of events (cultural and historical), microcomputer software, and a range of video products to name a few. We have begun piecemeal to acquire these but they present an entire range of problems in terms of systems (e. g. , VHS or Beta, PAL or other video systems) to actually use them. This takes collections into new areas and is virtually impossible to undertake on a single institution basis. The Malaysian Resource Center represents one approach at Ohio University. Also reflecting the new roles, in 1984 an alumnus presented the Library with a sizeable collection of Southeast Asian artifacts, reflecting the art and artisanship of Southeast Asian peoples. ② These, together with previous gifts of regalia of daily life, are being prepared for exhibit as an adjunct of our Southeast Asian Collection.

8. New Responses. Two years ago, Bill Frederick called for the establishment of a national institute of advanced studies for Southeast Asia. In the absence of any response, he has now stimulated the formation of one such institute at Ohio University. Sri (or SRI—Southeast Asia Research Institute) is still in its developmental phases. Part of its purpose is to respond to some of the new challenges discussed above which fall outside some of the traditional roles and missions of Southeast Asia Collections. It is too early to provide a detailed description. Our purpose in noting it here is that attempts are being made to respond in new ways to the challenges identified above.

Conclusion

In focusing on Ohio University and especially the library, we have responded to the topic which we were asked to address. We are proud of some of the things that we have accomplished, disappointed in what has not, and cowed by what remains. In focusing on Ohio University, our

---

① Examples of printed materials which assist in identifying and obtaining materials include the Library of Congress, *Accessions List, Southeast Asia* (Jakarta: Library of Congress Office) and *The John M. Echols Collection on Southeast Asia Accessions List* (Ithaca: Southeast Program, Cornell University). Similar information but with articles and analytic entries can be found in some country newsletters. We are most conversant with the "Malaysia/Singapore/Brunei Bibliography", begun by the Collection at Yale University but produced in recent years by the Ohio University Southeast Asia Collection, in *Berita; Newsletter of the Malaysia Singapore/ Brunei Studies Group* (Philadelphia: John Lent for the M/S/B Studies Group).

② The catalog for that collection is: Lian The-Mulliner, *Southeast Asia Through Ethnic Art: The Russell R. Ross Collection at Ohio University* (Athens: Ohio University Library 1984).

intention is not to claim particular contributions but to begin what we hope will be an ongoing communications process among the few institutions in the country concerned with Southeast Asia and the many more researchers concerned with the field.

APPENDIX A
OHIO UNIVERSITY THANKS THE DONORS TO THE TUN ABDUL RAZAK CHAIR

Corporate Contributors
Leadership gifts
Goodyear Malaysia Berhad
Esso Companies in Malaysia
American International Group
IBM World Trade Corporation
NCR Malaysia Sdn. Bhd.
RCA Send Irian Berhad
RJ. Reynolds Tobacco Co. Sdn. Bhd.
3M Malaysia Sdn. Bhd.
Johnson & Johnson Sdn. Bhd.

Major Gifts
General Instrument Sdn. Bhd.
Colgate-Palmolive (Malaysia) Sdn. Bhd.
Warner-Lambert (Mfg) Sdn. Bhd.
Caltex OH Malaysia Ltd.
The Chase Manhattan Bank, N. A.
Citibank, N. A.
Ford Motor Company of Malaysia Sdn, Bhd.

Special Gifts
Monsanto Fund
CPC (Malaysia) Sdn. Bhd.
Gillette Companies in Malaysia
Mobil Oil Malaysia Sdn. Bhd.
Uniroyal Malaysian Plantations Sdn. Bhd.
Union Carbide Malaysia Sdn. Bhd.
Ogilvy & Mather (M) Sdn. Bhd.
Burson-Marsteller (Malaysia) Sdn. Bhd.
Bristol-Myers (Malaysia) Sdn. Bhd.

APPENDIX B

About the Tun Abdul Razak Chair

In March of 1980, the Malaysian Ministry of Education announced in Kuala Lumpur and Washington D. C. the establishment of the Tun Abdul Razak Chair in Southeast Asian studies at Ohio University. Jointly endowed by a US $350,000 grant from the Government of Malaysia and by matching funds generously contributed by public-spirited American firms with operations in Malaysia, this Chair represents an extraordinary nation-to-nation commitment in higher education.

Under the agreement with Ohio University, Malaysia annually nominates prominent visiting scholars from a wide variety of academic fields to go to Ohio University to teach, to conduct research, and to travel to academic and other meetings around the nation. As intellectual envoys to the United States from Southeast Asia, these scholars will leave a lasting legacy in America: a new appreciation of our similarities, a new respect for our differences.

The first holder of the Tun Razak Chair, the world-renowned Islamic scholar, Professor Syed Mohd. Naquib al-Attas, served with distinction during the academic year of 1981 – 1982. He measurably advanced the purposes of the Chair's founders which are to expand American knowledge of the cultural, economic, social, and political life and history of Malaysia and Southeast Asia.

Professor al-Attas made substantial progress on a book of commentary on the great Islamic thinker, Al-Raniri, which will give new insight into the history of Southeast Asia and the impact of Islam in the Malay world. He taught courses, lectured in other parts of the nation, advised Ohio University librarians in their quest to strengthen further an already first-rate Southeast Asian collection, and served as an advisor/consultant to Malaysian and American students and scholars. The second distinguished Tun Razak Professor, soon to be announced, will build upon the foundation of excellence laid by Professor Naquib al-Attas.

The concept of the Razak Chair grew out of the vision and cooperation of many individuals and organizations. Without the inspiration and support of Tun Dr. Hussein Onn, Datuk Seri Dr. Mahathir, Datuk Musa Hitam and other Malaysian leaders, the project could not have been realized. The generous support of the civic-minded American companies being honored here tonight is an essential link in this unique partnership in international education. The leaders of these U. S. firms, here and at home, see this liaison as a natural corollary to their economic partnership with the people and government of Malaysia.

By every measure, the Tun Abdul Razak Chair is a remarkable success. Ohio University is proud to be part of this innovative program in Malaysian-American relations and understanding.

第二部分 目录控制

Section II Bibliographic Control

Scholarly Publications:
Considerations on Bibliographic Control And Dissemination①

This paper discusses certain factors affecting the publishers' responsibilities in catering to the academic community. These factors and responsibilities relate to the process of information transfer, and in following the suggested procedures publishers will find that benefits are opened to themselves as well as to their clientele. Addressed to publishers of scholarly material, it is hoped that this paper can encourage greater cooperation among all publishers, their distributors, and their customers. It may be that publishers, in universities especially, are already aware of the factors under discussion, and have effective procedures of their own. They should be further encouraged, therefore, to take a lead in their countries to ensure wider implementation of the procedures presented here.

Scholarly publications are expensive and have a limited if assured appeal; as contributions to knowledge they have nonetheless a world-wide appeal. It is therefore important for their publishers to make contact with their potential audience as quickly and as efficiently as possible. Publishers in the scholarly field have a duty, in terms of the spread of knowledge and of the educational, intellectual, and research aspects of national development, to contribute to the efficient transfer of information. It is library and documentation services that are of major concern in this process, but the procedures to be implemented will bring publishers closer to the research function of libraries and their users.

Through UNESCO, many basic recommendations regarding national libraries, deposit, and Universal Bibliographic Control (UBC) have recently seen widespread implementation, followed now by the review of bibliographic standards. The implications for publishers need to be adumbrated too.

International Standard Book Numbers (ISBN)

The ISBN scheme grew out of the need to standardize the various systems of numbering that publishers had been utilizing over many years to control and simplify the files identifying their books. It was first put into practice in Britain in 1967. In 1969 the International Standards Organization, with the approval of 23 countries, ratified the scheme, and ISO Standard No. 2108 – 1972 (E) was drawn up to coordinate and standardize the use of book numbers. Different countries (such as Britain and Australia②) have their own national ISBN agencies. The International ISBN Agency was set up in the Library of State of the Prussian Cultural Foundation in 1972. Its task is to co-ordinate the work of the national ISBN agencies, and to extend the scheme to non-participating countries, where cooperation amongst publishers, publishers' associations, and national bibliographic services should be instrumental in establishing eventual participation.

The ISBN itself is a ten-digit number divided into four parts (the letters ISBN should precede):

---

① Co-author: Stephen W. Massil
② The Australian Standard Book Numbering Agency has issued the following pamphlet: *International Standard Book Numbering in Australia*. 3rd ed. Canberra: Australian Standard Book Numbering Agency, National Library of Australia, 1973. ISBN 0 642 99004 2.

(a) group identifier
(b) publisher prefix
(c) title number
(d) check digit (for computer manipulation)

A number is unique to a title in a particular edition, and is unchangeable. The number appears on the back of the title page and perhaps on the book-jacket and elsewhere. It is used in all publicity and listings. The advantages for publishers, suppliers, and libraries are great, since they provide an efficient and economical method of communication amongst them.

International Standard Serial Numbers (ISSN)

Similar in concept and purpose to the ISBN for books, the ISSN for periodical and serials publications in the widest sense has arisen in direct response to the needs of UBC, and the system has been integrated with UNISIST activities (UNESCO's World Science Information Programme) in its International Serials Data Systems (ISDS) network. Again, centers for registering titles are being set up either nationally or regionally, and the resulting files are being coordinated by an International Centre in Paris.① In countries where centers are operating, publishers should seek their ISSNs from these. Otherwise they should notify the International Centre for the numbers to be assigned. Publishers may already have been notified by R. R. Bowker of ISSNs allocated. These appear in *Ulrich's International Periodicals Directory*② and *Ulrich's Irregular Serials and Annuals*,③ and the numbers have been included in the ISDS base file.

The ISSN is an eight-digit divided into two parts separated by a hyphen (and preceded by the letters ISSN); the eighth digit is a check-digit. The number is not publisher-oriented and relates to a particular title uniquely. (In Ulrich's, country or group identifiers precede the ISSN as printed, and do not form part of the ISSN). The number should appear on the cover or title-page of every issue, and in all publicity and listings. Monographs that are published in series need to show their respective ISBN and the ISSN of the series.

Bibliographic Control

Once the framework for the numbering systems has been set up in each country, the onus on publishers in complying with the requirements will be slight. There will be advantages in continuity of identification and ordering, and in other respects, if publishers can reserve numbers at the pre-publication stage; it is especially important to have the ISSN on the first issue as well as on subsequent ones. Adherence to the systems and standards④ will achieve a great step forward in respect of bibliographic control. This has nothing to do with censorship and regulation of the press (in the countries where publishers are obliged to obtain licenses, a virtue could be made of the arrangement to ensure allocation of the standard numbers by this means). Its purpose is to achieve awareness of what materials have been published, and to disseminate as much information concerning them as possible and as rapidly as possible.

The prime authority for bibliographic control should be vested in national bibliographic services, which in many countries are now operated within the national library. The main means at the disposal of the national bibliography for achieving this control is in most countries some sort of copyright deposit legislation⑤ whereby publishers are liable to deposit at least one copy of every

---

① ISDS International Centre, 20 Rue Bauchaumont, 75002 Paris, France. It publishes: *Bulletin de l'ISDS / ISDS Bulletin*, v. 1, no. 1 (1974). ISSN 0300-3000.
② 15th ed. New York, 1974.
③ 2nd ed. New York, 1973.
④ Following the ISBN and ISSN standards, there are the *International Standard Bibliographic Description for Monographs and for Serials*, *ISBD* (M) and *ISBD* (S) (London: IFLA Committee on Cataloging, 1974), which are being discussed by the national libraries of the world. These do not affect publishers directly, but they should be sufficiently aware of them in the interest of clear presentations of their title-pages and publicity materials.
⑤ E. g., Singapore. *Laws, statutes Chapter 224. Printers and Publishers Act.* Revised ed. 1970.

publication (issued for sale) with the national library (in Britain, the obligation is for six copies, one each to a group of institutions). In its turn the national bibliography is deputed to publish a listing of items received in this way; the work of the national library is severely hampered when the legislation is not strict, and where publishers are lax.

The importance of the measures for bibliographic awareness and control should be compounded by the attempts made by the Library of Congress in its shared cataloguing programme of the last fifteen years, and by the presence of its acquisitions agents — one for south-east Asia, for instance, based in Jakarta — in different parts of the world. The National Library of Australia also has an acquisitions office in Jakarta. Their acquisitions go to build up "area" collections in their respective libraries, and the listings published[1] are relied upon by other libraries for selection and other purposes. Local national bibliographies[2] are used in other parts of the world for the same purposes.

There should be a clear duty for publishers of scholarly material, which may have relevance for world knowledge as well as "area" study, to comply with deposit laws in terms of the needs of national development; the benefit of publicity via the national bibliography, and dissemination of this and other listings abroad, should also be an incentive.

Cataloguing In Publication (CIP)

A further development to consolidate bibliographic control, undergoing development in Britain, the U.S.A., and most actively in Australia in particular, is the procedure whereby publishers notify the national bibliography as early as possible of the publications they are planning, not merely so that the ISBN can be assigned and registered well in advance but so that preliminary cataloguing data can be prepared and printed in the book itself. This, of course, is an experiment geared to library needs, with the supremacy of centralized cataloguing as a goal, but the CIP information also ensures advance appearance in the National Bibliography itself.

Publishers of scholarly works are probably in the best position to co-operate with national bibliographic services in this part of the world, and to undertake such an experiment here. Some such development may seem worth initiating.

Serials

The remarks on bibliographic control apply equally to books and serials. Certain desiderata more specific to serials publishing, especially as they are more likely in the scholarly context to be published by societies and institutions than by commercial publishers, need to be treated separately.

It should be standard practice for each article in a journal to be preceded by a brief abstract or summary. Contents pages should be clear. There should be a title page (or its substitute — a cover or masthead) conveying both the title, the details of the issuing body and editorial board, numbering statement, and frequency. If an ISSN has been assigned, this should appear in the requisite place, and the ISDS key title statement associated with this number may also appear with lesser prominence. Style of presentation is optional, but references and abbreviations in articles and citations should follow recognized standards. A regular index should also be supplied with each completed volume or group of volumes. These details may be obvious, but there is a need to mention them. Standards of editing of scientific journals in South-East Asia have recently been the subject of a series of UNESCO courses. One of the special emphases of these courses was bibliographic control. Copies of the draft lecture notes[3] are available from the UNESCO Field

---

[1] E. g. Accessions List: *Indonesia, Malaysia, Singapore and Brunei*. Library of Congress. National Program for Acquisitions and Cataloguing (Jakarta: Library of Congress Office). ISSN 0041–7742.

[2] E. G. *Singapore National Bibliography*, 1971. Singapore: National Library, 1974.

[3] H. Grunewald, *A Short Course on Scientific Editing*; *Lecture Notes.* Jakarta: UNESCO Field Science Office for Southeast Asia, 1974.

Science Office for Southeast Asia.

Regarding the use of English, the titles of serials and of articles should be given in English in parallel with the vernacular, and those in non-Roman scripts should be transliterated as well. There should be a separate contents page in English, and abstracts of articles should also be given in English.

Regarding the titles of serials, it is library experience that these change often and sometimes quite arbitrarily. Under the ISDS scheme, each change of title requires a new ISSN, and it is quite understood that interested content changes require title changes, that variations, splits, and mergers occur under publishing conditions which need to be reflected in bibliographic systems. Nevertheless, it is recommended that publishers resist as sternly as possible the impulse to change the titles of their serial publications. [1]

Conclusion

Scholarly publishing is the most important wave of the information explosion. The measures for achieving bibliographic control described here are practical, and simple to put into effect. Publishers of scholarly material should take the lead, together with the national libraries, in coordinating the necessary procedures amongst themselves and in the publishing community at large. The benefits to publishers from their participation in this effort will be seen to be quite as great as any accruing to other components of the information process, and in particular the so-called "information gap" will be marginally narrowed.

---

[1] A group calling themselves Librarians United to Fight Costly, Silly, Unnecessary Serial Title Changes (LUTFCSUSTC) at Michigan State University Library, East Lansing, Mich., is the subject of a letter from D. C. Taylor, in *Library Association Record*, v. 76 no. 1, 1974.

国际图书刊物统一编号及著录的标准化①

一、前言

近几年来,世界各国的图书馆界,因鉴于图书刊物统一编号及著录标准化的重要性,在国际图书馆协会联盟(International Federation of Library Associations 以下简称"图协联盟"),国际文献联盟(International Federation of Documentation),国际标准化组织(International Standards Organization),及联合国教育、科学与文化组织(United Nations Educational, Scientific and Cultural Organization 以下简称"联教组织")等机构的倡导与实际推动下,陆续地制定了下列四项国际标准,由美、英、法、德、加、澳洲等国家率先领导,付诸实施:

1. 国际标准图书编号——ISBN(International Standard Book Number)②
2. 国际标准刊物编号——ISSN(International Standard Serial Number)③
3. 国际图书著录标准——ISBD(M)(International Standard Bibliographic Description for Monographs)④
4. 国际刊物著录标准——ISBD(S)(International Standard Bibliographic Description for Serials)⑤

根据最近的资料,这四种标准已受到世界各国图书馆界及出版界广泛的重视,很多国家且已正式采用这些标准。台湾地区亦曾为图协联盟会员之一,对于国际合作向来极为重视,应即采取步骤,将这些标准译成中文,向区内广为介绍;并由台湾"中央图书馆"及图书馆学会,会同有关机构拟订实施办法,及早付诸实施。本文因受篇幅限制,只能将此四种标准的来龙去脉做一个简要的报导。

二、国际标准图书编号"ISBN"

图书编号的作用大致有二:从出版界的观点来看,图书编号可以简化图书发行、宣传、推销、记录及管理等手续,为此之故,很多出版商或书商为了业务上的需要,早已实行了各自设计的编号。从图书馆的观点来看,图书编号可以简化图书采访、登录、出纳及管理等工作,尤其是近年来,因计算机的应用已日渐增广,图书编号遂成为简化计算机作业,简化数据储检及流通的重要方式之一。为使图书编号在全世界一致化,以发挥其最大的效能,美国早在1960年即有此建议,但最先付诸实行者还是英国。现行的国际标准图书编号是经英国福斯特(F. G. Foster)教授设计,由英国出版者协会(The Publishers'

---

① 本文的合作者为杨黄晴女士(美国新汉普夏大学助理教授,服务于该校图书馆编目部)。
② *International standard book numbering in Australia* / Australian Standard Book Numbering Agency. 3d ed. Canberra: National Library of Australia, 1973. - 10p. ISBN 0-642-99004-2. Paperback: gratis.
③ *Guidelines for ISDS*: UNISIST International serials data system (*ISDS*) / International Centre for the Registration of Serial Publications-Paris: UNESCO, 1973. -58p. - (SC/WS/538) Paperback; gratis.
④ *ISBD(M)* -International standard bibliographic description for monographic publications / International Federation of Library Associations. 1st standard ed. London: IFLA Committee on Cataloging, 1974. — X, 36p. ISBN 0-903043-02-5 Paperback: £ 2.00.
⑤ *ISBD(S)* – International standard bibliographic description for serials / Recommended by the Joint Working Group on the International Standard Bibliographic Description for Serials, set up by the IFLA Committee on Cataloging and the IFLA Committee on Serial Publications-London: IFLA Committee on Cataloging, 1974, — X, 36p. ISBN 0-903043-03-3 Paperback: £ 2.00.

Association）在 1967 年底开始采用。此后，美、加、澳洲等国家相继起而仿行。经过了 23 个国家的批准，国际标准化组织乃于 1972 年，正式将该编号制度订为国际标准——ISO Standard No. 2108 – 1972（E）。为了执行及推广此一标准，一个永久性的国际 ISBN 机构（International ISBN Agency）在 1972 年设立，附设于柏林的普鲁士文化协会（Stiftung Preussischer Kulturbesitz）图书馆内，以统筹协调世界各国有关标准图书编号的事宜。至于实际分配号码给出版商的工作，则分由各国的 ISBN 中心负责。

国际标准图书编号是一种十位数的号码，每一个号码包括下列四个部分：

1. 地区或国家识别号码（Group identifier）
2. 出版商号码（Publisher prefix）
3. 书名号码（Title number）
4. 核对数字（Check digit）

前三部分的号码皆为阿拉伯数字，每一部分的数字长短不一，可以相对的增减，使总数字经常保持九位。第四部分是一个单位数，逢"10"时则以英文字母的"×"代替，每一部分间有一空隔以资区别。

地区或国家识别号码并非因国家而异，有些国家因语言相同，有时可共同用一个号码：如"0"即同时代表英、美、加、澳洲、新西兰及南非等国家。根据手头的资料，"2"代表法国，"3"代表德国，"82"代表挪威，"90"则代表荷兰。这些号码是由国际 ISBN 机构统一分配的。

核对数字则是从每一编号的九个数字中，根据特别公式推算而来，用以查核该号码是否被误记。此种核对的方式，以计算机行之，十分方便有效。

因为前三部分的号码皆可以相对增减，变化无穷，因此每一部分皆有足够的号码可资分配及使用，例如：

ISBN	0	471	84831	x
	美国	Becker & Hayes	书名	核对数字
ISBN	0	903043	02	5
	英国	图协联盟	书名	核对数字

在实施此一标准时，最好能参考澳洲的情形，在"中央图书馆"内附设一 ISBN 机构，以掌管出版商号码的分配及其他有关事宜。凡图书无统一编号者，"中央图书馆"应在列入图书目录时，代为编号。

三、国际标准刊物编号"ISSN"

刊物编号的目的和用途与图书馆编号大致相同，在执行的方法上亦无大差异。最初提议设此编号者也是美国。在 1968 年，美国标准局（American Standards Institution，现已改名为 American National Standards Institute）的图书馆工作、文献与出版业组（Committee Z 39 on Library Work, Documentation, And Related Publishing Practices）特别设立了一个项目小组来研究刊物编号的统一标准。为了使得此一标准能够国际化，美国标准局将此一标准的草案送交国际标准化组织的第四十六技术小组（ISO/TC/46）审议，于获得通过后，正式定为国际标准刊物编号。

当此标准正在草拟之时，联教组织与国际科学团体联合会（International Council of Scientific Unions）花了 4 年的时间，在 1971 年共同提出了"建立一个世界科学数据系统可行性的研究报告"。① 此一报告与其附带建议在同年为联教组织大会所通过,并被列为联教组织主要任务之一。为简称计,此一"世界科学数据系统"乃被定名为——UNISIST。

与此同时,联教组织与国际科学团体联合会的一个著录工作小组(Joint UNISIST/ICSU-AB Working Group on Bibliographic Description)亦提出建立一个"国际刊物数据系统(International Serials Data System)可行性的报告"②,获得 UNISIST 中央委员会通过,成为 UNISIST 的主要活动之一。在法国政府经费的补助下,一个刊物登录的国际中心(International Center for the Registration of Serial Publications)已于1972年底在巴黎成立,总管刊物登录及编号的事宜。根据该中心的指南——Guidelines for ISDS,世界各国或各地区应分别设立该国家或地区的 ISDS 中心,实际负责刊物登录及编号的工作。

国际标准刊物编号是一种八位数的号码,分成两个四位数,中间由一"连字符号"(Hyphen)连接。其第八位数字是核对数字。每一号码除代表一个刊物的名称之外,别无其他意义,例如:

ISSN 0024-2527 为 Library Resources & Technical Services 的标准号码。

ISSN 0301-4150 为 AGE Current Awareness Service 的标准号码。

各国家或地区的 ISDS 中心,在设置之初应先向巴黎的国际中心报备,取得一份该国或地区已编过号的刊物名单,并由该国际中心配给一批未用的号码做为编号之用。各国或地区的中心应按照规定,按时将刊物登记及编号的资料,向国际中心呈报,使国际中心能有一套完整的记录。在没有设立 ISDS 中心的地区,刊物的出版者可直接向国际中心申请编号。为便捷计,美国的保克公司(R. R. Bowker Co.)便曾事先获得国际中心的同意,将七万多登录在该公司出版的两种国际刊物名录上(Ulrichs'International Periodicals Directory 及 Irregular Serials and Annuals)的刊物予以编号。各国新设的中心,对此批号码应特别留意,以免重复。

目前台湾虽已退出联教组织,对 ISDS 的活动仍应参加,最好能在"中央图书馆"内附设一 ISDS 的中心来负责台湾刊物登记及编号的有关事项。

四、国际图书著录标准"ISBD(M)"

国际图书著录标准的起源,可以追溯到1961年图协联盟在巴黎召开的"国际编目原则会议"(International Conference on Cataloging Principles)。基于国际合作的精神,该会议通过了一项极为重要的"原则说明"(Statement of Principles)。希望能依此原则而达到各国编目的一致化。此原则已经译成中文,刊载于第十四期"中国图书馆学会会报"上。③

由于巴黎会议能在编目原则上获得各国同意,大会在结束前成立一个统一编目规则(Uniform Cataloging Rules)的委员会,来继续推广编目一致化的工作。该委员会后来蜕变为图协联盟的编目委员会(IFLA Committee on Cataloging),并于1969年在哥本哈根召开了一个"国际编目专家的会议"(International Meeting of Cataloging Experts)。参加此会议的专家们,大家均有四点同感:

1. 每一国家应设立一个国家目录或编目机构,以负责该国所出版图书的编目工作。

---

① *Study report on the feasibility of a world science information system* / by the United Nation Educational, Scientific and Cultural Organization and the International Council of Scientific Unions-Paris: UNESCO, 1971. -XII, 161p. (UNESCO/UNISIST/4) Paperback; gratis.

② *Report on the feasibility of an international serials data system* / M. D Martin & C. I. Barnes; prepared for UNISIST/ICSU-AB Working Group on Bibliographic Description-London: INSPEC, 1970. (DM/CB/284) Paperback.

③ 国际图书编目原则会议. 中国图书馆学会会报. 1962. 12. (14): 51-54, 40

此国家目录不仅供国内图书馆之用,同时亦供给国外图书馆之用。

2. 在著录上,所有的国家应采用划一的格式。

3. 每一国家的编目机构应设法将外国图书的编目数据供给国内的图书馆。

4. 有鉴于编目数据的交换终将会使用计算机,各国图书编目应考虑采用某些统一的标点符号,使计算机能自动识别著录的项目,以减省数据输入的费用。

基于这些共同概念,此会议特设一国际著录标准之工作小组,以两年的时间拟定了国际图书著录标准。此标准在 1971 年公布后,不到两年的时间,已获得英、德、澳洲、南非、法、保加利亚、加、美、南斯拉夫、苏俄等国家的支持与采用。经过若干澄清与修正,此标准的"标准本"于 1974 年,正式由图协联盟出版。

有关此标准的概况,于镜宇先生在第 25 期"中国图书馆学会会报"上曾附带提及。[1]于先生亦建议台湾图书馆界速将此一标准的全文及因其而修改的"英美编目规则"(Anglo-American Cataloging Rules)第六章等译成中文,以作为订定编目规则的参考。国际图书著录标准的要点有下列三点:

1. 规定著录所应包括的项目。

2. 规定这些项目的顺序。

3. 规定区分这些项目所特用的标点符号及间隔。

兹将著录的全部项目,顺序及标点符号列示于后:

正题书名 = 并题书名:别题/第一作者记载;第二或其他作者记载. —版本记载/第一版本作者记载;第二或其他版本作者记载. —第一出版地;第二或其他出版地:出版者,出版时间(印刷地;第二或其他印刷地:印刷者). —页数或册数:插图记载;大小和附件. —(丛书记载;次丛书记载;丛书或次丛书编号 ISSN)

批注

国际标准图书编号 装订:价格

在上列例子中,有些项目在实际使用时可以省略;但有些项目亦可因需要而重复一次或多次。例如有些书的并题书名不止一个。此外,国际图书著录标准是以书名开始,与台湾地区现行的编目格式相似,颇适合我们采用。

五、国际刊物著录标准"ISBD(S)"

国际刊物著录标准是由图协联盟的一个联合工作小组拟定。此一小组系由图协联盟属下的编目委员会及刊物委员会在 1971 年共同设立。举凡此一标准的目的、内容与要点等,皆与国际图书著录标准力求相似。此标准草案在 1972 年 6 月经拟定后即印发给世界各国有关人士以供批评及建议。根据各方的反应及多次的修正,此标准在 1973 年底经联合小组通过,建议各国采用。

有关国际刊物著录标准的全部项目,顺序及标点符号,请参看下列示例:

特殊标题 = 并行标题:副标题/作者记载. —第一出版地;第二或其他出版地:出版者,出版日期及编号(印刷地;第二或其他印刷地:印刷者). —插图记载;大小和附件. —(丛书记载;丛书编号:次丛书记载:次丛书编号)

批注

国际标准刊物编号:价格

---

[1] 于镜宇. 分类编目之改进计划. 中国图书馆学会会报. 1973. 12(25):8-9,16.

其中应注意的是特殊标题的选取,所谓特殊标题乃指刊物的主要标题,于登录时须特别留意。采用国际刊物著录标准最好能由"中央图书馆"率先领导,并将此工作与台湾地区的 ISDS 中心的工作合并在一起,以避免重复。

六、结论

　　以上四种国际标准,虽然都是在最近才公布,但已普遍为世界各国所接受及采用;对促进国际合作及知识流通产生极大的影响。以目前的趋势,图书刊物著录编号的统一化势在必行。由于计算机的应用,国与国间目录的交换与编目合作等会更趋密切。为了配合这种趋势,对于已公布的国际标准,图书馆界及出版界应及早采取步骤,付诸实施。

Cooperative Regional Bibliographic Projects in South-East Asia

Introduction

Regional cooperation on joint bibliographic projects has been a recent development in South-East Asia. Despite the seemingly late start, nearly all such projects are carefully planned and have received enthusiastic support from the participating countries. This trend toward regional cooperation stems from the recognition of its importance by library leaders in South-East Asian countries and is fostered by encouragement and financial assistance provided by foundations and several regional and international organizations.

This article intends to trace the development of seven cooperative regional bibliographic projects now in existence in South-East Asia. A detailed description of the current status and major activities of these projects is given, based on the latest information available.

The term "South-East Asia" is here meant to include that part of the Asian continent lying south of China and east of India, together with the Indonesian and Philippine archipelagos. Owing to political and military conflicts, many projects discussed in this paper are largely confined to the five ASEAN countries, namely Thailand, Malaysia, Singapore, the Philippines, and Indonesia.

Of the joint bibliographic projects to be discussed in this article, some are strictly South-East Asian, others are projects initiated in South-East Asia but covering the whole of Asia. Those strictly for South-East Asia are: (a) the Regional Microfilm Clearing-house; (b) the compilation of a master-list of South-East Asian microforms; (c) the ISDS Regional Centre for Southeast Asia.

Those covering the whole of Asia are: (a) the Asian Mass Communication Research and Information Centre (AMIC); (b) the Asian Information Centre for Geotechnical Engineering; (c) the Agricultural Information Bank for Asia;[①] (d) the Clearing-house for Social Development in Asia.

The Regional Microfilm Clearing-house[②]

The increasing activities in microfilming historical records, archival materials and other publications of importance to South-East Asia as a means of preserving national heritages and facilitating research prompted the establishment of the Regional Microfilm Clearing-house at the Institute of South-East Asian Studies (ISEAS), Singapore, in 1972.

Campaigning most actively for the establishment of the clearing-house, among others, was Mrs. P. Lim Pui Huen, Librarian of ISEAS, who presented a paper on Regional Cooperation in Microfilming Activities at the first General Conference of the South-East Asian Branch, International Council on Archives (SARBICA) held in Manila from 24 to 28 May 1971.[③] Based on her paper and the general awareness of the need, the resolution, "... that a joint SARBICA-CONSAL clearing-house of information pertaining to microform matters be established...", along with a set of guidelines for its implementation, was adopted by the SARBICA conference.

As a result of the resolution, Mrs. Lim was appointed Regional Microfilm Coordinator, and

---

① Because the Agricultural Information Bank for Asia (AIBA) was discussed in another article in the issue in which this was published [see Remedies V. Viloria, "The Agricultural Information Bank for Asia: Its Development And Activities", *UNESCO Bulletin for Libraries*, Vol. 31, No. 6 (Nov. – Dec. 1977), pp. 331 – 339], the portion of the original manuscript relating to AIBA was omitted from the published article.

② The latest account of the clearing-house is in the paper written by Tan Sok Joo, "Regional Microfilm Clearing-house, 1972 – 1975: a report to SARBICA and CONSAL", *Proceedings of the Third Conference of Southeast Asian Librarians*, held in Jakarta from 1 to 5 December 1975 (Jakarta: Pusat Dokumentasi Ilmiah Nasional for Ikatan Pustakawan Indonesia, 1977), pp. 34 – 51.

③ The paper was later published in the *Southeast Asia Microfilms Newsletter*, No 1, December, 1972.

the library of ISEAS was asked to act as the clearing-house responsible for the gathering, publication and dissemination of relevant information on all matters relating to the planning, coordination, production, distribution, bibliographic control and use of South-East Asian microforms. In doing so, the clearing-house should "serve as liaison between interested parties within and without the region and promote efforts for cooperative programs and the sharing of experience and expertise". ①

Since its inception, the clearing-house has undertaken the following important work:

1. The compilation of the *Directory of Microfilm Facilities in Southeast Asia*. As the first order of business, the clearing-house conducted a survey of the existing microfilming facilities in South-East Asia. The results of the survey were published in 1972 as ISEAS's *Library Bulletin*, No. 3. A second edition with much updating was published in 1973 as ISEAS's *Library Bulletin*, No. 7. The directory lists the equipment of each institution, its microfilming programs, and guides to its collection.

2. The publication of the *Southeast Asia Microfilms Newsletter*. Under the editorship of Mrs. Lim six issues of the newsletter were published between 1972 and 1974. Since June 1975, the newsletter is managed by an editorial board, comprising Mrs. Lim and three other members. Under the new arrangement, the newsletter is published twice a year by ISEAS for SARBICA and GONSAL, and printed and distributed by the SARBICA secretariat in Kuala Lumpur.

Thus far the newsletter has disseminated information on serial and other titles filmed or acquired, sets collated for filming, purchases and evaluations of new equipment, microfilm consortia formed, regional cooperative projects, publications available about micrographics and microform applications, etc.

3. Searching out holdings of important or rare research materials for filming. The latest and most significant example of this is the attempt to microfilm national official gazettes of South-East Asian countries. This project is a cooperative effort undertaken at the request of the Library of Congress and the New York Public Library in making national official gazettes of the world available in microform.

As a first step in this attempt, the clearing-house began compiling a checklist of all national and state or other local gazettes, if any, of the region. A preliminary checklist was issued in December 1975 which contains holding information, both hard copies and microforms, of 84 gazettes published in Brunei, Burma, Democratic Kampuchea, Indonesia, Lao People's Republic, Malaysia, Papua New Guinea, the Philippines, Singapore, Thailand, Timor and the socialist Republic of Viet Nam.

The Master-list of South-East Asian Microforms②

Although, to some extent, this regional project is closely related to the Regional Microfilm Clearing-house project, it is a separate project which reports to SARBICA and CONSAL. Since SARBICA has a permanent secretariat and was the one that negotiated with the International Development Research Centre (IDRC)③ Canada for the funding of the master-list project, it is therefore responsible for the administration of the project.

The idea of compiling a regional master-list of microforms was first proposed by SARBICA in

---

① Tan Sok Joo, *op. cit.*, p. 1.

② The recent development of this project is described in the report by Winarti Partaningrat, "*Progress Report on a Joint SARBICA-CONSAL Project: the Compilation of a (Regional) Masterlist of Southeast Asian Microforms*", Proceeding of the Third Conference of Southeast Asian Librarians, held in Jakarta from 1 to 5 December 1975, (Jakarta: Pusat Dokumentasi Ilmiah Nasional for Ikatan Pustakawan; Indonesia, 1977), pp. 52–66.

③ IDRC is a public corporation created by an Act of the Canadian Parliament in 1970. Although most of its funds come from Parliament it is an autonomous body with a twenty-one member Board of Governors drawn from several countries. The aim of IDRC is "to help developing regions build up their own research capabilities and the innovative skills needed to solve their problems". Information sciences is one of the five programme divisions of IDRC and it has had a significant impact on the development of information systems for the benefit of developing countries.

1972. At almost the same time, a similar recommendation was made by the Permanent Committee on Socio-culturai Activities of the Association of South-East Asian Nations (ASEAN) calling for the compilation of a catalogue of microfilmed materials to facilitate the exchange of such materials among ASEAN countries. In 1973, the proposal of SARBICA was endorsed by CONSAL at its second conference.

With the cooperation of CONSAL, a proposal for financial support of the project was drafted in 1974 by Mrs. Hedwig Anuar, the SARBICA chairperson, and was submitted to IDRC for funding. ① In 1975, a grant was awarded by IDRC which enabled the project to commence in May 1975. Miss Winarti Partaningrat, the former director of the Indonesian National Scientific Documentation Center, was appointed Editor, while Mrs. Lim of ISEAS serves as the Project Director. The main objective of the master-list project is to "collect information regarding South-East Asian documents and publication already reproduced on microform in the region..." . ②

It is planned that within the two-year funding period, a 3-in. by 5-in. index card file containing complete bibliographic information on all South-East Asian microforms will be set up in the Project Office. This file will then be published. After this, the National Library of Singapore will assume responsibility for continuing the project so that supplementary volumes of the master-list can be brought out at regular intervals.

The ISDS Regional Centre for South-East Asia③

The latest regional bibliographic project, which was initiated in 1973 by Thailand and has had strong support from UNESCO and other South-East Asian countries, was formally established in March 1976 in Bangkok.

ISDS (International Serials Data System) is an important component of UNESCO's UNISIST program. ④ The major aims of ISDS are "to provide a reliable registry of world serial publications covering the full range of recorded knowledge" and to assign "to each serial published under a given title, a unique and unambiguous numeric code identifier, the International Standard Serial Number (ISSN)". ⑤

In order to attain these aims and to carry out its intended activities, a two-tier organizational structure consisting of an international centre and a network of national and regional centers has been adopted. Through an agreement between UNESCO and the French Government, the International Centre for the Registration of Serial Publications was established in Paris in 1973. Since then, pursuant to resolution 2.141 (c) adopted by the sixteenth session of the UNESCO General Conference, a number of national centers and one regional centre have been established, mostly in developed countries. ⑥

Many countries in South-East Asia felt that for reasons of economy, manpower, technology and regional cooperation, a regional centre instead of separately founded national centers would be more desirable and advantageous. Because of this, at the request of Mrs. Maenmas Chavalit, Director of the National Library of Thailand, a consultant was provided in November 1975 by

---

① Hedwig Anuar, *Proposal for the Compilation and Publication of a Masterlist of Southeast Asian Microforms*, Singapore: SARBICA, 1974, p. 4.
② *Guidelines for the Compilation of a Masterlist of Southeast Asian Microforms*, Singapore: The Project Office, 1975, p. 4.
③ Information concerning the background of the regional centre is contained in the UNESCO mission report and recommendations prepared by Hwa-Wei Lee, *The Possibility of Establishing a Regional Centre for the International Serials Data System in Thailand*, Paris: UNESCO, 1975, p. 42. (SC – 76/WS/7.)
④ UNISIST is a UNESCO programme concerned with international co-operation in the field of information, particularly with a view to promoting systems interconnection and facilitating access to the world information resources.
⑤ *ISDS Bulletin*, Vol. 1, No. 1 (1974)
⑥ Thus far, fifteen countries have announced the establishment of their national centers: United States, United Kingdom, Australia, Canada, Federal Republic of Germany, France, Argentina, Japan, Finland, Yugoslavia, Nigeria, Tunisia. Netherlands, Sweden and Brazil. Not all of these national centers are operational. The first regional centre was established in Moscow; it consists of the U. S. S. R., Bulgaria, Czechoslovakia, the German Democratic Republic, Hungary, Mongolia, Poland and Cuba.

UNESCO to undertake a one-month exploratory mission in South-East Asia to examine the feasibility of establishing such a regional centre. After meeting with library officials in Thailand, Malaysia, Singapore, Indonesia and the Philippines, a positive recommendation was made and, based on the recommendation, a special fund was provided by UNESCO to convene an organizing meeting① in Bangkok in March 1976. The organizing meeting was attended by representatives from the five above-mentioned countries and by M. Rosenbaum, Director of the international centre.

To participate in the ISDS regional centre, each member country has designated a national centre which is responsible for reporting all serials published in the country in accordance with the Guidelines for ISDS. ② Upon receiving such reports on standard forms the ISDS Regional Centre for Southeast Asia, which was established in Bangkok under the auspices of the National Library of Thailand, will assume the following responsibilities:
  1. Check for the completeness of the bibliographic information required.
  2. Assign an ISSN for each serial publication reported.
  3. Help national centers to promote the use of ISSN in their countries.
  4. Create and maintain a computerized regional serials data bank.
  5. Report newly registered serials to the international centre.
  6. Publish a regional list of serial publications and separate national lists of new serial titles.
  7. Answer inquiries concerning serial publications.
  8. Provide training opportunities to serials librarians and documentalists in the region.

The cost for operating the regional centre is to be shared by the cooperating countries, but, for an initial period of five years, financial support from outside sources is also needed. A request for such support has been submitted to IDRC for consideration.

Asian Mass Communication Research and Information Centre (AMIC)③

To serve as a regional clearing-house for mass communication in Asia, AMIC was established in 1971 in Singapore under the joint sponsorship of the Friedrich Ebert Stiftung, a German foundation,④ and the Singapore Government. In addition to its clearing-house functions, AMIC also aims at the promotion of teaching, training, and research in mass communication in Asia. At the international level, AMIC is one of six regional mass communication centers whose work is encouraged and co-ordinated by UNESCO.

The activities of AMIC may be grouped under three broad headings: research and training program, publication program and documentation program. It is the documentation program that is the focus of this article.

To facilitate the dissemination of information on mass communication in Asia, five major bibliographic projects have been undertaken by AMIC. Each of these is described briefly below:

AMIC Documentation List. This annotated list comprised of selected recent acquisitions by AMIC is published as a regular feature in AMIC's quarterly journal, *Media Asia* (No. 1, 1972). In its columns "Cues" and "Findings", Media Asia also carries popularized "rewrites" of important research reports and findings of interest to its readers.

AMIC Communication Bibliographies Series. This annotated subject bibliography series is issued from time to time in support of other activities organized by AMIC. The first one, issued in 1973, was on broadcasting in Asia.

---

　① The final report is available from the National Library of Thailand.
　② International Centre for the Registration of Serial Publications, Guidelines for *ISDS*, Paris: UNESCO, 1973, SC/WS/538).
　③ Lena U Wen Lim, "Asian Mass Communication Research and Information Centre", *Information*, December 1974, p. 318 – 19.
　④ The Friedrich Ebert Stiftung (FES) is an independent German foundation established in 1925 as the cultural legacy of Friedrich Ebert (1871 – 1925), the first President of the Weimar Republic. FES receives grants from both governmental sources and private donations. In the sphere of international co-operation, FES devotes itself to adult education, assistance to trade union training and co-operatives, aiding improvements in social structure, and use of mass media in education and training.

Asian Mass Communication Bibliography. The activities leading to the publication of various country sections of this bibliography are a cooperative project, sponsored, co-coordinated and initiated by AMIC in 1973. This project, which involves the compilation of separate country bibliographies, each by a national team, to be published separately but under a unified title, includes Hong Kong, India, Indonesia, Republic of Korea, Malaysia, Nepal, Pakistan, the Philippines, Singapore and Sri Lanka.

List of Theses, *1971. Studies in Mass Communication in Asia*. These annual lists are to include bibliographic information on all theses dealing with various aspects of mass communication in Asia completed either in Asian universities or elsewhere in the world.

In addition to its bibliographic publications, AMIC provides a document delivery service whereby it supplies upon request photocopies, microfilms, microfiches or translations of any material in its collections.

Asian Information Center for Geotechnical Engineering (AGE) [①]

The Asian Information Center for Geotechnical Engineering (Asian Geotechnical Engineering for short, abbreviated AGE) was founded in January 1973 at the Asian Institute of Technology in Bangkok under the joint sponsorship of the institute's Division of Geotechnical Engineering and the Library and Information Center.

The idea of establishing AGE was conceived at a meeting held in Bangkok in July 1971 of the representatives of the national societies of soil mechanics and foundation engineering in Asia. Arising from a generally felt need for a relevant, timely and responsive information service on geotechnical engineering especially tailored to the needs of Asian engineers, the meeting passed a resolution requesting the Asian Institute of Technology to establish and operate AGE for the purpose of selecting, acquiring, analyzing, storing, retrieving, publicizing and disseminating useful information on Asian geotechnical engineering for the benefit of all those who are concerned. Recognizing the significance of geotechnical engineering work in relation to social and economic development in Asia as well as the importance of providing an information service on a regional basis to serve the needs of geotechnical engineers and specialists, a grant was made by the International Development Research Centre to support the operation of AGE for a three-year period.

Some major activities of AGE are as follows:

1. To seek, select, and acquire both published and unpublished literature on geotechnical engineering which is relevant to Asia, with particular emphasis on literature published in Asia, preferably in English, but materials of importance in other languages are also included.

2. To establish both a card-index file and a machine-readable database for the relevant literature completely indexed and abstracted for easy retrieval. Both the International Geotechnical Classification System (IGC) and the soil Mechanics Thesaurus are used.

3. To prepare periodic directories of geotechnical engineers, specialists and organizations in Asia as well as reports in their ongoing projects.

4. To disseminate information on available literature and survey results through the following publications:

AGE Current Awareness Service—a quarterly publication informing readers of recent geotechnical engineering publications and contents of selected geotechnical engineering journals received at AGE.

Asian Geotechnical Engineering Abstracts—a quarterly publication consisting of abstracts of available publications and reports in geotechnical engineering in or about Asia.

AGE Conference Proceedings List—an annual list of conference proceedings on various

---

[①] This part of the article is based on an earlier paper by the present author, "The Experience of a Specialized Information Service in Asia—AGE", presented at the Round-table Conference on Documentation Problems in Developing Countries held in Khartoum, Sudan, on 10 – 11 April 1975. The conference was organized by FID/DC and the FID National Member in Sudan.

subjects of geotechnical engineering in AGE's collection.

AGE Journal Holdings List—an annually revised list of geotechnical engineering journals held at AGE.

Asian Geotechnical Engineering in Progress—an annual publication which will provide information on current design, construction and research projects in geotechnical engineering being undertaken in Asia.

5. To provide the three "R" services (Reference, Reprography, and Referral) to members and other users. It is planned that at some future date, the centre will also publish state-of-the-art reviews and bibliographies on subjects of interest to geotechnical engineers.

6. To cooperate with other information and documentation services on, or related to, geotechnical engineering both in and outside Asia to enhance information resources and service on geotechnical engineering on a global basis through reciprocal arrangement and systems interconnection.

The operation of AGE has been guided by two committees: the Policy Advisory Committee and the Technical Committee. An effective link between AGE and its users has been established through appointed liaison officers in many of the Asian countries.

In order to find the pattern of information usage by geotechnical engineers in Asia, a questionnaire survey was conducted among AGE users in March 1974. Findings concerning the general characteristics of AGE users, their information channels, the library facilities available to them, the types of technical information they often require, their appraisals of the AGE publications and services were reported in the paper "User and Use Analysis: A Case Study of the Information Utility by Geotechnical Engineers in Asian Countries."[1]

To evaluate the role of AGE now and in the future, a Workshop on Geotechnical Information Systems was held at AGE from 5 to 9 April 1976. The workshop was cosponsored by IDRC and AGE and had forty-two participants including members of the Policy Advisory Committee and the Technical Committee, liaison officers and representatives of other geotechnical information services from Australia, France, Federal Republic of Germany, Norway, Sweden, and the United States.

Clearing-house for Social Development in Asia[2]

The recent establishment of the Clearing-house for Social Development in Asia which is located in Bangkok is due largely to the Friedrich Ebert Stiftung in cooperation with the National Research Council of Thailand.

Recognizing the need for relevant information on social development in Asia by planners, policy-makers, government officials, researchers and others who are interested in the social development in various countries or regions of Asia, a feasibility study for the establishment of a regional clearing-house for such information was conducted in 1972 – 1973 by Erwin Kristofferson, then the regional representative for Asia of FES. During the course of this study, it was found that the idea of establishing a Clearing-house for Social Development in Asia was highly favored by many Asian countries.

Subsequent to the study, Preparatory Meeting of Experts was held in Bangkok in April 1973 and an information specialist, Dr Gottfried Volker, was sent by FES to take charge of the preparatory work. Through his efforts, an organizing meeting was held in Bangkok in February 1975 which resulted in the formation of an interim Governing Council and a Standing and Advisory Council. Since then the following activities have been undertaken by the clearing-house either through its own staff or local consultants contracted by the clearing-house:

1. A regional survey on the demand for and supply of information in Asia has been carried out

---

[1] This paper by the author was presented at the thirty-seventh Annual Meeting of the American Society for Information Science, Atlanta, Georgia, 13 – 17 October 1974, and was published in *Information Utilities*: *Proceedings of the 37th Annual Conference of the American Society for Information Science*, pp. 133 – 6, Washington D. C. : ASIS, 1974.

[2] Clearing-house for Social Development, Annual Report, February 15, 1975 – April 30, 1975, Bangkok, 1976, p. 8.

in Singapore, the Philippines, Thailand, Malaysia and Indonesia. Findings of the survey have been published in the Clearing House Journal.

2. A regional bibliographical study on social development data in the five ASEAN countries has also been conducted. All relevant materials which are available in these countries were collected, abstracted and indexed using the OECD Macrothesaurus. Results of the study have also been published in the Clearing House Journal.

3. The clearing-house is working on a number of selected topics which are important to the region: "Women Participating in Family Income", "Formal Associations and Development". and "Migration and the Impact on Social and Economic Development".

4. The preparation of a regional card catalogue on social development, comprising both published and unpublished materials, is in progress. All materials, including reports of ongoing research, are classified according to the OECD Macrothesaurus system and given four entries: author, title, subject and country. Relevant summaries are entered back of each card.

5. The Clearing House Journal reports on the findings of both the regional survey and the bibliographic study, along with any other relevant information. There are two issues to each volume. Each issue is devoted to a special country or topic; for example, Vol. II, No. 1 (February 1976) was devoted to "Social Development in the Philippines".

In addition to the above activities, the clearing-house also plans to conduct seminars and to publish occasional papers on subjects of significance to social development. Translation of selected literature from Asian languages into English is also contemplated.

According to the planning documents, the clearing-house will eventually become an independent, self-supporting regional institution. For the initial five years, it will be completely funded by FES. After that, the support from FES will be phased out gradually and the cost of operating the clearing-house will be shared by member countries.

Conclusions

This article has described in some detail six of the seven ongoing regional bibliographic projects in South-East Asia: three strictly South-East Asian in scope and coverage and four others covering some other Asian countries as well.

It is of interest to note that six out of the seven projects have been funded by two foundations: (a) the International Development Research Centre funds the master-list of South-East Asian microforms, the Asian Information Center for Geotechnical Engineering, the Agricultural Information Bank for Asia, and partly the ISDS Regional Centre for Southeast Asia; (b) the Friedrich Ebert Stiftung funds the Asian Mass Communication Research and Information Centre and the Clearing-house for Social Development in Asia.

The generous financial support provided by IDRC and FES has made it possible to develop cooperative regional bibliographic projects in South-East Asia. This support has encouraged countries to work together in joint bibliographic projects.

Two regional professional organizations—CONSAL and SARBICA—although they have met infrequently in the past, have, nevertheless, provided a forum for librarians, documentalists and archivists in South-East Asia to discuss problems of mutual concern and to work out cooperative projects.

UNESCO's UNISIST program—with its emphasis on the needs of developing countries—has been instrumental in the establishment of the ISDS Regional Centre for Southeast Asia. The Organization, through both its UNISIST and NATIS programs, has also greatly assisted countries in South-East Asia in the setting up or strengthening of their national library and information infrastructures, as well as in the training of librarians, documentalists and archivists, and in the promotion of closer regional cooperation.

Recent developments in several of the international information systems such as the International Nuclear Information System (INIS), the International Information System for the Agricultural Sciences and Technology (AGRIS), and the Development Sciences Information

System (DEVSIS) have encouraged many of the countries in South-East Asia to participate in these international information systems by prompting bibliographic information relating to their countries, in standard format, to their international databases. Such participation is very important both in terms of helping the countries in South-East Asia to improve their bibliographic apparatus and in making their bibliographic information more readily available world-wide. It is only through cooperation in bibliographic projects that there can be true sharing of information among all nations.

第三部分 国际合作

Section III International Cooperation

An Approach to Regional Cooperation in Scientific and Technical Information Services for Southeast Asia[①]

Introduction

The developing countries in Southeast Asia, especially Malaysia, Singapore, Indonesia, the Philippines, and Thailand, are in a stage of rapid economic, socio-political, and industrial development. In order to expedite the development process, seeking to close the technological gap between the "developing" countries and the "developed" countries instead of widening it, as it has been the case in the past, an expanded, more responsive scientific and technical information service is urgently needed.

The relationship between "development" and "information" can be seen as mutually dependent. This is especially so in the development of science and technology. There is a positive correlation existing between the degree of industrial and technological development and the level of information requirement. The higher the degree of development, the greater the need for information services, and vice versa. It is also predictable that more development in science and technology will generate more need for information and more readily available information will stimulate and accelerate further scientific and technical development.

Aware of the full impact of scientific and technical information in national development, in recent years, many countries in Southeast Asia have taken effective measures toward setting up national documentation centers or strengthening their national libraries for the purpose of improving the scientific and technical information services in their respective countries. These attempts were made either under the assistance and encouragement of UNESCO or under their own initiative. It seems to be the time to promote the idea of regional cooperation as a necessary step for the developing countries in Southeast Asia to join forces for better information services throughout the entire region. Effective regional cooperation will serve to complement the national efforts and plans rather than to be a substitute for them. The cross fertilization of this parallel approach both at the national level and at the regional and international level will be mutually beneficial.

The Necessity for Regional Cooperation

The needs for regional and international cooperation in meeting the scientific and technical information requirement is no longer a questionable supposition. Many international organizations, both inter-governmental and non-governmental, have been in fact eagerly pursuing and promoting this objective. Among them are UNESCO, the International Council of Scientific Unions (ICSU), the International Federation for Documentation (IFD), the International Standards Organization (ISO), and the International Federation for Information Processing (IFIP), to name just a few.[②]

[①] This article is based on a paper delivered by the author at the Conference on Scientific and Technical Information Needs for Malaysia and Singapore held in Kuala Lumpur on 24 – 26 September, 1971 under the joint sponsorship of the Library Associations of Malaysia and Singapore.

[②] F. A. Sviridov, "International Trends in Documentation and Information Services", *Library Trends*, V. 17 No. 3 (January 1969), pp. 326 – 338.

Recently, there have been a few regional organizations taking concrete moves toward regional cooperation in scientific and technical information policies and cooperative activities. The most notable and successful one is NORDFORSK (the Scandinavian Council for Applied Research) founded jointly by the four Scandinavian countries: Denmark, Finland, Norway and Sweden, and also Iceland. Since 1952, NORDFORSK has had a special committee on technical information, Scandinavian Committee for Technical Information Services (NORDinfo), which has tried to act as a policy-formulating body in the technological information field, and it has initiated several cooperative projects. ①

The Organization for Economic Co-operation and Development (OECD) has also set up an office within its Science Directorate to help in developing and coordinating the science information policies among its member-countries. In 1969, the eight member-countries of the Council for Mutual Economic Assistance (CMEA) also established an International Centre of Scientific and Technical Information in Moscow for the purpose of coordinating the science information policies of member countries. ②

Several factors and recent developments have provided a favorable environment for regional cooperation. They are: 1) The universality of scientific and technical knowledge and the desire for information transfer across national boundaries; 2) the recent technological advancement in computer technology, reprography, telecommunications; and 3) the development of "UNISIST".

1. The Universality of Knowledge And the Desire for Information Transfer.

It has been said that knowledge has no national boundary. Knowledge is built on knowledge. ③ Therefore it is an international asset and resource. This is very true in science and technology. Scientific and technical knowledge flourishes only when it is freely exchanged and readily available among the researchers and technologists in the world. The transfer of scientific and technological information from developed countries to the developing countries is of particular importance and is viewed as one of the prerequisites by which a developing nation can narrow the gap between the "have" and the "have-not" nations of the world.

2. The Advancement of Communication Technologies And Information Transfer.

Information transfer is as old as civilization. Several major innovations in the past have accelerated the pace of such transfer. The creation of written languages, the invention of paper and printing, the growth of presses and publications, the development of modern transportation arid communication systems, etc. have all contributed to the transfer of information and have accelerated the growth of the world's knowledge. The most recent and significant developments which serve to revolutionize information handling and service are: 1) the development of computer technology and its potential application in information processing, 2) the improvement in the reprographic techniques, and 3) the advancement in telecommunications. These new technological developments have both directly and indirectly affected the process of information collecting, analyzing, indexing, handling, retrieving and disseminating. They have brought about drastic change both in the concept and in the practice of library and information services.

The computers, which have the power and versatility to process data with high speed and precision, are increasingly being used in libraries and information centers as an effective means to cope with the proliferation of today's information. Although the computers are without doubt a powerful tool which can be employed by the librarians, documentalists, and information specialists to cope with the problem of the "information explosion", it is expensive in terms of hardware

---

① Bjorn V. Tell, "Scandinavian Developments in Documentation and Information Services", *Library Trends*, V. 17 No. 3 (January 1969), pp. 289 – 298.

② United Nations Educational, Scientific and Cultural Organization/International Council of Scientific Unions, *UNISIST: Synopsis of the Feasibility Study on a World Science Information System* (Paris: UNESCO, 1971), p. 26. The eight countries are Bulgaria, Czechoslovakia, German Democratic Republic, Hungary, Mongolia Poland Rumania and USSR.

③ *Ibid.*, pp. vi – vii.

acquisitions and software developments. For the developing countries in Southeast Asia, an elaborate information system operated by computers with an extensive storage of bibliographical data prepared both externally and internally can only be achieved by a joint force of as many countries in the region as possible.

The improvement in reprographic techniques such as microfilming and various methods of copying and duplicating have enabled the wide dissemination of information some of which may not be available or accessible otherwise. It has made it possible for the libraries and information centers in many countries to interchange reproduced information on request.

The spectacular advancement in telecommunications, particularly satellite communications, is another reason for regional and international cooperation. The satellite communications can overcome the geographical barriers which formerly prohibited the free flow of information. The capability of communication satellites to transmit voice, teletype and facsimile signals to a distant place without recourse to telephone lines has a distinct advantage over other communication media. A combination of telephone, teletype, radio, and satellite communications can provide an effective network of national, regional, and world information systems which will greatly facilitate interlibrary communications and cooperation and bridge the distance gap.

3. The Development of UNISIST. ①

Another important recent development having significant meaning for regional and international cooperation is the joint feasibility study on a world science information system undertaken by UNESCO and ICSU. The report of the study which has just been published reaffirms the belief that a world-wide information system is both desirable and feasible. The broad principles embodied in the study are quoted below: ②

— the unimpeded exchange of published or publishable scientific information and data among scientists of all countries;

— hospitality to the diversity of disciplines and fields of science and technology as well as to the diversity of languages used for the international exchange of scientific information;

— promotion of the interchange of published or publishable information and data among the systems, whether manual or machine, which process and provide information for the use of scientists;

— the cooperative development and maintenance of technical standards in order to facilitate the interchange of scientific information and data among systems;

— promotion of compatibility between and among information processing systems developed in different countries and in different areas of the sciences;

— promotion of cooperative agreements between and among systems in different countries and in different areas of the sciences for the purpose of sharing workloads and of providing needed services and products;

— assistance to countries, both developing and developed, wishing access to contemporary and future information services in the sciences;

— the development of human and information resources in all countries as necessary foundations for the utilization of machine systems;

— the increased participation of scientists in the development and use of information systems, with particular attention to the involvement of scientists in the evaluation, compaction, and synthesis of scientific information and data;

— the involvement of the coming generation of scientists in the planning of scientific information systems of the future;

— the reduction of administrative and legal barriers to the flow of scientific information

---

① UNISIST is an acronym which stands for the feasibility study and for the recommended future program to implement its recommendations. *Ibid.*, p. v.

② *Ibid.*, pp. vi – vii.

between and among countries.

While the UNISIST feasibility study was in progress, a conference focusing on the application of science and technology to the development of Asia convened in New Delhi in August 1968. The conference considered the development of information and documentation facilities and the organization and promotion of international and regional cooperation as two of the priority areas where action is needed. Among other recommendations, the conference recommended to participating governments for priority action in Asia "the development of information and documentation facilities through strengthening existing centers; establishing new centers and links between national centers; rationalizing existing systems and making maximum use of modern techniques of reproduction, abstracting and data processing; considering the establishment of one or more regional information clearing-houses."①

Besides the foregoing factors and developments which have provided the necessary impetus for regional and international cooperation, there are also many specific reasons calling for effective and immediate regional cooperation in Southeast Asia. The two most important reasons are:

First, the countries in Southeast Asia generally suffer from a scarcity of library and information resources and services, inadequate funds necessary for their support, and a shortage of trained librarians, documentalists, and information specialists. In order that the limited resources may be best utilized to meet the developing needs, a pooling of the available resources in the region through voluntary cooperation and a carefully worked out system of coordination is needed.

Second, the close approximation of social and economic conditions prevailing in the countries of Southeast Asia and the intimate relationship and geographical distance among them provide a favorable environment for regional cooperation. It is now time to undertake some concrete actions.

Possibilities and Important Considerations in Regional Cooperation

There are a score of possibilities for cooperation on a regional basis all of which are fundamental in the realization of a region-wide information system and, when implemented, would yield good results.

1. Establishment of subject oriented or discipline oriented bibliographical data centers in a few selected libraries and documentation centers or in a single location where both strong library facilities and computer capability exist. Externally generated databases in machine-readable form are to be acquired and the subject coverage of each database should as far as possible not be overlapped or duplicated. These centers should be considered as regional information centers in the particular subjects or disciplines in which each of them specializes.

2. Establishment of communication linkage between the bibliographical data centers and other national libraries, documentation centers, and selected academic and research libraries in the region. Satellite communications should be employed as soon as possible to provide an effective linkage not just among the national centers in each of the participating countries within the region but also with other major libraries and documentation centers in countries outside the region. Other media of communication such as telephone, teletype, and facsimile transmission should be developed to interconnect each of the national centers with the libraries and documentation centers in their respective countries.

3. Each of the bibliographical data centers should also maintain a region-wide union list of serials, reference works, etc. in the subject or discipline in which each of them specializes. The frequently updated computer printout of such lists should be deposited in other bibliographical centers, national libraries, and documentation centers.

4. Each of the bibliographical data centers should also collect, analyze, index, abstract, and store the scientific and technical publications and reports, both published and unpublished, by the participating countries in the region. Agreement may be worked out so that at least one copy of

---

① Conference on the Application of Science and Technology to the Development of Asia, New Delhi. August 1968, *Science and Technology in Asian Development* (Paris: UNESCO, 1970), p. 215.

such publications and reports can be deposited in the bibliographical center which specializes on the subject or the discipline.

5. Each of the bibliographical data centers should serve as a clearinghouse for announcement, reproduction, and dissemination of the scientific and technical publications and reports collected or deposited in the center.

6. Each of the bibliographical data centers should maintain effective contact and close cooperation with other national, regional, and international centers throughout the world.

7. A regional coordinating council for scientific and technical information needs to be established to plan and coordinate regional cooperation and other activities. The council should seek to identify the needs, and establish priorities and guidelines in regional cooperative programs and activities. The functions of the council should also include the following:

a) To encourage the publication of national bibliographies, union list of serials, union catalogs, etc.;

b) to formulate policies which will facilitate exchange of publications, interlibrary loans, photoduplications, and reference and referral services among participating countries;

c) to hold regional conferences for the communication and exchange of ideas among the librarians, documentalists, and information specialists;

d) to conduct short courses and in-service training programs at the advanced level for training or upgrading the professional staff in library and information services;

e) to establish standards and uniform formats for bibliographic records and other library and information services;

f) to provide consultation services to national libraries, documentation centers and other libraries in the development of scientific and technical information resources and services. There is a special need for consultation service in the planning and design of computerized library and information systems; and

g) to consider the financial matters of joint activities.

The possibilities elaborated above are all basic and necessary for the region. The establishment of a region-wide subject or discipline oriented bibliographical data center or centers is not impractical if each of them evolves from an existing center or library within the region. The utilizing or reprocessing of bibliographical tapes produced by the existing abstracting and indexing services in the developed countries is an economic necessity for the developing countries. For example, at present no one country in Southeast Asia can afford to produce the Chemical Abstracts itself with the limited financial, technical, and human resources at its disposal. The regional centers can, however, supplement the acquired databases by adding to them the locally indexed and abstracted inputs produced from local scientific and technical publications and reports.

To successfully carry out the possible activities already mentioned, there are a few basic considerations which must be kept in mind.

1. Regional cooperation should be based on the voluntary participation of national libraries, documentation centers, and major academic and research libraries within the region. The network of regional information systems should be flexible in structure as suggested in the UNISIST report.①

2. The establishment of regional information centers should be in the spirit of cooperation instead of competition. Unnecessary duplication of efforts should be avoided.

3. Regional cooperation should be planned according to the specific conditions and requirements of the region. It should be tailor-made rather than transplanted.

4. It is recommended that the make up of the "region" should not be strictly defined. Although initially the cooperation may be confined to Malaysia, Singapore, Indonesia, the Philippines, and Thailand, other countries in the region are welcome to join if they so desire.

---

① United Nations Educational, Scientific and Cultural Organization/International Council of Scientific Unions, *op. cit.*, p. 19.

AIT'S Role in Regional Cooperation

In considering the scientific and technical information needs of the region and the cooperative efforts to provide for it, it is desirable to examine the unique role the Asian Institute of Technology (AIT) plays in the region and its plan to build up strong library and information resources which, when fully developed, will suffice to serve as a regional information center.

The Asian Institute of Technology located centrally in Bangkok, is a regional graduate school of engineering. It has an international faculty and its students come from 18 countries in Asia to study in the Diploma, Master's and Doctoral programs and to do research. Its graduates stay in Asia to apply their newly gained knowledge to the development of this vast region — only 4 percent have left Asia to work in the West. The AIT is uniquely chartered as a private non-profit regional institution and is recognized as an "international organization" in every respect.

Since its inception in 1959 AIT has grown steadily and its sphere of activities in Asia has widened greatly — both geographically and in services and programs offered. [1] Its objectives are to provide:

1. Educational opportunities at the master's and doctorate levels.

2. Through post-graduate diploma courses and short-term institutes, opportunities for practicing engineers in the region to keep abreast of technological developments and their application to the needs of the region.

3. Stimuli for the development of research oriented specifically to the needs of the region by the establishment of a major research center within AIT.

4. Opportunities for faculty members from other educational institutions to study and conduct research at AIT.

5. A focus for the development of engineering education to meet the unique needs of the region.

6. Mechanisms for the introduction into the region of the latest developments in technology and for the development of their application to its needs.

7. A center for the development of equipment for research and instructional laboratories.

8. An outstanding library to serve the needs of both AIT and the region.

9. A major computing center, designed and operated to serve AIT and other institutions in the region.

10. A regional focal point and catalyst for the development of professional activities, including conferences and seminars, and a center for the publication of technical information for the region.

The fields of study presently offered at AIT encompass the following divisions:
- Environmental Engineering
- Geotechnical Engineering
- Structural Engineering and Mechanics
- Systems Engineering and Management
- Transportation Engineering
- Water Science and Engineering

Additional fields will be added according to the needs of the region:
- Agricultural Engineering (to commence in January 1972)
- Electrical Engineering — Power Systems (to commence in August 1972)
- Computer Science
- Economic Geology
- Chemical Engineering
- Food Technology

---

[1] Before 1967, AIT was known as the SEATO Graduate School of Engineering. It is now totally independent from SEATO.

Mechanical Engineering

It is anticipated that by 1980 AIT will become a complete institute of technology with a total enrollment of 1,000 graduate students.

In order that AIT can achieve its long-range goals and broad objectives, a new campus on a site of 400 acres 42 kilometers north of Bangkok is being constructed. The total capital investment for the new campus will be in the amount of 20 million U. S. dollars. The first phase of construction costing 6.2 million U. S. dollars will be completed in August 1972. A 1.6 – million U. S. dollar Library and Computer Center Complex which will occupy 100,000 sq. ft. of space is being planned for 1974.

Pursuant to the objectives, particularly number 8, the Institute has, ever since its conception, devoted a large portion of its resources to the development of a well stocked library. According to the long-range projection of the library, its collection of books will be expanded from 30,000 volumes at present to 300,000 volumes in the 1980s. During the same period, its journal titles will be increased from 1,000 to 5,000.

The long-range development plan of the AIT Library also includes the following which are significant to regional cooperation:

1. To establish a computer-based bibliographical data bank.

Because of the critically high cost in cataloging, indexing, and abstracting of books, documents, technical publications and reports, journal articles, and papers of conference proceedings, the library seeks to utilize the existing cataloging, indexing, and abstracting services available in machine-readable form as the major input of its data bank and to supplement them with its own selected bibliographical data cataloged and indexed from its own collections.

Based on the recently published survey of scientific and technical tape services,① there are 55 known bibliographical data sources now available on magnetic tapes which can be obtained either by subscription or by special arrangement. ② A few of the widely known tape services are listed below:

Chemical Abstracts — Condensates.

Engineering Index — Compendex.

Institute of Electrical and Electronics Engineers — IEEE

REFLECS (Retrieval from the Literature on Electronics and Computer Sciences).

Institution of Electrical Engineers — INSPEC Tape Service.

International Atomic Energy Agency — INIS Output Tape.

U. S. Government Research and Development Reports (USGRDR).

U. S. Library of Congress — MARC Distribution Service.

Initially AIT will seek to acquire bibliographical data in engineering and related subject areas such as CA Condensates, EI Compendex, INSPEC, USGRDR, HRIS, and CAIN, and to add others later as may be needed. Close coordination will be undertaken with other libraries and documentation centers in the region that may also plan to establish such bibliographical data banks in other subject areas so that unnecessary duplication of efforts and subject coverage can be avoided.

Besides the above databases, the AIT Library also plans to make use of the MARC (Machine Readable Cataloging) tapes of both the U. S. and U. K. to aid in book selection, acquisition, cataloging, processing, SDI (selective dissemination of information) service, and current and retrospective bibliographical search, etc. Once they are in operation, most of these services will

---

① Kenneth D. Carroll, *Survey of Scientific-Technical Tape Services* (New York: American Institute of Physics, 1970), p. 64. (PB 196 154)

② Although the survey by Carroll does not include those tapes made by government sources not available to the general public (e. g., NASA and DDC – U. S. Defense Documentation Center), it also omits a number of other tape services known to exist (e. g., MIT INTREX—Information Transfer Experiment—tape, Highways Research Information Service—HRIS, MEDLARS—Medical Literature Analysis and Retrieval System of the U. S. National Library of Medicine, and CAIN—Cataloging and Indexing—tape of the U. S. National Agricultural Library).

undoubtedly be made available to other libraries and documentation center as well as to industries, government agencies, and individual researchers and engineers on a cost-sharing basis in order to bring down the unit cost. This experiment will begin as soon as there is access to a large computer system capable of processing the magnetic tapes and the required financial support which is being sought by the Institute becomes available.

2. To experiment with satellite communication for immediate interconnection with major libraries and national documentation centers in and outside the region.

There is now a very promising experiment underway at the University of Hawaii called "Pan Pacific Education and Communication Experiments by Satellite" (PEACESAT). The essence of this experiment is to use the ATS (Applications Technology Satellite) geostationary satellite owned by the U. S. National Aeronautics and Space Administration (NASA) as a relay to interconnect institutions of higher education in the Pacific basin for purpose of two-way voice, teletype, and facsimile communications. The University of Hawaii has developed a very effective low-cost ground station capable of transmitting and receiving the three types of information. We are now making contact with both the University of Hawaii and NASA for participation in the experiment and in the use of ATS satellites. Once the arrangements are made, we plan to set up a ground station in Bangkok with communication linkage with the Library of the University of Hawaii and other major libraries in California, U. S. A., in Australia, and in New Zealand where such ground stations will he installed. This communication network when established will greatly facilitate the flow of scientific and technical information into the region. Furthermore, if the cost of such equipment is low enough, a regional network of ground stations can be strategically located with interconnections of at least one library or documentation center in each country.

3. To plan and design a computerized library system providing the necessary support for the two major undertakings mentioned. Currently, two such sub-systems employing an IBM 1130 computer system are already in operation—one in journal listing and control and one in acquisitions and accounting. ① Restricted by the limited capacity of the present computer, further computer applications will have to wait until a large computer system is installed on the campus.

Planning And Implementation Strategy

In view of the future plans of the AIT Library and the two projected major undertakings which will have a region-wide implication and significance, it is necessary that a regional coordinating council be founded to coordinate the program and development of the AIT Library in relationship with the national libraries, documentation centers, and major academic and research libraries in the region and to plan for other cooperative activities among the libraries and documentation centers.

It is suggested that the council members should consist of national representatives as well as representatives from UNESCO, FID/CAO (Commission for Asia and Oceania of the International Federation for Documentation), ASPAC (The Asian and Pacific Council), ASAIHL (The Association of Southeast Asian Institutions of Higher Learning), SEAMEO (South East Asian Ministers of Education Organization), and AIT who are interested in and concerned about regional cooperation. It is further suggested that a planning committee for the establishment of the proposed "Regional Coordinating Council" be founded as soon as can be arranged under the sponsorship of UNESCO and AIT. The planning committee should consist of one representative from each of the participating countries such as Malaysia. Singapore, Indonesia, the Philippines, and Thailand plus one each from UNESCO and AIT.

The time has come for concrete action in regional cooperation. The developing countries in Southeast Asia will be greatly benefitted by the joint force of their national libraries, documentation centers, and academic and research libraries in searching for effective ways and means to share

---

① Detailed description of these two operations are reported in the author's article "Library Mechanization at the Asian Institute of Technology", *International Library Review*, V. 3 No. 3 (June 1971), pp. 257 – 270.

their information resources and services in science and technology for the betterment of life and the well-being of their people. This spirit of cooperation is imperative if the scientific and technical information needs of the region are to be fulfilled.

Regional Cooperation for ISDS

Introduction

Perhaps the most significant development in the library and documentation field, world-wide, during the 1970s is the major surge of international cooperation in information transfer and sharing through the standardization of bibliographic description and improved tools for systems interconnection. The role played by UNESCO to spearhead this movement has won great acclaim the world over, but the success of this development is also the result of the cooperation and support of many other international organizations such as the International Council of Scientific Unions (ICSU) which, in collaboration with UNESCO, jointly sponsored the inquiry into the feasibility of a World Science Information System (UNISIST)①.

The International Federation of Library Associations (IFLA), long active in international cooperation, contributed to the standardization of bibliographic description which culminated in the publication of ISBD (M)② and ISBD (S)③ and in the establishment of an Bibliographic Control (UBC)④ among all nations.

To establish the foundation necessary for effective Universal Bibliographic Control and information transfer, in September 1974, UNESCO together with IFLA, FID (International Federation of Documentation), and ICA (International Council of Archives), convened an Intergovernmental Conference on the Planning of National Documentation, Library and Archives Infrastructures in Paris. ⑤ At this conference which was attended by delegates from 86 countries, a new program called "National Information System" (NATIS) was launched. This string of developments beginning with the UNISIST program has turned the pages of library history to an exciting new chapter.

The UNISIST program which was formally established by UNESCO in 1972 at its 17th Session of the General Conference grew out from the feasibility study undertaken jointly by UNESCO and ICSU from 1967 to 1971 and the recommendations made at the Intergovernmental Conference that convened in October 1971 specifically to consider the program proposal put forth in the study report.

While the long-range goal of the UNISIST program is to develop international networks of information services in the various sectors of sciences, it also establishes five intermediate objectives on which many program recommendations are based. These objectives are:

1. To undertake activities for improvement of the tools of systems interconnection.

2. To provide assistance for strengthening the functions and improving the performance of the institutional components of the information transfer chain.

3. To help in the development of the specialized manpower essential for the planning and operation of information networks, especially in the developing countries.

---

① *Study Report on the Feasibility of a World Science Information System by the United Nations Educational, Scientific and Cultural Organization and the International Council of Scientific Unions* (Paris: UNESCO, 1971). (UNESCO/UNISIST/4)

② International Federation of Library Associations. ISBD (M) —*International Standard Bibliographic Description for Monographic Publications*. 1st standard ed. (London: IFLA Committee on Cataloguing, 1974). ISBN 0-903043-02-5.

③ *ISBD (S) —International Standard Bibliographic Description for Serials, Recommended by the Joint Working Group on the International Standard Bibliographic Description for Serials set up by the IFLA Committee on Cataloguing and the IFLA Committee on Serial Publications* (London: IFLA Committee on Cataloguing 1974). ISBN 0-903043-03-3.

④ Dorothy Anderson, *Universal Bibliographic Control*, Intergovernmental Conference on the Planning of National Documentation, Library and Archives Infrastructures, Paris, 23-27 September 1974. (Paris: UNESCO, 1974). (COM-74/NATIS/Ref. 3)

⑤ *Final Report, Intergovernmental Conference on the Planning of National Documentation, Library, and Archives Infrastructures, Paris, 23-27 September 1974* (Paris: UNESCO, 1975). (CQM/MD/30)

4. To encourage the development of scientific information policies and national networks.

5. To assist Member States, especially the developing countries, in the creation and development of their infrastructure in the field of scientific and technical information.

Under these five broad objectives, a variety of programs have been planned or are being carried out by the Division of Scientific and Technological Information and Documentation of UNESCO which acts as the executive office for the UNISIST program.

What is ISDS?

The International Serials Data System (ISDS), an important component of the UNISIST program, was established in 1972 after its original proposal which was contained in the "Report on the Feasibility of an International Serials Data System, and Preliminary System Design"① was approved by the UNISIST Central Committee, and recommended to UNESCO for implementation. The system as outlined in the report envisions a two-tier organizational structure consisting of an International Centre (IC) and a network of national and regional centers (NC and RC) jointly responsible for the creation and maintenance of computer-based data banks, which hold essential information for the identification of serials.

According to the first issue of the *ISDS Bulletin* published in 1974, "The aim of ISDS is to provide a reliable registry of world serial publications covering the full range of recorded knowledge. It is responsible for assigning to each serial published under a given title, a unique and unambiguous numeric code identifier, the International Standard Serial Number (ISSN)."

Through an agreement between UNESCO and the French Government, the International Centre for the Registration of Serial Publications was established in Paris with funds provided by the two founding bodies.

The operation policy of the ISDS network is based on a set of common rules and standards which cover the ISSN, rules for ISSN assignment, the content of ISDS data files on international, national and regional levels, the use of standard data element specifications, tagging schemes, character sets and magnetic tape formats for interchange and integration purposes. Detailed descriptions of the structure, policies, procedures and specifications of ISDS are given in the Guidelines for ISDS which is available in English, French, Japanese, Russian and Spanish.②

Since the success of the ISDS network depends to a large extent on the establishment of national or regional centers in every part of the world and the effective coordination of their activities, the UNESCO Member States and associate members were invited in November 1972 by the Director General of UNESCO to establish such centers. To date, 19 national centers and one regional centre have been declared. The 19 national centers are: U.S.A., U.K., Australia, Canada, Federal Republic of Germany, France, Argentina, Japan, Finland, Yugoslavia, Nigeri, Thailand, Tunisia, Holland, Sweden, Brazil, Indonesia, and the Philippines. The one Regional Centre in Moscow consists of the U.S.S.R., Bulgaria, Czechoslovakia, the German Democratic Republic, Hungary, Mongolia, Poland and Cuba. More than half of the national centers have already begun operation.

Why a Regional Centre?

Although three national centers in the Southeast Asian Region have been declared, none is in operation as yet. While planning is still in progress for some, it is felt that, perhaps, the concept of having a regional centre in Southeast Asia should be explored and their advantages be examined. Some of the advantages are:

1. From the economical point of view, because the number of current serial publications in

---

① In M. D. Martin and C. I. Barnes. *Report on the Feasibility of an International Serials Data System*, prepared for UNISIST/ICSU-AB Working Group on Bibliographic Description. (London: INSPEC, 1970). (DM/CB/284)

② *Guidelines for ISDS: UNISIST, International Serials Data System (ISDS)*. International Centre for the Registration of Serial Publications. (Paris: UNESCO 1973) (SC/WS/538)

most of the Southeast Asian countries is relatively small, it will not pay for each country to develop and maintain a computer-based serial data bank separately. The regional centre is economically feasible when, particularly, if the use of a computer is considered.

2. In terms of funding, the regional centre will have far more leverage than a national centre in seeking financial supports.

3. The regional centre also provides an answer to the scarcity of trained manpower in the Region. In addition, the proposed regional centre can provide training opportunities for serial librarians in the Southeast Asian countries.

4. The establishment of a regional centre will help those countries that may otherwise not be able to participate in ISDS for some time to come.

5. With a computer-based serial data bank, a variety of services can be provided as a by-product to the participating countries, e. g., the printing of new serial titles, both regional and national at desired intervals.

6. The computer-based serial data bank can be easily duplicated to provide each participating country a ready-made serial record in machine-readable form whenever needed.

7. The regional centre could serve as a catalyst for further cooperation in the Region.

How to Proceed?

With the many advantages given in the preceding section of this paper, it seems clear that the establishment of a regional centre in Southeast Asia is highly desirable. But the question immediately coming to mind is "How is this to be done?" To answer this, UNESCO, at the request of the Royal Thai Government, has engaged the author, the former Director of the Library and Information Center, Asian Institute of Technology, to return to Southeast Asia for a three week mission to prepare a program proposal for the potential pilot project.

In order to carry out his mission, the author plans to visit Thailand, Malaysia, Singapore, Indonesia, and the Philippines between November 21 and December 14, 1975. The visit would have the following six objectives:

1. To assess the present situation of serial publications in these countries.

2. To evaluate the current status of bibliographical control for serial publications in these countries.

3. To identify the national body and, possibly, the individual person (s) responsible for the bibliographical control of serial publications in each of these countries.

4. To negotiate with appropriate authorities in each of these countries for their participation in the proposed regional centre.

5. To solicit inputs from various sources for the establishment of the centre.

6. To hold an open discussion on the preliminary plan of the Centre at the Third Conference of Southeast Asian Librarians to be held in Jakarta from December 1 to 5, 1975.

It is hoped that at the conclusion of the visit, a detailed program proposal can be prepared based on the data gathered and the feedbacks received during the discussions.

To facilitate such discussions, it is felt that a written outline of the preliminary plan as conceived by the author should be made available as a base for discussion. A sketch of this preliminary plan which covers such considerations as objectives, organization, operation, and financing is presented below.

The Preliminary Plan

1. Objectives:

A. To establish a computer-based regional serials data bank for serials published in each of the participating countries using the ISDS format and ISSN.

B. To serve as a regional node of the ISDS International Centre by putting the local data into the data bank of the International Centre and by acting as a liaison between the International

Centre and the representatives of participating countries in the Region.

  C. To improve the bibliographical control of serial publications in each participating country.

  D. To facilitate the information transfer on serial publications both within and beyond the Region.

  E. To foster a spirit of cooperation among participating countries.

2. Organization:

  A. It is proposed that the Regional Centre be established in Thailand under the auspices of its National Library. The Director of the National Library also serves as the Director of the Regional Centre.

  B. The countries interested in participating in the Regional Centre may do so on a voluntary basis.

  C. Each participating country should designate a national agency to act as the national representative for the Regional Centre. The national agency should be the one which has a general responsibility in the handling of serial publications of the country, such as the national library.

  D. There should be an advisory committee consisting of 5 to 10 members with one representative nominated by each national agency and 1 to 3 technical experts appointed by the Director. The committee should meet once a year to consider policy, procedure and budget of the Centre.

  E. A full-time executive secretary should be appointed by the Director to take charge of day-to-day operations.

  F. The Centre should have an adequate number of staff to handle the flow of work.

3. Operations:

  A. The national representative in each participating country should supply information on serial publications of its country at least once a month, on the standard worksheet adopted by the International Centre and in accordance with the rules set out in the Guidelines for ISDS and its supplements. A photocopy of the cover and the title page of each serial publication should accompany the worksheet.

  B. The Regional Centre will check the correctness of each worksheet and will assign an ISSN to each serial publication. The national representative will be notified of the ISSN assigned and should in turn inform the publisher concerned and persuade him to use the ISSN in all issues of the serial publication.

  C. The national representatives should prepare promotional materials and conduct workshops for serial publishers in their respective countries to acquaint them with the purpose and intend of ISSN.

  D. The Regional Centre will be responsible for the development of a computerized system to handle the input, merge and update of all serial records and to generate magnetic tapes for submission to the International Centre.

  E. The Regional Centre will provide the national agency of each participating country with a periodic printout of the complete regional record together with a separate national list of new serial titles.

  F. The Regional Centre will act as a regional clearinghouse on information concerning serial publications. It should maintain a complete list of serial records of the International Centre and the necessary reference and bibliographic tools on serials.

  G. An annual workshop for the national representatives will be conducted in Bangkok in conjunction with the annual meeting of the advisory committee to familiarize them with the operations and latest development of both the International Centre and the Regional Centre.

  H. In cooperation with library schools and other educational institutions the Regional Centre may conduct in-service training programs, short courses, seminars, etc. on bibliographic control of serial publications and other related subjects.

4. Financing:

A. Because the Regional Centre is conceived as a regional pilot project of UNESCO, it is proposed that for the initial period of five years the financial support for the Regional Centre is to be sought from UNDP or from other funding sources.

B. Budget requests of the Regional Centre for the first two years of operation should include such line items as:

Salaries and fringe benefits for the Executive Secretary and other staff members.
—Meeting expenses of the advisory committee.
—Expenses of the annual workshop for national representatives.
—Travel expenses for the Director and the Executive Secretary to attend regional and international meetings on ISDS.
—Cost of developing a computerized system and computer time.
—Equipment and supplies.
—Postage, telegraph, TWX, etc.
—Miscellaneous.

C. Long-range financial requirement of the Centre should be reviewed by the advisory committee which is responsible for the establishment of fiscal policies and the approval of future budgets.

Conclusions and Recommendations

This paper has reviewed the recent major developments in international cooperation with particular reference to the UNISIST program and ISDS. A proposal is made to establish a Regional Centre for ISDS in Southeast Asia as a pilot project of UNESCO. To facilitate discussions in connection with the UNESCO sponsored mission, the author has drafted a preliminary plan for the establishment of the Regional Centre to be used during his three-week visit to Thailand, Malaysia, Singapore, Indonesia, and the Philippines. Communications to the author on any aspects of the preliminary plan are most welcome.

In order that the Regional Centre can be established at the earliest date possible it is recommended that:

1. All countries interested in participating in the regional project are urged to designate a national agency which will then appoint one of its staff as national representative,

2. The National Library of Thailand is requested to take immediate action to convene a planning meeting for the Regional Centre and to establish an ad hoc committee for the organization of the Regional Centre. All national representatives should be invited,

3. UNESCO is requested to act swiftly on the program proposal and to provide funds for the planning meeting to be held in Bangkok early in 1976,

4. The final program proposal should be submitted to funding sources as soon as possible, and

5. Besides the five countries already identified, other Southeast Asian countries that are interested in participating in the Regional Centre are requested to inform the ad hoc organization committee about their intents.

It is hoped that the participants of the Third Conference of the Southeast Asian Librarians would give their endorsement and support to this regional project which shares the same aspiration as the conference: to further library development through regional cooperation.

Educating for International Interdependence:
The Role of the Academic Library — Ohio University and Malaysia①

We are pleased to address you today both because of the fond memories that we have of visiting Malaysia and working with many fine librarians from Malaysia in regional programs and because of the special relationship which exists between our Library and Malaysia. We do not have to remind many of you that this conference coincides with the inauguration of the Malaysian Resource Center in the Southeast Asia Collection of Ohio University Libraries. We will return to that subject later.

Before beginning our remarks, we should commend the Minister and his predecessors. The academic libraries, library collections, and the librarians of Malaysia set a standard which other nations in the region struggle to approach. This is particularly noteworthy when one recalls that, with one exception, the development of universities in Malaysia, and previously in Malaya, has been accomplished during the past twenty-five years. We trust, that in discussing the role and contributions that the Ohio University Library has made and can make, that we do not convey the idea that academic libraries within Malaysia have done less than an outstanding job, and certainly the strong support of the government and the respective universities over the past quarter century have made this possible.

We do believe that there is a role, and even a responsibility, for academic libraries in the United States in cooperating with students, scholars, colleagues, institutions, and governments in Third World nations. In reviewing the possible themes that we would like to discuss today, we have decided to focus on two. ②

We have chosen these complementary themes because we believe that they are of considerable importance but also because they reflect particular strengths and contributions of Ohio University Library, and thus we are able to discuss practice rather than theory. In brief, the themes are:

1. affording opportunities for continuing education and growth among professional librarians in Malaysia (exemplified in the international internship program pioneered by Ohio University Library and its Southeast Asia Collection in 1979), and

2. the two-fold task of providing appropriate resources for students from abroad in the U. S. and for increasing awareness among Americans of other nations and cultures with which they share the planet (of which the new Malaysian Resource Center marks a new direction).

International Library Internships

We have described our international library internships in some detail elsewhere③ and today will confine our remarks to a few highlights and a brief consideration of the relevance of this program for today's theme, "Higher Education and Economic Development in Malaysia — Thinking Ahead," and for libraries in Malaysia, particularly libraries serving institutions of higher education.

In Asia, and in Malaysia in particular, librarianship has generally been recognized as an

---

① Co-Author: K. Mulliner. Paper presented to First Tun Abdul Razak Conference on Southeast Asia Studies, "Higher Education And Economic Development in Malaysia — Thinking Ahead", at Ohio University, May 10, 1985.

② A wider range of activities was described in K. Mulliner, Hwa-Wei Lee, and Lian The-Mulliner, "International Information Exchange and Southeast Asia Collections —A View from the U. S.", *Journal of Educational Media Science*, Vol. 18, No. 2 (Winter 1980), pp. 3 - 18; reprinted in this volume.

③ Hwa-Wei Lee, "International Library Internships: An Effective Approach to Co-operation", *International Library Review*, Vol. 17 (1985), pp. 17 - 25; reprinted in this volume. Also, K. Mulliner and Hwa-Wei Lee, "International Exchange of Librarians and the Ohio University Internship Program", *College & Research Libraries News*, Vol. 43, No. 10 (November 1982), pp. 345 - 348; reprinted in this volume.

important professional activity. An active undergraduate library science curriculum is offered at the MARA Institute of Technology. Recognition of the importance of qualified professionals has led to programs to send those who will occupy professional positions in the libraries for schooling in the U. K., U. S., Australia, and elsewhere. The result is a well-trained cadre of librarians.

It is perhaps this success that creates the challenge which we address through the international library internship program. As in other high-technology fields (yes, today librarianship is certainly a high-technology endeavor), change is the one constant with which we live in library and information science. As a result, the professional education which librarians received a decade ago now is dated, and education from earlier, no matter how germane at the time, seems almost quaint. Of course, professional activities help compensate for this — the Congress of Southeast Asian Librarians (CONSAL), of which we have been fortunate to attend meetings, is a particularly valuable interchange within the region[①]— and it would be possible to send the librarians back to school.

As neither is completely satisfactory (conferences are too brief for real hands-on experience and schooling is too lengthy, costly, and also lacking in practical experience), the international library internship program addresses a real need in providing opportunities to work with the latest in library and information technology in a library setting. Briefly, professional librarians at the middle-management level spend three to six months undertaking a personally tailored program of practical experience. Usually, interns will divide their time roughly in half between working in their particular areas of responsibility (i. e., cataloging, acquisitions, or reference) and half their time spending brief periods in all of the other library departments. This permits the development of the specific skills and knowledge needed for an individual's immediate responsibilities and also a greater understanding and appreciation of the activities of the other departments in the library and how these mesh to support the library's mission — providing perspectives which will prepare them for greater management responsibilities in their home institutions.

For librarians and library science faculty from Southeast Asia, our internationally recognized Southeast Asia Collection, headed by Ms. Lian The-Mulliner, affords additional opportunities to work with many of the same materials and languages which they will encounter in their home institutions.

In addition to our outstanding Southeast Asia Collection, Ohio University Library can offer ample opportunity to become familiar with the latest in library and information technology, to investigate how such technology impacts on library organization and management, and to discuss with librarians familiar with the region how such technology might fit into the Southeast Asian context. Of course, it is up to each intern to draw on her or his own special knowledge of the context in which she works to interpret the information given. The goal is not to provide pat answers and uncritical adoption of Western answers to an Asian environment but rather to provide stimulating experiences and professional guidance to assist the interns in determining such answers for themselves.

Beyond our valuable staff who bring human qualities as well as an awareness of Asia and Southeast Asia, Ohio University Library has other advantages which make it an ideal site for such a program. We would be remiss if we did not mention the support and assistance which the Library receives from our University President, our Provost and other senior administrators, our outstanding Center for International Studies under Dr. Felix Gagliano and the International Student and Faculty Services Office as well as the faculty, staff and students of the University in general.

In assisting the interns to explore the applications of technology to library services, we have a relatively long history in such applications. In the 1960s, we were a founding member of OCLC

---

① The published proceedings of the recent meetings are informative. D. E. K. Wijasuriya, Yip Seong Chun, and Syed Salim Agha (eds.), *Access to Information: Proceedings of the Fifth Congress of Southeast Asian Librarians, Kuala Lumpur, 25 – 29 May 1981* (KuaJa Lumpur: CONSAL V, 1982), and *The Library in the Information Revolution: Proceedings of the Sixth Congress of Southeast Asian Librarians, Singapore, 30 May – 3 June 1983* (Singapore: CONSAL VI, 1983).

(now the Online Computer Library Center but then the Ohio College Library Center), a national and international library network with 6,000 member libraries and which, within its database, contains almost 12 million library records and is adding over 1 million more each year. In 1971, Ohio University Library was the first member institution to input a record online into that system. Today, with OCLC, we are able to share the demanding tasks of cataloging with all other member institutions, to identify which other member institutions may have a copy of a book or article which our library users may need, and online to ask that, or several, institutions to lend it to us. Conversely, all of the other member institutions are able to identify the materials which we have and to request to borrow them from us — a valuable plus for the Malaysian Resource Center and one of which I hope all of the Malaysian and American visitors from other institutions in this country are aware. The networking through OCLC is a striking example of cooperation to share scarce resources and to maximize the effectiveness of skilled personnel.

In serving our local users, we have an automated library system based on the Virginia Tech Library System (VTLS), known locally as ALICE, which provides an automated circulation system, an online public access catalog for users, and all of this is based on our computerized cataloging through OCLC. Other enhancements to automate serials control and acquisitions are expected in the next year. ① This system also permits users of terminals from anywhere on campus or microcomputers in their homes to access the public catalog to identify materials. As this is not a library meeting, we will not amplify on our pride and joy with the system.

Augmenting the system to identify the latest information available, we offer computerized searching of most indexes using microcomputers to download the information identified. Beyond these, microcomputers are used for a large and growing number of administrative and routine tasks. The import, for the intern, is that there is ample opportunity to encounter and work with virtually the gamut of computer applications to library service.

We will mention only one additional strength of the internship program, that of location. The Columbus, Ohio, area is a major center of information technology today. OCLC is headquartered just outside in Dublin, Ohio, and Chemical Abstracts, which is in the forefront in providing online information services, is in Columbus as are Battelle and a range of other information services and companies. Major library and information science academic programs are available at Indiana University, Kent State University, the University of Kentucky and the University of Pittsburgh. In describing the information-rich environs, we cannot neglect Athens and the Ohio University' campus. Here the intern encounters a cosmopolitan university with a large international student enrollment and a university and community committed to international understanding, all of this in a beautiful and relatively safe environment, some distance from the distractions of urban centers.

Lest we wax poetic, let us conclude the discussion of the international internship program with some realities. In the past six years, internship training has been provided to more than 20 professional librarians from all of the ASEAN countries (except Brunei and Singapore), from Taiwan, the People's Republic of China, Papua New Guinea, and Saudi Arabia. Support for the program has been provided by UNESCO, the Asia Foundation, the U. S. Agency for International Development, the U. S. Department of Education, and from the interns' home governments and institutions. We would add that while we have direct costs which must be met, the costs are only a fraction of what it would cost for a formal educational program abroad and the results, based on the evaluations which we have received from the interns and their home institutions, have been impressive. To date, we have only had one participant from Malaysia, but we would hope that such an opportunity might be extended to others in the future.

---

① The system and our experiences are described in Hwa-Wei Lee, K. Mulliner, E. Hoffmann-Pinther, and Hannah McCauley, "Alice at One: Candid Reflections on the Adoption, Installation, and Use of the Virginia Tech Library System (VTLS) at Ohio University;" paper presented at the Integrated Online Library Systems Second National Conference, September 13 – 14, 1984, Atlanta, Georgia. Published in the *Proceedings* (Canfield, Ohio: Genaway and Associates, 1984), pp. 228 – 242; reprinted in this volume.

Malaysian Resource Center

Earlier this morning, we had the pleasure of attending, with our distinguished guests from Malaysia, the opening of the Malaysian Resource Center within the Library's Southeast Asia Collection. All of you have received a brochure describing the Center and its projected activities. Without repeating that information, we will make two points.

The first is that today's ceremony was an impressive step, but only one of many which have gone before and many that will follow. Since its creation in 1967, the Southeast Asia Collection has, in less than two decades, grown into a major national and international resource for research on Southeast Asia (in this, it is not unlike the nation of Malaysia which traces its prominence to *Merdeka* [independence] only a decade earlier than the Collection). Some years ago, the Southeast Asia Collection undertook a serious assessment of its national and international role. It was recognized that publications from and about Southeast Asia were ballooning to an extent that no academic library in the U. S. could hope or afford to collect everything from and about every country in the region. The wisdom of this analysis was attested to at a meeting this past March in conjunction with the national Association for Asian Studies Annual Conference in Philadelphia, in which representatives from the eight academic research libraries with Southeast Asian Collections and the Library of Congress discussed ways in which responsibilities might be shared.

In its decision to concentrate its collection development efforts, the Southeast Asia Collection considered its historical, local, and national roles. Historically, when the Collection was created concurrently with the Southeast Asia Studies Program (under the direction of Professors Norman Parmer and Paul van der Veur), the Program and the Collection focused on Malaysia and Indonesia. Locally, the University has developed significant ties with Malaysia (personified today in holder of the Tun Abdul Razak Chair in Southeast Asian Studies, Datin Professor Fatimah Hamid Don) while the Southeast Asia Studies Program (now Center) has built on those beginnings to also develop strengths on the Philippines. Nationally, the Collection observed that, while Cornell had unapproachable strengths for Indonesia and most other countries in the region were receiving major attention from one or more of the other collection, no Collection had identified Malaysia and its neighboring states of Brunei and Singapore as foci. As a result, in the past decade, the Southeast Asia Collection has concentrated on these nations with secondary emphasis on the Association for Southeast Asian Nations (ASEAN) and its other member nations.

For Malaysia, as the occasion of our discussion, this means that Ohio University receives as much and usually more materials from Malaysia than any other academic institution in the U. S. We believe that it is safe to say, despite the outstanding growth and development of libraries in Malaysia, only the National Library and libraries serving some of the major universities in Malaysia, have larger collections on Malaysia than Ohio University.

With this background and with Ohio University Library's commitment to resource sharing, the Malaysian Resource Center is a logical step. In part it recognizes the reality that the Southeast Asian Collection should be a primary source for anyone seeking research materials on Malaysia. It also represents a long standing commitment to service beyond the immediate users at Ohio University. Companies and U. S. government officials are increasingly aware that we may be the only institution with particular Malaysian materials. We would add that the service which they receive is also an important attraction.

Beyond those who need materials for research, academic, policy, or financial interests, there are millions of Americans who know little about Malaysia and whose lives are the poorer for that ignorance. Within the Center for International Studies, there have been, and continue to be, active programs to increase international awareness in the schools of Southeastern Ohio and to engage in citizenship awareness to make the wider population more cognizant of the cultural richness of the world. While the Malaysian Resource Center will not, with the simple cutting of a ribbon, banish the ignorance in this country of Malaysia and things Malaysian, it is a further step on the road. It will support the outreach program of the Center for International Studies and similar programs elsewhere in the U. S. It is lighting a candle rather than cursing the darkness.

We are particularly pleased that the Malaysian Resource Center will offer films, tapes, and other materials beyond those usually thought of as information. It is consonant with the role of the library as a repository of the human record, not just the written record. Such materials offer the opportunity of reaching citizenry with a wide range of interests, who may be little interested in a scholarly tome but will find relaxation and common threads of human experience in a noblat record or a Shahnon Ahmad novel. We are sure that scholars, with the increasing attention given to popular history, will also find a rich repository in the future.

The second quality of the Malaysian Resource Center directly addresses the theme of this gathering. The more than 15,000 Malaysians studying in institutions of higher education in North America represent a serious challenge and responsibility for the academic community. Some of us who are older may recall schooling during a colonial era. The curriculum frequently focused on the colonial center with more information provided about the towns and provinces in the West than about neighboring kampongs and states. Not that such learning is necessarily bad, only that when it displaces students' awareness of their home history, heritage, and neighbors, something has been lost. This is not unlike what Malaysian students encounter when enrolled in academic institutions in North America. Few will find many courses on Asia, not to mention Southeast Asia. We are more fortunate at Ohio University, with its strong Southeast Asia Studies Center and numerous faculty who have taught and done research in Malaysia, but students should not expect that all of their American teachers will be familiar with the Malaysian and Southeast Asian situations.

If this is the case in general, it is much more true for students enrolled at other North American universities in specialized fields of knowledge such as science, engineering, education, and business, as so many Malaysians do — recognizing the economic development needs of Malaysia. Even if few Malaysian courses are offered, there is an alternative. As a student climbs the educational ladder, there are increasing opportunities for individual research and exploration, for testing the theories and lessons presented in class in contexts of the student's choosing.

The Malaysian Resource Center and the strength of the Southeast Asia Collection provide the substance for such testing, using Malaysian data and contexts. It is important to recognize that the mission of the Malaysian Resource Center is national. It serves not only the students and faculty at Ohio University or the citizenry of Southeastern Ohio. It is available to students and faculty across North America (the OCLC systems helps make this possible) attending or affiliated with American institutions. As an anonymous example, there is a Malaysian studying taxation at a major institution in a neighboring state. The student contacted our Collection to ask about property taxes in Malaysia, based on what the student is learning in courses in that institution. Based on the subsequent materials borrowed, it is evident that the student has discovered that Malaysia has a very different approach than that in the U. S. Multiply this example by hundreds and thousands and the potential value of the Malaysian Resource Center for Malaysia becomes clearer.

Certainly, not every student from Malaysia will want or need to use Malaysian materials. But it is important for the student, and for Malaysia in the longer run, that such materials be available and that Malaysian students be encouraged to take advantage of them. We would only add that we are already very pleased to help make our resources available to numerous Malaysians from other institutions who come here to do research during academic vacations. We would welcome more.

We are very pleased with the support and the materials of the Malaysian Embassy. We look forward to a continuing mutually beneficial association. We hope that the Minister and other government officials in Malaysia can help to identify Ohio University as a repository, if not a depository, for Malaysian materials. We also encourage the Embassy and the Malaysian Students Department to assist us in making Malaysian students in the U. S. more aware of the Malaysian Resource Center, of the materials in our Southeast Asia Collection, of our willingness to help and to share these materials, and of the advantages to the students and to Malaysia resulting from this effort.

As we closed the initial section with a discussion of realities, perhaps that is a fitting theme for the conclusion of the paper as well. While we have dealt at length on the strengths of the Malaysian Resource Center (current and potential) and of the Ohio University Library's Southeast Asia Collection, we hardly need remind everyone that such strengths do not come cheap. In the past two decades, the Collection has achieved its present stature as a result of substantial support from Ohio University, from the Library, and from the U. S. Government. Since the establishment of the Tun Razak Chair, some funding is also provided to assist us in strengthening our holdings of Malaysian materials and to address the research needs of the Tun Razak Professor. At the same time, publishing costs and the quantities of materials available in Malaysia and from other countries on Malaysia are rising.

We have emphasized the positive points in the growth of the Southeast Asia Collection. There have been other times, in the mid - 1970s, when Ohio University faced severe financial crises. Those are painful to remember and, we hope, behind us. Still, it was instructive. As a result of that experience, we are aware that public budgets are subject to many factors. To prevent such pain in the future, the Library is pleased to announce that, with the support of the President and the University administration and the Development Office, we have launched a campaign to provide an endowment for the Southeast Asia Collection of $1 million. We have already received initial gifts of more than $100,000 toward that goal. We believe that, with this endowment, we can assure that the next two decades of the Southeast Asia Collection and of the Malaysian Resource Center will be as fruitful as the past.

第四部分 国际交换与馆员培训

Section IV International Exchanges and Internships

International Exchange of Librarians And the Ohio University Internship Program[1]

Introduction

"International exchange of librarians" is often interpreted as those bilateral arrangements between institutions to exchange librarians on a short-term basis. The details of such arrangements vary from agreement to agreement and, as a rule, are expected to work out to the mutual advantage of both institutions and of the individuals. But, practically speaking, not all exchanges are bilateral nor on a one-to-one basis. Some may begin as unilateral and later become bilateral as a result of the relationships established while others may lead to multilateral or other asymmetrical relationships. No matter the form, it is likely that exchanges will require considerable negotiation, patience, and time to finalize a multitude of details. This paper will illustrate the above points by discussing some of the exchange opportunities available for American librarians and then by focusing on the library internship programs offered by the Ohio University Libraries.

Opportunities for American Librarians

Many of the exchange arrangements among American librarians and their foreign counterparts result from personal contacts. While this means that those individuals with international connections are most likely to develop further contacts, those wishing to join the international library community are not excluded. One of the media for initial contacts which has been little utilized is the advertisement section of professional journals.[2] This year, in response to an ad in *College & Research Libraries News*, April 1981, p. 108, placed by a French librarian, a colleague is arranging to switch jobs with his French counterpart. The realization of such exchanges requires not only the willingness of both individuals to agree to mutually satisfactory arrangement but also the strong yet flexible support of their respective library and institutional administrations. This latter is individual; therefore, special administrative actions may be required to make an exchange possible.

In addition to personal contacts, a variety of other approaches may also prove fruitful. The Fulbright Exchange Program and the Peace Corps, for examples, are two of the best known programs administered by the U.S. government. The Fulbright Program offers opportunities for teaching or research in professional fields, including library science, in many parts of the world — both developed and less developed. The Peace Corps, which lists library science as a programming emphasis is suitable for both young and experienced librarians interested in library service in less developed countries. Opportunities for Peace Corps Volunteers with library background or expertise include teaching, consulting, and service. Although monetarily the Peace Corps may not be the most attractive, the experience itself can be both challenging and rewarding. Two of my colleagues on a field trip to Southeast Asia last year reported encountering Peace Corps

---

[1] Co-Author: K. Mulliner. This paper was originally presented to the American Library Association International Relations Round Table at the Annual Conference in Philadelphia, Pa., on July 12, 1982.

[2] Also potentially valuable are the exchange notices sometimes carried in the *IFLA Journal*.

Volunteers working in libraries and teaching in library science programs. For such positions the Peace Corps offers a standard of living comparable to locally employed peers within libraries and other institutions. And, while it is not stressed by the Peace Corps, Volunteers receive a "readjustment allowance" of $175 for each month that they serve at the end of their assignments, reflecting a level of savings that many of us in the U. S. wish we could maintain.

Funded by U. S. government agencies and private foundations, the Committee on Scholarly Communication with the People's Republic of China (a joint standing committee of the American Council of Learned Societies, the National Academy of Sciences, and the Social Science Research Council) maintains a number of exchange programs with the People's Republic of China. The Committee has a program for American graduate students and postdoctoral scholars to carry out long-term study or research in affiliation with Chinese universities and research institutes; a short-term reciprocal exchange of senior-level Chinese and American scholars; a bilateral conference program; and an exchange of joint working groups in selected fields. Although American librarians have not actively participated in these programs, a visit by a group of Chinese librarians to this country was among the first exchange visits under the auspices of the Committee.

For experienced librarians and library educators, opportunities for short-term consulting or teaching assignments are frequently available through the U. S. Agency for International Development, the U. S. International Communication Agency (Ed.: since reverted to the more familiar U. S. Information Agency), the United Nations, UNESCO, the World Health Organization, and others. Some comparable opportunities may also be available through foundations and foreign governments and institutions. With the financial support of the Asian Development Bank and other international agencies, many universities in the developing nations of Asia are embarking on long-term development projects which will require the services of library consultants.

With rising standards of living in many developing countries, some can now offer salaries and employment attractive to librarians from the U. S. In Asia many American librarians are known to be (or to have been) employed in Hong Kong, Malaysia, Singapore, Taiwan, and Thailand, all of which have a strong demand for experienced librarians as they modernize their library services. There is a shortage of trained librarians in many of these countries.

Internships for Asian Librarians

To provide experience in modern library practices and concepts for middle and upper-level professionals in some Asian nations, Ohio University inaugurated a library internship program in 1979, initially at the request of Chulalongkorn University in Bangkok, Thailand. Since its inception, the program has been designed to serve two distinct groups of librarians from East and Southeast Asia. The first is comprised of middle or upper management personnel who have been working for several years and are now in need of upgrading their knowledge and skills, particularly with regard to the applications of technology to the information field. This group has since been broadened to include library science faculty, to provide them with practical experience to enhance their teaching capabilities. The second group includes recent graduates from professional degree programs in the U. S. and has aimed at providing hands-on experience with automated systems prior to returning to their home institutions to assume responsible positions.

The geographical preference indicated in this program arises from the strong ties of the Ohio University's Southeast Asia Collection with libraries and librarians from East and Southeast Asian countries. Thus far, three librarians from Thailand, one from Indonesia, and five from Taiwan have completed internships ranging from two to six months (although three months has been the preferred minimum). Among the interns, three are library science faculty and six hold responsible library positions at the middle management level or higher. Three of these also teach part-time in the library science programs of their institutions.

The success of these programs has attracted UNESCO funding for two of the library school faculty last year and two more this fall, each for three months. Another program, which is being carried out in cooperation with the Graduate School of Library and Information Science of Simmons College with partial funding from UNESCO, provides graduate library education at Simmons and practical training at Ohio University for a staff member from the Institute of Scientific and Technical Information of China (ISTIC). This program is especially tailored to combine education and training to meet a special need.

The internship programs at Ohio University Libraries[①] have, among others, the following special features:

1. As much as possible, the training program for each intern is planned to suit the individual needs of the intern and his/her institution. It takes into consideration the intern's educational background, previous training and experience, and career goals.

2. The length of an internship, normally three to six months, proves to be mutually beneficial for the interns and for the Ohio University Libraries. It provides sufficient time for the interns to be trained in their chosen areas of specialization plus it affords an overview and some experience in library management and departmental operations. During the internship period, the Library in return receives the services of the interns. Their area and language expertise are welcome additions to the Southeast Asia Collection and the Cataloging Department. The internships also include attendance at selected library workshops and conferences as well as visits to major libraries in the eastern United States. For instance, within easy driving distance is Columbus, the home of OCLC, Chemical Abstracts Service, and Ohio State University. Several library schools (including Kent State, Case Western Reserve, Pittsburgh, and Indiana) are also conveniently accessible.

3. Although the internships stress modern library concepts and the practice includes computerization and networking such as OCLC online cataloging and interlibrary loan systems, database searches, etc., special attention is given to the applicability of the technologies to the interns' home countries. The Library's Southeast Asia Collection, one of the best in the U. S., provides an ideal learning environment for the interns to relate their training to familiar materials and situations.

4. Complementing the Southeast Asia Collection, Ohio University Libraries also has a number of staff members familiar with library development in Asian countries. These professionals are able to guide and advise the interns with regard to their individual needs. Additionally, Ohio University has strong ties with a number of educational institutions in Asia, particularly Malaysia. This is evidenced in the recent joint gift by the Malaysian government and U. S. corporations to establish the endowed Tun Abdul Razak Chair for Malaysian Studies at Ohio University. These associations which span diverse faculty and administrators contribute to a cordial and supportive working and learning environment for the interns.

Adequate financing is of course essential to implementation of the intern program. Essentially, there are three types of direct costs involved:

1. **Travel Expenses.** These include the international travel to Ohio and return, local transportation for visits, and the costs of participating in conferences and workshops. Depending on the distance to the home country, the number of visits to be made, there can be considerable variation in cost, but $3,000 should be considered an absolute minimum for interns from Asia (based on mid-1982 air fares).

2. **Living Expenses.** These include room and board, insurance, and personal and incidental expenses. For a rural locale such as Athens, Ohio, $600 per month is adequate for subsistence. Obviously, this figure depends on local costs and must be adjusted for inflation.

3. **Administrative Expenses.** These include the travel expenses (but not salaries) of library staff who will accompany the intern (s) for visits and conferences as well as the cost of telephone and telex usage, postage, photocopying, and database searching. To this should be added

---

[①] The article by Ron Coplen and Muriel Regan, "Internship Programs in Special Libraries: A Mutually Beneficial Experience for Librarian and Student", *Special Libraries* 72 (January 1981): 31-38, capably highlights many of the general characteristics of internships and thus the discussion here focuses on characteristics special to international exchanges.

receptions and official entertainment. The minimum estimate for these expenses is about $1,000.

Applying these figures to a three-month internship, the direct costs would be about $5,800. The estimated indirect cost to the University for staff time spent programming, coordinating, supervising, training, and counseling plus overhead will amount to about $1,500 each month for each intern. These indirect cost can be partially and justifiably returned by assigning the intern to work approximately one-half time in a library department. This benefits the intern by deepening his/her understanding of how the library really works and how things are accomplished but at the same time contributes to the library's productivity. An important mutual benefit which cannot be monetized is the exchange of ideas between the interns and the library staff through daily contacts. ① Funding for the internship programs with the Ohio University Libraries has come from a number of sources. These have included full support from UNESCO for four library school faculty from Southeast Asia, shared UNESCO and home-institution support for a technical librarian from China, support for travel and living expenses for five librarians from Taiwan by their universities and information agencies with Ohio University underwriting the administrative costs, and other combinations. U. S. Federal funding under Title VI (Foreign Language and Area Studies) also partially supported two interns from Thailand and, beginning in October 1982, intern support was included in our Title II-C (Strengthening Research library Resources) project for cataloging Southeast Asian materials. In this project, the intern from Southeast Asia will profit from the opportunity to work in a modern automated library and the Library will profit from having a professional librarian with linguistic and cataloging skills not available in the U. S.

Despite the importance of outside funding, the success of the programs relies on the strong commitment by Ohio University, and particularly its top administration, to international cooperation. And, as is evident above, the support from UNESCO, both financially and through encouragement, has also been vital in the program's growth.

In summarizing the internship programs, we consider them to have special merit. They are relatively inexpensive in comparison with formal library science education programs and have far more substance than study tours. The programs are particularly advantageous for professional librarians from Third World nations as they are afforded concentrated training and experiences which provide both depth and breadth within a relatively short period. As these individuals occupy or will be occupying responsible positions within the library profession in their own countries, the opportunity to use and understand contemporary technological applications and management processes can impact on the advancement of entire nations.

Conclusions

International exchanges have many benefits. In the long run, they not only benefit the individuals but also foster inter-institutional cooperation, information sharing, networking, and standardization on a global basis. Library internship, such as those at Ohio University, fulfill an important need. This is evidenced by the growing number of requests received and the availability of external funding. The fact that many institutions are willing to send their librarians to Ohio University Libraries for internship training at their own expense manifests the value of such short-term training. It is hoped that more libraries in the U. S. will open their doors to foreign librarians either on exchange or on internships. Standing in the forefront of modern library developments, the U. S. has much to offer in librarianship. Yet, at the same time, there is much that U. S. librarians and libraries can learn from others through such interchanges.

---

① The benefits to the institution hosting an intern, described in the Coplen and Regan article, *Ibid*., p. 32, are all applicable to the international context and often heightened as a result of the cross-cultural dimension of the interaction.

International Library Internships:
An Effective Approach to Cooperation[①]

Introduction

Cooperation for library development in the Asian and Pacific Region takes many forms. Such diversity is necessary to address the varying needs and levels of development among and within the countries in the Region. One important area for cooperation is the education and training of library and information professionals. Adequate manpower resources are crucial for library development at a time when the importance of information for national development is widely acknowledged. I have found, in my years of professional involvement in the Region, that the pace of library development in a given country is often dictated by the quality and quantity of its library professionals. Without these, little happens.

Given this need, the development of professional manpower in library and information science is a fertile area for cooperation between the developed countries and the developing nations. As pioneers and leaders in library education, American and Canadian library schools have led in educating large numbers of information professionals from the Asian and Pacific Region. In the past two decades, Great Britain and other European countries also have been educating increasing numbers of library and information professionals. More recently, Australia and a regional program in the Philippines have made significant contributions as well. Most of the graduates who have returned to their homes hold responsible positions in libraries and information centers. Many are contributing to national library development in their respective countries. Yet, despite these educational opportunities, the number of trained professionals is still far short of actual needs.

In addition to formal library education, which requires the greatest investment in time and money, there is an urgent need for a diversity of training programs and professional opportunities, ranging from short courses, seminars, workshops and conferences to exchanges of personnel, professional visits, and internships. All of these provide training and retraining for library and information workers not only in the "basics" needed in their jobs but also in the new concepts, skills, and technologies in this rapidly changing profession of librarianship. Nothing can compare with a formal library education — the value of which is beyond doubt — yet there is a definite need to supplement or complement it with a variety of training programs especially designed and tailored to the needs of the individuals involved. Unlike formal library education which often is bound by a fixed program of study and course sequences, training programs can be far more flexible and responsive to individual needs.

Recognizing this, since 1979 the Ohio University Library has been offering internship programs to library and information professionals from the Asian and Pacific Region.

Origin of the Internship Program

The internship program at Ohio University was begun in response to a number of requests from libraries and information centers in Indonesia, Taiwan, and Thailand. A number of factors made this possible, including:

— the support of the Ohio University administration and its strong commitment to international education and cooperation;

[①] Revised version of a paper originally presented to the Joint Annual Program of the Asian/Pacific American Librarians Association and the Chinese-American Librarians Association, June 28 – 29, 1983, in conjunction with the American Library Association Annual Conference, Los Angeles, California.

— the University's long standing association with educational programs in Malaysia and the University's Center for Southeast Asian Studies which originally stimulated the development of the Library's internationally recognized Southeast Asia Collection,

— the interest and enthusiasm of the library staff especially those in the Southeast Asia Collection which provides an excellent home base for many of the interns, and

— the financial support of the Division of General Information Programme of UNESCO for several of the interns and the support of other funding sources including the interns' own institutions.

One additional factor of importance was my own working and teaching experience in Southeast Asia between 1968 and 1975 when I was seconded by the U. S. Agency for International Development to work as the Director of Library and Information Center at the Asian Institute of Technology (AIT) in Bangkok, Thailand. My close involvement in library development during those seven years led me to recognize the importance of internship programs. In fact, back in 1970, I started an internship program at AIT for several librarians from Indonesia and other libraries in Thailand. The current internship program at Ohio University could properly be seen as a continuation of this earlier program.

Purpose of Internships

Since its inception, the prime purpose of our internship program has been to provide practical experience in a major American library for selected library and information professionals from the Asian and Pacific Region on modern concepts and developments in library and information services. Given our strong Southeast Asia link, (although one of our most recent programs was the training of two Saudi Arabian professionals in the management of a micrographic department for the National Center for Financial and Economic Information) our special focus has been Southeast Asia.

Three main groups of library and information professionals have benefitted from the training. The first group consists of middle— and upper-level professionals who received formal library education or training several years ago and now need to update their knowledge and skills for our rapidly changing profession. The second group consists of mostly younger faculty members of Southeast Asian library schools who wish to refresh their library skills with the hope of integrating theory and practice through the internship. The third group consists of new graduates of American library schools from the Asian and Pacific region who, before returning to their home countries, would like an opportunity to apply what they have learned in the context of a major American library. Of the 15 interns who have participated in the program, the majority divided almost equally between the first two groups. Some of the first group have dual responsibilities, i. e., in addition to working in the library, they also teach part-time in library schools at their home institutions. Thus far seven countries have been represented in the program. They are Thailand, Taiwan, Indonesia, Malaysia, the Philippines, People's Republic of China, and Saudi Arabia.

Structure of Internships

As was mentioned earlier, nearly all training is individually designed so that each intern has a tailor-made program to suit his or her special background and needs. In order to provide the utmost care in the training of each intern, we prefer no more than two interns at any one time. In fact, our experience has been that it is desirable to work with a single intern, although there are definite advantages in terms of mutual support in having a peer intern to whom to turn. Also, there needs to be a sufficient lapse of time between programs to give the participating staff a break. This is necessitated by the considerable time participating staff must give in the training and supervising of the interns.

While finalized only after his/her arrival and after a face-to-face meeting, much of the preparation for the program takes place several months in advance through correspondence. Once the specific background and needs of an intern have been identified, an appropriate library staff member is assigned as the training coordinator to oversee the entire training of the intern from arrival to departure. This staff member will be assisted by others as required. Our experience further suggests that three to six months are desirable to permit sufficient hands-on experience. A longer time period also permits the intern to make a greater contributions to the primary mission of the library. Six months is recommended for those interns whose English language proficiency requires a longer adjustment period. To give each intern greater awareness of various library practices, visits to other libraries in the vicinity are arranged. Depending on funding, visits to OCLC and Chemical Abstracts, which are located in Columbus, Ohio, and attendance at relevant library conferences, workshops, seminars, etc. are often a part of the program as well. For library school faculty members, a visit to the nearby library schools such as Kent State, Case Western Reserve, Pittsburgh, Kentucky, and Indiana may be added if so desired.

Scheduling of the training normally takes two forms. One is a stationary assignment in which an intern is assigned to one or two library areas (or departments) for half of each day during the entire internship period. This assignment is made according to each interns needs for in-depth training in a given library or information service. The other form is a rotating assignment in which, during the other half of each day, the intern is assigned to a different library area for a period ranging from one to ten days each. This is designed to give the intern overall experience in a wide range of library operations. Some of the interns who have specific training objectives may be asked to carry out a project under the supervision or guidance of experienced staff members, in addition to the two forms of assignments.

It is of interest to note that among the areas most interns have wished to learn are:

1. Modern organization and management of a library or information center including particularly the many aspects of human resources management;

2. applications of modern technologies to library and information services including computerized online cataloging and interlibrary loan, such as the systems provided by OCLC, and online searching of remote databases through Dialog, SDC, BRS, MEDLINE, etc. (our local online public access catalog and circulation system became available only this summer);

3. networking of library and information services; and

4. the applicability of the above for the intern's home institution.

The last is of utmost importance in our view since unless most of the practical experience gained by the interns can be applied in their own environment, there is little value in the internship program. At the same time, the interns must be expected to interpret what they learn rather than expecting to be able to directly transplant each technological application.

Costs of Internships

To insure the success of the internship program, adequate funding for the following three types of direct costs① must be secured:

1. <u>Travel Expenses</u>. These include international travel to Ohio and return, local transportation for visits, and the costs of participating in conferences and workshops. Depending on the distance to the home country, the number of visits to be made, and the number of conferences to be attended, there can be considerable variation in cost, but $3,500 should be considered a minimum for interns from Asia (based on 1983 air fares).

2. <u>Living Expenses</u>. These include room and board, insurance, and personal and incidental expenses. For a rural locale such as Athens, Ohio $600 per month is adequate for subsistence. Obviously, this figure depends on local costs and must be adjusted for inflation. Expenses for interns accompanied by family members would be higher.

3. <u>Administrative Expenses</u>. These include the travel expenses (but not salaries) of library staff who will accompany the intern (s) for visits and conferences as well as the cost of

---

① Adapted from Hwa-Wei Lee and K. Mulliner, "International Exchange of Librarians and the Ohio University Internship Program," *College & Research Libraries News*, Vol. XLIII. No. 10, November 1982, pp. 345–348; reprinted as the proceeding article in this volume.

telephones, textbooks and reading materials, telex, postage, photocopying, and database searching. To this should be added receptions and official entertainment. The minimum estimate for these expenses is about $1,000 for a three-month training with an increment of $150 per additional month — depending on activities.

Applying these figures to a three-month internship, the direct costs would be about $6,300 (or $8,650 for six months).

The estimated indirect cost to the University for staff time spent programming, coordinating, supervising, training, travelling, and counseling plus overhead will amount to about $1,500 each month for each intern. Although part of this indirect cost may be recovered from the work performed by the interns during their internship, that part not recovered can be considered as a contribution made by the Ohio University Library to international cooperation. It is our hope that more libraries in North America, particularly those with area resources and expertise, will consider offering internship training to library and information professionals from the Asian and Pacific Region. Currently, because of the success of our internship program, we receive more requests than we can possible handle.

Funding Sources

Financial support for the direct costs of the internship programs has come from a number of sources. Most important of these has been from the General Information Programme of the United Nations Educational, Scientific and Cultural Organization (UNESCO). The two Saudi Arabian interns were supported by their Government through the U.S.-Saudi Arabian Joint Commission on Economic Cooperation. Others were financed by funds made available through U.S. federal grants, that the Library was awarded under Titles II-C and VI of the Higher Education Act or by the interns' home institution.

It is necessary for the interns' home institutions to convince their government of the importance of a library internship and to seek financial support for it as well. Beyond this, Third World institutions should recognize their unique ability to inaugurate programs. Many international and bi-lateral agencies are more responsive to requests from recipient institutions than to proposals from the West. In this regard also, recognition by Third World governments of the importance of libraries and information centers for development efforts will affect the willingness of aid-granting and technical assistance agencies to support internships.

Program Review and Evaluation

To assure continuing flexibility in the programming and scheduling for an intern, I conduct a monthly review with the intern and his/her program coordinator. The review often leads to program modifications and improvements. In addition to periodic program reviews, two separate evaluations are carried out at the end of each internship: one by the intern using a standard evaluation form and one by the training coordinator. Although we have received highly satisfactory and complimentary evaluations from most of the interns, we actively seek their suggestions for the refinement of the program. Many of the suggestions have been adopted in subsequent programming and training. Some of the more important suggestions include: improved housing arrangements, assigning a staff member for each intern throughout the internship, preferred timing of internships during the year, and the value of some of the visits and the lack of value of others. Another form of evaluation which we hope to conduct is to ask for an evaluation by the intern's home institution of the effects of the training on an intern's performance after return. The findings could provide useful information and insights from a different perspective.

Summary and Recommendations

This paper thus far has described in some detail the internship program of Ohio University which has proven both popular and successful. Among the special features of the program are its flexibility and adaptability. Each intern receives an individually designed program based on his/her background and needs. In describing the program I have briefly traced its origin, purpose, format, costs, sources of funding, program review and evaluation, etc. Based on our experience, I would like to offer a few recommendations for the continuation of the program and for those others who may want to do the same.

<u>First</u>, I hope to see more libraries offering this program. There is an urgent need to upgrade and improve the knowledge and skills of a large number of library and information professionals in the Asian and Pacific Region in view of rapid social, economic and technological changes. The need for improved library and information services is increasingly recognized. It is an opportue time for library and information professionals to take part in the development and to gain recognition for their services.

<u>Second</u>, although there may be no monetary advantage for libraries to offer internship training, the experience itself can be richly rewarding. From my own experience, shared by my Ohio University colleagues, I have learned a great deal from each intern and have made lasting friendships with many of them. In fact, among other contributions, each intern has brought to our library a rich cultural experience and an opportunity to view our operations and procedures from different perspectives. Not unimportantly, they also pave the way for further inter-institutional cooperation and meaningful information exchanges for our Southeast Asia Collection.

<u>Third</u>, in order that more internships can be made available to the large number of library and information professionals who need them, expanded sources of funding are needed. In addition to increasing current financial support from international organizations and foundations, there is a need for greater awareness by governments of the value of internship programs as an important component for development. Such awareness, of course, must be followed by financial commitments. This applies to nations in the Region and to nations providing development assistance. Sending library and information professionals abroad for internship training should be strongly supported by the home institutions as well.

<u>Fourth</u>, in the selection of interns, particularly from non-English speaking countries, a moderate level of English proficiency should be required as this will facilitate the learning process and assure maximum benefit from the short-term training.

<u>Fifth</u>, another factor affecting the results of internships is the desire and determination to learn by the interns. It is very important that each intern be made aware early in his/her training that the responsibility to learn rests on the intern. The staff members assigned to coordinate the internship training should also be carefully selected and matched. They should have the professional ability, cultural sensitivity and commitment to do justice to the program. A successful internship program is often the result of good planning and team work. It requires the support and participation of a major segment of the library staff who will not only help the interns in their training but also will go out of their way to make the interns feel welcome and at home.

<u>Sixth</u>, the commitment from the intern's home institution must extend beyond financial support. Unless the institution is prepared to capitalize on what the intern has gained, our time and effort might be more usefully directed to other areas. Important to this process is not only providing opportunities for the returned intern to apply what she/he has gained but also to share the lessons with others. Even with major expansion in internship opportunities, adequate addressing of the regional needs for professional development demands that those individuals selected serve not only as practitioners but as teachers for their colleagues after returning. Teaching in this instance refers to professional development programs rather than necessarily to a classroom role.

In conclusion, the internship program at Ohio University has offered a new approach to cooperation. Both the interns and we have learned from and about each other and ourselves. The experiences have been mutually rewarding.

第五部分 图书馆与资讯服务

Section V Library and Information Services

User and Use Analysis:
A Case Study of the Information Utility by Geotechnical Engineers in Asian Countries

Introduction

The need for engineering and technical information in Asia is increasingly felt as the pace for economic and industrial development is accelerated. Engineers and technical experts in Asia are often frustrated by the inaccessibility of relevant information at the time of need. Although to some degree this situation is also true in the developed world, it more seriously affects progress in the developing countries where both expertise and financial resources are in critically short supply.

As a regional institution for advanced engineering education and research, the Asian Institute of Technology (AIT) is deeply involved in the technical development of the Asian region and it is this involvement which has led AIT to an awareness of the urgent needs of Asian engineers for relevant information. To this need, AIT has, since its inception, given top priority to the development of a first class library and information center within the Institute. Steps have been taken to expand this facility into a regional information center for engineering and related fields, embracing the collection, organization and dissemination of useful technical information.

To experiment with the setting up of a regional information service, a very important but highly specialized field — Geotechnical Engineering, has been chosen for the pilot project. The idea of establishing a regional information center for geotechnical engineering was conceived at the meeting held in Bangkok in July 1971, of representatives of national societies of soil mechanics and foundation engineering in Asia. One of the resolutions of the meeting requested AIT to establish and operate the specialized information center for the benefit of all those who are concerned with geotechnical engineering in Asia. The importance of this undertaking was recognized through a grant awarded by the International Development Research Centre of Canada to partially support the operations of the Center for the initial three-year period. As a result, The Asian Information Center for Geotechnical Engineering (Asian Geotechnical Engineering for short, abbreviated AGE) was founded in January 1973 within the AIT Library and Information Center in collaboration with AIT's Division of Geotechnical Engineering. The operation of AGE is guided by a Policy Advisory Committee whose members are either leading subject specialists or information experts and a Technical Committee whose members are largely from AIT. At least one liaison officer from each Asian country has been appointed to provide close linkage between AGE and its users.

Major Functions of AGE

Serving as a clearing house in Asia for information on all aspects of geotechnical engineering such as soil mechanics, foundation engineering, engineering geology, rock mechanics, earthquake engineering and other related fields, the Center undertakes the responsibility to collect all relevant information and data useful to the region, to design a computer-based information storage and retrieval system, to disseminate such information through its publications and reproduction services, and to provide the three-R service (reference, referral and reproduction).

The three present publications of AGE are:

AGE Current Awareness Service. A quarterly publication informing readers of recent geotechnical engineering publications and contents of selected geotechnical engineering journals received at AGE.

Asian Geotechnical Engineering Abstracts. A quarterly publication consisting of abstracts of available publications and reports on geotechnical engineering relevant to Asia.

AGE Journal Holdings List. A list of geotechnical engineering journals held at AGE.

Other publications soon to be published are:

AGE Conference Proceedings List. A list of conference proceedings on various subjects of geotechnical engineering in AGE'S collections.

Asian Geotechnical Engineering Directory. A bi-annual publication to consist of information on various organizations and individuals who are doing geotechnical engineering work in Asia or work relevant to Asia.

Asian Geotechnical Engineering In Progress. A semi-annual publication to consist of information on current design, construction and research projects in geotechnical engineering being undertaken in Asia.

Users of AGE

Basically, AGE'S services are available at a subsidized cost to all who are concerned with any aspect of geotechnical engineering work in Asia. Regular users of AGE are encouraged to join AGE either as an individual member or as an institutional member in order to receive the wide range of information services at a very low annual fee.

As of April 15, 1974, 33 individuals and 41 institutions, mostly in Asia, had joined AGE as fee-paying members. In addition, there were 50 complimentary members consisting of those who serve either on the Policy Advisory Committee and the Technical Committee or as liaison officers. Table 1 gives the breakdown of the membership.

User and Use Analysis

In a continuing effort to make AGE more responsive to the information needs of its members, this study was conducted in March 1974. A total of 88 questionnaires was sent to all individual and institutional members in Asia as well as to all liaison officers. Before the middle of April, 36 questionnaires were returned constituting 40.9% of the total number of questionnaires sent. Results and findings derived from the returns in conjunction with other membership data previously gather by AGE are presented in the remaining part of this paper.

User Analysis

There are a few general characteristics of AGE's membership that can be summarized below. These include all individual members and one representative from each institutional member.

1. A majority are middle-aged, 46.15% between 31 and 40 and 23.08% between 41 and 50. All are college graduates with 46.43% having a Master's degree and 17.85% having a doctoral degree.

2. A very high percentage of them (79.4%) are either chief engineers or are holding senior executive and teaching positions.

3. As shown in Table II, a high percentage of both individual and institutional members are from engineering and consulting firms.

4. One phenomenon among individual members is the large number of engineers working in foreign countries. Of the 33 individual members, 11 are working in countries other than their own. For example, one Thai works in China, two Chinese work in Indonesia one Australian works in Nepal, three Americans, one Dutch and one Indian work in Singapore, one Japanese works in Thailand, and one Indian works in the U. S.

TABLE I: AGE MEMBERSHIP

country	Indiv. Member	Instn. Member	Complimentary Policy	Technical	Liaison	Total
Bangladesh	0	0	0	0	1	1
Burma	0	0	0	0	1	1
China, ROC	3	15	1	0	2	21
Guam	0	1	0	0	0	1
Hong Kong	1	5	0	0	1	7
India	1	3	2	0	3	9
Indonesia	4	1	1	0	1	7
Iran	0	0	0	0	1	1
Israel	0	0	1	0	1	2
Japan	3	2	2	0	2	9
Korea, South	2	0	0	0	1	3
Malaysia	3	1	1	0	1	6
Nepal	1	0	0	0	0	1
Pakistan	0	1	0	0	1	2
Philippines	2	0	0	0	1	3
Singapore	5	0	1	0	1	7
Sri Lanka	0	1	0	0	1	2
Thailand	6	8	4	11	0	29
Asia Totals	31	38	13	11	19	112
Outside Asia						
Australia	0	2	2	0	0	4
Belgium	0	0	1	0	0	1
Brazil	0	0	1	0	0	1
Denmark	0	1	0	0	0	1
Un. Kingdom	0	0	1	0	0	1
United States	2	0	2	0	0	4
Non-Asia Totals	2	3	7	0	0	12

TABLE II: SOURCES OF FEE-PAYING MEMBERS

Sources	Individual No.	%	Institutional No.	%
Engineering & Consulting Firms	21	63.64	19	46.34
Universities &				

(Continuing)

Sources	No. Individual	%	No. Institutional	%
Research Organizations	9	27.27	7	17.07
Government Agencies	2	6.06	15	36.59
Unknown	1	3.03	0	0.00
Total	33	100.00	41	100.00

Use Analysis

In regard to information seeking behavior, library facilities, and types of information often required, a rather uniform pattern was found among the population surveyed. No significant deviation can be detected either among the two membership groups and liaison officers or among those with different types of employment. Also differences in countries, nationalities, ages, education, and experience do not seem to affect the general pattern in any significant way.

Channels for Technical Information

The frequently used channels for technical information a shown in Table III are the "reading relevant literature" particularly in books, journals, proceedings, reports and papers, "visits and field trips" and "membership in professional societies".

When asked to indicate the three most important channels, an overwhelming majority (77.8%) indicated "reading of relevant literature" as the most important channel while a clear majority each (27.8% and 33.3% respectively) indicated "contacts with specialists in the same institution" and "attending conferences, seminars, workshops, etc." as the second and third most important channels.

TABLE III: CHANNELS FOR TECHNICAL INFORMATION

Channels	Frequently Used	Casually Used	Not Used	No Answer
Personal contacts and correspond. with outside persons	12	22	2	0
Contacts with specialists in the same institution.	14	16	3	3
Attending conferences, seminars, workshops, etc.	4	30	2	0
Reading relevant literature in:				
Books	30	6	0	0
Journals	26	10	0	0
Proceedings	22	12	2	0
Reports/papers	24	10	2	0
Patents	0	10	16	10
Documents	8	16	6	6
Visits and field trips.	20	16	0	0
Membership in professional societies	20	14	0	2
Enrolling for further studies.	2	4	26	4
Use of current awareness services, indexing and abstracting services, bibliographies, etc.	8	20	8	0
Others.	0	0	2	34

Library Facilities Available

In regard to personal library facilities, 11% rated their personal libraries as "adequate", 38.9% rated theirs as "average" or "inadequate". The highest number of books reported is 4,330 volumes while the lowest is 20 (the average is 490.7 and the median is 100). The highest number of journal titles reported is 114 while the lowest is 2. The number of journals currently received range from 2 to 27 with an average of 3 titles on geotechnical engineering. The geotechnical engineering journals most frequently owned are: *Geotechnical Engineering*, *Geotechnique*, and the *Journal of the Soil Mechanics and Foundations Division*, *Proceedings of the American Society of Civil Engineers*.

When asked about library facilities of the employer institutions, 11% rated theirs as "adequate", 55.6%, as "average" and 11% as "inadequate". The number of books ranged from a maximum of 200,000 volumes to a minimum of 60 volumes (the average is 32,582 and the medium is 7,000). The number of journal titles ranged from 2,600 down to 20. 38.9% of the libraries have Engineering Index, 27.8% own Geotechnical Abstracts and the *GEODEX Retrieval System for Geotechnical Abstracts*, and 22% have their own indexing systems.

For other library and information facilities available, 27.8% rated those they use as "average", 38.9%, as "inadequate" and 27.8% gave no answers.

When asked how much of the information needs of each member has been met from the various library facilities available, the answers for the majority are that the personal libraries satisfy from 25% to 50% of their information needs while very little help was received from other library facilities.

TABLE IV: PERCENTAGE OF INFORMATION NEEDS SATISFIED

Library Facility	0 – 25%	25 – 50%	50 – 75%	75 – 100%
Personal	4	14	8	4
Employer's	16	4	6	0
Others	22	2	2	0

Types of Technical Information Often Required

Concerning the types of technical information often required by members, a great majority indicated "Practical information" as most often required. This is followed by "Site investigations", "Field performance data" and "Engineering design and construction details".

Table V shows not only those types of technical information which are often required but also those types of technical information which are not often required by the members.

Evaluation of AGE

The effectiveness and usefulness of AGE in meeting the information needs of its members were evaluated in terms of its publications and services.

AGE Publications

The appraisal of two of the published AGE publications were conducted through the questionnaire. The majority of responses were favorable. One suggestion for the Asian Geotechnical Engineering Abstracts was to give more coverage to the practical aspects of geotechnical engineering relating to Asia.

TABLE V: TYPES OF TECHNICAL INFORMATION REQUIRED

Types	Most Often	Average	Not Often	No Answer
Theoretical work.	2	10	14	10
Research findings or reports.	6	12	8	10
State-of-the-art review.	8	8	10	10
Practical information.	26	6	0	4
Field perFformance data.	20	12	0	4
Site investigations.	24	8	0	4
Engineering design and construction details.	18	8	2	8
Bibliographies, indexes, abstracts, etc.	4	8	16	8
Others.	0	0	4	32

TABLE VI: APPRAISAL OF AGE PUBLICATIONS

AGE Current Awareness Service

	Good	Average	Poor	No Answer
Coverage	18	14	2	2
Arrangement	14	20	0	2
Timeliness	16	16	2	2
	Very Useful	Moderate	Not Useful	No Answer
Overall	14	16	2	4

Asian Geotechnical Engineering Abstracts

	Good	Average	Poor	No Answer
Coverage	16	12	2	6
Arrangement	12	16	2	6
Timeliness	16	12	2	6
	Very Useful	Moderate	Not Useful	No Answer
Overall	6	20	4	6

AGE Service

The finding was that 33.3% of the members have used the reproduction service of AGE at least once, 22.2% have used the reference service, and 5.6% have used the referral service. In all cases, the ratings for the services received by those who used them were considered "satisfactory". For those members who have not used AGE's services, the following reasons were indicated:

1. There has not been a need for such services yet. (16 indicated)
2. Because of the distance which prevents direct access to such services. (12 indicated)
3. Because of the long time required to receive such services, it would not help to solve immediate problems. (6 indicated)
4. Did not know that such services are available. (2 indicated)
5. Because of the difficulty in paying for such services. (2 indicated)

Summary and Conclusions

The study on information utility by geotechnical engineers in Asia based on the analysis of data provided by the AGE members points out the following facts which are worthy of attention:

1. The majority of information users in geotechnical engineering are from engineering and consulting firms or are those who are engaged in such work. They are in the middle age bracket, well trained, and holding senior or executive positions.

2. There seems to be a rather uniform pattern among them in their information seeking behavior. For example, the frequently used channels for information by the majority of respondents are reading of relevant literature from books, journals, proceedings, reports and papers.

3. The library facilities available to them are generally "average" or "inadequate" to meet their information needs. Only one third of them have access to the *Engineering Index* and other specialized indexing and abstracting tools. As a consequence, few use these tools regularly for finding information. They are confined to their personal libraries for up to 50% of their information needs.

4. The types of technical information often required are practical in nature. Theoretical work, bibliographical publications, research reports, and state-of-the-art review are less often required.

5. The responses to two of the AGE publications are generally favorable with a greater number considering *AGE Current Awareness Service* as more useful than *Asian Geotechnical Engineering Abstracts*.

6. Although the reasons given for the low level of use of AGE services by members are mainly the lack of needs and the factors of time and distance, some marketing efforts are necessary to convince the members and other potential users of AGE's ability to supply needed information as quickly and as economically as possible.

7. The user and use analysis contained in this study has been confined mainly to the members of AGE. Further study is needed to include the uses made by non-members.

AGE has been in existence slightly more than one year. The two publications mentioned in this study have just completed their first annual volumes. Many of its services are beginning to become known among potential users in Asia. The continued growth of its membership and services used should be closely monitored to provide additional information on the pattern of information needs and uses of engineers in the developing countries of Asia.

The Application of Information Technology to Close the Information Gap[①]

Introduction

One of the most pressing problems facing the developing nations in Asia today is the inability of their libraries and information centers to respond effectively and expediently to the wide range of information needs which are required for national development.

It has been observed that there exist two types of "information gap" in Asia. One is the lack of immediate access to the ever widening frontier of new knowledge resulting from the rapid advancement of science and technology in the developed world. Another is the lack of an effective mechanism to uncover useful indigenous information available within one's country or in the region.

A great deal of human and financial resources have been wasted in Asia as a direct result of these two types of "information gap". The perpetuation of this situation has rendered the works of Asian scientists, research workers, and technical specialists both inefficient and ineffective.

Recognizing such a serious problem, most of the Southeast Asian nations already have taken steps to correct it. This is shown in the findings of a 1972 UNESCO report[②] which states:

> In each country visited there is active interest in the development of scientific and technical information, and plans for improvement of the present system. In Indonesia, a Ford Foundation mission recently advised on the establishment of a national network of science information centers to be co-coordinated by the National Scientific Documentation Centre, and the Government has requested UNDP (United Nations Development Programme) consultant services to assist in the actual planning. In Malaysia a mission was carried out in late 1971 under British Council sponsorship to advise on "Scientific and Technical Library and Information Services in Malaysia" In Singapore there has been no direct follow-up on the 1969 UNESCO sponsored "Proposals for the setting-up of a Scientific and Technical Information Centre", but there is active interest in revising this study to bring it in line with the changing situation in Singapore. In the Philippines the NSDB (National Science Development Board) is setting up a new National Science Information Centre which will serve as the national co-coordinating body and as the linkage to regional and international networks or systems. The Government has requested UNDP advisory services in planning the Centre. In Hong Kong the Committee for Scientific Co-ordination has set up a Sub-Committee on Scientific and Technical Information to consider the establishment of a "Centralized Technical Information Service." In Thailand the Thai National Documentation Centre (TNDC) which is already well established is planning further services, and the Asian Institute of Technology has advanced plans for development of a complete information service on a regional level. In all countries the value of regional linkages was recognized and the concept of a regional information network in science and technology was strongly supported.[③]

In Taiwan, a Science and Technology Information Center has been founded and is in operation under the "National Science Council". A plan to form a nation-wide library and

---

① Based on an earlier paper presented by the author at the Regional Seminar on Information Storage, Retrieval and Dissemination organized by Asian Mass Communication Research and Information Centre in cooperation with National Research Council of Thailand, Bangkok, March 26 – 30, 1973. It was brought up to date as of June 1974.

② *Report of UNESCO Fact-Finding Mission on the Regional Information Network for Science and Technology in Southeast Asia.* 1972. 20 p. (SCP/425/2 – 25)

③ *Ibid.*, p. 4.

information network was proposed by this author in early 1974. ① It is hoped that this plan will be considered for adoption.

In the field of social sciences, a study was made by Mr. Erwin Kristoffersen, former regional representative of the Friedrich-Ebert-Stiftung which resulted in a well documented proposal to establish a Clearing House for Social Development in Asia as an effective measure to meet the information needs in the social sciences. ② The study pointed out the serious deficiencies existing in the exchange and dissemination of indigenous information in the social sciences, much of which is vital for developmental planning.

In the light of these two studies and the important groundwork they have laid, I would like to direct attention to the possible tools made available by recent advancements in information technology which can be applied to improve library-information services in the region.

Information Technology

Information technology is a term referring to those technologies which can be applied to library-information work. There are many such technologies available at present. They generally come under the labels of 1) Reprography, 2) Computers, or 3) Telecommunications.

Each of these three actually represents a variety of applications and different degrees of sophistication. They may work independently or together in either simple or complex library and information systems. Just as with other tools, not all the technologies are suitable for all situations and at all times. It is necessary that we give our attention to those technologies which are considered relevant to each of our particular environments.

Reprography

Despite the fact that "Reprography" is a relatively new term, this technology is already under widespread use by many libraries and information centers in this region. Unlike the newness of the name, reprography consists of many not-too-new techniques such as microfilming and various methods of copying and duplicating.

The techniques of reprography are very important for the developing countries in that:

1) they enable a wider dissemination of information some of which might not be available or accessible otherwise;

2) they have made it possible for libraries and information centers to interchange reproduced information;

3) various microforms are by far the most economic means for information storage and for dissemination to distant places by mail; and

4) the computer-output-microforms (COM) reduces the problem of storage and dissemination for the large amount of computer generated data including library catalogs and union lists of serials. The process of transferring bibliographical data from the magnetic tape output on to microfilm is relatively simple and economical.

Computers

Although the use of computers in library-information work has found wide acceptance throughout the world, it has just begun in Southeast Asia. The computer is a very promising tool in that it has the power and versatility to process data with high speed and precision. The main obstacles standing in the way of wider application by libraries and information centers in Asia are the factors of high cost, especially in the initial stage, the language barriers and the lack of trained

---

① Hwa-Wei Lee, "Proposal for the Establishment of a National Library And Information Network", *Central Daily News*, Feb. 26 – 27, 1974 (In Chinese); reprinted in this volume.

② Erwin Kristoffersen, *Clearing House for Social Development in Asia*; *Project Proposals And Report on the Findings of a Feasibility Study* (Bangkok: Friedrich-Ebert-Stiftung, Bangkok Office, 1972). p. 35.

staff. The language barriers are beginning to be overcome as more and more input and output devices for non-Roman languages have been developed and are being put into operation, e. g. , Thai and Japanese. The other obstacles can be overcome by methods of sharing and pooling of available resources. One feasible approach is to set up cooperative information processing centers for libraries and information centers that wish to participate in it. This type of center can be established in large libraries or information centers which have easy access to computer facilities.

The essence of this setup is to share the costs of not only the use of a computer system and the developing of the software necessary for its support, but also the pooling together of specially trained personnel. By means of this arrangement, even small libraries and information centers can have the benefit of sharing a computer with large libraries and information centers. The work which can be best handled by such centers would be:

1) Establish and maintain a national (or regional) data bank on indigenous publications. A by-product of this data bank is the publication of national (or regional) bibliographies.

2) Establish and maintain a national (or regional) data bank on major library collections in the country (or region). A by-product of this data bank is the publication of a national (or regional) union catalog and separate book catalogs for each participating library or information center.

3) Establish and maintain a national (or regional) data bank on periodicals and serial publications held by major libraries and information centers in the country (or the region). A by-product of this data bank is the publication of a union list of periodicals and serials and separate lists of holdings for each participating library or information center.

4) Establish and maintain a national (or regional) data bank for scientific and technical literature of relevance to the country (or the region). A by-product of this data bank is the publication at regular intervals of abstracting journals. A score of other services such as SDI service, current awareness service, and retrospective search of the data file can also be initiated.

5) Establish and maintain a national (or regional) data bank on such vital information as census data, demographic data, land use data, hydrological and meteorological data, inventories of communications and transportation, industrial and housing facilities, geological and natural resources, etc. , and relevant economic and sociological data.

6) Act as a centralized processing center for the acquisitions, cataloging, and processing of books, journals and other materials for the libraries and information centers that want to participate in such labor — and cost-saving operations. There are a wide range of activities that can be channeled through such a central processing service.

7) Some of these centers may also consider the possibility of acquiring the MARC (MAchine-Readable Cataloging) tapes of both the U. S. Library of Congress and the British National Bibliography for local storage and manipulation. Arrangements may also be made to have either direct or indirect access to some of the major databases in the developed countries by means of modern telecommunications.

8) The various data banks or processing centers may be integrated within a national (or regional) library and information system or network. Other activities of such a system or network are:

A. Develop a library of computer programs for various library-information work.

B. Provide consulting services to libraries or information centers in the application of appropriate information technology.

C. Provide various computer services to individual or special library-information projects.

D. Conduct short courses, seminars and workshops for the training and up-grading of librarians and information scientists in the use of computer and other information technology for library-information work.

Telecommunications

Telecommunications is an important part of the new information technology which holds great promise for improving library-information services in Asia.

An effort has been made by the United Nations Economic Commission for Asia and the Far East (ECAFE) to make the countries of Asia into an "Asian Telecommunity." The program intends to develop in every Asian country a telecommunication network and to link the various national networks from Iran to Indonesia by a system of modern communication services provided at the most economical rates. It, when fully realized, will undoubtedly accelerate the interchange of information amongst the libraries and information centers in the region by making possible information transmission and facsimile reproduction at high speed and at low cost. It will also facilitate the development of national library-information systems and regional library-information networks similar to those systems and networks already in operation in many parts of the world. One such example is the ESRO system which was reported by Isotta. ①

ESRO system is the information system for the Space Documentation Service of the European Space Research Organization located in Darmstadt, Germany. The ESRO system was designed on the concept of a centralized file maintenance and software responsibility, coupled with decentralized searching of the files by remote terminals sited in the member states. The total configuration consists of the central computer facility in Darmstadt, together with its own local terminal; a single leased line to Paris where two terminals are installed; a party-line connection from Paris to St. Mary Cray in Kent where a terminal is installed at the Technology Reports Centre; a party-line connection from Paris to Bretigny, where a terminal is installed at the Centre Nationale D'Etudes Spatiale; a terminal in the ESRO establishment in Noordwijk, Holland; and another terminal in the ESRO establishment in Frascati near Rome. ②

This type of system can be adopted in Asia if the "Asian Telecommunity" becomes a reality and the cost of telecommunications is substantially reduced.

Another important recent development in telecommunications which has an encouraging implication for Asia is the ability to transmit information among widely dispersed points of the world via satellites. The capability of communication satellites to transmit voice, teletype and facsimile signals to a distant place at the speed of light has a distinct advantage over other communication media for inter-continental communications. An inter-connection of computers, telephones, teletypes and communication satellites can provide a most effective network of national, regional and world information systems.

A highly sophisticated network system which saw the interfacing of all these was demonstrated at the 35th annual meeting of the American Society for Information Science held in Washington, D. C. on October 23 – 26, 1972. The system demonstrated was called the "International Information Retrieval Network", Through the several on-line terminals located on the conference grounds, participants of the annual meeting were able to query not just the many databases on computers located several hundred miles away in different parts of the U. S. A. but also the data files of the ESRO in Darmstadt, Germany via the INTELSAT IV communication satellite. The demonstration featured several recent innovations:

1) International communications via satellite.
2) Remote video and printing terminals.
3) On-line, interactive retrieval systems using both natural-text and index—based techniques.
4) Networking.
5) Access to multiple databases.

The demonstration showed that international networks are technologically feasible, economically conceivable, and usable with minimal instruction. ③

Another less sophisticated but operating system using only teletype machines and the

---

① N. E. C. Isotta, "International Information Networks: 1. The ESRO System" *Aslib Proceedings*, V. 24, No. 1 (January 1972) pp. 31 – 7.
② Ibid., p. 33.
③ From "A World of Information", program of the 35th annual meeting of *ASIS*. p. 8.

INTELSAT IV F – 2 satellite is the satellite linkage between John Crerar Library (JCL) in Chicago, U. S. A. and Consejo Nacional de Investigaciones Cientificas y Tecnicas (C. N. I. C. T.) in Buenos Aires, Argentina. The basis of the system consists of some fourteen technical libraries in Argentina which are linked by Telex to cache other and to C. N. I. C. T. in Buenos Aires. When an institution cannot fill its needs from its own collection, a message is sent to C. N. I. C. T. which then attempts to locate the needed item in one of the other libraries by use of the Union Lists and catalogs. If this is unsuccessful, the request is then transmitted to JCL and the latter provides a microfilm copy by return airmail. The costs of photocopies and the relay messages are borne by the National Academy of Sciences in the U. S. [1]

The JCL/C. N. I. C. T. system is a good example of what the developing countries can do to close the information gap existing within and among countries. Financial assistance of this kind is probably available from many international or foreign aid organizations.

AIT's Plans

As a regional institution for advanced engineering education and research, the Asian Institute of Technology (AIT) is deeply involved in the technical development of the Asian region and it is this involvement which has led AIT to an awareness of the urgent needs of Asian engineers for relevant information. To meet this need AIT has devoted a large portion of its resources to develop an outstanding library and information center within the Institute. Steps have been taken to expand this facility into a regional library and information center for engineering and related fields, embracing the collection, organization and dissemination of useful technical information. The recently founded Asian Information Center for Geotechnical Engineering, under the joint sponsorship of the AIT Division of Geotechnical Engineering and the Library, is an example of one such endeavor.

To improve library-information service in the region, especially in the application of the latest information technology, AIT is in a very unique position. We are now in the process of undertaking five major steps which, if successful, will undoubtedly have a far reaching effect on the development of a regional library-information network. These steps are (1) expanding computerized library-information service with a regional outlook, (2) establishing the Asian Information Center for Geotechnical Engineering, (3) leading a project for a computer-based union list of serials in Thailand, (4) collaborating with the National Library of Australia to set up a regional MARC data processing and distribution center, and (5) planning for an information transfer experiment via satellite between AIT and the Knowledge Availability Systems Center (KASC) of the University of Pittsburgh.

1) Expanding computerized library-information service:

With the installation in January 1974 of a large computer system (CDC 3600) at AIT to replace the currently overloaded IBM 1130, the Library plans to greatly expand its existing computerized systems in acquisitions, accounting, serials listing, etc. while converting them from IBM 1130 to CDC 3600. The existing applications which began in 1969 were reported in the *International Library Review*. [2] As a part of this plan, a library systems analyst from the U. K. has been employed to undertake the designing and implementing of the expanded operations. This specialist, Mr. Stephen W. Massil, from the University of Birmingham joined AIT Library as the Associate Director in September 1973. Mr. Massil has been actively working with the Birmingham Libraries' Cooperative Mechanization Project which utilizes MARC records in three libraries (Aston and Birmingham Universities, and the Birmingham Public Libraries) on a cooperative basis. Work

---

[1] From the letter of William S. Budington, Executive Director and Librarian of the John Crerar Library dated August 30, 1971 and from correspondences with Miss Judith A. Model of the National Academy of Science in 1973.

[2] Hwa-Wei Lee, "Library Mechanization at the Asian Institute of Technology," *International Library Review*, V. 3, No. 3 (June 1971), pp. 257 – 270.

of the Project has been reported regularly in Program. ① It is hoped that with the background of this specialist on library cooperative mechanization, many of our new programs will have a broader perspective and regional outlook and will tie in with the regional library-information network development.

2) Establishing the Asian Information Center for Geotechnical Engineering (AGE):

To experiment with the setting up of a regional library-information service, we have selected a very important but highly specialized field—Geotechnical Engineering, as our pilot project. The idea of establishing AGE was conceived at the meeting of representatives of national societies of soil mechanics and foundation engineering in the Asian region which convened in Bangkok in July 1971. Through one of the resolutions of the meeting, AIT was requested to undertake the task of establishing and operating AGE for the benefit of engineers in Asia. The importance of this undertaking was recognized through a grant awarded by the International Development Research Centre of Canada to partially support the activities of the Center for the initial three-year period. Because of this support, AGE was formally established in January 1973.

Serving as a clearing house in Asia for information on all phases of Geotechnical Engineering such as soil mechanics, foundation engineering, engineering geology, rock mechanics, earthquake engineering and other related fields, the Center will undertake the responsibility to collect all relevant information and data useful to the region, to design a computer-based information storage and retrieval system, to disseminate such information through its publications and photocopying and microfilming services, and to provide the three-R services (reference, referral and reproduction).

The detailed information concerning the data files, the publications, and the services of the Center are contained in an introductory brochure published by the Center. ② Subscriptions to the service have come from 17 countries, mostly from Asia.

3) Leading a project for a computer-based union list of serials in Thailand:

The project for a computer-based union list of serials in which all major libraries in Thailand will participate has been undertaken since February 1974. Data input is in accordance with the UNISISTs Guidelines for ISDS. ③ The input data are being keypunched and will be stored in AIT's CDC 3600 computer for many of the possible uses envisioned by the participating libraries. It is further planned that such a machine readable union list of serials will found the base of a national center, or eventually a regional center or network, for the International] Serials Data System (ISDS).

4) Collaborating with the National Library of Australia to set up a regional MARC data processing and distribution center.

Considerable progress has been made in the setting up of a regional MARC (MAchine Readable Cataloging) data processing and distribution center at AIT in collaboration with the National Library of Australia which would provide search service of the MARC files it owns and operates including both the U. S. and the U. K. MARC tapes plus the Australian MARC tapes at request to participating libraries in Southeast Asia channeled through AIT. During the process, AIT will maintain a computerized MARC file of library collections represented by the participating libraries in lieu of a union catalog. Local inputs in MARC format can be entered into the file to form the base for a national MARC database of various Southeast Asian countries. National bibliographies and other desired products can be produced from such database as needed. Detailed

---

① The most recent is: D. G. R. Buckle and others, "The Birmingham Libraries' Co-operative Mechanization Project: Progress Report, January 1972 – July 1973", *Program*: *News of Computers In Libraries*, V. 7, No. 4 (October 1973), pp. 196 – 204.

② *Introducing Asian Information Center for Geotechnical Engineering* (Bangkok: Asian Institute of Technology, 1973). p. 9.

③ International Centre for the Registration of Serial Publication, *UNISIST*: *Guidelines for ISDS* (Paris: UNESCO, 1973). p. 58.

explanations of this project is given in two recent papers by Massil. ①

5) Planning for an information transfer experiment via satellite between AIT and the Knowledge Availability Systems Center of the University of Pittsburgh:

This experiment which is now being planned is patterned after both the ESRO system and the JCL/C. N. I. C. T. system already described. The Knowledge Availability Systems Center (KASC) is one of the six NASA Regional Dissemination Centers in the U. S. Under the directorship of Professor Allen Kent who is also the Chairman of the Department of Information Science at the University of Pittsburgh, KASC has not only the expertise in information/ computer/ communications areas but also the immediate access to almost every important computerized database in science and engineering. The linkage to KASC via satellite will be a great advantage for both AIT and the region in that we will have remote, immediate access to the many computerized databases which are vital to our information requirement and yet, too expensive for us to own. It is our plan that subsequent arrangements will be made with all parties concerned to supply information drawn from KASC through AIT to other libraries and information centers in the region. This experiment will commence as soon as funds for its support are available.

These above mentioned recent developments will have an important effect on the overall improvement of library-information service in the region. The advancement of information technology definitely offers excellent possibilities for rapid improvement. It is of prime importance that the libraries and information centers in Asia will take full advantage of this development to close the "information gap" existing between the developed world and the developing world and to become a true partner in national and regional development.

---

① Stephen W. Massil, "The co-operative use of MARC tapes", a paper presented at the Conference on National and Academic Libraries in Malaysia and Singapore, Pulau Pinang, March 1 – 3, 1974. p. 8; and Stephen W. Massil, "Local and regional use of MARC in Southeast Asia," a paper submitted to the IFLA Committee on Mechanization, May 1974. p. 5.

The Experience of a Specialized Information Service in Asia — AGE[①]

Introduction

The many documentation problems in developing countries often stem from similar causes. These problems show a remarkable unity of focus despite the scattered location of developing countries over the various parts of the world. In seeking appropriate solutions to these problems which in some cases may require separate approaches for peculiar circumstances, an identification of these prevailing problems and their causes is the necessary first step. This paper intends to identify some of the documentation problems and difficulties encountered by the Asian Information Center for Geotechnical Engineering (AGE) in its first two years of operation and to suggest necessary actions needed for their remedies.

AGE

The Asian Information Center for Geotechnical Engineering (Asian Geotechnical Engineering for short, abbreviated AGE) was founded in January 1973 at the Asian Institute of Technology, a Bangkok based regional post-graduate school for engineering and related sciences. AGE is jointly sponsored AIT's Division of Geotechnical Engineering and the Library and Information Center. In general, the term "Geotechnical Engineering" comprises five subject areas:

Soil mechanics
Foundation engineering
Rock mechanics
Engineering geology
Earthquake engineering

The idea of establishing AGE was conceived at a meeting held in Bangkok, July 1971, of the representatives of the national societies of soil mechanics and foundation engineering in Asia. Arising from a generally felt need for a relevant, timely and responsive information service on geotechnical engineering especially tailored to the needs of Asian engineers, the meeting passed a resolution requesting the Asian Institute of Technology to establish and operate AGE for the purpose of selecting, acquiring, analyzing, storing, retrieving, publicizing, and disseminating useful information on Asian geotechnical engineering for the benefit of all those who are concerned. Recognizing the significance of geotechnical engineering work in relation to social and economic development in Asia as well as the importance of providing information service on a regional basis to serve the needs of geotechnical engineers and specialists, a grant was made by the International Development Research Centre (Canada) to support the operations of AGE for a three-year period.

Among the major activities of AGE are:

1. Searching, selecting, and acquiring both published and unpublished literature on geotechnical engineering which are relevant to Asia. Emphasis is given to literature originating in Asia, preferably in English, but materials of importance even in other languages are also included.

2. Establishing both an index card file and a machine-readable database for the relevant literature completely indexed and abstracted for easy retrieval. Both the International Geotechnical Classification System (IGC) and the Soil Mechanics Thesaurus are used.

[①] Presented at the Round Table Conference on Documentation Problems in Developing Countries held in Khartoum on 10 – 11 April 1975. The conference was organized by FID/DC and the FID National Member in Sudan.

3. Disseminating information on available literature through the following secondary publications:

AGE Current Awareness Service: A quarterly publication informing readers of recent geotechnical engineering publications and contents of selected geotechnical engineering journals received at AGE.

Asian Geotechnical Engineering Abstracts: A quarterly publication consisting of abstracts of available publications and reports on geotechnical engineering in or about Asia.

AGE Conference Proceedings List: An annual list of conference proceedings on various subjects of geotechnical engineering in AGE's collections.

AGE Journal Holdings List: A list revised annually of geotechnical engineering journals held at AGE.

Besides these four publications, a SDI service by computer is currently being developed and is expected to be ready for service early in 1976.

4. Conducting periodic surveys on geotechnical engineers, specialists, and organizations in Asia as well as their on-going projects and works in progress. Results of these surveys are published in the following two publications:

Asian Geotechnical Engineering Directory: A biennial publication to consist of information on various organizations and individuals who are doing geotechnical engineering work in Asia or work relevant to Asia.

Asian Geotechnical Engineering in Progress: A semi-annual publication to consist of information on current design, construction and research projects in geotechnical engineering being undertaken in Asia.

5. Providing the three "**R**" services (**R**eference, **R**eprography, and **R**eferral) to members and other users. It is planned that at some future date, the Center may also publish state-of-the-art reviews and bibliographies on subjects of interest to geotechnical engineers.

6. Cooperating with other information and documentation services on or related to geotechnical engineering both in and outside Asia to enhance information resources and service on geotechnical engineering on a global basis through reciprocal arrangement and systems interconnection. Discussions on this have been in progress with Geotechnical Abstracts, Inc. (Germany); the Division of Applied Geomechanics, Commonwealth Scientific and Industrial Research Organization (Australia); the Swedish Geotechnical Institute; etc.

Basically, AGE's collections, database, publications, and services are available to its "individual members" and "institutional members". With the financial support generously provided by IDRC, AGE is able to keep the fees for the two kinds of membership at a very low level with a special rate to Asians in order to give them the maximum benefit at a cost the majority of them can afford. As of December 31, 1974, AGE had a total of 149 members; 52 are institutional members and 97 are individual members. They represent 17 Asian countries and 8 non-Asian countries. It is hoped that the number of members will be greatly increased in the years ahead so that AGE could eventually support itself through membership fees and incomes drawn from publication sales and service charges received from non-members.

In order to find the pattern of information usage by geotechnical engineers in Asia, a questionnaire survey was conducted among AGE members in March 1974. Findings concerning the general characteristics of AGE members, their channels for information, the library facilities available to them, the types of technical information they often require as well as their appraisals of the two quarterly AGE publications: The AGE Current Awareness Services and the Asian Geotechnical Engineering Abstracts, and other services provided by AGE were reported in the paper entitled "User and Use Analysis: A Case Study of the Information Utility by Geotechnical

Engineers in Asian Countries."①

A follow-up study on the usage of all six AGE publications and the three "R" services by AGE members is being undertaken at present also by means of questionnaire. The second study is designed to seek answers to the following questions:

1. How appropriately have AGE publications and services served the needs of its members?
2. How would they rate the relative importance among the six AGE publications and among the various services?
3. What tangible effects have these publications and services had upon the members?
4. What improvement is needed in the existing publications and services?
5. Are there other publications and services which the members would like AGE to provide?
6. Does AGE meet their general expectation as a regional information center for geotechnical engineering?
7. What are some of the effective ways AGE can get more new members?
8. What are some of the effective ways AGE can obtain more technical literature from the member's country?

The answers to these questions are very important for the planning and future programming of AGE during its next phase of development.

Documentation Problems

The common problems for documentation in developing countries as were experienced by AGE included language differences, bibliographical control, availability, currency, and information consciousness. A brief discussion of each of these problems together with their implications and possible solutions are presented below:

1. The language differences:

This problem is not unfamiliar to documentalists in that there are many little known languages with which very few documentation services, including AGE, have the capability to deal. Being a regional post-graduate school, the students and faculty members of the Asian Institute of Technology come from 22 Asian countries. This gives AGE the advantage of accessible linguistic assistance whenever needed. But even so, for practical reasons, AGE's collection is predominantly in English with a very small percentage of relevant literature in other languages. This practice is dictated by practicality and user demand rather than by the proportion of the literature available. This act of "discrimination" in the search and selection of relevant literature has restricted the coverage of AGE's collection.

In order to improve this situation, it is felt that the following measures should be taken by authors and editors of technical publications in every country, but particularly in those countries whose languages are less commonly known.

—For the authors, it will be very useful if they can supply the titles of their papers in a widely used language, preferable in English, in addition to their own. Furthermore, it will be very helpful if they can also prepare an abstract with key words or descriptors in such a language to accompany each of their papers.

—For the editors of proceedings, serial publications, and journals, they should either require their author to provide title, abstract, and key words in a widely used language in addition to their own or help them in providing these as a standard feature. A bi-lingual title page and table of contents will facilitate literature search and simplify the documentation process.

---

① Hwa-Wei Lee, "User and use analysis: A case study of the information utility by geotechnical engineers in Asian countries," Paper presented at the 37th Annual Meeting of the American Society for Information Science, Atlanta, Georgia, October 13-17, 1974, preceding paper in this collection.

2. Bibliographical control:

The lack of a comprehensive bibliographical control of publications and literature generated in most of the developing countries in Asia presents another serious problem for documentation work. Although the number of national bibliographies published by developing countries in Asia is increasing, a majority of them are neither complete nor current. This is also true in regard to indexes to journal literature and technical papers prepared by many of the Asian countries. Up until recent years scholars and researchers both in Asia and elsewhere have relied heavily on published library catalogs, international indexes and bibliographies produced by developed countries as the main sources for publications and literature of developing countries. Because of the inadequate coverage of these externally published bibliographical tools, many of the works of Asian origin are not included and therefore are unknown to others. From the AGE's experience, there is a very large amount of relevant literature on geotechnical engineering in most of the Asian countries which has not been listed anywhere.

In terms of the importance of indigenous material for engineers in Asia and the demand for it as shown by 58% of the photocopying requests received by AGE in 1974 which were for materials generated in Asia, a major effort should be made by as many Asian countries as possible to provide full bibliographical coverage of publications and literature originating in each of their countries.

The steps to be taken to remedy this problem include the publication of a national bibliography and national indexes by designated agencies such as the national library and the national documentation center or other suitable agencies in each country. The coverage of both should be as complete and current as possible. This must be supported by appropriate depository laws which govern not just trade publications, but also documents, reports, and technical literature by a variety of sources.

The basic principles of Universal Bibliographic Control (UBC) which were proposed by FID and endorsed at the Intergovernmental Conference on the Planning of National Documentation, Library and Archives infrastructures, convened by UNESCO on September 23 – 27, 1974 should be implemented by each country to the fullest extent possible. The tools for standardization such as ISBD (M), ISBD (S), ISDS Guidelines, etc. should be adopted. Efforts should be made to participate in various international information systems such as INIS, AGRIS and DEVSIS so that a worldwide coverage of useful information in fields of importance can be made possible through international cooperation.

3. Availability:

The problem of availability or to put it more accurately "unavailability" of many indigenous publications and report literature is another headache for documentalists in Asia. Based on AGE's user survey, the most frequently required technical information by geotechnical engineers are field performance data, site investigation information, and engineering design and construction details. But, according to AGE's experience, much of this information is not published for wide distribution and is, therefore, very difficult to obtain.

The original sources for report literature of this kind, either published or unpublished, are government offices responsible for engineering works, academic and research institutions involved in engineering research and projects, and engineering and consulting firms. They have large amounts of report literature, but most of it is not easily available due to government red tape or unnecessary restrictions imposed by some of their issuing bodies. Furthermore, many international or inter-governmental organizations, various foundations, and a score of foreign-aid agencies of the aid-given countries also generate a considerable number of documents and reports. It takes an extraordinary effort, frequently involving personal knowledge and contacts, to acquire some of this information which often proved to be most useful to engineers.

The experience of AGE serves to illustrate a serious need existing in developing countries where a great deal of financial and human resources could be saved or be channeled to better use if much of this report literature, not just that on engineering, could be deposited in national documentation centers of the respective countries and be adequately listed. The operation may be patterned somewhat after the National Technical Information Services (NTIS) of the U. S. to which all publications and reports of government funded or sponsored research and development projects must be deposited. By means of weekly announcements and monthly indexes, and supported by reprographic services, all such publications and reports are made easily available at low cost. It would be more advantageous if the national documentation center or an appropriate agency in every country could expand its coverage to include not just government related publications and reports but others as well, that originate in its country.

4. The Currency Problem:

A serious obstacle which prevents the inflow of useful information to the developing countries is the lack of convertible currency or foreign exchange in most of the developing countries. Because of this problem, both individuals and institutions in developing countries are unable to purchase needed publications, to subscribe to essential journals, to join professional societies, to obtain reprographic services, or to take advantage of specialized information services available to them from sources outside their countries. The use of UNESCO coupons has not functioned well as they, also, are difficult to obtain. There are also regulations on import controls which serve to discourage foreign publications from entering some countries or to step up their prices.

From AGE's experience, the currency problem has made it very difficult if not impossible for some individuals and institutions in Asian countries to join AGE or to use AGE's services despite the nominal rate of charge made possible by an IDRC grant.

To simplify this problem, permission has been granted by AGE to its members and users in those countries where foreign exchange is hard to obtain to pay their membership fees or service charges in local currencies to the appointed AGE liaison officer in their country. The local currency collected is to be used by the liaison officer to purchase local publications for AGE and to pay for packing and mailing costs. But even this provision is considered illegal in some countries. This unfortunate situation is not only responsible, in part, for the slow growth of AGE's membership, but also restricts many Asian users from taking advantage of the services provided by AGE.

Unless the governments can take affirmative action to ease the regulations on foreign exchange, particularly when it is used for the acquisition of publications and technical information, the information users of these countries will continue to be impoverished information-wise.

5. Information Consciousness:

Documentation services exist for their users. In the developing countries, the needs of information users are sometimes hidden or invisible at first but reveal themselves in an accelerated rate of use once started. Because of this, the temporary absence of visible needs should not be taken to mean that documentation services are not needed or at least not urgent. The main cause for the hidden needs stems from the long absence of adequate library and information services in most of the developing countries. People simply become accustomed to this situation and learn to get along without the benefit of information. This situation has resulted in a vicious circle of slowness in national development as well as in an "inferior" state of documentation service.

In order to improve such a situation, a special effort must be made to break the vicious circle by establishing a few model documentation services in developing countries or by improving their existing documentation services within the national documentation, library and archives infrastructures. These documentation services should serve to stimulate an "information consciousness" among the people they serve and to unearth the hidden needs.

One of the heartening experiences of AGE thus far has been the seeing of the changes taking place in the use pattern of its users. Those AGE users who have used AGE's service once tend to make more and frequent uses thereafter. This proves that once a confidence is established, an increased information use can be expected. The awakening of "information consciousness" is therefore a major task of any documentation services in the developing countries.

Conclusions

This paper has presented a brief description of a regional documentation service—the Asian Information Center for Geotechnical Engineering—and some of the documentation problems it has encountered. Since the causes of these problems are quite similar among developing countries in different regions of the world, the solutions to these common problems may also be unified. It is hoped that this paper will bring about further discussions on other documentation problems and their possible solutions so that a joint effort could be developed to improve documentation services in the developing countries.

Approaches to Development of Water Resources Scientific Information Systems[①]

Easy access to the wide range of scientific information on water resources is a basic necessity for policy makers, planners, managers, scientists, engineers, and researchers, as well as for private citizens who are concerned with various aspects of water resources planning, development, and management in their efforts to ensure an adequate supply of clean water for mankind's consumption.

Because of the interdisciplinary nature of water resources information and the needs of a diversity of users, there has been an increasing demand for specialized, mission-oriented information systems at local, state, national, and international levels covering the whole spectrum of water resources activities.

The international model described in the first paper "An International Model for the Transfer of Water Resources Information" is an excellent design for a global information system on community water supplies and sanitation. In order to complement that presentation, this report will concentrate on the discussion of approaches to the development of water resources information systems on the local, state, and national levels, with particular consideration given to the applicability of these approaches in developing countries. Also to be examined is the current trend toward the development of national and international information systems along with the possibility for interconnection of existing information systems into large national and international networks utilizing the latest computer and telecommunication technologies available.

Conceptual Information System and Some Operational Definitions

During the past thirty years there has been a great proliferation of both published and unpublished materials in the form of books, journals, reports, proceedings, documents, patents, specifications, data sheets, charts, etc. Many of these also appeared in a variety of media from paper copies and microtexts to punched cards. The body of information has greatly expanded and the demand for information by users has vastly increased. This has placed undue pressure on various information systems to expand subject, language, and geographical coverage, to deepen content analysis, to share resources with other information systems through cooperation and networking, and to make resources and services readily available and accessible.

Although it has been observed that many scientists and researchers still rely on their personal contacts and direct correspondence as the primary approach to obtain new information, this one-to-one approach in information transfer as shown in Figure I is no longer adequate to meet the information needs of today's world.

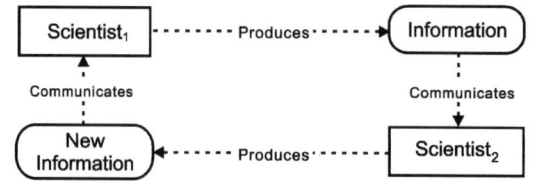

Figure I. Information transfer in a one-to-one communication mode

Because more information is transmitted through various communication channels in ever increasing speed and frequency, it is becoming difficult for scientists and researchers to keep up.

[①] Co-Author: Marjorie H. Rhoades

To find the information available in one's field, as well as to obtain it when needed, necessitates the services of well-established information systems and the aid of up-to-date, comprehensive bibliographical apparatus which includes card catalogs, book reviews, indexing and abstracting publications, selective dissemination of information (SDI), and on-line bibliographical databases. A diagram showing the transfer of scientific information through a multitude of communication channels including the various information systems and a wide range of primary and secondary publications is provided in Figure II. ①

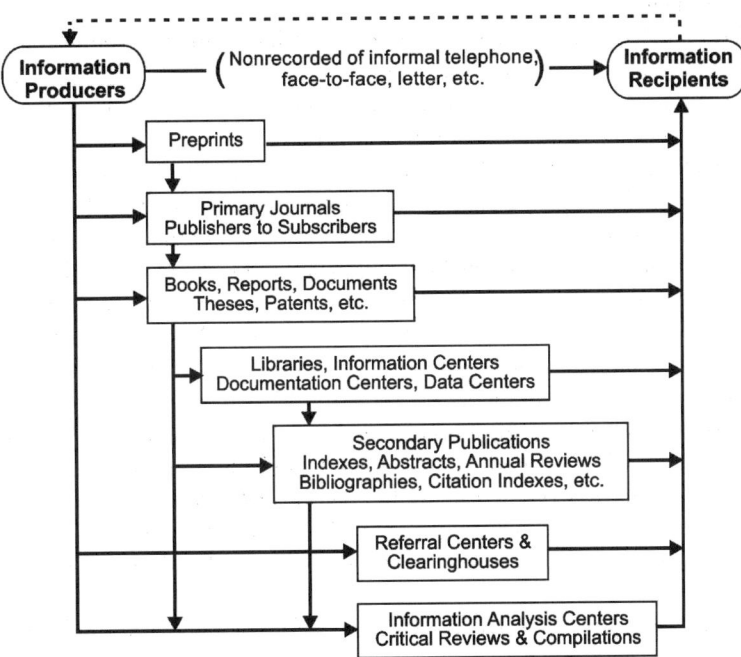

Figure II. Information transfer through a multitude of channels

From these diagrams one can derive a simple definition for the term Information System, that is:

Information System refers to the methods, materials, media producers, and recipients involved in an organized way to effect information transfer within a specific field, activity, or organization. ②

INFORMATION here is defined as knowledge, intelligence, facts, or data which can be used, transferred, or communicated. It has four basic qualities: namely, 1) existence, 2) availability, 3) language (or a recognizable representation) and 4) meaning. It is the quality of "meaning" that differentiates information from DATA. The distinction between information and KNOWLEDGE is in the degree of permanency. KNOWLEDGE is generally longer in life and more persistent. The term DATA is regarded as raw facts or observations and is often characterized by a tendency toward numerics or quantification. One can also say that quantified DATA intellectually processed become INFORMATION and produce KNOWLEDGE.

The Variety of Information Systems

Information systems exist to effect information transfer in an organized way. In order to maximize the effect for various user groups or organizations which may have different information needs and requirements, a variety of information systems each with some special emphasis has

---

① Both Figures I and II have been adapted from Herman M. Weisman, *Information Systems, Services and Centers* (New York: Becker and Hayes, 1972), pp. 24 & 30.
② Ibid., pp. 14 – 16.

developed. In general, there are a number of basic functions and services which are common to all information systems, but because of the differences in their emphases, five forms of information systems can be identified:
1. Libraries (including special or technical libraries)
2. Information or documentation centers
3. Specialized data centers
4. Referral centers or clearinghouses
5. Information analysis centers

A LIBRARY is probably the best known form of an information system. The major functions of a library consist normally of collecting, cataloging, preserving, circulating, and providing reference service. In special and technical libraries, collections may be limited to a special field with greater emphasis on unpublished materials of current value.

An INFORMATION CENTER (better known in Europe and some other countries as a DOCUMENTATION CENTER) is to some extent similar to a special or technical library in its collection emphasis and subject scope. Unlike libraries which see the preservation of the world's knowledge as their long-term goal, information centers are more concerned with current information contained in technical literature and unpublished materials. In general, an information center also pays more attention to content analysis and in-depth indexing. Many information centers employ the aid of a computer to process information for bibliographical search and retrieval, and for providing SDI and other specialized services.

Although it is not uncommon for libraries and information centers to also engage in data collection and service on a limited scale, the collecting and managing of a large data file is often the function of a SPECIALIZED DATA CENTER which in some cases, also performs the activities of an information analysis center by compiling and repackaging specialized data into a more compact and useful form. Many water related data centers are already in existence nationally and internationally.

A REFERRAL CENTER or a CLEARINGHOUSE may have some of the features of an information center, but its main task is to disseminate current information on on-going projects and research activities or to make referrals. The chief concern, then, for a referral center is in the information sources rather than the contents.

The primary function of an INFORMATION ANALYSIS CENTER is to collect and analyze all relevant information on a topic or a group of chosen topics, repackaging them into compact reports for the convenience of their users. The staff of an information analysis center often consists of highly qualified subject specialists working in a team with librarians and information scientists.

It is important to note that although information systems can be roughly grouped into the five forms, a clear distinction between each group and the others is not easy in that many of them do have overlapping functions, activities, and services. The difference among them is a matter of degree or emphasis rather than substance. Some information systems may very well by design consist of more than one of the forms described.

The National Referral Center of the Library of Congress is a good example of a library that provides referral service as a part of its total services. The National Technical Information Services (NTIS) combines the forms of a documentation center and a clearinghouse. In addition to being a depository for federally funded research and technical reports, it also indexes and abstracts them and prepares them for computer research (NTISearch), publishes a semi-monthly *Government Reports Announcements* and Index and a companion *Weekly Government Abstracts*, and sells photocopies or microfiche copies of such reports on demand. Currently, about 6,000 profiles are run daily by all organizations using the NTIS database.

Some information centers are known to be established within libraries. Vice versa some libraries may also be founded as a section of a large information center. As stated earlier, many data centers also function as information analysis centers. One of these is the National Oceanographic Data Center which performs the activities of an information analysis center in addition to being a specialized data center. An example of a clearinghouse is the Smithsonian Science Information Exchange which collects and disseminates information about ongoing or current research.

Developing an Information System

  No matter in what form an information system may be, the general approach to developing an information system in an organization or an agency normally would consist of four basic phases: the background study phase, the system design phase, the development phase, and the operation phase. Each of these phases can be further divided into a number of activities which could be used as a checklist by information system planners.

I. The Background Study Phase:
  A. The goals and mission of the "parent" organization.
  B. The definition and characteristics of potential users.
  C. The information needs and requirements of both the organization and users.
  D. Existing information facilities and resources, both internal and external.
  E. The objectives, scope, and services of the planned information system.
  F. Other influencing and constraining factors:
    1. Attitude of the top management.
    2. Characteristics of the organization.
    3. Anticipated source and level of financial support.
    4. Availability of computer and telecommunication facilities.
    5. Trained library and information personnel.

II. The System Design Phase:
  A. Analysis of the findings of the background study.
  B. Decision on the form (s) of information system.
  C. Determination of the organization structure.
    1. Placement of the information system within the structure of the "parent" organization.
    2. Centralization vs. decentralization.
  D. Selection of the mode of operation.
    1. Manual vs. mechanization.
    2. Self-sufficient vs. interdependence.
  E. Definition of the scope of collection.
    1. Subject coverage.
    2. Language coverage.
    3. Geographical coverage.
    4. Medium coverage.
    5. Time coverage.
  F. Determination of resources required.
    1. Facilities.
    2. Equipment.
    3. Materials.
    4. Personnel.
    5. Cooperation and integration with existing activities.
  G. Design of system and operating procedures.
    1. System configuration.
    2. Record and data elements.
    3. Indexing and abstracting standards.
    4. Thesauri development.
    5. File structure and database format.
    6. Storage and retrieval considerations.
    7. Photoduplication and reproduction techniques.

        8. Interconnection with other information systems and networks.
    H. Cost estimates.
    I. Establishment of a time schedule for system development and implementation.
    J. Approval of the system design by the management.
III. The Development Phase:
    A. Dry run check-out of system and operating procedures.
    B. Set up pilot operation.
        1. Recruit and train staff.
        2. Acquire materials and equipment.
        3. Prepare physical facilities.
        4. Pilot operation.
        5. Provide user training.
        6. Evaluate design and procedures based on pilot operation.
        7. Revise as necessary and as feasible.
IV. The Operation Phase
    A. Implement by set stages.
    B. Check and evaluate each implemented stage and revise as necessary.
    C. Full operation of system.
    D. Periodic review.

Emerging Trend Toward National Systems and Networks

From the many papers in this session of the Conference, we are able to learn about the operating details of an assortment of information systems in water resources, some large, some small; some world-wide, some local; some in developed countries, several in developing countries. In addition, we learn about the recent trend in many countries toward the establishment of national information systems and networks in water resources.

Uncoordinated though they are, there is an abundance of information systems in water or water related fields in many of the developed countries. Giving the United States as an example, according to the 1966 *Directory of Information Resources in the United States*: Water, there were 800 non-commercial organizations that are doing research or collecting data on water.① Many of them have their own information systems. In order to coordinate information services and data collecting activities within each country for the purpose of sharing resources and reducing unnecessary duplication, a new trend emerging in recent years is toward the establishment of national water resources information systems and networks.

Unlike that which has been the case in the United States, Canada, and some other developed countries, water resources information systems in many developing countries are understandably less well developed. The lack of needed information and data for water resources planners and others is undoubtedly a hindrance to the planning and development of sound water resources programs in these countries. Not only are the water resources information systems poorly developed, the whole of scientific information systems in many developing countries also are undernourished.

There is an encouraging sign, however, that because of the rapid economic, social and political developments in many developing countries coupled with a succession of national development plans, an awareness of the importance of library and information services in national development is increasingly seen. Through the promotion and assistance of United Nations Educational, Scientific and Cultural Organization (UNESCO), attempts have been made by some countries to develop and strengthen their national information systems and infrastructures.

Similar assistance has also been provided by other international and inter? governmental

---

① U. S. Library of Congress, National Referral Center for Science and Technology, *A Directory of Information Resources in the United States*: Water (Washington, D. C.: Government Printing Office, 1966). p. 248.

organizations, private organizations and foundations, and governments of developed countries through their technical assistance programs to help developing countries establish viable information systems. The inclusion of an information transfer package as a major component of many technical assistance programs is of great significance in helping developing countries develop the capability for self reliance.

Because of this impetus, activities have begun in many developing countries to publish national bibliographies, to inventory periodical and serial holdings and to coordinate resources development and sharing among the national library, national documentation center, major academic and research libraries, public and private libraries, and special libraries. An increasing number of indigenous publications which were unknown or unaccountable before are now included in national bibliographies and periodical indexes.

Despite the many improvements, a serious problem remains in the area of unpublished materials. In the fields of development literature under which water resources is also a part, according to the recent report on the preliminary design of an international information system for the development sciences,[①] 60 percent of the relevant literature is unpublished material which is usually very difficult, if not impossible, to obtain. Consequently, this type of material is inadequately covered by published bibliographies and indexes. The report compares this type of material to the submerged part of an "iceberg" (Figure III). Only 40 percent of the total development literature is "visible". A majority of them are journal articles (22 percent) and books (18 percent).

To increase the accessibility to the 60 percent of invisible information requires the improvement of national information systems in each of the developing countries. The designation of a national center for water resources information and data from the existing information systems in the country is highly desirable. The national center should have the following basic responsibilities:

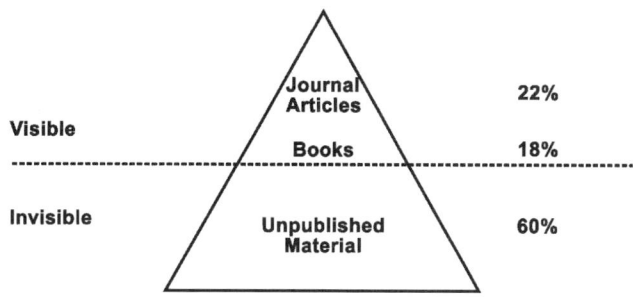

Figure III. The development literature "iceberg"

1. coordinates the information gathering, data collection, and services of existing water resources information systems in the country;

2. creates and maintains a national bibliographical database in water resources information and data;

3. serves as a special node on water resources information in the national information network; and

4. acts as the national focal point for the exchange of water resources information with other countries and for possible future inter-connection with international information systems or networks.

---

① DEVSIS: *The Preliminary Design of an International Information system for the Development Sciences*; prepared by the DEVSIS Study Team... (Ottawa: International development Research Centre, 1976), p. 18. (IDRC-065e)

International Cooperation and Networking

In the international arena there is an increasing number of information systems which have been established to serve the information needs of a worldwide user community interested in water or water-related subjects.

The first is the development of an acceptable model for the establishment of international, mission-oriented information systems based on the following principles①:

1. decentralization of the task of identifying and recording information as it is produced, each participating nation (or region) being responsible for reporting what is produced in its own territory;

2. centralized merging of material reported by the different input centers, the task being performed in an international agency through international financing;

3. output products tailored to the needs of advanced institutions with computer facilities, as well as printed (or microfilmed) indexes and abstracts that can be used by institutions without such facilities, and individual scientists;

4. service for photocopies or microfiches to ensure availability;

5. products available at low cost and all charges payable in local currencies;

6. international management, based on consultation with all participants;

7. engagement of governments to ensure official support and the availability and infusion of relevant government publications and reports; and

8. utilization of an internationally accepted standard bibliographical format to permit future interconnection among various international information systems.

Thus far, two operational international information systems have built on this model. They are the International Nuclear Information System (INIS) and the International Information System for the Agricultural Sciences (AGRIS). In fact, it was INIS that first developed and refined such a model. Other international information systems which will probably follow the same principles and are in the proposal and planning stages are in such fields as development sciences (DEVSIS), population and demography (IDEMIS or POPINS), science policy (SPINES), industrial technology (UNITIS), informatics (WISI), and architecture and urbanism (ARCHIS) .② It is entirely possible that under the auspices of an appropriate UN department or agency we can add water resources (WATIS) to the list. The task of setting up an international water resources information system is not insurmountable in that there already exist a number of well established national focal points in many countries. The extensive machine-readable database now developed by WRSIC and its collaborating agreements with many countries might easily be extended into an international system.

The second is the development of machine-readable bibliographical databases in almost all the major fields of science and technology during the last ten year. As the number and size of these databases have expanded very rapidly, there is a corresponding sharp increase in the number of searches. The increase in use coupled with the improvement made in telecommunication has resulted in a continued reduction in cost per use. This, in turn has further stimulated the use of machine-readable databases by an ever larger number of users. Several important impacts of this development have been observed:

1. more on-line terminals have been established at an increasing number of locations to facilitate the use;

2. more effective communication techniques;

3. improved standardization and cooperation among database producers;

---

① John E. Woolston, "International Information Systems: Their Relation to Economic And social Development", paper presented at International Symposium on Information systems: Connection and Compatibility, Varna, Bulgaria, Sept. 30 – Oct 3, 1974. (IAEA – SM – 189/I) pp. 1 – 2.

② DEVSIS, *op. cit.*, p. 38.

4. expanded bibliographical services;
5. increased demand for document delivery service, interlibrary loan and photocopying service;
6. greater needs for resources sharing and networking among information systems.

The estimated number and size of databases available through Lockheed's DIALOG and the rates of both the increase in search and the decrease in cost as shown in Table I are astonishing.

Table I. The Growth of Lockheed's DIALOG[1]

Year	No. of Databases	Size of Databases	Rate of Increase in Searches	Rate of Decrease in Cost
1965	1	200,000	—	—
1970	—	—	100	100
1973	11	2,100,000	2,000	40
1975	30	8,000,000	15,000	20

The total number of on-line searches made in the U. S. A., exclusive of OCLC and MARC on-line cataloging uses, is estimated at 270,000 in 1972, 700,000 in 1974, and 1,000,000 in 1975.[2] If the current effort to lower the tariff rate for information transmission is successful, the cost of search will be even cheaper and the use will be expected to increase even more.

The third is the development of large information networks both nationally and internationally to interconnect existing information systems, databases, and computers through telecommunication linkage. Because of advances in computer and telecommunication technologies, the forming of interactive information networks becomes technically and economically feasible. Great advantages can be gained by using communication satellites to link geographically dispersed information systems into a resource-sharing network at a much reduced cost. A recent cost evaluation shows that through the use of communication satellites, the cost of long distance lines has dropped dramatically. For example, in 1974, a leased voice-grade line from New York to Los Angeles cost $2,200 per month via land links; it now costs only $1,000 per month utilizing a communications satellite link.[3]

By means of information networks, extensive information resources and computer facilities became accessible to more users in wider geographical areas thereby distributing expenses for computer and database operations to a large group of users resulting in sizable cost reduction. Developing countries and some small countries that formerly could not afford to have their own computers and machine-readable databases will now be able to share such resources and facilities with developed countries without incurring high investment costs.

The large national and international information networks now in operation are ARPANET established by the Advanced Research Projects Agency of the U. S. Department of Defense and the Space Documentation Service (SDS) of the European Space Agency. Currently under planning by the Commission of the European Communities is a large multinational and multilingual information network called EURONET, or the European Network.[4] The experience gained from these networks

---

[1] Lee G. Burchinal, "Bringing the American Revolution On-Line Information Science And National R & D", *Bulletin of the American Society for Information Science*, V. 2, No. 8 (March 1976), p. 27.

[2] Martha E. Williams, "The Impact of Machine-readable Data Bases on Library and Information Services", *Information Processing and Management*, V. 13, No. 2 (1977). p. 101.

[3] D. M. Audsley, "One-Line Networking Between Information Centers in Europe", In NATO Advisory Group for Aerospace Research and Development, *National and International Networks of Libraries, Documentation and Information Centers*, papers presented at the Technical Information Panel Specialists' Meeting held in Brussels, Belgium, October 2 – 3, 1974 (Paris: UNESCO, 1975). (NTIS AD – A009 426) pap. 7, p. 6.

[4] John Page, "International STI Networks: Promises and Problems." *Bulletin of the American Society for Information Science*, V. 2, No. 4 (Nov. 1975), pp. 12 – 13.

will be very useful to the planning and design of other information networks elsewhere.

With the trend toward development of a national water resources information system in many countries and with the availability of a machine-readable database created by WRSIC, it is possible now that through the spreading of national and international information networks, one can have easy access to the water resources database from many parts of the world. The time is right also for the national water resources information systems to consider the possibility of forming a global information system on water resources based on the INIS model.

Challenges for the Library and Information Profession

The thirtieth anniversary marks a major milestone for the Library Association of China. Its many important contributions to the promotion of modern library and information services in Taiwan deserve special recognition and applause. Without the catalyst of the Association, the recent collaboration with the National Central Library to develop a computerized Chinese MARC database and information system which encompass a wide range of programs and activities could not have been accomplished within a short four-year period. Besides the library automation project, the Association has excelled in many other areas such as: legislative action; the development of library standards; the promotion of better library services; the enhancement of library education, training, and research; consultation; international cooperation; publications; etc. This short essay on challenges for librarianship[①] in coming years, with particular reference to Taiwan, is dedicated as a tribute to the Association on the occasion of its thirtieth anniversary.

Although the year 2000 still seems far away, it is only a short seventeen years from now. If one looks at the long history of librarianship or of our civilization, seventeen years is a brief period indeed. Moreover, with the magnitude and range of changes taking place in our society — the so called "Information Age", one can be sure that the pace and scope of change in library and information services will be even more drastic in the coming years than in the past. It will be fun in the year of 2003 to look back 20 years to see how the profession has progressed at the 50th anniversary of the Association.

The shifting of our society from an industrial base to an information base in the recent past has been depicted in some detail by John Naisbitt in his best seller, *Megatrends*. He advises that "innovations in communications and computer technology will accelerate the pace of change..."[②] One such change with major impact on the future of library and information services is electronic publishing, storage, and dissemination of information. Such a change, although still in its early stage of development, has prompted some highly respected futurists in our profession to predict the early disappearance of printed materials as well as the demise of the libraries as we know them today.

From this scenario this essay intends to examine the current societal and technological changes that affect librarianship and to suggest a possible strategy for coping with these changes.

Unlike the predictions of Professor F. Wilfrid Lancaster in many of his publications that, with the further development of electronic publishing, the future society will be paperless and that "the library as we now know it — a building housing physical artifacts — will cease to exist..."[③] This author has another view. It is my belief that, despite the great potential of electronic publishing which will affect our society as well as our profession, information in printed forms will continue to exist into the 21st Century. People will read more as the educational level rises, as work becomes more knowledge-based, and as the quality of life and leisure time further increase. The front page of the September 8, 1983, New York Times carried the headline — **Americans in Electronic Era Are Reading as Much as Ever** — and cited evidence to support the claim. It reported that about 50,000 book titles will be published this year, the most ever, and that book sales, bookstores, library circulation, and newspaper readership are all growing.[④]

Referring to the immortality of libraries, Dr. Richard De Gennaro feels that:

---

① The word, "librarianship", is used in its broadest sense to encompass the entire realm of the library and information science profession.
② John Naisbitt, *Megatrends: Ten New Directions Transforming Our Lives*, (New York, Warner books, 1982), p. 19.
③ F. Wilfrid Lancaster, "Electronic publishing: Its impact on the distribution of information," *National forum, The Phi Kappa Phi Journal*, Vol. LXIII, No. 3 (Summer 1983), p. 5.
④ Edward Fiske, *New York Times*, 8 September 1983, p. 1.

We need to lay to rest the simplistic idea that electronic technology in the hands of information entrepreneurs is going to put an end to libraries. Libraries are here to stay, but by no means are they going to stay the same. Their basic functions will remain, but the ways and means they use to perform those functions will change in varying degrees and at varying speeds for different kinds of libraries in different countries. ①

Dr. De Gennaro's position has a large following in the profession. As living institutions, libraries adapt to societal and technological changes. "Libraries are becoming more, not less, important in our information society even though their relative share of the total information market is declining," further remarked de Gennaro. ②

For libraries to assume this even greater role in the information society they must prepare themselves for the many challenges that lie ahead. Among these are:

1. The challenge of information explosion and pollution.
2. The challenge of new information technology.
3. The challenge of the changing roles of libraries (and information centers).
4. The challenge of new professional competencies required.
5. The challenge of global interdependence.

Each of the challenges is discussed below, as well as the associated problems and possible strategies for coping with these.

Information Explosion and Pollution

One significant characteristic of an information society is the increasing number of information occupations. According to Naisbitt, in 1950 only about 17% of American workers held information jobs. By 1982, this reached 60%. Most of these workers, be they scientists, researchers, teachers, lawyers, librarians, programmers, secretaries, bankers, clerks, accountants, stock brokers, managers, insurance agents, bureaucrats, etc., spend their time creating, processing, or distributing information. Now, more than ever before, we are experiencing the impact of the information explosion and pollution. ③ For example:

— Between 6,000 and 7,000 scientific articles are written each day.

— Scientific and technical information now increases 13% per year, which means it doubles every 5.5 years.

— But the rate will soon jump to perhaps 40% per year because of new, more powerful information systems and an increasing population of scientists. That means that data will double every 20 months.

— By 1985 the volume of information will be somewhere between 4 and 7 times what it was only a few years earlier. ④

Such a phenomenal growth of information, unless effectively handled and organized for easy access, will soon drown us in a flood. Uncontrolled information can usefully be considered as trash which pollutes our environment.

In the case of journal publishing, there were about 1,000 journals in 1850. Today, the number has surpassed 100,000. Each day new journals are born. Managing growing, fast-changing journal publications long has been a headache for the serials librarians, not to mention users. Control of the contents of journals is an even greater problem than the management of the titles. Indexing and abstracting publications created to provide bibliographic control and access to the journal articles have in themselves become too bulky to be handled manually. To keep up with editing and publishing of these indexing and abstracting publications back in the 1960s, many of

---

① Richard De Gennaro, "Libraries, Technology, and the Information Market-place", *National Forum*, *The Phi Kappa Phi Journal*, Vol. LXIII, No. 3 (Summer 1983), p. 31.
② Ibid.
③ Naisbitt, *Megatrends*, p. 14.
④ Ibid., p. 24.

the publishers began to rely on computers for sorting, composing, and type-setting. A by-product of this was the computerized bibliographic databases which were later made searchable online and thus came the online revolution.

By searching these online databases, users can locate a large number of citations, many of which would otherwise be unknown. However, locating the bibliographic information is still much easier than actually obtaining the publication. This has substantially expanded the work of many libraries and information centers to trace needed information and obtain it for users. The rising cost of publications and limited library budgets mean that no library today can meet all of the needs of its users — especially when such needs have mushroomed through the proliferation of online databases and users who have become aware of the potentialities of new information technology. Cooperative acquisition and collection development, bibliographic control and union listing, interlibrary loan, and resource sharing are some of the necessary means currently employed by libraries in many countries to cope with this situation.

A welcome trend in document delivery in recent years has been the supplying of needed texts by database vendors and others at the time of online search. Orders can be placed online and copies of the texts can be sent by mail. Although the cost may be a little high for average users, with technological advances, it may become a cost-effective, common practice in the foreseeable future. Even online delivery, whether real time or through down loading, is finding a market. Such services, including on-demand publishing — if not, overpriced, can indeed save the libraries and information centers the cost of subscribing to and maintaining large numbers of infrequently used journals and back volumes. This, of course, poses an entirely different set of problems for journal publishers. The wave of this information explosion and pollution is now heading toward the less developed countries. Some of the experiences now sweeping through the U. S. A. will soon reach Taiwan.

As one of the fastest developing newly industrialized nations in Asia, Taiwan has enjoyed a high standard of living. Most of the population is educated, skilled, and industrious. Telecommunication systems are well developed. The publishing industry and the book trade are relatively active. Libraries and information centers of all types are in the process of modernization. The recent Government policy in terms of economic development is to transform the national economy from an industrial to a high technology base. Such a transition requires a strong support from the library and information profession. Already, under the leadership of the Library Association of China, in collaboration with the National Central Library, an ambitious Chinese Library Automation Planning Project was launched in 1980 with the following objectives. [1]

1. To develop the Chinese MARC format for the cataloging of Chinese materials.

2. To design an automated library and information system for the processing of library materials.

3. To create databases for Chinese materials and to bring in selected databases from abroad.

4. To establish a national information service center and a network of libraries and information centers to support the needs for national development.

To achieve these objectives is by no means simple, but with the determination, dedication, and cooperation of the library and information workers, many of these have either been realized or are well under way.

New Information Technology

In retrospect, the information explosion of the last two decades was largely responsible for the rapid development of information technology. Much of the advancement in computer technology, electronic technology, and telecommunications has found its way into the information fields through increasing market demands. The creation of large computerized databases, some of which are the

---

[1] National Central Library, *The Library Automation in the National Central Library*, *R. O. C.* (Taipei: 1983), p. 1.

by-products of computerized typesetting of indexing and abstracting publications, has made the most noticeable progress. From literature citations, to abstracts, to numeric data, and to the full text of documents; more and more databases of various types are now available for online remote access, thanks to the advancing information technology.

Two important recent developments in computerized databases are the home information service and the document delivery service.

1. Examples of home information service: Prestel, the pioneer of home information service in Great Britain is an interactive system made available by the British Post Office in 1979. The system enables home, library, and business users to have access through their television sets, modified for videotext, to a variety of computer-based information services for a fee. CompuServe, a private system designed for owners of home, business, and office computers is now available in many parts of the United States. CompuServe claims to serve 70,000 customers and to be adding 7,000 new users each month. It provides access to news stories of Associated Press, the Washington Post's Electronic Newsletter, price quotes and trading volume of more than 9000 stocks, Standard & Poor's descriptive and financial information on more than 3000 companies, airline schedules and fares, the Travel America service for making reservations, games, electronic mail, etc. Depending on the time of day, speed of transmission and particular database the cost of each connected hour varies from US $6 to US $15.

2. Example of document delivery service: The Original Article Text Service (OATS) offered by the Institute for Scientific Information in the United States is one of the many commercial document fulfillment services now available. OATS enables users to order articles online through DIALOG'S DIALORDER Service, SDC's ORBDOC, the ISI Search Network, and soon, BRS.

Parallel to the development of computerized databases and their online access is the quiet evolution in electronic publishing. Already many books, journals, and technical publications are typeset by computers with full text stored in disks. Two important future possibilities of electronic publishing are on-demand publishing and electronic delivery.

1. On-demand publishing. The rising cost in publications, coupled with the information boom, have led some publishers to consider the desirability of on-demand publishing. Storing publishable materials on disks in a central facility and printing only on request is one way to slow proliferation of publications. A variation of on-demand publishing is the electronic journal described by Eugene Garfield as a personalized SDI journal. [1] Manuscripts for such a journal may be written, edited, and refereed through a computer-based network without ever producing a paper copy. The final text will be stored in disks and will be disseminated to subscribers whose interests match the subject matter of the texts.

2. Electronic delivery. This is a logical extension of electronic publishing — electronically stored full text of any publication, either in full or in part, can be transmitted to requesters or subscribers. In a more recent article, Mr. Garfield reported other plans for electronic delivery of full texts currently under consideration: [2]

a) Article Delivery Over Network Information Service (ADONIS). This service has been proposed by a consortium of publishers, including Blackwell, Elsevier, Pergamon Press, Springer, and Academic Press to provide a user with a copy of the needed journal article stored on videodisc. The copy may be sent by mail or a telecommunications channel to a printing facility at the user's location.

b) Automated Retrieval of Text from Europe's Multinational Information Service (ARTEMIS). Proposed by the Commission of the European Communities, the service calls for storing the full text of documents on magnetic tape and transmitting them via telephone lines to computers at printing centers where the full text would be either reproduced and sent through the

---

[1] Eugene Garfield, "ASCAmatic — The Personalized Journal," *in his Essays of an Information Scientist*, Vol. 1 (Philadelphia: ISI Press, 1977), p. 22.

[2] Eugene Garfield, "Document Delivery-Systems in the Information Age", *National Forum*, *The Phi Kappa Phi Journal*, Vol. LXIII, No. 3 (Summer 1983), pp. 8 – 10.

mail or relayed directly to the requester.

Although both of these systems, among others, are still in the early stages of planning, they point out some of the possible courses of action for electronic document delivery in the future.

In Taiwan, applications of the new information technologies are rising since overcoming seemingly insurmountable difficulties in inputting and outputting Chinese characters and processing them by computer. The development of Chinese MARC and other computerized databases in Chinese language is well underway. What is needed is a national library and information system which will include the development of a computerized national bibliographic database and network of library and information centers to share online cataloging resources through interlibrary loan, and eventually, document delivery. Existing databases, both domestic and foreign, should be accessible online in all major cities. The development of domestic databases should be coordinated to avoid unnecessary duplication of effort and overlap of coverage. Microcomputers should be used by libraries and information centers for local applications. Care, however, should be taken to assure hardware compatibility, and both hardware and software should support common protocols, and standards[①] to facilitate future interconnection. Specialized or mission-oriented libraries and information centers can form their own networks to share resources.

The availability of highly reliable and efficient postal service make document delivery within the Taiwan by mail the most effective. Electronic mail service can be easily established also, as microcomputers and terminals are becoming widely available in offices and homes. Modern telephone service also makes this and regular telephone communication fast and easy. Telecommunication links with other countries, especially the United States via satellite, are very convenient also. These all combine to provide the Taiwan with advanced information services from abroad as needed.

Changing Role of Libraries and Information Centers

As dynamic institutions, the role of libraries and information centers changes with time. Change is a process in which an institution rejuvenates itself to meet new demands and challenges. Libraries and information centers, although differing in function and role, share many similarities. Libraries have existed within information centers and information centers can be established within libraries. In the information society, a library and an information center are like a person's two hands. Without being handicapped, each needs the other to do a better job. Regardless of the name, a library or an information center must be capable of performing a variety of functions to meet the wide range of user needs. Public libraries should be an integral part of their community and act as community centers to provide informational, cultural, educational, social, and recreational services. Academic and research libraries should include in their role the preservation and dissemination of scholarly information to expand the frontiers of knowledge. National and state (provincial) libraries should play leadership roles in the promotion of library cooperation and services and in the development of library and information systems and networks. School libraries should be not only the learning resources center but the center of learning. Special libraries and information centers should be providers of managerial and technical information geared to the specific needs of the parent organization. Major centers among these should serve as network and resource nodes in the national system.

In Taiwan, the change in the roles of libraries and information centers will likely be even more drastic and necessary in the next few years as a result of social and technological transformations. Moreover, libraries and information centers have much catching up to do because of inadequate earlier modernization. The recent surge of computer applications, in varying degrees of sophistication, in many libraries and information centers has helped to shake some old concepts

---

① Such as the International Standards Organizations (ISO) open systems interconnection (OSI) — thus the ISO OSI model. A good discussion can be found in Michael Witt, "An Introduction to Layered Protocols", *Byte*, Vol. 8, No. 9 (September 1983), pp. 385–398.

and practices. More and greater changes are still needed to meet the increasing information demands of a fast developing nation. The Government's policy of fostering the development of high technology in place of labor-intensive industries affords new opportunities for libraries and information centers to fill new roles.

New Professional Competencies

As a result of the information explosion and technological changes which have brought fundamental changes in the library and information profession, there has been concern in recent years about the professional competencies needed for library and information workers in the information age. To prepare future professionals, the following competencies are suggested:
1. The foundations of librarianship (including information science).
2. Subject specialization and language facility.
3. Human relations and communication.
4. Information technology and applications.
5. Management theory and practice.
6. Business knowledge and marketing.
7. Fund raising and grantsmanship.

Depending on the level and variety of responsibilities, not all these competencies need be uniformly required. For example, in large library or information center, there will be a range of positions varying in level and type. Library education should be sufficiently diversified to prepare various library and information workers needed. For top managers, advanced post-graduate, interdisciplinary programs may be needed. For middle-and upper-level professionals the program should be at the graduate level with electives for different specializations. For technical and clerical staff, four-and two-year programs at the undergraduate level should be considered as the minimum. While the emphasis of the undergraduate programs should be aimed at some degree of competency in technical skills, graduate programs focus on fundamentals (i. e., basic values) as advocated by Prof. Herbert White[1] rather than specific applications (i. e., certain skills). Because of rapid changes in technology, most of the latest applications should be given encouragement and high priority by the management. Librarianship, like engineering, cannot afford to neglect continuing education.

In addition to working in the libraries and information centers, new opportunities exist for competent professionals to work as information consultants or specialists in government agencies, business and industrial firms, and other organizations. These consultants, or specialists, can work either independently or in conjunction with other librarians to provide special information service to senior executives, decision-makers, and researchers.

Seeing the opportunity for business ventures, many entrepreneurial library and information professionals have set up private, for profit, offices to sell information services to institutions, business firms, or others who are in need of information.[2] The education or training of these information entrepreneurs does not differ much from those working in libraries and information centers except, perhaps, for an even greater emphasis on business and marketing.

Extending library education from the undergraduate level to graduate level and widening the curriculum to include information science and other subjects are some of the encouraging trends already underway in Taiwan. The annual workshops for library support staff sponsored and organized by the Library Association of China have provided much needed educational opportunities for large numbers of para-professionals in library and information centers to acquire or update knowledge and skills for their work. The challenges for library education in Taiwan in the coming years are many. These may include continued revision of the curriculum to reflect the new

---

[1] Herbert S. White, "Defining Basic Competencies", *American Libraries*, Vol. 14, No. 8 (September 1983), p. 521.

[2] See Barbara B. Minor (ed.), *Information Broker/Free-Lance Librarian: – New Careers – New Library Services: Workshop Proceedings* (Syracuse: School of Information Science, Syracuse University, 1976).

emphases and needs in information science, improvement in the quality of instruction and the teaching faculty, recruitment of capable students from a variety of subject backgrounds — especially science and technology, and exploration of new frontiers in the field through interdisciplinary and multidisciplinary research. Library education in the era of information technology should be aimed at educating leaders and innovators rather than at training practitioners and followers.

One of the major obstacle to recruitment is the low status and low pay given library and information professionals. Although this may be seen as a universal problem, solutions to it must be sought from within each country. The establishment of required professional competencies may improve the professional image and attract promising people to the ranks. In the long run, the profession should strive for excellency in its services. Making library and information service indispensable is a certain way to command respect, to positively project the image, and to claim greater rewards.

Global Interdependence

"Knowledge knows no national boundary." This common belief of the scholarly world has gained new life through the development of information technology. By means of satellite communication the geographic distances among nations have shrunk. Online databases are now accessible throughout the world if one can afford the cost, which is seldom totally prohibitive. However, barriers to the free flow of information across national boundaries are still pervasive as countries seek to restrict certain information from others for reason of national security or technological competition. There are other barriers such as high telecommunications tariffs, lack of foreign exchange, inadequate telecommunication facilities, language, etc. The lack of information, particularly the information needed for national development, has been one of the characteristics of underdeveloped countries. These countries are often referred to as "information poor" countries as distinct from those which are "information rich".

In recent years, several developments have stimulated transborder information flow.

1. World-wide marketing efforts of indexing and abstracting services.

2. Broadening the coverage of many databases to include information from the Third World countries.

3. Availability of online databases from remote access via satellite, regardless of distance.

4. Increasing recognition of the importance of information for national development by developing countries.

5. Concerted efforts by many developing countries to develop a national information infrastructure, with the technical assistance of the United Nations Educational, Scientific and Cultural Organization (UNESCO).

6. Development of international cooperative information systems such as the INIS (International Nuclear Information System), AGRIS (International Information System for the Agricultural Sciences and Technology), DEVSIS (Development Sciences Information System), ISDS (International Serials Data System), INDIS (Industrial Development Information System), etc. which encourages the participation of both developed and developing countries to share information among one another. ①

7. Increasing opportunities for library and information professionals to be educated or trained abroad. International and regional conferences, seminars, short courses, etc. are being held in many parts of the world with large participation from developing countries.

8. Development of international standards governing information transfer. ②

---

① For detailed descriptions of these international systems, see *International Cooperative Information Systems*; Proceedings of a Seminar Held in Vienna, Austria, 9–13 July 1979 (Ottawa: IDRC, 1980).

② See *ISO Standards Handbook* 1: *Information Transfer*, [texts of ISO Standards] (Geneva: International Organization for Standardization, 1977).

9. Promotion of world-wide programs in Universal Bibliographic Control (UBC) and Universal Availability of Publications (UAP) by IFLA (International Federation of Library Associations and Institutions).

At the Intergovernmental Conference on Scientific and Technological Information for Development (UNISIST II) held in Paris in 1979, the following basic belief was reaffirmed:

> Information, the product of the scientific and technological efforts made by the whole of humanity, is an essential resource to which all countries should have free access, and consideration should be given to the way in which scientific and technological information fits into the development process.
>
> The more readily a society can obtain access to abundant and varied information, drawn from worldwide sources, the freer it is to make choices suited to its own style of development and to the goals that it has set. [1]

In moving from industry to high technology, Taiwan should be strongly interested in exchanges of publications and information with other countries. Efforts by individual libraries and information centers should be encouraged and coordinated wherever appropriate to assure maximum impact. The establishment of Chinese bibliographic databases in MARC format will facilitate the exchange of bibliographic records with other countries. Special information centers should concentrate on selecting, evaluating, and repackaging suitable information for dissemination. Depending on the users, some of the information may be translated into Chinese for wider readership. Collaboration with and contributions to international information systems and major databases to expand coverage of Chinese materials will be mutually beneficial. Many of the specialized regional information resources and databases, such as those established and maintained by the Asian Institute of Technology in Bangkok, Thailand, can serve as models for developing further regional and national databases and information services. [2] Cooperation with these existing databases deserves special consideration.

Although political pressure from the People's Republic of China (PRC) has caused many inter-governmental and international agencies to exclude the Taiwan from participation, Taiwan should not be discouraged by such unfair political tactics. Unofficial contacts with international organizations and participation by individual library and information professionals in international and regional conferences should be increased. The political conduct of the PRC often is self-defeating in international meetings.

In conclusion, the author wishes to again extend his congratulations to the Library Association of China on its thirtieth anniversary. As a life member of the Association, I share both the pride in its past accomplishments and the challenges that lie ahead. The Association can be only as good as its members. The challenges described in this essay can be effectively met with the combined wisdom and strength of the Associations membership acting in unison.

---

[1] W. Lohner, "Intergovernmental conference on Scientific and Technological Information for Development (UNISIST II): Main Issues and Results", in *International Cooperative Information Systems: Proceedings of Seminar Held in Vienna, Austria, 9 – 13 July 1979* (Ottawa: IDRC. 1980). P. 21.

[2] An autonomous regional institution for postgraduate education in engineering and technology, the Asian Institute of Technology in Bangkok has established four specialized information centers to serve information needs in Asia: the Asian Information Center for Geotechnical Engineering (AICGE), the International Development Information Center (IDIC), the Renewable Energy Resources Information Center (RERIC), and the Environmental Sanitation Information Center (ESIC).

第六部分 图书馆自动化

Section VI Library Automation

The Information Technology — New Tools And New Possibilities for Information Storage, Retrieval and Dissemination

Introduction

One of the most pressing problems facing the developing nations in Asia today is the inability of their libraries and information centers to respond effectively and expediently to the wide range of information needs which are required for national development.

It has been observed that there exist two types of "information gap" in Asia. One is the lack of immediate access to the growing body of knowledge accumulated because of the rapid advancement in science and technology. Another is the lack of an effective mechanism to uncover useful indigenous information, to collect it from widely scattered sources, to index it for easy retrieval, and to publicize it for and to disseminate it to the potential users. It is an unfortunate fact that even among the Asian countries themselves, there is very little cooperation and interchange of useful information between the libraries and information centers.

A great deal of human and financial resources have been wasted in Asia as a direct result of these two types of "information gap". The perpetuation of this situation has rendered the works of Asian scientists, research workers, and technical specialists both ineffective and inefficient because of the amount of unnecessary duplication of efforts.

Recognizing such a serious problem, many Asian nations already have taken steps to correct it. This is shown in the findings of a recent UNESCO report:[①]

>   In each country visited there is active interest in the development of scientific and technical information, and plans for improvement of the present system. In Indonesia, a Ford Foundation mission recently advised on the establishment of a national network of science information centers to be coordinated by the National Scientific Documentation Centre, and the Government has requested UNDP consultant services to assist in the actual planning. In Malaysia, a mission was carried out in late 1971 under British Council sponsorship to advise on "Scientific and Technical Library and Information Services in Malaysia". In Singapore, there has been no direct follow-up on the 1969 UNESCO sponsored "Proposals for the Setting-up of a Scientific and Technical Information Centre", but there is active interest in revising this study to bring it in line with the changing situation in Singapore. In the Philippines, the NSDB is setting up a new National Science Information Centre which will serve as the national coordinating body and as the linkage to regional and international networks or systems. The Government has requested UNDP advisory services in planning the Centre. In Hong Kong the Committee for Scientific Co-ordination has set up a Sub-Committee on Scientific and Technical Information to consider the establishment of a "Centralized Technical Information Service". In Thailand the Thai National Documentation Centre (TNDC) which is already well established is planning further services, and the Asian Institute of Technology has advanced plans for development of a complete information service on a regional level. In all countries the value of regional linkages was recognized and the concept of regional information

---

① *Report of UNESCO Fact-Finding Mission on the Regional Information Network for Science and Technology in Southeast Asia*. 1972. p. 20. (SCP/425/2 – 25).

network in science and technology was strongly supported. ①

For the social sciences, a comparable study was made by Mr. Erwin Kristoffersen, regional representative of the Friedrich-Ebert-Stiftung which has resulted in a well documented proposal to establish a Clearing House for Social Development in Asia as an effective measure to meet the information needs in the Social Sciences. ② The study pointed out the serious deficiencies existing in the exchange and dissemination of indigenous information in the social sciences much of which is vital for developmental planning. The following paragraphs are quoted from the findings:

> The objective need for an improvement in the exchange of information in the field of social development has often been mentioned, even in such documents as the "Jackson Report", and was discussed along with proposals for the improvement in various official and unofficial meetings.
>
> Interviews during the course of the feasibility study of various institutions further established the fact that the exchange of information was either completely lacking or had considerable gaps within and between agencies and different government departments. Institutes and universities only in a very few cases had regular channels to receive and to disseminate information. Non-governmental agencies and organizations were found to be almost totally excluded from the regular flow of information.
>
> As this was found regarding "official information". a regular exchange of "unofficial information" between the mentioned institutions was not to be found at all.
>
> In certain instances the situation was better on the international level, but worse than expected in respect to regional exchange. Compilation of information was usually undertaken on an ad hoc basis. Mailing lists for the regular dissemination of own material hardly existed.
>
> If the premise is accepted that regional exchange of information is a condition of development promotion the objective need has clearly been established. ③

In the light of these two studies and the important groundwork they have laid, I would like to direct my talk to the possible tools made available by recent advancements in information technology which can be applied to improve library-information services in the region.

Information Technology

Information technology is a term referring to those technologies which can be applied to library-information work. There are many such technologies available now-a-days. They generally come under one of the following three labels:

1) Reprography
2) Computers
3) Telecommunications

Each of these three actually represents a variety of applications and different degrees of sophistication. They may also work independently or together in a complex information system. Just as with other tools, not all the technologies are suitable for all situations and at all times. It is necessary that I speak only of those technologies which are considered relevant to our particular situation and requirement at the present time. As I am not a technical expert, I speak only as a librarian.

Reprography

Despite the fact that "Reprography" is a relatively new term, this technology is already under widespread use by many libraries and information centers in Southeast Asia. Unlike the newness of the name, reprography consists of many not-too-new techniques such as microfilming and various

---

① Ibid., p. 4.

② Erwin Kristoffersen, *Clearing House for Social Development in Asia*; *Project Proposals and Report on the Findings of a Feasibility Study* (Bangkok: Friedrich-Ebert-Stiftung, Bangkok Office, 1972). p. 35.

③ Ibid., p. 14.

methods of copying and duplicating.

The techniques of reprography are very important for the developing countries in that:

1) they enable a wider dissemination of information some of which might not be available or accessible otherwise;

2) they have made it possible for libraries and information centers to interchange reproduced information;

3) various microforms are by far the most economic means for information storage and for dissemination to distant places by mail; and

4) the computer-output-microforms (COM) reduces the problem of storage and dissemination for the large amount of computer generated data.

Computers

Although the use of computers in library-information work has found wide acceptance throughout the world, it has just begun in Southeast Asia. The computer is a very promising tool in that it has the power and versatility to process data with high speed and precision. The main obstacles standing in the way of wider application by libraries and information centers in Asia are the factors of high cost, especially in the initial stage, and the lack of trained staff. These two obstacles can be overcome by setting up either national data processing centers within each country or multinational (or regional) data processing centers within a number of cooperating countries. The former can be affiliated with either the national library, the national documentation center, an institutional library or a special information center, whichever has the computer capability. The latter can be attached to a regional or international organization that is so equipped.

The essence of this setup is to share the costs of both owning or sharing a computer system and developing the software necessary for its support, and pooling together the trained personnel. By means of this arrangement, even small libraries and information centers can have the benefit of sharing a computer with large libraries and information centers. The work which can be best handled by such data processing centers would be:

1) Establish and maintain a national (or regional) data bank on indigenous publications. A by-product of this data bank is the publication of national (or regional) bibliographies.

2) Establish and maintain a national (or regional) data bank on major library collections in the country (or region). A by-product of this data bank is the publication of a national (or regional) union catalog and separate book catalogs for each participating library or information center.

3) Establish and maintain a national (or regional) data bank on periodicals and serial publications held by major libraries and information centers in the country (or the region). A by-product of this data bank is the publication of a union list of periodicals and serials and separate lists of holdings for each participating library or information center.

4) Establish and maintain a national (or regional) data bank for scientific and technical literature of relevance to the country (or the region). A by-product of this data bank is the publication at regular intervals of abstracting journals. A score of other services such as SDI service, current awareness service, and retrospective search of the data file can also be performed.

5) Establish and maintain a national (or regional) data bank on such vital information as census data, demographic data, land use data, hydrological and meteorological data, inventories of communications and transportation, industrial and housing facilities, geological and natural resources, etc., and relevant economic and sociological data.

6) Act as a national (or regional) processing center for the acquisitions, cataloging, and processing of books, journals and other materials for the libraries and information centers that want to participate in such labor-and-cost-saving operations. There are a wide range of activities that can be channeled through such a central processing service.

7) The center may also consider the possibility of acquiring the MARC (Machine-Readable Cataloging) tapes of both the U.S. Library of Congress and the British National Bibliography for

local storage and manipulation.

Arrangements may also be made to obtain the machine-readable database of MEDLARS (Medical Literature Analysis and Retrieval System of the National Library of Medicine, U. S. A.), CAIN (Cataloging and Indexing System of the National Agricultural Library, U. S. A.), ERIC (Educational Resources Information Center) tapes, etc. for local storage and manipulation.

Because of the high cost of leasing some of the commercially produced databases such as the Chemical Abstracts, the Engineering Index, the Historical Abstracts, the Psychological Abstracts, etc., it may not be financially feasible for national centers to invest a large portion of their funds to acquire or lease these databases except when there is a particular need for having any one of them.

8) Develop a library of computer programs for various library-information work including programs for automatic indexing, photocomposition, etc.

9) Provide consulting services to other libraries or information centers who are interested in establishing their own computer operations.

10) Provide various computer services to individual or special library-information projects.

11) Conduct short courses, seminars and workshops for the training and up-grading of librarians and information scientists in the use of computer and other information technology for library-information work.

Telecommunications

Telecommunications is an important part of the new information technology which holds great promise for improving library-information services in Asia.

An effort has been made by the United Nations Economic Commission for Asia and the Far East (ECAFE) to make the countries of Asia into an "Asian Telecommunity". The program intends to develop in every Asian country a telecommunication network and to link the various national networks from Iran to Indonesia by a system of modern communication services provided at the most economical rates. When fully realized, it will undoubtedly accelerate the interchange of information among the libraries and information centers in the region by making possible information transmission and facsimile reproduction at high speed and at low cost. It will also facilitate the development of national library-information systems and regional library-information networks similar to those systems and networks already in operation in many parts of the world. One such example is the ESRO system which was reported in a recent article by Isotta. [1]

ESRO system is the information system for the Space Documentation Service of the European Space Research Organization located in Darmstadt, Germany. The ESRO system was designed on the concept of a centralized file maintenance and software responsibility, coupled with decentralized searching of the files by remote terminals sited in the member states. The total configuration (Figure 1) consists of the central computer facility in Darmstadt, together with its own local terminal; a single leased line to Paris where two terminals are installed; a party-line connection from Paris to St. Mary Cray in Kent where a terminal is installed at the Technology Reports Centre; a party-line connection from Paris to Bretigny, where a terminal is installed at the Centre Nationale D'Etudes Spatiale; a terminal in the ESRO establishment in Noordwijk, Holland; and another terminal in the ESRO establishment in Frascati near Rome. [2]

This type of system can be adopted in Asia if the "Asian Telecommunity" becomes a reality and the cost of telecommunications is substantially reduced.

Another important recent development in telecommunications which has an encouraging implication for Asia is the ability to transmit information among widely dispersed points of the world via satellites. The capability of communication satellites to transmit voice, teletype and facsimile

---

[1] N. E. C. Isotta, "International Information Networks: 1. The ESRO System". *Aslib Proceedings*, V. 24 No. 1 (January 1972) pp. 31 – 7.

[2] Ibid., p. 33.

signals to a distant place at the speed of light has a distinct advantage over other communication media for inter-continental communications. An interconnection of computers, telephones, teletypes and communication satellites can provide a most effective network of national, regional and world information systems.

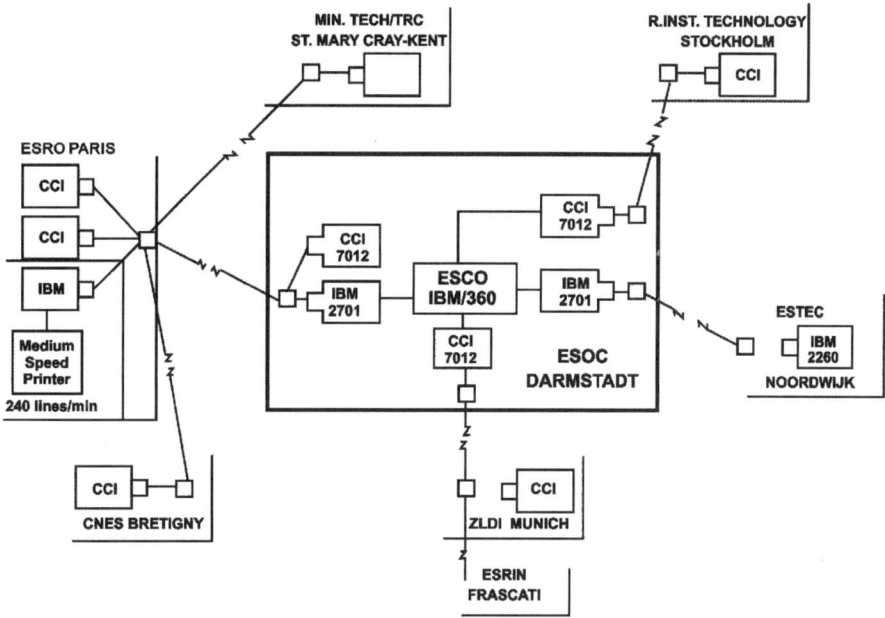

Figure 1 First European Network for the Dissemination of Scientific and Technical Information

A highly sophisticated network system which saw the interfacing of all these was demonstrated recently at the 35th annual meeting of the American Society for Information Science held in Washington, D. C. on October 23 – 26, 1972. The system demonstrated was called "International Information Retrieval Network". Through the several on-line terminals located on the conference grounds, participants of the annual meeting were able to query not just the many databases on computers located several hundred miles away in different parts of the U. S. A. but also the data files of the ESRO in Darmstadt, Germany via the INTELSAT IV communication satellite. The demonstration featured several recent innovations, including:

1) International communications via satellite.
2) Remote video and printing terminals.
3) On-line, interactive retrieval systems using both natural-text and index-based techniques.
4) Networking.
5) Access to multiple databases.

The demonstration showed that international networks are technologically feasible, economically conceivable, and usable with minimal instruction. ①

Another less sophisticated but operating system using only teletype machines and the INTELSAT IV F – 2 satellite is the satellite linkage between John Crerar Library (JCL) in Chicago, U. S. A. and Consejo Nacional de Investigaciones Cientificasy Tecnicas (C. N. I. C. T.) in Buenos Aires, Argentina. The basis of the system consists of some fourteen technical libraries in Argentina, which are linked by Telex to each other and to C. N. I. C. T. in Buenos Aires. When an institution cannot fill its needs from its own collection, a message is sent to C. N. I. C. T. which then attempts to locate the needed item in one of the other libraries by use of the Union Lists and catalogs. If this is unsuccessful, the request is then transmitted to JCL and the latter provides

---

① From "A World of Information", the program of the 35th annual meeting of ASIS. p. 8.

microfilm copy by return airmail. The costs of photocopies and the relay messages are borne by the National Academy of Sciences in the U. S. ①

The JCL/C. N. I. C. T. system is a good example of what the developing countries can do to obtain the needed information from developed countries. Financial assistance of this kind is probably available from many international or foreign aid organizations.

AIT's Plans

As a regional institution for advanced engineering education and research, the Asian Institute of Technology (AIT) is deeply involved in the technical development of the Asian region and it is this involvement which has led AIT to an awareness of the urgent needs of Asian engineers for relevant information. To meet this need AIT has devoted a large portion of its resources to develop an outstanding library and information center within the Institute. Steps have been taken to expand this facility into a regional library and information center for engineering and related fields, embracing the collection, organization and dissemination of useful technical information. The recently founded Asian Information Center for Geotechnical Engineering, under the joint sponsorship of the AIT Division of Geotechnical Engineering and the Library, is an example of one such endeavor.

To improve library-information service in the region, especially in the application of the latest information technology, AIT is in a very unique position. We are now in the process of undertaking three major steps which, if successful, will undoubtedly have a far reaching effect on the development of a regional library — information network. These steps are (1) expanding computerized library-information service with a regional outlook, (2) establishing the Asian Information Center for Geotechnical Engineering, and (3) planning for an information transfer experiment via satellite between AIT and the Knowledge Availability Systems Center (KASC) of the University of Pittsburgh.

1) Expanding computerized library-information service:

Within the next six months, a very large computer system (CDC 3600) will be installed at AIT to replace the currently overloaded IBM 1130. With the massive memory and the fast printing capabilities of a CDC computer system, we plan to greatly expand our present computerized library operations.

As a part of this plan, we have requested and received approval from the Government of the United Kingdom to provide us with a library systems analyst to help us in the planning and implementing of our expanded computer applications. This specialist is from the University of Birmingham and will join AIT Library in September. For the last six years, this specialist has been actively working with the Birmingham Libraries' Cooperative Mechanization Project which utilizes MARC records in three libraries (Aston and Birmingham Universities, and the Birmingham Public Libraries) on a cooperative basis. Work of the Project has been reported regularly in Program. ② We hope that with the background of this specialist on library cooperative mechanization, many of our new programs will have a broader perspective and regional outlook and will tie in with the regional library-information network development.

2) Establishing the Asian Information Center for Geotechnical Engineering (AICGE):

To experiment with the setting up of a regional library-information service, we have selected a very important but highly specialized field — Geotechnical Engineering, as our pilot project. The idea of establishing AGE was conceived at the meeting of representatives of national societies of soil mechanics and foundation engineering in the Asian region which convened in Bangkok in July

---

① From the letter of William S. Budington, Executive Director and Librarian of the John Crerar Library dated August 30, 1971.

② Most recent report of the Project is: E. H. C. Driver, D. G. R. Buckle, S. W. Massil, D. J. Wilkins & A. R. Hall, "The Birmingham Libraries' Cooperative Mechanization Project: Progress Report, June 1970 – January 1972," *Program: News of Commuters in Libraries*, V. 6, No. 2 (April 1972) pp. 120 – 6.

1971. Through one of the resolutions of the meeting, AIT was requested to undertake the task of establishing and operating AGE for the benefit of engineers in Asia. The importance of this undertaking was recognized through a grant awarded by the International Development Research Centre of Canada to partially support the activities of the Center for the initial three-year period.

Serving as a clearing House in Asia for information on all phases of Geotechnical Engineering such as soil mechanics, foundation engineering, engineering geology, rock mechanics, earthquake engineering and other related fields. The Center will undertake the responsibility to collect all relevant information and data useful to the region, to design a computer-based information storage and retrieval system, to disseminate such information through its publications and photocopying and microfilming services, and to provide the three-R service (reference, referral and reproduction).

The detailed information concerning the data files, the publications, and the services of the Center are contained in an introductory brochure published by the Center.①

3) Planning for an information transfer experiment via satellite between AIT and the Knowledge Availability Systems Center of the University of Pittsburgh:

This experiment which is now being planned is patterned after both the ESRO system and the JCL/C.N.I.C.T. system already described. The Knowledge Availability Systems Center (KASC) is one of the six NASA Regional Dissemination Centers in the U.S. Under the directorship of Professor Allen Kent who is also the Chairman of the Department of Information Science at the University of Pittsburgh, KASC has not only the expertise in information/computer/communications areas but also the immediate access to almost every important computerized database in science and engineering. The linkage to KASC via satellite will be a great advantage for both the AIT and the region in that we will have remote, immediate access to the many computerized databases which are vital to our information requirement and yet, too expensive for us to own. It is our plan that subsequent arrangements will be made with all parties concerned to supply information drawn from KASC through AIT to other libraries and information centers in the region. This sounds so much like a dream, but it is not far from reality.

Concluding Remarks

This paper only has scratched the surface of several recent developments which will have an important effect on the overall improvement of library-information service in the region. The advancement of information technology has definitely offered excellent possibilities for rapid improvement. It is of prime importance that the libraries and information centers in Asia will take full advantage of this development to close the "information gap" existing between the developed world and the developing world and to become a true partner in national and regional development.

Vigorous efforts should be given by all those who are concerned with the improvement of library-information service in the region to carry out the two-phase project proposed by the UNESCO Fact-Finding Mission:②

The first phase emphasizes (1) reinforcing national centers, (2) training information specialists, (3) training users of scientific and technical information, (4) improving and extending national information services, and (5) introducing the necessary compatibility elements and links between the national information centers.

The second phase constitutes the actual establishment of formal linkages between the centers into an operational regional network.

It is felt however that the regional network to be established should not be restricted to only scientific and technical information. Instead, it should link the major libraries and information centers in all subjects including the social sciences. The libraries and information centers of the

---

① *Introducing Asian Information Center for Geotechnical Engineering* (Bangkok, Asian Institute of Technology, 1973). p.9.

② UNESCO, *op. cit.*, p.1.

group of international organizations and agencies in the region constitute a very important resource in the social sciences. These information resources plus the proposed Clearing House for Social Development in Asia should not be left out of the regional network.

As far as AIT is concerned, as a regional institution committed to the development of Asia, we shall do whatever is possible to work for the early realization of the second phase of the project.

Recent Breakthroughs in Library Automation in Taiwan

Introduction

The utilization of computers for bibliographical control, information database management, and other library operations in Taiwan although not begun until 1973 has made remarkable progress within a relatively short span of time. Most significant of this development is the ability now to process materials and publications in Chinese scripts along with those in Roman alphabets. This major breakthrough in Chinese library automation was revealed recently at the International Workshop on Chinese Library Automation held in Taipei from February 14 to 19, 1981. The workshop, under the joint sponsorship of the Library Association of Taiwan, the American Council of Learned Societies, and China Committee for Scientific and Scholarly Cooperation with the U. S., attracted over 220 participants including 40 from such countries and territories as Australia, Belgium, Hong Kong, Japan, South Korea, Singapore, and the U. S. A. Representatives from the Library of Congress, the OCLC Online Computer Library Center, the Research Libraries Group (RLG), Washington Library Network (WLN), and several major East Asian libraries (Harvard, Hawaii, Indiana, Rutgers, Washington, and Yale) were among the American contingent.

Main Purposes of the Workshop

As stated in his opening address, His Excellency C. K. Yen, former Governor of Taiwan, pointed out the three main purposes of the workshop:
 1. to report and review the recent accomplishments in library automation in Taiwan;
 2. to seek advice on the refinement of these initial achievements, and
 3. to explore the possibility for international cooperation.

Guided by these goals, the workshop was divided into four consecutive sessions, each consisting of a number of papers.

Session I. The Chinese Language and Computers (Chaired by Dr. Shih-Chien Yang, Dr. Ching-Chun Hsieh, Dr. Chen-Chau Yang, and Mr. Karl Lo).

Session II. Chinese Cataloging Rules and the Chinese MARC (Chaired by Mr. James E. Agenbroad, Mr. John T. Ma, and Dr, Nelson Chou).

Session III. Library Automation Case Studies (Chaired by Dr. Tung-Sheng Fang, Dr. Hwa-wei Lee, and Ms. Barbara Roland).

Session IV. International Cooperation for Library Automation (Chaired by Mr. Eugene Wu, Dr, Robert M. Hayes, Ms. Margaret Chang Fung).

The following is a list of papers delivered at the workshop (papers by Taiwan participants identified by an asterisk) in the order of presentation:

 * "The design of the Chinese Character Code for Information Interchange — CCCII", by C. C. Hsieh, K. T. Huang, C. T. Chang, and C. C. Yang.

 * "The design of a cross-reference database for Chinese character indexing", by C. C. Yang, K. T. Huang, C. T. Chang, and C. C. Hsieh.

"Requirements definition for East Asian character support enhancements to Research Libraries Information Network" by John Haeger.

"Personal names and the Chinese Character Code for Information Interchange, volume 1 (CCCII/1) — Adequacy and implications" by James E. Agenbroad.

 * "The establishment of hsing-fu-writing and consideration for the Chinese language's input method" by T. Y. Kiang and T. H. Cheng.

 * "On the application of the basic component set of Chinese characters" by S. Lin.

* "Discussion on the arrangement of characters used in computers from the viewpoint of Chinese character structure and evolutionary changes" by H. T. Li and C. F. Chow.
* "A survey of various forms of Chinese characters" by C. K. Pan,
* "Discussion on hsing-mu in Chinese computers" by H. H. Chin and Y. S. Ho.
* "A comparative study of Romanization systems for the Chinese language" by T. J. Liu.
* "Study on the phonetics of characters used in computers" by J. C. Lin and H. Chou.
* "An introduction to a modified system of Chinese Romanization (named Huarwern)" by Shir-Jen Jang.
* "Information, computer and Chinese language" by Nelson Chou.
* "Chinese Cataloging Rules — A draft" by C. C. Lan, Working Group on Chinese Cataloging Rules.
* "The use of the Chinese MARC in North American Libraries" by Karl Lo.
* "Chinese MARC: Its present status and future development" by Lucy T. C. Lee, Working Group on Chinese MARC.

"Automated library networking: Possibilities for international cooperation" by Raymond DeBuse.

"The application of computer in Chinese information systems; a general survey" by T. S. Fang.

* "The Union List of Chinese Serials in Taiwan: A case report" by Rui-Lan Ku Wu.
* "The preliminary plan for the Index to Chinese Periodical Literature: A case report" by Rui-Lan Ku Wu.
* "The Agricultural Science and Technology Management System" by Wan-Jiun Wu.
* "Computer-microfilm retrieval system used for processing Chinese character criminal data in R. O. C." by Yung-Liang Loh.
* "Freedom Council Information Abstract" by Jack K. T. Huang.
* "The Chinese Education Resources Information System" by Margaret C. Fung.
* "International cooperation in library automation" by Henrietta D. Avram and Lenore S. Maruyama.
* "International cooperation in Chinese library automation: An American perspective" by Hideo Kaneko.
* "Library automation for Chinese collections in Western Europe: Potentials and problems" by John T. Ma.
* "A sketch for a computerized national library and information network" by Hwa-Wei Lee.
* "The development of Japan/MARC and Chinese character sets" by Tokutaro Takahashi and Toshikazu Kanaka.

Major Accomplishments Highlighted

Most important among these papers were the ones presented by participants from Taiwan which describe in detail the following major accomplishments in Chinese library automation:

1. The development of various Chinese computer input and output devices and the design of a comprehensive cross-reference index of varying coding systems for Chinese characters.
2. The compilation of a "Chinese Character Code for Information Inter-Change" (CCCII).
3. The complete revision of the Chinese Cataloging Rules (CCR).
4. The adoption of the "Chinese MARC Format" and development of a prototype online cataloging system.

It was astonishing to note that, through the cooperative efforts of a group of determined and dedicated librarians, computer and information scientists, and philologists in Taiwan, so much was accomplished in a record time of eight months! The three working groups which were responsible for much of the success are the Chinese Character Analyses Group, the Chinese Cataloging Rules Working Group, and the Chinese MARC Working Group. All three were founded to carry out the National Library Automation Plan (NLAP) under the direction of the Library Automation Planning

Committee (LAPC) which was established jointly by the Library Association of China and the National Central Library (NCL) in early 1980. The following briefly highlight the major accomplishments revealed at the workshop:

The development of various Chinese computer input and output devices and the design of a comprehensive cross-reference index of varying coding systems for Chinese characters.

Because of the complexity of the Chinese language and the large number of Chinese characters any computer system must deal with in processing, a variety of input and output devices has been developed by different organizations, computer companies, and vendors in Taiwan with the advice and assistance of many specialists in philology and computer science. Besides the several research papers focusing on the various approaches and/or problems in processing Chinese language materials that were presented at the workshop, at least 14 computer companies and vendors exhibited their Chinese input and output devices. Two of the companies: R. P. T. Intergroups International Ltd. and the Taiwan Automation Company, also displayed their prototype online Chinese MARC systems which were developed for the Chinese MARC Working Group. As observed, no attempt has been made as yet at this point of development to standardize the Chinese input and output devices since none is considered perfect. The keen competition among the computer firms in the development of a most efficient and cost-effective input and output device for the processing of Chinese language data is a very healthy thing, at least for the time being.

In coping with the various coding systems for computer input of Chinese characters, the design of a comprehensive cross reference index of these systems becomes very necessary in order to provide an effective means for identifying, finding or addressing a Chinese character by whatever coding system employed in computer input, be it based on radical, stroke count, stroke sequence, component expression (or radical expression), phonetic codes (such as kou-yu, Wade-Giles, Yale, pinyin, and Liu), telegraph code, three-corner code, four-corner code, or any one of the internal codes of various Chinese data processing systems.

Figure 1 is a block diagram of the cross-reference database for Chinese character indexing being developed by the Chinese Character Analysis Group which consists of many top philologists, librarians, and computer scientists in Taiwan. The four most active leaders of the Group are: Professors Chung-Tao Chang, Ching-Chun Hsieh, Jack Kai-Tung Huang, and Chen-Chau Yang. The database, when completed, will not only facilitate code conversions and cross-referencing but will also serve as an aid to further studies of Chinese characters.

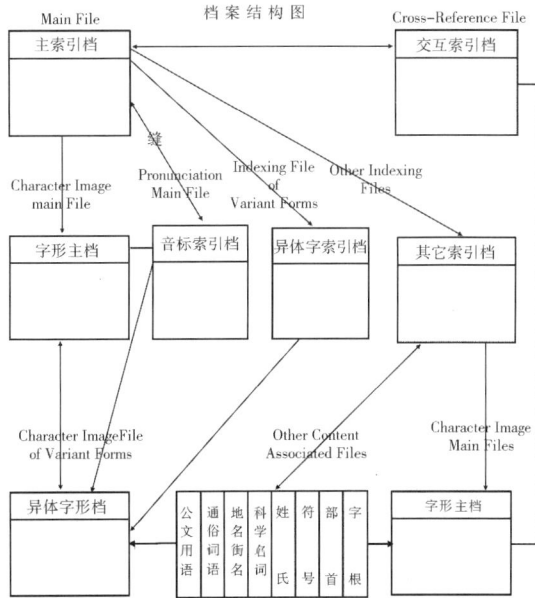

Figure 1. Block diagram of the cross-reference database for Chinese character indexing.

The compilation of a "Chinese Character Code for Information Interchange".
This project which was also carried out by the Chinese Character Analysis Group is probably one of the most important undertakings in the scientific analysis of the Chinese language in recent time by a team of over 200 specialists. The task of designing CCCII consisted of two major efforts: first, to construct a code structure which can accommodate all known Chinese characters and second, to organize and group them according to the code structure. So far, more than 30,000 Chinese characters, including 4,807 most commonly used ones; 16,197 less commonly used ones; and some 10,793 variant forms, have been identified, grouped and coded. It is of significance to note that the application of the Code is not confined to traditional forms of characters being used in Taiwan, Hong Kong and the overseas Chinese communities. Rather, it is also applicable to the simplified characters adopted in the Chinese mainland and Singapore and the Chinese characters in circulation in Japan and Korea. More will be added, as we were told, in the next two or three years to include languages of ethnic minorities such as Manchurian, Mongolian, Arabic and Tibetan as well as other rarely used characters. When this is done, the total number of coded Chinese characters may exceed 80,000.

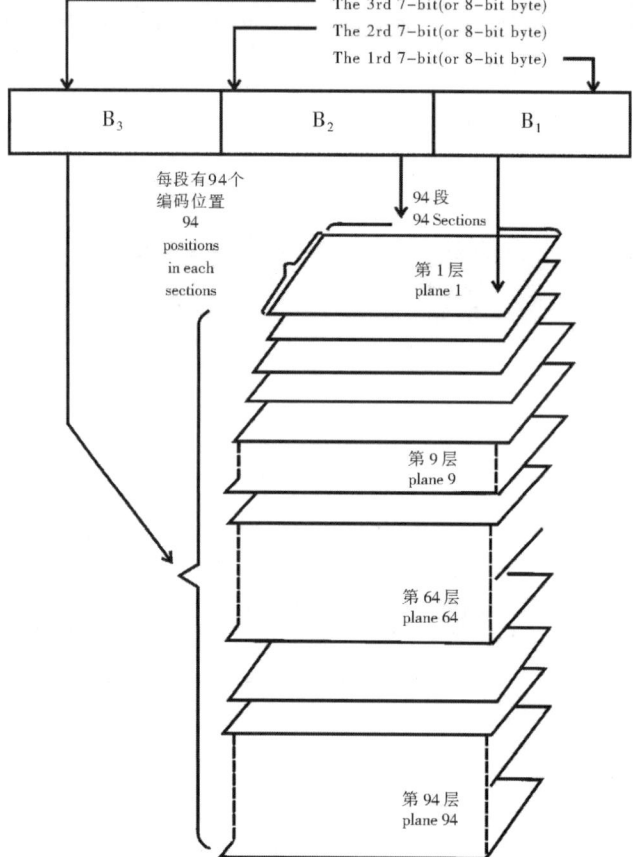

Figure 2. Three-dimensional structure of CCCII.

To achieve international compatibility for information exchange the Code was designed in complete accordance with the international standards of ISO – 646 (7-bit Coded Character Set for Information Processing Interchange) and ISO – 2022 (Code Extension Techniques for Use with the ISO – 7-bit Coded Character Set). Figure 2 shows the three-dimensional structure of CCCII. In it, each Chinese character is identified by a three 7-bit bytes. Vertically, the three-dimensional code structure consists of 94 planes. Horizontally, each plane has 94 sections and each section has 94 positions.

Of the first two published volumes of the Code (volume 2 is in two parts) the first volume, which represents plane one, consists of 4,807 most frequently used Chinese characters; 35 Chinese punctuation marks; 214 radicals; 41 Chinese numerical character; 37 Chinese phonetic symbols; and 4 tonal marks. The Chinese characters are arranged first according to the Kang Hsi radical sequence and then by stroke-count. Characters with the same radical sequence and stroke count are sub — arranged by stroke-order. The precedence of strokes is in descending order, is: 1) a dot; 2) a horizontal stroke; 3) a vertical stroke; 4) a stroke down to the left; and 5) a stroke down to the right.

The second volume of the Code is published in two parts. The first part consists of a revision of volume 1 with the addition of 16,197 less frequently used characters. The second part consists of 10,793 variant forms of Chinese characters.

Having variant forms is quite common to many Chinese characters. Usually many of the variant forms of a character have exactly the same pronunciation and meaning but differ in their stroke image. Although often interchangeable in writing, when used to name a person, place or thing, they are considered as different characters. In CCCII, the codes assigned to the variant forms of a character are designed to have identical two right-most bytes. In this way, the variant forms of a character are placed at the same section and same position but in different planes, below the normal form. This arrangement makes it easy to identify the variant forms of a character. An example of variant forms is shown in Figure 3.

The complete revision of the Chinese Cataloging Rules.

Taking over the work already begun by the Cataloging Committee of the Library Association of China, the Chinese Cataloging Rules Working Group, in May of 1980, began its task of revising the 1965 NCL Cataloging Rules for Books in Chinese. Under the leadership of Professor Chien-Chang Lan, the Group adopted the following guidelines for the development of the new rules:

1. The rules should be applicable to all types of publications, including print and non-print materials. The contents should range widely enough to meet the need of libraries, information centers, and any other institutions, and can be used in book catalogs, card catalogs, or machine-readable catalogs.

2. Description should based on the International Standard Bibliographic Description (ISBD).

3. The feasible part of the NCL cataloging rules should be retained; domestic circumstances and cultural tradition, be taken into consideration.

4. Merits of AACR2 (Anglo-American Cataloging Rules, second edition) and Nippon Cataloging Rules should be adopted.

异体字形 CCCII 编码结构实例

	60	60	60	60	60	60	60	60	60	B_2 2ed Byte
	49	4B	4C	4E	4D	4F	50	51	52	54	B_1 1st Byte
21	額	頤	顆	額	顏	題	顎	頛	類	願	normal form 此列为通用体
27	频	颐	颗	额	颜	题	颚	颣	类	愿	simplified form 此列为大陆简体
2D	頡	臣		頏	頵	題	頱		臂	煩	other variations 以下四列为同义片体
33	熲			頱		䐴					
39	炟				頵		釖				
3F	禎						鑙				

3rd Byte

B_3

Figure 3. Example of the table of variant forms and associated CCCII codes.

5. UNIMARC (Universal Machine-Readable Cataloging) should be consulted to make the rules applicable to library automation.

Immediately after the guidelines were set the Group went on to translate the AACR2 and the Nippon Cataloging Rules (1978 preliminary edition) into Chinese. This was followed by a drafting of rules and collecting of examples. By the end of 1980, the Group had completed the chapters on general rules and the description of books.

The adoption of the "Chinese MARC Format" and the development of a prototype online cataloging system.

This two-pronged project which was also completed in a record time of eight months was carried out by the Chinese MARC Wording Group under the leadership of Professor Lucy T. C. Lee. Aimed at facilitating international exchange and sharing of bibliographic information in machine-readable form the Chinese MARC Format follows closely the design and format of the UNIMARC and LC MARC II with only minor modifications necessary for the cataloging of Chinese materials.

In consideration of the needs of the non-Chinese speaking user and library environment, several major fields, such as title proper, statement of responsibility, physical descriptions, series, subject, etc., are designed in such a way that they can be recorded and searched in Chinese, English, or Wade-Giles romanization which is adopted as the standard transliteration. Some of the modifications and the reasons for doing so are given below:

1. Adding subfield identifier "$r" to the fields of 200, 225, and 5xx in order to make title proper and series title accessible by romanization. This provision is mainly for libraries abroad since very few libraries in Taiwan would have the need to access bibliographic records by their transliterations.

2. Adding subfield identifier "$u" to fields 3xx for libraries which use cataloging rules other than the Chinese Cataloging Rules to record notes in Chinese, English, or romanization.

3. Assigning subfield identifier "$g" to fields 600, 700, 701, and 702 to identify the dynastic era during which a Chinese individual lived either in the Ch'ing dynasty or earlier. The association of a personal name with the name of a dynasty when he lived is a ling observed tradition in Chinese bibliography and scholarship.

4. The UNIMARC undefined indicators are assigned new functions in Chinese MARC in the fields of 215 and 225 (e.g., physical description and series).

5. Field 501 (collective uniform title) and field 503 (uniform convention headings) which are not used in Chinese MARC are reserved in the Format with an asterisk for libraries adopting cataloging rules other than the Chinese Cataloging Rules.

The published Chinese MARC Format which was distributed at the workshop consists of two parts. Part one has four sections which explain the scope, the application, the definition of terms, and the structure of the communication format. Part two includes appendices for catalog card format, tape format, character set, Wade-Giles romanization system, etc.

In the development of a prototype online cataloging system the Working Group had the cooperation and support of two computer companies: R. P. T. Intergroups International Ltd. (Wang VS Model English/Chinese Computer) and the Taiwan Automation Company (CCRT 280 System), each developed a pilot system using the same 1,100 bibliographic records selected by the Group from the Chinese National Bibliography, the National Union Catalog of the Library of Congress, and the library catalog of the National Taiwan University. At the demonstration of the two online Chinese MARC systems during the workshop, the following operations were shown:

1. Computer-produced pages of the *Chinese National Bibliography*.
2. Computer-produced catalog cards.
3. Online display of Chinese bibliographic records.
4. Online query and search functions including input, update, delete, modify, search.

It was announced that beginning immediately all newly acquired titles of the National Central

Library will be input into the database. This will be joined by seven large libraries later in a shared cataloging mode. The distribution of catalog cards on the new format is scheduled for October 1981 and the test tapes, in 1982. The timetable may seem ambitious, but—if the past offers any indication— nothing is impossible!

Conclusion

The workshop was a great success judging from its superior planning, organization, programming, and most important of all, its substance. Without any doubt, a great deal of effort was put into the workshop by a large number of dedicated individuals. Most important among them are Professor Chen-Ku Wang, Director of the National Central Library; Mrs. Margaret Chang Fung, Director of the National Taiwan Normal University Library; and Professor Jack Kai-Tung Huang, Director of the Department of Computer Science, Ming-Chuan College. Many foreign participants, including even those who are familiar with library development in Taiwan, were surprised and impressed by the recent accomplishments in Chinese library automation. The purposefulness, determination, and team spirit of the Chinese librarians in Taiwan, together with the cooperation and support of computer scientists and philologists, were truly admirable and applaudable. It is obvious that additional work is needed to further refine some of the accomplishments and to continue the unfinished tasks. Such efforts will bring about even greater success in the years to come.

With regard to international cooperation, the sincerity and willingness of the libraries and librarians in Taiwan to share the fruits of their labor with others deserves special mention. The continued development of Chinese computer input and output devices and the plan of the National Central Library to produce and make available Chinese MARC records, both current and retrospective, will be of great value to every library with a Chinese or East Asian collection. The prospect for international cooperation in the sharing of Chinese MARC records has drawn closer the day when one can search bibliographic records in Chinese scripts through a terminal linked to—a database of a major bibliographic utility in any part of the world.

Alice at One:
Candid Reflections on the Adoption, Installation, and Use of the Virginia Tech Library System (Vtls) at Ohio University[①]

This report presents a mixed picture. In describing the accomplishments and disappointments in using a to-be-integrated library system, we hope that our experiences will interest and benefit others who are just embarking on the treacherous path of library automation. If we focus on the problems and possibilities encountered, it is because we think that these may be of greatest value. Today numerous publications offer detailed guides as to how to acquire and implement an integrated library system. We won't recapitulate these but rather will try to shed some light on what occurs when theory meets practice or when the irresistible ideal encounters immovable realities. Despite what follows, we are very pleased with our choice of the Virginia Tech Library System (VTLS), both in terms of services provided to our library users and our relationships with the vendors.

Background

Although the activities which culminated in our present use of VTLS began in 1978, our membership dating from more than a decade before in the then Ohio College Library Center (OCLC) greatly shaped our deliberations. On August 26, 1971, Ohio University was the first member institution to input, online, a record into the OCLC database (never mind that the system immediately crashed). Twelve years later, on October 11, 1983, Ohio University Libraries input the first record into the national online union catalog of its second ten million records (no. 10000001). As a result of this long standing commitment to entering our holdings in machine readable form and into the OCLC database, our attention was directed toward a system which would utilize these existing records.

Like many other academic libraries during the 1970s, particularly those in Ohio, we anticipated and awaited the development of subsystems by OCLC to handle acquisitions, circulation, serials control, interlibrary loans, etc. which would build on the successful online national network for shared cataloging. Although, after several delays, the highly successful interlibrary loan subsystem became a reality in 1978, the other subsystems were postponed or only partially implemented.

By 1978, the increasing capabilities and decreasing costs of minicomputers led many libraries to develop library systems at the local or regional levels which utilized the machine-readable cataloging records created for the OCLC database. It was widely recognized that circulation and online public access catalogs were prime candidates for such an undertaking. At this same time, many "turnkey" systems developed by commercial firms were introduced.

Within this environment, OCLC's failure to negotiate an agreement with GEAC and its on-again, off-again approach to developing circulation and online public access catalog subsystems induced Ohio University to explore alterative solutions. As the founders of OCLC, libraries in Ohio tended to look to OCLC for answers to automation needs. As a result, Ohio libraries (including OHIONET) have lagged behind in the development of local or regional systems in comparison with libraries in many other states.

For Ohio University, automating circulation was identified as the first priority. To explore and evaluate the possibilities, a Task Force on an Automated Circulation System was created in

---

[①] Co-Authors: K. Mulliner, E. Hoffmann-Pinther and Hannah McCauley.

September 1978, consisting of library and computer center staff with representatives of the faculty and the students. The Task Force was chaired by William Betcher, then Assistant Director for Public Services and subsequently Associate Director for Services. Its charges were:

— to conduct a feasibility study for an automated circulation system in the O. U. Libraries;
— to investigate various automated circulation systems available commercially and the possibility of developing a system locally (using university computer center personnel) patterned after Ohio State University (O. S. U.) Libraries' Library Control System (LCS);
— to gather cost information on various systems for comparison, and
— to submit a report with a set of recommendations.

Although directed toward an automated circulation system, the Task Force envisioned that the selected approach should include an online public access catalog or provide for inclusion of such in the near future.

O. S. U. 's LCS was identified as a strong contender in the early phases of the investigation because: 1) O. S. U. Libraries were willing to share the LCS software with us, and 2) utilization of LCS would lead to greater cooperation with our larger sister institution to the north. The investigation revealed, however, that adoption of LCS would require considerable, costly upgrading of the university mainframe and would require substantial staff support for the computer center. Money and personnel requirements dictated the abandonment of this option.

Throughout 1980 and 1981, the Task Force explored all then available turnkey circulation systems. Onsite visits, demonstrations, and consultations with user — institutions of various systems were arranged. In September 1981, the Task Force visited the Virginia Polytechnic Institute and State University in Blacksburg, and, shortly thereafter, the VTLS system was selected. In December of that year, Dr. Vinod Chachra and members of the VTLS team offered a presentation and demonstra? tion in Athens, Ohio.

The following factors were significant in the selection:

1. Provision for an integrated library system with a linkage to OCLC's online cataloging and the utilization of MARC records to create the local database.

2. Immediate availability of an automated circulation system and online public access catalog, with future expansion to include serials control, acquisitions, and management information. All of which complement the OCLC cataloging and interlibrary loan subsystems. Appendix A illustrates this interrelationship.

3. Ease of use of the system for both staff and patrons; subject search capability.

4. Reasonable costs for the software package and the annual maintenance fee compared with other available systems. (When we contracted for the software in 1982, the cost was $20,000 plus an annual maintenance fee of $3,000. The annual maintenance fee entitles us to all enhancements released during the year. Although the charges for these have risen, they are still extremely competitive.)

5. The quality and vision of the personnel on the VTLS team.

6. The degree of local control and flexibility allowed by the system, including local networking and short-form cataloging.

While the Task Force had primary responsibility for identifying systems, other staff were engaged in complementary activities before the selection of the system. Special funding was obtained from the university for a $125,000 two-year retrospective conversion project in 1979. An NEH Challenge grant provided $150,000 for cataloging the Special Collections backlog, and a $115,999 grant under Title II-C of the Higher Education Act supported cataloging of the backlog in the nationally important Southeast Asia Collection. It was also recognized that special funding would be required to acquire the system hardware and software. In 1981, $150,000 was raised from private sources to largely cover these costs.

With the selection of the system, hardware was simultaneously ordered: an HP 3000/40 minicomputer and three 404 megabyte disk drives as well as terminals, wiring, etc.

In planning for installation, it was decided to place the CPU and related hardware in the

University Computing Services (since renamed Computing and Learning Services) because that facility, unlike the main (Vernon R. Alden) library building, had secure space and the required environmental control. Moreover, Computing Services had the trained personnel to look after the hardware for the 102 hours 7 days per week that the library is open to the public. Capitalizing on existing excellent relations, Computing Services agreed to provide a separate room for the HP3000/40 and disk drives and to provide an experienced systems analyst to be responsible for the library system in return for which a.5 FTE position was transferred to Computing Services.

During the past two and one-half years, this arrangement has worked extremely well. Augmentation of the existing expertise in the University's Computing Services has assured the necessary technical support while freeing library staff to concentrate on library aspects of the applications. Building on this basis, further agreements with Computing Services provide for maintenance of the hardware and peripherals (other than the CPU and disk drives) at about one-half the cost of external maintenance agreements and service is readily available on site, an important consideration for an installation that is 75 miles from the nearest large city. Beyond maintenance and repair support, Computing Services is able to provide loan equipment (such as a terminal or modem) while repairs are being made.

Based on our experience, if at all possible, working closely with existing computer expertise within or available to the organization is the best approach. The savings in time and personnel as well as money can be better used to provide library services.

Installation

In March 1982, installation of the HP3000/40 began. With loading of our OCLC archival tapes scheduled for July, Murphy's Law made its first of many appearances. Virginia Tech had a new program (offering a segmented rather than a single unit database) which they promised with only a three-week delay. We should have known from our OCLC experience that enhancements promised by systems people are always late. It was late August before the new program was installed and archival tape loading could begin. Loading the tapes, which contained 356,000 records, extended until the end of March 1983. At the outset, six records were loaded each minute. By the end, this had slowed to 1.5 records per minute. The rate of loading is determined by the software — under the VTLS system, each character is interrogated in loading and then passed to the buffer. When the buffer is X% full (we had set it at 80%), the buffer process then writes the record to the database and establishes the chains. We learned, belatedly, that one ought to do a super-chain process and a Syst-Dump after loading each tape. The super-chain process is the only means of speeding up the loading process.

We also learned that at the beginning of the loading of the first tape the recovery system should be tested. We lost 4 – 1/2 weeks of work by not doing a "Syst-Dump and restore" to ensure the correct functioning of the recovery system.

During the installation phase, circulation personnel became concerned that insufficient items would be barcoded and linked to permit implementation of the circulation system. Within our libraries, collection development and ordering is handled by professional staff serving as subject bibliographers in their areas of expertise. It was agreed that, beginning in the summer of 1982, the bibliographers — with the assistance of other staff and student employees — would barcode the volumes in that part of the LC schedule which fell within their areas of responsibility. Dual barcodes were used, with one placed in each monograph and its twin placed on the back of the shelflist card. The cataloging department could then use a light pen to scan the barcode on the shelflist and link it to the bibliographic record in the database. Linking is necessary for circulation and also to indicate the location (s) of titles.

In retrospect, this immense effort— resulting in the bar coding of 289,000 volumes — was not needed to implement the circulation function. It proved more efficient to link each volume after it circulated. However, it permits linking of non-circulating titles (i.e., reference) and those which are yet to circulate without physically handling each volume. Linking is essential for maximum benefits from the online public catalog. This applies only to volumes in the collection before March 1983. Once the archival tapes were loaded, each addition to the collection is linked as part of the cataloging routine. One strength of the VTLS system is this interface which obviates the need to continue acquire and load OCLC tapes once the retrospective tapes have been entered.

While the barcoding was demanding of professional staff time, it served to greatly increase bibliographers' familiarity with the collection areas for which they were responsible. It also afforded the opportunity to systematically weed the collection for the first time in many years.

Inauguration and Upgrading

With the completion of tape loading, testing of the system and staff training began in earnest. Limited training had begun earlier for the circulation staff. It was evident that the system was ready for its debut, but it was also evident that the hardware and storage would soon be inadequate for our needs, not to mention meeting the needs for five years to come.

It should be stressed that, in planning and acquiring the system and the hardware configuration, we thoroughly established our wants and needs and refined these in terms of budgetary realities. Expert advice was sought and checked and double checked. But even before becoming officially available, response time problems and the need for greater database capacity and more terminals dictated the enlargement of the system.

While some library staff were preparing for the inaugural shower for our new automated system, others were in consultation with Hewlett Packard negotiating an upgrade. The inaugural cocktail party was held on July 15, 1983, to introduce the system to the campus community (and to thank the staff of the library and computer services as well as the numerous faculty and administrators who had contributed to the realization of the system). As utilized at Ohio University, the system was named ALICE. A name-that-system campaign was held among library staff which resulted in a host of acronyms. The librarian at a regional campus reminded us that the name need not be an acronym, as evident in the language Pascal. Almost synchronously, the name ALICE was suggested with allusions to the Wonderland which the system would open for library users. Clinching the argument, it was noted that in the song "White Rabbit," the Jefferson Airplane advised, "Go ask Alice, I'll think she'll know" — exactly the attitude we hoped to cultivate toward the new system.

Within the same time frame, negotiations were concluded with Hewlett-Packard to trade the HP3000/40 on the new HP3000/68 with an interim HP 3000/64 until the 68 became available. Three additional 404 MB drives were also acquired. Under a special offer then effect, an HP 125 microcomputer with software was added at no additional cost. This HP 125 gives us a backup to record check-ins and check-outs at circulation during times that the system is down.

After the inauguration, full implementation of the system began with the fall quarter of 1983/84. In October, the switch to the HP3000/64 was accomplished. In February 1984, this was converted to the 68 series with the addition of one extra block of main memory and disc caching.

The upgraded system has performed to our expectations. It has also greatly increased the terminal capacity. After one year, we have 9 terminals for cataloging and other exclusive staff use, 4 for circulation transactions, 3 ports for connection through the computer network or by dial access, and 25 public terminals — at least one of which is available on each of the main library's seven floors as well as in the separate music library.

This dispersal of public terminals has eliminated the central card catalog and the need for multitudinous departmental catalogs. On May 13, 1983, the main catalog was officially closed. Not only do users no longer need to check the main catalog, as a result of our cooperation with Computing and Learning Services, the library system is integrated into the intra-university computing network (diagrammed in Appendix B). Through communications controllers and a Gandalf Port Contention Controller, any of the hundreds of terminals spread across the campus (and on regional campuses) can access the library system. Moreover, the network permits dial access and thus the library system is accessible through a phone datalink for anywhere. One important impact is that the question of the number of public terminals needed is somewhat muted, virtually any terminal is a public terminal with access to the online public access catalog (including information on item availability).

Networking

With participation in the intra-university computer network, long-standing commitments to cooperation and service, the capabilities of the VTLS software, and as the only research library serving rural south and southeastern Ohio, it was probably inevitable that no sooner had ALICE become operational than explorations began for extending service to other libraries. This took two main thrusts: service to regional campuses and service to public libraries (through the regional network OVAL-Ohio Valley Area Libraries — comprised of eleven public libraries in ten counties). Complementing planning for extensions, Ohio University has been planning for a microwave system to serve regional campuses, technical colleges, and other colleges in the region. The availability of the library system has been an important addition to the planning for the interconnect system. The projected system is pictured in Appendix C.

While the microwave interconnect system will require special appropriations, planning has proceeded on extending service to the regional campuses and the public libraries, joint committees for each comprised of our staff and representatives of the participating institutions have been meeting regularly since October 1983.

As noted, dial access to ALICE on the Athens campus is currently available. Regional campuses currently utilize this facility as well as existing connections into the intra-university computer network to check our holdings for titles of interest. But planning is well underway to provide a separate but linked regional campus databases which will afford the regional campuses all of the facilities of the VTLS system. Equipment is currently being installed at the Lancaster campus as the prototype (other regional campuses are at Belmont, Chillicothe, Ironton, and Zanesville). Lancaster's retrospective OCLC tapes will be loaded into the regional campus databases (which affords all of the services of the main campus database). An existing microwave communications linkage is used, eliminating line charges.

Difficulties Encountered — Lessons Learned

Despite our general satisfaction and success in acquiring and implementing the VTLS system, the foregoing should indicate that the experience has not been without trials and tribulations. We share these with those who are contemplating or planning an integrated online system in the hope that they may be spared some grief.

1. Estimating equipment needs.

Attempting to specify the exact hardware configuration that will be needed while providing for system growth is difficult to say the least. In part this is a function of the pace of change in computer technologies. There is a reluctance to acquire equipment which will soon be outdated; however, even the most careful planning is no guarantee that this will not be the case. As funds for hardware purchases are not unlimited, specification and procurement require careful estimates. Hardware vendors, to remain competitive, may recommend smaller equipment with marginal growth potential. As noted, even as the system became operational, it was obvious that greater capacity was needed. Upgrading to the HP3000/68 nearly doubled our hardware costs and our maintenance costs. At the same time, it also became evident that the initial projection that three 404 MB disk drives would be adequate for one million bibliographic records was grossly overoptimistic. With 400,000 records loaded, we discovered that three additional 404 MB drives would be needed — at a cost of $65,000. Technology contributes to this. At the June 1984 users group meeting, Hewlett Packard reported that its five-year projection is that computing power will double and cost will be halved.

2. Estimating other costs.

Cost overruns in automated systems extend well beyond hardware, although hardware is a significant factor. Recognizing the potential for overruns, we added a fudge factor of 25%. Our experience indicates that even 50% is likely insufficient. While this consideration may pose some problems for larger institutions, for smaller libraries with limited funding such overruns could be critical.

3. Loading archival tapes.

Because of the nature of the VTLS database and limited guidance in setting parameters, we found that tape loading required much longer than predicted, with a severe reduction in loading speed as the database grew. Of course, this was a function of the proportion of our collection on tape. Having participated in OCLC for more than a decade and having undertaken several retrospective conversion projects during that time, the number of records which we had on tape greatly exceeded previous VTLS users.

4. Availability of the system during loading.

An automated system which is unavailable is worse than a return to a manual system. Backlogs are created at each step of the process which then must be processed. The unavailability of the system has resulted from installation of new equipment or the installation of new versions of the VTLS software. Such down time must be scheduled for slack times; for us this is during breaks between quarters. We hope that we have made a major step toward alleviating the problem of having to fully unload and load the system each time. "Adager," a utility for H-P's IMAGE system which allows database manipulation and modification without loading and unloading, has been ordered and we hope will eliminate much of this problem.

5. Securing the database.

In offering access to the system from many different locations in the library (several of which are uncontrolled), from any terminal on campus, and by telephone, library users have much greater access to the database. Unfortunately, this is true for experimenters or vandals as well as for the serious user. At the end of our Spring Quarter, we had a serious problem with a "Dr. Who," who was able to enter the circulation system and record 118 checkouts for books still in the library. We also had sporadic cases of other individuals, presumably computer science students, attempting to enter the system in statuses to which they were not entitled. This problem has been brought to the attention of Virginia Tech, which reports that new security measures will be available in the fall of 1984. Despite such efforts, this problem is likely to remain endemic. As people climb Mt. Everest because its there, students are likely to attempt to enter the database for the same reason. Our only solace is that, as yet, such unauthorized entries, seem prompted more by curiosity or a practical joke than malicious intent.

6. Turnover in VTLS personnel.

Perhaps a tribute to the success of the VTLS system is the extent to which the staff have moved to other, more responsible positions. An attraction of the VTLS system was that the people engaged in development and in support were familiar with libraries, and, for us, were familiar with large academic libraries. We found them helpful and congenial. Unfortunately, the meteoric rise in installations of the system since our original contract has brought many changes. Many of the people with whom we originally worked, and who made particular commitments to us, have since left Virginia Tech for other positions. As the number of using institutions grows, the personal contacts become more tenuous, and one is forced to formal means of registering complaints and suggestions. During the past year, Virginia Tech has developed a logging system for phoned-in problems, which has largely alleviated a lack of follow-up due to changing personnel or responsibilities.

7. Delays in developing promoted subsystems.

Delays in the development and introduction of subsystems and enhancements seems intrinsic to the library automation field. Virginia Tech is no exception. Of course, different institutions have different priorities, and those responsible for selling the system will tend to emphasize what the potential purchaser wants to hear. When we first acquired the software, we were told to expect serials control and acquisitions within a year. We now have had the system operational for a year and are still told to expect these two subsystems within a year. To be fair to the VTLS organization, they have concentrated on improving and enhancing the cataloging, circulation and online public access catalog components of the system (including authority control, word search, and Boolean operators). We agree that it is important to have this core to work as well as possible before diverting staff and resources to other development efforts — as long as the delay does not become unreasonable. Conversely, when users are told that an enhancement or subsystem will be available by a certain date, much frustration could be avoided if the vendor and systems people would strive to provide realistic projections and then to achieve those targets. This situation is akin to the "revolution of rising expectations" described for the Third World. While system users have far more capacity and benefits than previously, they have been led to expect even more.

Conclusion

At the tender age of one, ALICE is a well-behaved child whose growth threatens to exceed our wildest hopes and imagination. While there are things which we would do differently (as described above), selecting the VTLS system is not among them. Perhaps our pride shows. In recent months, we have received visits and telephone calls from libraries considering integrated systems. We have responded as fully and as honestly as possible. We are aware that several of these have since joined the VTLS family. In our own evaluation of alternative systems, we found discussions with users to be extremely valuable. Institutions considering VTLS should be aware that an active users group has been formed. Information on the Group and on the results of occasional surveys of users are available from the newly elected Chair: Jack Bazuzi of the Virginia State Library. We also remain willing to show off our one-year-old ALICE.

APPENDIX A
OCLC-VTLS COMPLEMENTARITY

The Development of
Local ALICE System in the 1980's

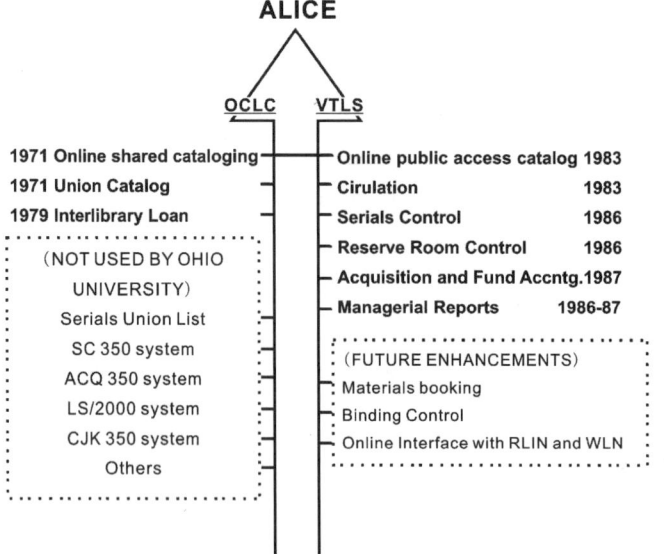

1. 图书馆学的世界观   137

APPENDIX B
ALICE IN INTRA-UNIVERSITY COMPUTING NETWORK

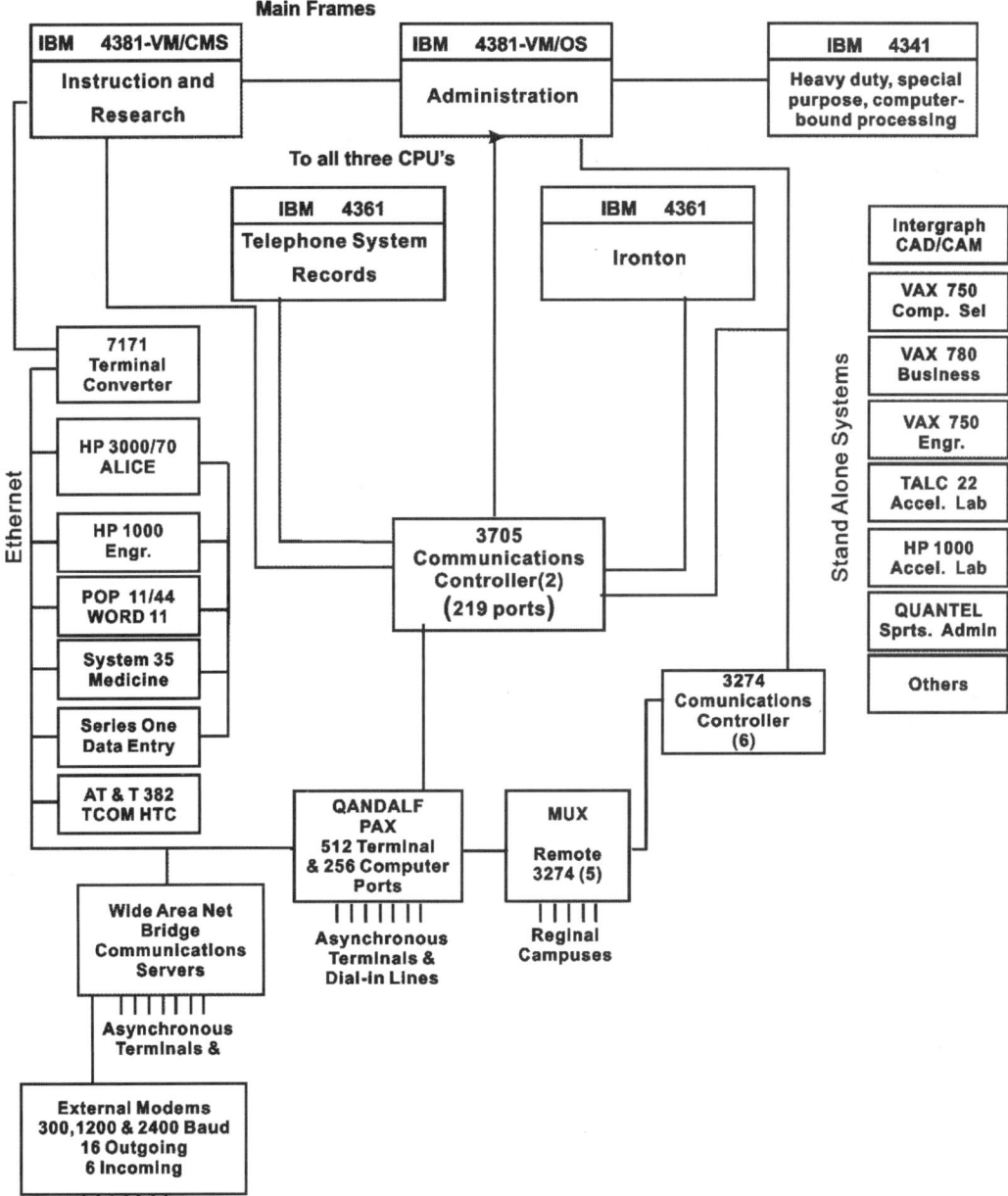

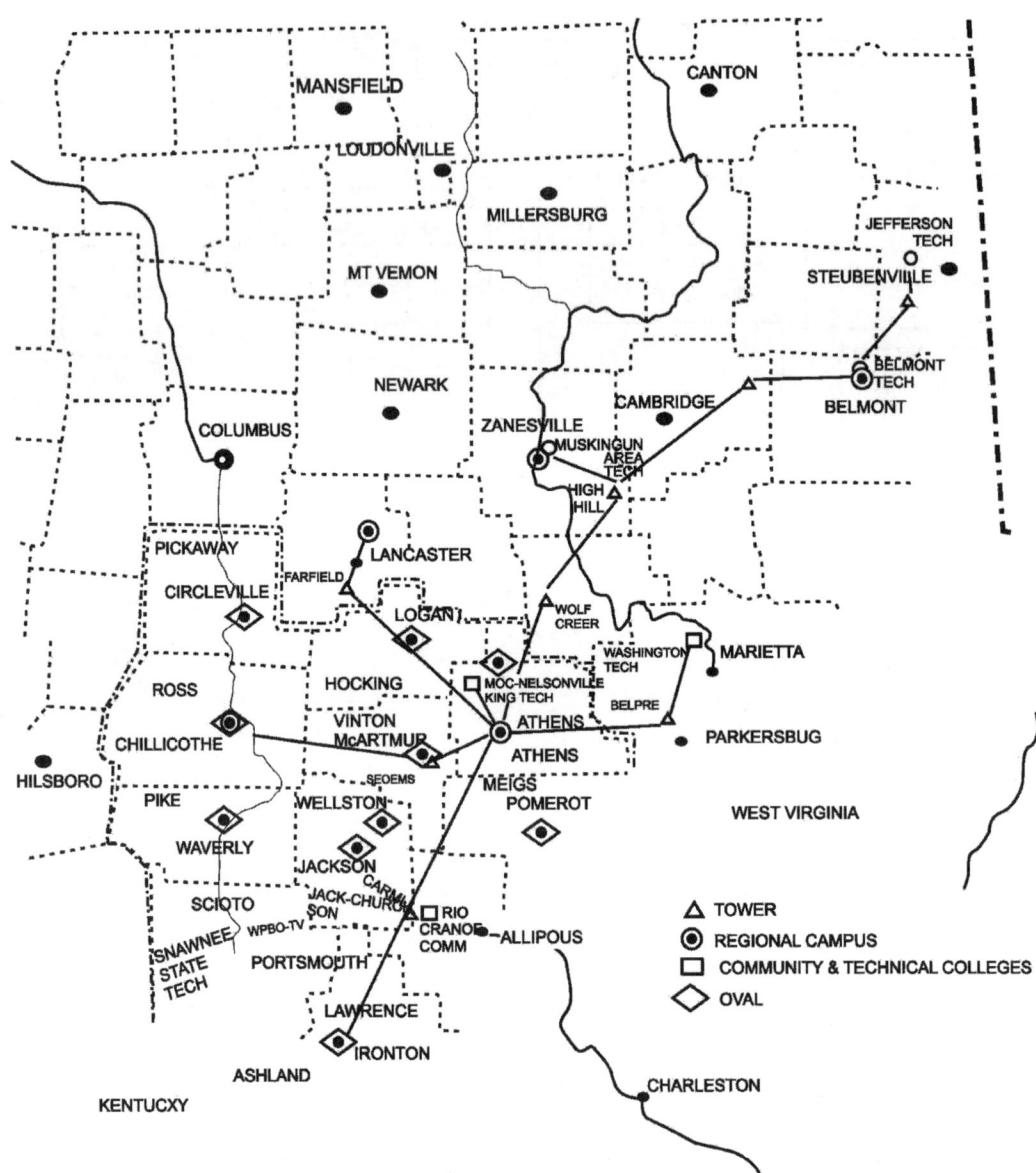

Trends in Automation in American Academic Libraries: Ohio University's Experiences①

Introduction

Historically American Libraries have been in the forefront in applying information technologies: from the origins of the Hollerith punched-card tabulating system in the latter part of the 19th century; through the growing use of micrographics in the 1930s; photocopying and data processing equipment in the 1950s; the wide-spread application of succeeding generations of computers and the accompanying developments in telecommunications in the 1960s and 1970s; to the mass storage as exemplified in optical discs in the 1980s. The pace of innovation accelerates as each new technology is adopted and refined. ②

A comprehensive state university of 24,000 students founded in 1804, Ohio University has a main campus in Athens, Ohio, and five regional campuses in surrounding Southeastern Ohio. Just as in many American academic libraries, Ohio University Library has been in the mainstream of information technology applications and library automation. Since the beginning of OCLC under its former name, the Ohio College Library Center, back in 1967, the Ohio University Library has been an active participant and supporter. The case history of Ohio University Library in the applications of information technology and in library automation can be seen as fairly representative of academic libraries in North America. For the past three decades, despite differences in strategy, approach, and timing among academic libraries, the general trend has been comparable to that which I will describe for Ohio University.

Significant Developments in the 1960s

In the 1960s, computers (then all mainframes) were too expensive for most libraries, and library applications software was generally unavailable, yet several major initiatives with far-reaching impacts on library automation were launched. These included the MEDLARS (MEDical Literature Analysis and Retrieval System) project of the National Library of Medicine, the INTREX (INformation TRansfer Experiment) project by the Massachusetts Institute of Technology, the design and implementation of the MARC (MAchine Readable Cataloging) format by the Library of Congress, and the establishment of the Ohio College Library Center (OCLC) by a group of academic libraries in Ohio, including Ohio University. At about the same time, Stanford University initiated its BALLOTS (Bibliographic Automation of Large Library Operations using a Time-sharing System) project which evolved into the Research Libraries Information Network (RLIN). Another important trend in the 1960s was the beginning by many abstracting and indexing services to use computers in photo composition and typesetting of printed publications — making possible machine-searchable databases.

The MEDLARS Project and subsequent medical information network developed by the National Library of Medicine has benefited immeasurably medical and health sciences libraries and the professionals whom they serve. The INTREX project, from 1965 to 1973, reaffirmed the design concept that large libraries could become information transfer systems. But, as we assess

---

① This a substantially revised and updated version of an earlier paper, Hwa-Wei Lee, "Applications of Information Technology in an American Library — The Case of Ohio University Libraries", presented at the First Pacific Conference on New Information Technologies for Library and Information Professionals, June 16 – 18, 1987, in Bangkok, Thailand. It appeared in the Proceedings (West Newton, Mass: MicroUse Information, 1987), pp. 144 – 164.

② Stephen R. Slamon, "Library Automation". In Encyclopedia of Library and Information Science (New York: Marcel Dekker, 1975), V. 14, pp. 338 – 445.

the importance of the major developments in the 1960s, the most significant and far-reaching were probably the design in 1965 of a MARC format for bibliographic data (which is machine-readable, largely interchangeable, and internationally acceptable) and the establishment in 1967 of OCLC. The beginning distribution on magnetic tapes of MARC-formatted cataloging records by the Library of Congress undoubtedly affected the design of OCLC and its first computer-based shared cataloging and union catalog system. Other than these major applications, library automation in the 1960s tended to replicate manual processes including the use of computers for the production of catalog cards, accession lists, serial holdings, and the like.

The Mushrooming of OCLC in the 1970s

The founding of OCLC in 1967 by a small number of academic library members of the Ohio College Association and the Inter-University Library Council—which consisted of library directors of state-supported universities in Ohio, followed sixteen years of study and deliberation and also involved the Ohio Library Association. ① Only after the successful implementation of the MARC project in November 1966, cooperative, shared cataloging on a centralized computer system became practical.

Through the foresight of the Ohio academic librarians and the effective leadership of Mr. Frederic G. Kilgour, Executive Director of OCLC from its inception in 1967 to his retirement in 1980, OCLC grew by leaps and bounds from a small organization of two staff members, with an initial budget of $67,000 and 54 participating libraries in Ohio to a complex organization of over 885 staff members, with a budget of $95.7 million in 1988 and a growing membership of 9,400 libraries of all types in the U.S. and 26 other countries. [Diagram I]. Initially OCLC provided a computer-based cataloging system in batch process. This was upgraded to a real-time, online, interactive mode in 1971. On August 26, 1971, Ohio University Library entered the first member-produced cataloging record online. Although the system immediately crashed, Ohio University Library ended that day with 147 titles cataloged. During the first two days an average of ten titles per terminal hour were entered.

The instant success of the OCLC shared cataloging system attracted other Ohio libraries and, soon, libraries in other states. Reflecting broader library membership and geographical distribution, OCLC in 1977 changed its name to OCLC, Inc. In 1981, with the adoption of a new governance structure, the legal name became the OCLC Online Computer Library Center, Incorporated. ②

Most significant in OCLC's growth was the expansion of its cataloging database. From its 1971 beginning, the database reached its one millionth record in September 1974, a period of over three years. The second million records took 18 months to accumulate. As the number of members increased so did the rate of growth in the records. The most recent million records, to 19 million, in January, 1989 took only six months! This has made OCLC the largest and fastest growing bibliographic database in the world. [Diagram II]. According to OCLC, of the 19 million bibliographic records, 80 percent were contributed by OCLC members. The remaining 20 percent were provided by the Library of Congress, the National Library of Medicine, the National Agricultural Library, the National Library of Canada, the U.S. Government Printing Office, and, recently, the British Library. Benefiting from the size and currency of the database, OCLC users can locate cataloging records from OCLC for 94 percent of the items they catalog and thus need to perform original cataloging for only 6 percent of their materials. ③ This is a considerable savings in time and expense in cataloging by member libraries.

---

① Lewis C. Branscomb and A. Robert Rogers, "The Conception and Birth Pangs of OCLC-An Account of the Struggles of the Formative Years", *College and Research Libraries*, V. 42, No. 4 (July 1981), pp. 303–307.

② Kathleen L. Maciuszko, *OCLC, A Decade of Development, 1967–1977* (Littleton, Colorado: Libraries Unlimited, 1984).

③ *OCLC Annual Report, 1987/88* (Dublin, Ohio: OCLC, 1988).

Adding to OCLC's success is its online interlibrary loan system introduced in 1979. The system is built on the shared database which includes 298 million member-location symbols. OCLC reports that in 1987/88 more than 3.78 million interlibrary loans were transacted online in one year and more than 20 million interlibrary loan requests have been logged since 1979. At present, better than 90 percent of the requests can be verified online and 87 percent are filled. Facilitated by electronic library-to-library communication through the OCLC telecommunications system, interlibrary loan items are shipped by mail or UPS to borrowers within an average of four days.

Although in recent years OCLC's services have extended to many other areas including serials control, acquisitions and a decentralized, minicomputer-based local system — LS/2000, Ohio University has chosen to participate only in OCLC's online union catalog, shared cataloging, and interlibrary loan components. These, in our judgment, represent the services best offered centrally to facilitate resource sharing and take advantage of economies of scale. Other OCLC services are either less competitive or were offered too late.

While OCLC was concentrating on improving services at the national level in the late 1970s and early 1980s, many libraries were looking for local systems for local library functions. The trend in the late 1970s was to develop or purchase a local system for circulation, online public access catalog, etc., which could interface (often through tape loading) with the OCLC online union catalog and shared cataloging service. Such a system enables a library to participate in OCLC for shared cataloging and interlibrary loans while downloading the OCLC-created MARC catalog records into local computer storage to support activities in such areas as circulation, acquisitions, fund accounting, serials check-in, and online public access catalog.

The availability of the online public access catalog to replace the century-old card catalog and the COM (Computer-Output-Microform) catalog of the 1960s and 1970s is widespread in the 1980s. The OCLC online union catalog is, and will continue to be, the single most important cataloging and interlibrary loan tool, but its lack of subject access and cryptic search keys have made it unattractive as an online public access catalog, although this may be overcome with the refinements scheduled to be available late in 1989 or 1990. The declining cost and expanding power of minicomputers and microcomputers as well as the availability of software packages for library functions have lured many libraries to seek local alternatives either individually or in clusters.

The Development of the Local ALICE System in the 1980s[1]

In 1978, Ohio University opted to explore locally integrated library systems capable of interfacing with OCLC but operated independently on a dedicated minicomputer. The result has been the successful implementation of the ALICE system which became operational in July 1983. In September 1978, a task force to explore local library systems was formed to investigate possibilities and approaches. Consisting of library and computer center staff, faculty, and students, the task force sought an integrated system which would use OCLC for shared cataloging and interlibrary loans but would support, in modular form, circulation, and online public access catalog, acquisitions, and other library functions. The system should be based on a central database created from the OCLC MARC records with added holdings and location information as well as the barcode number. The task force considered circulation and an online catalog among the first priorities. Throughout 1980 and 1981, the task force studied nearly all available systems. On-site visits and presentations by vendors to the staff were arranged. In December 1981 the Virginia Tech Library System (VTLS), designed and developed by Virginia Polytechnic Institute and State University in Blacksburg, Virginia, was selected for the following reasons:

---

[1] Hwa-Wei Lee, K. Mulliner, E. Hoffmann-Pinther, and Hannah McCauley, "ALICE" at One: Candid Reflections on the Adoption, Installation, and Use of the Virginia Tech Library System (VTLS) at Ohio University. In Second National Conference on Integrated Online Library Systems, September 13 and 14, 1984, Atlanta Georgia. *Proceedings* (Canfield, Ohio: Genaway and Associates, Inc., 1984), pp. 228-242. Included as preceding article in this compilation.

1. Provision of an integrated library system with an online linkage to OCLC's cataloging and utilization of MARC records to create the local database.

2. Immediate availability of an automated circulation system and online public access catalog, with planned expansion to include serials control, acquisitions, and management information — all of which complement the OCLC cataloging and interlibrary loan subsystems.

3. Ease of use of the system by both staff and patrons. Searches can be by author, title, subject, call number, and, now, key words with Boolean operators.

4. Reasonable cost of the software package and the annual maintenance fee compared with other available systems. (When Ohio University contracted for the software in 1982, the cost was $20,000 plus an annual maintenance fee of $3,000. The annual maintenance entitles the library to all enhancements released during the year.)

5. The quality and vision of the personnel on the VTLS team (including a common experience in an academic environment).

6. The degree of local control and flexibility allowed by the system, including local networking and short-form cataloging.

Recognizing that an automated library system requires a database of machine-readable cataloging records, the library, in 1979, began a massive effort to convert pre-1971 cataloging records to machine-readable MARC format with grants and gifts totaling $400,000. As the first library to participate in OCLC, the Ohio University was fortunate to own a large machine-readable database for materials cataloged online since 1971. As a result of the conversion effort, when the VTLS System was installed in August 1982, nearly 400,000 catalog records-representing nearly one million volumes — were loaded from archival tapes. These comprised about 80 percent of the Library's monographs, excluding titles in governmental documents and a large portion of the microform, maps, and non-print collections which were indexed or cataloged manually.

Typical of designated depositories for U.S. government documents, the library maintains a separate collection arranged by the Superintendent of Documents (SUDOCS) classification number (based on issuing body rather than subject content) that relies on the printed *Monthly Catalog of the United States Government Publications* (and annual accumulations) augmented by Congressional Information Service indexes for access. At the same time that Ohio University was celebrating its centennial as a designated depository in 1986, we purchased retrospective cataloging records for U.S. Government documents on MARC tapes from the Government and have loaded these into the local database as an integral part of the online public access catalog. Similarly, MARC tapes available through OCLC are being acquired for major microform sets as a result of the ARL (Association of Research Libraries) -initiated Major Microforms Project.

With the signing of a contract with VTLS and the ordering and installation of a Hewlett Packard minicomputer (HP 3000/40) hardware and other peripheral equipment in the early part of 1982, a search for a name for the local system resulted in selecting ALICE, with a credit to Lewis Carroirs Alice in Wonderland and suggesting the wonderland which the system would open for library users. Clinching the argument, was the song, "White Rabbit", in which the Jefferson Airplane advised, "Go ask Alice, I think she'll know" — exactly the attitude we hoped to cultivate toward the new system.

With the strong support of the University's Computing and Learning Services, where the Library's HP 3000 system is housed, installation and tape loading went well. Barcoding a large portion of the library collection was time consuming, involving a majority of the library staff in 1982 and 1983. The completion of the tape loading in July 1983 enabled the library to formally inaugurate the online public access catalog and close its card catalog on July 15, 1983. Because creation of a patron file required additional preparation, the circulation function was implemented in September that year. By linking the library computer to the university-wide computer network from the beginning, the online catalog is accessible not only by library terminals located on every floor and in every service area of the main library building and the detached Music and Dance Library in the Music Building but also by terminals connected to the University network throughout the Athens campus. Dial access by microcomputers or terminals equipped with modems is also available regardless of location or distance. [Diagram in Appendix B of preceding article.] This is a feature only an online system can provide. Almost immediately, the libraries on the five regional campuses took advantage of this capability.

Because VTLS included networking in its design, the Regional Campuses located between 50 to 125 miles from Athens, have been able to network with the main library in the full use of VTLS for their library automation in a network environment. The Lancaster campus was the first to become a secondary account of VTLS, and by 1985, had every feature that is available in Athens. By sharing the central computer but maintaining a separate database, O. U. -Lancaster has its own database and holdings for its users yet, by a simple command, they can switch to our much larger database and holdings. Conversely, users in Athens can also view the Lancaster database. At the present time, we are replicating this on other campuses, some by dedicated telephone lines and others by microwave telecommunications. (See Appendix C in preceding article.)

Of course, every expansion of the local system requires the upgrading of the computer and peripheral equipment. Since the installation of a HP 3000/40 in 1982, we have upgraded to an HP 3000/64 in 1983, HP 3000/68 in 1984, HP 3000/70 in 1987, and, most recently, to an HP 3000/950 in 1989. The expansion of the CPU was accompanied by adding more and more storage capacities (from three 404 megabyte (MB) disc drives [totaling 1,212 MB] in 1982 to seven 404 MB and two 570 MB drives [totaling 3,968 MB] in 1987). The total value of the central hardware in 1989 approaches $500,000.

As the only major library in Southeastern Ohio, the Ohio University Library serves as the back-up resource library for public libraries in ten surrounding counties grouped under the Ohio Valley Area Libraries (OVAL). Through State Library funding, Ohio University Library provides reference and interlibrary loan services to OVAL libraries, amounting in 1988 to 1,912 reference responses and 6,007 loans of books or photocopies. Future interconnection of OVAL Libraries with Ohio University Libraries is feasible, based on a consultant study,[1] but depends on the wishes of the member public libraries.

The Growth of Online Database Searching

Paralleling the development of library automation since the 1960s has been the development of computerized databases by indexing and abstracting firms. Ohio University Library began online database search services in its Health Sciences Library in 1978. This was followed by a library-wide Computerized Information Retrieval Service (CIRS) inaugurated in 1979. Currently, we have online access to more than 400 databases in a variety of subject areas. In addition to those available through DIALOG, BRS, and STN, we have direct access to MEDLARS, Wilsonline, LEXIS/NEXIS, OhioPi (Ohio Public Information), and others. One-half of the cost for CIRS has been subsidized by the library to lessen the financial burden for students.

Our original hardware, a Texas Instruments terminal with no memory, an acoustic coupling, and 300 baud transmission speed, has been replaced by microcomputers. In 1983, the Library acquired an IBM-PC, equipped with a 1200 baud modem and Smartcom II as the communication software. This system permitted downloading of data and printing at a faster speed, and increased the cost effectiveness of searching, thus lowering patron costs. Additional hardware purchases, from 1984 to the present, have upgraded our systems to 80286 – chip based IBM and Zenith machines, a Macintosh, and an IBM-XT— all with hard disks and 2400 baud modems. Further, to provide faster and better reference service, guidelines were established for the use of CIRS for ready reference service at the discretion of the reference staff, free of charge.

---

[1] Jose-Marie Griffiths and Carolyn J. Goshen. *A Systems Analysis of the Ohio Valley Area Libraries (OVAL). Final Report* (Rockville, Maryland: King Research, Inc., 1985).

New and Emerging Information Technologies

In coping with the ever growing new and emerging information technologies which have flooded the market place, Ohio University Library has taken a number of steps to prepare itself for the inevitable. The future prospects are exciting and challenging. Among the steps taken are:

a. Expanding non-print collections to include many new formats.

Beginning in the 1960s the Library expanded its Microform Collection as more scholarly and research materials became available on that format. In the 1970s and 1980s, the federal government has published and distributed more and more of its publications in microfiche. To save space, money, and material, the library also decided early in 1979 to subscribe to both a paper copy and a microform copy of a number of selected journals and to discard the paper copy after the peak-use period. By 1986 the library collection in microformat exceeded that in print volumes (1,319,107 microforms vs 1,284,130 printed volumes). It is typical that in 1988 the library added 67,236 new microform units compared to 49,071 new printed volumes.

Microforms today are only one of many non-print formats: audio and video cassettes, audio and data compact discs, microcomputer floppy disks, optical discs, videodiscs, etc. To adequately service these newer formats, the Library has acquired a range of new equipment including digital image and optical character recognition (OCR) scanning equipment for conversion of print materials, image preservation, and desktop publishing.

b. Growing use of CD-ROM based information.

The coming of age for CD-ROM laser technology demands new knowledge, skills, and methods to handle the Read-Only-Memory (ROM) compact disc. To develop these, the Library has acquired several CD-ROM workstations which combine MS-DOS PCs and disc players. As of May 1989, 24 CD-ROM databases are offered (with more added regularly) including *ERIC*, *Books-in-Print Plus and Ulrich's Guide to Periodicals*, *PsycLit*, *Dissertation Abstracts* (from the 19th Century to the present), *MLA International Bibliography*, *Public Affairs Information Service* (PAIS), a variety of Wilson Indexes and the *Academic American Encyclopedia* by Grolier. Dedicated workstations provide access to *Compact Medbase*, *InfoTrac*, *and NewsBank*. Offering data rather than bibliographic information on CD-ROM are *Consu/Stats I* (U.S. government-produced consumer data), *Econ/Stats I* and *StatPak* (government statistical data), and *Compact Disclosure* on corporations. Thousands of public domain software and shareware programs can be downloaded by users from *PC-SIG*. By use of the CD-ROM based information, the library hopes to develop methods and procedures for the handling of such technology to the best advantage. It is anticipated that end-user searching on CD-ROM will ease the demand for online searching (CIRS) serving increasing numbers of users without the cost of online searching; however, teaching students and faculty to use the various search software and databases effectively has proven very demanding of staff time.

c. Use of a telefacsimile machine (fax) for document delivery, reference service, and communications.

Between June 1986 and June 1987 the Health Sciences Library of Ohio University was chosen by the State Library of Ohio to operate an experimental telefacsimile network for the transmission of biomedical information in a multi-type library environment. Seventeen Ohio libraries of various types participated in the experiment. The one-year project demonstrated the need, reliability, value, and speed of using telefacsimile for document delivery of health related and biomedical interlibrary loan requests. The FAX equipment installed at the 17 sites was the Pitney Bowes 8150, which cost $2,300 each.

While the state-funded library project was underway, the Vice Provost responsible for regional campuses placed Fax equipment in the library of each regional campus. Although primarily for use in information transmission by the deans of these campuses and the Vice Provost, the libraries regularly use it for document delivery and reference queries.

After the successful experiment on the use of a FAX machine, the library has expanded its scope to cover all library areas. The FAX machine is heavily used for interlibrary loans, routine telecommunications (especially overseas), and even to share memos and materials with other offices on campus (alleviating the need for messenger deliveries). As an example, as this paper was being written, we were able to respond to a query about non-Roman scripts in libraries from the Institute of Southeast Asian Studies in Singapore.

FAX has proven an easy and efficient means of communicating at any distance, rivaling regular mail in cost and surpassing it in speed, while eliminating the ubiquitous office problem of telephone tag.

d. Providing general public computer terminals and microcomputers for students and faculty in the library.

Since 1982, in cooperation with the University's Computing and Learning Services (UCLS), the library has provided space for a computer lab — the first of many of its kind established on the Athens campus. As of May 1989, the Lab offers 25 MS-DOS microcomputers, 13 Macintosh, 9 Apple II-Es, and 33 terminals connected to the University's Wide Area Network. The terminals in these labs provide additional means to access the ALICE online catalog, as well as other mini-and mainframe computers on campus.

e. Providing microcomputers for library departments and staff.

To facilitate office automation, more than 50 microcomputers have been installed in library departments over the last seven years — about one PC for every 1.5 regular staff. Microcomputers have been in use since 1982, but initial emphasis was on sharing. Staff members have been encouraged (and given numerous professional development opportunities) to learn the use of microcomputer for data and word processing. One local area network (LAN) is in occasional use and the Library has access to the University's wide area network (WAN). Many courses and workshops in the applications of microcomputer have been offered by UCLS and the Library. Several staff struggle to remain current with the technology and serve as resident experts for other staff. Applications include calculation of the Library's acquisitions formula using SuperCalc5, specialized departmental databases, a variety of special bibliographies, a remote bulletin Board (RBBS) for Health Sciences faculty, desktop publishing in both Macintosh and MS-DOS environments, and E-Mail (using BITNET and MCI Mail—the latter also providing telex facilities).

New Development at the State Level.

The information explosion confronts academic and research libraries with new challenges and opportunities, including space (shelving print materials, storage cases for other media, and floor space for workstations and other equipment required by newer media), identification (much of the most useful information is under-represented in bibliographic databases), and access (users can discover a variety of materials beyond the resources of any single institution). It was the space issue which prompted the State of Ohio to launch its first major new initiative since the founding of OCLC two decades earlier. Confronted with massive capital requests for new or enlarged library buildings on state-supported university campuses, the State Legislature of Ohio created a special committee to assess the space requirements of university libraries. That committee, from its inception, recognized that space was only one dimension of the problem. The Committee emphasized:

> ... [T]he academic library of today has a threefold purpose, serving not only as a storehouse of information, but also as a gateway to information held elsewhere, and as a

center for instruction about information. ①

Following the committee's report in 1987, ② the Board of Regents (the state-level policy agency for all state-supported post-secondary schools) established a number of task forces to begin planning for a statewide information access system, the Ohio Library Information System (OLIS). ③ That planning process is nearing fruition with a Request for Proposals (RFP) scheduled for June 15, 1989. A decision on vendor (s) is expected by December 1989, and the system is scheduled to be acquired with funding available July 1, 1990, and to become operational on July 1, 1991. The planning process has emphasized that this will be an information system for the 1990s and beyond. It is expected to join together, without replicating or replacing, local systems on the participating campuses. It will facilitate resource sharing among 15 state-supported universities and medical colleges and two private universities, including permitting users to initiate interlibrary borrowing requests without an intermediary. On a single terminal, the user will easily move from a local online public access catalog to a statewide union catalog. To make resource sharing a reality, a statewide document delivery system will bring the documents to the requester's institution in three days.

Most significant is the emphasis on information. In addition to the usual bibliographic information found in an online public access catalog (OPAC), the system offer a variety of indexing services to transparently provide the same access to journal articles and reports as to book and periodical titles, full-text services, data, and images. The system will also provide gateways to other information services which are not available within the system. Access is expected to be through microcomputers or, preferably, scholars workstations rather than terminals. With the anticipated innovations in the system, a phased approach is planned with attention to keeping the system open to further advances in the technology.

It would be premature to evaluate a system still in planning, but librarians, computer and telecommunications specialists, and faculty and researchers are working together to provide innovative service which may rival the earlier contributions of OCLC.

Summary and Conclusion

In reviewing library automation at Ohio University during the last three decades with particular regard to the use of computers, the picture matches nearly exactly that described by Richard DeGennaro in 1983:

"We are well into our third decade of library automation. The first decade, the 1960s, was dominated by primitive local systems. The second decade, the 1970s, was dominated by large multitype and multipurpose library networks. The current and third decade, the 1980s, will be sophisticated multifunction turnkey systems on mini-and micro-computers; and they will have lines to a variety of library and commercial networks on large mainframe."④

The general trend of moving from centralization in the 1970s to the decentralization in the 1980s, according to his reasoning, has been "shaped and driven by the cost and capabilities of the computer and telecommunications technologies..." of that time period. ⑤

Such has been our experience. Ohio University will seek to refine its local ALICE system and to fully implement all functions making it a completely integrated system. The exploration of the potentials and impacts of CD-ROM and other new information technologies will continue. As the

---

① Ohio Board of Regents, Library Study Committee. *Academic Libraries in Ohio*; *Progress through Collaboration*, *Storage*, *and Technology* (Columbus, Ohio: Ohio Board of Regents, 1987), p. vii.

② Ibid.

③ Hwa-Wei Lee, "Planning Process And Considerations for a Statewide Academic Libraries Information System in Ohio," paper presented at the Second Pacific Conference on New Information Technologies for Library and Information Profession – als, May 29 – 31, 1989, Singapore. The paper appeared in the *Proceedings* (West Newton, Mass. : MicroUse Information, 1989), pp. 203 – 210. Included in Section VIII of this compilation.

④ Richard De Gennaro, "Library Automation and Networking Perspectives on Three Decades," *Library Journal*, Vol. 108, No. 7 (April 1, 1983), p. 629.

⑤ Ibid.

cost for computers further decreases and their capacity expands, appropriate employment of new information technologies for library services is necessary to harness the changing information environment and demands in the years ahead.

If one were to add a fourth decade to De Gennaro's report, we will be serving users with greater computing power sitting on their desks than was available through the mainframes of the 1970s. We are preparing for a time, described by Jacques Vallee:

"'Think about it, man,' said a young enthusiast at the San Francisco home computer fair last year [1981], 'you could have the entire Library of Congress at your fingertips.'

'What would you do if you had the entire Library of Congress at your fingertips?' I asked him.

I am still waiting for an answer."①

Not only should we be able to answer the question in the next few years, we must answer it.

DIAGRAM I

Mushrooming of OCLC

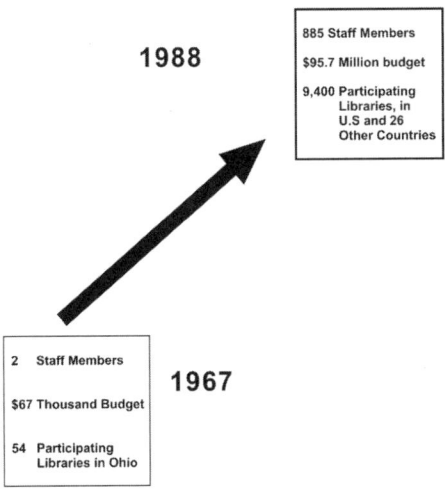

DIAGRAM II

Growth of OCLC Database

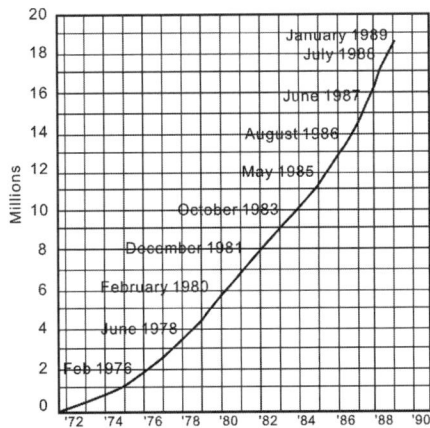

---

① Jacques Vallee, *The Network Revolution: Confessions of a Computer Scientist* (Berkeley: And/Or Press, 1982), p. 172.

第七部分 图书馆发展

Section VII Library Development

Fragmentation of Academic Library Resources in Thai University Libraries

Many of the academic institutions in the developing countries in Southeast Asia have been confronted with a serious shortage of library resources which are of vital importance for their national development. The shortage is generally blamed on the lack of adequate funds, a limited number of trained personnel, and the unavailability of suitable books and other library materials. It is true that most of the academic libraries I have visited in Southeast Asia are poorly funded as they often are not given top priority over the many competing demands which the university authorities must consider in the allocation of funds. The lack of a sufficient number of trained personnel is another factor contributing to the shortage of library resources, but this is due largely to the low pay and status of academic librarians who are generally considered inferior to their teaching colleagues. ① The number of suitable books — especially those with academic subjects and content, published in the native languages — is far short of demand. For academic books, university libraries must rely heavily on imported foreign books for which the high cost is often prohibitive for the average reader or even the academic libraries. In order to supply a sufficient number of textbooks which students often cannot afford themselves, many academic libraries must use a large portion of their inadequate book funds to purchase multiple copies of textbooks. ② The number of translated titles of foreign publications available is very small and frequently available only after a long delay. As a result, many academic libraries have mainly dated publications, rare and historical materials, multiple copies of textbooks, and only a small percentage of books that can be considered up-to-date and of current interest.

But this is not the most critical problem. Limited resources can be channeled into effective use. This problem of shortages in funds, personnel and books is common in the developing countries and we must learn to live with it while at the same time struggling for its improvement. The main problem lies not in the shortage of library resources but in the fragmentation of the limited resources among the many faculty libraries and departmental libraries in most Thai universities. This general practice of decentralization of library resources and services coupled with the absence of effective coordination and cooperation among the many decentralized library units has further complicated the existing problems.

According to a survey of the current status of faculty libraries and departmental libraries in Thai universities which I conducted recently it was found that many of the library resources in Thai universities have been divided among the many faculty libraries and departmental libraries with little or no coordination to make the total resources within each university available to the entire university community. With only a few exceptions, most of the central libraries which do exist are

---

① University librarians in Thailand generally do not have faculty status unless they also teach. It is quite common in the universities where library science courses are offered that librarians must teach in order to achieve faculty status, salary and promotion. The teaching load of an average of ten hours a week is too heavy for those who also have the responsibility of running their libraries. Consequently it is always the library service that suffers.

② It was reported that a library "buys as many as 50 copies of a textbook in the liberal arts because many students cannot afford to buy them." S. A. Barnett, E. L. Brown and C. W. Stone, *Developmental Book Activities and Needs in Thailand* New York: Wolf Management Services, 1967), p. 69.

very weak in resources and have no direct administrative authority over the faculty libraries. As a general rule, most of the faculties in Thai universities maintain their own faculty libraries. The university librarians (rightly these people should be called the librarians of the central libraries) often assume no responsibility in the overall planning and development of the library resources and services of their respective universities. The coordination of the various library units, using one university as an example, rests upon the office of the deputy rector for academic affairs instead of the university librarian. There is no centralized acquisition or cataloging. A union catalog of books and a union list of serials on a university-wide basis are not usually available for consultation. Many of the faculty libraries are not staffed by trained professional library staff and their materials are not properly catalogued and kept. The library hours are, in most cased, irregular and short, making them not easily accessible to the users. Because one faculty library does not know what the others are doing, unnecessary duplication in acquisition of library materials and journal subscriptions is often found on the same campus. To quote the observation of a foreign expert:

> The library situation is chaotic partly because the building and housing of collections is divided among the rival demands of faculty libraries, departmental libraries and the central library. There is great preference for faculty libraries, but no one of them is completely adequate for advanced study or research in the field. Departmental libraries tend to split up the fields which are represented in the faculty library. And the unanswered question is — What is the purpose of the central library? Sometimes the central library is referred to as though it is a place from which books may be borrowed for indefinite periods by faculty or departmental libraries, sometimes as though it is a repository for basic texts in courses. ①

This situation of fragmentation of library resources and services occurs not only in Thai universities, but also can be found in many of the other developing countries as well. As stated by an internationally known American librarian:

> Each of these separate libraries in a university may have its own rules and regulations, its own systems — or no system at all — of cataloging and classification, its own restrictions on use, and complete indepen? dence of any centralized administrative oversight. There is seldom cooperation among them for exchange of information, interlibrary loan, or coordinated acquisition. The role of the central library is often merely that of a dumping ground for those books which none of the other libraries wants, and it is therefore frequently the least-used by students of any of the university's libraries. ②

The preceding observations are by no means an exaggeration of the prevailing situation. My own survey, made recently, serves to support the above statements. A summary of the data obtained from the survey is presented below.

The survey was intended to include all Thai institutions of higher learning with university standing that confer degrees but excluding military academies (some of which are considered university equivalents). There are 11 institutions of higher learning in Thailand that fall into this category:

Asian Institute of Technology
Chiangmai University
Chulalongkorn University
College of Education
Kasetsart University
Khonkaen University
Mahidol University (formerly University of Medical Sciences)
National Institute of Development Administration
Prince of Songkla University
Silapakorn University

---

① Cited in Ibid. , Moody E. Prior, *Report on Graduate Education in Thailand*, *Bangkok*, as quoted by Barnett, Brown and Stone, p. 67.
② Lester Asheim. *Librarianship in the Developing Countries*, p. 6. (Urbana: University of Illinois Press, 1966)

Thammasat University

Among the 11 institutions named above: Two do not have faculty libraries (Asian Institute of Technology and the National Institute of Development Administration); two did not respond to the survey (Chiangmai University and Silapakorn University, both having faculty libraries); leaving seven institutions that provided meaningful data for this study. It is of interest to note that among the seven useful replies, two do not have a central library (College of Education and Prince of Songkla University). Other institutions varied, having from one to ten faculty libraries.

Chulalongkorn University	10 faculty libraries	(Two are off–campus.)
College of Education	6 branch libraries	(The college consists of 6 branches, separately located. Each branch has its own library. There is no central library.)
Kasetsart University	4 faculty libraries	(One is off–campus.)
Khonkaen University	1 faculty library	(It is off–campus.)
Mahidol University	7 faculty libraries	(Six are off–campus.)
Prince of Songkla	3 faculty libraries	(The University consists of three faculties located on different campuses. Each has its own library. There is no central library.)
Thammasat University	5 faculty libraries	(None is off–campus.)

According to the statistical information in Appendix I, the only central library having a considerable strength over its faculty libraries is the central library of Thammasat University which has a collection over 125,000 volumes. It is followed by the central library of Chulalongkorn University, Prasarnmitr Campus of the College of Education, and the Siriraj Medical Library of the Mahidol University, each having a collection of 76,477 volumes, 62,000 volumes, and 50,000 volumes respectively. If the resources of all faculty libraries are included, Chulalongkorn University should lead all others with a combined strength of 183,561 volumes compared to the 150,136 volumes which Thammasat University has.

One serious problem, readily evident in the data in Appendix I, is the rather short library hours most of the libraries are open for service. The longest library hours were reported by the Siriraj Medical library which opens 77 hours per week in comparison to the shortest hours reported by a faculty library which opens only 20 hours per week. A compelling fact is that many of the faculty libraries are accessible only during office hours when most students are attending classes.①

In regard to other questions asked in the survey, only the central library of Thammasat University has an overall jurisdiction and administrative control over the faculty libraries; three central libraries, Chulalongkorn, Kasetsart, and Thammasat, are reported to have maintained or are in the process of setting up a union catalog of all library books that are in the faculty libraries of their respective universities. Two universities, both Mahidol and Thammasat, have a union list of journals. Another one, Chulalongkorn, is in the process of setting one up. Concerning centralized library acquisition and cataloging, the central libraries of Khonkaen and Thammasat reported that they are 100% responsible for the acquisition and cataloging of library materials for their faculty libraries. The central library of Kasetsart University reported that they do the cataloging for one of their faculty libraries. The rest of the central libraries have nothing or little to do with the acquisition and cataloging of library materials for their faculty libraries.

If the faculty libraries were not under the administrative control of the central library. Librarians were asked what kind of machinery was available to coordinate the work of the various faculty libraries and the central library. Except for Thammasat where the central library does have the administrative control over its faculty libraries, most of the other institutions acknowledged having varying degrees of coordination between the central library and faculty libraries, one was by means of a library committee which consists of members from each faculty chaired by the deputy rector

---

① I was told that some of the faculty libraries do not allow students from other faculties of the same university to use their libraries.

for academic affairs with the librarian of the central library serving as secretary. But there were others in which there were only loose coordination between the central library and the faculty libraries.

Another question put to the librarians was: "Are you generally in favor of the present setup of your library and its relationship with the faculty libraries? If your answer is a no, what will you do?" Again, except for Thammasat, most of the libraries surveyed were not in favor of the present set up of their library and their relationships with the faculty libraries, but felt it would be difficult to seek changes in the present situation especially when the administration of many institutions is decentralized.

The last question sought any special comments librarians might have concerning the question of centralized library service versus decentralized library service. Despite the fact that most Thai university libraries are decentralized, the general feeling of the librarians was definitely in favor of a centralized library service, or at least, as put this way by a university librarian, "a coordinated decentralization."①

It seems to be the consensus of the respondents that the limited library resources in Thai universities can be put to better use only through effective coordination between the central library and the various faculty libraries and departmental libraries, but, in order to do so, the position of University Librarian must first be firmly established. This position should carry with it the responsibility and appropriate authority to coordinate the library resources and services within each of the universities. Far-sighted university administrators should stand behind the university librarian and the central library to provide them with whatever support necessary to work out an effective system of coordination between the central library and the various library units.

It is also desirable that small library units in each university be consolidated into large units or be combined with the central library with the exception of those library units located off the main campus. Minimum standards must be required for the creation of new faculty libraries before they are permitted to be established and to begin functioning.

A decentralized library system without an effective means for close coordination of the fragmented resources is not suitable for the universities in developing countries. There are additional reasons for this argument.

1) The majority of academic programs in Thai universities are at the undergraduate level where a basic collection of well selected books and journals may be required by several faculties because of the overlapping needs and the interdisciplinary areas of study. Unnecessary duplication of these publications could be avoided by having them in the central library. Also the use of a well stocked central library will have the advantage over a faculty library in providing the university students with a general and broad educational experience.

2) There are many common reference books and bibliographical works which are essential to provide good library services but are too expensive to be duplicated in the faculty libraries, especially when the funds for library materials are critically inadequate.

3) If faculty libraries are to serve as a useful aid in instruction and research it will require trained library staff to man their services. This will place a great strain on the small number of trained librarians available. If untrained staff are employed, they will not be able to handle the reference, documentation and technical services expected of them and, consequently, will reduce the usefulness of the library and make the collection inaccessible to its users.

4) It is also wasteful to require that all faculty libraries remain open for long hours and be

---

① "Coordinated decentralization" is a term borrowed from the Harvard University library system where effective measures have been taken to coordinate the many autonomous library units within the University. See Douglas W. Bryant, "Centralization and Decentralization at Harvard," Centralization and Decentralization at Harvard," *College and Research Libraries*, 3 (1961), pp. 328–334. It is of interest to note, however, that Harvard University Libraries have a combined strength of approximately 8,000,000 volumes with an annual expenditure in the neighborhood of US $8,000,000 in 1967 while the majority of libraries in Thai universities have fewer than 100,000 volumes and spend less than 20,000 US dollars per year for books and journals. If effective co-ordination of library resources and services is necessary for Harvard it will be even more so for the university libraries in Thailand. Richard DeGennaro, "Automation in the Harvard College Library", *Harvard Library Bulletin*, 16 (1968), p. 218.

staffed by trained librarians when a well planned central library can be kept open for service during evenings and weekends with only a skeleton of trained staff to man the key positions.

The decentralized library system, although able to be justified in a large library system where the total collection is very large and strong, is difficult to justify in a small library where the collection is both small and weak and where no effective means of coordination among the various units is available. The fragmentation of academic library resources is not only unable to meet the needs of an undergraduate education but is also inadequate to support the many graduate programs now being offered in many of the Thai universities. A recently published report, A Proposal for the establishment of the Graduate Programs in the Basic Science and Mathematics in Thailand, prepared by a team of experts appointed by the University Development Commission of the National Education Council clearly pointed out the serious deficiency of the many faculty libraries now in existence. [1]

To remedy the aforementioned deficiencies and, at the same time, to take into consideration the strong local tradition of having the academic faculties a considerable autonomy in managing their own academic affairs including the libraries, the following actions are recommended for consideration and possible adoption.

1) The position of the University Librarian (or the Director of University Libraries) should be established in each of the universities to plan and execute the overall development of library resources and services. It should be made clear that the university library consists of all the collections of books in the possession of university, wherever located.

2) The University Librarian should be vested with the responsibility of coordinating the various administratively and geographically decentralized library units so that they will be more responsive to the total needs of the university community. The University Librarian should be a member of the University Senate and have memberships in the committees which concern the academic programs so that he (or she) will be fully informed and involved in the academic development of the university.

3) The librarians of various faculty and departmental libraries should be recruited and recommended for appointment by the University Librarian in consultation with the dean of the faculty or the head of the department concerned. The librarian of the faculty or departmental library should be responsible both to the dean of the faculty or to the head of the department to which his (or her) library belongs and to the University Librarian.

4) There should be a University Libraries Administrative Council with members consisting of the university librarian, two or three senior members of the Central Library, and the librarians of the faculty libraries. The Council should meet regularly to discuss matters of concern to all library units in the university.

5) There should be a Library Advisory Committee for the University librarian consisting of one faculty member from each faculty appointed by the deans of their respective faculties and the University Librarian. The Committee should meet at least four times a year to advise the University Librarian on policy matters.

6) Although the selection of library materials for each of the faculty libraries should be the basic responsibility of the librarians in each of the faculty libraries, centralized acquisition by the central library is strongly urged to achieve economy in the operation and to avoid unnecessary duplications. Since mechanized library operations can be easily employed to obtain maximum efficiency, centralized acquisition and accounting, as well as centralized cataloging and processing should be contemplated to take advantage of modern technology. This would enable the librarians of the faculty libraries to have more free time for direct service to their readers.

7) A union catalog of books and union lists of journal holdings and serial titles should be established and maintained in the Central Library. Whenever it will be economically and

---

[1] Thailand, University Development Commission, *A Proposal for the Establishment of the Graduate Programs in the Basic sciences and Mathematics in Thailand* (Bangkok: University Development Commission, 1968), pp. 8–9, 17, 27–28, 44.

technically feasible, printed book catalogs, lists of journal holdings and serial titles should be made available in the faculty and departmental libraries for the convenience of all users.

8) Even though separate library budgets for each faculty library may still be maintained, the University Librarian must see to it that all libraries have received the adequate financial support each of them will require. Careful planning and coordination by the University librarian in consultation with the university officials, deans and the librarians of the faculty libraries is necessary to ensure that the overall goals of the library development in the university will be met. The financial norm that "the annual budget should constitute from 5 to 10 per cent of the total annual university budget" as recommended by the UNESCO Regional Seminar on Library Development in South Asia, 3 – 14 October 1960 in Delhi, India[①] should—as far as possible—be used as a guide for the budget preparation and request.

9) All professionally trained staff, whether they teach or not, should be accorded faculty status with appropriate faculty rank and salary as this will be necessary to attract the best qualified people into the academic librarianship and to enable the libraries to retain their competent staff. In order to enable the librarians to devote more time to their library work, the teaching loads for those who still work and teach should be reduced to a maximum of six hours per week with adequate time allowed for the preparation of lectures and other related instructional duties.

10) All faculty libraries should make their resources and services available not only to their own students and faculty members but also to those from other faculties within the university. Provision should be made also to enable qualified persons from outside the university to use the library collections.

11) A positive step that might be taken by the central library to reduce the number of excuses the faculties have for wanting to have their own faculty libraries is to seek immediate improvement of the resources and services of the central library by making their services more responsive to the specific needs of the faculties. Longer library hours, a more liberal loan policy for the faculty members, faster reference service and expert bibliographic assistance can all contribute to the prestige of a central library and help to earn the confidence and respect of the faculty members. The needs for faculty libraries arise when the service of the central library falls and vice versa.

12) A program of cooperative acquisition should be worked out among the library units so that each can concentrate their efforts in their fields of specialties, not competing to overlap in the subject coverage. Materials required for interdisciplinary areas should be left to the central library. In this way, a much stronger collection can be developed with minimum waste and duplication.

Just to improve the library resources and services within each of the universities is not enough. The developing countries with their limited library resources available must seek also a wider coordination and cooperation among all university libraries in each of the countries and among academic libraries, governmental libraries, public libraries, special libraries, and the National Library. When the voices of professional librarians are weak in the countries where library development is not considered a priority item, leadership from higher authorities in the educational administration is urgently needed to help the librarians in their respective countries.

In Thailand, for example, the National Education Council, a coordinating body for the planning and development of all levels of education, especially higher education, can help the university librarians by establishing a committee for university libraries to review the needs of academic libraries in the universities and to make recommendations for their improvement. Appropriate legislation and minimum standards for university libraries should be drafted and promulgated to guide the development of university libraries. There is an urgent need at present to provide for the newly established universities a set of guidelines for the organization and development of their library resources and services.

Nationwide projects among the university libraries in the preparation of a union catalog of all academic libraries, a union list of journals and serial titles, interlibrary loan, expanded

---

① "Regional Seminar On Library Development in South Asia", *UNESCO Library Bulletin* Vol. 15, No. 4 (1961).

photocopying service, centralized technical processing, free exchange of duplicate publications, etc. could be initiated and coordinated by the National Education Council in cooperation with the National Library and the Thai National Documentation Centre.

The recommendation made by the Wolf Management services on cooperative acquisition of library materials among university libraries and the proper role of the National Education Council is well taken and should be put into operation as soon as possible:

> The National Education Council should be encouraged to coordinate acquisition of materials among college and university libraries, to help prevent future expensive duplication of high-cost resources. Looking toward expansion of graduate level studies in Thailand, it is imperative that all library resources be reviewed and regarded more or less as a common reservoir. ①

In conclusion, the shortage of library resources in Thai universities resulting from inadequate funds, not enough trained librarians, and the lack of appropriate books, can nevertheless be improved by effective coordination and consolidation of the various library units with in each of the universities and by inter-university cooperation under the leadership of the National Education Council. The uncoordinated system of decentralization of library resources and services as those commonly found in Thai universities is too luxurious for a country where most of the university libraries are considered small and inadequate in their resources. Effective measures must be taken to pool the library resources together or the programs of instruction and research in Thai universities will be retarded by the inability of their academic libraries to respond effectively to meet the needs.

APPENDIX I

Statistical survey of library resources in the institutions of higher education in Thailand as of January 1970
Except as noted in footnote 4, statistical information was obtained from survey responses from all university librarians.

Name of Institution	Cataloged volumes	Current journals	Non-current journals	Professional staff	Clerical staff	Library hours per week
Asian Inst. of Tech. Chiengmai Univ. ②	23,236	714	64	3	5	72.5
Chulalongkorn Univ.						
Central Library	76,477	436	200	10	16	52.0
Faculty Libraries						
Architecture	2,267	19	...	1	2	45.0
Arts	6,977	5	...	1	1	20.0
Commerce & Accountancy	4,881	68	...	1	3	44.0
Education	34,292	86	...	4	10	70.5
Engineering	18,817	23	...	1	5	37.5
Medicine③	18,397	245	...	3	4	64.0
Political Sci.	4,804	51	...	1	3	54.5
Science	10,300	89	...	1	9	35.0
Veterinary Science[11]	4,020	300	...	0	1	55.5

---

① S. A. Barnett, E. L. Brown and C. W. Stone. *Developmental Book Activities and Needs in Thailand* (New York: Wolf Management Services, 1967). p. 72.

② No reply was received.

③ The faculty is located off the main campus.

(Continuing)

Name of Institution	Cataloged volumes	Current journals	Non-current journals	Professional staff	Clerical staff	Library hours per week
Mass Comm. & PR	2,329	35	1	1	1	68.0
College of Education[1]						
Prasarnmitr Campus	62,000	351	153	7	2	70.0
Patumwan Campus[2]	11,000	...	...	1	3	63.5
Kasetsart Univ.						
Main Library	30,325	333	474	3	20	64.0
Faculty Libraries						
Econ. & Public Administration	...	...	...	...	40.0	
Engineering[11]	...	...	—	...	...	40.0
Fisheries	...	...	...	...	...	40.0
Forestry	...	...	...	...	...	40.0
Khonkaen Univ.						
Main Library	3,817	154	198	1	13	76.5
Faculty Libraries						
Agriculture[11]	215	7	...	...	1	35.0
Mahidol Univ.						
Siriraj Medical Library[3]	50,000	450	...	9	6	77.0
Faculty Libraries						
Dentistry[11]	2,410	77	...	1	1	40.0
Medical Tech.	2,185	21	...	0	1	40.0
Pharmacy[11]	5,468	42	...	1	2	49.3
Public Health[11]	5,000	91	33	...	4	40.0
Ramathibodhi Hospital[11]	201	280	24	2	1	70.3
Science[11]	3,000	490	...	3	5	61.5
Tropical Med.[11]	1,420	92	54	1	2	35.0
National Inst. of Development Administration	37,204	597	321	14	17	40.0
Prince of Songkla Univ.[4]						

[1] The College has six branches, each has its own library.
[2] Information obtained from *A Directory of Libraries in Bangkok* (Bangkok: UNESCO Regional Office for Education in Asia, 1970).
[3] It serves as central library.
[4] There is no central library.

(Continuing)

Name of Institution	Cataloged volumes	Current journals	Non-current journals	Professional staff	Clerical staff	Library hours per week
Faculty Libraries						
Education	5,000	42	15	1	1	50.0
Engineering[11]	...	...	...	...	...	...
Science[11]	...	...	...	...	...	...
Silpakorn Univ.[10,13] Central Library	2,178	(51)		...	...	45.0
Faculty Libraries						
Archaeology	5000	...	...	(3)		35.0
Architecture	690	(8)		(2)		40.0
Painting & Sculpture	700	...	...	(2)		40.0
Tabkaew College	5,763	(53)		1	2	70.0
Thammasat Univ. Central Library	125,702	627	198	12	28	64.0
Faculty Libraries						
Commerce & Accountancy	1,530	16	11	1	3	40.0
Economics	9,404	80	...	2	7	64.0
Law	3,500	15		...	...	64.0
Political Science	6,000	70	...	1	...	40.0
Social Administration	4,000	53	...	1	2	64.0

A New Engineering Library Emerging in ASIA

Today most of the Asian countries are confronted with the serious problem of a "brain drain", which has gravely hampered the speed of their national development. Unless this situation can be rectified, the gap between the developed countries and the developing countries can never be narrowed. Dependence on foreign technical assistance will not solve the development problems of the region in the long run. Rather, the best brain powers of Asia must be employed for the development of Asia. This is one of the major concerns of Asian nations that are struggling for rapid socio-political, economic, industrial, and technological development as well as for educational and cultural upsurge. Without the "brain power", nothing can be achieved or take root.

There are many factors contributing to the problem of the "brain drain". The inappropriate education and training that many of the young aspirants of Asian countries receive in the developed countries is one such factor. The overtraining and sophisticated education some of them attain constitutes a waste rather than a gain in brain power for the developing countries — this has been referred to as "brain waste".

In order to overcome the problem of a "brain drain" or, in some cases, a "brain waste", a new regional postgraduate school, the Asian Institute of Technology, (AIT) has been founded. It was first established in 1959 as the SEATO Graduate School of Engineering in Bangkok. In 1967, it became completely indepenaent of the Southeast Asia Treaty Organization (SEATO). The A T is an autonomous, nonprofit, private, regional institution of advanced engineering education and research in Asia. It is governed by an international board of trustees with 22 trustee members from 13 countries serving as individual members rather than as representatives of their countries. As of September 1971, the AIT Board consists of members from the following countries: Australia, Republic of China, France, Indonesia, Japan, Malaysia, New Zealand, Pakistan, the Philippines, Thailand, the United Kingdom, the United states, and South Vietnam.

AIT Program

During the 1971 – 1972 academic year, 215 graduate students representing 18 Asian countries were enrolled in the three types of programs — the eight-month diploma program, the twenty-month Masters degree program, and the two-year Doctoral degree program. The majority of students are enrolled in the Master's degree program under one of the six academic divisions: Environmental Engineering, Geotechnical Engineering, Structural Engineering and Mechanics, Systems Engineering and Management, Transportation Engineering, and Water Science and Engineering. A new division in Agricultural Engineering will be added in January 1972, and in September 1972, another division, Electrical engineering — Power Systems is to be added.

According to the Master Plan, in 1980 AIT will become a complete institute of technology offering graduate programs in all engineering branches and related fields with a projected enrollment of 1,000. Besides the three types of programs already mentioned, the Institute will also provide in-service training and continuing education for a large number of practicing engineers, researchers, and engineering faculty of other universities through a series of seminars, workshops, conferences, and short courses. A number of short courses and conferences have already been organized and offered, but the scope of this type of continuing education will be greatly expanded in the years ahead to hasten the pace of technological development in the region by helping the engineers to keep abreast of the new knowledge available in their respective fields. The distinction of AIT's academic program, as has been demonstrated thus far, is not only to attain a quality engineering education of very high standard, which is necessary to attract the best engineering students in Asia, but also to provide an education that is relevant to the conditions and needs of the region so that its graduates can be best prepared to serve their countries.

The employment records on AIT graduates, now approaching 450, speak well of the Institute's accomplishment. Besides the 7 percent who went on for doctoral studies in the West and the 4 percent who sought employment outside Asia, the remaining 89 percent have stayed Asia to engage in various engineering works. Roughly over half, or 54 percent, of those who stay on are in government service, 24 percent work in private enterprise, and 22 percent teach in Asian universities.

AIT Library Activities

The fact that there are few adequate and up-to-date engineering libraries in Asia has prompted AIT to exert a major effort in building up a strong library resource in engineering and related subjects to serve the needs of both AIT and the region. Recent statistics reveal that the Library collection has now exceeded 35,000 books and over 1,000 journals. In addition to this conventional stock, the library also has a large number of microfiches, microfilms, technical documents and reports, maps, slides, and films. Close cooperation is maintained with other academic, research, and special libraries in Bangkok for interlibrary loan and photocopying services. For the necessary back up support, the Library has also made extensive use of the various services rendered by major libraries and documentation centers throughout the world, such as the Library of Congress, the National Library of Medicine, Linda Hall Library, and John Crerar Library in the United states and the National Lending Library for Science and Technology in Great Britain.

Although the primary function of the AIT Library is to support the instructional and research programs of the Institute, by virtue of the regional characteristics of AIT, the Library also has a regional dimension and obligation. In fact, the Board of Trustees sees the Library as a regional resource and has envisioned it as a regional library and information center in engineering and related fields. In doing so, a preliminary proposal was drawn up in February 1971 and was subsequently submitted to foundations and governmental and international agencies for financial support. Should the necessary funds be obtained, the regional library and information center concept will soon be implemented.

In preparing to assume the larger role, the Library has been actively taking part in many regional cooperative projects and activities and, at the same time, vigorously pursuing the course of expansion and innovation. Computer application in the housekeeping functions of the library was introduced in 1968. At present, it consists of the acquisitions and accounting system and the serials listing and control system.[①] Further applications are planned for the time when a larger computer system becomes available at AIT in place of the current IBM 1130.

The effective transference of scientific and technological knowledge from the developed countries to the developing countries depends to a large extent on the availability of a responsive information system or systems which have a large bibliographical database prepared both by external and internal sources. The AIT Library is currently investigating the possibility of setting up a bibliographical database using the MARC magnetic tapes and the *Engineering Index Compendex* as the major inputs.

To expedite the process of information transfer, consideration has also been given to satellite communications for linkage of national information centers in the various parts of Asia and with the major libraries in the developed countries. It is hoped that a regional network of library and information systems can be established through cooperative efforts, a preliminary discussion of such a possibility was to be held at the Conference on Scientific and Technical Information Needs for Malaysia and Singapore, in Kuala Lumpur, September 24 to 26, 1971. The Conference was jointly sponsored by the Library Association of Malaysia and the Library Association of Singapore

---

① For a detailed description of these two systems see the article by this author, "Library Mechanization at the Asian Institute of Technology", *International Library Review*, Vol. 3, No. 3 (June 1971), pp. 257 – 70.

with invited participants from other southeast Asian countries. ①

The Asian Institute of Technology is now temporarily located on the campus of Chulalongkorn University (the largest Thai national university) situated in the center of Bangkok. The Library of the Institute occupies a space of approximately 5,000 square feet. The rapidly growing collection and the heavy use both by AIT students and faculty and by outside patrons crowd the facility.

Fortunately, this situation will be eliminated in August 1972 when AIT will move from its present location to the new campus located 42 kilometers from Bangkok on 400 acres of land donated by the Thai Government. The new campus, now under construction, at a cost of US $20 million, when completed, will be among the best in Asia. The first phase of construction, costing more than $6.2 million, includes a major academic building — a part of which will temporarily house the library, an administration building, a campus services complex, dormitory rooms and dining facilities for 350 students, and five faculty residences. A permanent library building that will occupy 100,000 square feet of space is being planned for completion in 1974.

AIT Assistance to Other Libraries

The spirit of cooperation among libraries in Thailand and elsewhere in Asia is important for the development of better library service in the region. In pursuance of this aim, the AIT Library has been generously providing assistance to other libraries in many ways. For example, consultations were held on the establishment of the Asian Highway Technical Information Center and the reorganization plan of the Khonkaen University Library. Short training courses were conducted for library staff of the two organizations. A number of special demonstrations and lectures on computer applications were given to librarians of other libraries and to students in the several library schools in Bangkok. Exchange of duplicate books and journal files is undertaken from time to time with other libraries. Finally, the library has been actively participating in the cooperative projects of compiling a union list of serials and special bibliographies. The implementation of regional library services, if successful, will undoubtedly enhance the present role of the AIT Library to an even greater extent.

---

① By invitation, this author submitted a paper oil the topic of "Regional Cooperation in Scientific and Technical Information Services".

Principles of National Library And Information Policy

Introduction

The last quarter of this century has been described as the "information age" and our society, as an "information society". More than ever before, our world is becoming information dependent. The "information gap" between industrialized countries whose information needs have been better served and developing countries whose information needs have been less well served is becoming wider and more serious. There is also a growing concern for the disparity in communication and information capacities among different countries. To expedite the pace of social, economic, political, cultural, scientific and technological development, it is necessary to improve library and information services to provide the information required for development. The effort to raise the level of library and information services in every country, including Taiwan which is among the more highly developed countries of Asia, should be carefully planned and centrally coordinated at the national level to achieve maximum results.

Japan, in recent years, offers a successful model. The comprehensive National Information System for Science and Technology (NIST) plans and coordinates the information service activities of all branches and disciplines as well as the actual work done by the Japan Scientific and Technical Information Center (JICST) to collect, analyze, disseminate useful information for national development. An official white paper by the Japanese government in 1981 on the development of science and technology details the government's policies regarding scientific and technical information and compares these with other major industrialized countries. A Chinese translation is available. ①

In planning and coordinating library and information services at the national level, every country needs to formulate a comprehensive national library and information policy targeted at supporting national development objectives. Intended as an aid to national planning for a sound library and information policy, this paper discusses the origin, definition, objectives, importance, principles and issues regarding a national library and information policy in the hope of generating further thought and discussion on this vitally important subject.

Origin

Discussion and formulation of national library and information policies, either in full or part, have been underway in some countries since the 1950s, but treatment in library literature has been sporadic and incomplete. The systematic promotion of a comprehensive national library and information policy in every country has been a major goal of the United Nations Educational, Scientific and Cultural Organization (UNESCO) in the 1970s under its UNISIST program for a "world science information system". The emphasis is to provide effective coordination between the development of library and information services, especially scientific and technical information, and the information needs of national development.

A review of UNESCO's activities in the promotion of library, information, documentation, and archive services in every country provides interesting insights into several major developments under the UNESCO banner. ② The UNISIST program was officially launched in 1971 after a four-year feasibility study undertaken in collaboration with the International Council of Scientific Unions

---

① *White Paper on the Science And Technology of Japan*: *Comparison of Science And Technology with other Countries And the Policy Decision of Japan*. Science And Technology Series, No. 8 (Taipei: Science and Technology Information Center of the National Science Council, 1983.) (In Chinese).

② J. Stephen Parker, *UNESCO And Library Development Planning* (London: The Library Association, 1985).

(ICSU). The program administered by the Division of Scientific Documentation and Information in the science sector of UNESCO emphasized scientific and technical information. To carry out the program, each country was asked to establish a national UNISIST committee and to select a national focal point. In 1974 came the NATIS (National Information System) program administered by the Department of Documentation, Libraries and Archives in the culture section of UNESCO. The emphasis of NATIS was somewhat broader in scope. It encompassed library, documentation and archive services and focused on national planning and development. Both UNISIST and NATIS promoted the idea of establishing a national information policy in each country in the service of national development.

To eliminate the duplication of the two overlapping programs within UNESCO, a decision was made in 1977 to incorporate NATIS into UNISIST and to place it under the administration of a new division called the General Information Programme which reports directly to the Assistant Director-General for Studies and Programming in the UNESCO Secretariat.

The new division recognizes the interdependence of libraries, information centers, documentation services and archives that make up the backbone of library and information services. It seeks to harmonize on a national scale the coordination, planning and functioning of infrastructures as an important concept in developing and implementing national information policies. Such policies are best placed within the overall context of national development policies in other fields and embodied in national development plans to ensure adequate attention, publicity and support. Of the five main themes of the General Information Programme of UNESCO below, the policy consideration tops all others:

1. promotion of the formulation of information policies and plans at national, regional, and international levels;
2. promotion and dissemination of methods, norms, and standards for information, handling;
3. contributions to the development of infrastructures;
4. contributions to the development of specialized information systems in all disciplines; and
5. promotion of the training and education of specialists in and users of information.

A number of UNESCO publications have discussed national information policies in greater detail. [1]

Definition

Although the formulation of information policy and plans at the national level has been strongly promoted by UNESCO under its UNISIST program, the definition of information policy is often unclear. The emphasis has been on scientific and technical information rather than on a wider context of information which include libraries and information services covering all subjects as well as publishing and other scholarly communications and information dissemination.

A national library and information policy must be broad in scope and coverage. It can be considered as a conscious attempt to direct and improve, on a long-term basis, the structure, organization, program, resources, and services of the nation's library and information systems and networks comprised of libraries, information centers, documentation services, archives, and related activities. The inclusion of publishers and information industries, both in the public and private sectors, in policy considerations is highly desirable.

Put simply, national library and information policy can be defined as statements or general principles for planned and coordinated development of the nation's library and information services, including publishing and information industries, in accordance with the existing conditions in the country and its information needs for national development. The policy should

---

[1] D. J. Urquhart, *National Information Policy*, NATIS National Information Systems (Paris: UNESCO, 1976). COM 76/NATIS/6. John Gray, *Information Policy Objectives*; UNISIST Proposals (Paris: UNESCO, 1974). SC/74/WS/3. Ines Wesley-Tanaskovic, *Guidelines on National Information Policy: Scope, Formulation and Implementation* (Paris: UNESCO, 1985). PGI-85443/14. 264

address the key issues in library and information services and provide administrative guidelines for long-range management planning, decision-making, and implementation.

Objectives

In considering the formulation of a national library and information policy, several important policy objectives come to mind. These include:

1. The promotion of the free flow and use of human knowledge for the benefit of both individuals and society.

2. The requirement that information from all sources, especially from the public sector, unless classified or restricted, should be made available as a national resource.

3. The principle of free and unrestricted use of library and information services by the general public on a not-for-profit basis and for charging reasonable fees for specialized information services.

4. The provision of timely and relevant information for decision-making to decision-makers and researchers at all levels of government and in all sectors of the society.

5. The recognition of the important and mutually complementary roles played by libraries, information centers, documentation services, and archives in the selection, collection, storage, analysis, retrieval, and dissemination of information.

6. The design of appropriate administrative structures and mechanisms to effectively coordinate major programs and activities as well as to monitor and evaluate results.

7. The determination of source and level of funding to adequately support library and information services.

Besides the above policy objectives, the primary purpose of a national information policy, stated by Guinchat and Menou,[1] is to maximize the effectiveness of the national information system, and in particular:

1. to work out the information needs of different socio-professional groups;

2. to establish priorities in regard to these needs;

3. to decide how the national information systems should be organized, what services should be provided and how this is to be done;

4. to constantly monitor the capacity of the national information infrastructure (i. e., all the human, material and financial resources devoted to scientific and technical information) to cover these needs;

5. to decide what measures are needed to enable the national information system to perform its role; and

6. to decide how the national information system should be further developed.

In addition to these main guidelines, Guinchat and Menou[2] also identified a number of specific policies dealing with many aspects of scientific and technical information:

1. development and improvement of primary publications and, more generally, of the availability of information and data;

2. expansion of document holdings and collections of data, and improved access to them;

3. access to foreign collections of documents and databases;

4. development of translation services;

5. bibliographic control, indexing and analysis of documents produced in the country;

6. development of documentation services (referral, retrospective searches, current awareness, SDI, etc) and information services;

7. coordination between the various information units and specialized subsystems;

8. development and standardization of equipment for the processing and communication of information;

---

[1] CIare Guinchat and Michel Menou, General Introduction to the Techniques of Information and Documentation Work (Paris: UNESCO, 1983), p. 314. ⁵Ibid., pp. 314 – 315.

[2] Ibid., pp. 314 – 315.

9. standardization of information techniques and products;
10. development of specialized manpower and training facilities;
11. financing of units and the pricing of their services;
12. preparation of appropriate legislation and regulations for information activities;
13. promotion of services and user education;
14. encouragement of research and development in the information science;
15. closer cooperation with other countries and participation in international networks.

Although this list of objectives, guidelines, and specific policies is by no means complete or inclusive, it provides some excellent examples at what a national library and information policy should aim.

Importance

The preceding portion of this paper documented the need for a national library and information policy. Such a policy is important for the following reasons:

1. It calls attention to the vital roles played by library and information services in national development.
2. It provides a general statement of direction for the development of library and information services.
3. It helps the coordination of planning and implementation of library and information services at the highest levels of the government.
4. It appeals to the government for adequate funding of library and information services.
5. It makes possible integrating the policy into the national development plans.
6. It invites the participation and input in policy formulation by government leaders, planners, representative users of information, and library and information professionals.

The mere formulation of a library and information policy by a wide range of interested and concerned constituencies helps to familiarize them with the work of library and information professions and to rally their support. A national library and information policy is a way to make certain that the country's information needs, or at least its priority needs, are satisfied as far as possible and that all available resources are utilized with maximum economy and effectiveness. This can only he done through a collective effort in the preparation and implementation of policy decisions, joint actions, compromises, and the coordination of activities.

Principles

It has been said that national library and information policy should be formulated with the information needs and the specific information environment of the countries in mind. Beyond the policy objectives and guidelines already mentioned which should be taken into consideration in policy formulation, a new additional general principles should be observed.

1. It should be based on actual situations and existing conditions of each country.

The information needs and the strategy for meeting them will differ in every country depending on the level of development and the infrastructure available. Often, this difference is dictated by the social, economic and political systems of the county. Allocation of priorities is necessary in countries having limited library and information resources and infrastructures.

2. It should support the information needs in national development.

As much as possible, a national library and information policy should be in concert with the development goals of the country. It should consider the established priorities in the national development plans and their information requirements. For maximum impact, national library and information policy should be incorporated into the national development plans with steps for implementation.

3. It should be formulated by a national commission at the highest government levels and be implemented by a national coordinating agency.

The importance of library and information services to national development should be a sufficient reason for the appointment of a national commission to formulate the national library and information policy. In Taiwan's case, for example, the commission should have membership from the executive and legislative branches of the government, the Directors of the "Central Library" and the Science and Technology Information Center of the "National Science Council", representatives of the economic and cultural planning and development councils, the Library Association of China, the publishers association, and users. In addition to formulating policies, the commission may also be empowered to develop a comprehensive plan for the development of the nation's library and information services, that is, the means for implementing the policy. Such a plan may call for the establishment of a national coordinating agency to oversee and monitor the implementations of the plan.

4. The policy should result in a well developed program for the development of the nation's library and information services and the infrastructures necessary for their provision.

Because a national policy is considered as a statement or general principle for planned and coordinated development of the nation's library and information services, the design of a program and budget for the attainment of policy objectives should be the next step. The program may include both long and medium-terms and be implemented under the oversight and coordination of the national coordinating agency. Again, in the case of Taiwan, such a coordinating agency may best be placed within the National Central Library which has played a leading role in the overall library development of the country. Should this be considered, the status of the National Central Library should be raised accordingly. The placing of the "Central Library", as it is now, under the Department of Social Education in the Ministry of Education is viewed by many as inappropriate and too low to fulfill its role as the national library. In policy considerations, the place of the National Central Library in the Government's hierarchy should be reviewed and, hopefully, adjusted upward.

5. It should emphasize the interdependence of all types of library and information services.

Although libraries, information centers, documentation services and archives have distinct purposes and functions, especially those with special missions, they also have many things in common and often can not get along without the others. To enhance the overall library and information services in a country the diversity of types should be respected and fostered while their common bonds are strengthened. Special encouragement should be given to cooperation and mutual support among libraries and information centers across the separate systems or subsystems at every level. In the development of information systems, not only scientific and technical information are important, other fields such as business, economics, industry, etc., should receive equal attention. A harmonized development of all information resources and services, not just scientific and technical information, is an important reason that the national library should be considered as the national coordinating agency.

6. It should ensure maximum availability and convenience of use for all information.

The polity should make certain that diversified library and information resources are available to every user regardless of their location, vocation, education or wealth. A comprehensive plan for the division of responsibility in acquisitions, cataloging, analysis, indexing, abstracting, storage, and dissemination of useful information should be centrally developed and coordinated. The methods of cooperative acquisitions which have been successfully implemented in many countries should be employed at both local and national levels. In the use of information, all unnecessary restrictions and barriers should be removed to facilitate easy access to library and information services by all users.

7. It should consider the impact of new library and information technologies.

For effective and efficient handling of library and information resources, which are growing by leaps and bounds, to better serve the information needs of users requires the application of appropriate library and information technologies which include computers, telecommunication, micrographics, videotext, and a score of other new developments. Recent breakthroughs in computers capable of processing Chinese characters are of great importance for library and information services in Taiwan. In planning for library automation, the successful example of OCLC (Online Computer Library Center) in the U.S.A. in the area of online shared cataloging, union catalog, interlibrary loan, etc., can serve as a model. The formulation and standardization of procedures, formats, rules, codes, systems, etc., should be established at the earliest possible stage to facilitate systems development and interconnection. In planning for library automation and networking, central coordination beginning at the earliest stage is highly desirable to maximize the cost-effectiveness of such undertakings.

8. It should encourage active participation in international cooperation and programs.

The recent developments in the international arena led by UNESCO and other international organizations such as the International Federation of Library Associations and Institutions (IFLA), the International Council of Archives (ICA), the International Federation of Documentation (FID), etc., have expedited the growth of international cooperation in library and information services. Participation in international programs and other cooperative activities through bilateral agreements or multi-lateral arrangements should be encouraged as long as these are judged as beneficial to all parties.

The availability of remote online access via satellite of large, computerized databases in the U.S. and elsewhere in the world has opened up new opportunities as well as problems. Searches of bibliographic databases often generate large numbers of citations for which the documents are not available locally, and the costs of searches are expensive. To save communication costs, certain heavily used foreign databases can he either purchased or leased to run in local computers at major libraries and information centers which then make the databases available to local users. Creation of domestic databases, complementing but not duplicating those already available, should be initiated and the efforts coordinated.

9. It should plan for the manpower needs in library and information services.

Because the manpower needs are sufficiently diverse, both in terms of levels and specializations, a wide range of educational and training programs should be planned. These may include formal education at the undergraduate and graduate levels, as well as a variety of in-service training and/or continuing education programs. The policy should encourage the upgrading of library and information education at all levels and the provision of more opportunities for in-service training and continuing education. Position classifications and pay scales for library and information workers of all levels and specializations should commensurate with the qualifications required for each and with comparable professions to attract and retain talented and dedicated staff.

10. It should promote the importance of library and information services and user education.

The promotion of library and information services and the education of library and information users should go hand-in-hand as both will increase the rate and level of library and information use. It is generally recognized that unless the library and information resources and services are fully utilized, their true value will remain under appreciated.

11. It should provide the basis for appropriate legislative actions pertaining to library and information services and to publishing and related activities.

The policy should call for a review and update, if needed, of existing laws and regulations pertaining to library and information services and to publishing and related information activities. New laws should be enacted and regulations promulgated to enforce the policy and to guarantee the free and unrestricted access to public information through library and information services.

Issues

Beyond the major principles to be considered, some of the vital issues confronting policy makers in Taiwan are:

(1) What should be the proper governing structure for library and information services at the national level? Which is the most preferable: centralization, decentralization or coordinated decentralization?

(2) Should the National Central Library be the coordinating agency for the planning and development of the nation's library and information services?

(3) Where should the National Central Library be in the administrative structure of the central Government?

(4) Should scientific and technical information be the only concern of a national information policy or should such policy cover the whole realm of library and information services?

(5) Should library and information services be offered free or at a fee? This issue also touches upon the question of public sector versus private sector in information services, and the debate between the advocates of free enterprise and those of free access. Is it more important for the public to have access to the information than for a private organization to profit from it?

Because each of the above issues is sufficiently major, this paper can not adequately consider the ramifications of these issues from all points of view. They are raised here to stimulate further discussions by library and government leaders as well as others concerned in Taiwan. It is hoped, that from a careful consideration of these issues, some consensus can be reached and compromises made. The end result will be a sound policy providing administrative guidelines for long-range management planning, decision-making, and implementation for the nation's libraries, information centers, documentation services, and archives.

第八部分　图书馆联网

Section VIII　Library Networking

建立台湾图书资料网刍议

一、前　言

最近笔者有幸应邀回台湾参加第二届建设会议，对台湾近年来在政经建设及文教发展各方面所获致的重大成就，有极深刻的印象；对上上下下坚苦卓绝，努力建设的精神，尤感钦佩。在会议期间曾抽暇参观几所图书馆及新迁到南港隶属"国科会"的科技资料中心，借机向台湾图书馆的部分同仁及先进请教，所见所闻，获益匪浅。根据笔者愚见，深感台湾的图书馆及资料中心在最近几年来，在质与量方面都有显著的进步；但这种进步，若以当前经济建设发展过程中的需要来衡量，则又嫌不足。当此人类知识文化与科学技术正在突飞猛进的时代，图书馆与资料中心的任务与使命不但大为加重，其地位亦显著提高。愈是发展程度高的国家，对于图书资料的需要愈为广泛与迫切。台湾经济与科技的发展，目前已达到相当程度，对于图书资料的需求，今后将日趋迫切。

二、图书馆的功能与使命

图书馆负有保存及延续人类知识与文化的使命。"保存"人类知识与文化的遗产固属重要，但仅保存是消极的、被动的；图书馆更重大的使命是积极的"延续"人类的知识与文化，使其发扬光大，造福人群。要想达到这种"承先启后"、"继往开来"的功能与使命，一方面有赖于图书馆同仁在观念及方法上的革新；另一方面亦有赖于社会对于图书馆的重视与支持，使之能发挥其应有的功能。

自从第二次世界大战以后，由于知识的发展与科学的进步，促成了出版品的大量增加；由于出版品的剧增，有人比喻20世纪70年代为"资料爆炸"的时代。这种知识与资料的剧增，对于图书馆及资料中心的功能与使命产生巨大的影响。第一，在过去，学者专家们钻研学问可以不依靠图书馆来供应图书资料，现在已不复可能；第二，科学与技术的加速发展有赖于图书资料的适时供应与有效支持；第三，面对浩如烟海的新知识与出版品，即使大规模的图书馆，要想尽量搜集，亦感力不从心；第四，除了搜集之外，对于图书资料的整理、分类、储藏、检索、流通及使用等，旧的观念与方法已不足应付。基于以上几点改变，世界各国的图书馆都在迅速蜕变与创新，以求赶上时代，担当起新时代图书馆所应担负的任务。

三、当前的趋势

近几年来，由于前述因素的影响，世界各国图书馆的发展有以下五点趋势，颇值我们参考借鉴：

（一）馆际间分工合作的加强。图书馆馆际间可以合作的项目甚多，如图书互借，联合目录的设置，分类采购搜集，及统一编目等，在国内外的图书馆间已有很多先例，其中不乏有相当成效者。当此出版品汗牛充栋且价格急剧上涨之时，欲使有限的经费、人力与设备能发挥最大的效果，实有赖于图书馆间的密切合作，一方面互通有无，相互支持；一方面分类采购，避免重复。这种有计划的合作是充实全国图书资料的一项极重要的工作，亟待推广及加强。

（二）新方法及技术的采用。由于图书馆藏书不断增加，业务量加大及人员增多，许多图书馆已纷纷采用科学的管理方式来处理一般业务。此外，由于科学技术发达，许多新颖的技术已逐渐为图书馆所采用，以扩充服务项目，提高工作效率，充分发挥图书馆的效能。此种技术目前已被使用者有摄影技术、复印技术、视听技术、计算机技术、及电讯技术等，其中有许多可值我们采用者。这些新技术若由各图书馆个别使用，也许很不经济；但若由若干图书馆联合使用，则不仅经济有效，更能促进图书馆的效能。

（三）特殊资料中心的设立。特殊资料中心（Specialized Information Center）的设立系由特别图书馆（Special Library）演变而来，其性质较之特别图书馆尤为专门。对于特殊资料的储存及检索较特别图书馆更为讲究。有些资料中心还将有关资料加以精简化，再个别的提供给某些特约的使用者。特殊资料中心有的按学科而设，有的按任务而设；有的隶属于图书馆，有的单独设立，情况各异。许多国家更设有全国性的科技资料中心以统筹及协调全国的科技资料及有关活动。"国科会"的科技资料中心即为一例。

（四）大规模目录及资料库的建立。因为图书资料的大量增加，为求有效控制，许多国家的国家图书馆已开始建立国家目录，力求完整齐全。许多学术团体、政府及私人机构亦分别编印各种索引或摘要，以应所需。这种工作非常必要，但亦十分艰巨，因此非一般图书馆或资料中心可以个别承当。目前这种大规模的目录及索引，如英美的 MARC（Machine-Readable Catalog）和举世闻名的化学摘要（Chemical Abstracts）等皆已陆续使用计算机作业，以节省人力及增广用途。

（五）图书资料网的建立。图书资料网的建立是馆际合作的加强与具体化，其规模可大可小，其组织与性质亦按个别需要及特殊情况而定。大抵在纵的方面可按地域来分，在横的方面可按学科、使命或图书馆的类别来分。纵与横之间的联系与合作可以逐步发展，由小而大，由简而繁，最后达到世界性的图书馆网，以促进国际图书资料的自由流通。目前联合国文教组织正为推动此一构想而努力。依台湾目前的情况，我们亟应计划及建立一个统一的图书资料网，使台湾的图书馆及资料中心能按照台湾需要做全面性的发展，使得有限的资源能发挥最大的效用；对内可促进台湾的建设与发展；对外可增强国际合作与文化交流。

四、各国的先例

有关图书资料网的建立，世界各国不乏先例。以美国之富裕及其图书资料的完备，对图书资料网的建立尚且不遗余力，这种例子值得我们借镜。美国立国的精神是以地方分权为主，加以土地面积广大，故其图书资料网的建立多由各州开始，目前著有成效者计有：新英格兰图书馆网、柯罗拉多学术图书馆图书处理中心、俄亥俄学院图书中心等。近年来全国性的图书资料网亦逐渐分科设立，其进行已有相当成绩者计有：以国家医学图书馆为首的生物医学通讯网、以国家农业图书馆为首的农业科学资料网，由国会图书馆主持的国家采购及编目计划和全国刊物资料系统等。

除此以外，国会图书馆尚将全国图书目录的作业计算机化，其所创用的 MARC 格式，逐渐为世界各国所采用，促成了各国间国家目录计算机作业的格式划一。为了要进一步地促进全国各图书馆及资料中心的合作与发展，美国政府在最近还成立了一个全国图书馆及资料科学委员会，来计划及推行全国图书资料发展的工作。美国政府的商业部亦设立一所全国科技资料服务中心，来搜集全国的科技研究与发展报告，予以整理、分类与摘要，再编入分类索引半月刊及综合索引月刊，印发全国各地，使得有关科技的新知识资料能够迅速而广泛地被流传与使用。

在英国，建立一个全国图书资料网的计划目前正在实施中。除了地方性的图书馆以外，政府最近尚将历史悠久的大英博物馆图书馆与其他四所国立图书馆，一同归并入一个新的体制之中名之为大英图书馆，重新分划各图书馆的职责，将其性质重叠者予以合并或裁减，以建立一个切实有效的全国图书资料网。

在加拿大，1969年颁布的国家图书馆法授权国家图书馆馆长（National Librarian）以调协全国图书馆发展之责。对于全国图书资料网的建立产生了积极有效的作用。

在亚洲国家中，首先计划设立全国图书资料网者当以印度尼西亚为首。印度尼西亚政府在第一个五年发展计划（1969—1973年）中即特别强调改进科技资料供应与服务的重要性。由于图书馆界同仁的努力及国外专家的协助，一个全国图书资料网的建立计划已经拟定。因为印度尼西亚尚无一所国家图书馆，故有关全国图书资料的搜集及目录编印等工作，将交由四所已具有规模的图书馆去分别负责，并将此四所图书馆置于一个新设置的国家图书馆长之下，由其统筹计划及协调全国图书资料网的发展。

五、建立图书资料网的步骤

有鉴于当前世界趋势及台湾的需要，笔者认为建立一个统一的图书资料网实在是当务之急，刻不容缓。为了抛砖引玉，特将个人一点浅陋的构想提出来以请教于台湾图书馆同仁及学者专家。

（一）在台湾行政主管部门下设立台湾图书资料网计划执行委员会（以下简称委员会）。委员十五人，由行政主管遴聘，任期两年，连聘得连任。

1. 主任委员由现任"中央图书馆"馆长兼任。

2. 第一期委员中之半数，任期一年，以后每年得改聘委员会委员之半数。

3. 委员会之成员除"中央图书馆"馆长外，应包括科学、教育、经济、军事、交通等主管部门及科技资料中心等六单位之有关业务高级主管各一人，图书馆从业人员六人及出版界二人。

4. 委员会得依实际需要设立秘书处及有关科组以掌理计划、研究、发展、考核、及财政之责。

5. 委员会之经费得由秘书处按照需要逐年编列预算呈请行政主管部门支付。

（二）本委员会应尽速拟定台湾图书馆及资料中心的政策与发展计划，包括台湾图书资料网的建立，呈请行政主管部门核准后颁布施行。

（三）本委员会应负有督导台湾图书资料网建立与发展之责。

（四）本委员会应根据实际情况及需要将台湾各主要图书馆及资料中心之职责作下列重点分配，例如：

1. "中央图书馆"应有下列各项职责：

A、台湾图书目录中心。

B、台湾期刊目录中心。

C、台湾官书目录中心。

D、台湾图书期刊官书编目中心。

E、台湾联合图书目录中心。

F、国际图书之交换与合作。

2. 科技资料中心应有下列各项职责：

A、台湾科技资料之搜集、分类、储藏、检索、流通、使用等。

B、台湾科技资料目录中心。

C、台湾期刊联合目录中心。

D、国际科技资料之搜集与交换。

3. 工业技术研究院图书馆应为台湾工业技术之资料及服务中心。

4. 中山研究院应为台湾军事科学及技术之图书馆及资料中心。

5. 其他各图书馆应分别着重下列各学科之图书与期刊之搜集：

A、台大图书馆——自然科学、人文科学。

B、台大医学院——医学、生物。

C、台大法学院——法律及联合国文献等。

D、"中央研究院"傅斯年图书馆——历史、语言。

E、政大——社会科学。

F、师大——教育。

G、成大——工程。

H、台湾清华——原子能、核子科学。

I、交通——电讯。

J、中兴——农业。

K、台湾中大——地球物理。

L、"台北故宫博物馆"——古籍、珍本、档案等。

（五）本委员会应拟定台湾各图书馆馆际互借及资料流通之办法。寓辅助于奖励，应按每年出借图书之多寡订定经费辅助办法。

（六）本委员会应在台湾各地指定若干图书馆或资料中心，设立统一采购及编目中心，其经费不敷之数得由本委员会酌予补助。

（七）本委员会应在台湾各地选定若干地点适合的图书馆或资料中心，协助其装设电传打字机以建立馆际通讯网，加强馆际的联系。

（八）本委员会应考虑设立一计算机作业中心，专供各图书馆及资料中心之用。

（九）本委员会应根据台湾专业人才的需要，拟订长短程图书资料专业人员的培养与训练计划，协助及辅导各有关训练机构，以加强专业人员职前教育及在职训练。

以上各点构想仍以第一点为最重要，希望行政当局能采纳实施。有了委员会的组织，则其他计划及实行细则皆可由委员会成员集思广益，逐项加以制定，付诸实施。

六、结 论

加强图书馆及资料中心的效能，固有赖于政府的辅导、社会的支持，以提高其地位，增加其经费，改善其设备，增加其图书的搜集与收藏；但图书馆及资料中心本身对于观念与方法的革新，对于专业人员训练的加强，以及馆际间的合作等，亦不容忽视。除此以外，由于图书资料的急遽增加及社会对于图书馆及资料中心的需求日渐增多，欲使有限的经费、人力、与设备，得以发挥最大的效能，有赖台湾各图书馆及资料中心的同仁，明于本身职责之艰巨，在行政主管部门辅助与督导下，设立一统一的计划及协调的机构，以拟定台湾图书资料长短程的发展计划，并将台湾各图书馆及资料中心纳入一个整体的图书资料网内，使得台湾的图书馆及资料中心能配合台湾的需要作全面的发展。

Sharing Information Resources through Computer
——Assisted Systems And Networking

Introduction

Although information is regarded as an inexhaustible resource, making it fully available and easily accessible in meeting the diversified needs of its users requires that it be collected, organized, and shared. There is an economical reason, too, for the sharing of information resources, not only for the information "poor" countries, but also for the information "rich." With the continued rise in both the quantity and cost of publications, the shrinking of library budgets, and the constant broadening of user demands resulting from the expanding frontiers of knowledge, it becomes quite clear that finite library budgets have made it increasingly difficult to meet the infinite demands of users.

Library cooperation in sharing resources is not a new concept. In fact, many such activities have long been in existence: shared cataloging, reciprocal borrowing and photocopying, interlibrary loan, cooperative acquisitions, exchange of duplicates, cooperative storage and delivery, etc. Many of these cooperative activities have been discussed in the preceding sessions. This paper intends to discuss one of the recent developments in resources sharing: Computer-assisted information systems and networking.

Because of the introduction of computers and the rapid advancement in telecommunications technology, fast and cost-effective ways of sharing information and resources are now possible on a far greater scale than was known before. The development of computer-assisted information systems and networks is of great importance for world-wide cooperation in resources sharing involving both developed and developing countries.

The development of computer-assisted information systems and networks has three interrelated components: (1) the creation and growth of many machine-readable databases capable of on-line, interactive searching from remote terminals; (2) the development of computerized library networks connecting libraries and computer facilities and databases; and (3) the establishment of mission-oriented national and international information systems based on a well-conceived model developed for the International Nuclear Information System (INIS).

Each of these components will be discussed in some detail below. Particular attention will be given to their implications for developing countries. The future interconnection of information resources, databases, library networks, and international information systems to form a world-wide information network is a distinct possibility in the 1980s.

The Creation And Growth of Machine-Readable Databases

Because of the continued increase in the number of bibliographical records and in the cost and time required to prepare for their publication manually, many abstracting and indexing services and publishers have turned to computers for relief. The result has been a fast growth in the number and size of machine-readable databases in the last 15 years. The important by-products of these databases are their ability to provide a variety of bibliographical services such as on-line, interactive search and selective dissemination of information (SDI) service.

According to the 1976 estimate of the National Federation of Abstracting and Indexing Services, there were 2,500 indexing and abstracting services in existence world-wide; of these, about 200 were in machine-readable form, and most of these were capable of being searched from remote terminals.① Although most of the databases are for bibliographical information, there are others which cover news articles, full texts of legal cases and statutes, numeric data, and graphic representations.②

Despite their short history, machine-readable databases have become a major bibliographical and reference tool in the U. S., Canada, Europe, and some other parts of the world. To illustrate the phenomenal growth of machine-readable databases in the U. S., the experience of Lockheed Information System, a large commercial on-line database service center, is used. The table below shows that, beginning with only one database and 200,000 records in 1965, Lockheed now has nearly 30 databases containing a total of 8 million records. Using an index of 100 for 1970, in 1975 the search volume had grown to 15,000 and the cost had dropped to 20.

Table 1. The Growth of Lockheed's DIALOG③

Year	No. of Databases	Size of Databases	Rate of Increase in Searches	Rate of Decrease in Cost
1965	1	200,000	...	...
1970	...	...	100	100
1973	11	2,100,000	2,000	40
1975	30	8,000,000	15,000	20

The impact of the phenomenal growth of machine-readable databases has resulted in the following: (1) more on-line terminals established at an increasing number of locations to facilitate remote access; (2) more effective communication techniques; (3) improved standardization and cooperation among database producers; (4) expanded bibliographical services; (5) increased demand for document delivery service, interlibrary loan, and photocopying service; and (6) greater needs for resources sharing and networking among information systems.

Before leaving the discussion of databases, mention must be made of a particularly important one, the Machine-Readable Cataloging (MARC) created by the Library of Congress. The MARC format, designed to represent bibliographical data in machine-readable form, has since been adopted as the national and international standard. The MARC database has been used widely in the U. S. as a cataloging and bibliographical tool, as a source for interlibrary loan, acquisitions, and circulation, and for as many as a score of other applications. An increasing number of countries, including a few of the developing ones, are now producing their national bibliographies in MARC format. Many countries are also exchanging MARC tapes.

Because of the high costs involved in creating and maintaining machine-readable databases, it is considered impractical for most developing countries (and even some small, developed ones) to undertake such projects, except for producing their national bibliographies and periodical indexes in machine-readable format. They should, instead, make use of the large databases in developed countries, either off-line or through on-line terminals.

In recent years, UNESCO and some developed countries have conducted a number of experiments or pilot projects to test the usefulness of providing SDI service to researchers in

---

① Donald G. Fink, "The Impact of Technology in Library Science", *Special Libraries*, Vol. 68, no. 2 (February 1977), p. 78.

② Martha E. Williams, "The Impact of Machine-Readable Data Bases on Library and Information Services", *Information Processing & Management*, Vol. 13, no. 2 (1977), pp. 95–96.

③ Lee G. Burchinal, "Bringing the American Revolution On-Line Information Science and National R & D", *Bulletin of the American Society for Information Science*, Vol. 2, No. 8 (March 1976), p. 27.

selected developing countries. The results are generally favorable. ① However, because of the high telecommunication costs and use charges, the volume of searches to be made by developing counties may remain low unless there is a special reduced rate for users from the developing countries.

The Development of Computerized Library Networks

Another important phenomenon of recent times which facilitates the sharing of resources is the development of computerized library networks, through which machine-readable databases become a viable information resource accessible to a large number of users, both near and far.

According to the recent report by Susan K. Martin, there are twenty-five large library networks in the U.S., all relying on computers for resource sharing. If one adds the many other non-computerized library networks, there is hardly any library which does not belong to a library network. Some, in fact, belong to several networks for different purposes. Because of the proliferation of library networks, a Council of Computerized Library Networks was founded in 1973 to discuss the need for communication among networks. ②

Of the twenty-five computerized library networks, the most successful and best known is the Ohio College Library Center (OCLC). As the name implies, OCLC was first incorporated (in 1965) as a network for academic libraries in Ohio. It became on-line in 1971. Two years later, its membership was enlarged to include out-of-state libraries. Today it has over eight hundred libraries and fifteen hundred on-line terminals, representing almost every type and size of library in forty-two states. ③ The main operation of OCLC at present is the on-line shared cataloging and processing system. Other operations currently under development by OCLC are a serials check-in subsystem, an interlibrary loan subsystem, a circulation subsystem, and an acquisitions subsystem. In cooperation with the Council on Library Resources and the Library of Congress, 200,000 serial records will soon be made available through OCLC by the Conversion of Serials Project (CONSER).

While OCLC has scored an initial success in the U.S., the development of computerized library networks in other countries, particularly the developed ones, had also made good progress. Besides the many local and national library and information networks already in existence in many countries, a number of multinational information networks have been established. Two well-known ones are ARPANET and BSRO/SDS. The former is a computer-communication system developed cooperatively by more than two dozen research and development organizations under the sponsorship of the U.S. Advanced Research Projects Agency. At present, it embraces sixty-five digital computers in forty-five locations in the U.S., and extends to Norway and London. ④ The latter, the Space Documentation Service of the European Space Agency, is a star-shaped network with its central computer facility at Frascati, Italy, connected by private leased lines to terminals located throughout most of western Europe, including Spain and Scandinavia. The network is currently operating at a level of 25,000 searches per year of some twelve databases containing around 5 million bibliographical records. ⑤

Another large network, EURONET, created by the nine western countries of the European

---

① UNISIST Pilot Projects for the Establishment of SDI Services, "*UNISIST Newsletter*, Vol. 2, no. 4 (1974), p. 2;" Computer-based Information Services for Science and Technology, "*NAS-CONICET (Argentina) Science Cooperation Program: Report of Activities* (Washington, D. C.: National Academy of Sciences, 1976), pp. 36–43; Charles P. Bourne, "Computer-based Reference Services as an Alternative Means to Improve Resources — Poor Local Libraries in Developing Countries," *International Library Review*, Vol. 9, no. 1 (1977), pp. 43–50.

② Susan K. Martin, *Library Networks 1976–77* (White Plains, N. Y.: Knowledge Industry Publications, 1976), p. 41.

③ *OCLC Newsletter*, no. 106 (4 February 1977), pp. 1 & 4.

④ J. C. R. Licklider, "A Network of Computer and Information Systems," *National and International Networks of Libraries, Documentation, and Information Centers*, AGARD Conference Proceedings, no. 158 (Paris: NATO Advisory Group for Aerospace Research and Development, 1975), p. 21.

⑤ John Page, "International STI Networks: Promises and Problems", *Bulletin of the American Society for Information Science*, Vol. 2, no. 4 (November 1975), pp. 12.

Economic Community, is in the active planning stage and should become operational in 1978. This network is being planned according to a very broad concept, concerned not merely with the provision of a modern communication network, but also with a true sharing and coordination of information resources among the member countries. ① When established, it will have switching nodes in Frankfurt, London, Paris, and Rome and concentrators in Amsterdam, Brussels, Copenhagen, and Dublin.

For developing countries (and some small but developed ones), although local and national library and information networks have been developed largely without computers and sophisticated telecommunication systems, there is an increasing possibility that they may be connected to international networks through a designated national node in each of their countries. A recent example of this is Morocco, which has been connected to ESRO/SDS by a leased-line. ②

The so-called "network parasitology" concept employed successfully by Finland is another good example applicable to developing countries. Since 1971, the Helsinki University of Technology Library has been able to provide SDI and retrospective searches by using the computers and databases located at the Royal Institute of Technology Library, the Biomedical Documentation Center in Stockholm, and the Technological University of Denmark in Copenhagen. Each of the 120 SDI clients who pays about $100 for the annual subscription will receive approximately 100 SDI printouts during the year. By using telephone connections through the Tymnet link in Brussels to Palo Alto, California, the Helsinki Library can also perform on-line retrospective searches for its clients at an average cost of $30-40 per search. ③

Other instances of networking in developing countries that are worth mentioning are the telex networks established in several Latin American countries. The best known one is the Argentine Telex Network for Scientific and Technical Information, which was initiated in 1971 under the U. S.—Argentina Science Cooperation Program. The Telex network connects the principal libraries and documentation centers in Argentina. In addition, the network center in Buenos Aires is linked to a number of cooperating libraries in the U. S. and some other countries, with the purpose of improving access to and delivery of technical information resources within Argentina as well as from the U. S., and, eventually, from other countries in Latin America and Europe. ④

The Establishment of International Information Systems

While the development of both the machine-readable databases and the computerized networks is in progress, there is another important development being undertaken by several international and intergovernmental organizations to establish mission-oriented information systems on a global basis. The first of these is the International Nuclear Information System (INIS) established in 1970 by the International Atomic Energy Agency as a cooperative system to handle information related to the peaceful applications of atomic energy.

During the process of planning and designing INIS, several important principles were conceived and agreed upon by its planning team. These principles, which have since been adopted as a model for several other international information systems such as the International Information System for the Agricultural Sciences and Technology (AGRIS) and the International Information System for the Development Science (DEVSIS), are: (1) decentralization of the task of identifying and recording information as it is produced, each participating nation (or region) being responsible for reporting what is produced in its own territory; (2) centralized merging of material

---

① Ibid., p. 13.
② W. A. Martin, "Maximizing the Use of an Information Service in an International Environment," *Advancement in Retrieval Technology as Related to Information Systems*, AGARD Conference Preprint, no. 207 (Paris: NATO Advisory Group for Aerospace Research and Development, 1976), pp. 7, 2.
③ Elin Tornudd, "Benefits from Network 'Parasitology'", *UNESCO Bulletin for Libraries*, Vol. 30, No, 4 (July – August 1976), pp. 206 – 9.
④ "The Argentine Telex Network for Scientific and Technical Information", *NAS-CONICET (Argentina) Science Cooperation Program: Report of Activities*, pp. 1 – 35.

reported by the different input centers (national focal points), the task being performed in an international agency through international financing; (3) output products tailored to the needs of advanced institutions with computer facilities, as well as printed (or microfilmed) indexes and abstracts that can be used by institutions without such facilities, and by individual scientists; (4) back-up service of photocopies or microfiches to ensure availability of texts; (5) products available at low cost and all charges payable in local currencies; (6) international management, based on consultation with all participants; (7) engagement of governments to ensure official support and the availability and infusion of relevant government publications and reports; and (8) utilization of an internationally accepted standard bibliographical format to permit future interconnection among various international information systems. ①

The model stipulated above has many important features, some of which are of special benefit to developing countries. First, it makes each participating country responsible for reporting the relevant publications in its territory, thereby preventing duplication of effort and ensuring full coverage. Second, since each participating country is to bear the cost of initial reporting, countries with a larger volume of publication will pay more, while countries with a smaller volume will pay less. This apportionment of costs favors developing countries and therefore encourages them to participate. Third, the central processing of bibliographical records in an international center supported by international funding is more economical than for each country to attempt to process them locally. By means of central processing, bibliographical information from all participating countries can be quickly merged and made available worldwide. Furthermore, such processing helps to enforce accepted international standards in bibliographical format and reporting, and provides training opportunities for information workers in developing countries.

In promoting the establishment of international mission-oriented information systems and the application of methods, norms, and standards which will maximize the inter-compatibility of all systems and facilitate their interconnections, UNESCO has made a significant contribution through its UNISIST programs, whose aims are to coordinate existing trends towards cooperation and to act as a catalyst for the necessary development of a world-wide information network.

Conclusion

It is clear that a new era for resource sharing has arrived. To take advantage of machine-readable data bases and the opportunity for greater resource sharing through computerized networking and international information systems, great care must be given to standardization and system compatibility. The development of information infrastructure in each country is also a necessity for effective resource sharing.

Since knowledge has no boundaries, all countries should try to make the knowledge produced in their territories bibliographically accountable either by manual system or by computer. The imbalance of geographical and language coverage of existing machine-readable databases should be corrected to include more non-"west" publications.

While the bibliographical accessibility is bound to improve as a direct result of the development in computer-assisted systems and networks, several major impacts on library, documentation and information services in developing countries may also be expected. First is the likely increase in the demand for improved document delivery service. This has, indeed, been felt by libraries in those countries where on-line databases are used. The second is the growing language problem to be faced by libraries and their patrons because of the expanded language coverage by many databases. Both translation service and information on available translations will become necessary. The third is the need for training of database searchers and users. The fourth is the problem concerning the payment in "hard" currencies or in the form of UNESCO coupons.

---

① John E. Woolston, "International Information Systems: Their Relation to Economic and Social Development", paper presented at the International Symposium on Information Systems: Connection and Compatibility, Varna, Bulgaria, 30 September – 3 October 1974 (IAEASM – 189/1), pp. 1 – 2.

And, finally, even though the costs for international telecommunications and the charges for database use have declined in recent years, it is still considered very expensive for researchers in developing countries. A reduced rate or some kind of subsidy for users from nonprofit organizations in developing countries is highly recommended.

A Sketch for a Computerized National Library And Information Network

Introduction

Library and information services in Taiwan, has entered a new era with the successful development of computer terminals and software packages which are capable of processing both Chinese characters and the Roman alphabet. Although in the past several years the use of computers for library and information work in Taiwan has been making good progress, the applications were limited to library materials in the Roman alphabet. The complexity of the Chinese language makes transliterations into Roman script inadequate and unsatisfactory. Now that both Chinese characters and the Roman alphabet can be processed by computers at the same time, coupled with the encouragement of the Chinese Government to apply computers more widely in government, business, industry, education, and research, we can foresee an accelerated use of computers in library and information work in the coming year. The holding of this international workshop on Chinese library automation is an encouraging manifestation of this movement.

Over the years I have been watching the spread of library automation in Taiwan. In a paper I wrote in 1974,[1] I proposed the formation of a National Library and Information Network. The idea was prompted by the development of national library and information services in the U. S. A., Great Britain, Canada and other countries. At that time, OCLC was still a local system and on-line search of remote databases was still in its infancy. Networking without computer and telecommunication linkage was somewhat fragile. The recent advancement of computer and telecommunication technologies and their expanded applications in library and information work have, however, greatly improved the network environment, particularly the computerized networks.

Drawing from successful experiences in computerized library and information networks in the U. S. A., this paper seeks to outline a computerized National Library and Information Network in Taiwan. Since no two countries are alike and the specific network environments varies from country to country, the proposed network will be Chinese in character taking into consideration the special situation and needs in Taiwan. Due to the shortage of time in preparing this paper, only a sketch of the proposed network is presented. It is intended for preliminary discussions only. Hopefully, through discussions and further studies, more complete and refined design for a computerized National Library and Information Network may result.

Current Library Automation in Taiwan

The recent paper of Margaret C. Fung, "State of the Art: Library Automation in Taipei", offered a detailed account of the history, development and present status of library automation in Taiwan.[2] The paper also described some of the basic requirements in processing library materials in the Chinese language and the several approaches currently available for inputting.

Of all the library automation projects in Taiwan as described by Fung many have been developed by individual libraries with their particular needs in mind. Common among these are serial control systems, acquisition systems, and cataloging systems. In addition, a number of computerized databases have been built for the storage and retrieval of bibliographical and management information on some special subjects or areas.

---

[1] Hwa-Wei Lee, "Suggestions for the Establishment of a National Library And Information Network", *Central Daily News*, 26 – 27 February 1974. In Chinese.

[2] Margaret C. Fung, "State of the Art: Library Automation in Taipei", paper presented at the 46th General Conference of the International Federation of Library Associations and Institutions, Manila, Philippines, August 18 – 23, 1980.

Most important of the recent developments in library automation is the formation of the Library Automation Working Group with the aim of developing a national plan for library automation and implementing it. The Working Group, although not exactly the same as the one proposed in my 1974 paper, however, has a similar purpose in mind.

Already the group, which consists of librarians, information scientists, and computer scientists, has drawn up a Plan for a National Information Service System.① The plan was subsequently adopted by the National Central Library in April 1980 and is being implemented under its auspices with the assistance of the Working Group. The plan which has a completion date of 1983 consists of the following four stages:②

I. Automation for Chinese library materials.
1. Research on Chinese Machine-Readable Cataloging (Chinese MARC) format:
   1.1. Revision of the cataloging rules for Chinese library materials.
   1.2. Application for use in Taiwan of the International Standard Book Numbers (ISBN) and the International Standard Serial Numbers (ISSN).
   1.3. Compilation of a list of subject headings for Chinese library materials.
   1.4. Development of Chinese MARC format.
2. Development of a database for Chinese library materials:
   2.1. Development of Chinese MARC database.
      2.1.1. A union catalog of Chinese books.
      2.1.2. A union list of Chinese periodicals.
      2.1.3. A union catalog of other materials such as government documents, technical reports, research papers, etc.
      2.1.4. A retrieval system for Chinese library materials.
   2.2. Development of databases for Chinese library materials in various subjects.
      2.2.1. Compilation of a thesaurus.
      2.2.2. Compilation of indices and abstracts.
      2.2.3. Development of a retrieval system for subject databases.
3. Training of library and information service personnel.

II. Automation for Western library materials:
1. Development of Western MARC database:
   1.1. Acquisition of the U.S. Library of Congress MARC records (LC MARC) and others.
   1.2. Establishment of a database of other Western books not included in the LC MARC.
   1.3. Development of a union catalog of Western books.
   1.4. Making use of information retrieval systems developed by information networks abroad.
2. Development of various subject databases for Western library materials:
   2.1. Acquisition of selected subject databases from abroad.
   2.2. Development of subject databases locally by division of labor.
   2.3. Development of ail information retrieval system for subject databases in Western languages.
3. Training of library and information service personnel. (Same as 1.3.)

III. Development of library management systems:
1. Acquisition.
2. Circulation.
3. Library administration.

---

① National Central Library, *Plan for a National Information Service System* (Taipei: National Central Library, 1980). In Chinese.

② "Project for Library Automation", *National Central Library Newsletter*, Vol. 12 No. 2 (August 1980), pp. 117–119. In Chinese.

IV. Planning for a national information network:
1. Implementation of an on-line system.
2. Selective dissemination of information (SDI) service.

The above plan, although appearing to be quite ambitious, has had a number of projects in the first stage undertaken and now near completion. The ground has thus been laid for the planning and development of the projects in the latter stages. In the light of experience gained in library automation in the U. S. it is felt that the best approach to handle most of the projects in the latter stages is to implement them through the framework of a computerized National Library and Information Network using a combination of modified OCLC and Lockheed models.

Design for a Computerized National Library and Information Network

The geographical area in Taiwan seems to favor a single, unified National Library and Information Network in order to achieve the economics of scale as well as operation efficiency in library automation. With the advent of computer and telecommunication technologies which are increasingly available in Taiwan under the Government's encouragement and the successful development of input and output devices which can process library materials and information in both Chinese and Western languages, a computerized national network is not only possible now, but is necessary to take advantage of the gigantic power these technologies can offer in information processing, storage, retrieval, and transmission.

In designing such a computerized National Library and Information Network in Taiwan one must take into consideration the specific network environment there and profit from the experience of network development in other countries. For discussion purposes a few of the basic considerations for network development are given below:

I. In the building of an on-line national union catalog, some of the successful features of the OCLC model[1] can be adapted, they are:

1. The concept of on-line shared cataloging is probably the best way to build a national union catalog by dividing labor and pooling resources. (Approximately 84% of OCLC cataloging records are contributed by participating libraries, only 16% from LC MARC.)[2]

2. The concept of having one central database for all cataloged materials regardless of languages, forms, and types.

3. The concept of modulization in the systems design which enables the addition of other subsystems such as serial control, interlibrary loan, acquisition, circulation, etc. to enhance the usage of the on-line union catalog.

4. The concept of accessibility to the on-line union catalog and affordability by all types of libraries and information centers regardless of their sizes.

5. The ability of the shared cataloging system to provide custom-printed catalog cards, and other products to participating libraries.

6. The method of sharing the cost of operations by participating libraries as determined by the number of uses made by each.

7. The concept of open communication from the participating libraries to governance, and accountability from governance to participating libraries.

II. In addition to having an on-line national union catalog, the Network should endeavor to provide on-line access to as many domestic computerized databases as possible and to selected

---

[1] OCLC was founded in 1967 by the Ohio College Association and was originally called the Ohio College Library Center. As a result of its fast growth from a state network to a national network, its name was changed to OCLC, Inc. in 1977. Today OCLC operates an on-line computer network used by over 2,200 libraries in 50 states, Canada, and other countries. OCLC's database, the on-line union catalog, contains more than 6 million bibliographic records for books, serials, audiovisual materials, maps, manuscripts, scores, sound recordings, and other library materials. There are over 65 million location symbols. The database grows at a rate of about 25,000 records per week. Of these approximately 21,000 are provided by participating libraries; the remainder comes from the Library of Congress MARC records.

[2] LC MARC refers to the format of the Machine-Readable Cataloging (MARC) records of the Library of Congress.

foreign databases.

1. The development of separate, specialized, domestic, computerized databases should be encouraged but coordinated to avoid unnecessary duplication and overlap as well as to achieve the use of a standard format in input and in database structure.

2. By special arrangement and proper compensation the network should acquire the files of such domestic databases and should use the Lockheed, SDC, or BRS models[①] to make these databases available for on-line access. All databases built with a common standard format can be merged into one file to facilitate searches.

3. A cost analysis should be made to determine which of the following modes of operation for accessing foreign databases is more cost effective and efficient. Obviously, the projected volume of such searches is a major factor in the cost analysis.

   a. To subscribe or lease the tapes of selected foreign databases and store them in the networks computer for domestic access.

   b. To provide direct access via communication satellite to databases stored in Lockheed, SDC, or BRS.

   c. A proper combination of 1) and 2) above.

III. Since the National Central Library in Taipei has played a prominent role in the development of library and information services in Taiwan it seems to be logical and desirable to vest the responsibility of the governance of the computerized National Library and Information Network to the National Central Library which will then he responsible for seeking the funds necessary for the operation of the network and for coordinating the activities related to the development of the network. Some of the operational considerations of the network are:

1. The National Central Library should seek the advice of a network advisory board with two-thirds of its members elected by participating libraries and the other one-third appointed by the Director of the National Central Library, all to serve a three-year staggered term.

2. The National Central Library should develop and establish the appropriate administrative office to plan, develop, manage, and evaluate the national network.

3. Whenever appropriate, the National Central Library may delegate or contract other agencies to undertake specific tasks for the network. For example, the Scientific and Technological Information Center of the National Science Council may be asked to administer the computerized databases and information search service, the Library Association of China may be contracted to organize education and training programs for staff members of network libraries, and the nation's library schools may be involved in research projects concerning the network.

4. In view of the many long-term benefits of a computerized National Library and Information Network and its impact in furthering national development, the Government should endeavor to provide adequate funding for the establishment and operation of the network. The investment in this is very small indeed if compared with other government projects, but the return will be immeasurable and the effect will be far reaching.

Conclusion

This paper has thus far touched upon a very important part of library automation, that is networking. Because of the limited time available to write this paper, many thoughts expressed therein are very sketchy. It is my firm belief, however, the need for a computerized National Library and Information Network is self evident and the timing for its initiation is just right. It is hoped that some of the suggestions made here will lead to further discussions and actions. To set the course of library automation through a well conceived plan under the framework of a National Library and Information Network will undoubtedly expedite the process of development and achieve the optimum results.

---

① Lockheed Information Systems operates one of the world's largest online information services-Dialog-which manages more than 120 databases containing a total of 40 million bibliographic citations and abstracts. Other major vendors of computerized databases in the U. S. are SDC's Orbit, BRS, etc.

Planning Process And Considerations for a Statewide Academic Libraries Information System in Ohio[①]

Ohio: The Birthplace of OCLC

Cooperation for automation and resource sharing among academic libraries, especially the state-supported university libraries, has been firmly established in Ohio since the 1960s. The most important accomplishment was the establishment of OCLC in 1967. Originally, OCLC was the abbreviation for Ohio College Library Center, an entity founded by a group of academic libraries whose institutions were members of the Ohio College Association. Under the leadership of the Inter-University Library Council (IULC), an informal organization of the library directors of state-supported universities, initial funding was obtained from the Ohio Board of Regents, the planning and coordinating agency for all state-supported institutions of higher education. OCLC's success in creating a central bibliographic database of MARC (Machine-Readable Cataloging) records to facilitate online, shared cataloging by participating libraries induced many other libraries to join. Within fifteen years, OCLC had become a multi-type library network. The membership had grown from 48 in 1967 to 2,934 in 1982, covering every state of the Union.[②] The expanding membership caused OCLC to change its name and governance. Today, OCLC stands for the Online Computer Library Center. As of June 30, 1988, OCLC had 9,400 participating libraries of all type and sizes in 50 states and 23 other countries with 17,748,222 bibliographic records, making it the world's largest bibliographic database. In 1987–1988 alone, 21.9 million books and other materials were cataloged into the database, and 3.78 million transactions for interlibrary loan were handled.[③]

By the late 1970s and early 1980s, with the advances in mini-computer technologies, many libraries found it desirable to develop or acquire local library systems for other library functions not provided by OCLC. In 1988, there were 50 library systems vendors in the market,[④] most claiming to include a variety of integrated library functions. Additionally, many of these systems are capable of networking among a group of libraries on a local or regional basis. Even with local systems, most libraries still participate in OCLC for shared cataloging and interlibrary loans. In Ohio, for example, of the thirteen state-supported universities and two medical colleges, all of which are members of OCLC, one has a locally developed system and eight others have acquired local systems (Table I). Nearly all are capable of providing an online public access catalog (OPAC), acquisitions, fund accounting, circulation, and serials control.

Table I AUTOMATED LIBRARY SYSTEMS IN OHIO PUBLIC UNIVERSITIES

University of Akron	Virginia Tech Library System
Ohio University	Virginia Tech Library System
Youngstown State Univ.	Virginia Tech Library System
Bowling Green State Univ.	LS/2 (quasi-orphan)

---

① This article was written in the midst of the process, March 1989. As this volume is compiled, the process is nearing fruition and an "Afterword" is appended to update this report.

② Kathleen L. Maciuszko, *OCLC: A Decade of Development*, 1967–1977 (Littleton, Colorado: Libraries Unlimited, 1984), pp. 17 & 219.

③ *OCLC Annual Report, 1987/88: Furthering Access to the World's Information*. (Dublin, Ohio: OCLC Online Computer Library Center), pp. 4 & 20.

④ Roger A. Walton & Frank R. Bridge, "Automated system marketplace 1987: Maturity and Competition", *Library Journal*, Vol. 113, No. 6 (April 1, 1988), pp. 33–44.

(Continuing)

Univ. of Cincinnati	Washington Lib. Network (orphan)
Ohio State Univ.	LCS (locally developed)
Wright State Univ.	DRA (Data Research Associates)
Cleveland State Univ.	NOTIS (from Northwestern)
Kent State Univ.	NOTIS
Miami Univ.	No System (subsequently, Innovative Interfaces)
Central State Univ.	No System
Medial College of Ohio	No System
NEOUCOM	No System
Shawnee State Univ.	No System
Univ. of Toledo	No System (subsequently NOTIS)

To facilitate resource sharing, the thirteen university libraries have a reciprocal borrowing agreement allowing faculty and students at these universities to use each other's libraries. Interlibrary loan and photocopy requests among IULC libraries receive priority attention and are free of charges. Those libraries with a local system allow the other libraries remote dial-up access. Through OCLC these libraries all have access to the bibliographic records of the others; however, such records do not indicate the number of copies in a given library nor circulation status. Information on serial holdings is often incomplete or absent. Further, OCLC's massive database does not yet allow for subject, keyword, or Boolean searching. Most local systems provide these capabilities.

A New Initiative

In 1986, facing massive requests for new and enlarged library facilities on state-supported campuses, the state legislature mandated that the Ohio Board of Regents assess the need for space by the university libraries and possible alternatives. The Board created a seventeen-member Library Study Committee, chaired by Dr. Elaine Hairston, Vice Chancellor for Academic and Special Programs of the Board of Regents, consisting of a university president, a provost, two vice presidents, two deans, two library directors, a professor, and OCLC researcher, a publisher, and four additional Board of Regents senior staff officers. The Committee decided early in its deliberations that its charge would require assessment of "the role of the academic library... in its broadest contemporary sense" and that it "should consider such opportunities for improving the quality of libraries as might appear in the context of its considerations."[①]

In its published report of the year-long study, the Committee felt that:

> This wider perspective is necessary because the academic library of today has a threefold purpose, serving not only as a storehouse of information, but also as a gateway to information held elsewhere, and as a center for instruction about information (p. vii).

Accordingly, the Committee's recommendation centered on three broad areas:

1) Collaboration, which encompasses a range of issues such as collaborative acquisitions, shared access, and shared storage;

2) Technology, including high density means of publication such as the existing microform and the emerging compact disk;

3) Alternative storage, including the various methods of maintaining rarely used materials in

---

① Ohio Board of Regents Library Study Committee, *Academic Libraries in Ohio: Progress Through Collaboration, Storage, and Technology. Report of the Library Study Committee* (Columbus: Library Study Committee, Ohio Board of Regents), p. vii.

a warehouse environment.①

The principal recommendation for collaboration was to implement "as expeditiously as possible a statewide electronic catalog system". The project, initially the Ohio Library Access System (OLAS) was later named the Ohio Library and Information System (OLIS). Collateral recommendations included retrospective conversion of remaining paper catalog records to MARC format, the development and implementation of a statewide delivery system for library materials, and a plan for a cooperative preservation program.

Ohio Library Information System: The Rationale

Soon after the release of the Committee Report, the Ohio Board of Regents acted to begin planning for a statewide electronic library system. They commissioned a feasibility study② and an evaluation of centralized vs. distributed approaches to the statewide system,③ established a steering committee and three task forces (one each for systems managers, librarians, and users), held a working conference featuring reports of experts on multi-campus systems from seven different states, drafted a Planning Paper and held regional hearings, and prepared a "Request for Information" (RFI) document. A chronology of events from the formation of the Library Study Committee to the issuance of the RFI is recorded in Table II and the planned implementation dates in Table III.

Table II HISTORY OF OHIO LIBRARY AND INFORMATION SYSTEM

1986	Capital Budget Estimates for Library Buildings for Biennia 1987 – 1992: $121.7 million total
1986	Library Study Committee Mandated by State Legislature in Capital Budget Bill
Fall 1986	Library Study Committee Formed by Board of Regents (including Ohio University President as member)
Sept. 1987	Library Study Committee Report, *Progress Through Collaboration, Storage, and Technology*, issued. Recommendations under heading "Collaboration": 1. Five-year plan to implement statewide electronic library system 2. State funding to convert existing catalog records to machine readable format 3. Development of state distribution system for library materials
Fall 1987	Ohio Board of Regents commissions a feasibility study of statewide system from RMG Associates
Winter 1988	Elaine Hairston, then Vice Chancellor of Ohio Board of Regents (since Chancellor) meets with library directors from state supported universities and Steering Committee appointed
March 1988	Board of Regents establishes three task forces: Systems Managers, Librarians, and Users. Ohio University representatives include Kent Mulliner and Larry Buell (replaced by George Hinkle) on Systems Managers, Betty Hoffmann-Pinther on Librarians, and Dr. David Hendricker on Users
Apr. – Aug. 1988	Task Forces work toward planning document and RFI (Request For Information) from potential systems vendors
July 1, 1988	Board of Regents receives Capital Budget Appropriation of $2.5 million
Summer 1988	Board of Regents commissions an evaluation of centralized vs. distributed approach to Statewide system, then known as OLAS (Ohio Library Access System)
September 1988	Working Conference in Columbus, Ohio (Videotape of Proceedings available) — Draft of Planning Paper prepared

---

① Ibid.
② RMG Consultants, *Alternative Approaches to Linking State University Automated Library Systems for the Ohio Board of Regents* (Chicago, IL: RMG Consultants, 1988).
③ Bernard Hurley, *Centralization vs Decentralization for Large Library Systems in a Changing Technological Environment: A position paper for the Ohio Board of Regents* (Berkeley, California: Hurley Consulting Corp., 1988).

Table III OHIO LIBRARY & INFORMATION SYSTEM PROJECT PLANNING TIMETABLE

July 1, 1988	Capital Appropriation of $2.5 million available
Sept. 1988	Consultants (Library Systems—Greg Byerly of Kent State Univ. &Computer Systems—Carroll Notestine, retired from Ohio State Univ.) hired
Dec. 5–9, 1988	Regional hearings on OLIS Draft Planning Paper
Dec. 16, 1988	Final OLIS Plan and draft RFI [Request For Information] circulated to campuses
January 1989	RFI sent to vendors & meetings with vendors
March 15, 1989	Vendor Responses to RFI due
May 1, 1989	Draft RFP [Request for Proposals] circulated to campuses
June 15, 1989	RFP sent to vendors
July 1, 1989	Operating Funds for 1989–1991 available
Sept. 4, 1989	RFP responses due
Sept. 15, 1989	Capital budget request for 1990–1992 prepared
Sept. 22, 1989	Acting Director and initial support staff hired
Dec. 1, 1989	Vendor(s) selected
July 1, 1990	Capital budget for 1990–1992 available
August 1, 1990	Operating budget request for 1991–1993 prepared
July 1, 1991	Operating budget for 1991–1993 available

First Phase of Implementation Begins

The Planning Paper, issued on November 2, 1988,[①] was divided into the following sections:
* Goal Statement
* Need for an Ohio Library Information System
* Assumptions
* Governance issues
* Tentative project timetable.

Because the currently installed six different local systems at the nine IULC libraries are not compatible, direct communication among them is impractical. OLIS will connect local systems at the thirteen state universities, plus the two medical colleges. OLIS is conceived as a multi-dimensional information system which will integrate traditional catalog and circulation functions for a statewide system with a document delivery service to make the information resources readily available for users from each participating university and beyond.

The Ohio Board of Regents emphasized the importance of the system by incorporating OLIS into its Selective Excellence initiatives—nationally acclaimed challenge grants to encourage outstanding programs specifically funded by the State of Ohio. Although OLIS will directly benefit the faculty, researchers and students of the state-supported universities initially, the system will be available to all citizens in Ohio and later may be expanded to include other institutions of higher learning and other types of libraries.

The Planning Paper[②] identifies the following reasons for creation of OLIS:
* Access to the diverse resources of IULC libraries
* Enhance interlibrary loan and inter-institutional borrowing

---

① OLAS Steering Committee, *Ohio Library Access System Planning Paper* (Columbus, Ohio: OLAS Steering Committee, Ohio Board of Regents, 1988).

② Ibid., pp. 4–5.

* Cooperative collection development and management
* Access to centrally maintained databases and other information resources
* Research for further improvement of information access.

Basic Assumptions for System Design

The heart of the Planning Paper treats basic assumptions,[1] which outline the bases for system design and specifications. Four categories of assumptions are identified:
* General assumptions
* Access and use assumptions,
* Functional assumptions, including:
  * Catalog creation and maintenance
  * Document delivery and circulation
  * Acquisitions and serials
  * Collection development and maintenance
  * Online public access catalog
* System assumptions.

Some important assumptions are summarized below:

1) A decentralized (or distributed) model with individual local systems linked to a central system is preferred. Fig. 1 shows one such model which links each local system to a central system via a Linked System Protocol (LSP) or internal protocols.

Figure 1 PREFERRED SYSTEM CONFIGURAION

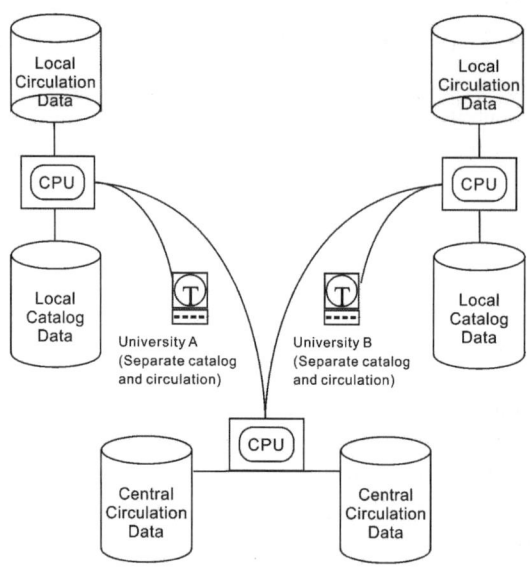

Central System Linked via LSP or Internal Protocols To Local Catalog and Circulation

2) The System will be designed with one standard command structure for all users. It is an end-user driven system.

3) The local online catalog will serve as the first database for bibliographic searches before searching the centrally maintained database.

4) Access to circulation information in the online catalog is considered an essential element of the system. Although all Ohioans will have access to the system, users affiliated with participating institutions will be able to directly initiate request for document delivery from any of the libraries.

---

[1] Ibid., pp. 5–16.

5) The system will have a wide variety of search capabilities including keyword and Boolean operators.

6) OLIS will not be an interlibrary loan system, but an intra-system circulation and document delivery network. A statewide circulation policy shall reflect this philosophy.

7) Effective and expeditious document delivery will be provided as an integral part of OLIS.

8) Besides traditional bibliographic information, OLIS will provide direct access to the full text of journal articles or the tables of contents of individual publications.

9) OLIS will provide capacity for collection and use analysis, cooperative collection development, preservation, etc.

10) Updates and transactions to local nodes and the central database will occur simultaneously in real time.

11) The selection of a system is neither a simple procurement process (e.g. acquire an existing system based on responses to RFP) nor an entrepreneurial development process (e.g., design a totally new system) but a combination of both: the selection of a vendor (s) to work with Ohio to design a system that will support state-of-the-art capabilities and use.

12) OLIS will move toward full implementation in stages which are governed by local constraints and interests.

13) The development process will be participatory and widely discussed.

14) Participating institutions will be involved in the governance of OLIS.

The Road Ahead

At the time of this writing (March 1989), the Request for Information (RFI) document has gone out to some 50 vendors and interested parties. The responses are due on April 15. In the meantime, the Task Forces are working on functional specifications which will be included in the Request For Proposal (RFP) document to be issued on June 15. Specialized consultative working conferences on the functional specifications are scheduled for late April and a second general working conference is scheduled on May 2 – 3 to consider the vendor responses to the RFI and to finalize the RFP.

Although the final shape of OLIS is still unclear, all involved in the process are encouraged by the progress thus far and remain optimistic about the future. Many questions remain, some of which will not be answered until the vendor and system have been selected and the governance structure and funding clarified.

A major question is not only what will be the system architecture, but whether there is a system that will do all that is expected. There are also concerns about whether the new system and its various components to be selected will indeed perform better than the existing local systems in all major functions. Can transition be accomplished with minimal interruption of services? Will the governance structure be able to balance central management and local will? How will OLIS be financed after the initial capital funding by the State and will there be some kind of compensation or incentives for libraries which have invested funds in their local systems? Virtually all involved are concerned that OLIS should be viewed not as a means to reduce future library funding but rather as increasing the effectiveness and richness of library resources and services to benefit all library users. Moreover, the beneficiaries should include not only users at the state-supported universities but all other Ohioans who may use them.

Document delivery, cooperative collection development, retrospective conversion, preservation, regional depository facilities for less used research materials, and the application of new technologies are all complements of the new system which, if effected correctly, will raise academic libraries in Ohio to new plateaus of excellence as they enter the 1990s.

The major academic libraries in Ohio are once again undertaking a giant step together after the success of OCLC. The results may be equally as far reaching as the first one.

Afterword — December 1990

The statewide system is on the verge of realization. After a number of name changes [from Ohio Library Access System (OLAS) to Ohio Library & Information System (OLIS) to OhioLINK], implementation planning is underway. Because the goal is to serve academic and research users throughout Ohio, two private institutions (the University of Dayton and Case-Western Reserve University have been added to the project.

From the responses to the RFP, eight vendors were invited to present two-day demonstrations in February 1990 which were attended by steering committee, task force, and library subcommittee members as well as representatives from each institution in various functional areas (cataloging, circulation, reference, etc.). The eight vendors were: Ameritech/OCLC, CARL (Colorado Academic and Research Libraries), DRA (Digital Research), GEAC, Innovative Interfaces Inc., NOTIS, Unisys, and VTLS (Virginia Tech Library System). Following the demonstrations, the four most promising vendors were invited for further presentations and a representative expert committee made site visits to academic institutions using the four systems. These were CARL, DRA, Innovative Interfaces, and VTLS. These four were then ranked and negotiations were begun with the preferred company. [Editor's further update: In March 1991, a contract was approved with Innovative Interfaces Inc.]

It is anticipated that OhioLINK will be implemented in two phases. The first, April 1991 – June 1992, will include a number of local sites and commencement of work on the central site. In phase II, July 1992 – June 1994, the remaining sites will be installed. In addition to the local and central sites, implementation includes installing a variety of online databases (in addition to the holdings of the participating institutions), ① a physical document-delivery service (likely through a commercial delivery service), an electronic document delivery system (using high quality transmission and recovery of fax and digital information), and ongoing research and installation of scholars work stations to take full advantage of OhioLINK's capabilities.

Throughout the planning process, emphasis focused on hardware and software selection. Only when this process was completed in mid – 1990 did discussions turn to issues of governance. About one-half of the provosts (chief academic officers) of the participating institutions serve on the Governing Board, with rotating terms. Advising the Board are a Policy Advisory Committee (comprised of representative provosts, academic administrators, faculty, library directors, and library systems managers) and a Library Advisory Committee (comprised of the library directors of all participating institutions). The Library Advisory Committee is served by a number of sub-committees to provide advice on uniform policies in functional areas. An Executive Director is responsible for operations.

---

① Ohio Board of Regents, *Connecting People, Libraries & Information for Ohio's Future* (Columbus: Ohio Board of Regents, 1989).

Bibliography

Below lists the professional writings of Hwa-Wei Lee in chronological order. Items marked by an asterisk " * " are the ones included in this book.

* "Africana at Duquesne University Library", *African Studies Bulletin* Vol. VI, No. 3 (October 1963), pp. 25 – 27.

* "Africana — A Special Collection at Duquesne University", *The Catholic Library World*, Vol. XXXV, No. 4 (December 1963), pp. 209 – 211.

"Educational Development in Taiwan Under Nationalist Government, 1945 – 1962", (Unpublished Ph. D. dissertation, University of Pittsburgh, 1964).

"Report of the Workshop on Admission of Students from Taiwan and Hong Kong", *Chung Kuo I Chou* (China Newsweek), No. 834 (April 18, 1966), pp. 12 – 15. (In Chinese)

"The Recent Educational Reform in Communist China", *School and Society*, Vol. XCVI, No. 2311 (November 9, 1968), pp. 395 – 400.

"Computer Application in Library and Information Services: The Current AIT Experiments and Future Plans", paper presented at the First Computer Applications Symposium jointly sponsored by the Computer Science Laboratory, Chulalongkorn University and U. S. Educational Foundation in Thailand, Bangkok, June 23 – 25, 1969.

"Asian Institute of Technology", *The Scooper Monthly*, October 1969, pp. 76 – 81. (In Chinese)

"Planning for Computer Applications in the AIT Library", paper presented at the 1969 annual conference of the Thai Library Association, Bangkok, December 15 – 19, 1969.

* "Fragmentation of Academic Library Resources in Thai University Libraries", *International Library Review*, Vol. III, No. 2 (April 1971), pp. 155 – 167.

"Library Mechanization at the Asian Institute of Technology", *International Library Review*, Vol. III, No. 3 (July 1971), pp. 257 – 270.

"Regional Cooperation in Scientific and Technical Information Service", *Proceedings of the Conference on Scientific and Technical Information Needs for Malaysia and Singapore*, Institute Teknoloji Mara, Kuala Lumpur, September 24 – 26, 1971. Kuala Lumpur: Persatuan Perpustakaan Malaysia and Library Association of Singapore, 1972, pp. 97 – 105.

* "A New Engineering Library Emerging in Asia", *Libraries in International Development*, No. 41 (December 1971), pp. 103.

* "The Information Technology—New Tools and New Possibilities for Information Storage, Retrieval and Dissemination", paper presented at the Regional Seminar on Information Storage, Retrieval and Dissemination, organized by Asian Mass Communication Research and Information Centre in cooperation with the National Research Council of Thailand, Bangkok, March 26 – 30, 1973. p. 10.

"Partner for School Library Development in Thailand", *T. L. A. Bulletin*, Vol. XVII, No. 5 (September/October 1973), pp. 443 – 448.

* "Proposal for the Establishment of a National Library and Information Network", *Central Daily News* (Taipei), February 26 – 27, 1974. (In Chinese)

"Possibilities in Employing Computer and Other Information Technologies to Further Library and Information Services in Southeast Asia", *Network*, Vol. I, No. 3 (March 1974), pp. 10 – 12, and 24 – 28.

With S. W. Massil, *Library Automation at the Asian Institute of Technology—Bangkok*. The Larc Reports, V. 7, No. 3. Peoria, Illinois: The Larc Press, 1974. p. 35.

"Regional Cooperation in Scientific and Technical Information Service", In *A Survey of Automated Activities in the Libraries of Asia and the Far East*. (World Survey Series, Vol. 5). Peoria, Illinois, The Larc Press, 1974, pp. 11 – 17.

* "The Application of Information Technology to Close the Information Gap", paper presented at the First Conference on Asian Library cooperation, Tamsui, Taipei, August 19 – 22, 1974. 12p.

* "User and Use Analysis: A Case Study of the Information Utility by Geotechnical Engineers in Asian Countries", *Information Utilities: Proceedings of the 37th Annual Conference of the American Society for Information Science*, Atlanta, Georgia, October 13 – 17, 1974. Edited by Pranas Zunde. Washington, D. C., 1974, V. II, pp. 133 – 136.

With S. W. Massil, *Proposal for Library Development at Prince of Songkla University in Southern Thailand*. Prepared at the request of the University Development Project Office, Prince of Songkla University. Bangkok: Asian Institute of Technology, 1974. 23p.

* With S. W. Massil, "Scholarly Publications: Considerations on Bibliographic Control and Dissemination", *Scholarly Publishing in Southeast Asia*, Proceedings of the Seminar on Scholarly Publishing in Southeast Asia, sponsored by the Association of Southeast Asian Institutions of Higher Learning, University of Malaya, Kuala Lumpur, January 16 – 18, 1975. Edited by Beda Lim. Kuala Lumpur, 1975, pp. 212 – 218.

* With J. C, Yang, "International Standard Numbering for Books and Serials and the Standardization of Bibliographic Descriptions", *Journals of Library and Information Science*, V. I, No. 1 (February 1975), pp. 60 – 66. (In Chinese)

* "The Experience of a Specialized Information Service in Asia — AGE", paper presented at the Round Table Conference on Documentation Problems in Developing Countries, Khartoum, Sudan, April 10 – 11, 1975 sponsored by FID/DC and FID National Member in Sudan. Published in *Journal of Library and Information Science*, V. 1, No. 2 (Oct. 1975), pp. 82 – 93.

"Recent Important Developments in the Library World", *Bulletin of the Library Association of China*, No. 27 (December 1975), pp. 34 – 36. (In Chinese)

* "Regional Cooperation for ISDS", *Proceedings of the Third Conference of Southeast Asian Librarians*, Jakarta, Indonesia, December 1 – 5, 1975. Edited by Luwarsih Pringgoadisurjo and Kardiati Sjahrial. Jakarta: PDIN-LIPI for Ikatan Pustakawan Indonesia (Indonesian Librarians Association), 1977, pp. 159 – 166.

The Possibility of Establishing a Regional Centre for the International Serials Data System in Thailand. (SC –76/WS/7), Paris: UNESCO, 1976. 43p.

"The Third Conference of Southeast Asian Librarians", *Leads*, V. 18, No. 1 (March 1976), pp. 3 – 4.

"Proposal for the Establishment of an ISDS Regional Center for Southeast Asia in Thailand", *Leads*, V. 18, No. 2 (July 1976), pp. 4 – 5.

* "Cooperative Regional Bibliographic Projects in Southeast Asia", paper presented at the Library Seminars of the International Association of Oriental Librarians held in conjunction with the 30th International Congress of Human Sciences in Asia and North Africa, Mexico City, August 3 – 8, 1976. 17 p. Published in *UNESCO Bulletin for Libraries*, V. 31, No. 6 (Nov. – Dec. 1977), pp. 344 – 351, 370.

* With Marjorie Rhoades, "Approaches to Development of Water Resources Scientific Information Systems", *Water Knowledge Transfer: Proceedings of the Second International Conference on Transfer of Water Resources Knowledge*, Colorado State University, June 29 – July 1, 1977. Fort Collins, Colorado: Water Resource Publications, 1978, Y. 2. pp. 625 – 644.

* "Sharing Information Resources Through Computer-assisted Systems and Networking", *Resource Sharing of Libraries in Developing Countries* Proceedings of the 1977 IFLA/UNESCO Pre-Session Seminar for Librarians from Developing Countries, Antwerp University, August 30- September 4, 1977. Munchen, K. G. Saur, 1979, pp. 208 – 216. Also published in *Journal of Library and Information Science*, V. 4, No. 1 (April 1978), pp. 14 – 24.

"Impacts of International Information Systems on NATIS", paper presented at Fourth Congress of Southeast Asian Librarians, Bangkok, June 5 – 9, 1978. Published in the *Proceedings*, *Regional Cooperation for the Development of National Information Services*. Bangkok: Thai Library Association, 1981, pp. 133 – 146.

"Online Revolution and Libraries", *Library Planning and Media Technology*. Library Workshop Proceedings, November 28 – 30, 1979. Taipei: National Taiwan Normal University Library, 1980, pp. 14 – 17. (In Chinese)

"The Current Status of Academic Library Administration in the U. S. ", paper presented at the Annual Meeting of Directors of Academic and Research Libraries, Taipei, December 1, 1979. 10 p. (In Chinese)

* With K. Mulliner and Lian The-Mulliner, "International Information Exchange and Southeast Asia Collections—A View from the U. S. ", presented at the 1980 Meeting of the International Association of Orientalist Librarians, Manila, August 17 – 23, 1980. 17 pages. Published in *Journal of Educational Media Science*, V. 18, No. 2 (Winter 1980), pp. 3 – 18.

* "A Sketch for a Computerized National Library and Information Network", paper presented at the International Workshop on Chinese Library Automation, Taipei, February 14 – 19, 1981. 11 pages.

Acquisitions From the Third World, Editor and Compiler, with K. Mulliner, special thematic issue of Library Acquisitions: Practice and Theory, V. 6, No. 2 (1982), pp. 79 – 238.

* With K. Mulliner, "Library Acquisitions from the Third World: An Introduction", *Library Acquisitions: Practice and Theory*, V. 6, No. 2 (1982), pp. 79 – 85.

* "Recent Breakthroughs in Library Automation in Taiwan", *Journal of Educational Media Science*, Vol. 19, No. 2 (Winter 1982), pp. 119 – 136.

* With K. Mulliner, "International Exchanges of Librarians and the Ohio University Internship Program", paper presented to the International Relations Round Table of the American Library Association at the ALA Conference in Philadelphia, July 1982. Published in *College & Research Libraries News*, V. 43, No. 10 (November 1982), pp. 345 – 348.

* "Challenges for the Library and Information Profession", *Bulletin of the Library Association of China*, No. 35 (1983), pp. 235 – 246.

* "International Library Internships: An Effective Approach to Cooperation", paper presented to the annual program of the Asian/Pacific American Librarians Association and the Chinese-American Librarians Association, in conjunction with the annual American Library Association conference, Los Angeles, June 28 – 29, 1983. Published in *Areas of Cooperation in Library Development in Asian and Pacific Regions*, Athens, Ohio: Chinese-American Librarians Association, 1985, pp. 21 – 27, and, in a revised form, in the International Library Review, Vol. 17, No. 1 (1985), pp. 17 – 25.

Areas of Cooperation in Library Development in Asia and Pacific Regions. Papers presented at the 1983 Joint Annual Program of the Asian/Pacific American Librarians Association and Chinese-American Librarians Association, June 28 – 29, 1983, Los Angeles, California. Editor, with Sally C. Tseng and K. Mulliner. Athens, Ohio: Chinese-American Librarians Association, 1985. 63p.

* With K. Mulliner, E. Hoffmatin-Pinther, and Hannah McCauley, "ALICE at One: Candid Reflections on the Adoption, Installation, and Use of the Virginia Tech Library System (VTLS) at Ohio University", paper presented at the Integrated Online Library Systems Second National Conference, September 13 – 14, 1984, in Atlanta, Georgia. Published in the *Proceedings*, Canfield, Ohio: Genaway & Associates, 1984, pp. 228 – 242.

With M. Beckman and Jianyan Huang, "Management of Scientific and Technical Information Centers: Aspects of Planning a Course Sponsored by IDRC (Canada) and ISTIC (China)", paper presented at the International Federation for Documentation (FID) Pre-Congress Workshop on Curriculum Development in a Changing World, The Hague, September 3 – 4, 1984. 19p.

Lecture Notes and Suggested Readings on Modern Library Management and Automation.

Athens, Ohio, 1985. 87p.

* With K. Mulliner, "Educating for International Interdependence: The Role of the Academic Library—Ohio University and Malaysia", at the First Annual Tun Abdul Razak Conference in Malaysia, Athens, Ohio, May 10, 1985. 9p.

* With K. Mulliner, "Funding for the Southeast Asia Collection and Research Resources at Ohio University", paper presented at the Annual Meeting of the Association for Asian Studies in Chicago, Illinois, March 21, 1986.

"International Exchanges and Internships for Librarians", paper presented at the LACUNY [Library Association of the City University of New York] Institute' 86, New York City, April 4, 1986.

"Current Status and Trends of American Libraries", *Newsletter of the Library Society of Fujian Province*, No. 25 (1986), pp. 14 – 38.

* "Principles and Issues on National Library and Information Policy", *Papers of the Library Cooperation and Development Seminar*, August 17 – 18, 1986. Taipei: National Central Library, 1987; pp. 5. 1 – 5. 22. Also published in *Journal of Library and Information Science*, V. 13, No. 1 (April 1987), pp. 1 – 16.

"Applications of Information Technology in An American Library—The Case of Ohio University Libraries", published in First Pacific Conference On New Information Technology for Library and Information Professionals, June 16 – 18, 1987, Bangkok, *Proceedings*. Edited by Ching-Chih Chen and David I. Raitt. West Newton, MA: MicroUse Information, 1987, pp. 155 – 164.

"Library Automation at Ohio University Library: Past, Present and Future." In *Collection of Essays Honoring Chiang Wei-Tang on His Ninetieth Birthday*. Taipei, Library Association of China, 1987. pp. 47 – 72.

* "Trends in Automation in American Academic Libraries: Ohio University's Experience", by Educational Resources Information Center, ED 315 081, ERIC Clearinghouse, May 1989. 20p.

"Major Milestones in American Library Automation Since the 1960s", *National Central Library News Bulletin*, Vol. 11, No. 4 (Nov. 1989), pp. 4 – 7. (Speech delivered at the National Central Library in Taipei on June 2, 1989). (In Chinese)

* "Planning Process and Considerations for a State-Wide Academic Libraries Information System in Ohio", Second Pacific Conference on New Information Technology for Library and Information Professionals and Educational Media Specialists and Technologists, Singapore, May 29 – 31, 1989. Published in Proceedings, edited by Ching-chih Chen and David I. RaiU. West Newton, MA: MicroUse Information, 1989, 203 – 210. Also published in *Journal of Educational Media & Library Sciences*, V. 27, No. 2 (Winter 1990). pp. 127 – 138.

New Concepts and New Technology in Library Services. Library Lecture Series. , No. 10. Kaohsiung, Taiwan: National Sun Yat-sen University, 1989. 25 p. (In Chinese)

Final Report of the 1NNERTAP Project Review. Consultant Report on the Information Network on New and Renewable Energy Resources and Technologies for Asia and the Pacific, commissioned by the International Development Research Centre. Ottawa, Canada: IDRC, 1990. 33p.

(Published by Student Book Company, 1991, Taipei)

2. 现代化图书馆管理[①]
On Modern Library Management

编者的话
Editor's Comments

  当我在草拟这丛书的书名时，一位在念图书资讯学的同学曾建议我用"图书资讯科学"做书名，她的意思很明显：一是她认为"图书资讯学"是一种"科学"；二是用了"科学"两个字，便可以在一般社会人士心目中提高这门学问的身价，因而便可使更多人愿意学习这门学问，从而献身图书资讯事业。这位同学的看法，不但反映了一般社会人士对"图书资讯学"的看法，也多多少少说出了她自己和很多图书资讯从业人员的心态。这个普及的心态来源，背景很是复杂。简单地说，一方面是因为近百年来自然科学在社会进化过程中的冲击性；另一方面，是因为从事图书资讯事业的人们对这门学问的认识有偏差，我很能了解并同情这个建议。考虑再三，我仍然用"图书资讯学"做书名，我觉得，"学"字本身便已经有了"系统化研求"的涵义，而且在一般社会人士的心目中，既然已将"科学"二字当作"自然科学"的专用词，又何必在已经复杂已极的现代名词中，为大家更增添不必要的混淆？巴特勒先生（Pierce Butler）说得好："不管如何，一个词的意义决定在社会的采纳与否，而不在逻辑性地下定义。"[②] 再说回头，要改变一般社会人士对这门学问的看法，不是硬用"科学"一词便可以达到的，一切还得看这门学问是不是值得人们冠以"科学"这个词，还得看我们从事这项事业的人是否值得人们重视。我感谢这位同学的建议，但也不想为不采纳这个建议而致歉。

  知识的成长是社会进步的原动力，而图书资讯却是知识成长必备的要素。知识是人们日积月累的经验和研究的成果，这些知识的结晶便储藏在图书资讯中。图书资讯学是研究：

  （1）目前及以往图书资讯的型态；
  （2）搜集它们的方法；
  （3）整理它们的过程和方法；
  （4）传播它们到需求者的方式、过程和途径。

  根据上述四项研究成果来改进一切图书资讯的作业程序，并推测、试拟未来图书资讯作业的方向与方法，所以，我们也可以说图书资讯学是社会进步、文化发扬的基石。

  参照国内需求，这套丛书先出十一本作第一辑：
  （1）《图书资讯学导论》周宁森著

[①] 该书作为周宁森主编的《图书信息学丛书》由台北市三民书局于1996年出版。
[②] Pierce Butler. *An Introduction to Library Science* Chicago：University of Chicago Press, 1933, p. 2.

（2）《资讯政策》张鼎钟著
（3）《图书资讯组织原理》何光国著
（4）《图书资讯之储存及检索》张庭国著
（5）《现代化图书馆管理》李华伟著
（6）《图书馆际合作与资讯网之建设》林孟真著
（7）《美国国会图书馆主题编目》陈麦麟、林国强合著
（8）《图书馆与当代资讯科技》景懿频著
（9）《图书资讯学专业教育》沈宝环著
（10）《法律图书馆》夏道泰著
（11）《文献计量学导论》何光国著

  本丛书的作者都是当代图书资讯学的精英，内容均能推陈出新，深入浅出，特地在此向他们致最高的敬意和最深的谢意，若有疏漏之处，都是编者一人的责任。

  最后，我要向三民书局刘振强先生致敬，像这样专业性的学术丛书是注定了要蚀本的，刘先生为了国家民族的远景，毅然斥资去做这项明知无利可图但影响深远的事，实在不由人不佩服。

主编

周宁森

于新泽西州

周　序

Preface by Zhou Ning-Shen

和华伟兄初次相识是在台北故宫博物院；那是 1973 年。故宫的蒋复璁院长宴客，请的是当年国建会的成员，华伟兄便在其中。那年"国建会"的总领队是普林斯顿大学葛思德东方图书馆馆长童世纲先生。如果我记得不错，华伟那时是从泰国来的。我是因缘附会，正好在台北南港"中央研究院"参加"第一届国际中文电子计算器会议"，便也被邀雁行之列。在宴会中，华伟兄和我并未曾深谈。如今，童世纲先生墓木已拱，华伟兄和我也都年逾花甲。但是华伟兄仍然朝气蓬勃，在事业的大道上勇往迈进，令人佩服。

第二次见到华伟是 1984 年。我应邀去台北参加"第一届亚太地区图书馆学会议"。在去台北的飞机上与华伟兄不期而遇，才知他已返回美国服务，也是去台北参加同一会议的。我们在飞机上交换阅读了彼此的论文。他对我那篇"语音识别"的论文赞扬不止，使我顿生知己之感；彼此都觉相"知"恨晚。那年在台北，我二人同受"国科会"之托，共同审查了"国科会"所属的科技资料中心的日常作业；并合写了一篇书面建议给"国科会"。

当我受命编这一套丛书时，华伟兄便是最先进入我心目中的执笔人之一。因为，我知道华伟兄不但博学深思，更是说"一"不"二"的信人。

上周我接到华伟兄的书稿，一口气读完后，对华伟兄的认识又深了一层！华伟兄的这部大作不但深入浅出、思维细密、巨细无遗，可作为图书馆管理学的课本；更是图书馆从业人员应参考的经典之作。这部书足以传世。

周宁森
1995 年 4 月 25 日于新泽西

王　序

Preface by Wang Zheng-Gu

　　《现代化图书馆管理》一书是李华伟博士的近著。李博士在图书馆界是一位学养深厚、经验宏富的图书馆学者和管理专才。早在 1959 年即献身于图书馆工作,首先在美国匹兹堡大学及都肯大学担任专业馆员及部主任,1964 年获得匹兹堡大学哲学博士学位,1966 年即担任宾州爱丁堡大学图书馆馆长及该校图书馆系助理教授,1968 年应美国国际发展总署之聘前往泰国担任亚洲理工学院图书馆及资讯中心主任,前后 7 年,对于国际图书馆事业的合作与发展贡献良多,1975 年任满返美,在科罗拉多州大学担任教授及图书馆副馆长。1978 年李博士膺任美国俄亥俄大学图书馆馆长兼教育学院教授职务,任内多方参与国际图书馆界活动,曾被推选为国际图书馆协会联盟(IFLA)大学暨研究图书馆委员会委员,美国图书馆协会及俄亥俄州图书馆协会理事。李博士在他服务图书馆期间,一直关切于国内图书馆事业的发展。多年来,他奔走于海峡两岸,教学、讲演及参加各有关会议,宣扬图书馆经营的新理念。中国图书馆学会为表扬他所展现的"全心奉献,全力投入"的图书馆专业精神,于 1989 年第 37 届年会中特颁赠图书馆事业特殊贡献奖,以示敬意。

　　这本专著可说是李博士结合了图书馆学与管理科学理论和实务的一本精心之作。管理学是一门近百年间发展的学科,而应用在图书馆方面则是在 1960 年代以后的事。一如管理学家杜拉克(Peter F. Drucker)所说,在过去五十年间,世界上已开发国家都已转变成为一"机构性社会",任何重要的社会任务,都由一些大型的组织来担任。而这些机构所发挥的效能之高低,将直接影响到整个社会生活、福利和安全。因此,管理学之应用亦日益广泛。以图书馆而言,在过去的发展中,由于社会和民众的需要,多朝向合作化经营与制度化管理迈进。诸如各馆间的结合,大单元体制的建立,目标管理观念的推行,甚至营销观念的做法,或多或少地受到了企业管理制度的影响。图书馆在机构性社会中,无疑的有其重要的地位,其服务成效势必成为图书馆发展之关键,而科学化管理制度也将为图书馆经营管理者必须研究的一门知识。

　　图书馆管理的著述,一方面着重理论的阐发,另一方面着重管理实务的佐证与融合,两者缺一均属不可。如仅重理论,将徒托空谈,而无补实际;反之,如仅重实务,又被认为墨守成规,而了无新意。本书是著者参酌管理学的理论,并结合三十多年来管理图书馆的经验所撰述的。书中首先就现代化的任务与使命加以阐释,继而依次就 20 世纪西方管理学的发展、图书馆的规划、组织、人力资源、领导与作业、控制与评估等分章剖析,最后以跨世纪的图书馆发展作为结论。著者在绪论中曾提到"在民主、自由、开放及重视基本人权的社会中,图书馆在组织、收藏、管理、流通、服务各方面应具备崇尚民主、发展民智、服务社会,并保持公正不偏的精神"。这可以说是图书馆在管理理念上所应秉持的原则。在各章分论中,内容精详,并附有美国图书馆管理作业的实例,其中如俄亥俄大学组织、职责、人员、经费及馆藏等章则统计,多为一般著作中所罕见的实际参考资料。尤其著者在本书后章所介绍的观念,管理的意义在"修己安人",管理的基本精神在"中道",更说明著者所倡导的现代化图书馆管理应该是科学化、制度化与人性化的管理方式,而所期望的图书馆是一所开放的、自由的、为社会大众提供公正服务的资讯和教育中心。

  本书的出版，不仅介绍了现代图书馆管理的新观念，更提供给图书馆界有关管理实务的参考资料，谨借此机会向图书馆界推介，并向著者致贺。

王振鹄

1995 年 6 月

自 序

Author's Preface

这本关于现代化图书馆管理的书是我在大学图书馆担任行政工作之余,断断续续地花了近五年的时间把它完成的。在这段时间里,因为朋友的催促和工作上的需要,我道不自量力地把过去所发表过的六十多篇文章选了一部分,由台湾的学生书局出版了《图书馆学的世界观:1963—1989 论文选集》(1991) 及我与同事盖瑞·汉博士 (Gary Hunt) 合著了一本 90 年代图书馆如何募款的书,《Fundraising for the 1990s: The Challenge Ahead》(1992)。另外,因为我近十多年来几乎每年都应邀前往祖国大陆各地短期讲学,特此撰写了一套关于《现代化图书馆管理及自动化》的讲义,由于这些原因,这本书被拖延了五年才得与读者见面。为此,我必须向台湾的三民书局刘振强先生、编辑部各位先生(女士)及负责主编"图书资讯学丛书"的周宁森博士致歉,并对他们的耐心和宽容表示由衷的感谢。

自从 1957 年由台湾来美国匹兹堡大学深造,到现在这一段将近四十年的岁月里,我很少用中文写作,因此写这本书对我是一个考验,也是驱策我重新复习中文写作的一个良好机会。正好乘逢甲大学图书馆胡凤生副馆长在俄亥俄大学教育学院攻读博士的机会,请她抽空校对了一遍。我的学生助理杨阳小姐是一位品学兼优的研究生,在她的帮助下,使用计算机的中文软件系统为我整理文稿。对她们两位的贡献,我也一并致谢。

从 1959 年开始,在我从事图书馆工作三十多年的时间里,有幸正好赶上了图书馆经历最剧烈变动的一个时期,因为人类资讯知识的突飞猛进,计算机技术、电讯技术、密集储存技术、多媒体技术及电子出版技术的快速发展;加上现代管理学的进展和国际计算机资讯联网 (Internet) 的畅通,使得图书馆在过去四十年的变化和影响比过去四百年还要巨大而深远。图书馆和资讯中心已从传统式以纸张印刷品为主的"纸张图书馆"(Paper-based Library)进展到 70 年代的"自动化图书馆"(Automated Library),八十年代的"网络化图书馆"(Networked Library),及 90 年代的"电子化图书馆"(Electronic Library)。因为国际计算机资讯联网的畅通,21 世纪的图书馆和资讯中心将无疑地朝向"虚拟图书馆"(Virtual Library) 这个方向发展。虚拟图书馆是融合了各期图书馆的特色和优点,破除了图书馆人为的栅篱,使得图书资讯的服务能无远弗届,不受空间和距离的限制。这本探讨现代化图书馆管理的书是尽可能地配合这个发展的趋势。

为了完成这本书,我得到了很多朋友和亲人的鼓励和帮助,其中最值得感谢的是我的贤内助,Mary F.(Kratochvil)Lee,她的了解、同情、忍耐和牺牲使我能够没有后顾之忧,安心著作。

最后,本书在付梓之前能得到我平生最钦佩的良师益友——前"中央图书馆"馆长及现任台湾师范大学教授——王振鹄兄的过目匡正及赐赠序文,使我倍感荣幸和感激。

李华伟　谨识
1995 年 4 月于美国俄亥俄州雅典城

第一章　绪　言

Chapter 1　Introduction

第一节　现代化图书馆的任务与使命

在 20 世纪科学进步，教育普及，知识发展，文化昌明的时代，图书馆的发展也日新月异。不仅各类型图书馆的发展越来越普遍，藏书越来越丰富，服务的对象与项目越来越扩充；图书馆本身的组织与分工也随同变得更复杂而细密，图书馆的任务与使命亦不断增强。这本关于现代化图书馆管理的书是根据作者在美国大学图书馆从事行政工作三十多年的经验，加上对近代管理学在理论与实践上的体会，特就当前图书馆在发展中的实际需要写出来，借以抛砖引玉，向国内外从事或研究图书馆行政的专家们请教，希望探讨的结果，能对促进图书馆管理的现代化有所裨益。

为了配合社会的需要，图书馆因性质及服务对象不同而有下列分类：

1. 国家图书馆
（1）一般的（包括具有国家图书馆实质的美国国会图书馆）。
（2）专门的（如美国的国家医学图书馆、国家农业图书馆）。
2. 公共图书馆
（1）公立图书馆。
（2）私立图书馆。
3. 大专院校图书馆
（1）大学图书馆。
（2）学院及专科院校图书馆。
4. 中小学图书馆，学习资源中心，或教育媒体中心（Learning Resources or Educational Media Center）
5. 特别（专门）图书馆
（1）机关、公司图书馆。
（2）医学图书馆。
（3）法律图书馆。
（4）研究机构图书馆。
（5）科技资讯中心（"Information" 一词有多种不同的翻译，包括资讯，情报或信息，本书则采用台湾通用的"资讯"）。
（6）特殊资料或数据中心（Data Center）。

即使图书馆有上列各种类别，其共同任务和使命可以归纳如下：

一、任务
（1）图书资讯的选择、采购、整理、分类、编目、典藏及维护。
（2）图书资讯的流通和使用。

（3）读者服务，指导和教育（包括对新移民、文盲、老弱残废、贫民等）。
（4）馆际合作和资源共享。
（5）为配合社会发展所需，针对促进教育、文化、政治、经济及工商业发展等所提供的特殊服务。
（6）图书馆员工素质的提升，包括对在职训练和继续教育的加强。
（7）对图书馆和资讯服务理论与方法的研究，以及对新技术的发展、引进和使用。

二、使命

（1）人类知识和文化的收集、保存、传递和发扬光大。
（2）人类精神和文化生活的充实。
（3）配合国家与地方的建设与发展。
（4）满足社会大众对资讯、职业、教育、休闲和文化生活的需要。
（5）配合时代改变，科技进步，知识发展所因应的各种新服务及措施。

在一个民主、自由、开放及重视基本人权的社会，图书馆在其组织、收藏、管理、流通、服务各方面，应具备崇尚民主、发展民智、服务社会和保持公正不偏的精神。

第二节 各类图书馆的功能

前面已经说过，图书馆因性质及服务对象不同而有不同的类别，这种类别的形成是为配合社会需要，加强服务功能而产生，兹将各类图书馆的功能略为叙述于下：

一、国家图书馆

国家图书馆，顾名思义，即为一国最大的国立图书馆。目前世界各国大多设有国家图书馆，赋予不同程度的权责和使命。美国的"国会图书馆"（The Library of Congress）及日本的"国家议会图书馆"（National Diet Library）在实质上担当了国家图书馆的功能与使命。在美国，除了国会图书馆以外，还有国家医学图书馆（National Library of Medicine）和国家农业图书馆（National Agricultural Library）。这两个图书馆虽然是国家级的图书馆，但是都是专门性图书馆。它们的任务、使命与地位都与国会图书馆不同。

近三四十年来，很多国家因重视科技的发展与需要，在联合国教育科学和文化组织（United Nations Educational, Scientific and Cultural Organization，UNESCO）的倡导下，纷纷设立全国性的科技资讯或文献中心，隶属于国家科学委员会或类似机构之下，专门负责有关科技资讯与文献的工作。

也有些国家在国家图书馆之外，分设国家档案馆（National Archives）专门收藏中央政府各机构重要的公文资料。

各国的国家图书馆，虽然因历史及文化背景的不同，而有不同的任务，但一般来说，多半有下列几项不同程度的共同职责：

（1）领导及协调全国图书馆事业的发展。
（2）收集本国及有关本国的出版品。可经由出版法或版权法的规定，收藏国内出版商送缴的书刊及非书刊资料。很多国家并订有出版品贮存法，规定任何私人或公家机构出版品皆须送缴一至数本至国家图书馆收藏。法国早在 1617 年即订有此贮存法。

（3）经由与国内各图书馆协调与合作的方式进行合作采购世界各国的书刊资料。

（4）建立全国图书目录或书目资料库，将全国出版品迅速编目入库以利查索和使用（有些国家图书馆还提供编目服务和编目资料给国内外图书馆）。美国国会图书馆从 1942 年开始发行国家联合目录（National Union Catalog）。

（5）领导，协调或协助建立全国图书资讯服务，以加强馆际合作，资源共享，自动化，网路化，图书资讯的保存与维护，国际的合作、联系与支持。

（6）代表国家参加国际图书资讯会议及合作项目。如参加国际机读编目格式（UNIMARC），国际标准图书编号（ISBN），国际标准连续性出版物编号（ISSN），国际标准书目著录（ISBD），国际出版品流通计划（UAP），国际书目控制（UBC）等活动。

二、公共图书馆

公共图书馆虽有公立与私立之分，而公立图书馆之中又有省、县、市、乡、镇等不同层次，但其服务读者及为社会大众提供图书资讯的宗旨大致相同。一般公共图书馆的服务对象及层面虽然有差别，但其主要权责计有：

（1）收藏各种能配合社会需要的图书资讯，包括本地的历史、文化、文献和地方志等。

（2）举办各种活动以造成读书风气，鼓励民众使用图书馆。

（3）提供参考咨询服务，为一般读者解答日常生活中各种实际问题；对本地区工商业、政府及其他机构提供专门性咨询服务。

（4）与其他图书馆合作协调，互相支持，并建立地区性图书馆网络，促进资源共享及提高与增广图书馆服务的层面。

（5）与其他文化机构合作协调，为当地居民提供各种文化活动，以充实精神生活，扫除文盲，提高民智及服务社会。

为了能使图书馆服务更为普及，很多公共图书馆，尤其是在大城市或地区宽广的地方，在辖区内选择适当地方设立分馆（Branch Library）；或使用专门设计的车辆或交通工具，作为巡回图书馆（Mobile Library）；更有些图书馆对行动不便或缺乏交通工具的读者提供邮寄图书服务。美国的很多公共图书馆更不断地创新立异，建立各种专为老弱残废及对在牢狱里犯人的服务。近些年来，为了服务新移民及扫除文盲，很多图书馆亦因此增设新的服务项目。

三、大专院校图书馆

大专院校的目的主要在于教学、研究与社会服务。其图书馆的任务亦以支持教学、研究与服务为主。有规模的综合性大学，其图书馆收藏极为丰富，尤其是着重于各学科领域的研究资料与文献，因此有时被称为研究图书馆（Research Library）。专科院校的图书馆在收藏上则比较专门，多数以实用为主。有些专门院校的图书馆特别注重对于视听媒体（Audio-Visual Media）和综合媒体（Multimedia）的收藏和使用，因此有的定名为教育媒体中心（Educational Media Center）或学习资源中心（Learning Resources Center）。一般大专院校图书馆与公共图书馆的显著不同点为：

（1）大专院校图书馆藏书包括过去与现在的出版品与非书刊资料，比较重视研究的价值和需要。公共图书馆则重视新出版的畅销书刊及当代名著，藏书多以读者的兴趣为导向。

（2）一般大专或研究图书馆多以藏书量的多少为衡量，而一般公共图书馆多以借阅次数的多少为衡量。

有一些著名的公共图书馆，历史悠久，藏书丰富，且拥有多种特藏，在藏书上可以媲美规模大的大学或研究图书馆，如美国的纽约公共图书馆（New York Public Library），波士顿公共图书馆（Boston Public Library）等。另外还有一些著名的大学图书馆，其藏书量及经费远超越大多数其他国家的国家图书馆，如美国的哈佛大学（Harvard University）及英国的牛津大学（Cambridge University）图书馆等，是世界上第一流的研究图书馆。

四、学校图书馆

中小学及一般职业训练学校近年来已逐渐设立校内图书馆或学习资源中心，作为学生学习及教师准备教学之用。有很多国家设有学校图书馆标准，规定学校图书馆馆员除了具备教师资格之外，还要受过图书馆专业训练。在世界各国图书馆发达的地方，学校图书馆与公共图书馆有密切合作的关系。

五、特别（专门）图书馆

特别图书馆的种类很多，包括了政府机关、工商企业机构的图书馆、医院图书馆、一些特殊性质的专门图书馆、资讯中心及资料库（Data Center）等。这些图书馆规模大小不一，有系公营的，可开放给社会大众使用。有的是私营的，对外不开放。担任特别图书馆的馆员，一般除了要具备图书馆学及资讯科学的专业知识外，还须受有特殊学科的训练，俾能提供专门性质的参考咨询服务及建立专门的资料库以供读者所需。

第三节　图书馆的发展趋势

图书馆的起源和发展在中西历史上都非常早，有了文字及符号的记载，就有了图书馆。随着人类文明的进展，图书馆的发展也有着显著的改变，尤其是20世纪以来，图书馆学与资讯科学已变成一门学科，图书资讯的服务也变成一种专业。图书出版业的发展、科学技术的进步及人类知识的迅速累积交互影响，促成了"资讯的爆炸"（Information Explosion）。图书馆的图书资讯收集不仅在量的方面加速增长，在种类上亦不断改变，从手抄本到印刷品到电子出版物，从文字图片到视听媒介到多元媒体，从幻灯片到录像带，从缩微片到光盘，举凡书刊、资料、档案、文献，不论是何种媒体，只要能符合读者需要及具有资讯价值，皆可收藏。

为了要使各种收藏能便于读者查检及使用，很多第二手文献处理（如目录、索引等）及第三手文献处理（如摘要、提纲等）皆应时而生。图书馆的目录由最通用的卡片式逐渐演变成了计算机处理的在线目录。由于计算机系统的发展，图书馆开始使用它来建立图书馆目录资料库及其他作业，如采购、编目、图书管理流通、连续出版品及期刊的控制及行政管理等。

在60年代中叶，图书馆自动化受当时大型计算机系统的影响及限制，有集中发展之势。美国国家医学图书馆首先使用计算器来建立医学文献分析及检索系统（Medical Literature Analysis and Retrieval System，MEDLARS）。紧接着，美国国会图书馆也开始设计及推广机读式编目的标准格式(Machine Readable Cataloging, MARC format),将图书馆编目的资料用机读编目的格式做成磁带分送大型图书馆试用。随着机读编目的发展,在美国俄亥俄州的一些大学图书馆藉此机会设立了俄亥俄学院图书馆中心(Ohio College Library Center, OCLC),以合作的方式聘请了当时的图书馆自动化专家 Frederick G. Kilgour 来主持其事,买了一部大型的计算器,开始合作编目,利用国会图书馆的磁带目录及其机读编目的标准格式,加上参与馆所输入的编目资料,建立目录中心。先是分线作业(Batch Process),然后在 1971 年开始进入联机操作(Online Process)。因为在 70 年代上半期,中小型计算机还在雏形时期,大型计算机价格偏高,而适合图书馆使用的软件还付诸阙如,有待发展。因此,在图书馆自动化方面一般皆认为应集中发展,不宜个别单独进行。OCLC 的成立,为图书馆自动化,尤其是合作编目,建立联合目录,开辟了一个可行的途径。很多图书馆都纷纷加入,由俄州扩充到邻近各州,进而在短短十年的时间扩充成了一个全国性的系统。在 1977 年,OCLC 的简称已不再代表俄亥俄学院图书馆中心。到了 1981 年,OCLC 的新名称是图书馆计算机在线中心(Online Computer Library Center)。参加的图书馆已由当初俄亥俄州五十四所大学与学院图书馆扩充到四千多所各类型的图书馆。根据 1994 年 6 月的统计,OCLC 的成员已超过一万八千所图书馆,分布在美国各州及世界上六十多个国家和地区。OCLC 的经费已由最初的每年六万四千美元增加到每年一亿三千二百万美元,工作人员亦由最初四个人增加到近千人。OCLC 最成功的服务项目是合作编目、联合目录及馆际互借。OCLC 的目录资料库目前是世界最大的,每年增加二百多万新书的目录①。参与图书馆在编目时可以很容易地在 OCLC 的资料库中发现近 94% 的新书已经编好了,不用重新编目。这种人工及时间的节省,不仅降低了图书馆在图书编目方面的开销,而且大大改善了图书馆对读者服务的形象,使新购的书刊能够很快地上架以便于读者的使用。因为 OCLC 的编目资料库越来越丰富,使得找书非常容易。OCLC 在 1979 年开始提供全国性的馆际互借服务系统,将过去以人工操作的诸多不便及缺点,进行划时代的革新,效果卓越。

类似 OCLC 的图书资讯网系统还有研究图书馆资讯网(Research Libraries Information Network, RLIN)。在 1970 年代末,RLIN 将中、日、韩文图书资料纳入系统。这个资讯系统与 OCLC 是美国最大的两个资讯网;现今均已扩充至世界性的系统。

表 1-1、1-2、1-3、1-4 分别显示了 OCLC 在一些重要服务项目上的绝对优势。

在 60 年代另外一个大进展是很多出版文摘(Abstract)和索引(Index)的机构,像美国化学文摘服务公司(Chemical Abstract Service),开始使用计算机作业,以缩短人工整理资料及排版的时间。由于大批资料贮存在计算机内,在线检索的服务遂附带产生,大规模的资料库服务中心也应时成立。像 Dialog 和 BRS 等,个别拥有众多的资料库以供图书馆及个人做在线检索之用。目前,因通讯网络的发达,分布在世界上各个角落的图书馆都可以由多种卫星频道直接检索近千种的资料库,除了目录资料外,很多资料库还贮存了文献、数据及其他资料,检索便捷,大大增加了资讯的有效利用。

到了 70 年代下半期,因中型计算机(Minicomputer)的普遍化,不但性能扩大,而且价格降低。很多图书馆及一些厂商开始设计及推广以中型计算机为主的图书馆自动化系统,以供各图书馆或地方性网络之用。OCLC 虽然在合作编目,建立全国目录库,及馆际互借上为图书馆提供了极大的方便及革新,但在发展全面性图书馆自动化系统方面,还不

---

① Furthering Access to the World's Information; OCLC Annual Report 1993-1994. (Dublin, Ohio: OCLC, Online Computer Library Center, 1994.) p. 48.

及一些图书馆及个别厂商所发展系统的成效。例如迄至 1988 年底，OCLC 的全国目录还不能提供主题标目（Subject Heading）及关键词（Keyword）检索，因此无法完全取代传统式的卡片目录。在提供图书馆采购、流通及期刊控制系统方面，OCLC 亦步调迟缓，不够积极。为此之故，在 70 年代末和 80 年代初期，很多图书馆除了仍使用 OCLC 做合作编目、联合目录及馆际互借外，在其他方面开始使用自己发展的或一些厂商发展的系统来实现图书馆的全面自动化。以俄亥俄大学为例，在 1980 年即决定使用 VTLS 系统来配合 OCLC 的不足以建立在线公用目录（Online Public Access Catalog），图书流通、图书采购和期刊控制等一贯性的系统①。

表 1-1　OCLC 在 1993—1994 会计年度的服务统计②

参与图书馆	18,168 所
分布国家和地区	61 个
使用在线编目的书刊量	23,200,000 件
使用磁带输入编目的书刊量	18,500,000 件
编目卡片印制量	42,200,000 件
编目磁带订购量	34,200,000 件
目录资料库新增书目	2,200,000 件
目录资料库书目统计	29,000,000 件
馆际互借系统使用次数	7,031,066 次
经费总额	$132,446,700
资产价值	$174,791,000

表 1-2　OCLC 目录资料库按媒体的分类③

种类	由国会图书馆提供的书目	由参与图书馆提供的书目	国会图书馆提供经参与图书馆修正	总数
书籍	3,747,067	18,765,505	2,105,345	24,617,917
连续出版物	167,455	1,316,095	46,616	1,530,166
视听媒体	94,976	623,999	23,542	742,517
地图	146,189	194,330	2,918	343,437
文献原稿	70	223,897	262	224,229
录音唱片	79.021	795,657	54,567	929,245
乐谱	32,887	651,220	49,166	733,273
计算机存盘	1,400	52,068	145	53,613
总计	4,269,065	22,622,771	2,282,561	29,174,397
百分比	6.83%	80.39%	12.78%	100%

---

① Hwa-Wei Lee and others. "ALICE at One: Candid Reflections on the Adoption, Installation, and Use of the Virginia Tech Library System (VTLS) at Ohio University," 收录于李华伟著，《图书馆学的世界观：1963—1989 论文选集》（台北市：学生书局，1991），pp. 211-223.

② Furthering Access to the World's Information; OCLC Annual Report 1993-1994. (Dublin, Ohio: OCLC, Online Computer Library Center, 1994.) pp. 6-7.

③ Furthering Access to the World's Information; OCLC Annual Report 1993-1994. (Dublin, Ohio: OCLC, Online Computer Library Center, 1994.) p. 8

表1-3　OCLC目录资料库按出版年代的分类①

2000B.C 到 1B.C	286
1A.D – 1449	1,777
1450 – 1699	290,606
1700 – 1799	448,050
1800 – 1899	2,384,591
1900 – 1909	656,417
1910 – 1919	656,364
1920 – 1929	802,071
1930 – 1939	938,664
1940 – 1949	969,067
1950 – 1959	1,488,651
1960 – 1969	2,783,068
1970 – 1979	5,292,870
1980 – 1989	6,911,824
1990 –	2,542,024

表1-4　OCLC目录资料库按语言分类②

英文（English）	19,115,219
法文（French）	1,782,141
德文（German）	1,760,926
西班牙文（Spanish）	1,282,735
俄文（Russian）	589,667
意大利文（Italian）	517,828
中文（Chinese）	407,142
日文（Japanese）	336,004
拉丁文（Latin）	284,221
葡萄牙文（Portuguese）	258,803
荷兰文（Dutch）	172,078
希伯来（犹太）文（Hebrew）	151,192
波兰文（Polish）	143,496
阿拉伯文（Arabic）	142,778

---

① Furthering Access to the World's Information, OCLC Annual Report 1993 – 1994. (Dublin, Ohio: OCLC, Online Computer Library Center, 1994.) p.9
② Furthering Access to the World's Information; OCLC Annual Report 1993 – 1994. (Dublin, Ohio: OCLC, Online Computer Library Center, 1994.) p.26

(Continuing)

瑞典文（Swedish）	120,602
丹麦文（Danish）	81,403
印度尼西亚文（Indonesia）	78,001
韩文（Korean）	75,934
捷克文（Czech）	74,835
匈牙利文（Hungarian）	67,855
挪威文（Norwegian）	53,706
土耳其文（Turkish）	49,467
塞尔维亚罗马字体文（Serbo-Croatian Roman）	44,513
希腊文（Greek-Modem）	44,513
保加利亚文（Bulgarian）	39,207
罗马尼亚文（Romanian）	37,097
乌克兰文（Ukrainian）	36,860
泰文（Thai）	35,533
芬兰文（Finnish）	35,471
印度文（Hindi）	34,257
波斯文（Persian）	30,534
意第绪文（Yiddish）	29,344
塞尔维亚斯拉夫语文（Serbo-Croatian Cyrillic）	23,344
越南文（Vietnamese）	22,924
其他三百三十六种文字	

在80年代初期，除了中型计算机大受一般图书馆欢迎之外，微型计算机（Microcomputer）亦开始出笼，为一些小型图书馆提供了自动化的好机会。微电脑除促成小型图书馆自动化外，还因其价格便宜，在中大型图书馆中亦被普遍采用。这些微电脑除了用在在线检索以外，还用在字处理、小型资料库的建立、采购、会计等方面。OCLC亦将微机改装成联机操作的工作站（Work Station）。

到了80年代中期以后，密集光盘（CD-ROM）开始进入图书馆市场，渐有取代由人工检索印刷出版的大型资料库的趋势。因密集光盘的储存量大、造价低、机器检索方便、可供使用者自己动手检索等优越条件，极受图书馆及读者欢迎。密集光盘虽然目前多用为储存目录资料，但其他方面的应用，如全文储存、影像储存等，前途无限。除了光盘之外，电讯传真（Telefascimile）亦在80年代后期因技术的改进及读者对文献传递的需要很快地普遍化。

根据1994年一篇有关图书馆自动化系统市场的调查报告，在1993年有58家厂商在美国及世界各地的六万三千九百三十六所图书馆中装置了他们的系统。其中成长率最快的是在1990年以后。表1-5显示以中型计算机（Minicomputer System）为主的一些主要厂商。表1-6显示了以微电脑（Microcomputer System）为主的一些主要厂商①。

90年代的图书馆将会受到资讯技术快速发展的更大影响和后果。因为计算机在图书馆中的使用更加普遍和成熟，加上通讯网路及电子出版的发展，促进了图书馆馆内与外间的联网及书刊文献的电子传递，使得图书馆之间的资源共享和互通有无更能名符其实，达到优惠读者的效果。近两、年来所发展的国际计算机资讯联网（Internet）更缩短了图书馆与图书馆、图书馆与读者及图书馆与资讯之间的地理差距，使得"虚拟"图书馆（Virtual Library）的理想可以及早实现。因为国际计算机资讯联网的发展，世界上很多国家——包括美国在内，都纷纷开始规划以资讯高速公路（Information Superhighway）为主干的国家资讯基础建设（National Information Infrastructure）。21世纪的图书馆不管是以何种形式出现，在促进知识发展、资讯传递、生活素质和文化水平上会担负更重要的任务与使命。

表1-5 以中型计算机为主的主要厂商及其已安装的系统数量

厂商	数量
GEAC	1,070
Dynix	1,040
DRA	418
Innovative	369
Info Dimensions	263
IME	259
SIRSI	251
Sobeco	249
VTLS	191
General Auto	182
NOTIS	179
Gaylord	162
Comstow	66
Best Seller	58
ILS	32
CARL	30
NSC	28
Georgetown	25
Gateway	22
CMDS	14
COBit	10
总数	4,892

① Jose-Marie Griffiths and Kimberly Kertis. "Automated System Marketplace 1994," Library Journal, Vol. 119, No. 6 (April 1, 1992), p. 59.

表 1-6 以微机为主的主要厂商及其已安装的系统数量

厂商	数量
Follett	21,300
Winnebago	16,480
Inmagic	9,351
Caspr	3,721
Mcgraw Hill	2,700
Data Trek	2,606
IME	2,070
Dynix	470
Brodart	256
ILS	253
VTLS	92
Ringgold	33
总数	59,322

第四节 图书馆管理的现代化

为了要充分适应资讯社会的发展和读者的需要，配合因新技术所提供的机会和冲击，及利用现代管理学的观念和方法，图书馆的管理应不断地调整和革新，使之能赶上时代，发挥图书馆在资讯社会中应有的功能，以造福社会及人群。

因为各国的国情不同，加上各种各类图书馆及资讯中心内外环境的差异，其组织与管理有显然的分歧。在组织上，有些国家的图书馆及资讯中心系统分明，职权集中，由中央伸延到地方，如苏联及中国大陆。但亦有些国家，尤其是美国，则正好相反。若仔细分析比较，两者各有其利弊。但不管是任何体制，图书馆和资讯中心内部的组织与行政应能掌握现代化的精神，力求主动、革新，以迎合时代潮流及变更。在管理上更能采用新的观念，强调服务的目的与社会的使命，重视情境因素的互动关系，尊重个别的差异和需要，运用科学和民主的方法，采取协调合作的精神来达成图书馆的各自功能。

图书馆管理的现代化，除了其他的因素外，也受到近代管理学发展的影响。越是规模大的图书馆，越感到现代化管理的需要，因此对于管理学方面最近的发展极为重视。本书的第二章特把西方管理学在 20 世纪以来的一些重要发展予以介绍及分析。

"管理"这个名词，在西方管理学上一般是指对人、事、物等组成系统的活动、发展和变化进行有目的与有意识的控制行为。美国的史蒂芬·罗宾士（Stephen P. Robbins）在他的《管理概论》一书中指出："管理"为有效地透过一个组织中的成员去完成一些工作的过程[①]。很多管理学家把这些过程分为规划、组织、用人、领导与控制，而称之为管理的五大功能。在实行上，这些管理功能具有连贯性，而且是周而复始、持续不断的。

---

① Stephen P. Robbins.《管理概论：理论与实务》. 李茂兴，译. 台北：晓园出版社，1989，p.4.

图1-1显示这些管理功能的连贯性。现代的"管理学"即是研究这些现象与规律的科学,它涉及了行为科学、社会学、心理学、人类学、经济学、技术科学、工程学、应用数学、系统论、信息论与控制论等学科的领域,是一门高度综合性的交叉学科。

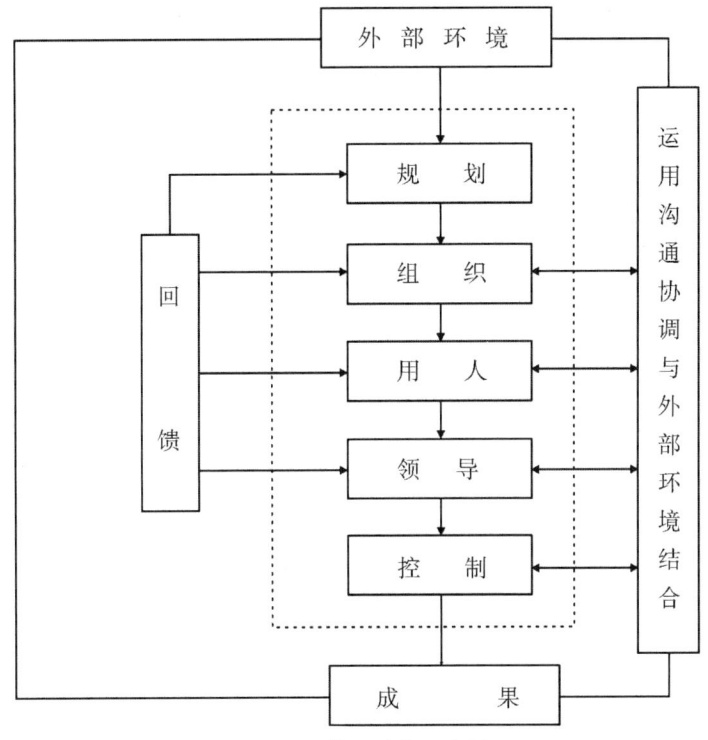

图1-1 管理功能程序图

紧接着第二章以后,本书的第三、四、五、六、七各章将分别讨论规划、组织、用人、领导及控制这五项管理功能在图书馆中的应用。本书的第八章除了总结之外,将试图预测今后图书馆发展的重点和方向,以供读者参考及探讨。因为中外文化背景的不同,特将中国式管理的意义、目的、基础、精神、原则、方法和境界等与西方管理学说加以比较,以求能综合中外优点,以建立适合于中国国情并合乎现代化需要的中国式管理。

在20世纪即将结束,21世纪即将来临的这个跨世纪的阶段,因为人类知识资讯空前未有的突飞猛进,以及计算机、电讯、电子出版、密集储存、国际互联网等新兴技术的发展和冲击,图书馆正面临一个需要重新定位的重要关头。无疑地,21世纪的图书馆将是一个充满生机、积极主动、融合了传统式以印刷品为主体的"纸张"图书馆及60年代以来新发展的"自动化"、"网路化"及"电子化"的图书馆,形成了跨世纪无远弗届和无所不在的"虚拟"图书馆。

第二章　二十世纪西方管理学的发展

Chapter 2　The Development of Management Science in the West in the Twentieth Century

第一节　历史背景——从古代到工业革命

有效的管理概念及方法早在两千年以前即已存在，这在中西方的历史上已有事实证明。像中国的长城，埃及的金字塔，印度的古王宫等，都是经过周详的计划，经由严密的组织，动员大量的人力，投注大量的资源，采用精密的技术，经过长时间的努力所完成的浩大工程，至今仍旧存在，令人景仰。即使如此，管理学成为一门学科，还是近百年来的事。在此之前，18 世纪经济大师亚当·史密斯（Adam Smith）在他的《国富论》（Wealth of Nations）一书中特别提到"分工"在工业生产上的经济效益。他以制造大头针为例，认为经由分工可以增加工人对机器操作的技术与熟练度，省下因转换工作所浪费的时间，从而增加了生产力。当时起源在英国的"工业革命"，以机械替代人力，以工厂替代家庭生产，使得一些生产企业规模扩大。美国的洛克菲勒（Rockefeller）和卡尼基（Carnegie）分别垄断了石油及钢铁工业等。工业革命和大型企业的发展使当时社会对管理学的理论和方法重新进行研究与探讨，从而建立了 20 世纪西方的管理学。

第二节　各学派理论的兴起和整合

在 19 世纪后期，以弗端里克·泰勒（Frederick Taylor）为首的科学管理学派提出了以科学方法找出各种劳动或生产过程的"最佳方式"。自此以后，很多其他学派相继出现，造成了管理学理论百家争鸣的现象，从不同的论点及方法上，企图充实管理学的内涵。史蒂芬·罗宾士（Stephen P. Robbins）将这些学派归为七类，把它们演进的时期用图表显示于下①：

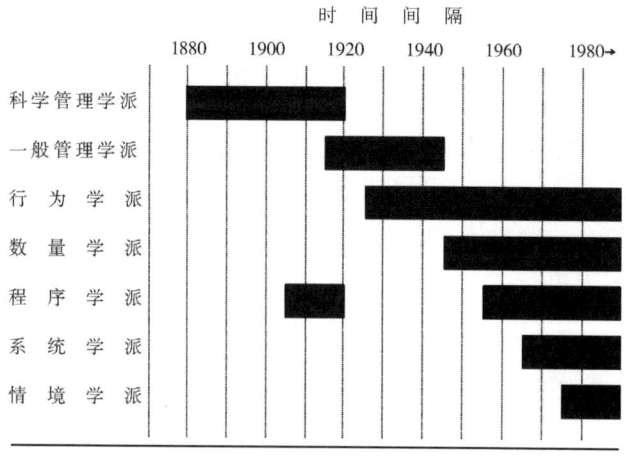

图 2-1　主要管理学派演进的时期

---

① Stephen P. Robbins.《管理概论：理论与实务》，李茂兴，译.（台北市：晓园出版社，1989），p. 39.
——*Organization Theory*: *Structure*, *Design*, *and Applications*. 3rd ed.（Englewood Cliff, N. J.: Prentice-Hall, 1990.）

以下将这些学派的主要代表人物及其观点做简单的介绍。

一、科学管理学派

在 20 世纪初最早发展的管理学理论是由弗端里克·泰勒（Frederick Taylor）所提出的"科学管理"理论[1]。泰勒是美国宾州钢铁公司的机械工程师，根据他的观察，认为工人工作的分配和程序缺乏科学分析，因此没有标准，效率低，造成严重的人力浪费。为了要改善这种情况，他花了近二十年的时间研究每项工作的"最佳方式"，提出了下列四项管理原则：

（1）用科学方法去分析各项工作中的每一动作细节，以确定最佳的操作方式，摒弃旧式的经验法则。

（2）对于工人的选用、训练、分配和报酬应采用科学方法。

（3）以诚恳的态度与工人合作，以确保所有的工作方法与程序均能符合科学原则。

（4）工作的分配与责任的分担在工人与管理者之间应该是平衡合理的。管理者应该负责管理上的工作。

因为泰勒长期的努力，加上他在 1911 年出版的专著《科学管理原则》一书，使得他的管理理论得到普遍的重视，因而被后人奉为科学管理之父。

受泰勒长期影响的一对夫妇，法兰克与莉琳·吉伯斯（Frank & Lillian Gilbreth），后来亦献身于科学管理的研究，以减少无谓的身体动作，设计最适当的工具与设备，来谋求最佳的工作绩效[2][3]。

另外一位曾跟随泰勒研究过的莫里斯·古克（Morris Cooke），曾把科学管理的一些原则应用到大学与政府机构的行政组织上[4][5]。

二、一般管理学派

如图 2-1 所显示，从 1915 到 1945 年之间是一般管理理论的发展时期，因为这一派学者把研究的重心放在整个组织上，因此他们被称为"一般管理学派"。

这一学派的主要代表有法国的亨利·费尧（Henri Fayol）和德国的麦克斯·韦伯（Max Weber）两位。

亨利·费尧是法国一家大型煤矿公司的主管，因此他的研究是根据自身经验把注意力放在经理人员的工作上。他的十四点具有弹性的管理原则（Principles of Management）被认为是可以普遍使用，放之于四海而皆准的。

（1）专业分工：可使员工对自己的工作熟能生巧，增进效率，提高生产力。

（2）职权：根据职位的不同，每位员工应有明确的责任及相应的权力。

（3）纪律：组织的规定，必须大家遵循，并切实执行。

（4）指挥统一：每位员工只接受一位主管的命令。

---

[1] Frederick Winslow Taylor. The Principles of Scientific Management. (New York: Harper & Row, 1911.)
——*Scientific Management, Comprising Shop Management, The Principles of Scientific Management and Testimony before the Special House Committee.* (New York: Harper & Row, 1947.)

[2] Frank B. Gilbreth. Motion Study' a Method for Increasing the Efficiency of the Workman. (New York: D. Van Nostrand, 1911.)

[3] ——and Lillian M. Gilbreth. *Fatigue Study: The Elimination of Humanity's Greatest Unnecessary Waste, a First Step in Motion Study.* 2nd ed. rev. (New York: Macmillan, 1919.)

[4] Morris Cooke. *Academic and Industrial Efficiency.* (New York: Carnegie Foundation for the Advancement of Teaching, 1910.) Bulletin No. 5.

[5] ——*Our Cities Awake.* (New York: Doubleday, 1918.)

(5) 指导统一：组织中有共同目标的单位应受同一主管及同一计划所指导。
(6) 团体利益至上：个人利益必须服从整个组织的利益。
(7) 酬劳公平：薪资应根据每人工作难易及多寡而定。
(8) 集权：员工在决策过程中参与的程度应以实际的情况而定。
(9) 层级节制：重视从上层主管到基层员工的指挥链（Chain of Command）。
(10) 秩序：一切作业要按照计划执行，井然有序。
(11) 公正：经理人对待部属应该关心及公平。
(12) 员工职位稳定：高流动率会导致低效率，人员编制任用应求稳定。
(13) 创造进取：在工作的计划与执行时，允许员工有创造进取的机会。
(14) 团队精神：以促进员工的合作及向心力。

除了以上十四点管理原则之外，费尧也是首先将"规划"、"组织"、"指挥"、"协调"及"控制"，当做一个贯联的管理程序来解释管理工作的五个主要功能①。

麦克斯·韦伯是德国的一位社会学家。他所提出的"职权结构"理论和"层级组织"（Bureaucracy）的型态，具有专业分工、层次分明、照章行事、不讲人情的特点。这些理论与组织形态已成为设计一般大型组织结构的重要参考。下面是韦伯理想中的层级组织②：

(1) 专业分工：将各项劳动及工作按专业性质予以明确地划分。
(2) 层次分明：将一般职位按照等级纳入组织，使低层次接受高层次的指挥与控制。
(3) 公开甄选：员工的选用及分配是按照各人的学识、技术、经验、能力及工作的需要，经过正式甄选的方式来处理。
(4) 循章办事：员工的工作及行动应该按照组织的规章及决定以达到一致性的要求。
(5) 不讲人情：在执行上尽量避免人情的考虑及私心的因素。
(6) 掌握方向：按组织的目标及计划行事，以求达到最好的成果。由于一般管理学派及科学管理学派为现代管理学说奠定了大部分的理论基础，因此这两派的开拓者，都被称为管理学的"古典理论家"（Classical Theorists）。

三、行为学派

行为学派尊重人为因素在组织机构中的关键性。这一学派的主要代表有胡果·宾士德堡（Hugo Munsterberg），玛丽·帕克·弗列特（Mary Park Follett），歇斯特·巴纳德（Chester I. Barnard），埃尔顿·梅友（Elton Mayo），克里斯·亚吉利斯（Chris Argyris），亚伯拉罕·马斯洛（Abraham Maslow），道格拉斯·马葛瑞格（Douglas McGregor）和兰西斯·李克特（Rensis Likert）等多位。

胡果·宾士德堡在1913年所出版的《心理学与工业效率》一书中开创了工业心理学的领域③。他认为对于人类行为的研究，有助于了解个别差异。透过对工作所做的科学分析及由心理测验对员工个别差异的了解，有助于对员工的甄选，工作的分配，以导致效率的增加。这个观念显示了科学管理与工业心理学两者之间的关联性。

玛丽·帕克·弗列特是位社会心理学家，她体认到个体行为在组织中的作用。她首先强调组织的基础在于群体伦理，而非个人主义。个人的潜力如果不经由群体活动中发挥出

---

① Henri Fayol. *Industrial and General Administration*. (Paris: Dunod, 1916). Translated by Constance Storrs (London: Pitman, 1949). Revised by Irwin Gray (New York: Institute of Electrical and Electronics Engineers, 1984).
② Max Weber. *The Theory of Social and Economic Organizations*. Translated by A. M. Henderson and Talcott Parsons. Edited by Talcott Parsons. (New York: Free Press, 1964).
③ Hugo Munsterbert. *Psychology and Industrial Efficiency*. (Boston: Houghton Mifflin, 1913).

来，那么就只是隐含未发的潜力而已，不会有什么作用①。因此，管理工作是在于协调和整合群体的努力。机构的管理人员要依靠本身的知识、技术与能力去领导部属，而不应仅依赖正式职权或职位。弗列特这种充满人性的理论直接影响到一般组织机构对于激励、领导以及职权的看法。这与日本目前的管理风格——非常强调群体的合作与团队精神——有颇多吻合之处。

歇斯特·巴纳德曾是新泽西州贝尔电话公司的总裁。他在1938年出版的《主管的功能》一书中认为组织是个社会化系统，它是由一群有社会互动关系的人们所组成②。组织的成功不仅要依靠员工之间的合作，而且也关联到与外界人群与机构所维持的良好关系。健全的管理要兼顾一个组织内外环境各种互动关系的协调与平衡。

哈佛大学心理学家埃尔顿·梅友之所以成名是因为他在1927到1932年这五年间在美国芝加哥西方电气公司的霍桑工厂所进行的霍桑实验（The Hawthorne Studies）③。这一实验开始时是为了研究工作环境和生产力之间的关系。在两个选定的工作群体中，以照明、温度以及其他工作条件为工作环境的变量，一个实验群体在变量很大的环境下工作，另一个群体在变量很稳定的环境下工作。研究者起初假定个人的生产力与变量的强弱有关联，但是实验的结果却不尽然。例如当照明强度增加时，两个群体的生产力都提高；当照明强度减弱时，两个群体的生产力依然持续上升；只有当照明度减到和月光那般暗淡时，生产力在变量大的那个群体才会下降。梅友这个实验指出，照明度和群体的生产力之间并没有直接关系，相反的，群体内部的社会化规范或标准是影响工人生产力的关键因素。当两个群体的工人觉察到他们被注意时，他们的生产力会发生提升的效果。梅友实验的结论中指出了下列几项解释：

（1）行为与情绪之间有密切的关系。
（2）群体的影响力对于个人的行为有重大的作用。
（3）在决定员工的个人产能时，群体的标准很有作用。
（4）在决定产能时，金钱跟群体标准、群体情绪以及安全感比较起来，是较不重要的因素。

事实上，霍桑实验并非没有缺点。它在进行的程序、结果的分析及结论等方面都曾受到批评④。但即使如此，这个实验激起了管理学上对人性因素研究的兴趣和重视。从历史的角度看，霍桑实验推动了人际关系运动。在霍桑的时代里存在着一个普遍的看法，认为人跟机械没有什么两样，把工人放在工厂里，加上必要的工具及原料，就可以产生一定数量的成品。这种错误观念的改变，颇受霍桑实验的影响。霍桑实验说明人非机械，在科学管理中所强调的"最佳工作方式"必须参入"群体行为"才能有效。这些群体行为包括了激励、咨询、领导及沟通等人际关系的技巧。

---

① Mary Park Follett. *The New State: Group Organization the Solution of Popular Government.* (London: Longmans, Green & Co., 1918).
——*Dynamic Administration. The Collected Papers of...* Edited by Elliot M. Fox, & L. Urwick. 2nd ed. (New York: Hippocrene Books, 1982).
② Chester I. Barnard. *The Functions of the Executives.* (Cambridge, Mass.: Harvard University Press, 1938).
③ Elton Mayo. *The Human Problems of an Industrial Civilization.* (New York: Macmillan, 1933).
④ Henry A. Landsberger. *Hawthorne Revisited.* (Ithaca, N.Y.: New York State School of Industrial Relations, Cornell University, 1958)
Alex Carey. "The Hawthorne Studies: A Radical Criticism" *American Sociological Review*, Vol. 32, No. 3 (June 1967), pp 403-416.
Berkeley Rice. "The Hawthorne Defect: Persistence of a Flawed Theory," *Psychology Today*, Vol. 16, No. 2 (February 1982), pp. 70-74.

在 20 世纪 50 年代末与 60 年代初,克里斯·亚吉利斯[①]、亚伯拉罕·马斯洛[②]、道格拉斯·马葛瑞格[③]和兰西斯·李克特等的管理著作陆续问世[④]。他们对人性的看法颇为接近,认为要提高员工的绩效,管理者应使工作涵盖更多的人性的一面。他们主张:

(1) 让员工能充分地参与和他们工作有关的决策。
(2) 管理人员应给予员工更多的信任与信心。
(3) 尽量使员工的目标和组织的目标趋于一致。
(4) 容许员工自我监督其工作以代替外在的控制等。

除此之外,马斯洛的"需求层次"理论有助于对激发员工动机及提高工作积极性的了解。马葛瑞格的"X 理论"与"Y 理论"也对管理者的领导方式从行为科学的观点予以分析。

四、数量学派

管理上"数量方法"包括统计的应用、最适当模型、资讯模式以及计算机仿真等,例如线型规划就是其中的一种技术,可以用来改善资源分派的选择。数学及统计学的数量方法在二次世界大战中,曾用来解决军事上的重要策略问题,这种数量方法后来也应用到民间组织的管理上而成为管理科学或作业研究(Operation Research)。

使用这种方法最有名的是罗勃特·麦克纳玛拉(Robert McNamara)与查理士·松顿(Charles Thornton)。麦克纳玛拉脱离军职后先投效于福特公司,以统计方法改进了福特公司的决策程序,后来在担任美国国防部长时,利用"成本—效益"的分析法(Cost-Benefit Analysis)将资源分派决策加以数量化。松顿在脱离军职后数年之间创立了规模甚大的理顿工业公司(Litton Industries),他也是把数量技术应用到公司的重要决策上。这一派的倡导者认为管理是一种逻辑程序,可以用数学符号及关系来表示。

数量方法虽然对管理决策,特别是在规划与控制方面极为有用,但因为大多数管理者对于数学和统计学感到陌生,缺乏建立数量模型的抽象能力,因此真正能使用者为数不多。另外,亦有人认为数量方法虽然提供了一项简化及解决复杂问题的有力推理工具,它还不够称为一个新的学派。

五、程序学派

因为以上各种学派各有其长处,但每派大多只能涵盖整个管理学领域的一部分。因此在 60 年代初期,赫洛·孔兹(Harold Koontz)著文指出各种学派的分歧处,建议将当时处于"管理理论丛林"(Management Theory Jungle)的分歧局面予以整合[⑤]。他将早期由亨利·费尧提出的管理程序——即规划、组织、指挥、协调和控制等五项功能加以发挥。他认为只有把各种管理学派的理论整合归纳于这些程序之中,才能使各种分歧的理论走出"丛林",变成一个综合的管理理论。孔兹的想法后来被接受为"程序学派"。

---

① Chris Argyris. *Personality and Organization: The Conflict between System and the Individual*. (New York: Harper & Row, 1957).
② Abraham Maslow. *Motivation and Personality*. 3rd ed. New York: Harper & Row, 1987.
③ Douglas McGregor. *The Human Side of Enterprise*. New York: McGraw-Hill, 1960.
④ Rensis Likert. *New Patterns of Management*. New York: McGraw-Hill, 1961.
⑤ Harold Koontz. "The Management Theory Jungle," *Journal of the Academy of Management*, Vol. 4, No. 3 (December 1961), pp. 174 – 188.
——. ed. *Toward a Unified Theory of Management*. New York: McGraw-Hill, 1964.

六、系统学派

把组织当作一个系统架构来分析是在 60 年代中期开始。支持系统学派者认为组织是由各种相关要素组成，包括个体、群体、态度、动机、正式结构、互动关系、目标、职位以及职权等。管理者的工作在于确保组织中每一部分能够相互支持，密切配合，以达成组织的目标。除了体认到组织内部各项活动的相互依赖性，系统学派还强调组织与外在环境的互动关系。一般管理学者认为，系统学派虽有其优点，但在发展上还不足以成为各管理学派的整合性架构。

七、情境学派

情境学派（Contingency or Situation Management）是企图整合管理理论的另一派别。这一学派认为因为人类社会及生活的复杂性及多变性，所以没有一个单一原则能放之四海而皆准。

像一般简单的原则：如果 X→就 Y（例如：如果想提高生产力"X"，就应该采取分工"Y"），情境学派把以上的原则加上一个"Z"变项（或情境决定因子）：

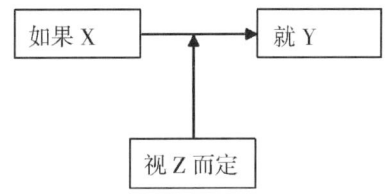

情境学派的研究者目前至少已确认出 100 个以上的变项，下面是几个在组织中常见的变项：
（1）组织的大小及复杂性。
（2）技术更新的快慢性。
（3）外在环境的不确定性。
（4）员工的个别差异性。

对于一个管理者而言，他（她）的任务就是要提供并维持一个良好的组织环境，以便组织中的每位成员可以在一起工作以达成组织所择定的使命与目的。在设计一个有绩效的内部组织环境时，每一位管理者都必须考虑到组织内外部各种可能变项的影响。

从以上所列举的各个学派可以大致看出近代西方管理思潮的演进。总而言之，各派的管理思想有其优点及贡献，也有其以偏概全之处。在采用时，必须取长补短，视实际情况灵活运用。要是再能配合上适于中国文化和国情的管理思想（请参考本书第八章第四节），相信会有更好的效果。

第三节　管理学理论在图书馆中的应用

自从 20 世纪初开始，各种图书馆因社会的需要而急遽发展。有许多大型的图书馆因规模日趋庞大复杂，对图书馆的组织与管理开始采用现代化管理学的理论与方法。

在 1930 年，唐纳·孔尼（Donald Coney）建议将科学管理的观念与方法运用到大学图书馆的组织与行政上。这包括图书馆功能的分类，目标的建立，生产力的提高，工作的专门化和标准化,和员工的有效使用等①。1952 年,在他另一篇有关图书馆管理的文章里,孔尼指出,图书馆的行政人员一般多缺乏管理学的知识和观念②。以劳伦斯·克拉克·蒲威尔(Lawrence Clark Powell)为例,他认为处理图书馆行政必须有天赋的心智与精神,再加上管理学上的一些"雕虫小技"(a knack for gimmicks and gadgets)③。这种轻视管理学的论调,即使在 50 年代左右,在一般的图书馆中还极为普遍。

当图书馆的管理观念及方法还在蜕变的过程中,在大型企业组织中,现代管理学得以逐渐发展趋于成熟,有些结果被引用到图书馆的管理上。其中,较受重视的理论有三:

(1) 图书馆结构的观点
(2) 图书馆人际关系的观点
(3) 图书馆政治运用的观点

一、从结构的观点

根据早期科学管理及一般管理学派的观点,这一派强调组织的重要性,视组织为有理性的系统。它的假设如下:

(1) 图书馆与其他组织一样,它的设立和存在是为了要达到某种预定的目的。
(2) 这个组织的结构及其内部程序包括规划、沟通、决策、协调和控制,受制于它的目的、规模大小、技术和环境。
(3) 组织的行为基本上是理性的,它受组织的目的、规模、技术、环境和结构的影响远较组织中个人的需要为大。

二、从人际关系的观点

这一派非常重视员工的个人需要,在工作安排上尽可能要设法配合。他们在某种程度上也相信组织是理性的,但认为组织与员工的需要能够一致才能和谐互惠。这一派的假设是:

(1) 一个组织的存在主要在满足员工的需要。
(2) 组织的每位员工能重大地影响到组织的目的(Goals)、目标(Objectives)和程序(Processes)。
(3) 员工们要依赖组织来满足个人需要和获得生活的意义。
(4) 假如个人的需要能附和组织的需要,不但个人感到满足,组织的目的也能达成。

三、从政治运用的观点

这一派较适合于政府机构和非营利的组织,因为它重视以协调方式来处理组织内部的冲突(Conflict)现象,并能在分配有限资源时考虑到权力(Power)影响的因素。它认为员工虽有不同的价值观,但在必要做决策时,能够取得协调。权力和冲突是政治派用来研究一个复杂机构非常重要的变量(Variables)。这一派的基本假设有:

(1) 一个机构内最重要的决策是如何分配有限的资源。

---

① Donald Coney. "Scientific Management and University Libraries", in G. T. Schwenning, ed. *Management Problems.* (Chapel Hill: University of North Carolina Press, 1930.) pp. 169 – 198.

② Donald coney "Management in College and University Libraries", *Library Trends*, Vol. 1, No. 1 (July 1952), pp. 83 – 94.

③ Lawrence Clark Powell. "The Gift to Be Simple" in John David Mar-shall, ed. *Of, By, and For Librarians.* (Hamden, Connecticut: Shoe String Press, 1960.) p. 266.

（2）一个机构的决策是经由各种内部协调的结果。

（3）在一个机构内，各位员工和各单位都有不同的价值观、信念和对现实的看法。

（4）机构的目的是多重的，而有些甚至于是相互冲突的，决定机构的目的要经由继续不断的协商和谈判。

结构观点的理论有助于我们了解组织的目的、技术和结构间的关系。其缺点在于忽视人在机构中的地位及权力和冲突在组织中的因素。人际关系观点的理论虽然强调人在组织中的重要性，但却忽视结构的约束和权威等作用。另一缺点是它与结构派一样，不重视有限资源的分配、权力或冲突等关键。政治运用的观点强调组织内外各种政治因素的作用，利用协调的方式以化解矛盾与冲突，达成明智的决策，使有限资源得到合理的分配。因为上列三种观点都对图书馆的管理有相当的影响，应该综合采用，并因情况不同而做适当的选择[①]。

[①] Beverly P. Lynch, ed. *Management Strategies for Libraries*. (New York: Neal-Schuman, 1985.) pp. ix – xviii.

第三章　图书馆的规划

Chapter 3　Library Planning

在本书第一章第四节已提到现代管理学中的五项管理功能——规划、组织、用人、领导及控制。因为"规划"（Planning）是一个机构在选择方向（Direction），拟定目的（Goals）及目标（Objectives），和决定如何行动时的主要作业程序，它在五项功能中占有先导的地位。赫洛·孔兹（Harold Koontz）等在他们合著的《管理理论》一书中用下列图形来显示规划是管理的基础①。

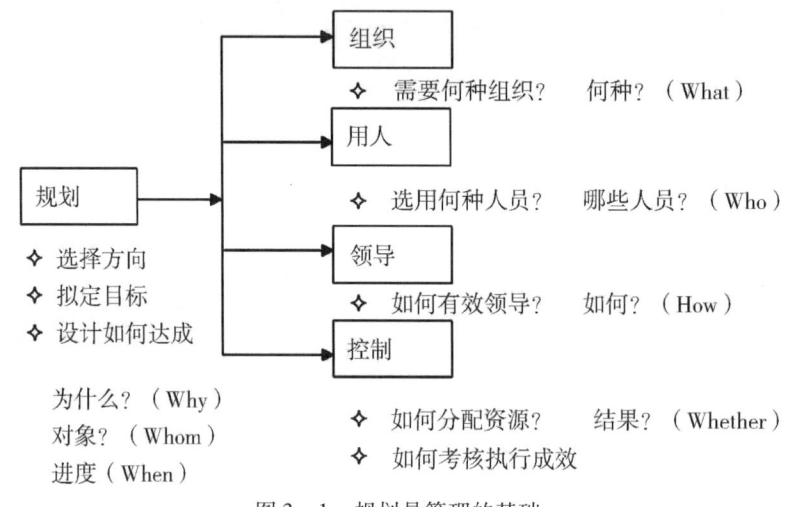

图 3-1　规划是管理的基础

从图 3-1 中可以看到每一管理功能都有它特殊的任务：
1. 规划的任务是说明一个机构存在的原因，它的服务对象是谁，和作业的进度。
2. 组织的任务是决定一个机构所需具备的结构。
3. 用人是指选用哪些员工和如何分配工作，以达到人尽其才的效能。
4. 领导是决定如何执行。
5. 控制是要考核执行的成效作为下一步的参考。

第一节　规划的定义与目的

在一个机构里，上下各层次及左右各部门都应该按照所拟定的规划来作业。规划是一个机构根据其使命（Mission）、本身的优点和特色及历史渊源，再经由审察分析内外界情况、机会及需要，以建立中、长程目的（Goals），近程目标（Objectives），和发展达成每

---

① Harold Koontz, Cyril O'Donnell, Heinz Weihrich. 《管理精论》，苏永成，译. 台北：台北国际商业出版社，1987，p. 79.

项目标的各种策略（Strategies）及行动（Actions）的作业。行动这一词，亦有用计划方案（Programs）、任务（Tasks）等来称呼者。在执行一个规划时，一个机构必须衡量其经费来源，拟定预算（Budget），并制定有关的政策（Policies）、规则（Rules）、标准（Standards）及程序（Procedure）。关于规划的一般次序可以用图 3 - 2 来说明。

规划的第一步是将一个机构的"使命"用简明的文字加以叙述。使命说明（Mission Statement）是在阐明一个机构存在的理由，它应该明确地指出一个机构该做些什么？为谁做？有何利益？它的内容包含机构的优势、工作范围、服务重点、主要对象和预期的效果。每一个机构在拟定计划、分配资源及做决策时都应当以它的使命说明作为最高指导原则。

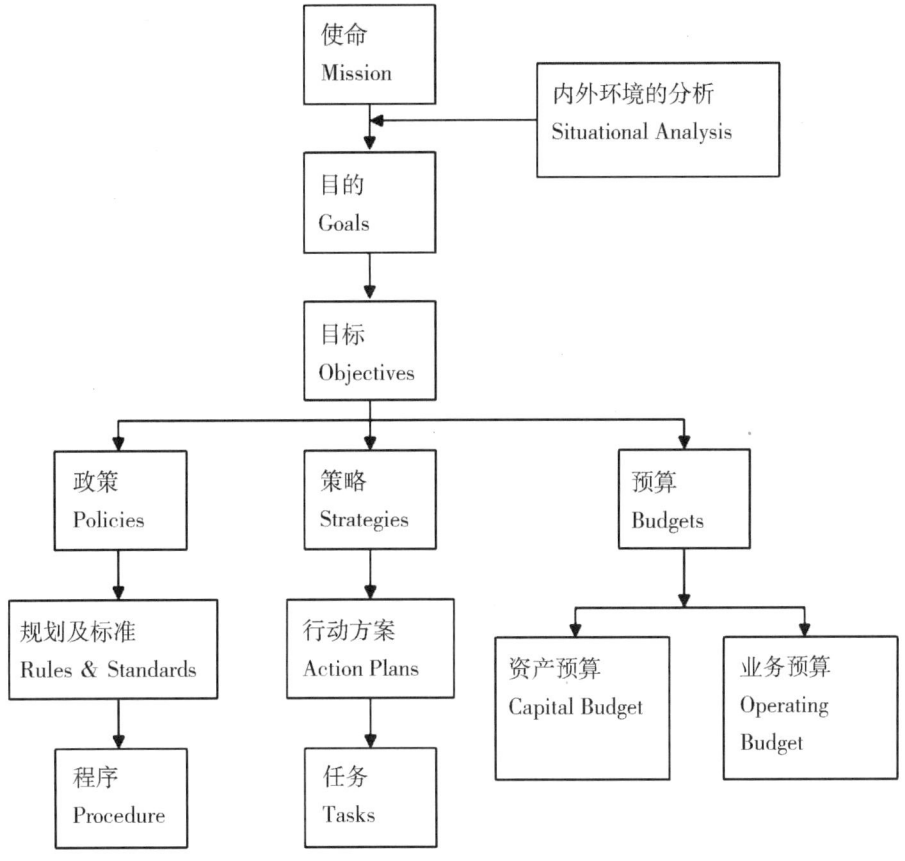

图 3 - 2 规划的次序

"目的"与"目标"这两个常用词在中文的意义上没有明显的差别，但在英文的意义上，目的（Goal）是比较长期的，而目标（Objective）则是比较短程的。从图 3 - 2 来看，规划不仅是要建立目的及目标，而且要设法达成。因此它是既有"目的"（要完成什么），又有"手段"（如何去完成）。

规划的作用是为一个机构的全体员工指示行动方向，使大家能为共同的目标而努力。在绝大多数的机构里，目前所面临的困难是如何将有限的资源做最合理及有效的分配与应用。规划可以在众多要做的工作中，分别轻重前后，帮助一个机构在这一方面做理性的选择及决定。因此亦有人把资源的适当分配当作规划的主要作用。规划做得好的话，可以减少工作上不必要的重复及浪费，增加机构的全盘效率。因为规划是前瞻性的，它也表示了一个机构力求创新的愿望。

一个可以执行的规划必须要有经费的支持。根据经费的来源，给予适当的分配和使用，这是预算的功能。预算有业务预算（Operating Budget）与资产预算（Capital Budget）两种。业务的预算包括员工的薪金及福利、办公费用、一般器材、日常用品、家具、出差费、邮电费、维修费、保养费及书刊资料费等经常性的开支。资产的预算包括建筑、重大翻修、贵重器材、自动化系统的装置或更新等大项的开销。有关预算的详细讨论请看第七章第二节"财务的控制"。

第二节　规划的种类及步骤

一、规划的种类

规划的种类很多，一般有长、中、短程之分。

1. 长程规划（或称"策略性规划"——Strategic Planning）

一般是五年以上，用以决定一个组织的长程目的、政策、策略及估计达成目的所需的资源。长程规划是具有前瞻性的，应能对组织之目的与手段做较大幅度的调整，视所有事物为变量，不受旧有承诺及传统的限制。

2. 中程规划

一般是二年至五年，是对达成某些选定项目所做比较具体及经过协调的规划。所需资源也按照预定的策略予以分配。中、长程规划可以使规划者往远处看，预测可能发生的变化及其冲击作用，借以拟定适当的对策。

3. 短程规划

一般是二年以下，包括了在已定的目标下进行工作及资源的分配、进度表和考核的依据等。有些短程规划亦被称为"营运性规划"，它的时间较短，是以季、月或周来衡量。营运性规划又可分成"单一用途规划"及"常备性规划"两种。前者是为了完成一项特定目标所拟定的。如图书馆为要装置一个光盘检索网路所拟定的计划，此计划在达成预定的目标以后即告结束。后者是用来处理一再发生的情况。例如有关图书馆的图书流通，资讯服务的政策、手续及规定等。短程规划应该与中、长程规划尽量协调和配合，以促成长程目的的达成。

二、规划的步骤

因为规划的拟定往往受内外在环境因素的影响，因此当这些因素变动时，一个规划也应该予以适度的修正。

根据图3-2的次序，规划的步骤可以分为下面几点：

1. 确定规划的前提

（1）简单明确地阐述一个机构的使命

每一个机构都有它存在的主要原因及对其所在地社会的责任。一个图书馆的使命说明应该包含它的存在理由、服务对象及社会责任等。阐明一个机构的使命是要让全体员工对于其本身的工作"建立共识"，有了这个明确的共识，大家才会有共同的使命感和价值观。以俄亥俄大学图书馆为例，它的使命说明是：

"作为一个资源共享、资讯、知识及思想传递的中心，俄亥俄大学图书馆通过它的馆藏、服务及对其他合作机构的参与，为俄亥俄大学、俄亥俄州东南地区及美国国内和国际学术界提供服务。为了支持大学的教学和研究，图书馆与大学各部门保持密切联系及磋商，以发展、维护及扩大图书馆的馆藏。全馆馆员负责组织及保存馆藏；引进适用的技术；协助读者能充分使用本地及全国各地区的图书资源及服务；经由与教员的合作将资讯查检和分析技能融合于大学部学生及研究生的课程之中；协助教员有效使用各种教学媒体增进优质教学；训练学生成为经验丰富的资讯使用者并能终生得益。"

美国国会图书馆馆长杰姆士·比林顿博士（James H. Billington），在新上任不久即开始一连串的规划活动。他希望在2000年，亦即是国会图书馆成立二百周年，完成他的革新计划。以下是他在1989年所宣布的国会图书馆的使命：

    A. 收集及维护一个包括人类知识、资讯及表达全球性的馆藏。
    B. 使得所有的馆藏及人力资源能够继续及有效地提供美国国会所使用。
    C. 使得所有资源能够充分的开放和为美国的人民及其他的图书馆服务。
    D. 促进和庆祝所有人民及所有科学的智慧创造自由。

在他的补充说明中，比林顿强调以上四点的先后次序、重要性、及关联性。他认为馆藏的发展最重要，其次是为国会服务，再其次是为美国人民及其他图书馆服务，最后才是为有创造性的社会大众（The Creative Community）服务。

（2）内外环境的分析。

一个机构在明确地决定其使命后，下一步就是要自我检查是否有能力达成使命。这种自我检查包括了对内部情况及外在环境各种影响因素所进行的研究和分析。图书馆内部情况的影响通常有下列几种：

    A. 经费及拨款的情况。
    B. 馆藏的成长率及特色。
    C. 人员的编制及素质。
    D. 组织及分工。
    E. 图书馆的建筑、面积及设备。
    F. 读者服务的项目及优缺点。

图书馆外在环境的影响大概包括了：

    A. 整个小区的经济情况。
    B. 上级机构对图书馆的支持。
    C. 其他相关机构对有限经费来源的竞争。
    D. 小区对图书馆的重视程度。
    E. 读者的需求及水平。
    F. 出版界的情况。
    G. 资讯技术的发展与使用。
    H. 图书资讯网路与馆际合作。
    I. 政府的规章法令。
    J. 大众传播，尤其是电视娱乐节目的影响。

因为能影响图书馆的内部情况和外在环境的各种因素经常在变动，所以在做规划时应对这些变量予以定期的研究与分析。在大型图书馆中，这种研究分析的资料可以从读者意见调查、小区分析、内部报告、预算及开支，和各种统计数字中取得。对于所收集的各种资料，规划人员应该进行下列四项分析：

A. 图书馆的长处或优势（Strengths）。
B. 图书馆的弱点（Weaknesses）。
C. 图书馆面对的机会（Opportunities）。
D. 图书馆遭遇的威胁（Threats）。

每一个图书馆有其特有的长处或优势，包括藏书特色、服务项目、人员、设置、经费、资讯技术、上级机构或社会的支持等。如何发挥或突显这些优点，使能出类拔萃，以加强其优势作用，是规划时一个极重要的考虑方面。

同样地，每一个图书馆多少会有一些内部的缺点，这些缺点若能及早发觉，予以改善，可以减少恶性蔓延，提高员工士气，改进工作效能。

有很多时候，在图书馆所处的环境里，可能会有特别的机会出现，像政府或基金会的特别补助、私人捐款、新技术的开发、与邻近图书馆的合作等。这些机会若能及时把握和采用，可以扩大图书馆的资源，发挥员工的潜能，增加图书馆的服务项目，及提高图书馆的地位。

此外，因为图书期刊费用的上涨，经费的紧缩，馆舍和书库的饱和，新技术及新媒体开发所带来的问题，传统图书馆观念亟需变革等等不利因素的影响，使图书馆遭遇到前所未有的威胁。为了维持生存，迎合新的资讯需要，图书馆必须提出应变的对策，力求更新。

2. 决定目的

在规划时第二个步骤是决定图书馆的目的。图书馆的目的应该是图书馆使命的延伸，它是达成使命的重要指标。在拟定目的时，除了应考虑到图书馆内在的因素，还应注意下列各点：

（1）它应该与图书馆的使命配合一致。
（2）它是比较广义的。
（3）它是可以衍变成具体可行的目标。
（4）它是可以达成的。
（5）它的表达是简明清晰的。

以俄亥俄大学图书馆的目的为例，该馆1994年及未来的目的一共有十二项：

（1）提供有效的、经济的及高质量的图书馆服务。
（2）寻求适当的财力支持，使图书馆能达到配合高质量教学活动所必须的数量和质量标准。
（3）经过加强的馆员发展计划及其他继续教育的机会，以促进馆员的成长。
（4）将图书馆使用的知识和大学部学生、研究生及专业教育结合起来，为学生的终生学习打下基础。
（5）分析图书馆现有图书资源，制定合理的增长和发展计划。
（6）推广读者对图书馆馆藏、服务及学校其他资讯资源的了解和使用，使得读者能独立的使用更多的资源。
（7）保持优美、舒适、安全及合适的学习环境。
（8）改善现有的设备及器材，并设计新的设备，以便利多种媒体的教学。
（9）协助教师使用教学媒体及技术，鼓励使用这些媒体及技术以满足学生学习的需要。
（10）用及时和有效的方式，采用先进和经济的方法，来维护图书馆的馆藏，以保持图书馆所收藏研究资料的完整齐全。
（11）通过本馆的馆藏、服务和馆员发展计划，积极支持对国际社会和相互依赖教育的承当。

（12）通过本馆的馆藏、服务和有关人事措施，充分支持学校对社会平等和人权政策所采取的坚决维护态度。

这些"目的"是从该大学的十年计划中及其他文件的有关部分中摘出。它们的先后次序是每一年由全体馆员投票决定，依据其公认的重要性来排列。

3. 制定目标

一旦有了使命及明确的目的，下一个步骤即是经由全体员工的参与来制定整个机构的近程目标。在前节中所提到的使命和目的虽然也需要逐年检讨及做必要的修正，它仍然是比较长期的而且是原则性的，只有目标才是具体的及指望能在一两年内可以完成的。在制定一个机构的使命及目的时，其作业大多由上层主管负责，依据机构设立的主要原因及大方向，并审度内外在环境因素及员工的意向来决定，中下层员工的参与程度较小。在制定目标、策略及行动时，中下层员工参与程度应该大量地增加。从图书馆的观点来看，它与一般企业机构有不同之点，因为它是服务性及非营利性的，虽然在经营上图书馆也要讲求现代化的管理及效率，但它与企业机构比较起来应该是非常民主及透明的。因此在制定目标时，图书馆的主管不仅要允许员工参与，而且应该创造机会，鼓励员工积极地参加。早先的科学管理学派虽认为"规划"与"执行"应该分开，但晚近的观念认为员工的参与不但可以提高士气，增加效能，而且有助于规划的执行。

在一个大型的图书馆里，有的特设有规划与发展（Planning and Development）部门或指定专人来负责全馆的规划作业。在这些馆里，正式的参与人员包括上级机构的代表、正副馆长、预算人员、各部门主任、图书馆决策和咨询委员会的成员、特设的规划小组组员及其他馆员。大学图书馆还可以包括各学院院长、系主任、教授和学生代表、社会人士等。在小型图书馆里，有时由馆长自行负责，或由一个特设的委员会来规划。

因为目标是目的的延伸，因此在每一个目的之下可以有不同数目的目标（或子目的）。在拟定目标时，通常应顾到下列七点：

（1）它是否可以付诸实施？
（2）它是否提供多种实施的途径？
（3）它是否够明确？
（4）它的结果是否可以衡量？
（5）它是否有时间限制？
（6）它是否有适当的难度及具有挑战性？
（7）它是否支持本机构的价值观念及目的？

在一个组织里，除了整体的目标外，各部门或各位员工可能有个别的目标。这种不同层次的目标有时会彼此不兼容，因而造成组织间、群体间，甚至个人间的矛盾和冲突。在制定目标时，应注意协调和沟通，鼓励员工的参与，使得整体的目标能为全体员工所了解和接受，各部门及各人的目标应该能配合组织的目标，各层次的目标能够连贯一致，以发挥整体的效果。

在近三十年来，很多机构采用"目标管理"（Management by Objectives）的方式来动员每一位员工以达成所定的目标。本章的第三节将对目标管理的方式及优缺点加以阐述。

4. 策略及行动

在制定比较具体可行的目标以后，下一步骤就是要选择达成每一目标的最佳策略及拟定各种行动的方案。这些策略及行动方案应该由各负责执行的部门来拟定，经由上级同意后，认为与整个机构的使命、目的及目标配合，然后付诸实行。每一项行动方案最好还能包含达成目标的时间、进度及可资衡量的指标。

一般说来，每一行动方案（Action Plan）还可以分解成一系列的行动。为了慎重起见，在采取行动前，亦有先进行小规模的先导实验（Pilot Study or Pretest），以确定该方案的可行性（Feasibility），使能发现问题，及时加以修正，再正式开始实施。在拟定新的行动方案时，应同时提出所需人员、设备及其他开销的预算和实施时的工作分配及进度表等。

5. 政策、规则、标准及程序

政策、规则、标准和程序是将规划付诸实行时的重要规范，它的目的不在约束，而是对各层次的员工在他（她）们各自的权责范围内对经常出现的情况所能自行做主的授权。它亦能协助各层次的管理人员在遭遇困难时，知道应采取何种措施，或选择解决问题的途径。好的政策及规则要有员工参与，共同制定。它可以引发员工的积极主动性及促成各单位间工作的和谐一致性，以求有效地达成机构的目的和目标。在一个大学图书馆里，它的政策与规则必须与大学的政策与规则配合，不相抵触。以有关人事甄选、任用、考核、升迁的政策和规则为例，图书馆的政策与规则应以大学的政策与规则为准，只有在执行的细节上加以补充，使得大学的政策和规则在执行时更能符合图书馆的情况和需要。在图书的采购及期刊的订阅方面，虽然因情况特殊与一般采购手续不同，也必须在大学或上层机构所定的采购政策及规则以外另定办法，由上层批准后执行，使得图书馆的各种采购业务在合乎学校规定的范围内，能够机动有效地执行。

在拟定一个政策时，一般要包括下面五个部分：

（1）政策的说明（Statement）——要说明制定政策的原因。
（2）政策的范围（Scope）——指出政策所包含的范围及针对的情况。
（3）政策的内容（Contents）——申述政策的要点。
（4）执行的程序（Implementation Procedure）——解释在执行时的细节。
（5）生效日期及如何修改（Effective Date and Revision）——注明生效的日期及修改的办法。

规则和政策比较起来，政策是比较原则性的及可以变通的；而规则是比较严谨的，没有什么伸缩性。例如不准在图书馆内吸烟的规定和对借书过期不还罚款的规定，一旦颁布了就要严格执行。除非有特殊的原因，一般是不可通融的。

程序是指在执行政策与规则时所定出的细节，有时它会被包括在政策和规则之内，亦有的是由执行单位另外拟定的。

第三节 目标管理（Management by Objectives）

当一个机构完成其规划的作业以后，下一步就是要把这个规划付诸实施。在最近四十年来，我们常听到"目标管理"这个名词。目标管理的定义虽然因人而异，颇不一致，但其主要作用是把一个机构所定的大目标融合在管理系统之中，使得机构的大目标能够透过各个部门，各位员工的个别目标，在有系统的协调、配合、执行和考核之下，能够如期完成。完好的目标管理可以激发员工的自我动机，创造激励的环境，加强机构的决策分权，改善对工作的评估，持续并提升工作的成效，及促成目标的达成。

一、目标管理的过程

目标管理的过程一般可归纳于下：

（1）在制定机构的规划时，应尽量鼓励员工的参与。

（2）在规划制定以后，应使用各种有效方法，让全体员工知道。

（3）根据所制定的大目标，经由协调及辅导，建立各部门的子目标及行动方案和每位员工的个别目标。这些部门的目标应该有达成的期限和进度表。

（4）授权每一部门及每位员工，让他们有充分的自主权来执行他（她）们的行动方案及达成他（她）们的目标。

（5）上级主管尽力协助及支持下层的工作，以鼓励代替控制，而且重视绩效的回馈。

（6）以员工执行其个人所定目标的成效作为年度考核的依据。

（7）在执行过程中及年终考核时能根据实况对各层次的规划与目标予以修正。

图3-3以流程的方式说明目标管理的开始、执行及用于评估上的程序。

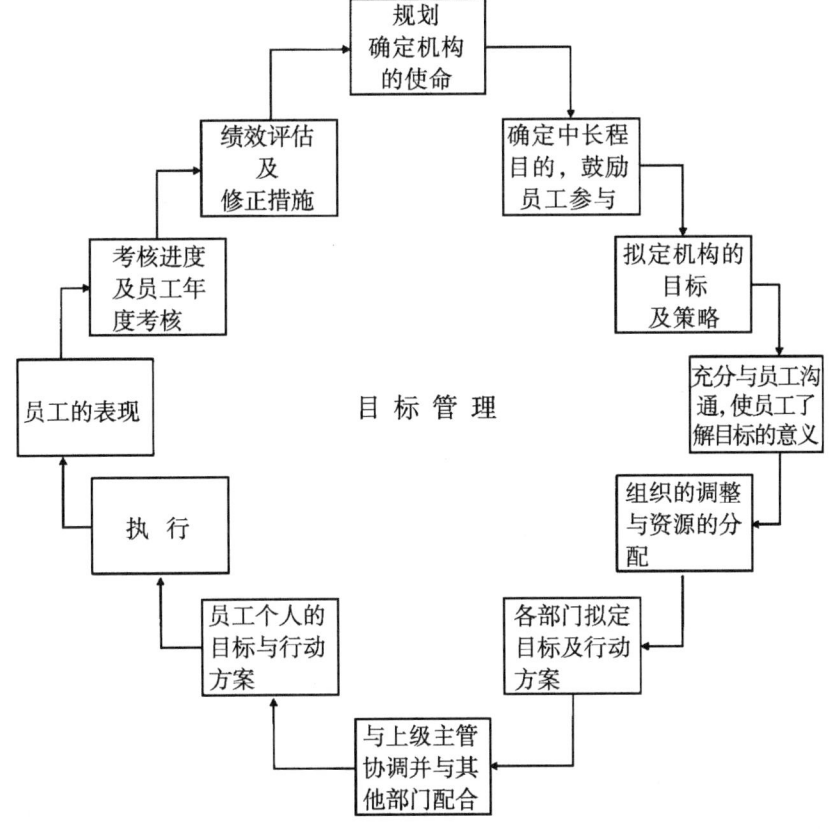

图3-3 目标管理的流程图

大型的图书馆在采用目标管理时，还要注意到各部门及每位员工个人的目标与其他部门及其他员工的目标之间的关联性。例如，期刊装订的时间表与读者使用这些期刊最频繁的时期，编目部对于一些急用书刊的加速处理程序，采访部与编目部的作业流程等，会牵涉两个或多个部门之间的协调和配合，需要上级的管理者将众多相关的子目标与工作方案等，根据其完成的时间和先后次序，构成一个相互联结的工作网，使得每项工作完成的时间能与相关的工作呼应及配合。每一个工作网之下还可以再分解成相互联结的小工作网，以提高整个机构的工作效能。

二、目标管理的优点和执行上常见的一些偏差

经过多年的实施,目标管理的优点远超过它的缺点。一般说来,目标管理的特点是,由主观变为客观,由整体变成个体,由无形变为有形(数据)。其精神在"引力"而非"推力"。它的优点有:

(1)驱使每个机构对确定其目标的认真和重视。
(2)鼓励员工参与目标的制定,激励员工的积极性。
(3)有了目标的导向,使得管理更上轨道。
(4)可以推动分权管理,改善上下层的关系,加强员工的责任心。
(5)可以加强机构内各部门的协调、配合与系统化。
(6)可以协助建立有效控制工具,及时矫正执行上的偏差。
(7)可以结合规划、执行与考核为一体。

在执行目标管理时常见的一些偏差:

(1)很多机构在执行目标管理前,没有充分与员工沟通及使员工了解目标管理的理论基础是建立在自我控制和自我导向的观点上,很多员工对此不够了解。
(2)有些机构没有制定明确的使命、目的和目标。
(3)要制定真正可以验证及适当难度的目标并不容易。
(4)有些员工的表现,如奉公守法、早到迟走、工作认真、团体精神等,不能用数据来衡量。若过分重视考绩的结果,会造成对短期目标的强调,及对长期目标的轻视。
(5)过分强调可验证的目标也会造成重量不重质的结果。

以上这些偏差,若能在运用时加以注意,设法改进,则目标管理还是利多弊少的一种管理方法。

第四节 策略性的规划(Strategic Planning)

在本章的第二节中讲到长程规划时曾提到策略性的规划,因为在近二三十年来,社会的变迁极为剧烈,新技术的发展突飞猛进,传统式的规划方式已不够应付各种剧变的需要。新的、能够面对将来的规划必须具有策略性的眼光及思想。这种策略性的规划在大型企业中已被普遍采用,但政府机构和非营利组织(包括图书馆)对此还刚刚开始起步。

一、什么是策略性的规划

现任密西根大学图书馆馆长唐纳德·雷吉士博士(Donald E. Riggs)在1984年出版了一本《图书馆管理者的策略规划》的书,对策略性规划的重要性及如何在图书馆中使用,首先予以完整及有系统性的介绍①。一般说来,策略性的规划是要使一个机构了解它现在所处的地位及情况,确认它将来希望达到的境界,以及设计如何达到此境界的最佳途径。策略性规划的过程包括了使命的说明、策略、目的和目标的拟定,并对可供选择的途径(Alternatives)、应变的措施(Contingency)、政策、资源分配、执行和评估等所做的考虑。因为策略规划是长程的,它是具有前瞻性及冒险性的。它的冒险(Risk-taking)是经过慎重考虑各种情况及应变措施后才大胆地决定。好的策略规划还有赖于管理者具备"策略性

---

① Donald E. Riggs. *Strategic Planning for Library Managers*. Phoenix, Arizona: Oryx Press, 1984.

的思想"(Strategic Thinking)及"策略性的眼光"(Strategic Vision),敢于大胆假设,而且眼光远大。

策略性规划有它长程的目的,亦有它近程的目标,在执行时它要评估执行的结果,随着内外界环境的变动,予以适当地修正。策略性规划与传统性规划的主要不同点在于策略性规划是"由远而近",而传统性规划是"由近而远"。"由远而近"的方式是先有一个长远的目的,再由此规划如何达成目的的步骤及策略。"由近而远"的方式则是以推演的方式,从近程目标向前推进,以达到远程的目的。传统式规划与策略性规划的主要不同点可由图3-4看出。例如说,用传统式规划来制定的目的多半是过去和现在目的的延伸,不会有大的突破。而策略性规划的远程目的是按照对将来所希望达成的设想来制定,不受过去和现在的限制。两者之间的差距(Gap)显示了传统式规划与策略性规划可能导致的不同结果。策略性规划的优点是能突破现状,面对将来,以策略性的手段来扩大图3-4中成果的差距。

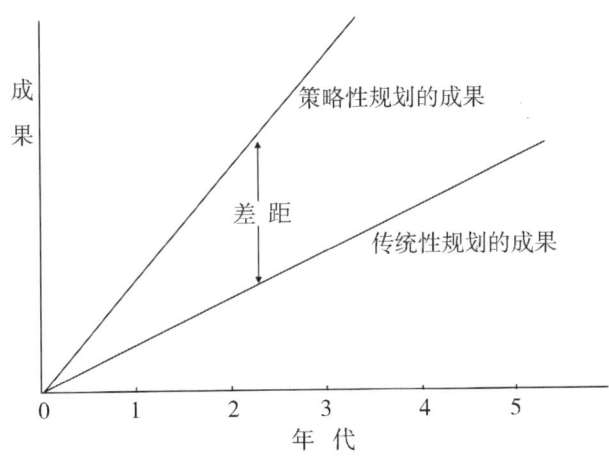

图3-4 策略性规划与传统性规划两者间成果的差距

与一些受传统影响较大的机构一样,图书馆是一个比较保守的机构,它受古老制度、方法与思想的影响,喜欢因循旧规,趋于被动,不容易突破现况,更谈不上冒险。在目前的资讯社会里,图书馆在众多的竞争因素下,若不力求更新,迟早会被其他机构所取代。为了确保图书馆的存在,使它能在资讯社会中发挥更大的功能,它的规划必须是建立在"将来"的基础上,并根据此"将来"的目的,来拟定达成此目的的最佳途径及应该采取的策略。

当一个机构发觉有下列任何一种情况时,这是应该进行策略性规划的时机:
(1)原先设立的宗旨,因环境的改变而逐渐消失。
(2)经费来源愈来愈减少,大家已对这个机构失去兴趣。
(3)很多工作已被别的机构抢去。
(4)员工缺乏主动性,士气低落。
(5)机构的前途显得变幻无常,飘摇不定。
(6)机构的目的不明确,失去了方向。

当然,策略规划不应该是到了病入膏肓时再做。一个健全的机构也可以采用它来发展长期的策略,以确切掌握未来的方向。一个好的策略规划必须是面对将来的(Futuristic),以服务对象为主导的(Client-driven),重视行动的(Action-oriented),有弹性的

(Flexible)及对文化敏感的(Culturally Sensitive)。它应该了解机构本身的任务(Mandate)、长处(Strength)、短处(Weakness),觉察到可能的威胁(Threats)和机会(Opportunities),认知各种约束(Constraints)和参数(Parameters),利用集体规划的方式,来导致机构的革新。因此,策略规划不仅可以"应变",而且可以"防患于未然",发挥"洞悉先机"的效果。

二、如何进行策略性的规划

要做好一个切实可行的策略性规划,图书馆的馆长应该身先士卒,亲自领导和参与。在大的图书馆中,馆长可以设立一个包括副馆长、各部门主任、员工代表及社会代表(在大学图书馆则为学校行政、教授和学生代表等)的规划小组,由馆长亲自主持。经由馆长对策略性规划的重视,和所显示的认真态度,才能激发大家对规划工作的热忱与关注。这个小组可以先从下面四个基本问题的探讨着手:

1. 图书馆的现况如何?
2. 图书馆对将来有何期望?
3. 哪些可能的障碍将会影响图书馆对将来的期望?
4. 图书馆应采取哪些行动来达成图书馆的目的及目标?

在寻求解答这些问题之前,馆长及其助手应大量收集有关资料及统计数字,供规划小组分析研究。

图书馆的策略规划有的是包括在上级机构的策略规划作业之内,亦有的是由图书馆自己主动规划。前者的好处是图书馆部分的规划已与上级机构的规划配合,在执行时易于得到上级的支持。后者则应力求与上级机构的规划程序配合,以争取上级的认可与支持,在这种情况下最好能有上级代表参与图书馆的规划小组。

要做好策略性的规划是需要馆长及规划小组的成员投注相当多的时间和精力,有些图书馆则以工作忙无暇规划为借口,尽量拖延。也有些馆长认为"没有目标,就没有失败(No Objectives, No Failure);没有方向,就不会走失(No Direction, No Loss)"。这种借口与"多做多错;少做少错"的想法是造成一个图书馆管理失败的致命伤!实际上,基于策略规划的重要性,不管图书馆馆长及其他部门主管有多忙,皆应排出时间来规划。只有图书馆馆长以身作则,才能鼓励员工积极参与。

三、策略性规划的流程

在制定策略规划时,本章第二节所提到的基本步骤可以参考及采用。克伦·博劳奔(Kieran P. Broadbent)在他一篇文章中为策略规划的程序提出以下说明[①]:

1. **使命说明**(Mission Statement)

这应该是用简明的文字来说明一个机构存在的原因、任务、服务对象,及对社会的责任等。

2. **策略分析**(Strategic Analysis)

这是要找出各种足以影响一个机构作业的因素,包括这个机构本身的"长处"及"弱点"和外在的"机会"及"威胁",以决定所须选择的某些策略及这些策略的比重。

---

① Kieran P. Broadbent. "Strategic Planning: An Essential Process for Research and Information Centers", Paper presented to the Consultancy on Strategic Information Planning International Workshop and Seminar, Ljutijana, Slovenia, pp. 14–17 (April 1992).

机构本身的优缺点可以从下列情况看出：
（1）组织文化
（2）共同价值观
（3）领导的风格
（4）员工的素质
（5）组织的结构
（6）财务状况
（7）其他资源

机构外在的机会和威胁可以从下列各点显示出来：
（1）社会文化因素
（2）政府的政策和措施
（3）经济情况
（4）技术发展
（5）竞争
（6）环境
（7）服务对象
（8）人口成分和动态
（9）生活方式

3. **目的及目标**（Goals and Objectives）

制定目的及目标的用意是在决定一个机构的大方针及希望达到的成果。

4. **作业计划**（Operational Plan）

这种计划多半是中、短程的，它的内容应该包括有：
（1）作业的细节
（2）执行的人员
（3）资源的分配
（4）与其他单位的协调
（5）预计的成效
（6）考核的指标
（7）作业的进度
（8）完成的时间

5. **执行**（Implementation）

有了计划之后就要付诸实施。一个考虑周详的计划会减少执行上所产生的枝节及偏差。为了要使执行能够顺利，一个机构必须做好下列的准备：
（1）建立团队精神（Teamwork）
（2）有适当的组织（Structure）
（3）有良好的沟通（Communication）
（4）激发员工的动机（Motivation）
（5）提高士气（Morale）
（6）加强工作的训练（Job Training）
（7）有效的资讯系统（Information System）

6. **评估**（Evaluation）

有系统的考核各种预订的指标，才可以获知执行的成效及需要改进之处。

因为当前的图书馆是处于一个急遽变动的环境中，它必须采用策略规划的方法来建立一个在"比较上占优势"（Comparative Advantage）和"竞争上露锋芒"（Competitive Edge）的机构。图3-5显示了策略性规划的流程。它说明策略规划是要经由很多人的深思熟虑，和大家参与的复杂过程才产生的。

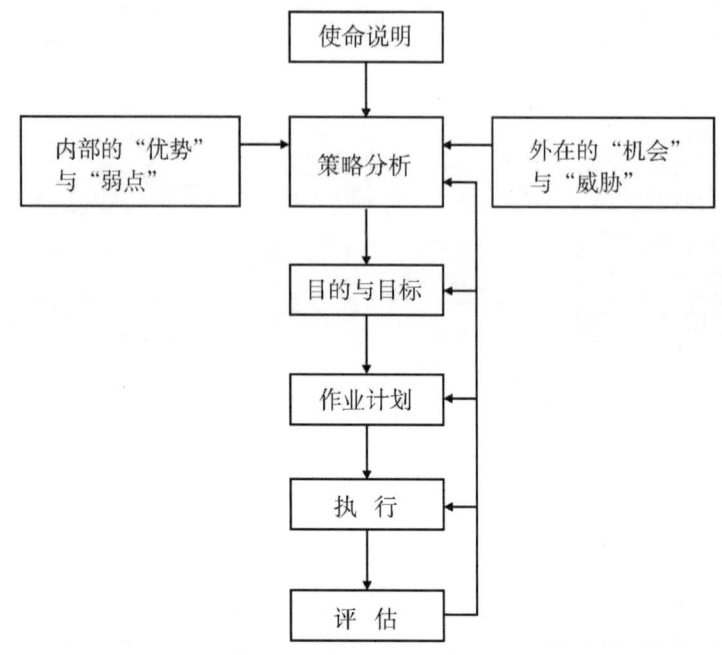

图3-5　策略性规划的流程

第四章　图书馆的组织

Chapter 4　Library Organization

前两章讲到管理的功能时曾提到在规划的功能之后紧接着的就是组织的功能。一个机构在认同其特殊使命，拟定其目的及目标，和决定采取行动之后，下一个步骤就是要设计一个适当的组织和建立一个有效的结构，以充分使用及分配现有或预计可以取得的资源，来达成机构的使命、目的和目标。

本章试将组织的涵义、基本原则、组织的环境、组织的设计及结构和组织的发展等专题从图书馆的观点加以探讨。

第一节　组织的涵义

组织在英文中有"名词"与"动词"之分。从名词的定义来讲，组织（Organization）是一个以人为主的社会团体或机构。它的成立是为了达到某些共同和明确的使命与目的。在这个团体或机构存在的过程中，它是一个随着环境及需要的变动而自行调整的有机系统（Organic System）。从动词的定义来讲，组织（Organize）是一种行动。它包括了一个机构中全部人员如何通过分工合作和分层负责来有效地发挥整体功能，以达成预定的目的。一个有效的机构应该是具备高度弹性的有机组织。

根据以上两种解释，组织大约有下列四点涵义：

1. 一个组织或机构的存在，必须有共同的使命和目的，它的结构是为达成此目的而设计的。

2. 它是一个有机体的系统，重视分工合作及经由有协调的交互影响活动，以满足员工的需要（Needs）和期望（Aspiration）。

3. 它的存在是为了制造产品（Products）或提供服务（Services）。

4. 它的结构要能配合环境的变迁随时调整和更新。

一般来说，组织的形式是根据其功能而定（Form Follows Functions）。近代的系统理论把组织当作一种输入—转变—输出的模式，着重工作的流程和结果。

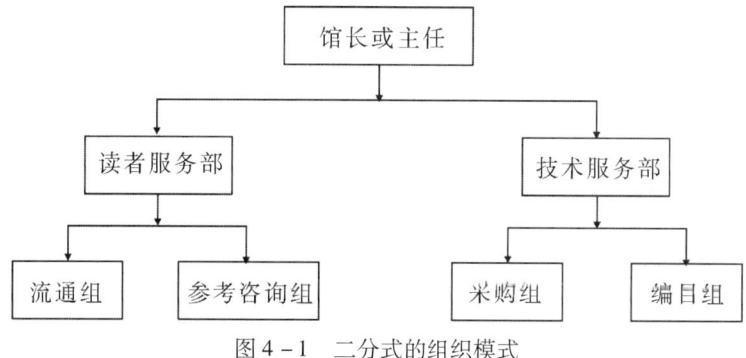

图 4-1　二分式的组织模式

不论是什么机构或团体，它的组织往往受到外在环境与内在因素的影响。由于"组织"与"环境"的交互作用，因此组织多具有动力（Dynamic）或流动（Fluid）的特性。现代化的图书馆因为受到环境变化和复杂性的影响，它的组织结构也是经常在调整和更革。数十年来沿用的"二分式"或"三分式"的组织在大型图书馆中已经被一些其他的组织模式所取代。图4-1及4-2显示中外图书馆沿用已久的基本组织模式。

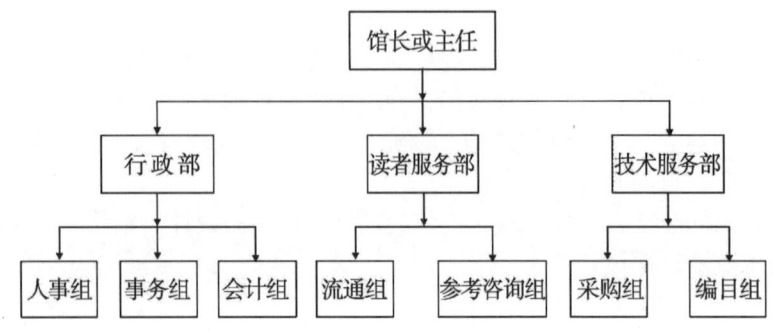

图4-2　三分式的组织模式

从图4-1和图4-2两种模式来看，很多图书馆还可以根据其规模的大小和性质的差异加设副馆长、馆长助理、人事管理员、会计员、分馆主任等职位。在各部门之下还可以根据不同的功能增设期刊组、视听资料组、自动化组、文献组、档案组等。

第二节　组织的基本原则

组织的设计和结构也有一些基本原则可以遵循。在第二章讲到近代西方管理学的发展时我们曾经讨论到科学管理学派和一般管理学派一些大师的理论，其中有亨利·费尧的十四点具有弹性的管理原则，在这些原则中至少有四点是特别适用在组织上的。

一、统一指挥（Unity of Command）

这一原则是指在一个组织中每一位员工最好只有一位直接指挥的上司。这种单一的指挥，虽然在命令的下达，或上下沟通时较为容易，但有时不易做到。例如在矩阵式（Matrix）的组织中（下面将会讨论到），或在需要横向沟通协调时，指挥的单一化有时反而会碍事，缺乏弹性。

二、专业分工（Specialization or Division of Labor）

在每一个稍有规模的组织里都有很多不同的任务需要专业分工。若能够将全部员工根据其知识、技术、能力、兴趣、性格和特点予以适当的分配和安置，不仅可以人尽其才，增进工作效率，增加员工的满足感，同时更能提高工作质量，降低生产成本。

分工与专业化虽在求人尽其才，但日久不变，亦会有其缺点。例如说像分工太细，容易使每位员工的工作变成重复单调、缺乏适应力、不易接受革新的措施，有时还会造成本位主义的心理，不能与其他单位合作，漠视整体的目标和需要。

三、层级节制（Scalar Principle or Chain of Command）

这是指一个机构内部上下层级和从属的关系。在每一个组织较为严密的机构里都存在着这种层级节制的现象。中国传统观念中所谓"上下有序"也是建立在层级节制的原则上。与层级节制有关的组织原则尚有"线的功能"与"幕僚功能"两种：

1. 线的功能（Line Function）是指上级主管对下属具有指挥与管辖之权。在一个图书馆里，馆长之下有副馆长、部门主任、组长及所隶属的员工。他（她）们之间的从属关系是直线的。

2. 幕僚功能（Staff Function）是指担任参谋作业，无指挥及管辖权的幕僚人员，如馆长助理、人事管理员、会计员等。担任这些工作的人多半只对馆长负责，执行所交付的任务，对其他部门无直接的关系。

四、控制的幅度（Span of Control）

根据早先管理学的理论，每一位主管所直接管辖的部属应该在五人至八人之间。这个数目虽然可因许多因素而变通，但它的存在影响到一个机构中层级多寡的程度。在控制幅度窄的机构里，它的层级可能会比较多，因而形成了高的组织（Tall Organization）。在控制幅度宽的机构里，它的层级可能会比较少，形成了平坦的组织（Flat Organization）。这说明了组织层级多少与控制幅度大小的相互关系。一般来讲，组织的层级不宜太多，因为多了会造成高度官僚化，形成沟通上的困难，人员的滥用，以致影响到工作的效率和经济的效益。

虽然控制的范围有其理论的根据，但在人数限定上，其他的因素亦不可不顾。这些因素包括有：

（1）工作性质及复杂程度。
（2）部属的能力。
（3）部属彼此间的距离等。

第三节　组织的环境

任何一个机构都有它内外在的环境。组织与环境的交互影响形成了一个组织的气候——或者可以称为组织的文化（Organizational Culture）。这种组织文化就像人的个性（Personality）一样，反映了一个机构的特征。它影响到机构的价值观、认同感、组织形态、作业方式和规范、领导风格和员工的表现等。

一、组织文化的特性

组织文化一般说来有七种比较明显的特性[①]：

1. **员工自主性**
指一个机构中员工能自发自动，积极工作，革新应变的程度。

2. **结构管制性**
指使用规章制度及直接监督来控制员工的程度。

---

① Stephen P. Robbins.《管理概论：理论与实务》，李茂兴，译. 台北市：晓园出版社，1989，p. 47.

3. 上级支持性

指管理人员对部属的关怀和支持的程度。

4. 认同感

指员工对于整个机构的认同程度。

5. 绩效奖赏

指对员工的成就给予奖赏的程度。

6. 冲突的容忍性

指员工在群体关系中所表现出对冲突矛盾采取容忍的程度。

7. 风险容忍度

指一个机构能够承担风险的程度。

经由上述七个特性在不同程度上的混合形成了一个机构的组织文化。这种组织文化一旦形成则不大容易改变，除非是内外环境发生剧烈的变动。

每一个图书馆也多少有它自己的组织文化，健全的组织文化需要留意培养，不健全的组织文化则需要仔细诊断其病因，使能对症下药，早日康复。作为一个图书馆的馆长必须能激发员工的积极性、自发性、认同感、向心力和服务心等以造成合作、和谐、进取和追求团体荣誉的组织文化。

二、组织的外在环境

一个机构的外在环境包括了能够影响这个机构的各种外在因素。根据其影响力或相关性的大小，外在环境可以分成"一般环境"（General Environment）与"特定环境"（Special Environment）两种。特定环境对一个机构的影响较之一般环境是比较直接而且明显的。以图书馆为例，它的一般环境包括了当前政治、经济、社会、教育、科技发展、文化水平等情况。美元在世界市场上的贬值会造成国外书刊价值的提高而影响到图书馆的采购。政府税收的减少会影响到公共图书馆的经费。计算器与电子通讯技术的发展加速了图书馆自动化和网路化的进展。这些都是一般环境可能造成的影响。图书馆的特定环境包括每个图书馆个别的上级机构，它所服务的小区和读者，它可能面对的一些地方上的压力团体（如工会、极端保守团体等）、有关的法令规章（如图书馆法、版权法等）、书商、图书馆间的合作网路（像 OCLC）等。

图书馆的外在环境，根据其变化或复杂的程度，还可以分成"环境的不确定性"（Environmental Uncertainty）和"环境复杂度"（Environmental Complexity）两种。处在这种变化较大而复杂性又高的环境里，图书馆的组织应力求机动以加强应变力。

美国图书馆行政专家贝波丽·玲曲（Beverly P. Lynch）认为不论是那一种图书馆，其内部组织和决策多少会受到外在因素的影响。她认为图书馆是一个"开放系统"（Open System），与周围环境有密切的交互往来关系。它从周围的环境中取得所需的资源（Resources）与动力（Energy），将之转变成产品（Products）或服务（Services），以回馈于社会。

要了解图书馆的外在环境，玲曲认为下面四个步骤极为重要[①]：

（1）要了解环境的特质（Nature）。

（2）要了解图书馆与它的特定环境中其他机构的关系。

---

① Beverly P. Lynch. "The Academic Library and Its Environment", In *Management Strategies for Libraries: A Basic Reader*, edited by her. New York: Neal-Schuman, 1985. pp. 223 – 224.

（3）要了解图书馆与其他图书馆间的交流合作。
（4）要了解环境对图书馆内部结构和操作的影响。

除此之外，图书馆亦应确定它本身工作的范围（Boundry）。以俄亥俄大学图书馆为例，该馆除了首先要为本校师生提供各种配合教学研究所需的图书信息和咨询服务之外，同时亦要在可能的范围内对本小区的居民、附近中小学师生、俄州东南部地区的公共图书馆和医疗卫生机构及其他州立大学师生等，依已定的合作协议或承诺，提供图书馆服务。因为俄亥俄大学图书馆的东南亚藏书和其他一些特藏是在美国或世界上卓有名望的，因此它对俄州以外的读者或图书馆也提供对这些特藏的服务。这种服务范围的延伸，可因每个图书馆的实际情况及能力而定。

第四节　组织的设计和结构

本章前三节已将组织的涵义、基本原则和组织环境加以叙述，下面将接着讨论组织的设计和结构。

组织设计（Organization Design）是指如何经由设计以建立最合适当前情况及需要的结构。它是将组织内的员工及其他资源做合理的分配和利用，使一个机构能成为一个灵活、协调、有效率的有机体，并使每位员工能各尽所能，发挥个人的专长，在工作上经由分工合作及协调配合，以达成机构的使命和目的。因为环境及需要的不时更变，一个组织的结构也要随时调整，以保持"日日新"的形态。组织设计因此是一个持续不断、随时更新的过程。

组织设计是要考虑到一个机构内部应该设立那些部门，应有多少层级，如何分工和专门化，纵横职位的分布，各个职位的权责，直线与幕僚的功能，各个部门间的交互关系，权力的集中与分散，委员会与任务小组的运用等。一个健全的组织既要有适度的集权化、制度化和标准化，又要兼备相当的分权化、应变力和有机性。

长期以来，图书馆被视为一个比较简单及稳定的机构。但是在最近二三十年来，由于知识信息的快速发展、科学技术的日新月异、图书馆收藏、服务项目及规模的不断扩大、社会大众对资讯服务要求的提升、图书馆本身的自动化、电子化和网路化等，使得图书馆的组织发生重大的变动。图书馆所面临的"环境不确定性"和"环境复杂性"较之以前任何一个时期更为明显。因此图书馆的组织设计也变得更有挑战性。

一、组织的部门化和层级化

组织的部门化是将一个机构内的员工依工作的需要而按分工的原则分成若干部门，每一部门由一位主管来领导，在大的机构里，每一部门之内还可以再分为若干层级。这种部门化和层级化可以用金字塔形的组织结构来显示，像前面图 4-1 和图 4-2 组织模式就是很好的例子。

一般图书馆在划分部门时大多采用下列几种方式：
1. 依功能分——如采购、编目、流通、参考咨询等。
2. 依服务性质分——如行政、读者服务、技术服务等。
3. 依读者分——如儿童馆、青少年部、大学部、研究图书馆等。
4. 依位置分——如总馆、分馆等。

5. 依学科分——如社会科学、自然科学、人文、工程技术、医学、法律、教育、农业等。
6. 依资料分——如地图、缩微片、视听资料、期刊、政府出版物等。

在规模较大的图书馆组织里，很多会同时采用多种划分的方式。以图4-3俄亥俄大学图书馆为例，我们可以看出它是采用了至少五种不同的方式。

一般来说，大学图书馆在美国的校园里具有较高的地位，几乎有一半的图书馆馆长拥有院长（Dean）级的身份。常见的称号有院长级图书馆馆长（Dean of Libraries），大学或学院图书馆馆长（University or College Librarian），图书馆馆长（Director of Libraries or Library Director）。以上的名称中所用的图书馆复数（Libraries）是指主管全校的图书馆，包括了总馆和分馆。除此之外，有很多馆长还兼管校中的教学媒体中心（Instructional Media Center）、学习资源中心（Learning Resources Center）或视听教育中心（Educational Media Center）。这些中心尽管名称不一致，但多半提供视听媒体及设备供师生使用。有的还协助教师或研究人员制作视听教材，包括电影、录像、幻灯片、挂图、计算机协助教学及多媒体等。最近十几年来，有些馆长还升任主管图书馆、计算机中心、教学媒体中心的助理副校长（Assistant Vice President）或副教务长（Associate Provost）。

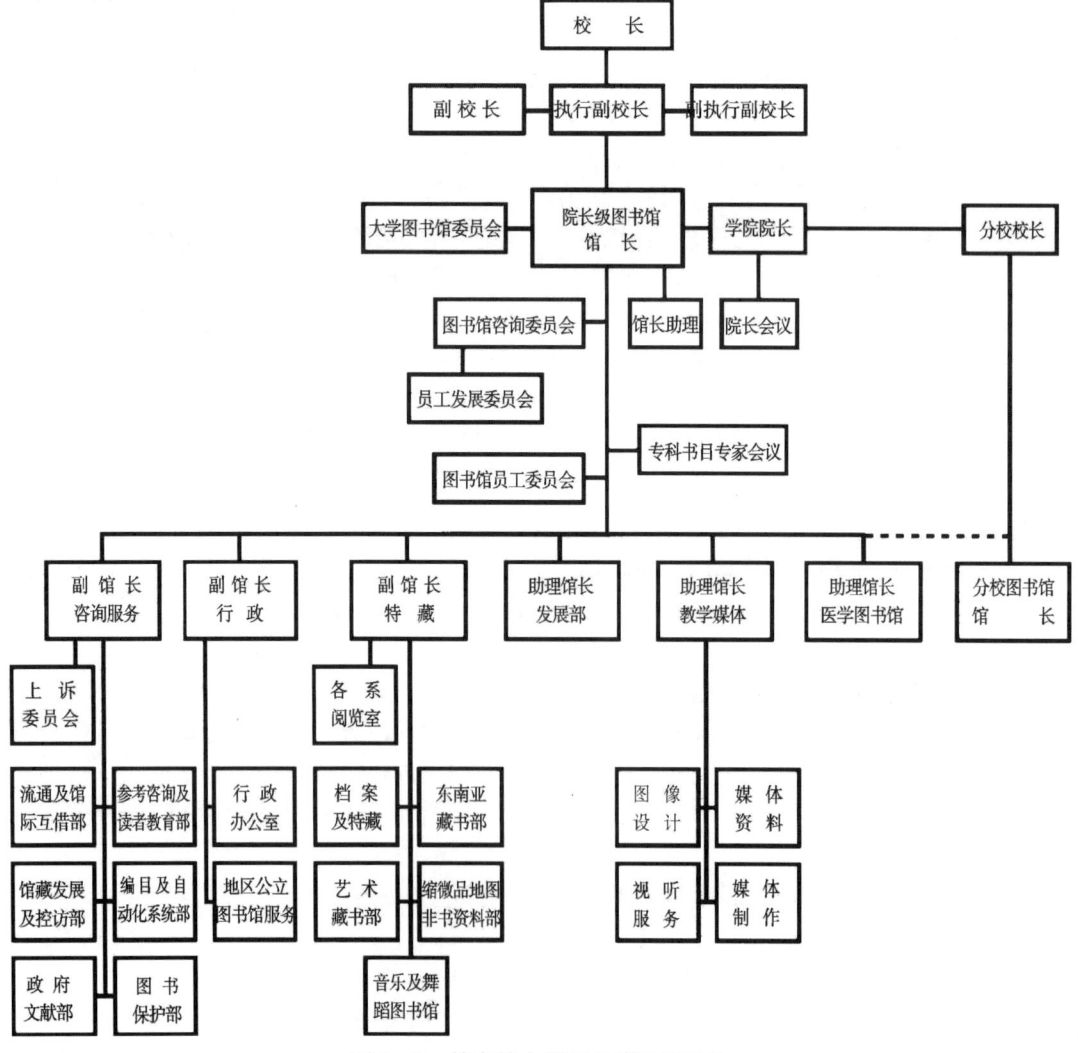

图4-3 俄亥俄大学图书馆组织结构

从俄亥俄大学图书馆的组织结构看，该校的图书馆馆长直属于执行副校长（Provost）之下，是院长会议（Deans Council）成员之一。在馆长之下有三位副馆长（Associate Dean），两位助理馆长（Assistant Dean），一位馆长助理（Assistant to the Dean）。

三位副馆长的职务划分系按服务性质：一位管行政（包括预算控制、人事管理及馆舍维护）；一位管服务（包括读者服务与技术服务的六个部门：像藏书发展及采购，编目及图书馆系统，流通及馆际互借，参考及读者教育，政府出版物，图书维护）；另一位管特别藏书（包括档案及特藏，艺术、音乐及舞蹈，东南亚，缩微片、地图，非书刊资料等五个部门）。

两位助理馆长一位管医学图书馆，她的职务是按学科分；一位管教学媒体中心，他的职务是按资料分。

在两位副馆长（服务和特别藏书）和一位助理馆长（教学媒体）管辖之下有十五个部门，其中按功能分的有八个：

（1）藏书发展及采购。
（2）编目及图书馆系统。
（3）流通及馆际互借。
（4）参考及读者教育。
（5）图书维护。
（6）媒体制作。
（7）视听器材服务。
（8）总图设计。

其中按学科分的有三个：

（1）艺术。
（2）音乐及舞蹈（属分馆之一）。
（3）东南亚。

其中按资料分的有四个：

（1）政府出版物。
（2）档案及特藏。
（3）缩微片、地图和非书刊资料。
（4）视听资料（主要是影片、录像、光盘等）。

前述的音乐及舞蹈图书馆因为是单独设在音乐大楼，因此它与另外五个分校的图书馆及两个系阅览室又可以是按位置来划分的。

俄亥俄大学图书馆是一个比较集中的图书馆，除了音乐及舞蹈图书馆、五个分校图书馆和两个系阅览室外，其余的都集中在总馆之内。总馆的面积有285,745平方英尺（合26,546平方米），可以容纳1,400,000册图书及3,200位读者。

二、集中或分散

组织设计的另一个考虑是"集中"或"分散"。这两种形式的图书馆各有其利弊，值得加以探讨。

集中（Centralization）的图书馆是将全馆的图书、人员及其他资源集中在一个总馆之内，由一位馆长总揽全责，为全体读者服务。这种形式在很多大专院校图书馆、公共图书馆或专门图书馆中被普遍采用。

分散（Decentralization）的图书馆是在总馆之外另行设立若干分馆。这种情况在大的校园里、地区或公司机关里也是常见的。美国的哈佛大学图书馆就是一个分馆林立的分散型图书馆。在很多国家的大学图书馆里，我们也经常看到有很多单独设立、各自为政的院系馆。

以上两种组织形式虽然各有利弊，但是从最近的趋势来看，越来越多的大学图书馆趋向集中式，设法把一些小馆合并起来，以减少分馆的数目。相反的，很多大的公共图书馆为了便利读者及各小区的发展和需要，逐渐增设分馆。这种现象显示了大学图书馆与公共图书馆在藏书和服务的性质上有所不同。以下仅将集中与分散两种形式的优缺点加以比较：

1. **集中式的优点**

（1）图书资源及服务集中在一个场所对一般读者极为方便，尤其是可以把一些重要和昂贵的参考工具书集中在一处，由专业馆员指导读者如何使用。

（2）图书资源、人员和设备的重复可以减少以节省经费和避免不必要的浪费。

（3）总馆开放的时间可以较任何分馆长久，而且服务的项目更为齐备。

（4）各学科的书刊资料放置在一处有利于现代跨学科研究（Cross Disciplinary Studies）和科际研究（Interdisciplinary Studies）的需要。

（5）增进图书馆管理和各部门间协调的便利及效率。

2. **集中式的缺点**

（1）在一个规模大、藏书丰富的图书馆，因为内部结构复杂，对一些普通的读者来讲，会感到不易使用。为了弥补这个缺点，有些大学图书馆在馆内另设大学部图书馆（Undergraduate Library），精选适合大学部学生程度的十多万册图书、三、四千种期刊和一些非书刊资料，专供本科生使用。

（2）不管是大专院校、市区或公司机关，要是它的地区很辽阔，而图书馆的使用者又很分散，除非安排有很好的交通工具，否则会造成对读者的很大不便。最近十余年来，因为图书馆的自动化和网路化，再加上电子通讯的逐渐普遍，图书馆与远距离读者的联系会比以前便捷。

3. **分布式的优点**

（1）有些性质特殊的图书馆，如法律、医学、音乐、盲人等，比较适于单独设立。

（2）分散型图书馆因它的地点与它所服务的读者较为接近，容易了解读者的需求并建立与读者的良好关系。

（3）在大学内的一些院（系）图书馆因为在藏书和服务上能针对各该院（系）的需要，在使用上亦较方便，因此颇受本院（系）师生的喜爱。

（4）院（系）图书馆员可能具备该学科的专门知识，能够了解该院（系）师生的需要，以提供相应的服务。

4. **分布式的缺点**

（1）一般分馆所收藏的书刊资料，不仅收藏量小，而且收藏面也比较狭窄，不够读者使用。

（2）人员、书刊和设备会有不必要的重复，从整个图书馆的经济效益来看将是比较浪费的。

（3）除非总馆有充裕的经费，或分馆自有其经费来源，否则的话很多分馆会遭遇到人员不够，馆员素质差，开放时间短，及参考工具书缺乏等问题。

（4）大学图书馆的分馆虽然对本院（系）师生较为方便，但对外系读者则颇不方便。

在一个分馆较多的校区里一个读者往往要跑好几个分馆才能找齐所需的资料。这种不便有时会使读者放弃使用别的分馆，造成学习和研究上的缺陷。

（5）分馆型的图书馆与现代跨学科或科际性的学习研究趋势不能配合。

（6）图书馆的组织太分散，在管理、协调和合作上将会非常困难，影响到整个图书馆的效率。

（7）有些管理不善的分馆，图书馆的书刊会变成少数教授和学生的私人收藏，不易收回。

从以上的比较看来，两种形式的图书馆组织各有利弊。总体言之，规模大、服务对象和地区分散、经费充裕的图书馆可以酌量设立一些分馆。这些分馆应由总馆统一规划、管辖和协调，力求能保持划一的服务标准——包括人员素质、训练和配置、开放时间、设备、藏书、流通规则等。反之亦然，凡是规模小、服务对象和地区集中、经费不充裕的图书馆应尽量减少设立分馆，使能集中人力、财力和物力来提高图书馆服务的水平。

在大城市中的公共图书馆，为了加强对市民的服务，可在居民集中的地区设立小区分馆。这些分馆有的还能按照当地的特殊情况建立具有特色的服务项目。公共图书馆与大专院校图书馆因为在性质上的差异，因此在藏书、服务和组织上有所不同。这些不同点在本书第一章第二节讲到各类图书馆的功能时已加以比较。

三、矩阵式的组织（Matrix Organization）

前面所讲的功能式结构具有专业化的优点，但实行久了，会变得僵硬，缺乏弹性。为了纠正这个缺点，很多大型的生产企业机构开始采用矩阵式的组织。这种组织是把一个机构中的员工按工作或生产的需要分成若干方案（Project）或产品（Product）小组（Team），各由一位组长负责（如图4-4中的甲、乙、丙、丁各组）。这些小组在执行任务时，得接受一些依功能而设的专业部门或人员的指导和协助（如图4-4中的A，B，C，D各部门）。

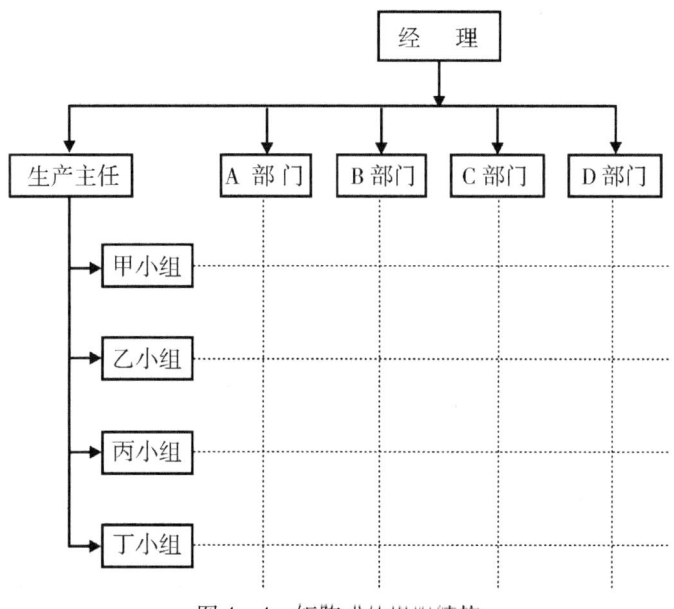

图4-4 矩阵式的组织结构

在图 4-4 里的部门组织是比较固定的，像人事、会计、采购、推销、自动化、研究与发展等。小组的组合则非常灵活，每个小组的人数及专长系按需要而定。当一个新的任务开始时，经理可以从其他小组中调出一批人员来组成一个新的小组。在任务完成后，小组的人员可以回归原组或被派到其他一组。

矩阵式组织有它的优缺点：它的优点是能够采用功能性分工的长处，在员工的调派上保持机动性，可以有效地利用现有人力资源来执行上级交代的各种任务或方案。它的缺点是指挥的不统一，容易使员工有不知所从之感。另外，要是调派太频繁的话，也会造成员工的不安全感，影响到工作的情绪。

俄亥俄大学图书馆的编目及图书馆系统部（Cataloging and Library Systems Department）早在 1984 年即开始试用这种矩阵式组织。因为效果很好，一直沿用到现在。这种结构的好处是在分派工作时能够根据作业的需要及员工的专长，分成若干方案小组，如图 4-5。每个小组的人数是按方案的大小而定，有的方案延续多年，有的只有几个星期，小组的人员可按需要而调整。当一个新的任务被交代下来时，编目部的主任可以从现有各小组中调出一批人员来成立一个新的小组。等到任务完成时即行解散，它的员工可以回到原先的小组或被派到另一个小组。至于编目部的几位专业图书馆员，他（她）们的工作分配则是按照各人的专长，每人负责指导、训练和协助各方案小组中所属的工作。

四、对角线的考虑（Diagonal Consideration）

前面所讨论的各种组织设计方式多半是从一个机构中纵与横的关系来考虑（Vertical and Horizontal Considerations）。本节将列举一种建立在对角线基础上的组织设计方式。这种方式能使得组织结构上纵与横的各层级单位除了有上下、左右的联系外，还可以有交叉的联系，加强了一个机构内部的协调和沟通。

对角线的考虑是指在一个机构内依不同需要所设立的会议（Council），委员会（Committee）和任务小组（Task Force）等。会议多半是较上层次的咨询机构，而且有相当的权力。委员会和任务小组的设立则是针对某些特殊任务或活动，而且常是跨越部门的。委员会有长期性的常设委员会（Standing Committee）或短期的特别委员会（Ad Hoc Committee）。有些委员会还设有一个或多个附属委员会（Subcommittee）。任务小组与特别委员会性质相似，多半是为了完成某一特殊任务而设立，一旦任务完成，即可解散。在一些人数较多的会议里，为了要对会议的议程或讨论项目预先有所准备，可以设立指导委员会（Steering Committee）。

以上这些组织方式与机构的董事会或理事会（Trustees or Board）又有不同。董事会或理事会是一个机构的上层组织，它的权限极大，举凡一个机构的重大计划、方针、政策、预算、一级主管的任用等都要由董事会或理事会的批准或同意。

不论是董事会或一个附属委员会，它在成立时都应该有一个章程（Constitution），法规（Rules and Regulations）或附则（By-laws）。这些章程、法规或附则应该明确地将这个董事会、会议、委员会或任务小组的组织、任务与权限加以说明。

从俄亥俄大学图书馆的组织结构（图 4-3）上我们可以看出下列五个不同性质的会议和委员会：

（1）院长会议（Deans Council）。

（2）大学图书馆委员会（University Library Committee）。

（3）图书馆会议（Library Council）。

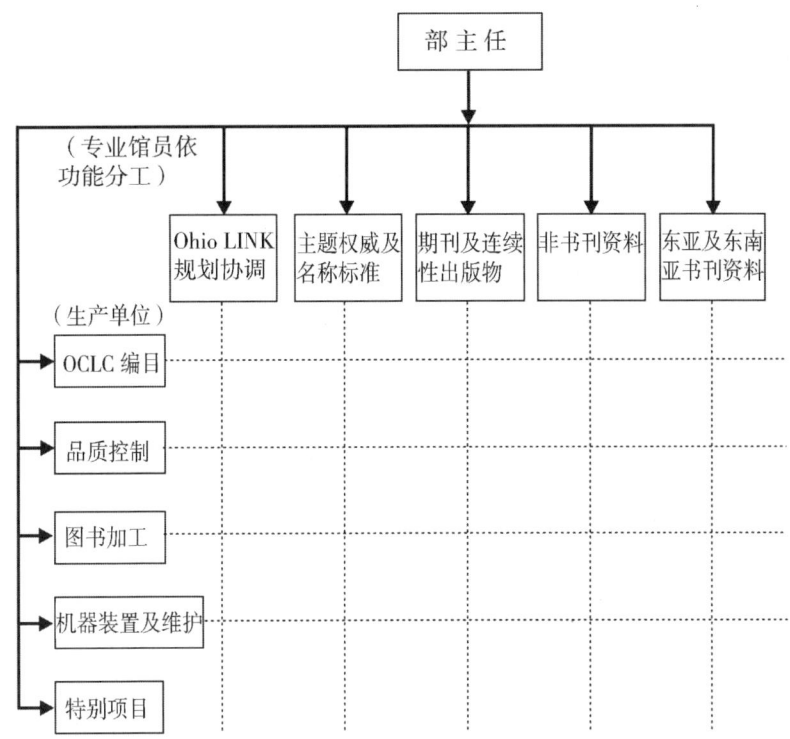

图 4-5　俄亥俄大学图书馆编目及图书馆系统部矩阵式组织结构

（4）书目专家会议（Subject Bibliographers Council）。
（5）员工发展委员会（Staff Development Committee）。

以上这些是比较正式的，所以列入组织结构中，还有一些经常性和临时性的，没有一一列入。

院长会议是由十个学院及五个分校的院长所组成。图书馆馆长也是该会议的成员之一。这个会议是由执行副校长（Provost）所主持，每月开会一次。举凡校内有关教务的计划与决策在执行之前多半都要经过这个会议的讨论。

大学图书馆委员会的委员是经教授评议会（Faculty Senate），行政人员咨议会（Administrative Senate）和学生咨议会（Student Senate）分别推荐，由校长聘请的八位教授、两位行政人员及三位学生所组成。学生的任期系一年一聘，教授及行政人员的任期是三年一聘，图书馆馆长是当然委员（Ex Officio Member）。这个委员会每年至少集会三次，其目的在向校长、执行副校长及馆长提供意见；担任馆长的咨询机构，并促进图书馆与教授、行政人员及学生的联系与沟通。大学图书馆委员会在很多大学中都有设立，但其组织和职权很少有完全相同的。

图书馆会议是馆内参与式管理（Participative Management）的最高机构。这个委员会每两周集会一次，其成员包括馆长一人，副馆长三人，助理馆长二人，再加上由馆员推选出来的六位任期两年的代表。凡是图书馆内的重要决策，包括长、短程计划，一般的政策、规章、条例和重大事项等都要经由这个会议的商讨，做成建议，送交馆长做最后决定。有些牵涉到大学的决策，馆长可以提请大学图书馆委员会参加意见，或向执行副校长请示及报备。

书目专家会议是由负责选购各学科图书期刊及其他资料的专业图书馆员所组成，每月开会一次来协调全馆的馆藏发展及其他有关事宜。在俄亥俄大学图书馆内，每一位专业馆员除了他（她）本身的职务外，还要按其个人的学科专长兼负下列书目专家的责任：

1. 藏书发展

与所负责的各学系教授代表建立联系，了解各系教学和研究的需要，拟定个别的藏书发展政策，分配图书期刊购买经费，选择所要购买的书刊及其他资料等。

2. 与各学系保持联系

负责图书馆与各系的沟通。

3. 图书馆教学（Library Instruction）

利用各种机会教授并协助各系师生如何使用图书馆的资源。

4. 参加每月的书目专家会议

5. 提出年度报告

会议的召集人是馆藏发展及采购部主任。这个会议之下还有一个指导委员会，它的目的是在拟定全体大会的议程及讨论项目，有时还预先准备计划或提案以供全体会议时讨论，使得大会能顺利进行，不致花费太多时间于一些讨论项目，并能得到较好的效果。指导委员会的七位委员是由全体大会选出，任期一年，其中一位固定委员及召集人是馆藏发展及采购部的主任。

员工发展委员会是直属于图书馆会议之下的一个常设会议。它的目的是在规划及执行有关提高员工素质、专业知识和技能的各种在职训练和继续教育。这个委员会的八位委员是由图书馆会议提名，由馆长聘定，每人任期两年。主管行政事务的副馆长和员工联谊会的副主席是当然委员。

除了以上这些比较正式的会议和委员会之外，俄亥俄大学图书馆还设有以馆长、副馆长、助理馆长、馆长助理和办公室秘书所组成的执行委员会（Executive Committee）；以各部门主任所组成的部主任联合会议（Joint Department Heads Meeting）；各部门内部的会议（Department Meetings）；全馆的馆员大会（Staff Meeting）等定期会议以加强内部各部门间的协调和沟通，以促进员工对于馆务在规划、决策和执行上的参与。

为了加强馆员员工的联谊及社交活动，俄亥俄大学图书馆也设有一个图书馆员工联谊会（Library Staff Association）。这个联谊会的活动很多，在建立员工间和谐、友善、关怀、互助的关系上贡献极大。

五、权威与授权

组织设计的另一个考虑是权威与授权。以下试将权威的一些类型和授权的一些步骤及情境因素加以讨论。

1. 权威与层次（Authority and Hierarchy）

权威与层次在组织中是一个常见的现象，所谓"分层负责"是也。权威的观念形成是来自于组织中从属的关系（Scalar Chain）。中国的传统观念"上下有序"也是建立在权威的基础上。在管理学中最引起争论的莫过于"权威"的观念，因为权威常有被滥用之虑。

权威是指影响或指挥他人的力量。一个主管因他（她）在一个机构中的职位而获得了某些合法的权力，可以用来指挥属下，令他（她）们服从。这种权威虽然因层次不同而有别，但它必须建立在合理的基础上。换言之，权威之是否被尊重或接受，视其是否被用得合理和适当。因此权威的"接受者"实际应该是权威的"决定者"。这个道理，在一个民主的社会里，是很显然的。

因为职位的划分与不同，权威可以分成直线、幕僚、功能性三种不同的类型：

(1) 直线权威（Line Authority）。这是指上司与部属之间在指挥链（Chain of Command）上所建立的权威关系。这种关系只要上级用得合理和适当，一般都会被下属所接受。以俄亥俄大学图书馆为例（见图 4-3），图书馆馆长之上依序有执行副校长和校长，馆长之下依序有副馆长、各部门主任及员工等。这种从属的关系形成了直线型的指挥链。

(2) 幕僚权威（Staff Authority）。在一些机构里，因为工作上的需要，往往会增设一些幕僚的职位，如馆长助理、人事管理员、会计师、法律顾问、公关人员等。像馆长助理这个职位，可以算是典型的个人幕僚（Personal Staff），他（她）的存在主要在协助或处理馆长所交付的事务，没有直线权威。其他如人事管理员、会计师等则属于专业幕僚（Specialized Staff），他（她）们的存在是在提供各种专业技能来支持各直线管理人员或部门的工作。这些专业幕僚可以提供建议或协助，但没有指挥权。建议的执行必须透过主管的同意，经由指挥链，由各直线管理人员来实施。

(3) 功能性权威（Functional Authority）。在规模大的机构里，有的专设有人事、会计、资讯、公关等部门。这些部门对于各个直线单位可以行使功能性的权威。这种权威的行使是有限制的，往往仅包含某些特定的工作范围，它的目的是在促进这些事务的协调划一和执行的效率。

2. 授权（Delegation）

授权是指在一个机构里，根据权威的类型和指挥链的关系，把一些职责（Responsibilities）分配给各层次和部门的主管并授予适当的权威，使得各位主管对他（她）的工作负起责任（Accountability），能以分工合作、分层负责的方式来达成机构的使命和目的。

任何一个大而复杂的机构里都需要有职务分配（Allocation of Duties）和授权。最高主管虽然要对整个机构的成败负责，每一层次的主管也应该对他（她）的部门或单位的表现负责。为此，在指派工作时应该明确地把权威与责任交代清楚，使部属能充分地了解授权的幅度、担负的职责及预期的绩效。一般说来，机构的规模愈大，作业愈复杂，技术性愈强，部属的素质愈好，上级对部属愈信任的话，其授权的程度也愈高。

也有些主管喜欢自己总揽全权，紧握不放；或者是对部属不够信任，怕授权太多会失去对部属的控制。有些部属因为怕失败受责不敢承担较大的职责；或者是满足现状，觉得已有足够的工作，不愿接受更多的职责。以上这些情况会造成授权的障碍。为了要破除这些障碍，上级主管应该设法创造一种互相信赖，上下和谐，不怕冒险犯错的组织文化。另外，对于工作努力、绩效优越的部属，也应该给予适当的奖励。这种奖励不一定必须是金钱的，举凡褒奖、晋升、更好的工作条件、更有挑战性的职责或同事的认可等都能发生鼓励的作用。

六、非正式的组织

本章以上各节所讲的组织是属于正式的组织（Formal Organization），本节将讨论非正式的组织（Informal Organization）。在每一个机构里都会存在着非正式组织的现象。这种现象的形成是因为在一般组织里都经常会有一些颇得人望、受人拥戴的人才。这些人虽然不一定拥有因职位而赋予的权威（Authority of Position），但在许多员工的心目中，他（她）们具有相当的影响力，因而拥有因领导能力而赋予的权威（Authority of Leadership）。他（她）们关心这个机构的发展和成就，因为这是与大多数员工有切身关系。有些非正式组织只是员工间一种社会性的群体活动,包括了社交活动、讯息沟通和相互督促等人际关系。非正式组织假如运用得当的话,可以对一个机构的管理发生积极的作用。反之,要是运用不当的话,会对一个机构的管理造成不利的阻碍。这就是所谓"成事不足,败事有余"。为了防患未然,机构的主管应该尽早发觉这种非正式组织的存在,设法引导它们参与机构内各种"参与式管理"(Participative Management)的渠道,让它们的力量能发挥正面的作用。

七、参与式的管理

近代的图书馆,随着它急遽的发展,其组织趋向庞大、复杂和官僚化。这种官僚化的缺点是:分工过细、流于呆板、缺乏协调、少应变力、本位主义、控制多于启发、忽视员工兴趣与要求及着重短期效果而忽略了长期目标等。为了防患官僚化的毛病,很多图书馆采用了参与式的管理,以鼓励各级员工参与图书馆的管理和决策的过程,使图书馆的行政能够民主化、透明化和人性化。

一个成功的参与式管理需要由馆长带头做起,将图书馆的行政、财务、人事等业务尽可能的公开,广辟各种讯息沟通的渠道,建立各种馆员参政的机会。从图书馆的规划开始,鼓励员工参与目的与目标的拟定。经由各种会议、委员会或任务小组,使馆员能够充分地参加各级决策的过程,以建立各种行动方案,付诸实施。理想的参与式管理是建立在一个和谐、合作、信赖的团队精神上。实际经验证明当员工能参加制定与他(她)们工作有关的决策时,他(她)们工作的积极性会显然地提高。参与式管理的另一个优点是它对组织人性化(Humanize the Organization)的重视。组织的人性化包括了:

(1)把员工当作成熟和负责的人来看待。
(2)重视员工社会的需要。
(3)改善工作环境和员工福利。
(4)强调工作的保障。
(5)奖励重于惩罚。
(6)鼓励自动自发的精神。
(7)加强意见及讯息的沟通。

参与式管理虽有它的优点,但反对者亦提出它的一些缺点:

(1)在一个组织里喜欢参与的人总是那么几个人,只有他(她)们得到参与的好处,其他的人得分担他(她)们的工作。
(2)参与式管理很浪费时间,参与多了会减少整个机构的生产力。
(3)参与的人并不一定有决策的专门知识,他(她)们所做的决策并不是最明智的。
(4)参与式管理的极端是无政府主义,它造成了"人人决策,无人负责"的后果。
(5)参与决策的过程并不就是决策,最后的决策还是要由主管决定。

以上这些批评,也有它的道理,可供采用参与式管理者的参考。基于这些批评,有的管理者采用比较折衷的"咨询式管理"(Consultative Management)。它是用咨询的方式,加强管理者与员工的双向沟通,鼓励员工表达他(她)们的意见,了解员工的观点和想法,然后由管理者做出能反映大多数意见的决策。

第五节　组织发展

组织发展（Organization Development，简称 OD）是在 20 世纪 60 年代后期开始在美国及一些西方国家流行。它是使用行为科学的一些方法，有计划地来改进一个机构及加速其发展的过程。前面讲过，每个机构都需要能顺应周围环境的改变而做适当的调整和更新。组织发展是为这种自我更新的需求提供了一个有效的方法。它的目的是在帮助一个机构预计所需采取的行动，解决现有的困难，充分使用人力资源，改善内部沟通，实现机构目标和提高工作效率。组织发展在美国大的企业或政府机关里使用得比较多，但很少被图书馆所采用。即使如此，它的一些基本观念和方法值得我们学习和了解。

一、组织发展的定义

关于组织发展的著作很多，因此对它的定义各人看法有所不同，归纳起来大致包含了下列五点[①]：
1. 它是一个有计划的"介入"（Intervention）过程。
2. 它是用在整个机构的发展上。
3. 它是由最高级主管来亲自主持。
4. 它是使用行为科学方法的一种行动研究（Action Research）。
5. 它的目的是在促成机构的自我更新，以提高机构的效率和增进机构的健康。

这里所讲的"介入"是指由外界的专家来指导和协助组织发展的计划与行动。

另外也有人认为组织发展是顺应环境改变的一个措施。它是为了改变一个机构的信念（Beliefs）、态度（Attitude），价值观（Values）和结构（Structure）等所采用的一种复杂的教育策略。它的目的在使一个机构能顺应（Adapt）新的技术、市场、挑战和各种足以令人晕眩的高速改变[②]。

组织发展专家温多·法兰曲（Wendell L. French）认为除了以上各家的定义外，组织发展是一个长程的努力，应该持续不断地进行[③]。

二、行为科学的方法

对组织发展影响最多的有三个行为科学的方法[④]

1. 感受性的训练（Sensitivity Training）

这种方法亦被称为"T 组"的训练（T-Group Training）。它是由在美国国家训练实验室（National Training Laboratories），应用行为科学研究所（Institute for Applied Behavioral Science）的科特·李文（Kurt Lewin）和他的助手们所发展出来的。在 40 年代后期这种方法曾经被用在分析一个小组中各人的人际关系及交互影响。在训练员的指导下，小组中的

[①] Richard Beckhard. *Organization Development: Strategies and Models*. Reading, Mass.: Addison-Wesley, 1969, p. 9.
[②] Warren G. Bennis. *Organization Development: Its Nature, Origins, and Prospects*. Reading, Mass.: Addison-Wesley, 1969, p. 2.
[③] Wendell L French, & Cecil H. Bell, Jr. *Organization Development*. Englewood Cliffs, N. J.: Prentice-Hall, 1973, p. 15.
[④] W. Warner Burke. "Organization Development", In *AMA Management Handbook*, 2nd ed. edited by William K. Fallon. New York: AMACOM, 1983, pp. I-66 - I-68.

成员互相交换各人在小组中的行为和感受,由此而学习到个别行为及小组行为的成长。在1950年代后期,这种方法被用在组织发展上,企图改变组织的管理模式和其他特性。目前所用的"建立团队"(Team Building)的介入方法即是由感受性训练演变而来。

2. **社会与技术的系统**(Sociotechnical Systems)

这个方法是由在英国伦敦的塔威斯多克研究所(Tavistock Institute of London)两位研究员:以内克·推师特(Eric Trist)和肯尼·本福士(Kenneth Bamforth)首先使用。塔威斯多克研究所是专门研究人际关系的训练及组织的改变,尤其是重视社会关系和技术要求在改变一个组织的发展时对于员工的影响。推师特和本福士认为每一个机构同时也是一个技术与社会的系统。在改变一个机构时,决不能忽视技术与社会两者的影响。目前组织发展在改变一个机构时所采用的职位重新设计(Job Redesign)、建立自主的工作小组(Autonomous Work Group),及生产机构的结构设计等介入方法皆多受此影响。

3. **测量的反馈**(Survey Feedback)

这种采用问卷(Questionnaire)法来诊断和治疗一个机构的一些毛病的方法是在50年代由密西根大学(Michigan University)社会研究所(Institute for Social Research)的兰西斯·李克特(Rensis Likert)、佛罗益·孟(Floyd Mann),和他们几位助手所发展出来的。使用问卷法来测量员工的态度和士气在当时虽然不是没有人用,但企图以它的结果来改变一个机构倒是很新颖的。

特别是孟,他设计了一种"群体解决问题"(Group Problem Solving)的方法让一群在一起工作的员工能够一起分析测验的结果而用之来解决工作上的实际问题,这种测量反馈成了组织发展中常用的一种方法。

三、组织发展的程序

一般来讲,组织发展大概有下列7个步骤①:

1. **开端**(Entry)

决定要使用组织发展的方法时多半是因为一个机构的主管和员工共同意识到某些问题的存在而希望藉由组织发展来改善现状或组织文化。当这种情况出现时,机构的主管应设法邀请一位组织发展的顾问专家来与员工接触。这位顾问最好是从外面请来,他必须在初步的接触中很快地获得员工的信任,以建立互相合作的良好关系。经过对现有及其他可以获得资料的分析,这位顾问可以大致地发现问题的症结及是否适用组织发展的方法来解决。以上两项任务相当重要,而且也事关组织发展的成败。但是,要保证组织发展能够有效,各级主管和员工还需要预先做好心理准备,全力支持及参与。

2. **定约**(Contracting)

当顾问选定以后,双方应该定一个书面协议,说明聘用的时间、酬劳、工作的范围、双方应该履行的任务、沟通的方式、保密的要求及预期的结果等。

3. **资料的收集**(Data Collection)

以下是组织发展在收集资料时常用的四种方法:

(1)观察(Observation)有经验的顾问可以藉他(她)敏锐的观察力来鉴定一个机构的内部是否融洽、合作、团结、开放或有效率等。

(2)文献(Documents)研究一个机构的各种文献记录,包括年度报告、缺席统计、

---

① W. Warner Burke. "Organization Development", In AM A *Management Handbook*, 2nd ed. edited by William K. Fallon. New York: AMACOM, 1983, pp. I-68-I-72

申诉案件、会议记录等等，可以了解机构的作业情况。

（3）问卷（Questionnaires）采用标准或特别设计的问卷来调查员工的观感、态度和对一些问题看法。

（4）会谈（Interviews）这种最常用的方法可以是个别的面谈亦可以是小组的会谈。个别面谈可以比小组会谈获得更多每个人的意见，但小组会谈比较节省时间而且在大规模的机构里亦属必须。不论是面谈和会谈，一般包含了下面四个问题：

A. 什么是机构的优点、长处，或好的特质？
B. 什么是机构的缺点、毛病，或必须改进之处？
C. 什么是您工作最满意或重视的地方？
D. 什么是您工作上的阻碍或限制？

A、B 两个问题是针对着机构的优、缺点；C、D 是针对着各位员工工作上的长、短处。凡是优越的地方，应该给予肯定和鼓励，凡是有问题的地方则应该设法改进。

4. 诊断（Diagnosis）

在资料收集之后，下一步骤是分析和诊断，以便鉴定一个机构的健康情况，加强保健，或对症下药。在诊断时应当避免先入之见，尽量要公正、客观。为此，在诊断前应先选定一些客观的模式作为诊断时的比较或依据。这种模式应该是一个开放式的系统（Open System），它包括了输入（Input），内部作业（Throughput）及输出（Output）。

5. 反馈（Feedback）

除了诊断之外，顾问还需要把资料分析的结果做成摘要，供机构的员工参考和反应。这种摘要一般有三个部分：

（1）会谈的摘要先要按照问题的次序排列。有些回答最好能逐字引用，相同回答的次数也应该注明。

（2）会谈的资料可再按机构的功能来分列。这种分列法最好经过事先的磋商，一切以对事不对人为原则。

（3）最后一部分是将顾问的观察、印象和反应做一总结。这一部分与前面的不同处在前者不参入顾问的意见，而这一部分是顾问自己的意见。

6. 介入（Intervention）

介入虽然是指在发觉问题的存在以后所采取的有计划的行动和改进措施，实际上当一个机构在决定采取组织发展时也就是介入的开始。

有效的介入必须符合三个条件：

（1）具备正确的讯息。
（2）提供给机构各种可能采用的改进措施。
（3）在机构选择了所要采用的改进措施以后，协助其建立执行的决心。

一些常用的介入方法包括了：

（1）团队的建立（Team Building）
（2）冲突的处理（Conflict Management）
（3）测量的反馈（Survey Feedback）
（4）结构的改变（Structure Change）
（5）事业前程规划与发展（Career Planning and Development）
（6）训练（Training）
（7）咨询（Consultation Process）

（8）高质量工作环境的设计（Quality of Work Life Projects）

7. 评估（Evaluation）

评估虽然是组织发展的最后一个步骤，但是在评估时常会发觉一些可以用来做诊断的新资料，因此藉由评估的结果又可以引发下一个回合的组织发展活动。

为了要比较组织发展的成效，有的评估活动在资料收集时即预先进行一个初步的测量。等到介入以后再重复这个测量以比较两个测量的结果。有些在组织发展各阶段所收集的资料，如员工缺席率、人事变动率、申诉率、生产率等，都可以加以分析比较。组织发展的过程和循环性可以从图4-6中显示出来。

四、组织发展的评论

以上所讲的组织发展，虽然有它的一些理论根据和优点，但是也有人批评它不够科学和缺乏能证明它的确有效的实例[①]。但是从它所采用的方法来看，组织发展还是一个可以用来诊断一个机构内部的问题和企图改变组织文化的一种有计划的行动和程序。倡导使用组织发展的人认为在一个庞大的机构里，为了要使这个机构能顺应环境的改变和需要，进行有计划地和顺从员工意见的改革，只有采用组织发展的方法才能客观、公正地深入员工之间去调查他（她）们的意见和感受，激发员工自发、自动和合作的精神，以期共同解决内部问题，改善组织文化，和增进员工个人的成长及对工作的满意度。

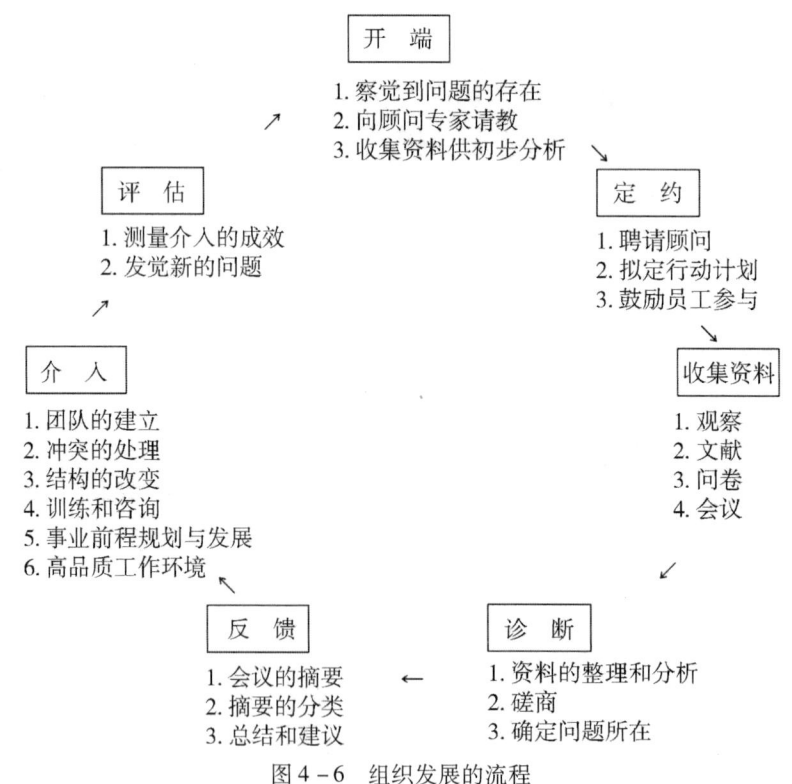

图4-6 组织发展的流程

---

① Patrick E. Connor. "A Critical Inquiry into Some Assumptions and Values Characterizing OD", *Academy of Management Review*, Vol. 2, No. 4 (October 1977), pp. 635–644.

第五章　图书馆人力资源管理

Chapter 5　Management of Human Resources in Libraries

要把一个图书馆办好，除了要有周详的规划，健全的组织和充裕的经费之外，还需要有适当数目及具备各种专长的工作人员。一般来说，图书馆的员工可以分成两种：一种是接受过高级专业教育的专业人员，一种是具备一般教育及技术训练的技术人员。这种区分在大型的图书馆中比较明显，但在小型的图书馆中则比较模糊。大的图书馆因为分工比较细密，每位员工都有明确的职责。小的图书馆有时只有两三位员工，要把每人的职责分得很细，反而不灵活也不切实际。有些图书馆，除了正式编额的员工之外，还任用一些无薪酬的义务工作人员（Volunteers），以弥补工作人员的不足。很多大专院校及中学图书馆中也经常雇用学生担任部分时间（Part-time）的工作。

图书馆人力资源的管理（Human Resource Management），虽然是管理上五个功能之一，但实际上是最重要的。因为"人"的管理是最复杂，也是最困难的，它直接地影响到一个机构的效果和成败。本章以下各节将分别讨论有关人力资源管理的五个主要项目：

（1）人员的甄选和任用。
（2）薪酬、福利和安全。
（3）员工的训练和发展。
（4）考绩。
（5）激发动机。

第一节　人员的甄选和任用

人员的甄选（Recruitment）和任用（Placement）在大的机构里多半由专设的人事部门来处理。在小的机构里，有时只有一位人事管理员来负责有关人事的业务。有的图书馆是由一位副馆长兼管人事业务。关于人员的甄选和任用一般要经过下面几个程序：

一、人力资源规划（Human Resource Planning）

一个图书馆的人力资源规划应该是该馆整个规划的一部分。根据这个规划以建立图书馆的组织架构及人员编制。也有些图书馆，它的组织与人员编制是由政府主管单位以法令来规定，看起来虽然标准划一，但实行时缺乏伸缩及应变力。

二、工作分析（Job Analysis）

根据图书馆的人力资源规划，每一个职位都应该经由"工作分析"来决定其职称、等级、隶属、最低学历要求、专长及职责功能等，这些资料构成每一职位的"工作说明书"（Job Description）。因为每个职位常有改变，必须定时检查及修正，以保持其内容确实无误。工作说明书除了每一二年定期查核一次外，每当员工出缺需要填补时，主管人事的部门应会同该职位的隶属单位的负责人共同查核并做必要的修订。另外，每一位员工若觉得自己的工作与工作说明有显著不同时，亦可申请查核、修订。凡是经过修订的工作说明书，其职称及等级亦可能由人事部门根据职位分类标准予以调整。在进行工作分析时，一般有四种方法：

（1）由直属主管或人事管理员根据人员的编制及工作需要拟定各个职位的工作说明书。这种方法多运用于新设立的职位或在职位出缺需要填补时。

（2）由直属主管用"观察"或"约谈"的方式来分析一个职位的工作。

（3）由员工填答有关工作内容的"问卷"（Questionnaire）。

（4）由员工自己"记录"每天的活动，交给直属主管查阅。

工作说明书的格式很多，一般应包括下列各点：

（1）工作职称

（2）工作单位

（3）直属主管

（4）部属

（5）职位编号

（6）等级

（7）功能

（8）职责（可以加注每一职责所占时间的百分比）

（9）最低学历要求

（10）专长

（11）其他

工作说明书和职务问卷的主要用途有三：

（1）用来对每个职位的评审和分类并决定其在一个机构中的相关位置。

（2）使每位员工能了解自己职位的职务（Duties）和责任（Responsibilities）。

（3）提供所需资料以作为决定与劳工市场（Labor Market）足以竞争的薪酬。

在做职位评审和分类时，一般有三个标准，每个标准依其不同的难度，给予适当的点数。

（1）所需的知识（Knowledge）包括教育程度和实际经验。

（2）决策的范围（Scope of Decision Making）包括人际关系的范围、管理的层次、预算的控制、经费的多寡以及权责的大小。

（3）解决问题的复杂度（Complexity of Problem Solving）包括决策的难度和影响程度。

三、甄选（Recruiting）

当一个图书馆开始招募与选用员工时，它必须根据工作说明书拟定招募广告。为了要甄选最合适的人才，对于专业人员的职位最好能公开招募。美国的图书馆一般都采取下列几种招募的方法：

（1）在图书馆学专业的刊物及全国性报纸上刊登广告。

（2）将招募的通知分送到有关的图书馆或图书馆团体请推荐合适人选。

（3）利用各种图书馆会议的"求职"和"求人"服务，与求职者做初步的接触及会谈。

（4）在图书馆内选拔人才调任（Transfer）或升任（Promotion）。调任有时是配合内部的改组或是员工的发展计划。只要是在同等级内调动（Lateral Transfer），馆长可以有权决定。升任会牵涉机会均等的考虑，有时也需要经过内部的公开甄选。

招募人员的广告一般包括下列各点：
（1）工作职称（若是临时性职位，应该注明聘用时间的长短）
（2）职责
（3）资格及专长
（4）待遇及福利
（5）职位等级
（6）申请手续
（7）截止日期
（8）图书馆的简介

对于技术人员（非专业人员）的招募，一般多就地取才，在图书馆所在地附近公开招募。有的公立大学或公家机关的图书馆对于技术人员的招募须按州或地方政府的人事任用规定办理。

为了保持甄选过程的公开和公正，很多图书馆会为每一个招募的职位建立一个临时的甄选委员会（Search Committee）。这个委员会的成员和人数是按职位的高低而有所不同。甄选大学图书馆馆长的委员会可能包括一位副教务长，一位院长，几位教授和一些图书馆馆员的代表。人数可以超过十人以上。甄选专业馆员的委员会可能仅包括该部门的主任和其他两三位馆员。

这种甄选委员会的任务一般有下列几项：
（1）刊登广告。
（2）制订客观的甄选标准。
（3）审查应征者的申请资料。
（4）初步甄选几位合格者。
（5）背景调查。
（6）将初步选出三至五人的名单提供给馆长核定后定期约请面谈。
（7）安排及进行面谈。
（8）根据面谈的结果，把最合适的人选按名次排列建议给馆长做最后决定。

以上任务是用于甄选专业馆员的，在甄选馆长时最后核定者在大专院校里多半是主管教务的副校长或教务长。在公共图书馆多半是主管该馆的地方政府部门主管或图书馆的董事会。在甄选馆员时，馆长的任务有下列几项：
（1）核定工作说明书。
（2）决定职位等级和待遇。
（3）设立甄选委员会并指派该会的召集人。
（4）核定初选人名单，确定选择过程公正无私。
（5）单独面谈。
（6）核定最后名单并向上级主管人事的单位报备。
（7）与选定的馆员联系，商讨待遇及开始上班的日期。
（8）发聘书及签订合约。

以上各项任务，每个机构多有不同之处。因国情不同，中外各国在执行上也有相当的差别。有些馆长的任务可以授权人事部门协助及办理。

对于应征者或申请人来讲，一般的申请手续包括有：
（1）申请信——要说明为何申请及具备何种适合的专长和学经历。
（2）履历书——要将个人的求职目的、学经历、专长、及其他有关的资料详细列出。
（3）推荐人名单或推荐信——依照征人广告的要求提供。
（4）学历证明——依照广告的要求提供。

四、考试（Testing）

台湾地区目前采用考试的方法来授予担任公职的资格，像"普通考试"、"高等考试"、"公务人员任用资格考试"等。通过这种考试者才拥有被聘任的资格。亦有些国家，只承认经过认可或政府承认的图书资讯学院所颁授的学位。在美国，只有经过美国图书馆学会所认可的一些学校的硕士学位才算数。

对于具备一般教育及技术训练的技术人员，有些图书馆在选用时，给予某种特殊的考试，以鉴定这些人员的技术程度，作为选择的根据。有一种常用的考试叫做"工作抽样法"（Model Sampling）。这是根据工作分析的结果把一些有代表性的基本技能选出来让应征者试作一下，以观察其成绩。就像让应征秘书的人试用计算器字处理的技术写一封简单的回信一样，从而判断应征者是否具备字处理的基本知识、语文能力、及知道一般书信的格式。很多大机构的人事部门也有定期的考试以储备各种可能需要的人才。

有一些企业机构在甄选员工时，采用标准化的智力测验、性向测验或能力测验等。因为这些测验的准确性（Validity）和可靠性（Reliability）曾经受到批评，而且有人认为这种考试的内容，对一些种族有歧视之嫌，故近年来已很少使用。

五、背景调查（Background Checking）

当甄选委员会将申请者按其提供的资料加以分析选出其中五至十位最合适者之后，下一步是进行背景调查。基本上这种调查的方法有三：

1. 向申请者所列的推荐人联系，分别请他（她）们写推荐信或在长途电话中向他们探问有关申请者的情况，包括查核申请者在履历表中所填资料的真实性及其他有关问题。因这些推荐人是由申请者提供的，一般的结果多半是对申请者有利的。

2. 直接用信件或电话向申请人过去或现在雇用机构或单位负责人查询申请者的工作情况。这种调查的结果可能会受雇主对申请人喜恶的影响，但也可能是比较公正的。

3. 向申请者的毕业学校查核在学成绩及所获的学位。这是在防患申请者提供伪造的成绩单或毕业文凭。经过背景调查，甄选委员会可以把复选的人数减少到三至五位，提请馆长批准后约请到馆中面谈。因为约请面谈的旅费及膳宿费用照理应当由征人的图书馆负担，在人数上会有所限制。为节省经费起见，有的图书馆可能在五个人当中约请最合适的三位面谈，假若面谈后对前三位不尽满意的话，可以再邀请后两位面谈，以做出最后决定。

六、面谈（Interviewing）

面谈是甄选过程中极为重要的一个步骤。有些应征人在书面的资料上看起来也许十分优秀及合适，但是在面谈时可能会发觉事实并不尽然。有些应征者可以在提供的资料中把他（她）的长处特别强调，把短处加以隐瞒。可是在面谈时，有些会显露真面目：像多话、爱批评他人、喜欢抱怨、不修边幅等。虽然面谈多少会受一些主观、先入为主等因素的影响，但是经过精心规划及有组织的面谈，其可靠性仍然是很高的。

面谈时应该注意下列几点：
（1）熟知职位说明及工作的细节。
（2）先行构思的一组适当的问题。
（3）决定评估的表格。
（4）面谈中要注意观察应征者行为、举止、态度和反应。
（5）面谈时最好不要记笔记，等面谈结束后再补记谈话要点及印象。
（6）面谈时不宜太严肃，使应征者能够畅所欲言，没有拘束感。

对于职位高的专业人员，像馆长、副馆长、部门主任等，在面谈是可以先行规定要作一个专题演讲，以便观察应征者的专业知识、经验、见解及口才等。对于职位低的专业人员在面谈时可以安排合适的工作示范，以便观察应征者对所申请职位的知识、技能和熟练程度。

在面谈之后甄选委员会应将评估的表格及参与面谈各人的意见加以整理和分析，向馆长报告及推荐，以便馆长做最后决定。这种推荐的名单可以是依先后次序排列，也可以仅列举各人的优缺点，让馆长决定最后名次。

七、用人（Hiring）

除了决定最合适应征者的先后名次，馆长还要查核整个甄选过程是否公正无私及符合政府法令和上级的规定。有些图书馆在用人之前还需要得到上级的同意或批准。

当以上的查核认为满意后，馆长或人事管理员即可以把结果通知名次最高的应征者并与其商讨薪酬、开始工作的日期及其他有关雇用的手续等事项。等到双方同意以后，图书馆必须以书面的方式与当选者签约。假如名次最高的应征者因任何原因放弃此机会，馆长可以依次聘用第二位或第三位应征者。

万一甄选委员会对所有的申请者均不满意，也可以向馆长建议重新刊登广告，再来一次。这个广告的内容可以酌量修改，以便能有更多合适的申请者。

第二节　薪酬、福利和安全

在聘用一位员工时，一个机构必须先有一个薪酬的标准。这种标准的制订是要根据下面几种考虑：
（1）职位的高低和责任的轻重。
（2）工作的繁简及技术性的强弱。
（3）人力市场的需求和供应。
（4）机构的财务情况和能力。

除了薪酬之外，员工比较关心的还有职位保障、福利制度、训练、动机、考绩和劳资关系等。本节将分别讨论到薪酬标准的建立和员工的福利制度，至于人员的训练、考绩和动机等将在第三、四、五各节分别说明。

一、薪酬的标准

薪酬标准的建立一般是根据职位的分类和等级。一个公平合理的薪酬制度应该具备下列几点:

(1) 凡是需要相似技术、努力程度、责任和工作情况的职位应该列入相同的等级及得到同样的薪酬。

(2) 它必须是公平合理,不受种族、肤色、宗教信仰、性别、原先国籍、年龄、退伍军人身份或残疾等因素的影响。

(3) 它应该比得上其他类似机构的薪酬标准。

为了要建立这些标准,每个机构应该把所有的职位按照工作分析及职位说明书划分成不同的类别和等级。以美国的大学图书馆为例,一般的员工可分成专业人员及技术人员两大类:

1. 专业人员

绝大多数的专业人员是具备图书资讯科学硕士学位以上的专业图书馆员。也有一部分是具备其他硕士以上学位的专业人员,如计算机学、会计学、档案学、教育媒体技术、公共关系、人事行政等。在美国的大学图书馆里,很多专业图书馆员除了具备图书资讯科学的学位外还具备有其他学科的高级学位。这种双学位的要求是为了配合大学图书馆工作的需要。这种情况在医学图书馆、法律图书馆及一些以学科为主的特别图书馆中尤其普遍。在一般公共图书馆中,很多只规定要具备图书馆资讯科学的硕士学位。

专业人员的等级每个图书馆都有不同。以俄亥俄大学为例,有下面七个不同的等级:

(1) 初级馆员是在获得图书资讯硕士学位或其他相关学位后,刚开始在图书馆工作的专业人员。

(2) 中级馆员是具备两个硕士学位或已在图书馆工作五年以上,成绩优越的专业人员。

(3) 小部门主任。除了具备中级馆员资格外,还担任十位员工以下的部门主任。

(4) 大部门的主任。除了具备中级馆员资格外,还担任十位员工以上的部门主任。

(5) 助理馆长。必须具备部门主任的资格和三年以上的行政经验。

(6) 副馆长。必须具备部门主任的资格和五年以上的行政经验。

(7) 馆长。必须具备助理馆长或副馆长的资格和十年以上的行政经验。很多大学图书馆(包括俄亥俄大学在内)还规定馆长要有相当于副教授以上资格及拥有相关的博士学位。

在美国的大学图书馆中专业馆员很受重视。有很多大学将图书馆专业人员视同教学人员,授予与教员相同的等级,如讲师(Instructor)、助理教授(Assistant Professor)、副教授(Associate Professor)和教授(Professor)。在这种情形之下,这些馆员的任用资格、升迁以及是否能获得"永久聘用"(Tenure)要比照教员的标准和考核方法,包括:

(1) 学位。因为图书馆学的硕士学位在过去是"终极学位"(Terminal Degree)。图书馆员只要有硕士学位就可以升迁这种情况目前已不存在。因此若要升到副教授或教授需要有两个以上的硕士学位。

(2) 教学的成绩。图书馆员通常可以用图书馆工作的成就来替代。

(3) 研究成果与著作。这对图书馆员来讲比较困难,因为教员除了教学之外,有时间作研究及写作,而且有寒暑假及休假时间;但是图书馆员却没有这些便利。

(4) 服务。这是指图书馆员对社会及在他(她)专业领域内所作的贡献。

按照以上的标准和考核办法,很多馆员只能升到助理教授,并且不容易得到"永久聘用"

的资格，这对图书馆的专业馆员来说是比较不利的。另外，有些拥有高级学位的低级馆员，为了要升级，只顾研究和写作，不管工作好坏或职位高低都可以升到教授，取得高薪及"永久聘用"资格。反之，有些高级主管因为没有高级学位，没有时间研究和写作，即使工作努力，成绩良好，反而升不上去。这种不合理的情况虽然可以设法避免，但终究是一个缺点。

在另外一些大学图书馆中，包括俄亥俄大学在内，则采用其他不同的方法。这些方法是特别为图书馆专业人员设立适当职位等级。这些等级可以比照教员的等级和待遇，但它的考核、升迁和永久聘用是按照图书馆本身的工作和标准来制定的。

美国的研究图书馆协会（Association of Research Libraries）在1991年曾经做了一个图书馆馆员是否具备教员身份、名称和等级的调查。根据从该会一百零七个会员图书馆所收回的九十九份资料，我们可以获得下列的实况[①]：

（1）馆员是否具有教员身份及可以申请"永久聘用"？
* 三十五个图书馆（34.6%）的答复是肯定的。
* 三十一个图书馆（30.7%）有专业馆员身份，可以继续聘用，但非"永久聘用"。
* 九个图书馆（8.9%）有教员身份，可以继续聘用，但非"永久聘用"。
* 一个图书馆（1.0%）有专业馆员身份，但可以"永久聘用"。
* 二十三个图书馆（22.8%）采用其他方法。

在其他的方法中，有的馆采用两种聘用方法，一个是教员身份，一个是专业馆员身份。前者可以申请"永久聘用"，后者则是继续聘用。有的图书馆准许在三年之后更改身份，也有的在初聘时，先以专业馆员身份试用三年，在三年以内表现良好的话，可以转到教员身份。

（2）申请"永久聘用"的规定。大多数可以申请"永久聘用"的图书馆规定其具有教员身份的馆员必须对下列三个审查标准提出有力的证据或说明：
  A. 图书资讯工作的成绩（Practice of Librarianship）。
  B. 研究与著作（Research and Publications）。
  C. 服务（Service）。

在三十五个具有教员身份及可以申请"永久聘用"的图书馆中：
* 有十六个把上面三个标准等量使用。
* 有十九个特别强调在图书资讯工作方面的卓越表现。
* 有五个不要求研究与著作的成果。
* 有两个规定要有图书馆硕士以上的学位。

有关研究与著作的标准，一般颇不划一。有的规定最少要有二至三篇文章，一本书及四个书评。

"永久聘用"的资格审查一般是在聘任后的第五年开始，在第六年结束以前能够通过的话，即可获得"永久聘用"，否则会被解聘。

2. 技术人员

除了专业人员之外，另一类极为重要的图书馆工作人员是技术人员。技术人员的学历虽然没有专业人员所要求的那样高，但他（她）们所担任的工作并不简单，而且有时候要经过相当长时间的在职训练。这些人员的职位、名称、等级和薪酬是按照每个图书馆或其所在机构的人事任用办法所规定。俄亥俄大学图书馆的技术人员有下面几种类别及等级。

[①] Jack Siggins (comp.). *Academic Status for Librarian in ARL Libraries*. SPEC Kit 182. Washington, D.C.: Office of Management Services, Association of Research Libraries, 1992.

其中有些类别是专为图书馆而设的，其他的类别则是采用大学一般所通用者。

图书馆的技术人员职称和等级：

职称	等级
图书馆办事员（Library Clerk）	50
图书馆助理（Library Assistant）	56
资深图书馆助理（Senior Library Assistant）	62
图书馆职员（Library Associate）	65
资深图书馆职员（Senior Library Associate）	68
图书馆技术员（Library Specialist）	71

除了以上冠以图书馆的职称之外，俄亥俄大学图书馆还有以下一些其他的职称：

职称	等级
打字员（Typist）	50
资深打字员（Senior Typist）	53
秘书（Secretary）	62
资深秘书（Senior Secretary）	65
办事员（Clerical Specialist）	56
高级办事员（Clerical Supervisor）	62
记账员（Account Clerk）	62
高级记账员（Account Clerk Specialist）	65
办公室机器操作员（Office Machine Operator）	53
资深办公室机器操作员（Senior Office Machine Operator）	56
视听器材技术员（Audio Visual Specialist）	65
摄影师（Photographer）	65

二、员工的福利制度

除了薪酬之外，员工最关心的就是他（她）们的福利。根据美国的雇主福利研究所（Employer Benefit Research Institute）在1992年所做的一个调查，75%被调查的员工认为员工福利的好坏是他（她）们在应聘时一个极为重要的考虑。从1990年的57%，到1991年的70%，这个百分比几乎每年都在增加[1]。这种对福利制度的重视，一方面是因为医疗保险费用的直线上升，使得每位馆员都希望他（她）的雇主能提供医疗保险。另一个原因是更多的人认为雇主有责任改善员工的福利，使每个人都能安心工作，进而改善生活的质量。

一个机构的福利制度大概包含了下面几种：

1. **医疗保险（Health Care Insurance）**

医疗保险的种类很多，方法也不一，有的不包括防治牙病和眼睛的查验及配眼镜。有的规定每人每年要支付一部分费用，其余的再由保险公司支付，也有的要病人自付一部分的药品费。

---

[1] Joseph S. Piacentini, & Jill D. Foley. EBRI *Databook on Employee Benefits*. 2nd ed. Washington, D.C.: Employee Benefit Research Institute, 1992.

2. **退休后的福利**（Retirement Benefit）

这包括由雇主支付全部或部分的社会福利金（Social Security）和退休基金。

3. **各种休假**（Leave Provision）

休假有"年假"（Annual Leave）、"病假"（Sick Leave）、"个人假"（Personal Leave）、"进修假"（Sabbatical Leave）、"公假"（Official or Administrative Leave）及"留职停薪假"（Leave without Pay）等多种。除此之外，一年还有十多天的法定假日（Holidays）。

4. **教育福利**（Educational Benefits）

有很多大学图书馆准许员工在公余免费选课或读学位，这种教育福利有时还包括配偶和子女在内。

5. **生命保险**（Life Insurance）

根据薪酬的百分比，但总数不超过一个固定数目。（例如像年薪的两倍，但不得超过十万元等）

6. **因公受伤或因长病而无力工作的保险计划**（Long-Term Disability Plan）

由保险公司支付60%左右的薪酬一直到六十五岁退休。

7. **其他**（Others）

这些其他的福利包括了新聘人员搬迁补助、托儿所、健身运动、戒除烟酒及吸毒等恶习，及使用学校设备和参加康乐活动的优待折扣等。

美国的研究图书馆协会在1993年对该会一百一十九个会员图书馆做了一个馆员福利的问卷调查，以下是七十一个图书馆的回答[①]：

* 100%的图书馆都提供医疗保险。

* 86%提供有选择的牙病保险。

* 91%提供生命保险。

* 68%支付社会福利的保险金。

* 88.6%支付一部分退休金的保险金。

* 平均年假是每年二十二个工作天（或每月有14.6小时）。

* 平均病假是每年十四个工作天（或每月有9.2小时）。

* 大多数都有进修假、公假、留职停薪假及法定假日。

* 44%的大学有收费的托儿所。

* 77%准许员工免费选课（平均每年9.6个学分）。

* 36%优待员工眷属及子女入学（其中52%全免费，27%半免费，21%可安排免费进入其有相互协议的学校）。

因为员工福利项目的增多及医疗保险费用的大量增加，使得一般机构用在员工福利的开销逐年增加。以俄亥俄大学图书馆为例，1992—1993年，员工的薪酬与福利一共是3,931,761美元，其中薪酬是2,762,995美元（占70.27%），福利是1,168,766美元（占29.73%），福利的开销是薪酬的42.30%。与1982—1983年相比，当时的薪酬与福利一共是1,779,380美元，其中薪酬是1,470,255美元（占82.63%），福利是309,095美元（占17.37%），福利的开销是薪酬的21.02%。十年之间的变化如此之大实在惊人。这种趋势若是不加以控制，将会造成福利费用的比重逐年增加，使图书馆其他经费的比重相形之下逐年减少。长此下去会迫使图书馆裁减员工，加雇部分时间临时员工（Part-time Temporary

---

① Teri R. Switzer. *Benefits for Professional Staff in ARL Libraries*. SPEC Kit 197. Washington, D.C.: Office of Management Services, Association of Research Libraries, 1993.

Staff)以减少福利的费用,或者将一些工作,像图书编目等发包给馆外的机构去做。

三、员工的安全与保健(Employee Safety and Health)

除了薪酬和福利之外,员工另外一个最关心的问题就是工作环境的安全。有了一个安全的工作场所,可以使员工安心地工作,保护员工的健康,进而提高了工作的效率。

早在1970年,美国国会即通过了一个"职业安全和保健法案"(Occupational Safety and Health Act),由总统签署后生效。该法案的目的在于确保全国男女员工有一个安全和健康的工作环境。为了执行这个法案,美国的劳工部特别建立了一个职业安全和保健行政总署(Occupational Safety and Health Administration)来制定各种法规与标准,由分布在全国各地的检查员负责执行。根据这个行政总署的规定任何雇用十一人以上的机构、工厂或企业,必须将因职业而意外受伤或生病的个别记录向该署就近地区的办事处申报,以便调查、统计及设法改善和避免再发生。

该署的检查员亦可以依法进行检查,将不符标准和需要改进之点以书面形式通知被检查的机构,限期改善。不遵从者可以根据情况的轻重予以罚款或送上法庭审判。

1. 造成意外事故(Accidents)的原因

一般来说,因意外而受伤的原因有偶发事件(Chance Occurrences)、不安全的情况(Unsafe Conditions)和不安全的行为(Unsafe Acts)三种:

(1)偶发事件。这种事件大多数是在很偶然的情况之下发生,像某一位员工因不慎踩到自己的鞋带而跌跤受伤,这种事件实非机构之过,与工作环境无关。

(2)不安全的情况。这种发生意外的情况多半是可以改善或设法避免的,像下列的一些例子:

  A. 走道的光线不够或是灯泡烧坏了没有及时更换
  B. 家俱的摆布阻挡了通道
  C. 机械的安装和维护不良
  D. 通风设备不够
  E. 化学原料的随便存放

这样的情况实在很多,而且不胜枚举,应该随时注意,定时检查,以求改善。

根据一些研究的结果认为另有两种情况与意外事件有关联,一种是工作时间,另一种是心理的气候。

  A. 工作的时间,譬如说,很多意外事件是发生在下午或晚班的时间。当员工工作五、六个小时以后,因为疲倦(fatigue)的关系,会影响到注意力,而容易有意外。现在很多机构都规定每工作两个小时需要休息十五至二十分钟。

  B. 心理的气候(Psychological Climate),这是指一个人的心理状况与意外事件的关联。当一位员工在工作不顺心及情绪不好时,或周围环境的噪杂等情况下也会容易出意外[①]。

(3)不安全的行为,不安全的"行为"或"举动"多半是人为的。它的造成通常是大意和不小心,有时与不安全的情况无关。下面是一些常见的原因:

  A. 工作时漫不经心、开玩笑、恶作剧、斗嘴等。
  B. 不按照规定的方式操作。

[①] Dove Zohar. "Safety Climate in Industrial Organization: Theoretical and Applied Implications", *Journal of Applied Psychology*, Vol. 65, No. 1 (Feb. 1980), pp. 96–102.

C. 乱丢东西。
D. 操作机器超速或太慢。

也有些人，天性使然，容易出错，有经常闯祸的倾向（Accidental prone）。心理学家阿波是（A. G. Arbous）和柯力取（J. E. Kerrich）还为此作过研究，认为的确有这种人[1]。但后来的研究认为眼力不好的人[2]，年龄在十七到二十八岁之间的年轻人[3]和知觉能力比动作技巧慢的人[4]，比较容易出意外。

2. 如何避免意外事件

为了避免或减少意外事件，美国国家安全委员会（National Safety Council）提出了三个"E"的方法，即工程设计（Engineering）、教育（Education）和执行（Enforcement）。

（1）工程设计即是要建立安全的工作环境。
（2）教育即是要教育员工有关安全的措施。
（3）执行即是要将安全规则严格执行。

除此之外，最重要还在于如何改善不安全的情况和减少不安全的行为。

要减少不安全的行为，格雷·德色勒（Gary Dessler）建议以下几种方法[5]：
（1）使用各种测验以选择员工及分配工作。

有些标准测验可以测定各人的情绪稳定程度、肌肉协调程度及视觉技巧等。
（2）加强宣传以提高员工对安全的重视和警觉。
（3）有计划地安全训练。
（4）严格执行各种安全措施。
（5）上级主管应该以身作则，特别强调对安全的重视。

近年来，人类工程学（Human Engineering）在工业工程中占有很重要的地位，它的主要任务是：
（1）设计适合员工使用的工具与设备等以加强员工的安全和效率，减少意外事件的发生。
（2）创造适合员工的工作环境，使每人都能够很舒适、愉快和安全地工作。

人类工程学的应用是在考虑到人与机器设备的配合问题，员工的生理限制，人与环境的关系和安全的措施。它的目的是将可能由于人的疏忽所造成的意外事件减至最低的程度。

3. 员工的健康措施

员工的保健工作十分重要。健康的员工不仅可以减少医疗保险的开销而且还可以增加生产力。有很多机构还为员工提供健身设备、运动和有益的康乐活动，鼓励员工参加，以减少员工因过分操劳或顾虑所产生的重压感（Stress）或精疲力竭（Burnout）。

（1）重压感。重压感可因很多原因引起，有些是完全与工作相关的。但有重压感的员工，他（她）的健康、心理状况与工作多半都会受到影响。据研究，最能引起重压感的原因依次有下列多种[6]：
A. 夫、妻或亲人的死亡。

---

[1] A. G. Arbous, and J. E. Kerrich. "The Phenomenon of Accident Prone-ness", *Industrial Medicine and Surgery*, Vol. 22, No. 4 (April 1953), pp. 141–148.
[2] Ernest McCormick, and Joseph Tiffin. *Industrial Psychology*. Englewood Cliffs, N. J.: Prentice-Hall, 1974, p. 523.
[3] Ernest McCormick, and Joseph Tiffin. *Industrial Psychology*. Englewood Cliffs, N. J.: Prentice-Hall, 1974, pp. 524–525.
[4] Milton Blum and James Nayler. *Industrial Psychology*. New York: Harper & Row, 1968, p. 522.
[5] Gary Dessler. *Personnel Management*. 4th ed. Englewood Cliffs, N. J.: Prentice-Hall, 1988, pp. 670–671.
[6] R. A. Alkov. "The Life Change Unit and Accident Behavior," *Lifeline*, (Norfolk, Va.: U. S. Naval Safety Center) Vol. 21, No. 5 (Sept.–Oct. 1992).

B. 婚姻问题：如结婚、离婚、分居、怀孕、性生活不调等。
C. 经济问题。
D. 工作问题。
E. 人际关系。
F. 健康问题。
G. 假日及生活习惯的改变。
H. 其他。

以上第四项与工作有关的重压感（Job Stress）可因下列原因而引起：

A. 上下班的时间、工作的安排。
B. 居住远近及交通问题。
C. 工作质量的要求与时限。
D. 工作的保障。
E. 对工作是否胜任的程度。
F. 与上司和同事的关系。
G. 与顾客或服务对象的关系。
H. 个性与工作。

有些具有强烈工作意愿（Workaholics）的员工非常忠于职守，工作认真努力，按期或提前完成所交代的任务。长久下来，若是没有适当的休闲活动以资调剂，有时也会变成工作的重压感。长期在重压感的压力下，对个人来讲会有下列的影响：

A. 忧虑不安（Anxiety）。
B. 沮丧（Depression）。
C. 愤怒（Anger）。
D. 导致心脏病症（Cardiovascular）或高血压（Hypertension）。
E. 头痛（Headache）。
F. 容易出意外事故（Accidents）。
G. 吸用毒品（Drug Abuse）。
H. 酗酒（Alcoholic）。
I. 饮食不正常（Over or Under Eating）。
J. 人际关系不好。

对一个机构来讲，有重压感的员工也会造成下列的影响：

A. 工作效率与质量显然地下降。
B. 缺席率（Absenteeism）显然地增加。
C. 人事变动（Turnover）加多。
D. 有较多的诉苦（Grievances）事件。

亦有专家认为：适度的重压感可以增加员工的生产力和效率。对于工作不力的或能力不相配的员工，增加重压感可以迫使这些人去找另外的工作[①]。

要减少对工作的重压感，有些方法可以采用：这包括了适度的饮食、睡眠和休闲活动，时间的有效利用（Time Management），调换工作（Job Transfers），和寻求专家指导（Counseling）。卡罗·欧伯（Karl Albrecht）对于减少工作上的重压感有以下的建议[②]：

---

① Andrew DuBrin. *Human Relations: A Job Oriented Approach*. Reston, Va.: Reston, 1978, pp. 66–67.
② Karl Albrecht. *Stress and the Manager*. Englewood Cliffs, N. J.: Spectrum, 1979.

A. 与上司、同事及下属建立和谐合作的关系。
B. 不要从事能力所不及之工作（Don't bite off more than you can chew）。
C. 了解上司的困难并帮助上司了解你的困难。
D. 对重要任务应主动地提出完成的时间，不要让上司为你决定。限时完成的时间应该是相互认为合理的。
E. 对可能出现的情况或任务，能够洞察在先，早做准备，不致临时手忙脚乱，穷于应付。
F. 不管多忙，每一天都要抽出一些时间做休闲活动。
G. 利用休假时间完全与工作脱离，以调解身心。
H. 做主管的要能够充分授权，尽量减少对一般琐碎业务（Trivia）的操心。
I. 每天要安排一些不受干扰（Uninterruptibility）的时间以便能专心致力于重要的工作。
J. 对于棘手的问题不要逃避或拖延，应尽快把它处理掉。

（2）精疲力竭

精疲力竭多半与工作的压力有关。有些人太专注于工作，终日忙碌不停，没有其他的消遣和娱乐，置家庭及亲友不顾，长久下来，很容易导致精疲力竭。最容易造成精疲力竭的人多半是"工作狂"（Workaholic）之类。

精疲力竭的征象根据赫伯特·福劳登伯格（Herbert Freudenberger）的分析，有下列几种[①]：

A. 无法放松（Relax）。
B. 个人情绪受工作所支配。
C. 对所努力的工作突然觉得失去意义。
D. 愈做愈没有兴趣。
E. 愈来愈觉得需要用吸烟、喝酒或用镇定剂等来支撑。
F. 脾气变得暴躁，容易激怒（Irritable）。

要避免达到精疲力竭的境界，可以尝试以下几种方法：

A. 打破旧习，设法改变工作以外的休闲活动。
B. 定时度假或出外旅行，使能更换环境，舒畅心情。
C. 重新评估工作的目标和方式，应量力为之。
D. 减少工作上的重压感。

可是即使如此，一般机构都多少遭遇到员工酗酒、吸用毒品等问题。据美国人事行政协会（American Society for Personnel Administration）的估计，在一般的机构中大约3%到6%的员工有此问题。

尤其是酗酒，大约50%的酗酒者是女性，25%是白领阶层，50%有大学教育程度。另外，据专家估计约50%的问题员工是酗酒者，因为他（她）们经常缺席，工作效率低，质量差，与同事相处不好，而且容易发生意外，造成机构的重大损失。

对于吸用毒品者来讲，他（她）们的问题也是相当严重的，因为吸用毒品的花费很大，这些员工有时会偷窃、贪污、贩毒等。

对付酗酒及吸用毒品的员工的对策不外是惩戒、解职、内部辅导和送到外面的专门机构去治疗四种：

（1）惩戒（Disciplining）。这多半是对初犯者所使用的。惩戒是一个警告，假如再犯

---

① Herbert Freudenberger. *Burn-out*. Toronto：Bantam Books, 1980.

的话会解职。惩戒可以与内部辅导和送到外面的专门机构去治疗配合，使得初患者能及时得到治疗，以戒除恶习。

（2）解职（Discharge or Dismissal）。这是用来对付知错不改或积习难改的员工。

（3）内部辅导（In-house Counseling）。有很多机构专设有"员工协助活动"（Employee Assistance Program），由有经验的医疗人员和心理专家来治疗酗酒、吸用毒品或有心理病症的员工。

（4）外面的专门机构（Outside Agency）。这种专门机构包括诊所、医院、精神病医师、心理学专家和"无名酗酒者组织"（Alcoholics Anonymous）等。

为了防患酗酒及吸用毒品，每一个机构都必须有严格禁止的明文规定，用时还需要有一批受过专门训练的中上级部门主管能够从行为上觉察到酗酒或吸用毒品的员工，以采取适当的处置。

第三节　员工的训练和发展

由于科技的进步一日千里，图书馆员工的工作及他（她）们所使用的技术也不断的改变和更新，因此每一位员工都应该接受新知识和新技术的训练，使能跟得上时代的进步。除了训练之外，图书馆还应该协助员工在事业前途上的发展，让员工能认清自己在图书馆中的地位、未来的出路、升迁的机会等。一个完善的员工训练和发展措施不但可以增进员工的知识和技能、改变员工的行为和想法，并且可以激励员工努力向上，加强工作绩效，让员工认识自我的兴趣、潜能及未来发展的目标。

员工的训练和发展应包括新任用的和已在职的员工。对于新任用员工的训练一般有"认识环境"（Orientation）和"工作训练"（Work Training）两种。对于已在职员工的训练和发展一般有"在职训练"（In-service Training），"职外训练"（Off-the-job Training），"继续教育"（Continuing Education），"休假进修"（Sabbatical, Professional Leave or Study Leave），和"事业前途发展"（Career Development）等。

一、新任用员工的训练

新任用的员工刚上班时，对于新的工作环境感到生疏和顾虑，应该给予一个有规划的"认识环境"的训练。这种训练的目的在于减少新任用员工心理上的不安，使他（她）们能够很快地熟悉新的工作环境，顺利地开始工作。

1. 认识环境

认识环境的训练应由主管人事的部门制定办法、内容和执行细则，然后会同该员工的单位主管共同执行。认识环境的内容应包括：

（1）机构的历史、使命、目的和目标。

（2）机构的组织和重要的主管人员。

（3）要是一个机构已经有了"组织介绍"（Introduction of the Organization）或"认识环境手册"（Orientation Handbook）之类的书刊，应该给每位新任的员工一本，并将主要的内容加以解释。

（4）向新任员工解释他（她）们的职位说明，在所属单位中的位置，和所属单位的介绍。

（5）介绍一般人事规则包括员工福利，上、下班及休息时间，工作时数，支薪手续，工作要求，各种假期，请假手续，试用时期，考绩办法等。

（6）带新任员工参观工作场所（如休息处、布告栏、意见箱、餐厅、厕所所在地），并介绍给有关主管及同事。

（7）其他事项（如使用公家电话的规定）。

虽然不一定每个机构都编印有"认识环境手册"，但越是大的机构，越需要有这种手册，将所有的人事政策和规则收集在一起，以便员工的阅读和参考。

在进行"认识环境"时，最好能有一个"清查单"（Checklist）来避免对于重要事项的遗漏。这个清查单在"认识环境"完成以后送缴人事部门查存。

一个详细的"清查单"应该包括下列项目：

（1）职务介绍
——职务说明
——训练计划
——部门的目的和目标
——部门的组织
——部门的分工

（2）环境介绍
——部门的同事
——工作的场所
——工具、器材和办公用品的领用
——布告栏
——意见箱
——休息室、餐厅、洗手间
——医务室
——紧急情况的应变措施

（3）介绍资料
——认识环境手册
——其他资料

（4）工作时间
——上、下班时间
——吃饭及休息时间
——参与馆内活动

（5）假期
——年假
——病假
——个人假
——法定假日
——留职停薪的规定

（6）薪酬和福利
——发薪日期及领薪手续

——薪给标准和等级
——加班费
——试用时期的考绩
——医疗保险
——退休金制度
——其他福利
（7）权利及义务
——按时上、下班
——出席率
——工作态度
——行为和外表
——道德规范
——安全
——申诉的程序

2. **工作训练**

在认识环境以后，下一个步骤是工作训练。新任用的员工也许已有工作的经验，但不一定是完全一致的。而且每一个机构的工作程序多少有不同的地方，因此，对新员工的工作训练极为重要。

进行工作训练多半在新员工的单位内进行，由单位主管派一位老练的员工负责。必要时也可以与其他有关单位协调，共同进行。训练时间的长短要看每一个工作的情况来决定。新任员工所具备的技术、经验和能力也影响到训练的方式和时间的长短。对于有经验的新员工，应该尽可能地聆听他（她）们的意见，设法采纳。

二、已在职员工的训练与发展

对已在职员工的训练有很多种，它的目的在于增进员工知识和技能，使员工更能适应变迁中的工作环境及所需的新技能。在一般的情况下，"在职训练"和"职外训练"是机构的责任，必须由机构免费提供并准许员工利用工作时间去学习。"休假进修"和"事业前途发展"是员工与机构两者共同的责任，其费用及时间应该由员工与机构共同负责。至于"继续教育"一项，虽然很多机构都鼓励员工去参加，而且有时也给予资助及工作时间上的方便，但其责任在于员工自己。除非是机构规定和指派员工去参加，继续教育的费用及时间多由员工自己负责。

1. **在职训练**

这是指让员工在工作时间内所参加的各种与工作有关的训练，包括了某些技术技能、管理技能、人际关系、解决问题的能力、工作轮调、见习和促进身心健康的方法等。有些训练是针对一两个人特别设计的，也有些是由人事处或由员工组成的员工发展委员会 (Staff Development Committee) 根据员工的意见和需要所设计，由员工自己选择参加。

"工作轮调"（Job Rotation）也是在职训练的一种，使得员工能有机会学习并尝试另外一个职位的工作。这种轮调大多是横向或在同等级中进行，它可以帮助员工了解各部门间的关系，学习新的技能和拓广工作的视野。

另外一种在职训练是"见习"（Internship），这是让一些具有能力而且表现良好的员工能跟从某一位上级主管见习一个时期，作为将来有机会升迁时的准备。

2. 职外训练

这是指派选或鼓励员工前往参加某些讲习会、研讨会、会议、讲座、展览及示范等，以学习新的知识和技术。这种学习机会多半在机构以外的地点举行。员工的交通、膳宿、注册等的开销由机构支付，其所用时间算为出公差。

3. 休假进修

很多机构，尤其是大学图书馆，订有办法，准许专业人员在工作若干年以后（一般是七年一次），可以申请休假进修半年（全薪）或一年（半薪）。申请人必须提出与工作有关的进修或研究计划，再由最高主管批准。

4. 事业前途发展

为了使长期任用的员工有机会继续发展他（她）们的事业前途并求配合一个机构现在和将来人力资源的需要，每一个机构都应该有计划地辅导员工去拟定个人的事业前途发展计划。这种计划的范围，不只包括工作上的知识和技能，也包括生活上、益智上、语言上、人际关系上的各种学习，以充实员工的生活及一般的能力。以下是一些有助于事业前途发展的措施：

（1）加强对员工的辅导。这种辅导包括了：

A. 向员工讲解事业前途发展的措施和重要性。
B. 与个别员工讨论他（她）们对自我前程所拟定的目标和期望。
C. 评估他（她）们的计划是否切合实际并与机构的人力资源规划相呼应。
D. 讨论机构本身如何配合。
E. 建议员工如何利用各种训练和进修机会自我充实，以为将来的升迁做好准备。
F. 指出那些是员工可以把握的晋升机会。

（2）让新进的员工尝试多种工作机会以发觉最适合及最能胜任的工作。

（3）尽早给予员工较具挑战性的工作。史蒂芬·罗宾士在他的《管理概论》一书中指出"初期就担任较挑战性工作的员工，以后的工作成绩会比较好"[①]。

（4）有些职位出缺时，应尽可能先在机构内部公布，鼓励合格的员工申请。

以上所提到的各种方式是属于"员工发展"（Staff Development）一类，下面我们将接着讨论"继续教育"（Continuing Education）。

5. 继续教育

员工的继续教育有助于提高员工素质，是一件好事，值得鼓励。但是"继续教育"与一般的"员工发展"有时是有区别的。

一般说来，继续教育是指员工本身为了求知欲的驱使，希望能充实自己，为制造升迁或更好的就业机会，而决定在工作之余前往进修或研究。继续教育的方式包括：

（1）正式攻读学位或仅选修一些课程。
（2）参加函授教育和终生教育。
（3）参加讲习班、研讨会或一般学术会议。
（4）休假进修或专题研究。
（5）与其他机构进行人员交换或见习。

这种学习的结果也许与员工的工作有间接的联系，但不是非有不可的。相形之下，员工发展则是与工作有直接关联的特殊训练，有时是由机构的单位选派或指定参加。简而言

---

① Stephen P. Robbins.《管理概论：理论与实践》，李茂兴，译. 台北：晓园出版社，1989，p.243.

之，继续教育是以员工个人的需要为主，而员工发展是以机构的需要为主。

从图书馆的立场来讲，馆员的素质愈高愈好，这不仅是为了吸收新知识，加强对读者的服务，而且也提高了图书馆的地位。为此之故，在不影响正常工作的情况之下，图书馆应对有志进行继续教育的员工给予鼓励及协助，必要时还可以给予部分资助，以示奖励。在员工完成高等学位或有研究成果时，也应该给予表扬。有些图书馆还为此订有加薪或升迁的办法。

第四节 考 绩

人力资源管理另一个重要的环节是员工的考绩（Performance Appraisal），本节将分别讨论考绩的作用、方法、问题及解决之道。

一、考绩的作用

员工的工作表现和敬业精神直接影响到整个机构的成效。因为每个人的学识、能力、技术、为人和努力的程度有所不同，要想赏罚分明，必须有适当的考绩措施，以作为升迁、调职、降级、解职、加减薪、训练、员工发展等的依据。

员工考绩的作用一般有以下各点：

（1）增进一个机构的效率以达成机构的目标。
（2）协助员工的自我发展及成长，使能更胜任所担任的工作。
（3）为员工提供有关各人在工作上的表现和成就的评估和及时的回馈。
（4）辅导员工改进工作上的缺点。
（5）作为决定薪酬及升迁的依据。
（6）加强员工与上司之间的沟通与了解。

考绩工作要做得好，必须有周详的规划和公正无私的执行。人事部门首先要制订有关考绩的办法和条例，训练员工有关考绩的技术和要点，然后在实施时能够进行监督和辅导。

在实施考绩时一般有下列三个步骤：

（1）确定每位员工的工作及标准，使每位员工与其直属上司有相同的了解。
（2）使用预先决定采用的考绩表格来衡量每位员工的工作表现和工作标准的差距。
（3）将考绩的结果与个别员工进行讨论，好的地方要给予赞赏，有缺点的地方应该共同讨论改进的办法。

二、考绩的方法

常用的考绩方法可以分成四类：考绩的评分表、执行考绩者、考绩的面谈及考绩的次数。

1. 考评的评分表

考绩时采用的评分表，每个机构都有所不同。但一般多包括各种可以用来鉴别员工在工作表现上的一些重要特征。以俄亥俄大学图书馆为例，该馆对专业图书馆员的评分包括了下列十项特征：

　　＊ 工作的质与量（Quality and Quantity of Work）
　　＊ 专业的知识与技能（Knowledge of Work and Skills）

* 适应力（Adaptability）
* 可靠性（Dependability）
* 判断（Judgment）
* 主动性和理解力（Initiative and Perception）
* 合作和人品（Cooperation and Personal Qualities）
* 行政和管理的能力（Administrative/Supervisory Ability）
* 对图书馆专业和大学内部的服务（Service to Library Profession and University Service）
* 专业的发展（Professional Development）

对于每个特征在评鉴之前，每位被考绩的员工应该和他（她）的顶头上司（亦即评鉴者）将每个特征的重要性依下列比重选择适当的分数，例如：

* 不重要（Unimportant）　　　　　　　　　　1分
* 有几分重要（Somewhat Important）　　　　2分
* 重要（Important）　　　　　　　　　　　　3分
* 相当重要（Quite Important）　　　　　　　4分
* 非常重要（Extremely Important）　　　　　5分

对于图书馆的部门主任以上职位来讲，行政和管理能力应该是"非常重要"，但对初级馆员来讲，可能是"不重要"或"有几分重要"。

在评鉴时，每个特征的评分亦可以有下列几种区分：

* 无关（Not Applicable）　　　　　　　　　　0分
* 很差（Poor）　　　　　　　　　　　　　　　1分
* 低于平均水平（Below Average）　　　　　　2分
* 普通（Average）　　　　　　　　　　　　　3分
* 很好（Good）　　　　　　　　　　　　　　　4分
* 杰出（Outstanding）　　　　　　　　　　　5分

每个特征的评分（Score）乘上它的比重（Value）加起来的总分（Sum），再除去比重的总分（Value Total），即是各人评鉴的平均分数（Average Score）。这种平均分数也可以视为各人的绩效分数（Merit Rating），作为加薪多少的参考。表5-1是这种评分表的一个样式。

俄亥俄大学图书馆的评分表除了使用上面的打分方法外，在每个特征之下还鼓励评鉴者加注适当的评论。在评分表的最后一部分，评鉴者还可以做书面的总结。

为了加强考绩的公正和客观，评鉴者在评鉴以后要请他（她）的上司复阅一下，这位复阅者亦可以在评分表上加注复阅的意见。

经过了复阅，评鉴者必须把评分表让被考绩的员工过目及签字表明已看过。员工在看过他（她）的评分表之后，也可以在评分表上加注意见，然后将评分表交回人事部门归档或进行必须的措施。

除了以上所用的评分表之外，有的机构也采取一些其他不同的方法：像严重事件记录法和叙述法等。

(1) 严重事件记录法（Critical Incident Recording）。这种方法是由上司将员工在工作上所发生的特别事件，不管是好的或是坏的，分别记录下来，然后在考绩时逐一提出，作为勉励和改进的依据。这种用实例来评鉴的方法，有下列几种优点：

A. 依赖平时的观察，以实例为证，比较客观。

B. 使用文字记录，有助于日后的回忆。
C. 对于经常发生的事件，可以推究其原因，设法改进。若能将这种方法与评分表合并使用会增加评分表的客观性。

表 5-1 考绩评分表的样式

比重分	特征	评分	总分
_____	工作的质与量	_____	_____
_____	专业的知识与技能	_____	_____
_____	适应力	_____	_____
_____	可靠性	_____	_____
_____	主动性和理解力	_____	_____
_____	合作和人品	_____	_____
_____	行政和管理的能力	_____	_____
_____	图书馆专业和大学内部的服务	_____	_____
_____	专业的发展	_____	_____
总比重分		总评分	总积分

总积分/总比重分＝平均分数（或绩效分数）

（2）叙述法（Narrative Method）。这种方法是将每位员工的表现，根据其职责、工作的目标和标准，加以叙述，最后做成总结及评论。因为叙述法是根据评鉴者的个人观点及喜恶，缺乏客观性，而且有时以偏概全，失却公正。有些比较忙的上司也可能随便写几句，敷衍了事。叙述法若能作为评分表法的补充，像用在评分表上的总结，还是有它的优越之点。

2. 执行考绩者

执行考绩的人在绝大多数的情况下多半是被评鉴者的直属上司。这种情况是合乎情理的，因为直属上司应该是最能了解属下的工作和绩效，但是在某些特殊的情况之下，执行考绩者可能是同僚（Peer）、评鉴小组或被考绩者的自我评鉴。

在一些大学图书馆里，对于有教员身份（Faculty Status）的专业图书馆员通常是采用同僚或评审小组的评鉴。这种评鉴方式有它客观的优点，但有时也会偏向于人缘好及会作公共关系的人。对于一些不善于自我表扬，但工作努力，有良好成果的员工不一定完全公平。因为同僚和评审小组的人员对于某一位员工的工作能力和绩效不一定有充分的了解，有时候只看到一些外表。当一位下属对他（她）上司给的考绩感到有偏见或不公平时，也可以由图书馆的馆长设立一个评鉴小组来考绩。

也有些评鉴者在执行考绩之前先请被评鉴者来个自我评鉴以作为考绩时的参考。格雷·德色勒（Gary Dessler）在他《人事管理》一书中指出自我评鉴的缺点是每个人都有倾向把自己评得太好，这是很多有关研究的共同结论[1]。

3. 考绩的面谈

考绩时的面谈是考绩中一个极为重要的部分，需要预先做好下列三项准备：

---

[1] Gary Dessler. *Personnel Management*. 4th ed. Englewood Cliffs, N.J.: Prentice-Hall, 1988, pp. 511-512.

（1）整理及研究有关资料，将有关被评鉴者的工作说明、目标及标准、过去的考绩等资料先行温习一遍。

（2）把面谈的日期和时间在一个星期以前告诉员工，让他（她）们也有时间为考绩而准备。

（3）要有足够的及对彼此都方便的面谈时间，面谈的地点应该是不易受干扰的地方。

在进行面谈时要注意下面五个要点：

（1）向员工解释面谈的目的和方式，鼓励员工发言，注意倾听。

（2）着重面谈的积极性及建设性，一切以对事不对人为主，强调解决问题的途径。

（3）对员工的成就和杰出的表现应该给予适度的认定和称赞。

（4）在意见或看法不同时，应尽量鼓励双方了解彼此的观点。

（5）商讨下一步的行动或改进方案。

对于因考绩不佳或其他原因而动怒的员工应该用冷静而理智的态度去对付。根据一些心理学家的研究，动怒是一种正常的防御性行为，评鉴者应该以对事不对人的态度，避免用"你怎么会如此无能，连这种工作都做不好？"这种有破坏对方自尊心或有损人格的批评。最好的方法是举出一些实例与员工商讨如何改进，并提供必要的支持和协助。在员工很激动和愤怒时，应该给他（她）一个冷静下来的时间和过程，让他（她）能恢复理智。

4. 考绩的次数

正常的考绩次数应该是一年一次，但也有很多例外，比如是对新聘人员，还在试用中的员工，有的是三至六个月考绩一次，一直到正式任用时才改到一年一次。有些正式任用的员工因表现不好，他（她）的上司可以在正常的考绩次数之外，另定每三个月一次的特别考绩，以观察员工在工作上的改进，在经过三次特别考绩及书面的告诫之后，要是没有显著的改进，这位员工可能被调职、降级和解聘。

在馆员具有教员身分的大学图书馆中，除了一年一度的考绩之外，馆员在任期满六年时规定要经过升等和"永久任用"的考绩。这种考绩事关个人的去留问题，极为重要。本章第二节讲到专业人员的薪酬时，已经详细说明过这种考绩的标准与程序，在此不再重复。

三、问题及解决之道

考绩有其积极的作用，执行得好的话，能够发挥奖惩的功能，提高员工的生产力及服务水平。以下仅将考绩工作经常遭遇的一些问题及其解决之道加以讨论。

1. 如何能确定及划一考绩的标准

要想使考绩能够公平、客观及公正，考绩者对于被考绩者的职责必须事先了解并且彼此同意，对于考绩评分表上各项特征的定义及评分标准也应该有详细及具体的说明，尽量使工作的绩效数量化以增加考绩的客观性。初次担任考绩的上司应该经过讲习或训练，使能充分了解考绩的意义及方法，不让个人的喜恶和成见掺入考绩的结果。

2. 如何加强考绩的作用

一般考绩虽然是一年一次，但是考绩的工作应该是持续不断，经常进行的。员工表现良好或有特殊贡献时，应及时奖励及表扬。员工表现欠佳或患有过错时，也应该立即警告并采取改善措施。这些适当的奖惩要随时进行，不要等到一年一度的考绩时才提出来。

3. 如何避免太宽或太苛的考绩者

除了划一考绩标准和加强对考绩者的训练之外，考绩者的上司在复审时应该注意到太宽或太苛情况的纠正。图书馆的馆长或人事部门的负责人也可以用比较的方式来核查是否有太宽和太苛情况的存在。有些考绩者因为怕得罪属下和引起下属的不满，故意把每位员工的考绩提高，造成考绩的不公平；也有些考绩者对某些员工有偏见也许会评审得太苛。对于这种情况，考绩者的上司在复评时可以察觉，被考绩者也可以经由申诉的手续，提出复审的要求，由馆长设立一个复审委员会来进行复审。当然，也有些员工自己认为十全十美，对任何批评都不接受，即使得到很好的考绩仍然觉得不满意。对于这些员工只有设法开导，必要时也可以经由复审委员会复审。

4. 如何把考绩工作认真做好

这需要馆长以身作则，率先领导，不马虎，不敷衍。考绩要与图书馆（最好也是员工）的目的和目标相配合。

第五节 激发动机

激励员工以提高工作效率、积极性及敬业、乐业的精神，使每位员工能充分发挥他（她）的能力，是人力资源管理中极为重要的一部分。在任何一个机构里，我们常可以观察到有些员工不但工作努力，而且力求上进。根据很多心理学家的分析，这些员工是因为某种需要的驱动而努力工作，以求达到他（她）心目中认为有价值的一些目标。如何能树立有价值的目标，以驱动员工的需要及努力工作的愿望，这是激发动机所要讨论的。

有关激发动机（Motivating）的研究，从五十年代到现在出现了许多不同的理论，它们分别是需求层次理论、X 和 Y 理论、双因素理论、三需求理论、目标设定理论、强化理论、公平理论和期望理论。以下特分别予以讨论[①]。

一、激发动机的各种理论

1. 需求层次理论

根据亚伯拉罕·马斯洛（Abraham Maslow）的研究，认为人的需求有五个明显的层次，因此提出了"需求层次的理论"（Hierarchy of Needs Theory）。这个理论认为人类有下面五个层次的需求[②]：

（1）生理的需求（Physiological Needs）——最低层的。这种需求包含饥饿、口渴、居住、异性吸引和其他生理上的需要。

（2）安全的需求（Safety Needs）——次低层的。这种需求包含工作的保障、安全感、医疗保险、收入足以安家维生等。

（3）社会的需求（Social Needs）——中间层。这种需求包含了友谊、相亲相爱、归属感、社会关系等。

（4）尊重的需求（Esteem Needs）——中上层。这种需求包含了内在的尊重如自尊、自爱、自信、自行约束、上进心和成就感等；及外在的尊重如社会地位、为人敬爱、奖励和声望等。

（5）自我实现的需求（Self-Actualization Needs）——最高层。这种需求包含了充分发

---

① Stephen P. Robbins.《管理概论：理论与实践》，李茂兴，译. 台北：晓园出版社，1989，pp. 295–318.
② Abraham Maslow. *Motivation and Personality*. New York: Harper & Row, 1954.

挥自己才华及达成自我完成的满足感。有了这种需求的人会不断提高个人的目标，自发自动地去努力达成。

马斯洛认为一般人在低层次需求满足后，才能往上一层次的需求努力，一个机构要鼓励员工努力工作，应当尽力满足员工生理和安全的需求，然后鼓励员工去追求社会尊重和自我实现的需求。低层次的需求在满足后，往往就不会再有激励的作用，只有高层次的需求所导致的驱动力才是持久不断的。马斯洛的理论虽然被广泛的采用，但缺乏事实的证明。有些人的行为是很复杂的，在同一个时间可能有多种不同层次的需求，不一定是要等到下一层次的需求满足后才去追求上一层次的目标①。

2. X 和 Y 理论

这个理论是由道格拉斯·马葛瑞格（Douglas McGregor）所提出。根据他对管理员工的观察，马葛瑞格假定人性可以分成 X 与 Y 两种倾向②：

X 型的员工，根据假设，有下列特征：

（1）这种人天生不喜欢工作，会借口逃避。

（2）要迫使这种人就范，必须用威胁、高压、控制和惩罚的手段。

（3）这种人不会主动地负起职责，需要有他人指挥。

（4）X 型员工重视工作上的安全因素，没有特别奢望或雄心。

Y 型的员工，根据假设，有下列特征：

（1）这种员工视工作为日常生活中一个重要的部分。

（2）乐于接受交付的责任，努力去达成。

（3）能自发自动。

（4）能发挥团队的精神和群体的力量。

马葛瑞格的两种假定与中国传统哲学上"性善"与"性恶"的说法有相似之处。他本人相信 Y 理论比 X 理论好，因此主张采用以下的方法来激励员工：

（1）鼓励参与决策的过程。

（2）赋予相当的权责及挑战性的工作。

（3）培养良好的群体关系。

3. 双因素理论

心理学家费瑞克·贺兹伯格（Frederick Herzberg）所提出的双因素理论是指保健因素（Hygiene Factors）和激励因素（Motivators）两种③。他用问卷让员工描述关于工作上感到满足及不满足的情况，将答案分类后所归纳出来的十六个项目用图表来显示（图 5-1）。贺兹伯格的结论是：员工所感觉到的满足与不满足的情况可以显然地分成两类：感到满足的一类多半属于成就感、认同感、工作本身、责任感、发展和成长等内在的因素。感到不满足的一类多半属于机构政策与行政管理、上司、与上司的关系、工作环境、薪酬、与同事的关系、个人生活、与部属的关系、身份和安全感等外在的因素。

从图 5-1 来看，导致工作满足的内在因素跟导致工作不满足的外在因素是截然不同的。贺兹伯特将导致满足的因素划分为"激励因素"，将导致不满足的因素归类为"保健因素"。改善导致不满足的"保健因素"后，虽然会减少员工的不满足感，但不一定就能

---

① Mahound A. Wahba, and Lawrence G. Bridwell. "Maslow Reconsideration: A Review of Research on the Need Hierarchy Theory", *Organizational Behavior and Human Performance*, Vol. 15, No. 2 (April 1976), pp. 212–240.

② Douglas McGregor. *The Human Side of Enterprise.* New York: McGraw-Hill, 1960.

③ Frederick Herzberg, Bernard Mausner, and Barbara Snyderman. *The Motivation to Work.* 2nd ed. New York: John Wiley, 1959.

够激励员工。只有提高能导致满足的"激励因素",才能使员工感到真正的满足①。

贺兹伯格的双因素理论与传统观念上认为"满足"的反面就是"不满足"的逻辑持不同的看法。贺兹伯格的研究认为"满足"的反面不是"不满足",而是"非满足";"不满足"的反面不是"满足",而是"非不满足"。用这种方法来说明双因素的不同作用是比较清楚及说得过去的。

4. 三需求理论

三需求理论(Three Needs Theory)是由约翰·埃金生(John Atkinson)和戴维·麦克里伦(David McClelland)等多人所提出,这三种需求分别是②③:

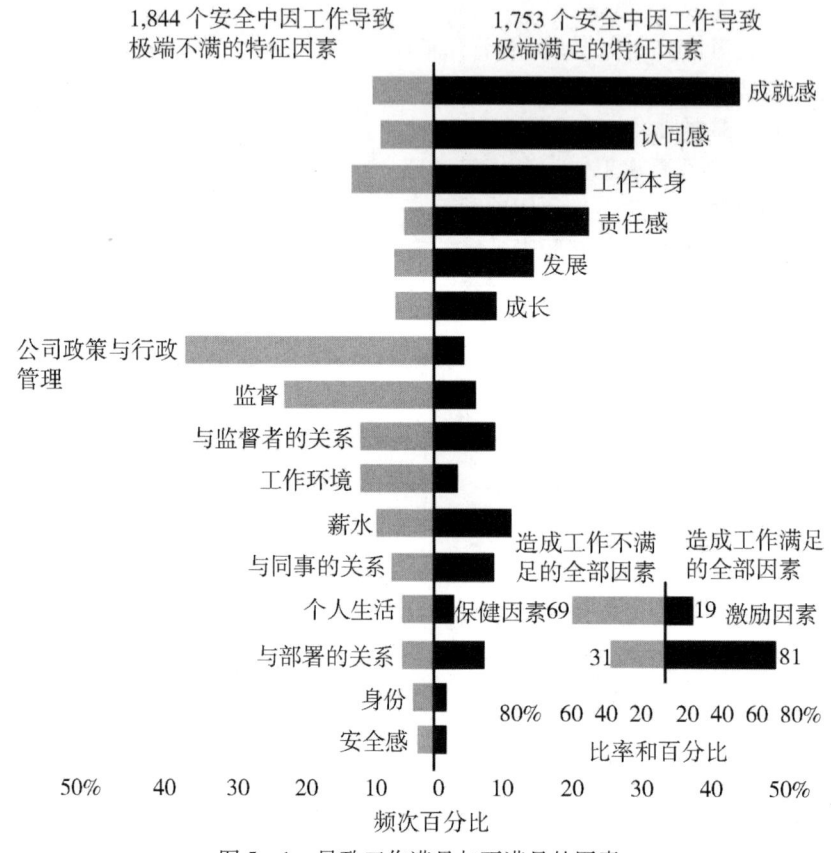

图 5-1 导致工作满足与不满足的因素

(1) 成就感的需求(Need for Achievement)
(2) 权力的需求(Need for Power)
(3) 结盟感的需求(Need for Affiliation)

成就感需求的理论认为人之所以努力工作往往是要满足个人的成就感,并非仅仅为了报酬或其他外在的诱因。追求成就感的驱动力会驱使个人尽力把工作做得更好和更有效率。驱动力的大小与成就感需求的强弱成正比。从麦克里伦的研究中发现具有高成就感需求的人通常不喜欢选择成功胜算相当低的任务,因为他(她)将无法从中获得成就感的满

---

① Frederick Herzberg. "One More Time: How Do You Motivate Employees?" *Harvard Business Review*, Vol. 47, No. 1 (Jan. /Feb. 1968), p. 57.
② John W. Atkinson, and Joel O. Raynor. *Motivation and Achievement*. Washington, D. C.: Winston, 1974.
③ David C. McClelland. *Power: The Inner Experience*. New York: Ir-vington, 1975, p. 427.

足。同样的，他（她）们也不喜欢选择成功胜算相当高的任务，因为这将会缺乏挑战性。当成功或失败的机会几乎相当时，这种任务最具吸引力，并且能考验个人努力的程度，进而从中获得成就感的满足。具有高成就感需求的人，假如能给予适当难度的责任，鼓励他（她）们设立具有适度挑战性的目标，在工作中能够经常地对他（她）们的绩效给予评审和回馈，将可以协助他（她）们在众人之中脱颖而出。

权力的需求是一种追求影响力的欲望。有高权力需求的人往往有很强的驱动力，希望能够升迁到更高、更有影响力的地位。这种人有关心自己的影响力胜过关心自己的绩效的倾向，喜欢处于具有竞争性和身份地位导向的环境中。

结盟感的需求是一个让别人喜欢和接受的欲望。具有高度结盟需求的人较喜欢友好、合作和互助的工作环境，对于竞争的场合设法避免。

5. 目标设定理论

目标设定（Goal Setting）理论认为朝一个目标的工作意图是激励作用的一个主要来源。经由员工参与而设定具有适当难度及挑战性的目标是股激励的作用力，可以增加员工的努力程度和工作的绩效。有关目标管理及参与式管理的好处已分别在本书第三章第三节及第四章第四节中加以说明[①]。

6. 强化理论

强化理论（Reinforcement Theory）与目标设定理论的假设正好相反。目标设定理论是采用认知法（Cognitive Approach）的观点，认为个人的行动是由他（她）的意图所引导，是一种内心认知的过程。强化理论是采用行为法（Behavioristic Approach）的观点，认为个人的行为可用强化作用来操纵，是由外在环境所引发的。这种理论主张在个人有良好行为或工作表现时，应立即给予鼓励和积极的回馈，以增加这种行为和表现重复发生的机率。鼓励和回馈都是行为的强化剂（Reinforces），能够用来控制和影响个人的行为。反之亦然，惩罚也是强化剂的一种，可以用来减少或改正不好的行为。强化理论的缺点是只注意行为的外表，忽视了个人的内心状态，因此只能当作众多激励作用的一种[②]。

7. 公平理论

公平理论（Equity Theory）也是激励作用的一种。一个人的工作分配、责任、薪酬、升迁是否公平，往往会影响到这个人的工作情绪及努力的程度。用来衡量是否公平的方式很多，有的是以自己为主，首先衡量自己从工作中所得到的结果（Outcome or Rewards）与所付出的投入（Input or Contribution）是否相当？在自我衡量之外，一般人多喜欢拿自己的所得与他人的所得比较。这种比较有的仅限于自己的工作部门，但也有的要延伸到其他部门，甚至于其他机构。当个人对这种衡量的结果认为满意时，他（她）的工作态度和情绪会比较积极。当这种衡量的结果是不满意时，很多人会因此闹情绪，影响到工作的表现、出勤率和整个部门或机构的士气、和谐、合作和绩效。

采取公平、公正和公开的人事管理制度，使员工感觉到机会均等，赏罚分明，报酬合理等，因此也是有激励作用的[③]。

[①] Gary P. Latham, and Gary A. Yukl. "A Review of Research on the Application of Goal Setting in Organizations", *Academy of Management Journal*, Vol. 18, No. 4 (Dec. 1975), pp. 824–845.
[②] Stephen P. Robbins. 《管理概论：理论与实践》，李茂兴，译. 台北：晓园出版社，1989, pp. 295–318.
[③] John E. Dittrich, and Michael R. Carrell. "Organizational Equity Perceptions, Employee Job Satisfaction, and Departmental Absence and Turnover Rates", *Organizational Behavior and Human Performance*, Vol. 24, No. 1 (August 1979), pp. 29–40.

8. 期望理论

期望理论（Expectancy Theory）是由威克脱·乌龙（Victor Vroom）首先提出，他的很多假设得到了实证研究的支持①。这个理论的基本假设是：对个人的激励，单靠提供能满足这个人某些需求的诱因是不够的。虽然诱因的吸引力大小会有关系，但除非这个人相信有能力能做到，否则他（她）是不会轻易心动的。从以上的假设可以推演出期望理论的三个变量：

（1）吸引力——指预期中努力所得的结果，在个人心目中的重要性。

（2）绩效与报酬的关联性——要有多少绩效才能获得预期的结果？

（3）努力与绩效的关联性——要付出多少努力才能达成所需的绩效及是否有此能力？

这三个变量的相互关系可以从图5-2中看出。

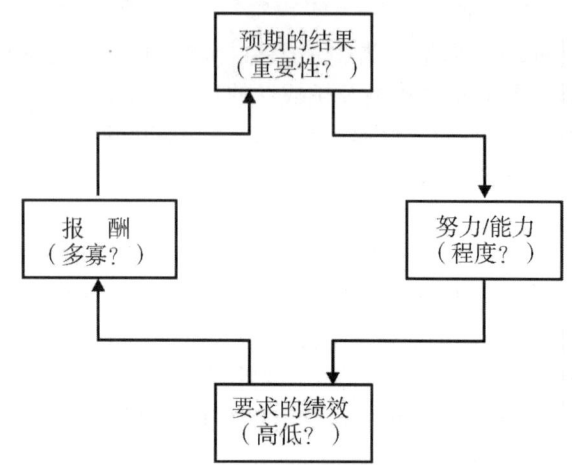

图5-2 期望理论的模式

预期的结果的重要性因人而异。正面的结果可以包括薪酬、福利、工作保障、友谊、信任、运用个人的才智等。负面的结果包括排挤、冲突、惩罚、疲劳、挫折、厌倦、忧虑、不安、不受重用、解职等。愈是重要的结果，愈是有吸引力。为了要获得预期的成果，员工会根据吸引力的强弱、个人能力程度及所要求绩效的高低来调整其努力的程度。期望理论是个情境模式，以上所提的三个变量会影响各人的激励作用。只有个人对于自己的绩效、报酬和结果的预期才能决定努力的程度。

二、从理论到应用

上一节介绍了当前管理学上关于激励作用的八个理论，接着我们将要讨论这些理论的实际应用。

1. 一般注意之点

（1）了解个别的差异。这是在强调激发动机时，要采用适合于个别差异不同的诱因。

（2）要人尽其才。要挑选适当的人来担任适当的工作，使每个人都能充分发挥他（她）的才干，例如说，具有高成就需求的人比较适合担任一个独立部门的主管。

（3）使用目标管理。根据目标设定理论，每位员工应该参与目标的设计并且具备适合个人能力和挑战性的个人目标。经由评估，上司应及时提供回馈，让员工知道他（她）工

---

① Victor H. Vroom. *Work and Motivation*. New York: Wiley, 1964.

作的绩效，以增进他（她）们对达成目标的信心。

（4）奖赏的方式要因人而异。因为每位员工有不同的需求，做主管的应该了解这种差异，在奖赏时使用最有激励作用的方式，像加薪、升迁、授权、参与决策等。根据强化理论和期望理论的原则，使报酬能跟绩效一致。罗宾士分析了近八十篇研究探讨各种激励方法对员工影响的报告而得到以下的结论：

A. 用金钱为诱因可以增加生产力的 30%。

B. 用目标设定的方法可以提高 16% 的生产力。

C. 设计工作使其丰富化可以提高 8% 到 16% 的生产力。

D. 让员工参与决策使生产力增加 1%。

罗宾士的分析说明金钱的奖赏还是最重要的①。

（5）考绩方式要公平合理。奖赏的方式虽然要因人而异，但作为奖赏根据的考绩方式必须要公平无私，使员工信服。一个机构的主管或人事部门负责人应该把机构的薪酬政策、考绩规则、奖赏方法等向员工公布及沟通。每年的加薪幅度，其中多少是基于生活指数调整，多少是基于良好的绩效，都应该让员工知道。

（6）提供一个令人愉快的工作环境。期望理论虽然重视报酬，但也强调人的行为的最终动机是追求快乐和满足感。提供一个令人愉快的工作环境其本身就有激励的作用。下一节所讨论的"高质量工作生活"（Quality of Work Life，或简称 QWL）就是要给人一个愉快的工作环境。

2. 界定"高质量的工作生活"

高质量的工作生活在美国的大型企业里开始流行是在七十年代。它的定义是指"在一个机构里员工可以满足他（她）们重要个人需求的程度"。一般来说，高质量的工作生活包括了下面六项②：

（1）对待员工能够公正、公平和同情。

（2）让员工有机会充分使用他（她）的技能及达到完全的自我实现。

（3）员工之间的沟通是开放的及可以信赖的。

（4）让员工有机会积极地参与有关他（她）们工作的重大决定。

（5）适当的及公平的薪酬。

（6）有一个安全及健康的工作环境。

为了要提高工作生活的质量，一个机构的上层主管一定要确认具有这种高质量工作生活的价值和达成的决心。用来提高质量的方法很多，包括了目标管理（Management by Objectives），以员工小组为中心的高质量工作生活计划（Team-centered QWL Programs），质量圈（Quality Circle），全质量管理（Total Quality Management），和其他的一些措施，以下将分别介绍这些方法：

3. 实行目标管理

在本书第三章讲到图书馆的规划时，我们已将目标管理的意义、过程及优缺点加以分析讨论，在此不再重复。

目标管理有以下三个基本因素，对于提高一个机构内部工作生活的质量具有积极的激励作用。

（1）设立目标——鼓励员工参与制定整个机构及自己部门目标的过程，并对自己工作

---

① Stephen P. Robbins.《管理概论：理论与实践》，李茂兴，译. 台北：晓园出版社，1989，pp. 295 – 318.
② Gary Dessler. *Personnel Management*. 4th ed. Englewood Cliffs, N. J.：Prentice-Hall, 1988, pp. 457 – 460.

的要求有充分的了解。
(2) 及时回馈——尽快地让员工知道他（她）们努力的绩效，以增加强化作用。
(3) 鼓励参与——让员工参与制定他（她）们自己的工作目标，可以激发他（她）们工作的热诚，满足他（她）们较高层次的需求。

4. 推动以员工小组为中心的（Team-centered）"高质量工作生活"计划

这种激励员工的方式在20世纪70年代即已在大型企业中被采用。美国的通用汽车公司（General Motors）是采用这个计划的创始者。对于工厂中生产和装配在线的工人来说，这种方式可以改善枯燥无味及纯机械式的工作环境，使员工有机会参与工程设计，借重他（她）们丰富的工作经验，来改进作业的过程，兼顾员工的舒适与生产的需要，以求改善员工的工作环境，并能提高生产效率和质量。

顾名思义，以员工小组为中心的QWL计划是在大型企业中设立一些小组（task force）来设计或规划如何改进某一生产部门的工作环境。这些小组的成员包括了员工代表、工会代表、工厂管理者、工程技术人员等。小组的建议将会送给上级主管优先考虑，以便采用和做相应的措施。

也有些员工小组被赋予相当的自治（Self-management）权以决定自己的生产进度表、工作的分配和时数，和自选小组成员等来达成上级规定的工作指标。超过生产目标及合乎质量要求者会有适当的奖励。

5. 建立"质量圈"

质量圈（Quality Circle）的观念和作法最早是由美国的专家在日本试用及推广的。第二次世界大战以后，日本的经济及工商业可以说是百废待举，产品质量非常差，无法进入世界市场。当时治理日本的盟军统帅麦克·阿瑟将军（General Douglas MacArthur）特地请美国政府派了一位质量管理专家——爱德华·德明博士（Edward Deming）——在1948年前往日本协助。经过了数年的努力"德明轮子"（Deming Wheel）的观念在日本被普遍接受及实行。"德明轮子"是指质量之轮的运转要经过下面几个步骤：

(1) 由众人参与的计划。
(2) 收集资料。
(3) 分析。
(4) 工作的设计。

除了德明博士之外，另外一位美国专家，邱仁博士（J. M. Juran）在1954年前往日本讲授"全质量控制"（Total Quality Control）的方法，也得到日本人的欢迎，对激励员工、提高生产力及质量改良方面产生了积极的作用，使日本产品在世界市场上极有竞争力。由于质量圈在日本的施行极为成功，七十年代以后传回美国，被很多机构所采用。

什么是质量圈？根据唐纳·第俄（Donald Dewar）的解释，它是由五至十位在同一单位工作的员工，经过特别训练以后所成立的一个小组，每周定期聚会一小时，用来探讨在工作上的一些问题并设法自己解决[①]。在大的企业里，有的同时会设有上百个质量圈。成立质量圈一般有计划、训练、起步及作业四个步骤，以下将分别讨论：

(1) 计划。在开始计划之前，一个机构的最高主管必须先决定要在机构里实行质量圈的组织。随着这个决定，下一步是要设立一个规划委员会及选择一位外面的顾问专家来指导。有些机构会在内部选一位适合的辅导人员（Facilitator），给予特别的训练来担任顾问

---

① Donald Dewar. *The Quality Circle Guide to Participation Management*. Englewood Cliffs, N. J.：Prentice-Hall, 1980.

专家的工作。规划委员会的委员人数应视机构的大小而定，一般不超过十五人。委员们应包括来自机构各部门的员工、工会代表及一两位高级主管。规划委员会刚开始时的主要任务是要决定质量圈的基本目标，像减少错误和改进质量的指针，有效的协调合作，增加工作的参与，激励动机，及预防问题的发生等。当然，这个委员会也可以对员工的薪酬、福利、人事管理的政策和措施等进行讨论和建议改善。

规划委员会的下一步骤是要选出两、三个单位作为试验的质量圈并指定每个质量圈的领导人（Leader），通常这些领导人应该是由每个质量圈所在的工作单位的负责人来担任。

（2）训练。被指定的领导人在顾问专家或指导人员的协助下开始学习质量圈的理论和实施，这种为期三四天的训练包括了个案的研究（Case Studies）及作为一个领导人所必须具备的一些常识和技巧。

（3）起步。由部门主管、各单位负责人及指定的质量圈领导人，在顾问专家或指导人员的协助下，向这些单位的员工讲解质量圈的优点及一般介绍，鼓励员工自动申请加入。在领导人与个别员工联系及知道他（她）们要参加的意图后，这些供试验的质量圈就可以设立。顾问专家和指导人员在这时也要开始提供有关质量圈的各种训练，使参加质量圈的员工能够开始行动。

（4）作业。有关作业的行动包括发掘本单位里各种工作上的问题，选择值得优先考虑的问题，分析有关资料，了解问题所在，建议解决之道，和建议的处理等五个步骤。在通常情况下，最能激励员工的方式不外让员工有机会参与改善他（她）们工作的程序和方法。质量圈的优点是在提供这种参与的机会，使员工觉得他（她）们的意见得到重视，而且显示了上级对下属的倚重和关心。

质量圈的理论基础来自于马斯洛、马葛瑞格、贺兹伯格等的动机理论，尤其是要满足员工的上层需求。借由学习、沟通、回馈、责任感、表扬等方式使员工在参与中对工作感到满足。这种激发动机的方式不一定要依赖金钱的诱因，它可以使员工的积极性长久维持下去，视工作的成果和个人的努力为最大的奖赏。

在八十年代，有些人认为质量圈的流行只是一时的风尚，不久就会烟消云散，这种看法是不很确实的。从激励动机的观点，质量圈之所以被普遍接受是因为它对人为因素和组织文化的适当重视。质量圈的推行能够成功有赖于下列几个条件[①]：

（1）机构主管的支持及有力的领导。
（2）团体的精神和小组的动力（Group Dynamics）。
（3）强调目标的选择及对问题的认定、调查和解决。
（4）有充分的信息及资料以供分析研讨。
（5）着重在结果（Results）。
（6）员工主动参加（Volunteer Membership）。
（7）有效率的沟通渠道。
（8）员工和主管皆须接受训练。
（9）开放、相互信赖、合作及积极参与的组织文化。

6. 推行"全质量管理"

"全质量管理"（Total Quality Management）虽然也是由德明、邱仁等专家首先提倡及推广，并且与"质量圈"的发展有密切的关联，但它们在本质上有所不同。质量圈的参与

---

① Daniel Sell and Mary Ellen Mortola. "Quality Circles and Library Management", *Community and Junior College Libraries*, Vol. 3, No. 3 (Spring, 1985), pp. 79–92.

者是各个小单位的基层员工，它的目的是改进这个单位的产品和服务的质量。全质量管理的参与者是整个机构的员工，它的目的是为了满足这个机构服务对象（Customers）的要求。很多美国的大型企业在八十年代初期即开始以"高质量"的产品和服务为标榜。美国的海军总部是最早使用"全质量管理"这个称呼的。在1988年，美国的国防部开始采用全质量管理并要求与该部有合作关系的厂家和机构也要推行全质量管理。根据1991年的一篇报导，不仅是一半以上美国最大的一千家企业已采用了全质量管理，美国政府的很多机构及二十多所大学也开始采用①。

在图书馆中，全质量管理开始被采用是在1990年以后。洛桑娜·欧尼娥（Rosanna M. O'Neil）在她1994年刚出版的《全质量管理在图书馆中》一书中收集了有关美国、英国及澳大利亚一些图书馆实施全质量管理的论文②。其中最具影响力的是密西根大学图书馆馆长唐纳德·雷吉士（Donald E. Riggs）所写的两篇③。

（1）什么是全质量管理。全质量管理的定义大概可以归纳如下：

"它是为了要达到顾客的最高满意程度所进行的长期的、全面的和彻底的内部改进；使整个机构各个功能和过程从规划、组织、执行、服务到考核能够做到整体的配合，进而形成人人参与及追求高质量服务的组织文化。"

图书馆是一个服务的行业，它的服务对象是读者，如何满足读者求知的需求是图书馆的主要任务。全质量管理虽然是一个新称呼，但它的精神在图书馆中早已施行，全质量管理可以加强图书馆的服务水平，使用全质量管理的观念和方法与图书馆重视服务的目的是贯联的。

（2）全质量管理的特征。根据全质量管理的各种论著，全质量管理有下列五个特征：

A. 它是基于一种新的管理概念所导致的组织文化的改变（Cultural Change），这种概念是采用持续的改进来满足顾客的要求。
B. 这种管理概念所形成的管理行为（Management Behavior）包括了以身作则，设计高质量的生产或服务过程，使用优良的工具，鼓励沟通，提供回馈，及建立相互依赖和支持的工作环境。
C. 改变的方式（Mechanisms of Change）包括有训练、沟通、认可（Recognition）、协调合作和使顾客满意的计划。
D. 在执行（Implementing）时要确定机构的使命，预期的成果，顾客和服务的对象，了解顾客的要求，设计产品和服务的标准和品质，和采取必须的行动。
E. 测量达成高质量与不达成高质量的差价和后果。

（3）实行全质量管理的要点。推行全质量管理虽然有不同的途径和方法，但是有些基本的共同点，德明把这些归纳成十四个要点。他认为这些要点代表了全质量管理的精髓，无论是什么样的机构都可适用④。

A. 要有一个与机构目标一致的计划（Consistency of Purpose）
一切行动要以机构的使命说明为指标，员工对于机构的使命要有明确的了解。

---

① Ted Marchese. "TQM Reaches the Academy", *AAHE Bulletin*, Vol. 44, (Nov. 1991), pp. 3–9.
② Rosanna M. O'Neil. *Total Quality Management in Libraries: A Sourcebook*. Englewood, Colorado: Libraries Unlimited, 1994.
③ Donald E. Riggs. "TQM: Quality Improvement in New Clothes", *College and Research Libraries*, Vol. 53, No. 6 (Nov. 1992), pp. 481–482.
Donald E. Riggs. "Strategic Quality Management in Libraries", *Advances in Librarianship*, Vol. 16 (1992), pp. 93–105.
④ W. Edwards Deming. *Out of the Crisis: Quality, Productivity and Competitive Position*. Cambridge, Mass.: Massachusetts Institute of Technology, 1986.

B. 改善质量应当由采用新的观念开始。培养认真负责的精神，不马虎，不敷衍，改善工作的技能和程序，不容许错误的发生。
C. 停用依靠对产品的查验作为提高质量的方法。提高质量有赖于对整体作业过程的改进，不单凭对产品的查验。最好能利用统计分析和各种图表的方法来发觉问题的所在，进而采取改进的措施。
D. 在选购材料时不要以价格作为决定的因素。低价格的材料很可能是低质量的。
E. 对于作业过程的改进应该持续不断。不要满足现状，要具有"日日新"和"更上一层楼"的精神。
F. 加强对员工的训练。只有不断提高每位员工的技能才能改善工作的质量及制造良好的成品（或提高更能满足顾客的服务）。
G. 培养领导才能。鼓励员工自发自动，充分发挥各人的才干，建立敬业乐业的精神。
H. 驱除恐惧感。增强员工的信心，使他（她）们勇于面对困难，设法自行解决。
I. 撤除各部门间的障碍。鼓励不同部门的员工能互相合作，彼此配合，以发挥团队的精神。
J. 少用口号（Slogans）、劝诫（Exhortations）和指标（Targets），这些方法多半是无效的。
K. 取消数量定额（Numerical Quotas）制度。为了达成预订的产额，员工会忽略了对质量的重视。
L. 使员工对自己的技艺（Workmanship）感到自豪。提供高质量的材料、装备、工具和工作环境，使员工能发挥所长，得到成功的满足。
M. 创造自我改善（Self-improvement）的机会。使每位员工都能在工作中成长，吸收新知，和学习新的方法。
N. 建立全质量管理的制度，全力推动。有计划地实行全质量管理，让全体员工都能参与。

（4）实行全质量管理的好处。前面讲过，全质量管理不是一个时髦的口号，它的目的是在满足顾客或服务对象的需求；它的方法是动员全体员工从改良工作的过程着手，在整个制度和系统上进行改革，以制造高质量的产品和提供最能令顾客满意的服务。在做生意的观点上认为只有优良质量的产品，保证满意的服务，才能建立信誉，争取更多的顾客，占据更大的市场和销路，为公司增加营利。这种观念可以同样使用在非营利的机构。以图书馆来说，要想争取更多的经费，单作公共关系是不够的，还应当从改善服务上着手，使读者感到满意才行。

第六章　图书馆的领导和作业

Chapter 6　Leadership And Operations in Libraries

　　将一个机构的计划付诸实行，以达成其预期的目标，是管理过程中一个主要的环节。这种管理的作业包括了领导、指挥、监督、决策、应变、沟通及化解冲突等。二十世纪以来，很多管理学上的研究很注重领导者所具有的各种特征和才能，亦有很多研究特别强调领导者的风格和情境因素的交互作用。六十年代以后，因为受到民主观念的影响，"领导"、"指挥"和"监督"等词被认为有一种具有权威作用的涵义，不符合民主的精神，必须改为"执行"、"作业"或"运作"，以表示上下一致，分工合作，以团队的精神共同的达成组织的目标而努力。

　　不管是"领导"或者是"作业"，这个管理的功能一般包含了"领导才能"（Leadership）、"决策"（Decision Making）、"沟通"（Communication），和"冲突的化解"（Conflict Resolution）等。本章将分别将这些运作的功能加以探讨。

第一节　领导才能

　　即使是在一个民主的社会里，每一个有效能的机构都必须有它的领导者，否则的话，这个机构将会变得"群龙无首"、"不知所从"的状况。当此人类知识和资讯技术急遽发展的时代，我们所面临的环境可以说是"变幻莫测"和"瞬息万变"，很多现有的机构，包括图书馆在内，已经遭遇到严重的考验。这些机构必须有卓越的领导者，能够团结员工，把握机会，发挥潜能，塑造一种适合环境的组织文化，以完成机构的使命和目的。在图书馆里这些领导者包括了馆长、副馆长、部门主任及各级主管等，他（她）们的行政地位和职权虽然是根据组织的结构和规章而定，但每人应当不仅以管理者（Manager）自居，采用因其职位和任务所授予的权责，更要发挥各人的影响力或魅力来激励员工，以发挥最高度的整体工作效能。这种影响力是指个人的领导才能，"管理者"与"领导者"的主要差别也就是在此。

　　国内的图书馆学大师沈宝环教授在他的大作《图书馆事业的领导问题》中对于领导的定义有详细的解释，并列举了中外的一些论述，对于"管理者"与"领导者"的分野提出以下精辟的看法[①]：

　　（1）领导者的着眼是长程的，而且过去、现在、未来兼顾。管理者所主要关切的是现状，即令有改变意图也只是近程或中程的。

　　（2）领导者的考虑是全盘的，着眼的观点是广博的。管理者的眼光多数是局部的，以自己负责的单位或机构为主。

　　（3）如果以军事学的术语来表示，领导者的立场是战略性的，管理者的立场是战术性的。

---

　　① 沈宝环，《图书馆事业的领导问题》，《当代图书馆事业论集：庆祝王振鹄教授七秩荣庆论文集》。台北：正中书局，1994，pp. 11 – 32.

（4）管理者以一己的利害、成就为主要考虑，领导者是大我无私，经常为考虑培养后进，以达到世代交替的目的。

对于领导者才能的研究大致经过三个阶段，每一阶段有它代表的理论观点：（1）特征的理论（Trait Theory），（2）行为的理论（Behavioral Theory），（3）情境的理论（Situational Theory）。以下将把这三种理论加以介绍及分析。

一、特征的理论

早期对于领导才能的研究认为成功的领导者必须具备某些个人特征（Individual Traits），希望把这些特征加以区别和确定。从各种研究中提到的特征很多，凡是好的个人特征都可以列入，这些包括了智力（Intelligence）、决心（Determination）、热诚（Enthusiasm）、友善（Friendliness）、自信（Self-assurance）、主动（Initiative）、勇敢（Bravery）、精力充沛（Energetic）、诚笃（Integrity）、支配欲（Taking Control）、强壮（Strength）、督导能力（Supervisory Ability）、诚恳（Sincerity）、诚实（Honesty）、专业知识（Professional Knowledge）等。但是经过实际观察，发觉许多这些特征与领导才能的相关系数相当低微，例如智力、支配欲、自信、精力充沛和专业知识是五种与领导才能呈正相关的特征，但它们的相关系数仅介于 + 0.25 到 + 0.35 之间，这说明了特征可能是领导才能的部分因素，除了特征之外还有其他影响因素①。

二、行为的理论

这个理论着重于领导者的行为模式（Behavior Pattern）或风格（Style），这与特征理论特别强调个人的特征有显著的不同。行为理论一派认为领导者的行为大致可以归纳成三种不同的模式，即独裁专制的（Autocratic），协助的（Supportive），和体制的（Structured）。

以下将分别予以解释。

1. **独裁专制的模式**

这种模式的领导者会使用他（她）的权力来命令和指挥部属及采用奖赏和处罚的方式来驱使部属去努力工作。

2. **协助的模式**

这种领导者会设法建立一个以员工为主导的（Staff-oriented）社会气氛（Social Climate），使得每位员工都能自发自动的去尽其所能，努力工作。

3. **体制的模式**

这种领导者要尽力设立一个以任务为中心的（Task-oriented）工作体制，用分工合作和分层负责的方式，订定工作的要求和标准，以达成机构的目标②。

这三种行为模式，经过实际观察，也发觉不能放之四海而皆准。俄亥俄州立大学和密歇根大学对于行为理论的研究在早期颇受重视，特此加以介绍③。

1. **俄亥俄州立大学的研究**

俄亥俄州立大学在 20 世纪 40 年代后期开始研究领导者的行为，在这个研究的过程中

---

① Stephen P. Robbins.《管理概论：理论与实务》，李茂兴，译. 台北：晓园出版社，1989, p. 321

② Victor H. Vroom. "The Search for a Theory of Leadership," In *Contemporary Management*: *Issues and Viewpoints*, ed. by Joseph W. McCuire. Englewood Cliffs, N. J.：Prentice-Hall, 1974, p. 396.

③ Ralph M. Stogdill. *Stogdill's Handbook of Leadership*：*A Survey of Theory and Research*. Revised and expanded ed. by Bernard M. Bass. New York：Free Press, 1981.

俄州大学的研究者将一千多种员工所能描述的领导行为归纳成"体制型"和"体谅型"两大类：

（1）体制型。这一型的领导者会将各项任务指派给部属，期望他（她）们的工作绩效能维持在某一水平之上，并能按期完成。在执行的过程中领导者可能会界定自己与部属之间的关系，试图规划各项工作的程序，工作间的交互关系，和达成目标的行为。

（2）体谅型。这一型的领导者能够与部属建立互相信赖的关系，尊重员工的意见，关心他（她）们的福利、地位和满足感。体谅程度高的领导者给予部属易于亲近的感觉，会帮助部属解决个人的困难。

根据对这种分类所进行广泛研究的结果，发现体制和体谅程度两者都高的领导者，其部属的绩效和满足感会比体制和体谅有一项低的领导者来得高。这说明"体制"和"体谅"两种领导行为并不是互不兼容的，两者必须适当的配合使用，才能得到较好的效果。

2. 密西根大学的研究

密西根大学的调查研究中心在研究高效能领导者的行为模式时，也发觉有"员工导向"（Employee-oriented）和"生产导向"（Production-oriented）两类：

（1）员工导向。是指领导者重视人际关系，关心部属的需求，并了解部属当中存在着个别差异的因素。

（2）生产导向。是指领导者强调工作的技术与任务的如期完成，视部属为达成机构目标的手段。

这个研究的结论强烈地赞成员工导向的领导者，认为这种领导者与较高的群体生产力和工作满足感有关联性；反之，生产导向的领导者则与较低的群体生产力和工作满足感有关联性。

除了以上两个研究之外，罗伯·伯雷克（Robert Blake）和珍·莫顿（Jane Mouton）两位也以类似的两种构面的理论提出了"管理方格"（Management Grid）的解说[①]，这个解说是将"关心部属"（Concern for People）和"关心生产"（Concern for Production）两个构面各分成九个不同程度的管理风格，如图6-1所显示，9×9共有81个方格，在这些方格中有五个是显然不同的，例如：

（1，1）式的管理风格是既不关心部属又不关心生产。
（9，1）式的管理风格是过分强调生产和效率，完全忽略了部属的感受和士气。
（1，9）式的管理风格是过分关心部属的感受和士气，完全忽略了生产和效率。
（5，5）式的管理风格兼顾了生产和效率以及部属的感受和士气。
（9，9）式的管理风格是高度地兼顾了生产和效率以及部属的感受和士气。

从以上五个方格中所显示的领导风格中，（9，9）式可能是最理想的而（1，1）式可能是最不理想的。这种假说有它的优点，但它的缺点是没能将不同的情境因素会对这些风格的影响加入考虑，因此还不足以解释领导才能的全部现象。

三、情境的理论（Situational Theory）

为了弥补上两个理论的不足，情境理论认为除了各种特征与行为风格之外，还需要考虑到领导者与其工作情境中各个变数的交互作用。这种变量包括了工作的性质、复杂度、技术面、经费、员工素质、计划的完善、上司的态度、群体的规划、外在的威胁与压力、

[①] Robert R. Blake, and Jane S. Mouton. *The Managerial Grid.* Houston: Gulf Publishing, 1964.

组织的形态与文化等。

根据一些专家的研究，情境理论也有几种比较重要的模式：（1）专制—民主的连续模式。（2）费德勒模式。（3）路径—目标模式。以下将分别介绍：

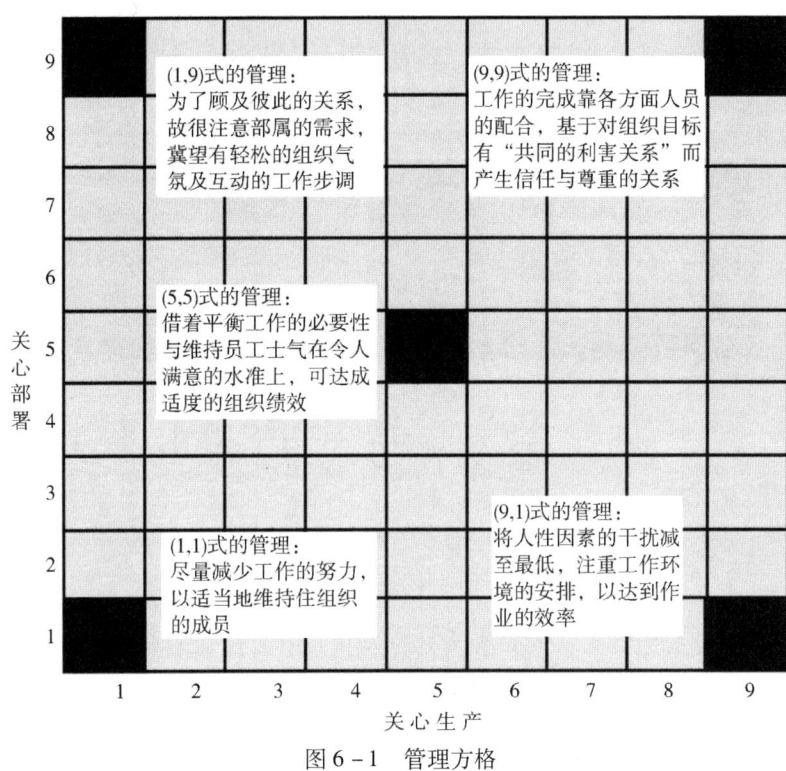

图 6-1　管理方格

1. 专制—民主的连维模式（Autocracy-Democracy Continuum Model）

这一模式认为"专制"与"民主"是沿着光谱中众多情况的两个极端而已。在专制的一端，领导者自己做决策，然后交给下属去执行及完成。在民主的一端，领导者与部属共同做决策，组织中每一位员工都拥有公平的投票权。在这两个极端之间有许多其他不同程度的风格。它的选择视领导者、员工和情境而定。图 6-2 显示这种连续模式中的各种不同的领导风格[①]。

有关这个模式的研究者多对参与式的领导风格给予肯定。他们的结论是："参与式的领导风格比非参与式的领导风格更能增加部属的满足感。"但是，他们亦认为专制式或民主式的领导风格虽然关系到部属的满足感，但却跟生产力没有明显的关系[②]。

2. 费德勒模式（The Fiedler Model）

这一模式是由佛列·费德勒（Fred Fiedler）发展出来的。费德勒认为有效能的群体绩效决定于两个因素能否有适当的配合。

第一个因素是情境对于领导者的风格与其部属间的互动关系。

第二个因素是情境对于领导者所施予控制和影响的程度。

费德勒采用问卷的方法设计了一个测量工具，可以用来衡量一个领导者是属于"任务

---

① Robert Tannenbaum, and Warren H. Schmidt. "How to Choose a Leadership Pattern?" *Harvard Business Review*, Vol. 56, No. 2 (March – April, 1958), pp. 95 – 101.

② W. Clay Hammer, and Dennis W. Organ. Organizational Behavior: *An Applied Psychological Approach*. Dallas: Business Publications, 1978, pp. 396 – 397.

导向"(Task-oriented)或"人际关系导向"(Human-relation Oriented)的领导风格。然后,他又提出了三种情境构面:

(1) 领导者与部属的关系——部属对于领导者信任,有信心,以及尊敬的程度。
(2) 任务结构——工作指派程序化的程度。
(3) 职位权力——领导者对于聘用、解聘、升迁、加薪等情形的影响程度。

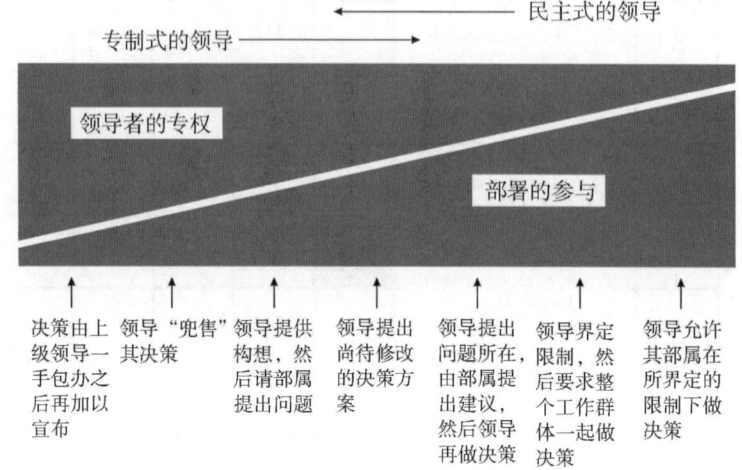

图6-2 专制—民主连续模式

以上三个构面的程度愈高即表示领导者的影响力愈大。从图6-3来看,费德勒的三项情境组合可以有八种结果。这是根据他在研究过一千二百个机构之后所得到的结论。

(1) 任务导向的领导者在情境组合对他最有利以及最不利的情形下,绩效较好(在Ⅰ、Ⅱ、Ⅲ、Ⅷ的情境组合之下)。

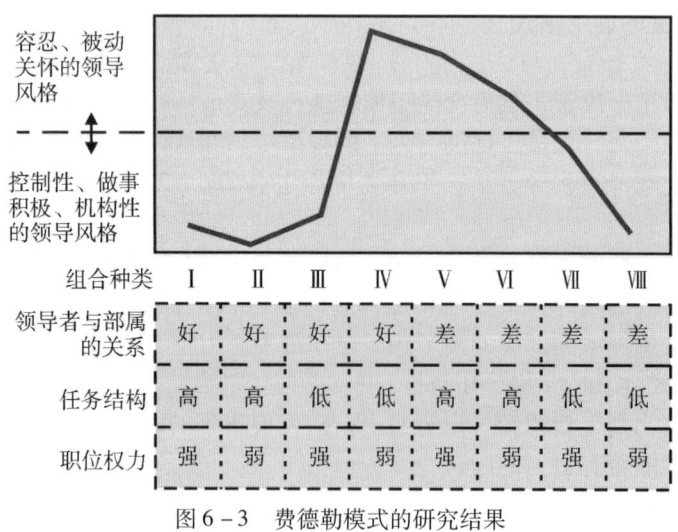

图6-3 费德勒模式的研究结果

(2) 人际关系导向的领导者在情境组合适中的条件下,绩效较好(在Ⅳ、Ⅴ、Ⅵ、Ⅶ的情境组合之下)①。

费德勒的权变模式虽然对领导效能的解释比在他以前的各家理论更为完善,但仍然有

---

① Fred E. Fiedler. *A Theory of Leadership Effectiveness*. New York: McGraw-Hill, 1967.

许多缺点：

（1）情境变项相当复杂，像决定领导者与部属关系的好坏，任务结构化程度的高低，和职位权力的强弱，都不是很容易给予精确的评估。

（2）模式中忽略了部属的特征。

（3）没有考虑到领导者或部属的各种技术能力。

（4）费德勒在研究中所得到的相关系数相当低，在统计上都不够显著。

（5）他所用的问卷背后的逻辑推理也不容易了解，后来的研究指出其分类并不稳定[1]。

3. 路径—目标模式（Path-Goal Model）

这一个情境模式是由多伦多大学的罗伯·豪斯（Robert House）教授所指出，用来探讨"努力与绩效"及"绩效与目标"间的关联，以及"体制"与"体谅"两种领导行为构面的作用。它结合了上一章所讨论过激励的期望模式与前述的俄亥俄州立大学对于"体制"与"体谅"的研究。豪斯的模式认为领导者应负有下述的责任：

"……增加奖赏部属的频率与种类，使得"工作—目标"的过程能顺利达成。清理沿途的路径，减少过程的障碍与陷阱。增加在过程中部属感受到满足的机会，使部属能在上述奖赏的路径中畅行无阻[2]。"

因为此一理论用到"清理路径"、"满足需要"和"目标达成"等词句，故称为"路径—目标"模式。对于"体制"和"体谅"的作用，豪斯的模式中有两项一般性的主张：

（1）部属接受领导者的行为而且感到满意的程度是决定该领导者的行为是否可以作为能够在现在或将来满足其需求的来源。

（2）领导者的行为是否能产生激励作用取决于下面两个因素：

A. 部属的需求能否满足，要看他（她）们工作的绩效而定。

B. 领导者提供各种训练、指导、支持和奖赏：改善部属的工作环境，以为有效能的绩效奠定基础。

图6-4显示在领导者的行为与部属的绩效之间的关系外，还有两组情境变项：一是部属的个人特质。二是环境压力与任务的要求。

由于以上两项主张和情境变项，豪斯提出以下的几点假设：

（1）对于那些认为奖赏来自于自身行为表现的部属，领导者应该多采用"体谅"。

（2）对于那些认为奖赏来自别人所赐部属，领导者应该采用"体制"。

（3）对于高度职权化的部属，应该采用"体制"。

（4）当部属认为其能力已超过任务的需求时，"体制"的程度要减少。

（5）当任务之例行性、群体规范以及控制活动都已经使得目标和达成目标的路径明朗化时，"体制"的程度要降低。

（6）当部属对自己的工作感到不满、疲乏、挫折或有逼迫感的时候，领导者应多给予"体谅"，并减少"体制"的程度[3]。

从豪斯的假设，我们可以看出领导者对于"体制"和"体谅"模式的运用应考虑到各种情境因素，例如说："体制"在任务结构化程度高的情况下，对于部属最有用；在任务结构化程度低的情况下就比较无效。"体制"在任务模糊不清和令人不安的时候，能使

---

[1] Stephen P. Robbins.《管理概论：理论与实务》，李茂兴，译. 台北：晓园出版社，1989, pp. 328-329.
[2] Robert J. House, and Terence R. Mitchell. "Path-Goal Theory of Leadership", *Journal of Contemporary Business*, Vol. 3, No. 4 (Autumn, 1974), pp. 81-97.
[3] Stephen P. Robbins.《管理概论：理论与实务》，李茂兴，译. 台北：晓园出版社，1989, p. 330.

部属得到较高的满足感；但是在任务结构化程度相当高的情况下，则没有多大用处。当任务不明确时，部属希望领导者能指示达成目标的途径；而任务在相当例行性的情况下，部属较需要的是领导者的关怀。

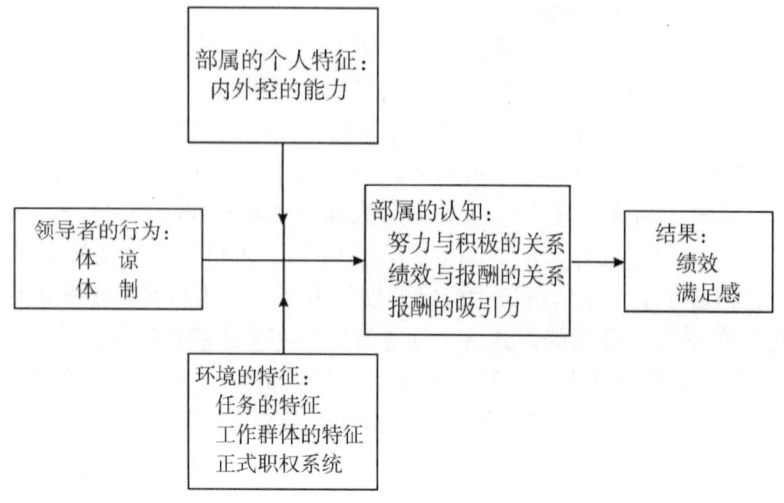

图 6-4　路径—目标模式中各种影响因素

第二节　决　策

在日常的生活中，每一个人或群体都会遭遇到许多需要作决策的情况。这些情况有的是"例行性"的，可以根据已有的准则或以往的经验，很快地做出决策；也有很多是"非例行性"的，必须经过深思熟虑，或者是集思广益，考虑出各种可能的应对之策及其不同的后果，从中选出一个最合适可行者。一般来讲，个人的决策比较单纯及快捷，多半由决策者自己承当后果之责。群体的决策是必须由众人所参与，过程比较复杂，其后果多半需由群体的领导者负责。一个好的领导者应当把成功的果实让大家共享，而自己承当不成功的责任和后果。

一、决策的定义和步骤

管理学家彼特·杜克尔（Peter Drucker）把决策视为一种"判断"（Judgment），就是从众多可以解决某一问题的"可行方案"中（Alternatives）选择一个最适当的[①]。

以图书馆为例，假设某一天下午忽然停电了，自动化系统无法操作，除了走道、楼梯和电梯有紧急发电系统可以照明外，其他的地方光线暗淡。馆长面临这种情况应该如何应付？在正常的情况下，每个图书馆都会有预先定好的紧急情况应变办法，其中包括有对临时断电的各种应变措施，诸如：

1. 分配专人或部门负责检查是否有人被困在电梯里？
2. 馆长办公室应负责打听停电的原因及可能修复的时间，并将情况随时向各部门通报。
3. 各部门应斟酌情况，使用储备的电筒及蜡烛等。

---

① Peter F. Drucker. *The Effective Executive*. New York：Harper & Row，1967），p. 143.

4. 如停电时间不超过两小时的话，图书馆照常开放，但停止出借图书。各部门的工作人员应指导读者前往光线较好的地区。

5. 如停电时间会超过两个小时的话，图书馆应暂时关闭，馆员应指引读者平安地离开，除了少数员工必须留下，其他的可以提前下班。

6. 在供电回复后，图书馆继续开放的各种措施。

以上这些应变措施是例行性的，可以按照预先定好的办法或过去的惯例来做决策，并以最快的方式采取行动。

但是有很多非例行性的情况必须经过比较复杂的决策过程。例如像图书馆如何进行内部改组及人员调动？如何选择一个新的自动化系统？如何加强员工的在职训练？图书馆应否购买或租用复印机的设备？图书馆应否开始对外募款等特殊情况？都需要有员工参与考虑和决策。在这过程中，资讯的收集和分析，内部的沟通，群体动力的运用，对于各种可行性方案的讨论、评估和最后的选择等，虽然要花费较多的人力、时间和开销来进行决策，但若能得到好的结果，仍然是非常值得的。

对于非例行性情况的决策，一般有以下所列举的一些步骤：

1. 确定问题的所在。
2. 进行对问题的分析和了解。
3. 建立决策的各种准则和比重。
4. 列举可以解决问题的各种可行方案。
5. 根据决策的准则以衡量各个方案的利弊及名次。
6. 选择一个最佳的方案。
7. 执行所选择的方案。
8. 评估执行的结果。

现代化的管理主张一个机构的领导应该把决策的权责尽可能地分配给各级主管并要求这些主管鼓励属下的员工参加决策的过程。不论是上级的领导或是各级的主管，作为一个决策者，必须有能力去鉴别例行性和非例行性的情况，以便采取相应的措施。对例行性的问题，一般可遵照现行的规章或办法处理。对非例行性的问题，则需采取以上所列举的决策步骤。

在大的机构里，例行性问题的处理多半是由中、下级的主管负责；非例行性问题的处理多半是中、上级主管的责任。这种分工的方式可以使上级主管有较多的时间和精力去处理比较困难和复杂的非例行性问题。

二、个人决策的重要因素

决策有个人决策和群体决策两种，它们的使用视情况而定。能够影响个人决策的因素一般有下列五种：

1. 经验

无疑地，经验是影响决策的重要因素。对于例行性的问题，有经验的决策者可以当机立断，迎刃而解。也有的能够从过去的错误中吸取教训，不再重蹈覆辙。经验丰富的决策者其所做决策的正确性也较高。对于非例行性的问题，有时单凭过去的经验是不够的。必须把经验与其他的因素配合，才会做出较好的决策。

2. 专业知识和技能

有效的决策也必须依赖决策者所具备的专业知识和技能。因为在搜集资讯、分析问题及寻找各种可以解决问题的方案时,专业的知识和技能有时会比经验更重要。

3. 判断

判断是指能够正确评估资讯的能力。有良好判断力的人,除了经验与专业知识之外,还需要有清晰的理解和推理能力,能够在复杂的情况中洞察问题及机会的所在,并在众多的解决方案之中选择其中最佳者。

4. 创造力

创造力,是指一个人能够突破现状提出崭新构想和解决问题方法的能力,有创造力的决策者可以在工作中力意创新,开拓新境界;在决策时能够提出各种崭新的解决方案,以供评估及选择。创造力与标新立异有所不同,它是一种丰富的想象力,能够"标新",但不在"立异"。

在决策理论里,经验与创造力彼此之间的消长关系有时会存在着矛盾的现象。有经验而资深的主管,有时会过分依赖经验来决策。没有经验的资浅的主管,有时反而能在决策过程中掺入新的构想。下一节所要讨论的群体决策可以用来消除这种矛盾的现象。

5. 数量分析技能

虽然数量分析的方法在图书馆中很少被采用,但它仍然是一个辅助决策的有效手段,应该推广。具有这种技能的决策者(或他们的助理人员)必须具备有相当的数学和统计学的知识,能够了解线性程序(Linear Programming)、等候理论(Queuing Theory)、几率理论(Probability Theory)和网路分析(Network Analysis)等方法。近几年来,因为计算机的普遍使用,很多数量分析的工作可以运用计算机来处理,这比过去用人工计算方便及快捷得多。

三、群体决策

在一个以员工导向并采用参与式管理的机构里,群体决策(Group Decision-making)比个人决策(Individual Decision-making)更受员工的欢迎,并有提高士气的作用。群体决策是由机构或者某个部门里的员工所组成的委员会或小组来参与决策的过程。以下试将群体决策利弊加以分析。

1. 群体决策的利弊

群体决策的好处大约有下面几种:

(1) 能够集思广益,从多方面来考虑一个问题,进而获得更多的资讯、知识和多样化的解决方案,使决策能符合大多数员工的愿望。

(2) 能够增加决策的接受性,有助于意见的沟通和决策的执行。

(3) 符合民主的精神,增加决策的合法性。

(4) 能够避免个人决策容易受自私、人情和个人权力等因素的影响。当然,群体决策的一些瑕疵也经常受到批评,例如:

(1) 要花费较多的时间在沟通和寻求妥协,才能做到符合众意的决策。

(2) 不是每位员工都具备参与的愿望及决策的技能,有时会被少数员工所操纵。

(3) 因为群体压力(Group Pressure)的因素,使得很多决策趋向于保持现状及保护各部门员工的既有利益,不利于创新或突破。

(4) 会导致责任不清的现象。群体决策的执行和后果虽然最后还是要由机构的主管来承担,但一般参与决策的员工有时对此没有清楚的了解。群体决策虽然有其利弊,但在一般情况之下还是利多于弊,值得提倡。

2. 群体决策的一些方法

为了针对或减少前面所提到群体压力的不良影响，有些比较有效的方法可以被考虑采用。

（1）脑力激荡（Brain Storming）的方法。这种方法是让一个人数不多的小组成员聚在一起，由主持人将问题述说清楚，然后让每个人提出各种可行的方案。在这段时间里，不允许有任何评语或讨论。主持者将所有被提出的方案都记录下来，等每人都有机会发言后，再逐一予以分析和讨论，以求获得共识，选出最佳的方案来供决策和执行。脑力激荡的好处是在鼓励各人提出创新性的解决方案，从不同的方案中引诱出其他的方案，即使有些可能是荒谬和不切实际的想法，也在鼓励之例。

（2）名义上的（Nominal）群体技术。这种方法与脑力激荡大致相似，它的四个主要步骤是：

A. 每位参与的员工先将各自对于某一问题的意见写在纸上。

B. 接着由每位参与者轮流报告自己的意见，分别记录在一张贴在墙上大家都可以看到的大纸或黑板上面。

C. 在所有的意见记录完毕以后，全体参与者开始进行讨论每一个意见，并加以评估。

D. 各参与者以独立的方式给每个意见打分数，积分最高的意见就是大家所共识的最佳方案。

（3）德耳菲（Delphi）技术。这个方法除了参与者不参加开会和面对面的讨论外，其他与名义上群体技术无甚差别，以下是它的五个基本步骤：

A. 使用专门设计的问卷，让每位参与者针对某一问题提出可能的解决方案。

B. 每位参与者以不记名的方式完成第一次问卷。

C. 将第一次问卷的回答加以整理，把集中的答案印发给参与者。

D. 根据第一次问卷的答案，让每位参与者再一次解答原先的问题以观察是否可能引发新的解答，和改变原先的想法。

E. 重复前两个步骤，一直到有了一致的解决方案。

德耳菲技术的好处是不需要参与者聚集在一起开会，可使远道的参与者一齐参加，但它的缺点是无法获得像名义上群体技术那么多的解决方案，因为有些想法是需要经过面对面讨论之后才能激发出来的。德耳菲技术的另外一个缺点是主持人所花的时间和精力比别的方法要多。

四、图书馆的决策

以上各节所讨论的决策定义和步骤，个人和群体的决策等，是一般性的原则和方法，但是在实际实行时，可因人、时、地等因素而有所不同。

图书馆是个非营利而且以服务为主的机构，它的价值观念与很多其他的机构有所差异。例如说图书馆中有些专对公司、商家所提供的特殊参考资讯服务是否应当酌量收费？当图书馆应读者要求向收费的资料库进行检索时，这种费用应该由谁来出？等问题，这种决策牵涉到图书馆的历史传统、使命、经费来源、政府法令等，必须特别慎重考虑。

另外，图书馆的员工素质比较高，有很多知识渊博、学有专长的专业人员，在这种机构里，群体决策的效果会比少数人决策来得好。

第三节 沟　通

能影响一个机构作业成败的因素虽然很多，但讯息的沟通（Communication）是其中最主要的因素之一。作为一个主管，他（她）的大部时间和精力是用在沟通上。前两节所讨论到领导和决策，它的成功与否也有赖于沟通。图书馆目前所处的时代是一个"资讯主导时代"（Age of Information Dominance），这个时代的特征是"资讯爆炸"（Information Explosion），资讯技术的突飞猛进，和社会大众对于讯息的需求正在急遽地增长。在这种情况之下，图书馆的使命极为艰巨，其人际间和组织内部的沟通，比过去任何时期来得重要。本节将就沟通的定义和途径，组织的沟通，不同层次的沟通网路，及如何克服沟通的阻碍等问题加以讨论。

一、沟通的定义和途径

沟通最基本的定义是意思的"传达"和"了解"。成功的沟通不只是讯息的传递，而且要使对方了解讯息的原意。在传递的过程中要尽量避免因各种噪音（Noise）的干扰所可能造成对讯息原意的歪曲。

了解（Understanding）并不意味着"同意"（Agreement）。良好的沟通可以增进彼此的了解，但不一定保证双方能同意某一个观念。即使如此，多一点了解，可以化除误会，进而建立双方的相互尊敬。为了要获知对方了解的程度及减少讯息的误传，"回馈"（Feedback）是极为必要的，一个完整的沟通必须包括讯息接受者的回馈。图6-5显示了讯息沟通的基本途径。

讯息从来源传达到接受者的途径中要经过"编码"（Encoding），传递管道（Delivery Channel），及"解码"（Decoding）等过程。编码和译码不仅仅是指在电讯传播时所采用的密码，它还包括了运用书面（Written）、口语（Oral）或非语言（Non-verbal）的沟通技巧，个人的态度和形象，双方的知识程度，和社会文化背景等的传递方式。以最常用的文字、口语和动作为例，当我们说话时，这些话就是讯息的编码；当我们书写时，这些文字就是讯息的编码；当我们画图时，这些图画就是讯息的编码；当我们以操作表达时，则脸部表情和手势等也都含有某些特殊意义。在很多情况之下，因为沟通双方的知识程度和社会背景有所不同，可能会使传达的讯息在编码及译码时受到歪曲，因而造成误解。

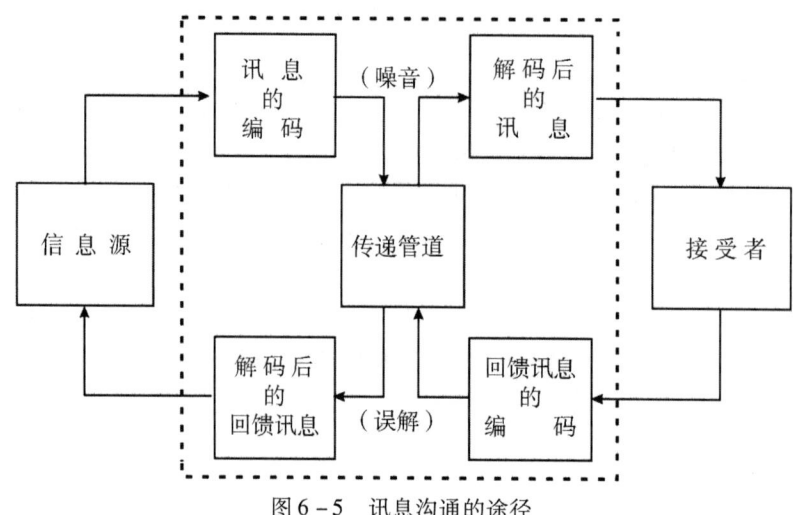

图6-5　讯息沟通的途径

管道是讯息传递的中介,其中最常用的有书面和口语两种。口语有面对面的交谈、开会和电话、闭路电视等。书面除了备忘录(Memorandum),信件(Letter),报告(Report),通告(Announcement),新闻信(Newsletter)等之外,现在又加上电讯传真(Telefacsmile,或简称 FAX),电子信件(Electronic Mail),电子通告(Electronic Bulletin),录像(Video)和种种日新月异的电子媒介(Electronic Media)等。虽然我们目前还不能确定使用电子媒介作为传递中介的效果,但是根据以往的经验,用时使用口语和书面两种方式比仅仅使用其中之一来得有效[①]。

二、组织内部的沟通

上一节所讨论的是一些人际沟通的基本方式和途径,本节将接着讨论组织内部的沟通(Organizational Communication)。一般来说,组织沟通较人际沟通复杂得多。在组织之中除了有正式沟通和非正式沟通的区别外,还有垂直流程、水平流程和交错流程等不同的沟通管道。

1. 正式与非正式沟通

在一个图书馆里,正式沟通是指按照图书馆的组织结构所进行的沟通。当主管对员工,员工对主管,主管对主管,员工对员工,或馆员对读者因执行公务时所进行的沟通都可以视为一种正式的沟通。

非正式的沟通多半是不按照正常轨道或程序所进行的沟通。它的目的不仅是在满足员工之间的社会关系和友谊,有时还可以用来弥补正式沟通的官僚式缺点。例如某一位员工在遭遇一个难题时打一个电话向另一个部门中的朋友求助,这种方式有时在几分钟内就可以把问题解决,不像在正式沟通上要逐层上报或向别的部门协调所花费的时间和精力。因此,非正式沟通的使用有时会比较迅速有效,对于正式沟通有辅助的作用。

另外一种非正式沟通是属于"谣传"(Grapevine)之类。它在所有的机构中都是十分活跃的。一个对美国海军人员的研究发觉谣传(或道听途说)是讯息传递最迅速的手段。表 6-1 显示从四千名海军人员的调查中,谣传占据了 38% 讯息的来源[②]。因为谣传在机构中的普遍存在,而且传递迅速,有时谣传的讯息是员工对某些措施或情况的反应,具有回馈的作用,因此,值得管理者的重视。

2. 沟通的管道

组织沟通的管道一般有垂直(Vertical)、水平(Horizontal)和交错(Cross)三种。垂直管道又可以分成向上(Upward)和向下(Downward)两种。

表 6-1　讯息传递最迅速的方式

传递方式	调查结果的百分比
谣传(或道听途说)	38%
直属上长	27%
官方的备忘录	17%
广播新闻	7%

---

① T. L. Dahle, "An Objective and Comparative Study of Five Methods of Transmitting Information to Business and Industrial Employees", *Speech Monograph*, Vol. 21, No. 1 (March 1954), pp. 21-28.

② Harold Sutton, and Lyman W. Porter. "A Study of the Grapevine in a Government Organization", *Personnel Psychology*, Vol. 21, No. 2 (Summer, 1968), pp. 223-230.

(Continuing)

传递方式	调查结果的百分比
电台的指挥系统	4%
公布栏	4%
其他	3%
	100%

（1）沟通。这是指一位主管依着职权指挥链对部属执行着指挥、目标管理、协调、辅导和评估等沟通活动。这种沟通可能包括各种口头或书面的方式。

（2）向上沟通。这是指部属依循组织层级向上级主管提出各种有关工作的报告和讯息。低层员工向上沟通的内容和范围要看组织文化而定。在一个采用高度参与式管理及具有一个和谐的组织气氛的图书馆里，各级部属提供讯息的意愿会很高，对于图书馆的规划、决策、运作及评估会发生良好的作用。反之，在一个高度集权的环境里，员工只肯被动地提供一些与控制功能有关的讯息。

（3）水平或横向（Lateral）的沟通。这是指一个机构中属于同一层级的员工间所进行的沟通，这种沟通方式很多是非正式的沟通，但也有一些是正式的。有些图书馆有意以平面式的组织来取代层级式的组织，就是要加强水平的沟通，加速讯息的横向传递。也有一些图书馆将工作上有关联性的部门整合成一个较大的工作单位，由一位部门主管担任协调者（Coordinator）或团队领导（Team Leader）的职务。

（4）交错沟通。这是指在不同职权指挥链的不同层级和部门的员工可以直接进行正式或非正式的沟通。正式沟通多半是以跨部门的委员会和项目小组等方式来进行。

以图书馆的员工发展委员会（Staff Development Committee）为例，这个委员会的成员可以包括主管人事行政的副馆长，员工联谊会的主席，及由员工推选出来的三至五位代表。在必要时，这个委员会还可以邀请馆外的专家担任顾问或指导。

三、不同层次的沟通网路

我们若将以上四种沟通管道加以分析，可以组合成五种不同的基本网路（Network）。从上图6-6的假设中可以看出这些网路的不同形状。

（1）链状型代表五层的垂直层级，其沟通方向只有上、下两途。

（2）Y字型代表四个层级，若将Y字型倒过来看我们可以看到两位部属向一位主管报告，在这之上还有两个层级。

（3）轮状型只有两个层级。中间一位是主管，其余四位是部属，所有的沟通都要经过这位主管，部属与部属之间没有正式的互动关系（Interaction）。

（4）环状型代表三个层次的两种可能情况：一个是有一位主管与两个不同层级的四位部属沟通；另一个是由两位主管与部属之间的垂直沟通。这种网路允许每一位员工都能与邻近的同事产生互动的关系。

（5）交错型是允许各层级的员工能够自由地与其他的员工进行沟通。这种形状的沟通最适合于交错式委员会或项目小组的运作。

以上五种不同形状的网路各有利弊，它们在使用上的效能可以用以下四个标准来衡量：

（1）传递的速度。

（2）正确性。

(3) 出现领导人物的几率。
(4) 员工的士气。

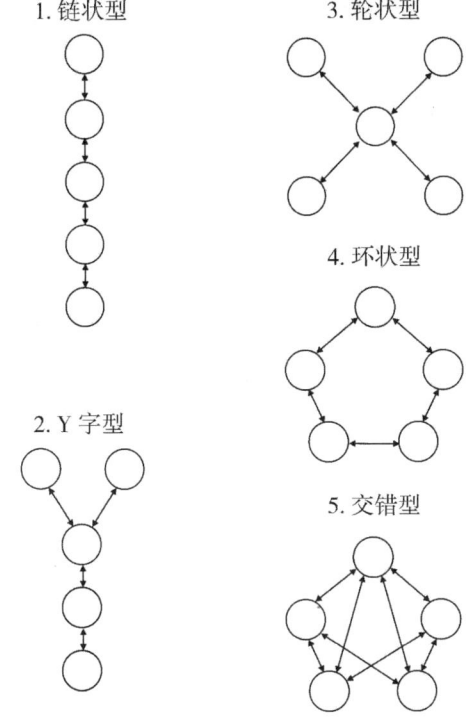

图6-6 各种沟通网路的图形

根据这些标准,若以讯息传递的速度来看,轮状型和交错型最快,环状型最慢;若以讯息传递的正确性来判断,链状型、Y字型和轮状型最高,环状型最低;若以出现领导人物的几率来衡量,轮状型最高,环状型和交错型最低;若以提高员工士气来评审,环状型和交错型最有效,轮状型最无效。表6-2显示了对于这些沟通网路的不同效能。

表6-2 各种沟通网路效能的衡量

衡量标准	链状	Y字型	轮状	环状	交错型
传递速度	适中	适中	快	慢	快
正确性	高	高	高	低	适中
出现领导人物	适中	适中	高	低	低
提高士气	适中	适中	差	好	好

四、沟通的障碍及如何克服

前面已经讨论过讯息沟通的途径和各种不同的沟通方式和网路,本节将接着讨论在沟通时经常会遭遇的一些障碍及如何克服的一些方法。对于这些障碍的了解和克服可以减少对讯息的误传和歪曲,使人际和组织沟通能够达到积极的效能。

关于最常见的沟通障碍,一般有下面七种:

1. 过滤作用（Filtering）

有些人有意把讯息当作权力或操纵的手段，以过滤的方法把该传递的讯息加以扣留、修改或延误。这种行为的动机有的是藉此表示自己的重要，也有的是为了要蒙蔽他人，自我渲染，或隐瞒自己的过失。

在一个机构里，讯息过滤的程度有时也会受到层级结构和组织文化的影响，层级较多的机构和好大喜功的组织文化对于讯息过滤的程度也较大。

2. 选择认知作用

有选择性的认知是人之常情，在沟通的过程中每个人都会依据自己的兴趣、知识、经验、文化背景、需求和偏好等因素选择并解释有关的讯息。

3. 情绪作用

每一个人对讯息的感受会受到当时情绪的影响。因为情绪的好坏会影响到个人对于一个讯息的理解和反应，因此在动怒时最好不要对某些讯息加以解释和处理。

4. 语言作用

即使是使用同一语言文字，但是因为各人不同性别、年龄、种族、教育程度和文化背景等因素的影响，在语意上会造成若干差别，导致了沟通上的误会。

5. 非口语的作用

非口语虽然也是沟通的一个方式，但是它的清晰度比口语差，容易造成误解。

6. 讯息的过度负荷（Information Overload）

讯息太少虽然不好，但讯息太多也会造成沟通的障碍。目前一般机构的各级主管每天所需要过目或处理的讯息有时有过多之感，其中有些是重要的，但也有些是不重要的，却仍然需要花时间去处理。这种讯息的过度负荷会影响到行政和决策的效率，有时甚至于造成讯息的轻重倒置。

同样地，很多主管为了要找寻工作上所需要的讯息，有时要面对浩瀚的资讯海洋，像从中去捞针一样地找寻一点一滴的有用讯息。

7. 时间的压力

良好的沟通必须有充分的时间，但是在实际情况中很多沟通工作都在时间的压力下匆忙或草率的进行，影响到沟通的效果。

为了要克服以上七种在沟通时可能遭遇到的障碍，有些相应的对策可以采用：

1. 讯息管制

这里所讲的"管制"（Control）并不是指"限制"（Restriction），而是要建立一个有效的"资讯管理系统"（Information Management System）。这个系统的作用是尽可能地将所有的讯息予以分类，分配给各有关部门和层级的主管负责，使得讯息的传递、接受、处理和流通能够适当地分配，以舒解讯息的过分集中，缓和少数人的过度负荷，同时避免重要的讯息被积压或遗漏。

另外，要求员工在使用书面和口头沟通时，应该简明扼要，最好不要越级。在用书面沟通时，长篇的报告或计划书都应该附有摘要（Summary），而且标明"特急"、"急件"或"普通"等识别的标签。

为了增加直接沟通的时效，每一个机构中的大小部门都应该每天或每周定时举行会议，由主要干部和员工代表参加以进行口头上的沟通，传达及交换有关讯息，并讨论业务上的大小问题。这种汇报的形式有时可以用"执行委员会"（Executive Committee）。部主任会议（Department Heads Meeting），或其他名称的会议来进行。对于重大的事件或决策，主管也可以在适当时机召开员工大会，亲自向员工报告，进行讨论，并听取员工的意见。这种直接沟通的方式可以弥补因执行分层负责所造成上下意见不能沟通的弊病。

2. **使用明晰的文字和语言**

在使用口语或是书面沟通时要尽量使用简明易懂并适合接受者语言能力的字句，以加强对方的了解。有时亦不妨使用不同的表达方式来重复沟通的讯息。对于重要和复杂的讯息若能同时使用口头和书面的沟通，往往可以获得较好的效果。

利用回馈的方式也可以确定对方了解的程度，以减少沟通过程中的误传。在使用口头沟通时，可以顺便问对方是否了解，或从对方的表情和反应来判断了解的程度。

3. **注意倾听**

倾听（Listening）与听（Hearing）有主动与被动之别。倾听不只是被动地听而且是主动地思考对方话中的意义。注意倾听必须全神贯注，因此比较费力。根据研究，一般人用英文讲话的速度大约是每分钟一百五十个字，但是倾听者的接受量可以超过每分钟一千个字。这种速度的差异可以允许倾听者做心智上的思考。

作为一个好的倾听者，是良好沟通的必备条件。以下一些建议有助于培养注意倾听的能力。

（1）尽量多听少说，千万不要中途打断对方的说话。在适当时可以提出问题，表示注意倾听。

（2）制造一个轻松和谐的气氛，使对方能畅所欲言。

（3）在对方讲话时表现出有兴趣的态度，要专心聚神，有耐性。

（4）要有接受批评或不同意见的容量，不轻易生气。

（5）等听完对方的话后，再进行讨论。

4. **注意非口头的暗示**

这种暗示在沟通时占有很大的分量，千万不要忽略。

5. **控制情绪**

激动的情绪能使人无法明智地表达自己的意向或歪曲了对外来讯息的理解。在沟通时最好是要在双方情绪都平稳的状况之下进行。

6. **广设沟通管道**

虽然作为非正式沟通管道之一的谣传是不可能完全避免的，但是为了要减少因误用谣传所导致的不良效果，每一个健全的机构应该尽力的广设各种正式的沟通管道，以便利正确的讯息传递和回馈。一些主管借着控制讯息来显示自己权威的心态应该改变，使能造成一个讯息畅通、和谐互信的组织气氛。

第四节 冲突的化解

一、冲突的定义和来源

在任何一个机构里，因为员工对于一些问题在认知或看法上有所不同，因此导致了冲突（Conflict）。这种认知上的不兼容，有时会引起敌对、不合作、互不相让、罢工或暴动等行为。在正常情况下一般主管用在冲突化解上的时间仅次于用在沟通上的时间。良好的人际与组织沟通其实也是化解冲突和减少因冲突所造成负面结果的一种方法。

在图书馆中,冲突的发生也在所难免,例如在争取经费分配时,采访部门认为增加图书采购经费应该被优先考虑;编目部门认为增加编目人员以减少新购图书被积压应该是最重要的;而参考咨询部门则认为增加国际计算机资讯联网(Internet)的设备和使用不应迟缓。诸如此类的情况,可以用"不胜枚举"或"俯拾皆是"等词来形容。越是规模大的图书馆,因认知或看法不同所造成的冲突会越多。举凡目标的订定、组织的结构、资源的分配、工作的协调、人员的安排和任用等,都可能导致不同程度和不同性质的冲突。罗宾士把冲突的来源归纳成下面四种[1]:

1. 不兼容的目标(Goal Incompatibility)
2. 结构关系(Structural Relationship)
3. 稀少资源(Scarce Resources)
4. 沟通上的歪曲(Communication Distortion)

除此以外,人际或行为的因素(Interpersonal or Behavioral Factors),像个别性格及思想的差异等,也是造成冲突的重要原因。

二、有关冲突的不同学说

虽然能导致冲突的原因很多,但是对如何处理和化解冲突的方法,管理学家也有一些不同的看法:

1. 传统的学说

在20世纪40年代以前,这一派的看法相当盛行。它认为冲突是机构中一种不正常,而且有害的现象,应该防止或消除。

2. 行为学说

这一派的主张盛行于20世纪40年代至70年代之间。它认为机构中冲突的发生是极其自然而无可避免的,在很多情况下也未必是不利的,因此应当善于处理,将冲突合理化,把有害的冲突控制在可以容忍的程度之内。

3. 互动学说

这一派的学说在20世纪70年代以后开始流行,它认为适当程度的冲突利于一个机构的改革和创新,可以促进机构目的的达成,应该予以鼓励。这种具有建设性的冲突,可以视为"良性的"冲突。相对地,一个没有冲突,过于稳定和宁静的机构,会缺乏竞争性和创造力,不适于生存在一个急遽变化的环境中。

根据冲突的互动学说,冲突不是要"化解",而是要适度地"调整"。这种调整就是要建立一个适当的冲突标准,然后将实际发生的冲突标准与预期的适当冲突标准相比较。当实际冲突标准高于或低于适当的标准时,管理者必须采取相应的措施去降低或提高实际的冲突,使得这些冲突能够维持在某种预期的适当程度。

三、冲突的调整和处理

关于化解冲突的方法很多,亚仁·菲立(Alan C. Filley)将这些方法归纳成两败俱伤(Lose-Lose)或不分胜负(No Win-No Lose),一赢一输(Win-Lose),及两全其美(Win-Win)三种[2]。他的分类可以加以如下的修正和补充:

---

[1] Stephen P. Robbins. *Managing Organizational Conflict: A Nontraditional Approach*. Englewood Cliffs, N. J.: Prentice-Hall, 1974, pp. 11-14.

[2] Alan C. Filley. *Interpersonal Conflict Resolution*. Glenview, IL.: Scott, Foresman, 1974, pp. 9-11.

1. **两败俱伤**（Lose – Lose）**或不分胜负**（No Win – No Lose）

这种化解冲突的方法是让冲突的双方都落入一种不是两败俱伤就是不分胜负的局面，使得冲突的双方都得不到好处，整个机构亦因此受到负面的影响。这一类所使用的方法包括了下面各种：

（1）退而求其次的妥协（Compromise）

（2）让第三者去仲裁（Arbitration）

（3）私下的承诺（Side Payment）

（4）疏通（Smoothing）

（5）拖延（Delaying）

（6）抑压（Denial）

（7）逃避（Escape）

（8）不过问（Noninvolvement）

2. **一赢一输**（Win – Lose）

这种化解的方法在表面上有一方是赢家，但实际上输的一方并不一定就会心甘情愿的接受，因此也不是很好的办法。促成一赢一输的方法也有以下几种：

（1）上级以命令来强制实行（Forcing）

（2）少数服从多数（Majority Ruling）

（3）少数操纵多数（Minority Ruling）

3. **两全其美**（Win – Win）

这种双方都是赢家的方法是化解冲突的上策。它的策略是使冲突的双方能够将注意力集中在共同的目标上，使得大家的利益一致。这种策略的主要手段有二：

（1）解决问题（Problem Solving）

（2）建立超乎寻常的目的或目标（Superordinate Goals）

在采用"解决问题"的策略时首先要确定冲突的来源，然后将这些原因当作问题来解决，不逃避，不妥协，也不拖延。

"超乎寻常的目的或目标"是指大于一个机构内各个冲突单位的个别目标。在建立超乎寻常的目标时要采用参与式管理及目标管理的方式让各部门的员工能体会到他（她）们的个别目标虽然重要，但最终的目的还在实现机构的大目标。达成这些大目标是大家的责任，必须以群策群力、分工合作的方式来促其实现。这种情况不一定就是要"牺牲小我，完成大我"，而是要使小我的目标与大我的目标能够兼容并顾，相辅相成，以达到两全其美的结果。

菲立曾经请七十四位主管描述他（她）们自己及上司处理冲突的方法，依次将其中五种最常用而有效的方法开列如下[①]：

（1）对持（Confrontation）或面对冲突

（2）疏通（Smoothing）

（3）妥协（Compromise）

（4）强制实行（Forcing）

（5）不过问（Noninvolvement）或撤退（Withdrawal）

以上第　项的"对持"或"面对冲突"若能采用"两全其美"的策略来处理应该是

[①] Alan C. Filley. *Interpersonal Conflict Resolution.* （Glenview, IL.：Scott, Foresman, 1974）. P – 31.

最理想的。担任主管的人要对这种策略的精意有深切的体会，并能适当地运用，将可以提高员工的积极性、创造力、团体精神、良性竞争及向心力，以增进机构的效能和达成机构的目的。

　　因为冲突对于一个机构有它正面的和负面的影响，有效的管理者必须能够将机构内部的冲突保持在一个适当的水平，并将其不利的影响减少到最低程度。

第七章　图书馆的控制与评估

Chapter 7　Control And Assessment in Libraries

第一节　控制的意义和重要性

"控制"（Control）是管理的五大功能之一。控制虽然会有监督和管制的意思，但它的用意不在于操纵员工，而是要使一个机构的各种内部作业能按照原先的计划，以分工合作、协调配合的方式，如期完成，以达成机构的目的和目标。有效的控制能协助员工知道他（她）们工作的进度和效果，及时地矫正执行上的偏差，以增加整个机构的效能。控制的另外一个主要作用是评估一个机构内部整体和各项作业的正确性和效能。以图书馆为例，控制是用来保证高质量的资讯服务，以满足读者与社会对于讯息的需求的一个手段。

控制虽然是管理过程中的最后一个环节，它的作用在规划时即已开始，而且涵盖在每一个过程之中。本章所讨论的控制将包括财务的控制，作业的控制，管理资讯系统的建立，和管理效能的评估。关于人力资源的控制，在第五章"图书馆的人力资源管理"中已经概括了。

第二节　财务的控制

一、财务资源管理（Financial Resources Management）

财务资源与第五章所专门讨论的人力资源管理（Human Resources Management）同为现代化管理的两大课题。任何机构皆需要具备这两种资源才能开展业务，进行规划、组织、执行和控制的作业，以达成组织的使命和目的。

财务资源管理包括了"开源"及"节流"的种种措施。前者是指一个机构对于所需经费的争取，后者是指一个机构对于所获得经费的有效使用。

1. 图书馆经费的来源

图书馆是一个非营利的机构。除了在企业机构内设立的特别图书馆和讯息中心外，一般图书馆的经费来源大概有下面几种：

（1）政府机构拨付的经费。这是专对国家图书馆、公立图书馆和公立的大专院校图书馆而言。

（2）学校或上级主管机构的拨款。这是指一般的大专院校和中小学图书馆等。有些学校在所收的学杂费中包括了图书馆的经费或使用费，作为图书馆经费的部分来源。

（3）地方的税收。这是专对公立图书馆和一些中小学图书馆而言。

（4）捐款。很多图书馆都得益于私人、基金会，和企业界各种不同名目的捐款。在图书馆普遍遭遇到经费短缺的情况下，这种经费来源的重要性已受到广泛的重视。本书作者与盖瑞·汉（Gary A. Hunt）合写了一本图书馆在20世纪90年代如何对外募款的书，1992年在美国出版，欢迎阅读、参考及指教[①]。

[①] Hwa-wei Lee, & Gary Hunt. *Fundraising for The 1990s: the Challenge Ahead. A Practical Guide for Library Fundraising*. Canfield, Ohio: Genaway & Associates, 1992.

（5）政府或基金会的特殊奖金或项目辅助。要得到这种奖金或辅助，图书馆必须提出针对性的申请书，并要经过征选的过程才能获得。

（6）图书馆在业务上的收入。这包括了利息、基金孳息、有偿服务、场地租金、罚款等。

为了大力争取充裕的经费，图书馆必须采取各种有效的措施，其中最主要的还是在尽力发挥图书馆的服务功能，满足读者和社会对于资讯的需求，使图书馆的重要性能被上级机构及社会所肯定。另外，图书馆对现有经费的有效使用，也是获得上级机构及社会的信任和赞助的一个方法。

2. 图书馆财务的控制

对于图书馆经费的控制，一般包括了预算（Budgeting），会计（Accounting），稽核（Auditing），和成本效益分析（Cost-Benefit Analysis）等作业。预算的制作多半要配合一个机构的会计年度，一年或两年作一次，它是将规划付诸实行的一个必须有的步骤。以下将特别予以讨论。

二、预算的作业

图书馆的预算作业要看图书馆的组织、规模和它与上级机构的关系而定。一般来说，图书馆的预算是经由对经费来源的估计，及与上级机构协商后所订定的经费分配和开销的计划。它的目的是在有效地使用预期的经费，以配合图书馆长、中、短程的规划，达成图书馆的使命和目的。因此，在实际上，预算不仅是规划的延伸，它把有限的资源根据各项作业的轻重，加以分配，而且也是一种控制的机能，用来保证资源的有效利用。

1. 预算的种类

和一般政府机关及非营利机构相似，图书馆的预算可以分成下列三种：

（1）业务预算（Operating Budget）。顾名思义，业务预算是一种一般性的作业预算，它包含了人事经费、办公经费、图书经费等项目。以俄亥俄大学图书馆为例，业务预算可以根据俄大预算表 1,000 至 9,000 的分类法细分如下（表 7-1）：

表 7-1　俄亥俄大学图书馆 1994-1995 会计年度业务预算分类

分类	用途	1993-1994 预算	1994-1995 预算
1,000,S	薪金	$2,743,024	$2,886,950
2,000,S	福利	$1,067,575	$1,102,442
小计	薪金及福利	$3,810,599	$3,989,392
3,000,S	办公用品	$78,240	$75,000
4,000,S	出差	$10,871	$10,000
5,000,S	通讯	$59,100	$54,100
6,000,S	租金及维修	$88,000	$114,000
7,000,S	其他费用	$101,564	$94,000
8,000,S			
9,000,S	图书、期刊及器材	$2,178,900	$2,401,763
小计	3,000,S 至 9,000,S	$2,516,675	$2,748,863
总计		$6,327,274	$6,738,255

注：以上的大项分类还可以细分成很多小类。

(2) 资产预算（Capital Budget）。资产预算与业务预算不同之处在于前者不是一年一度的预算，它的经费拨款是要满足远程的需要，像图书馆购买土地作将来发展之用，馆舍的建筑、增建或大翻修，购买自动化系统或设备，新增或更换书架和家俱等较大的开销。这些经费的争取要经过详细的规划和早期与上级机构的沟通。有些建筑新馆的资产可以有较长的时间去支配使用，不像业务预算一样要受会计年度的限制。

(3) 专门的预算（Special Budget）。这种预算是指除了一般经费来源以外的专款预算，像捐款以及政府或基金会的特殊奖金和项目辅助等。有很多这些专款可以当作正常经费一样包括在业务预算中，也有些专款必须另列预算，分别控制。

在制作以上的预算时，图书馆的馆长或负责财务或预算的主管应该亲自参与，各部门的主任也应该根据图书馆的规划项目提出经费的要求。这些项目的重要性及先后次序的排列，可以由一个有代表性的员工委员会用圈选的方式来决定。为了统一预算制作的标准和格式，图书馆的上级机构要预先颁布预算制作的指引（Guideline）和说明（Instruction）以便各预算制作单位的遵循。例如像平均年薪增加4%，医疗保险增加3%等已知或已经决定的标准，也应该及早宣布。做好的预算必须由上级机构的主管批准后执行。由于会计年度中途经费的增减和项目的变动，以上的预算也可以在必要时予以调整或修改。

2. 预算的方法

除了以上三种预算的种类，在制作预算时还有很多不同的方法可以采用。在一般情况之下，有很多预算的制作采用了不止一种的方法，以下是对于一些最常用方法的介绍：

(1) 分项预算（Line Item Budget）。这种方法最常使用在编列业务预算上。表7-1中所列举的预算分类就是一种典型的分项预算，以本年度和上一年度的预算和实际开销为基础，分项预算是逐项的决定下一年度的经费分配，有的酌量增加，有的保持现状，也有的予以裁减。这种决定多半是参考实际的需要、规划的重点和经费的来源。

(2) 总额预算（Lump-sum Budget）。这种方法是由上级机构给予一个下年度的经费总额，然后任由执行预算的单位去决定如何分配。根据上级所给予的经费总额，执行预算的单位可以用分项预算或其他方式来决定经费的各种用途。

(3) 公式预算（Formula Budget）。这种方法是用某种公式来决定经费的分配。例如某些公立图书馆的经费是按照管辖地区的人口和地区的大小而定。有些大学图书馆的经费是按照该大学学生人数与其不同程度和学科来决定。

(4) 规划—方案—预算系统（Planning - Programming - Budget System，或简称PPBS）。这种方法是以执行某些按照规划的方案为预算的重点。这些方案是以目标为导向的，而且也可能是跨部门的。在设计这些方案时，不仅要遵循着机构的使命和目的，同时要考虑到它的成本效益。"规划—方案—预算系统"在六十年代被美国的联邦政府所采用，名噪一时，但是不久即烟消云散。目前有些机构仍然采用这种方法的精神，鼓励各部门之间以协调合作的方法，提出跨部门的方案。俄亥俄大学每年都在新增经费中拨出一部分供校中各部门提出方案来申请。俄大的图书馆每年亦利用这种机会提出各种方案，例如像1993年与计算中心共同提出的推广使用Internet的教学方案，在1994年与一些学院共同提出的加强多媒体教材的设计、制作和使用方案等，都得到了校方的特别拨款。

(5) 履行预算（Performance Budget）。这种方法是将一个机构中一些工作项目依据其履行的次数以估计每次履行所需的费用。将履行这些项目的费用加在一起便是一个机构的总预算。以图书馆为例：采访部的预算可以从每年购买多少新书，订阅多少期刊，和处理多少赠书等来决定；编目部亦可以从每年要编上多少书刊，建立多少书目等来决定其预算；流通部可以从每年外借多少各类的图书资料或将之归架等的数量来决定其预算；参考咨询部更容易从各种履行的服务项目中拟定其经费的所需。履行预算的特点是必须先计算出每一项目的单元价值（Unit Cost）。像参考资讯在解答读者讯问时每一分钟的费用是多少和每一次成功的馆际互借要花多少钱等。

（6）零基预算（Zero-base Budget）。这种方法的预算与前面所介绍过的分项预算在作法上和观念上截然不同。分项预算一旦决定以后，往后每年的预算是增是减，都是将以前的预算作为基准（Base Budget）。零基预算是不以过去的预算为根据，每一会计年度开始前各部门要分别列举每一项要做的工作及其所需费用，报给上级裁决。上级在做决策时通常会考虑到每项工作的重要性、成本效益及经费情况以决定何者可以做，何者可以延缓，何者可以不做。零基预算首先是由美国德州仪器公司在七十年代采用。在 1977 年得到美国卡特总统的青睐，因此在联邦政府中用过一阵。这种预算方法因为有些不合实际的地方，在 1981 年里根总统主政时被停止使用，里根还批评这种方法在很多方面是累赘的，并无助于降低联邦政府的开销[①]。

三、会计和稽核

会计是财务管理的主要手段，它是将一个机构的资产、债务、收入、支出和盈余等加以详细记载及做成各种报表，使得一个机构的财务状况能够一目了然，以确保经费的使用得当。这种账目记载和会计报表的格式目前已逐渐标准化。

图书馆会计工作的繁简是根据它的组织结构与规模大小而定。有些图书馆的会计是由它的上级机构负责，也有些图书馆自行设立会计部门，由专业的会计人员负责。作为图书馆的主管和部门主任都应该具备一般的会计常识及财务分析的能力，能够有效地执行图书馆财务资源管理。

因为经费来源和用途的不同，有很多图书馆必须有不同的经费项目（Fund Accounts）。最常见的项目有以下几种：

1. **有限制的或无限制的经费**（Restricted or Non-restricted Funds）

有些经费，包括一些私人捐款，是专为某些特殊用途而设，像图书馆的购书经费，有时不能用在别的用途上。

2. **现行的经费**（Current Funds）

这是指本会计年度的一般经费，它可以包括各种来源的专用或非专用款项，及有限制或无限制的款项等。

3. **捐赠的基金**（Endowment Funds）

这是指不立即用掉的大额捐款。根据捐款者的愿望和机构自己的决定，这些钱可以储存起来，只动用孳生的利息；或者在储存一段预订的时间后用掉。基金的用途有的是有限制的，但也有的是无限制的。

4. **不动产的经费**（Plant Funds）

这种经费是专用于土地的购买、房舍的修建、设备和器材的添置等。

5. **托管的基金**（Agency or Fiduciary Funds）

这种基金包括了养老金（Pension Fund），信托的金钱（Trust Fund），或其他代为保管的基金。图书馆之友会的经费等也可以算是托管基金的一种，它不是图书馆的钱，但是由

---

① "Zero-Base Budgeting is Abandoned by Reagan", *Wall Street Journal*. August 10, 1981, p.8.

图书馆代为管理。

为了查核一个机构的会计工作是否完备、正确及经费是否使用得当，一般都有内部稽核（Internal Audit）和外部稽核（External Audit）两种程序。

1. 内部稽核是由机构自己的财务或会计人员来查核各种经费的收支情况，使用的手续，账目的记载，开销的是否得当及单据是否齐全等。这种稽核是经常性的，有问题时会立即纠正或建议修正的措施。

2. 外部稽核是由上级机构或独立的会计公司来查核一个机构的整体财务状况及其会计工作的是否完善。这种稽核有很多是配合年度的财务报告。

以上两种稽核程序都是控制的有效方法，确保财务管理的健全和合法。

四、成本效益分析

成本效益的分析是第二次世界大战时的产物，曾经用在美国国防经费的评估与控制上，在20世纪60年代颇为盛行。这种分析是将每一项活动的成本与其预期的效益加以比较，以决定是否合算及可行。比较精密的分析必须以数据为依据，其结果才会可靠。目前因为计算机的普遍使用，对于数据的分析比过去容易及省时。在图书馆的日常作业中有很多情况可以采用成本效益的分析来做决策。

例如，像图书馆的馆际互借，假设每一次的实际平均费用是十五美元，假如有一本常用的书，在一年之内要向别馆去借三次，倒不如去买一本来得便宜及方便。

亦有些图书馆为了向读者催付在美金三元以下逾期还书的罚款，其所花的人工及手续费会远超过三块钱，是否值得？若是从成本效益的观点来看，凡是罚款在三元以下者，不必立刻催付。使用自动化的图书流通系统，读者在下次借书时，计算机系统会显示读者还有未清的罚款，那时候再催还欠款。另外，图书馆也可以等到读者欠款超过十元美金时再采取行动。

除成本效益的分析之外，在管理学上还有两个常提到的概念。一个是"成本—效果的研究"（Cost – Effectiveness Studies），另一个是"成本—效率的研究"（Cost – Efficiency Studies），以下试将这两个概念的不同意义加以解释。

1. **成本—效果的研究**

成本—效果是指如何在某一个成本之下获得最佳的结果，以图书馆的购书经费为例，如何能善用这笔钱来购买到最多量的，而且是适当的书刊，这是成本—效果研究所希望能达到的目标。

2. **成本—效率的研究**

这种研究是着重在如何以最低的成本来达到某种预期的结果。以图书馆的编目工作为例，如何能以最经济有效的方法把全年的新购书刊全部编目完成，这是成本—效率研究所希望找到的答案。

以上两种不同概念，虽然彼此的着重点有所不同，但两者的目的都是在善用一个机构的财务资源，以达到最好的效果。在图书馆的日常作业中可以使用成本效益分析的个案可以说是不胜枚举。把各种有关数据，用计算机来分析比较，已经是越来越普遍。

第三节　作业的控制

上一节所讨论的财务控制是要确保一个机构对于它的财务资源能够适当的分配和使用，使得它的作业能够按照机构的目标和计划如期完成。作业的控制和财务的控制实际上是一体的两面，就像人的双手和双足一样，有着相辅相成的作用。

在第一章已经讨论过，图书馆的目的与功能虽然会因它的种类不同而有差别，但它的主要使命和任务大致上是一致的。为了要达成每一个图书馆的目的与功能，它必须拟定长、中、短程的计划和策略，进行组织和分工，取得适当的人力与财务资源，然后在有效的领导和协调之下开展业务及提供服务。作业的控制就是要保证业务的开展和服务的提供能够遵循机构的使命和目的，保持高度的质量和效能，并能如期完成。

最常使用在作业控制上的方法有甘特图表和网式图形等，以下将分别予以介绍。

一、甘特图表（Gantt Chart）

甘特图表是由科学管理大师弗端里克·泰勒的助手亨利·甘特（Henry L. Gantt）所创用。这个图表是将一个作业计划的各种项目与它进行的进度表用简单的图形来显示，以便于追踪及控制。以图 7-1 为例，这个甘特图表的水平轴是表示一个作业的进度，它可以用周、月或季来做单元。这个图表的垂直轴则代表这个作业各个部分。图 7-1 是假设某一图书馆进行自动化系统更新的一个作业计划。在进行过程之中，已完成的进度可以用不同的颜色或阴影来表明。例如，当进行到第七季时，发觉员工训练和分期安装较预订的计划分别迟了三个月和一个半月。这时候，主管图书馆自动化系统更新计划的人必须设法加速作业，以求赶上，或者是修改作业计划，将完成的日期往后推延。

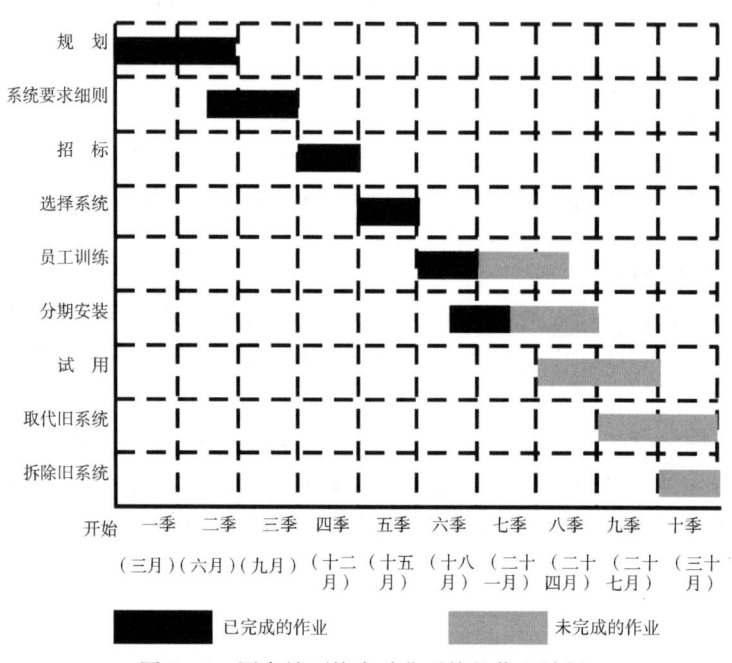

图 7-1　图书馆更换自动化系统的作业计划

二、网式图形

网式图形有两种模式,都是在 20 世纪 50 年代末期开始用来控制大型而复杂的作业计划。一个是"要径法"(Critical Path Method,或简称 CPM),另一个是"计划评核技术"(Program Evaluation and Review Technique,或简称 PERT)。采用网式图形的方法一般有以下的步骤:

1. 对执行某一计划的重要活动加以分析。
2. 决定这些活动的先后次序及彼此之间的互动关系。
3. 用流程图的方式来表明整体计划的各个活动。
4. 估计每个活动所需的时间。
5. 设定每项活动开始和完成的日期及整体计划的进度。

要径法与计划评核技术的共同点是两者都采用流程图的方式来表明整体计划的各项活动,如图 7-2 所显示:每一个圆圈代表一个活动的起点,它的数字表示活动的次序;每一个箭头代表活动的过程(用字母表示)和所需的时间(用数字表示)。在这个图中我们可以看到第六个活动完成后,才能进行第七个活动。另外,我们还可以看到有些活动可以同时进行。整体计划从开始到完成最长要二十六周的时间。因为计划的执行要依靠上级的经费补助,因此 C 和 F 的这条途径极为重要,可以被视为"要径"(Critical Path)。要是 C 和 F 可以缩短四周的话,整个装置也可以早四周完成,因为 A,C,F 这个途径估计需要十七周,而 A,B,E,G 和 A,D 这两个途径各需十三周就够了。

以上这个例子只是一个很简单的作业计划。实际上,要径法和计划评核技术是十分适用于规模庞大而复杂的活动。

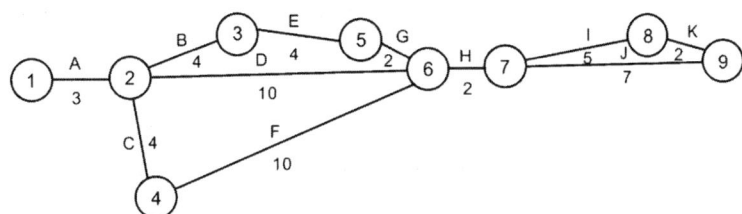

①—A	估计所需费用	(3 周)
②—B	拟定招标的计划	(4 周)
②—C	向上级申请经费辅助	(4 周)
②—D	图书馆自筹不足的经费	(10 周)
③—E	招标及议价	(4 周)
④—F	得到上级的辅助	(10 周)
⑤—G	选择包商	(2 周)
⑥—H	与包商定约	(2 周)
⑦—I	包商动工	(5 周)
⑦—J	使用临时的集会场地	(7 周)
⑧—K	验收及试用	(2 周)
⑨	装置完成	

图 7-2 会议室装设视听音响设备流程图

第四节　建立管理资讯系统

要做好控制及评估的工作，必须要有正确的资讯。为了能有效地掌握所需的资讯，每一个机构都应该建立一个完善的管理资讯系统（Management Information System），以收集、整理、分析和及时提供有助于规划、决策、执行、解决问题、控制和评估的讯息。

一个完整的管理资讯系统应该包括人事、财务、作业和成果等各种文字和数位化的讯息。数位化的讯息可以从日常的统计报表和定期的调查及问卷等方式中取得。目前有很多有关这方面的计算机软件系统已经被开发出来，可以用来处理管理资讯。

为了加强管理资讯系统的功能，图书馆首先应当把一些常用的统计报表标准化，使得各馆所收集到的管理资讯能够标准一致，相互比较。美国的联邦政府教育部、美国图书馆协会，及研究图书馆协会等机构都定期向所属图书馆收集统计资料，经过统计和分析之后，建立资料库及印刷发行。这种大规模而且有系统的收集，有助于图书馆统计资料的标准化，对于图书馆事业的发展，极有贡献。

除了这些有代表性的主要统计资料外，每个图书馆还要根据各自业务的需要，有系统地收集其他的统计资料。本章的附录收集了俄亥俄大学图书馆有关人事、经费、服务项目、馆际互借和藏书发展的统计表格以供参考。

一个健全的管理资讯系统应该配合一个机构的组织，以分工合作的方式来建立。机构的各级主管需要参与管理资讯系统的设计并决定何种资讯必须收集，因为收集、整理及分析资讯很花时间，凡是没有必要的资讯应该不去收集。有些资讯只对某一部门有用，不必纳入整体机构的管理资讯系统。管理资讯的收集有时也要经过浓缩与淘汰的过程。浓缩是将所收集的资讯加以整理、归并和简化，以保留其精华。淘汰是剔除无用和过时的资讯，有些图书馆长年累月的收集了很多统计资料，但是置之不用，这是非常浪费时间及人力的。要避免这种情况，各级主管应该定期检讨各种长久以来所收集资讯的使用率和价值，对无用的资料应该与上级或其他部门协调后，停止收集。另外，因为政府法令的改变及新兴情况的需要，有些新的资讯必须开始收集，管理资讯系统应该能灵活地配合这种需要，适时地予以调整。

总结以上的讨论，有效的管理资讯系统必须具备以下一些特征：
（1）正确性。
（2）时效性。
（3）经济性。
（4）标准化。
（5）弹性。
（6）可了解性。
（7）全面性。
（8）分工合作。

在使用管理资讯系统时，各级主管应该兼顾"质"与"量"的成果。很多管理资讯过分偏重数量的成果而忽略了对质量的重视，使得员工趋向于追求急功近利的狭隘标准。

管理资讯系统的另外一个重要作用是能及时地发出警号，使管理者发觉作业的偏差而能迅速地采取修正措施。以某一个图书馆的编目部为例,在正常情况下,该部门每年平均编目的书刊是四万五千种,当这个平均数目在某一年突然降低了 10% 以上时,管理资讯系统应该立即通知上级主管以便查明原因所在并采取适当的对策。

第五节　管理效能的评估

前面各节所讨论的财务控制、作业控制和管理资讯系统,其作用是在确保一个机构的作业能按照规划去执行,以达成机构的使命与目的。这一节所要讨论的评估(Evaluation and Measurement)是要以客观和可信的方法来确定执行的程度和所获致的效果是否与所定的目标符合。

从系统的观念来看,图书馆的本身也是一个系统,它的作业流程可以分成投入(Input)、执行过程(Processes)、输出(Output)和结果(Outcome)四个程序。

图书馆的投入包括了人力、馆舍、经费和设备等。图书馆的执行过程包括了图书采购、整理、编目和收藏等。图书馆的输出包括了读者服务、资讯检索、图书流通、讯息文献的传递等。以上这些活动都可以分别加以评估,以决定其满足读者对讯息需要的结果如何。有很多国家已分别订定各类图书馆的标准。这些标准可以用来作为评估的一种依据。以美国为例,美国图书馆协会曾经先后订定了大学图书馆标准[1],学院图书馆标准[2],公共图书馆的评估[3],学术图书馆的评估等[4]。主张图书馆评估最有力的权威,兰卡斯特教授(F. W. Lancaster),也在他的著作中提出了对于图书馆各种活动评估的方法和实例[5]。

一、评估的目的

在兰卡斯特所著《假如你要评估你的图书馆》一书中,他认为评估至少有下面四个目的[6]:

(1) 要找出现行服务的水平点和标志(Benchmark),以作为日后评估的比较。
(2) 要与其他图书馆比较彼此的成果。
(3) 要证明图书馆存在的价值及其成本效益。
(4) 要诊断图书馆作业的缺点,以便采取改善的措施。

他特别推崇印度图书馆学者阮冈纳赞(S. R. Ranganathan)在 1931 年所提出来的《图

---

[1] American Library Association. Association of College and Research Libraries. "Standards for University Libraries", *College and Research Libraries News*, Vol. 40, No. 2 (1979), pp. 101 – 110.
American Library Association. Association of College and Research Libraries. University Library Standards Review Committee, "Standards for University Libraries: Evaluation of Performance," *College and Research Libraries News*, Vol. 50, No. 8 (1989), pp. 679 – 691.

[2] American Library Association. *Association and College of Research Libraries*. "Standards for College Libraries, 1986", College and Research Libraries News, Vol. 47, No. 3 (1989), pp. 189 – 199.

[3] Eruest De Prospo, Ellen Altman, & Kenneth E. Beasley. *Performance Measures for Public Libraries*. Chicago: American Library Association, 1973.

[4] Nancy A. Van House, Beth T. Weil, & Charle R. McClure. *Measuring Academic Library Performance: A Practical Approach*. Chicago: American Library Association, 1990.

[5] F. W. Lancaster. If You Want to Evaluate Your Library... 2nd ed. Champaign, IL.: University of Illinois Graduate School of Library and Information Science, 1993.
Sharon L. Baker, & F. W. Lancaster. *The Measurement and Evaluation of Library Services*. 2nd ed. Washington, D.C.: Information Resources Press, 1991.

[6] 同 F. W. Lancaster (1993), pp. 8 – 9.

书馆学的五个法则》[①]：
(1) 书是为了要用的（Books are for use）。
(2) 每位读者能够找到他（她）所要的书（Every reader his book）。
(3) 每本书要有它的读者（Every book its reader）。
(4) 节省读者的时间（Save the time of the reader）。
(5) 图书馆是一个生长的有机体（Library is a growing organism）。

根据"书是为了要用的"法则，图书馆对于藏书和服务的评估应以满足读者的需要为着眼点，每本藏书的使用次数越多，这本书的成本效益越大。

"每位读者能够找到他（她）所要的书"是要评估图书馆能够满足读者需要的程度。除了提供需要的书刊之外，图书馆是否能满意地答复读者的询问和提供所需的讯息也是需要评估的。

"每本书要有它的读者"是指图书馆所收藏的书必须有使用的价值。这是要评估图书期刊的使用率。另外，图书馆也应该把收藏的书刊向读者介绍，以增加书刊的使用和流通率。

"节省读者的时间"是一般图书馆所经常忽略的一个问题。很多图书馆员认为提供读者所需要的资讯是图书馆的职责，但没有考虑到如何去方便读者，节省读者的时间，使读者能够在最快速的境况下获得所需的讯息。在评估时，这两种情况都应该予以考虑。

"图书馆是一个生长的有机体"是在表明图书馆应该不断的配合各种内外在情境的改变，力求调整及创新。一个故步自封，不思改革的图书馆将无法生存在急遽改变中的资讯社会。因此对于图书馆的评估也要重视图书馆对新观念、新方法和新技术的接受程度和适应能力。

阮冈纳赞的法则虽然早在六十多年以前资讯社会观念还没有发展的时候即已提出，他对图书馆的任务和使命的真知灼见，为当前图书馆的评估提出了明确的指标。图书馆的评估不仅是要决定究竟"做得有多好？"（How is it doing?）还要找出"做得对不对？"（Is it doing what it should be doing?）。光是做得好，但是做得不对，等于是前功尽弃。只是做得对，但是却做得不好，则等于没有做。因此在评估时应该兼顾不但要"做得好"而且是"做得对"。

二、评估的项目

图书馆的评估可以从很多方面来进行。兰卡斯特在他的书中把图书馆的评估分成文献传递服务、参考咨询服务及其他等三大类，每一类之下列举了许多评估的实例。

1. **文献传递服务**（Document Delivery Services）
(1) 藏书质量和内容。
(2) 藏书使用情况。
(3) 对于期刊的选订和使用。
(4) 对于书刊的剔旧和图书馆空间的使用。
(5) 图书目录的使用。
(6) 库藏的研究。
(7) 影响文献传递成败的因素。

2. **参考咨询服务**（Reference Services）
(1) 问题的解答。

---

① S. R. Ranganathan. *The Five Laws of Library Science.* 2nd ed. Madras：Library Association, 1957.

(2) 资料库的检索。
(3) 对读者的教育。
3. **其他**（Other Aspects）
(1) 资源共享。
(2) 成本—效率的考虑。
(3) 成本—效益的研究。
(4) 连续性的质量控制。

对于以上每一项作业的评估，兰卡斯特都举出很多实例作为参考[①]。

在兰茜·文豪斯（Nancy A. Van House）等所著的《学术图书馆作业测量》一书中对图书馆的评估分成一般的，书刊的在库（Availability）和使用，设备和图书馆利用，和资讯服务等四大类。他们的评估特别着重在图书馆对读者所提供的服务。

1. **一般的**（General）。一般满意程度的调查（General Satisfaction Survey）
2. **书刊的在库和使用**（Materials Availability and Use）
(1) 书刊流通（Circulation）。
(2) 书刊在馆内的使用（In-Library Materials Use）。
(3) 全部书刊的使用率（Total Materials Use）。
(4) 书刊在库的情况（Materials Availability）。
(5) 获得所需书刊的时间（Requested-Materials Delay）。
3. **设备和图书馆的利用**
(1) 入馆人数或次数（Attendance）。
(2) 馆外的使用（Remote Use）。
(3) 全部使用次数（Total Use）。
(4) 设备的使用率（Facilities Use Rate）。
(5) 各服务台的使用（Service Point Use）。
(6) 图书馆大楼的使用（Building Use）。
4. **资讯服务**（Information Services）
(1) 参考咨询服务的记录（Reference Transactions）。
(2) 对参考咨询服务满意程度的调查（Reference Satisfaction Survey）。
(3) 在线检索服务的评估（Online Search Evaluation）。

兰茜·文豪斯等在他们的书里专为以上的各种评估设计了一套立即可以采用的标准调查和问卷表格。这些评估的工具是要达成以下几个要求[②]：
(1) 测量图书馆各种活动的影响、效率和效果，以作为决策及资源分配的依据。
(2) 以数量方法来向上级机构和社会解释图书馆的功能和成效。
(3) 帮助各部门主管在适当的周期来测量作业的水平，以便比较及采取改进的措施。
(4) 它是以读者及服务为导向的（User-and Service-Oriented）。
(5) 为图书馆的规划提供有用的数据资料。
(6) 可以很方便及经济有效地为各学术和研究图书馆所采用。

---

① 同 F. W. Lancaster (1993), pp. 1–313.
② Nancy A. Van House, Beth T. Weil, & Charle R. McClure. *Measuring Academic Library Performance: A Practical Approach*. (Chicago: American Library Association, 1990). pp. VII & IX.

三、评估的步骤

在进行评估时，一般常用的步骤大致可以归纳为以下各种：

1. 选择评估的项目

上一节已经列举了许多可供评估的项目，在设计评估时应根据一个机构和部门的需要，选择一个和多个评估的项目。

2. 决定评估的目的

在进行评估之前，一般要考虑到评估的目的是什么？有的评估是在测量一个机构的作业是否正确，是否配合或遵循机构的使命和目的；有的是在测量作业进度成效，及读者满意的程度。前者是要判断"做得对不对"，"该不该做"；后者是要鉴定"做得好不好"，"好到什么程度"。

3. 设立评估的标准

为了使得评估能够客观和正确，每个机构或部门应该设立评估的准则和目标，并将一些专门名词、工作和读者分类等不同定义加以确定。

例如以"图书在库率"（Materials Availability）和"图书获得率"（Material Accessibility）两个容易混淆的术语来评估："图书在库率"是指读者要在图书馆中找到某一特定书刊的几率；而"图书获得率"是指除了这本书是否在书库里之外，还涉及图书馆开放的时间，图书归架的速度，图书目录的完备，流通系统的效率，和读者使用图书馆的能力等其他影响的因素。在评估图书使用情况时，这两个术语的定义必须要明确地界定。

4. 设计评估的方式

评估的方式一般有调查、问卷、观察、面谈和对资料报表的分析等多种。在征求读者对图书馆各项作业的意见和满足程度时，调查、问卷及面谈是三个最常用的方法。

关于问卷的设计、测试、抽样、时间的选择、分发、整理、统计、分析和总结等过程的讨论，有很多专门的书籍可供参考。一些社会科学研究法的书对于"问卷"的方式多有详细的说明。

5. 资料的收集、整理和分析

在收集资料时，图书馆内部的沟通十分重要。员工必须了解评估的积极用意，并需参加有关调查、问卷及面谈的技术训练。资料收集到后的整理，目前可以利用计算机来处理。负责资料整理和分析的人员必须懂得使用各种用在计算机上的统计分析软件来进行各种分析比较，并将结果用图表显示及文字说明。

6. 诊断及采取改进措施

评估的目的是在诊断一个机构的健康情况。就像每个人的定期体检一样，它的目的在于保健。当诊断发觉有病状时，就应当设法治疗，使能及早恢复健康。当图书馆在评估时发觉有某些缺点，就应该采取必要的措施去改进。

附录1 俄亥俄大学图书馆人员统计表（1978-1979 至 1993-1994）

Fiscal Year	STAFF				PART-TIME STUDENT ASSISTANT HOURS						Grand Total
	Contract		Classified		Staff FTE	Operating	Non-Operating	Work-Study	Total Hours	Student FTE	Staff/ Student FTE
	Oper.	Funded	Oper.	Funded							
1978-79	24.11	0.50	53.0	0.00	77.61	33,977	n/a	41,120	75,097	36.11	113.72
1979-80	24.11	1.17	53.0	0.57	78.85	35,356	n/a	44,156	79,512	38.23	117.08
1980-81	25.11	2.08	53.0	4.39	84.58	28,713	n/a	50,961	79,674	38.30	122.88
1981-82	25.44	3.92	53.0	6.11	88.47	25,742	11,052	49,734	86,528	41.60	130.07
1982-83	26.28	5.45	53.0	6.72	91.45	31,220	10,597	50,265	92,082	44.27	135.72
1983-84	26.94	3.17	52.5	4.13	86.74	37,009	9,908	58,456	105,373	50.66	137.40
1984-85	29.28	1.25	48.0	.63	79.16	36,748	8,611	56,965	102,324	49.19	128.35
1985-86	29.28	1.75	48.0	3.51	82.54	40,586	11,469	59,365	111,420	53.57	136.11
1986-87	30.28	2.00	48.0	1.90	82.18	49,087	15,981	54,583	119,651	57.52	139.70
1987-88	28.77	1.57	52.0	3.40	85.74	44,494	11,583	56,640	112,720	54.19	139.93
1988-89	30.20	2.65	53.5	3.15	89.50	50,060	9,553	53,111	112,724	54.19	143.69
1989-90	30.90	3.52	54.0	3.89	92.31	48,694	9,494	53,108	111,296	53.51	145.82
1990-91	32.60	3.98	52.5	4.45	93.53	51,824	15,542	43,343	110,709	53.22	146.75
1991-92	37.46	3.45	57.5	7.50	105.91	56,385	15,924	55,839	128,148	61.61	167.52
1992-93	39.66	5.25	56.5	5.60	107.01	51,812	25,631	60,270	137,713	66.21	173.22
1993-94①	57.25	6.92	70.4	2.10	131.67	90,983	15,989	65,700	172,672	83.01	214.68

① Includes University Center statistics

附录2 俄亥俄大学图书馆经费开支表 (1993-1994)

Object Code	Descriptor	Operating	Rotaries	Grants	Endowments	Gifts	Grand Total
1110-1190	Contract salaries	1,742,896	1,150	100,054	16,698	1,482	1,862,280
1700	Classified salaries	1,560,599	9,935	35,010	7,268		1,612,812
1520	Student wages	298,221	44,678	14,382			357,281
Subtotal:	Salaries/Wages	3,601,716	55,763	149,446	23,966	1,482	3,832,373
2000's	Benefits	1,390,411	4,395	55,985	3,812		1,454,603
Total:	Salaries, Wages, Benefits	4,992,127	60,158	205,431	27,778	1,482	5,286,976
3000's-9000's	Supplies, Travel, Communication, Service Contracts, Equipment	954,975	222,112	66,222	13,318	6,931	1,263,558
9570	Binding	68,029					68,029
9530	Serials	275,765			102		275,867
9550/9560	Periodicals	1,465,109			51		1,465,160
9580/9590	Books & Other	916,502	(459)	10,348	113,219	33,625	1,073,235
Subtotal:	Acquisitions	2,657,376	(459)	10,348	113,372	33,625	2,814,262
9950-9951	Miscellaneous transfers	(3,704)	(47,086)			(450)	(51,240)
GRAND TOTAL		8,668,803	234,725	282,001	154,468	41,588	9,381,585

附录3　俄亥俄大学图书馆主要服务项目统计表
(1978 – 1979 至 1993 – 1994)

Academic Year	Number of User Visits	Number of Checkouts	—Materials Used—		Total Usage	Tours & Lectures (Persons)	Reference Questions Asked	CD-ROM① Searches	ALICE Searches
			Number Used on Reserve	Number Used in Library					
1978 – 79	1,037,741	259,170	120,142	498,857	878,169	4,874	137,209		
1979 – 80	1,148,664	244,444	127,938	343,092	715,474	5,695	110,472		
1980 – 81	1,254,556	196,586	154,830	398,896	750,312	4,602	145,525		
1981 – 82	1,402,974	218,468	173,996	436,037	828,501	4,029	164,221		
1982 – 83	1,472,580	200,971	194,750	466,216	861,937	4,776	169,300		
1983 – 84	1,456,674	214,906	183,664	425,391	823,961	4,163	165,656		
1984 – 85	1,355,260	256,486	183,223	452,841	892,550	3,983	128,401		
1985 – 86	1,326,072	285,244	177,757	449,072	912,073	3,575	193,425		
1986 – 87	1,356,288	258,671	153,169	530,842	942,682	3,274	189,347		
1987 – 88	1,385,369	280,963	210,396	508,081	999,440	5,633	169,911	5,312	
1988 – 89	1,372,975	265,391	234,759	538,732	1,038,882	5,948	167,391	6,457	
1989 – 90	1,369,016	265,334	250,225	447,373	962,932	8,220	139,828	12,592	1,134,580
1990 – 91	1,344,287	281,426	288,841	437,245	1,007,512	8,985	170,965	23,858	1,502,935
1991 – 92	1,354,406	328,237	321,673	507,978	1,157,888	9,408	170,262	111,353	2,145,239
1992 – 93	1,273,182	314,808	302,289	506,340	1,123,437	10,396	142,841	132,456	2,443,526
1993 – 94	1,274,054	324,561	315,832	525,184	1,165,577	13,403	153,819	177,772	2,583,143

① CD-ROM searches do not include searches conducted on InfoTrac before February 1994, Newsbank or Government Document Specialized Databases.

附录 4 俄亥俄大学图书馆馆际互借统计表
(1978 – 1979 至 1993 – 1994)

| | Inter library Borrowing | | | | | | Interlibrary Lending | | | |
| | | | Univ. Centers | | Libraries-General | | Medical | | OVAL | Total |
Academic Year	Requests	Filled	Requests	Filled	Requests	Filled	Requests	Filled	Filled	Filled①
1978 – 79	6,088				4,621				n/a	4,621
1979 – 80	6,642				5,602		51		4,524	10,177
1980 – 81	9,314				5,183		1,752		5,708	12,643
1981 – 82	8,445				5,177		2,361		6,287	13,825
1982 – 83	8,878				6,088		2,467		6,466	15,021
1983 – 84	9,171				6,487		1,825		6,487	14,799
1984 – 85	9,359				7,518		1,830		6,487	15,835
1985 – 86	8,719				9,488		1,666		6,833	17,987
1986 – 87	8,574				10,497		3,678		6,207	20,384
1987 – 88	8,705				11,844		3,715		5,907	21,466
1988 – 89	8,739	7,180			14,389	6,677	4,084	2,689	5,1%	14,562
1989 – 90	9,460	6,927			14,702	6,508	4,442	3,052	4,070	13,630
1990 – 91	10,411	7,845	3,339	2,681	10,956	4,814	4,284	2,970	3,911	11,6952
1991 – 92	11,070	8,691	3,903	3,463	14,196	6,451	7,033	4,407	3,674	14,5322
1992 – 93	13,020	9,513	3,741	3,361	15,624	7,175	7,970	5,199	2,490	14,8642
1993 – 94	12,245	9,647	4,319	3,797	15,894	7,591	8,471	5,711	1,921	15,223②

① Total column is for requests for 1978 – 1988 and for fills for 1989 – 1994.
② Total does not include loans to University Centers (Regional Campuses).

附录5 俄亥俄大学图书馆馆藏统计表（1978-1979 至 1993-1994）

Fiscal Year	Books & Bound Serials (Volumes)	Gov. Doc. (Volumes)	Total	% of Incr	Microforms (Units)	% of Incr	Other① (Pieces)	% of Incr	Current② Periodical (Titles)	% of Incr
1978-79	743,368	306,780	1,050,140		640,663		265,539		5,542	
1979-80	769,732	337,945	1,107,677	5.5%	679,877	6.1%	272,507	2.6%	5,754	3.8%
1980-81	813,314	361,485	1,174,799	6.1%	754,768	11.0%	272,973	.2%	6,022	4.7%
1981-82	876,794	375,648	1,252,442	6.6%	820,622	8.7%	276,620	1.3%	6,004	-0.3%
1982-83	912,884	230,461③	1,143,345	-8.7%	1,062,283	29.4%	309,303	11.8%	8,003	33.3%
1983-84	952,263	239,052	1,191,315	4.2%	1,137,833	7.1%	327,087	5.7%	8,857	10.7%
1984-85	985,227	249,471	1,234,698	3.6%	1,233,129	8.4%	334,578	2.3%	9,426	6.4%
1985-86	1,029,869	254,261	1,284,130	4.0%	1,319,107	7.0%	346,538	3.6%	9,705	3.0%
1986-87	1,074,050	260,862	1,334,912	4.0%	1,411,636	7.0%	353,324	2.0%	9,968	2.7%
1987-88	1,119,744	264,239	1,383,983	3.7%	1,478,872	4.8%	364,084	3.0%	10,261	2.9%
1988-89	1,161,186	269,753	1,430,939	3.4%	1,626,815	10.0%	307,927	1.9%	10,326	0.6%
1989-90	1,203,215	274,456	1,477,671	3.3%	1,738,726	6.9%	244,332④	-34.1%	10,705	3.7%
1990-91	1,254,832	279,394	1,534,226	3.8%	1,823,172	4.9%	250,482	2.5%	10,938	2.2%
1991-92	1,308,676	284,125	1,592,801	3.8%	1,956,851	7.3%	300,247⑤	9.9%	11,083	1.3%
1992-93	1,354,885	288,067	1,642,952	3.1%	2,067,207	5.6%	307,290	2.3%	11,217	1.2%
1993-94	1,398,433	292,089	1,690,522	2.9%	2,179,780	5.4%	311,218	1.3%	11,414	1.8%

① Other includes maps, discs, tapes cassettes, photographs, films exhibition catalogs, drymounts, posters, scores, and Multi-media kits. Excluded from these are OU archives, manuscripts, and local government records.

② Figures include current titles received in Documents and Southeast Asia Collections.

③ The volume count of government documents was revised based on a complete inventory and weeding. Because many titles are bound in one volume, the count by volumes is less than the count by title.

④ The Slide Collection was returned to the College of Fine Arts, 132,143 slides, therefore, the number of "Other" was reduced in 1989-1990.

⑤ An increase of 49,765 items was due to the assimilation of the Instruction Media Services collections along with gifts of photograph collections from School of Theater and the College of Osteopathic Medicine.

第八章　跨世纪的图书馆发展

Chapter 8　Library Developments into the Next Century

这本探讨现代化图书馆管理的书融汇了作者多年来从事图书馆行政工作的经验和体会，希望能发生抛砖引玉的作用，激发读者的共鸣，在当前的资讯主导时代中，共同为改善图书馆管理的质量及加强图书馆服务的功能而努力。

在距离 21 世纪只有六年时间的今天，因为人类知识资讯空前未有的突飞猛进，以及计算机、电讯、综合媒体、电子出版、密集储存、国际联网等新兴技术的急遽发展，在这些众多冲力影响之下，图书馆正面临着一个急遽蜕变和重新定位的紧要关头，有些未来学的学者甚至预测以书刊印刷品为主的传统图书馆将会很快地为时代所淘汰而消失踪迹。

从图书馆的历史和近四十年来的发展来看，图书馆为了迎合时代潮流、知识资讯的爆炸和资讯技术的发展，正在不断地蜕变和革新中。从 20 世纪初开始，图书馆已经从旧式专为少数人服务的藏书楼走向为平民大众服务的图书馆。公共图书馆的兴起和成长，充分地显示了这个发展趋向。到了四十年代，科技资讯的发展促成了特殊图书馆和科技资讯中心（或文献资讯中心）的设立和茁壮。到了 60 年代，因为计算机技术的普遍化，使得以印刷的书籍资料为主的传统图书馆（Paper-based Library）开始朝向自动化图书馆（Automated Library）发展。到了 70 年代中叶，因为电讯技术的发展，促成图书馆的网路化（Networked Library），加强了图书馆之间的合作和资源共享。到了 80 年代中叶，因为电子出版及密集储存技术的发展，使得很多出版物开始以电子、光盘和综合媒体等形式出现，为图书馆的电子化（Electronic Library）开拓了新的境界。到了 90 年代，由于计算机、电讯、电子技术和综合媒体的结合使用，加上了国际计算机资讯联网（Internet）的发展，使图书馆摆脱了传统的枷锁，能从各自孤立和局限的服务模式转变成资源共享和无远不及的"虚拟"图书馆（Virtual Library）。表 8-1 表明了图书馆发展的几个重要转折点（Turning Point）。

表 8-1　20 世纪以来图书馆发展的重要转折点

1900——由为少数人服务的藏书楼变为大众化的图书馆。国家图书馆、公共图书馆、大专院校图书馆等都开始快速地发展。
1940——特殊图书馆和科技资讯中心开始发展茁壮，形成各类图书馆中重要的一支。
1960——由以印刷品及人工为主的"纸张图书馆"开始向"自动化的图书馆"发展。
1970——开始向"网路化的图书馆"发展。
1980——开始向"电子化的图书馆"发展。
1990——因为国际计算机资讯联网的普遍化，使得图书馆开始向"虚拟的图书馆"发展。
2000——结合了纸张图书馆、自动化图书馆、网路化图书馆、电子图书馆及虚拟图书馆特色的综合图书馆。

从上面各期发展的大势来看，图书馆并没有故步自封，漠视大环境中各种发展所造成的机会和挑战。事实上，从 20 世纪 60 年代以来，图书馆在新兴资讯技术的发展和使用方面采取了主导的作用。即使是受到了人力和财力等因素的限制，还能在适当时期，率先使用新兴的资讯技术，改进及加强为读者和社会的服务。

在结束本书之前，本章将讨论未来几年三个对图书馆有重大影响的发展：①国际计算机资讯联网，②综合媒体技术，③资讯高速公路；然后就这些发展对图书馆现代化的管理和跨世纪的挑战加以分析和评论，以作为本书的总结。

第一节　国际计算机资讯联网（**Internet**）的发展及影响

在 20 世纪 90 年代最具影响力的一个发展无疑地应该是国际计算机资讯联网。它对加强图书馆无远弗届的资讯服务和实现虚拟图书馆这一理想提供了强有力的条件。早在六十年代美国国防部的高深研究计划总署（Advanced Research Projects Agency，ARPA）即已开始建立一些大型计算机的联网，称之为 ARPANET。这个方法在 80 年代为美国国家科学基金会（National Science Foundation）所采用。美国国家科学基金会的联网——NSFnet 是将美国各地的一些大学、研究机构及政府部门的计算机网路——其中包括有很多超型计算机（Supercomputers）和特别的计算机软件——衔接成一个全国性的计算机资讯网路以便利科技研究人员互通信息、交换研究成果及达成资讯共享的目的。

由于 NSFnet 的发展，很多其他的国家也开始仿效，并设法与美国联网，因此产生了 Internet 或者是网路的网路（Network of Networks）。目前，它是联结了世界上成千上万计算机网路的国际网路。根据 1993 年 7 月的统计，与 Internet 联网的计算机已超过一百七十万台，这些计算机分布在世界上六十多个国家，几乎每十分钟就会有一个新的网路与 Internet 联网。近千万的 Internet 使用者可以在各自不同的计算机硬软件上采用共同通讯协议，即是 TCP/IP—Transmission Control Protocol/Internet Protocol，来与其他计算机的使用者沟通和交换资讯。作为一个国际联网，Internet 的特点是自由组合，有政府赞助但不受政府的管制。到目前为止，以美国为例，参加这个联网的费用是由各个计算机网路每年担负很小的一笔年费，使得这个网路的每位使用者可以每天二十四小时免费使用。世界上很多与 Internet 联网的大学图书馆已经将它的在线图书馆目录和一些电子化的数据库开放给 Internet 的使用者。很多在台湾、香港和美国的图书馆都已如此做，除了图书馆的目录和数据库之外，从 Internet 上还可以查检到大量的宝贵资料，不论是科技工程、医药卫生、文史哲学、政治经济、教育娱乐、艺术音乐等方面的资讯都可以找到，绝大多数不仅是免费的，而且还可以利用文件传输协议（File Transfer Protocol，FTP）的设计将之从不同的计算机储存内拷贝到自己的计算机储存内以供使用，真正做到了古语所说的"秀才不出门，能知天下事"的假想。因为使用 Internet 是免费及无所不及的，图书馆可以用它做文献传递，提高了馆际互借、资源共享和国际学术交流的时效。在国际计算机资讯联网快速发展的今天，越来越多极为方便的用户接口（User Interface）和引导工具，像 Archie（一种有寻找档案功能的系统），Gopher（一种阶层式的查看系统），World Wide Web（一种能联结各种声像资料—Hypertext—的网路系统），及 Mosaic（一种能在 Gopher 上查询资料的系统）等，已被不同的使用者开发出来供大家使用。

美国的 Internet 因为得到国家科学基金会的经费支持，所以能够几乎是免费地让大家使用。但正因如此，使用者越来越多，由当初仅供科研人员使用扩充到人人都可使用，造成现有网路的超量负荷。尤其是很多营利性质的商业机构也加入使用。由于这个原因，国家基金会有意将 Internet 开放给私人企业去投资发展。

第二节 多媒体（Multimedia）技术的发展

随着计算机的发展，多媒体技术也跟着向前突飞猛进。多媒体技术与过去各种单独的视听影像技术有所不同，它是以计算机操纵（Computer-mediated），经过数位化（Digitized）的各种文字、声像、图画的综合体。这种数位化以后的文字、声像、图画、录像可以用在配备有多媒体功能的计算机上，亦可以储存在光盘上流通，还可以藉国际计算机资讯联网上特殊的广世网（World-Wide Web）软件来交流。由于多媒体在教育、资讯、商业和娱乐上的优势，它将会大量地发展而变成图书馆收藏及提供资讯服务的一种新的形式。

根据《英文中国纪事报杂志》(The Free China Journal) 最近的报导，台湾在多媒体计算机的生产、研究和发展上在世界上是非常领先的。在 1993 年，台湾多媒体计算机的生产量是二万八千台，到了 1994 年，多媒体计算机的生产也惊人地增长了二十六倍到了七十二万八百台！大约 10% 左右是供应区内市场的需要，其余的则外销世界各国，大约一半的区外市场是美国。除了多媒体计算机外，其他的生产像声卡（Sound Cards）、录像卡（Video Cards）、光盘驱动器（CD-ROM Drives）、高频度电视（High Definition TVs）、声像服务器（Video Servers）、声像电话（Video Telephones）、计算机游戏及以光盘为媒体的百科全书、字典、教材、地图、游戏、音乐、卡拉 OK（Karaoke）等可供多媒体计算机使用的产品，也像雨后春笋一样地大量涌现。1995 年 1 月 9 日至 15 日在台北举行的国际音响、录像、电子和多媒体的商展上，大约有三分之一的新产品是跟多媒体有关的[①]。

因为多媒体的发展和普遍化，图书馆的收藏、设备与服务也应该有相应的调整以配合时代的需要。

第三节 资讯高速公路（Information Superhighway）的发展

为了要迎合国际计算机资讯联网所造成资讯传递大量增长的需要，美国的国会在 1992 年首先考虑到建立全国资讯高速公路及国家教育与研究网路（National Education and Research Network，NERN）的迫切性。美国现任副总统澳尔·郭（Al Gore）在他担任国会参议员时，即是推动建立全国资讯高速公路和国家教育与研究网路最得力的一人。

建立全国资讯高速公路是加强国家资讯基础建设（National Information Infrastructure）的一个主要部分。目前美国政府的立场是经由国会立法，在政府主导及协助下，由私人企业以公开竞争方式去开发。

台湾地区最近亦由资讯发展推动小组成立了"资讯通讯基础建设计划"的研究小组，对下面五个主题进行前瞻性、宏观性及策略性的探讨，这五个主题分别是[②]：

[①] The Free China Journal, Vol. 12, No. 3 (Jan. 25, 1995), p. 8.
[②] 《台湾之信息超级公路—NII》，《美中科学通讯》(Midwest Science News), Vol. 2, No. 4 (December 1994), p. 3.

（1）策略研究。
（2）行政机关需求。
（3）新兴运用。
（4）负载分析。
（5）产业发展。

这个小组在 1994 年 5 月提出了以下十点综合建议，经行政主管部门批准在同年 6 月开始施行①。

（1）成立推动组织。在行政主管部门成立任务编组，作跨部会协调；民间则成立民间咨询委员会以资沟通与配合。
（2）推广与沟通。加强对社会的宣传，以求扩大使用的层面，建立共识。
（3）落实自由化。除网路基本建设由政府负担外，其余则开放给民间自由竞争。由行政主管部门制订办法确保公平合理，并确定进行的时间表。
（4）修订相关的法则。
（5）支持相关的技术研究和发展。
（6）办理实验性先导计划。
（7）加强频谱有效运用。
（8）建立网网相连的环境，使资源互通，减少浪费。有线电视亦并入整体考虑。
（9）提前公布采购，以带动区内产业发展。
（10）采用地区与国际接轨标准。

据调查，目前台湾地区已经建立的网路有以下各种②：

行政主管部门——行政资讯网路。
内政主管部门——户政兵役系统网路与资料库。
卫生主管部门——医疗网路。
交通主管部门
电信：
——语音网路
——数据网路
交通：
——公路监理网路
财政主管部门
海关：
——通关网路
金融：
——金融网路
经济主管部门
——加值网路
——商业自动化网路
教育主管部门——教育网路

---

① 《台湾之信息超级公路—NII》，《美中科学通讯》（*Midwest Science News*），Vol. 2, No. 4（December 1994），p. 3.
② 陈世敏，《台湾信息/传播的产管学三结合》，《美中科学通讯》（*Midwest Science News*），Vol. 2, No. 4（December 1994），p. 29

科学委员会——科技资料网路

新闻主管部门——有线电视网路

交通主管部门的电话局为了配合通讯技术的发展及资讯社会的需求,对台湾现阶段资讯通信建设特别提出了以下的策略①:

1. **网路光纤化**

提供高质量、高速率、大容量的传输电路,以配合未来资讯网路基础建设的需要。

2. **交换宽带化**

将数据网路由"讯框传送"(Frame Relay)改换成"异步传送"(Asynchronous Transfer Mode, ATM)。传输速度将由1.544 Mbps增至2.488 Gbps。

3. **服务整合化**

整合语音、数据、影像、视讯、CATV及多媒体等,提供整体性服务。

4. **应用普及化**

续建资讯接取网路,分封交换网路、网际资讯网路,在台湾之十六话价区均建立网路节点,以达成资讯应用普及化的目标。

5. **联机国际化**

将以上各种网路与国际联机,以增进资讯通讯的国际交流。

6. **资讯生活化**

加速资讯通讯网路的基础建设,促进资讯充分流通,提供全民便捷价廉的通信服务,以达到资讯生活化的境界。

由以上三个最新的发展来看,在未来五年跨世纪的重要关头,图书馆面临着重大的挑战。对于要对21世纪的图书馆重新定位,每一位图书馆的从业人员都应该了解本身的艰巨责任和使命,使未来的图书馆能够配合新资讯技术的发展与人类社会对图书馆的不同期望。本章的最后两节将分别将现代化图书馆管理的要点加以总结,并将未来数年图书馆所会遭遇到跨世纪的挑战加以讨论。

第四节 有效的图书馆管理

根据前面各章的讨论,有效的图书馆管理很明显包括了规划、组织、人力资源、作业和控制评估五个有贯联性的程序。在解释管理的定义时,本书的第一章曾经提出:有效的管理是凭借着规划、组织、领导和决策的作业,及控制评估的手段来分配及善用机构的人力、财力和物力,以达成一个机构的任务和使命。在20世纪90年代的今天,因为人类知识的大量增长和资讯技术的突飞猛进,有效的图书馆管理是要配合时代的发展和需要,透过对于人力、物力和财力的妥当分配和充分运用,经由上述五个管理程序,以发挥各个图书馆的功能。

管理学概念在中国的发展虽然比西方早了两千年,但是管理学成为一个学科来研究,还是近百年来在西方开始的。本书的第二章就20世纪西方管理学的发展加以介绍,其中简略地讨论了西方各学派理论的兴起和整合,从最早的科学管理学派和一般管理学派的理

---

① 电信局,《台湾信息通信网络建设计划》,《美中科学通讯》(*Midwest Science News*), Vol. 2, No. 4 (December 1994), pp. 26-27.

论到后来的行为学派和情境学派。近十几年来，因为日本的工业发达及产品的价廉物美，横扫国际市场，引起了西方管理学者对于日本式管理的好奇和探究[1][2][3]：像"质量圈"（Quality Circle）和"全质量管理"（Total Quality Management）等方法已被美国很多的企业和机构所采用。关于中国式的管理，国内很多管理学家也著书提倡，曾仕强教授所著《现代化的中国式管理》一书对于中国式管理的意义、目的、基础、精神、原则、方法、特色和境界提出了极为精辟的见解，是一本值得大家阅读的佳作[4]。因为管理离不开文化，而各国文化背景不同，所以有美国式管理、日本式管理和中国式管理的不同。曾教授中国式管理的要点是：

一、管理的意义是修己安人

"修己安人"来之于《论语》。修己的功夫包括了"格物、致知、诚意、正心及修身"。安人的行为包括了"齐家、治国、平天下"。管理的活动始于"修己"而终于"安人"。为了配合现代的需要，曾仕强主张在安人的行为中加入"立业"一项使成为"齐家、立业、治国、平天下"。孔子认为人性是纯的，无所谓善恶，像一张白纸一样可以由环境所塑造。这就是所谓"性相近，习相远也"。"修己以安人"是指管理者应该以身作则，树立良好的榜样，这样才能做到"其身正，不令而行；其身不正，虽令不从。"

二、管理的最终目的在安人

"修己"是"安人"的先决条件，但是如何把"安人"的工作做好才是管理的最终目的。"安"是人生的基本要求，马斯洛的五个需要层次中也列有"安全"的需要。孔子所指的"君子不忧不惧"就是让员工处于一个"无忧无惧"的环境中，能够身安心乐，而又安分乐业，要能做到如此，管理者必须采用以下几种方式：

（1）诚心待人。
（2）合理待遇。
（3）适当关怀。
（4）合适工作。
（5）安定保障。
（6）相互尊重。
（7）适时升迁。
（8）创业辅助。

三、管理的有效力量是感应

这是指采用中国传统道德哲学中的"仁"和"爱"来对待员工，以激发员工的善意感激。做到仁者无敌，相亲相爱，"己欲立而立人，己欲达而达人"的崇高理想。

---

[1] Richard Tanner Pascale, and Anthory G. Athos. *The Art of Japanese Management*: *Application for American Executives*. (New York: Simon & Shuster, 1981). p. 20.

[2] Peter F. Drucker. *Managing in the Non-Profit Organization*. (New York: Harper Business, 1990). pp. 127-128.

[3] William G. Ouchi. *Theory Z*: *How American Business Can Meet the Japanese Challenge*. (Reading, MA.: Addison-Wesley, 1981).

[4] 曾仕强：《现代化的中国管理》，经济日报丛书，台北：经济日报社1987年版，第202页。

四、管理的基本精神在中道

中国的儒家思想讲求中庸之道。中国式的管理实际上就是多元中道的管理，它重视管理的合理化，强调和谐共存，兼顾个人与团体利益的平衡，一切要做到"恰到好处"，避免"过犹不及"。西方管理常用"二分法"或对立冲突的眼光来考察事理现象，因此强调监督、制衡。中国管理的目的在安人，一切以和谐并行、协和一致及相辅相成为重。

五、管理的最佳原则是"情、理、法"

"情、理、法"在中国管理思想中有它的先后次序。"理"居于中有驾驭"情"与"法"的作用，使得管理"合理化"。所谓"有理走遍天下，无理寸步难行"和"变法三千，道理一个"就是这个意思。"法"是"制度化"的一个手段。因为法是人订的，可以依"理"来修改，使能因时制宜，以求"不固而中"。"情"是指发乎仁心而中节的情。以真挚、关怀和珍惜的爱心来对待部属和同事是一种"安人之道"，也是管理的"人性化"。因此"情、理、法"也就是管理的人性化、合理化和制度化。

六、管理的基本方法是"经权法"

经权法是常道与变通的法则。"经"指的是"经常不变的法则"，所谓"万变不离其宗"，或孔子所说"吾道一以贯之"就是这个意思。"权"是"通权达变"，是"经"在万殊之事中的运用，即所谓"一本万殊"、"变中有常"之意。一个机构要能"守经达变"才能历久而常新，配合时代的改变。经权法比西方的"权变理论"（The Contingency Theory）更为完备。

七、管理应该发挥象棋的十二特色

1. 天人合一

象棋中每一枚棋子都有其特定才能和意向，但是一盘棋的输赢仍然取决于下棋人的布局与棋力。"顺天应人"是管理的一个基本观念。

2. 确立制度

象棋有它完备的制度供下棋的人遵守，一个机构的管理也是一样。

3. 公平竞争

象棋的游戏应该是一种君子之争。正常的公平竞争是促成进步的良好动力。

4. 组织精简

象棋的组织十分精简，每一成员有其明确的职责。

5. 各施所长

象棋重视人尽其才，各施所长的原则。

6. 互依互赖

象棋中每一个成员除了可以单独作战以外还需要分工合作，发挥相互支持的作用。

7. 无为而治

象棋中的车、马、炮、士、相、兵等各有所为，唯有将、帅不仅无为而且需要其他成员的保护。这是"无为故能使众为"的一个管理特色。

8. 民主自治

象棋所表现的领导方式是十分符合民主原则的。每一枚棋子都不勉强其他棋子来顺从它；大家都遵守规则行动，而且各自负责，即使将、帅也是一样。

9. 竭尽全力

象棋中的每一枚棋在下棋者的指挥下能够竭尽心力，赴汤蹈火，义无反顾，努力达成各自的特殊任务。

10. 贯彻始终

在每次战役中，每枚棋子都会奋不顾身，努力以赴，不惜以身相殉，贯彻始终。

11. 千变万化

中国先哲自古即认为"变"是宇宙中不变的事实。孔子说："逝者如斯乎，不舍昼夜。"象棋棋子不多，规则简单，但是在下棋时，却可以千变万化，虚虚实实，使对手难于捉摸。

12. 和平融洽

象棋是君子之争，下棋的双方都希望获胜，但必须在和平融洽的气氛下进行，胜不骄败不馁，保持心平气和及虚怀若谷的良好棋品。

八、管理的最高境界在"无为而治"

无为而治是发挥"无所为而为"的精神以达到"知其不可而为"的境界。无为不是"一事不作"或"一事无成"，而是放手支持部属去做。部属的有为，正是主管的无为。无为而治的现代化功能是要使机构内的员工都能自发自动地发挥潜能，以达成工作的目标。

在他的书中，曾教授特别强调，"关于欧美的管理科学，我们要在自己的管理哲学思想系里来接受，来批判，积极吸取其精华，以期迎头赶上。"因此他建议在建立中国式管理时应该追求"固有传统"、"西洋精华"和"自我创造"的三结合①。表8-2是曾教授对中、日、美三国不同管理的特色加以比较。

本书的第三章到第七章分别讨论到管理的五个功能，规划功能的一章中包含了规划的定义和目的，规划的种类及步骤，目标管理，和策略性的规划。组织功能的一章中包含了组织的涵义，组织的基本原则，组织的环境，组织的设计和结构，和组织的发展。人力资源管理的一章中包含了人员的：甄选和任用、薪酬、福利和安全、员工的训练和发展、考绩和激发动机。作业功能的一章中包含了领导才能、决策、沟通和冲突的化解。控制与评估功能的一章中包含了控制的意义和重要性、财务的控制、作业的控制、建立管理资讯系统和管理效能的评估。

有效的图书馆管理应该要融会贯通以上各章所讨论过的要点，掺入中国式管理的特质，使能附和中国的文化背景和国情，达成维护固有传统，吸收西洋精华，和力求自我创造的中国式管理的模式。自我创造是一种"吸收后的超越能力"，能够自我创造，才能达到《大学》一书中所谓"苟日新，日日新，又日新"的境界。

---

① 曾仕强：《现代化的中国管理》，经济日报丛书，台北：经济日报社1987年版，第202页。

表8-2 比较中、日、美三国不同管理特点

综合气氛	综合特征	成员投入	成员特征	成员动态	评估标准	控制形态	领导形态	组织形态	计划形态	升迁要件	行为特征	理论基础	思想基础	
紧张忙碌地把工作做好	重绩效	部分投入	专业性	一生在不同机构从事同一工作	重结果不重过程	局部	指挥型	砖型	偏重打固定靶	能力本位	依据是非判断	个人主义	制衡思想	美
辛苦劳累地把工作做好	重利益	全部投入	一致性	一生在不同机构从事同一工作	结果重于过程	全面	协调型	石壁型	偏重打活动靶	年资序列	绝对服从上级	集团主义	大和思想	日
安心愉快地把工作做好	重安人	情境转移	交互性	一生在不同机构从事不同工作	过程重于结果	全面无形	无为型	树状	偏爱打飞靶	情境配合	合理追求圆满	交互主义	太极思想	中

第五节　跨世纪的挑战

在20世纪即将结束，而21世纪即将来临的今天，因为受了知识爆炸、资讯技术发展和资讯社会的需求种种影响，图书馆遭遇了空前未有的激荡和挑战。在采用第三章所提到的策略规划时，图书馆应审度当前的情况，检讨本身的优势和弱点，把跨世纪的挑战当作是一个良好的机会来看，建立有远见的眼光（Vision）和价值观（Value），为达成图书馆的时代使命，制定远、中、短程目和计划。

由于电子书刊和多媒体资料的发展，传统式以纸张、印刷品为主的图书馆虽然不会消声灭迹，但是必须作相应的改变，使得图书馆的收藏多样化。由于知识的爆炸及书刊资料的增价远超过图书购买的能力，馆际互借、电子传递及以分工合作方式来发展图书馆的馆藏亟待加强。过去以馆藏的多少来衡量图书馆的强弱的观念将会改为以图书馆能够获得读者所需要资讯的能力来衡量图书馆的好坏，这就是所谓以"获得率"（Access）来取代"拥有量"（Ownership）。当然"获得率"高的图书馆还应当保持某种水平的"拥有量"

才能满足馆际合作、资源共享的要求。

另外一个重大的挑战是书刊资料的数位化（Digitized）。由于计算机技术、密集储存技术和馆际联网的发展，越来越多的书刊资料将以数位的方式出现。从现在的国际通讯联网中 Internet 已经可以获得大量的数位资料。美国的国会图书馆在 1994 年 10 月正式宣布要带头发动一个国家数位化资讯图书馆（National Digital Library）的计划。在这个计划之下，国会图书馆将联合一些大型的研究图书馆以分工合作的方式把重要的藏书及其他媒体改变成数位化影像（Digitized Images），经过国际计算机资讯联网，以供全国各地的图书馆及一般人民使用。目前很多图书馆已表示要参加这个跨世纪的计划。在经费方面，很多大企业家及基金会已答应提供资助。这个计划的目的除了要以数位影像的方式来保存人类知识的资产，同时也在促成虚拟图书馆这个理想的早日实现。

当然，在推行将大量书刊资料转成数位影像以供读者使用的同时，有关知识产权的保护问题随着发生。对于以数位影像、电子出版及多媒体的专利权和翻印权究竟如何处理还有待政府的立法。除了知识产权之外，使用这些资料的费用如何决定？对于图书馆会发生何种影响等？是否会造成资讯使用者之间贫富差异的不公平现象？（Disparity Between the Information Rich and Information Poor）诸如此类的很多问题，也有待对于今后发展的观察和大家的探讨。

前面已经讨论过的虚拟图书馆将是 21 世纪图书馆的特色，它综合了纸张图书馆、自动化图书馆、网路化图书馆及电子化图书馆的优点，扩大了图书馆的资源，使得图书馆的服务能无远不及，超越了时空的限制，真正做到了馆际的资源共享，撤除了图书馆间人为的栅篱和障碍。

在推广虚拟图书馆这个概念时，传统图书馆的管理也遭遇到了严重的考验。为了迎合虚拟图书馆的发展，图书馆的组织必须打破金字塔式传统的架构而趋向扁平化，以任务编组取代阶层组织，用充分授权的方式来缩短决策的过程，给员工更多发挥集体智能的弹性空间，以促成图书馆内部的灵活、机动、民主和参与。图书馆的人力、财力和物力也应该按照策略性的规划，予以重新分配和组合，使得有限的资源能够获得最妥当及高效率地使用。对于人力资源的管理应该特别注重员工的素质，加强在职训练及继续教育，培养员工的领导才能和应变能力，并善用激励和沟通的方法来提高士气，发挥团队精神，提高工作效率。随时注意情境变素的影响，调整图书馆运作，加强图书馆的馆际合作，改进图书馆与其他相关机构的配合，以评估的方式来保持高质量的服务，以满足读者的需求和服务社会的宗旨。

总之，21 世纪的图书馆是多姿多彩的、充满生机及创造性的图书馆。我们必须以崭新的眼光和做法，利用各种新兴的资讯技术、媒体和服务方式去塑造一个合乎时代需要，而且具备各种功能的新型图书馆。

（该书由台北市三民书局于 1996 年出版）

3. 20世纪90年代图书馆募款所面对的挑战
实用指南：从新手到专家
Fundraising for the 1990s: The Challenge Ahead A Practical Guide for Library Fundraising: From Novice to Expert.[①]

前 言
Foreword

Fundraising for the 1990s: The Challenge Ahead is an important addition to the collection of any fundraising practitioner. While it has been written especially for the librarian or for the Library Development Office whose responsibility is to seek funds for this very special and difficult professional field of work, its constituency is much broader.

Rather than being written by fundraising consultants or philanthropic theoreticians, Drs. Lee and Hunt have spent years in the "front lines" learning the science as well as the art of fundraising. *Fundraising for the 1990s* provides the eager-to-learn novice with an excellent blueprint with which to build a campaign. However, it is a comprehensive refresher "how to" manual reminding the experienced development officer of the solid concepts which must be employed if private or government funds are to be successfully sought. Every well executed annual fund drive or capital campaign is underpinned by the tenets described within this text.

To the novice I say: "Welcome aboard to an increasingly important and competitive career choice. It is one which you will find rewarding, satisfying and most fulfilling. This book, along with hard work, dedication and a strong personal faith in the mission of your library will provide you with a road map to successful fundraising."

To the seasoned professional, *Fundraising for the 1990s* will reinforce all the correct strategies, decisions and plans you have made throughout your career. It is the adherence to these proven truths which have set you apart from those who never achieved the level of your success, and never knew why.

Jack Ellis
Vice President for Development
Ohio University

---

① Co-author: Gary A. Hunt. Published by Genaway & Associates, Inc. 1992.

第一章 绪 论

Chapter 1 Introduction

Fundraising is a common activity in America for not-for-profit organizations and for charitable purposes. In fact, generous donations and gifts for good causes have long been encouraged by our society. It shows the generosity and philanthropy of the American people.

The earliest recorded fundraising activity in this country can be traced to 1641, when the Massachusetts Bay Colony sent three clergymen to England to seek an endowment for Harvard College.[1] Even though one of the clergymen involved wound up on the scaffold in England, another returned with £ 500. A little more than one hundred years later, in 1751, Benjamin Franklin raised £ 2,000 to establish a hospital for "poor sick persons" in Philadelphia. The various techniques he employed at that time were similar to those used today. Franklin even appealed to the Pennsylvania Assembly to match his £ 2,000 and got it. This successful effort is regarded as the first known challenge grant[2].

Since 1950, more and more fundraising campaigns have been launched, many with very ambitious goals. The Museum of Modern Art in New York began a capital campaign in the late 1970s with a goal of $20 million and had raised $117 million eight years later. In 1986, Princeton University completed a $410.5 million capital campaign. In February 1992, Stanford University closed its $1.1 billion campaign with $1.3 billion in pledges and gifts. Columbia, Cornell, Harvard, New York, Notre Dame, Pennsylvania, and Yale Universities (to name just a few) all got into the act for big money. The largest known campaign goal is the five-year, $1.5 billion goal announced by Yale in May 1992[3]. Currently the New York Public Library is in the middle of a $200 million campaign, the largest on record for a library.

Confronted with static or constricted public funding, fundraising programs and activities have become increasingly important for a variety of organizations—intensifying competition for a share of available funds and making the process more complex. An increasing number of libraries are adding to this congestion. Both on-going annual fundraising activities and major capital campaigns are becoming an integral part of library programs. Larger libraries have established development offices and hired professional fundraisers to carry out the development tasks. Some college and university libraries rely on the assistance and support of institution-wide development offices.

Fundraising can be defined as programs and activities planned and undertaken to raise funds for a stated purpose. There are two broad types of fundraising: **annual giving** and **capital campaigns**. Annual giving is a regular, on-going activity. Capital campaigns are major one-time (although possibly successive) efforts to raise large amounts of money for a special purpose (or purposes) over a specified period of time. Table 1 – 1 identifies some of the major differences between the two types of fundraising.

As a result of the expanding role of fundraising activities, a body of knowledge, techniques, methods, and approaches has been developed, refined, and perfected over the years. Many successful fundraisers have become professional "development" experts. Although there is still no formal academic degree program for the education and training of professional fundraisers, many seasoned professionals have found majors and courses in public relations, marketing, journalism, advertising, communication, business or even psychology, sociology, creative writing, law, and

---

[1] Scott M. Cutlip. *Fund raising in the United States: its role in America's philanthropy*. (New Brunswick, NJ: Rutgers University Press, 1965.) p. 34.

[2] Maurice Gurin. "The changing capital campaign." *Fund Raising Management*, v. 18 No. 4 (June 1987), p. 29.

[3] Julie L. Nicklin. "Yale opens a campaign for $1.5-billion, largest drive in U. S. higher education." *The Chronicle of Higher Education*, 13 May 1992, p. A32.

others to be useful preparation. Many professional associations have been formed, and the number of professional publications has grown in recent years. (For a list of such associations, see Appendix I. For a list of professional journals, see the section on "Sources and Suggested Reading" at the end of this book.) The demand for development consultants has prompted the growth of an increasing number of consulting firms on fundraising.

It is a fact of life, however, that—despite the growing number of professional fundraisers and development officers—a large number of people are drafted into the fundraising arena, largely of necessity and without adequate preparation. These include library deans/directors, library trustees/board directors, senior library administrators, public relation staff, and volunteers who find themselves facing the challenge to raise funds. Like it or not, they must roll up their sleeves and prepare to enter the arena.

Table 1 – 1 Differences Between Annual And Capital Fundraising①

Annual	Capital
* Ongoing	* Intensive
* Continuous in an annual cycle	* With a set time period (normally 1 to 5 years)
* Smaller dollar goal	
* Relatively low-key	* Large dollar goal
* Small number of staff	* High profile
* Fewer volunteers	* Larger number of staff
* Programs with limited scope, such as:	* Many volunteers
	* Expanded programs with a complex organization (often including out side consultants), for example:
— mailings	
— major gifts	
— phonations	— annual giving programs
— planned giving	— campaign publicity
— special events	— campaign relations
	— computer operations and systems development
	— corporate and foundation relations
	— major gifts and constituent programs
	— phonation
	— planned giving
	— proposal writing
	— prospect management and special projects
	— prospect research
	— stewardship and donor relations

This practical guide is not written for seasoned fundraisers or development professionals, but for novices who need a "how to" or "do-it-yourself" type of approach. Unlike most published guides on fundraising, which were written by development professionals, this is written by librarians and intended for librarians, library trustees, and volunteers.

Both co-authors were first exposed to fundraising almost a decade ago. Ohio University launched its first, modest major capital campaign between 1977 and 1979 to raise $14 million. As the first University in the Old Northwest Territory, the institution planned its campaign to coincide with the 175th anniversary of its founding in 1804. Under the able leadership of President

---

① Adapted from Jean A. Crawford and Judith A. Potts. "How to survive a capital campaign. *Fund Raising Management*, v. 17, No. 5 (July 1986), p. 40.

Charles J. Ping and Vice President for Development, Mr. Jack Ellis, "1804 Fund Campaign" goal was surpassed and nearly $23 million was raised.

Of this amount, some $400,000 was raised for the Library to establish the 1804 Special Library Endowment. The annual income from this endowment, a guaranteed six percent of the endowment's market value (under the University's "spending policy"), has enabled the Library to purchase major collections of scholarly and research value which are too expensive for regular subject allocations in the annual acquisitions budget. With a sound investment plan, the market value of the endowment in July 1991 reached $600,000. Since its inception, the endowment has made possible several major purchases, including the extensive research files, manuscripts, and collections of the famed journalist and writer, Cornelius Ryan; the large collection of the British scholar and book collector, Edmund Blunden; a special music score collection; a number of major microform sets, and others.

Following that campaign, the Library applied for and was awarded its first Challenge Grant of $150,000 in 1980 from the National Endowment for the Humanities to strengthen library collections in the humanities. With the help of the University's Development Office, the Library raised the $450,000 matching requirement in only three years, one less than the four years allowed. Eventually, some $683,000 in private contributions were raised in response to the Challenge. Encouraged by the results of this first Challenge Grant, the Library applied successfully in 1988 for a second Challenge Grant from the National Endowment for the Humanities. This time the grant was for $750,000, and the matching requirement was $3 million. The fundraising effort was timed to coincide with a second major capital campaign by the University. Included within the $100 million institution-wide goal for "The Third Century Campaign" was a $6 million goal for the Library—twice the NEH Challenge Grant matching requirement.

From the experiences we have gained writing two successful grant proposals for the National Endowment for the Humanities Challenge Grant program, raising required matching dollars, and conducting a $6 million major capital campaign, we have advanced from the stage of "fledgling neophyte", but are still some distance from being "expert". By working closely with the Development Office of Ohio University, we have gained much valuable knowledge about the theory and practice of fundraising and development work. Through this practical guide, we hope to share our experiences with those in the fundraising arena, whether they are novices or further along the path to becoming experts.

This practical guide contains eight chapters. Following the introduction, Chapter 2 describes the planning process for successful fundraising. Chapters 3 and 4 discuss the potential sources of financial support available in the public and private sectors, respectively. Chapter 5 covers the programs and activities for successful fundraising. Chapter 6 provides two case studies: one based on annual giving and the other on a major capital campaign. Chapter 7 covers the important but sometimes overlooked subject of donor stewardship. The final chapter, chapter 8, is a conclusion.

We recognize that libraries come in various types and sizes with a multitude of structures; therefore, a general guide for fundraising may not whet everyone's appetite or meet the widest range of needs. Although the co-authors have gained their experience in a public-university-library setting, we have tried to include those techniques, methods, and approaches which have general applicability or which are more easily transferable from one type of library to another.

Even though there are a large number of philanthropic foundations, corporations, and donors who are willing and capable of giving, they must be carefully approached and solicited before gifts are made. The 1990 national philanthropic statistics showed that Americans gave more money to fundraising requests than they spent on gas and oil. More than $122.5 billion was given to philanthropy, while $93.8 billion was spent on fuel!

Because more and more nonprofit organizations, including libraries, are engaged in fundraising, most of the better known funding sources are flooded by calls, letters, visits, and requests. It is no longer adequate in fundraising to merely demonstrate one's needs. Instead, one must first convince the prospective donors of the organization's value and worth and then detail the beneficial results the gift would have to the larger society. It is of utmost importance, therefore, for every organization that is considering fundraising to examine its own credibility and worth. Successful fundraising is often built on the positive image, reputation, trust, and social value of an organization.

Even though grants by foundations, corporations, and organizations both in terms of number and dollar amount awarded, have been significant, the importance of individual donors should never be overlooked. Generous gifts by individual donors often make up the major portion of any capital campaign. Based on the experience of the Ohio University Third Century Campaign thus far, about 65 percent of all giving is from individual donors while foundations, corporations, government and organizations make up the remaining 35 percent. ①

In a typical major fundraising campaign, so-called "megagifts" are viewed as far more significant than small gifts. Most fundraising literature emphasizes the "Rule of Thirds," that about one-third of the funds will come from the top ten to fifteen gifts; one third will come from the next 100 to 125 gifts; and the remaining one-third will come from all other gifts. ② Another rule-of-thumb is the commonly observed lopsided ratio in fundraising that 80 percent of the revenue from fundraising comes from 20 percent of the donors. ③ For a successful fundraising campaign, it is clear that participation by a few of these "heavyweights" or "pacesetters" is crucial. These individuals should be identified and, preferably, interviewed and enlisted before setting goals.

Another important factor is the cost of any fundraising program. It is a truism in the development world that "it costs money to raise money." One expert reports that many established educational institutions surveyed consider 12 percent of the dollar amount raised to be a reasonable cost figure. ④ He identifies the costs by types of funds sought as follows (by program and range of costs for each dollar raised):

● Annual funds programs, 11 – 37 cents.
● Major gifts, 5 – 11 cents.
● Corporate gifts, 3 – 11 cents.
● Deferred gifts, 0.6 – 3 cents.
● Foundation gifts, 0.5 – 2 cents. ⑤

From the above, annual giving programs are clearly the most expensive to conduct while foundation gifts cost the least to raise. For capital campaigns, he projects the costs at 4 to 7 percent during the program's life span, recognizing that start-up costs are high and that costs should decline each year once a campaign is well underway. ⑥

Besides the up-front investment of funds there is also a need for commitment and teamwork by the governing body, parent organization, senior administrators, staff, and volunteers in a major capital campaign. Fundraising is necessarily time-consuming. It will take up a good portion of the time and energy of those involved. Teamwork can maximize the coordinated efforts and achieve greater efficiency in the deployment of available resources. There is a high correlation between the degree of institutional commitment and overall success.

Now, if after reading all this you are still interested in fundraising and want to give it a try, please read the chapters in the rest of this guide and get into the action. We wish you good luck, success, and, above all, fun! The challenge of fundraising is real, but the rewards may be very much worth the effort.

---

① Campaign tops $87 million mark. "*News From the Ohio University Third Century Campaign*: *More Than a Margin*, v. 2, No. 1 (April 1992), p. 1.

② Jerold Panas. *Mega gifts*: *who gives them, who gets them*. (Chicago: Pluribus Press, 1984) p. 173.

③ Don Ryan and Richard Murdock. "Identifying and nurturing core donors." *Fund Raising Management*, v. 16, No. 12 (February 1986), p. 21.

④ Thomas E. Broce. *Fund raising*; *the guide to raising money from private sources*. (Norman, OK: University of Oklahoma Press, 1979) p. 188.

⑤ Ibid.

⑥ Ibid., p. 189. Also in Harvey J. Jacobson. "15 ways to measure fund raising program effectiveness". *Fund Raising Management*, v. 13, No. 10 (Dec. 1982), p. 25.

第二章 募款规划

Chapter 2 Planning for Fundraising

I. Are You Ready for the Challenge?

A library considering starting a capital campaign from scratch would be well-advised to begin by developing an effective annual giving program. But even before taking this step, one must begin with careful and detailed planning. In his program on "Going After Capital Funds: The Process, The Players and Their Roles" for the Fund Raising and Financial Development Section of the ALA Library Administration and Management Association several years ago, Dwight Burlingame posed seven critical questions for self-examination by libraries before launching into any kind of fundraising activity:

Seven Questions

1. Does your library enjoy a strong institutional image with a plan for the future? People only give to strong causes.

2. Giving is a habit. Do you have a stable giving program with the support of a few large donors and good volunteers?

3. Do you have a strong research/records department and, related to that;

4. Have you researched the top one-fifth of your prospects? They will account for as much as 80 percent of the campaign goal amount. Prospects can be drawn from four groups:
- Past and current donors;
- users of the library;
- past and present members of your organizational "family", i.e. Board, Friends and staff;
- the philanthropic community.

5. Do you have staff and money committed to the campaign?

6. Have you involved your board? Is leadership available? Strong and determined leadership will inspire others to commit to a cause.

7. Are you convinced you have a case and are you prepared to develop a case statement? The case statement is the single most important document of the campaign. It details the need, goals, plans, personnel, and all other elements a donor needs to be aware of before making a commitment to the cause.

Burlingame cautioned that if your library cannot answer a resounding "yes" to each of these seven questions, you should not proceed until you can.

To plan for an annual giving program, each library needs to consider the questions candidly and seriously. While a "yes" may not be possible at the beginning, it should be planned that—by implementing an annual giving program-a library will be able to answer "yes." Undertaking an annual giving program is, therefore, a useful way to prepare for a major capital campaign later.

In developing a case statement, a library must realistically assess its needs against regular sources of funding, take a hard look at the climate, readiness and potential donors for fundraising, and, by weighing all these factors, set the goal for either an annual giving program or a capital campaign.

II. Where is Your Team?

Fundraising is time consuming and requires a concerted team effort. Besides the library director, who must be prepared to commit between ten and twenty percent of her/his time, another senior library staff member should be assigned the responsibility to plan, coordinate, and implement the fundraising program. This individual, reporting directly to the library director, may be someone holding a staff position such as "Assistant to the Director" or a "Deputy Director". In a large library, there may be a full-time position for a "Development Officer" with the title of "Director for Development" or something similar. For a large public library, there may be a "Public Relations" position which is assigned some fundraising responsibilities or a "Director of Development" position dedicated to fundraising exclusively. In a college or university, there may already be an institution-wide "Development Office" headed by a "Vice President for Development" or a "Director". The office may have several development staff, with one of them assigned to take charge of library fundraising activities either on a full-or part-time basis. In the latter case, the library director or his designate should work closely with the development staff in all fundraising activities.

The Development Office

Using Ohio University as an example, a strong Development Office, headed by a Vice President for Development, has been in place for several decades. The office was much expanded three years ago to prepare for the undertaking of the major capital campaign— "The Third Century Campaign" — with a goal of $100 million. As a result, the university library was given the opportunity to share a full-time professional development officer with two colleges (the College of Fine Arts and the College of Health and Human Services). In addition to one-third time of this "Assistant Dean for Development," both the Dean of Libraries and the Associate Dean of Libraries for Subject and Special Collection spend approximately one-fifth of their time on the capital campaign—trying to raise $6 million for the library. Another senior staff, the Head of the Archives and Special Collection, serves as the Executive Secretary of the Friends of Ohio University Libraries. Among the members of the library management team, several have outstanding skills in grantsmanship and proposal writing. In addition to two successful Challenge Grants and one major program grant from the National Endowment for the Humanities, within the last decade the library has also been awarded six large grants from the Department of Education under the Title II-C, Strengthening Research Library Resources, of the Higher Education Act. These individuals, especially the Assistant to the Dean, have been responsible for the drafting of many proposals. The total time and effort committed by the library staff is therefore very substantial.

Even though the library would have liked to have a full-time development staff, the budget and cost-benefit considerations of both the Development Office and the three University units ruled out this possibility. It is felt, however, that a minimum of a half-time person is necessary for each unit during a major campaign period. In the cost sharing of the Assistant Dean for Development position, the Development Office is responsible for 62% of the salary and fringe benefits, while the two colleges and the library each share one-third of the remaining 38% of the salary and fringe benefits. The three units also divide the full cost of travel and office supplies. Furthermore, the library makes available one-fourth of a secretary's time to the work of the Assistant Dean.

Administratively, the Assistant Dean for Development reports directly to the Director of Major Gifts Program in the Development Office and has his office there. He meets at least once a week with each of the three deans and is invited to attend any meetings of the deans' executive committees. In Appendix I we have included the job description of the shared Assistant Dean for Development.

There are many benefits to be gained from working closely with a well established Development Office, such as that at Ohio University.
   1. The library has received much useful advice on the basics from the fundraising professionals.
   2. The library has received various support services from the Development Office:
   A. Overall planning in relation to the Third Century Campaign.
   B. Publication of the Library's case statement.
   C. Research on potential donors.
   D. Database for various categories of potential donors.
   E. Annual giving programs.
   F. Corporate and foundation relations.
   G. Review of proposals written by library staff.
   H. Statistical reports.

3. Referral of unassigned donors and gifts to the library.

One important component in the make up of the fundraising team is the "volunteers". No fundraising program can be successful without the effective support of many individual volunteers. Three groups of volunteers must be recruited for any fundraising program. These are:

1. Individuals who are highly respected and highly placed leaders of the community, of various professions, or in the nation.

These volunteers may not have time to actually participate in committee work or in solicitation on the library's behalf, but should be willing to let the library use their names and connections to induce others to make gifts to the library. At appropriate occasions, they may help to make key personal contacts for major gifts. Often they will set an example by their own significant gifts appropriate to their financial situations.

2. Well-known and willing individuals who have a strong feeling for the library and are able to act in a leadership role in the library's fundraising program and to serve on committees. They may also set an example by making major gifts to the library.

3. Other individuals who are supporters of the library and are willing to volunteer their time and energy for the library's fundraising program.

In colleges and universities, many outstanding volunteers can be recruited from the faculty and alumni with a history of strong support for the library. In public libraries, excellent volunteers are often found among community leaders, past and current board members, and frequent library users. A good fundraising team is therefore made up of library staff, development officers, and volunteer leaders, all marching in unison with a common belief, a strong commitment and a contagious enthusiasm to raise funds for a noble cause.

III. Can You Count on Your Friends of the Library Group?

An important channel for recruiting volunteers is a Friends of the Library group. Increasingly, such groups have been founded in libraries, regardless of type and size, throughout the country. Although fundraising may not be the sole purpose or priority of the "friends," it is the place where some of the best volunteers can be identified and recruited.

In writing for the inaugural issue of the newsletter of the Friends of the Library of Ohio University, a founding member of the organization described his vision of a "friend of libraries" as "anyone who delights in reading; anyone who believes in the importance of books, recorded information, ideas, knowledge; anyone who perceives the value for human culture of a sense of historical time, a connected understanding of the past, a broad sense of the present, a factually anchored perception of the future—any or all of these—is a potential friend of libraries." ①

In the same article, he offered several reasons for having a library friends group. "The major purpose of the Friends of the Library of Ohio University is to aid the library to reach its full potential. Basically, the Friends aim to promote understanding of the library—its importance as an educational, cultural, and research center; its aims; its resources; its services; its strengths; its weaknesses; its problems; its needs. Second, through better understanding, the Friends intend to foster a favorable climate for improving public, private, and institutional support of the library. Third, the Friends hope to stimulate and encourage gifts to the library, either needed books and manuscripts or funds for their purchase." ②

What a Friends Group Can Do

To assist in fundraising, a friends group can be very helpful through its programs and activities. Among the things that friends can do in fundraising are:
- Recruiting volunteers within and beyond the membership;
- promoting the library within the community;

---

① Frank B. Fieler. "Friends." *Gatherings for the Friends of Ohio University Library*, No. 1 (August 1979), p. 3
② Ibid.

● sponsoring fundraising events such as book sales, receptions, special banquets, etc.;
● encouraging members and others to donate significant collections to the library;
● making annual gifts to the library for selected collection areas and/or services;
● establishing memorial collections or endowments.

Perhaps the most successful friends group in the country is the Brandeis University National Women's Committee. Since its inception in 1948, the Women's Committee has raised over $42 million for the Brandeis University Library. In Chapter 6, a case study written by Bessie Hahn, Director of Library Services at Brandeis University, provides detailed information on the outstanding work of this very active and highly visible friends group. For an example of the Bylaws of a Friends organization, see Appendix II at the end of this book.

IV. How Necessary Is a Feasibility Study?

A critical step in planning for fundraising is a feasibility study. Generally speaking, such a study has two dimensions. The first is an **internal evaluation**, called in some fundraising literature an "Internal Program Audit". The second is an **external evaluation**, referred to as a "Market Survey".

An internal program audit, according to one authority, is a formal, comprehensive evaluation of an institution's development program and its relationship to the people in the institutional areas that it touches. [1] The same authority sees a market survey as a test of an institution's philanthropic potential. [2] The survey is often done by carefully executed interviews of a broad range of individuals representing major constituencies.

Internal Program Audit

To begin the feasibility study, a library should first establish an internal committee or task force. Depending on the type of library, the membership of the committee should include most of the following: library director, the chair of the board or library committee, the chief development officer, the public relations officer, the coordinator of fundraising, a library trustee or college/university trustee, community leaders, prospective donors, and volunteers. If an outside consultant is to be used, the consultant should be selected by the committee and should work closely with the committee.

For undertaking the internal program audit, the committee or the consultant should gather all relevant information and data, then study and analyze it in order to assess a library's fundraising program and preparedness.

For a thorough and comprehensive audit of the fundraising structure and capability, a careful examination of the following is recommended: [3]

1. Articulation of the case for support.
2. Assessment of fundraising progress over the last five years.
3. Review of current operating goals and priorities for development, including current and past years' activities, current staffing structures and personnel, and the breadth of institutional resources.
4. Examination of the annual giving participation level in terms of both percentage and overall dollars.
5. Review of the current relationships within the organizational structure between other components of the advancement effort, if any, and the development program. [4]
6. Review of the depth and breadth of local, community, and state corporate and foundation support, solicitation progress in those areas, and utilization of board relationships and volunteer-

---

[1] Dove, *op. cit.*, p. 25
[2] *Ibid.*, p. 18
[3] John Grenzebach and Associates, Inc. "Description of the development program audit provided by John Grenzebach and Associates, Inc." [Corporate report] (Chicago: 1986). pp 1 – 4
[4] It is noted that in several instances the word "advancement" is used interchangeably with the word "development" to describe fundraising activities. The term "development", however, is common in most fundraising literature.

based activities with these corporations and foundations.

7. Examination of the specific corporate and foundation relations programs: identification, analysis, research, cultivation, and solicitation of gift prospects; management and tracking mechanisms employed with these programs.

8. Identification of the strengths and weaknesses of board members and other top leadership.

9. Examination of institutional support groups, if any: the strength of various fundraising boards, the quality of the program (s), their relationship (s) to the institution.

10. Review of the current levels of involvement of the chief executive officer, the board, and other high-level institutional officers in advancement activities—in particular, their current level and expertise in solicitation activities.

11. Review of the involvement and understanding of institutional administrators with regard to the development program and public relations, the needs determination process, and a designation of special gift opportunities and major gifts-targeted solicitation.

12. Examination of the formal relationship and level of cooperation of the development program with other components of the institution.

13. Review of research, records, and system support functions.

14. Review of the quality of proposal preparation and internal proposal review.

15. Review of the planned giving program and how it is incorporated into the development program—number of mailings, request procedures, record keeping, planned gift proposals presented to gift prospects.

16. Examination of the donor relations program-acknowledgment strategies, cultivation events, gift clubs, and donor recognition activities.

17. Review and/or structuring of a detailed annual operating plan for development, which specifies monthly, quarterly, and annual goals together with reporting mechanisms and review methods.

18. Other special aspects of the institution that require review or examination.

Because of the complexity and extensive involvement of the internal program audit, especially if a library or an institution is to undertake a major capital campaign, it is recommended that an experienced outside consultant be engaged to conduct the audit.① Depending on the size of the institution and the scope of the campaign, more than one consultant may be needed. The use of outside evaluators is often favored as they can provide objective assessment and impartial recommendations. Many of these consultants also have broader expertise and experience to contribute and share.

Based on the audit, the consultant (s) should prepare a written report with findings and recommendations. An exit meeting of the consultant (s) and the governing board, the library director, and members of the feasibility study committee should be held to allow for an oral presentation of the report for discussion.

The Market Survey

In the conducting of a market survey, the following are suggested as part of the process to be employed by an outside consultant.②

1. Develop the design of the survey.
2. Assemble and evaluate the list of prospects to be interviewed.
3. Draft and review the interview contact letter and needs statement.
4. Develop interview strategies.
5. Draft the interview questionnaire.
6. Assemble and mail any ancillary marketing materials that may be required.
7. Establish the interview schedule and execute it.
8. Correlate and analyze the information obtained.
9. Prepare the survey report and recommendations based on the findings.

---

① Dove, *op. cit.*, p. 28.
② *Ibid.*, p. 20 and Grenzebach, *op. cit.*, pp. 3 – 4.

10. Present both a written and an oral survey report.

Even though the main purpose of a market survey is to obtain an accurate assessment of the feasibility and possible goal of a fundraising program, there are other benefits that can be realized through a well-conducted survey:

1. It helps to inform the potential donors about the true values and pressing needs of the library.

2. It is a good way to uncover new leaders and supporters.

3. The findings can provide useful feedback about the perceptions of the library among community leaders and others important to the library.

For best results, the selection of individuals to be interviewed is crucial. They should include a cross section of board members, faculty, staff, alumni, friends, community leaders, and other constituents who may be potential donors or who may influence others to work and give. Preferably, all of these individuals should have some degree connection to or familiarity with the library. Normally, interviews of between 50 and 70 well-chosen individuals will provide fairly accurate information. To complete this number of interviews, the list of selected names should probably be twice that number. Before the interview, each person should receive an initial contact letter and brief case statement describing the programs and funding needs of the library. This is followed up by a telephone call to schedule the survey interview. A confidential interview is then conducted by the consultant or by the development staff. Besides the face-to-face interviews, other forms of survey, such as telephone interviews, focus groups, and direct-mail questionnaires can be used as supplements.

Written Report

The findings of the market survey should be communicated in a written report which should cover the following points. [1]

1. Suggested goal for the campaign, if such a campaign is feasible.

2. The anticipated strengths and weaknesses of the campaign identified by the survey.

3. A recommended strategic plan for the campaign.

4. The potential leadership available as compared to the leadership required to make the campaign successful.

5. A list of major donor prospects.

6. A recommendation on services needed to establish and carry forward the campaign and a proposed campaign structure.

7. If it is not feasible to conduct a campaign, recommendations for upgrading the institution's development performance and potential so that it will become feasible.

8. A draft letter expressing appreciation to those who have been interviewed.

9. Significant development information obtained through the survey interviews but not necessarily pertinent to the campaign's feasibility.

The combination of findings from the internal and external evaluations will provide an accurate and perceptive assessment of the library's financial needs and potential for fundraising. If the recommendation is positive, the findings will also lay the ground work for action with a maximum possibility for success.

To help set the goal for a capital campaign more precisely, the consultant should work out a gift table. As shown in Table 2-1 (the gift table of Ohio University's $100 million campaign), a gift table is a projection of the amount of funds that can be raised based on the number of gifts in different categories and levels. For example: in the **Leadership** category, Ohio University expects to raise one $10,000,000 gift, two $5,000,000 gifts, four $2,500,000 gifts, eight $1,000,000 gifts, and twenty $500,000 gifts, for a total of $48,000,000; in the **Major** category, the University anticipates raising forty $250,000 gifts and seventy-five $100,000 gifts, for a total of $17,000,000; in the **Special** category, two hundred $50,000 gifts and 550 $10,000 gifts, for a total of $15,500,000; and all others under $10,000 for a total of

---

[1] *Ibid.*, pp. 4-5.

$19,000,000. The grand total is $100,000,000. These figures were not simply made up by someone. They are based on the best analysis of all relevant data collected during the feasibility study.

As the percentage of each category indicates, leadership gifts make up 48% of the total goal and major gifts constitute 17% of the total goal. The two will account for 65% of the $100 million. This combined percentage is necessary to project the campaign's success.

Table 2-1 Example of a Gift Table

THE OHIO UNIVERSITY
THIRD CENTUBY CAMPAIGN
GIFT TABLE
$100 MILLOON GOAL
(Pro Forma Table of Required Campaign Gifts for
Comprehensive University Campaign)

	Number of Gifts	Gift Level	Total $ Required	Cumulative Total	
Leadership Gifts	1	$10,000,000	$10,000,000	$10,000,000	
	2	5,000,000	10,000,000	20,000,000	
	4	2,500,000	10,000,000	30,000,000	
	8	1,000,000	8,000,000	38,000,000	
	20	500,000	10,000,000	48,000,000	48%
Major Gifts	40	$250,000	$10,000,000	$58,000,000	
	75	100,000	7,500,000	65,500,000	65%
Special Gifts	200	$50,000	$10,000,000	$75,500,000	
	550	10,000	5,500,000	81,000,000	81%
General Gifts, Annual Support and All Other Gifts	all others (100,000+)	up to $10,000	$19,000,000	$100,000,000	100%

Table 2-2 Example of a Monthly Gift Report

THE OHIO UNIVERSITY THIRD CENTURY CAMPAIGN GIFT REPORT
June 30, 1992
Donor commitments By Level
(Gift Table)

	Required Level	Number	Total	Actual Campaign Number	Actual Campaign Total	Monthly Number	Changes Total
Leadership	$10,000,000+	1	$10,000,000	1	$10,000,000		
	5,000,000+	2	10,000,000	1	7,000,000		
	2,500,000+	4	10,000,000				
	1,000,000+	8	8,000,000	14	17,363,115	1	$850,000
	500,000+	20	10,000,000	15	9,195,221		
			48,000,000		43,558,336	1	850,000
Major	250,000+	40	10,000,000	30	9,786,032	2	720,033
	100,000+	75	7,500,000	61	8,466,253	2	238,403
			17,500,000		18,252,285	4	958,436
Special	50,000+	200	10,000,000	86	5,474,190	5	334,535
	10,000+	550	5,500,000	515	10,145,255	33	519,012
			15,500,000		15,619,445	38	853,547
Other Campaign and University Gifts	Up to 10,000	all others	19,000,000	124,809	16,140,031	2,897	310,550
Total			$100,000,000	125,532	$93,570,097	2,940	$2,972,533

Table 2-3 Example of a Quarterly Graphic Chart

The Ohio University
THIRD CENTURY CAMPAIGN

5-year Graph Illustrating Progress
Toward Goal Attainment by Quarter
June 30, 1992

[Graph showing $ Commitments (millions) over quarters 1-21 from 1988 to 1993, with data points:
$12,736,174 (10-1-88)
$16,829,315 (12-31-88)
$24,162,213 (3-31-89)
$31,280,479 (7-31-89)
$38,258,442 (9-30-89)
$41,808,228 (12-31-89)
$44,609,218 (3-31-90)
$52,070,140 (6-30-90)
$55,722,688 (9-30-90)
$68,000,000 Kickoff (10-5-90)
$71,145,935 (12-31-90)
$72,714,837 (3-31-91)
$76,663,976 (6-30-91)
$80,570,039 (9-30-91)
$81,146,281 (10-31-91)
$85,520,551 (12-31-90)
$86,575,607 (1-31-92)
$93,570,097 (6-30-92)]

Once a campaign is started, the Gift Table can be extended to become a monthly Gift Report. Table 2-2 shows the June 30, 1992 Gift Report of Ohio University's Third Century Campaign entering its 46th month. On a quarterly basis, the amount of gifts can be graphically charted to show the progress of the campaign. Table 2-3 is an example of a chart to show campaign progress.

A good feasibility study can prevent one from entering a campaign with an impossible goal, the wrong leadership, or a case one cannot sell. [1]

Because a complete and detailed feasibility study is involved, time consuming, and consequently expensive, a scaled down version is often employed for less ambitious fundraising campaigns. For libraries with a good ongoing program of annual and planned giving and a well established development office, a feasibility study may not be necessary. A large amount of information that a feasibility study would gather may already be known. The decision whether or not to conduct a "textbook" type feasibility study has to be made by the individual library or institution based on its own particular situation.

V. What Constitutes a Good Case Statement?

In the previous sections, frequent reference was made to a "case statement" because a case statement plays a key role in fundraising, especially in a capital campaign. The development of a case statement should begin early in the planning phase of a fundraising program. Either a fairly

---

[1] Bronson C. Davis. "The possible dream: base your campaign formula on a feasibility study". *Currents*, v. 12, No. 10 (Nov/Dec 1986), pp. 20-26.

late draft or a completed case statement should be ready by the time a feasibility study is to be conducted. But what is a case statement, anyway? What purpose does it serve? How is it written? Who is responsible for writing it? How does it differ from other fundraising literature? And how should it be used?

Purpose of the Case Statement

In general, a case statement can be defined as a basic articulation of the purpose, needs, goals, and benefits of an intended fundraising program. Often it includes a general description and a brief history of the library (or the institution of which the library is a part). It is designed to show that a particular library has a compelling case, not merely needs, for fundraising and support. Some of the common elements of a good case statement should include:

1. A mission statement.
2. A message or messages of endorsement and commitment from the top leadership (university/college president, chair of the library board, community leaders, etc.).
3. A brief history and major accomplishments.
4. The significance of current and new program initiatives.
5. The vision for program excellency.
6. Plans for the implementation.
7. Additional funding needed to achieve program excellence.
8. Distinctive value and benefits of these programs.
9. Cause and reasons for giving. and,
10. Key leaders in the fundraising campaign.

Mary Helene Pendel believes that a case statement must:

1. Serve to justify and explain the institution, its program and needs, so as to lead to advocacy and actual support.
2. Attempt to win the reader with the vision of the leadership of the institution and reassure the reader of the wisdom and responsible nature of its management.
3. Characterize the organization so that it is distinctive in the eyes of the reader (this does not necessarily mean unique).
4. Be positive, forward looking, and confident, with all the facts and projections reasonable, clear, vital, and accurate.
5. Carefully set forth the fundraising plans in terms of policy, priority, and enduring benefits. (The following questions must be anticipated from the reader: Why this institution? Why now? Why me? How?) The case must be clear and concise, even though it may, in fact, be lengthy.
6. Be a substantial plan for the future, not a burdensome revisiting of the past, no matter how honored or glorious. In a real sense, it is a prospectus. It invites investment. ①

Outline for a Case Statement

A recent fundraising book for academic and research libraries suggested an outline for a case statement which is very similar to the one quoted by Dove from the initial work of D. M. Thompson and others. A revised version of Thompson's outline is given below:②

1. Preface or Summary
   This section should express the essence of the case and state overall goals to be achieved.
2. Mission of the Library
   A. Role in society

---

① Mary H. Pendel. *What is a case statement?* (Arlington, VA: Thompson and Pendel Associates, 1981)
② Mary Bailey Pierce, "Fundraising/development plan," In: Barbara I. Dewey (ed.). *Raising money for academic and research libraries: a how-to-do-it manual for librarians.* (New York: Neal-Schuman Publishers, 1991), pp. 4 – 5. The earlier versions will be found in Dove, *op. cit.*, and in D. M. Thompson, *Typical outline for the case statement.* (Arlington, VA: Frantzreb, Prey, Ferner and Thompson, 1978)

  B. Philosophy of purpose
  C. Mission, goals, and program
  D. Salient factors in its history
  E. Factors that appeal to
   a. Users of library services
   b. Institutional family
   c. Governing board members and volunteers
   d. Friends and communities
   e. Past and current donors
   f. Potential leadership and funding sources
3. Record of Accomplishment
  A. Service growth
  B. Service users-meeting their needs
  C. Institutional family
   a. Nature and quality
   b. Role in teaching, research, policy, preservation, collection, services
  D. Community service
  E. Improvements in environment and physical facilities
  F. Financial growth
  G. Philanthropic support—distinctive gifts
  H. Where the institution stands today
4. Directions for the Future
  A. Distinctions that must continue to endure
  B. New directions
  C. Objectives, curriculum, programs, services
  D. Service users
  E. Financial policies and needs
  F. Physical facilities and new technologies
5. Urgent and Continuing Development Objectives
  A. Priorities and costs
   a. Endowment for
    a) Collection development
    b) Special projects/programs
    c) Preservation and conservation
    d) Staff development
    e) Library beautification
    f) Technology enhancement
    g) Building maintenance
    h) Facility maintenance
   b. New buildings
   c. Redevelopment of present facilities
   d. Property acquisition
   e. Debt reduction
  B. Master Plan
6. Benefits to the Community for the Investment
7. Plan of Action to Accomplish Future Objectives
  A. Goals
  B. Programs
   a. Support current operations
   b. Support capital expansion
   c. Support special programs or projects

            d. Role of estate planning
    C. Organization
    D. Timing
    E. Resources
        a. Constituent sources
        b. Range of gifts needed-gift table
        c. Opportunities for memorials and tributes
        d. Methods of giving
8. The Institution's Sponsorship
    A. Membership of the board and administration
    B. Members of the development and leadership teams
    C. Sponsoring body or bodies, if any

The above outline for a case statement is a suggestion of possible contents. The inclusion or omission of any of these elements is a decision to be made by each library based on its specific situation and needs.

Publishing the Case Statement

In writing a case statement, a team approach is recommended. The initial draft should be prepared by a library staff member assigned by the library director. It should then be reviewed by the library management for refinement. A professional writer from the development office or a professional firm specialized in writing case statements may be obtained to edit the draft and to prepare it for publication. It has been the view of development professionals that the final product of a case statement, including its art work, photography, printing, and paper, should be well done at all costs. Although the co-authors agree that such a publication, which is the basic document for the campaign, should be in the best form possible, we don't feel the need for going overboard. Extravagance in campaign spending may be seen by donors and volunteers as an unnecessary waste of the hard-raised money.

第三章 捐款的来源：公共部门

Chapter 3　Sources of Funds: The Public Sector

Introduction

So you have determined that a major campaign is feasible. You have assessed your market niche, developed a clear focus for the campaign, and written a convincing case statement. Specific dollar goals have been established. Now you are ready to begin looking for sources of potential support to meet those goals.

These will tend to fall into four broad categories: (1) **government agencies**, including federal, state and local funding sources; (2) **private foundations**, including independent foundations, community foundations, and operating foundations; (3) **corporations and businesses**; and (4) **individuals**, including alumni, faculty, staff, friends, and other persons with a connection to your organization.

According to figures released by the American Association of Fundraising Counsel, total private giving (excluding government agencies) amounted to an estimated $122.57 billion in 1990. More than 83 percent, or $101.8 billion, was given by living individuals. Another $7.79 billion came in the form of bequests. Foundations contributed $7.08 billion and corporations $5.9 billion.[①] From these statistics it is clear that of the three major categories of private support—foundations, corporations and individuals—the last is by far the most important. Your own time and energy should be allocated accordingly: most of it should be devoted to identifying, cultivating and soliciting individual prospects for both direct gifts and so-called "planned gifts", including bequests.

In this chapter we will tell you how to identify potential government sources of external support for your library's fundraising program. Next we will examine the much more lucrative private sector. In both cases we will describe specific information sources, printed and computerized, that can help you find a match between your needs and the grantmakers/donors that have the power to meet those needs. We will talk about some of the major trends in the grantmaking and donor communities that you should be aware of. We will tell you how to assess whether a particular foundation, corporation or individual is worth the effort to pursue.

Time and energy are limited commodities in any fundraising effort. It is important to invest them where they will have the highest potential to pay dividends for your library. That means being smart right at the beginning, as you are trying to identify your prospects.

I. Seeking Federal Grants

Due to our nation's unique division of authority between federal, state and local units of government, the world of tax-supported grants for libraries has become a very complex subject. The peculiar jargon of grant-making can also pose difficulties for the novice (or even an expert!), so perhaps we should start by briefly describing some of the common types of grant programs that you will encounter at all levels.

Types of Grants

Block grants are made directly by the federal government to states or localities, which then have the authority to award the money to eligible organizations to carry out activities consistent with

---

[①] *Annual register of grant support: a directory of funding sources, 1992*. 25th edition. (Wilmette, IL: National Registry Publishing Co., 1991), p. xiii.

the authorizing legislation. The Library Services and Construction Act is a good example of a block grant program. State library agencies are asked to formulate a "state plan," and federal funds are then allocated to the agency, which makes awards and administers the grants in accordance with the plan.

Formula grants are awarded on the basis of a set of objective criteria, often derived from census data and typically including such factors as population characteristics, the number of people served, income, or need as determined by statistical models. The authorizing legislation will spell out the formula to be used. Formula grants are not so much "grants" as we generally use that term, as they are a method for allocating funds. Titles I and II of the Library Services and Construction Act (see below) are formula grants.

Categorical grants are designed to meet a specific need or to serve a particular group. The programs conducted under LSCA Title IV, "Library Services to Indian Tribes and Hawaiian Natives", are examples of categorical grants.

Project grants are made on the basis of the merits of the proposal, which is usually judged in competition with other proposals of a similar kind. They differ considerably from block, formula, and categorical grants, which are less competitive and more mechanical in their operation. Outside experts are often used to evaluate applications, but the agency itself exercises broad discretion in selecting the projects to be funded and the amounts awarded. Another characteristic of project grants is that they are supposed to achieve significant practical benefits while employing established methods and conforming to accepted standards. Innovation and discovery are not generally expected or even desired in a project grant. Most of the federal grant programs available to libraries (including those offered by the National Endowment for the Humanities and by the U. S. Department of Education under provisions of the Higher Education Act) belong to this category.

Demonstration grants are awarded to test novel approaches to solving problems. They should benefit the target group being served, but unlike project grants their main purpose is to prove the effectiveness of the new methodology and promote its wider use by other organizations. Pilot projects being proposed for a demonstration grant should be based on sound research. A good example of a demonstration grant is the Department of Education's HEA Title II-D program to promote library technology.

Research grants differ from both project grants and demonstration grants in that they are not awarded to produce a direct benefit or to field test a new methodology. Instead, they are intended to support the gathering, interpretation, and analysis of information in order to arrive at new understandings of fundamental issues and problems. The results of a research grant, when successful, will sometimes lead to both demonstration and project grants. Research grants for libraries are less common than other types, although the NEH Office of Preservation and Access will support basic research that shows promise of leading to new and better techniques for preserving library materials.

Matching grants require that the recipient devote some of its own resources to supporting the activity being underwritten by the grant. In fact, most government grants have matching requirements, which must be met by either "hard" contributions of actual cash, "soft" or "in-kind" contributions of labor, equipment, and supplies, or a combination of the two. The amount of matching support required differs widely from one program to the next, but it must be carefully considered before moving ahead with an application.

Challenge grants are made contingent on the grantee raising additional support from private, non-governmental sources in order to trigger release of the original award. In the case of the NEH Challenge Grant program, first-time recipients are required to raise three dollars in private contributions for every one dollar in federal funds. Second-time recipients are asked to raise four dollars for each federal dollar awarded.

Federal Grant Programs for Libraries

Federal support for libraries takes two broad forms: (1) direct funding of the so-called "national libraries" (including the Library of Congress, the National Archives, the National Library of Medicine, the National Agricultural Library, and certain Presidential Libraries); and (2) grants-in-aid programs available on a competitive basis to other libraries, public and academic, throughout the United States. (Interestingly, the national libraries are generally excluded from support under these grants-in-aid programs.) We will spend most of our attention describing these federal grant programs for libraries.

In terms of library support, the most important federal grant-making agencies are: the National Endowment for the Humanities, the Department of Education (under provisions of both the Higher Education Act [HEA] and the Library Services and Construction Act [LSCA]), the National Historic Publications and Records Commission, the National Science Foundation, the National Library of Medicine, and the Council on Library Resources.

It is important to work from current information, even in the earliest "brainstorming" phase of developing your proposal. Completely new funding initiatives are sometimes announced. Existing programs may be redirected, scaled back, combined with others, or eliminated. Two of the best sources of information on the ever-changing federal scene are the monthly "Washington Hotline" column in *College and Research Libraries News* and the more detailed but irregularly published *ALA Washington Newsletter*. Here you can follow the course of congressional and executive action on grant programs relevant to libraries, including appropriation levels and policy changes, even before they become law.

With the caveat that specific programs are always subject to change, we offer a rundown of the most important federal grants currently available to libraries. Further information regarding each of the agencies and programs mentioned below can be obtained by writing to the offices listed in Appendix VIII.

National Endowment for the Humanities:

State Programs ($26.9 million for fiscal year 1992)

Block grants are given to state humanities councils to foster greater public access to the humanities and to provide a focus for discussion, analysis, and implementation of effective and continuing public activities in the humanities. The various state humanities councils are listed in the *Annual Register of Grant Support*, together with a description of their programs. (See Appendix VIII.) Requests for guidelines and applications for grants should be made directly to the state councils.

Division of Preservation and Access ($20.8 million in fiscal year 1992)

Library and Archival Materials: grants support the microfilming of important research collections at single institutions and by consortia; research on preservation technology or procedures; projects to increase public understanding of preservation.

National Heritage Preservation Program: grants support housing and storage of objects, improved climate control, installation of security, lighting, and fire-prevention systems.

U.S. Newspaper Program: grants for statewide projects to identify, catalog, and preserve (through microfilming) endangered newspapers of importance for humanities research.

Division of Public Programs

Humanities Projects in Libraries and Archives: grants for projects that will enhance public understanding of the humanities through the use of books and other materials held by libraries and archives. Grants are awarded both for planning activities and to implement programs. ($2.8 million awarded in FY 1990.)

Humanities Projects in Media: grants to support planning, scripting or production of television and radio programs in the humanities. ($9.6 million in fiscal year 1992)

Division of Research Programs ($19.9 million in fiscal year 1992)

Grants are made in six major areas, of which two are of special interest to libraries:

Texts: support for the preparation of authoritative, annotated editions, translations into English of important works, and subventions to support the publication costs of books in the humanities.

Reference Materials: grants for preparing reference works, bibliographies, bibliographic data bases, descriptive catalogs, indexes, union lists, and other guides to humanities documentation; and projects that improve the ways in which libraries, archives, and other repositories make research documentation available. Projects must be national or international in scope, not limited to institutional collections, which are supported by the Division of Preservation and Access.

Division of Education Programs

Higher Education in the Humanities: support for institutes for college and university faculty, workshops, national conferences, curriculum development efforts, or projects to foster the reinvigoration of humanities teaching; cooperative efforts are encouraged among faculty and administrators within a single institution; among faculty and administrators from a group of institutions, or to support projects that improve the humanities preparation of new teachers and educational leaders. ($7.4 million in fiscal year 1992)

Office of Challenge Grants ($16 million for fiscal year 1992)

Institutions wishing to develop new sources of financial support for programs in the humanities may request challenge grant assistance. One dollar of federal support will be provided for every three or four private dollars raised, depending on whether the institution is a first or a second time applicant. Both federal and private matching funds may be used in flexible ways to meet institutional needs, such as establishing or increasing endowment, construction, renovation, equipment purchases, or the retirement of debt. A maximum of $1 million in federal funding can be requested.

Department of Education:

Higher Education Act (HEA)

Title II-A, College Libraries: grants to institutions that demonstrate the greatest need based on criteria established by the Secretary of Education. (Not funded since FY 1984)

Title II-B, **Library Career Training Program**: supports training in librarianship through fellowships and other educational assistance. Promotes library and information science research, development, and demonstration projects. ($651,000 in fiscal year 1991)

Title II-C, **Strengthening Research Library Resources**: provides assistance to major research libraries for collection development, bibliographic access, and preservation. ($5.7 million in fiscal year 1991)

Title II-D, **Technology**: grants for technological equipment and other purposes to meet special needs and to promote resource sharing. ($3.9 million appropriated for FY 1991)

Library Services and Construction Act (LSCA)

Title I, **Public Library Services**: formula grant funds allocated to the States to provide improved public library access for persons who, by reason of distance, residence, handicap, or other disadvantages, are not able to benefit from basic public library services. ($83.8 million appropriated for FY 1991)

Title II, **Public Library Construction**: formula funds distributed through designated state library administrative agencies for approved public library construction projects.

Title III, **Interlibrary Cooperation and Resource Sharing**: funds are allocated to the designated state library administrative agency for projects that promote resource sharing and cooperation among all types of libraries through the development of cooperative library networks and cooperation among public, academic, school, and special libraries. ($19.9 million appropriated for FY 1991)

Title IV, **Library Literacy Program**: grants to state and local public libraries to coordinate and plan library literacy programs and to arrange for the training of librarians and volunteers to carry out such programs. ($8.1 million in fiscal year 1991)

Title IV, **Library Services for Indian Tribes and Hawaiian Natives Program**: basic grants and special project grants to develop and improve public library services to eligible Indian tribes and Hawaiian native organizations. ($2.4 million in fiscal year 1990)

National Library of Medicine:
   Health Science Information Resource Program: Grants to facilitate access to and delivery of health science information via pathways using the most effective computer **and telecommunications technology**; grants to utilize and improve the infrastructure for the transfer of health science information via technological means. ($1.8 million for fiscal year 1991)
   Medical Library Assistance Program: Project grants to improve health information services by providing funds to train professional personnel, strengthen library and information resources, support biomedical publications, and conduct research in information science and in medical information. (est. $21.8 million for fiscal year 1992)

National Historical Publication And Records Commission:
   Historical Records Grants and Historical Documents Publications Grants: support for the collection, preservation, arrangement, description, editing and publication of historical records and archives. ($5 million in 1991)

Institute of Museum Services:
   This independent federal agency serves museums in all disciplines including art, history, historic sites, natural history, and science-technology centers. If yours is one of those unusual institutions operating as both a library and museum, it may qualify for support under one or more of the following programs:
   General Operating Support: competitive awards for one year to support ongoing institutional activities. Amounts are limited to 10 percent of the museum's non-federal operating budget. ($17.3 million in fiscal year 1989)
   Conservation Project Support: grants of up to two years' duration for conservation treatment of both living and non-living collections, condition and environmental surveys, and research and training. ($3.2 million in fiscal year 1989)
   Professional Services Program: grants support one year demonstration projects designed to improve museum services. ($250,000 in fiscal year 1989)
   Museum Assessment Program I & II: non-competitive grants of $1,400 each are awarded to conduct either (I) an independent professional assessment of museum operations and programs; or (II) an independent professional assessment of a museum's collection care and maintenance. Such assessments can be valuable tools in developing a case statement for private support to improve conditions. ($400,000 in fiscal year 1989)

II. State And Local Grants for Libraries

State and local government support for libraries is too multifaceted a topic to be covered in this book, since every state and locality has its own unique programs for libraries. Public libraries, consortia made up of public libraries, and networks that support public libraries, can often look to some kind of state library administrative agency for assistance. This organization is generally responsible for managing whatever categorical, formula, or project grants for public libraries happen to be funded by state appropriations. It will also be responsible for administering federal block grants awarded under the Library Services and Construction Act. Public librarians interested in learning about state supported grant opportunities (as well as LSCA funds) should contact their state library agency for information.

In the realm of state-assisted higher education, an office or board is generally established with varying degrees of power over such matters as annual operating budgets, capital construction, curriculum, labor relations, and other issues affecting the state's system of higher education.

Lately there has been a tendency for these statewide coordinating bodies to involve themselves more directly in library affairs. In most states they are responsible for approving library construction projects. Sometimes they provide formula grants of various kinds directly to libraries in the system, as well as offering project grants in such areas as acquisitions, automation, retrospective conversion, and preservation. Even challenge grants are being offered in some states, particularly for purposes of creating endowed chairs.

III. Dealing with Government Granting Agencies

There are a few generalizations you can make about government granting agencies. They tend to prefer long, detailed proposals with plenty of documentation. Once a grant has been awarded, they often impose rather elaborate reporting requirements. Moreover, there is little connection between the amount of money available and the amount of information required for the initial application and in subsequent reports. For this reason, some jaded experts have found it to their advantage not to deal at all with a government agency when small amounts of money are involved. If you are going to get swamped by lots of paperwork, it might as well be for a big payoff!

Some agencies present a human face and appreciate being consulted directly about grant proposals. The National Endowment for the Humanities, for example, is conducted more like a large private foundation than a government bureaucracy. But other federal and state agencies are much more impersonal. They may not welcome telephone calls and in-person visits to discuss proposals. In fact, they may actually prohibit such contacts.

Finally, the matching requirement is a feature of nearly all government grant programs. It is their way of leveraging the expenditure of tax dollars and demonstrating fiscal responsibility to politically sensitive legislatures. Of course we have all read about the tricks recipients play to live within the matching requirements and even make money on government grants. Total project costs are sometimes inflated to show a large "soft" match. Staff time on the project is exaggerated. Indirect costs are pumped up even more. Lately there has been an effort to crack down on these kinds of abuses. In general, you will have much less flexibility dealing with a government agency than with a corporation or foundation, where often a phone call can clear up any problems. We mention this early because it may affect the extent to which you want to include government granting agencies in your fundraising plans.

第四章 捐款的来源：私人来源

Chapter 4　Sources of Funds: The Private Sector

I. Foundations

There are more than 30,000 private foundations in the United States, and in 1989 they awarded some $6.7 billion in grants to eligible organizations. A much smaller number of company-sponsored foundations gave another $5 billion, bringing to $11.7 billion the total amount of yearly support provided by this important source of funds. Even though foundations of all kinds account for perhaps 10 percent of total charitable giving on an annual basis, they devote around one third of their funds to higher education, giving them a disproportionate impact in this sector.[①] And since most of that support is directed to **private** colleges and universities, their importance is even greater for this group of institutions. As the generous grants listed in Table 4-1 demonstrate, foundations offer a potential source of support that should not be overlooked in your development program.

What is a Foundation?

Foundations are non-profit, non-governmental entities established under section 501 (c) (3) of the Tax Code for the purpose of supporting educational, cultural, religious, health-related, and other causes, primarily by awarding grants to eligible non-profit organizations. They derive their funding from a combination of invested principal, donor contributions, and (in the case of many corporate foundations) operating income from the parent organization. In order to maintain their favored status under the Internal Revenue Act, foundations are required to distribute a certain percentage of their invested assets to eligible recipients each year. Currently the so-called "payout requirement" is set at 5 percent. This should be a source of reassurance to you as an applicant. It helps to remember that even though competition for foundation grants can get pretty fierce at times, they do want to give their money away. In fact, they must give it away or face stiff penalties under the tax laws. Your job is to convince them that your library and the project you want to carry out are worthy of support. Think of a relationship with a foundation as a partnership. They have the money. You have the ideas, the service mission, and the human resources to actualize their philanthropic impulses, giving them concrete form.

Table 4-1　The Largest Foundation Grants to Libraries in 1989/90
(Source: *The Foundation Grants Index*, 1992)

$3,000,000 from the Houston Endowment to the Houston Public Library (TX) for increased automation and collection enhancement.	$500,000 from the Aaron Diamond Foundation to the New York Public Library (NY) for a cataloging project.
$830,000 from the W. K. Kellogg Foundation to the New York Public Library (NY) to prepare leaders for library information systems and develop software for an integrated, interactive computer-based network.	$354,955 from the William E. Simon Foundation to the Richard Nixon Library and Birthplace (CA) for general operating expenses.
$650,000 from the Champlin Foundations to the Providence Public Library (RI) for renovations and central site software.	$310,329 from the Benedum Foundation to the West Virginia Library Commission (W. VA) to strengthen public libraries in the state.

---

① *The foundation grants index*, 1990/91. 19th edition. (Washington, D. C.: The Foundation Center, c1990), p. x

(Continuing)

$515,000 from the H. J. & Drue Heinz Foundation to the New York Public Library (NY) for general support and an endowed book fund.	$300,000 from the Morgan Guaranty Trust Company of New York Charitable Trust to the New York Public Library (NY) for capital support.
$504,825 from the Abell-Hanger Foundation to the Permian Basin Petroleum Museum, Library and Hall of Fame (TX) for general operating support and as a challenge grant for permanent endowment.	$275,000 from the Andrew W. Mellon Foundation to the National Szechenyi Library (Budapest, Hungary) for acquiring books, periodicals, computers, software and other equipment.

Types of Foundations

The world of foundations can be broken down into four basic categories:
- Independent foundations, including general purpose and special purpose foundations;
- company sponsored or corporate foundations;
- community foundations;
- operating foundations.

An **independent foundation** is usually created by an individual, a family, or a group of individuals to carry out their philanthropic wishes in perpetuity. They are governed by boards of directors and may (depending on size) employ a paid staff. (In fact, only about 1,200 of the very largest foundations have paid staff.) Most independent foundations have broad charters that legally permit them to support a variety of different causes and organizations. Among the best known of these "general purpose" foundations are the Ford Foundation, the Kellogg Foundation, the Mac Arthur Foundation, the Carnegie Foundation, and the Rockefeller Foundation. There are also a number of "specialized" foundations established to provide funding for particular areas of need. Examples include the American Heart Foundation, the Asia Foundation, or the Council on Library Resources.

The fact is that almost all foundations, even those that supposedly exist "for purposes of general charitable giving", are highly selective in where they put their money. Most limit support to a few organizations and causes that were important to the original founders, or that have gained the interest of the current directors. Many tend to focus their generosity on certain geographic areas, again concentrating on places where the founders have lived or conducted business or otherwise come to feel personal ties. As a general rule, the smaller the foundation, the more rigid, unchanging and parochial its funding priorities will tend to be. Conversely, the better known foundations with assets above $25 million are less likely to be geographically limited in their giving programs and much more willing to take up new causes, set their own agenda based on changing perceptions of societal needs, and make grants to deserving organizations based on the merits of their programs. The problem is that everyone knows this and floods the top national foundations with requests. Although there are approximately 30,000 foundations in this country, about 5,000 provide 90% of the funding.

Corporations manage their charitable support through foundations, direct giving programs, or both. The largest organizations will sometimes establish a **company-sponsored foundation**, otherwise known as a **corporate foundation**. Prominent corporate foundations include the Procter & Gamble Foundation, the Scripps-Howard Foundation, and the Exxon Foundation. Although legally separate and run by their own boards, corporate foundations are still closely tied in with their parent companies. To the extent that the foundation has invested assets (as opposed to annual allocations from the company), it will subject to the same payout requirement as a private foundation: 5 percent of the annual average market value. Direct giving programs, on the other hand, are unregulated and function at the discretion of the corporation. They are not obligated to give any particular dollar amount. A company with a foundation may also operate a **direct giving program**, sometimes sharing the same staff and office space. But the vast majority of companies, even the largest ones, do not operate foundations at all. They prefer to channel their philanthropic support exclusively through direct giving programs. For this reason, we will devote a separate section of this chapter to corporations as prospects for library fundraising.

Community foundations are established with the explicit aim of supporting worthy causes in a particular city or region. Examples include the Cleveland Foundation, the San Francisco Foundation, or the Kanawha Valley Foundation in West Virginia. Although they are generally organized by a few leading local citizens, their assets often consist of many different trust funds contributed over the years by residents of the community. Some of these individual endowments may be designated for a particular charity, others may be restricted to a certain category of need (e.g. child welfare), while others can be used at the discretion of the board within the guidelines of the foundation. Community foundations are exempt from the payout requirement, but they are required to receive continuing donations. So they generally publish lots of attractive literature, conduct well publicized annual giving campaigns, and actively seek major gifts and bequests from prominent citizens of the localities they serve. The important thing to remember about community foundations is that they are always local in their interests. How "local" is local? Depending on the foundation, it might be defined as the city limits, a metropolitan area, a county, or a region. Consult the printed guidelines or, if possible, talk to staff to see if your library fits.

Operating foundations exist to support a specific non-profit organization, whether it be a hospital, a college or university, a performing arts group, or a social service agency. In effect, they function as the fundraising arm of the parent organization and exist to serve its own programs. While their charters may permit them to make outside grants, support of this kind is rare. On the other hand, your own college or university may well have an operating foundation that it runs in close collaboration with its office of development, alumni affairs, or institutional support. In that case, you must regard the foundation as a prime candidate to provide financial support for library programs. It will also be a key ally in your effort to secure funds from the outside.

The Competition for Funds: Why Research is Needed

The best known foundations receive thousands of funding requests each year, many of them from deserving applicants with compelling needs. There are 873,000 tax-exempt organizations in the United States that rely on charitable contributions for support. So for every single foundation, there are 30 potential applicants. For each of the top 5,000 foundations, which account for 90 percent of the funding, there are 175 eligible applicants. All told, foundations receive almost 1 million funding requests every year. Perhaps no more than 6 or 7 percent are approved.

What are the reasons for this high failure rate? Foundation executives complain that often the proposals they receive fall completely outside their expressed areas of interest. Most foundations are restricted in their giving. They restrict to certain geographic areas; they restrict by the population served; they restrict by subject area. Although libraries have traditionally looked to foundations to support construction projects, many foundations will not contribute to capital campaigns. Others will not contribute to endowment.

It is a sad fact that most of the proposals submitted to foundations give little indication that the applicant has taken the trouble to become aware of their priorities, their restrictions, or their capabilities. Requests are routinely made for prohibited items, or for dollar amounts far beyond what the foundation is able to give. **The first rule in gaining foundation support is to select the right foundations to approach.** Doing your homework in advance will not guarantee success for your proposal, but at least it will help it to gain a fair hearing. The experts agree that it is better to concentrate on a few good foundation prospects than to waste time and postage on a "scatter gun" approach.

How to Find Information on Foundations

The task of locating foundations likely to support your library is made much easier by the existence of The Foundation Center. Created and supported by the foundation community itself, The Foundation Center operates offices in New York City, Cleveland, and San Francisco. Through its extensive publications program (including both printed sources and online databases), together with its network of 127 depository libraries, the Foundation Center does yeoman's work in collecting and disseminating good, current information about foundation activity in the United States and (to a lesser extent) abroad.

Most of the tools you will use to identify foundations of possible interest for your library fundraising effort are published by The Foundation Center. But there are other organizations, including the Taft Corporation, the Council on Foundations, and the Council for the Advancement and Support of Education, that distribute valuable information. A selective list of "Sources of Information on Foundations" appears in Appendix IX. Before starting your research, you should also consult Foundation Fundamentals, the latest edition of which is cited in our bibliography. It provides an excellent introduction to the process, together with specific instructions on using the resources of The Foundation Center.

In reviewing the information sources listed in Appendix IX, you will notice that some describe what foundations **say they do** (directories), while others reveal **what they actually have done** (indexes to grants awarded). Most experienced researchers like to begin with the grant indexes, developing a long list of foundations that have made awards in their field of interest, then work back to the directories to learn more in detail about those organizations. But both kinds of information are important. For instance, Foundation X might say nothing at all about libraries in its statement of purpose published in *The Foundation Directory*. Yet a check of *The Foundation Grants* Index reveals that it has made several large grants to libraries in recent years. Certainly you would not want to overlook Foundation X as a potential prospect.

By the same token, the directory entries for Foundation Y might indicate a willingness to support libraries, while a check of the grant indexes fails to turn up any such gifts. What is the explanation? Worst case scenario: Foundation Y has lost interest in libraries but neglected to update its mission statement. Best case scenario: Foundation Y would love to support libraries but hasn't found the right proposal yet. In either event, you would want to put Foundation Y on your "long list" of potential prospects for further review.

In order to close the gap between theory and practice—between what grantmakers say they do and what they actually do—the Foundation Center has begun to publish a series of guides combining both kinds of information and focusing on particular subject areas. The *National Guide to Funding for Libraries & Information Services* profiles some 367 foundations and 28 direct corporate giving programs that either (1) show a significant interest in libraries in their stated purpose or (2) have actually made grants to libraries of $5,000 or more in the latest reporting year. So long as it remains current, *The National Guide* is perhaps the best place to begin looking for foundations that might support your own library's programs. But remember that even this source, convenient as it is to use, does not exhaust all the potential foundation and corporate assistance available to libraries. Nor does inclusion in the guide by any means ensure that a particular foundation is a good prospect to support your library.

No matter how up-to-date the indexes and directories you happen to be using, they at best tell you what foundations are doing right now. Even when using a *COMSEARCH Printout* or a Dialog online search, you are learning about grants that have already been awarded. But foundations do get involved in new areas of grantmaking, and sometimes learning about it after the fact is just not good enough. The foundation may have already chosen the specific organizations it wants to support under the new initiative. By the time you apply, it may be ready to move on to a completely different area. If the J. P. Moneybags Foundation intends to launch a program next year "to improve access to information through library automation and networking", wouldn't it be better to know about it before any awards are made? That way you have a chance to get in on the ground floor with a good proposal.

There is no easy-to-use, one-stop resource for finding out what foundations are planning to do in the future, but the periodicals included in "Sources for Further Reading" can certainly help. They contain feature articles, organizational profiles, statistics, interviews with foundation executives, and other information that can keep you abreast of new trends in philanthropic giving and provide an edge on the competition. Once you learn about a new initiative, you can subject the foundation to the same research process that you would apply to organizations already making grants in that area.

The Research Process

The purpose of your research is to find one or more foundations that will be interested in your library and its programs. You will start by developing a preliminary "long list" of foundations that have some potential to support your campaign. Through further research you will narrow the list down to a select number of prospects that are clearly worth pursuing.

At this point it is helpful to pull into focus the needs assessment and case statement that we discussed in Chapter 2. What are the major goals and dollar targets of your fundraising effort? What population groups are served by your library? What kind of support are you seeking: capital funds for construction? endowment? seed money for an experimental program? equipment? If the funds are needed for acquisitions, preservation, or technical processing, what are the major subject areas involved? Who will benefit if the project is successful: students? community residents? faculty? national scholars in a particular discipline? a minority group?

Once you have your goals clearly in mind, there are two basic approaches to identifying foundation prospects: by **subject area** or by **geographic giving pattern**. The approach you select will depend on the goals you have established for the library fundraising effort and on the specific projects you want to get funded. Of course there is nothing wrong with pursuing both approaches, but recognize that they will yield different results. Major private foundations are interested in the project and will want it to impact on a national level. Local and regional foundations are mainly interested in the community you serve. Corporate foundations might be interested in either or both, especially if the parent company employs a lot of people in your service area.

Perhaps your case statement includes a variety of needs, ranging from big-ticket items (building a new library) to comparatively small ones (installing a group of personal computers for CD-ROM database searching). A major project that will cost lots of money and has national importance should point you in the direction of the large, national, private or corporate foundation sector. To develop a preliminary list of prospects, follow a **subject approach** using resources like the *Foundation Grants Index Annual* and the guides to large grantmakers such as *The Foundation Directory or the Taft Foundation Reporter*.

On the other hand, a more modest project that will primarily benefit a local constituency might be a good candidate for a local or regional foundation. In that case, you will employ the **geographic approach**, trying to identify grantmakers with a particular interest in your area and the people you serve. Corporations with operations in your city or region will be possible candidates, along with community foundations. Since you are not looking for huge amounts of money, do not neglect to consult sources that cover a larger range of smaller foundations, such as The *Foundation Directory*, *Part 2*, the *National Data Book of Foundations*, or even some of the state and regional guides listed in Foundation Fundamentals.

As you gather more information about particular foundation prospects, you should ask yourself the following questions about each of them:

1. Is the foundation really committed to supporting library programs?
2. Is it likely to support institutions in your state or region of the country?
3. Is the dollar amount of your proposal within the range of the foundation?
4. Are there any restrictions against support of the kind you need?
5. Does the foundation tend to support all the costs for a particular project, or does it prefer to see cost-sharing? Are you prepared to meet the cost-sharing requirement?
6. What is the typical project duration for this foundation, and does it match your own needs?
7. Does the foundation have deadlines, or does it review proposals as they are received?

As you ask these questions, certain foundations will be eliminated from your preliminary list, leaving you with a group of high priority prospects. These are the organizations worth researching in greater depth. You will want to write away for their published reports and guidelines, if available. Based on what you learn about the foundation and its priorities, you may decide to refine your basic idea, packaging it in ways that appeal more strongly to the interests of the foundation.

When the time finally comes to present your proposal, let the foundation know you have done your homework. Tell them in no uncertain terms what has led you to think they should be interested in your library and what it wants to accomplish.

Trends in Foundation Giving

For every foundation you find with an expressed commitment to libraries, there will be many more with an interest in promoting research and scholarship in certain subject areas: through research grants to scholars, fellowships for talented graduate students, conferences and seminars, publication subventions, and the like. These foundations need to be reminded that library resources are an integral part of the research process.

Let's say that the I. M. Rich Foundation has announced a grantmaking program "to improve teaching and research on the Arab-speaking world through a series of endowed chairs, faculty development grants, and graduate stipends at selected doctoral granting universities." This kind of initiative should be jumped on if you already have comprehensive or research level collection in some aspect of Arabic civilization. You can make the argument that library and information resources need to be acquired, cataloged, and made accessible both to local and to national scholars over bibliographic networks.

In fact, whenever you have an outstanding academic program on your campus, you should try to enter into a partnership with its leading faculty and administrators to approach funding sources with joint proposals that combine direct support for research and curriculum development with library enhancement. This is always a good strategy to follow: find out who's getting the external funding and try to get in on their act.

Many foundations are interested in providing assistance to certain demographic groups: e. g. hispanics, blacks, senior citizens, teenagers, etc. In that case you need to match your library user population to the group the foundation wants to benefit. Certainly there are creative ways for libraries to focus on programs serving particular demographic groups. Such programs have been developed more aggressively by the public libraries, but there are many academic libraries that also serve minority populations, linguistic minorities, handicapped persons, and other people with special needs. Again, a foundation that has never thought about supporting libraries but has an expressed interest in continuing education and the adult learner might be convinced to underwrite a special project to develop library instruction programs focused on this particular group.

Pilot projects are becoming increasingly popular with foundations. They are looking for good demonstration projects that they can fund for one, two or three years and will then be taken over and funded from regular sources. One-time awards are common. There are many opportunities in this area for projects designed to test emerging library and information technologies. For example, the University of Iowa Libraries recently received a $752,432 grant from the Roy J. Carver Charitable Trust to develop an "Information Arcade" where faculty and students can use multimedia workstations for research, classroom instruction, and independent learning. Located in a prominent area of the main library, the new facility will contain more than 55 state-of-the-art computer stations providing access to communications networks as well as both bibliographic and full-text databases.[①]

Tax supported organizations are increasingly looking to foundations for support. Many foundations have tended to exclude tax supported organizations. Often this limitation will not

---

① Article in *The University of Iowa Libraries Bulletin*, May 1992.

appear as a hard and fast rule in the guidelines, but if you look at the pattern of actual grants to educational institutions, they end up being concentrated exclusively in the private sector. From the point of view of the foundation community, this preference is justified. After all, annual foundation support amounts to only about 1 percent of the federal budget in dollar terms. They don't want to use their assets just to supplement existing government programs, no matter how worthwhile they might be. Foundations want to direct their money where it will make a difference, perhaps by providing an alternative to government sponsored programs or by helping to launch an experimental pilot project that tries to address problems in innovative ways.

In response, public colleges and universities are trying to make the case that they are semi-private in nature. They point to the fact that in most cases state subsidies cover only a portion of the total educational costs and that tuition and fees (in addition to private support) are important sources of income. It remains to be seen how effective this strategy will be. But if your library is located at a public institution, you might want to try this gambit in approaches you make to foundations.

II. Corporations and Businesses

Corporate philanthropy has been officially encouraged by the federal tax code since 1935, when the deduction rate of 5 percent of net pre-tax earnings was established. The Tax Reform Act of 1981 increased this figure to 10 percent. Some corporations do contribute at the 5 percent level, and "Five Percent Clubs" have been formed in a few major cities to honor these generous companies. ① Almost none make use of the full 10 percent allowed under IRS guidelines. In fact, corporate giving has historically averaged only in the 2 percent range. Statistics collected by the Council for Aid to Education show that the average U. S. corporation gave only 1.96 percent of its pre-tax earnings to charity in 1990. The highest figure ever recorded was 2.31 percent in 1986. ②

The gap between what corporations can deduct from taxes and what they actually contribute to qualified charities can be explained by a number of factors. There are many competing demands on net earnings, including capital reinvestment, product research and development, wage and benefit increases for employees, and dividend increases for shareholders. Strong pressure from any of these quarters will tend to reduce whatever commitment a corporation might feel to support external causes, no matter how worthy. Anyone trying to secure a major corporate gift needs to understand this situation and market the proposal in ways that appeal to its self interest. More about this later.

The largest single determinate of corporate philanthropy is profitability. Companies that aren't making money are unlikely to give it away. And remember that the size of a corporation is no indication of its current profitability. A Fortune 500 company is quite capable of losing money. For instance, Ford Motor Company lost $2.3 billion in 1991. Determining profits should be part of your preliminary prospect research with corporations. A lot of time can be wasted planning an approach to that major company headquartered in your state, only to find out it has been losing money two years in a row. Neither its employees nor its shareholders are going to tolerate giving away money under those circumstances. On the other hand, if you can identify a company expecting to earn a big windfall profit in the year ahead, it might be very much to your advantage to approach them early with a well-reasoned gift proposal. The only exception to the "current profitability rule" would be in the case of a corporate foundation with a large endowment, so that its grant making activity does not depend on annual contributions from the parent company. These sources of support tend to be less sensitive to current economic conditions.

But most corporations channel all their philanthropic support through **direct giving programs**

---

① Aldo C. Podesta. *Raising funds from America's* 2,000,000 *overlooked corporations*. (Hartsdale, NY: Public Service Materials Center, c1984), p. 24. The cities are: Baltimore, Maryland; Birmingham, Alabama; and Louisville, Kentucky.

② Jennifer Moore. "Corporate Giving: Still Stalled." *The Chronicle of Philanthropy*, v. iv, No. 1 (October 22, 1991), p. 1 *passim*.

that rely on current revenues from the company itself. In addition to making cash gifts, corporate direct giving programs will also work with deserving applicants to arrange in-kind contributions of equipment, professional expertise, volunteer time, or office space. During bad economic times, the corporation may be much more inclined to offer in-kind support than to make a large gift of cash.

Identifying Corporate Prospects

In Appendix X we have listed some of the most useful sources of information on company-sponsored foundations and corporate direct giving programs. We have also included such standard business references as Business Periodicals Index and Compact Disclosure to remind you how important it is to obtain an up-to-date picture of how the company is doing in terms of profitability, return on investment, and projected revenues.

How do you go about culling the good prospects from this seemingly endless list of corporations? There are three kinds of connections that can exist between your library and a corporation. When all three come together at once, your chances of success are excellent. But at least one of the following links should be established before moving to the cultivation and solicitation stage.

First, look for a **conceptual relationship** between the company's business interests, broadly defined, and your own library programs.

Second, look for **geographic proximity** between your library and the company's headquarters, or failing that, a significant regional office, factory, or service area.

Third, look for **personal contacts** between your own volunteer leaders and top officials in the company.

Conceptual Relationships

Corporations can be quite narrow in their philanthropic practices. They see philanthropy as part and parcel of their corporate planning objectives. They are not so much involved in making judgments about worthy appeals as they are in the business of implementing a policy, and you can bet that the policy has been designed to further corporate ends in some fashion. What we will say in Chapter 5 about the need to carefully screen your prospects is especially relevant when it comes to corporate appeals. It is important to establish a clear link between what your library is doing (or wants to accomplish with corporate assistance) and the needs of that particular company. From this conceptual link, you must then try to build a genuine **strategic partnership** with the company.

This connection can be as simple as generating favorable publicity for the corporate benefactor. If your library is well thought of in the community, if people have warm feelings about who you are and what you do, then a local company may want to become associated with that positive reputation by supporting your programs, especially the most popular ones. This strategy can work surprisingly well, but only if you already enjoy high visibility and a positive public image. And it will only work for a truly local business or corporation that wants to promote good public relations in the community.

Do not neglect the "embarrassment factor" when it comes to targeting corporate prospects. If a company has a public relations problem, perhaps you can help it to overcome the problem. Who do you think are the major corporate donors to mainstream environmental groups? Oil companies, of course. Why not look to paper manufacturers to help solve the massive preservation problems faced by libraries? They may not be taking the same kind of heat over acid paper as the coal-burning utilities are feeling over acid rain, but at least they can be made to understand the situation. A high visibility project to restore, say, a rare Audubon elephant folio, might have considerable public relations value to a high-end paper manufacturer whose market niche is based on a reputation for quality. This is the kind of relationship between a genuine library need and corporate self-interest that you need to discover in order to be consistently successful with this type of prospect. Another such strategy would be to target television stations or cable outlets for support of a young adult literacy program.

If your library is part of a larger institution of higher learning, look at the areas on campus that have attracted corporate support in the past. Often the purposes for which money has been awarded will fall into one of two categories: (1) improving the labor pool available to the corporation by better educating students in certain skills and disciplines; or (2) performing research that could one day lead to product development, but may be too speculative right now to undertake in the company's own laboratories.

With a little imagination, academic libraries can position themselves to appeal to both of these traditional areas of corporate involvement. In terms of educating our future work force, libraries serve as laboratories for students to develop the kinds of information seeking skills they will need to become lifelong independent learners. On most campuses, the library is where a majority of students encounter for the first time the kind of networked computing environment that is becoming such an important feature of our lives. Certainly there are opportunities here to establish creative corporate partnerships, not only with local companies that employ many of our graduates but with those that develop and produce the information products used in business, industry and the professions.

A good example of a library-corporate partnership focusing on research and development is the pilot project conducted jointly by Xerox Corporation and Cornell University Library to test a system for high speed, on demand digital scanning of deteriorated books and other documents. A project staff of preservation librarians and systems analysts from Cornell worked with engineers at Xerox to determine whether digital scanning technology, coupled with high speed laser printing, could be made to produce paper facsimiles at comparable cost and with superior quality to microfilmed images, while yielding such value added benefits as computer storage, searching capabilities, and portability over networks. ① The results of the experiments suggest it will be possible to scan and digitize deteriorating library materials and offer the contents over high capacity networks. Clearly such a development could have commercial applications for Xerox.

If you are unable to develop a direct cooperative venture between your library and a corporation, try to piggy-back on top of academic departments that are successful at attracting their backing. A major contracted research project may require library materials that you do not currently own. If you can get your institutional grants administrator or contracted research office to agree, it is an excellent idea to review proposals before they are submitted to funding in the first place. The review might include an assessment of current library strength in the research area of the proposal, and if resources are inadequate, a plan for improvement. Then the budget could be built into the grant proposal itself. Graduate programs in certain disciplines are supposed to be supported by the external funding they generate. The library acquisitions funding needed to bring specific components of the collection up to "research" level should be similarly supported from sponsored research funds.

Trends in Corporate Giving

Because of the current recession, many major corporations are not increasing their giving budgets to keep pace with inflation. There was dramatic growth during the decade of the 1980s: from \$2.5 billion in 1981 to \$5.2 billion in 1986. But since then corporate philanthropy has failed to keep pace with inflation. Last year's (1990) total of \$6 billion actually represents a decrease in constant dollar terms. ②

In this competitive environment, it helps to be aware of the new directions in corporate giving so that you can market your library in ways that will appeal to their interests. Following are some

---

① Anne R. Kenney and Lynne K. Personius. "Update on digital techniques". *The Commission on Preservation and Access newsletter.* No. 40, Nov. /Dec. 1991. [Newsletter insert].

② Jennifer Moore. *Op. cit.*, p. 1.

of these recent trends:
- Corporations are looking for projects that will yield high visibility for themselves and generate concrete accomplishments.
- There has been a tendency to award larger grants, which reduces overall number of grants that can be made.
- Corporations are less likely than ever to fund organizations approaching them for the first time. They are looking for the tried and true.
- There is a tendency to avoid projects with multiple sponsors, so that the corporation can get all the credit for a particular project.
- They are looking for measurable results.
- They are making more grants for activities in areas near company headquarters; fewer grants go to areas of regional operations.
- They are providing more non-cash gifts, such as equipment or volunteer services.
- They are funding projects that have broad popular appeal with consumers, employees, and community residents. Environmental issues and school reform are hot topics at the moment. Increases in these categories have eroded support for higher education and arts organizations.
- There is more aid for pre-college education. During the decade of the 1980s, this category grew from 4 percent of the total educational giving of corporations to 11 per cent.
- Many corporations have decided to stop giving altogether to capital campaigns.

A possible way around these negative trends? Solicit smaller companies that haven't given in the past. When the topic of business philanthropy is raised, we tend to think automatically in terms of the high visibility Fortune 500 corporations. It's true that these outfits are likely to have the largest and most organized charitable giving programs. But for precisely that reason they also receive the lion's share of funding requests—thousands more than they can accommodate each year. It can be well worth your time to look beyond the Fortune 500 companies to identify small but profitable businesses active in your own community: retailers, wholesalers, small manufacturers, service firms, real estate, finance and insurance firms, banks, doctor's offices, attorneys, hotels and motels, accounting firms, local or regional utilities, to name just a few. Most academic libraries have plenty of reference tools that can lead you to these potential sources of support.

Corporations Are People Too

Remember that even though corporations and foundations may appear impersonal, they are made up of human beings like yourself; and it is human beings who will make the decision whether or not to fund your proposal. There is much more room for the personal touch in working with foundation or corporation prospects than is true in the case of a government agency. As you reach the final stage of the research process with a high priority corporate or foundation prospect, you should take the trouble to learn about the people who run the organization and make the real decisions. Check the *Taft Foundation Reporter* for information on the donors, directors, and officers. If the foundation is not listed there, check their names in biographical directories like *Who's Who in Finance and Industry* or *Dun & Bradstreet Online*. Find out if any of the officers and directors are alumni of your college or university. Find out if anyone on your major gifts committee knows any of the influential people at the foundation.

Make up a single alphabetical list of all of these individuals, providing a little background on each, and circulate it to members of your major gifts committee, the development office, the trustees, and other volunteer leaders that you rely on for advice and help in the campaign. If you have a friend of the library (or of the college or university of which you are a part) who in turn knows the CEO of a corporation on your prospect list, do not be shy about asking him or her for help. It might be no more than writing a cover letter for your application. It might be calling for an appointment with the executive. Ideally, it could mean accompanying you to the appointment and helping to present the proposal. It might mean calling with a word of support after the proposal has been presented. Make use of your influential campaign volunteers to the fullest extent possible when dealing with the corporate world. They are the ones who have credibility with their fellow leaders in the business community.

III. Individuals — The Most Important Prospects of All

Individual donors account for the vast majority of the charitable dollars contributed each year, and your fund raising plan needs to emphasize them. Some librarians resist the logic of devoting more time to individuals than to other kinds of prospects. They actually seem to prefer the impersonality of government agencies, foundation staff, or corporate giving officers. These organizations are in the business of giving money away, so there is no embarrassment in asking. That is what they expect you to do. And the asking is more likely to be done by means of a written proposal, rather than in a face-to-face meeting. Some of us are more comfortable working with ideas on paper than with people.

You mustn't let these attitudes lead you to ignore individuals as prospects for support. Studies have shown that in the long run they will provide most of your dollars. They will be much more loyal than corporations or foundations, which tend to follow their own agendas. They are more likely to make unrestricted gifts that can be applied to your areas of greatest need. But most important, individual donors can help you obtain other gifts from their own friends, relatives, or business contacts. Every personal contribution your library receives has a potential multiplying effect that can extend for a lifetime.

There is one very significant trait of individual donors that you must always bear in mind: some have a whole lot more money than others. A few will be capable of making that $1 million leadership gift. Indeed, it was recently announced that businessman W. T. Young had pledged $5 million to the University of Kentucky Library campaign. That is the kind of personal gift that we all dream about, and in Chapter 6 U. K. Library Director Paul Willis tells us how it was secured. But of course most individual donors will be able to provide far less: it might be only $100, or $1,000, or $10,000, or perhaps as much as $100,000.

It is important to recognize the widely divergent giving capabilities of individual donors, so you can target your efforts where they do the most good. A capital campaign is an intensive, time-limited project to raise a specific sum of money. To be successful, you must manage your own time carefully. That means following the gift table pyramid structure outlined in chapter two, dividing prospects up into categories by expected giving levels, and then devoting most of your efforts to securing those leadership and major gifts. In the case of government agencies, foundations or corporations, it will be fairly easy to assign them to a giving level, and it will generally be high on the pyramid. After all, grants of $100,000 and more are not at all uncommon. It is easy to justify spending the time needed to secure such a gift for your campaign.

In developing a pool of individual prospects, your effort must be not just to find as many people as possible to support the campaign, but to select from this larger group the very best prospects for concentrated attention. What makes the process frustrating is that (unlike government, foundation or corporate grant-makers) it is difficult to know what an individual's giving capacity might be. There are techniques for making these kinds of judgments, and in the next chapter we will describe a few of them. For now it is enough to emphasize that you want to identify the potential leadership donors right at the outset, so you can begin working to secure their support early in the campaign, preferably even before it is announced to the public. Next you will turn your attention to the so-called "major gifts" level on the pyramid, and so on, as the campaign moves through its various phases to a conclusion.

So where do you start looking for those individual donors? More than likely they are going to come from one or more of the following categories:

1. Prior donors.
2. Friends members and volunteers.
3. Alumni, their spouses, and business associates.

4. Faculty members.
5. Library users.
6. Collectors and book dealers.
7. Related organizations.
8. Student groups (such as fraternities and sororities).
9. Graduating and reunion classes.

Prior Donors

It is an axiom of fundraising that those who have already given to your cause are the most likely to give in the future. Sometimes there is a tendency to think that prior donors have "done their part" and should be excused from the current campaign. That is a big mistake. Always enlist the support of your existing donors, when you are lucky enough to have them!

All the textbooks say you are supposed to build a major capital campaign on the foundation of a successful annual giving program. What often happens in practice is that a college or university is able to meet that test and decides to launch a campaign. But in the meantime the library itself has little to show in the way of annual support. Many a director has been invited to participate in a capital campaign without having any cards to lay on the table in the form of major donors with a history of giving to the library. That kind of situation calls for some innovative strategies for identifying people around whom you can build a viable campaign.

Friends Groups

A friends group might be a good place to start. But again it will not yield too many great prospects unless it has reached a certain size and maturity, with a pattern of year-to-year increases in annual giving. If you have a friends organization like the University of Illinois Library, which includes some 4,000 members contributing \$330,000 a year,① then you are blessed with a built-in pool of individual prospects for your capital campaign. In a case like this, key members of the friends group should already have been included in the pre-campaign feasibility study. These are the very persons you will now target as campaign leaders. That means, in the first place, discussing with them in specific terms their own "lead gifts" to the library. But it also means recruiting them to serve on your major gifts committee where they will help you to identify, evaluate, and solicit other prospective donors. (In our next chapter, "Organizing for Success," we will discuss this process in some detail.)

But let's face it, few friends groups can compare with the one at the University of Illinois Library, or the Yale Library Associates, or the Brandeis National Women's Committee. Most are modest affairs that do not generate much in the way of annual giving. Often they consist of faculty members and townspeople of modest means, few of whom are in a position to play major roles in a successful capital campaign. At least one fundraising expert, Duke University Library Director Jerry Campbell, has gone so far as to say publicly that friends groups cost more than they are worth.② In any case, it is true that many libraries have all but ignored their established friends organizations when undertaking a major capital campaign. Make a realistic assessment of your own friends group in terms of its ability to substantially assist with the campaign. Then, if necessary, do not hesitate to turn outside this circle of past supporters to find persons of "influence and affluence" for leadership positions.

Alumni

Unlike other parts of campus, the library does not have its own alumni. This is becoming an even greater handicap than in past years, since the trend these days in university capital

---

① Joan M. Hood. "Library friends." In: Barbara I. Dewey, op. cit., p. 13.
② Jerry Campbell. "Identification and cultivation of potential donors." Presentation at ACRL/FFDS Preconference, "Implementing Successful Capital Campaigns for the Establishment of Endowment Funds in Libraries." Chicago, June 21-22, 1990. [Author's notes]

campaigns is to emphasize so-called "constituent" fundraising. This approach is based on the theory of market segmentation. Instead of trying to sell the whole institution as one undifferentiated mass, why not divide it up into its constituent parts and appeal to those with a special connection to each area? Typically college deans are encouraged to form their own alumni societies, publish newsletters, and establish boards of visitors composed of prominent alumni whose "expertise" is sought in guiding educational programs. Once the fundraising drive is launched, these organizational structures can be placed in service of the campaign. Each college or school becomes directly involved in the cultivation and solicitation process, targeting appeals to its own graduates. Not only does this approach leverage the efforts of the central development office by enlisting the help of college deans, school directors, and department chairs, but it draws upon the special identification graduates are supposed to have with their own academic program.

In theory, constituent fundraising produces better overall results (broader participation and more dollars) than the earlier centralized approach. But it can easily work against general university services, such as the library, that lack a clearly defined constituency. In order to avoid being frozen out of the process, library directors need to be more aggressive than ever in pursuing influential alumni. Some of the strategies include:

Argue the library's right to have access to the top donors. Here is where the most important allies you can have are the president and the chief development officer. Only they can give you access to the coveted top donors. This is a key issue for the library. You have to be prepared to go right to the top and demand at least a fair share of the really good prospects for the library.

Raid other colleges for their alumni. If you are part of a college or university, learn as much as you can about the key people on the board of trustees, the alumni association, external boards of visitors, and (of course) major donors to other programs.

Ask permission to pursue wealthy non-givers. Every college or university has a pool of well-to-do alumni who, for whatever reasons, have never given a dime to the institution. These may not be prime prospects, so why not ask the development office to let you pursue them? What has anybody got to lose? And it just could happen that the library will succeed where others have failed. In Chapter 8 we will share a stunning success story involving a so-called "non-giver."

Graduate student alumni are being targeted by many academic libraries for their capital campaigns. This group differs from undergraduate alumni in several important respects. They are much less inclined to be interested in college athletics, which right away cuts out the biggest competitor for all alumni dollars. During their years on campus, graduate students probably spend more time in the library (or the research laboratory) than anyplace else. They have a good understanding of the importance of the library and can be convinced to support it. Finally, former graduate students receive less attention from development personnel, who have learned from experience that the undergraduate alum is more likely to feel institutional loyalty.

Former student library employees are another category of alumni that may deserve special attention. Libraries are among the largest student employers on most campuses. These student employees have spent a great deal of time in the library. Often they develop close ties with their supervisors. Some libraries have begun to claim them as their own "alumni." If they worked in the library and had a positive experience, they may be willing to give to you in preference to their college or academic department.

Faculty Members

Faculty members (both current and emeriti) should be high on your list of potential supporters. More than anyone else, they understand the importance of library resources to the research process. Faculty often spend their entire working careers at a single college or university. Many develop an emotional attachment to the institution that encourages them to take the long view of things and prompts a desire to leave a part of themselves behind for future generations. These kinds of feelings make faculty members excellent prospects for library endowment campaigns, which offer less glamour and more immediate results than other types of capital campaigns.

The problem, of course, is that for years low faculty salaries have made it impossible for them to participate as major donors. In terms of immediate cash gifts, most faculty members are still likely to be fairly limited in what they can contribute. But by employing some of the creative planned and deferred giving methods described later in this chapter, it is well within the realm of possibility for many older faculty members to give upwards of $100,000 or more to your campaign. Best of all, you as director know the faculty on a personal level better than you know any other class of individual prospect. And it is relationships that ultimately raise money.

Many faculty members spend years of effort building up their personal research collections, which can in turn become valuable gifts-in-kind to the library. Although there may be a good deal of duplication between a faculty convenience collection and the library's holdings, it is generally worthwhile to examine even these kinds of collections carefully for useful items. Duplicates from a private library are usually in better condition than their counterparts in your circulating collection, and for that reason may be worth adding. In other cases the collections assembled by faculty members are highly specialized and constitute an impressive addition to the library's more general coverage of a particular field.

Library Users

Even library users should be considered potential prospects, assuming they are satisfied with the service they have received. (If they are not satisfied, you had better think long and hard about launching a campaign in the first place. It might be better to concentrate on improving the library's image with its constituents.) In the 1985 ALA Yearbook it was reported the public library in Virginia Beach had received the entire estate of a local couple who had been "heavy library users" and "wanted to give the city something for everyone."①

Collectors and Book Dealers

Among the university's alumni and friends, there are bound to be at least a few who have invested considerable wealth and personal taste collecting rare books, examples of fine printing, historical manuscripts, posters, prints and broadsides, or other similar kinds of material. Such persons should be identified and cultivated early in a capital campaign. They are natural allies of the library, which can not only serve as the eventual repository for their collections, but can also make the case that resources will be needed to properly organize, catalog, house and exhibit those collections to best advantage. One way to identify collectors in your vicinity and learn of their interests is to cultivate local book dealers. A dealer who also happens to be an alumni (or with whom the library does a substantial amount of business) can be a valuable source of information.

Related Organizations

One of the best techniques (also suggested by Jerry Campbell of Duke University Libraries) is to steal lists. Ask your friends to supply membership lists of organizations to which they belong. Obtain lists of major donors to other philanthropic causes in the community.② Look for people involved in library-related fields, such as publishing, information technology, museums, the arts, education, and the like. Be a joiner. Affiliate with local service clubs, business councils, community associations, and cultural organizations. Use every opportunity to meet people of "influence or affluence," seeking always to interest them in the library's collections, services, and programs.

Student Groups

Student groups, including Greek organizations, honor societies, and other special interest

---

① Clyde C. Walton. "Gifts, bequests, endowments." *ALA yearbook of library and information service*; 1985, p. 133.
② Jerry Campbell, *Ibid.*

clubs, can often be enlisted on behalf the library's campaign. It is unlikely that you will be able to raise big dollars directly from the students themselves. But their visible support and energy as volunteers can be an invaluable asset in selling the library to others. You need to convince alumni and other prospects that the library is an important part of the educational process—that it really matters to students. At the University of Kentucky Library (whose $20 million capital campaign is profiled in chapter 5), the Panhellenic Council organized a walk-a-thon with a goal of $10,000. Some 800 sorority members participated in the event, which was widely publicized in the local media. ① Although the actual dollars raised might not seem all that significant in the context of such a big campaign, the message was worth a million! Remember this when it comes to planning special events and tours for donors, preparing publicity materials about the campaign, or conducting telephone solicitations, and seek help from student organizations.

Graduating and Reunion Classes

Despite what we have just said about students being unlikely to make large gifts as individuals, they have been known to raise significant amounts of money by acting together. In recent years there have been senior class gifts in the five-digits at several schools, including Indiana University and the University of Iowa.

Class reunions provide another opportunity for groups of former students to benefit the library. In many cases, the organizers of these events are looking for attractive gift ideas. If you are engaged in a capital campaign, find out the size of recent reunion gifts and develop a few ideas to fit within that dollar framework. Once you have prepared your list, ask the alumni office for a chance to share it with the reunion leaders. The results can be quite gratifying. At Ohio University, where the authors of this book have gained their own fundraising experience, the Class of 1952 gave $12,500 as its 35th reunion gift to furnish a new lounge in the library. For its 50th reunion gift, the University of Pennsylvania's class of 1932 established a $100,000 acquisitions endowment. ② The North Carolina State Class of 1932 raised $32,000 for library acquisitions at that institution. ③

IV. Types of Giving
Direct Giving

There is an old wisecrack that pretty well sums up two basic kinds of giving: "You can pay me now, or you can pay me later!" In the world of development, "pay me now" translates into "direct giving". It refers to a situation when the gift is made immediately, or within a short timeframe, from the donor to the charity. Planned or deferred giving, on the other hand, is an arrangement in which the donor agrees to "pay later", sometimes many years later. Normally you will prefer to receive a direct gift, whether it consists of cash, securities, real estate, or other tangible property. But there can be circumstances (as described below) when a planned or deferred gift offers advantages to donor and charity alike.

Cash gifts

In any campaign, the most valuable gifts are those that are made in cash and paid in full to the charitable institution. Direct cash giving provides you with the desired resources right away, allowing you either to invest them in an endowment or spend them to produce immediate benefits for your patrons. Only slightly less desirable is the so-called "life of the campaign pledge", in which a donor agrees to make a gift of cash payable in several installments over a relatively brief period, (say three to five years), so that the pledge is redeemed in full by the end of your capital campaign.

---

① *Library Hotline*, January 16, 1989, p. 5.
② Clyde C. Walton. "Gifts, bequests and endowments". *ALA yearbook of library and information service*; *1984*, p. 150.
③ Clyde C. Walton. "Gifts, bequests and endowments". *ALA yearbook of library and information service*; *1986*, p. 152.

Gifts of appreciated securities

If a donor owns stock that has appreciated in value, he or she can transfer ownership in the security to a qualifying charity. Not only does this avoid a taxable gain on the appreciated value, it generates a tax deduction equal to the full value of the security on the day it was transferred. This can be an attractive way for certain high income donors to make an even larger contribution to your campaign than would be possible by other means. Here's how it works. Assume that a donor in a 33 percent marginal tax bracket owns 1000 shares of a stock purchased five years ago for $30,000 and currently worth $60,000. By transferring those shares to a qualifying charity, the donor can claim a $60,000 deduction, which at the 33 percent rate translates into a tax savings of $20,000. The effective cost to the donor for making this $60,000 gift is only $10,000: the original $30,000 investment minus the $20,000 in tax savings.

Gifts of real estate

These gifts are tricky to handle because of all the risks commonly associated with real estate. Before accepting ownership of any donated property, it is essential to conduct a thorough examination of its market value and liquidity, together with any outstanding mortgages, taxes, liens, legal claims or other potential problems that could generate unwanted costs and/or complicate its sale. In fact, if the real estate is to be sold and converted to cash, then you are better off letting the donor do it. Of course in the case of a highly appreciated piece of real estate, the donor may want to do just the opposite in order to avoid a taxable capital gain. Unless you have a development office that is used to handling gifts of real estate, it is probably better to turn it down.

Gifts of tangible property

Libraries have a unique opportunity to seek out gifts of books, manuscripts and other valuable material for the enhancement of their collections. But beware the donor who attaches unacceptable conditions to a potential gift-in-kind. The library must be free to exercise the same judgment in disposing of a gift collection that it would employ in spending actual funds to purchase materials. If the materials are out of date, out of scope, in poor physical condition, or otherwise inappropriate, the gift should be politely refused. An alternative, of course, is to accept the gift with the understanding that it will be sold for cash or exchanged for items that the library needs. Most donors appreciate being dealt with in an honest and forthright manner.

Be especially skeptical of the donor who vastly over-values his personal heirlooms and wants you to provide handsomely for their display, hinting that a more substantial gift may someday result if you are able to meet the test. The provost at a well-known midwestern university once opined that what the school most needed was a "Vice-President in Charge of Saying 'No' to Gifts." What he meant by this is that too often gifts are accepted not because they are valuable in themselves, but for some ulterior motive: typically a hope that today's unwanted gift will lead to future largesse. Somehow it almost never works out that way!

Planned Giving

It should always be your goal to encourage donors to make their gifts promptly, during the life of the campaign if at all possible. But you will often encounter situations when the donor is unable to handle a large gift right the moment. Perhaps the donor is "cash poor", with lots of assets tied up in real estate, investments, or business ventures that cannot be liquidated for quite some time. Perhaps there are current expenses that need to be met, or family obligations expected to arise in the future that require the donor to retain control of assets until reaching a later stage in life. Perhaps that prospective donor who has assembled a fine book collection over the years is still enjoying it too much to consider parting with it for the time being. In cases like these, you need to be aware of some of the basic planned giving concepts, so that you can tailor a proposal to meet the particular financial abilities and current life situation of your donor prospect.

As a library director you cannot be expected to become a true "expert" about all the intricacies of planned giving. On larger campuses there should be someone (perhaps even a full-time planned giving officer) who can provide advice on these matters. In fact, some of the more elaborate planned giving vehicles, like pooled income funds or charitable remainder trusts, will only be available at institutions with mature development operations able to accept and manage gifts of this kind. (If you are not among these, consult a local attorney who specializes in estate planning.) But as the library director, you should be familiar in a general way with the most common types of planned giving arrangements and understand their advantages to both donor and charitable institution.

The most important point to remember about planned (or deferred) giving is that it provides an opportunity for the donor to leverage the size of his or her gift. Either it allows a gift to be made at some future point that cannot be secured right now, or it permits the donor to make a much larger gift than would otherwise be possible. In fact, many donors will be surprised and delighted to learn what they can do with a little financial ingenuity. Planned giving enlists time as your ally, making it possible for both donor and charity to realize their dreams.

Extended Pledges

The most familiar way to increase the size of a gift beyond what a donor might normally be able to consider is simply to stretch it out over an extended period of time. While $10,000 may look like a great deal of money to many potential donors, the idea of paying $1,000 a year for ten years (or less than $100 a month) will probably appear much less daunting.

Bequests

Sometimes considered the second-class citizens of fundraising, because they do not generate an immediate payoff for the charity, bequests are nonetheless an indispensable part of any planned giving program. You should have in place a low-key, repetitive, tasteful but persistent program for encouraging bequests. Frank A. Logan, director of bequests and trusts for Dartmouth College, has noted that as the baby-boom generation approaches retirement, there will be an unprecedented opportunity to generate bequest gifts. "There is a golden age out there. You have this build up of assets that have to go somewhere. These people have to be reminded that you can't take it with you."①

Life Insurance

A term life insurance policy, with your library made out as beneficiary, could be an attractive way for a younger donor to leverage a relatively small current cash outlay into a gift of sizeable proportions. For example, a healthy 40 year-old non-smoker can purchase a $50,000 term life insurance policy for about $5,000. Of course you will not receive the benefit of that gift for many years, and for exactly this reason many development officers discourage this type of planned giving. It is probably better for the institution to get $5,000 right now, as opposed to receiving $50,000 in forty years or more. But depending on what formula your development office uses to establish the value of life insurance gifts, the donor could be publicly credited with a major gift to the campaign. This is a good vehicle for younger, prestige-minded donors who want to establish themselves in the philanthropic community.

Pooled income funds

Under a pooled income arrangement, donors give cash or securities to a fund set up by a charity, which invests the assets in a portfolio. Donors get charitable tax deductions and receive income from the fund proportionate to the shares they own in it, much like a mutual fund. In fact, some charities offer a "family" of several different pooled income funds, each having its own investment objective and asset mix.

---

① Quoted in the *Chronicle of Philanthropy*, October 22, 1991, p. 23.

Charitable remainder trusts

A charitable remainder trust is an agreement by a donor to place assets in trust for a designated period of time. During the trust term, the donor (or other beneficiaries) receive annual distributions from the trust assets. At the expiration of the trust term, the assets pass to the designated charity. The benefits are that (1) the donor is entitled to an income tax deduction; (2) distributions can be assured for the life of the donor, his wife, or children for a period of years; (3) it allows non-income producing property to be converted to income producing assets without incurring a capital gain; (4) it eliminates the need for the donor to manage the assets; (5) the potential taxable estate of the donor is reduced by the amount of the donation; (6) it can be a "win/win" proposition for both the donor and the charity.

Charitable lead trusts

With this vehicle the donor places assets in trust for a designated period, during which time annual distributions from the corpus are paid to the charitable organization. (Hence the term "lead" trust, since the benefit to the charity accrues from the very beginning of the arrangement—unlike a "remainder" trust, in which the benefit is postponed.) At the expiration of the trust term, the assets revert to the donor, designated heirs, or an estate. The benefits are that (1) the donor is entitled to current income tax deductions at a time when income may be relatively high and the deductions are therefore more valuable; (2) the assets are later recovered by the donor (or heirs) at a time when they will presumably be more needed.

Charitable annuity trusts and charitable uniterm trusts

These terms really describe the way in which the assets are invested: either to produce a fixed annual payment (annuity) or a flexible yield that can fluctuate based on market conditions (Uniterm). Annuity trusts and uniterm trusts can be established either for remainder or lead charitable trusts.

Conclusion

As one expert has said: "Planned giving is the branch of giving that spends most of its time listening to donors and thinking about long-term gifts, building endowments, and strengthening the institution."[①] Over the next two decades there will be unprecedented opportunities in the planned giving area. Tens of millions of "baby boomers" will be reaching their maximum earning years and approaching retirement. These are the very people who attended colleges and universities during the great expansion period of the 1960s and 1970s. They comprise a big portion of your alumni base, but many have not yet participated significantly in either annual giving drives or capital campaigns. In the meantime, inflation in real estate values (and in mortgage payments) has left many of these prospects cash poor but with greatly appreciated assets. Over the years ahead there will be a massive shifting of these accumulated assets. A well orchestrated planned giving program can reap big dividends for your library.

---

① *Ibid.*, p. 23.

第五章 为募款成功所建立的组织

Chapter 5　Organizing for Success

I. What is the Appropriate Organization for Fundraising?

In Chapter 2 on "Planning for Fundraising", mention was made of the importance of teamwork. An effective team often is made up of the top executive of the institution, the library director, board directors, development staff, community leaders, volunteers, friends of the library, and others. In university settings, faculty members and senior university administrators are among the strong library supporters and volunteers. To achieve maximum results from the joint talent, commitment, efforts, and enthusiasm of the fundraising team, an appropriate and effective organization is essential.

The organization of the development office and its team varies greatly from one library to another, depending on the organizational structure of a library, the particular program of fundraising, and the extent of the campaign.

For an academic library in a major university, the library may have its own development staff, either under the jurisdiction of the university's development office or responsible to the library director. In either case, a close coordination of the efforts must be maintained between the university's development office and the library. Taking a look at the organization chart of the Development Office of Ohio University in Table 5-1, one can see how a well established development program is organized. As indicated in Chapter 2, Ohio University is currently undertaking a major fundraising campaign with a goal of $100 million. The campaign has required an expansion of staff size from less than 10 to over 40.

Even with such a large and complex organization, the library must also contribute a great amount of staff time and financial resources to support the fundraising activities. In addition to the one-third time of an Assistant Dean of Development assigned to the library, the Dean of University Libraries, the Associate Dean for Subject and Special Collections, the Assistant to the Dean, the Head of Special Collections and Archives, and a number of other library staff all have devoted various amounts of time to the campaign. We fully realize that such a level of commitment and spirit of cooperation are of utmost importance for a successful campaign.

3. 20世纪90年代图书馆募款所面对的挑战 实用指南：从新手到专家 367

Table 5-1 Organization Chart of Ohio University's Development Office

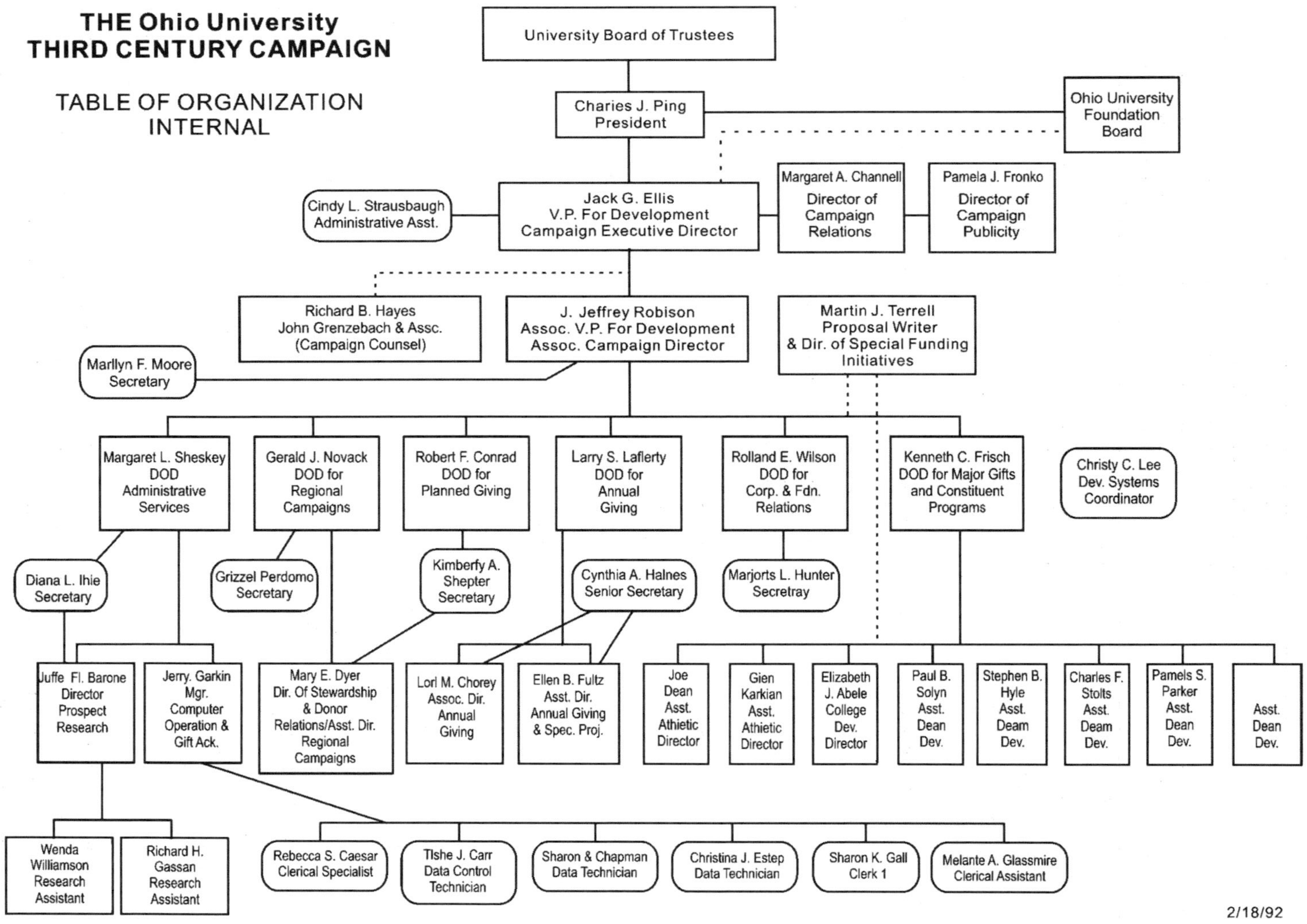

Table 5–2 Organization for Fundraising at the University of Kentucky Library

```
                Library Associates Executive Board
                     Director of Libraries
                              |
                    Fundraising Coordinator
                              |
   ---------------------------+---------------------------
   |                          |                          |
Director                   Director                   Director
Support Services           Gifts Program              Public Relations

Prospect evaluation        Foundations                News bureau
Gift records               Corporations               Publications
Prospect records           Individuals                Special events
Acknowledgments                                       Marketing
Special reports                                       Proposal preparation
```

NOTE: Directors should be Library staff members because of the tremendous amount of work to be done.

Table 5–3 Organization Chart of Development Office at a Medium-Sized University

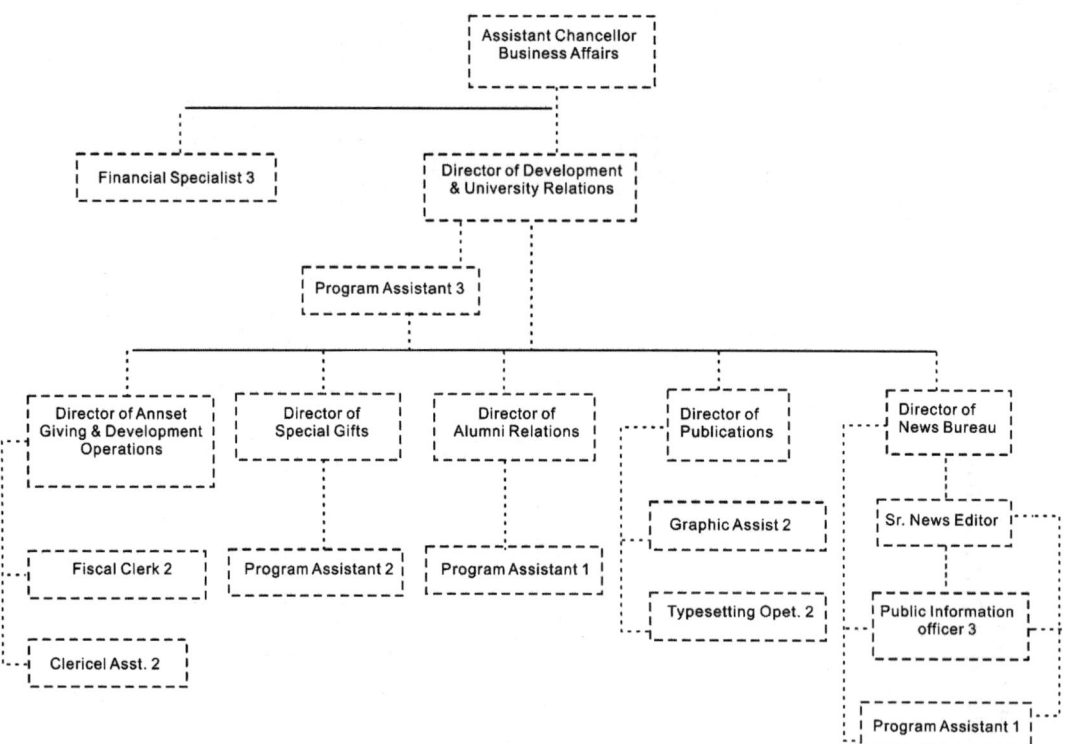

Table 5–2 outlines the organization of a $20 million capital campaign at the University of Kentucky Library, which is more fully described in Chapter 6. Here the fundraising operation is conducted from within the library itself, with a very substantial contribution of its own staff time. By contrast, in colleges or universities of smaller size, there may only be one or two development officers for the entire institution. In such a case, the fundraising for the library may be an integral part of the institution. The library director may be consulted and asked to participate by the development office. An example of the organization of the development office at this type of institution

II. How Do You Organize for a Major Capital Campaign?

Besides the organization of the development office, the assignment of development staff, the assignment of fundraising responsibilities to library staff, and the recruitment of leaders and volunteers, there is a need to design a structure to facilitate cooperation and communications among all the participants in a fundraising program. The structure for a major capital campaign may be quite complicated given the extent of involvement and the limits on time. The External Organization Chart of Ohio University's Third Century Campaign in Table 5 – 4 is an example of the type of organizational structure needed to undertake a major capital campaign.

Table5 – 4   External Organization Chart of the Ohio University Third Century Campaign

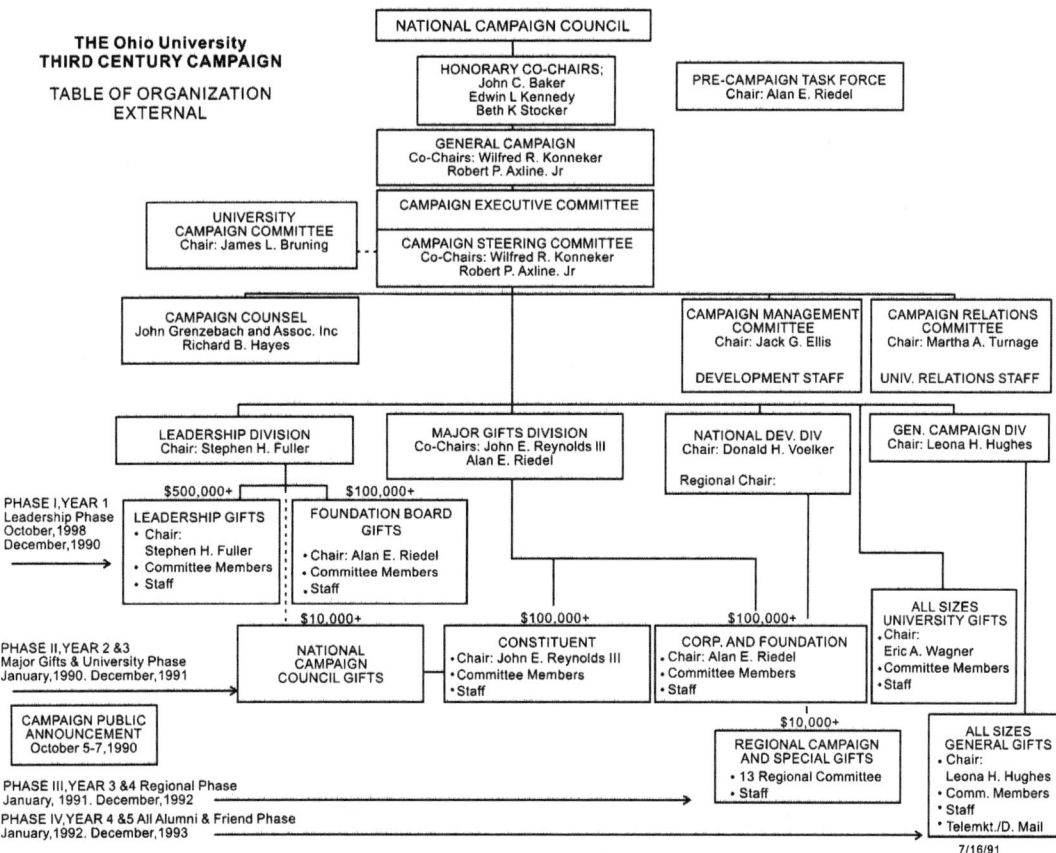

As shown in the external organization chart, there is a hierarchical structure of committees under a **National Campaign Council**. The council has a number of honorary co-chairs, including a past university president and two distinguished alumni—each of whom has made a multi-million-dollar gift to the campaign. The **Council**, under the co-chair of two distinguished alumni, has a **Campaign Executive Committee** and a **Campaign Steering Committee**. Both the university president and vice president for development are members of the Campaign Executive Committee. To assist the **Council**, there are three university committees, four divisions (each with its own subcommittees), and a number of special committees:

University Committees
- **University Campaign Committee** — chaired by the Provost
- **Campaign Management Committee** — chaired by the Vice President for Development
- **Campaign Relations Committee** — chaired by the Vice President for University Relations

Divisions
- **Leadership Gifts Division**
  — Leadership Gifts Committee (for gifts of $500,000 +)
  — Ohio University Foundation Board Gifts Committee (for gifts of $100,000 +)
- **Major Gifts Division**
  — Major Gifts Committee (for gifts of $100,000 +)
- **National Development Division**
  — Regional Campaign and Special Gifts Committee
  — General Campaign Division
  — All sizes General Gifts Committee

Special Committees
- **Constituent Unit Committees** (each college, the library, athletics, etc.)
- **Corporate and Foundation Committee**
- **All Sizes University Gifts Committee**

The membership of each committee often consists of development staff, institution administrators, and volunteer leaders. The typical duties and responsibilities, using the Constituent Unit Committee as an example, are shown in Table 5 – 5.

The recruitment of volunteer leaders for various committees is not easy but is absolutely essential. Because these volunteer leaders will be asked to not only contribute their time but also their money, every library needs to have a few of these committed individuals.

Table 5 – 5 Duties and Responsibilities of the Constituent Committee Members

Objective: To join together with five to ten other alumni and friends of the college/unit to seek campaign gift commitments toward the constituency goal from major prospects rated $100,000 + including alumni, friends, corporations and foundations.

Primary Responsibilities:
  A constituent committee member will be asked to help by soliciting prospects—individuals by and large—who are rated for outright and/or deferred gifts of $100,000 to $499,000. This activity will comprise Phase II of the Ohio University Third Century Campaign and should be completed within 24 months, running January 1990 – December, 1991. Other responsibilities include:
  1. Participating in all constituent committee meetings to be called by the constituency chair two or three times a year, not likely to exceed six meetings.
  2. Attending the first two all-important constituency committee meetings held:
  July 28, 1990 which will also serve to bring together committee members from all constituencies during the Ohio University Foundation Board annual meeting weekend.
  October 5 & 6, 1990 the campaign kickoff gala weekend which announces the campaign publicly and recognizes all campaign volunteers.
  3. Contributing strategies for cultivating and soliciting prospects.
  4. Considering a campaign major gift commitment of their own outright over a five year period or through some combination of outright and deferred commitment. It will be important for all committee members to make their own campaign commitments as soon as possible, recognizing the importance of doing so before beginning to solicit others.

III. Do You Have a System for Prospect Identification?

Once the organization is in place, the next big step is the identification and evaluation of all donor prospects. The system of prospect identification includes finding, researching, and rating any potential donor, who may be an individual, a corporation, a foundation, or a government agency. It has been noted earlier that individual donors are the single most important category of donors. In a typical campaign they may contribute up to 80% of the goal.

Because the evaluation of corporate, foundation, and government funding sources has been well covered in the preceding chapters, this section focuses on the more complicated task of assessing individual prospects to determine how much they can contribute to your campaign.

All individual prospects may be divided into a number of categories by the level of giving. The following four categories are used in the Third Century Campaign of Ohio University:

A. **Leadership gift prospects**: These are prospects who can give above the $500,000 level.
B. **Major gift prospects**: These are prospects who can give between $100,000 and $499,999.
C. **Special gift prospects**: These are prospects who can give between $10,000 and $99,999.
D. **General gift prospects**: For all those who can give up to $10,000.

Because, as indicated from experience in most major campaigns, nearly 90% of the funds raised come from fewer than 10% of all donors, it is of utmost importance to identify the top 10% prospects early in the campaign. This top 10% is made up of all the **leadership**, **major**, and **special** gift prospects.

As mentioned in Chapter 4, colleges and universities often find their best donor prospects among alumni and friends. Those who have given in the past are more likely to give again and at a higher level for a compelling cause. Both retired and current faculty and staff are also strong donor prospects. In a major capital campaign, academic libraries often have to compete with academic departments in the same institution to claim alumni or others as donor prospects. One way of doing this is by showing the past giving record of those who have previously supported the library. If a library has already had an annual giving program, the identification of donor prospects is much easier. A strong Friends of the Library group will also be very helpful.

In public libraries, donor prospects, in addition to library patrons, board directors, and friends, may include community and civic leaders, businesses, etc.

To identify the right prospects and establish for each the potential level of giving, the development office of an institution or a library must be equipped to research the list of individual prospects using a variety of information and reference resources. (For list of information sources for individual prospects, see Appendix XI.) An experienced reference librarian will make an excellent researcher on prospects. A common problem that should be corrected is that researchers in a development office often have no background in library reference work and do not know many of the reference sources available in the library. It is advisable that researchers in the development office and the library's reference librarians team up to get as much information as possible for each of the key prospects. Since many of the prospects have had a connection with the institution or library, some of their personal information which may be hard to find elsewhere is actually in the institutional records. Following is a list of essential information to be gathered for each prospect.[1]

— name, nickname (including Mr., Mrs., Ms., Dr., Prof., etc.)
— addresses
— telephone and FAX number(s)
— business title, address, and phone, FAX, E-mail numbers
— marital status
— number, names, and ages of children
— date and place of birth
— education (secondary and higher/academic areas/degrees)
— spouse's name
— spouse's education and business
— family connections to the organization
— family connections to other organizations

---

[1] Based on F. Mark Whittaker, "Prospect research, evaluation, cultivation, and solicitation". Outline of presentation at annual CASE conference, Philadelphia, Pa., March 1983. Quoted by Dove, *op. cit.*, p. 93.

- job history
- honors and achievements
- clubs and organizations
- political affiliation
- religious affiliation
- personal interests
- estimated net worth
- net salary
- stock holdings
- directorships
- family foundations
- favorite charities
- gift record
- names of secretaries
- attorney
- banker
- close friends

Based on the information gathered, the development staff will be able to identify prospects for the **leadership**, **major**, and **special** groups and begin the process of evaluation and rating. In the rating of donor prospects, the development staff should as much as possible include appropriate members of various committees. The knowledge of individual prospects by friends, peers, or acquaintances who serve as volunteers often enhances and validates staff efforts.

A number of formal approaches are used to best estimate the giving potential of a prospect. [1]

i. Group Discussion

In this approach, evaluators engage in a round-table discussion until they agree on a rating. The group session is conducted by a group leader. A development staff member should be present to record the observations but should make no comment that could influence a rating. The success of this approach depends, to a large extent, on the group leader's ability to initiate discussion and the group's willingness to participate openly and forthrightly.

ii. Group/Individual Rating

Each member is given a rating book and works individually, without discussion, to rate the prospects and offer appropriate written comments. A development staff member collects the rating books at the end of the session and tabulates the information. Despite the shortcoming of preventing evaluators exchanging information within the group, the advantage is that the confidentiality afforded may encourage each evaluator to provide more pointed and useful comments.

iii. Individual/One-on-One

A development staff member meets individually with the evaluators and verbally goes through the prospect list, recording pertinent comments on the evaluation form. The advantage of this approach is the freedom of expression for each evaluator, who is not required to put anything in writing. The disadvantage is the large amount of time required by development staff to meet with more than one evaluator for second and third opinions.

iv. Individual/Solitary

Evaluators are given a list of prospects and rating instructions and left on their own to complete the task by a set date. The advantage of this approach is that it gives the evaluator time

---

[1] *Ibid.*, pp. 99 – 101.

to reflect and to substantially consider the rating and comments for the ones they know. The disadvantage is that an evaluator may at times put off doing the evaluation and not meet the deadline.

Regardless which approach is employed, at least three evaluations for each prospect are considered desirable. The results, if all within close range, give a better estimate of the giving potential of a prospect. Even though there is no completely reliable yardstick to measure an individual's giving potential on the basis of accumulated assets and income, the income asset gift rating formula in Table 5-6[①] provides a useful framework for making decisions.

Table 5-6   Income/Asset Gift Rating Formula

Annual Income	Accumulated Assets	Gift Potential	Rating
$1 million +	$10 million +	$500,000 +	500K +
$500,000 to $1 million	$5 to $10 million	$250,000 to $500,000	250K
$250,000 to $500,000	$1 to $5 million	$100,000 to $250,000	100K
$100,000 to $250,000	$1 million -	$50,000 to $100,000	50K
$50,000 to $100,000	$500,000 -	$10,000 to $50,000	10k

IV. How Important Is Prospect Cultivation?

In any fundraising program, cultivation of donor prospects plays an important part in getting results. Prospect identification and evaluation serve only to ascertain those individuals who have the ability to give; however, without the proper cultivation, most prospects may not have the desire to give. Once a strong prospect is identified, evaluated, and rated, she or he should be assigned to a development staff. Each development staff will then choose among the most promising prospects assigned and work out a personalized cultivation strategy. The actual cultivation may involve the library director, other library staff, and volunteers. In some fundraising literature, the use of two weighting systems is suggested as a means for designing the strategy for cultivation. One system is based on the **giving capacity** and another on the **interest level** of the prospect. These weighting methods are given in Table 5-7 and Table 5-8 respectively.

Table 5-7   Weighting Method for Giving Capacity

Estimated Giving Capacity	Weight
Up to $1,000	1
$1,001 to $10,000	2
$10,001 to $50,000	3
$50,001 to $100,000	4
$100,001 and up	5

In general, the higher the combined weight of the two methods, the greater the likelihood of giving. Cultivation should begin with prospects who have the highest weights in both the **Giving Capacity** and **Interest Level**. For prospects weighted high in **giving capacity** and low in **interest level**, proper cultivation may move the **interest level** up.

[①] *Ibid.*, p.102. This rating formula has been revised and updated by the co-authors.

Table 5-8 Weighting Method for Interest Level

Description of Prospect	Weight
Clearly turned off, no record of interest	1
Minimal interest, occasional donor, attends meetings infrequently	2
Moderately active or formerly very active	3
Very active, major donor, gift club member, committee person	4
Member of governing board, other boards, or executive groups	5

There are many approaches to cultivation, but some are better than others. While cultivation by providing information, such as newsletters, special-status letters from the chief executive of the institution, case statements, and fundraising brochures, is important, personal cultivation is much more effective and often essential. Invitations to informal activities, such as a party or dinner at the home of a volunteer, small luncheons with campaign leaders, cultural and sports events at the institution, friends programs and gatherings, all can help build a good relationship with the donor prospect.

Other effective means of cultivation, in order of impact, include: an invitation to a leadership retreat, a visit by the chief executive, appropriate recognition and honor, attendance at a special event on site, attendance of a special event off site, sharing firsthand of priority information, a visit by a volunteer, a letter from the chief executive, a visit by a staff member, a phone call from the chief executive, a phone call from a volunteer, invitation to a major event, a letter from a volunteer, a phone call from a staff member, a letter from a staff member.

There are various suggestions as to the desirable number of contacts and the optimal length of the cultivation period. Normally, an average of 10 visits over a period of 12 months is considered a norm in cultivating a major donor prospect. These, again, must be adjusted from case to case. There are no substitutes for sincerity, trust, honesty, care, mutual respect, friendship, good interpersonal relationship, sound judgment, and patience.

V. What Are the Best Methods of Gift Solicitation?

Once a good personal relationship characterized by mutual respect has been established and the donor prospect has been fully informed of the fundraising program, the next step is gift solicitation.

In planning for gift solicitation, a personalized proposal is prepared which should match the prospect's interest and the institution's need. The proposal should ask for a specific amount, which should be the largest gift possible by the prospect. Before requesting a meeting with the prospect, a team of two persons should be selected to present the gift proposal.

In making arrangements for a face-to-face meeting, it is not uncommon for a prospect to decide that a meeting is unnecessary because he/she knows all about the fundraising and has already decided on a gift amount. Even in this case, you should still request a meeting by saying something along the following lines:

"My responsibility as a volunteer is to personally visit each prospect I have agreed to contact. I certainly don't intend to pressure you, but I would appreciate the chance to talk with you in person about the library and to tell you why I believe the fundraising is important. How about getting together on...?"[1]

When meeting with the prospect, try to convey the purpose of your visit with your own enthusiasm and commitment. The conversation should include a brief account of the fundraising—

---

[1] Adapted from *The Ohio University Third Century Campaign volunteer manual*. (Athens, Ohio: Ohio University Foundation, 1988), p. 22.

its goals, its leadership, significant gifts already received or pledged, the perceived benefits, etc. If you are a volunteer, it wouldn't hurt to give the reason for your involvement and to mention your own gift commitment. Don't dominate the conversation. Let the prospect ask questions. Explain to the prospect that gifts to the library can be made in the form of cash, appreciated securities, real estate, insurance, or bequests or other kinds of deferred gifts. Even though tax incentives are not usually the primary motive for making a charitable contribution, some donors may consider a larger gift if they know there are tax advantages.

In the gift proposal, if a large gift is asked, a named gift appropriate to the level of giving may be suggested. It may be naming a library building, a wing, a room, a collection, an endowment, memorial or tribute fund for a specific purpose, an automated library system, or other suitable recognition. An archetypical example was the naming of the Library at New York University as the Elmer Holmes Bobst Library in recognition of an $11 million gift from the pharmaceutical magnate. Subsequently, the name was carried to its automated system, Bobcat-for the Bobst Library Computerized Catalog. More will be said on the subject of donor recognition opportunities in Chapter 7.

Except for capital construction or facility renovation in which cash gifts are preferred, the library may accept the following methods of giving:
- Cash, one-time
- Cash on term basis, 3 – 5 years
- Cash on term basis, plus bequest
- Cash plus some asset, such as
  — securities
  — life insurance
  — real property
  — personal property
- Cash plus some asset, plus one or more deferred gift devices
  — annuity
  — wealth-replacement trust
  — unitrust

Throughout the solicitation process, which may require more than one meeting, do not give up in the face of an initial negative response. If it becomes clear that the proposed amount is beyond the prospect's giving capacity or interest, one should be prepared to negotiate a lesser gift or adopt one of the above-listed methods of giving, with or without cash. The library should be grateful for whatever amount a donor wishes to give in the end.

A gift is not official until it is documented or a gift agreement form is executed and signed by the donor. An example of the gift agreement form used by Ohio University is shown in Appendix III. Examples of a prospect entry form, a cultivation/solicitation plan, and a contact report are shown in Appendices IV through VI.

第六章 两个募款成功的计划

Chapter 6 Two Successful Fundraising Programs

CASE STUDY NUMBER 1:
CREATING A SUCCESSFUL ANNUAL GIVING PROGRAM:
THE BRANDEIS UNIVERSITY NATIONAL WOMEN'S COMMITTEE

By Bessie K. Hahn, Director of Libraries
Brandeis University

I. Brandeis University

Brandeis University is located in Waltham, Massachusetts, just over 10 miles west of Boston. Since its founding in 1948, the University has grown to become one of the few private universities of distinction established in this century. It has sought, from its inception, to be that *rara avis* of American education, a university which combines graduate instruction and advanced research with a first class liberal arts college. When Brandeis became a member of Phi Beta Kappa in 1961, only thirteen years after its founding, it was the youngest institution in more than a century to receive such recognition. In 1985 Brandeis was honored as one of the major research universities in the nation with a membership to the Association of American Universities.

The principal components of the University are the undergraduate College of Arts and Sciences with an enrollment of 2,900 students, the Graduate School of Arts and Sciences with 650 students, and the Florence Heller Graduate School for Advanced Studies in Social Welfare with 100 students. The University offers 20 graduate programs, 17 of which lead to Ph. D. degrees.

The Brandeis University Library

The Brandeis University Library had its beginnings in a stone stable. From a collection of 2,000 books the Library's holdings have grown to over 900,000 volumes, 800,000 pieces of microform, 300,000 government documents and 7,500 serial titles. The collections are now housed in three separate locations: the Main Library, the Gerstenzang Science Library and the Intercultural Library. The Main Library consists of the Bertha and Jacob Goldfarb Library, which contains the humanities and social science collections, as well as one of the most important Judaica collections in the country; the Leonard L. Farber Library, completed in 1983, which houses music and fine arts materials, serials and microforms, and a multi-level undergraduate study center; and the Rapaporte Treasure Hall, which holds such notable collections as the Leonardo da Vinci Collection, the Vito Volterra History of Science Collection, and the Spanish Civil War Collection. The Gerstenzang Science Library contains collections in the physical and natural sciences and mathematics. The Intercultural Library, established in 1989, promotes minority cultures and multi-culturalism.

Brandeis is a member of the Research Library Group. It is also a founding member of the Boston Library Consortium, whose membership includes 10 other institutions: Boston College, Boston Public Library, Boston University, MIT, University of Massachusetts/Amherst, University of Massachusetts/Boston, Massachusetts State Library, Northeastern University, Tufts University and Wellesley College.

The Library has received a number of major grants from federal agencies in recent years, including a National Endowment for the Humanities challenge grant in 1989 that will result in the establishment of a $3.2 million endowment for the humanities collections; two Title IIC grants from the U. S. Department of Education; and matching grants from the National Endowment for the Arts and the National Science Foundation. The Library also works closely with the University Development office on corporate and foundation grants. But the mainstay of the Library's development effort is fundraising through the **Brandeis University National Women's Committee**, which has raised over $42 million since its founding 43 years ago.

II. The Brandeis University National Women's Committee

The Brandeis University Library has from the very beginning been intertwined with an organization affectionately referred to on campus as "The Women's Committee." Evidence of the work of the Women's Committee is present everywhere in the libraries. Upon entering the Main Library, visitors are immediately aware of a dramatic Tribute Wall in the entrance foyer inscribed with the names of many major contributors to the Women's Committee. As the visitors browse through the open stacks, they take notice of the numerous plaques decorating the end panels, recalling the generosity of those members of the Women's Committee who have over the years made significant contributions to the development of the Library's collections. And the majority of the books have bookplates recognizing the donors as members or friends of the Women's Committee.

In 1948, at the request of the founding fathers of Brandeis University, a group of eight women, representing a variety of Jewish Women's organizations, came together to create a new organization that would take responsibility for providing books for the University Library. At the time, the Library was housed in a converted barn, and boasted a collection of a few thousand outdated books on medicine and veterinary medicine, entirely inappropriate for a liberal arts college. The Brandeis University National Women's Committee was thus born. Though affiliated with the University, the Women's Committee was to be a national, autonomous nonprofit membership organization whose mission was for the complete support and maintenance of the University Library. This idea of supporting the library of a Jewish-sponsored non-sectarian university generated tremendous excitement among Jewish women, and seven local chapters in New England and New York were formed from the very start. By 1952, when the University graduated its first class, the number of chapters had already reached 73. In recognizing the Women's Committee as an important constituency for this young university, its National President becomes a member of the University Board of Trustees during her term of office.

One of the first activities of the fledgling organization was to establish a "Book Fund" to supply books to the Library. New and innovative programs were introduced with the arrival of every new National President and administration, many of which are still on the roster of current activities. More will be said on these programs later on in the chapter.

The Women's Committee has not limited its activities to just putting books on the shelves. Six years after it came into existence, it supplied the funds for a three-story addition to the stable. By the time it celebrated its 10th anniversary, it had raised another $1 million toward the new Goldfarb Library. In the early 80's, half of the cost of automating the Library was underwritten by the Women's Committee. Fundraising for "Library Work Scholars" and "Preservation" has been exceedingly successful in recent years. The former program raises funds for supporting student workers in the Library; the latter subsidizes ongoing operating expenses incurred by the in-house Preservation unit. Another important component of their fundraising program has been the development of library endowment funds, beginning with the Library Trust, which provides income for library operations and general maintenance.

Mission

The purpose of the Brandeis University National Women's Committee is to provide financial support and growth for the Brandeis University Libraries, which serve a community of students and scholars, in education and research, united by their commitment to the pursuit of knowledge. The National Women's Committee offers its members opportunity for intellectual pursuit, continuing education, community service, social interaction, personal enrichment, and leadership development. The members act as emissaries to support and enhance the image of Brandeis, a Jewish-sponsored, non-sectarian university where excellence is the tradition.

From this mission statement, it can be seen that the primary function of the Women's Committee is to provide support and growth for the Brandeis Library. Equally important, however, are services to its members. The goal of the Women's Committee as a membership and social organization is then to also create opportunities and programs for its members in continuing education, community service, and leadership development.

Membership

To date, the Women's Committee has some 55,000 members in 115 chapters throughout the U. S. Most of the members are not in any way connected to the University prior to their joining the Women's Committee; in fact, most of them have never even visited the campus. In the early years, Jewish women were attracted to the Women's Committee by the idea of supporting the country's one and only Jewish-sponsored non-sectarian university, and raising money for its library was an important reason for joining. Many of these women had not had the opportunity for a college education, but were bright and thirsty for knowledge. The Women's Committee gave them the chance to be directly involved with the development of a university. Nowadays, besides being supportive of Jewish concerns, more women are attracted to the Women's Committee because it is a service organization with excellent programs designed to serve the social and intellectual needs of its members. Offerings such as study groups and lectures by Brandeis faculty members, special interest programs, and social interactions with other women may have attracted more members than the expressed cause of supporting the Brandeis University Library, especially among younger women between the ages of 25 and 35.

The membership base consists primarily of women over the age of 50, many of whom are full-time homemakers, or retired. They tend to be long-standing members, many of whom have been leaders within their local chapters and on the national level for over 20 years. As can be expected, member recruitment has paralleled the changing national demographics of the Jewish population. In areas with older Jewish populations, such as Florida, membership in the Women's Committee is also growing steadily. In other areas where there are proportionately more younger Jews who are, more often than not, working professionals with heavy family responsibilities, a different strategy is needed to attract them to the Women's Committee.

Organizational Structure

The Chief Executive Officer of the Brandeis University National Women's Committee is the National President, elected for a term of one year but eligible for election to the office for three consecutive years. The National President oversees an Executive Committee and a National Board. The Executive Committee consists of 11 elected officers, 14 former national presidents, 38 appointed national chairs, and 8 regional presidents elected by their respective regions. The National Board includes members of the Executive Committee, plus other honorary and elected directors. All elected officers are dues paying volunteers. This volunteer governing structure is supported by an Executive Director and a national professional staff organized into Executive, Administrative, Membership and Chapter Program Services, Public Relations, Development, and Accounting departments. There is also limited professional field staff support.

Chapters and Regions

The Women's Committee is a conglomerate of local constituent organizations, known as "chapters," chartered by the National Board. Currently there are 115 chapters scattered throughout United States. A chapter may be chartered in any community with a minimum of 75 members. Each chapter adopts its own bylaws, as long as they are based upon the pattern of the national bylaws. There are two categories of membership: annual or life members. Annual dues are at three levels: $25, $35 and $50; dues for life membership is $250.

Local chapters are grouped into eight regions: Florida, Mid-Atlantic, Midwest, New England, New Jersey and Southern Connecticut, New York, Northwest, Southwest, and Western. Regional officers are elected to assist local chapters in promoting the aims and programs of the organization. Often, regional workshops for chapter officers are held to provide leadership training and to develop program and fundraising skills.

Incentives And Reward System

The success of the organization has traditionally been based on a chapter goal system for fundraising and membership. The national Board endorses annual national goals which are prepared by the national Executive Committee in consultation with regional presidents. Each chapter negotiates with the National Board its financial and membership goals, the levels of which depend on the demographics of its location and its past performance.

Since the work is carried out by volunteers, the only reward members can expect is the recognition and admiration of their peers. Chapters are recognized for achieving various financial goals as well as membership retention, renewal, and new member recruitment. Those chapters that have achieved total financial and membership goals are recognized with the Presidential citation at the organization's annual national conference. Chapter presidents are presented with a handsome bust of Louis D. Brandeis; like an "Emmy" or "Oscar," it has become the organization's most coveted "Louis" award. Another top award for exceptional achievement is the "Chapter of the Year" award, given to a chapter that exceeds its goals and is truly representational of the Women's Committee's mission. And, recognizing that local chapters must also contribute to the welfare of their own communities, community service awards are given to those with innovative community projects. In fact, service to community has become extremely active and visible in some local chapters. The Desert Chapter of Palm Springs, California, was saluted by President George Bush as the 717th Daily Point of Light for the Nation in March, 1992, for its 200 – volunteer tutoring program.

The National Office

Under the direction of the Executive Director, the National staff assists the lay leadership by developing and communicating the organization's priorities and goals to its membership, working with national chairs to implement their various programs, and providing the membership with information about the University and its Library.

Since the membership is scattered throughout the country, communication with and among its members is one of the biggest challenges faced by the Women's Committee. A number of publications have been created to widely and regularly publicize Library achievements, major academic and research developments on campus, the organization's priorities and issues, and its activities on the chapter, regional, and national levels.

Publications And Public Relations

A national newspaper, *Imprint*, is the major publication for informing the membership of Brandeis events and Women's Committee activities. Published quarterly, the *Imprint* also serves effectively as a promotional tool for fundraising programs. Another quarterly publication, *President to s*, is sent to chapter presidents to highlight important areas in which to focus their energies and to keep them abreast of current issues affecting the Women's Committee and the University. Monthly informational mailings are sent to chapter presidents and chairs with suggestions for programming, fundraising, and membership activities.

Local chapters are encouraged to produce their own newsletters and press releases. Four times a year, the National Office distributes sample press releases featuring university, library, and Women's Committee news for local placement. A recent public relations guide gives further tips on writing news releases, news placement, and speech making. The National Office also provides local chapters with professionally designed brochures and boiler-plate material that they can incorporate into their own publications.

The National Office utilizes all types of marketing techniques to advance its cause and visibility. National telethons, direct mailings, televised appeals, training films, and other modern-day marketing tools are regularly employed for major fundraising events and for publicizing the work of — and the fun associated with membership in — the organization.

Leadership Development

Another important function of the National Office is leadership development. The future of the organization is dependent on the quality of its prospective leaders. The Women's Committee has not left the development of future leaders to chance, but has developed methods to identify and train them. A national leadership development program provides formalized training of national leaders who in turn train volunteers at the regional level. Workshops in fundraising techniques, business planning, and leadership skills are conducted in tandem with national business meetings, and every opportunity is created to help more members gain a working knowledge of the organization. Another training program brings to the annual conference "leadership interns" who have taken some leadership responsibilities on the chapter level and have the potential and expressed commitment to assume increased leadership roles. For some of these members, the very idea that they might have leadership potential is received with both fear and exhilaration. Having the chance to learn has brought forth many a latent talent, so it is easy to understand the enduring loyalty of these members for the organization which has nurtured them.

Donor Recognition

As many members are also major donors, their gifts are acknowledged and publicized in a variety of ways. Individual plaques on a Tribute Wall in the Library Foyer and on library shelves, and book plates in individual volumes, are all permanent reminders of donor generosity in the Library. Specially designed sculpture pieces, jewelry, and limited edition art work are treasured by donors, often serving as conversation pieces and bringing attention to the Women's Committee.

The University makes additional recognition of the contributions of leading members of the Women's Committee. The incumbent National President is automatically a member of the Board of Trustees; others are invited to serve as Brandeis Fellows or President's Councilors; and honorary degrees were conferred on a few of the most outstanding "Women."

Most of the awards are presented during the annual National Conference when about 300 volunteer leaders from national, regional, and local chapters convene on campus in June. For them, the annual conference is a reunion with friends from far away places. It is an occasion to learn more about the Library, to exchange ideas, and to improve leadership and fundraising skills. There is friendly competition for eleventh-hour fundraising activities, but most of all, it is a time to celebrate successes resulting from a year's hard work, and to bring back to their chapters mementos and reminders of their achievements.

Major Fundraising Programs

Sources of revenue from local chapters include membership dues, contributions toward the "Book Fund", book sales, and other fundraising events.

Book Fund

With the objective of "Building Volumes for Tomorrow," the Book Fund is in reality many categories of giving. Donations may range from $5 to $25,000 or more, and may be designated for general books, special book collections in a subject area, journal subscriptions, or endowments for journals. Book Fund contributions are used by many donors to commemorate special occasions — such as birthdays, graduation, weddings, etc. —of their family members or friends.

Book Sales: "New Books for Old"

Local chapters hold book sales annually. The most famous and the largest of the book sales is sponsored by the North Shore Chapter in Chicago, an annual event that attracts thousands of collectors, dealers and book lovers from all over the country. The Chapter works all year round to collect as many as 400,000 books for the sale. It has its own warehouse where hundreds of volunteers process and sort the books into 40 categories. Over the years the group has gained extensive knowledge in recognizing rare, first editions and other collectible works. The actual nine-day sale takes place in a shopping center under a 26,000 square foot tent. On opening day, customers line up before dawn with their chairs, radios and picnic baskets as if they were waiting to purchase rock concert tickets. The 1991 event netted over $120,000 for the Library.

Book Stores

Several chapters have opened permanent bookstores instead of conducting annual book sales. The Greater Boston Chapter's "Brandeis Bookstall" is open six days and two evenings a week and staffed by volunteers working on four-hour shifts.

Other major fundraising programs are for more specific goals. The **Benefactors' Choice Acquisitions** is an annual fund for the purchase of rare materials and expensive scholarly works that cannot be supported by the Library's general operating budgets. The **Annual Giving Program** is currently being used for the support of preservation efforts in prolonging the useful lives of books in the general collection. Contributions to the **Library Work Scholar Fund** underwrite the salaries of students who work in the Library and are on financial aid. This Fund is for both annual and endowment giving. The **CALL Brandeis Fund** (CALL: Computer-Assisted Library Link) appeals to those who wish to support the technological needs of a modern-day library. Efforts to build an endowment for the Library started in 1977 with the establishment of the **Library Trust Fund**. The following pages give examples of how the Women's Committee has publicized these programs.

Campaign for Brandeis

In 1986, the Women's Committee decided to participate in the University's first capital campaign, setting a goal of $2.4 million to enhance the Library's ability to meet the challenges of the Age of Information: expansion and preservation of collections, adoption of new information technologies, professional development of staff, as well as support for the Audiovisual Center and University Archives. Matching an $800,000 challenge grant from the National Endowment for the Humanities became a major component of the Campaign when the Library received the award in 1989, and the Women's Committee agreed to raise half of the required $2.4 million.

The Campaign was an opportunity for the Women's Committee to accelerate its development activities in major donor solicitations, planned and deferred gift options, and fundraising among corporations and foundations. It has also brought more coordinated planning and collaboration between the Women's Committee and the University Development Office. The solid donor base built during the campaign and the experience and confidence gained from its success will spur the organization to greater ambition in the coming years.

Member Service Programs

As a membership organization, the need to provide interesting and meaningful programs is as important to the Women's Committee as raising funds for the Brandeis Library. Group travel, visits to museums, concerts, and insurance programs are some of the more usual services offered by the Women's Committee. Unlike other fundraising organizations, however, the Women's Committee considers continuing education opportunities for its members as its highest service priority. Taking advantage of the availability and willingness of the Brandeis faculty, the Women's Committee has created programs such as "Study Groups" and "University-on-Wheels" that local chapters can offer.

Study Groups

A study group is a "self-study" adult education program on a specific topic in which participants are given a syllabus and reading list. The participants meet regularly once or twice a week for several months with a knowledgeable discussion leader to go through the material. Brandeis Study Groups' syllabi have been prepared by University faculty exclusively for the Women's Committee, and are available to local chapters at nominal cost. A chapter may offer as few or as many different courses as it deems appropriate.

University-on-Wheels

During school intersession (January) each year, different groups of Brandeis faculty travel thousands of miles to different parts of the country, bringing the University and their expertise to chapters and regions. While they may specialize in many different fields, their lectures often carry a common theme. For example, the theme for the 1992 University-on-Wheels is "the American Political Scene." Lectures for this series include, among others, "Unraveling the American Tapestry: The Search for Western Culture Beneath Diversity," offered by an anthropologist; "The 1992 Presidential Campaign: Issues We Won't be Hearing About," by an American Studies faculty; "Justice in America: The New Supreme Court" by a political scientist; and "What if You Turned on the Television and Lincoln and Douglas Were Debating?" by a professor of English.

The Library and the Women's Committee

In its partnership with the Women's Committee, the Library's primary role is to communicate to the "benefactor" organization its needs and aspirations. The University Librarian acts as the principle link to the Women's Committee, keeping the latter's leadership abreast of new developments in the library and information fields, the challenges libraries face, and the direction the Brandeis Library should take. She participates in the University-on-Wheels program, traveling and bringing the Brandeis Library message to numerous chapters around the country. Other key library staff are also frequently involved in special projects. They are called upon to supply background information and draft case statements for the Women's Committee's capital campaigns and major donor solicitations. They regularly contribute articles to the Imprint, publicizing Library projects and activities. In addition, tours, demonstrations, and workshops are incorporated into the Women's Committee conference programs to familiarize the membership with the inner workings of the Library.

The staff have invested a great deal of time on the Women's Committee, but in return they have gained the kind of knowledge and experience that will serve them well in their professional lives. Before they can articulate their vision and goals for the Library, they must first learn to plan and prioritize. Before they can successfully explain themselves to people
unfamiliar with the library profession, they have to learn to avoid library jargon and be succinct and clear in their presentations. Before they can prepare fundraising case statements, they must be familiar with the academic programs the University offers and the specifics of faculty research. Working with the leaders of the Women's Committee has definitely improved the Library staffs organizational, fundraising, and communication skills.

III. The Future

Between 1948 and 1991, the Women's Committee raised more than $42 million for the support of the Brandeis University Library. Its network of local chapters has penetrated into hundreds of communities, and the programs these chapters sponsor have enriched the lives of thousands of people. In spite of unprecedented success as a "friends of the library" organization, there is nevertheless a general feeling among its leaders that the Women's Committee will not realize its full potential unless it develops new techniques and strategies to accommodate the changing demographics and life styles of its volunteers. The strategic decisions on membership, programs, and fundraising for the next decade are therefore linked to developing the most effective ways to utilize the volunteer and professional network.

Membership is a major source of revenue for the organization. The Women's Committee is developing new strategies to retain existing membership and to expand into new membership markets including alumni; parents, spouses, and children of current and former members; and other ethnic groups. Increased efforts will also be made to develop and train new leaders.

The membership expects a broad range of educational opportunities. The current programs, such as Study Groups and University-on-Wheels, do not lead to an end product. There is no obvious incentive for a member to continue after one or two study groups. A continuing education program with a degree certificate might offer such an incentive.

Increased fundraising for the Library is naturally the ultimate goal for the Women's Committee. In addition to continuing its support of the general operating expenses of the Library, the Women's Committee will in the next decade increase its efforts in building endowments for collections, especially in the sciences and social sciences, and raising funds for the adoption of new technologies.

The Women's Committee is an integral part of the University, and has from time to time raised funds for University causes other than the Library. Also, the reality of library fundraising is that some donors may choose to fund research and academic programs directly instead of giving to the Library. The development strategy is to approach these prospective donors with an integrated package covering both library and program needs. The Women's Committee expects to continue this dual fundraising track in the future.

Conclusion

The Women's Committee has brought goodwill to Brandeis University and generous

financial support to its Library. On the other hand, members of the Women's Committee also feel rewarded for their work by their "pride in affiliation" with one of the youngest and finest private universities in the country. Whether an organization such as the Women's Committee would work equally successfully for other libraries is an often-asked question. Several ingredients combine to make the Women's Committee unique and successful. Some campuses may very well have these ingredients for the establishment of a similar "friends of the library" organization.

The Women's Committee was built upon **ethnic pride**. So far, the majority of the members have come from the American-Jewish community. In spite of their different financial status and social background, the members nonetheless share a common cultural background and ideals. The call to create and build a library for America's one and only Jewish-sponsored, non-sectarian university strongly appeals to their pride in being the "People of the Book." More than any other ethnic group, the Jewish people also have a stronger tradition of giving.

The Women's Committee provides **services to its members**. While its primary goal is still the Brandeis Library, it has become an enormous service organization, providing the social and intellectual stimulation its members seek. The emphasis on spotting talent and developing leaders for both local chapters and national administration has provided opportunities for self-fulfillment that would not have been possible for many a homemaker or retiree. A growing cadre of Brandeis members are participating in significant local community service projects related to educational and literacy programs as well as elder care services, adding another dimension to their Brandeis affiliation.

The Women's Committee has had the foresight to constantly **recruit and groom** its members as they advance through the leadership ranks. The organization has been fortunate to attract generations of talented and motivated women who were willing to accept its challenges of leadership, but its volunteer leadership could not have achieved the level of sophistication and cohesiveness without the support of the National Office and its professionally trained staff. It has enabled thousands of women to develop intellectually and enhance their personal skills. It has successfully integrated the needs of the organization with the interests of the individual member.

Acknowledgement

The author is grateful to Harriet Winer, Executive Director of the Brandeis University National Women's Committee, for her many insightful comments on this chapter and for her tireless effort on behalf of the Brandeis Library.

CASE STUDY NUMBER 2:
BUILDING AND ENDOWMENT CAMPAIGNS:
A $20 MILLION EFFORT AT THE UNIVERSITY OF KENTUCKY LIBRARY

By Paul A. Willis, Director of Libraries
University of Kentucky

Introduction

The University of Kentucky plans to construct a new central and life sciences library which is scheduled to open in the fall of 1995. It is expected to be approximately 387,000 square feet and the cost is estimated at $58 million. A campaign for private funds to support this construction project had a goal of $12 million and this was reached. The remaining funds will be sought from the state legislature.

In addition to the building fund drive, a campaign to add $8 million to the book endowment ran simultaneously for a total fund drive of $20 million. The book endowment drive started first as is explained below.

Brief History of Library Buildings

Until 1909 the University of Kentucky did not have a central library. The President maintained his private collection in the administration building, where his secretary checked out books to students. Small collections existed in some of the colleges and departments, and at the Agriculture Experiment Station. The President persuaded Andrew Carnegie to give funds for a library on the campus in Lexington, although the public library in town was also constructed with Carnegie funds. The first building dedicated for library use was 56 × 56 feet and was opened in 1909 at a construction cost of $26,000. The President's secretary became the University's first librarian. She later earned a library science degree.

In the heart of the Depression, the second central library was opened. A 90,000 square foot building which had been constructed at a cost of $450,000 was dedicated in 1931, and the building was funded without a state appropriation of funds. Instead it was funded with University reserves. Margaret I. King, the first librarian, moved into this building and served as librarian until 1949. When she retired after 40 years of service, the building was named for her. This building, which still functions as the main library, is a fixed stack structure and it was designed to be a closed stack facility. But it became part of an open stack library in 1963 when a 65,000 square foot addition was opened. The addition cost approximately $2 million.

The eight levels of fixed stacks make the original part of the building rather inflexible, and the addition was designed in such a way that it is difficult to arrange services in the building to suit patron needs. This situation was compounded when in 1974 a second addition was built at the front of the main building and connected by a bridge. This addition has 84,000 square feet and was built for about $4 million.

I. Building Project Summary

When a new President was appointed to the University in 1990, he reviewed plans for a third addition to the King Library complex. The first critical and bold decision which he made concerning library operations was to seek funding for a totally new facility at a new location. A detailed review by the President and his Cabinet preceded this decision, which was made in spite of the fact that it obviously increased the cost of the building project.

The University has branch libraries and reading rooms in 14 different locations on the main campus. Space needs at most of these facilities are critical, so the overall building plan addresses these needs as well. The Medical Library had a request pending for a new library at the same time that the new main library was being discussed. A decision was made at the President's Cabinet, and supported by the Chancellor of the Medical Center, to integrate the two projects. In part, this approach was taken because it would be difficult to get state funding for two library projects on the same campus. But it was also recognized that the newer information technology might allow traditional library services to be re-designed. The new building is being programmed to serve as a central and life sciences library; incorporating not only the Medical Library, but the Agriculture Library and Biological Sciences branch.

It is recognized that some type of library service must remain in the Medical Center teaching hospital, which will be a few blocks from the new building. An "Information Center" is being planned to remain in part of the present Medical Library space. In fact, information centers are being planned for the other colleges as well. All will be designed in close consultation with the faculty and students from each college.

The first Information Center opened on campus in January 1992 in an addition to the College of Business and Economics Building. It is exclusively non-print, but the business librarian has access in the information center to most major on-line services and CD products in the relevant subject areas. A rapid document delivery service operates from the King Library where the print collection is housed. The information center also has 100 personal computers and serves the computing lab needs of the College. It is anticipated that the operation of the Business and Economics Information Center will serve as a model for the information centers to be created at the Medical Center and Agriculture Center, after the new central and life sciences library opens in 1995 (if all schedules are maintained).

The building will house central library services and collections in the social sciences, humanities, and life sciences. It is expected that it will seat 3,000 and (by maximizing compact shelving) will hold over 2,000,000 volumes. A decision has been made to utilize compact shelving extensively, as opposed to maintaining part of the collection in remote storage. (A year or so ago, the Library began storing part of the collection in an underground storage facility about an hour away from campus. This is a professionally managed service and meets quite well the storage needs for uncataloged collections. But when the local newspaper issued a story about the Library putting books and journals "in a cave," it caused many individuals to realize that a new library must be needed!)

There are those who question the need for a new building with this much square footage. They argue that electronic storage and other information technology developments reduce the amount of space required in an academic library. I think that one must consider the fact that approximately 25 square feet must be programmed for each reader using a book. But when space is added for a reader using a terminal and perhaps a printer or other electronic machine, the square footage must be increased. Training facilities are also in demand when information resources are in non-traditional formats. Other factors (such as the need to store computer tapes) modify the use of library space, but do not necessarily reduce the need for it. Since it is impossible to anticipate what the newer technology will bring during the useful life of a new library building, it is being programmed to have open and flexible space. Not only will this allow library services to be provided in an efficient and effective manner, but it will allow modifications and space reconfiguration with minimal expense. The floor weight capacity will be designed to handle compact shelving in any area.

A building of about five stories is desired. Given the slope of the anticipated site, the main entrance may be on the middle level. With a concentration of public services on the entry level, many users will have their needs met on this floor or one level up or down. The principal programming guide is to view the arrangement of services from the perspective of a patron with a need for information who is at the front door. The number of service points will be kept to a minimum, with perhaps a central service area which will be the only service point staffed during periods of low use. The arrangement of collections or services by distinctions which may not be meaningful to patrons will be avoided whenever possible. An example of this is arrangement or segregation by publisher, such as government information. An effort is being made not to program services and departments as they now exist, but to program services as noted above with an administrative structure to be developed after the services are designed; an administrative structure which will support the services program. In addition to providing traditional library services, the building will reflect the latest in library and information technology. The new facility will serve as a base for electronic support to classrooms, offices, labs, and dorms. Remote access and document delivery will be readily available, and it is anticipated that those who use the new building will come because they wish to and not because they have to do so.

The second phase of the building program is to renovate the oldest part of the King Library for Special Collections and Archives. The fixed stacks in this building suggest a continuing library use, and it will make a very attractive Special Collections building. The 1963 addition to the King Building will have a separate entrance and serve as a physical sciences and engineering library. This part of the building will function totally independently from the other part. The present branch libraries in the physical sciences and engineering will be centralized in this facility and most of the academic departments in these areas are located nearby—some in adjoining buildings. The 1974 wing will be converted into a fine arts library consolidating the present Art, Music, and Music Listening Center facilities. The fine arts departments are next to this wing of the library. This centralization of most of the branch library collections will free considerable space on campus for reassignment to the academic departments. Much of the branch library space to be vacated is former classroom, lab, or office space which is needed by the departments. If a "net cost" of the library building program is calculated by subtracting the "value" of the space to be freed, it becomes a much reduced number.

State-wide Role of Library

The University of Kentucky is the flagship institution of higher education in the state. It has the largest library collection and has participated in all state network and collection sharing arrangements. Interlibrary loan activities increased dramatically when the main library's automation system was linked to that of the Community College system in Kentucky. The University of Kentucky operates 14 community colleges with an enrollment of about 45,000 across the state. A FAX network and dedicated staff is critical to the success of the interlibrary loan activities from the Community College Libraries to the main Library. I mention this because the new President of the University of Kentucky was formerly the Chancellor of the Community College system. In that capacity, he automated their libraries and worked with the main library staff to link the individual computers and to create the FAX network and special staffing. The President was in a position to see the importance of library and information services to the individual community colleges, which for the most part are located in rural parts of the state. He understands how technology impacts the delivery of information services. This, I believe, influenced the name of the building portion of the library campaign. The new facility is referred to as "The Commonwealth Library" to emphasize the state-wide (Kentucky is officially the Commonwealth of Kentucky) role of the new facility. This is the central factor in seeking support for the new building: it will enhance library and information services not only on the Lexington Campus, but to those libraries and individuals from around the state who use the collections and services of the libraries on the main University of Kentucky campus in Lexington. Equalizing access to information throughout the state is a goal for the new library, recognizing that the building is just one part of the University's information infrastructure with the other central parts being communications and computer facilities. The Library's catalog is mounted on an IBM 3090 in the University's Computing Center, and remote access is encouraged for other institutions in the state. Databases are also mounted on the mainframe (e.g. ERIC), and these will be shared in the future as licensing and other arrangements are finalized. Some donors and legislators are influenced by the state-wide mission of the Library and its potential to work in cooperation with other libraries in the state to increase the sharing of information to the most rural parts of Kentucky. This is viewed as critical for professionals practicing in small communities, and the value of information to economic development is generally recognized.

II. Library Campaign

The Library Campaign at the University of Kentucky has two parts which need explanation. In 1989 an article appeared in the local newspaper about library budget problems and journal cancellations which were then underway. The article caught the attention of a former student employee in the Library who had recently moved back to Lexington in his capacity as a top administrator at the new Toyota plant in an adjoining county. After a visit to the Library by several Toyota officials, an unrestricted gift of $1 million was made to the Library and a Toyota Book Endowment Fund was created. Not long after that a Challenge Grant for $750,000 was received from the National Endowment for the Humanities to create a humanities book endowment. This campaign was underway when the decision was made to seek funds for a new library facility. Combining the two efforts has proved to be a sound decision, since the building project appeals to some donors and the collection endowment appeals to others. Another fortuitous event occurred in the fall of 1990, when the Library sought a donor to underwrite a kick-off dinner for the endowment drive. The coaches and Athletic Director served as leaders in the campaign and made several public service announcements for the Library. The dinner was designed to generate momentum for the fundraising efforts. A local horseman, Mr. John R. Gaines, and his wife agreed to support the dinner. This initial involvement caused Mr. Gaines to become interested in the Library endowment drive and our plans for a new building. Eventually he agreed to work with the President in a co-chair capacity on a campaign to complete both fundraising drives. Starting in the fall of 1990, Mr. Gaines worked full-time on the $20 million library campaign, visiting potential donors, writing the Campaign literature, and working with both the library staff and the University Development Office.

It was thought that in order to attract the attention of potential major donors and the Kentucky legislature (where most of the building money would come from) a so-called "Family Campaign" would be appropriate. A consultant was employed to assist the University in the campaign starting with the Family Campaign. It focused on students, faculty, and staff including retirees. The student campaign started first and generated much attention for the Library. The faculty/staff/retiree campaign was designed to be a personal solicitation effort with a ratio of 1 solicitor for every 5 employees. It was truly a peer-to-peer effort.

Since the University of Kentucky has about 12,000 employees (including the Community College system), many people served as solicitors in the campaign. This required many training sessions, tours of the Library, talks, etc. on the part of the Library and Development Office staff, as well as by the campaign leadership. A highly respected faculty member was selected to head the Family Campaign, and a representative committee worked with him in the design of the campaign. Video presentations were prepared and special campaign literature written. The goal set for the family campaign was the level of participation and not the amount of money raised. Still, this part of the campaign did raise substantial funds. The ability of faculty and staff to participate by way of payroll deduction was important to its success. During the entire campaign it was the President who was the key. He made numerous talks around the state and to alumni groups throughout the country. In nearly every speech he made on or off campus during this period of time, he made it clear that the new library building and endowment were his first priorities. This obviously was important to potential major donors.

Student Role

The student part of the campaign got an early start and was lead by the existing Student Development Council, which is part of the University Development Office. The President of the

University Student Government Organization was a key figure in the student campaign. One of the advantages of the student activities in advance of other concentrated fundraising was that it increased the awareness on campus, in the community, and in the state at large about the needs of the Library and the campaign. The main focus of the student effort was the book endowment. They called their campaign "Pack the Stacks" and made an effort to get every graduating student to donate $35 to the endowment. It was estimated that this was the cost of an average book. For each $35 donated, a bookplate was placed in a book noting the name of the donor or other person the person chose to honor. Many student organized events were conducted, including a phone-a-thon and a campus-wide "University Day", in which one of the student leaders from Tiananmen Square, Chi Ling, and Betty Boa Lord were brought to campus for a program which 1,500 people attended.

Major Donors — Individual and Corporate

The Development Office worked closely with the President and John Gaines to prepare a list of major donors to contact. The President was involved in all solicitations, and in most cases handled this himself. Toyota made a second million dollar gift earmarked for the building. Local businessman and UK graduate W. T. Young made a $5 million gift for the new building and the University plans to name the building for him. A list of naming opportunities was prepared. This was useful on occasion, but most donors were either interested in the project or not without great attention being given to the naming opportunities list. Several major Kentucky corporations made significant gifts to the project.

Alumni

The Library in conjunction with the Development Office solicited the alumni for the endowment, but the Alumni Association developed plans to organize a major fund drive starting in 1992 to benefit the Library.

Other Factors Contributing to Success

The Library has a full-time Fundraising Coordinator, who is essential to the fundraising activities in the Library. She is responsible for coordinating activities with the Development Office and for planning and implementing fundraising events which the Library did on its own. (An organization chart for the University of Kentucky Library appears in Chapter 5, Table 5 - 2.) The work of the Development Office was critical to the success of the Library Campaign, as were the efforts of other University departments such as Public Relations, which handled the preparation of media and other information about the campaign. History will record that the turning event for the University of Kentucky Library came in 1989 when Toyota Motor Corporation made a million dollar gift to the Library. That started a sequence of events which lead to the creation of a major book endowment and plans for a $58 million building. Although many individuals played key roles in the campaign, none equaled that of the President. He made it his number one priority and worked tirelessly for the campaign for several years. Without the commitment of the President and his dedicated personal efforts to raise the needed funds, the campaign would never have been the outstanding success that it was.

第七章 对捐款者负责及对捐款的管理

Chapter 7 Donor Stewardship

Introduction

If it is true that human relationships motivate philanthropy, especially when it comes to major gifts, then **donor stewardship** can be thought of as the art of sustaining those relationships over time. We have all had the experience of meeting someone who makes a terrific first impression, only to disappoint us later on with his lack of attentiveness, reliability or follow through. What happens in the realm of personal friendship also applies to development. From the donor's point of view, charities all too often behave like inconstant friends: full of consideration at the outset, decidedly nonchalant after the gift has been made.

From the fundraiser's perspective this kind of behavior is also understandable—up to a point. Sometimes we have to work so hard cultivating a donor and securing the gift that it is only natural for us to relax a little bit afterwards. Besides, there are always new donors to cultivate, new proposals to be written and presented, new fundraising goals to be met. In the rush of a major capital campaign, it is easy to forget about those who have already made their commitment.

You should resist that temptation at all costs! Failure to satisfy your existing donors risks losing a very precious resource. Never underestimate the value of your current donors. They are important to you in many ways. First, if you treat them well they can generally be counted on to give more in the future. Second, having supported your library themselves, they are your most persuasive advocates when it comes to securing gifts from others. Third, prospective donors are impressed by the effort you make to honor those who have already given. At least some will be motivated to give precisely because they want that kind of recognition and sense of belonging for themselves.

The Meaning of Stewardship

The word "steward" comes from the Anglo-Saxon stiweard (sti, an enclosure or hall + weard, a ward or keeper) and refers to a person placed in charge of a large household or country estate. It implies both responsible management of resources and a sense of hospitality: the ability to make people feel at home, part of a family, comfortable and contented. These are the kinds of feelings you should try to evoke in all donors, from the moment they begin to support the library. You want them to feel like true participants in the enterprise, and you want them to understand that their gifts are really making a difference.

An effective stewardship program involves an interwoven network of activities aimed at making donors feel involved in a community of informed and valued persons whose assistance is enabling the library to achieve its full potential. We have said earlier that capital campaigns are generally built on the foundation of a successful annual giving program. This means that there is really no hard and fast distinction between stewardship and cultivation. Since you will rely to a considerable degree on support from prior donors, at least in the early stages of the campaign, the stewardship they have been receiving in the past blends seamlessly into the cultivation process for the new campaign.

The heart of good stewardship is a sound **campaign communications and promotion strategy**, designed to keep your various publics regularly informed about the progress of the campaign and to support particular objectives. Campaign publications can take the form of printed materials (newsletters, promotional brochures, press releases) as well as multi-media productions (slide shows or video). **Special events** are also a form of stewardship, although these too will often include both past donors and important prospects who have not yet made a contribution. Gala events are often held to launch a campaign, as well as to celebrate its successful conclusion. In the period between, it is common to bring together the volunteer leadership with the campaign staff at regular intervals for events that combine a little business, a little education or consciousness raising about the institution, a little companionship, and a little entertainment. Stewardship has traditionally meant **donor recognition programs** designed to honor those who have actually supported the campaign. Effective stewardship must rely on a good **donor information and gift accounting systems.** In recent years, several excellent automated systems have been developed to accomplish this task more efficiently than has ever been possible before. And of course taking care of your donors must always include sound **management of funds**, both those invested for endowment and those that have been contributed for spending on particular projects. Finally, a truly successful campaign should always lay the groundwork for future fundraising. In our last section we will discuss the concept of a **constituent society** for the library, similar to those that are being developed for academic colleges and schools on many university campuses.

I. Campaign Communications and Promotion

You will need to develop a communications and promotions strategy for your campaign, whether or not it is part of a larger institution-wide effort or focused on the library alone. In the former case, guidelines may be issued from the central development office. At smaller institutions, or where the library is running a capital campaign by itself, you will need to work out your own approach to communications and promotion, in cooperation with development, alumni affairs, and public relations personnel on campus. **Communications** refers to the periodic announcements, articles, personality profiles, and campaign updates that are released either for the general media or for in-house publications, like the alumni newsletter or the president's quarterly letter to contributors. **Promotion** refers to one-time-only publications, such as brochures or campaign videos, that are specially designed for the campaign and are targeted at specific groups of potential donors.

The objectives for the communications/promotions strategy should include:
1. Publicizing the campaign's goals and objectives;
2. Reporting on the campaign's progress;
3. Recognizing campaign leadership, volunteers, and donors;
4. Providing promotional materials to support donor solicitation efforts;
5. Producing appropriate printed materials for special campaign special events.

i. Campaign Communications

The media selected for publicizing the campaign will vary according to content and objective. Internal media include the university alumni newsletter, college-based newsletters, faculty staff newsletter, the student newspaper, and of course any publications put out by the library itself. External media include newspapers, magazines, house organs, radio, and television. In the case of a major university-wide capital campaign, it is not uncommon for the institution to develop a separate publications program devoted specifically to the campaign itself. Typically this might include a quarterly or semiannual newsletter, together with an annual report listing all donors and highlighting major success stories about the campaign.

Of course if your library already publishes its own newsletter, you will want to use it to the fullest extent possible to promote the goals of the campaign. But remember that a newsletter intended for donors is more than just a handy communications tool. It must be designed and printed with an eye toward producing a certain image. In other words, it must be of consistently high quality in both content and appearance. Quite a few libraries, especially among the top ARL institutions, are producing impressive (and expensive) publications, printed on glossy paper with full color photography and the like. Fortunately, the advent of desktop publishing makes it possible to produce acceptable (if not lavish) results at much lower costs. If your own resources will not permit you to achieve at least that level of quality, it is best to rely on the various university-wide publications as your primary vehicle for campaign communications.

Although this chapter is about stewardship, with its emphasis on building good relations with donors, it is also important to inform other constituencies, such as university administrators, faculty, and library staff, about the success of the campaign. In developing publicity about your fundraising efforts, do not forget to send it to both external and internal outlets.

Whether using your own newsletter, an institutional publication, or external media outlets, there are several important points to bear in mind about publicizing gifts to the library:

1. Be certain that the gift is in-hand, or at least committed in writing, before making a public announcement.

2. Secure the donor's permission to publicize the gift. Remember that donors have a right to privacy! Always ask if they mind publicity, and scrupulously follow any restrictions they ask you to observe. Some foundations require that any press releases about their grants be cleared in advance by staff. Others ask to be provided with copies of what appears in print.

3. Publicize the largest gifts first, in the early stages of the campaign, in order to build momentum and encourage a higher standard of giving by your remaining prospects.

4. Publicize smaller gifts in strategic ways: to encourage particular constituencies; to overcome a lull in the campaign; or to keep morale high.

5. Match the level of publicity to the level of the gift.

6. Timeliness is critical to the success of media relations. Top priority should be given to the public announcement of major gifts, as soon as they are received and the necessary permissions obtained.

Work with the public relations staff at your institution, if you are lucky enough to have them. They will have far more experience than you placing stories in local, state, and national media. If your efforts are part of a larger, institution-wide capital campaign, there may be staff specifically assigned to handle campaign relations, as well as guidelines on the timing of announcements and coordination with other units on campus. The PR staff can help with press releases or even organizing a press conference to announce the occasional mega-gift to the library.

Whether you are writing press releases yourself or relying on someone else for that service, it is a good idea to develop a checklist of the standard elements to include. For example:

1. Impact of the gift on the library;
2. quotes from the donor;
3. a brief profile of the donor;
4. quotes from the library director and/or senior administrators on the impact of the gift;
5. a brief statement about the goals of the campaign, its timetable, and progress to date;
6. a one-or two-sentence statement on who to contact for further information on the campaign.

To gain maximum benefit from grants and major gifts, you will want to publicize the news as broadly as possible. Depending on the size of the award (or its impact), it might even be appropriate to notify such outlets as the *New York Times*, *The Chronicle of Higher Education*, CBS, NBC, ABC, and CNN. Even smaller gifts may interest a national media outlet if they come from an unusual source or are made to support an especially innovative project, with a compelling human story behind it. (On the other hand it is a waste of time, paper, and postage to send releases on ordinary gifts to the major media outlets.) Certainly state and local media should be given the opportunity to publicize gifts to the library, since their impact will most often be local in nature.

In developing your publicity strategy, try to be attentive to the donor's needs and desires. Announcements in *College & Research Library News* or the *Wilson Library Bulletin* are fine, but they are really designed to enhance your own reputation (and that of your library). From the donor's standpoint, it is much more important to be recognized in a general media outlet, whether national or local. If the donor lives in a distant part of the country, he may want to have his gift publicized in his own local paper, as well as in the university's alumni newsletter. Perhaps he will want it mentioned in a professional journal, company newsletter, or association magazine that circulates among his associates. It doesn't hurt to ask. Business and corporate contributors want to have their generosity publicized where it can be noticed by customers, employees, voters and politicians.

ii. Promotional Materials

The central promotional piece for your fundraising effort is the **campaign brochure**. Experienced fund raisers are fond of saying that "a fancy brochure never raised a dime." It is certainly true that a brochure **by itself** is not going to produce many gifts. You should conceive of it as just one of several components in the cultivation and solicitation process, to be used in conjunction with personal meetings, formal presentations, written proposals and other tools of persuasion at your disposal. Some fundraisers conceive of the brochure as a "door opener," a way to capture the prospect's interest and to suggest possible areas of giving for later discussion. Others like to leave it with the donor after the first meeting, as a kind of reminder and to provide an excuse for later follow up. ("Have you had a chance to read about what we are trying to accomplish in the library?")

In terms of content, the brochure should closely follow the **campaign case statement**, the elements of which were discussed in chapter two. But depending on the money you have to spend, it will most likely be an abbreviated version of the original case statement, focusing on the services you provide and how the requested funds can help you perform them better. It will outline your fundraising priorities and describe specific recognition opportunities for donors. And unlike the case statement, most campaign brochures are heavily illustrated. In fact, the layout, graphic design, and photography will be as important as the written content. The brochure should be effective but not too lavish. Some donors are put off by a piece of literature that appears overly expensive.

More and more companies and non-profit institutions are using **promotional videos** to sell products, motivate employees, and solicit donations. According to the Direct Marketing Association, a trade organization in New York City, video tapes lend themselves to upscale products and generate response rates of from 2 to 13 percent.① The San Diego Zoo sent videocassettes to 900 of its top prospects in a 1990 campaign to raise $1 million. Miami University Library has produced an effective eight-minute video as part of a $100 million university-wide capital campaign. A national fundraiser has found that when prospects have been "softened up" by an advance video, the size of the average gift increases for smaller donors and the response rate increases for larger ones. A videocassette is still new enough to command the attention of prospects. Most will insert it in their VCR and watch out of curiosity. Printed brochures, on the other hand, are all too often discarded without being read.

The great advantage of video is that it can convey human faces and the unique sense of place behind your institution. It is more effective in communicating emotion than conveying hard facts or complex thoughts. Alumni who have been out of school for a long time, who perhaps live some distance away, can be drawn back to the campus and into the library. The **disadvantage** of video is its high cost. The going rate for basic but professional quality video is still around $1,000 per minute of finished product, or between $8,000 to $10,000 for a standard length production of no more than ten minutes. If your institution has a telecommunications program or an in-house video production unit, you may be able to cut those costs quite a bit. On the other hand, if you employ a lot of expensive techniques, like multiple cameras or aerial shots, the costs can easily run two or three times above the standard rate of $1,000 per minute.

Before deciding whether a promotional video would be an appropriate tool for your campaign and worth the substantial investment, you should answer a few fundamental questions:

1. Why is it needed? What is the over-arching goal of the video?
2. How will the video be used? Will you show it only once as part of a gala event? Will it be

---

① Article in Columbus (Ohio) *Business First*, September 23, 1991, p. 30.

used repeatedly for group presentations, such as civic clubs and alumni chapter meetings? Or will people watch it at home? The style, tone, and content of the video must be dictated by the context in which it is used.

3. Who will watch the video? People who already know something about the library and its programs? People who know about your parent institution, but are not familiar with the library? Complete strangers? Mostly alumni? Mostly business or community prospects?

4. When will it be used? Will it launch the library campaign, give it a mid-term boost, or wrap it up? A video designed for one point in your campaign may not be nearly as effective at another.

5. What are the basic objectives? Is the video intended purely for cultivation of donors? Or do you want it to include the hard sell? List no more than a half dozen major points you want to put across.

6. Who supplies the program content? Will a library staff member provide an initial script?

7. What is the approximate length? (Don't count on holding the viewer's attention, for more than ten minutes, unless you have a very interesting story to tell!)

8. How long do you want the video to be useful? The more specifically geared to the needs of your campaign, the quicker it will become outdated. There could be similar limitations with a high tech focus. A modular approach to program content offers the greatest flexibility over time.

Once you have worked your way through these seven points and can answer them to your satisfaction, you are ready to bring in the video production experts (whether from on campus or from the outside) and start work on your project. For further reading on this topic, we recommend a publication of the Counsel for the Advancement and Support of Education called, *Electronic Advancement: Fund Raising*. It consists of a 202 – page book together with two 60 – minute VHS videocassettes containing ten examples of successful fundraising videos. For ordering information, call CASE Publications at (800) 336 – 4776 or (703) 204 – 0411 in Virginia.

II. Conducting Special Events

Special events provide an opportunity to bring people into your library who might not otherwise be aware of what it has to offer. They can also be an occasion for your regular users to see the library in a new way, associating it with a touch of elegance and class. Special events include regular, recurring events, such as library tours, a book sale, or a Friends meeting. Or they can be unique, one-time-only affairs designed to celebrate some accomplishment, such as the opening of a new wing, the acquisition of a noteworthy special collection, the launching of a major capital campaign, or recognizing donors at the conclusion of a campaign.

It is important to distinguish between fundraising events designed to generate money and so-called "friend raisers" that are intended to share information and promote goodwill. If your library does not have a well formed constituency, it may be necessary to hold a friend raiser in order to educate some of your prospective donors about your programs. The Tulsa County Public Library held a series of VIP breakfasts to acquaint community business leaders with its needs in preparation for a fundraising campaign. Knowing that their invited guests were busy people, as careful about spending their time as spending their money, the library settled on the breakfast format, which proved to be highly successful. [1]

April L. Harris has developed a useful list of questions you should ask about any proposed special event. Does the event:

- Support the library's and/or the institution's mission?
- Help achieve specific goals?
- Showcase resources unique to your library?
- Help friend raise or fund raise?
- Generate goodwill?

---

[1] Sul H. Lee (ed.). *Library fund-raising: vital margin for excellence*. (Ann Arbor: Pieran Press, 1984), p. 31.

● Consistently comply with the library and/or institutional image?
● Match available resources?①

Harris also emphasizes the importance of placing special events within the context of an overall master plan for promoting public relations. The random event scheduled in response to a unique development is less effective than a well planned series of events that build on each other and achieve cumulative impact.

i. The Campaign Gala

It has become traditional to mark at least the public announcement of major capital campaign with some kind of gala event in which the sponsoring organization really outdoes itself to impress its constituency. In his essay on "Public Relations" in Dewey's *Raising Money for Academic and Research Libraries*, William R. Mott outlines the conceptual steps to follow in planning such an event:

● What kind of event will launch the campaign?
● Who will announce the campaign?
● On what occasion will it be announced?
● How will different prospect groups be informed—major library donors, other library donors, major institutional donors, other university donors, current and former library staff, students, parents, alumni, current and former faculty?
● What intermediate goals will be used for special events?
● What concluding event might be appropriate?
● Do you have the capacity to organize major special events, or will you need help?②

There are pros and cons to the idea of holding lavish events for donors, especially in an academic environment. Proponents argue that in many communities, donors have come to expect them. If you fail to provide a lavish banquet at a downtown hotel, or an afternoon outing at a wealthy donor's estate, or an evening of ballroom dancing, or a chance to meet Paul Newman—then your campaign will just not be taken seriously. You are missing an opportunity to impress donors with the stature of your institution and convey an aura of glamour and excitement.

On the other hand, these events are expensive, even when the participants are asked to purchase tickets. Costs can range anywhere between $10 per head for a simple reception with hot and cold hors d'oeuvres and cash bar, to $50 and more for a reception, open bar, and full banquet dinner. In some high-priced metropolitan areas, the costs can be even higher. Special events also absorb huge amounts of staff time and energy. And they inevitably give rise to criticism from certain quarters that the institution is wasting its money entertaining wealthy people while more pressing needs remain unmet. Following the excesses of the 1980s, there seems to be a trend developing in the philanthropic community against gala events. In fact, the political climate on some campuses could make the whole idea of a campaign gala untenable from the outset.

If your fundraising effort is part of an institution-wide campaign, then the decision to hold a gala event, together with most of the operational details, will be left to others. At the very minimum, you should insist on having input on the guest list, so that library supporters can be invited to attend. Make sure that you and your key staff are able to be on hand. If seating is assigned, try to see to it that at least some of the top institutional donors are placed with library staff and supporters. Generally these events will feature a speech by the president outlining the case for support and announcing the goals for the campaign. It is important that the library be mentioned in that speech, which in one version or another might be given on several important occasions, and you should not feel shy about urging this on your president.

---

① April L. Harris. "Special events and their role in fund raising". *Journal of Library Administration*; 1990; 12 (4); pp. 39–51.
② William R. Mott. "Public relations." In: *Dewey, op. cit.*, p. 82.

ii. Other Special Events

In addition to gala events designed to launch or conclude a major capital campaign, there are other types of activities that can be useful in promoting the library among actual or potential donors. Often these kinds of special library events are employed as part of a campus wide program directed at alumni and friends.

a. Alumni events are a familiar enough occurrence on most college and university campuses. Whether taking the form of class reunions, homecoming weekends, chapter programs, or so-called "alumni colleges", the library should plan to participate. This might take the form of tours, exhibits, an open house with demonstrations, a book sale, a lecture, or a performance of some kind.

b. Exhibitions provide an occasion to do something attractive for your donor prospects, especially when the library can boast some truly distinguished special collections or has acquired an outstanding new collection worthy of attention.

c. Concerts and performances can be used to generate goodwill and may be especially appropriate for certain types of libraries. Peter A. Munstedt, the Conservatory Librarian at University of Missouri-Kansas City, reports on a highly successful benefit concert organized by the Conservatory's Music Library Committee. Performers were selected from alumni of the conservatory, who had fewer concretizing opportunities than students and faculty. The event could be coordinated with the annual alumni dinner held in September. "Encore 88" was a success, with an audience of over 200 attending. This event netted only $600, but the library improved its image and standing in the community. While performing arts faculty are perhaps the best suited to hold this kind of event, there are other possibilities. An English department might organize a poetry reading in conjunction with a special poetry collection. The business college might provide a financial planning workshop in conjunction with demonstrating a new investment related CD-ROM database owned by the library. ①

d. Tours of the library should be offered as a regular feature of your public relations program. If there are groups of alumni and friends on campus for any occasion, the library should be on their itinerary—or at the very least an optional item for any free time available to the participants. You should arrive at an understanding with your president, college deans, the development office, and other key players on campus that the library welcomes visiting dignitaries and is prepared to provide professional, informative, and interesting tours of its facilities—on short notice if necessary!

e. Anniversary events correspond to some significant date in the life of the library, one of its departments, or the parent institution. It may be twenty years since your building was occupied. In 1986 Ohio University Library celebrated the one hundredth anniversary of its status as an official depository for United States government documents. Officials from the GPO were on hand to present a certificate, congratulatory letters from senators and congressmen were read, and a program was conducted with invited speakers, including the Archivist of the United States. These occasions provide an excuse to bring constituents into the library to celebrate and to be educated through formal presentations, exhibits, tours, and the like.

f. Dedication ceremonies are another good way to draw people into the library who might not otherwise pay it much attention. Of course the construction of a new building or a major addition will always call for some kind of official ceremony. But do not neglect the opportunity to highlight such accomplishments as the installation of a new integrated system, or the opening of a media demonstration lab, or even a significant renovation project.

g. New collections can also be recognized by dedication ceremonies. At Ohio University Library, special events were held to mark receipt of the Cornelius Ryan World War II Collection in 1981, the Edmund Blunden Collection of Romantic Literature in 1982, the Beeler Collection of Medieval History in 1987, and the E. W. Scripps Journalism Archive in 1989. On these occasions

---

① Peter A. Munstedt. "Library benefit concerts: blood, sweat, and cash". *College & Research Libraries News*; March 1989, pp. 204 – 5.

the donor/collector (if living), together with his family and friends, will be asked to attend as honored guests. The program should balance scholarly appreciation of the collection with personal reminiscences. Depending on the importance of the collection and the availability of funding, your dedication program might be quite simple—no more than an hour or two—or it might become much more elaborate. In the case of the Scripps Archives dedication, the program took the form of a two-day conference on "The Life and Times of E. W. Scripps". More than thirty family members were present, together with local faculty and invited journalism history scholars from around the country.

h. Millionth volume celebrations are familiar fare for most larger academic libraries. Of course depending on the size of your collection, it could just as well be a "Hundred Thousandth Volume" or a "Five Millionth Volume" observance.

i. Open houses are a good way to highlight new library products, equipment, and services, especially for important constituents who may not be regular visitors. Some libraries conduct open houses in conjunction with campus-wide events, such as a homecoming weekend, in order to reach a broader audience.

III. Donor Recognition Programs

The library's donor recognition program should be both traditional and distinctive, reflecting the history of the institution and yet standing apart from other recognition programs on campus. Fortunately, the library offers a number of unique opportunities for recognizing all its donors, great and small. Fundamental to any good donor recognition program is the timely acknowledgement of all gifts. The next most important thing is to create appropriate naming opportunities for your donors. Finally, you want your donor recognition program to incorporate the concept of progressivity, so that donors are motivated to advance from one level of giving to the next.

i. Gift Acknowledgment

The core of stewardship is the recognition of specific donors for their generosity to the library. In most cases this process will begin with letters of acknowledgement. How many should you write? One fundraising expert recommends that gifts be acknowledged no fewer than seven times.[①] Under this so-called "Rule of Sevens", the donor might receive immediately upon making a gift one letter from the development office, another soon after from the library director, another from the president of the friends of the library or chairman of its campaign committee, together with an official gift receipt (for tax purposes) from the treasurer. If the contribution has been made in support of a particular area of the library, a brief note from the appropriate department head or subject bibliographer might be in order, letting the donor know exactly what has been done with the gift. Eventually a student or faculty member will benefit from the gift, and in that case a personal note from the library patron will be more effective than almost any kind of acknowledgement you can devise. Finally, each donor should be recognized by name in some type of annual report, whether published by the library or by the development office.

In the case of major donors or those who have established permanent endowments, you should go still further. An annual letter from the director summarizing the benefits to the library is an excellent way to keep in contact and encourage continued interest in your programs. You might want to consider sending your top few donors a small but attractive gift each year, perhaps at the holiday season, with a brief note of appreciation. But take care not to overdo this practice. If they begin to receive lavish gifts in the mail, donors will wonder how the library is spending its money. Remember that good stewardship also involves the prudent and responsible handling of funds!

The library director should take the time to meet with key donors from time to time, either by traveling to their homes or by inviting them to campus for a visit. These are people with whom you need to establish a good personal relationship, one that involves them as partners and advisers in

---

① Jerold Panas. "Yours for the asking". *National Association for Hospital Development Journal*; Fall, 1986.

the library enterprise. It is especially appropriate to invite key representatives of the foundation or corporation to visit the library for an on-site examination of the projects they have funded. Some directors are concerned that giving grantmakers too much personal attention may encourage them to meddle in library management issues. This rarely happens with library donors, and when it does, it can usually be handled diplomatically.

Sometimes donors will act as though they are not interested in being singled out for praise. Of course you should always listen to what donors say. But be careful not to take their protestations of modesty at face value. You should gently but persistently probe the donor's feelings on the subject of recognition. If public mention of their gifts makes them uncomfortable, then by all means respect their requests for anonymity. But most donors will be pleased to receive tasteful and sincere appreciation. Many will be flattered by more overt kinds of recognition. Good treatment of donors has a double payoff. First, it makes the specific donor being recognized feel good. Second, it impresses other would-be donors to see you making a fuss over a gift. They imagine what it would be like for themselves be on the receiving end of that kind of recognition.

ii. Handling Gifts-in-Kind

Libraries often receive contributions of books, magazines, sound recordings, manuscripts and other tangible property. These so-called "gifts-in-kind" present special challenges in donor stewardship. First, you need to decide whether to accept the gift at all. Often the materials will simply not be appropriate for addition to the library's collection. For example, duplicate works will normally be rejected, along with materials that have become dated (unless rare), fall outside the scope of your collecting policy, or are in poor physical condition. It is good stewardship to offer alternative means for disposing of items not selected for the collection: through sale by a friends group, with the proceeds applied to future acquisitions; through exchange of material for other items for which the library has a more pressing need; or through donation to another institution. In this way the donor can always be assured that the gift will benefit the library in some way.

A donor wishing to claim tax deduction for a gift of books or other library materials will need to assign them a dollar value and fulfill certain other requirements. Since libraries are often asked to help with this process, you should obtain current copies of the following IRS publications, both for your own information and to share with donors:

Form 8283 — **Noncash Charitable Contributions**
Publication 526 — **Charitable Contributions**
Publication 561 — **Determining the Value of Donated Property**

If the amount of claimed deductions for **all noncash gifts** exceeds $500 in a given tax year, donors must complete IRS Form 8283 and file it with their tax return. For example, if a donor gives $100 worth of books to your library, together with $500 worth of used clothing to the Salvation Army, then Form 8283 must be completed in order to claim the full $600 deduction for noncash gifts contributed during that year.

Under current IRS guidelines, the donor can employ personal research to establish a value for any gift whose claimed value does not exceed $5,000. It is perfectly appropriate to assist the donor with information from sources such as *Books in Print*, *Bookman's Price Index*, *Book Auction Records*, *American Book Prices Current*, or listings in individual dealers' catalogs. But make it clear that the ultimate responsibility for establishing the value must be borne by donor, not the library. It's a good idea to sit down with the donor and review IRS Publication 561 (Determining the Value of Donated Property), particularly the section on books and other collections.

Generally, if the claimed deduction is more than $5,000, the donor must have an expert appraisal made by a qualified appraiser and attach a summary to the tax return. In these cases you should at least be prepared to help the donor locate a "qualified" appraiser. Ask for referrals from other libraries, or from groups like the Antiquarian Bookdealer's Association of America. You may also want to consult a standard directory such as *Sheppard's Book Dealers in North America*, but remember that not all dealers are qualified (or willing) to perform appraisals. The safest approach is to find someone with previous experience appraising similar material for tax purposes. Unfortunately, the guidelines prohibit using the same dealer from whom the donor has purchased his or her collection. (Too close a relationship with an interested party.) They also prohibit using any dealer who conducts most of his or her appraisals for your particular library. (Same reason.) Consult IRS Publication 561 for further stipulations regarding the qualifications of the appraiser.

Sometimes a question arises over who should pay the appraisal fee: the donor or the library. The IRS guidelines state that the fee cannot be based on a percentage of the appraised value, but they are silent on the issue of which party should pay. Most libraries ask donors to pay for their own appraisals, since it is they who will presumably derive a tax deduction. (The appraisal fee is itself a deductible business expense, in most cases.) From a stewardship standpoint, you are under no obligation to defray the appraisal costs. Do so only for compelling reasons.

iii. Naming Opportunities

In any capital campaign, it is important to offer opportunities for donors to designate named gifts for themselves and for others they wish to honor. Typical opportunities range from the library building itself, to parts of buildings (rooms, wings or additions), to endowed positions (directorship, curatorship, subject specialist), to departmental collections or parts of collections, to endowed funds for acquisitions, preservation, professional development, automation, or just about any other legitimate purpose—all the way down to individual book volumes that have been acquired with donated funds.

The simple bookplate has long been a staple of gift recognition programs in academic libraries. For a rather small amount, donors can permanently affix their own name (or that of a loved one) to a book that will be read by generations of students and faculty. In fact there are few opportunities as attractive as this for the donor of modest means who makes a gift of $100 or less to the annual giving drive or to a capital campaign. Every library should have a standard gift bookplate: one for regular gifts and another for memorial gifts. In the case of larger gifts, sufficient to create an endowed fund, you should work with donors to design a customized bookplate.

Most development offices or university foundations will set a minimum threshold gift needed to create a named endowment: typically around $35,000. You might need to negotiate separate guidelines for library endowments. Development officers are attuned to raising endowments for faculty chairs or for student financial support. In each case, a sizable amount of annual support must be generated in order to underwrite those programs. Based on an assumed 6 percent return, a principal of at least $1 million is needed to support an endowed chair. Depending on whether you are a public or private institution, between $50,000 and $150,000 is required to create a named full-tuition scholarship. But library collection support can be broken down into much smaller increments, allowing for a wide range of affordable naming opportunities for your donors. For example, a library endowment of $10,000 will only generate around $600 each year. But if those funds are used to purchase books and periodicals in a particular discipline, they will be more than welcomed by most academic libraries. It can be an advantage to your campaign if the library is allowed to offer named endowment opportunities at a "bargain" rate.

At Ohio University Libraries, where the authors have gained their experience, named endowment opportunities for acquisitions begin for as little as $15,000, and we will allow donors up to five years to achieve that goal. Of course in order to name an *entire collection or department* for a donor, much higher levels should be established. For example:

Items and Conditions	Targeted Amount
Named acquisitions endowment in a particular subject area	$15,000
Named component of a collection, for example: medieval history	$100,000 or ten times the annual cost of acquisitions, whichever is greater

(continuing)

Items and Conditions	Targeted Amount
Named collection, for example: history	$500,000 or ten times the annual cost of acquisitions, whichever is greater
Name departmental collection: that is, one that includes its own staff and facilities	$1,000,000 or five times the annual cost of both acquisitions and staff support, whichever is greater

As to buildings and other facilities, it is not uncommon for trustee action to be required in order to name them. The point is that you should develop a policy at the outset of the campaign—and then stick to it! Your general naming guidelines for new library construction and renovation projects might look something like this:

Items and Conditions	Targeted Amount
New library construction, if entirely funded from private sector	No less than 51% of the cost of construction
New library construction, if major portion (more than 51%) is to be funded by the state and/or other public sources	Cost difference between government allocations and overall cost of construction, but not less than 33% of overall cost
Library renovations, when entire cost is to private sector be funded from private sector	Generally, 100% of renovation cost; a lesser amount if renovation cost is above $2 million but no less than 51% of overall cost
Library renovations, when state and/or public sources are paying part of the cost	Difference between government allocations and overall cost of renovations, but no less than 33% of overall cost
Components of the library structure (reading room, media laboratory, classroom, auditorium, office, seminar room, reception areas, etc.)	150% of actual square footage construction cost (the additional 50% is endowment for upkeep purposes)
Courtyards, gardens and other landscaping	150% of cost (the additional 50% is endowment for upkeep purposes)

iv. Donor Societies

Most colleges and universities with mature development programs have established a system of donor societies organized into tiers based on the level of giving. For example, at Ohio University there are five such societies:

Trustees' Academy — for donors whose gifts and pledges total at least $10,000 over a period of ten years;
Putnam Society — for donors who have given at the annual level of $1,000;
1804 Society — for donors whose annual contributions range between $500 and $999;
Lindley Society — for donors whose annual contributions fall between $250 and $499;
Cutler Society — for donors whose annual contribution range between $100 and $249.

If your institution has created a series of donor societies, you should make certain that contributors to the library are properly credited and inducted into the appropriate group. In the case of cash gifts, this does not normally present any problems. But gifts-in-kind to the library are often overlooked by central development offices, either because they are not reported at all or because of the difficulties in establishing a dollar value that would allow assignment to the proper society. Part of practicing good stewardship with respect to gifts-in-kind involves setting up a procedure to ensure they are properly reported and credited for donor recognition purposes.

v. Honor Wall Plaques

At some point in the campaign you should consider setting up a permanent display to recognize those who have contributed to its success. Variously referred to as "honor walls", "donor walls," or "memorial walls", these recognition units are a familiar site in most hospitals and in many academic buildings, including an increasing number of libraries. There are several companies in the business of designing and fabricating honor wall systems. Some will be found listed in periodicals like *CASE Currents and The Chronicle of Philanthropy*. To identify others, enquire at local organizations that have recently installed structures of their own. Most sales persons will be happy to work with you to design a system that fits your needs. You should be prepared to answer the following basic questions:

1. Are you looking for a closed-end unit that will honor only those who have contributed to this capital campaign, or do you want it to be expandable to accommodate additional names in the future?

2. If the campaign is not over, or if you intend the system to be an open-ended one, are their enough gifts already in hand to justify installing it now? Nothing looks worse that a whole lot of blank name plates. It makes your fundraising program look like a failure!

3. What are your gift categories (in dollar amounts), what are you going to call them (Leaders, Benefactors, Patrons, Supporters, etc), and how many donors do you need to recognize in each?

4. How much are you willing to spend? Honor wall systems can range all the way from $500 for an off-the shelf plaque to $50,000 or more for a large, dramatic, customized architectural structure employing the finest materials and workmanship. For a price in the $2,000 to $3,000 range you should be able to buy an attractive system able to handle up to 100 donors in several categories.

5. Are your donors and potential donors likely to spend much time in the library? If the answer is yes, you may want to invest more in the system than would otherwise be the case.

6. Does the installation need to be completed in time for a dedication ceremony or other campus event? If so, allow plenty of time.

IV. Donor Information And Gift Accounting Systems

Most of the fundraising techniques we have discussed so far will depend for their success on a reliable donor records system. Sometimes we think of donor record keeping as a practice that begins only after a gift is made. No doubt this is the most critical aspect: it is absolutely necessary to maintain a good accounting of contributions once they are "in the door". That is why we have chosen to discuss the issue in this chapter on stewardship. But an effective donor records system should do much more than tell you who has given how much for what purpose. At each stage of the development enterprise from the moment a prospect is identified, through the initial research, the volunteer/staff assignments, the correspondence, proposal writing and personal contacts, to the eventual gift or pledge receipt and subsequent administration of a stewardship program—your tasks will be made much easier if you record what has been done in a form that can be easily retrieved to support the next step in the process.

Anyone familiar with the world of library automation will quickly recognize that we are talking about an **integrated systems** approach to donor records. Over the past decade the development function has become progressively more computerized on most campuses. The trend started with batch processing of alumni records, mailing lists and gift transactions performed on a mainframe in the computer center. Next came word processing, first on dumb terminals connected to the mainframe, then on personal computers. With the evolution of not just word processing, but also relational databases and fund accounting software—all in a desktop computer environment—it became possible to place powerful and flexible tools directly in the hands of those who perform the day-to-day work of development. Today there are a number of fundraising and planned giving software products on the market. Some of the better known are listed in Appendix XII.

i. Features

You may decide to acquire your own donor information software; or you may decide to share a system already in use by development and alumni affairs—assuming you can gain access to it. Perhaps planning is now underway to select such a system, and the library has been asked for input. Whatever the situation, you should have some knowledge of the features that are typically included in the best modern donor information and gift accounting software packages. In this way you can make informed judgments on how well the library's needs are being served by the current procedures, compared to what is available on the market.

The modules in a fully integrated system include: donor information, prospect tracking, gift accounting, planned giving analysis, and word processing/mailing list management. The following section provides in highly abbreviated fashion a list of desirable features in each of these modules:

a. Donor information module

SALUTATIONS

There is nothing more important in donor stewardship than getting the salutation right and keeping it right. Is it "Dear Mr. and Mrs. Smith?" Or "Dear Bob and Mary?"

NAME

MULTIPLE ADDRESSES

Generally there will be at least two: a home and a business address. Find out which one the donor wants you to use for correspondence and other mailings. The system should be able to tag this **preferred address**. Many donors (especially retirees) will also have a second home where they spend a part of the year. If they follow a regular schedule between residences, the system should be able to record that information as well.

MULTIPLE PHONE NUMBERS

Same comments apply as above.

PROSPECT CATEGORY

The usual prospect types include: students; alumni (with degree [s] and date [s]); friends; faculty/staff; corporations; foundations; units of government; and affiliated organizations.

MARITAL STATUS (and name of spouse)

NUMBER OF CHILDREN (and names)

BIRTH DATE

Important not only if you want to recognize the donor's birthday, but for purposes of determining the value of bequests, annuities, trusts, and certain other deferred gifts.

BIOGRAPHICAL SUMMARY

Place of birth; schools attended and degrees held; military service; places prospect has lived; foreign travel; hobbies and special interests of any kind.

EMPLOYMENT SUMMARY

Companies the prospect has worked for, with dates and positions held. Does the current employer have a matching gifts program? Cross-link the company name with a separate company file, so you can quickly find out which donors/alumni are employed by a particular company.

AFFILIATIONS

Membership in civic organizations, service clubs, churches, political parties, honorary societies, etc.

GIVING SUMMARY

Dates, amounts, and designations of all previous gifts, pledges, and pledge redemptions by this donor, together with any matching or memorial gifts made in connection with this donor, cross referenced in each case from the primary donor.

PROSPECT RESEARCH RESULTS

Estimates of income and assets, evaluation of real estate holdings, assessment of giving potential by volunteer committees and/or through application of a rating formula.

b. Prospect tracking

CLEARANCE PROCEDURES

Does the library have permission to solicit a gift, in a certain amount, from this particular prospect? In most campus-wide campaigns, a "clearance procedure" will be established to resolve conflicting claims by different units and avoid multiple solicitations of the same prospect.

SOLICITATION PHASE

At what stage of the process are you with the prospect: identification, cultivation, solicitation, gift commitment, gift received, or stewardship?

STAFF/VOLUNTEER ASSIGNMENTS

Who has been assigned to work the prospect?

APPOINTMENTS

Record in advance any planned meetings with the prospect.

CONTACT RESULTS

Record of meetings and/or telephone conversations with the prospect.

FOLLOW-UP

What is the next step with this prospect? When and by whom shall it be accomplished?

c. Gift accounting

DAILY GIFT TRANSACTIONS

Type of gift (cash, pledge, deferred, in-kind)

Solicitation code: what generated gift

Date gift was made

Amount of the gift

Joint donor

Matching gift

Account number to which gift should be credited Memorial gift

ACCOUNT CASH SUMMARIES TO BUSINESS/TREASURER'S OFFICE ABILITY TO PERIODICALLY RECONCILE ACCOUNTS

CAMPAIGN SUMMARIES

Cumulative amounts raised

—by donor category (alumni, foundation, etc.)

— by goal (acquisitions, endowment, etc.)

—by type of gift (cash, in-kind, etc.)

— by phase (cultivation, solicitation, etc.)

Monthly/quarterly changes

— by donor category (alumni, foundation, etc.)

—by goal (acquisitions, endowment, etc.)

— by type of gift (cash, in-kind, etc.)

—by phase (cultivation, solicitation, etc.)

COMPLETE GIFT HISTORY

Pledge credit, including multiple pledges

Campaign credit, including multiple campaigns

Record credits in donor information file

PLEDGE BILLING, including multiple pledges

CORPORATE MATCHING GIFT BILLING

d. Word processing

The donor information system should interface with one of the more widely used word processing programs, such as WordPerfect or MacWrite. In this way, elements from the database can be easily incorporated into form letters, correspondence, mailings and proposals created for the prospect, while (conversely) these written materials can be filed in the system under the prospect's name for future retrieval and use.

e. Planned giving analysis

This is really a species of financial software used to calculate such things as allowable deductions, future principal value and the annual payouts of annuities, trusts and other planned giving vehicles. These functions do not necessarily have to be integrated into the overall system, since they will normally be used only for a small number of prospects in the final stages of structuring a planned gift arrangement. Some vendors, like Blackbaud MicroSystems, offer planned giving analysis as a separate module to run alongside their donor information and fund accounting packages. Others, like Crescendo, Planned Giving Manager, or TrustProcessor, are stand alone products. (See Appendix XII.)

ii. Management issues

You will need to decide which records should to be kept by the library, as opposed to the development and financial offices. Of course if you are going it alone, with no help from either a central development operation or the institution's financial office, the issue will be simplified. You must implement your own comprehensive donor information and gift accounting system. More likely you will at least be getting help from the financial office to record cash gift transactions, handle endowment investment and income distributions, and manage the monthly fund accounting that accompanies these activities. Generally the library will want to set up enough redundant procedures so that (for example) cash gifts, expenditures, and account balances can be periodically reconciled with whatever external reports it is receiving. This is standard practice in library management. Indeed, most libraries have well established procedures in place for sharing relevant financial information with their campus business offices on a "need to know" basis.

The situation is somewhat different with respect to information compiled by development or alumni offices. There is less of a tradition in place for sharing, updating, and correcting data about current or prospective donors—even with other units on the same campus. In part, this attitude stems from legitimate concerns to protect the confidentiality of sensitive donor/alumni information. In part, it reflects the organizational realities of development offices, most of which are just not equipped to deal with outside queries. The willingness to share information may be there, but the ability to do so on a timely basis is sometimes lacking. You will need to make a judgment based on conditions at your campus. Whether you rely on the development office or institute your own procedures, the goal is to have available all the information required to serve both your existing and prospective donors as efficiently as possible.

V. Management of Funds

i. Gift Acceptance Policy

It is in the nature of capital campaigns that they have both a designated dollar goal and a fixed time frame within which the goal is supposed to be reached: for example, $100 million over five years. In order to keep track of your progress, it is necessary to establish guidelines specifying: (1) when to start counting gifts toward the campaign and when to stop; and (2) what gifts to count and (if other than a straight cash gift) what method of calculation to apply; and (3) how to document gifts. All of these matters should be spelled out in a written *gift acceptance policy*. Such a policy not only enables you to measure precisely the over all success of the campaign, it also provides guidance to donors as to whether a particular gift will be counted toward the effort and in what amount.

a. When to Start Counting

Normally the termination date of a capital campaign will be less ambiguous than the beginning date. That is because most major campaigns involve several years of advance planning before they are officially launched. During this planning period, several of your top prospects may have made substantial gifts that preclude them from any further participation in the campaign. Others may have made gifts in anticipation of the campaign, with the explicit understanding that they would be counted. In either case, your gift acceptance policy should indicate clearly how these "early" gifts will be treated for campaign purposes. Many colleges and universities begin counting virtually all gifts made to the institution for two or even three years before the public announcement of a capital campaign. The decision will depend primarily on how much you expect to need those gifts in order to reach or surpass the goal.

b. What Gifts to Count

The Council for the Advancement and Support of Education (CASE) has established guidelines on "Management Reporting Standards for Educational Institutions" that define how to calculate the value of different types of gifts for campaign purposes. The following procedures, which are quoted directly from Ohio University's gift acceptance policy, are consistent with those standards and can be used to formulate your own regulations in this area:

1. Cash — counted at face value.

2. Pledges — counted at face value when properly documented during the campaign, with full payment completed within five years of the pledge date.

3. Securities — counted at averaged market value on the date the donor gives the securities to The Ohio University Foundation or other recognized University repository.

4. Real Property, Personal Property, Equipment, and other in—kind gifts — counted at the fair market value determined by a qualified third-party appraiser, subject to IRS rules and the completion of Form 8283 where needed.

5. Charitable Remainder Trusts, Pooled Income Funds and Gift Annuities — counted at fair market value of assets given. In the event that such a gift's principal is invaded to honor commitments to the donor, only the remaining interest will be counted.

6. Charitable Lead Trusts — counted at the cumulative value of the annual gifts received during the Campaign period, or the net present value of the entire gifts flow determined at the date of gift, whichever is larger.

7. Insurance — Gifts of Insurance will be counted in accordance with the following guidelines:

a. For fully paid-up policies on the lives of donors 65 years old or older, count at full value of death benefit.

b. For fully paid-up policies on the lives of donors less than 65 years old, count at cash surrender value or discounted value as if death benefit amount was placed in a five per cent unitrust for a number of years equal to the difference between the donor's age and 65, whichever is greater.

c. For new or existing policies, count at the cash surrender value of the policy when donated, plus the premium payments made within seven years of the pledge date.

d. For death benefits of policies realized during the Campaign, count at full value.

8. Life Estates — counted at the fair market value of the property donated on the date of the gift.

9. Government Matching Funds — given that matching funds from Federal or State are donative in nature and not linked to contractual or proprietary interest of the state, such funds will be counted in the Campaign.

10. Estate Distributions — counted at fair market value when distribution is documented.

11. Bequest Provisions — counted in the Campaign according to the following guidelines:

a. Must be documented by copy of estate document, portion thereof, or the completion of a bequest provision statement.

b. Must be a specific or residual bequest.

c. For donors 65 years of age or more, will be counted at the specific amount or the estimated residual amount subject to documentation by the donor.

d. For donors 64 years of age or less, bequest will be counted at the specific amount or the estimated residual amount subject to documentation and may be discounted at the discretion of the Executive Committee for the years between the donor's age and age 65 as though the bequest amount were transferred to a five per cent unitrust.

12. Grants — national or international in origin, grants provided from the corporate or foundation sector or by a government or government agency, when consistent with the goals of the Campaign, will be counted in the campaign total.

c. How to Document Gifts

The gift acceptance policy should specify the documentation required for each type of gift. Normally written documentation of some kind will be needed before any gift can be counted toward the campaign total. For outright gifts or multi-year pledges of currently expendable funds, the documentation may be as simple as a signed and dated official pledge card or letter of intent. For a gift of tangible property, you need copies of the appraisal (if it was required to be performed), together with IRS form 8283 recording the fair market value of the gift. Depending on their nature and complexity, planned gifts may require such items of documentation as: formal contracts and letters of agreement; instruments of transfer; copies of bequests or bequest clauses along with a standard statement certifying the estimated amount of a residual share; insurance policies; or copies of trust instruments and supporting trust data.

ii. Endowments

Because of their permanent nature, endowments need to be handled with special care and foresight. Remember that an endowment can remain in existence for twenty, fifty or one hundred years, long after its originators have departed the scene. Generally speaking all gifts for endowment should be accompanied by written guidelines signed by both the donor and the library director. This document should indicate the basic purpose for which the endowment is being established, who will hold the principal, how it will be invested, what spending policy will be followed, and how the expendable income will be used.

It can be argued that building the library's permanent endowment will yield greater long terms benefit than raising money for current spending. Similarly, a gift to unrestricted library endowment represents the best kind of fund raising of all. If a donor's wishes do require that restrictions be imposed, then the broadest possible statement of purpose is to be preferred when drawing up the endowment guidelines. (For example: collection enrichment, preservation, staff development, etc.) In establishing a new restricted endowment, it is important to convince the donor that modifications should be allowed over the years to meet changing conditions.

Most likely the library's various endowed accounts will be managed as segments of a larger, pooled endowment principal held by the institution's 501 (c) (3) organization. Contributions are typically combined together and invested under the direction of a treasurer, a finance committee, or perhaps one or more independent investment managers selected by the foundation. This means that the library will generally have no direct voice in deciding how to invest the principal, reviewing investment performance, or determining how much to allocate each year for spending. In such cases, the investment vehicles and spending policy cited in your endowment guidelines will simply be those which are adopted by your underlying institutional foundation or 503 (c) (3) organization.

Still, you should have a basic grasp of how endowments operate, if only to remain on top of things and be in a position to plan intelligently. Ideally, an endowment should yield a total return (income plus capital appreciation) that will enable its managers to accomplish two goals: (1) make annual allocations for spending sufficient to fund the activities for which it was created, and (2) reinvest enough to principal so as to compensate for the ongoing effects of inflation. This should be an issue of some interest to librarians, since annual increases in the cost of books and periodicals have consistently exceeded both the widely followed Consumer Price Index as well as the Higher Education Price Index. A little reflection will show that any endowment whose principal fails to grow will be yielding progressively less each year in actual buying power.

In the old days university endowments were invested almost entirely in high quality government and corporate bonds. But experts claim that the best total returns over time are to be found in common stocks, and so today most endowment portfolios keep at least some exposure to the equity markets. There are various mechanisms for ensuring that a balance is achieved between current spending and maintenance of principal in constant dollar terms. Since the value of the endowment portfolio can fluctuate quite a bit from year to year (or even month to month) depending on the behavior of financial markets, these formulas are usually based on multi-year rolling averages, with inflation factors keyed to such measures as the CPI or the Higher Education Price Index. In periods when return on investment is high and inflation moderate, it is easy to satisfy the demand both for spendable income and reinvestment for the future. At other times a compromise must be struck. For instance, in one year it may be necessary to eat into principal in order to fund programs. But in another year one may have to reduce current spending below desirable levels in order to restore the *corpus*.

Whoever determines the amount of annual spendable income, the library needs to have procedures in place for making sure that it is properly spent, in accordance with the guidelines, and the results reported to donors. Given the permanent nature of endowments, combined with the transient nature of staff, this can be more difficult than one might assume. Unless good records are maintained, an endowment established many years ago can easily be forgotten once all those who were involved in its creation have departed the scene. The income may continue to arrive each year, but the purpose of the endowment and the identity of the donor are lost in the obscurity of time. To prevent this from happening, clear responsibility should be assigned for maintaining the underlying documentation about each endowment, spending the income in an appropriate and timely manner, and reporting the results to donors and their descendants. A sample internal policy on library endowments is included in Appendix XIII.

VI. Constituent Societies

In chapter 4 we discussed the trend toward so-called "constituent fundraising" on college and university campuses, noting that in many ways this new approach works to the disadvantage of organizations (such as the library) which lack a natural base of alumni. To compensate for this disadvantage, it is essential for library directors to seize the opportunities afforded by a major capital campaign to build a cadre of individuals, foundations, and corporations whose primary loyalty will be the library itself and who can be expected to take an interest in its welfare even after the campaign has ended.

Most capital campaigns draw the library director and development staff into an intense whirl of fundraising activity, meeting people of wealth and influence from the community, the region and across the nation. From these contacts you will assemble a major gifts committee. As the gifts begin to materialize, you will involve these new friends in your stewardship program, recognizing their support in appropriate ways and inducting them into gift societies. You will correspond with them on a regular basis, at least annually, to keep them informed of how their funds are being used and how the library is doing.

But to be truly successful as a fundraiser, you must take one further step. **You must create a visible, permanent organizational network** among these supporters that will outlast the current campaign and provide them with an ongoing sense of affiliation with the library itself. At the larger universities, many academic colleges and departments have already organized national "boards of visitors", consisting of prominent alumni who are brought back to campus on a regular basis to be updated on the direction of the program and consult with the dean. These same individuals are available to transition to a fundraising mode when planning starts for the next capital campaign.

As you carry out the activities of your campaign, always try to work as a network builder. Find ways to draw your supporters together to meet one another. Convey a sense that you value their participation in library affairs beyond just giving money. When the campaign is over, it will be a simple matter to convert your major gifts committee into a "board of visitors" or a "national advisory council". Then you will have created the nucleus of a local, regional, or national support network both to increase annual giving levels during the post-campaign years and to lay the groundwork for the next big capital campaign.

Of course the top priority of any stewardship program is to maintain the interest and loyalty of those who have made large gifts in the current campaign. But don't lose sight of the need to cultivate the medium-sized donor. In many cases these will be the individuals who, in another decade or fifteen years, will be in a position to make major gifts. There can be an advantage to getting in early with these promising prospects, at a time when they are receiving less attention from other charities and from competing units on your own campus. In the world of fundraising, nothing is more important than keeping your sights focused on the long-term. After all, there will always be other campaigns!

第八章 结论

Chapter 8 Conclusion

I. Fundraising for the 90s: The Challenge Ahead

Fundraising has already become a fact of life for many libraries, and it appears that the climate of the 1990s will enhance this trend. Universities across the United States can expect severe budgetary constraints in the years ahead. Colleges and universities have a limited number of income sources: state support, tuition, government contracts, and private fundraising. All four are coming under pressure right now, and the pressure is not going to let up. Last year, for the first time in over 30 years, the total amount of money states allocated to higher education was less than in the preceding year: a drop of about $80 million nationally. As a percentage of overall state spending, the amount given to colleges and universities has been shrinking since 1982. In response, tuition has been going up—by 13 percent, on average, at four-year public institutions last year.① But legislatures are feeling the pressure from students and parents to limit tuition increases. In Ohio, for example, tuition hikes by public universities were capped at 7 percent last year. Private institutions are legally free to raise tuition at will; but they must contend with the discipline of the educational marketplace, where higher tuition drives potential students to seek lower cost alternatives. For nearly all colleges and universities, public and private, there will be mounting pressure to close the gap between conventional revenues and expenditure needs through even greater efforts at fundraising.

In this endeavor one institution will be forced to contend with another. Libraries will be placed in the position of competing both with external rivals (for government, foundation, and corporate support) and with other units on the same campus (for support by alumni and friends). Unfortunately, academic librarians must confront this challenge with some distinct disadvantages. Many college and university development officers do not view the library as an especially attractive "sell" for donors. After all, it cannot claim any alumni of its own. In the language of a political campaign manager, support for libraries tends to be "broad, but shallow". Everyone has warm feelings about us, but few are passionately motivated to give. Most can be easily drawn to support other candidates with a stronger, more direct appeal. Librarians must also combat the "Bottomless Pit Syndrome": the perception that no amount of money is ever enough to purchase all the books, all the periodicals, all the media resources, and all the databases we claim to need. Donors, like chief academic officers, want to know what their dollars will accomplish in concrete terms.

Good comparative data on library fundraising is in short supply, and few organizations are willing to publicize their failures. But the authors have found plenty of anecdotal evidence to suggest that all too often libraries do not fare well in university capital campaigns. Sometimes no dollar goal at all is established for the library. In other instances, the library portion is set very low as a percentage of the total campus goal. In still other cases, one hears of capital campaigns that have ended triumphantly, but with the library left far short of achieving its own goal.②

---

① Anthony DePalma. "Bad times force universities to re-think what they are". *New York Times*, (February 3, 1992), Section A, p. 1.

② Perhaps it would help our case if university development officials were made aware of a study conducted by James L. Boyle and reported in *The Chronicle of Philanthropy*, vol. Ⅲ, no. 16 (June 4, 1991), p. 18. According to Boyle, the more library books an institution has for each student, the greater its alumni contributions are likely to be. "The library collection was the strongest predictor of both the rate of giving by graduates and the average size of their gifts."

II. Twelve Principles for Successful Fundraising

In the preceding chapters we have attempted to arm you with all the tools you need to win at the fundraising game. Let us summarize the points we have made in twelve basic principles.

1. Develop a positive image.

Successful fundraising is built on a positive image, reputation, trust, and perceived value to the community. Do everything possible to put the library in the consciousness of the appropriate constituencies before attempting a major capital campaign. Develop your annual giving program, both as a means of testing the waters and promoting the library's reputation. Always remember that success attracts money. Avoid talking about what you need. Instead, stress your accomplishments. In the donor's mind, libraries do not have needs. People have needs that libraries can satisfy.

2. Find your market niche.

It is of utmost importance for any organization considering a major fundraising effort to begin with a careful self-examination of its own worth and unique contributions to society. Discover what it is that you do especially well. Identify the accomplishments that make you stand out from other libraries, as well as from other units on campus. A good feasibility study is one way to gain this kind of knowledge. Use the feedback from both the internal and external audit to sharpen your market definition and develop a compelling case statement. At the very least, this process of self-examination should prevent the library from entering a campaign with an impossible goal, the wrong leadership, or a case that cannot be sold.

3. Pick the best volunteer leadership possible.

The quality of your volunteer leadership can make or break a campaign. Strong leaders make their own commitments first and then convince others to follow suit. Strong leaders enjoy the respect of their peers. It will pay big dividends later on if, at the outset of your campaign, you make an effort to find leaders who have either "influence" or "affluence," preferably both. This is a time when you may need to call upon the president and the chief development officer for their assistance in recruiting the best possible leadership. If you have a friends organization, make a hard-nosed, realistic assessment of its ability to contribute to the success of your capital campaign. If necessary, do not hesitate to bypass the group in setting up a separate campaign volunteer structure.

4. Target prospects carefully.

Although support from foundations, corporations, and public agencies will play a role in your campaign, it is individual donors who are likely to count most. Many fundraising experts hold to the so-called "rule of thirds," while others cite the 80 percent / 20 percent ratio. The point is that most of your support in dollar terms will come from a small handful of top donors. You need to identify these key prospects early and then focus your efforts on this group, avoiding distractions. Be realistic in targeting your prospects. It is better to work with a small number of carefully chosen and well researched prospects than to follow a "scatter gun" approach. Remember that a capital campaign is an intensive, time-limited effort to raise a specific sum of money. To be successful, you must manage your own time efficiently. That means following the gift table structure and concentrating your attention on the top prospects.

5. Be prepared to spend time and money on fundraising.

It is a fact of life in development work that it costs money to raise money. Depending on the type of fundraising involved, it will cost you anywhere between 3 to 37 percent of each dollar raised. Annual giving programs are the most expensive (from 11 to 37 percent), while capital campaigns will generally cost from 4 to 7 percent during their life span. If the library is participating as part of a larger, campus-wide capital campaign, some of these costs may be centrally budgeted and supported by the institution's development office. There may be opportunities to share certain personnel and project costs with other units on campus. But there is no escaping the fact that the library will have to spend a considerable amount of its own staff time and money if it wants to be a real player in the fundraising game. Since a large portion of these costs are incurred early in a campaign, before the results have begun to materialize, there can be moments of high anxiety when it appears that you may be wasting valuable resources. Successful fundraising requires risk taking and a certain amount of courage, not the least of which involves standing up to the doubters among your own colleagues and staff.

6. Concentrate on relationships.

No rule is more important than this one. It is relationships that raise money, especially when it comes to major gifts. To be successful, you must be personally involved in the fundraising effort. You need to spend enough time with your volunteer leaders and top prospects to get to know them and allow them to know you. The personal touch is critical whether we are speaking about corporate and foundation fundraising, or appeals directed to individuals. In the case of corporations and foundations, a word of support from a well placed volunteer can help gain a hearing for your proposal. In the case of individual donors, do everything possible to create and sustain a bond of personal friendship, respect, and trust. Nothing else will work better than this.

7. Make the ask.

When all the planning is done, when all the case statements have been written, when all the brochures and mailings have been sent—eventually somebody is going to have to ask someone else for money! Be sure to make the ask. Explaining what you need the money for is not asking for a gift. Presenting a proposal is not the same as asking for a gift. If you don't ask, you won't get. It's as simple as that! Psychologically this is the most difficult part of fundraising for most of us, and the reason is simple: nobody likes to risk rejection. But if you have done your homework, and if the prospect has been properly cultivated, the solicitation itself will not be a surprise.

8. Listen and be patient.

If you get a "no", listen carefully. Is the prospect saying no because he or she is not sufficiently interested? In that case you may need to get the person more involved in your program. Is it because the prospect cannot afford to give what you are asking? If so, suggest alternatives: for example, a multi-year pledge or a planned gift of some kind. One of the most tricky issues in fundraising is knowing when to give up on a prospect and when to persist. No one wants to waste time and energy on a prospect who is clearly not going to come through with a gift. On the other hand, you should never quit on a prospect as long as there is at least some hope. In many cases the situation will be ambiguous. The prospect will tell you that now is not the right time for a gift, or that obligations elsewhere preclude a major commitment. In these cases you need to rethink your strategy with this particular prospect and try again later on. Remember that the average length of time between initial cultivation and a gift is twenty-four months. Often it will take much longer. So be flexible, tenacious, and above all patient.

9. Never ask anyone to support a cause you don't support yourself.

Your prospects are going to want to know what you and your staff have done to support the library's fundraising effort. It is important to make your own commitment to the campaign early. The same principle applies to staff, especially those who will be directly involved in working with prospects. Outside donors will understand that librarians are not able in most cases to make major gifts. It is the rate of participation that counts, not the dollar volume raised.

10. Provide return on investment.

After a gift is made, donors want to know what impact it is having on the operation of the library. You should set up a stewardship program that offers regular feedback to donors on the benefits that are being gained as a result of their generosity. Those who have established endowments should receive at least one report each year on the materials acquired, or services provided, from the endowment income.

11. Never forget a donor.

Once a person has made a commitment to your library, it is critical that he or she be cherished as part of a family of supporters. Remember that prior donors make the best prospects for future gifts. You must establish a system for remaining in touch with all donors, great and small. Depending on the level of their past support, recruit them into a friends of the library group, a giving society, or a volunteer council of some kind. Communicate with them through newsletters, correspondence, personal visits, and organized events.

12. Keep your sense of humor.

Maintaining good relations with the institutional development office will pay the library big dividends. But there will be occasions when you need to push them to give the library a fair shake. You need to play by the rules, but don't be afraid to step on some toes when the occasion demands it. In any capital campaign there will be moments of high pressure, when tempers run short and conflict occurs. There will be donors with big egos, volunteer leaders whose feelings get hurt, deans who get angry at you for poaching their prospects. Pride leads to empty purses. There is no room for inflated egos and arrogance in fundraising. A sense of humor will help you get through those tough times and keep your program on track to success.

III. Putting It All Together

We end this book with a true story that will underscore some of the points we have been making and will hopefully encourage you to apply your own skills to the adventure of fundraising.

John Smith (the name and a few other details have been changed to protect his anonymity) graduated from Ohio University in the 1930s with a degree in engineering. Soon after, he moved to Texas and established an electrical contracting business. Over the years his business grew and prospered with the construction boom in that state. Mr. Smith was known and remembered at Ohio University through his participation in local alumni chapter activities. But he had never returned to campus, nor had he made a financial contribution to the university of any kind. In the parlance of development professionals, he was a "non-donor." Yet the regional campaign committee in Texas had assigned Mr. Smith a rating of 4. He was in their view capable of making a major gift of at least $100,000. In other words, the ability was there; but the willingness might be questionable.

In the meantime, the library had reached the conclusion that it needed to expand its list of major gift prospects in order to have any hope of successfully completing its $6 million campaign. Most of the best alumni prospects were already claimed by other units on campus, typically by the college or school from which they had graduated. So we tried a strategy that other libraries had followed with some success: we sought permission to pursue a group of six highly rated prospects who had never given any money to the university and were therefore not claimed by anyone else. Mr. Smith was among this group of six.

Once permission was granted, we wasted no time in cultivating these new prospects, who were living in various locations throughout the country. Our Assistant Dean for Development called each of them and requested an appointment. All but one agreed to meet with him, including Mr. Smith. On that first visit the conversation was kept to general matters about the university, the library and the Third Century Campaign. But our representative learned a great deal about Mr. Smith. He was indeed capable of making a major gift and was favorably disposed toward Ohio University. He learned that Mr. Smith was about to retire and in the process of planning to remove funds from a profit sharing plan, but that he had concerns about the tax ramifications of any action he might take.

The situation appeared promising enough to arrange for a return visit a few months later with the Dean of Libraries. After an enjoyable morning of conversation and lunch at a local restaurant, the Dean asked Mr. Smith if he would consider a gift of $100,000. Mr. Smith looked a little puzzled at first and then replied that he and wife were thinking of a much larger gift, possibly as much as one million dollars! "Would that be all right?" he asked.

Needless to say, this was perfectly agreeable to the Dean and his assistant, who promptly put Mr. Smith in touch with Ohio University's Director of Planned Giving for a detailed analysis of his financial condition and an evaluation of various tax strategies. Less than a month later, the planned giving expert traveled to Texas and spent half a day with Mr. Smith. The result was an agreement to establish a charitable remainder trust with a transfer of some $1.2 million in assets from the prospect's profit sharing plan. The trust will pay 6 percent annually to Mr. Smith and his wife for the remainder of their lives. In the meantime, they will receive a charitable deduction of almost $400,000 which can be used to offset the capital gains incurred as a result of cashing in the profit sharing plan and liquidating other assets associated with his former business. At the end of the trust term, the library will receive the original corpus plus any accumulated growth over and above the 6 percent annual payout to Mr. Smith and his wife. Truly this is a "win / win" situation for everyone concerned!

Of course not all your attempts at fundraising will have such happy endings, but the story of Mr. Smith is a true one that should serve to remind you of several points. First is the critical importance of the individual donor with an attachment to your institution. Although John Smith was a so-called "non-giver", he thought enough of Ohio University to be receptive to a major gift appeal. Moreover, when the gift came, it was made without conditions as to its eventual use. (This is rarely the case with government, corporate, or foundation contributions.) The story also illustrates the importance of using your top representative (in this case, the Dean of Libraries) to actually make the ask. It is doubtful whether this prospect would have responded favorably to an appeal by any lesser person. The fact that we were then able to bring in an expert in planned giving to close the negotiations was also critical to the outcome. Creative planned giving mechanisms, such as charitable remainder trusts, have become an essential part of the fundraising arsenal.

But most of all the story of John Smith illustrates the element of serendipity—the unexpected stroke of good luck and perfect timing-that all experienced fundraisers have encountered at some point in their careers. It reminds us that an outstanding gift can materialize where and when you least anticipate it, if you will just keep trying. Good luck in your own fundraising efforts!

附录1: 主管发展副院长的工作描述

Appendix I: Job Description of an Assistant Dean for Development

OHIO UNIVERSITY
ASSISTANT DEAN FOR DEVELOPMENT
Serving the Colleges of Fine Arts, Health and Human Services And
the University Libraries

Ohio University, approaching its third century of service to Ohio and the nation, is seeking applications and nominations for the position of Assistant Dean for Development. The successful candidate will become a staff member in an expanding development office which is currently preparing for a $100 million campaign.

Ohio University is a major research institution with 22,000 students, 850 faculty, a private support base of $7 million per year, $29 million in sponsored research and $55 million in endowment. The University is composed of ten colleges and has five branch campuses in Southeastern Ohio.

—The COLLEGE OF FINE ARTS provides academic programs and professional training in the visual and performing arts through the Schools of Art, Dance, Music, Theater, Film, Comparative Arts and Visual Communication. The college was formally established in 1936 and is the forerunner for all other colleges of fine arts in the state of Ohio. While serving the needs of 1,000 fine arts majors, the college provides an opportunity for all students to obtain a broad cultural education.

—The COLLEGE OF HEALTH AND HUMAN SERVICES, the newest college at Ohio University, is made up of five schools: the School of Health and Sports Sciences, the School of Hearing and Speech Sciences, the School of Home Economics, the School of Nursing, and the School of Physical Therapy. More than 100 faculty and staff in the College provide students with a unique blend of didactic instruction and clinical education and field experiences. To provide such experiences locally, the Schools operate a variety of facilities such as the Child Development Center, the Speech and Hearing Clinic, Therapy Associates, and several recreational facilities, including a golf course, ice arena, and Aquatic Center.

— The UNIVERSITY LIBRARIES, with 1.4 million print volumes, 1.6 million microforms, and 18,000 serial subscriptions, employ the latest information technologies including an integrated online library system linked to the international OCLC bibliographic network. Special research collections covering Southeast Asia, journalism, literature, history of science, and osteopathic medicine have attracted many federal and foundation grants, including a current $750,000 NEH Challenge Grant.

The successful candidate will report to the Director of Development for Major Gifts and Constituent Fund Raising and will serve as the primary development officer for the Colleges of Fine Arts, Health and Human Services, and University Libraries. The development officer's prime responsibility will be for the identification, cultivation, solicitation, and stewardship of major gift prospects for the colleges and the University Libraries. Additional responsibilities include staffing the college volunteer committees, overseeing the colleges annual giving program and assisting with college constituent activities.

The University is seeking individuals who have a minimum of a bachelor's degree and one to three years of fund raising experience. Although preference will be given to candidates with fund raising experience, related experience in higher education, business, promotions or sales will be considered.

Good oral and written skills will be required. The candidate must also have the ability to get along with people, a willingness to travel and a general knowledge of higher education.

Compensation will be in the range of $28,000 to $35,000 per year or commensurate with experience. Please submit a letter of application, a resume, and three references. Applications or letters of nomination should be postmarked by November 17, 1989.

Ohio University is an Affirmative Action, Equal Opportunity Employer. Applications from women, minorities, and persons with disabilities are encouraged.

附录 2：俄亥俄大学图书馆之友章程

Appendix II: By-Laws of the Friends of the Library of Ohio University

ARTICLE I
NAME

Section 1. The name of this organization shall he the Friends of the Libraries of Ohio University.

ARTICLE II
PURPOSE

Section 1. The purpose of the Friends of the Libraries shall be to maintain an association of persons interested in books, whose goals are to strengthen the Libraries, enhance the collections and promote their usefulness.

Section 2. This organization does not contemplate pecuniary gain or profit to its members. No part of the income or monies of this organization shall inure to the benefit of any member, and no part shall be devoted to influence legislation or to carry on propaganda.

ARTICLE III
MEMBERSHIP

Section 1. The membership year shall be from January 1 to December 31.

Section 2. Any individual, business, or corporate body interested in the purposes of this organization may become a member upon payment of a contribution prescribed by the Board of Directors suitable to the following categories:

a. Student
b. Senior (aged 82 and above)
c. Individual
d. Family (two persons or more)
e. Contributing
f. Supporting
g. Patron
h. Corporate and Benefactor

Section 3. Membership may be extended by a simple majority vote of the Board of Directors for a gift of materials in lieu of monetary contributions.

Section 4. Membership in the Manasseh Cutler Society, the Jacob Lindley Society, the 1804 Society, and the Trustees Academy will be extended concurrently to members of this organization whose annual contributions are at the equivalent level of support specified for membership in those organizations.

Section 5. Gifts in excess of $5,000 may be designated for an endowment fund to be named at the discretion of the donor and proceeds from such funds may be designated for specific purposes within the jurisdiction of the Libraries.

Section 6. Life membership may be conferred by unanimous vote of the Board of Directors for extraordinary gifts of money, equipment, books, collections, or other library material; or for unusual service to the Libraries.

Section 7. Except for life members, a member who has not made a contribution in two years shall be classified as inactive.

ARTICLE IV
PRIVILEGES

Section 1. All active members have the right to attend meetings and to participate in the activities of the organization.

Section 2. Members shall have early admission to book sales held by the organization; and enjoy borrowing privileges and use of all public services in accordance with the regulations of the Ohio University Libraries.

Section 3. Members may receive publications from time to time prepared and sent under the jurisdiction of the Board of Directors.

ARTICLE V
OFFICERS

Section 1. The officers of this organization shall be a President and a President-elect, who serves as Vice-President.

Section 2. The President-elect shall succeed the President in the event a vacancy occurs. In this event, the President-elect position shall be filed through majority vote by the Board of Directors.

Section 3. The officers shall perform the duties prescribed for them in the parliamentary authority adopted by this organization.

ARTICLE VI
EXECUTIVE SECRETARY & TREASURER

Section 1. The Executive Secretary shall be appointed by the Director of Libraries in consultation with the Board of Directors.

Section 2. The Executive Secretary shall serve as Treasurer of the organization, keep up-to-date financial records, and make payments as approved by the Board of Directors.

Section 3. The Executive Secretary shall maintain official records and membership lists, prepare the annual report, send out mailings, act as secretary of the Board of Directors, and perform such other duties as the Board of Directors shall deem appropriate and necessary.

Section 4. A headquarters off site and clerical services shall be furnished to the organization by the Alden Library.

ARTICLE VII
BOARD OF DIRECTORS

Section 1. The Board of Directors shall be composed of the President, the President-elect, and seven members. The Director of Libraries and the executive Secretary shall serve as non-voting members.

Section 2. The Board of Directors shall manage the affairs of the organization, provide guidelines for the use of general funds, and receive special gifts in accordance with the policies of the Libraries. Such acts shall be by a majority vote after a quorum is reached.

Section 3. The Board of Directors shall meet on call of the President, the Executive Secretary or by the request of any two members of the Board. A simple majority of voting members of the Board, with either the President or President-elect presiding, shall constitute a Quorum.

Section 4. The Board of Directors is empowered to fill by appointment the remaining portion of any term vacated by a member or the President-elect.

ARTICLE VIII
COMMITTEES

Section 1. The organization shall have an Executive Committee chaired by the President and consisting of the President-elect, one chairperson, appointed by the President, or a standing committee, and the Executive Secretary.

Section 2. The organization shall have the minimum number of standing committees as follows: (1) Membership, (2) Program, and (3) Publications. The Executive Secretary shall be a non-voting member of all standing committees.

Section 3. The chairpersons of the standing committees shall be appointed by the President and shall serve from one annual meeting to the following.

Section 4. Ad hoc committees may be named and their chairpersons appointed by the President.

ARTICLE IX
MEETINGS

Section 1. The annual meeting of the organization shall be held prior to the conclusion of the spring session of the academic year, the time and place to be determined by the Board of Directors.

Section 2. Special meetings of the organization may be called at any time by the President, the Executive Secretary, or by any two members of the Board of Directors.

Section 3. Ten members present, in addition to a quorum of the Board of Directors, shall constitute a quorum, and every member shall be entitled to vote on all matters brought before the organization. All decisions shall be by majority vote.

ARTICLE X
ELECTION OF MEMBERS OF THE BOARD OF DIRECTORS

Section 1. All members of the Board of Directors shall serve without compensation.

Section 2. The officers and other voting members of the Board of Directors shall be elected at the annual meeting as the positions become vacant. The President and President-elect shall be elected in even years and serve for two years from the annual meeting at which they are elected until the annual meeting held in the second following year. The other voting members of the Board of Directors shall serve for three-year staggered terms from the annual meeting at which they are elected until the annual meeting held in the third year following that date.

Section 3. A nominating committee of three, appointed by the President, shall present at least thirty days before the annual meeting names for nomination for election to the Board of Directors.

Section 4. Nominations may be made from the floor providing the nominee has given his consent and willingness to serve if elected.

ARTICLE XI
FUNDS AND LIABILITY

Section 1. Funds designated to the Friends of the Libraries of Ohio University shall be directed to and deposited through the Ohio University Foundation. Direct disbursement of said funds shall be authorized by the Board of Directors of the Friends of the Libraries to the Ohio University Libraries and shall be used solely for the purpose provided in Article II. Contributions made as provided herein are deductible for federal income tax purposes, in accordance with the Internal Revenue Service Code and regulations. The Director of Libraries shall have the authority to make nominal expenditure of funds. All other disbursements of funds shall be by action of the Board of Directors.

Section 2. No member of this organization shall be liable except for unpaid contributions; and no personal liability shall in any event be attached to any member of this organization in connection with any of its undertakings.

ARTICLE XII
PARLIAMENTARY AUTHORITY

Section 1. The rules contained in Robert's Rules of Order Revised shall govern this organization in all cases in which they are applicable, and in which they are not inconsistent with these By-Laws.

ARTICLE XIII
AMENDMENT

Section 1. These By-Laws may be amended at any annual or special meeting of the organization by a two-thirds vote of members present, provided notice was given at the previous meeting or by mail at least thirty days in advance of the meeting.

Approved by Board 13 April 1988
Approved by the Membership 2 June 1988

附录 3：俄亥俄大学三百周年庆典捐赠协议

Appendix III: The Ohio University Third Century Campaign Gift Agreement

I/We hereby pledge a total of $ _____ to the Ohio University Third Century Campaign.
_____ This gift is for unrestricted use by the University
_____ This gift is to be used for _____
I/We will fulfill my/our commitment to OHIO UNIVERSITY in the following manner:

PLEDGE YEAR ONE　　　　　　　　　$ _____
PLEDGE YEAR TWO　　　　　　　　　$ _____
PLEDGE YEAR THREE　　　　　　　　$ _____
PLEDGE YEAR FOUR　　　　　　　　 $ _____
PLEDGE YEAR FIVE　　　　　　　　　$ _____

I/we will begin gift payments in the month of _____, 19 _____
Please send a pledge reminder: 　　　　I/We plan to make this gift in the following manner:
_____ Quarterly _____ Semi-Annually　 _____ Life Insurance _____ Gift Annuity
_____ Annually _____ It is not necessary _____ Charitable Trust _____ Pooled Fund
　　　　　to send a pledge reminder.　 _____ Cash, Securities, or Real Estate
_____ Other _____

Signature (s) _____
Date
Please acknowledge and credit this gift as follows:
_____
Name (s)　　　　　　(Please Print)
_____
Address

The Ohio University Foundation
P. O. Drawer 869
Athens, OH 45701-0869
(614) 593-2636 · (614) 593-2486

附录4：参加俄亥俄大学三百周年庆典活动报名表

Appendix IV: The Ohio University Third Century Campaign Prospect Entry Form

Submitted by: _____ Date: _____
PROSPECT NAME (Degree/Year): _____
Type of Prospect (please circle): Individual. Corporation. Foundation. Other
Home Address. _____
Phone: _____
Position: _____
Company: _____
Address: _____
Phone: _____
Additional qualifying information: _____
Should the prospect be cross-referenced with another individual or organization? (Please list):
Rating (Total Ask Amount): $ _____
Unit (1): _____   Designation: _____   Amount: $ _____
Unit (2): _____   Designation: _____   Amount: $ _____
Unit (3): _____   Designation: _____   Amount: $ _____
Status (please circle): Prospect / Cultivation / Solicitation / Pending / Stewardship (See reverse side for descriptions) Status Comments:
Recommended Assignments:
University _____
Development _____
Volunteer (s) _____
Statement of Purpose (proposed cultivation / solicitation plan): _____
(Attach additional sheets as needed)
<u>PLEASE RETURN THIS FORM TO THE OFFICE OF PROSPECT MANAGEMENT</u>

附录 5: 俄亥俄大学三百周年庆典认捐表

Appendix V: The Ohio University Third Century Campaign Cultivation / Solicitation Plan

(Prepared by Development Officer. Must be approved before prospect is released for contact.)

Submitted by: _____ Date: _____
Prospect Name: _____
Rating (ask amount): $ _____
Proposed Interest: _____
Strategy (show minimum of 4 contacts):

Date (mm/dd/yy)	Activity	With Whom?
_____	_____	_____

Proposed volunteer (s) for tills cultivation. If not already recorded:
(1)
(2)
(3)
Proposed date of solicitation:
Proposed solicitation team:
    University _____ _____ _____
    Development _____ _____ _____
    Volunteer (s) _____ _____ _____
Approval:
_____ Date: _____
(Senior Development Campaign Officer)

PLEASE RETURN THIS FORM TO THE OFFICE OF PROSPECT MANAGEMENT

附录6：俄亥俄大学三百周年庆典活动联系报告

Appendix VI: The Ohio University Third Century Campaign Contact Report

Office Route

_____ Ellis
_____ Robison
_____ Prospect Res.

Development/Alumni Officer _____ Contact Date _____
Contact made by _____ Report Date _____
Contact Name: _____ Business Phone: _____
Title: _____ Home Phone: _____
Firm: _____ ☐ Alumni (degree __ yr __)
　　　　　　　　　　　　　　　　　　　　　☐ Friend
Address: _____
　　　　　　　　　　　　　　　　　　　　　☐ Parent
City: _____　　　　　☐ Corporation
ACTIVITY TYPE STATUS　　　　　　　　　☐ Foundation
☐ Phone　　　　☐ Identification　　　　☐ Other
☐ Personal Visit　☐ Cultivation
☐ Alumni Event　☐ Solicitation (Amount _____ Purpose _____)
☐ Campus Visit　☐ Pending
☐ Other:　　　　☐ Stewardship
Summary: _____
Status Change: _____
Next Step: _____
Next Date: _____
Report: _____

CONFIDENTIAL TO: The Ohio University Foundation
P. O. Drawer 869
Athens, Ohio 45701-0869
(614) 593-2636 - (614) 593-2486

附录 7：专业募款机构

Appendix VII: Professional Fundraising Organizations

(Source: *Encyclopedia of Associations*, 26th Edition – 1992)

AMERICAN PROSPECT RESEARCH ASSOCIATION
1600 Wilson Blvd., Suite 905
Arlington, VA 22209　　　　　　　Phone: (703) 525 – 1191

　　Facilitates education and dissemination of information about prospect research; encourages professional development and cooperative relationships among members. Bestows awards; provides placement and speaker referral services.

ASSOCIATION OF BLACK FOUNDATION EXECUTIVES
1828 L Street NW
Washington, D. C. 20036　　　　　Phone: (202) 466 – 6512

　　Encourages greater recognition of the economic, educational, and social issues facing blacks in the grantmaking field. Promotes support of blacks as grantmaking professionals. Seeks to increase the number of blacks entering the grantmaking field and helps members improve their job effectiveness.

COUNCIL FOR ADVANCEMENT AND SUPPORT OF EDUCATION
11 Dupont Circle NW, Suite 400
Washington, DC 200036　　　　　Phone: (202) 328 – 5925

　　Institutional members are colleges, universities, and two-year colleges, as well as independent elementary and secondary schools. Individual members typically work in alumni affairs, publications, public relations, development, and institutional advancement. CASE offers its members professional training seminars and publications. Maintains a small reference library containing case studies, papers, campus publications, etc. Monitors federal legislation of interest to members. Gives annual awards. Conducts research projects. Maintains a National Clearinghouse for Corporate Matching Gift Information (202 – 328 – 5900). Publishes *Currents* (monthly) and the *CASE Directory* (annual). Holds annual conference (with exhibits) in July.

DIRECT MAIL FUNDRAISERS ASSOCIATION
445 W. 45th Street
New York, NY 100036　　　　　　Phone: (212) 489 – 4929

　　Works to help members in their professional efforts; promotes and supports the direct mail fundraising industry; functions as information clearinghouse; offers workshops, seminars, and awards. Publishes a *Membership Directory* and a quarterly *Newsletter*.

THE GRANTSMANSHIP CENTER
650 South Spring Street, Suite 507
PO Box 6210
Los Angeles, CA 90014　　　　　Phone: (213) 689 – 9222

　　Trains people from nonprofit public and private agencies to develop their fundraising skills. Offers workshops in grantsmanship, proposal writing, and fundraising. Conducts over 200 programs annually. Publishes the *Whole Nonprofit Catalog: A Compendium of Sources and*

Resources for Managers and Staff of Nonprofit Organizations (quarterly).

NATIONAL COUNCIL FOR COMMUNITY DEVELOPMENT
41 E. 42nd Street, Suite 1500
New York, NY 100017　　　　　　Phone: (212) 682 – 1106
　　Promotes economic development and develops fundraising activities within communities. Conducts training programs. Publishes *Developments* (irregular).

NATIONAL NETWORK OF GRANTMAKERS
2335 18th Street, NW
Washington, DC 20009　　　　　　Phone: (202) 483 – 0030
　　Members are staff/trustees of corporate and independent foundations; religious giving programs; philanthropists; staff of nonprofit organizations serving grantmakers. Provides a communications link of sharing information and ideas on grantmaking; acts as a voice for social justice issues within the grantmaking community and other sectors, including government, business, labor and education. Sponsors workshops for grantmakers. Publishes *The Network Newsletter* (quarterly), as well as the *Grantseekers Guide* and other brochures.

NATIONAL SOCIETY OF FUND RAISING EXECUTIVES
1101 King Street, Suite 3000
Alexandria, VA 22314　　　　　　Phone: (703) 684 – 0410
　　Members are engaged in the direction and execution of fundraising programs for nonprofit organizations, agencies, churches, counseling firms, and institutions in the education, health, and welfare areas. Encourages research and training in fundraising through formal course work and continuing education. Holds workshops and seminars dealing with all phases of fundraising. Gives awards; compiles statistics; maintains a speakers' bureau; and offers a placement service. Publishes *ESS Employment Opportunities* and *NSFRE News* (monthly). Holds annual conference, with exhibits.

附录 8：政府资助相关信息

Appendix VIII: Sources of Information on Government Grants

General Directories:

Annual Register of Grant Support: A Directory of Funding Sources. 1992. 25th edition. (Wilmette, IL: National Register Publishing Co., 1992.) Annual directory of grant support programs offered by government agencies, public and private foundations, corporations, community funds, unions, educational and professional associations, and other groups. Primary organization is by subject category.

Federal Register. Some programs, like DOE'S HEA grants, publish their guidelines and applications procedures in the *Federal Register*, along with announcing changes or planned changes, or possible changes in the program.

Publications & Guidelines on Specific Programs:
National Endowment for the Humanities:
Office of Publications and Public Affairs
National Endowment for the Humanities
1100 Pennsylvania Avenue, N.W.
Washington, D.C. 20506
(202) 786-0438
Request a publication called *Overview of Endowment Programs*. Application guidelines are available for each of the six divisions and for the Office of Challenge Grants.

U.S. Department of Education:

Library Programs
Office of Educational Research and Improvement (OERI)
555 New Jersey Avenue
Washington, D.C. 20208-5571
(202) 219-1315
Fax: (202) 219-1466
For HEA Title II-B: request *Library Programs: HEA Title 1I-B Library Career Training Program*; abstracts of funded programs.
For HEA Title II-C: request fact sheet; application package; abstracts of 1989 funded projects.
For LSCA Title IV: request annual publication, *Library Literacy Program: Analysis of Funded Projects.*

National Historical Publications and Records Commission:

National Archives Building, Room 697
Washington, D.C. 20408
(202) 501-5600
Fax: (202) 501-5005
You can request guidelines, annual reports, a quarterly newsletter called *Annotation*, special reports, and a publications catalog, *Historical Documentary Editions: A Price List.*

National Library of Medicine:

Extramural Programs
National Library of Medicine
8600 Rockville Pike
Bethesda, MD 20894
(301) 496-4221
Fax: (301) 402-0421
Request National Library of Medicine Grant Programs. Request a fact sheet and application information for the Health Sciences Information Resource Grants. Consult 42 Code of Federal Regulations 52 and 45 Code of Federal Regulations 92.

Institute of Museum Services:

IMS Program Office
1100 Pennsylvania Avenue, N. W.
Room 510
Washington, D. C. 20506
(202) 786-0539
Funding requests are made on the official IMS application form, obtainable from the address listed above.

Periodicals:

Federal Grants and Contracts Weekly. Washington, D. C.: Capitol Publications, Inc.
ALA Washington Newsletter. Washington, D. C.: American Library Association; irregular
College & Research Library News; monthly. See especially the "Washington Hotline" column.
Humanities Magazine. Washington, D. C.: National Endowment for the Humanities.

附录 9：基金会相关信息

Appendix IX: Sources of Information on Foundations

Directories:

Taft Foundation Reporter — National Edition (Washington: The Taft Group; Annual): A highly selective directory providing in-depth coverage of the very largest private foundations. Arranged alphabetically by foundation name, with indexes by state, type of grants awarded, field of interest, and by individuals, including donors, family of donors, officers, directors, etc. This is the only reference that provides biographical information on the people who make decisions at foundations.

Taft Foundation Reporter — Regional Editions (Washington: The Taft Group; Annual): Contains the same information as in the national edition listed above, but divided into nine smaller editions covering different parts of the U. S.

Source Book Profiles (NY: The Foundation Center; Serial): Annual subscription service providing detailed information on the 1,000 largest private foundations. Updates notify the subscriber of significant changes in giving interest, personnel, and addresses.

The Foundation Directory (NY: The Foundation Center; Annual): Geographically organized by state, this annual directory profiles 7,600 of the largest U. S. foundations: those with assets of at least $1 million or annual giving of at least $100,000. Each entry provides the name and address of the foundation, together with a statement on its financial data, purpose and activities, types of support available, limitations, officers and board members, number of staff, and publications. Indexed by subject area, type of support, foundation name, and by state and city.

The Foundation Directory, Part 2 (NY: The Foundation Center; Biennial): Provides information similar to that contained in the Foundation Directory, but for mid-sized foundations: those with annual contributions in the $25,000 to $100,000 range. There are five indexes, providing access by location, officers and trustees, types of support, and over 200 specific subject areas.

National Data Book of Foundations: A Comprehensive Guide to Grantmaking Foundations. (NY: The Foundation Center; Annual): Gives brief information on over 30,000 foundations. The most comprehensive coverage available. Listed by state, but with no subject indexing. Introduction provides statistics on foundation giving for the year covered.

Indexes to Grants Awarded:

The Foundation Grants Index, 20th edition, 1992 (NY: The Foundation Center; Annual):

The most recent compilation covers some 46,431 grants awarded by 472 foundations having a total value of $3.25 billion and representing about 44 percent of the total dollars awarded by private and community foundations in 1989. [Note that there is about a two-year time lag between the year cited in the title and the actual time period being covered.] The organization is by state, then alphabetically by foundations located in that state. Following a brief statement of the purpose and funding limitations of the foundation, each of its grants is listed. Entries contain the recipient's name, city and state, amount given, and the purpose of the award. There are indexes by grant recipient name, subject, type of support, location, and recipient category (e. g. colleges and universities, arts and humanities organizations, libraries, etc.). Using this tool, for example, you can identify awards made to libraries for, say, endowment, by each state in the country. Information contained in this source is updated every three months in *The Foundation*

Grants Index Quarterly.

COMSEARCH Printouts (NY: The Foundation Center; published on demand): A series of computer generated printouts based on *The Foundation Grants Index* database. As of this writing, *COMSEARCH Printouts* are available for 26 broad topics (including "Libraries and Information Science"), for 28 specific subject fields within those broader topics, and geographically for 2 cities, 11 states, and 7 regions of the U.S.

DIALOG Online Search: Both *The Foundation Directory* and *Foundation Grants Index* databases can be searched through DIALOG, available to many libraries. Advantages of a DIALOG search are convenience, speed, and currency. The databases are continuously updated based on new information submitted to the Foundation Center. If cost is a factor, searches can be limited by year to include only the most recent information not contained in the printed sources.

Directory And Index:

National Guide to Funding for Libraries & Information Services (Washington: The Foundation Center, cl991.): Combines information from *The Foundation Directory* and *The Foundation Grants Index Annual* (see below) to profile some 367 foundations and 28 direct corporate giving programs that either (1) show a significant interest in libraries in their stated purpose or (2) have actually made grants to libraries of $5,000 or more in the latest year of record.

State & Regional Directories:

There are scores of state and regional directories of foundations and other funding sources issued by a variety of publishers. Both quality and currency can vary widely. The 1991 edition of *Foundation Fundamentals* lists 81 such directories.

附录 10：募捐社团相关信息

Appendix X: Sources of Information on Corporate Prospects

Directories:

Taft Corporate Giving Directory (Washington, D. C.: Taft Group; annual): Detailed profiles of 571 of the largest corporate giving programs in the U. S. Each company listed makes annual contributions of at least $500,000. Covers direct giving programs as well as grants by corporate foundations. Ten indexes allow access by headquarters state, operating locations, grant type, and recipient type.

The Corporate Fund Raising Directory (Washington: Public Service Materials Center; Annual): Alphabetical directory of Fortune 500 companies with corporate giving programs. Entries provide information on application procedures, contact persons, primary areas of interest, geographic preferences, and previous grants. Indexed by location of corporate headquarters, by geographic preference in giving, and by areas of interest (including both "colleges and universities" and "libraries").

Corporate Foundation Profiles (NY: The Foundation Center; Irregular): Descriptions of 234 company-sponsored foundations, taken from the Source Book Profiles described in Appendix IX.

Dun's Million Dollar Directory (Parsippany, NY: Dun's Marketing Services; annual): Profiles more than 160,000 businesses that meet one of the following criteria: (1) 250 or more employees at one location, (2) $25 million or more in sales volume, (3) net worth greater than $500,000. More than 140,000 of the listings are privately owned businesses, providing information that is difficult to obtain elsewhere in so convenient a format. Available in print format, on CD-ROM and on magnetic tape.

Moody's Industrial Manual (NY: Moody's Investors Service; annual): Covers the larger companies, and is especially useful for companies that have merged with or been acquired by others.

Mergers and Acquisitions (Philadelphia: MLR Enterprises, bimonthly): Tracks mergers and acquisitions, generally providing selling prices. If you have a prospect who has recently sold a business, this is a good source from which to obtain the purchase price.

International Directory of Corporate Affiliations, *1992* (Wilmette, IL: National Register Publishing Company; annual): Allows you to look up a corporate subsidiary, division, or affiliate and trace the reporting hierarchy in its parent company, whether based in the United States or abroad. A special section at the beginning covers recent mergers, acquisitions, and name changes.

CD-ROM Databases:

Compact D/SEC (*Disclosure*): The Disclosure Database contains financial and management information on over 12,000 **public companies**, derived from annual and periodic reports filed with the U. S. Securities and Exchange Commission (SEC). These are larger U. S. companies, having at least 500 shareholders of one class of stock and at least $5 million in assets. Excluded are management investment companies, real estate, limited partnerships, or oil and gas drilling funds.

Business Periodicals Index: Offered by H. W. Wilson Company, the BPI is good for basic literature searches in the field of business.

Business NewsBank: CD-ROM index to the microfiche publication of the same title, containing articles in business trade journals, city and regional magazines and newspapers. Highly useful for obtaining information on smaller concerns.

Online Services:

Dun & Bradstreet United States (DBJJS): Available through STM Systems, this database contains information on more that 1.1 million U.S. business establishments with 10 or more employees. For each establishment, provides information about the CEO, description of the business, number of employees, and sales volume. Comprehensive coverage of smaller U.S. companies, but the service is expensive: up to $30 for each profile requested, in addition to the $125 initiation fee and connect time.

*Biz * File (Business Phone Directory)*: Available through CompuServe, this national database provides phone numbers and (in most cases) addresses for thousands of companies throughout the United States.

SEC Filings: Available through Dialog, this database provides detailed financial information on the 12,000 U.S. corporations required to file financial information with the Securities and Exchange Commission. More up-to-date and more complete than the information found in Compact Disclosure, which does not include the full SEC report.

附录 11：募捐个人相关信息

Appendix XI: Sources of Information on Individual Prospects

Directories:

Who's Who in Finance and Industry (Wilmette, IL: Marquis Who's Who; annual): Biographical information on 25,400 North American and international business professionals in the fields of accounting, advertising, banking and finance, communications, construction and engineering, industrial and commercial firms, insurance, investment companies, retail trade, transportation, utilities, and other sectors of the business community. Other biographical directories in the Marquis series include regional guides for the East, Midwest, South and Southwest, and the West, together with profession-based guides directories for advertising, law, entertainment, science and engineering industries. The annual *Index to Marquis Who's Who Books* can be used to locate entries in any of these publications.

People in Philanthropy (Washington, D. C.: Taft Corporation; 1984): Divided into four sections: Wealthy People, Foundation Donors, Foundation Officers, and Corporate Officers. Each section contains biographical sketches (some—in all) providing information on current employment, education, philanthropic affiliations, and business affiliations. Indexed by state of birth and by alma mater, allowing you to identify people who have geographical ties to your region and school ties, either with your institution or with volunteers on your committee. The chief drawback of this source is that it lists only very prominent and wealthy people, many of whom are being constantly solicited for funds and may be difficult to contact.

Biography and Genealogy Master Index (Detroit: Gale Research; semiannual): Indexes many biographical guides, covering both current and older listings.

CD-ROM Databases And Online Services:

Newsbank: This product, familiar to most librarians, contains a valuable "Names in the News" feature that permits you to obtain up-to-date information on prominent individuals in business, politics, and the professions.

*Phone * File*: Available through CompuServe, this national database of telephone directories allows you to search a surname by state and city, providing a list of names, telephone numbers, address, and how long each listed person has been living at that address.

Public Records:

Property Records: Most county courthouses have an auditor's office that maintains property records for both commercial and residential real estate. Most are willing to provide information over the telephone, including the appraised or (in some cases) the market value. Unfortunately, the appraisal values are often not very current; and you need to be sure you understand the method of valuation being used in each case. This information can be helpful in estimating a prospect's net worth. If you know that the prospect has recently sold a property, the selling price can usually be obtained as well.

Probate Records: The county probate courts house records on estates undergoing probate. You will need to know the approximate date of death and the jurisdiction in which the estate is being probated. You are generally looking for the inventory of the estate and its disposition. The research must be performed in person, since the information is often difficult to extract from the records, and few courts will respond to either written or telephone inquiries. A note of caution: most people assume (incorrectly) that this kind of information is private and may be offended if they learn it has been shared with another party.

附录 12：募捐软件产品

Appendix XII：Fundraising Software Products

Fundraising Software

Product Name：Benefactor
Vendor：Datatel
Hardware Platform：Prime
Address：4375 Fair Lakes Court
Fairfax, VA 22033
703 – 968 – 9000 or 415 – 957 – 9002

Product Name：Fund-Master
Vendor：Master Software Corporation
Hardware Platform：N/A
Address：8604 Allisonville Road, Suite 309
Indianapolis, IN 46250
(317) 842 – 7020

Product Name：Advance
Vendor：Business Systems Resources (BRS)
Hardware Platform：DEC
Address：1000 Winter Street
Waltham, MA 02154
617 – 890 – 2105

Product Name：Mac Vantage
Vendor：MacVantage, Inc.
Hardware Platform：Macintosh
Address：120 Montgomery Street, Suite 1260
San Francisco, CA 94104
415 – 397 – 6249

Product Name：Quodata
Vendor：Quodata
Hardware Platform：DEC
Address：266 Pearl Street
Hartford, CT 06103
203 – 728 – 6777

Product Name：The Raiser's Edge
Vendor：Blackbaud MicroSystems, Inc.
Features：Donor information, fund accounting, planned giving
Hardware Platform：IBM & compatible
Address：160 E. Main Street
Huntington, NY 11743

1 – 800 – 443 – 9441
516 – 385 – 1420

Product Name: Commtact
Vendor: Campaign Associates, Ltd.
Hardware Platform: Macintosh
Address: 491 Amherst St.
Nashua, NH 03063
603 – 595 – 8774

Product Name: N/A
Vendor: The Iowa System
Hardware Platform: N/A
Address: 180 North Riverside Dr., Suite 309
Iowa City, IA 52244 – 2808
800 – 959 – 2999
317 – 842 – 7020

Product Name: Iowa State Alumni/Development System
Vendor: University Systems Technology
Hardware Platform: N/A
Address: ISIS Center, ISU Research Park
2501 N. Loop Dr., Suite 616
Ames, IA 50010
1 – 800 – 237 – 9613

Product: Alumni/Development System (ADS)
Vendor: Information Associates
Features: Biographical, financial, trucking, giving clubs, membership
Hardware Platform: N/A
Address: 3000 Ridge Rd. East
Rochester, NY 14622
716 – 467 – 7740

Product Name: N/A
Vendor: American Management Systems, Inc.
Features: Packaged and customized software for alumni/development operations
Hardware Platform: N/A
Address: 1777 N. Kent Street
Arlington, VA 22209 703 – 841 – 6000

Product Name: SHY System
Vendor: Jeffrey R. Shy Associates, Inc.
Features: Alumni/development information and word processing systems
Hardware Platform: Available for IBM-compatible microcomputers, Wang and DEC minicomputers, and IBM mainframe computers
Address: 5252B Olde Town Rd.
Williamsburg, VA 23185
804 – 253 – 2988

Product Name: N/A

Vendor: Computer Management & Development Services (CMDS)
Features: Development and alumni fundraising, tracking, and reporting
Hardware Platform: IBM System 36 and IBM AS400
Address: PO Box 1184
Harrisonburg, VA 22801
703-434-5499

Product Name: Matchmaker
Vendor: Heritage Computer Systems
Hardware Platform: IBM PC or compatible
Address: 4020 North 20th Street
Phoenix, AZ 85016-6024
1-800-752-3100

Planned Giving Software

Product Name: Planned Giving Manager
Vendor: PG Calc
Hardware Platform: N/A
Address: 129 Mount Auburn Street
Cambridge, MA 02138
617-497-4970

Product Name: Crescendo
Vendor: Crescendo Software
Hardware Platform: IBM PC or compatible
Address: 1601 Carmen Dr., Suite 103
Camarillo, CA 93010
805-987-0567

Product Name: TrustProcessor
Vendor: BancCorp Systems, Inc.
Hardware Platform: IBM PC, System 36, AS400
Address: PO Box 50597
Amarillo, TX 50597

附录 13：俄亥俄大学图书馆：馆内政策与程序

Appendix XIII: Ohio University Libraries: Internal Policy & Procedure

SUBJECT: LIBRARY ENDOWMENTS

PURPOSE: To specify the Library's policies and procedures and for managing its endowed accounts.

POLICY: The library has established a series of restricted endowed accounts with the Ohio University Foundation in order to provide a permanent source of income for acquisitions and other designated activities. It is the policy of the library to expend endowment income in a timely manner to carry out the wishes of donors, as expressed in the endowment guidelines and other available documentation. To that end, the Dean of Libraries will assign responsibility for each endowment to a specific staff member, who will develop a budget, make expenditures, and report results, following the procedures and timetables outlined below.

PROCEDURES:

1. The administrative office will maintain files for each endowment containing the guidelines, amendments to the guidelines, correspondence with donors/originators, and other relevant materials.

2. The AD for Special Services will maintain a document listing each endowment and summarizing pertinent information, including its purpose, implementation procedures, staff assignments, and principal donors. (See attachment A.)

3. By May 1 of each year, the AD for Special Services will notify staff members of the amounts available for expenditure in endowments under their control.

4. For endowments requiring that an annual budget be prepared, the responsible staff member will submit a proposed budget no later than June 1 for review and approval, through channels, by the Dean.

5. By July 1 of each year, the responsible staff member will prepare a brief report for the AD for Special Services accounting for the expenditure of endowment income over the preceding twelve months and outlining what has been accomplished. This information will be forwarded to the Dean, for inclusion in an annual letter to major donors, and to the Head of Collection Development and Acquisitions.

引用资料及建议阅读书目

Sources and Suggested Reading

NOTE: Directories and indexes to sources of government, foundation and corporate support will be found in Appendices VIII — X.

Bibliographies

Cresap, Marlys. "Alternative sources of income for libraries: a bibliography." Iowa Library Quarterly; Winter 1987; 24 (4): 35 – 43. [Reprinted in *Unabashed Librarian*; 1988; (66): 6 – 8.]

Georgi, Charlotte and Terry Fate. *Fund-raising, grants, and foundations: a comprehensive bibliography.* Libraries Unlimited; 1985; ISBN: 0 – 87287 – 441 – 9.

Lists 1500 titles on fundraising, grants and foundations under three sections: (1) Reference Information Sources, including associations, national, state and local directories, government publications, on-line sources, etc.; (2) Subject Information Sources, covering such items as computers, foundations, publicity and public relations; and (3) Basic Fund Raising Library, listing books and articles that are the best in the field, according to the compiler.

Hayes, Sherman. "Fundraising: a brief bibliography." *Journal of Library Administration*; 1990; 12 (4): 135 – 152.

Peterson, Lorna. *Fund raising for libraries.* Vance Bibliographies; 1989; ISBN: 0 – 7920 – 0348 – 9.

Books

Bonnell, Pamela G. *Fund raising for the small library.* Chicago: American Library Association, Library Administration and Management Association, 1983.

Boss, Richard W. *Grant money and how to get it.* New York: Bowker, 1980.

Breivik, Patricia S. *Funding alternatives for libraries.* Chicago: American Library Association, 1979.

Broce, Thomas E. *Fund raising: the guide to raising money from private sources.* Norman, OK: University of Oklahoma Press, 1979.

Burlingame, Dwight F. and Lamont J. Hulse (eds.). *Taking fundraising seriously: advancing the profession and practice of raising money.* San Francisco and Oxford: Jossey-Bass Publishers, 1991.

Corry, Emmett. *Grants for libraries: a guide to public and private finding programs and proposal writing techniques.* Littleton, CO: Libraries Unlimited, 1986.

Cutlip, Scott M. *Fund raising in the United States: its role in America's philanthropy.* New Brunswick, NJ: Rutgers University Press, 1965.

Dermer, Joseph and Stephen Wertheimer, eds. *The complete guide to corporate fund raising.* New York: Public Service Materials Center, 1982.

Nine essays by various authors representing both the corporate and professional fundraising environments. Contents include: Corporate Giving in America—An Overview; Organizing a Corporate Campaign; The Five Elements Most Essential in Conduction a Successful Corporate Campaign; My Guide for Securing Corporate Gifts; Corporate Support and the Capital Campaign; Corporate Support for Higher Education; Corporations and the Smaller Institution; Corporate Fund Raising from the Viewpoint of the Arts; Everything You Always Wanted to Know about Corporate Giving.

Dewey, Barbara I. , ed. *Raising money for academic and research libraries: a how-to-do-it manual for librarians.* New York and London: Neal-Schuman Publishers, Inc. , 1991.

Directory of new and emerging foundations. New York: The Foundation Center, 1991, ISBN: 0-87954-396-5.

Dolnick, Sandy, ed. *Friends of the library sourcebook.* Chicago: American Library Association, 1980.

Dolnick, Sandy, ed. *Fundraising for nonprofit institutions.* Greenwich, CT & London: JAI Press, 1987. ISBN: 0-89232-387-6.

Sixteen essays by various authors on such topics as: assessing the community, federal grants, foundations, and friends groups. Includes ten case studies in different non-profit settings.

Dove, Kent E. *Conducting a successful capital campaign.* San Francisco & London: Jossey-Bass, 1988. ISBN: 1-55542-104-0.

Duronio, Margaret A. and Bruce A. Loessin. *Effective fund raising in higher education.* San Francisco and Oxford: Jossey-Bass Publications, 1991.

Electronic advancement: fund raising. (Fairfax, VA: Counsel for the Advancement and Support of Education, 1991).

Book with accompanying 60-minute videocassette examines the theory and use of video for fundraising purposes, with several good examples.

External fund raising / systems and procedures exchange center (SPEC Kit #48). Washington, D. C. : Association of Research Libraries, 1978.

Flanagan, Joan. *The grass roots fundraising book.* Chicago: Contemporary Books, 1982. ISBN: 0-8092-5746-7.

Fund raising in ARL libraries / systems and procedures exchange center (SPEC Kit #94). Washington, D. C. : Association of Research Libraries, Office of Management Studies, 1983.

Harvey, John F. and Peter Spyers-Duran. *Austerity management in academic libraries.* Metuchen, NJ and London: Scarecrow Press, 1984.

Holtz, Herman. *The consultant's guide to proposal writing.* 2nd edition. New York: John Wiley, c1990.

Krummel, D. W. , ed. *Organizing the library's support: donors, volunteers, friends.* Urbana-Champaign, IL: University of Illinois Graduate School of Library Science, 1980.

Lauffer, Armand. *Grantsmanship and fund raising.* Beverly Hills, London and New Delhi: Sage Publications, c1984.

Lee, Sul H. (ed.). *Library fund-raising: a vital margin for excellence.* Ann Arbor, MI: Pierian Press, 1984.

Lefferts, Robert E. *Getting a grant in the 1990's: how to write successful grant proposals.* New York: Prentice-Hall Press, 1990.

Guides the would-be proposal writer through the process and provides a list of resources.

Library development and fund raising capabilities / systems and procedures exchange center (SPEC Kit #146). Washington, D. C. : Association of Research Libraries, Office of Management Studies, 1988.

Lord, James Gregory. *The raising of money.* Cleveland: Third Sector Press; c. 1983; 6th printing, 1987. ISBN: 0-939120-02-X.

Discusses the psychology of fundraising: why people give, how to tap into their emotions, what to avoid.

Margolin, Judith B. *Foundation fundamentals: a guide for grantseekers.* 4th edition. New York: The Foundation Center, 1991. ISBN: 0-87954-392-2.

Updates earlier editions by Carol Kurzig (1981) and Patricia Read (1986).

Murray, Vic. *Improving corporate donations: new strategies for grantmakers and grantseekers.* San Francisco and Oxford: Jossey-Bass Publishers, 1991.

Panas, Jerold. *Mega gifts: who gives them, who gets them.* Chicago: Pluribus Press, 1984.

Pendel, Mary H. *What is a case statement?* Arlington, VA: Thompson and Pendel

Associates, 1981.

Pray, Francis C. *Handbook for educational fundraising*. San Francisco: Jossey-Bass, Inc., 1981.

Rosso, Henry A. *Achieving excellence in fund raising: a comprehensive guide to principles, strategies, and methods*. San Francisco and Oxford, Jossey-Bass Publishers, 1991.

Rowland, A. Westley (ed.). *Handbook of institutional advancement* (2nd ed.). San Francisco & London: Jossey-Bass, 1986.

Shellow, Jill R. *The grantseekers guide: national network of grantmakers*. Mt. Kisco, NY: Moyer, Bell, 1985.

Smith, Craig W. and Eric W. Skjei. *Getting grants*. New York: Harper and Row, cl980.

Steele, Victoria and Stephen D. Elder. *Becoming a fundraiser: the principles and practice of library development*. Chicago and London: American Library Association, 1992.

Swan, James. *Fundraising for the small public library: a how-to-do-it manual for librarians*. New York: Neal-Schuman, 1990.

Helpful ideas on recruiting and training volunteers, motivating boards, brainstorming, planning, and using community resources.

Thompson, D. M. et al. *Typical outline for the case statement*. Arlington, VA: Frantzreb, Prey, Ferner and Thompson, 1978.

Warner, Irving R. *The art of fund raising*. Toronto and NY: Bantam Books, 1984.

Articles

Berry, John N. "The fundraising trap". *Library Journal*; June 15, 1986 (111): 4.

Major fundraising efforts require heavy investments of money and staff and trustee time. Often they fail to raise the targeted amounts. Fundraising, particularly for capital projects and special purposes, is a legitimate source of support. But the demand to raise private funds must not become a substitute for adequate tax support for libraries.

Bob, Murray L. "Confessions of a grantsperson: a lighthearted look at some serious money". *Library Journal*; June 15, 1988, 113: 26 – 29.

Bohlen, Jeanne L. "Foundations, private". *ALA Yearbook of Library and Information Services*; 1989: 115 – 116.

Annual review of foundation grants to libraries.

Bohlen, Jeanne L. "The foundation connection". In: Dolnick, S. *Fundraising for nonprofit institutions*: 47 – 72.

Role of foundations in charitable giving; services provided by the Foundation Center Network; categories of foundations; conducting preliminary research (checklists are included); sources of information.

Booth, Martha. "PR notes: proposals, grants, public relations". *The Southeastern Librarian*; Fall 1988, 38: 129 – 132.

One of the best ways for a library to generate good PR is to publicize newly awarded grants and contracts. Outlines procedures to be followed after the award letter has been received.

Borland, Anne and Smith, Oliver. "Foundations, private". *ALA Yearbook of Library and Information Services*; 1990: 117 – 118.

Annual review of foundation grants to libraries.

Boykin, Joseph F. "Fundraising and financial development— major gift solicitations". *ALA Yearbook of Library and Information Services*; 1988, 13: 146 – 147.

Bradbury, Dan. "Fundraising and financial development." *ALA Yearbook of Library and Information Services*, 1987: 144 – 147.

Annual review of fundraising activities in public and academic libraries, including: friends groups, special events, direct appeals, capital campaigns, corporate and foundation grants.

Bradbury, David J. "Seven strategies for effective fundraising." *Bottom Line*, 1988 (4): 11 – 14.

Brownlee, Elaine U. and Neal J. Ney. "Alice B. Toklas and the libraries: building a successful friends group". *Library Journal*; February 1, 1988, 113: 41 –42.

Burlingame, Dwight F. "Library capital campaigns". *Journal of Library Administration*, 1990, 12 (4): 89 –101.

Burlingame, Dwight F. "The small library and fund-raising for automation". *Library Hi Tech*, 1989, 7 (2): 49 –51.

Small libraries can take advantage of alternative funding sources to address their automation needs. Careful planning is needed to identify funding sources. Clear and confident communication of needs and objectives required.

Caddell, B. "Some thoughts on fundraising". *Unabashed Librarian*, 1988 (665): 5.

Campbell, Jerry D. "Fundraising" *Show-Me Libraries*, August 1987 (38): 17 – 24. [Reprinted from North Carolina Libraries, Winter 1986.]

Director of Duke University Libraries shares keys to his own fundraising success.

Chenault, Libby. "Applying for foundation grants". *North Carolina Libraries*, Winter 1986, 44: 216 –224.

Components of a typical grant proposal; how foundations evaluate proposals; guide to North Carolina foundations; selected reference sources on foundations.

Clark, Charlene K. "Getting started with annual funds in academic libraries: setting the stage for annual giving." *Journal of Library Administration*, 1990, 12 (4): 73 –87.

Clark, Charlene. "Private support for public purposes; library fund raising." *Wilson Library Bulletin*, February 1986, 60 (6): 18 –21.

Outlines a fund raising strategy based on experience of the Sterling C. Evans Library of Texas A & M University.

Clark, Charlene. "Public relations". *Texas Library Journal*, Summer 1985 (61): 46 –47.

Texas A & M University Library decides to make fund raising a high priority.

Clay, Edwin S. "Fund raising by strategic design". *The Bottom Line*, 1987, 1 (3): 25 –27.

Crawford, Jean A. and Judith A. Potts. "How to survive a capital campaign". *Fund Raising Management*, July 1986 (17: 5).

Curtis, Eileen A. "Fund raising by direct mail". *The Unabashed Librarian*, 1984 (51): 3 –4. [Reprinted from College & Research Libraries News, October 1984.]

Davis, Bronson C. "The possible dream: base your campaign formula on a feasibility study". Currents, Nov/Dec 1986 (12): 20 –26.

Davis, Nancy M. "Fund-raising success: knowing why people give". *Association Management*, November 1988, 40: 120 –127.

Psychology of fundraising, especially from the corporate sector. Tips from fundraising guru Barry Nickelsberg, Director of The Funding Center.

Drabenstott, Jon, ed. "Funding library automation". *Library Hi Tech*, Spring 1986, 4 (13): 111 –120.

Fieler, Frank B. "Friends". *Gatherings for the Friends of Ohio University Library*, August 1979, 1: 3.

Finger, Diane. "Brother, can you spare a dime?" *Public Relations Journal*, June 1988, 113: 18 –19.

Fontaine, Sue. "Ideas for library fundraising: plagiarize and localize". *Show-Me Libraries*, 1986 (August): 9 –13.

Fontaine, Sue. "The role of public relations in fund raising". *Journal of Library Administration*, 1990, 12 (4): 15 –38.

"Forming a friends group. In: *The library trustee*. (4th ed.). Chicago: American Library Association, 1988: 204 –206.

Forsythe, Patricia H. "An endowment campaign for a public library." *Journal of Library Administration*, 1990, 12 (4): 103 –119.

"Friends of Broward County Library: developmental study". In: Dolnick, S. *Fundraising for nonprofit institutions*: 251-260.

Sample feasibility study conducted by American City Bureau/Beaver Associates on behalf of the Friends of the Broward County Library in Pompano Beach, Florida, to assess the prospects of conducting a capital campaign with a target of between $1.5 and $2 million.

"Glittering fund raiser at University of Delaware". *Library Journal*, July 1985 (110): 18.

Gurin, Maurice G. "The changing capital campaign." *Fund Raising Management*, June 1987 (18: 4).

Gurin, Maurice G. and Jon Van Til. "Understanding philanthropy: fund raising in perspective". *Journal of Library Administration*, 1990, 12 (4): 3-14.

Haeuser, Michael. "What friends are for: gaining financial independence". *Wilson Library Bulletin*, May 1986: 25-27.

Informative account of a highly successful friends group at a small midwestern liberal arts college.

Hall, Holly. "Choosing the right consultant". *Chronicle of Philanthropy*, February 26, 1991, 3 (9): 22-27.

Detailed discussion of how Colgate University went about the process of selecting a consultant for a major capital campaign.

Hall, Richard B. "Trends in financing public library buildings". *Library Trends*, Fall 1987, 36: 423-453.

Harris, April L. "Special events and their role in fund raising". *Journal of Library Administration*, 1990, 12 (4): 39-51.

Hobart, D. L. "The importance of being in earnest: the trustee as fundraiser". *Bookmark*, Summer 1987, 45: 211-15.

Hodge, James M. and David B. Richardson. "The role of planned giving". *Journal of Library Administration*, 1990, 12 (4): 121-134.

Hood, Joan M. "An academic library's approach to fundraising". In: Dolnick, S. *Fundraising for nonprofit institutions*: 203-221.

University of Illinois Library expands private support by launching a friends organization, formation of an undergraduate library friends division, sponsoring two publications, recruiting volunteers, and conducting an annual fund solicitation employing direct mail, phonations, personal solicitation, and a series of "development luncheons.".

Huntley, Mary Deanne. "Why a PR firm". *Illinois Libraries*, 1987, 69: 59-60.

Jacobson, Harvey J. "15 ways to measure fund raising program effectiveness". *Fund Raising Management*, Dec. 1982 (13: 10).

Kirby, Christine L. "Preparing grant proposals for automation funding". *Bulletin of the American Society for Information Science*, August/September 1986, 12: 17-18.

Kletzien, S. Damon. "Foundations, private". *ALA Yearbook of Library and Information Services*, 1984: 144-146.

Review of private foundation grants to libraries.

Lau, Shuk-fong. "Ten ways to raise library funding". *Journal of Library and Information Science (USA/Taiwan)*, April 1986, 12 (1): 41-50.

Ten methods for raising money are outlined: direct mail, phonation, flea market, friends of the library, gifts and exchange programs, annual giving, special events, foundation grants, corporate grants, and service fees.

Little, Paul L. and Sharon A. Saulmon. "Gifts, donations, and special collections". *Public Libraries*, 1987, 26 (Spring): 8-10.

"Mathematics faculty teach extra classes to support their library." *Cornell '91*. [alumni magazine] Ithaca, NY: Cornell University, 1991.

Math faculty teach extra classes, designating their compensation for support of a departmental library. Some $82,500 has been raised by 10 faculty, and alumni have contributed $6,000.

McGovern, Gail J. "Alternative funding sources: local fund raising; demonstrating the value of". *The Bottom Line*, 1987, 1 (3): 32 –33.

McGovern, Gail. "Alternate funding sources: the inside track; what the experts say about seeking alternative funding". *The Bottom Line*, 1987, 1 (4): 30 –31.

McGovern, Gail. "Alternate funding sources: direct mail campaigns". *The Bottom Line*, 1987, 1 (1): 35 –37.

McGovern, Gail. "Alternative funding sources: tapping into local grants". *The Bottom Line*, 1988, 2 (3): 33 –34.

McGovern, Gail. "Alternative funding sources: how to deal with rejection... and improve your grant success rate at the same time". *The Bottom Line*, 1989, 2 (2): 28 –29.

Miller, Robert C. "Endowment funding in academic libraries: pitfalls and potential". *The Bottom Line*, 1987, 1 (1): 23 –27.

Moran, Irene E. "Writing a winning grant proposal". *The Bottom Line*, 1987, 1 (2): 13 –17.

Munstedt, Peter A. "Library benefit concerts: blood, sweat, and cash". *College & Research Libraries News*, March 1989, (3): 205 –206.

Describes a music library benefit concert presented at the University of Missouri-Kansas City.

Nelson, Venesse C. "Buried alive in gifts". *Library Journal*, April 15, 1988, 113: 54 –56.

"Nixon library fundraising quickly tops $22 million". *Library Journal*, October 1, 1986, (111): 25.

Panas, Jerold. "Yours for the asking". *National Association for Hospital Development Journal*, Fall, 1986.

Founder of one the nation's largest fund raising firms gives general advice: rule of thirds; importance of leadership gifts; donors give "because it feels good;" stress your mission; be sure to listen and wait for prospect to show enthusiasm; for big donors, a verbal presentation is more important than printed materials; best prospects are those who already give; important to find best volunteer possible.

Prentice, A. E. "Gifts, grants and bequests". *Library Trustee*, 1988.

Prentice, Ann E. "Financial support for libraries: fund raising and fees". *ALA Yearbook of Library and Information Services*, 1986: 248.

Ryan, Don and Richard Murdock. "Identifying and nurturing core donors". *Fund Raising Management*, Feb 1986 (16: 12).

Stam, David H. "Finding funds to support preservation". In: The Library Preservation Program. *American Library Association*, 1985: 80 –83.

Strand, Bobbie J. "Finding and researching major donor prospects". Journal of Library Administration, 1990, 12 (4): 53 –71.

Streit, Samuel A. "All that glitters: fund raising for special collections in academic libraries". *Rare Books and Manuscripts Librarianship*, Spring 1988, 3 (1): 31 –41.

Among important matters requiring consideration are budget relief, donor identification, cultivation and solicitation. Success will go to institutions that balance tenacity, creativity, and resilience with good organization, coordination of effort, and careful management.

Switzer, Daniel E. "The role of marketing in fundraising." In: Dolnick, S. *Fundraising for nonprofit institutions*: 1 –18.

Based on experience with a Milwaukee art museum, the author discusses the importance of market analysis in planning an annual giving campaign. Topics include: establishing mission and goals, situation analysis, fundraising objectives, strategies, recognition, special events.

Thomson, Ruth G. "A primer on federal assistance grants." In: Dolnick, S. *Fundraising for nonprofit institutions*: 33 –45.

Helpful hints on preparing successful proposals for federal funding. Lists sources of information on available federal assistance.

Tomer, Christinger. "Developing financial support for library preservation: an alternative approach." *Journal of Academic Librarianship*, July 1985, 11 (3): 133 –135.

To meet the costly challenge of preservation, research libraries should forge cooperative arrangements with publishers and information processing organizations to reissue endangered materials in an appropriate format and at low costs.

VanNatten, Janet. "Are fund raising feasibility studies feasible?" *The Unabashed Librarian*, 1986, (59): 19 – 20.

Hiring a professional consulting firm for a building campaign in a New Jersey town.

Walters, Suzanne and William L. Funk. "Corporate connections in Denver". In: Dolnick, S., *Fundraising for nonprofit institutions*: 243 – 249.

Denver Public Library establishes a partnership with United Bank of Denver. Contains some useful tips on corporate solicitation in general.

Walton, Clyde C. "Gifts, bequests and endowments". *ALA Yearbook of Library and Information Services*, 1984 – 1988.

This annual review of major cash and in-kind gifts to libraries appeared in the ALA Yearbook from 1984 through 1988.

Waters, Richard L. "Funding a major building project: the Dallas story". In: Dolnick, S. *Fundraising for nonprofit institutions*: 173 – 183.

Dallas Public Library constructs a new $24.7 million, 646,000 square foot Central Library facility through a "public-private partnership" involving a capital improvements bond election and a private fundraising campaign with a target of $9 million.

Whittle, Susan S. "How to assess your community". In: Dolnick, S. *Fundraising for nonprofit institutions*: 19 – 31.

Public library context, but many comments can apply to academic library setting. Author stresses importance of knowing demography of library users, identifying supporters, recruiting leaders, reasons people give, making the "ask".

"Wilson Foundation makes grants". *Wilson Library Bulletin*, February 1989, 63: 7.

Wright, Robert. "The foundation game". *New Republic*, November 5, 1990.

Annuals and Periodicals

Chronicle of Philanthropy. Washington, D. C.: Chronicle of Philanthropy, biweekly except the last two weeks of August and December.

Feature articles and regular departments cover the spectrum of private giving in the U. S. and abroad.

Currents. Washington, D. C.: Council for the Advancement and Support of Education; monthly, except August and December.

Foundation giving 1991: yearbook of facts and figures on independent, corporate, and community foundations. New York: The Foundation Center, 1991. ISBN: 0 – 87954 – 397 – 3.

Foundation News. Washington, D. C.: Council on Foundations; bimonthly) (check to see if the Foundation Grants Index Quarterly is published in this periodical)

Giving USA; annual.

Yearbook published by the American Association of Fund Raising Counsel.

Grants for libraries and information services. New York: The Foundation Center; annual.

Covers grants to nonprofit organizations in the U. S. and abroad to public, academic, and special libraries.

The Grantsmanship Center NEWS; bimonthly.

Contains information on grants available in both the public and private sector.

Guide to corporate giving; irregular.

Describes 711 major American corporations, with special emphasis on those supporting the arts.

Local/State Funding Report. Published by Government Information Services, 1611 North Kent Street, Arlington, VA 22209.

Tax Exempt News. Published by Capitol Publications, Inc.

Whole Nonprofit Catalog; semiannual. Published by The Grantsmanship Center. Contains feature articles, lists of resources for fundraisers.

NOTES ON CONTRIBUTORS

Hwa-Wei Lee, Dean of University Libraries at Ohio University, has had more than ten years of experience in fundraising. In addition, he has been a successful proposal writer for various types of grants throughout his thirty-year professional career. In collaboration with the coauthor, Dr. Gary Hunt, Associate Dean of University Libraries, and other colleagues of Ohio University Libraries, Dr. Lee has been awarded two Challenge Grants for a total of $900,000 from the National Endowment for the Humanities since 1984 and raised nearly $3.5 million in private matching funds in response to the challenges. His grantsmanship has also netted nearly $2 million from both international and national sources. Most noticeable of these have been seven consecutive grants from the highly competitive Title II-C of the Higher Education Act for the strengthening of research library sources administered by the U.S. Department of Education. When he came to Ohio University fourteen years ago, the library's endowment funds totaled less than $20,000. These have grown to over $2.5 million in 1992. It is anticipated that by the time the major capital campaign now being undertaken by Ohio University is over in 1993, the library's endowment funds will reach $4 million.

A native of China, Dr. Lee did his undergraduate study at the National Taiwan Normal University, where he received his B. Ed, degree. In 1957, he came to the U.S. as a graduate student and received all his graduate degrees (M. Ed., M. L. S., and Ph. D.) from the University of Pittsburgh. While a graduate student, he was recruited by the University of Pittsburgh Libraries and began his library career in 1959. Since then, he has held various library administrative and faculty positions at University of Pittsburgh, Duquesne University, Edinboro University of Pennsylvania, Asian Institute of Technology (Bangkok, Thailand), and Colorado State University. His work in Bangkok from 1968 to 1975 was sponsored be the U.S. Agency for International Development.

Long active in international librarianship, Dr. Lee has traveled extensively in Asia and other parts of the world. He was frequently sought as a library consultant by foundations, foreign universities and governments, UNESCO, FAO, International Development Research Center of Canada, etc. His publications include the recently published book, *Librarianship in World Perspective: Selected Writings, 1963 – 1989*, and some sixty journal articles, consultant reports, and conference papers.

Among the numerous honors received are the American Library Association's John Ames Humphrey/Forest Press Award for significant contributions to international librarianship in 1991 and the Ohio Librarian of the Year in 1987 by the Ohio Library Association.

Gary A. Hunt is Associate Dean of Libraries for Special Collections at Ohio University, where he is responsible for managing a division consisting of the departments of Archives & Special Collections, the Fine Arts Library, the Music/Dance Library, the Southeast Asia Collection, Microforms/Maps/Non-Print Materials, Chemistry/Physics and Mathematics/Computer Science. He shares responsibility for external fundraising on behalf of the library, including annual giving, Friends of the Library activities, and coordination of a $6 million capital campaign. He has authored numerous successful grant proposals, including two National Endowment for the Humanities Challenge Grants (the maximum number allowed any single recipient) and two NEH Humanities Projects in Libraries proposals.

Born in California, Dr. Hunt received his undergraduate degree from the University of California at Berkeley; his Ph. D. in English and American Literature from Brandeis University; and the MLS from Simmons College. He taught English at several universities in Massachusetts before joining the staff of Boston University Library in 1976. Since his arrival at Ohio University in 1979, he has been active in professional library activities, helping to found the Ohio Preservation Council in 1982 and serving as a panelist and reviewer with the National Endowment for the

Humanities. In 1982 Dr. Hunt won election as Vice-President/President-Elect of the Academic Library Association of Ohio, a chapter of ACRL.

Bessie King Hahn has been the University Librarian at Brandeis University since 1981. First trained as a biochemist, she received her MLS from Syracuse University and stayed on to become the Libraries' first Life Sciences Bibliographer and then Department Head for Science and Technology. From 1978 to 1981, she held the position of Assistant Director for Reader Services at the Milton S. Eisenhower Library of the Johns Hopkins University.

Besides her interest in library development, Ms. Hahn has also been active in ALA and the Chinese-American Librarians Association (CALA), working on issues ranging from bibliographic instruction to minority concerns to women administrators. She served as president of CALA in 1982–1983. Currently she is president of the Boston Library Consortium.

Ms. Hahn has lectured extensively in The People's Republic of China on library management and information technology. She was offered an honorary adjunct professorship for her contributions to the modernization of the Shanghai Jiao Tong University Libraries. Currently she is under contract with a Taiwan publisher to complete a book on library technologies.

Paul A. Willis is Director of University Libraries and Professor of Law at the University of Kentucky in Lexington, a position he has held since 1973. Mr. Willis earned his A. B. from the University of Kentucky in 1963; his MLS from the University of Maryland Graduate School of Library and Information Services in 1966; and his J. D. from the University of Kentucky College of Law in 1969. He has written extensively on law librarianship, legal education, and methodologies of legal research.

4. 巴布亚新几内亚高等院校间的图书馆发展、资源共享和联网
Library Development, Resource Sharing, and Networking Among Higher Education Institutions in Papua New Guinea[①]

最终报告与建议
Final Report and Recommendations

执行摘要
Executive Summary

In accordance with the project proposal for resource sharing and networking of higher education information resources in Papua New Guinea (PNG) drawn up by the Commission for Higher Education (CHE) and the Library Council (LC), this consultant was engaged by the Asia Foundation to undertake a survey of higher education information resources in Papua New Guinea and to prepare a report with recommendations for the upgrading of resources according to acceptable norms, effective sharing of resources through phased introduction of automation and networking, and the creation of a database of information resources.

In a visit to PNG from the 17th of August to the 6th of September 1991, the consultant met with many educational officials, administrators, teachers, and librarians and visited a large number of colleges and universities and their libraries—as many as could be arranged within the time allowed—throughout the Country: Port Moresby, Goroka, Lae, Madang, Mt. Hagen, Rabaul, and Wewak. In addition, he visited the National Library and its National Archives and Public Records Services, the libraries of the Department of Agriculture and Livestock and the Department of Health, the libraries of the PNG Forest Research Institute and the PNG Institute of Medical Research, several provincial public libraries, the libraries of a national high school and a provincial demonstration high school, the Liklik Buk Information Center of the Appropriate Technology Development Institute, and the Library of Melanesian Institute. Altogether, a total of 41 libraries of various types in seven cities were visited during the three-week consultancy (listed in Appendix 1).

Based on the survey of this wide-range of libraries and-information resources and taking into consideration of the national environment and needs of PNG, the consultant developed his preliminary report and recommendations as defined in the terms of reference. The report identified both the strengths and weaknesses in information resources and proposes a strategy for building centers of excellence as possible nodes for automation and networking. The preliminary report, issued on 20 September 1991, was distributed widely in PNG by the Library Council for review and comments. After studying the many comments and suggestions received, the consultant

---

[①] This report is at the Request of Commission for Higher Education and Library Council of The Government of Papua New Guinea, December 1991, printed at the National Research Institute Printshop, 1991.

prepared this final report with modified recommendations—some of which have been substantially strengthened.

In view of the difficult economic and financial situations the Country is facing and the inadequate support that most of the libraries receive, the task of building adequate library and information resources to meet the needs of education, research, and service is monumental to say the least Some of the problems are further compounded by the over-proliferation of small colleges, which inflates costs and reduces operational efficiency—a fact recognized in the 1990 National Higher Education Plan.

It is hoped that the recommendations in this report will contribute to development of a workable plan which will generate a coordinated and determined effort for a phased introduction of library networking employing appropriate computer and information technologies for effective sharing of resources and much improved library services. Major government funding, is needed to strengthen the resources of the six major libraries as the building blocks of a proposed Papua New, Guinea, Library and Information Network (PNGLINET). Further government funding is also recommended for libraries in other institutions of higher education where the library resources are grossly inadequate.

The six major libraries, each with special subject strength, are identified below:
— University of PNG's Main Library
— PNG University of Technology Library
— National Library & National Archives
— University of PNG Medical Library
— University, of PNG Goroka Teachers College Library
— Administrative College Library

The pooled strengths of these libraries via a coordinated program for resource development and sharing and a computerized networking will provide the necessary backbone for PNGLINET which will be accessible by various libraries and users throughout the nation.

主要建议
Key Recommendations

National Approaches

1. The CHE Secretariat should add a senior position, Library Services Coordinator, to plan and coordinate the development of library and information resources in institutions of higher education in PNG.

2. The Coordinator should be advised by the Library Council and should work with the Department of Education, the National Library (or the yet to be established Office of Libraries and Archives), and other related government departments for the improvement of library and information resources in the nation's higher education institutions.

3. The Library Services Coordinator should draw up national development plan for university and college libraries taking into consideration the recommendations made in this report.

4. The National Library Service should play a key role in the development of libraries in government agencies, community and high schools, as well as public libraries in the National Capital District and in all the provinces which complement and support the development of libraries in higher education institutions.

5. The "Basic-Standards for College Libraries" developed by the National Library Service (see Appendix 2) need to be re-examined and revised to upgrade minimum requirements for space, collections, services, staff, and funding as well as to add certain performance measurements. Different minimum standards may be needed for the various type of colleges.

6. A formula for funding libraries should be developed to ensure that, even in difficult economic times, the libraries will not be stripped of minimum funding. The suggested criterion is that a minimum of 5% of the institution's operating budget should be spent for library resources (books, journals, audio-visual material etc.). To correct the long time neglect of the many college libraries in recent years, special funding from the Government should be specifically designated for library improvement.

Development of PNGLINET

7. Adequate funding should be provided to those libraries which have been identified as having collections of major strength and recognized as centers of excellence. These national information resources within the education sector include the Main Library and Medical Library of the University of Papua New Guinea (UPNG), the Library of the University of Technology (Unitech), and the UPNG Goroka Teachers College. These libraries, each with strengths in certain subject areas—together with the National Library and the Administrative College Library—should be considered as the major building block s of a proposed Papua New Guinea Library and Information Network (PNGLINET).

8. As shown in Diagram I, "Building Blocks for a National Network of Library and Information Resources in PNG", each of these libraries could serve as the resource center for other libraries in the same field of specialization.

— The Main Library of UPNG should serve as the national resource center for Humanities, Law, Sciences Social Sciences, and PNG collection.

— The Medical Library of UPNG should serve as the national resource center for Medical and Allied Health Sciences.

— The Library of Goroka Teachers College of UPNG should serve as the national resource center for Education, Behavioral Science and Curriculum Materials.

— The Library of Unitech should serve as the national resource center, for Agriculture, Business, Engineering, and Technology.

— The National Library should serve as the national resource center for all government departments, as well as all public and school libraries in the Country. It should also be the main center for all government publications, official depository for PNG publications, and the National Audio-visual Materials Center.

— The Library of Administrative College should serve as the national resource center for Management Science, Public Policy and Administration, and Development Information.

9. To house the growing library and information resources in these key libraries, adequate and functional library buildings with sufficient space for growth should be planned and constructed. These buildings should have temperature and humidity control to protect the collections and to provide a comfortable environment for their users. In preparation for computerization, adequate wiring for computers and electronic equipment (with provision for future growth and changes) should be included. Ample seating, preferably including a number of individualized study carrels, should be provided. Presently, all of the key libraries in higher education institutions need additional space. Special government funding is strongly recommended.

10. For economical storage and preservation of less used research materials which must be retained, a central storage facility with high density compact shelving should be built to be used by all libraries. Multiple copies of storage items can be given to interested libraries or discarded. The collections in the facility should be identified in both the local catalog and the online union catalog for easy search and retrieval whenever needed. The planning for such a facility should begin as soon as possible by the Library Services Coordinator.

11. A well developed library systems software capable of networking for the key libraries identified in Recommendation 7 should be selected and installed. Three-year capital funding totaling K900,000 should be appropriated to purchase both the software and hardware for the six

resource libraries in a network environment, and an annual operating budget of K100,000 (with inflationary adjustment each year) should be provided to maintain the network and make it accessible by computers from remote locations.

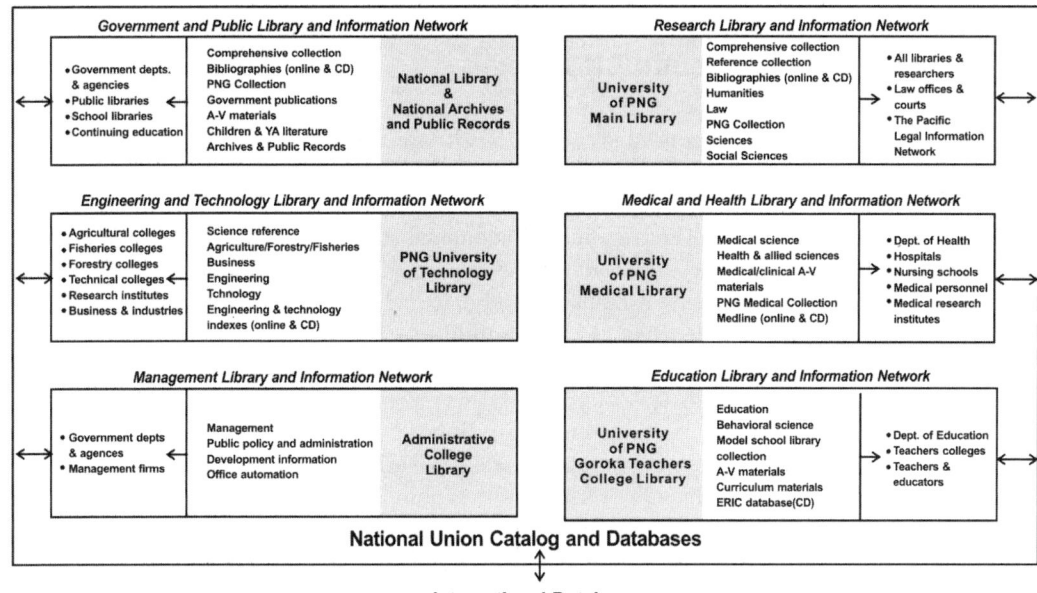

Diagram I: Building Blocks for a National Network of Library and Information Resources in PNG
Papua New Guinea Library and Information Network (PNGLINET)

12. There should be a national database of the library and information resources in the computerized PNGLINET using the MARC international format for bibliographic records. The National Library Service should establish a PNG MARC for use by all libraries for shared cataloging to create the online national union catalog arid bibliographic database. It is recommended that the PNG MARC closely adhere to a major international standard, such as LC MARC, UK MARC, or AUSMARC, to facilitate utilization of records prepared elsewhere with little or no conversion required.

13. The online national union catalog should contain the complete library and information resources (including books, serial titles and holdings information, audio-visual materials, indexed journal articles, archival materials, local databases, etc.) of the key libraries.

14. PNGLINET should serve as the gateway to library and information resources outside the country. PACESAT and other advanced telecommunication technologies should be used to access world-wide databases, including Australian Bibliographic Network, the OCLC Online Computer Library Center, Medline, Dialog, etc.

15. At the appropriate stage of development for PNGLINET, a governing structure should be put in place to ensure full participation of all major resources libraries. The exact form of the governing structure and its composition should be decided by CHE in consultation with other related government agencies. The Library Services Coordinator may serve as the Executive Director of PNGLINET for day-to-day operations with an adequate operating budget and staffing.

16. The selection of a fully developed and proven software package for the PNGLINET should be done by a committee of all participating libraries with the advice of an experienced and unbiased consultant. The needs and requirements of the network should be communicated through a "planning document" and a "request for proposal" prepared by the Committee.

17. For the development of information resources and services within each of the six sub-networks in Diagram I, there is a need to create a position of system librarian in each of the six resource libraries.

18. Once PNGLINET becomes operational, provision should be made to extend access to other libraries. Procedures for inter-library lending and document delivery will need to be established. Opportunities—with central funding—should be made available in stages for libraries wishing to join PNGLINET as full participants.

College and Other Academic Libraries

19. Because the library and information resources in most of the colleges are generally inadequate, major augmentation is needed to bring each to a minimum acceptable standard.

20. The transition of the community-school teachers colleges from a two-year certificate program to a three-year diploma program requires that the libraries of these colleges be greatly improved. Major remedial infusions of funding for additional staff and information resources should be considered a high priority for a period of five years. Minimum quantitative standards and performance measurements should be established and enforced. The recommendations made at the Library Workshop, 18 – 24 March 1990, by the participants from all teachers colleges under the sponsorship of the Teacher Education Division of the Department of Education were well thought-out and should be implemented.

21. Most of the libraries in nursing schools, technical colleges, and other special colleges show signs of long-standing neglect and generally are impoverished. Major efforts and actions are urgently needed to improve them. In working with appropriate government departments, the Library Services Coordinator of CHE should develop guidelines and minimum standards for these libraries and seek annual funding for them.

22. To realize economies of scale cost-effective operation, many of the small colleges with inferior programs and library resources should be merged into larger units or be incorporated with the universities or better established institutions.

23. Staffing goals should be a minimum of one trained librarian (with a library diploma or certificate) and two library technicians for every teachers college library and minimum of one trained librarian and one library technician for each of the technical, nursing, and special colleges. These goals should be achieved before 1997.

24. The position classification and salary scale for library staff should be uniform and comparable to teaching staff with equivalent educational requirements and qualifications. There need to be clear career paths for promotion and movement for both professional and support library staff. The staff classification and fringe benefits in college libraries should be made equitable with university libraries.

25. Opportunities for in-service training and continuing education should be made available to college librarians to acquire new knowledge and skills for modern library and information services. There should be funding and provision for educational leaves by CHE to library staff through open selection. The existing programs in the UPNG Department of Library and Information Studies should be expanded, with necessary funding, to meet such needs.

26. For each teachers college library, a minimum of 300 new books, and 20 audio-visual materials of relevance to the curriculum should be added to the collection each year and at least 50 journal subscriptions maintained. For each technical, nursing and special college library, the minimum requirement should be adding 150 new books and 10 audio-visual materials of relevance to the curriculum each year and maintenance of 25 journal subscriptions. These materials should be carefully selected (rather than happenstance gifts), to support the curriculum and should be cataloged for easy access. Funding for acquisitions arid cataloging are critically needed to remedy the outdated collections found in most of these libraries.

27. Centralized acquisitions and cataloging for college libraries should be explored to afford savings in both manpower and costs. For example, many library vendors abroad can provide attractive discounts for volume acquisitions. They can also provide cataloging service at little or no additional cost. With the establishment of PNGLINET, centralized and shared cataloging services can ease the manpower scarcity in small libraries. The National Library in recent years has

provided central acquisitions and cataloging service for public and school libraries. This useful service can perhaps be expanded to tertiary libraries.

28. To make better use of audio-visual materials, all college libraries should have a room equipped with appropriate A-V equipment. Teachers should be encouraged to use the room and to incorporate A-V materials into their instruction. The room and equipment should be well maintained. The strong A-V collection of the National Library should be expanded and used as the resource collection to augment local collections.

29. Many of the library buildings in colleges badly need repair or expansion. Many require new and additional equipment and furniture. A survey should be conducted by the Library Services Coordinator to determine such needs, and funding for the improvements should be provided.

Complementary Library and Information Services Nationally

30. The Library Services Coordinator of CHE should develop a system for the collection of annual statistics and other relevant information. These data should be stored in a computer and analyzed for management purposes. A directory of library and information resources in higher education institutions should be published annually.

31. Similarly, statistical data and other relevant information for all government, public, special, and school libraries should be collected and kept by the National Library. Statistics for college and university libraries collected by CHE may also be included. A national, directory of these library and information resources should be published regularly. Such data compilations are valuable planning and management tools locally, regionally, and nationally.

32. To encourage and provide incentives for sharing resources, those libraries with a net inter-library lending (i. e., number of items loaned to others minus number of items borrowed from other libraries) should be reimbursed for the cost of handling and mailing from a special fund established by the Government.

33. The National Library Service and the Department of Education should promote indigenous publications in all subjects, especially for children and young adult audiences.

34. Instruction in library and learning skills should be a part of the regular college curriculum and available to all students. This is especially important for students at teachers colleges. They will be transmitting these skills to future generations. It is recommended that CHE and the Department of Education develop necessary guidelines and implementation plans.

35. Teachers college libraries should have a model collection for school libraries similar to that maintained by the National Library Service. It is important that future teachers become familiar with such a collection. Separate funding should be provided by the Department of Education to establish and maintain such a collection in each teachers college library upon request.

36. The Goroka Teachers College Library should establish and maintain a model collection for high school libraries. Future high school teachers should be familiar with such a collection. They should also familiar with the selected annual booklists for high schools prepared by the National Library.

37. Based on local circumstances, the library in some of the UPNG Extension Centers located in a province could ideally be established as a cultural center combining the public library, the vocational center library, and the University Center Library into one joint facility. Since the funding of all three is borne by the provincial government, such a shared facility will eliminate unnecessary duplication and be more cost-effective. Both the National Library Service and UPNG Library should assist in the design and establishment of these cultural centers. Cooperation with other libraries in the vicinity of the cultural center should be encouraged also.

报 告
Report

1. BACKGROUND

Education is critical to nation building. For the development of future leaders in the increasingly complex society of Papua New Guinea, higher education is key in providing much-needed human resources. According to the 1990 National Higher Education Plan, greater effort must be made by all sectors of the higher education community, including libraries, to define detailed requirements, based on the visions of the Plan. To adequately support the activities in teaching, research, and service, the libraries in all institutions of higher education must develop strong resources arid services appropriate to the mission of the respective institutions—regardless whether public or private, large or small, urban or rural, and multi-or single-purpose. The quality of education in the institutions of higher education is largely dependent on the strengths of the available library and information resources.

In this endeavor, finding a cost-effective systematic, and coordinated way to develop the required library and information resources—which builds on existing strengths, minimizes unnecessary duplication, establishes common standards, encourages cooperation and resource sharing, plans for phased introduction of automation and networking, and finally, creates a national database of library and information resources—the Commission for Higher Education and the Library Council of Papua New Guinea developed a project proposal for "Resource Sharing and Networking of Higher Education Information Resources in Papua New Guinea" and sought the support of the Asia Foundation to engage a consultant, Dr. Hwa-Wei Lee, Dean of University Libraries, Ohio University (Athens, Ohio 45701, U.S.A.). to conduct "a survey of higher education information resources in Papua New Guinea with a view towards identifying collection strengths; upgrading resources in keeping with academic norms; preparing guidelines for the phased introduction of an automated network and creation of a centralized database of institutional resources."

The work of the consultant was undertaken from the 17th of August to the 6th of September, 1991. Working under the guidance of the Commission for Higher Education (CHE) and the Library Council (LC) and with the able assistance of Dr. John Evans, Head of the Department of Library and Information Studies, University of Papua New Guinea (UPNG), the consultant met with education officials, administrators, teaching staff, and librarians in related government offices and representative institutions in many parts of the Country, including, Port Moresby (the National Capital District), and other major cities and regions such as Goroka, Lae, Madang, Mt. Hagen, Rabaul, and Wewak. The extensive travels by airplane, car, bus, and walking were eye-opening and at times personally risky. The report that follows is based on the study and analysis of the data collected and interviews conducted. It also take into consideration the report of a parallel study on public library development conducted in 1990 by Dr. D. E. K. Wijasuriya, former Director — General, National Library of Malaysia, under the auspices of the Library Council.

The consultant wishes to acknowledge his deep gratitude to the Asia Foundation, Commission for Higher Education, Library Council, Department of Education, the Department of Library and Information Studies of UPNG, and all of the individuals whom he met throughout the assignment for their useful advice and support. He is especially indebted to Dr. Naomi T. Martin, Chair of CHE, Mr. Ruben San Mateo, Executive Director of the Secretariat and Deputy Chair of CHE, and Dr. Moseley Moramoro, OBE, Chair of the Library Council, for their visionary leadership in the development of higher education libraries and information resources as necessary for quality education. Mr. Neil Nicholls, the National Librarian, Ms. Florence Griffin, UPNG Librarian, Mr. Deveni Temu, Unitech Librarian, Ms. Margaret Obi and Mr. Ismeal Isikel, both of the UPNG Department of Library and Information Studies, Mr. David Austin Principal of Madang Teachers College, Mr. Richard Green, Principal of Mt. Hagen Technical College, and Mr. John Thomas, Deputy Librarian of Goroka Teachers College are also to be thanked for their extraordinary assistance.

Upon the completion of his fruitful visit, to Papua New Guinea, the consultant submitted a preliminary report to the Commission for Higher Education, the Library Council, and the National Library Service in late September for review and comments. The report to the Library Council was further copied for wide distribution to all those individuals visited and consulted in PNG. Based on the comments and suggestions received this final report is prepared for possible adoption by the Commission for Higher Education and for necessary follow-up actions by all those concerned.

2. TERMS OF REFERENCE

As stated in the Project Proposal, the precise TERMS OF REFERENCE for the consultancy were:

"To undertake a survey of higher education information resources in Papua New Guinea; suggest norms for the upgrading of resources; develop guidelines for more effective resource sharing through the phased introduction of automation and networking and the creation of a database of information resources."

The JUSTIFICATION for the project, as stipulated in the proposal was:

"At the present time the major information resources of Papua New Guinea for tertiary level teaching, research and developmental purposes are found largely in the country's higher education institutions."

"While there are collection strengths and centers of excellence, these are not widely known or utilized outside the institution's immediate community of users. At the same time, there are also deficiencies in resources as well as some overlap and duplication."

The proposed survey therefore will not only identify collection strengths and centers of excellence but will suggest norms for the upgrading of resources and the development of an environment for cooperation and resource sharing through the phased introduction of automation and networking.

The eventual creation of a centralized database of information resources would be of great benefit not only to higher education institutions but also to public and private sector agencies and their key role in the development process.

"Higher education information resources which are coordinated, further upgraded and conveniently accessible can provide effective support for key development sectors in Papua New Guinea as well as more effectively serve teaching and research requirements."

The proposal further specified the BENEFITS expected as follows:

"(1) Strengthening support for quality academic programs.

(2) The identification of resources and highlighting of collection strengths and deficiencies.

(3) The development of norms for the progressive and systematic upgrading of resources.

(4) The development of guidelines to facilitate more effective resources sharing through automation and networking.

(5) The creation of a database of information resources."

3. PROJECT ACTIVITIES

Thanks to the arrangements made by Mr. Ruben San Mateo of CHE and Dr. John Evans of the LC, the consultant met with Mr. J. Tetaga, the Secretary of the Department of Education and several of his deputies before setting out to visit 26 of the 62 institutions of higher education, all with programs of post-grade 10 level (but excluding the 4 national high schools which provide

grade 11 and 12 level courses), as defined by the Commission in its National Higher Education Plan of 1990. The following is the list of the institutions visited:
    Universities (2 of 2):
        Papua New Guinea University of Technology (Lae)
    Matheson Library
        Liklik Buk Information Center
    University of Papua New Guinea
        The Michael Somare Library (Main Library at Port Moresby)
        Medical Faculty Library (Taurama)
        The Library of Goroka Teachers College (Goroka)
        Two of UPNG's 10 extension studies centers (Madang and Rabaul)
    Teachers Colleges for Community Schools (7 of 8):
        Balob Teachers College (Lae)
        Gaulim Teachers College (Rabaul)
        Holy Trinity Teachers College (Mount Hagen)
        Kabaleo Teachers College (Rabaul)
        Madang Teachers College (Madang)
        St. Benedict's Teachers College (Wewak)
        St. Paul's Teachers College (Rabaul)
    Technical Colleges (4 of 6):
        Goroka Technical College (Goroka)
        Lae Technical College (Lae)
        Madang Technical College (Madang)
        Mt. Hagen Technical College (Mt. Hagen)
    Nursing Schools (3 of 11):
        Lae School of Nursing (Lae)
        Nazarene College of Nursing (Mt. Hagen)
        Rabaul School of Nursing (Rabaul)
    Allied Health Sciences (1 of 2):
        College of Allied Health Sciences (Taurama)
    Agriculturial Colleges (2 of 4):
        Highlands Agricultural College (Mt Hagen)
        Vudal Agricultural College (Rabaul)
    Other institutions (2 of 8):
        Administrative College
        Port Moresby In-service College
    Additionally, the consultant also visited the following 15 non-academic libraries:
        National Library Service (Port Moresby)
        National Archives and Public Records Services (a branch of the National Library; Port Moresby)
        The Library of the Department of Agriculture and Livestock (Port Moresby)
        The Library of the Department of Health (Port Moresby)
        The Library of the PNG Forest Research Institute (Lae)
        The Botany Library of the Botany Branch of PNG Forest Research Institute (Lae)
        The Library of the PNG Institute of Medical Research (Goroka)
        The Library of the Melanesian Institute (Goroka)
        The City Public Library of Port Moresby (Port Moresby)
        Goroka Public Library (Goroka)
        Lae Public Library (Lae)
        Madang Public Library (Madang)
        Rabaul Public Library (Rabaul)

Goroka Demonstration High School Library (Goroka)
Passam National High School Library (Wewak)

Appendix 1 provides a complete list of the individuals consulted and/or interviewed by the consultant.

4. FACT FINDING

Through visits to 41 libraries, the consultant found that the best libraries were in the main libraries of the two national universities (University of PNG and PNG University of Technology), the National Library Service, UPNG Medical Library, UPNG Goroka Teachers College Library, and the Administrative College. Despite some necessary overlaps in basic collections among these six centers of excellence, each has its own special areas of subject specialization and collection strength.

UNIVERSITY OF PAPUA NEW GUINEA

Started in 1966, the Main Library (Michael Somare Library) of the University has the Country's best and largest library collection. It contains about 400,000 volumes of books and subscribes to 1,500 journals. The collection is strong in general reference, humanities, law, New Guinea Collection, Sciences, and Social Sciences. The library is a member of the Asia-Pacific Information Network in the Social Sciences (APINSS), a UNESCO sponsored project. The library building is centrally located on the campus. It is a modern, air-conditioned building with adequate seating and is open to both university and non-university users. About 1,500 users entered the library daily. The library uses a microfiche catalog which is generated by the ADLIB system of Britain on a Prime Computer. The circulation module of the ADLIB system was installed this year and is being tested. Sets of the microfiche catalog have been distributed to other libraries. The Library also provides online search of DIALOG databases and two CD-ROM databases (Book in Print and ERIC). Two distinct collections can be considered as centers of excellence. They are:

(1) The 30,000-volume Law Collection, and within it is the special collection of the laws of the 19 Pacific island governments which is the cornerstone of the Pacific Legal Information Network (PALIN), a project supported by the Asia Foundation.

(2) The New Guinea Collection contains well over 82,000 volumes and is regarded as the premier research collection in the world for materials relating to PNG and Irian Jaya. It collects everything from books, pamphlets, and journals to theses, government and consultancy reports, microforms, newspapers, photographs and slides, maps, posters, stamps, offprints, church, mission and private records, and contemporary work of art. The catalog has been automated which also includes indexing to over 50,000 articles and monographs relevant to PNG and its environment.

The Medical Library, with its strong collection of some 46,000 volumes of books and approximately 380 journal titles, is a de facto national medical library in every sense. Its collection is strong in Medical Science and the Allied Health Sciences. Seventy percent of its clientele are health personnel located in hospitals and health centers throughout the Country. Since 1981, at the recommendation of the Department of Health, the Library has been designated by the World Health Organization as the National Focal Point Library in PNG for health sciences. It has online access to the Medline Database in the National Health Library in Canberra, Australia via microcomputer and modem. The searches, including photocopies, are free under an agreement between the Australian Government and the World Health Organization. The Library's microfiche catalog is generated by the ADLIB System. Presently, the Library is in the process of setting up a CD-ROM system for the Cambridge database. In recent years, the library has deposited a selected collection of medical Reference and key texts in 20 major hospitals around the nation for use by doctors and health personnel.

The Goroka Teachers College is an integral part of the University. It differs from other teachers colleges in that it is the only one educating secondary-school teachers while the others train community school teachers. The College Library has one of the best collection on education and behavioral science, consisting of 80,000 volumes of books and bound serials, 300 current journals, and 2,000 audio-visual materials. The library uses the automated cataloging system of the Main Library and has its own Bibliofile and ERIC CD-ROMs for searching. It also has one of the best equipped media centers and is capable of making instructional video. The Library sees itself as the resource center for the Highland region.

PAPUA NEW GUINEA UNIVERSITY OF TECHNOLOGY

Founded in 1967, Unitech Library is the second largest library in the country with its 120,000 volume collection, 2,000 current Journal titles, and 2,400 audio-visual materials. The modern library building is spacious, air-conditioned, and carpeted providing a pleasant environment. In addition to the strength of its reference and general collections, the library collection is especially strong in Agriculture, Business, Engineering, and Technology. The Library's catalog is on CD-ROM—one of the very few in Asia—produced by the Brodart Company in the U.S. The catalog is updated twice a year. The Library also provides online computer searching of various databases free of charge and has available several CD-ROM databases.

THE NATIONAL LIBRARY SERVICE

The National Library Service was created in 1975 by Cabinet directive. At that time, the National Archives (although created as a separate archival activity in 1962) became a branch of the National Library. The National Library and the National Archives and Public Records are housed in separate buildings but located next to each other. The collections of the National Library consist of 45,000 books, 400 current journals, and some 4,500 films and video cassettes. Besides being the official depository for PNG publications, the Library's reference collection, PNG collection, and film collection are considered as major national resources. The National Archives maintains valuable government records dating as far back as 1884. As a service to the nation, the National Library publishes the *Papua New Guinea National Bibliography* (bi-annual), the *National Union List of Serials*, and a number of directories and booklists. It also serves as the National ISBN Agency. Despite the government decisions for decentralization and funding cuts, the National Library has continued to provide vital services to public and school libraries in the provinces through centralized technical services, community school library book subsidy scheme, matching grants for high school libraries, and seminal grants for the College of Distance Education and vocational center libraries. It also provides online searching of a wide range of databases for libraries. These databases include both those created by the National Library itself and those can be accessed through the National Library of Australia. A number of databases on CD-ROM (Bookbank, Books in Print Plus, Bibliofile, and ERIC) are also available for use free of charge.

ADMINISTRATIVE COLLEGE

Founded in 1963, the library of Administrative College is one the oldest libraries in PNG. The building is air-Conditioned and adequate in space. The collection of 46,240 books, 646 current journals, and over 300 audio-visual materials is particularly strong in Government, Management, Public Administration, and Office Automation.

Other than the above major library and information resources, there are also a small number of special libraries with reasonably good collections, including:

The Department of Agriculture and Livestock Library
PNG Forest Research Institute Library
PNG Institute of Medical Research Library
Port Moresby In-service College Library

The collections in these libraries have fewer than 40,000 volumes and fewer than 200 current journal subscriptions.

For the rest of the libraries in institutions of higher education, the picture is unfortunately very sad, due to decreasing government funding in recent years.

Although varying greatly in quality and quantity among themselves, the libraries in the ten teachers colleges for community school teachers, as shown in Appendix 4, are considered slightly better than those in the agriculture/fisheries/forestry colleges. The libraries in the technical and nursing colleges are even worse (see Appendix 5). Many do not measure up to the high school libraries that this consultant visited.

In general, the collections of these libraries are largely outdated because few recent books of relevance have been purchased. The only new stocks have been gifts (mostly from the Asia Foundation, British High Commission, church agencies, etc.). Few of the libraries can afford to subscribe journals. Many do not have any audio-visual materials or the equipment with which to use them. The library rooms in most cases are small and in need of repair. With the exception of teachers colleges, many college libraries do not have a full-time trained librarian to run the library. There is clear evidence of neglect by the college administration in the wake of funding cuts.

With the exception of the Port Moresby In-service College which has a larger library collection, Appendix 4 shows that, among the other 9 teachers colleges, the library collections of books range between 2,719 and 32,000 volumes and current journal subscriptions between 7 and 41. Only one reported to have about 100 A-V materials. The library's annual materials budgets range from K700 to K4,800 and the number of library staff between 0.5 and 3. Four of the nine use personal computers for cataloging and two also use them for circulation and online search. Eight of the colleges are affiliated with a church organization. Some of these libraries are staffed by foreign, volunteers and receive occasional donations of funds or books from foreign sources.

Evident in Appendix 5, the conditions are even worse for most of the government-run colleges. Most have neither library staff nor funds for library materials.

There are many reasons for the desolate situation in which most of these libraries find themselves. Common explanations include:

1. decreasing government funding,
2. lack of economies of scale: too few students and programs in each college,
3. absence of trained librarians,
4. low pay and low status of library positions which causes frequent turn-over,
5. heavy losses of newly acquired library materials due to lack of adequate supervision and security measures,
6. lack of support by college administrations and inadequate concern by teachers, and
7. outdated methods of instruction and learning.

The result of these inadequate library facilities is the obvious poor quality of college education which can, at best, be described as secondary education.

In talking with principals and teachers, the consultant was encouraged by expressions of strong desires to improve the current situation. For the teachers colleges, in particular, the introduction of a three-year diploma program in place of the former two-year certificate program has brought recognition of the need to upgrade library resources and facilities. This was expressed in a resolution adopted by the principals at the 1990 Annual Principals Conference. The resolution stated:

> "The Annual Principals' Conference requests that the Association for Teacher Education, in collaboration with the Commission for Higher Education, submit a project for upgrading resources in libraries and develop computer link-ups amongst all college and university libraries in Papua New Guinea. This upgrading is essential to the implementation of the three year diploma programme."

With reference to library proposals from technical colleges, Mr. T. Poesi, Assistant Secretary Technical Education of the Department of Education, acknowledged in a letter to Dr. John Evans dated May 1991, that "Most colleges have voiced their dissatisfaction over the present state of their library facilities, and express a strong desire to improve them."

On behalf of agriculture colleges, Mr. Samuel Lahis, Director of Agricultural Education and Training Department of Agriculture and Livestock, also expressed the need for special funding to improve library resources and facilities.

It is clear from the data and foregoing expressions of concern that all the college libraries in Papua New Guinea are in need of adequate funding from the Government. Such funding should be sustained throughout the 1990s and be specifically ear-marked for use exclusively for the libraries to support a minimum level of adequacy in staffing, collection development, and service.

5. CHALLENGES AND OPPORTUNITIES

Despite the gloomy conditions which prevail among college libraries, there are many bright spots in overall library development. The emphasis on quality higher education to meet the manpower needs of the nation, as emphasized in the 1990 National Higher Education Plan, sets the direction for improvement of libraries serving higher education. The survey of higher education information resources in PNG undertaken by this consultant identified six strong centers of excellence with little overlap and great complementary strengths. The possibility and potential for a national network of library and information resources is present and ready. Since most of the cataloging records in the six major resource libraries are already in machine-readable format, a unified national bibliographic database can be created relatively easily. The good telecommunications system available in the country lends itself to computer networking. There is also an admirable spirit of cooperation among, libraries to share resources and to make their collections and services available to others.

In Diagram I: "Building Blocks for a National Network of Library and Information, Resources in PNG", this consultant presents a plan for the formation of PAPUA NEW GUINEA LIBRARY AND INFORMATION NETWORK (PNGLINGET). The national network is built on six foundation blocks. Each block is itself a sub-system of a special area encompassing a group of libraries and users.

— The University of PNG's Main Library could serve as the resource center of the RESEARCH LIBRARY AND INFORMATION NETWORK which would provide information services in Humanities, PNG collection, Sciences, and Social Sciences. The Law Library could be the resource center for law libraries and legal information users.

— The University of PNG's Medical Library could serve as the resource center of the MEDICAL AND HEALTH LIBRARY AND INFORMATION NETWORK providing services to personnel in the Department of Health, hospitals, nursing schools, medical research institutes, and others.

— The University of PNG Goroka Teachers College Library could serve as the resource center of the EDUCATION LIBRARY AND INFORMATION NETWORK providing services to officials in the Department of Education and to teachers and students in other teachers colleges.

— The National Library Service and its National Archives and Public Records could serve as the resource center of the GOVERNMENT AND PUBLIC LIBRARY AND INFORMATION NETWORK providing services to government departments and agencies, public and school libraries, and citizenry.

— The PNG University of Technology Library could serve as the resource center of the ENGINEERING AND TECHNOLOGY LIBRARY AND INFORMATION NETWORK providing service to businesses and industries, research institutes, and the agriculture, fisheries, forestry, and technical colleges.

— The Administrative College Library could serve as the resource center of the MANAGEMENT LIBRARY AND INFORMATION NETWORK providing services to government department and agencies and to management firms.

The interconnection of these six sub-networks by computers and communications links will form PNGLINET. The effective networking of these six separate but inter-related sub-networks requires that a common computer software and hardware system be selected and used for all.

Considerable coordination will be needed in planning and developing PNGLINET. This may require the establishment of a network planning committee with its members appointed by CHE to include the chief librarians of the six major resource libraries, the head of the UPNG Department of Library and Information Studies, and representatives from the Departments of Education, Finance and Planning, and Personnel Management. The Committee should preferably chaired by Mr. Ruben San Mateo, Executive Director of the Secretariat and Deputy Chairperson of CHE.

Within CHE, a new position of Library Services Coordinator should be created to work with the libraries in the higher education sector. The position should have sufficient rank and authority to carry out its functions. Improving library and information resources in higher education institutions will require dramatic efforts to compensate for past deficiencies and to lay the foundation, for networking and resource sharing. The following are suggested as immediate responsibilities for the CHE Library Services Coordinator:

1. Seek adequate government funding for the major resources libraries in the higher education sector: first, by restoring the previous funding level and second, by developing a formula whereby libraries receive a fixed percentage of an institution's operating funds for materials acquisition, staffing, and equipment. Capital funding for those libraries in need of building expansion or rehabilitation or a new building should be considered as a high priority.

2. Develop separate library standards for teachers colleges, technical colleges, nursing colleges, and others according to program needs. Adequate government funding from appropriate sources should be required for these colleges to meet the standards.

3. Serve as the staff officer of the network planning committee to develop system requirements and specifications which can then be written into a PLANNING DOCUMENT and a REQUEST FOR PROPOSAL

4. Prepare a policy statement on resource sharing among higher education institutions to be endorsed by CHE.

5. Review the other recommendations made by this consultant and plan to implement those deemed appropriate.

Improvement of library and information resources and the development of PNGLINET require not only the support of the Government but also close cooperation among those in the library profession. Although the National Library Service is only one of the six major library resources in the country, it has a significant role to play in the formation of the PNGLINET. The responsibilities of the National Library Service in this endeavor should be recognized and properly defined.

The Library Council of PNG which was established by Cabinet directive in 1975 should, according to its charge, advise the Government on the importance of establishing PNGLINET and should actively solicit necessary government support in all sectors and at all levels.

At the time of the consultant's visit to Papua New Guinea, an unfortunate disagreement intensified between the National Library Service and the Library Council over the exact roles and responsibilities of each. On the positive side, both wish to exert more influence on national planning and development of library and information services; however, this conflict serves to undermine the goals both wish to pursue for the good of the country. Historically, both the National Library Service and the Library Council were established by Cabinet directives in 1975. In recent years, the National Library Service has sought to establish an Office of Libraries & Archives as a means to expand the authority of the National Library in the development of library and information services for the whole country. This approach, however, has not been supported by the Library Council for fear of over-centralization and bureaucratization. It is necessary that a reasonable solution to this controversy be found soon by the Government.

6. RECOMMENDATIONS AND JUSTIFICATIONS

In line with the project proposal and the terms of reference, the consultant submits the following recommendations, each with its justification, for review and possible a adoption by the

Commission for Higher Education and the Library Council of Papua New Guinea.

National Approaches

1. The CHE Secretariat should add a senior position, Library Services Coordinator, to plan and coordinate the development of the library and information resources in institutions of higher education in PNG:

Justification: Improving libraries in the 62 institutions of higher education involving many government departments and each of the 19 provincial government will require a full-time position with sufficient rank within the Secretariat of CHE.

2. The Coordinator should be advised by the Library Council and should work with the Department of Education, the National Library (or the yet to be established Office of Libraries and Archives), and other related government departments for the improvement of library and information resources in the nation's higher education institutions.

Justification: The Library Council was created by a Cabinet directive in 1975 to advise the Government on library and information services as well as cooperation among PNG libraries. The same directive also established the National Library Service. Both have significant roles to play in the overall improvement in the nation's library and information resources. The recent decision (118/90) by the National Executive Council to establish an Office of Libraries and Archives may result in the re-structuring of the National Library Service. The Coordinator should work with the new Office when it begins to function as well as with other related government agencies for broader interactions.

3. The Library Services Coordinator should draw up a national development plan for university and college libraries taking into consideration the recommendations made in this report.

Justification: There should be a plan for phased implementation of the recommendations made in this report after its acceptance and approval by CHE.

4. The National Library Service should play a key role in the development of libraries in government agencies, community and high schools, as well as public libraries in the National Capital District and in all the provinces which complement and support the development of libraries in higher education institutions.

Justification: In addition to the strength of its collections as major library and information resources in the nation, the National Library Service also provides valuable services to government agencies, community and high schools, public libraries, and the general citizenry.

5. The "Basic Standards for College Libraries" developed by the National Library Service (see Appendix 2) need to be re-examined and revised to upgrade minimum requirements for space, collections, services, staff, and funding as well as to add certain performance measurements. Different minimum standards may be needed for the various types of colleges.

Justification: The current standards should be enhanced to recognize the different library requirements for teachers colleges, technical colleges, nursing colleges, etc. and to include output performance measurements to encourage and assess qualitative improvement of these libraries.

6. A formula for funding libraries should be developed to ensure that even in difficult economic times, the libraries will not be stripped of minimum funding. The suggested criterion is that a minimum of 5% of the institution's operating budget should be spent for library resources (books, journals, audio-visual materials, etc.). To correct the long time neglect of the many college libraries in recent years, special funding from the Government should be specifically designated for library improvement.

Justification: The fact that most colleges currently provide little or no funding for acquisition of new library materials needs to be corrected. The identification of a fixed percentage of a college's operating budget for library acquisitions as an absolute minimum is necessary in times of financial crisis. The recommended level, 5%, is still less than the 6% committed at the University of Technology.

Development of PNGLNET

7. Adequate funding should be provided to those libraries which have been identified as having collections of major strength and recognized as centers of excellence. These national information resources within the education sector include the Main Library and Medical Library of the University of Papua New Guinea (UPNG), the Library of the University of Technology (Unitech), and the UPNG Goroka Teachers College. These libraries, each with strengths in certain subject areas—together with the National Library and the Administrative College Library—should be considered as the major building blocks of a proposed Papua New Guinea Library and Information Network (PNGLINET).

Justification: Adequate funding for the six major resource libraries should be considered a wise investment for the nation's future. There is little unnecessary duplication in the information resources in these libraries. Each tends to complement the others.

8. As shown in Diagram Ⅰ, "Building Blocks for a National Network of Library and Information Resources in PNG", each of these libraries could serve as the resource center for other libraries in the same field of specialization.

— The Main Library of UPNG should serve as the national resource center for Humanities, Law, Sciences, Social Sciences, and PNG collection.

— The Medical Library of UPNG should serve as the national resource center for Medical and Allied Health Sciences.

— The Library of Goroka Teachers College of UPNG should serve as the national resource center for Education, Behavioral Science and Curriculum Materials.

— The Library of Unitech should serve as the national resource center for Agriculture, Business, Engineering, and Technology.

— The National Library should serve as the national resource center for all government departments, as well as all public and school libraries in the Country. It should also be the main center for all government publications, official depository for PNG publications, and the National Audio-visual Materials Center.

— The Library of Administrative College should serve as the national resource center for Management Science, Public Policy and Administration, and Development Information.

Justification: Assigning special responsibilities to each of the six major resource libraries to serve as a building block in the formation of a national network of library and information resources affords a rational and cost-effective way to build a comprehensive information reservoir.

9. To house the growing library and information resources in these key libraries, adequate and functional library buildings with sufficient space for growth should be planned and constructed. These buildings should have temperature and humidity control to protect the collections and to provide a comfortable environment for their users. In preparation for computerization, adequate wiring for computers and electronic equipment (with provision for future growth and changes) should be included. Ample seating, preferably including a number of individualized study carrels, should be provided. Presently, all of the key libraries in higher education institutions need additional space. Special government funding is strongly recommended.

Justification: For the key resource libraries to properly carry out their responsibilities and fulfill their roles within the system, adequate and appropriate building facilities are needed.

10. For economical storage and preservation of less used research materials which must be retained, a central storage facility with high density compact shelving should be built to be used by all libraries. Multiple copies of storage items can be given to interested libraries or discarded. The collections in the facility should be identified in both the local catalog and the online union catalog for easy search and retrieval whenever needed. The planning for such a facility should begin as soon as possible by the Library Services Coordinator.

Justification: A central storage facility for less-used library materials is an economical way to cope with the continual growth in library and information resources in the major resource libraries.

Such a storage facility can be constructed at comparatively low cost to achieve considerable savings in per unit storage cost.

11. A well developed library systems software capable of networking for the key libraries identified in Recommendation 7 should be selected and installed. Three-year capital funding totaling K900,000 should be appropriated to purchase both the software and hardware for the six resource libraries in a network environment, and an annual operating budget of K100,000 (with inflationary adjustment each year) should be provided to maintain the network and make it accessible by computers from remote locations.

Justification: The experiences of developed countries in recent years have indicated that for effective networking of library resources, it is preferable to select one proven system for use by all libraries in the network. A number of library systems now available are capable of creating a central database while permitting each library to maintain a high degree of local autonomy.

12. There should be a national database of the library and information resources in the computerized PNGLINET using the MARC international format for bibliographic records. The National Library Service should establish a PNG MARC for use by all libraries for shared cataloging to create the online national union catalog and bibliographic database. It is recommended that the PNG MARC closely adhere to a major international standard, such as LC MARC, UK MARC, or AUSMARC, to facilitate utilization of records prepared elsewhere with little or no conversion required.

Justification: The creation and maintenance of an up-to-date online union catalog using standard MARC format is a high priority for effective sharing of library and information resources. The OCLC Online Computer Library Center's online shared cataloging system offers a desirable model for development.

13. The online national union catalog should contain the complete library and information resources (including books, serial titles and holdings information, audio-visual materials, indexed journal articles, archival materials, local databases, etc.) of the key libraries.

Justification: To maximize the usefulness of the union catalog, as many types of library and information resources as possible should be included. Other libraries should be encouraged to participate in the online national union catalog (See Recommendation 18).

14. PNGLINET should serve as the gateway to library and information resources outside the country. PACESAT and other advanced telecommunication technologies should be used to access world-wide databases, including Australian Bibliographic Network, the OCLC Online Computer Library Center, Medline, Dialog, etc.

Justification: Access to and searching of remote databases and information resources worldwide are already available in many of the key resources libraries. These should be expanded to take advantage of new developments in computer and telecommunication technologies.

15. At the appropriate stage of development for PNGLINET, a governing structure should be put in place to ensure full participation of all major resources libraries. The exact form of the governing structure and its composition should be decided by CHE in consultation with other related government agencies. The Library Services Coordinator may serve as the Executive Director of PNGLINET for day-to-day operations with an adequate operating budget and staffing.

Justification: This governing structure is necessary to ensure a smooth operation of PNGLINET. Adequate funding and staffing should be provided by the Government for effective implementation.

16. The selection of a fully developed and proven software package for the PNGLINET should be done by a committee of all participating libraries with the advice of an experienced and unbiased consultant. The needs and requirements of the network should be communicated through a "planning document" and a "request for proposal" prepared by the Committee.

Justification: With a number of excellent software packages now available, selection should be done openly, objectively, and rationally (offering opportunities for meaningful inputs by the institutions to be included). The needs and requirements of the network should be carefully documented. The service of an experienced consultant for the entire PNGLINET project is highly recommended to speed up the process and avoid costly mistakes.

17. For the development of information resources and services within each of the six sub-networks in Diagram I, there is a need to create a position of system librarian in each of the six resource libraries.

Justification: These positions are needed to develop and implement each of the sub networks under the overall network plan. Training or retraining of existing staff with knowledge and experience in library automation should be considered in meeting this staffing need.

18. Once PNGLINET becomes operational, provision should be made to extend access to other libraries. Procedures for inter-library lending and document delivery will need to be established. Opportunities-with central funding—should be made available in stages for libraries wishing to join PNGLINET as full participants.

Justification: There is a difference between "access" and "participant". To realize the maximum benefit of PNGLINET, it should be made accessible to any institution with means to access the network and use the resources. For the network and resources to expand, all libraries should be allow to participate as full members. As PNGLINET matures, it should become a network of all libraries and information resources in the country.

College and Other Academic Libraries

19. Because the library and information resources in most of the colleges are generally inadequate, major augmentation is needed to bring each to a minimum acceptable standard.

Justification: The obvious inadequacies of the college libraries, documented in Appendices 3, 4 and 5, justify the urgency of remedial measures.

20. The transition of the community-school teachers colleges from a two-year certificate program to a three-year diploma program requires that the libraries of these colleges be greatly improved. Major remedial infusions of funding for additional staff and information resources should be considered a high priority for a period of five years. Minimum quantitative standards and performance measurements should be established and enforced. The recommendations made at the Library Workshop, 18 – 24 March 1990, by the participants from all teachers colleges under the sponsorship of the Teacher Education Division of the Department of Education were well thought-out and should be implemented.

Justification: The resolution adopted at the 1990 Annual Principals' Conference of the teachers colleges further expressed the grave need for upgrading library and information resources in these colleges.

21. Most of the libraries in nursing schools, technical colleges, and other special colleges show signs of long-standing neglect and generally are impoverished. Major efforts and actions are urgently needed to improve them. In working with appropriate government departments, the Library Services Coordinator of CHE should develop guidelines and minimum standards for these libraries and seek annual funding for them.

Justification: As a result of the lack of funding and staffing, compounded by a long period of neglect, most of these libraries have little left to be called a library. The quality of education in these colleges is clearly in doubt. There is definite need for greater attention from the respective government departments to provide adequate funding for library improvement.

22. To realize economies of scale for cost-effective operation, many of the small colleges with inferior programs and library resources should be merged into larger units or be incorporated with the universities or better established institutions.

Justification: This action is necessary to rectify some of the problems found in PNG colleges. It is recognized, however, that many of these colleges are run by different church agencies and may find merger impractical or unacceptable.

23. Staffing goals should be a minimum of one trained librarian (with a library diploma or certificate) and two library technicians for every teachers college library and a minimum of one

trained librarian and one library technician for each of the technical, nursing, and special colleges. These goals should be achieved before 1997.

Justification: Without at least one qualified librarian in each college, little improvement can be anticipated. Many of the weakest libraries visited by the consultant had no full-time librarian responsible for book selection, ordering, cataloging, advising users, teaching library skills, etc. This situation must be rectified as soon as possible. Some colleges have employed a lecturer-librarian to oversee the library. This is acceptable if the lecturer librarian has the required librarian qualifications and devotes at least two-thirds time to library work.

24. The position classification and salary scale for library staff should be uniform and comparable to teaching staff with equivalent educational requirements and qualifications. There need to be clear career paths for promotion and movement for both professional and support library staff. The staff classification and fringe benefits in college libraries should be made equitable with university libraries.

Justification: The disparities in position classification and salary for library staff are found between university libraries and the National Library, between universities and colleges, and between librarians, and teachers in colleges. Staff members of the National Library also receive no. housing. This causes, morale problems and discourages the recruitment of the best people to the library profession.

25. Opportunities for in-service training and continuing education should be made available to college librarians to acquire new knowledge and skills for modern library and information services. There should be funding and provision for educational leaves by CHE to library staff through open selection. The existing programs in the UPNG Department of Library and Information Studies should be expanded, with necessary funding, to meet such needs.

Justification: The improvement of library and information services in the nation requires a steady supply of well educated and trained library personnel at every level. It also requires programs and opportunities for in-service training and continuing education to upgrade the knowledge and skills in a rapidly changing profession. The UPNG Department of Library and Information Studies has done an outstanding job but is in need of greater financial support.

26. For each teachers college library, a minimum of 300 new books, and 20 audio-visual materials of relevance to the curriculum should be added to the collection each year and at least 50 journal subscriptions maintained. For each technical, nursing, and special college library, the minimum requirement should be adding 150 new books and 10 audio-visual materials of relevance to the curriculum each year and maintenance of 25 journal subscriptions. These materials should be carefully selected (rather than happenstance gifts) to support the curriculum and should be cataloged for easy access. Funding for acquisitions and cataloging are critically needed to remedy the outdated collections found in most of these libraries.

Justification: About 90% of the collections in college libraries were found to be outdated. These minimum requirements will assure new and relevant materials for the libraries (and the faculty and students whom they serve) which are badly in need, of major infusions of new resources. The rationale for not basing the recommended annual additions on student numbers is because of the small enrollment of many colleges. The reading requirements of a college of 60 students will not differ much from a college of 200 students in terms of the range of library resources needed. In recognition of the differing needs of teachers colleges and other types of colleges, at least two standards are suggested.

27. Centralized acquisitions and cataloging for college libraries should be explored to afford savings in both manpower and costs. For example, many library vendors abroad can provide attractive discounts for volume acquisitions. They can also provide cataloging service at little or no additional cost. With the establishment of PNGLINET, centralized and shared cataloging services can ease the manpower scarcity in small libraries. The National Library, in recent years, has provided central acquisitions and cataloging service for public and school libraries. This useful service can perhaps be expanded to tertiary, libraries.

Justification: Centralized acquisitions can reduce costs and facilitate the cataloging process. Centralized cataloging helps to standardize cataloging practices while facilitating the creation of a national bibliographic database.

28. To make better use of audio-visual materials, all college libraries should have a room equipped with appropriate A-V equipment. Teachers should be encouraged to use the room and to incorporate A-V materials into their instruction. The room and equipment should be well maintained. The strong A-V collection of the National Library should be expanded and used as the resource collection to augment local collections.

Justification: A functional college library should also be the learning resources center where a wealth of audio-visual materials are available for teaching and learning. Ideally, such a resource center should be an integral part of the library, and the instructional program.

29. Many of the library buildings in colleges badly need repair or expansion. Many require new and additional equipment and furniture. A survey should be conducted by the Library Services Coordinator to determine such needs, and funding for the improvements should be provided.

Justification: Sufficient library space and adequate library facilities will enhance the library's ability to provide quality services. Based on the survey results, a five-to ten-year plan should be developed for phased implementation.

Complementary Library And Information Services Nationally

30. The Library Services Coordinator of CHE should develop a system for the collection of annual statistics and other relevant information. These data should be stored in a computer and analyzed for management purposes. A directory of library and information resources in higher education institutions should be published annually.

Justification: Gathering and analyzing useful statistics and information is necessary for planning and management. The publication of resources directories would make these resources better known and better used.

31. Similarly, statistical data and other relevant information for all government, public, special, and school libraries should be collected and kept by the National Library. Statistics for college and university libraries collected by CHE may also be included. A national directory of these library and information resources should be published regularly. Such data compilations are valuable planning and management tools locally, regionally, and nationally.

Justification: It is a basic function of the National Library to gather this type of information and disseminate it through the publication of directories and other guides.

32. To encourage and provide incentives for sharing resources, those libraries with a net inter-library lending (i.e. number of items loaned to others minus number of items borrowed from other libraries) should be reimbursed for the cost of handling and mailing from a special fund established by the Government.

Justification: It has been a common and effective practice in many countries to compensate and encourage resource libraries to lend more of their materials to other libraries. The reimbursement method enables these libraries to partially offset the costs of lending materials to others.

33. The National Library Service and the Department of Education should promote indigenous publications in all subjects, especially for children and young, adult audiences.

Justification: This is needed to preserve and develop appreciation of the rich cultural traditions of the country through the promotion of indigenous literature and publications.

34. Instruction in library and learning skills should be a part of the regular college curriculum and available to all students. This is especially important for students at teachers college. They will be transmitting these skills to future generations. It is recommended that CHE and the Department of Education develop necessary guidelines and implementation plans.

Justification: Library literacy is an important part of education and will foster independent studies and lifelong learning-essential skills in an age of rapid technological change.

35. Teachers college libraries should have a model collection for school libraries similar to that maintained by the National Library Service. It is important that future teachers become familiar with such a collection. Separate funding should be provided by the Department of Education to establish and maintain such a collection in each teachers college library upon request.

Justification: This will help prepare future school teachers to make better use of school libraries and resources in their teaching. Such a model collection should be available to students in the demonstration school of each college.

36. The Goroka Teachers College Library should establish and maintain a model collection for high school libraries. Future high school teachers should be familiar with such a collection. They should also familiar with the selected annual booklists for high schools prepared by the National Library.

Justification: The value of high school libraries, for both resources and services, should be instilled early in the minds of the future teachers. The creation of a sense of appreciation for reading and awareness of the world of printed materials suitable for high school students should be an important part of teachers' education.

37. Based on local circumstances, the library in some of the UPNG Extension Centers located in a province could ideally be established as a cultural center combining the public library, the vocational center library, and the University Center Library into one joint facility. Since the funding of all three is borne by the provincial government, such a shared facility will eliminate unnecessary duplication and be more cost-effective. Both the National Library Service and UPNG Library should assist in the design and establishment of these cultural centers. Cooperation with other libraries in the vicinity of the cultural center should be encouraged also.

Justification: In some provincial towns where the public library, the vocational center library, and the University Extension Centers are in close proximity. All are poorly funded by the provincial government. Combining these will enrich the resources and services available to the community.

附录1：咨询和面谈的人士

Appendix 1：Individuals Consulted/Interviewed

In Port oresby：

The Commission for Higher Education（P. O. Box 5117，Boroko）
Dr. Naomi T. Martin，Chairperson.
Mr. Ruben San Mateo，Executive Director of the Secretariat and Deputy Chairperson
The Library Council
Dr. Moseley Moramoro，OBE，Chair
Dr. John Evans，Executive Secretary
Department of Education（P. S. A Haus, P. O.，Boroko）
Mr. J. Tetaga，Secretary for Education
Mr. M. B. Peril，Deputy Secretary
Mr. P. Baki，First Assistant Secretary-Standards
Mr. W. Penias，First Assistant Secretary-General Educational Services
Mr. L. Taita，First Assistant Secretary-Special Educational Services
Mr. C. Runawery，Assistant Secretary-Policy Planning and Budget
Port Moresby In-service College.
Mr. J. Schofield，Principal
Ms. Taita Aihi，Librarian
University of Papua New Guinea
Administration：
Dr. John D. Lynch，Vice-Chancellor，
Prof. Api. C. Maha，Dean，Faculty of Education
Mr. Md. Abdul Mannan，Director，Plannmg & Implementation Unit
Mr. Gervk John，Acting Director，Extension Studies
Michael Somare Library
Ms. Florence J. Griffin，University Librarian
Mr. Elesallah Matatier，Periodicals Librarian
Mr. Joe Naguwean，New Guinea Collection Librarian
Mr. Joe K. Nom，Acting Archivist
Mr. Kametan Parkop，Library Officer
Ms. Eve Rannells，Liaw Librarian
Medical Library
Ms. Rhonda Lakele Eva，Medical Librarian
Department of Library and Information Studies
Dr. John A. Evans，Head
Mr. N. Amarasinghe，Senior Lecturer
Ms. Margaret Obi，Senior Lecturer
Mr. Ismael Isikel，Lecturer
Mr. Sam Kaima，Lecturer
Ms. Leah Kalamoroh，Teaching Fellow
National Library
Mr. Neil Nicholls，National Librarian
Mr. Daniel Paraide，Deputy National Librarian
Mr. Jim Maguire，Government Libraries Advisor
Ms. Nancy Lutton，Chief Archivist

Department of Agriculture and Livestock
Mr. Samuel B. Lahis, Director, Agricultural Education and Training
Ms. Bonnie Ontimo, Librarian
Department of Health
Ms. Rose Puipui, Librarian
College of Allied Health Sciences
Ms. Iboda Gibalu, Librarian
Department of Fisheries and Marine Resources
Mr. Ovia Tarube, Principal Education & Training Officer
Administrative College
Mr. Muepen Forepe, Assistant Librarian

In Rabaul:

UPNG East New Britain University Center
Ms. Mary Toliman, Director
Nonga School of Nursing
Sister Lucy Kotap, Principal
Gaulim Teachers College (United Church)
Samson Lowa, Principal
Ms. Eare Forova, Librarian
Kabaleo OLSH Teachers College (Catholic)
Mr. William Laisuit, Deputy Principal
Rabaul. Public Library
Ms. Jessie Kuamin, Book Mobile librarian
St. Paul Teachers College (Catholic)
Mr. Kubod Laiew, Deputy Principal
Mr. Joe Lipu, Lecturer and Librarian
Vudal Agriculture College
Mr. Pisou Popen, Principal
Mr. John Duigu, Deputy Principal
Ms. Flora Ungaia, Librarian

In Lae:

Balob Teachers College (Lutheran)
Mr. Kiane Towandong, Principal
Mr. Bert McNair, Deputy Principal
Mr. Anson Dom, Acting Librarian
Mr. Tymil Lyakin, Lecturer-Librarian
Forest Research Institute Library
Ms. Miriam Baru, Librarian
Lae Public Library
Mr. Bonny Ikon, Acting Head
Ms. Miriam Daniel, Library Officer
Ms. Lucy Sevese, Library Officer
Mr. Hinagere Upeguto, Library Officer
Lae School of Nursing
Mr. Deveni Temu, Volunteer
Papua New Guinea University of Technology
Prof. S. H. Pearse, Vice Chancellor
Mr. Deveni Temu, University Librarian

Ms. Selina Owen, Deputy University Librarian
Mr. Lucas Dosung, Chief Cataloger
Barrah I-Nuli, Librarian (Cataloging)
Ms. Geeta Parmeshwar, Assistant Librarian (Cataloging)
Raphael Topagur, Assistant Librarian
Ms. Mary Yamega, Assistant Librarian
Liklik Buk Information Center
Ms. Juanita Sabva, Information Assistant
Lae Technical College
Mr. Ebe V. Maeale, Principal
Mr. Ernie A. Saldia, Deputy Prihcipai (Academic)
Mr. Tini Wowis, Librarian

In Wewak:

St Benedict's Teachers College (Catholic)
Mr. Andrew Simpson, Principal
Mr. Leonard Kinminja, Deputy Principal
Sister Bonnie Clarke, Librarian
Passam National High School
Mr. L. R. Dissanayake, Lecturer-Librarian

In Madang:

Madang Public Library
Ms. Elizabeth Bomai, Provincial Library Officer
Madang Teachers College
Mr. David Austin, Principal
Ms. Gandy Yakam, Lecturer-Librarian
Ms. Emma William, Library Technician
Madang Technical College
Mr. Patrol Maino, Principal
UPNG Madang University Center
Mr. Greg Murphy, Director

In Goroka:

UPNG Goroka Teachers College
Mr. Fred Iakopya, Acting Pro-Vice Chancellor and Principal
Ms. Rena Khan, College Librarian
Mr. John Thomas, Assistant Librarian
PNG Institute of Medical Research
Ms. Barbara Joyce, Acting Librarian
Melanesian Institute
Ms. Monica Tiotam, Librarian
Goroka Public Library
Mrs. Mamera Fore, Librarian
Miss Janet Omahe, Assistant Librarian
Goroka Technical College
Mr. Bruce Jowa, Principal
Mrs. Dora Nugi, Librarian

In Mount Hagen:
 Highlands Agricultural College
 Mr. Phillip B. Senat, Deputy Principal
 Mr. Edward Edawi, Librarian
 Holy Trinity Teachers College (Catholic Church)
 Br. Peter Gilfedder, Principal
 Br. William Shaw, Lecturer-Librarian
 Ms. Kaipi Ogil, Librarian
 Mt Hagen Technical College
 Mr. Richard Green, Principal
 Nazarene College of Nursing (Nazarene Church)
 ST. Carol Bett, Nursing Tutor/Acting Principal

附录2: 巴布亚新几内亚的国家图书馆服务
Appendix 2: National Library Service of Papua New Guinea
BASIC STANDARDS FOR COLLEGE LIBRARIES

Role

The principal function of any library in an educational institution is to support and complement the curriculum. The college library has an additional role in fostering the reading habit which students may have discovered at community school. The library will often be the students only access to books and reading material. Students need this access if they are to maintain their literacy skills and if the reading habit is not to be lost irrevocably. Libraries should not be looked upon as an extra. They should be seen as an integral part of the college structure. The students learning process should not be united to the purely vocational skills taught at the college.

1. Library Facilities

A library room a least the size of a classroom that can be used for library activities.

ⅰ) Every college should have as a minimum provision the basic works and supply high library building.

ⅱ) Study space for 25 students or 10% of the enrolment whichever is greater.

2. Stock Provision

A minimum level of book provision should be 5 good quality books per student. The material must be selected very carefully in order that it best meets student needs. The National Library Service is prepared to assist in selecting suitable materials.

3. Library Use

ⅰ) A minimum of one hour per week per class.

ⅱ) Library to be open for pupils at lunch time and for one hour after classes.

4. Staffing

ⅰ) That a qualified librarian that is someone holding a Diploma in Library Studies or the equivalent should be employed to run the library.

ⅱ) As an interim measure one instructor to be appointed teacher librarian to look after book ordering, planning library activities and fund-raising.

ⅲ) All instructors to be involved with the library with each instructor taking his/her class into the library for at least one hour each week.

5. Training Instructors

ⅰ) All college instructors should receive a thorough training in organizing and using a library whilst at college.

ⅱ) Attendance at provincial workshops held by regional school library advisers should be obligatory for the designated instructor from each college involved.

6. Book Funds

To build and maintain a collection of 5 books per head at least K10 per head per year would be needed. The library should be funded jointly by the National Department of Education and the college itself.

附录3：六所主要图书馆的图书资讯资源

Appendix 3: Library and Information Resources in the Six Major Libraries

Library	Location	Agency	Collections			Material Budget	No. of Staff	Computer Applications
			Books	Journals	A–V			
National Library	Port Moresby	Education Department	45,000	400	4,500	N/A J	80	Cataloging, Nat'l Bib., CD-ROM Search-Bookbank, BIP Plus, Bibliofile, ERIC, Online Search-Dialog, Local Databases
University of PNG Main Library	Port Moresby	Comm. for Higher Educ.	400,000	1,500	N/A	K590,000	N/A	Cataloging, Circulation, COM, Microfiche Catalog, Online Search-Dialog, Local Databases
Medical Library	Port Moresby		46,000	380	N/A	N/A		Cataloging, COM microfiche catalog, Online Search of Medline
Goroka Teachers College	Goroka		80,000	300	2,000	K70,000	13	Cataloging, COM Microfiche Catalog, CD-ROM Search-ERIC plus Bibliofile, Online Search-Dialog
University of Technology	Lae		120,000	2,000	2,400	N/A		CD-ROM Catalog, Online Search, CD-ROM Search
Administrative College	Port Moresby	Personnel Management	46,240	646	305	K27,000	12	Nil

附录4：师范学院图书馆的图书资讯资源

Appendix 4: Library and Information Resources in the Teachers College Libraries[①]

Library	Location	Agency	Collections			Material Budget	No. of Staff	Computer Applications
			Books	Journals	A–V			
Balob T. C.	Lae	Lutheran/Anglican	19,500	30	N/A.	K 3,000	2	Cataloging and word processing
Dauli T. C	Tari	Evangelical Alliance	32,000	25	100	K 1,900	3	Nil
Holy Trinity T. C.	Mt. Hagen	Catholic	12,000	41	N/A	K 4,800	2	Cataloging, Circulation, and Online Search
Gaulim T. C.	Rabaul	United Church	4,000	4	N/A	K 2,000	2	Nil
Kabaleo T. C. (for Women)	Rabaul	Catholic	5,000	8	N/A	K 700	0.5	Nil
Madang T. C.	Madang	Dept. of Educ.	24,000	26	N/A	K 2,500	2	Cataloging
Port Moresby Inservice College	Port Moresby	Dept. of Educ.	40,000	82	N/A	K 6,900	5	Nil
St. Benedict's T. C.	Wewak	Catholic	3,000	28	N/A	K 2,000	2	Cataloging, Circulation, and Online Search
St. Paul's T. C. (for Men)	Rabaul	Catholic	2,719	7	N/A	K 2,000	1	Nil
Sonoma Adventist T. C.	Rabaul	Seventh Day Adventist	5,300	17	N/A	K 1,500	0.5	Nil

---

① Notes: All these colleges have an enrollment from a low of 119 to a high of 327. The average is 178. Students are admitted after the completion of 10th grade and the duration of study has just been expanded from two years to three years.

附录5：其他院校的图书资讯资源

Appendix 5：Library and Information Resources in Other College Libraries

Library	Location	Agency	Collections			Material Budget	No. of Staff	Computer Applications
			Books	Journals	A – V			
Agriculture/Fishery/Forestry:								
Highland Agri. Coll	Lae	Agri. Dept.	3,000	15	N/A	0	1	Has PCs in Library
Popondetta Agri. Coll.	Popondetta		10,160	35	N/A	0	1	Nil
Sepik Agri. Coll. (closed in –1990)	Maprik		8,503	N/A	N/A	K–3,000	1	Nil
Vudal Agri. Coll	Rabaul		7,000	N/A	N/A	K 200	3	Nil
National Fisheries Coll.	Kavieng	Fisheries Dept.	6,077	N/A	82	0	2	Nil
PNG Forestry. College	Bulolo	Forestry Dept.	16,000	N/A	N/A		1	Nil
Nursing:								
Lae School of Nursing	Lae	Health Dept.	N/A	N/A	N/A	0	0	Nil
Nazarene School of Nursing	Mt. Hagen	Nazarene Church	1,000		N/A		0	Nil
Rabaul School of Nursing	Rabaul	Health Dept	N/A	N/A		0	0	Nil
College of Allied Health Sci.	Port. Moresby	Health Dept.	1,400	0	N/A	0	1	Nil
Technical:								
Goroka Tech. Coll.	Goroka	Educ. Dept,	1,500	0			0	Nil
Lae Tech. Coll.	Lae	Educ. Dept.	7,110,	1	0	0	1	Nil
Madang Tech. Coll.	Madang	Educ. Dept.	N/A	N/A	N/A	0	0	Nil
Mt. Hagen Tech. Coll	Mt. Hagen	Educ. Dept.	2,500	0	0	0	0	Nil
Others:								
Civil Aviation Training Coll.	Port Moresby.	Civil Avi. Dept.	1,700	40	0	K 5,000	1	Nil
Divine, Word Inst.	Madang	Divine Word Inst.	17,000	40	N/A	K12,000	2.5	Nil
Elcom Training Coll	Port Moresby	Elect. Comm	1,500	62	450	0	1	Nil
Pacific Adventist Coll.	Port Moresby	Seventh Day Adventist	25,653	152	1,400	K20,000	5	Catalog Cards & labels,
Police Traininjg. Coll.	Port. Moresby	Police Dept	9,890	25	N/A	K 6,500	2	Nil
PNC Defence Force Coll	Lae	Defence Dept	5,716	N/A	0		1	Nil

附录 6: 参考文献

Appendix 6: References

Bacchus, M. Kazim. *Educational Policy and Development Strategy in the Third World.* Aldershot, Avebury, 1987. 233 p.

Baker, Leigh R. *Development of University Libraries in Papua New Guinea.* Metuchen, N. J.: Scarecrow Press, 1981. 399 p.

Bray, Mark. Education and Decentralization in Less Developed Countries: A Comment on General Trends, Issues and Problems. With Particular Reference to Papua New Guinea. Comparative Education, V, 21, No: 2 (1985), pp. 183 – 195.

Bray, Mark. *Educational Planning in a Decentralized System*: The Papua New Guinean Experience. Port Moresby: University of Papua New Guinea-Press, 1984. 159 p.

Butler, Alan. "PNG information Network: A Brief Report on, Progress." 1985. 2 pp.

Butler, Alan. "Training Librarians in the University of Papua New Guinea," *Information development.* V. 2, No. 4 (Oct. 1986), pp. 231 – 233.

Calvert, Philip: "In Defence of Standards: High School Library Standards in Papua New Guinea." Information Development, V. 2, No. 4 (Oct. 1986), pp. 234 – 241.

Commissions for Higher Education. National Higher Education Plan. Port Moresby Commission for Higher Education, 1990. 95 p.

Diagnostic Studies on Educational Management Country Studies: Papua New Guineas. Bangkok: UNESCO Regional Office for Education in Asia and the Pacific, 1984. 27 p.

Eva, Rhonda Lakele. "Prospects of Developing a Medical Library Network in Papua New Guinea." Masters thesis presented to the Department of Information and Library Studies, University College of Wales, 1991. 143 p.

Jackson, Miles M. *Teachers College Libraries in Papua New Guinea. A Report for the Asia Foundation. The Library Services and the Teacher Education Divisions of the Department of Education, Government of Papua New Guinea.* Honolulu: Graduate School of Library Studies, University of Hawaii at Manoa, 1981. 45 p.

Kakaw, Otto. "National Libraries, in a Time of Change: Viewpoint From a Developing Country—Papua New-Guinea." Paper presented at IFLA General Conference, Sydney, Australia, 1988. 15 p.

Library Workshop, 18 – 24 March 1990. [Report]. Port Moresby, Teacher Education Division, National Department of Education, Ministry of Education, 1990. 75 p.

Lim, Edward Huck Tee. "Strategic Plan for the Automation of the National Library of Papua New Guinea: Consultancy Report." Melbourne, 1990. 41 p.

Lim, Edward Huck Tee. "The Training Needs in Information Technology of the Staff of the Department of Library and Information Studies, University of Papua New Guinea: Consultancy Report." Melbourne: 1990. 15 p.

McNamara, Vin. *The Future Direction of Community School Teacher Education.* Teacher Education Research Project, The Unit Four Task Force Report Port Moresby: Department of Education, 1989. 113 p.

National Archives and Public Records Services of Papua New Guinea. *An Introductory Brochure.* Boroko, 1988. 11 p.

National Library Service of Papua New Guinea. *A Report, 1978 – 1985.* Waigani: National Library Service, 1986. 48 p.

National Library Service of Papua New Guinea. *Papua New Guinea Directory of Information Sources in Science and Technology.* Compiled by Jim Maguire. Waigani: National Library Service,

1991, [20] pp.

Ngabung, Paul. "Papua New Guinea." *In Funding For Higher Education in Asia and the Pacific: Strategies to Increase Cost Efficiency and Attract Additional Financial Support*, Bangkok: UNESCO Principal Regional Office for Asia and the Pacific, 1991. pp. 195 – 209.

Papua New Guinea. "National Library and Archives Bill 1990." Draft of 29/5/91. Port Moresby, 1991. 13 p.

Papua New Guinea. "National Policy on Library and Information Services." Draft 5 – 1.07.91. Port Moresby, 1991. [28] pp.

Swatridge, Colin. *Delivering the Goods, Education as Cargo in Papua New Guinea*. Manchester: Manchester University Press, 1985. 163 p.

University of Papua New Guinea. *Project: Strengthening of Extension Studies Programme in the University of Papua New Guinea*. Port Moresby: UPNG, 1991. 37 p.

University of Papua New Guinea, Extension Studies. *Handbook of Courses*. Port Moresby: UPNG, 1991. 34 p.

Wijasuriya, D. E. K. *A Library Development Plan for Papua New Guinea*. Port Moresby: 1990. 113 p.

(Printed at the National Research Institute Printshop, 1991).

5. OCLC 联机与光盘编目概论（节选）[①]
OCLC Compact Disk and Online Cataloging (extract)

第二章 图书馆编目的自动化
Chapter II Automated Cataloging in Libraries

At the request of Prof. Diao Weihan, I am very pleased to write this chapter on the history of library automation with a special focus on the development of automated cataloging in libraries since the 1960s. In this chapter, I will briefly review the history of library automation, describe the importance of cataloging in the total arena of library automation, take a special look at the demand for and education of cataloging librarians, and, finally, project the future development of library automation as we enter into the 21st century. Since I have been a library administrator for most of my forty years of library career, I will take a macro-view of the subject and leave the theoretical and technical details of automated cataloging to Prof. Diao. Since in Chapter One, Mr. Andrew Wang of OCLC well and completely described the OCLC Online Computer Library Center and its key services in online cataloging, resource sharing, and CatCD, I will try not to overlap with his writing on the significant works done by and contributions of OCLC in the development of automated cataloging.

2.1 Historical View of Library Automation

2.1.1 Pioneering concept in library automation

True library automation did not begin until the dispersion of modem computers. However, the earliest concept of an automated library was described by Vannevar Bush, Director of the U.S. Office of Scientific Research and Development, as early as 1945 before computers were born. Writing in the *Atlantic Monthly* in July 1945[②], Bush pioneered the concept of an automated library which he described as a "Memex" (or a memory extender).

> Memex is a device in which are stored books, records, and communications and which is mechanized so that it may be consulted with exceeding speed and flexibility... On the top are slanting translucent screens on which material can be projected for convenient reading. There are a keyboard and a set of buttons and levers.[③]

Although Bush foresaw microfilm as the storage medium, he had already envisioned the possibility of an automated or virtual library with machines providing information retrieval. In fact about the same time as his writing, development of early models of computers was underway at both the University of Pennsylvania in the U.S. and the University of Manchester in England. In 1947, the Bell Labs invented the transistor which allowed a large amount of information to be handled by small, inexpensive devices that eventually replaced vacuum tubes. This major breakthrough enabled the development of small-sized computers with greater speed and capacity

---

[①] 该著作由刁维汉、王行仁、李华伟编著，华东师范大学出版社 1999 年出版，所节选的第 2 章由李华伟编写。
[②] Bush, Vannevar (1945). As We May Think. *Atlantic Monthly.* 1945, 176 (1): 101–108
[③] Ibid., p. 107.

some decades later.① Since then, progress in computer development, including programming languages and software, advanced rapidly.

While the first generation of computers was under development, the Library of Congress began to mechanize its operations. In the 1940s, it installed an electrical accounting equipment for use in billing and payroll and in the tabulation unit of the Card Division. In 1948, it participated in the first public transmission of data by Ultrafax in which television and photography were combined to transmit information through the air at 186 000 miles a second. On October 21, 1948, Ultrafax transmitted the entire 1047 pages of the novel *Gone with the Wind* across the city of Washington from the old Wardman Park Hotel to a screen in the Library's Coolidge Auditorium in two minutes and twenty-one seconds. In January 1958, The Library took its first major steps toward a general program of automated information retrieval with the establishment of its Committee on Mechanized Information Retrieval.②

In the 1960s, computer technology and availability had advanced to the point that it was possible to build library applications.

2.1.2 Early developments in the 1960s

In the 1960s, several library projects in the application of computers were undertaken and many of them had significant impacts on library automation thereafter.

At the Library of Congress, the *Annual Report of the Librarian of Congress* for 1961 stated that "a completely new mechanized approach may be the ultimate answer, but there are possible intermediate systems that could eventually mature into full consideration."③ A report. *Automation at the Library of Congress*, written by a team of experts led by Gilbert King was issued in late 1963.④ In 1964, an IBM 1401 computer was leased and installed and in 1965, a 110-page report authored by Henriette D. Avram, titled "A Proposed Format for a Standardized Machine-Readable Record", was widely distributed and became the basis for the MARC (Machine-Readable Cataloging) Format. Between 1966 and 1968, sixteen major American libraries were invited to participate in the MARC Project and to receive reels of tape containing bibliographic records on a weekly basis. These libraries could use the tapes to catalog their books and to print their own catalog cards. Based on experience from the pilot project. LC designed an extended character set for roman alphabet languages and adopted a refined. MARC Ⅱ format. Toward the end of the 1960s, LC also launched a "retrospective conversion" project to convert its earlier cataloging records to machine-readable form.

While much of the excitement was at LC, there were other significant developments in various parts of the U.S. The formation of the Ohio College Library Center (known as OCLC) in 1967 by a group of colleges and universities in Ohio was one of most successful examples. Detailed discussion of OCLC's development, accomplishments, and contributions were given by Andrew Wang in Chapter One.

Two other notable developments in the 1960s were the creation of the Medical Literature Analysis and Retrieval System (MEDLARS) by the National Library of Medicine and the use of computers by major indexing and abstracting producers, such as the Chemical Abstracts Service and Engineering Index, to store and manipulate very large indexing and abstracting databases and to produce printed indexes and abstracts in a timely manner.

2.1.3 The development of online and shared cataloging

On August 26, 1971, the Ohio University Libraries entered the world's first cataloging record

---

① Duval, everly K. and Main, Linda (1992). *Automated Library Systems: A Librarian's Guide and Teaching Manual*. Weastport, CT and London: Meckler, pp. 16–17.

② Rohrbach, Peter T, (1985). *Find: Automation at the Library of Congress, the First Twenty-five Years and Beyond*, Washington, DC: Library of Congress.

③ Ibid., (1985).

④ Ibid., (1985).

online into OCLC's new system. The event marked a beginning in online and shared cataloging by a group of libraries at different locations regardless of distance. Shared, online cataloging has many obvious merits:

* It creates an online union catalog with holdings information for each library that owns a publication. Such a union catalog will facilitate easy identification of needed publications for interlibrary loans (resource sharing).

* Once a bibliographic record is entered, it can be used by other libraries for copy cataloging and thereby reduces duplication of effort, speeds up cataloging, and saves much of the cataloging costs.

* It standardizes cataloging formats and procedures and promotes the exchange of bibliographic records.

* Machine-readable records will form the basis for other computerized library functions such as circulation, acquisition, serials control, and an online public access catalog (OPAC).

* The OPAC platform can also be used by other compatible electronic databases for the convenience of information search and retrieval.

2.1.4. The development of Online Public Access Catalogs (OPACs)

In the 1960s, a number of libraries began experimenting with the concept of an online public access catalog. These early attempts provided very limited access and were unable to replace the time honored card catalogs. However, in subsequent decades, more and more refined OPACs came into being. In the early 1970s, Ohio State University Libraries had already introduced a fairly sophisticated online circulation system and from this it developed one of the first OPACs with a broad range of access points in the mid 1970s. Through its OPAC, accesses were available by author, title, a combination of author and title, and call number. Subject access was added in 1978, and provisions for cross-references were in planning. Refinements were made, and strategies became more complex as the system was revised and updated with advanced technology. Eventually, an online authority structure was devised, and a cross-reference display was included. These developments foreshadowed the intense activity of online public access catalog development in libraries in the 1980s. ①

The early development of an OPAC at Ohio State University Libraries was considered as an outgrowth of its circulation system. However, OPACs developed in other libraries took different paths. For examples, the OPACs of the Minnesota State University System Project for Automated Library Systems (MSUS/PALS) and the MELVYL of the University of California System wide Division of Library Automation were new designs, each with its own unique strengths. This development enabled an OPAC to become the core component of an integrated library automation system that included acquisitions, serials, cataloging, and circulation.

Throughout the 1980s, a number of user studies were conducted to determine the needs and expectations of OPAC users. The most notable of these were studies sponsored by the then Council on Library Resources (now named. Council on Library and Information Resources) in 1982. Through system monitoring, patron interviews, self-administered surveys of users/nonusers of online catalogs, system simulation, online controlled retrieval tests, and data collection by staff and expert observations, various aspects of user behavior were carefully examined. After analyzing such components as language used, screen design, access points, format, and contents of records to be displayed, the studies groups made the following eight recommendations: on the basic,

---

① Miller, Susan L. (1980), The Ohio State University Libraries Online Catalog. In: *Closing the Catalog*. Edited by D. Kaye Gapen and Bonnie Juergens. Phoenix, AZ: Oryx Press, pp. 79 – 84.

features of OPACs. ①②③④

* Author-title-subject access;
* Bibliographic details and availability for interlibrary loans;
* Attached printers;
* Dial-up access from a personal computer outside the library which frees the user from visiting the library;
* Access to all formats, i. e. books, periodicals, musicals, etc. ;
* Contents, i. e. , summaries and abstracts;
* browsing capability, and
* Boolean searching capability.

Almost all the above features and more are available in OPACs today. With the advance of the Internet, the World-wide Web (WWW), and other new technological changes in recent years, we have seen and can expect more refinements to make OPACs easier and friendlier to use by non-trained users.

2.2 The Importance of Cataloging in Library Automation

2.2.1 Cataloging has been the center piece of library automation

It has long been recognized that shared cataloging is a key component of any integrated library automation system; moreover, an examination of existing systems reveals that the work done in cataloging creates the necessary bibliographic record for other system components from acquisitions to circulation, to serial control, and, most important, to the online public access catalog. A well constructed bibliographic database in standardized machine-readable format facilitates information search and retrieval in addition to the use of the record as a basis for acquisitions arid serial control.

With the implementation of automated library systems, the overwhelming majority of libraries have sought to convert all their bibliographic records from non-machine readable form—such as catalog cards, book catalogs, or microform catalogs—to machine-readable form. This operation is called "retrospective conversion." For a library with a large collection, such conversion may be very costly and time-consuming but is considered necessary to enhance the value of an online public access catalog.

2.2.2 The rise of bibliographic utilities

To facilitate online cataloging, establish online union catalogs, and conduct retrospective conversion, a number of so called "bibliographic utilities" came into being. The best known of these is OCLC-an unquestionable true pioneer in online shared cataloging.

As defined by William Saffady, "bibliographic utilities" are organizations that "maintain large bibliographic databases and offer various products and services to subscribers who access them on an online, timesharing basis. The databases maintained by most bibliographic utilities are essentially online union catalogs."⑤ In general, the bibliographic utilities acquire their cataloging records in machine-readable form in the following three ways:

(1) From the Library of Congress and other national libraries through subscriptions,

(2) cataloging records input online by member libraries, and

---

① Matthews, Joseph K. (1982) A Study of Six Online Public Access Catalogs: A Final Report Submitted to the Council on Library Resources. Grass Valley, CA: J. Matthews & Associates, Inc.

② Cochrane, Pauline A. and Markey, Karen (1983). Catalog Use Studies Since the Introduction of Online Interactive Catalogs: Impact on Design for Subject Access. *Library & Information Science Resarch*, 1983, 5 (4): 337 – 363

③ Markey, Karen (1983). *Online Catalogs: Users' Problems and Needs. Final Report to the Council on Library Resources.* Dublin, OH: OCLC, Inc.

④ Duval and Main (1992), pp. 136 – 137.

⑤ Saffady, William (1994) *Introduction to Automation for Librarians.* 3rd ed. Chicago, IL: American Library Association.

(3) cataloging records tapeloaded by cooperating libraries.

Because the cataloging records maintained by bibliographic utilities also include library holding symbols, they can support interlibrary loan activities. Judged by the date of establishment and the number of participating libraries, OCLC is clearly the earliest and largest bibliographic utility. However, there are several other major bibliographic utilities in the United States and Canada. Some of the more important ones are described below. ①

(1) RLIN — the Research Libraries Information Network.

Established in 1978, RLIN — a bibliographic utility and online information retrieval system operated by the Research Libraries Group (RLG) — was an outgrowth of BALLOTS (Bibliographic Automation of Large Library Operations Using a Time Sharing System) developed by Stanford University. BALLOTS was itself an outgrowth of the Stanford Physics Information Retrieval. System (SPIRES) which was developed as an interactive online system in 1967. When BALLOTS became available as a shared cataloging service to other California libraries in 1976, it was regarded as a potential West Coast alternative to OCLC.

Founded in 1974 as resource-sharing consortium, the initial membership of RLG consisted of Harvard, Columbia, Yale, and the New York Public Library. Later, Harvard was replaced by Stanford which became the host institution for RLIN. Currently, it has more than 50 general members and 70 special members. In addition, some 1000 search-only accounts have been established1 for individual as well as institutional users.

(2) Utlas — the University of Toronto Library Automation System

Utlas was developed at the University of Toronto. Its origin can be traced back to 1963 when the University began examining the potential of computers for library operations. The name "Utlas" — University of Toronto Library Automation System—was first used in 1971. Soon after, its service was expanded to include public and academic libraries in Canada and some other countries. In 1985, Utlas was acquired by International Thomson, a Canadian-based multinational company with broad interests in publishing and information services and renamed Utlas International Canada. In 1992, it was acquired by ISM Information Systems Management Corporation, Canada's largest computer service bureau.

Utlas' offering is called CATSS, an acronym for Cataloging Support System. As with other competing services, it provides time-shared access to a large database of bibliographic records. Unlike OCLC, Utlas is not a membership organization; libraries become Utlas customers by signing a computer services contract. Currently, it has contracts with more than 600 institutions representing more than 2500 libraries. Approximately 90 percent are Canadian libraries.

Similar to OCLC and RLIN, Utlas also has extensive databases for publications in the Chinese, Japanese, and Korean languages. The Chinese CATSS was installed in 1989 at the National Central Library in Taiwan and has been used by 15 libraries there. It is based on the Chinese MARC format and supports a larger repertoire of characters than its North American and Japanese counterparts.

(3) WLN — the Western Library Network

WLN, previously known as the Washington Library Network, was founded by the Washington State Library in 1972. Currently, as a private, not-for-profit corporation, it has more than 750 subscribing libraries of all types and sizes, nearly 40 percent of which are in the state of Washington while the remainder were dispersed across Oregon, Idaho, Montana, Alaska, California, Arizona, and British Columbia. Like the other bibliographic utilities, the WLN database is an online union catalog. It contains bibliographic records plus information about participants' holdings.

---

① Ibid., pp. 232 – 252.

2.3 The Demand for and Education of Cataloging Librarians

2.3.1 The important role played by cataloging librarians in library automation

In traditional cataloging, most of the work was done manually and painstakingly by trained librarians who were classified as cataloging librarians or simply catalogers. To be a good cataloger one must possess a good knowledge of cataloging rules, classification schedules, and standardized subject headings. Before typewriters were introduced, neat handwriting was considered a necessity in order to hand-print the catalog cards. Later, this skill was updated to typing and keyboarding. Many libraries collecting foreign language materials also required their catalogers to have a working knowledge of one or more foreign languages. In large libraries, catalogers might also be grouped by their subject expertise.

Since technology which has ushered libraries into the computer age, more and more libraries have begun automated cataloging. This arose from the installation of an in-house-automated cataloging system and/or by participation in online cataloging through one of the bibliographic utilities.

Regardless of the changes from traditional cataloging to automated cataloging, the role of catalogers in intellectual analysis and organization of recorded human knowledge has not altered. The key difference now lies in the growing sophistication of tools deployed and the resulting speed and efficiency.

Another change resulting from shared online cataloging has been to allow professional catalogers to delegate much of the copy cataloging to clerical staff so that the professionals can devote more time to original cataloging and to dealing with more difficult cataloging problems. Using Ohio University Libraries as an example, by drawing on the massive number of bibliographic records in the OCLC online union catalog, about 94% of the new acquisitions can be quickly and cheaply cataloged by means of copy cataloging by trained clerical staff.

2.3.2 Job descriptions for cataloging librarians

A quick glance of the "Positions Open" section of two randomly selected issues of library journals [*American Libraries* (April 1998) and the *College and Research Libraries News* (December 1997)] identified a total of 12 openings for catalogers and four openings for technical services librarians out of 149 library positions listed in the two issues or 10.73% of the total openings.

In the job descriptions for catalogers, the following were the common requirements.

(1) An ALA-accredited MLS degree. (ALA—American Library Association).

(2) Relevant professional cataloging experience.

(3) Working knowledge of AACR2, MARC formats, LC Classification Schedules, LC Subject Headings, OCLC, and LC rule interpretations.

(4) Knowledge of serials cataloging.

(5) Experience with name authority creation and maintenance.

(6) Familiarity with ANSI (American National Standards Institute) holding standards.

In addition, other qualifications were identified as desirable.

(1) Reading knowledge some modern foreign languages.

(2) Familiarity with a local integrated library system.

(3) Knowledge of CONSER (Conversion of Serials Records) serials practices.

(4) Experiences in training staff.

(5) Knowledge in a subject area in addition to library and information science.

The specific duties in these job openings are revealing.

(1) Retrospective conversion and reclassification of serials and some monographs, including many foreign language materials.

(2) Preparation of non-CONSER serial records for CONSER authentication or creation of new

serials records for the CONSER database.

(3) Creation/revision of NACO (Name Authority Cooperative) headings.

(4) Editing existing records in local databases.

(5) Service as a resource person for clerical copy catalogers and database maintenance staff in matters relating to cataloging and authorities.

(6) Responsibility for original and complex copy cataloging of monographs and serials in all formats.

(7) Bibliographic problem resolution.

(8) Participation in the development of cataloging policies and procedures.

(9) Participation in library committees, teams, and task forces as required.

Expectations identified for candidates further illuminate the role of the professional cataloger.

(1) Commitment to high accuracy and output.

(2) Ability to work effectively in a changing organization and to provide leadership in the transition to a networked environment.

(3) Good communication, organizational, and interpersonal skills.

(4) Strong analytical, computer, and problem-solving skills.

(5) Strong service orientation.

(6) Demonstrated flexibility, initiative, and creativity.

(7) Demonstrated ability to work with staff, students, and faculty of culturally diverse backgrounds.

(8) Demonstrated commitment to professional development and service.

(9) For a department head's position, these were extended to demonstrated managerial, planning, leadership, communication, and interpersonal skills.

2.3.3 The education and training for cataloging librarians

In a typical cataloging department, there are at least three types of staff positions:

(1) Department head and assistant head (if a large department).

(2) Professional catalogers.

(3) Support staff (Paraprofessional and/or clerical staff).

From the job descriptions, all required a Master of Library Science degree from an accredited library science program. In the United States of America, about 50 library schools (some identified by different names) offer a Master of Library Science (or comparable) degree and are accredited by the Committee on Accreditation of the American Library Association.[①] A minimum of one to two years of full-time study is needed to complete a Master of Library Science degree. In addition to the basic educational requirement, many academic libraries in the U.S. also prefer professional catalogers (and other professional librarians) to have additional education in a subject area as well as competency in one or more foreign languages.

For a department head or assistant head, some years of relevant administrative experience may be required in addition to an MLS degree.

For support staff, the requirements vary considerably from library to library. In many cases, even though the minimum qualifications for entry-level positions may be very low, i.e., a high school diploma or an associate (two-year) degree, those with higher level of schooling, including university-level education are likely to be preferred. It is not uncommon to find that a notable percentage of the support staff possess college and graduate degrees.

Because of the rapid technological changes taking place in libraries, nearly all libraries offer on-the-job training and other programs for staff development on a regular basis. Staff members are also encouraged to attend professional meetings, seminars, workshops, or other continuing education opportunities for professional growth and self improvement.

---

① Library School and Training Courses. In: *American Library Directory* 1998 – 1999 (1998), 2. New Providence, NJ: R. R. Bowker. pp. 2567 – 85.

2.4 The Future of Library Automation

2.4.1 Keeping pace with rapid technological advances

From the sporadic applications of computers in only a few libraries in the 1960s to the widespread use of sophisticated computer and information technologies by libraries in the late 1990s, there have been dramatic changes in library operations and services from a paper-based library before the 1960s, to the beginning of automated libraries in the 1970s, to the networked libraries in the 1980s, and to electronic and virtual libraries in the 1990s.

Simply, looking at library catalogs and cataloging work reveals changes from handwritten catalog cards to typed cards, to mimeographed cards, to photocopied cards, to papertape-generated cards, to computer-printed and sorted cards—all within a very brief span of time. When OPACs began to replace the timehonored card and other forms of catalogs such as book catalogs, microfilm or fiche catalogs, and CD-ROM catalogs in early 1980s, even computer-printed cards quickly disappeared.

For cataloging, online shared cataloging has quickly gained prominence. New technologies have enabled libraries to greatly refine their automated systems and improve services. Not only have OCLC and other major bibliographic utilities expanded their technical capabilities, local and networked library systems have developed complementary capabilities. In the U.S., the pace of change is unprecedented. All libraries seem to be continually playing a catch-up game with no institution ahead of the technological advances. The latest developments in the Internet, WWW, electronic publishing, digitization, hypertext, expert systems, and artificial intelligence continues this process and further alters the way libraries operate.

In the Internet and WWW environment, the rich and wide variety of electronic information held on the Internet must come under some sort of bibliographic control it if its full potential is to be realized. Libraries just now have only begun to tackle the problems associated with the capturing, cataloging, and archiving of these information resources for easy access by their users.

2.4.2 New opportunities and challenges as we enter into the 21st century

As we approach the new century, we can be sure that, more opportunities and challenges are in the store for us with the continuing advances in computer, information, and telecommunication technologies.

First, all of the current automated library systems will become more mature, versatile, interactive and user friendly. We need to be a smart shopper, user, and master of the new technology.

Second, since catalogers will he more directly involved in the design and improvement of future OPAC and automated library systems, they should try to better understand the needs of end users. As suggested by Dr. Ling Hwey Jeng, catalogers "should be at the front line talking to end users, observing their searching behavior. They must begin to make creative use of research and studies already done, in and outside traditional cataloging literature." [1]

Third, more libraries will join local, regional, national, and international consortiums in a multi-faceted network environment for greater and more efficient resource sharing.

Fourth, libraries will need to transform themselves in a proactive manner to stay in business in the technology-driven environment. We are in the driver's seat and may control our own destiny but must be prepared to do so.

Fifth, information explosions resulting from the exponential growth in human knowledge will continue and will place greater demands on libraries to be more in tune with all the changes happening within and around them.

Sixth, there is a real need to better educate a new generation of library and information

---

[1] Ling Hwey Jeng (1997). Knowledge, Technology, and Research in Cataloging. *Cataloging and Classification Quarterly*. 1997, 24 (1/2): 125

professionals with all the necessary intellectual and technical competencies. All libraries should be staffed by trained and well-qualified library and information professionals, not by bureaucrats or incompetents. Opportunities for continuing education and training must be provided.

Finally, all levels of government and all parent organizations of libraries should recognize the importance of libraries with appropriate financial support. Investing in libraries is the same as investing in the nation's future.

6. 知识管理的理论与实践（节选）[①]
The Theory And Practice of Knowledge Management（extract）

第十四章　知识管理与图书馆在 21 世纪所扮演的角色
Chapter 14　Knowledge Management and the Role of Libraries in the 21st Century

第一节　21 世纪知识管理的发展趋势

20 世纪末，知识管理已变成在企业界一个时髦的述语，企业界首先意识到知识在知识时代"全球经济"中的重要性。在新知识经济中，特别是当人们能共享及创造性地使用知识时，知识就是力量。拥有并不断地更新相关及策略性的知识会使企业在竞争上获得优势。

信息和知识的管理长久以来被当作图书馆的首要职责，图书馆员和信息专业人员被训练成为信息和知识查询、选择、获取、组织、储存、再包装、传播和服务的专家。图书馆员有必要重新评估他们在知识和信息管理方面的优势和不足，在知识管理的进展和执行方面起带头作用。图书馆在 21 世纪的一个重要使命是在支持、促进和推动知识的更新，改革和更广义的创新知识以造福人类。

知识管理不仅仅是信息和数据的管理，也不仅仅是指信息技术。知识管理的一个目标是识别有用的、相关的知识，去组织，吸收及综合知识，及促进创造性地使用知识。信息技术为实现这一目标提供了技术工具。因为知识是通过人们的大脑来加工、使用、更新、扩展，是人类智慧的产物，所以人是知识管理的最重要部分。

知识时代的到来

20 世纪的后半叶，科技更迭的速度大大地加快并带来人类知识以指数速度的增长，亦即信息爆炸！可以肯定地说，这种变化速度会持续到 21 世纪，我们的生活和社会将越来越以知识为主导。虽然许多几乎是史无前例的变化来源于技术革命，特别是计算机领域、通讯领域和网络技术领域的变化，我们必须清楚地了解所有这些技术的突破都是人类知识、才能、创造与智慧发展的结果。人们才是技术变化的驱动力。正因为如此，我们必须保证技术的发展会造福于人类，并引导我们进入 21 世纪数字化和网络化的"知识时代"。

什么是知识时代？其一般的特质为何？这些问题需要下定义并获得解答。

[①] 该著由李华伟、董小英、左美云合著，华艺出版社 2002 年出版，为丘东江主编《21 世纪图书馆学丛书》之一，所节选的第 14 章由李华伟撰写。

丹尼尔·贝尔（Daniel Bell）对知识的定义是："知识是一组对事实或想法经过组织的陈述，呈现一合理的判断或一项实验结果，这些判断或实验结果是以某种有系统的形式经由某种通讯媒体传播给其他人。"① 至于信息的定义，马克·波拉特（Marc Porat）认为："信息就是经过组织与沟通的数据。"②

史蒂芬·埃布尔伦（Stephen Abram）把"知识的创造及使用过程看作从数据转变为信息，信息转变为知识，及知识驱动与支持人类的行为和决策的一个连续的流程。"以下是他对于数据、信息、及知识所下的定义。③

▶ 数据是没有加工过的事实，它自身没有预设的内涵或意义，采用标准化及质量控制的程序以使得数据能够被有效地及有信心地使用是数据管理成功的主要因素。

▶ 信息是赋有特殊内涵的数据或知识的有形体现……通常以书刊文章，或学习等与使用者有关联的产品出现。信息在沟通上的有效体现是它成功的主要因素。同样的数据可以用许多不同的方式来体现以满足不同使用者的需要。信息的价值在于它能够及时的满足使用者的特殊要求。

▶ 知识是信息在个人的角色、学习行为及经验的内涵之内。信息与个人的看法能够调和是知识成功的主要因素。知识之所以有价值是当它使用在适当的环境内涵之下。信息转变成知识的主要步骤是学习、认知、过滤、评估及平衡。

在知识时代，我们看到人类的知识以史无前例的速度累增，它影响到我们的生活及社会的每一个方面。由于人类的智力、创造力和智慧，我们的知识界每一小时、每一分、甚至每一秒都在增长。据估计，世界各地每年出版学术刊物大约有 850,000 种，年增长率为 2.5%。连续性出版品从 1972 年的 70,000 种增加到 1997 年的 118,500 种。全球每两分钟就有一篇科技论文完成。这种人类"显性"知识快速积累只是能够看得到的一个更大的、存在人的大脑及经验里的"隐性"知识冰山所露出水面的一部分。这是知识时代的基本特性，知识时代这个词强调知识（显性知识和隐性知识）在新世纪所扮演的角色。

近年来计算机、通讯与网络等科技的进步是知识扩充的一个重要理由。我们越能快速传递信息与知识，知识就越发达。在 7 世纪的中国和 15 世纪的欧洲所发明的印刷术大大地促进了人类知识的保存与传播。但是，只有在 1884 年，也就是 156 年前，当山谬·摩尔斯（Samuel Morse）发明了电传，才使信息的传播速度比一匹马或一个人所能跑的速度快。

现今，随着因特网（Internet）及万维网（World Wide Web）的来临，我们处在一个真正意义的地球村里，在这里，信息及知识能以光速的速度传播，不受距离或其他因素的限制。④

知识管理的发展

早在 1965 年，彼德. 杜鲁克（Peter F. Drucker）就指出知识将要代替土地、劳力、资金、机械等等，而成为主要的生产力。他的远见当时并没有得到适当的重视。直到 1991

---

① Bell, Daniel. *The Coming of Post-industrial Society: A Venture in Social Forecasting*. New York: Basic Books, 1973. P. 175.

② Porat, Marc. *The Information Economy: Definition and Measurement*. Washington, D. C.: U. S. Department of Commerce, Office of Telecommunications, 1977 (Publication 77-12), p. 1.

③ Abram, Stephen. "Post Information Age Positioning for Special Librarians: Is Knowledge Management the Answer?" Information Outlook. (June 1997), pp. 20-21.

④ Lee, Hwa-Wei. "Library in the Digital and Networked Knowledge Age of the Twenty-first Century". Published in Proceedings of 21st Century Public Libraries—*Vision and Reality*. Taichung, Taiwan: National Taichung Library, 2000, pp. 44-45.

年,当 Ikujiro Nonaka 提出了"隐性"知识和"显性"知识的概念,以及在《哈佛商业评论》上发表的"螺旋式知识"理论时,知识为主导的竞争时代才真正到来。1993 年,杜鲁克在他的《后资本主义社会》① 一书中阐述了知识工作者的支配地位,使得知识的重要性成为全球讨论的话题。从此知识管理变得越来越受重视,越来越多的关于如何提高知识管理的书和文章出现了。② 比尔.盖茨(Bill Gates)在他 1999 年出版的《数字化神经系统》一书中进一步指出知识和网络将会成为所有未来企业的基础。利博维茨(Jay Liebowitz)在他最新发表的《建立组织智能:知识管理导论》一书中指出:

"在走向现代知识管理的行动中,很多机构正设法平衡其组织内部的知识和其顾客及股东(stake holders)之间外部知识的关系。他们设法扩大其自身的组织智能来保证其竞争能力。

"知识管理的结果是为更好地平衡内部知识和外部知识而创造一个重视机构无形知识财产的程序。因此,知识管理指的是知识的创造、保护、获取、协调、统合、查寻以及传播。其目的是在建立一个知识共享环境,在这个环境中知识共享是力量,而不像老格言说的那样知识是力量。"③

知识管理的定义

由于知识管理仍然是一个比较新的概念,不同的作者从不同的角度给予不同的定义,对于"什么是知识管理?"简妮佛·罗利(Jennifer Rowley)所给的定义为:

"知识管理是对一个有志于扩展其目标的组织在知识财产方面的开发和发展。需要管理的知识包括显性的,记录的知识,和隐性的,主观知识。管理是一个要经过所有与知识的识别、共享和创造的有关过程。这需要知识库的创立和维护系统,及知识共享和组织学习的培养和促进。那些知识管理很成功的组织通常把知识当作一种资产来发展该组织的模式和价值,这些模式和价值又反过来帮助知识的创造和共享。"④

罗利的定义是以四种不同的知识管理观点为基础的。这四种观点是由托马斯·达文波特(Thomas H. Devenport)等人对许多知识管理计划进行研究之后所确定的。通过分析这些计划的具体目的,达文波特等人把知识管理分为四大类:⑤

(1) 创建知识库:知识库可以以文件形式储存知识和信息,这些知识库分为三类:
▶ 有可以储存外部知识的知识库,诸如具有竞争力的智能。
▶ 有可以储存经过整理后内部知识的知识库,诸如研究报告和以产品为导向的市场资料,如技术和方法。
▶ 有可以储存非正式的,内部的或隐性知识的知识库,诸如"知道怎样做的秘诀(know-how)"的讨论数据库。

(2) 改进知识的获取和传播:这里强调的是连通性、获取和转移。
▶ 像电视电话会议系统、文件扫描和共享的工具,以及电讯网络等主要技术。

(3) 改善知识的环境:建立一个有利于更有效地知识创造、传播和使用的环境。尤其

---

① Drucker, Peter Ferdinand. *Post-Capitalist Society*. New York: HarperBusiness, 1993.
② 勤业管理顾问公司,《知识管理的第一本书》,刘京伟,译. 台北:商周出版,成邦文化发行, 2000, pp. vi-vii.
③ Liebowitz, Jay. *Building Organizational intelligence: A Knowledge Management Primer*. Boca Raton, FL: CRC Press, 2000, pp. 1.
④ Rowley, Jennifer. "What is Knowledge Management?" *Library management*, V. 20, No. 8 (1999), pp. 416-419.
⑤ Davenport, Thomas H, DeLong, D. W., and Beers, M C. "Successful Knowledge management Projects." *Sloan Management Review*, V39, No. 2 (1998), pp. 43-57.

是针对那些与知识有关的组织模式和价值。
- 加强共享那些与客户建立关系与接触中所得来的知识。
- 奖励那些能为组织的结构知识基础作出贡献的人。
- 执行决策的审核计划以便评定工作人员是否及如何把知识运用到重要的决策之中。
- 要知道成功的知识管理有赖于其组织结构和文化背景。

(4) 把知识当作资产来管理：认清知识对一个组织的价值。

然而，其他人却寻求用发展过程的观点来定义知识管理。例如：简·达菲（Jan Duffy）把知识管理定义为"通过重用组织的智慧和经验来推动革新的过程"[1]。甘勒集团（Gartner Group）把知识管理定义为"一个以整合及协作方式来促进信息资产的创造、捕获、组织、获取和使用过程的一种学科"[2]。

下面是一组由加拉更（P. Galagan）提出的知识管理程序：[3]
- 创造新知识
- 利用从外部资源所获得的知识。
- 用文件、数据库、软件等形式来表现知识。
- 把知识渗透到加工过程、产品或服务之中。
- 把现有的知识传遍整个组织。
- 在做决策时要使用到所有可能得到的知识。
- 通过组织文化和奖励来促进知识的成长。
- 测量知识资产的价值和知识管理的效果。

从以上所描述的计划观点和操作程序，我们可以对知识管理当前的范围和内容有一个基本的了解。

知识管理的发展趋势

由于英国图书馆和资讯委员会的资助，一份关于《知识管理基本技能的调查：培训的要点》的中期报告于 1999 年 1 月发表。该报告揭示了知识管理发展的几个趋势。[4]

第一，绝大多数的组织都在谈论识别可做到的知识管理活动的必要性，这些活动会对企业有影响，使他们集中精力从事这些活动。

第二，知识管理不再只限于大型企业集团使用了，现在无论是公立的还是私立的组织，都在想办法怎样才能从知识管理的一些概念中受益。

第三，知识管理没有固定的蓝图，它是一种各自设计的活动，必须要反映出其组织，在市场的独特位置以及其文化特点。

第四，最高层组织领导的决心是知识管理得以成功的基本要素。

第五，知识主管（CKO）的角色正在被更清楚地定义为领导的角色，一般是有时限的，要能掌握方向，把握时机，使管理变革能顺利地通过关键时期。

---

[1] Duffy, Jan. *Harvesting Experience: Reaping the Benefits of Knowledge.* Prairie Village, KS: ARMA International, 1999 Also From her article, "Knowledge management: To Be or Not to Be?" *Information Management Journal*, V. 34, No. 1 (Jan. 2000), pp. 64–67.

[2] Bair, Jim "Knowledge Management is About Cooperation and Context". Gartner Advisory Services Research Note. May 14, 1999.

[3] Galagan, P. "Smart Companies (Knowledge management)" *Training and Development*, V. 51, No. 12 (1997), pp. 20–25.

[4] Abell, A. and Oxbrow, N. *Investigation of underpinning Skill for Knowledge Management: Training Implications, Interim Report.* London: TFPL, Inc. 1999

第六，知识管理已经标明的角色很有可能会是现有角色的改头换面，或成为现有职位之外加角色，或者被定义为新角色，由现有的职员来承当。然而，有许多新角色正在形成，例如：知识分析家、知识建筑师、知识管理者、知识经纪人、知识审计员、知识领航员、知识保护人；等等①，其中许多角色都是由前图书馆馆员和信息专家接任的。

第二节　图书馆和信息专业的变化

当企业界在新知识经济和数字化时代中进行变化的时候，各种类型的图书馆也在经历着猛烈的改变。从20世纪60年代起，每五年到十年，图书馆和信息专业就会发生一次显著的变化，60年代以前，大多数图书馆以纸张或者印刷式资料为主，发展的步伐缓慢，而且平静。然而，到了60年代，我们就看到了图书馆自动化的开始、机读目录格式的标准化，以及图书馆合作机构（OCLC—俄亥俄州学院图书馆中心）的建立。在七十年代，开始出现联机信息查寻和检索，CD-ROM也开始使用。80年代，图书馆网络开始普遍化，图书馆的集成自动化系统也趋于成熟。90年代，电子出版、多媒体、因特网、数字化得到重视。当我们进入21世纪时，图书馆向着综合的、虚拟的、及数字化方向迈进，数字化的世界深深地受着因特网（Internet）、万维网（World Wide Web）和知识时代的影响。元数据（Meta data）、都柏林核心集（Dublin Core）、网上资源合作编目（Cooperative Online Resources Catalog）以及知识管理都受到图书馆和信息专业内外的广泛关注。

图书馆面临的主要挑战

在快速变化的时期，图书馆和信息领域面临着许多挑战，例如：②
- ▶ 因科学和科技发展及其交互影响的结果造成了人类知识的快速成长。
- ▶ 丰富的信息资源，不论是好的或不好的，在因特网上都可以取得。
- ▶ 图书馆规模、功能、资源、服务及复杂性的增长。
- ▶ 各层次教育的发展，世界经济的成长，文化及生活水平的提升，出版、通讯与大众媒体的蓬勃发展。
- ▶ 大学里新的课程、学科及研究领域在不断地增加。
- ▶ 因特网的快速成长、普遍化及全球化使学术交流与出版的形式有很大的改变。
- ▶ 图书馆数据费用暴增，特别是科学、科技及医学方面的期刊出版品。这些出版品逐渐为少数具有财力及以争取高利润的国际出版商集团所垄断。
- ▶ 在保护版权及知识产权中增加对"公平使用"原则的限制，带给图书馆负面的影响。
- ▶ 多元化信息类型不断增长。
- ▶ 图书馆馆藏及服务国际化。
- ▶ 图书馆馆藏从"拥有"到"获取"的本质正在改变中。
- ▶ 图书馆的经费缩减或增加的不足。
- ▶ 图书馆系统的需求、维护及升级的费用很高。快速的科技发展似乎也使计算机及网络系统很快就过时，而经常性的更新费用尚未成为图书馆编列预算考虑的因素。

---

① Liebownz, Joy (2000), p. 58.
② Lee, Hwa-Wei. (2000), pp. 52–53.

- ▶ 大众要求更有效率的管理。
- ▶ 对图书馆自动化、馆际合作、资源共享、员工发展、读者教育、现代化管理及服务品质等要求投注更多的心力。
- ▶ 对图书馆员的信息技能和知识管理的要求不断增加。
- ▶ 读者的需求及期望不断扩增，而图书馆满足这些需求的能力却不断下降。
- ▶ 对信息素养及终身学习的重要角色不断提升。
- ▶ 快速的改变所不断提升的压力。
- ▶ 政府及社会大众对图书馆的重要性不够重视。
- ▶ 图书馆面对不确定的未来所带来的威胁。

21世纪的这些挑战中，许多是世界各地图书馆所共同面临的问题，但有些问题会比其他问题更严重一些，或者在某些国家会比其他国家更显得突出一些。

由于信息爆炸，因特网和万维网的扩展，我们的社会面临着更多的问题。问题之一是当我们淹溺在信息的汪洋大海里，我们仍然缺乏所需求的知识。另一个问题是"信息拥有"和"信息缺乏"之间距离的加大，这也是区分"信息富有"和"信息贫乏"的个人和国家的标志。这些问题对那些注重信息品质和平等使用知识的图书馆来讲是非常严重的。

第三节 图书馆在新世纪所扮演的角色

面对这一大串的挑战，图书馆必须采取恰当的因应措施。有些措施需要图书馆联合起来，同心协力去迎接这些挑战。例如：[1]

- ▶ 为了改进图书馆的合作、服务、及资源共享等业务，图书馆应组织地方性、区域性、国家性、国际性及专门性的图书馆网，以满足读者的各种需求。OCLC及OhioLINK是两个最成功的范例，后面将详细介绍。
- ▶ 在图书馆各自的特殊任务、目标及需求的基础上，每个图书馆应该规划独特的资源发展计划，将各种可获得的信息类型及其他合作图书馆现有馆藏资源的长处均列入考虑。
- ▶ 充分发挥计算机、信息、通讯及网络等科技的潜能，经由计算机化及网络化作业改善图书馆的服务、资源及管理。
- ▶ 强力支持 Internet 2 及下一代 Internet 的发展，使信息资源的发展、搜集、典藏、传播及学术交流更快速、更有效率。
- ▶ 图书馆人员应该经常并有系统地在 Internet 上探寻有用的信息资源并让使用者易于取得这些资源。
- ▶ 图书馆应该使用联盟的力量以获得购买图书及其他图书馆数据更好的价格，并向电子数据库、电子期刊及其他数字化资源出版商取得较有利的使用权协议。
- ▶ 图书馆应该结合力量发展或寻求学术交流新的替代方案，并免受商业出版商不合理的抬价与使用限制。SPARC（Scholarly Publishing and Academic Resources Coalition—学术出版与学术资源联盟）这个机构的创立就是一个很好的例子。

---

[1] Lee, Hwa-Wei. (2000), pp. 53-55.

SPARC 是由研究图书馆学会的会员所发起，这个学会的 122 个会员来自美加两国主要的国家图书馆、研究图书馆及大学图书馆。

▶ 图书馆应合作或联合策划，对无版权限制或已取得版权所有者同意的馆藏进行有选择性地数字化。这些数字化的馆藏将有助于实现 21 世纪数字图书馆的理想，并以过去无法达成的方式将图书馆带给远距离的读者。
▶ 为了提高馆员的技能与素质，图书馆应该对继续教育与馆员的训练给予高度重视。
▶ 图书馆应该采取有效的措施来招聘具备信息及应用技能的新馆员以为读者服务。
▶ 为使读者具备在知识时代生活所需之信息寻求技能，图书馆应该对读者教育投注更多的关注。
▶ 图书馆应该更进一步加强其终身学习场所的功能。公共图书馆更是适合扮演社区成人继续教育中心的任务。
▶ 图书馆应该采用新的管理原则与实务作法，特别是知识管理。
▶ 图书馆应定期评估其任务、目标、策略方向，并为组织更新与再生检视其组织架构。
▶ 图书馆必须通过建构一个改进信息收集、组织及对读者服务的持续过程来证明他们的价值与用处。唯有如此，才能获得读者的尊重及赢得政府与社会的支持。
▶ 图书馆应该努力成为一个学习的组织。
▶ 图书馆应该规划适当的活动来服务社区内较少获得服务的民众，包括贫民、未受教育者、少数族裔、新移民、老年无依者及残障者。
▶ 生活在 21 世纪相互依赖的世界，图书馆必须将其馆藏、活动及服务国际化。
▶ 图书馆必须采用知识管理的概念，及采取具体的步骤来推行。
▶ 图书馆必须尽可能地进行研究与发展计划，来提升图书馆学与信息科学的知识理论与实务作法。

图书馆在 21 世纪所扮演的新角色应该是社区的智慧公共食堂，借用奠基石的原则，那就是说：在图书馆里"人民与理想在真实环境与虚拟环境中交互相应，以扩展学习及创新知识。"①

OCLC——图书馆计算机联网中心

原 OCLC，俄亥俄学院图书馆中心（Ohio College Library Center），是由俄亥俄州学术图书馆在 1967 年成立。当时成立的主要目的是发展一套计算机系统，使参与的图书馆能做联机合作编目，并建立联机联合目录，通过馆际互借分享图书馆资源。在 OCLC 成立之前，大多数的图书馆必需对每一件图书馆所收藏的数据进行原始编目，这是费时、费力且费钱的作业。图书馆参与联机合作编目，能减少重复原始编目，同时能以最经济效益的方式产生联机馆藏联合目录。在 1960 年代后期与 1970 年代初期之间，很少图书馆负担得起大型计算机的费用，也很少馆员能操作大型计算机。为图书馆作业之需所撰写的计算机软件也未存在，OCLC 的创立是俄亥俄州学术图书馆为迎接当时的挑战所迈进的革命性的一步。OCLC 在 1971 年成功地进行联机编目之后，吸引其他州的图书馆跃然加入，在几年之内，OCLC 的参与图书馆已经遍及美国，也因此促使 OCLC 在 1977 年改变其管理架构及名称为 OCLC 公司（OCLC, Inc.），1981 年则更改其名称为 OCLC—图书馆计算机联网中心

---

① 由研究图书馆学会及 OCLC 所组织，在 1999 年 9 月 24 - 25 日，80 位大学图书馆的馆长在柯罗拉多州的奠基石城举行了为期两天的大学图书馆策略会议。这个会议为了要扩大 21 世纪数字知识时代图书馆的远景，特别提出了三个基本原则……后来被称为奠基石原则。

（Online Computer Libraiy Center）。在管理架构改变后，使俄亥俄州以外的图书馆也能成为 OCLC 的会员图书馆，具有使用者委员会代表的身份及参加董事会选举的权利。

根据 OCLC 最近发布的消息，截至 2000 年 6 月 30 日止，在 76 个国家及地区有超过 37,000 个图书馆是 OCLC 各种服务的使用者。他们之中有 8,859 个图书馆是 OCLC 的会员图书馆。这些图书馆通过 OCLC 联机及批次加载的方式进行编目作业，他们使用 OCLC 的 WorldCat 系统内的书目纪录进行数据编目，若在数据库内找不到相对应的书目纪录，则输入原始书目纪录。

OCLC 的在线目录称为 WorldCat 是目前世界上最大的书目数据库。截至 2000 年 6 月 30 日止在 WorldCat 有 42,476,614 笔书目纪录。OCLC 的会员图书馆以每 15 秒新增一笔纪录的速度每年新增大约有两百万笔纪录。这些纪录包含超过 7.6 亿个馆藏，400 种语言，及跨越超过 4,000 年的知识记载。①

OCLC 是以进一步检索世界知识及降低图书馆的费用为目的而成立。因为是非营利的机构，OCLC：
- ▶ 是经费完全自足，不依赖外来支持，
- ▶ 对图书馆的收费是依据各馆使用 OCLC 的服务及对 OCLC 的贡献而定，
- ▶ 通过使用者委员会及顾问委员会与 OCLC 会员图书馆一起检讨收费价格，
- ▶ 寻求降低图书馆每一单元运作成本成长的速率，
- ▶ 对于参与原始编目及资源共享的图书馆给予补偿，
- ▶ 支持研究、学术及教育，
- ▶ 寻求增加检索及使用世界各地不断增加的信息。

除了各种编目服务外，OCLC 也提供一些非常有用的网上参考服务，其中最重要的是 OCLC FirstSearch 服务，这项服务提供超过 2,700 种电子期刊及 56 种数据库供检索，并且超过 5,500,000 篇的全文文献也可透过 FirstSearch 在网上取得。使用者可在这个数量不断增加且含有馆藏讯息的数据库系统提出馆际互借的需求。OCLC 自 1978 年开放馆际互借服务以来，已处理超过 100,000,000 件馆际互借服务。②

OCLC 研究部（OCLC Office of Research）于 1978 年成立，是世界上专对图书馆及信息科学进行研究的主要中心之一，致力于带领图书馆勇敢地面对知识时代所面临的问题与挑战加以研究。过去 10 年间，OCLC 投资超过一亿美元来研究及发展新的服务项目。

自从 1997 年以来，OCLC 的一项新服务是建立 OCLC 学院（OCLC Institute）为图书馆在 21 世纪地球村及数字环境中提供高级教育与交换知识的机会。OCLC 学院所提供的课程，最受欢迎的是：
- ▶ 资源共享的持续与创新，
- ▶ 知识获取管理，
- ▶ 知识管理：方法与系统，
- ▶ 快速改变时代的科技计划，
- ▶ 元数据（Metadata）在知识管理中的应用。

仅在 1999 年，就有 52 种高级研习会在 OCLC 俄亥俄州哥伦布市总部、美国其他地区及世界几个地区举行。目前 OCLC 学院正在招募有意愿扩展新课程的兼任教师。2000 年的

---

① OCLC **Annual Report** *1999/2000*. Dublin, Ohio: OCLC Online Computer Center, 2000. pp. 1, 2, 6 - 7, 46 - 47 页。
② *An Overview of OCLC Services: Look What You're Doing Now... With OCLC*. Dublin, Ohio: OCLC Online Computer Library Center, 1999.

重点工作是将教育及训练的课程延伸到亚洲地区。

在迈入 21 世纪之际，OCLC 在 2000 年 7 月 1 日推出另一项新的服务，称为联机资源编目合作计划（Cooperative Online Resources Catalog，简称 CORC）。2000 年 1 月，超过 200 所各类型图书馆，包括 30 所非美国图书馆，已参与这项计划的发展与测试。这项计划为合作图书馆建立电子资源提供新开发的国际标准和描述语工具：如元数据（Metadata）和都柏林核心集（Dublin Core）等。

OhioLINK（Ohio Library and Information Network，俄亥俄图书馆和信息网络）

在俄亥俄州，学术图书馆的创新与合作精神已远近驰名，而 OCLC 于 1967 年成立可谓迈开了一大步。尽管 OCLC 在改进世界书目纪录的发展与检索方面有相当的成就，但在俄亥俄州的学术图书馆界仍觉得有必要成立一个全州性的学术图书馆联盟，以便全州图书馆在图书、资源与信息服务的其他方面有更密切的合作。俄亥俄州大专院校董事会（Ohio Board of Regents）① 于 1986 年指定一个特选的小组委员会，经过一年的研究后，发表一份报告《俄亥俄州学术图书馆的进步：经由合作、储存与科技》（Academic Libraries in Ohio：Progress Through Collaboration, Storage, and Technology）。② 这份报告建议：

▶ 尽速建立全州电子目录系统，包括将仍存留之一些卡片式目录回溯转换成机读目录格式，

▶ 发展及建立一套全州各参与图书馆之间的数据快速传递系统，

▶ 规划一个合作的图书文献储存计划。

从这份初期的报告及由俄亥俄州大专院校董事会所成立的推动委员会（Steering Committee）所采取的一连串行动下，OhioLINK 带着雄心大志于 1989 年筹组成立。创始之初，有 18 个单位加入，其中 13 个是综合性的州立大学，2 个大型私立大学，2 个州立医学大学及俄亥俄州图书馆。截至 2001 年 5 月，参与的单位数已扩增到 79 个，包括全州所有二年制的州立社区学院及技术学院，及大多数私立学院及大学。

OhioLINK 是建立在俄亥俄州学术及研究网（Ohio Academic and Research Network，OARnet）的网络架构上，是一个具集中式计算机系统的分布式图书馆网，它的计算机系统连接到各参与单位的计算机系统。通过规划，集中端（central site）及分散端（local site）都备有同一的计算机硬件及软件平台，使能达到最大极限之联结能力与兼容性。在集中端，有一个具有流通功能及实时显示每一件图书馆数据馆藏现况的网上联合目录。OhioLINK 的特点之一是允许任何一馆的读者可向其他所有的图书馆借书，包括所在图书馆未收藏或无法取得的图书数据之借阅要求。读者可以通过校园网络或 Internet，在办公室、实验室及家里提出借阅馆藏数据的需求，贷方图书馆将数据收集后经由特殊安排的传递服务送到读者所在图书馆，目标在 48 小时内完成传送，也就是多数的馆际互借可在二至三天内完成，这对读者而言是一大便利且无需花费金钱。目前 OhioLINK 的集成式网上联合目录包含超过 700 万种的图书数据，约有 3100 万册/件，而百分之五十六的资料是不重复的。这个目录服务全州大约有 500,000 名学生及 50,000 名教职员。在 2000 年，查询联合目的次数达到 2,250,000 次并且有 550,000 件的馆际借阅要求。

---

① 俄亥俄州大专院校董事会是隶属州长之下负责规划及监督全州州立大专院校有关一般政策及经费的州立协调机构。

② Ohio Board of Regents. Library Study Committee. *Academic Libraries in Ohio：Progress Through Collaboration, Storage, and Technology. Report of the Library Study Committee*, Columbus, Ohio：Ohio Board of Regents, 1987.

过去几年间，除了很受欢迎并且使用率高的馆际借阅服务外，OhioLINK 也推出其他的合作活动来扩展分享电子资源，并且开创其他服务，兹举其荦荦者如下：
- 采购多种高度需求的电子书目数据库及全文数据库，
- 增加全文电子数据库的数量，特别是电子期刊；
- 以联盟采购的力量与出版商协商，取得较大的折扣或达成有利的使用权协议；
- 采用全州购书的计划（a state wide approval plan），避免各馆采购不必要的复本；
- 扩大在线馆际借阅数据的范围，从图书到其他可外借的数据类型，例如微缩数据、录像带及 CD；
- 发展一套较完整的检索引擎，使易于同时检索多种数据库；
- 成立电子期刊中心（Electronic Journal Center），管理日益增加的电子期刊；
- 在俄亥俄州超级计算机中心（Ohio Super computer Center）成立一个可扩展储存空间的数字媒体中心（Digital Media Center），供各会员图书馆储存他们所开发的电子馆藏、及其他非营利机构或商业公司开发的电子资源。
- 改善校外远距检索 OhioLINK 的资源。

由于 OhioLINK 展示其利益及整体经济效益，在俄亥俄州政府及俄亥俄州大专院校董事会的支持下，每年可获得足够的经费。多数的经费用在支持集中作业、传递服务及主要书目、参考与全文数据库的采购、软件的持续发展、新开创事项及其他等方面的支出。1999 年初，会员图书馆投票表决每年从每个图书馆的图书采购经费中征集一部分基金供集中采购之用。

为了进行合作储存计划，建造了五座大型区域储存中心并且已在运作中。这些储存中心很有计划地设立在俄亥俄州的中部、东北部、西北部、东南部及西南部，供全州州立大学及学院储存较少利用的馆藏数据。各中心高密度及低成本的储存设备舒缓了多数校园中总馆及分馆拥挤的书架空间，使这些图书馆能为他们的读者提供较好的服务。所有存放在储存中心的资料开放现场使用，也可以提借，在读者提出借阅需求当天或次日便将数据还回原图书馆或送到其他 OhioLINK 的会员图书馆供使用。

第四节 图书馆和知识管理的关系

作为一个学习组织（Learning Organization），图书馆应该在知识管理中起带头作用。与那些把知识管理运用于竞争优势的其他企业组织不同，除了一些专门图书馆（例如公司的下属图书馆，这类图书馆可能被称为企业图书馆，特种图书馆或知识中心）之外，大多数的公共图书馆、学术性图书馆和研究性图书馆都具有不同的使命和价值观。它们不像一些专门图书馆仅仅为了竞争、为了内部使用，以及有限度地同外界共享知识，公共图书馆、学术性图书馆和研究性图书馆的最重要使命就是为其读者扩大知识的获取。由于使命的不同，图书馆的知识管理目标要定得更高。下面是图书馆该怎样在所有关键的管理和服务领域来改善其知识管理。

知识资源的管理

由于各种知识按指数速度增长，这就需要图书馆的资源获取策略从纸张印刷型发展到电子和数字型能够与它们的使命和职能保持一致。因为受到有限的资金、人员和空间的限制，图书馆必须要仔细地分析其使用者的需求，寻找发展一个合作选购的计划来满足这些要求。

从"拥有"（Ownership）到"获取"（Access），从"万一"（Just in Case）到"及时"（Just in Time）这种概念的变化应该是一个健全的资源发展策略目标。

应该发展和维护一个集成的网上公共获取目录（OPAC—Online Public Access Catalog）。该目录应具有馆内的知识和馆外的知识，以及印刷的和其他形式的知识。OPAC要包含众多的，有用的网站和知识资源，还应该安装一个定期检查和更新这种资源系统。

除了显性知识，图书馆要想办法获取所有对读者和图书馆内部操作有用的隐性知识。图书馆的网站应该作为所有筛选过的和相关的知识的窗口，不论是显性的和隐性的，现场的和远距离的，及各种形式的资源。[①]

作为知识管理活动的一个部分，勤业管理顾问公司（Arthur Anderson Business Consulting）设计了一个利用率非常高的网站："知识空间"（Knowledge Space）。知识空间提供三种类型的知识：

▶ 新闻：公司的主要新闻和分布在世界各地工作人员所感兴趣的热门话题。
▶ 资源：它包括"全球最好的作业"（Global Best Practices），"咨询网"（Ask Network），和"礼区资源"（Community Resources）。
▶ 连接：专供组织内部结构及跨部门的各个特别兴趣小组彼此交流和讨论之用。

"知识空间"所提供的资讯经常更新，他们鼓励用户反馈各种意见。[②]

图书馆也可以发展它们自己的独特"知识空间"。全体工作人员可以通过图书馆的内部网络，了解本馆战略性计划文件、年终报告、小组（Team）及部门报告、会议和委员会备忘录、统计分析、项目专款的申请书、政策和程序、操作手册、"成功的经验"（best practices）、"失败的教训"（lessons learned）、内部通告、图书馆新闻、员工活动、培训和职员发展机会等等。

人力资源管理

图书馆的馆员和用户拥有大量的专家们所具有的知识。在大学和研究机构，这种专门知识更多，应该编入目录和索引，并且不断地更新，使其通过图书馆创建并维护的电子数据库可以检索及找到。

图书馆馆员的知识以及所积累的经验构成了各类图书馆的智慧资产，应该受到重视和共享。使能形成一种共享知识和专业技术的组织文化，并实施恰当的奖励和鼓励。一个强调合作、共享和革新的组织文化环境只有在图书馆馆长的有力领导下．及在图书馆馆员达成共识的前提下，才能建立起来。

作为一个学习的组织，图书馆应该拨出一些年度经费来为全体员工提供继续教育和在职培训。知识必须不断地更新和扩充以防止其老化或停滞不前。

图书馆还应该鼓励老馆员把丰富的知识和经验传授给新馆员，建立一个辅导（Mentoring）制度来帮助新馆员向有经验的馆员学习，在方便的时候，定期安排非正式的

[①] 达菲在1999年为隐性知识下定义为"个人的，没有经过文献化的知识；受内涵影响的、由动力所创造及驱动的、内部化的及以经验为基础的；经常存在人的大脑中、行为上及概念里。"她把显性知识定义为"经过文献处理及公开的、结构的、内容固定的、外在的及有意识的知识。"

[②] Arthur Anderson Business Consulting (2000), pp. 225–229.

研讨会和餐叙（brownbag），让大家可以在那里交流"成功的经验"，吸取"失败的教训"，相互学习特殊的经验和知识。还可以在图书馆内部网页上建立特别兴趣小组和聊天室。

作为年终考绩的一部分，那些通过写作、出版、讲座、或辅导的方式来与他人共享自己的隐性知识和经验的馆员要受到适当的表扬和奖励。

因为资深的馆员已经积累了许多宝贵的经验，图书馆应该注重创造一个良好的工作条件和环境，使这些有经验的馆员能够愿意留任。

资源共享和联网合作

图书馆具有悠久的资源共享和联网合作的历史。自从20世纪60年代以来，计算机、电讯、网络化、数字技术的迅速发展加快了这方面的扩张。图书馆通常会因为各种合作项目以及资源共享而同时成为几个合作网的成员单位。其中最好的例子是OCLC（图书馆计算机联网中心）和OhioLINK（俄亥俄图书馆和信息网络）。

信息技术的发展

想要推动知识管理的执行，就必须有一个计划周详，可操作的知识管理系统，来使用最新的信息技术。

在网络环境中，参加同一联盟的图书馆要协调选择一个通用的系统，使合作图书馆之间能够最大限度地连通及兼容。

应该使用图书馆内部的互联网络（Intranet），通过文件/产品的共享，以及教训（lessons learned）和最好的经验（best practices）的。收集与出版来支持知识管理。

互联网络的功能也应该用来为用户、知识者（教授、研究员和课题专家等）、出版商、政府机构、商业和工业以及其他组织之间作为知识交流之用。

用户服务

了解用户至为重要，应为当务之急。用户信息可以从用户的注册数据库、流通和馆际借阅记录、最常问的参考咨询问题、电话和电子信件服务、电子刊物和数字化资源的使用等的统计分析中得来，但是，要注意不能侵犯各图书馆用户的隐私权。

所有的用户服务项目都应该符合个人的需要，新出版物的自动通知（new publication alert）及挑选的信息提供服务（selective dissemination of information）也要符合用户的兴趣。可以通过定期的用户调查来收集用户的满意程度和要求，调查结果可以用来计划，及重新设计图书馆的服务。"最好的经验"数据库要经常维护、分析和共享。

结　论

尽管知识管理已经成为管理上新近的"口头禅"，它是否会像以前的许多"口头禅"一样逐渐消失，将取决于我们怎样让它起作用。在企业界，知识管理一直被当作各个组织能够获得超越其对手的竞争优势，增加其产品的价值，赢得其客户最大满意程度的主要策略。

图书馆界可以向企业界学习。知识管理对图书馆向对企业界一样地重要，只是图书馆不存在竞争、所有权和想办法赚钱的问题。事实上，图书馆在显性知识的管理上已有长期的、丰富的经验，现在我们需要把我们的专长延伸到如何管理隐性知识。这不仅仅是为了满足图书馆用户的需求，也是为了改善图书馆本身的作业。任何一个想要成功地执行知识管理的图书馆都要有一个强有力的领导和具有洞察力的上层行政部门，这将有利于促成该组织的知识共享。随着图书馆进入21世纪的知识时代，我们不应该坐视知识管理的发展，而是要用专业知识和经验来武装自己，做知识管理的驾驭者。

在企业组织所新创立的职位之中，如：主要知识官员（Chief Knowledge Officer）、知识管理专家、知识经理等，主要知识官员常常是一个公司的高级主管，一个比主要信息官员（Chief Information Officer）高的职位。在过去的二十年中，许多主要信息官员的职位是由受过信息技术训练的人来做，而不是由受过图书馆和信息专业训练的人来做，因为主要信息官员更具有技术性。现在，除非我们想要躲避21世纪图书馆在知识管理方面所担当的新角色，否则，随着知识管理的到来和主要知识官员职位的设立，具备远大目光，领导才能，及专业知识的图书馆员及信息专家应该是最适合主要知识官员职位的。

为了要执行知识管理，各种类型的图书馆——包括学术和研究图书馆、特别图书馆、政府机构图书馆、信息中心、知识中心等，都应该与"图书馆学院"（不论它现在用的是什么名字）共同来设计新的课程，进行新的学习与研究，发展新的理论与实践，及培养更好的、现在的和将来的知识专业人员以迎接一个更为广大的求职市场的挑战与机会。

最后，绝对不要把知识管理当作知识控制来看。乔格·温·克罗福（Georg Von Krogh）等在他们合著的《促进知识创造》（Enabling Knowledge Creation）一书中特别强调"知识的创造"而反对"知识的控制"。在知识创造的过程中，每一个图书馆都应当动员所有的能力与资源作为知识创造的促成者及协助者。①

引用文献：

1 Abell, A. and Oxbrow, N. *Investigation of Underpinning Skill for Knowledge Management*: *Training Implications*, *Interim Report*. London: TFPL, Inc. 1999.

2. Allee, Verna. *The Knowledge Evolution-Expanding Organizational Intelligence*. Boston, Butteiworth–Heinemann, 1997.

3. 勤业管理顾问公司，《知识管理的第一本书》，刘京伟，译. 台北：商周出版，成邦文化发行，2000, pp. vi – vii.

4. Bair, Jim. "Knowledge Management is About Cooperation and Context". *Gartner Advisory Services Research Note*. May 14, 1999.

5. Bell, Daniel. *The Coming of Post-Industrial Society*: *A Venture in Social Forecasting*. New York: Basic Books, 1973.

6. Boisot, Max H. *Knowledge Assets*: *Securing Competitive Advantage in the Information Economy*. New York: Oxford University Press, 1998.

7. Borghoff, Uwe M. and Pareschi, Remo (eds). *Information Technology for Knowledge Management*. Berlin: Springer, 1998.

8. Brendan, Loughndge. "Knowledge Management, Librarians and Information Managers: Fad or Future." *New Library World*. V. 100, No. 6, 1999, pp. 245 – 253.

9. Carbeunm Alberto "How Does Knowledge Management Influence Innovation and Competitiveness?" *Journal of Knowledge Management*. V. 4, No. 2, 2000, pp. 87 – 98.

10. Davenport, Thomas H., DeLong, D. W., and Beers, M. C "Successful Knowledge Management Projects". *Sloan Management Review*. V. 39, No. 2, 1998, pp. 43 – 57.

---

① Von Krogh, Georg, Ichijo, Kazuo, and Nonaka, Ikujiro. *Enabling Knowledge Creation*; *How to Unlock the Mystery of Tacit Knowledge and Release the Power of Innovation*. New York: Oxford University Press, 2000.

11. De JagCT, Martha. "The KMAT Benchmaikmg Knowledge Management". *Library Management*. V. 20, No. 7, 1999, pp. 367 – 372.

12. Devlin, Keith J. *Infosense: Turning Information Into Knowledge*. New York: W. H. Freeman, 1999.

Drucker, Peter Ferdinand. *Post-Capitalist Society*. New York: HarperBusiness, 1993.

13. Duffy, Jan. Harvesting *Experience: Reaping the Benefits of Knowledge*. Prairie Village, KS: ARMA International, 1999.

14. "Knowledge Management: To Be or Not to Be?" *Information Management Journal*. V. 34, No. 1, Jan. 2000, pp. 54 – 67.

15. Galagan, P. "Smart Companies (Knowledge Management)". *Training and Development*. V. 51, No. 12, 1997, pp. 20 – 25.

16. Gumbley, Helen. "Knowledge Management". *Work Study*. V. 47, No. 5, 1999, pp. 175 – 177.

Huseman, Richard C. and Goodman, Jon P. *Leading with Knowledge: The Nature of Competition in the 21st Century*. Thousand Oaks, CA: Sage Publications, 1999.

17. Ishikawa, Akira. "Knowledge Management, Autopoiesis and Apoptosis". *Kybernetes*. V. 28, No. 6/7 (1999), pp. 821 – 825.

18. Lee, Hwa-Wei. "Libraries in the Digital and Networked Knowledge Age of the Twenty-first Century". *Proceedings of 21st Century Public Libraries — Vision and Reality*. Taichung, Taiwan: National Taichung Library, 2000, 1 – 43 – 1 – 67.

19. Liebowitz, Jay. *Building Organizational Intelligence A Knowledge Management Primer*. Boca Raton, FL: CRC Press, 2000.

20. O'Dell, Carla and Grayson, C Jackson, Jr. *If Only We Knew What We Know: The Transfer of Internal Knowledge and Best Practice*. New York: The Free Press, 1998.

21. *An Overview of OCLC Services: Look What You're Doing Now... With OCLC* Dublin, OH: OCLC Online Computer Library Center, 1999.

22. Pfeffer, Jeffrey and Sutton, Robert I. *The Knowing – Doing Gap: How Smart Conpanies Turn Knowledge Into Action*. Boston, MA: Harvard Business School Press, 2000.

23. Porat, Marc. *The Information Economy: Definition and Measurement*. Washington, D. C.: U. S. Department of Commerce, Office of Telecommunications, 1977 (Publication 77 – 12).

24. Rowley, Jennifer. "What is Knowledge Management?" *Library Management*. V. 20, No. 8 (1999), pp. 416 – 419.

25. Snkantaiah, T. Kanti and Koenig, Michael E. D (eds). *Knowledge Management for the Information Professional*. Medford, NJ: American Society for Information Science, 2000. (ASIS Monograph Series)

26. Teece, DavidJ. *Managing Intellectual Capital: Organizational, Strategic, and Policy Dimensions*. New Yoik: Oxford University Press, 2000

27. Tisscn, Rene, Andnessen, Daniel, and Deprez, Frank Lekanne. *Value-Based Knowledge Management*. Amsterdam: Addison Wesley Longman, 1998.

28. Von Krogh, Georg, Ichijo, Kazuo, and Nonaka, Ikujiro. *Enabling Knowledge Creation:*

How to Unlock the Mystery of tacit Knowledge and Release the Power of Innovation. New York: Oxford University Press, 2000.

29. Wiig, Karl M. "Knowledge Management: An Introduction and Perspective". *Journal of Knowledge Management* V. 1, No. 1 (Sept. 1997), pp. 6 – 14.

30. _____. "Knowledge Management: Where Did It Come From and Where Will It Go?" *Expert Systems With Applications*. V. 13, No. 1 (1997), pp. 1 – 14.

7. 亚太地区图书馆发展的合作领域（节选）
Areas of Cooperation in Library Development in Asia and Pacific Regions (extract)[1]

合作的新途径：图书馆员培训

Library Internships: A New Approach to Cooperation

Introduction

Cooperation for library development in the Asian and Pacific Region takes many forms. Such diversity is necessary to address the varying needs and levels of development among and within the countries in the Region. One important area for cooperation is the education and training of library and information professionals. Adequate manpower resources are crucial for library development at a time when the importance of information for national development is widely acknowledged. I have found, in my years of professional involvement in the Region, that the pace of library development in a given country is often dictated by the quality and quantity of its library professionals. Without these, little happens.

Given this need, the development of professional manpower in library and information science is a fertile area for cooperation between the developed countries and the developing nations. As pioneers and leaders in library education, American and Canadian library schools have led in educating large numbers of information professionals from the Asian and Pacific Region. In the past two decades, Great Britain and other European countries have also been educating increasing numbers of library and information professionals. More recently, Australia and a regional program in the Philippines have made significant contributions as well. Most of the graduates who have returned to their homes hold responsible positions in libraries and information centers. Many are contributing to national library development in their respective countries. Yet, despite those educational opportunities, the number of trained professionals is still far short of actual needs.

In addition to formal library education, which requires the greatest investment in time and money, there is an urgent need for a diversity of training programs and professional opportunities, ranging from short courses, seminars, workshops and conferences to exchanges of personnel, professional visits and internships. All of these provide training and retraining for library and information workers not only in the "basics" needed in their jobs but also in the new concepts, skills, and technologies in this rapidly changing profession of librarianship. Nothing can compare with a formal library education—the value of which is beyond doubt—yet there is a definite need to supplement or complement it with a variety of training programs especially designed and tailored to the needs of the individuals involved. Unlike formal library education which often is bound by a fixed program of study and course sequences, training programs can be far more flexible and responsive to individual needs.

---

[1] This book is a proceedings of the 1983 Joint Annual Program of the Asian/Pacific American Librarians Association and Chinese-American Librarians Association June 28 – 29, 1983 Los Angeles, California, edited by Sally C. Tseng, Hwa-Wei Lee and K. Mulliner, and published by Chinese-American Librarians Association in 1985.

Recognizing this, since 1979 the Ohio University Library has been offering internship programs to library and information professionals from the Asian and Pacific Region.

Origin of the Internship Program

The internship program at Ohio University was begun in response to a number of request from libraries and information centers in Indonesia, Taiwan and Thailand. A number of factors made this possible, including:

- the support of the Ohio University administration and its strong commitment to international education and cooperation.
- the University's long standing association with educational programs in Malaysia and the University's Center for Southeast Asian Studies which originally stimulated the development of the Library's internationally recognized Southeast Asia Collection,
- the interest and enthusiasm of the library staff especially those in the Southeast Asia Collection which provides an excellent home base for many of the interns, and
- the financial support of the Division of General Information Programme of UNESCO for several of the interns and the support of other funding sources including the interns' own institutions.

One additional factor of importance was my own working and teaching experience in Southeast Asia between 1968 and 1975 when I was seconded by the U.S. Agency for International Development to work as the Director of Library and Information Center at the Asian Institute of Technology (AIT) in Bangkok, Thailand. My close involvement with library development during those seven years led me to recognize the importance of internship programs. In fact, back in 1970, I started an internship program at AIT for several librarians from Indonesia and other libraries in Thailand. The current internship program at Ohio University could properly be seen as a continuation of this earlier program.

Purposes of Internships

Since its inception, the prime purpose of our internship program has been to provide practical experience in a major American library for selected library and information professionals from the Asian and Pacific Region on modern concepts and developments in library and information services. Given our strong Southeast Asia link, (although one of the most recent programs was the training of two Saudi Arabian professionals in the management of a micrographic department for the National Center for Financial and Economic Information) our special focus has been on Southeast Asia.

Three main groups of library and information professionals have benefited from the training. The first group consists of middle-and upper-level professionals who received formal library education or training several years ago and now need to update their knowledge and skills for our rapidly changing profession. The second group consists of mostly younger faculty members for Southeast Asian library schools who wish to refresh their library skills with the hope of integrating theory and practice through the internship. The third group consists of new graduates of American library schools from the Asian and Pacific Region who, before returning to their home countries, would like an opportunity to apply what they have learned in the context of a major American library. Of the 15 interns who have participated in the program, the majority divided almost equally between the first two groups. Some of the first group have dual responsibilities, i. e., in addition to working in the library, they also teach part-time in library schools at their home institutions. Thus far seven countries have been represented in the program. They are Thailand, Taiwan, Indonesia, Malaysia, the Philippines, People's Republic of China, and Saudi Arabia.

Structure of Internships

As was mentioned earlier, nearly all training is individually designed so that each intern has a tailor-made program to suit his or her special background and needs. In order to provide the utmost care in the training of each intern, we prefer no more than two interns at any one time. In fact, our experience has been that it is desirable to work with a single intern, although there are definite advantages in terms of mutual support in having a peer intern to whom to turn. Also, there needs to be a sufficient lapse of time between programs to give the participating staff a break. This is necessitated by the considerable time participating staff must give in the training and supervising of the interns.

While finalized only after his/her arrival and after a face-to-face meeting, much of the preparation for the program takes place several months in advance through correspondence. Once the specific background and needs of an intern have been identified, an appropriate library staff member is assigned as the training coordinator to oversee the entire training of the intern from arrival to departure. This staff member will be assisted by others as required. Our experience further suggests that three to six months are desirable to permit sufficient hands-on experience. A longer time period also permits the intern to make a greater contribution to the primary mission of the library. Six months is recommended for those interns whose English language proficiency requires a longer adjustment period. To give each intern greater awareness of various library practices, visits to other libraries in the vicinity are arranged. Depending on funding, visits to OCLC and Chemical Abstracts, which are located in Columbus, Ohio, and attendance at relevant library conferences, workshops, seminars, etc. are often a part of the program as well. For library school faculty members, a visit to nearby library schools such as Kent State, Case Western Reserve, Pittsburgh, Kentucky, and Indiana may be added if so desired.

Scheduling of the training normally takes two forms. One is a stationary assignment in which an intern is assigned to one or two library areas (or departments) for half of each day during the entire internship period. This assignment is made according to each intern's needs for in-depth training in a given library or information service. The other form is a rotating assignment in which, during the other half of each day, the intern is assigned to a different library area for a period ranging from one to ten days each. This is designed to give the intern overall experience in a wide range of library operations. Some of the interns who have specific training objectives may be asked to carry out a project under the supervision or guidance of experienced staff members, in addition to the two forms of assignments.

It is of interest to note that among the areas most interns have wished to learn are:

(1) Modern organization and management of a library or information center including particularly the many aspects of human resources management;

(2) applications of modern technologies to library and information services including computerized online cataloging and interlibrary loan, such as the systems provided by OCLC, and online searching of remote databases through Dialog, SDS, BRS, MEDLINE, etc. (Our local online public access catalog and circulation system became available only this summer);

(3) networking of library and information services; and

(4) the applicability of the above for the intern's home institution.

The last is of utmost importance in our view since unless most of the practical experience gained by the interns can be applied in their own environment, there is little value in the internship program. At the same time, the interns must be expected to interpret what they learn rather than expecting to be able to directly transplant each technological application.

Cost of Internships

To insure the success of the internship program, adequate funding for the following three types of direct costs must be secured:

(1) **Travel Expenses.** These include international travel to Ohio and return, local transportation for visits, and the costs of participating in conferences and workshops. Depending on the distance to the home country, the number of visits to be made, and the number of conferences to be attended, there can be considerable variation in cost, but $3,500 should be

considered a minimum for interns from Asia (based on 1983 air fares).

(2) **Living Expenses.** These include room and board, insurance, and personal and incidental expenses. For a rural locale such as Athens, Ohio, $600 per month is adequate for subsistence. Obviously, this figure depends on local costs and must be adjusted for inflation. Expenses for interns accompanied by family members would be higher.

(3) **Administrative Expenses.** These include the travel expenses (but not salaries) of library staff who will accompany the intern (s) for visits and conferences as well as the cost of telephones, textbook and reading materials, telex, postage, photocopying, and database searching. To this should be added receptions and official entertainment. The minimum estimate for these expenses is about $1,000 for a three-month training with an increment of $150 per additional month—depending on activities.

Applying these figures to a three-month internship, the direct costs would be about $6,300 (or $8,650 for six months).

The estimated indirect cost to the University for staff time spent programming, coordinating, supervising, training, traveling, and counseling plus overhead will amount to about $1,500 each month for each intern. Although part of this indirect cost may be recovered from the work performed by the interns during their internship, that part not recovered can be considered as a contribution made by the Ohio University Library to international cooperation. It is our hope that more libraries in North America, particularly those with area resources and expertise, will consider offering internship training to library and information professionals from the Asian and Pacific Region. Currently, because of the success of our internship program, we receive more requests than we can possibly handle.

Funding Sources

Financial support for the direct costs of the internship programs has come from a number of sources. Most important of these has been from the General Information Programme of the United Nations Educational, Scientific and Cultural Organization (UNESCO). The two Saudi Arabian interns were supported by their Government through the U.S.-Saudi Arabian Joint Commission on Economic Cooperation. Others were financed by funds made available through U.S. federal grants, that the Library was awarded under Titles II-C and VI of the Higher Education Act or by the interns' home institutions.

It is necessary for the interns' home institutions to convince their governments of the importance of a library internship and to seek financial support for it as well. Beyond this, Third World institutions should recognize their unique ability to inaugurate programs. Many international and bilateral agencies are more responsive to requests from recipient institutions than to proposals from the West. In this regard also, recognition by Third World governments of the importance of libraries and information centers for development efforts will affect the willingness of aid-granting and technical assistance agencies to support internships.

Program Review and Evaluation

To assure continuing flexibility in the programming and scheduling of an intern, I conduct a monthly review with the intern and his/her program coordinator. The review often leads to program modifications and improvements. In addition to periodic program reviews, two separate evaluations are carried out at the end of each internship: one by the intern using a standard evaluation form and one by the training coordinator. Although we have received highly satisfactory and complimentary evaluations from most of the interns, we actively seek their suggestions for the refinement of the program.

Many of the suggestions have been adopted in subsequent programming and training. Some of the more important suggestions include: improved housing arrangements, assigning a staff member for each intern throughout the internship, preferred timing of internships during the year, and the value of some of the visits and the lack of value of others. Another form of evaluation which we hope to conduct is to ask for an evaluation by the intern's home institution of the effects of the training on an intern's performance after return. The findings could provide information and insights from a different perspective.

Summary and Recommendations

This paper thus far has described in some detail the internship program of Ohio University which has proven both popular and successful. Among the special features of the program are its flexibility and adaptability. Each intern receives an individually designed program based on his/her background and needs. In describing the program I have briefly traced its origin, purpose, format, costs, sources of funding, program review and evaluations, etc. Based on our experience, I would like to offer a few recommendations for the continuation of the program and for others who may want to do the same.

First, I hope to see more libraries offering this program. There is an urgent need to upgrade and improve the knowledge and skills of a large number of library and information professionals in the Asian and Pacific Region in view of rapid social, economic and technological changes. The need for improved library and information services is increasingly recognized. It is an opportune time for library and information professionals to take part in the development and gain recognition for their services.

Second, although there may be no monetary advantage for libraries to offer internship training, the experience itself can be richly rewarding. From my own experience, shared by my Ohio University colleagues, I have learned a great deal from each intern and have made lasting friendships with many of them. In fact, among other contributions, each intern has brought to our library a rich cultural experience and an opportunity to view our operations and procedures from different perspectives. Not unimportantly, they also pave the way for further inter-institutional cooperation and meaningful information exchanges for our Southeast Asia Collection.

Third, in order that more internships can be made available to the large number of library and information professionals who need them, expanded sources of funding are needed. In addition to increasing current and financial support from international organizations and foundations, there is a need for greater awareness by governments of the value of internship programs as an important component for development. Such awareness, of course, must be followed by financial commitments. This applies to nations in the Region and to nations providing development assistance. Sending library and information professionals abroad for internship training should be strongly supported by the home institutions as well.

Fourth, in the selection of interns, particularly from non-English speaking countries, a moderate level of English proficiency should be required as this will facilitate the learning process and assure maximum benefit from the short-term training.

Fifth, another factor affecting the result of internships is the desire and determination to learn by the interns. It is important that each intern be made aware early in his/her training that the responsibility to learn rests on the intern. The staff members assigned to coordinate the internship training should be carefully selected and matched. They should have the professional ability, cultural sensitivity and commitment to do justice to the program. A successful internship program is often the result of good planning and team work. It requires the support and participation of a major segment of the library staff who will not only help the interns in their training but also go out of their way to make the interns feel welcome and at home.

Sixth, the commitment from the intern's home institution must extend beyond financial support. Unless the institution is prepared to capitalize on what the intern has gained, our time and effort might be more usefully directed to other areas. Important to this process is not only providing opportunities for the returned intern to apply what she/he has gained but also to share the lessons with others. Even with major expansion in internship opportunities, adequate addressing of the Regional needs for professional development demands that those individuals selected serve not only as practioners but as teachers for their colleagues after returning. Teaching in this instance refers to professional development programs rather than necessarily to a classroom role.

In conclusion, the internship program at Ohio University has offered a new approach to cooperation. We and the interns have learned from and about each other and ourselves for mutually rewarding experiences.

(Published by the Chinese-American Librarians Association for the Asian/Pacific American Librarians Association and the Chinese-American Librarians Association, 1985.)

8. 台湾的教育发展（1945—1962）
Educational Development in Taiwan, China (1945 – 1962)[①]

foreword

The writer heartily acknowledges his appreciation to all those who have given their generous assistance and guidance during the time this research was in progress. Particular gratitude is due to Dr. William H. E. Johnson, major advisor and Chairman of the Department of Educational Foundations, who gave constant encouragement and valuable advice. Thanks are rendered also to Dr. Ryland W. Crary and Dr. Robert E. Mason, Professors of Education, Dr. Harold Lancour, Dean of the Graduate School of Library and Information Sciences, Dr. Andrew D. Osborn, Professor of Library Science, and Dr. Shun-hsin Chou, Professor of Economics—all members of the dissertation committee—for their suggestions which guided the formation and development of this study. The writer is likewise indebted to Dr. Samuel C. Chu, Associate Professor of History, who recently spent one year in Taiwan as a Fulbright research fellow, for his reading of the manuscript and to Mr. Harold Chou, former instructor of Chinese Language, Hong Kong University, for his assistance in the romanization of Chinese transliteration. The writer is also under obligation to Mrs. Mary Kratochvil and Miss Anna Marie Carrier for their typing of the preliminary and final manuscripts and to Dr. Theodore T. Polk, Director of Graduate Study in Education, for his indispensable editorial counsel and guidance. Instrumental in enabling the writer to pursue his study in the United States was Rev. Paul L. Offenhiser, who raised the scholarship grant to finance the writer's first year of graduate study at the University of Pittsburgh. To him, the writer extends his deepest appreciation. The writer also wishes to thank his wife, Mary, for her patience and forbearance throughout the years of his doctoral study.

I. Introduction

A. Background of the Problem

In recent years, many researchers interested in comparative education have directed their attention to the study of educational development in Mainland China while, at the same time, very few have given attention to the study of the educational development in Taiwan. In view of the peculiar circumstances under which the Kuomingtang retreated to Taiwan in 1949, and of the rapid social and economic progress subsequently achieved by the Kuomingtang administration, it is rather surprising that so little study has been directed toward the educational program in Taiwan. The educational advancement achieved despite the enormous difficulties encountered could be an exemplar for other developing countries seeking an alternative to the Communistic solution.

[①] This is Dr. Hua-Wei Lee's dissertation for the degree of Doctor of Philosophy, the School of Education, University of Pittsburgh, 1964. The original title is the Educational Development in Taiwan under "Nationalist Government", 1945 – 1962.

There are a few publications dealing directly with the educational program in Taiwan,① but most of them have nothing more than a factual account of what is in existence, with no effort made to give insight into the background upon which the present educational experiment is based. A few studies, however, do deviate from the above conventional approach. One is devoted to the study of differing mental characteristics of students from the mainland and Taiwanese students.② Two others, in which education is considered a prime mover in economic development, offer suggestions to accelerate economic and social progress through education.③ These studies contribute to our knowledge of some of the special aspects of Nationalist education, but they do not meet the need for an overall scrutiny of the present educational program. This research is undertaken in an attempt to fill the need for study of education in Taiwan with broader perspective and in reasonable breadth and depth.

1. The Setting: Geographical, Historical, Economic, Social, Demographical and Political

Taiwan, which is better known to the West by its Portuguese name "Formosa" or "Ilha Formosa", is an island located in the Western Pacific, less than 100 miles east of the south China coast. The main island covers 13,808 square miles, and is about 250 miles in length and between 60 and 80 miles in width. For a long time this island was inhabited only by native aborigines. Later, it was also the home of Chinese and Japanese pirates. Chinese settlement in Taiwan dates back as far as the 12th century, but not until the 17th century did large groups of Chinese begin to cross the Taiwan Straits.

The Dutch invaded the island in 1624. At that time there were an estimated 30,000 settlers. Two years later the Spaniards also landed and occupied coastal areas in the northern part of the island until 1641, when they were driven out by the Dutch. In 1661, Ch'eng-kung Cheng, known to the West as Koxinga, recaptured Taiwan from the Dutch and used it as a base against the Manchus (or Ch'ing dynasty) in his attempt to restore the Ming dynasty. Under Cheng's rule, mainland refugees flocked to the island, giving Taiwan a Chinese majority in population and culture.

The Manchus conquered the island in 1683 and in the following year made the island a prefecture of Fukien Province, In 1886, it was formally made a province of China, but was ceded to Japan at the end of the first Sino-Japanese War in 1895. Those Chinese residing on the island attempted armed resistance to Japanese rule, proclaiming Taiwan a Republic, but this resistance was suppressed by Japanese force before the end of 1895. During the half century of Japanese occupation, there were repeated uprisings. The revolutionary movement continued despite brutal

---

① In Chinese: China, "Ministry of Education", Chiao Yü Kai K'ang Chung Hua Min Kuo San Shih Chiu Nien Chih Wu Shih Nien [A General Survey of Education, 1950 – 1961] (Taipei: 1961); China, "Ministry of Education", Chung Kuo Chiap Yü Nien Chien [Educational Yearbook of China] (3rd ed.; Taipei: Cheng Chung Shu Chu, 1957); Tsun-sheng Wu et al, "Chung Hua Min Kuo" Chiao Yü Chih [Education in "Taiwan"] (2 vols.; Taipei: Chung Hua Wen Hua Chu Pan Shih Yeh Wei Yüan Hui, 1955); Chien-sheng Shih et al, Chung Kuo Chiao Yü Hsien K'uang [The Present Status of Chinese Education] (4 vols.; Taipei: Chung Hua Wen Hua Chu Pan Shih Yeh Wei Yuan Hui, 1958); Taiwan, "Department of Education", Shih Nien Lai Ti Tai-wan Chiao Yü [Education in Taiwan in the Past Ten Years] (Taipei, 1955); Taiwan, "Department of Education", Taiwan Sheng Wu Shih Nien Kuo Min Chiao Yü Chi Chung Teng Chiao Yü Tiao Ch'a Pao Kao Shu [Report of the 1961 Survey of Elementary and Secondary Education in Taiwan Province] (Taichung, 1962); Chih-ting Wang, Tai-wan Chiao Yü Shih [The History of Taiwan's Education] (Taipei: Taiwan Shu Tien, 1959);

In English: China, "Ministry of Education", Education in Taiwan Purina the Past Ten Years (Taipei: Taiwan Book Company, 1955); China, "Ministry of Education", Education in "Taiwan" (Taipei, 1958); Abul Hassan K. Sassani, Education in Taiwan (Formosa), U. S. Office of Education Bulletin 1956, No. 3 (Washington, D. C.: Government Printing Office, 1956); Taiwan, "Department of Education", Education in Taiwan (Taichung, 1961).

② The "Taiwanese" not including the native aborigines, are ethnically Chinese differing from "mainlanders" only in that they were born and lived in Taiwan prior to 1945.

③ William G. Rodd "A Cross-Cultural Study of Taiwan's Schools" (unpublished PhD dissertation, Department of Education, Western Reserve University, 1958); Donald Murray Foster, "Education as an Instrument of National Policy for Economic Development in "Taiwan" (unpublished Ed. D. dissertation, Stanford University, 1962); Stanford Research Institute, Education and Development: The Role of Educational Planning in the Economic Development of "the Republic of China", prepared for Taiwan by Henry F. McCusker, Jr., and Harry J. Robinson (Menlo Park, California: The Institute, 1962), Vol. I.

attempts at suppression by the Japanese.

Following the Cairo Conference of 1943, a joint declaration issued by the heads of government of China, Great Britain, and the United State called for the return to the " Republic of China " of all the Chinese territory taken by Japan. On the basis of this wartime agreement, to which the Soviet Union subsequently subscribed, Taiwan and the nearby "Pescadores" were restored to China and made into a Chinese province after Japan's surrender in 1945.

While the initial response of the Taiwanese to the reestablishment of Chinese rule was one of rejoicing and enthusiasm, the first postwar administration of Taiwan under General Yi Ch'en proved to be inept and corrupt, giving rise to profound public discontent which erupted into a popular uprising on February 28, 1947.

Alarmed by the fast deteriorating situation on the island, the Kuomintang introduced a series of measures aimed at soothing public sentiment and correcting previous mistakes. When the Chinese Mainland was changed greatly in 1949, the Kuomintang (or the Nationalist Party) moved to Taiwan. Mr. Chiang assumed personal control and General Ch'eng Ch'en, Chiang's trusted lieutenant, was appointed governor. Determined to convert the island into an anti-Communist bastion, the Kuomintang began to embark upon a program of governmental reorganization and economic development the latter being greatly facilitated by large scale United States aid. ①

The Kuomingtang administration has had pronounced success in economic development. In agriculture, it has successfully carried out an agrarian reform, improved production techniques, and raised farm output. In industry, it has not only rehabilitated all the industries devastated during World War II, but has also built many new industries providing numerous new products to supply enough for both the domestic market and for export. Because of economic progress, per capita income has shown remarkable and uninterrupted increase, accompanied by a rising standard of living which is now among the highest in Asia. ② Such achievements are spectacular when it is taken into consideration that they have been made against great odds because of the adverse existing conditions such as that of the rapid annual population increase of 35 per 1,000③—one of the highest in the world, the limited resources available, and the costly but indispensable maintenance of the armed forces necessary for the island's defense.

The prevailing social conditions are no less influential. As a result of industrialization, Taiwan's society is experiencing a transformation from the traditional agricultural society. The concomitants of urbanization and the breakup of the traditional family system—with no ready substitutes for traditional beliefs, attitude, and moral standard—has created a grave problem of readjustment. The social impact of the population explosion, resulting from improved health conditions and a high birth rate, constitutes another threat. Surplus labor and the problem of unemployment go hand in hand.

The conflicts between the Taiwanese and Mainlanders have been greatly exaggerated by many. Although many did exist during the early period of the Kuomingtang administration, they have now gradually been resolved. This has come about through education and improved living conditions for a majority of the common people. There is no discrimination in any sense between these two ethnically identical groups of Chinese people. Many special measures have even been taken to protect the Taiwanese interest. One example is the quota system in the provincial colleges under which Taiwanese students enjoy a fixed high admission quota of 70 percent while students from the mainland compete through the entrance examination to be among the remaining 30 per cent admitted. ④

---

① The brief historical developments of Taiwan are drawn largely from the *China Yearbook, 1961 - 1962* (Taipei: China Publishing Company, 1962), pp. 118 - 19. For description of early history of Taiwan see Heng Lien, Tai-Wan T'ung Shih [A General History of Taiwan] (2 vols.; Taipei: Chung Hua Ts'ung Shu Wei Yüan Hui, 1958).

② C. T. Yang, *Economic And Social Development in "Taiwan" During the Past Decade* (Taipei: "Ministry of Economic Affairs", 1960), p. 1.

③ Chung Yang Jih Pao (Central Daily) September 9, 1962, p. 2.

④ Lih-Wu Han, *Taiwan Today* (Taipei: Hwa-Kuo Publishing Company, 1951), p. 156.

Besides the high population growth rate, another demographic factor having serious effect on education is the relatively larger proportion of young and unproductive manpower in the population. Official statistics disclose that 46 per cent of the total population in Taiwan is of age 14 or under (or 54 per cent of age 19 and under)① —a figure nearly double the corresponding figures for the United Kingdom and far in excess of those for the United States. ②

In the political sphere, the change from colonial rule to nationalist rule naturally affects Taiwan's society and education. As in most colonies, the people of Taiwan during the Japanese occupation were not only denied any political rights to administer their own affairs, but were also heavily taxed and closely regulated in matters of economic interest. The Japanese had instituted a few reforms in education, but these were aimed at cutting off the cultural tie between the people of Taiwan and those of the China mainland. They suppressed all learning of Chinese culture and entirely replaced the Chinese language with the Japanese language. This was done by education and by a well-devised system of social rewards. There were dual school systems for Taiwanese children and Japanese children, but few Taiwanese were granted the opportunity of advancing beyond primary school. Even if they were fortunate enough to be admitted to a secondary school or an institute of higher learning, they were confined to taking vocational training or to majoring in limited fields such as agriculture and medicine. ③

The colonial system was abolished after Taiwan was restored to China in 1945. After the provincial maladministration of the first few postwar years, many reforms were undertaken by the Kuomingtang administration. After 50 years of non-participation in the affairs of the government, Taiwanese were again invited to take part in political life and economic development. At present, they have been given a great deal of local autonomy with the Kuomingtang administration playing a decreasingly important part in the local affairs of the island. ④

The Kuomintang is the ruling party in Taiwan. There are two other political parties which are too small to be of any influence. ⑤ The Kuomintang is keenly concerned about education. The educational aims of Taiwan as adopted by the Kuomintang administration in April, 1929 were actually drawn up by the Kuomintang at its "Third National Congress" held in March of the same year. "The Congress" made the San Min Chu I (The Three People's Principles) the guiding principles of Chinese education. ⑥ There are still other factors which surpass in importance those already mentioned. The war conditions existing across the Straits and the determination of Kuomintang leaders to counter-attack the mainland and to rebuild the country based on the principle of San Min Chu I are more decisive factors than any previously mentioned. They are in fact, the basic factors behind all other factors.

2. Educational Development Since 1945

As social, economic, and political conditions make headway toward national reconstruction, education is also moving forward to contribute its share. During the 17 years since the retrocession of Taiwan, education has been working closely with all other forces in the society and correspondingly undergoing stages of change in its emphasis.

The first stage was between 1945 when Taiwan was returned to China and 1949 when the Kuomingtang administration retreated to Taiwan. During this period three major tasks were emphasized: (a) to replace the Japanese educational system with the Chinese educational system; (b) to replace the Japanese language with the Chinese national language; and (c) to reorientate

---

① *Taiwan Statistical Data Book*, 1963 (Taipei: Econcanic Research Center, Council for U. S. Aid, 1963), p. 160.
② The percentages of the total population at age 14 or under in the United Kingdom is 23.3 and in the United States it is 31.1, *Ibid*.
③ U. S. Office of Naval Operation, *Taiwan*, Civil Affairs Handbook (Washington, D. C., 1944), pp. 33 – 37.
④ Stanford University, China Project, *Taiwan* (HRAF, Sub-contractor's Monograph No. 31; New Haven: Printed by HRAP, 1956), p. 15.
⑤ The two parties are the Young China Party and the China Democratic Socialist Party.
⑥ Hang-chen Sun, "Chiao Yü Cheng Ts'e Yü Hsueh Chih" [Educational Policy and School System] Chung Hua Min Kuo Chiao Yü Chih, op. cit., pp. 10 – 11.

the people to Chinese culture.

The line between the second and third stages is difficult to draw; however, there have been two distinctive emphases since 1949. At first the main emphasis in education concentrated on making Taiwan a Nationalist base to hold back any other parties infiltration or aggression. In compliance with this, the program of planned education guided by the San Min Chu I was introduced. It was further reinforced after 1953 when the series of four-year economic plans were adopted. The Kuomingtang administration's efforts, however, were not aimed at merely making Taiwan into a model province, but were also directed toward preparing for recovery and reconstruction of the mainland. For this reason, when implementation of the first programs were well under way, the Administration launched many long-range programs to train the people for this second plan to recover and reconstruct the mainland. ①

The joint efforts of the Administration and the people in improving education has not been without fruition. The yearly educational statistics published have shown steady improvement in both quantity and quality. In the school year of 1961 – 62, for example, there were a total of 2,523,242 students enrolled in schools of all levels. When compared with the population of 11,149,000 there was more than one student for every five persons. The percentage of school-age children actually enrolled in school amounted to 96 per cent. ② Among all elementary school graduates, 52.33 per cent entered junior high schools; 81.85 per cent of all junior high school graduates entered senior high schools; and 76.75 per cent of all senior high school graduates entered institutes of higher education. ③ The ratios of school enrollment at all levels are comparable to many economically advanced countries.

Although the qualitative advance cannot be expressed in figures, the progress can be seen in the following major changes: normal schools have ascended to the junior college level; many secondary school teachers are now equipped with post-graduate training; the number of supplementary teachers has been reduced to a minimum; the educational status and living conditions of teachers at all levels are being raised; teaching programs and methods are being improved; curriculum standards are being revised to meet the new needs of the individual and society; and more laboratories and libraries are being established or strengthened.

Despite all of the progressive changes, education in Taiwan has met with both praise and criticism by those seriously concerned with the quality of education. Attempts are being made to overcome the shortcomings of education through the joint efforts of parents, teachers, and educational authorities. It is important at this stage to evaluate objectively the meaning and scope of the educational program of Taiwan—both its achievements and its shortcomings—through carefully conducted investigation and analysis of available data. It is hoped that the findings of this study will provide, for those who are interested in comparative education in general and in Chinese education in particular, a sound background of understanding of Chinese education in Taiwan.

B. Statement of the Problem

The problem of this study is to trace the development and direction of the present educational program in Taiwan and to determine, to the extent possible, the influential factors that have shaped the course of development and directed its trends.

---

① The Eighth National Congress of the Kuomintang, convening October 20, 1957, adopted a detailed platform which "emphasizes the fact that all the political, military, economic, social, overseas affairs and educational policies pursued in the free area aimed at building Taiwan into a model province dedicated to the Three Principles of the People; at laying a firm foundation for national recovery and at completing reparations for counter measures to destroy communism and achieve final victory." See *China Yearbook, 1961 – 1962, op. cit.*, p 100.

② The highest enrollment rate of all school-age Taiwan children during the 51 years of Japanese occupation was 71.3 per cent in 1943. See Wang, *op. cit.*, p. 46.

③ *China Yearbook, 1962 – 1963* (Taipei: China Publishing Company, 1963), pp. 512 – 15.

C. Elements of the Problem

The elements to be investigated are the historical background of Taiwan's education, the changes that have taken place after the Kuomingtang Administration resettled in Taiwan and the subsequent developments in educational thinking, administration and finance, school organization, primary education, secondary education, higher education, teachers' education, and social education. Since education is a product of time and environment, particular situations and factors that have existed in Taiwan and have shaped the educational development are to be carefully analyzed.

D. Sources of the Study

The validity of this study rests upon the sources and materials used. It is based primarily upon a carefully conducted investigation and analysis of the available original sources, such as Chinese administration documents and reports by both the Kuomingtang Administration and the provincial government, Chinese newspapers, educational laws and regulations, publications of learned educational societies in Taiwan, etc. Reliable secondary sources are consulted and used as supplements whenever the original sources are unavailable or insufficient.

The Oriental collections of the Library of Congress, the East Asian Library and the Teachers College Library of Columbia University, and the New York Public Library possess the main stock of the source materials which have been consulted as frequently as this research required. Inter-library loan has been used for those materials not available in the above libraries but which are located in libraries throughout the United States.

The writer has developed a small but important collection of many original source materials through his personal contact with educators in Taiwan, notably Dr. Chen-hsing Yen, the former Commissioner of Education of Taiwan Provincial Government, Dr. Yuan-tsai Tu, President of the Taiwan Provincial Normal University, and Mr. Chi-lu Huang.

Furthermore, since the writer lived, was educated, and taught in Taiwan during more than half of the period under study, he has utilized his background, common knowledge, and personal observations and experiences to assist him in the process of this study.

E. Method of Study

In general, the study is pursued and developed through the use of the historical-analytical method. ① It proceeds by locating all pertinent documents and records, determining the authenticity and meaning of the sources through the processes of external and internal criticism, putting together in a logical way the evidence derived from the documents and records, and then forming conclusions which offer sound generalizations with respect to the problem under study. The whole study is undertaken in the spirit of critical inquiry.

Throughout this study all Chinese characters, both personal names and bibliographic notations, except those well known in conventional forms (e. g. Taiwan for T'ai-wan; Chiang Kai-shek for Chiang Chieh-shih), are romanized in accordance with the Wade—Giles System of transliteration. ②

F. Justification of the Study

The undertaking is a difficult task since it requires extensive research in numerous original documents representing many fields of knowledge, such as geography, history, sociology, economics, politics, and international relations. To the best knowledge of the writer, no previous doctoral research on the Chinese Nationalist education program in Taiwan has been attempted with such a wide scope. It is hoped that this study will prove to be valuable in providing depth to our

---

① Carter V. Good, *Introduction to Educational Research* (New York: Appleton-Century-Crofts, 1959), pp. 115–58.
② For explanation of the Wade-Giles System, see U. S. Army Map Service, *Key to Wade-Giles Romanization of Chinese Characters* (Washington, D. C.: Government Printing Office, 1944).

understanding of the present educational development in Taiwan.

G. Delimitations and Limitations

1. Delimitations of the Study

a. The study of the Kuomingtang educational program in Taiwan is delimited from 1945 onward with emphasis on the changes and developments since 1949, after the Kuomingtang Administration moved to Taiwan.

b. Although the study is designated to present the educational program in Taiwan in depth, it is primarily an interpretation of facts with value judgments by the writer kept at a minimum.

2. Limitations of the Study

a. One grave limitation of this study is the unavailability of some source materials which may prevent this study from being as complete as the writer would wish. Due to the cost of printing, many Chinese administration documents are handwritten or mimeographed, making them difficult of access outside the country.

b. This study is further limited by lack of direct observation since 1957, when the writer left Taiwan for the United States.

c. Another limitation may result from the writer's personal involvement with the country and its educational system even though he has tried to be extremely careful in refraining from emotionalism, propagandizing, and prejudices.

d. There may be possible exaggeration or coloration contained in many official documents. Attempts are made to check some basic elements through interviews with students and educators newly arrived from Taiwan, and through correspondence with educators still in Taiwan.

II. Historical Background of Taiwan's Education

When political changes are taken into account, the educational history of Taiwan can be roughly divided into three epochs: The epoch of traditional education before 1895, the epoch of colonial education from 1895 to 1945, and the epoch of Nationalist education from 1945 to the present. Since the present Chinese Nationalist education is an outgrowth and an amalgamation of educational developments in mainland China prior to 1945 and developments on Taiwan, itself prior to 1945, it is necessary to present a brief sketch of these two historical sources. This investigation will provide a sound background for a more thorough understanding of the educational program of Kuomingtang Administration in Taiwan during the present epoch.

A. Traditional Education in Taiwan up to 1895

For the purpose of this study, the educational history of the traditional period can be further divided into the following periods: The early education of the aborigines as provided by Dutch and Spanish missionaries, the emergence of Chinese education in Taiwan, traditional Chinese education in Taiwan under the rule of the Ch'ing dynasty, and the early attempts at the modernization of education.

1. The Early Education of Aborigines as Provided by Dutch and Spanish Missionaries

There is no reliable information pertaining to educational activities prior to the Dutch and Spanish expeditions in the second half of the seventeenth century. The Dutch, through their East India Company, are credited as being the first to introduce any type of formal education to the people of Taiwan. Since their colonial interest in trade and commerce could be carried out only through the cooperation of the local people, missionary work and education were established as a means toward this end.

As soon as the Dutch had become settled in the southern part of Taiwan in 1627, they sent out the first missionary, Rev. George Candidius, to establish contact with the people of Taiwan. Although the assiduous endeavors of Candidius were not favorably met by the Chinese of the island, they did penetrate to the aborigine tribes. A rough estimate by Wang is that in a little more than one decade after 1627, about 5,000 aborigines were converted to Christianity. ①

As the result of this successful expansion of missionary work, a number of schools were subsequently established affiliated with the churches. The Dutch missionary believed that "the schools where people learn to read and write will serve as a medium for the propagation of the tenets of the Christian faith."② The instruction of these schools was mainly in religious matters. The Lord's prayer and catechism translated into the Sin Kong dialect③ in the form of roman letters by Reverend Candidius were used as texts.

Since the primary objective of the Dutch East India Company was to extend its commerce and trade among the local people, the missionaries, in addition to their ecclesiastical and educational works, were obliged to serve the Company's purpose also. The Company's intention was to make religion and trade go hand in hand, the one serving the other. Arnold describes it thus:

> As soon as the Dutch missionaries and teachers had learned the language and customs of the natives, they became especially useful to the company as collectors of taxes, interpreters, judicial functionaries, and even as tradesmen. ④

While the Dutch were carrying out their activities in trade, religious work, and education among the aborigines in the south, the Spanish acquired a small territory in the northern part of the island which they occupied between 1626 and 1642.

Just as with the Dutch, the Spanish also found it easier to extend their trade relations among the aborigines rather than among the Chinese residents. They also employed religion as a means of enhancing their trade interest. They enlisted the Dominican friars to carry out missionary work among the peaceful savages of the plains in the vicinity of Keelung. Churches were established. "A school was opened on Palm Island, in Keelung Harbor, about the year 1630, and enrolled at one time as many as 400 pupils."⑤

Despite their ultimate goals the labors of the Dutch and Spanish among the aborigines had the following beneficial effects:

(a) It is generally agreed that both Dutch and Spanish missionaries helped to improve the social customs of the aborigines with whom they had contact though the inculcation of Christian living.

(b) They left to the aborigines a written language in the form of roman letters based on the phonetic sounds of the dialects.

It is recorded in one of the historical sources that about 145 years later there were many aborigines who could write their dialect in the form of roman letters and used pens made of sharpened quills in their writing, which went horizontally from the left to the right. ⑥

2. The Emergence of Chinese Education in Taiwan (1661 – 1683)

When the Manchus overthrew the Ming dynasty in 1644, many Ming loyalists sought refuge in China's southeastern coastal area. Many even courageously retained the title of Ming in fighting against the Ch'ing. Their resistance lasted for some 20 years. One of the celebrated resistance fighters was Ch'eng-kung Cheng (or Koxinga) who sailed with his troops to Taiwan in 1661 and with little difficulty drove out the Dutch. Though Ch'eng-kung Cheng never realized his cherished

---

① Wang, op. cit. p. 2.
② Julean H. Arnold, *Education in Formosa*, U. S. Bureau of Education Bulletin 1908, No. 5 (Washington, D. C. : U. S. Government Printing Office, 1908), p. 11.
③ A dialect spoken by the aborigines in the place of Sin Kong.
④ Arnold, op. cit., p. 14.
⑤ Ibid., p. 65.
⑥ Hung-chien Kao, Tai-Wan Fu Chih [Historical Record of Taiwan Prefecture] Vol. I, Historical Documents Series No. 65 (Taipei: Reprinted by the Bank of Taiwan, Bureau of Economic Research, 1958), p. 161.

dream of recovering the mainland, he succeeded in opening up the island for Chinese settlement.

After the sudden death of Cheng, his son and able successor, Ching Cheng, followed in his father's path and continued the fight. With the able assistance of his lieutenant, Yung-hua Chen, Ching Cheng established a system of government administration and set up schools, both of which followed the traditional Chinese pattern with the civil service examination as the core. ① There were three levels of schools: the district schools, the county and prefectural schools, and the college. The district schools were equivalent to primary schools, the county and prefectural schools were considered secondary schools, and the college, the institution of higher education. Those who completed the district schools or its equivalent might take the county examination. Passing of the county examination was a prerequisite for admittance to the prefectural examination, and passing of the prefectural examination was a prerequisite for admittance to the college examination. Those who passed the college examination received three years of education in the college where room and board were provided. Upon completion of the study they might receive immediate appointment to a government office. The county and prefectural schools were the places where one was prepared to take the college examination. The function of the whole educational program was to select the best scholars for government service. ②

Throughout Cheng's regime the educational program was mainly for the Chinese. No records show whether or not there was any educational program designed specifically for the aborigines.

Ching Cheng also died young, causing a great setback to the educational program he had worked so hard to initiate. In 1683, Taiwan submitted to Ch'ing's rule.

3. Traditional Chinese Education in Taiwan Under the Ch'ing (1683 – 1885)

As soon as the Ch'ing took possession of Taiwan, they made it an integral part of the Empire and for more than two centuries governed it as a prefecture of Fukien Province. However, since it was separated from the mainland by the Taiwan Strait and since there was a lack of sea transportation, Taiwan was cut off from the mainland and received very little attention from the Imperial Court.

In education, Ching Cheng's educational system was largely retained with little improvement. The system was retained because both Ching Cheng's education system and the Ch'ing's educational system largely followed traditional Chinese education which had been practiced in China for centuries. There was a difference between them, however, in that the Ch'ing system overemphasized the examination system and was more formal and pedantic in the content of the examinations. This undue emphasis and increasing formality hampered educational development. Public schools such as the prefectural and county Confucian schools became places where only monthly and yearly examinations were administered. Students successfully passing such examinations were elevated to upper grades and were given monetary rewards. No formal instruction was given in these schools. In the course of years of residence, students might avail themselves of the opportunity to take the civil service examination toward the second degree—Chü-jen (recommended man). ③

As the public schools did very little for education it was the private school such as the shu-yüan (academies)④ upon which education really depended both in Taiwan, and on the China mainland. However, the quality of their instruction was inferior when compared with the shu-yüan established several centuries earlier.

Both the prefectural and county Confucian schools were at the secondary school level and the

---

① Lien, *op. cit.*, pp. 211 – 12.
② Wang, *op. cit.*, p. 8.
③ In the Ch'ing dynasty, there were three main grades of examinations: the lowest in the prefectural capital after preliminary examinations in the district seat (*hsien*), the second in the provincial capital, and the third in the capital of the empire with reexamination in the imperial palace. See Wolfgang Franke, *The Reform And Abolition of the Traditional Chinese Examination System* (Cambridge, Massachusetts: Harvard University Press, 1960), p. 8.
④ Wang, *op. cit.*, pp. 14 – 17. There were 37 such academies in 1893.

academies, at the college level. For primary education there were the i hsüeh (philanthropic schools), the she hsüeh (tribal schools), and the szu shu or shu-fang (private schools). Except for the tribal schools which were mainly for the education of the aborigines, all the philanthropic schools and private schools geared their studies toward preparation for the civil service examination for the first degree—Hsiu-ts'ai (cultivated talent). ①

4. First Attempts at the Modernization of Education in Taiwan (1885 – 1895)

The Imperial Court did not fully realize the geographic importance of Taiwan until the Sino-French War of 1884 when the French army threatened the defense of the coastal provinces by occupying Keelung and the "Pescadores". After the war, the Court made Taiwan an independent province and appointed as governor one of the most able and trusted officers of the time, General Ming-ch'uan Liu.

Liu was both a soldier and a statesman, equipped with modern ideas and a creative spirit. He immediately dedicated himself to the task of the modernization of Taiwan through the building of forts, the construction of railroads, the installation of telegraph cables, the development of mining resources, and the establishment of a shipping company. Since all of these called for trained personnel and technicians, along with the traditional examination system, he established Hsi Hsüeh T'ang (School for Western Learning) in 1887 and Tien-Pao Hsüeh T'ang (Telegraphy School) in 1890. The curriculum of the School for Western Learning reflected Liu's desire to produce a group of broadly-educated graduates proficient in English, French, geography, history, mathematics, and science, as well as in the Chinese classics. ②

For the somewhat neglected aborigines, Liu set up an effective policy of pacification and civilization. In addition to the establishment of a department for the control of the training of the aborigines through cultivation and schooling, Liu also set up a new type of school called Fan Hsüeh T'ang (Aboriginal School) to teach the children of aborigines' headmen the Chinese language, customs and manners. They were also taken to see urban life and to make contact with Chinese people.

The modernization attempts of Liu brought Taiwan into a new era when for a while everything seemed to progress well. But this soon caught the attention of many conservatives. Opposition began to mount especially in the central government. Liu was finally forced to resign in 1891. One of his political rivals, Yu-lien Shao, an extreme conservative, became his successor. It did not take long for him to undermine Liu's modernization movement. All the new schools were closed including the one for the aborigines. Soon afterwards, in 1895, Taiwan was ceded to Japan.

B. Colonial Education in Taiwan Under the Japanese (1895 – 1945)

1. Aims of Japanese Education in Taiwan

The Japanese attitude toward Taiwan, as stated in an American official source, is a typical expression of many other similar observations. This American source states:

> Despite much verbal testimony to the contrary, the fundamental attitude of the Japanese toward Taiwan is that of a conqueror bent on the fullest possible exploitation of the resources of the island, both of material and of manpower, and the development of the island as a base for military operations, regardless of the consequences to and interests of the native Formosans. ③

In theory, an edict issued by the Emperor Meiji proclaimed that the Taiwanese, newly taken into the Empire, were to be treated equally as brothers. But in practice the colonial government of

---

① *Ibid.*, pp. 18 – 19.
② Samuel C. Chu, "Liu Ming-Ch'uan and Modernization of Taiwan," *Journal of Asian Studies*. XXIII (November, 1963), pp. 51 – 52.
③ U. S. Office of Naval Operations, *op. cit.*, p. 69.

Taiwan, although clothed in civil titles, was a military regime which ruthlessly exploited the island for economic profit and for military expansion.

The objectives of education in Taiwan under the Japanese clearly reflected the fundamental policy of Japanese colonial administration which can be precisely summarized in two words— repression and exploitation. ①

Coinciding with fundamental policy, education in this period was both discriminatory and limited. ② The objectives of education as desired by the Japanese authorities were understanding of the Japanese language, improvement in production, and loyalty to the Empire.

An analysis of available data drawn largely from Japanese sources such as the annual reports on education in Taiwan, and publications by the "Formosan Education Association"③ reveal that there were separate schools for Taiwanese and Japanese children. Although this dual-school system was integrated after 1922 for the "middle schools" and after 1941 for the "elementary schools", the former was strictly for the Japanese, since admission requirements were set too high for any Taiwanese to pass. As to the latter, there were still separate curricula in the "integrated" schools where Japanese speaking people took the No. 1 curriculum, and non-Japanese speaking people took the No. 2 curriculum. Beyond elementary schooling, opportunity for Taiwanese was limited to vocational or technical training.

2. Stages of Development in Education

For the convenience of study the educational development under the Japanese can be further divided into three stages. The first stage is between 1895 and 1919, the second stage, between 1919 and 1937, and the third stage, between 1937 and 1945.

a. <u>Educational Development between 1895 and 1919</u>. During the first stage, the Japanese were interested mainly in the political control and economic exploitation of the island. Very little attention was given to education. For the purpose of political control, however, in the first few years of occupation, they set up a few language schools "to teach local people the Japanese language to prepare them for local civil administration."④ These schools later became the "public elementary schools" for Taiwanese. Japanese children attended the "primary schools." The former was financed through local taxes and the latter, through government funds.

The "middle schools" were founded a few years later. They followed the elementary school pattern.

One significant contribution made by the Japanese was the founding of a medical school in Taiwan as early as 1899. It is interesting to note that although Taiwanese were barred in almost all of their educational advances, they were permitted to study medicine. This not only solved the problem of supplying a large number of urgently needed medical personnel, but also contributed to the general improvement in public health and in medical service in Taiwan in later years.

b. <u>Educational Development between 1919 and 1937</u>. Nearly a quarter of a century of despotic rule in Taiwan did produce some beneficial results; namely, law and order, economic development, elevated standards of living, and modern elementary education. However, it also incurred a rising political discontent among the Taiwanese. Partly due to her proximity to China and partly due to the overwhelming predominance of Chinese on the island, the Taiwanese never ceased to resist Japanese rule. The rising tide of nationalism after the First World War also helped to stir up discontent.

In order to lessen the agitation of the Taiwanese, in 1919, the Japanese took initial steps

---

① Stanford University, China Project, *op. ci.*, p. 27.
② Han, *op. cit.*, p. 141.
③ Taiwan, "Government-General", *Annual Report on Education in Taiwan* ("*Formosa*"), 1907 (Tokyo: 1907). Taiwan ("Formosan") Education Association, *Modern Taiwan* ("*Formosa*"), *with Special Reference to Education* (Taipei: 1923).
④ Tadao Yanaihara, <u>Jih-Pen Ti Kuo Chu I Hsia Chih Tai-Wan</u> [Taiwan Under Japanese Imperialism] Translated from Japanese by Hsien-wen Chou (Bank of Taiwan, Office of Economic Research, Taiwan Yen Chiu Ts'ung K'an, 39; Taipei: Bank of Taiwan, 1956), p. 73.

toward liberalizing the autocratic system of colonial government. A series of political reforms were undertaken under Baron Kenjiro Den, a liberal statesman who was the first civilian Governor-General of Taiwan. In the educational sphere, the government adopted the policy of offering to Taiwanese educational opportunities equal to those afforded Japanese residents. Baron Den said:

> It is eminently proper that we also grant them opportunities of education not inferior to those available to our own children; that we encourage them to develop; that we foster men of genius in all walks of life, thereby increasing the resources of our country. ①

In this spirit the Educational Ordinance of 1919 and the New Educational Ordinance of 1922 were promulgated. The 1919 ordinance was aimed at extending secondary education and technical training to Taiwanese to improve their technical competence. The 1922 ordinance was aimed at redefining the distinction between the "primary school" (Shogakko) and the "public school" (Kogakko) as being mainly on the basis of the degree of mastery of the national language (Japanese) rather than on racial discrimination. The 1922 ordinance provided for elementary schools of two categories:

(1) For those "who habitually speak the national language," to be known as primary school.

(2) For those "who do not habitually speak the national language," to be known as public school. ②

In regard to secondary and higher education, the 1922 ordinance required that both Japanese and Taiwanese be admitted to the same middle and higher schools and to the university.

Although the two ordinances seemed to be well intentioned, few Taiwanese ever benefited from them. At the elementary school level, very few Taiwanese could habitually speak the "national" language. At the secondary school level, even though there was only one type of school, undue emphasis on the use of written Japanese in the entrance examination made it difficult for Taiwanese to be admitted. "The percentage of Formosan students in middle and higher schools was low, in some schools averaging no more than 1 per cent of the total attendance."③ The Japanese denied discrimination pointing out the language requirement as an inevitable barrier.

The real liberalization in the sphere of education came after 1919 with the relaxation of the rule which restricted Taiwanese from pursuing secondary and higher education in Japan. After that many Taiwanese did manage to attend schools in Japan where they were treated better and were given more freedom in choosing fields of study that they had had in Taiwan. ④

Another important educational development in this stage was the establishment of the Taihoku Imperial University in 1928. Before then, the educational system in Taiwan lacked any provision for non-technical university education. The reasons for establishing this university were as follows:

First, perhaps the most important reason of all, was to provide an elaborate first-class research center for exploration of all problems involved in colonizing the lands and peoples of southeast Asia and the Indies.

Second, since the Japanese middle school graduates on the island were increasing in number, it was necessary to set up a university for them.

Third, the lack of any provision for higher education had made it necessary for many Taiwanese to pursue their studies in Japan or elsewhere, such as in Hong Kong or even in China, which caused increased concern to the Japanese authorities. The establishment of a university in Taiwan would help to stop many Taiwanese who could become discontented if given the opportunity to study away from the island and were exposed to diverse social and political environments that would give them an unfavorable attitude toward the one they had become accustomed to in Taiwan.

c. Educational Development between 1937 and 1945. The China "Incident" of 1937 duly effected the last stage of educational development. The last Governor-General, Admiral Kiyoshi

---

① Ralston Hayden, "Japan's New Policy in Korea and Formosa", *Foreign Affairs*. II (March, 1924), pp. 477 – 78.

② U. S. Office of Naval Operations, *op. cit.*, p. 34.

③ *Ibid.*, p. 35.

④ In Taiwan, the study of law and politics were prohibited. Taiwanese could advance themselves only in the fields of agriculture and medicine.

Hasegawa, upon assuming office on November 27, 1940, made a formal statement emphasizing Taiwan's importance as a base for the southward advance of Japanese interest. He also made clear the political and strategic necessity of furthering the assimilation of the people of Taiwan to convert a once hostile and alien group to loyalty and willingness to support the central government. ① This new emphasis brought about the following changes in education: (1) A complete elimination of the Chinese language from the curriculum, (2) close restrictions on the use of the Taiwan dialect, (3) use of elementary schools as a means of instilling Japanese ideas and affecting the general outlook of Taiwan youth, and (4) utilization of all social organizations and mass educational media including adult classes, youth institutions, newspapers, broadcastings, the worship of Japanese Shinto, etc., to carry out the program of assimilation.

During the Second World War, Japan's southward advance called for the services of many Taiwanese who possessed knowledge of both Japanese and Chinese to serve as interpreters, coolies, or as actual soldiers. The regulation prohibiting the learning of the Chinese language was removed. Courses in Chinese once again flourished in order to prepare a large number of Taiwanese for careers in occupied areas of China and southeast Asia.

d. The Decline of Private Schools. Another sector of educational development in the early part of Japanese occupation that is worthy of note is the private schools. There were two types of private schools: the traditional Chinese Confucian schools called shu fang, and the schools founded by Western missionaries. The former were the dominant force in education during the early years of the occupation, and played an important role in the preservation and dissimilation of Chinese culture. But unfortunately, they declined quickly in numbers and influence with the increasing restrictions and control placed upon them by the Japanese administration. ②

The important position occupied by the Confucian schools is attested to by the fact that at the time of annexation there were as many as 1,707 Confucian schools with an enrollment totaling 29,941. ③ The official statistics of the Japanese administration show that in 1899 there were still 421 such schools with an enrollment of 25,215. In 1939, however, the number of Confucian schools was reduced to 17 and enrollment dropped to 932. In 1940, by order of the government even the remaining 17 schools were closed. ④

The schools established by missionaries, although small in number, also met with strict control. Furnivall described their situation as follows:

> The missionaries, who were the pioneers of western education in Formosa, suffered a grievous blow when the growth of public education enabled the Japanese to order the closure of the elementary department in missionary schools. ⑤

3. Educational Administration And Finance

a. The Organization of Educational Administration. The educational administration in the colonial government was vested in the Governor-General who in turn delegated large portions of the power to the Department of Education. Although the status of the department during the colonial period underwent many changes,⑥ its function remained the same—to control "all educational organs whatsoever, including schools, libraries, museums, kindergartens, private teaching institutes..." ⑦

At the second level, the provincial governments, there was a section of education within the bureau of internal affairs whose function was to control all the provincial schools and supervise educational activities at the lower level: the cities and counties. At the lower level, a similar office

---

① U. S. Office of Naval Operations, *op. cit.*, p. 2.
② Arnold, *op. cit.*, p. 50.
③ Wang, *op. cit.*, p. 48.
④ Taiwan, Bureau of Statistics, Tai-Wan Sheng Wu Shih I Nien Lai T'ung Chi T'i Yao [Statistical Abstract of Taiwan for the Last 51 Years] (Taipei: 1946), p. 1236.
⑤ J. S. Furnivall, *Educational Progress in Southeast Asia* (New York: Institute of Pacific Relations, 1943), p. 99.
⑥ Wang, *op. cit.*, pp. 28 – 29.
⑦ U. S. Office of Naval Operations, *op. cit.*, p. 33.

was founded in each county and municipal government "responsible for educational affairs within their respective jurisdictions."①

The overall organization was highly centralized and was both authoritative and efficient.

b. Educational Finance. Before 1898, all the schools established by the Government-General for the purpose of imparting the Japanese language or of educating Japanese children were directly financed by the insular treasury. Since the promulgating of the first Formosan Public School Ordinance in 1898, all the language schools, except those for Japanese children, were changed to "public schools," and their costs were borne thereafter by local taxes. It is said in Arnold's book that additional public schools could be established only "in those districts in which provision was first made for their support."② In contrast, the "primary schools" for Japanese children continued to be supported by the Government-General until 1922. Since then, the financial obligation of supporting schools at various levels was divided among the central government (Government-General), the provincial governments, and the county or municipal governments.

4. The School System

The school system in Taiwan during this period also underwent many changes. Due to the discrimination practiced, the school system appeared to be complicated and somewhat chaotic. There were three courses that can be traced: one for Taiwanese, one for Japanese, and one for the aborigines. This section will be devoted to a brief description of the three courses from elementary education up to higher education.

a. Elementary Education. In elementary education the practice of discrimination was keenly felt. Before 1942, there were "primary schools" for Japanese, "public schools" for Taiwanese, and the "schools for aborigines." After 1942, the "primary schools" and "public schools" were all named "elementary schools" but still retained some segregation by adopting different curricula. (For a school system chart, see chart 1)

Chart 1 Colonial School System 1942 – 1945③

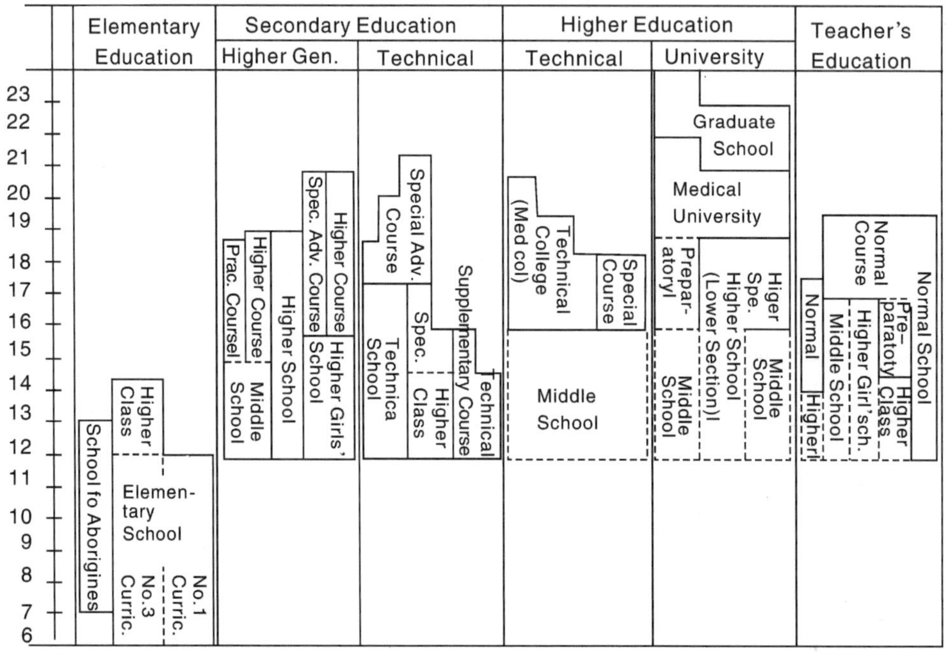

① Shigetaka Abe, "Education in Formosa And Korea", *Educational Yearbook*, 1931, p. 684.
② Arnold, *op. cit.*, p. 30.
③ Adapted from Taiwan, Bureau of Statistics, Tai-wan Sheng Wu Shin I Nien Lai T'ung Chi T'I Yao [Statistical Abstract of Taiwan for the Last 51 Years] (Taipei: 1946), P. 1208.

For most of the Taiwanese who studied the No. 2 curriculum, opportunity for further study was limited. The only door immediately open to them was the two year vocational training courses called "higher class" in agriculture, industry, or commerce which were affiliated with the elementary schools.

The road of schooling for the aborigines was short and narrow. Only four years of schooling was offered by the "schools for aborigines." These schools were run by the Department of Police with policemen serving as teachers. Their aim was to bring the aborigines under control and to open their lands to exploitation. Because schools were run by the police, the percentage of school age children (7 to 14 years of age) actually attending was much higher than the percentage for Taiwanese. Statistics show that in 1942 the percentages of school age children attending school were 86.1 per cent for aborigines and 61.6 per cent for Taiwanese and aborigines combined.① There was no compulsory education throughout the occupation period.

The percentage of school age children attending elementary schools reached 95.6 per cent for Japanese as early as 1919, and for Taiwanese, even in the peak year of 1943, only 71.3 per cent.②

b. Secondary Education. Secondary education consisted of "higher general education" and "technical education." The "normal schools" at the time of occupation were included with higher education and will be discussed separately.

(1) Higher General Education. There were two kinds of schools for higher general education: the "middle schools" for boys and the "higher girls' schools."③ Before 1922, both the "middle schools" and "higher girls' schools" were segregated. Those for the Japanese, established and financed by the Government-General were called "government middle schools" or "government higher girls' schools"; those for Taiwanese, established and financed by provincial governments were called "public middle schools" or "public higher girls' schools." In 1921, the revised Provincial Government Organic Law shifted the financial obligation of the government middle schools and higher girls' schools from the Government-General to the provincial government where the school was located.

The 1922 New Educational Ordinance further eliminated "government" or "public" from the names of the schools. The change in name was not accompanied by any change in practice. Schools formerly dominated by Japanese remained the same and admission of Taiwanese did not occur easily.

(2) Technical Education. In secondary education, the Japanese placed a great deal of emphasis on vocational training. According to 1944 statistics there were 22 middle schools, 23 higher girls' schools, and 27 technical schools. These figures did not include the 90 "technical supplementary courses" mostly affiliated with the elementary schools.④

The "technical supplementary courses" were primarily set up for Taiwanese.⑤ In the three other types of technical school (agricultural, technical, and commercial), Japanese were admitted much more easily than their fellow Taiwanese.

During the last two or three years of war, many short-term courses were established to train girl graduates to fill domestic posts in agriculture and commerce originally held by males.

c. Higher Education. Higher education under the Japanese, following the pattern of secondary education, could be divided into "university education" and "technical education."

Technical education was provided by five technical colleges one in each of the fields of

---

① Taiwan, Bureau of Statistics, op. cit., pp. 1241–42.
② After 1940 the percentage of school age Japanese children attending elementary schools reached 99.6 per cent. See Wang, op. cit., p. 46.
③ Separate schools for boys and girls in their teens or at the secondary education level has been a favored pattern in the Orient for centuries and is still adopted by the Chinese Nationalist.
④ Taiwan, Department of Education, Taiwan Sheng Chiao Yu Kai Ku'ang [A General Survey of Taiwan's Education] (Taipei: 1946), p. 18. As quoted by Wang, op. cit., p. 87.
⑤ The same source stated that in 1944 there were 15,828 Taiwanese enrolled in the technical supplementary course as compared to 2,234 Japanese.

medicine, economics (or commerce as it was called before 1943), agriculture and forestry, and industry plus a technical college for girls. The length of study in these colleges was three years except for the medical college where it was four years. Only middle school or technical school graduates might seek admission to these technical colleges.

University education had three levels: preparatory education, university education, and graduate studies. Preparatory education was provided either by the higher section of the Taihoku Higher School or by the preparatory courses affiliated with the Taihoku Imperial University.

The Taihoku Higher School established in 1922 was composed of a lower and a higher section. The lower section, equivalent to the middle school, admitted students who had completed the elementary school. The higher section, which was divided into "letters" and "sciences," admitted those who had completed either the lower section or a middle school. The graduates of the higher section were eligible for the University.

The preparatory course of the Taihoku Imperial University, founded in 1941, was also divided into the divisions of "letters" and "sciences." The length of their course of study was two years.

The Taihoku Imperial University, established in 1928, consisted of two faculties: letters and law, and science and agriculture. Later, along with a medical college, it added a college of engineering, the Research Institute on Tropical Medicine, the Research Institute of Southern Cultures and Resources, and a graduate school with a program of studies leading toward doctoral degrees.

　　d. Teacher Education. The Japanese were convinced that by controlling teachers' training they could control education. From the very beginning of the occupation, the Japanese tightened control of the teaching profession. Few Taiwanese were qualified or were trusted enough to be given the opportunity to teach.① In the early years, a majority of the teachers were recruited from Japan and were given assignments in Taiwan after a brief program of orientation.

The 1919 Educational Ordinance required the establishment of "normal schools" in Taiwan and in the same year a "Normal School Law" was promulgated which made the former normal departments within the language schools independent "normal schools" for the training of elementary teachers. For the secondary schools, teachers were largely recruited from Japan. In 1942, war conditions made it necessary to establish in the Taihoku Higher School an "Emergency Teachers Training Center" to train secondary school teachers. Students had to be graduates of either a normal school or a middle school. The fact that all normal school students received free education plus a monthly allowance and travel expenses during vacations was one of the significant factors which attracted promising youth, both Taiwanese and Japanese, to teaching as a profession.

C. Nationalist Education as Developed on Mainland China Before 1945

Following the examination of educational development in Taiwan, this section will examine Nationalist education in mainland China up to 1945.

1. Chinese Education before the Twentieth Century

In the study of educational development in mainland China before 1945 it is necessary to give a brief review of traditional Chinese education before the twentieth century. Historical documents reveal that although modern schools in China are a relatively recent development, traditional education in China is as old as Chinese civilization itself.

It is said in the section "Shun Tien" (Historical Events in the Time of Emperor Shun) of the Shang Shu (Book of History) that as early as sometime shortly before 2205 B. C., the Emperor Shun appointed Chi Minister of Teaching to superintend the teaching of the "five humanities."②

---

　　① Statistics show that between 1935 and 1944, there were 3,804 Japanese graduated from normal schools as compared with 925 for Taiwanese. See Wang, op. cit., p. 47.

　　② The "five humanities" are actually the five ethical principles that govern the relationships between human beings. See Feng-chieh Wang, Chung Kuo Chiao Yü Shih [History of Chinese Education] (2nd ed.; Taipei: Chung Cheng Shu Chü, 1954), p. 27.

And in the section "Wang Chih" (The Institutions of the Monarchs) of the Li Chi (Books of Rites)① it is also stated that between 2357 B. C. and 2206 B. C. there were schools named shang hsiang (higher schools) and hsia hsiang (lower schools). ②Education then was still in its rudimentary stages.

The historical documents also reveal that ancient China was governed by scholar-sages. "A governor is at the same time a teacher."③ Education was regarded as the foundation of the state and an important function of government. Because of this tradition the aspiration of Chinese intelligentsia was for government service. In order to select the ablest among the learned for official appointment, a means of close scrutiny was needed. This led to the formulation of the time-honored examination system. According to T'ung Chien Kang Mu (Outline of a Comprehensive History) an examination system was formally established in 606 A. D. by an imperial edict issued by the Emperor Yang of the Sui dynasty (589 – 618 A. D.).④ Originally, this system was merely a supplementary measure for the nomination system (hsüan chü) initiated in the Han dynasty (221 B. C. to 219 A. D.); however, it grew rapidly and superseded its predecessor. In the dynasties which followed, it became the most powerful institution and the most influential factor in Chinese education.

During most of the years when the examination system was in force, schools in China existed in name only. As already mentioned in the section "Traditional Chinese Education in Taiwan under the Ch'ing," public schools became places used only to register students and to administer examinations. The Confucian canons became the sole subject matter, and the so-called "eight-legged essay" became the only accepted style for literary expression.

The formality and narrowness of traditional learning not only discouraged independent thought but led the country into a period of retardation worse than the "Dark Ages" of Europe. From the sixteenth century on when the West underwent drastic changes in an effort to free itself from the past, China remained quite contented with her cultural inheritance, and state of stability and equilibrium. She lived in a world unto herself with little awareness of the progress the West had made in two or three short centuries.

The state of cultural and political isolation began to be challenged when China entered the nineteenth century. Beginning with the Opium War of 1842, China had a series of clashes with the West both culturally and politically. Since that time the traditional institutions of Chinese society has declined, including the examination system which was abolished in 1905.

Before the turn of the twentieth century, many farsighted Chinese officials including the enlightened young emperor Kuang Hsü initiated a series of reforms aimed at saving China from the "unprecedented crisis." Influenced by the popular thought of Chih-tung Chang, "Chung-hsüeh wei t'i, hsi-hsüeh wei yung," which may be translated, "Chinese learning for the fundamental principles, western learning for practical application,"⑤ emphasis of the reforms was placed on the learning of Western science and technology. This led to the establishment of new schools intended to replace the traditional examination system. However, the "Hundred Days' Reform" of 1898 led by Emperor Kuang Hsü was short-lived due to the strong opposition of the conservatives, but the tide of reform was inevitable. After the destructive Boxer Uprising of 1900, public sentiment forced the conservatives in the Imperial Court to give way to progressive forces. Many educational reforms initiated by Kuang Hsü were reenacted, the notable ones including: substitution of essays on historical and political topics for the traditional examination topics, establishment of schools of various grades throughout the country, adoption of a public school system in 1903, and final

---

① For a brief discussion of these ancient documents see Howard S. Gait, *A History of Chinese Educational Institutions*. Vol. I (London: Arthur Probsthain, 1951), pp. 6 – 24.
② Theodore E. Hsiao, *The History of Modern Education in China* (Shanghai: The Commercial Press, 1935), p. 4.
③ Also quoted from Shang Shu [Book of History]. See Feng-chieh Wang, *op. cit.*, p. 34.
④ *Ibid.*, p. 168.
⑤ Ssu-yü Teng and John K. Fairbank, *China's Response to the West; A Documentary Survey 1839 – 1923* (Cambridge: Harvard University Press, 1954), p. 164.

abolition of the examination system in 1905.

2. The Rise of Modern Education

With the abolishment of the examination system, the obstacles that once barred the progress of modern education were temporarily removed. The 1903 new school code which gave China the first modern public school system was now put to the test. Many new schools were established between 1905 and 1911. According to Kuo, there were 52,348 new schools of all types in 1910 with an enrollment totaling 1,625,534. ① To these figures could also be added the thousands of promising youth who flocked to Japan, America, and Europe in search of new knowledge.

The Revolution of 1911 brought China into a new era. A Republic was founded. Although the unification of China was not attained at that time, education was able to make slow but steady progress along the way toward modernization.

The Ministry of Education under the Republic immediately called a first educational conference to discuss the aims of education in a democratic nation and to revise the 1903 school system to make it less cumbersome and less wasteful. ② Four years of compulsory education was planned and the curriculum was modified to reduce the former undue emphasis placed upon the study of Confucian Classics. Educational opportunity for women was also extended.

Unfortunately, the founding of the Republic did not solve many of China's problems. Internally, political power was divided among the avaricious warlords who, with very few exceptions, were more tyrannical and corrupt than the Manchu administration. Externally, in addition to the unequal treaties which undermined the sovereignty of the Republic, the increasingly aggressive actions taken by Japan toward China presented a grave danger. The conditions prevailing in China greatly upset the intellectual class, especially those who returned from studying abroad. Believing that the weakness of China lay in the half-hearted Westernization, many of these intellectuals advocated ch'uan p'ang hsi hua (wholesale Westernization). They were instrumental in initiating the "New Thought Movement" in 1917. ③ At first, the movement was aimed at searching for "a new language, a new literature, a new outlook on life and society, and a new scholarship". ④ In 1919, it joined forces with the "May Fourth Movement," which originated as a patriotic student movement and merged into one multi-purpose "New Culture Movement." One of the significant contributions of this movement was the use of pai-hua or vernacular, in the place of wen yen or classical written language. This change enabled educators to start a large-scale mass education campaign and to effect a considerable increase in literacy.

During and after the "New Culture Movement," the development of Chinese education was strongly affected by the visits of many eminent educators from the West. The visits of John Dewey, Paul Monroe, Bertrand Russell, Hans Driesch, William A. McCall, and Helen Parkhurst, among others, all contributed to the development of the new education.

Dewey spent more than a year in China. His pragmatic philosophy of education aroused great interest and enthusiasm among the Chinese intellectuals. Dewey stated that all tradition must be subjected to critical examination in the light of experience, that there must be no disparity between school and life, and that learning is the result of active participation in the educational experience. Because of the influence of Dewey and the other Western educators, a new school system closely identified with the American pattern was in the making.

---

① Ping-wen Kuo, *The Chinese System of Public Education* (Contributions to Education No. 64; New York: Teachers College, Columbia University, 1915), pp. 107 – 10.

② The 1903 system was modeled after Japan's system which, in turn was copied from the French. The length of the school years from lowest primary through the university was 21 years. The 1912 school system resembled the American pattern and the length of schooling was shortened from 2 to 3 years. See Hang-chen Sun, *op. cit.*, pp. 33 – 38.

③ For historical backgrounds of the "new thought movement" see Shih Hu, The *Chinese Renaissance*, Chinese National Association for the Advancement of Education, Bulletin 6, II (Peking: 1923).

④ Far Eastern and Russian Institute, University of Washington, *A General Handbook of China*. Subcontractor's Monograph (New Haven: HRAF – 55, 1956), p. 587.

3. The "New School System" of 1922

The 1922 school system was the product of at least three national conferences, representing the concurrent and expert opinions of hundreds of prominent leaders of education from all parts of China. ①

The aims and standards of the new system, as finally promulgated on November 1, 1922, were sevenfold:

(a) To adapt itself to a changed and changing society;
(b) to promote the spirit of democracy;
(c) to develop individuality;
(d) to take into special consideration the economic status of the average citizen;
(e) to adjust education to the needs of life;
(f) to facilitate the spread of universal education, and
(g) to make itself flexible enough to allow for local variations. ②

All these aims, or "seven basic principles," advocated a new spirit in Chinese education. However, influenced by the prevailing thought at that time (wholesale Westernization), no mention was given to the place of traditional Chinese culture and heritage in modern education.

The 1922 "New School System" as shown in Chart 2 was an illustration of the 6 – 3 – 3 – 4 pattern. This system survived throughout the Nationalist period on the mainland with minor revisions and is still followed by the authority in Taiwan.

4. The Formation of Nationalist Education (1928 – 1937)

The domestic chaos and disunity of the post-revolution period in China was finally brought to an end through the successful Northern Expedition generated in Canton by the Kuomintang (or the Nationalist Party). By the end of 1928, all China was nominally united under Kuomintang rule and all avowed common allegiance to Sun Yat-sen's San Min Chu I (The Three Principles of the People).

In the same year the Kuomintang established a national government in Nanking. Aware of the importance of education in the national life, the government adopted a positive policy on education aimed at building up a national system of schools closely articulated to the needs of the nation. Under the Nationalist educational administration, all forms of educational work underwent a process of readjustment in order to conform to Dr. Sun's Three Principles. Under these guiding principles, the new education was called San Min Chu I education which, according to the proclamation of the First National Education Conference held in 1928, was to mean that:

> For the realization of Chinese nationalism, education is to aim at the revival of the national spirit, the advancement of Chinese culture, the elevation of the standard of morality, the training of physique, the spreading of scientific knowledge, and the cultivation of an aesthetic interest. For the realization of democracy in China, education is to aim at the diffusion of political knowledge, the cultivation of the ability of exercising political rights, the elucidation of the limit of freedom, the formation of law-abiding habits, the propagation of the intrinsic meaning of equality, the fostering of the virtue of social service, the training of organizing ability, and the promotion of a cooperative spirit. For the realization of socialism, education is to aim at the formation of working habits, the increase of productive skill, the extension of the application of science, the advocation of the equilibrium of economic profit, the advocation of international justice and the cultivation of human sympathy so that internationalism can be attained through racial self-determination. ③

---

① The conferences were the fifth, sixth, and seventh National Conferences of the Provincial and Special District Educational Associations held in 1919, 1920, and 1921 respectively. See C. W. Lush, *China's New System of Education*, Chinese National Association for the Advancement of Education, Bulletin 8, II (Peking: 1923).

② *Ibid.*, p. 1.

③ Hsiao, *op. cit.*, pp. 29 – 30.

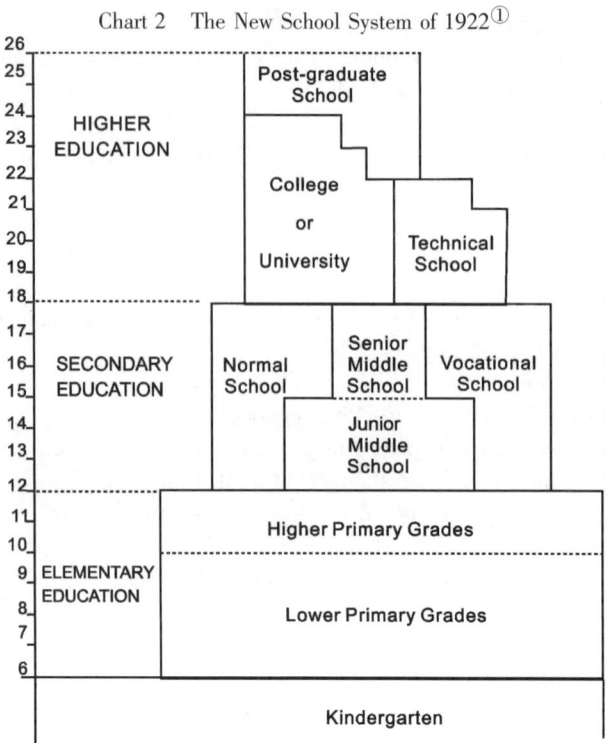

Chart 2 The New School System of 1922①

(The left column in the diagram represents the standard ages at which a student should enter the different grades. In practice, however, these are to be determined according to intelligence, record, and other considerations).

Concerned with the realization of Chinese nationalism, the Nationalists stand on the matter of Westernization was made quite clear. Different from the dominant thought at the time of the "New Culture Movement" which was that China should unconditionally or thoroughly adopt Western scientific knowledge and democratic institutions even if it meant at the expense of sacrificing traditional Chinese culture, the Nationalists adopted a policy which advocated preserving Chinese culture and at the same time revitalizing it through absorption of Western science and technology. This policy met with general acceptance. Based on this proclamation, the aims of education as formally adopted in 1929 were as follows:

> The educational aims of "the Republic of China" are to enrich the life of the people, to maintain and develop social life, to promote the livelihood of the citizens, and to continue to foster national life in accordance with the spirit of San-Min-Chu-I with a view to achieving the independence of the nation, the assertion of the people's rights, the attainment of the people's livelihood, and the realization of universal peace and brotherhood. ②

The Nationalist Government appeared at that time to be most keenly concerned with education. The government's efforts and achievements in the field of education were considerable when it is taken into account that at the same time it was engaged in the struggle to overcome the Communists and was trying to survive the economic crisis. Progress was made in the following categories: The four years of free compulsory education in the lower elementary school was enforced; the number of normal schools, agricultural and industrial schools, universities and colleges was more than doubled between 1928 and 1937; classes for adult education were established all over the country, the number of students rose from 206,021 in 1933 to 1,446,254

---

① Adapted from Lush, *op. cit.*, p. 11.
② Ch'ing-chih Ch'en, *History of Chinese Education* (Shanghai: The Commercial Press, 1936), p. 794.

in 1935; and by 1937 public libraries numbered 1,800.① TABLE 1 shows the increase of student enrollment at all levels between 1928 and 1935.

TABLE 1   THE INCREASE OF STUDENT ENROLLMENT BETWEEN 1928 AND 1935②

Year	Elementary School	Secondary School	College and University
1928	8,882,077③	234,811	25,198
1935	18,364,956	627,246	41,922

In a review of modern educational development in China, one cannot overlook the significant role played by the missionaries. For more than a century, the Christian missions conducted schools in China from primary to higher learning. Many of their schools were among the best in the country. Many of their graduates distinguished themselves in government and public service. Notable contributions of missionary schools include pioneer work in medical education, in the education of women, and in the introduction of Western subjects to the Chinese. Before 1927 the government did not have a definite policy governing the missionary schools, hence missionaries were free to make religious courses and workshops a required part of their educational program. During and after the "May Fourth Movement," public sentiment grew hostile to missionary education and evangelical work. After the Taiwan administration was established in 1928, a law was enacted requiring that all missionary schools be placed under the supervision of the Ministry of Education and be made to conform to the government regulations that no religious activities be allowed in primary schools, and that in the secondary schools and colleges, religious courses be on an elective basis.

5. Educational Development During the War (1937 – 1945)

The Sino-Japanese War interrupted many of the Nationalist educational programs which were in progress and brought great destruction to the educational institutions. Most of the institutions of higher education were moved into the interior where they continued to keep the light of education burning.④ The Taiwan administration undertook the responsibility of establishing some one hundred secondary schools to provide free education, room and board to students who fled from the Japanese occupied areas.⑤ Despite the war, education in unoccupied areas continued to make remarkable progress.

The popular slogan Chiao Yu Chiü Kuo (Education for National Salvation) was put into practice. The chief emphasis of education was to cultivate nationalistic thinking and to stimulate national spirit. In 1938 the Emergency session of the Kuomintang congress adopted a set of principles regarding the policy of K'ang Chan Chien Kuo (Resistance and Reconstruction). Four of these principles dealt with wartime education.

(a) Both the educational system and teaching materials shall be revised. A program of wartime education shall be instituted with emphasis on the cultivation of the people's morals, and the enhancement of scientific research, and the expansion of necessary facilities shall be effected.

(b) Technical personnel of all kinds shall be trained and given proper assignment in order to meet the needs of war.

---

① Far Eastern and Russian Institute, University of Washington, *op. cit.*, pp. 592 – 93.
② Feng-chieh Wang, "K'ang Chan Fu Yüan Shih Nien Chung Wo Kuo Chiao Yü Chih Chien T'ao" [An Appraisal of Chinese Education During the Ten Post-War Years] Chung Hua Min Kuo Chiao Yü Chih, *op. cit.*, p. 2.
③ Figure on enrollment of elementary schools for 1928 is lacking. The 1929 figure is used instead.
④ Altogether, 77 of China's 108 institutions of higher learning were moved into the interior, a few of them merged into two joint universities. See Hubert Freyn, *Chinese Education in the War* (Shanghai: Kelly and Walsh, 1940), p. 12.
⑤ In July, 1944, there were 50 national middle schools, 22 national normal schools, and 28 national vocational schools. See China, Ministry of Education, *Chinese Education Since 1937* (Chung-king: 1945), p. 5.

(c) Youths shall be given training to enable them to work in the war areas or rural districts.

(d) Women shall be given training so that they may be of service to social enterprises and thereby of help to the nation's war strengths. ①

Although the war was so destructive, it had far-reaching influences on the development of Chinese society and education.

(a) The migration of institutions of learning from the sea-coast to the interior had an important bearing on the future development of China's hinterland.

(b) The war helped to eliminate the strong provincialism among the Chinese through the large-scale migrational movement and the widened social contact.

(c) The hardship of wartime life and the struggle for survival changed the outlook of intellectuals.

(d) The war speeded up social change through the breaking up of family ties.

(e) The emergency war conditions called for a strong government and a centralized administration which in turn effected the educational administration.

(f) The war helped the Chinese people to strengthen their unity and to regain their self-confidence and national consciousness.

A few of the notable achievements in education during the war years were: Enforcement of universal compulsory education and technical education; emphasis on science education in schools of all levels. Equal attention was given to agricultural and industrial needs. The quantitative development of wartime education was also impressive. TABLE 2 shows the student enrollment at all school levels in 1944 in comparison with the 1936 figures. It is interesting to note that although the 1944 figure included only the unoccupied areas and the 1936 figure was for the whole country, yet the increase in enrollment for secondary education and higher education between 1936 and 1944 was quite substantial.

TABLE 2   THE INCREASE AND DECREASE OF STUDENT ENROLLMENT BETWEEN 1936 AND 1944②

Year	Elementary School	Secondary School	College and University
1936	18,364,956	627,246	41,922
1944	17,221,814	1,163,113	78,909
Per cent of increase	−6%	+85%	+88%

III. Postwar Rehabilitation of the Educational Program (1945 – 1949)

A. Postwar Conditions in Taiwan

1. Historical Retrospect

The people of Taiwan were not alone in their struggle to restore Taiwan to China during the 51 years of Japanese colonial rule. Shortly after Taiwan was annexed to Japan, Dr. Sun Yat-sen advocated, "Restoration of Taiwan, strengthening of China" as the primary goal of the Hsin Chung Hui, a revolutionary society which was the predecessor of the Kuomintang. ③ Inspired by this, the mainlanders had always stood ready to assist their compatriots in Taiwan in the struggle for liberation. At the end of the Second World War in accordance with the Cairo Declaration of 1943

---

① Hollington K. Tong (ed.), *China Handbook 1937 – 1945* (revised and enlarged edition with 1946 supplementary; New York: The Macmillan Company, 1947), p. 81.

② Adapted from Feng-chieh Wang, "K'ang Chan Fu Yüan Shih Nien Chung Wo Kuo Chiao Yü Chih Chien T'ao," *op. cit.*, pp. 2 – 3.

③ Yu-pang Lee, "Tai-wan Kuang Fu Yün Tung," [Restoration Movement in Taiwan] Hsin Sheng Ti Tai-wan [The New Born Taiwan] (Taipei: Hsin-Sheng Pao She, 1950), p. 95.

issued jointly by Generalissimo Chiang, President Roosevelt, and Prime Minister Churchill Taiwan was restored to China.

2. First Nationalist Administration in Taiwan

Although the general attitude of the Taiwanese of Chinese descent was one of joy and enthusiasm when the Taiwan administration took over, it was soon changed, for General Yi Ch'en,① the first postwar "Administrator General" of the provisional government, was a poor official. The new administration failed to retain the favorable attitude on the part of the Taiwanese who quickly became discontented with the corruption and inefficiency of the new bureaucratic administration. Not only was the administration unable to supply a sufficient number of competent officials to fill government positions, it also failed to take any action toward restoration of war-time damages or toward restoration of a normal life for the people.

All of this along with the oppression and economic decline led to the eruption of a popular revolt on February 28, 1947.② When order was restored, Yi Ch'en was replaced by Tao-ming Wei, a liberal statesman and distinguished veteran diplomat. Also, Taiwan was made a province and the provisional and administration was replaced by a Provincial Government with Wei as the first civil governor.

3. Political Reform after the "Event of February 28th"

During his short term in office, Wei made honest efforts to improve conditions. He brought many Taiwanese into government service and appointed Taiwanese to seven of the fifteen commissioner positions.③ The voice of the Taiwanese was heard in the Provisional Provincial Assembly which became a strong outlet for the local sentiment of the Taiwanese. Censorship was also officially lifted.④ Governor Wei attempted to keep the island free from the inflationary and disruptive forces that were at work on the mainland. Throughout Wei's term conditions improved slowly, but at a steady rate.

In January of 1949, when the Kuomingtang foresaw the possibility that Taiwan might be needed as a refuge, one of the ablest and most honest officials in the Taiwan administration, General Ch'eng Ch'en, was appointed to succeed Governor Wei. Ch'eng Ch'en concentrated on initiating a series of reforms aimed at making Taiwan a model province and a Nationalist stronghold.⑤

B. Rehabilitation of Education

Despite the totally unfavorable conditions existing during the postwar years, the rehabilitation of education in Taiwan was undertaken immediately and continued until temporarily disrupted by the "Event of February 28th." As announced on September 4, 1945, the three objectives of the new provisional government were: (1) no interruption of administration operation, (2) no closing down of schools, and (3) no slack in production.⑥ To attain the second objective, the educational authorities of the provisional government immediately engaged themselves in rehabilitation work. They found there were four major phases of rehabilitation desperately needed: the installation of the Chinese education system; the promotion of the Chinese language; the recruitment of Chinese teachers; and the adoption of a Chinese curriculum.

---

① Not to be confused with the Chinese Communist general whose name is pronounced and spelled in English in the same way.

② Joseph W. Ballantine, "*Formosa*": *A Problem for United States Foreign Policy* (Washington: The Brookings Institution, 1952), p. 62.

③ Fred W. Riggs, "*Formosa*": *Under Chinese Nationalist Rule* (New York: The Macmillan Company, 1952), p. 48.

④ Ballantine, *op. cit.*, p. 61.

⑤ Ch'eng Ch'en, "Chien She Tai-wan, Fan Kung Ta Lu," [Reconstruction of Taiwan, Counter-attack of the Mainland] Hsin Sheng Ti Tai-wan, *op. cit.*, p. 15.

⑥ Taiwan, Department of Education, Shih Nien Lai Ti Tai-wan Chiao Yü, *op. cit.*, p. 311.

1. Replacing the Japanese System with the Chinese System

In keeping with the educational administration on the mainland, the educational authority of the whole island was vested in the Department of Education, one of the several departments within the provisional (and later, the Provincial) government. The Department was subdivided into a secretariat, four divisions,① and one office each for inspection, auditing and statistics. Commissions were established to meet each of the emergent needs for recruiting teachers, compiling textbooks, promoting the Chinese national language (mandarin), and inspecting schools in the immediate postwar year.

At the local level, there was a "Bureau of Education" in Taipei city, and "Division of Education" in each of the other eight cities and eight counties. Both the Bureau and the Divisions consisted of two branches, "school education" and "social education".②

The new educational objective is set down in the five principles promulgated by the Department of Education were:

(a) To promote the "Three Peoples' Principles."

(b) To foster the nation's culture.

(c) To adapt education to the needs of the country in general and of the province in particular.

(d) To encourage academic pursuit

(e) To enforce equal educational opportunity.③

These were the principles that governed educational activities in the rehabilitation period. When putting these principles into practice, it was found that the school system of the colonial period was unsuitable, so a corresponding change in the school system took place.

a. Elementary Education. The discriminatory "higher classes" affiliated with the elementary school (which had kept Taiwanese from advancing beyond the elementary level during the colonial period) were now abolished. The former six years of elementary school was divided into four years of a lower elementary division and two years of a higher division. The 148 schools for aborigines were changed to elementary school which were undifferentiated from those for Taiwanese and were now staffed by qualified teachers instead of by the police.

b. Secondary Education. For the most part, the middle schools were unchanged except for the barriers preventing Taiwanese from entering were removed. Also, the number of years was extended to six, including three years of junior middle school and three years of senior middle school. The former "higher girls' schools" were changed to "girls' middle schools" and were elevated to the same academic level as the middle schools for boys. Technical schools were changed to 3-year junior vocational schools to which new 3-year senior vocational schools were added.

The complicated elementary teachers' educational program of the colonial period was also revised and simplified by setting up 3-year normal schools on the same level as the senior middle schools. To meet the urgent teachers' shortage, short-term teachers' training courses were inaugurated providing one year of special training for graduates of former 4 or 5-year middle schools. All of these changes except for the emergency measures, were intended to make the system in Taiwan conform with the Nationalist school system that was being practiced on the mainland.④

---

① The four divisions were: higher and normal education, secondary and vocational education, elementary education and local educational administration, and social education. *Ibid.*, p. 5.

② In the larger cities, the "school education" branch might be further divided into an elementary education branch and a secondary education branch. See *Ibid*

③ Ch'iao-shih Hsü, "Kuang Fu Ch'ien Hou Chih Tai-wan Chiao Yü [Education in Taiwan Before and After Japanese Occupation], Chung Hua Min Kuo Chiao Yü Chih. *op. cit.*, p. 14.

④ Hang-chen Sun, *op. cit.*, pp. 38–43. (As mentioned previously, the 1922 "new school system" was followed on the mainland. In 1932, minor revisions at the secondary level converted the comprehensive-type middle school into completely separate middle, vocational, and normal schools).

c. Higher Education. Technical colleges which were at the junior college level with three years of study were given college status and made into 4-year programs of study. Two-year junior college programs were still maintained by some of the colleges.

As might be expected, the former Taihoku Imperial University was transformed into the Taiwan University and Taihoku Higher School was made a 5-year Taiwan Provincial Teachers College.①

2. Replacing the Japanese Language with the Chinese Language

Changes in the school system during the rehabilitation period were accompanied by changes in teaching personnel, curriculum, and language studies. One of the greatest tasks of postwar rehabilitation fell in this area of language. The forceful assimilation program during the long period of Japanese colonization increased the difficulty of this task. Fortunately, the Japanese language stems from Chinese and retains to a certain degree some similarity; thus, the rehabilitation in language required a relatively short period of time.

As soon as the provisional government had been established, a "Commission for the Promotion of the National Language" was setup within the Department of Education. It was divided into three sections: survey and research, compilation and inspection, and training and information.

In each hsien (county) and municipality there was a "national language promotion center" under the jurisdiction of the local educational administration. The work of the centers is outlined as follows:

(a) Providing a national language institute for school teachers.
(b) Broadcasting model pronunciations of the national language.
(c) Discussing methods of promoting the national language.
(d) Compiling Taiwan dialect-national language bi-lingual textbooks.
(e) Experimenting in teaching methods and materials.
(f) Editing standard phonetic textbooks in the national language.
(g) Promoting the use of phonetic symbols.②

Other measures taken in the promotion of the national language included the testing of student performance in the national language and literature, and the placing of great emphasis on the studying of the national language in the normal schools and at the Taiwan Provincial Teachers College.

3. Replacing Japanese Teachers with Chinese Teachers

As shown in TABLE 3, during the Japanese occupation nearly 50.9 per cent of all elementary school teachers, 91.5 per cent of all secondary school teachers, and 77.5 per cent of all teachers in institutes of higher learning were Japanese. After the war when almost all of these returned to Japan, the problem of quickly securing replacements was immense.

TABLE 3 NUMBER OF TEACHERS IN TAIWAN IN 1944③

	Elementary Schools	Secondary Schools	Higher Institutions
Japanese	8,793	2,617	786
Taiwanese	8,456	243	225
Others	—	—	3
Total	17,249	2,860	1,014

① Hsü, op. cit., p.16.
② Ibid., pp.19–20.
③ Adapted from Hsü, op. cit., pp.16–17.

To solve the problem, the following three steps were taken by the government.

a. Recruiting offices were set up on the mainland with some 600 elementary teachers and 400 secondary teachers responding to the call.

b. A "Teachers' License Commission" was established to certify former local teachers who were qualified to teach. Through this, 670 secondary teachers out of 1,086 applicants, and 4,474 elementary teachers out of 7,592 applicants received certification.

c. Examinations were held and a short-term training program provided for those passing in order to enable former teachers of the shu fang (private Confucian schools) to teach elementary grades.

To guarantee an increasing supply of teachers, a long range teachers' training program was set up. This included the establishment of a Provincial Teachers College and several normal schools. ①

4. Replacing the Japanese Curriculum with a Chinese Curriculum

Rehabilitation work in this area of curriculum involved immediately abolishing the No. 1 and No. 2 curriculum in the elementary schools and establishing a unified curriculum which followed the standard curriculum as promulgated by the "Ministry of Education" of the Kuomingtang administration. In the middle schools, courses in morals, the Japanese language, history and geography, as well as in wu tao② were replaced with courses in the Three Peoples' Principles, civics, Chinese language, literature, history and geography, and physical education. At the Taiwan University, the lecture system was replaced by the credit system. Chinese language, literature, history and geography were made required courses.

Mandarin was made the teaching medium of all schools. Since the standard textbooks in use on the mainland were unsuitable for Taiwanese students, a "Commission for the Compilation of Teaching Materials to Be Used in Elementary And Secondary Schools" was established to select, compile, and revise texts in various subject areas. Textbooks especially for aborigine children were also compiled. ③

C. Effects of Political Changes in the Mainland

While the events described in the prior two sections were taking place in Taiwan, profound changes were also occurring in mainland China which led to the fateful defeat of the Kuomingtang by the Chinese Communists and to the final withdrawal of the Kuomingtang to Taiwan.

1. The "Civil War" in Postwar Years

The war between the Chinese Nationalists and the Communists had been off and on since the 1920's. The ideological differences ruled out any chance for a permanent peaceful settlement or for a genuine coalition government. After the failure of the postwar negotiations between the Kuomingtang administration and the Chinese Communists which had been arranged under American auspices, both sides claimed that they would wage "a war to the death" with the other. ④

In order to fulfill the Kuomintang's promise for a constitutional government after the Second World War, the Kuomingtang, supported by the Democratic Socialist Party and the Young China Party, called a Constituent National Assembly to adopt a constitution. The Chinese Communists and a third force, the Democratic League, refused to take part.

The National Assembly later convened on March 28, 1947 to elect Generalissimo Chiang as the first president of China. The constitutional government found itself faced with many grave

---

① *Ibid.*, pp. 16 – 18.

② Wu tao was the name for physical education in wartime Taiwan as well as in Japan in which two thirds of the program was militaristic.

③ Taiwan, Department of Education, Shih Nien Lai Ti Tai-wan Chiao Yü, *op. cit.*, pp. 3 – 4.

④ Ballantine, *op. cit.*, p. 80.

problems. The recurring armed clashes gradually grew into a full-scale civil war. To make it worse, the administration was very unstable. Low morals and corruption prevailed among ranking officials and officers. Besides this there was postwar inflation, peasant disaffection, and widespread distress among the middle class. All of these worked to the advantage of the Communists.

Although the Kuomintang was still the predominant force in the functioning of the constitutional government, it lost all its vitality. It was not a body of men willing to put national interest above personal gain; consequently, selfishness, nepotism, and corruption in their worst forms progressively weakened the administration.① By the end of 1949, the Chinese Communists succeeded in taking over the whole mainland, forcing the Kuomingtang to withdraw to Taiwan. Ballantine does well in analyzing the reasons underlying the downfall of the Kuomingtang on the mainland:

> The Chinese classics have taught that the Emperor ruled by the mandate of Heaven; that if he failed to rule with virtue, he forfeited this mandate; and that, in these circumstances, the people are justified in revolting. Some observers have attempted to explain the defeat of the government by reference to this doctrine. Such an explanation implies that there was a revolt, a successful revolt, of and by the people—which there was not. It is true that the people had lost confidence in the devotion of the government to their welfare and in its capacity to extricate the nation from the grave problems that beset it after eight long years of resistance to Japan. The articulate public had either become lukewarm in its support of the government or apathetic to the point of adopting an attitude of neutrality as between the Kuomintang and the Communists. Enthusiasm for the latter, however, was largely confined to student groups and to a section of the intellectuals. It is therefore inaccurate to describe the triumph of the Communists on the mainland as a successful popular revolution. Rather, the triumph has been that of a power group possessed of superior organization, discipline, and determination, more efficient and more ruthless than the government (also a power group), which it attacked.②

2. Taiwan Established as the Site of the Kuomingtang

Chiang Kai-shek foresaw the possibility of using Taiwan as a last base for recovery, so although he had temporarily retired from the presidency, he acted as party leader and began to direct removal of the government to Taiwan. In 1948 and 1949, about 2,000,000 mainland Chinese including 500,000 military personnel were moved to Taiwan.

With the removal of the seat of the government to Taiwan, two governmental mechanisms were established on the island. Taiwan continued to be a province of China with its own provincial government existing side by side with the government.

The Provincial Government was composed of a Provincial Council of 23 commissioners, among who were the heads of the various departmental units as ex-officio members. Administrative functions were grouped into ten departments: Civil affairs, finance, reconstruction, education, agriculture and forestry, social affairs, police affairs, communications, public healthy and the food bureau. There was also a Peoples' Political Council which later became the Provincial Assembly. It had no legislative power, but could make recommendations, hear reports, and interpellate officials of the Provincial Government.③

In preparation for local self-government, the administrative areas of Taiwan were redemacrated into five municipalities and 16 hsien (counties) on August 16, 1950, as follows:

a. The five municipalities were:

Kaohsiung, Keelung, Taichung, Tainan, and Taipei.

---

① George M. Beckmann, The Modernization of China and Japan (New York: Harper and Row, 1962), p. 509.
② Ballantine, op. cit., pp. 88 – 89.
③ China Handbook, 1951 (Taipei: China Publishing Company, 1951), pp. 338 – 39.

b. The 16 hsien were:

Changhua, Chiayi, Hsinchu, Hualien, I-lan, Kaohsiung, Miaoli, Nantau, Penghu (Pescadores), Pingtung, Taichung, Tainan, Taipei, Taitung, Taoyuan, and Yunling.

After 1945 the administration of the aborigines was transferred from the Police Department to the Department of Civil Affairs and the responsibility for educational matters and for health were taken over by the Department of Education and the Department of Public Health, respectively. The aborigines also were given representation in the Peoples' Political Council.

D. "Planned Education" And Its Implementation

Despite the prevailing difficulties both on the mainland and on Taiwan, educational rehabilitation in Taiwan was satisfactorily carried out. Several of the notable achievements were:

(1) Since 1946, tuition fees in all public schools from the primary grades to the college level have been waived in order to enable talented students to advance according to their ability without financial restraint.

(2) Since 1947, elementary school textbooks have been supplied by the government free of charge.

(3) Since 1947, the government has undertaken the responsibility for placement of all normal school graduates. This service was later extended to the graduate of the Provincial Teachers College.

(4) After the war, the government arranged to turn over some of the facilities formerly belonging to the Japanese to the various vocational schools to be used for practical training. Experimental farms were turned over to the agricultural vocational schools, factories, to the industrial vocational schools, shops, to the commercial vocational schools, a shipyard, to the maritime products vocational school, etc. [1]

The transition of education from the colonial system to the Nationalist system was largely completed by 1949. After that, because of the new situation created by the retreat of the government to Taiwan, a new epoch began with new needs and new challenges.

After 1949, many emergency measures were called for. In education, a program was needed which would fulfill the long range need for improvement of the island and the immediate need to protect Taiwan from Communist invasion or infiltration. To meet these needs the Department of Education, headed by Commissioner Hsüeh-ping Ch'en advocated a program called "planned education." In an article on *Planned Education in Taiwan* Ch'en highlights some of the basic elements of this new educational program. He quotes from a speech on the "Three Peoples' Principles and Planned Education," delivered at *The Placement Institute for Graduates of Secondary Schools and Colleges* by Ch'eng Ch'en concerning the meaning of "planned education":

> The planned education is an educational policy adopted according to the country's needs and theoretically in line with the educational thoughts of Dr. Sun Yat-sen and Chiang Kai-shek. It is aimed at the creation of a culture based on the Three Peoples' Principles and at the reconstruction of a country of the Three Peoples' Principles[2].

The speech also proclaimed the four major principles of the "planned education":

(1) The opportunity of receiving a fundamental education should be extended to all regardless of wealth or intelligence.

(2) Talented individuals should have an opportunity to advance themselves to the fullest extent at government expense.

(3) Those who complete an educational program appropriate to their ability should receive employment.

(4) The educational planning and development should correspond to the various needs of the

---

[1] Taiwan, Department of Education, *Shih Nien Lai Ti Tai-wan Chiao Yü*, op. cit., p. 8.

[2] Hsüeh-ping Ch'en, "Tai-wan Ti Chi Hua Chiao Yü" [Planned Education in Taiwan], Hsin Sheng Ti Tai-wan, op. cit., p. 75.

country. Attention should be directed toward the training of persons for production and reconstruction work and toward the upgrading of productivity and skills. ①

Based upon the above principles, Commissioner Ch'en outlined the educational objectives as "to foster national consciousness, to develop democratic spirit, and to facilitate reconstruction in people's livelihood."②

1. The Program And Methods of Implementation

To foster national consciousness, the teaching of Chinese history and Chinese geography received great emphasis. The nature of the war against international Communism and the reasons for the superiority of the Three Peoples' Principles over Communism were incorporated into the curriculum. Students also received training for meeting various wartime emergencies.

To develop democratic spirit, the principle of equality in education received top priority. Despite the shortage of educational funds, a large number of government scholarships were established to help deserving students at various school levels. ③ There were 200 full scholarships given each year to aborigines who graduated from elementary schools and wanted to study in secondary schools.

To facilitate reconstruction in people's livelihood, vocational education and technical training were emphasized. "Productivity and manual labor" in the school curriculum were enforced, requiring students, regardless of their major and level of schooling, to spend a few hours each week in the fields. The educational administration also intended to establish coordination among the "needs", the "training", and the "placement". In September, 1949, the first "Placement Institute for Graduates of Secondary Schools and Colleges" was held. Participating in the two weeks orientation program were 466 graduates who received placement according to their field of study and their own preferences. In June, 1950, the Provincial Government promulgated an "Outlines Governing Student Placement" which divided the placement procedures into three steps: (a) annual placement examinations, (b) placement institutes, and (c) appointments. Through this new procedure, 3,557 graduates received placement in 1950. ④

The implementation of this program called for increased expenditures. In 1944, one year prior to the Japanese surrender, the educational expenditure of the island was only 3.5 per cent of the total expenditure of the colonial administration. But in 1946, it increased to 8.4 per cent; and again in 1947, to 20.77 per cent; in 1948, to 25.79 per cent; and finally in 1949, it reached 28.0 per cent which made the educational expenditure the largest category among all major expenditures. ⑤

The above figures were for the provincial government. In the municipal and hsien governments, the educational expenditure also increased rapidly. It rose from an average of 4.04 per cent of the total local government budgets in 1946 to an average 32.98 percent in 1949. ⑥

2. Problems and Prospects

Under the program of "planned education" remarkable progress in education was achieved. However, it was not without problems, especially in the years of 1948 and 1949.

Perhaps the most serious problem faced by the educational administration was the sudden increase in student enrollment as a result of the large flow of mainland Chinese to Taiwan. It is estimated that more than 100,000 students fled to Taiwan in the years of 1948 and 1949. In order to accommodate these students, a two-shift system was adopted in the elementary schools, evening

---

① Ibid.
② Ibid.
③ In 1950, 9,229 full government scholarships, and 531 half scholarships were granted, making up 33 per cent of the education budget in the Provincial Government. Ibid.
④ Ibid., p. 76.
⑤ Ibid., p. 75.
⑥ Taiwan, Department of Education, <u>Shih Nien Lai Ti Tai-wan Chiao Yü</u>, op. cit., p. 178.

classes were added in the secondary schools, and a junior college in local administration was established. Even more serious, some 500,000 armed forces personnel who withdrew to Taiwan made school buildings their temporary barracks. Some schools had to temporarily close down, others managed to stay open with a two or three-shift system. This situation continued until 1950 when the construction of new barracks was completed.

Although the large flow of mainland Chinese who fled to Taiwan created some difficult problems, it also brought to Taiwan some beneficial results. Since the majority of refugee mainlanders were intellectuals, they helped to solve the teacher shortage in Taiwan. The Provincial Department of Education was able to promulgate a law in 1949, *Methods of Improving the Quality of Teachers in Schools of All Levels*, which set up a time table for gradually replacing the unqualified teachers with qualified ones. In-service training also was required for less experienced teachers.

IV. Educational Program of the Kuomingtang (1949 – 1962)

The year 1949 marked a turning point in the history of China. In that year, the whole of mainland China fell behind the "Bamboo Curtain" and the Kuomingtang were faced with reestablishing their administration in Taiwan. From past experiences, they recognized the critical weaknesses inherent in their system of administration and began immediate reforms aimed at general improvement on all fronts, but with party reform, reorganization of the armed forces, land reform, currency reform, and educational reform being given the most attention.

This chapter is intended to give an objective evaluation and appraisal of the Kuomingtang's program of educational reform since 1949. This is preceded by an analysis of the educational objectives and policies of the Kuomingtang, the predominant thought on education, the administrative mechanism and its legal basis, the financing of schools, and the development of the school system between 1949 and 1962.

A. Education as an Instrument of Kuomingtang's Policy

The ancient Chinese tradition of regarding education as an instrument of policy is evident from the saying "Government and education are one" (cheng chiao ho i).[①] The Kuomingtang was also keenly interested in closely linking education with policy. The aims of education as promulgated in 1929 made it clear that education in the Republic was to be based on the Three People's Principles:

> ... to enrich the life of the people, to maintain and develop social life, to promote the livelihood of the citizens, and to continue to foster national life in accordance with the spirit of San Min Chu I with a view of achieving the independence of the nation, the assertion of the people's rights, the attainment of the people's livelihood, and the realization of universal peace and brotherhood.[②]

In order to implement these aims, the local authority further promulgated eight guiding principles to be followed in putting these into practice.

(1) The curriculum and extra-curricular activities of all grades of school should be so coordinated that the subjects of history and geography should reveal the spirit of sovereignty and that practice in individual skills should lead to a better foundation for the people's livelihood.

(2) Popular education, according to the teaching of Sun Yat-sen, should emphasize the Chinese original virtues of loyalty, filial piety, kindness, love, faithfulness, and righteousness. It should also stress the teaching of industrial production.

(3) Social education should aim to acquaint the youngster with both urban and rural life, to give him a knowledge of home economics, to prepare him for citizenship, to foster in him

---

① Feng-chieh Wang, *op. cit.*, pp. 33 – 35.
② *Supra*, Chapter II, p. 51.

cooperation and the desire to protect public enterprises and properties.

(4) Collegiate and professional education should lay stress on scientific application and on the acquirement of scientific knowledge and technical skill.

(5) Teacher's education should aim to develop both physical and mental powers as well as moral and intellectual qualities in order to turn out competent teachers.

(6) Educational opportunities for both sexes should be equal with education for women stressing the development of female virtue and adjustment to better home and social life.

(7) Physical education should be emphasized in all grades especially those of the secondary and higher educational institutions where limited military training should be taught.

(8) The expansion of agricultural education should include methods of farm production, elevation of farmer's knowledge and skills, and promotion of farmer's cooperative enterprises. ①

In the preamble to the new Constitution adopted on December 25, 1946 and promulgated by the government on January 1, 1947, the National Assembly further confirmed that the basic principles on which the Republic was founded are based on the Three People's Principles. Article 1 of the "Constitution" states that " 'the Republic of China', founded on the Three Principles of the People, shall be a democratic republic of the people, to be governed by the people and for the people."②

In regard to "fundamental policies" toward "education and culture." "the Constitution" states in the following ten articles:③

Article 158. Education and culture shall aim at the development among the citizens of the national spirit, the spirit of "self-government", national morality, good physique, scientific knowledge, and the ability to earn a living.

Article 159. All citizens shall have equal opportunity to receive an education.

Article 160. All children of school age from 6 to 12 years shall receive free primary education. Those from poor families shall be supplied with books by the government. All citizens above school age who have not received primary education shall receive supplementary education free of charge and shall also be supplied with books by the Government.

Article 161. The governments shall extensively establish scholarships to assist students of good scholastic standing and exemplary conduct who lack the means to continue their school education.

Article 162. All public and private educational and cultural institutions in the Island shall, in accordance with law, be subject to "State" supervision.

Article 163. "The State" shall pay due attention to the balanced development of education in different regions, and shall promote social education in order to raise the cultural standard of the citizens in general. Grants from the "National Treasury" shall be made to frontier regions and economically poor areas to help them meet their educational and cultural expenses. The central government may either itself undertake the more important educational and cultural enterprises in such regions or give them financial assistance.

Article 164. Expenditures for educational programs, scientific studies, and cultural services shall not be, in respect of the "central government", less than 15 per cent of the total national budget; in respect of each province, less than 25 per cent of the total provincial budget; and in respect of each municipality or *hsien*, less than 35 per cent of the total municipal or *hsien* budget. Educational and cultural foundations established in accordance with law shall, together with their property, be protected.

Article 165. "The State" shall safeguard the livelihood of those who work in the fields of education, science, and arts, and shall, in accordance with the development of national economy,

---

① Sun, *op. cit.*, pp. 11 – 12.
② *China Yearbook, 1962 – 1963*, *op. cit.*, p. 913.
③ See the Constitution of "*Taiwan*", Chapter XIII, Fundamental National Policies, Section 5, Education And Culture. *Ibid.*, pp. 928 – 929.

increase their renumeration from time to time.

Article 166. "The State" shall encourage scientific discoveries and inventions, and shall protect ancient sites and articles of historical, cultural or artistic value.

Article 167. "The State" shall give encouragement or subsidies to the following enterprises or individuals:

1. Educational enterprises in the country which have been operated with good record by private individuals;

2. Educational enterprises which have been operated with good record by Chinese citizens residing abroad;

3. Persons who have made discoveries or inventions in the fields of learning and technology; and

4. Persons who have rendered long and meritorious services in the field of education. ①

This constitutional provision for educational policy is regarded as the legal basis for educational policy in Taiwan. On the mainland, however, general conditions made enforcement of "the Constitution" impossible. In Taiwan after 1949, though, general conditions improved rapidly that the Kuomingtang once again attempted to implement "the Constitution" whenever possible. Its efforts in the areas of "education and culture" were especially notable.

After a soul-searching period of self-criticism, the Kuomingtang concluded that past failures could be attributed largely to the failure of education. In a speech on the "Relationship between education and national reconstruction", delivered on September 3, 1951, Chiang Kai-shek stated:

> I feel that the most vital issue of our time that is worthy of study is the problem of education. Should we ever question why we were defeated on the mainland? One of the chief reasons for it was the failure of our education. As we know, all the failures in politics, in the military, or in economics are easily diagnosed and corrected. But failures in education are not easy to be noted. And very seldom will people be aware that our past failure resulted from our education. ②

As Chiang sees it, past failure in education was due to the half-hearted implementation of an education in line with the Three People's Principles. This half-heartedness left education like a ship sailing without a destination. To remedy this, Chiang asked all teachers and educational administrators to put forth every effort to carry out the new educational reform. In 1950, as a result of this appeal made by Chiang, the Kuomingtang adopted a platform which provided that in order to meet the needs of the time, the emergent objectives of education should be:

> To develop the moral character of the people in the direction of cooperation and fraternity, to denounce the false doctrine of class struggle so as to eradicate the contamination of Communism, to strengthen confidence in the final victory over Communism and Soviet imperialism, to render aid to displaced persons in educational, cultural and technical fields, and to guide and assist youth who are out of school to participate in the gigantic work of national salvation. ③

In June of the same year the "the Ministry of Education", in order to implement the educational platform, adopted a detailed program of education in the present anti-Communist period. This program, which consisted of 26 guiding principles with nine areas of emphasis, was entitled "Guiding Principles in the Implementing of Anti-Communist Education and Education for National Reconstruction". The nine areas of emphasis were as follows:

(1) Intensification of the Three People's Principles of education.

(2) Guidance of educationally displaced youth.

(3) Revision of the educational system.

---

① *Ibid*.

② Kai-shek Chiang, *Chiang Tsung T'ung Chiao Yü Yen Lun Lei Pien* [Classified Collection of Statements And Essays on Education by President Chiang], edited by Ch'un-hui Yuan (Taipei: Chung Yang Wen Wu Kung Ying She, 1958), pp. 122 – 23.

③ Tien-fang Ch'eng, *Educational Developments And Reforms in "Free China"* (Taipei: Ministry of Education, 1953), p. 4.

(4) Revision of the school curriculum.
(5) Encouragement of scholarly research.
(6) Transformation of social customs.
(7) Enlistment of specialists.
(8) Improvement of international cultural and educational cooperation.
(9) Preparation for educational rehabilitation in Communist occupied areas①.

To supplement this program, "the Ministry of Education" promulgated another set of laws in April, 1952 called the "Regulations Governing the Training for Students beyond the Junior Middle School Grades in Moral Training, the Military Arts, Physical Fitness, and Manual Skills during the Time of National Emergency."② This set of regulations clearly reflects the three main emphases that the Kuomingtang placed upon education.

(1) National spirit education (Min tsu ching shen chiao yü).
(2) Production and labor education (Sheng ch'an loa tung chiao yü).
(3) Combined literary and military education (Wen wu ho i chiao yü).

The first of the three emphases was aimed at instilling a sense of patriotism to safeguard the cultural heritage and resist Communist ideology. The second was aimed at fostering respect for manual labor so that students would become productive members of society. The third was aimed at training youth to meet the needs of the nation in both war and peace.

In compliance with the policy of the Kuomingtang, the Provincial Conference of Educational Administrators held in April, 1952 adopted an Education Reform Program which was put into practice through a set of ordinances promulgated by the Provincial Department of Education in 1952. These ordinances were:

(1) Guidelines for the enforcement of national spirit education in all schools of the Taiwan province. ③

(2) Guidelines for the enforcement of productive training and manual labor in all schools of the Taiwan Province. ④

(3) Guidelines for the revision of school curriculum in various grades of the Taiwan Province. ⑤

These ordinances describe in great detail the objectives, basic principles, items to be implemented, and methods of implementation, etc. No ordinance was issued regarding military training because it was administered directly by the China Youth Corps and was governed by the regulations promulgated by "the Ministry of Education" in 1952. ⑥

B. Educational Ideas of Dr. Sun Yat-sen and Chiang Kai-shek

In any study of the Kuomingtang educational program one cannot overlook the importance of the educational views of Dr. Sun Yat-sen and Chiang Kai-shek, for together their thoughts have shaped the course of educational development for nearly half a century.

1. Educational Ideas of Dr. Sun

As early as 1894, in his well-known letter to Hung-chang Li, Dr. Sun stated that among the four fundamentals of government, one is to fully develop the human talents (jen chin ch'i ts'ai). The method of attaining this goal, as he saw it, lay in education. He further stated that through proper education and fosterage, there should be no waste of human talent. ⑦ A year later in the

---

① Taiwan, Department of Education, Shih Nien Lai Ti Tai-wan Chiao Yü, op. cit., pp. 243 – 45.
② Ibid., pp. 246 – 49.
③ Ibid., pp. 249 – 52.
④ Ibid., pp. 252 – 56.
⑤ Ibid., pp. 256 – 59.
⑥ In 1960 all matters pertaining to military training of students were taken over by the "Ministry of Education". See China, "Ministry of Education", Chiao Yü Kai Ku'ang, op. cit., p. 166.
⑦ Tzu-shuang Chu, Chung Kuo Kuo Min Tana Chiao Yü Cheng Ts'e [Educational Policy of the Kuomintang] (Chungking: Kuo Ming T'u Shu Ch'u Pan She, 1941), p. 32.

Declaration of the Establishment of the Hsing Chung Hui (Society for Rebuilding China), he advocated the establishment of schools as one of the goals of the revolutionary society.① Although throughout his lifetime as a dedicated revolutionist, political ideologist and statesman, he did not write any book dealing especially with education, his educational views frequently appeared in his speeches, letters, and political writings. His educational blueprint and his regard for the importance of education in relation to a democratic government is evident in the following statements:

> The school is the source of civilization. Only after the successful establishment of schools can local self-government make progress. Close attention should, therefore, be directed to school education besides the four necessities of clothing, food, housing, and communications.②

All young men and women in a self-governing region have the right to free education, their tuition, books, clothing and board being supplied by public authorities. Schools are graded from kindergarten, primary school and middle school up to college. In addition, public lecture halls, libraries and night schools are to be provided for educating adults.③

Dr. Sun was not only a great statesman, but also a profound thinker. His Three People's Principles have been accepted as the fundamental doctrine in the making of the Constitution of Nationalist China. The genesis of the Three People's Principles can be found in the political and ethical teachings of ancient China. They also embody the best traditions of Western social and political institutions, modified to meet the existing conditions of modern China.④ In his own words in regard to the source of his thought including the Three People's Principles and his frequently cited dictum of "to understand is difficult; to act is easy", Dr. Sun said:

> The Principles which I have held in promoting the Chinese revolution were in some cases copied from our traditional ideals, in other cases modeled on European theory and experience and in still others formulated according to original and self-developed theories.⑤

2. Educational Ideas of Chiang

The importance of Chiang's educational views lies not only in his farsightedness on certain educational innovations, but also lies in the influential position he has held in China. At present, he is both the leader of Taiwan administration and the Tsung-Ts'ai (Director-General) of the Kuomintang. By virtue of the highly centralized government bureaucracy, his thought has profound and decisive influence on the important issues of the nation including educational issues, in which he has taken keen interest and on which he has placed great importance.

In an address entitled "Chiao Yü Chiu Kuo Yu Chiu Kuo Chiao Yü" (Education for the Salvation of the Nation and the National Salvation Education) he stated his convictions about education:

> I am convinced that in order to succeed in the revolution and to attain prosperity, the most urgent matter in any country or nation is the improvement of education. To explain more explicitly, the strength of a nation does not lie in her military might, but in her degree of cultural attainment and the educational enlightenment of her populace. Culture and education are the life stream in any country or nation and military might is merely a temporary characteristic of power. The former is growing and unlimited, the latter is instrumental and limited. The power of education therefore surpasses the power of any weapons.⑥

---

① Ibid.
② Yat-sen Sun, "First Steps of Local Self-Government" (1920), *Fundamentals of National Reconstruction* (Taipei: China Cultural Service, 1953), p. 72.
③ Ibid., pp. 70 – 71.
④ Chi-yun Chang, *The Essence of Chinese Culture* (Taipei: The China News Press, 1959), p. 165.
⑤ Yat-sen Sun, "History of the Chinese Revolution" (1923), *Fundamentals of National Reconstruction*, op. cit., pp. 76 – 79.
⑥ Chih-chih Chang and Chiu-yi Yao, Tsung Ts'ai Ti Chiao Yü Szu Hsiang [The Educational Thought of the Director-General] (Chung-King: Kuo Ming T'u Shu Ch'u Pan She, 1942), p. 44.

Chiang regarded himself as a follower of Dr. Sun's revolutionary doctrine and took it upon himself to propagate Dr. Sun's Three People's Principles, which in turn became the core of his own educational views. In an analysis of statements pertaining to education among Chiang's voluminous writings, the following five emphases are found:

(1) Education based on the best of Chinese tradition.
(2) Education centered on ethics.
(3) Education as a combination of literary knowledge and military training.
(4) Education in production and manual labor.
(5) Education by the "learning by doing" method.

Emphasis was placed on these five areas in an attempt to eradicate some of the most serious shortcomings either inherent in traditional Chinese culture or resulting from the too rapid movement for modernization. As modernization began, many Chinese were dazzled by the materialistic civilization of the West. They gave in to wholesale imitation of all things Western. No consideration was given to the fact that Western institutions were the products of totally different historical and cultural conditions and thus not completely suitable to the Chinese situation without some system of selection and adoption. This was accompanied by a lack of confidence in the place of the Chinese cultural heritage in modern living. To find an answer to the problem of finding the proper place for older time-proven traditions was Chiang's first emphasis.

The second emphasis was an attempt to bring more moral, physical, and civic education into the modern education, which tended to place greater importance on mere imparting of knowledge.

The six-arts curriculum of ceremonial, music, archery, charactering, writing, and mathematics in ancient Chinese education was a combination of literary education and military training which gradually was replaced by the civil service examination system where emphasis was on literary learning. The third emphasis was placed in order to reestablish respect for the military arts and to again strengthen individual physical fitness, and in turn, national strength.

The poverty and backwardness of Chinese society was largely a result of the traditional separation of school education and society, of learning and productive work or manual labor. The fourth emphasis attempted to remedy this by linking education with productive work and manual labor.

Perhaps the most important shortcoming of Chinese education was the lack of coordination between knowledge and action. The predominant thought of the past was "To understand is easy; to act is difficult." Dr. Sun replaced this with "To understand is difficult; to act is easy." Chiang went further to deliberate on his own "philosophy of action." In his own words, the essence of the word "action" is "an earnest action with a definite purpose and method resulting from analytical and critical studies."①

One of the most recent and most systematic expressions of Chiang's educational thought is found in his book under the lengthy title: Chapters on National Fecundity, Social Welfare, Education, and Health and Happiness published in 1953 as a supplement to Dr. Sun's lectures on the Principle of People's Livelihood which was left unfinished by Sun's untimely death on March 12, 1925. The third section of this book is devoted to the topic of education in which Chiang discusses in some detail the necessity for educational reform, the basic principles of education—including the subject matter, objectives, immediate task, the aim and effects of school education, etc., and various aspects in the implementation of education according to Dr. Sun's blueprint of the Principle of People's Livelihood. The essence of Chiang's educational ideas as expressed in this book is quoted as follows:

(1) In regard to the content of education:

... the subject matter to be taught has to include four aspects: intellectual, physical, moral, and social...②

---

① Chi-yun Chang, *op. cit.*, p. 187.
② Kai-shek Chiang, *Chapters on the National Fecundity, Social Welfare, Education, and Health and Happiness* (Taipei: China Cultural Service, 1953), p. 46.

The subject matters taught in ancient China were the six arts of ceremonial, music, archery, charactering, writing, and mathematics, which aimed at the training of a citizen whose body and mind should be developed in perfect balance, who should be as dexterous with his hands as he would be mentally alert, whose intellectual and moral qualities should be cultivated in equal measure, and who should embody in himself the attainments of a soldier as well as those of a man of letters.... We feel justified in saying that the ages of her greatness during the Han and Tang Dynasties were attributable mainly to this ancient type of education based upon the six arts. Unfortunately, when education became an adjunct of the system of state examinations beginning with the Sung Dynasty, most intellectuals began to bury themselves in tons of papers, learned to do mental instead of manual work, took delight in theorizing on the human mind and human nature without troubling themselves about the realities of life, and expatiated on the importance of civil affairs to the negligence of military training and national defense. The net result was the physical weakening of the individual together with the gradual and steady decline of the nation. ①

... Dr. Sun's lectures on the San Min Chu I are the foundation on which the fundamental principles and policies of Chinese education are built.

... I wish to follow faithfully Dr. Sun's teaching on education and to synthesize in the spirit of the ancient educational system based on the six arts, the intellectual, physical, moral, and social aspects of education and to make a fresh appraisal of the basic principles of Chinese education. ②

(2) In regard to the objectives of education:

... education should... teach them (youngsters) by planned instruction to cultivate their personality and develop their talents in the midst of a democratic life and enable them, both as members of their own families and as citizens, to engage in productive work and dedicate themselves wholeheartedly to the promotion of social progress and national regeneration. ③

(3) In regard to the school program:

It is the task of schools to see to it that students lead a full life, which should include:

①Physical and mental health.

②An ethical and moral life, which consists of belief in cooperation and mutual help as one's basic personal code, on the one hand, and in a harmonious living with members of one's family and with fellow-members of society, on the other.

③Family life, including such canastas duties as cleaning and dusting, and rules on the proper modes of speech and conduct.

④Occupational life, including productive techniques and the spirit of service.

⑤Life as a citizen, including essential knowledge about local, national, and world conditions as well as democratic habits.

⑥Ability to express oneself and do intellectual work, including the ability to make use of language in speech and writing.

⑦Profitable use of leisure, including the preservation of one's healthy appreciation of beauty, and attainment of a happy life. ④

(4) In regard to the coordination of educational plans and establishments:

As Chinese society is in process of being transformed, there is no one particular special pattern after which our educational plans can be modeled. The different grades of schools would have to teach the students not only to adapt themselves to the present social environment, but also so to mold their character and guide their conduct that they might readily fit into the emergent social order. This emergent social order would not be an imaginary mental product of the school authorities or the individual teachers, but would be the ultimate goal which we endeavor to attain

---

① *Ibid.*, pp. 47-48.
② *Ibid.*, p. 48.
③ *Ibid.*
④ *Ibid.*, pp. 49-50.

in our revolutionary efforts and the work of national reconstruction. That goal should be the common objective which all our political and economic planning and all our cultural and social policies should aim at and strive to realize...

It would be especially important for the great cities throughout the whole country to have libraries, science halls, antiquarian, historical, geographic, and art museums, and zoological and botanical gardens for the benefit of the general public... The central and local government should look upon these matters as of equal importance with school training. ①

The educational views of both Dr. Sun and Chiang advocated the adoption of Western scientific method and knowledge along with the preservation of the traditions which reflect the ethos of the Chinese culture. More recent developments, however, show signs of deviation from this. The most influential advocate of forgetting old traditions is the "Minister of Education", Chi-lu Huang, a top Kuomintang member and a loyal follower of Chiang. He has emphasized that national rejuvenation lies in the advance of Western science and technology and that "This goal cannot be achieved unless we stop clinging to our old traditions." ② This belief that the Chinese have attached too much importance to the past in the last two centuries, resulting in a stagnation of science and technology in China has been widely criticized. How much influence this new stand will have remains to be seen.

C. Educational Administration And the Theory of Equilibrium in Control

The line of educational authority in Taiwan is in the following order: "The Ministry of Education of the Kuomingtang administration"; the Department of Education of the Provincial Government; then the bureaus or sections of education of the hsien (counties) and municipal governments. Although the "Ministry of Education" is supposed to be the highest organ of educational administration in China, its present authority is confined to Taiwan Province and to a small part of Fukien Province consisting mainly of the islands of Kinmen (Quemoy) and Matsu, where the Nationalists also still maintain control.

The functions and organization of "the Ministry of Education" are governed largely by the "Ministry of Education Organic Law" of 1947 which was formulated in line with the constitutional requirement. Article 56 of "the Constitution" prescribes that members of the Executive Yuan (including the Minister of Education) shall be appointed by the leader of Taiwan administration on the recommendation of the "President of the Executive Yuan" (Prime Minister). "the Ministry of Education" is personally responsible to the Yuan and to his immediate superior officer— "the Prime Minister" —and together they share a joint responsibility to the Legislative Yuan. ③

Constitutional articles such as 37, 59 to 60, 71, and 95 to 97 also affect the Minister in his individual capacity or in his share in the collective responsibility of the Executive Yuan: (1) Laws and mandates are issued by the leader of Taiwan administration with the co-signature of "the Prime Minister" and "the heads of ministries or commissions concerned"; (2) the Executive Yuan presents the proposed budget for the next year to the Legislative Yuan and the budget statement of the preceding year to the Control Yuan; (3) when matters with which they are concerned are being considered in Legislative Yuan meetings. Ministers may present their opinions in person; (4) the Control Yuan may request Ministers to present their orders and related documents, investigate their activities, propose correct measures in case of "neglect of duty or violation of law" and "forward them to the Executive Yuan and the ministries and commissions concerned

---

① *Ibid.*, p. 51.

② An extract from the editorial of the leading English newspaper *China Post* (Taipei) as quoted by Asian Student, March 25, 1963, p. 7.

③ In accordance with Dr. Sun's conception of five powers, the Chinese Government, headed by a president who is elected by the National Assembly, is divided into five Yuans. These five Yuans are the highest organs of the State in their respective fields: Executive (administrative), Legislative, Judicial, Examination (civil service matters), and Control (consent, impeachment, ratification, and auditing).

directing their attention to effecting improvements."[1]

According to the "Ministry of Education" Organic Law of 1947, and the specialized laws and regulations such as the Regulations Governing Private Schools, the Normal School Law, the Technical School Law, and the University Law, etc., "the Ministry of Education" is vested with the authority to exercise jurisdiction over public and private schools and institutions of higher learning in conformance with national policy on education and in compliance with the requirements.[2]

After moving to Taiwan, the "Ministry of Education" in line with the general retrenchment policy of the administration, reduced the size of its organization to the present form which consists of: One minister, two vice ministers, one general secretary, and a number of secretaries, councilors, and inspectors; the departments of higher education, secondary education, elementary education, social education, and general affairs; the bureau of international cultural relations; the comptrollers' office, the personnel office; plus a number of committees. In 1954, under "the Ministry of Education" Dr. Chi-yun Chang, two councils—the National Academic Council and the Educational Research Council—resumed their activities as advisory organs to the Minister. The present organization of "the Ministry of Education" is shown in Chart 3.

Chart 3 Organization of the "Ministry of Education"[3]

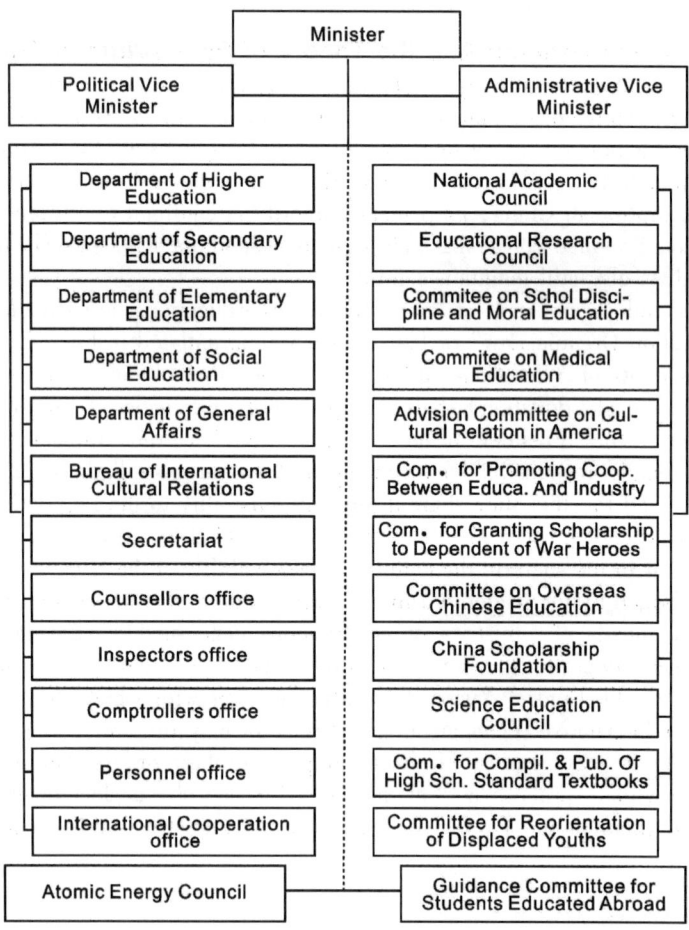

---

[1] Kathryn G. Heath, *Ministries of Education: Their Functions and Organization*, U. S. Office of Education Bulletin 1961, No. 21 (Washington: U. S. Government Printing Office, 1962), p. 214.

[2] *Ibid.*, pp. 216–17.

[3] Source: China, Ministry of Education, *Education in "the Republic of China"* (Taipei: Ministry of Education, 1960), p. 10.

In the Provincial Government, the Department of Education is the highest authority of educational administration within the province. The Commissioner of Education of the Taiwan Province is a member of the Provincial Government appointed by the government on the recommendation of the Governor and is under the control of "the Ministry of Education". Generally, he is more than just a link between the local and the central government, and within the framework of the law can do a great deal through his position and individual initiative. ①

The present organization of the Taiwan Provincial Department of Education as shown in Chart 4 is composed of one commissioner, one deputy commissioner, one secretary general, several secretaries, and a number of inspectors for each of the following six sections: (1) higher education, (2) secondary education, (3) vocational education, (4) elementary education, teacher's education, and local educational administration, (5) social education, and (6) general affairs. The legal foundation for the Department of Education is based on Provincial Government Organic Law.

Chart 4 Organization of the Taiwan Provincial Department Education ②

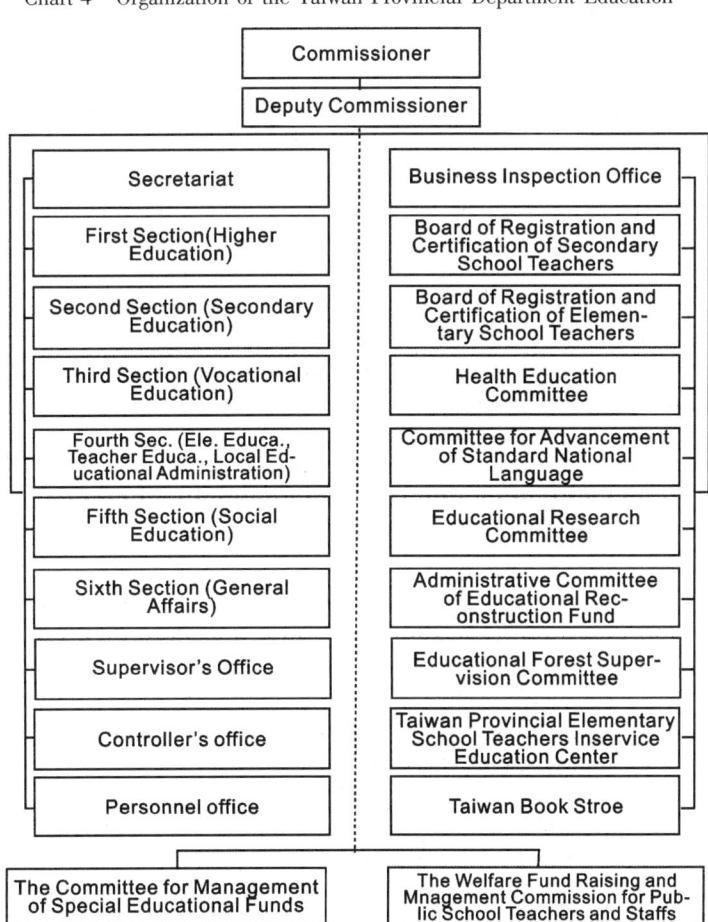

At the local level, there is a section of education in each hsien (county) and municipality. The secretary of education, appointed by the Provincial Government at the recommendation of the magistrate, is vested with the authority to administer local funds and to control schools at the

---

① Sassani, *op. cit.*, p. 23.
② Taiwan, Department of Education, *Education in the Province of Taiwan* (Taichung: Department of Education, 1960), p. v.

primary and secondary levels in his region. Since at present the hsien and municipality have become the unit of local self-government, their position and responsibilities have been greatly increased. The expanded educational program has put the major responsibility of elementary education in the hands of the local government which must find qualified educational administrators to fill various positions in the sections or bureaus of education.

Demarcation of powers among the various levels of government is also defined by the Constitution. Generally speaking, matters that are of national character fall within the jurisdiction of the central government, otherwise they are delegated to the provincial and hsien or municipal governments. For example, while "the Ministry of Education" exercises general supervision over the education of the entire country, in primary and secondary schools it exercises its powers only in policy-making, in the prescription of curricula, in the approval and compilation of textbooks and the approval of private schools, leaving the financing, building, maintenance and administration of these institutions to the local and provincial authorities. In securing a balanced development of the central government and local governments, Dr. Sun advocated the principle of equilibrium between the two. As early as 1922 in an article written for the thirtieth anniversary commemoration issue of the Hsin Wen Pao (News Press) entitled "Foundation for Rebuilding the Chinese Republic", he said:

> What are known as centralization of power and decentralization or even federal provincial autonomy are only hackneyed terms to facilitate argument whether gravity should be placed in the center or diverted to the periphery. Power, however, should not be distributed with the central or the local government as its objective. It should be distributed according to its nature. Power that should belong to the central government should be vested in the central government as to the case of military affairs and foreign affairs, which must be dealt with under one consistent, unified policy. On the other hand, power that should belong to a region should be vested in the local government as in the case of education and public health, as they may vary under different local conditions and circumstances. The matter needs further analysis, of course... in dealing with education, maritime districts may emphasize the science of sea products, while mountainous regions may put stress on mining and forestry. In such cases, freedom of action should undoubtedly be given to different regions. In other cases, however, the central government should exercise its authority and impose regulations. For instance, the school system and free education should be regulated on a national scale. In this way the central government must also be concerned in educational problems. So one single undertaking may be dealt with in one way by the central government and in another by local governments. When perfervid advocates of centralization, or decentralization, or even federal provincial autonomy, declare, as they often do, that this statement is a generalization or that statement is a particularization, do they not lose themselves in a fog of ambiguity?[①]

Dr. Sun's exponent as it appears in the article has been well incorporated into "the Constitution". The principle of equilibrium is the central core of Articles 107 to 111 of Chapter X of "the Constitution" which define the powers of the central and local government.

Close in line with this principle and despite the adverse circumstances existing in Taiwan where a government and a Provincial Government have jurisdiction over the same area, the demarcation of powers between them as prescribed in "the Constitution" has worked out quite satisfactorily, proving the applicability of Dr. Sun's principle of equilibrium.

D. The Finance of Education

One of the important features in the section of the Constitution dealing with the "Education and Culture" is the setting up of minimum requirements for educational appropriation in the national, provincial, and local governments. Article 164 of "the Constitution" stipulates that

---

① Yat-sen Sun, "Foundations for Rebuilding the Chinese Republic", written for the thirtieth anniversary commemoration issue of the Hsin Wen Pao (1922), *Fundamentals of National Reconstruction*, op. cit., pp. 113 – 14.

"Expenditures for educational programs, scientific studies, and cultural services shall not be, in respect of the Taiwan administration less than 15 per cent of the total national budget; in respect of each Province, less than 25 per cent of the total Provincial budget; and in respect of each Municipality or Hsien, less than 35 per cent of the total Municipal or Hsien budget..." ①

However, since the adoption of "the Constitution" in 1947, the National Government has not been able to fulfill the requirement of "the Constitution". This is due to the emergency situation confronting the government. A retrospective examination shows that on the eve of the outbreak of the Sino-Japanese War in 1937, the appropriation of the National Government for education was 4.29 per cent, which was the highest of the prewar years. During the War with Japan, because of the urgency of military needs, educational expenditures were reduced to an average of 2 per cent. After the war, the percentage of appropriation for education jumped to 5.14 per cent in 1946, and again to 10.89 per cent in 1948, one year after "the Constitution" was adopted. Because of the spread of civil war and the loss of territory, actual appropriation for 1949 came to only 1.56 per cent, and again dropped to 0.52 per cent in 1950②. Since 1950, the appropriation for education in the National Government has begun to climb again. It has shown a steady increase each year and reached 3.10 per cent in 1960. ③

In his "General Report of Government Operations", a speech delivered at the second Yangmingshan Forum,④ Yuan. Yun-wu Wang, gave as the reason for the Taiwan administration's inability to fulfill the Constitutional requirement; the high defense cost borne by the National Government which amounts to 75 per cent of the Taiwan administration's total appropriation. ⑤ He further disclosed that although the educational expenditure of the National Government was only 3.10 per cent of total Taiwan administration appropriation in 1960, it was the second largest expenditure of the Taiwan administration. ⑥

At the provincial and local levels, the Constitutional requirements have been met in Taiwan in recent years. TABLE 4 shows the actual educational expenditures at the national, provincial, and local levels and the percentage of the total expenditures at each of the government levels spent on education.

In TABLE 4 it is worthy of note that regardless of the fluctuation in the percentages, the educational expenditures of all levels show a rapid and steady increase over the years. It is easy to see that great strides have been made since 1946 when the percentage for the Provincial Government was only 8.41 and for the local government, an average of 4.04. ⑦

A breakdown of educational expenditures at various government levels taking 1961 – 1962 as an example shows that 46 per cent of the educational expenditures in the national government was spent on higher education, 74 per cent of the education expenditure in the provincial government was spent on higher and secondary education, and 71 per cent of the educational expenditure of the local government was spent on elementary education. An itemized summary of the use of educational expenditures at the various levels of government is shown in TABLE 5.

Despite efforts of the government to increase educational expenditures, the funds for education are still not sufficient to meet the increased cost of education at all school levels and the needs created by increased student enrollments. Because of insufficient funds, the government finds it economically impossible to keep up the same pace of recent years in its educational efforts.

---

① *Supra.* p. 77.
② "China; Educational Developments in 1951 – 1952," *International Yearbook of Education, 1952*, p. 83.
③ Yun-wu Wang, "I Pan Cheng Wu Pao Kao" [General Report of Government Operation] Chung Yang Semi-Monthly, Nos. 209 – 10 (September 1, 1961), p. 11.
④ Yangmingshan Forum, sponsored by the Taiwan administration, consisted of four phases. The first phase concerning economic and financial matters was held from July 1 to 7, 1961. The second phase concerning educational and cultural matters was held from August 25 to 31, 1961. Over 100 delegates, nearly half of them from overseas, attended each of the forums. See *China Yearbook, 1961 – 1962, op. cit.*, p. 1.
⑤ Yun-wu Wang, *op. cit.*, p. 11.
⑥ *Ibid.*
⑦ *Supra*, Chapter III, p. 72.

TABLE 4 EXPENDITURE ON EDUCATION AT VARIOUS GOVERNMENT LEVELS IN TAIWAN IN 1950 – 1962①

Government Level	1950	1951	1952	1953	1954 Jan. – June	1954 – 55	1955 – 56
National	6,567②	—	8,500③	8,368	15,912	41,286	73,330
Per Cent④	.52	—	.50	.50		1.09	—
Provincial	89,971	97,930	112,585	143,596	78,986	172,405	199,838
Per Cent	24.91	25.38	24.84	24.62	23.03	25.04	25.78
Local	58,638	107,380	179,533	196,368	130,592	366,413	400,095
Per Cent	37.46	33.44	34.14	34.71	34.93	35.52	37.36

Government Level	1956 – 57	1957 – 58	1958 – 59	1959 – 60	1960 – 61	1961 – 62
National	114,714	133,056	143,304	155,722	193,387	258,668
Per Cent	—	—	—	—	3.10	2.81
Provincial	257,341	303,494	325,361	367,819	405,543	533,615
Per Cent	24.15	27.18	27.90	28.66	26.85	29.54
Local	472,783	535,394	631,371	741,377	871,239	1,102,558
Per Cent	36.33	35.05	36.10	36.80	36.79	37.40

TABLE 5 ITEMIZED EDUCATION EXPENDITURES OF VARIOUS GOVERNMENT LEVELS IN 1961 – 1962⑤

Object of Expenditure	National Government	Per Cent	Provincial Government	Per Cent	Local Government	Per Cent
Administration	3,632⑥	1.40	2,875	0.54	—	—
Higher Education	120,950	46.76	107.102	20.07	—	—
Secondary Education	5,596	2.16⑦			254,998	23.13
Middle School			159,801	29.95		
Normal School			37,988	7.12		
Vocational School			95,100	17.82		
Elementary Education			11,444	2.14	786,418	71.33
Social Education	17,428	6.67	36,448	6.83	9,745	0.88
International Cultural Relations	36,284	14.03	—		—	
Others	74,958	28.98	82,957	15.53	51,597	4.66
Total	258,668		533,615		1,102,558	

In a recent speech of "Minister" Huang entitled "I ko ho yu chan shih yu p'ing shih ti chiao

---

① Source: Figures in this table were gathered by the author from a number of source including the *Educational Statistics of "Taiwan"*, 1960 – 1962, *China Yearbook*, 1950 – 1963, and *International Yearbook of Education*, 1950 – 1962, etc. The expenditures of the Provincial and local governments were readily available in almost all of the sources cited above; however, for the National Government, many figures were not available for security reasons.

② NT $ = New Taiwan dollar; NT $40 = US $1; Units: thousands.

③ with 1952 as base year (1952 = 100), the general price index of 1953 was 108.76 per cent; of 1954, 111.34 per cent; of 1955, 127.02 per cent; of 1956, 143.16 per cent; of 1957, 153.50 per cent of 1958, 155.64 per cent; of 1959, 172.43 per cent; of 1960, 1960.88 per cent; and of 1961, 203.25 per cent. The total increase over the ten-year period was 103.25 per cent. *China Yearbook*, 1963 – 1964 (Taipei: China Publishing Company, 1964), p. 303.

④ Percentage of the total expenditure of the respective government level.

⑤ Adapted from China, "Ministry of Education", *Educational Statistics of "Taiwan"*, 1960 – 1962, op. cit., pp. 71 – 73.

⑥ Unit: NT $ thousands.

⑦ Including elementary education.

yü tse hua" (An educational strategy suitable both in wartime and in time of peace), Huang warns about the extreme difficulty in the financing of education foreseeable in the years ahead. His warning is based on the fact that in 1952 the total educational expenditure was NT $300,618,000 and by 1962 it had reached NT $1,894,841,000, a six-fold increase in ten years. If the educational expenditure follows this rate of increase, in 1972 it will reach 12 billion New Taiwan dollars, an amount impossible for the government to bear.① It is quite clear that the present percentage of educational expenditures allocated by various government levels will not increase to any appreciable extent in the near future. This view is based on knowledge of the availability of economic resources in the country and of the many demands competing with education for a share of the government's income at various levels.

Possible solutions have been sought and a few immediate measures have been taken by the government, including the following four important steps:

1. The government is encouraging the establishment of private schools and the pooling of private funds to support education. Statistics for 1962 show that 55 elementary schools, 65 middle schools, 25 vocational schools, and 15 institutions of higher education in Taiwan were private establishments.②

2. The Provincial Department of Education began in 1955 to promulgate regulations governing the charging of tuition in public schools of secondary and higher levels. The present tuition rates for public and private secondary schools are given in TABLE 6.

For the purpose of comparison, the average cost of education per student at various school levels in 1962 is given in TABLE 7. A recent study conducted by Stanford Research Institute reveals that the major portion of these costs goes towards teachers' salaries. Teachers' salaries as a percentage of total cost per student vary from approximately 58 per cent (higher education) to 85 per cent (primary education), with an average of about 75 per cent.③

3. In order to raise educational funds to cover the expense of a long-term educational development program, the Provincial Government adopted a plan to raise the "Provincial Educational Reconstruction Fund" which had its primary goal set at NT $30,000,000.④ A special committee, the Taiwan Administrative Committee of the Educational Reconstruction Fund, was set up to administer the fund, which could be utilized as loans instead of subsidies for reconstruction purposes. The sources of the fund have been (a) special appropriation from the Provincial Government, (b) U.S. aid, (c) donations, and (d) others. Schools at any level either public or private which can raise funds covering half of the construction cost are eligible to make a loan. This program was put into operation at the beginning of the 1960 academic year.⑤

TABLE 6   TUITION AND FEES OF SECONDARY SCHOOLS IN TAIWAN EFFECTIVE SEPTEMBER, 1963⑥

Item	Public				Private			
	Middle Sch.		Voc. Sch.		Middle Sch.		Voc. Sch.	
	Junior	Senior	Junior	Senior	Junior	Senior	Junior	Senior
Tuition	60⑦	90	21	30	320	400	360	490

---

① Chi-lu Huang, "I Ko Ho Yü Chan Shih Yü P'ing Shih Ti Chiao Yü Tse Hua." An address delivered at the annual joint conference of ten educational organizations, Taipei, January 6, 1963.

② China, Ministry of Education, *Educational Statistics... 1962*, op. cit., pp. 5, 12, 20, and 42.

③ Stanford Research Institute, op. cit., p. 15.

④ A recent news release announced that the Joint Commission for Rural Reconstruction has agreed to loan NT $50,000,000 to the Provincial Department of Education for the Educational Reconstruction Fund. *Chung Yana Jih Pao* [Central Daily] January 5, 1963.

⑤ Taiwan, Department of Education, *Education in Taiwan*, op. cit., pp. 18-19.

⑥ Adapted from *Chung Yang Jih Pao* [Central Daily], August 18, 1963.

⑦ Unit: NT $

(continuing)

Item	Public			Private				
Curricular Materials	25	25	30	50	25	25	30	50
Laboratory	30	50	30	50	30	50	30	50
Physical Ed. ①	25	25	25	25	25	25	25	25
Library	20	20	20	20	20	20	20	20
Boy or Girl Scout	10	–	10	–	10	–	10	–
Productive Work	30	30	20	20	30	30	20	20
Misc. Fees②	90	90	100	100	175	180	185	190
Total③	290	330	256	295	635	730	680	845

TABLE 7 AVERAGE COST OF EDUCATION PER STUDENT AT VARIOUS SCHOOL LEVELS IN 1961 – 1962④

Level of Schooling	Average Cost per Student
Elementary School	393. 80⑤
Secondary Schools	
Middle School	1,447. 90
Vocational School	2,767. 00
Normal School	5,780. 20
University and College	10,400. 00

4. Since 1951 some of the financial difficulties of education have been lessened through the allocation of a part of the U. S. aid to China for educational purposes. During the 1961 fiscal year, U. S. aid to China amounted to US $52,100,000. Of this, US $ 50,000,000 was allocated to defense and US $2, 100, 000 to technical assistance. Education received its share of US $613,000 from the former and US $379,000 from the latter. ⑥

In addition to the above measures, the government also has sped up its economic development program in the hope that in the long run it will increase the government's revenue for supporting education.

E. The School System of Taiwan

The present school system of Taiwan follows largely the 6 – 3 – 3 – 4 plan which was first adopted in 1922. ⑦ Originally a transplanted form of the American system with a few influences from the European system, the basic structure has undergone little change in the course of 40 years of practice. The only major revisions of the 1922 system took place during the first few years after the adoption of the new educational aims in 1928. ⑧ At that time, serious shortcomings were found at the secondary school level where the "comprehensive high school," the product of a highly developed industrial society, was found to be unsuitable to the economically underdeveloped

---

① Only NT $10 is charged for evening students.
② NT $10 more is charged for Hsien secondary schools.
③ Children of servicemen pay only half.
④ Adapted from Chung Yana Jih Pao [Central Daily] October 2, 1962.
⑤ Unit: NT $
⑥ *China Yearbook*, 1961 – 1962, *op. cit.*, pp. 276, 363.
⑦ Supra, Chapter II, p. 48.
⑧ Supra, Chapter II, p. 50.

Chinese society and was therefore divided into separate "middle schools", "vocational schools", and "normal schools." The only other notable change was the replacing of the credit system and the elective curriculum in secondary schools with a fixed curriculum. Since then, only minor revisions have been made. The articulation of the entire school system may be seen in Chart 5.

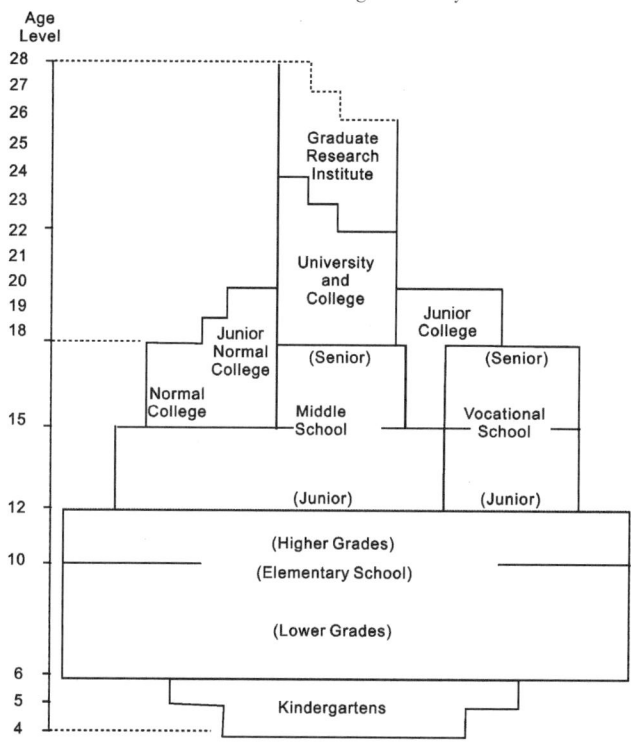

Chart 5 The Prevailing School System

In the main, the attendance at kindergarten is voluntary. Children between the ages of 4 and 6 are enrolled. The elementary school course of six years is compulsory and free for children between the ages of 6 and 12. The secondary schools are of three types: middle schools, vocational schools, and normal schools. The middle school is divided into junior and senior divisions, each requiring three years of study. Since 1950 there has been experimentation in Taiwan with a 4 – 2 plan to enable pupils who cannot afford the entire course to acquire at least four years of secondary education, and with a five year plan to shorten the length of study by eliminating the "double-cycle" junior and senior divisions. The vocational schools are specialized according to the occupation for which students are being prepared and usually follow the junior and senior divisions of the middle school course. The normal school for training primary school teachers formerly corresponded to the upper three-year cycle of the middle school with a course of study that combined general and professional subjects; but in 1960 the government adopted a new program aimed at gradually elevating all normal schools to the junior college level. The length of study may be either five years beginning at the senior middle school level or two years beginning at the college level. College and university education generally is for four years. Postgraduate work leading to a Master's degree requires two years of study. The doctorate program initiated in 1960 requires that candidates be examined before a national review board appointed by "the Ministry of Education".① The supplementary schools for adult education take two forms: the common supplementary school and the vocational supplementary school. Most of the supplementary schools are attached to the regular schools, but some have their own site, building and premises. They

---

① The "Organic Statute for Doctorate Councils" is appended in *China Yearbook, 1961 – 1962, op. cit.*, p. 936.

consist of primary, intermediate, and advanced classes. The primary class is equivalent to the fifth and sixth grades, the intermediate class, equivalent to the junior division of the secondary school, and the advanced class, equivalent to the senior division of the secondary school. The courses of study are 2 years, 3 years, and 3 years respectively.

One spectacular phenomenon of education since 1945 is the rapid increase of student enrollment at all school levels. Recent statistics show that in the 1962 – 1963 school year there were 722 kindergartens with an enrollment of 77,000 children in contrast to 95 kindergartens with an enrollment of 8,000 children in 1944, the peak year during the period of Japanese occupation. The increase is also significant at the elementary, secondary, and higher education levels. In the peak year during the period of Japanese occupation, there were 1,097 elementary schools enrolling 890,000 pupils, 75 secondary schools enrolling 46,000 pupils, and 4 colleges and one university with an enrollment totaling 2,100 students. In 1962, there were 1,948 elementary schools enrolling 2,087,055 pupils, 437 secondary schools enrolling 462,466 pupils, and 33 colleges and universities with an enrollment totaling 44,314 students. ① The enrollments for 1962 as compared with those for 1944 increased 9.6 times for kindergartens, 2.3 times for elementary schools, 10 times for secondary schools, and 21 times for colleges and universities. TABLE 8 shows the trend of increase in the number of schools and the student enrollment at all levels between 1945 and 1962 at five year intervals.

Excluding the kindergartens, the total number of students enrolled in 1962 reached 2,593,300. This means that students made up almost 23.26 per cent of the estimated total population (11,149,139)② —a relatively high percentage compared with other developing countries in Asia. ③

The increase in the proportion of students in the total population is also noticeable through the steady increase in the percentage of school-age children (from the ages of 6 to 12) actually enrolled in schools. It has risen from 71.31 per cent in 1944, to 79.98 per cent in 1950, to 92.33 per cent in 1955, to 95.59 per cent in 1960, and to 96.50 per cent in 1962. ④

The preceding section of this chapter has dealt with some of the remarkable quantitative developments of education in China in the past 17 years. In the following chapters an attempt is made to examine some of the qualitative developments in the various levels of schooling from primary education to secondary and higher education; and from teachers' education to social education.

TABLE 8   INCREASE IN THE NUMBER OF SCHOOLS AND IN STUDENT ENROLLMENT AT FIVE YEAR INTERVALS BETWEEN 1945 AND 1962⑤

School Level	1945	1950	1955	1960	1961	1962
Kindergarten	28⑥	28	413	675	679	722
School						
Student	5,634	17,111	46,390	79,702	78,261	77,000

① Chung Yang Jih Pao [Central Daily], October 23, 1963.

② The total population in Taiwan at the end of 1961 was 11,149,139 excluding aliens and servicemen, an increase of 356,937 over 1960. See China Yearbook, 1962 – 1963, op. cit., pp. 118 – 19.

③ According to data gathered by the Stanford Research Institute the recent enrollment figures (as percentages of total populations) for Asian countries are: Cambodia, 12 per cent; Hong Kong, 14 per cent; Republic of Korea, 18 per cent; Singapore, 20 per cent; Philippines, 17 per cent; Japan, 26 per cent; Thailand, 16 per cent; and Indonesia, 10 per cent. See Stanford Research Institute, op. cit., p. 18.

④ Data for years 1950, 1955, and 1960 are drawn from China, Chiao Yü Kai Ku'ang, op. cit., p. 7. For 1962, it is drawn from China, Government Information Office, Tai-wan Kuana Fu Shih Pa Nien [The Eighteen Postwar Years in Taiwan] (Shih Shih Ts'an K'ao Tzu Liao, No. 237; Taipei: 1963), p. 10.

⑤ Data for the years from 1945 – 1960 was drawn from China, Chiao Yü Kai Ku'ang, op. cit., pp. 2 – 3, 21 – 22, 25 – 26, 41 – 42, 51 – 52, 62, 79. Data for the year of 1961 was drawn from China, "Ministry of Education", Educational Statistics... 1962, op. cit., pp. 1, 4 – 5, 9, 12, 17, 20, 30, 36, 39, 42, 49. Data for 1962 was drawn from China, Government Information Office, op. cit., pp. 10 – 11.

⑥ No figure for 1945 is available; therefore, the 1946 figure is used instead.

(Continuing)

School Level	1945	1950	1955	1960	1961	1962
Elementary School	1,053	1,231	1,399	1,795	1,932	1,948
Student	850,097	906,950	1,237,904	1,879,428	1,997,016	2,087,055
Secondary-Middle School	137	128	146	244	280	318
Student	41,075	79,948	146,361	263,365	314,655	365,455
Vocational School	78	77	95	109	111	110
Student	24,444	34,437	60,397	84,337	88,335	91,693
Normal School	6	8	9	10	10	9
Student	3,409	5,651	6,792	7,572	6,572	5,318
Higher School	4	7	15	27	30	33
Student	2,022	6,665	18,174	35,060	38,403	44,314

V. The Development of Primary Education

A. Pre-elementary Education

According to the definition adopted by UNESCO in the second volume of the *World Survey of Education*, primary education is taken to mean "the first stage of formal education, for pupils ranging in age from childhood (5 to 7 years) to the onset of adolescence, who learn the fundamental skills, knowledge and attitudes which society expects to be the common possession of all citizens."① This definition of "primary education" seems to apply well to education in China where primary education comprises two stages: The "pre-elementary schools" mainly kindergartens; and the "elementary schools."

Pre-elementary education in China is of four types: kindergartens, nursery schools, children's homes, and orphanages. Only the kindergartens are directly under the supervision of the educational authorities, the others being under the direction of social welfare agencies of the government. Although at present the kindergarten is not in the realm of compulsory education, it has acquired a definite place in the school system and is regarded as a part of formal education.

The law governing the establishment of kindergartens was promulgated on December 20, 1943 while the leader of Taiwan administration was still in mainland China. It prescribed that kindergartens might be established privately or by provincial, hsien or municipal authorities, but that all kindergartens must be registered with the local educational authorities.② The law also provided that kindergartens might be either established independently or affiliated to elementary schools. The age of children to attend kindergarten, as stated in the law is between 4 and 6, but attendance is completely voluntary.

The curriculum standard for kindergartens was first promulgated by "the Ministry of Education" in 1929 and was subsequently revised in 1932, 1936, and lately, in 1953. The objectives of kindergartens as provided in the present curriculum standard are "to improve the physical and mental health of the children; to cultivate in them good habits; to help them to acquire the fundamental knowledge and skills necessary to their life and to promote their happiness

---

① *World Survey of Education*, II, *Primary Education* (Paris UNESCO, 1958), p. 11.
② China, Ministry of Education, Chiao Yü Fa Ling [Educational Laws and Regulations] (Taipei: Cheng Chung Shu Chü, 1953), pp. 211-12.

and welfare."① The standard also stipulates that equal stress should be given to the "teaching" and the "nurturing" of the children, that subjects and various activities should give the children a balanced development, and that both "games" and "music" should receive main emphasis. In recent years, because of the general improvements in living standards and in the employment of women, there has been an increased demand for kindergartens. In order to meet this demand, kindergartens, mostly private, have been widely established throughout Taiwan Province.

Although many kindergartens do have adequate facilities and physical plant, still others are far from being adequately equipped. Aimed at the general improvement of the facilities of kindergartens and at the protection of the children's health and safety, "the Ministry of Education" in 1961 adopted "Provisional Criteria for Kindergarten Equipment" which set up minimum requirements in regard to the selection of site, area and space, construction, playground, and the general arrangement, decoration, facilities, etc. ②

One serious problem hindering the further development of kindergartens is the shortage of qualified teachers. According to a report issued by the "Ministry of Education" concerning pre-elementary education, in 1961 there were only four classes for the training of kindergarten teachers supplying an average of 200 graduates each year. The number of kindergartens in Taiwan for the same year was 678. If one more teacher were to be added to every kindergarten each year, there would be a shortage of more than 400 teachers annually. This would not cover the turnover due to marriage, illness, or other such circumstances in which case substitute teachers are employed. Supplying enough teachers to meet the advancing demands for more pre-elementary education is a serious problem confronting the educational authorities. ③

One of the healthy developments along the lines of professional growth of kindergarten teachers is the recent organization of the Chinese Kindergarten Education Society, which had a membership of 300 in 1961. Some of the worthwhile activities of the Association included the establishment of a kindergarten education materials center for collecting materials in the field of pre-elementary education from other nations; the compilation and translation of pictorial books for children; an investigation of the existing conditions of the kindergartens in Taiwan; and the exchange of experiences through group discussions, lectures, etc. ④ The enthusiasm of the members of the society and the enriched programs have attracted a large membership and have produced active participation by the members. This in turn has created more and more interest in kindergarten education throughout the country.

B. The Legal Basis of Elementary Education

The second stage of the main body of primary education is elementary schooling which, according to the "Citizen School Law" (Kuo Min Hsüeh Hsiao Fa) promulgated by "the Ministry of Education" on March 15, 1944 is to provide "fundamental education to all children of school age from six to twelve and also to provide supplementary education (make-up education) to adults who have not received a fundamental education."⑤ Article 160 of "the Constitution" further stipulates that "those from poor families shall be supplied with books by the Government. All citizens above school age who have not received primary education shall receive supplementary education free of charge and shall also be supplied with books by the Government."⑥

The name "Citizen School" is to clearly indicate that the school not only provides the 6-years compulsory education for all school-age children, but also provides this free supplementary education for all citizens above school age who have not received a primary education. This is in accord with Article 26 of the Universal Declaration of Human Rights adopted by about 50 nations

---

① China, Ministry of Education, *Pre-school Education in "Taiwan"* (Taipei: 1961), p. 4.
② *Ibid.*, pp. 6 – 9.
③ *Ibid.*, pp. 15 – 16.
④ *Ibid.*, pp. 13 – 14.
⑤ China, Ministry of Education, Chiao Yü Fa Ling, *op. cit.*, pp. 207 – 08.
⑥ *Supra*, Chapter IV, pp. 76 – 77.

at the third session of the United Nations Assembly in December, 1948, which states that everyone has a right to education. This declaration set forth the idea that education, at least at the elementary level, should be free and compulsory.

"The aim of elementary education," according to the Citizen School Law "shall be to emphasize the cultivation of citizenship, the development of mental and physical health, and the acquirement of knowledge and skills necessary for making a living."① The organization of the elementary school as prescribed by law takes two forms: "The Central Citizen School" (Chung Hsin Kuo Min Hsüeh Hsiao) and "the Citizen School" (Kuo Min Hsüeh Hsiao). The Regulation Governing the Establishment of Citizen Schools and Central Citizen Schools enacted in 1945 stipulated that in each pao (unit of 100 families, or 10 chia) there should be a four-year "citizen school," (equivalent to the first four grades of an elementary school) but, if financially possible, preferably, a six-year "citizen school" (from first grade to the sixth); and in each hsiang (village) or chen (township) there should be a six-year "central citizen school" which, in addition to being a complete elementary school in itself, also is vested with the responsibility of supervising the surrounding citizen schools within its region.② The purpose of having separate establishments was to meet the needs existing in mainland China before the fall of the Kuomingtang administration when most of the rural areas could afford only four-year elementary schooling. But in Taiwan, since the regular six-year elementary school accounts for almost 100 per cent of all citizen schools, the four-year citizen school is practically nonexistent.

1. Compulsory Education

The regulations governing compulsory education were enacted in 1944. These regulations have since been somewhat modified. The latest compulsory school attendance regulation promulgated by the Provincial Government requires that compulsory education committees should be organized in each hsiang, chen, hsien, and municipality with chiefs or magistrates, legislators, and school principals responsible for enforcing attendance. With the assistance of the heads of the pao and the chia those parents or guardians who fail to send children to school are fined in accordance with the regulation.③ In addition to this, the regulation provided that each hsiang, chen, hsien, and municipality should allocate a part of its budget for financial assistance to children from needy families.④

The enforcement of compulsory education in Taiwan has been quite effective. This can be attributed largely to the administrative structure of the local self-government with the "pao-chia system"; however, the traditional reverence for education is also partially responsible.

2. Elementary School Curriculum

Being authorized to prescribe curriculum standards for all levels of schooling in China, "the Ministry of Education" adopted the first curriculum standards for elementary schools in 1929 with revisions in 1931, 1936, 1941, and 1948. The 1948 revision was done with great thoroughness and was the product of the combined efforts of many experts; however, after the Kuomingtang administration moved to Taiwan, the 1948 standards were found to be inadequate in meeting the multifarious needs of a time of national emergency. In order to meet the new needs "the Ministry of Education" in 1952 issued an order amending the 1948 standards, making revisions mainly in the subjects of "Chinese" and "general knowledge". The main features of the amendment were:

---

① China, "Ministry of Education", Chiao Yü Fa Ling, op. cit., p. 207.

② Pao, chia and hsiang, chen are the basic units of local administration in Nationalist China. Generally, each 10 families is designated as a chia and each 10 chia constitutes a pao. About 10 pao may form a hsiang (village) or chen (township) by their geographical locations. Although this scheme was originated as political units for local self-government, they are also used by educational authorities as units for school districts.

③ China, "Ministry of Education", Department of Elementary Education, Elementary Education in "Taiwan", 1962 (Taipei: 1962), p. 9.

④ Wang, op. cit., p. 198.

increased emphasis on the fight against Communism, increased emphasis on arousing a national spirit in the pupils and on training for productivity.

The prescribed curriculum for the elementary schools since 1952 is shown in TABLE 9.

TABLE 9 ELEMENTARY SCHOOL CURRICULUM[①]

Subject	Grade:	I	II	III	IV	V	VI
	Age:	6	7	8	9	10	11
1. Training of citizenship		120[②]	120	150	150	150	150
2. Games		180	180				
a. Music				90	90	90	90
b. Gymnastics				120	120	120	120
3. Chinese		420	420				
a. Speech				30	30	30	30
b. Reading				270	270	270	270
c. Composition				90	90	90	90
d. Writing				60	60	60	60
4. Arithmetic		—		180	210	210	210
5. General Knowledge		150	150	150	150		
a. Civics						30	30
b. History						60	60
c. Geography						60	60
d. Natural Science						120	120
6. Handicrafts		180	180				
a. Arts				60	60	60	60
b. Crafts				90	90	90	90
7. Extra-curricular activities		120	120	180	180	180	180
Total		1,170	1,170	1,470	1,500	1,620	1,620

"The Ministry of Education" not only sets the standards for curriculum but also sanctions textbooks prepared by private authors or by governmental bodies, provincial or central. This responsibility for examining textbooks is entrusted to the National Institute for Compilation and Translation which itself undertakes to publish certain textbooks in behalf of the Ministry.[③]

With the standards of curriculum revised, the elementary school textbooks also underwent corresponding changes. Two of the notable improvements in textbooks since 1952 have been the presentation of historical events in narrative style and the incorporation of materials relating to international understanding into the course of studies.

In recent years, as a result of accelerated changes in the economic development and in the

---

① Adapted from *World Survey of Education*, II, *op. cit.*, p. 246.
② Unit: Number of minutes per week.
③ *Ibid.*, pp. 246 – 48.

social life of the Chinese people during the process of rapid industrialization, the curriculum was again found to be inadequate. In view of the new needs, in 1959 "the Ministry of Education" made a complete appraisal of curricula in elementary and secondary schools and prepared to make extensive revisions of the 1952 curriculum standards. The Ministry established a Curriculum Development Committee composed of two sub-committees: One for the secondary school and one for the elementary school, each having educational specialists, curriculum experts, and experienced teachers and administrators as members.

Among the important innovations made by the sub-committee for the revision of elementary school curriculum was the decision to abolish the present double-cycled curriculum in the elementary school, (from the first grade to the fourth grade and from the fifth grade to the sixth) replacing it with a six-year single cycle curriculum from first grade through the sixth. Other improvements were the simplification of curriculum and the elimination of obsolete topics. ①

This revision is based upon two principles which have long been advocated in China, but have been somewhat neglected by educators:

(a) To reduce the study load of children at the elementary school level,
(b) To closely link education with life.

After extensive discussion and deliberation over a period of 20 months, the Committee came out with a draft of the new curriculum standards and a set of syllabi which were distributed in May of 1961 to schools, professional organizations, parents' associations, experts, and other interested persons for comment. In July, 1962, the Ministry, with the approval of the Executive Yuan, formally promulgated the new curriculum standards. Complete revision of textbooks according to the new standards was scheduled to start in the 1962–1963 academic year. ② The new standards are shown in TABLE 10.

TABLE 10 REVISED ELEMENTARY SCHOOL CURRICULUM③

Subject		Lower Grades		Intermediate Grades		Upper Grades	
		I	II	III	IV	V	VI
1.	Civics	150④			150		180
2.	Music and Games	180					
	a. Music				90		90
	b. Gymnastics				120		150
3.	Arts and Crafts	120					
	a. Arts			60		60	
	b. Crafts			90		90	
4.	Chinese	420			450		480
5.	Arithmetic	60			180	180	210
	Abacus					60	30
6.	General Knowledge	150					
	a. History				>60	60	
	b. Geography				90	60	
	c. Natural Science					120	
7.	Group Activities	120	180	150	240	180	240
	Total	1,200	1,260	1,440	1,530	1,710	1,770

---

① China, "Ministry of Education", Chiao Yü Kai Ku'ang, *op. cit.*, pp. 11–12.
② *Ibid.*
③ China, "Ministry of Education", *Elementary Education in "Taiwan"*, *op. cit.*, p. 26.
④ Unit: Number of minutes per week.

3. The Place of Private Schools in Elementary Education

The establishment of private schools is governed by the "Private School Law" which was promulgated in 1929 and subsequently revised in 1933, 1943, and 1947. Under this law matters regarding the establishment, change, and closing down of private schools at the college level are subject to the approval of "the Ministry of Education"; at the secondary level, the provincial government; and at the elementary level, the hsien or municipal government. The law further requires that all private schools should be placed under the supervision of the respective government levels, and their curricula, teaching materials and methods, examinations as well as administration should follow the same standards as those for the public schools. No teacher training institutions are permitted to be established privately. ①

In recent years as a result of the Government's policy of encouraging the establishment of private schools as well as public schools, the rules formerly restricting the establishment of private schools have been lifted and government subsidies made to private schools with good standing. The Provincial Educational Reconstruction Fund is also available for private schools to apply for loans. These measures have created a favorable atmosphere for the development of private schools in Taiwan. As a result, quite a number of private schools have been established in recent years, mostly at the secondary and higher education levels. At the elementary level, 95 per cent of all schools today in Taiwan are public institutions, so private schools constitute a very small portion of all elementary schools.

C. The Qualitative Development in Elementary Education

Significant improvements in the quality of elementary education in recent years are noted in the following areas: better qualified elementary school teachers, the improvement of teaching methods and materials, the experimentation in elementary education, and the enforcement of health education and medical care. Following is a detailed exposition of these qualitative developments.

1. Better Qualified Elementary School Teachers

To have better trained elementary school teachers has been one of the major concerns of educational authorities. The government has taken initial steps toward improving the competence of its teachers. The three-year normal schools from which most elementary school teachers in Taiwan have graduated not only were increased in number (from 3 in 1944 to 10 in 1961), ② but also were elevated in quality. In order to raise the status of normal schools from the equivalent of a senior middle school to the status of junior college, the course of study was lengthened from 3 to 5 years. ③ In addition to pre-service training, the government also provides various in-service training programs for both teachers and administrators.

The Provincial Department of Education took another major step by establishing the Provincial Elementary School Teachers' In-service Training Center in May, 1956 as a permanent institution for in-service training. In the six years since its inception in 1956, the center has conducted 47 classes in which 5,500 principals and teachers participated. Each class underwent one month's training in the Center's experimental school where the newest teaching methods are put into practice.

Other in-service training is offered by the normal schools through summer workshops and refresher courses. The "Ministry of Education" revealed that in 1961 about 70 per cent of the elementary school teachers in Taiwan were professionally trained, 25 per cent were high school graduates with teacher's certificates and 5 per cent had completed only 9 years of schooling. Nearly all of the teachers in the latter 30 per cent had received a four-week in-service training course. ④

---

① China, "Ministry of Education", <u>Chiao Yü Fa Ling</u>, *op. cit.*, pp. 25 – 30.
② *Supra.* Chapter IV, pp. 110 – 11.
③ China, "Ministry of Education", Department of Elementary Education, *op. cit.*, p. 18.
④ *Ibid.*, p. 19.

To enable qualified persons to teach, measures have been taken to issue certificates to those successfully passing the qualifying examinations held at regular intervals. For teachers and administrators who do not have an adequate professional educational background, a one-year course in the normal school is offered. Opportunities for professional growth are also given through programs such as the Sino-American education cooperation program which send teachers and administrators abroad for study or for observation.

Elementary school principals also must now meet minimum qualification standards. During his term as Provincial Commissioner of Education, Mr. Chen Liu was instrumental in the adoption of a minimum qualification standard requiring at least a normal school education with two years of successful experience of teaching or graduation from a teachers' college. ①

2. Improvement of Teaching Methods and Materials

The traditional emphasis on textbook study has gradually given way to more emphasis on the life of the child. Past overemphasis on the role of the teacher has also been replaced with child-centered methods. To a certain extent, children are encouraged to take the initiative under the guidance of the teacher. Teachers have become increasingly aware of the importance of the learning-by-doing method.

Although the curriculum is prescribed by educational authorities, teachers have a choice in the methods of instruction. This is especially true in the lower grades where the competition for entering junior middle school is not yet felt. In these grades teachers can fully utilize the school facilities and adapt their methods of teaching to the ability and growth of the pupils and to the nature of the subject matter.

In the past decade, a healthy trend in methodology has been the extensive use of audio-visual materials. Courses in audio-visual education have been added to the curriculum of the normal schools and the Normal University. All teachers are encouraged to make use of such materials as slides, filmstrips, recorders, mobile science laboratory units, and other educational equipment to supplement the traditional classroom teaching.

In 1955, an Audio-Visual Educational Center was established at the Provincial Taiwan Normal University. It was later reorganized and expanded to the National Educational Materials Center relocated in a new building especially constructed to meet its needs. The Center has five divisions, one of which is the Audio-Visual Division which is still housed at the Normal University. From the beginning, the Center has successfully met its overall objective of helping to improve teaching methods in elementary and secondary schools by providing audio-visual materials and by developing modern, dynamic curriculum materials and methods of instruction. It has also played a decisive role in the important process of evaluating and revising the curriculum of both elementary and secondary schools. ②

The chief functions of the Audio-Visual Division at the Normal University are:
(a) to circulate and repair audio-visual materials and equipment,
(b) to produce audio-visual materials for classroom use,
(c) to compile and publish an audio-visual education series,
(d) to give advisory opinions regarding audio-visual education,
(e) to coordinate audio-visual programs in schools,
(f) to provide in-service training for teachers in the use of audio-visual aids. ③

Through the technical and financial assistance of UNESCO's Technical Assistance Division and of the United States Mutual Security Mission to China, the work of the Center has produced far-reaching results through improvement of teaching methods and enrichment of teaching

---

① *Ibid.*, p. 17.
② U. S. Technical Cooperation Education Projects in "Taiwan", *The Road to Tomorrow, a Progress Report... 1952 1959* (Taipei: National Educational Materials Center, 1959), pp. 3 – 4.
③ China, "Ministry of Education", *Education in Taiwan*, op. cit., p. 87.

materials.

Educational authorities also attach great emphasis on the work of educational inspection in elementary schools. In addition to the regular inspection provided by scheduled visits made by school inspectors from provincial and hsien (or municipal) educational authorities, the local elementary school supervisors dispatched from the normal school of the region are also making regular visits. In recent years the Provincial Department of Education has founded a Visiting Supervisory Team for Elementary Schools which includes subject experts and experienced teachers to visit selected schools in each of the 16 hsiens and municipalities to demonstrate new teaching methods and materials and to hold meetings with teachers in the area to discuss problems concerning the improvement of teaching. The "Ministry of Education" also has set up a Science Education Advisory Committee for Elementary Schools to render special assistance in the teaching of science in elementary schools. ①

3. Experimentations in Elementary Education

In an effort to improve elementary education, the government has chosen several programs of experimentation. The major experiments have been on community-centered education, science education, the teaching of social science in a broad field curriculum, and the construction of intelligence tests. The following data on these experiments are largely based on a report issued by "the Ministry of Education". ②

a. Community-centered Education. Community-centered education in Taiwan was first undertaken in the middle schools in 1952 and was later extended to elementary schools. In 1955, four "citizen schools" were chosen to conduct such experiments and by 1956 one school in each hsien was designated to begin this experiment.

Theoretically, the ideal of community-centered education is not new in China. As early as 1920 Dr. Sun Yat-sen in his writing, "First Steps of Local Self-Government" stressed that the school is the source of civilization, that knowledge should be adapted to its practical use, and that education should be given not only to the young but to persons of all ages within the community. ③ In the years before World War II there was a period of such mass education and social reconstruction movements in China aimed at improving the living conditions of rural people. Unfortunately, it was interrupted by the war.

The present type of community-centered education is an idea reintroduced from the United States which had been previously successfully implemented in the Philippines. The emphasis of the community-centered school on a school program planned in direct relationship to its community is of significant importance for two reasons:

(1) It can contribute to better living in the community, and

(2) it can make the school program more vital and real, assuring children more meaningful experiences.

Because of these two advantages, community-centered education is being met with great enthusiasm in Taiwan. This is especially true in the rural school districts where the influence of the competitive entrance examination for entering junior middle schools, as will be discussed later, has little effect on the elementary school program which is thus relatively free to adapt curricula to local needs.

In order to train community-school teachers, the Provincial Department of Education, assisted by the United States International Co-operation Administration (ICA) Mutual Security Mission to China, ④ has conducted several summer workshops at the Provincial Elementary School Teachers'

---

① China, "Ministry of Education", Department of Elementary Education, *op. cit.*, p. 7.
② China, "Ministry of Education", Chiao Yü Kai Ku'ang, *op. cit.*, pp. 14 – 17.
③ *Supra*, Chapter IV, pp. 82 – 83.
④ Throughout this study the Agency for International Development (AID) is referred to by the name of its immediate predecessor, the International Cooperation Administration (ICA), a name used between June 30, 1955 and November 3, 1961, which is better known.

In-Service Training Center for the teachers and principals of participating schools. Also, courses on the principles and methods of community-centered schools are offered in all of the normal schools. Through this type of in-service training and course study, traditional ideas of teachers are changing.

Also, since the fundamental principles of community-school education are warmly supported by the general public, there is indication that this type of school will be voluntarily adapted by other schools. If it can escape the pressures exerted to prepare students only to pass the competitive entrance examination set for entering junior middle school, there is little doubt that the experiment would gain even greater success.

b. <u>Science Education</u>. As a part of the government's long-range science development program, an experiment in science education in the elementary schools has been adopted in order to improve the science education at the elementary level so that a social foundation for the development of science might be established.① The experiment was begun in 1957 under the direction of "the Ministry of Education" which appointed an advisory committee of specialists to take charge of the experimental design, compile the teaching materials and supervise implementation of the experiment. The 1952 curriculum standards require only the fifth and sixth grades to have separate courses in natural science. In the lower grades, natural science is included in the course on "general knowledge." This experiment is designed to teach natural science as a separate course in all the elementary grades. Initially, only three "citizen schools" in Hsinchu Hsien were chosen to take part, but the number has increased to 13, covering six hsien and municipalities and is expected to continue to be increased.②

Other activities which have aided the development of science education in elementary schools are as follows:

1. Revision of science textbooks and the compilation of teachers' manuals:

The textbook on natural science for use in the experiment are revised regularly to incorporate any new conceptions rising out of the experiment. In addition, the Advisory Committee compiles teachers' manuals for the texts.

2. "Mobile teaching aids demonstration units":

To provide teaching aids, the committee also designed "mobile teaching aids demonstration units" which contain teaching aids suitable to each of the lower, intermediate, and higher grades. The sixty units, 20 for each of the three levels, are housed in cars similar to mobile libraries for use in participating schools.

3. Seminars for teachers of natural science in elementary schools:

Three-week summer seminars have been conducted by several normal schools to discuss methods in the teaching of natural science.

4. Science education broadcast for children:

The increased interest of school children in natural science can be seen through the many problems raised in classrooms which are beyond the knowledge of elementary school teachers. In order to solve this problem, "the Ministry of Education" sponsors a weekly program called "Scientific World" which is aired on the Taiwan Broadcasting Stations. Teachers and children of elementary schools may send in their problems to the program and be answered by scientists. The questions and answers are then compiled every three months into a series, "The Scientific World of Children" which is distributed free to all elementary schools. This broadcast has proven to be a great success.

c. <u>The Teaching of Social Studies in the Broad Field Plan</u>. The teaching of social studies (general knowledge) in the upper grades (fifth and sixth grades) according to the 1952 curriculum standards is divided into three subjects: civics, history, and geography. Whether this specific subject plan of organization is superior to the broad field plan as being adopted in the

---

① China, "Ministry of Education", *Chiao Yü Kai Ku'ang*, *op. cit.*, pp. 14 – 15.
② *Ibid.*, p. 15.

lower grades (from first to fourth grades) is a question to which an answer must be sought.

In curriculum development there has been increasing evidence to show that the broad field plan has several principal advantages over the specific subject plan of organization. These are:

1. It avoids the extreme fragmentation of the specific subject plan and makes possible longer time assignments and larger units of study.

2. It avoids the extreme compartmentalization of the specific subject plan and makes possible organization of subject matter around a central topic or problem.

With this hypothesis, the educational authorities began in 1958 to undertake an experiment to determine the extent to which the broad field plan excels over the specific subject plan in the teaching of social studies.

The experiment was conducted by the Provincial Elementary School Teachers' In-Service Training Center in cooperation with four selected "citizen schools." Two classes, one experiment and one control, were chosen from both the fifth and sixth grades of each participating school. A set of four textbooks, one for each semester was compiled according to the principles of the broad field plan. The organization of subject matter was around eight central topics (or large units), two for each text. These textbooks were used for the experimental classes.

The primary result of the experiment as revealed by "the Ministry of Education" is highly in favor of the broad field plan. Since the experiment is still in progress, final results are not yet available. [1]

d. <u>The Construction of Intelligence Tests</u>. In order to provide a means for the measurement of the capacities of students so that teaching can be better suited to the needs of the students, both group tests and individual tests are being prepared by experts designated by "the Ministry of Education" and Chinese Association fox Mental Testing. The group tests for elementary students were completed by the end of 1960 and the preparation of individual tests based on the Stanford-Binet Intelligence Scale is still in progress.

4. The Enforcement of Health Education and Medical Care

One of the major responsibilities of elementary education is to develop good health habits in children. In Taiwan the health program in elementary schools has been successfully carried out as part of the national campaign for better health. Under the planning and supervision of the Committee for Health Education of the Provincial Department of Education, in collaboration with local educational authorities and assisted by public health agencies, a series of health programs have been implemented to schools throughout the island. The programs include: improving school sanitary installations, establishing and staffing school health clinics, giving regular physical examinations, providing remedial treatment of chronic diseases, arranging for immunizations, and developing programs for better nutrition.

Two main requirements of the 1962 minimum standards for elementary school buildings which attempt to alleviate health hazards are:

a. There should not be more than 50 pupils per classroom with 1.4 square meters allowed per child.

b. Sanitary facilities should include at least a health clinic, toilet, boiled drinking water, and a kitchen. All schools are also required to have an average of 4 square meters of outdoor space per child in city schools and 8 square meters per child in rural schools. If financially possible, bathing facilities should also be provided. [2]

In recent years it has become common practice to give a thorough physical examination to each child as he enters elementary school. A health record is then made for each child and kept on file. To it are added his weight and height measurements as taken at regular intervals and the

---

[1] *Ibid.*, p. 16.

[2] *Report on Educational Development of "Taiwan", 1961 – 1962*, Twenty-fifth International Conference on Public Education (Taipei: Ministry of Education, 1962), p. 16.

results of the physical checkups given at least once each school year. BCG tests, x-rays, vaccinations and inoculation are regularly given and results recorded. Dental examinations are also conducted once every semester or once every year.① This is all done in the school clinic which every school is required to have and to staff with a part-time doctor and a full-time registered nurse.②

Working in cooperation with WHO, the government has conducted a trachoma control program in elementary schools since 1954. As of June, 1962, a total of 1,895,574 people were given free treatment for trachoma in the areas where elementary school children were found to have trachoma. Of those given free medical treatment, 1,770,505 were completely cured.③

In addition to the above mentioned measures, the educational authorities are also conscious of the importance of health and nutrition education. The Provincial Department of Education with the assistance of the Joint Commission on Rural Reconstruction (JCRR) published a 12 volume set of textbooks called *The Healthful Life* for use in school health education.④ In order to make up for the deficiency in nutrition due to the over-milling and over-consumption of rice, a series of nutritional programs has been instituted with UNICEF daily providing skimmed milk. The school lunch program which originally began as an experiment has now been adopted and extended to many schools.

A general survey of the height and weight of school children conducted by the Elementary Teachers In-Service Training Center based on 400,000 elementary school children during the period of 1955 – 1959 shows the general improvement in children's health in the years under survey. The increase in height and weight for school children from 7 to 12 between 1955 and 1959 is shown in TABLE 11.

TABLE 11 FIVE-YEAR STUDY OF STUDENTS' HEIGHT AND WEIGHT IN TAIWAN BETWEEN 1955 AND 1959⑤

Year	Age					
	7	8	9	10	11	12
Height—Boys⑥						
1955	109.2	113.2	117.2	122.1	130.2	135.0
1956	110.3	116.2	119.4	122.4	133.2	136.7
1957	115.1	119.8	124.7	127.0	134.1	138.9
1958	115.58	120.16	124.98	129.86	132.24	135.02
1959	113.85	118.74	123.88	128.22	133.48	136.30
Girls						
1955	110.7	112.2	120.1	124.4	127.8	130.7
1956	111.5	114.7	123.0	125.9	130.2	130.5
1957	112.1	119.0	124.6	129.7	134.4	138.2
1958	114.54	119.72	124.68	129.5	132.96	136.06
1959	113.06	118.36	123.54	128.68	133.02	137.24

① China, "Ministry of Education", Department of Elementary Education, *op. cit.*, p. 10.
② *World Survey of Education*, *op. cit.*, II, p. 248.
③ *China Yearbook, 1962 – 1963*, *op. cit.*, p. 685.
④ The writer was one of the ten members selected by the Committee for Health Education to undertake the compilation of the textbooks during 1956 – 1957.
⑤ *Report on Education Progress of "Taiwan", 1959 – 1960*, Twenty-third International Conference on Public Education (Taipei: Ministry of Education, 1960), p. 14.
⑥ Unit: Milimeter

(Continuing)

Year	Age					
	7	8	9	10	11	12
	Weight—Boys①					
1955	17.5	19.7	21.5	23.4	25.7	28.4
1956	18.6	20.4	22.1	23.1	26.2	29.3
1957	20.2	22.0	23.2	24.5	27.1	28.3
1958	19.74	22.88	23.46	25.56	27.22	28.21
1959	19.31	21.48	23.38	25.26	26.56	29.42
	Girls					
1955	18.4	19.3	20.9	22.3	25.0	27.9
1956	20.5	21.8	21.7	23.4	25.3	28.0
1957	20.9	21.9	22.6	24.5	25.5	31.2
1958	19.70	21.24	23.12	26.06	27.11	28.11
1959	18.93	20.77	23.33	25.12	27.27	29.72

D. Problems and Trends in Primary Education

Although remarkable progress has been made in primary education, unsolved problems remain. This section will identify the most pressing ones and discuss their causes and impacts as well as possible solutions which the Taiwan administration is now exploring.

1. Effects of the Population Explosion

The first pressing problem facing elementary education is a result of the population explosion. In recent years the average rate of population increase in Taiwan has been 3.4 per cent, one of the highest in the world.② In addition, the school attendance rate of school-age children is also steadily increasing. These two factors combined with the limited amount of financial resources available has made it extremely difficult to expand the present school facilities to accommodate all children reaching the age of six.

The first step toward alleviating the problem was a survey on elementary and secondary education in Taiwan completed in October, 1961, from which the following statistics emerged:③

a. The number of graduating students in the 1961–1962 academic year totaled 260,427. The number of children reaching the school age of six in the 1962–1963 academic year was 409,678, an increase of 149,251 pupils. If the average size of a class were 50 pupils, 2,985 additional classes were needed; if the size were 60 pupils, 2,487 would be needed.

b. It was further disclosed that due to the rapid increase in student population, most classes in elementary schools were overcrowded. TABLE 12 shows that the average number of students in elementary school classes was 55.19 on the main campus and 40.04, in the school branches. TABLE 13 shows that there were 9,215 classes representing 24.79 per cent of the total number of classes with an enrollment of more than 61 pupils.

---

① Unit: Kilogram
② Taiwan, Department of Education, *A Survey Report on Taiwan Elementary And Secondary Education in 1961* (Taichung: 1961), p. 13.
③ *Ibid.*

TABLE 12   THE AVERAGE NUMBER OF STUDENTS PER CLASS IN EACH OF THE ELEMENTARY GRADES IN TAIWAN 1961 – 1962[①]

Grade	1	2	3	4	5	6	Total
Main Campus							
Classes	6,351	6,139	6,127	5,877	5,810	5,197	35,501
Medium	57.44	55.96	56.33	55.80	53.80	51.04	55.19
Branch							
Classes	507	404	307	226	128	101	1,673
Medium	46.55	43.40	41.06	39.33	32.15	27.60	40.04

Concurrent with overcrowded classes is the overcrowding of schools. The survey revealed that in some parts of the island, especially in Taipei City, there were schools with more than 60 classes, or with an enrollment of more than 3,000 pupils.

TABLE 13   THE VARIOUS SIZES OF ELEMENTARY SCHOOL CLASSES IN TAIWAN, 1961 – 1962[②]

Number of Pupils	Number of Classes	Percentage
Under 35	2,699	7.27
36 – 50	10,220	27.49
51 – 60	15,040	40.45
Over 61	9,215	24.79
Total	37,174	100.00

TABLE 14   THE SIZE OF ELEMENTARY SCHOOLS, 1961 – 1962[③]
(EXCLUDING BRANCHES)

Number of Classes	Number of Schools[④]	Per Cent	Number of Pupils	Number of Schools[⑤]	Per Cent
More than 60	53	3.08	Over 3,000	94	4.98
Less than 24	1,421	75.42	Under 1,000	1,222	64.86

c. Without taking into account the large number of classes which need to be added each year, there already exists a severe classroom shortage. This shortage can be readily seen in TABLE 15.

---

① *Ibid.*, p. 15.
② *Ibid.*
③ *Ibid.*, p. 82.
④ Of the branches, there are 466 schools or 93.20 per cent of the total number of branch schools which are composed of less than 6 classes. *Ibid.*
⑤ Of the branches, there are 436 schools or 87.20 per cent of the total number of branch schools which have an enrollment of 300 pupils. *Ibid.*

TABLE 15 SHORTAGE OF CLASSROOMS IN ELEMENTARY SCHOOL AS SHOWN BY THE NUMBER OF CLASSES IN THE "MULTI-GROUP SHIFT SYSTEM," 1961 – 1962①

Grade	Main Campus						Branch			
	Total	Full-day	Two-shift	Three-shift	Four-shift	Sub-Total	Full-day	Two-shift	Three-shift	Sub-Total
1	6,858	1,597	4,624	66	64	6,351	207	292	8	507
2	6,543	1,609	4,434	32	64	6,139	157	244	3	404
3	6,434	3,477	2,610	9	31	6,127	219	88	0	307
4	6,103	4,819	1,046	12	0	5,877	183	43	0	226
5	5,938	5,754	56	0	0	5,810	114	14	0	128
6	5,298	5,181	16	0	0	5,197	93	8	0	101
Total	37,174	22,437	12,786	119	159	35,510	973	689	11	1,673

which shows that it is not uncommon to have two, three, or even four classes of students use one classroom during separate sessions on the same day. In this "multi-group shift system" students stay at school for only one-half, one-third, or even one-fourth of the regular hours enjoyed by ordinary classes.

In addition to adoption of the "multi-group shift system," various locations are being utilized for instruction in the attempt to meet the need for more classrooms. Within the school, the library, offices, auditorium and gymnasium are used. Outside the school, use is made of public meeting places, temples and even private homes. Taking into account the number of classes held in other locations, the shortage of classrooms in 1961 – 1962 was 7,516. This does not include the 2,522 classes needed to be added to meet the natural increase in student population. ②

Measures, some temporary and others of a long-term nature, have been taken to cope with the actual problem of the population explosion but the task is not an easy one in view of the prevailing political, social, and economic conditions in Taiwan, The government's hands-off policy in matters concerning birth control has both political and social implications. Politically, the Taiwan administration contends that when the counter-attack on the mainland takes place, manpower will be a vital factor. Socially, the people still believe in large families, but lack any sense of public spirit about supporting educational endeavors which by tradition are "government business". Local communities will spend large amounts of money on festivals, but will seldom give financial aid to their schools. Thus, educational authorities have only limited financial resources at their disposal.

The following measures have been taken in an attempt to cope with the problems faced by these educational authorities.

a. The Provincial Department of Education enacted a law requiring all municipal governments to build one additional classroom for each new class and all <u>hsien</u> governments, at least two classrooms for every three classes. ③

b. In order to encourage local initiative in constructing more classrooms, beginning in 1957 the Provincial Department of Education has allocated each year a special fund for construction of classrooms wherever the local government or parents' association is willing to bear two-thirds of the cost and have the Department of Education subsidize the other one-third. Between 1957 and 1960 some 3,172 classrooms were constructed under this program. It is the government's hope that in the near future the multi-group shift system can be completely eliminated above the second grade level. TABLE 16 shows the number of classrooms constructed between 1957 and 1960.

c. At the end of 1957, the "Ministry of Education" also promulgated "Regulations Governing

---

① *Ibid.*, Part V, p. 11.
② *Ibid.*, p. 25.
③ *Ibid.*, pp. 2 – 3.

the Construction of Elementary School Buildings" which stipulates: (1) The maximum number of classes permitted in any elementary school is 36. School districts with schools containing more than 36 are required to establish new.

TABLE 16   THE CONSTRUCTION OF ELEMENTARY SCHOOL CLASSROOMS, 1957 – 1960[①]

School Year	No. of Existing Classrooms	Classrooms Added to Meet Increased Enrollments	Classrooms Added Through Subsidies	Total Classrooms
1957	19,724	1,066		20,790
1958	20,790	1,397	1,831	24,018
1959	24,018	1,783	438	26,239
1960	26,239	1,815	903	28,957
Total		6,061	3,172	

Schools or branches. These school districts may also be divided into smaller districts. (2) Based on its own particular needs each of the local governments is encouraged to draw up a long-range program for the development of elementary schools in its respective region and see that this program is fully carried out. (3) All elementary schools are asked to take good care of existing classrooms and make full use of them. (4) In anticipation of the further development of elementary education, each local government is requested to immediately seek new revenue for education and to establish funds for elementary education, and (5) private donations to support education should be encouraged.[②]

2. The Malpractice of "Malign Reviewing"[③]

The second pressing problem confronting elementary education is the much talked about "malign reviewing", a term used to describe the excessive preparation of the pupil for the competitive entrance examination for junior middle schools.

The causes of this malpractice are many, but the main reason is simply that there are more elementary school graduates than the limited number of junior middle schools can absorb. Other reasons of considerable importance are:

(a) Admission is based solely on performance in the competitive entrance examination.

(b) The traditional attitude of "promotionalism," that elementary education is the preparation for secondary education (mainly middle school) and that secondary education is the preparation for higher education (mainly the university), is still predominant.

(c) Society judges an elementary school by the number of its students who pass the entrance examination.

(d) Provincial middle schools are better equipped and staffed than the hsien or municipal middle schools and the latter are better than the private middle schools, thus creating a preference for admission to provincial middle schools.

(e) Teachers' salaries are very low, making it difficult for those who have large families to make ends meet. In order to make extra income most teachers are willing to teach overtime at the request of the parents.

(f) The custom of "reviewing" or "supplementary studies" in Taiwan dates back to the Japanese occupation when schools for Taiwanese children were far inferior to Japanese schools.

[①] China, "Ministry of Education", Chiao Yü Kai Ku'ang, op. cit., p. 3.
[②] Ibid.
[③] The term "Malign Reviewing" is the writer's own translation from the Chinese "E hsing pu hsi." Another translation by Miss Yah-chuan Wang, Head of the Department of Secondary Education in the Ministry of Education, is "vicious supplementary studies." See, for example, her "The Development of Junior Middle School Education in China," China Today, No. 4 (April, 1958), 37 – 38.

The "reviewing" became necessary in order for Taiwanese children to be able to meet the high admission requirements for the predominantly Japanese schools. This has made "reviewing" a general practice in Taiwan society. Many well-to-do families always have private tutors for their children in the after-school hours.

This is the background against which "malign reviewing" has gained an unshakeable place in elementary education and which is responsible for the malfunctioning of elementary education.

Under its influence, students beginning in the third or fourth grade are given excessive homework and assignments. Extra classes are added each day providing the material needed for students to pass the examination. Since the examination subjects consist only of Chinese, arithmetic, and general knowledge (civics, history, geography, and natural science), these have become the center of study. Despite the law strictly prohibiting over-emphasis on certain courses at the expense of others, still a few schools under the pressure of parents and society are compelled to teach only the 3 "basic" subjects. Students memorize only facts and recite them repetitiously, Many of these facts are beyond their comprehension and have no connection whatsoever with the students' lives or previous experiences. To compensate for the extra time and effort which the teachers have to put into this work, many schools openly charge students fees on a compulsory basis, defeating the axiom that elementary education should be both free and compulsory.

Perhaps the greatest injustice as a result of this malpractice is the lack of any provision to those graduates who either by their own choice or by failing to pass the examination do not enter the junior middle school. For this group of students the school has failed to provide the practical knowledge and skills that will enable them to make a living.① Another serious consequence of "malign reviewing" is the effect it has on the mental and physical development of children. The seriousness of this malpractice has caused quite a bit of concern among educators, educational authorities, and the general public. Many measures have already been taken to improve the situation, but recent reports show that there is still a long way to go before the problem can be completely eradicated. Following are some of the measures the government has already taken:

a. In order to control the content of all entrance examinations so that they do not become excessively difficult for the students, the government required that all tests should conform to and be within the limits of the textbooks compiled by the government. When this proved ineffective, the government reduced the number of subjects to be tested from three to two, eliminating "general knowledge" which generally requires excessive cramming and memorization. In addition to this the government made it illegal for teachers to teach overtime and to use school classrooms for such purposes in off-school hours. Also, school administrators were required to supervise their teachers to make certain that regular curriculum and class schedules are followed. Although these measures have not solved the basic problem, they did lessen the extent to which malign reviewing is done.

b. The second measure taken by the government has been to extend the school facilities at the secondary level. This has been done through the improvement of the facilities and teaching personnel of the local middle schools so that more applicants would be attracted to them rather than to the more preferred provincial middle schools. Also, two gradual changes were begun. Junior sections of the provincial middle schools were discontinued making the provincial schools solely senior middle schools, and the senior sections of the local middle schools were discontinued making the local middle schools solely junior middle schools. In this way competition between the two would gradually be eliminated and more important, education at the junior middle school level would be the responsibility of the local government, paving the way for the extension of compulsory education to 9 years.

c. The Taiwan administration's third measure was to improve teachers' welfare and raise their

---

① The percentage of elementary graduates wishing to enter junior middle school in 1960－1961 in main campus was 54. 19 per cent of the total graduates and the percentage of all elementary graduates who actually entered junior middle schools in the same year was 48. 46 per cent. In other words, about 51. 54 per cent of all elementary graduates were not enrolled in junior middle schools. See Taiwan, A Survey Report...op. cit., p. 14.

salaries; however, since almost all civil servants, including teachers, are underpaid, it is difficult for the government to make any substantial raises at present. Some financial relief has been achieved through the endeavors of the Provincial Department of Education which established a teachers' welfare fund in 1959 to make available loans, scholarships for teachers' children, retirement benefits, and assistance in case of accident.

3. Problems in Extending the Period of Compulsory Education

This problem is closely linked with that of eliminating "malign reviewing" since the successful implementation of the former would naturally eliminate the need for the latter. This task, however, is by no means an easy one. It calls for additional funds, staff, and facilities which are at present beyond that which the government is able to provide.

In September, 1955, the government adopted a "Program for the Development of Junior Middle School Education" which calls for more junior middle schools to be established by the local governments.① In March, 1956, the government further adopted a "Plan for Elementary School Graduates Entering Junior Middle School." Instead of making junior middle school compulsory for everyone, which was too large a task for the government, this second plan was to make it possible for those elementary graduates who wished to continue their education to be admitted to junior middle schools without an entrance examination. If this could be made possible, then the "malign reviewing" would no longer be needed.

Hsinchu Hsien was first chosen to try the plan and Kaohsiung City was added the second year. With the financial assistance of the Provincial Government, both the Hsinchu and the Kaohsiung local governments tried to provide enough schools to admit without examination all elementary graduates wishing to enter junior middle schools. The experiment met with considerable success. The preliminary results as reported by Mr. Chung-quen Liang, Chief of the Bureau of Education in Hsinchu Hsien, were as follows:

a. On the average, the scholastic achievements of the students at the junior middle schools who were admitted without examination compared favorably with those schools where students were admitted by passing the entrance examinational,②

b. the mental and physical well-being of the pupils showed marked improvement,③

c. local people paid more attention to educational problems and became more interested in educational undertakings. ④

The plan was intended to be implemented throughout the island within a 5-year period. It was unfortunate, however, that due to the change of Ministership combined with a shortage of funds, the experiment as well as the plan was suspended in 1959. Since then, the government has concentrated its efforts on the implementation of the "Program for the Development of Junior Middle School Education." One of the important steps taken toward this end was the requiring of local governments to establish at least one junior middle school in each village and township. This has helped to lessen the need for "malign reviewing" in the rural areas; however, in the large cities, the problem still remains.

VI. The Development of Secondary Education

According to the *World Survey of Education*, *Volume III*, *Secondary Education*, "secondary education" is interpreted as covering all types of education—general, technical, vocational,

---

① Taiwan, Department of Education, Shih Nien Lai Ti Tai-wan Chiao Yü, op. cit., pp. 287 – 90.
② Chung-quen Liang, Hsin-chu Hsien Shih Shih "Mien Shih Sheng Hsüeh" Ti Ch'eng Kuo [Achievements and Accomplishments in the Implementation of the Plan of "Admission Without Examination" in Hsinchu Hsien] (Taipei: Chung Hua Wen Hua Ch'u Pan Shih Yeh Wei Yuan Hui, 1960), pp. 4 – 23.
③ Ibid., pp. 80, 97.
④ Ibid., pp. 43 – 52.

teacher training or others—provided for young people between the approximate ages of 12 and 18.① At present in Nationalist China, secondary education covers three types of education—general, vocational, and normal—planned especially for young people of approximately 12 to 18 years of age. The legal basis for these three types of secondary education is prescribed by laws which will be analyzed in the following section.

A. The Legal Basis for Secondary Education

1. "Middle School Law"

In the section of Chapter II dealing with the development of the school system in China, it was mentioned that the 1922 New School System, which prescribed that secondary education was to follow the pattern of the American comprehensive high school, was amended in 1933. Since that time, secondary education has been provided by three separate types of schools— "middle schools," "vocational schools" and "normal schools" —each with its own special function and designed to meet a special need. Since the normal school will be included in the separate chapter on teacher education, this chapter is devoted entirely to the "middle school" and the "vocational school."

Three principal laws, one for each of the three types of schools, were promulgated by the government in 1932. Each makes certain fundamental stipulations regarding the objectives, organization and administration of its respective type of school. A set of regulations giving details regarding implementation supplements each of these laws.

The objectives of the "Middle school" as stipulated in Article 1 of the "Middle School Law" are:

> ...to be in accord with the overall educational aims of "the Republic", to extend the basic training achieved at the elementary school and to aim at the physical and mental development of the youth, the cultivation of good citizenship, and the preparation for advanced studies and useful employment.②

Article 2 of the law prescribes that the term "middle school" should include both the 3 year junior and the 3 year senior sections. When established separately, the school is called the junior or senior middle school accordingly; when established together, it is called a middle school. In Articles 3 and 4 it is prescribed that middle schools may be either private or public, the latter being established either by provincial, municipal, or hsien authorities. The fifth article requires that all middle schools be placed under the supervision and control of the provincial and municipal educational authorities. As directed in Article 11, graduation from an elementary school or its equivalent is required for entrance to the junior middle school and graduation from a junior middle school or its equivalent is in turn required for entrance to the senior middle school.③

2. "Vocational School Law"

The objective of the "vocational school" as stipulated in Article 1 of the "Vocational School Law" is "to cultivate in youth the knowledge of life and the skills of productivity."④ This also is to be pursued in accordance with the overall educational aims. The organization and administration are similar to those provided for the middle school; for example, the term "vocational school" should include both junior and senior sections. In the establishing of vocational schools, however, each school is to concentrate on only one type of occupation and be named accordingly; such as vocational-agricultural school, vocational-industrial school, vocational-commercial school, etc. Exceptions to this are allowed in those localities where a multi-subject vocational school is needed.

---

① *World Survey of Education*, Vol. III, *Secondary Education* (New York: International Documents Services, 1961), p. 10.
② China, Ministry of Education, Chiao Yü Fa Ling, *op. cit.*, p. 141.
③ *Ibid.*, p. 187.
④ *Ibid.*

Such schools are known simply as "vocational schools."①

B. The Qualitative Development of Middle Schools

1. School Organization and New Experiments

Middle school organization follows the 3 – 3 plan. Each school year begins on the first of August and ends on the thirty-first of July of the following year. Each of the two semesters of the academic year has 20 school weeks and each week, 6 school days. In addition to national holidays, there are spring, summer, and winter vacations, making a total of about 80 vacation days per year.

Besides the regular 3 – 3 plan, the government has conducted experiments with the 4 – 2 plan in two selected schools. The experiment is based on two assumptions:

(a) that the 3 – 3 plan represents some waste of time because of its double-cycled curriculums, and

(b) that the curriculum in the latter period of the middle school should be differentiated.

Following these assumptions, students in these two experimental schools are provided with a six-year course of studies that has no duplication. Fundamental subjects are taught the first four years with subjects grouped into either the division of arts or the division of sciences taught the last two years. The arts division has more courses in language and social studies; the science division has a heavier load in mathematics and natural science.②

Another experiment which eventually proved to be a failure was a 4 year middle school with a main emphasis on practical training. The experiment was conducted between 1952 and 1956 in 4 designated schools; however, partly due to the traditional low esteem for vocational training and partly due to the shortcomings in the design of the experiment, the plan was suspended.③

2. Curriculum Revision

Curriculum standards for middle schools were first regulated by law in 1929 with 7 subsequent revisions, the last major one in 1962. This latest revision originated in 1959 followed by the establishment of the Committee for the Revision of Curriculum Standards in Elementary and Middle Schools. The subcommittee for the revision of middle school curriculum standards adopted a draft of the new curriculum standards in October, 1960. After the final draft was promulgated in 1962, a three year period was allowed to complete implementation. The Ministry also designated eight middle schools to compile new teaching materials to comply with the new standards and to conduct experiments with the materials.④

For the purpose of comparison, it would be necessary to give examples of both the new and old curriculum standards and to compare the two programs of studies. Unfortunately, at the time of this study, the new programs of studies were not yet available, therefore only the programs of studies as based on the 1955 revision are listed. TABLE 17 gives the program for the junior middle school, TABLE 18 for the senior middle school.

The major points of emphasis in the new revised curriculum standards are analyzed below:

a. <u>Redefining Objectives</u>. The objectives of middle schools as stipulated in the "Middle School Law" do not differentiate between the functions of the junior and senior middle school. The new standards give each its own distinct objective. Those of the junior middle school are "to continue the fundamental education of the elementary school, aiming at the development of the body and mind of the adolescents, the fostering of citizenship and morality, the transmittance of the nation's culture, and the repletion of the basic knowledge and skills necessary for earning a

---

① *Ibid.*, pp. 187 – 88.
② China, "Ministry of Education", Chiao Yü Kai Ku'ang, *op. cit.*, p. 6.
③ *Ibid.*
④ Yah-ch'uan Wang, "I Nien Lai Ti Chung Teng Chiao Yü" [The Secondary Education in the Present Year], Chiao Yü Yu Wen Hua, No. 303 (February 15, 1963), 7 - 8.

livelihood. The overall objective of the junior middle school is to cultivate righteous and progressive citizens." The objectives of the senior middle school as adopted by the committee are "to cultivate the talented youth, to foster in him citizenship and morality, to offer him cultural and scientific education and military training to form a foundation for advanced studies of professional education, and to help him become the backbone of society."①

According to the new standards, the emphasis in the junior middle school is placed on education for life with a basic objective of providing for all adolescents a broad, general, and common education in the basic knowledge and skills as a basis for discovering and exploring their specialized interests, aptitudes, and abilities. This is align with the possible extension of compulsory education to the junior middle school. The emphasis of the senior middle school is clearly placed on education for the elite with a basic objective of differentiation of knowledge in order to prepare students for advanced undertakings.

TABLE 17　COURSES OF STUDY AND WEEKLY ACADEMIC HOURS FOR JUNIOR MIDDLE SCHOOL②

Subject	First Year		Second Year		Third Year	
	1	2	1	2	1	2
Chinese	6	6	6	6	6	6
Foreign Language (English)	3	3	3	3	4	4
Social Studies						
Civics	2	2	2	2	2	2
History	2	2	2	2	2	2
Geography	1	1	2	2	2	2
Mathematics	3	3	3	3	3	3
Natural Studies						
Physics and Chemistry			3	3	3	3
Natural History	3	3				
Physiology and Hygiene			2	2		
Physical Education	2	2	2 (1)③	2 (1)	2 (1)	2 (1)
Music	2	2	1	1	1	1
Fine Art	1	1	1	1	1	1
Manual Work (Home Economics)	2	2	2 (3)	2 (3)	(1)	(1)
Boy Scouting	1	1	1	1	1	1
Optional	—	—	—	—	−3	−3
Total	28	28	30	30	30	30

---

　① China, "Ministry of Education", Chiao Yü Kai Ku'ang, op cit., pp. 27 – 28.
　② China, "Ministry of Education", Department of Secondary Education, Secondary Education in "Taiwan" (Taipei: 1960), p. 15.
　③ The number of hours given in parentheses is for girl students.

TABLE 18 COURSES OF STUDY AND WEEKLY ACADEMIC HOURS FOR SENIOR MIDDLE SCHOOL①

Subject	First Year		Second Year		Third Year	
	1	2	1	2	1	2
Chinese	5	5	5	5	5	5
Foreign Language (English)	4	4	4	4	5	5
Civics	2	2	2	2		
Three People's Principles					2	2
History			2	2	2	2
Geography	2	2	2	2		
Mathematics	4	4	4	4	4	4
Physics					5	5
Chemistry			4	4		
Biology	3	3				
Physical Education	2	2	2 (1)②	2 (1)	2 (1)	2 (1)
Music	1	1	1	1		
Fine Art	1	1	1	1		
Manual Work (Home Economics)	2 (3)	2 (3)	2 (3)	2 (3)	(1)	(1)
Military Training	2	2	2	2	2	2
Optional	—	—	—	—	4	4
Total (Girl)	28 (29)	28 (29)	31 (31)	31 (31)	31 (31)	31 (31)

b. <u>Reinforcing Vocational Training and Reintroducing Elective Courses</u>. Two changes have been made in the junior middle schools. Practical courses such as industrial arts and home economics have been lengthened and more time is allotted in the third year for students to take courses of their choice from either the academic or the vocational courses.

The major change in the senior middle school has been the provision for elective courses for 2 hours each week in the second year and the time allotted for elective courses increased from 2 to 8 hours each week in the third year. Again, the elective courses may be either college preparatory or vocational training courses. ③

c. <u>Increasing Flexibility in Meeting Individual Needs</u>. In order to meet the varying needs and capabilities of pupils, increasing flexibility in the curriculum is being provided. In the junior middle school, there is greater flexibility in the teaching of foreign languages, mathematics, physics, and chemistry. In the senior middle school there is a notable emphasis on differentiation of curriculum through 2 courses of study, one emphasizing sciences and one emphasizing the arts. The differentiation is intensified in the second year and is increased by allowing more elective courses in the third year. In order that students be given a balanced course of studies, all are

---

① *Ibid.*, p. 16.
② The number of hours given in parentheses is for girl students.
③ *Ibid.*

required to take a certain number of courses in the other field of emphasis. ①

　　d. Intensifying Moral Education. The former courses in "civics" and "training for citizenship" have been combined into a course with equal emphasis on the study of moral principles on one hand and actual practice on the other. ②

　　e. Emphasizing the Teaching of Industrial Arts. To meet the needs of an industrial society the former "art crafts" course has been changed to "industrial arts" which is aimed at providing youth with the basic technical knowledge and skills necessary for modern life, fostering respect for manual labor, and instilling good work habits. ③

　　f. Eliminating Duplication in the Double-Cycle Curriculum. In the former curriculum there were many duplications in the teaching material of the junior and senior middle schools. In order to reduce the study load and make room for new material, great care was taken in formulating the new curriculum to avoid repetition and to seek better articulation of materials. ④

　　There are differences between the elementary and the secondary schools in the compilation of textbooks. In elementary schools almost all textbooks, except in music, arts, crafts, and gymnastics, are compiled by the Institute of Compilation and Translation and are distributed free to all elementary students In secondary schools, a great number of textbooks are compiled by the publishers in accord with curriculum standards; however, "the Ministry of Education" requires that all such textbooks also be approved by the Institute of Compilation and Translation. Its approval is effective for 3 years and can be extended after revision bringing the text up-to-date. Maximum price for each text is decided by the government on the basis of subject area and number of pages. ⑤

3. The Development of Science Education

　　Development of science education has been one of the government's main emphases in recent years. Measures taken by the government have included the establishment of a Science Education Council within "the Ministry of Education"; the promulgation of the "Plan for Developing Science Education in the Secondary Schools" which assisted by U. S. aid, has begun an ambitious revision of the current science texts; the improvement in the quality of science teachers; and the modernization of science facilities.

　　The major improvements in this regard have been in the following areas:

　　a. In-service training for science teachers at all levels has been provided to assure familiarity with and command of scientific advances and new teaching techniques.

　　b. Curriculum and textbook revision in senior middle schools has been undertaken to meet current needs in science education.

　　c. Adequate science equipment for secondary schools and for teacher training and higher institutions has been provided. ⑥

　　"the Ministry of Education" approached the science program first with an evaluation of the current status of science teaching, science curriculum, and science equipment in all senior middle schools which were chosen as the initial starting point for aid. Also, there were several science education conferences for senior middle school teachers held in 1958 and 1959 to arouse teacher interest and discover their needs. In 1959 a permanent in-service training center for middle school teachers was established at Taiwan Normal University with both long-term (17 weeks) and short-term (2 to 4 weeks) institutes in biology, physics, chemistry, and mathematics conducted for science teachers wishing to acquire new knowledge, to improve their teaching methods and materials and to exchange experiences with other teachers. Provisions also are made each year for

---

　　① *Ibid.*
　　② *Ibid.*
　　③ *Ibid.*
　　④ *Ibid.*, pp. 28 – 29.
　　⑤ *Ibid.*, pp. 29 – 30.
　　⑥ U. S. Technical Cooperation Education Project, *op. cit.*, pp. 47 – 48.

sending science teachers abroad for advanced training. In conjunction with these programs, the National Science Hall in Taipei undertook to display and demonstrate teaching aids and scientific experiments suitable for middle schools. ① To expand school science facilities, the government has appropriated a large sum of money each year beginning in 1959 to help middle and normal schools procure equipment and specimens to build up their science laboratories.

4. "Life-centered Education" and "Community-centered Education"

To try out new methods and to vitalize the existing curriculum in middle schools, the government has conducted the following two experiments.

a. "Life-centered Education." This experiment is intended "to replace traditional subject-centered education with a new method of education centered around real life."② The two basic principles of the experiment are to coordinate education with life and to link knowledge with application. Using these principles, the new curriculum adopted made social science subjects the core with other subjects centered around them. The whole curriculum is constructed according to large unit plans.

Beginning in 1953, classes in the junior section of the Provincial Chang Kung Middle School were designated for experimentation. The report on the experiment in progress by "the Ministry of Education" gives the following encouraging accounts:

(1) This experiment has served to arouse the interest of the students undergoing experimentation. It has further served to develop the individuality and personality of the said students at the same time they are being given balanced doses of knowledge and such knowledge has been well integrated and coordinated before given to them.

(2) The teaching methods, curriculum, materials of instruction, and guidance adopted in this experiment suit very well the needs of the students so as to achieve the following effects: realization of actual social conditions, development of national characteristics, cultivation of democratic spirit and habits, stimulation of creative interest, and accumulation of knowledge and skill.

(3) The spirit of the experiment meets very well the psychological requirements of the students undergoing experimentation so that it is a fit and proper continuation of the education that they have just received in the elementary schools. ③

b. "Community-centered Education." Another experiment also began in 1953 but with a much larger scope and a more penetrating influence is the experiment on "Community-centered education." The purpose and theoretical foundation for this type of education have already been expounded in the previous chapter. However, at the secondary school level, community-centered education has the following new emphases:

> It provides a comprehensive school program, attempting to meet a large variety of life needs. It also provides an opportunity for both out-of-school youths and adults desiring to improve their skills and culture. It encourages a cooperative and democratic attitude toward progress on the part of teachers, parents, children, and community. ④

In accordance with these new emphases, practical training courses in such schools have been improved and strengthened and principles and techniques of guidance have been introduced to alter the authoritative discipline-control attitude of teachers and to make the students better prepared for and adjusted to an ever changing environment.

The rapid increase in the number of schools to undertake such experiments between 1953 and 1962 is persuasive evidence of the general commendation of such schools. In 1953 there were only 2 community-centered schools, but as of June, 1962, there were a total of 51—18 middle

---

① *China Yearbook, 1962 - 1963*, op. cit., p, 518.
② China, Ministry of Education, Chiao Yü Kai Ku'ang. op. cit., p. 37.
③ China, "Ministry of Education", *Secondary Education... op. cit.*, p. 4.
④ U. S. Technical Cooperation Education Projects, *op. cit.*, p. 12.

schools, 2 normal schools and 31 elementary schools.① The results of the experiment as summarized by "the Ministry of Education" are:

(1) All the schools undertaking the experiment of community education have been able to make use of community contribution in resources to increase their facilities and buildings. And they have on the other hand been able to meet the needs of the community by offering the facilities of the schools for the use of the populace.

(2) With the change in instructional methods, the interest of the students are greatly enhanced. Guidance has taken the place of administration, management and discipline. The students have learned to manage and conduct themselves properly.

(3) It has been conducive to vocational training. The students are taught to use their hands as well as their brains. A balanced effect is thereby achieved.②

C. The Qualitative Development of Vocational Schools

The various functions of vocational schools as prescribed in the revised regulations of 1947 formulated in accord with Article 16 of the "Vocational School Law" are:

(1) Development of sound physique
(2) Cultivation of citizenship and morality
(3) Formation of good work habits
(4) Imparting of vocational knowledge and skills
(5) Improvement of vocational ethics
(6) Development of creativity and initiative.③

The regulations also further specify that junior vocational schools should acquaint youths with knowledge and skills of a relatively simple nature in order to develop their abilities in the common occupations while the senior vocational schools should acquaint youths with knowledge and skills of a more advanced nature so as to enable them to participate in actual production and management, and also to afford them a basis for further study or research.④

1. Types of Vocational Schools and Their Curriculum

Vocational schools specialize according to the occupation for which students are being prepared. At present the types include agricultural, commercial, industrial, home economics, fishery, nursing and midwifery schools. Some have both junior and senior sections either organized separately or combined.

By June, 1962, there were 111 vocational schools in operation—41 agricultural, 22 industrial, 30 commercial, 3 fishery, 9 home economics, 4 nursing and midwifery plus 2 others. Altogether there were 2,060 classes with 88,335 students and 7,027 teachers. These figures show a tremendous increase over those for 1944, the last war year, when there were only 27 schools, 322 classes, 14,628 students, and 675 teachers.⑤

Curriculum standards were last revised in 1952. The hours of instruction per week were reduced from 40 – 48 hours to 36 – 40 hours. Although schools may vary to meet specific needs, in general, in junior sections general subjects account for 40 per cent of the program and vocational subjects, 60 per cent. In senior sections 20 to 30 per cent of the program consists of general subjects, 30 per cent of vocational subjects, and 40 to 50 per cent of laboratory work.⑥ The general subjects for junior sections as shown in TABLE 19 include civics, Chinese, mathematics, foreign languages, history, geography, natural history, physics, chemistry,

---

① *China Yearbook, 1962 – 1963*, op. cit., p. 521.
② China, *Secondary Education*, op. cit., p. 5.
③ China, "Ministry of Education", Chiao Yü Fa Ling, op. cit., p. 188.
④ *Ibid.*
⑤ The 1944 figures are drawn from China, "Ministry of Education", Chiao Yü Kai Ku'ang. op, cit., p. 41, and the 1962 figures from China Yearbook, *1962 – 1963*. op, cit., p. 519.
⑥ China, "Ministry of Education', Chiao Yü Kai Ku'ang, op. cit., p. 43.

physiology and hygiene, music, fine arts, physical education, manual work, and boy scouts. For the senior section as shown in TABLE 20, they include Three People's Principles, civics, Chinese, mathematics, foreign languages, physical education, music, physics, chemistry, drawing, manual work, and military training.

2. Recent Reforms in Vocational Education

The traditional disdain for laboring occupations has been a major obstacle to the development of vocational education. In the past, vocational schools too often were staffed with unqualified teachers, had out-dated curriculums and provided very little suitable equipment. A large percentage of students were those who failed the entrance examinations for middle schools then enrolled in vocational schools only in order to stay in school longer. They were not genuinely interested in learning a trade.

Recently this situation has changed. Rapid economic development and industrialization have necessitated a thorough reform in vocational education. Substantial progress has been made, but the efforts in encouraging a change in public attitude must be deliberate, continuous, and extended over a long period of time. As in other countries, so also in China the attractive wages offered to skilled workers and technicians are influential in modifying public thinking, particularly that of the young people. Based on available data2 the following analyses have been made of some of the important recent reforms in various types of vocational schools.

TABLE 19 GENERAL SUBJECTS TAUGHT IN ALL JUNIOR VOCATIONAL SCHOOLS[①]

Subject	Agricultural			Commercial			Home Economic		
	1 yr.	2 yr.	3 yr.	1 yr.	2 yr.	3 yr.	1 yr.	2 yr.	3 yr.
Civics	×	×	×	×	×	×	×	×	×
Chinese	×	×	×	×	×	×	×	×	×
Mathematics	×	×		×	×	×	×	×	×
Foreign Language (English)	×	×	×	×	×	×	×	×	×
History	×	×		×	×		×	×	×
Geography	×	×		×	×		×	×	×
Natural History	×			×					
Physics and Chemistry		×				×			
Physiology and Hygiene	×				×				
Music	×	×		×	×		×	×	×
Fine Art				×	×		×	×	×
Physical Education	×	×	×	×	×	×	×	×	×
Boy or Girl Scouts	×	×	×	×	×	×	×	×	×
Manual Work				×	×				

---

① Data drawn from China, *Secondary Education... op. cit.*, TABLES 6, 18, 25.

TABLE 20 GENERAL SUBJECTS TAUGHT IN ALL SENIOR VOCATIONAL SCHOOLS[①]

Subject	Agricultural			Industrial			Commercial			Fishery			Nursing and Midwifery		
	1	2	3	1	2	3	1	2	3	1	2	3	1	2	3
Three People's Principles	×			×			×			×			×		
Civics		×	×		×	×		×	×		×			×	
Chinese	×	×	×	×	×	×	×	×	×	×	×	×	×	×	×
Mathematics	×	×		×	×	×	×	×		×	×				
Foreign Language	×	×		×	×	×	×	×	×	×	×		×	×	
Physical Education	×	×	×	×	×	×	×	×	×	×	×	×	×	×	
Music	×				×			×			×	×			
Physics		×		×						×			×		
Chemistry	×			×[②]						×			×		
Drawing				×	×		×	×	×		×				
Military Training	×	×	×	×	×	×	×	×	×	×	×	×	×	×	×
Manual Work							×	×							

a. <u>Industrial Vocational Education</u>. Reform in industrial vocational education in Taiwan began in 1952 when a specialist from Pennsylvania State University was invited to Taiwan to study the situation and to propose an orderly approach to the problem. The resulting report suggested a program which would simultaneously develop a teacher training institution and demonstrate in the schools a modern program of industrial vocational education.

Pursuant to the specialist's report, a contract was negotiated with Pennsylvania State University to initiate a program of teacher training as a permanent part of an existing institution then called Taiwan Teachers College, now Taiwan Provincial Normal University. As a direct result, a Department of Industrial Education was established at the Normal University. To secure information about industrial needs, a comprehensive survey was conducted in 1953 by the Normal University in collaboration with the Provincial Department of Education and with the assistance of a Pennsylvania State University team. As a result of this survey, the curriculum was reconstructed. The basic idea followed was the adoption of "unit-trade" courses to train skilled workers for industry. A curriculum laboratory was set up at Taiwan Normal University to develop the course of study for such training based on an analysis of the trade to be taught. The content of the course was worked out and arranged in the order in which it could best be taught, utilizing as many "live" projects as possible. Unit-trade courses for ten occupations were set up and demonstrated in eight industrial vocational schools. These included courses for training machinists, electricians, radio repairmen, auto mechanics, carpenters, pattern makers, foundry men, plumbers, printers, and sheet metal workers.[③] Several others in furniture making, designing, drafting, and welding were added later.[④]

There has been a satisfactorily close coordination between vocational schools and factories with many industries even participating in the planning and occasionally assisting directly by providing material and trained personnel.[⑤] To find a guide for further refinement, adjustment, and

---

[①] Data drawn from *Ibid.*, TABLES 7 – 12, 13 – 17, 19 – 22, 23 – 24.
[②] Only for Departments of Mining and Metallurgical Industry and Chemical Industry.
[③] *World Survey of Education*, III, *op. cit.*, p. 363.
[④] China, Ministry of Education, *Chiao Yü Kai Ku'ang*, *op. cit.*, p. 44.
[⑤] U. S. Technical Cooperation Education Project, *op. cit.*, p. 34.

possible extension of training plans, a second occupational survey of skilled and semi-skilled occupations was conducted in 1958.

b. <u>Agricultural Vocational Education</u>. Agricultural vocational education has also undergone improvements in curriculum, methods of teaching, facilities and equipment, and in teacher training. As well as constantly upgrading present farming methods, the agricultural vocational schools in each hsien are faced with providing a replacement supply of more productive farmers since more than half of the working force in Taiwan (1,780,900 out of 3,428,525) are engaged in farming① and the retirement of older farmers creates an annual demand for 24,000 new farmers. ②

Based on this need, alterations have been made in the traditional departmental course of study emphasizing comprehensive training in the knowledge of farming in general rather than specialization in a single subject. In the curriculum revisions, the vocational subjects in junior agricultural school have been simplified into courses in general agriculture, farm mechanics, and farm practice. At the senior level, schools are no longer divided into departments. Emphasis is again on general training with agronomy, horticulture, animal husbandry, forestry, processing of farm products, farm mechanics, and agricultural meteorology taught to all students. Where facilities permit, two or three elective courses designed to meet local needs were added in the last year. Throughout the course of study emphasis is put on practical training on the school farms. ③ In 1954, twenty-five agricultural vocational schools were selected as pilot schools to conduct experiments on this new type of curriculum. ④

To meet the need for a teacher training program, a Department of Agricultural Education was established in 1955 at the former Provincial Taichung Agricultural College, now called the Provincial Chung-Hsing University. It provides a four-year course of study to train competent teachers.

c. <u>Vocational Education in Other Occupations</u>. Along with the previously mentioned reforms in industrial and agricultural education, significant improvements are also being made in fishery vocational education and home economics education. In the fishery schools the government's efforts have been concentrated on improvement of educational equipment and facilities. A special appropriation was made in 1959 to purchase four new fishing boats for the three fishery vocational schools. Responsibility for supplying qualified teachers was vested to the Taiwan Provincial Maritime Junior College at Chilung.

Teacher training has received most of the government's attention in the area of home economics. A 1957 survey of the educational status of 175 home economics teachers in various secondary schools, including home economics vocational schools, showed that only twelve teachers had a broad four-year undergraduate education in home economics, the majority being middle school graduates from many other subject fields. ⑤ In response to this evident need for better prepared teachers, the Department of Home Economics which had been established at the Normal University in 1953 undertook the responsibility for providing better trained teachers and at the same time began to offer in-service training for those already holding teaching positions and to give advisory service to all secondary schools through cooperation with the Provincial Department of Education, "the Ministry of Education", and an advisory member of the U. S. ICA Mission to China. ⑥

3. The Development of Short-term Vocational Skill Training

This program was initiated for youths who either do not wish to continue or who fail the entrance examinations to various levels of schools in order to enable them to earn a living. In 1956 "the Ministry of Education" adopted a "Program of Vocational Training for Graduates of Middle and Elementary Schools" calling for industrial arts courses in middle schools and for vocational

---

① *China Yearbook, 1962 – 1963.* op, cit., p. 122.
② U. S. Technical Cooperation Education Project, *op. cit.*, p. 38.
③ *World Survey of Education*, III, *op. cit.*, p. 363.
④ China, *Secondary Education*, *op. cit.*, p. 8.
⑤ U. S. Technical Cooperation Education Projects, *op. cit.*, p. 18.
⑥ *Ibid.*, pp. 18 – 25.

schools and factories to utilize their training facilities to establish "vocational skill training centers" to meet the industrial demand for skilled workers in particular areas. Two such centers were put into operation on a trial basis in February, 1958 by the Provincial Taichung Senior Industrial Vocational School and the Provincial Taichung Commercial Vocational School. By June, 1962 there were 36 centers offering a total of 50 courses. Many of the centers are directly supported by or established in collaboration with local industries such as the Taiwan Power Company, the Taiwan Sugar Company, the Taiwan Cement Company and the Bureau of Telephone Communications. The programs offered by the centers are arranged to meet individual abilities. Middle school graduates might receive a six month to one year training program on specialized techniques in a unit trade; junior middle school graduates might receive a one year program in a practical skill; and elementary school graduates might receive a six month or one year program in a basic craft. ① As of February, 1962, 15,583 persons (8,965 male and 6,618 female) had completed their training and more than 77 per cent had found employment. ②

D. Nationalist Programs in Secondary Schools

Corresponding with the general call for mobilization of the country in what is still considered a time of national emergency, military training has been revived in all senior secondary schools, colleges and universities. There has also been vigorous development of political education among students through the activities of the China Youth Corps. Some of the important aspects of these two programs will be analyzed in this section.

1. Military Training

Military training in China has been deep-rooted in tradition. Chinese officials frequently make reference to ancient education which rightly consisted of both literary education and military training. The present system of military training for students in the senior section of secondary schools and in colleges was resumed in 1952 giving boys basic military training and girls training in nursing and auxiliary services. Initially, the program was administered by the China Youth Corps and was implemented on a trial basis in the normal schools. It later was extended to public and private senior middle schools and then to colleges and universities. In order to make the training a permanent and integral part of the educational system, "the Ministry of Education" took over the administration in June, 1960. ③

At present, the training is compulsory. It includes moral education, military techniques, life habits, and physical fitness. Senior middle school students receive 216 hours of training over a three-year period, or an average of two hours per week. In addition to the weekly two hour period of military training, male college students are required to take 12 weeks of concentrated training at a military base during the third summer vacation, making a total of 792 hours during the four-year college period. After completion of the fourth year, one year of R. O. T. C. and active duty follows.

Government authorities have reported the following gratifying results of the military training program:

a. A stronger patriotism among Chinese students as evidenced by the increased number of students choosing to go to military schools or to remain in the armed services.

b. An enrichment of the educational program through the amalgamation of literary education and military arts.

c. A transformation of the prevailing social attitudes to bring about a higher esteem for military training.

d. An imbuing of good habits (orderliness, cleanliness, alertness, and obedience to the law) and a cultivation of virtues (bravery, cooperation, and mutual assistance) in students.

---

① China, "Ministry of Education", Chiao Yü Kai Ku'ang, op. cit., pp. 66 – 67.
② Chung Yung Jih Pao [Central Daily], May 14, 1962.
③ China, "Ministry of Education", Chiao Yü Kai Ku'ang, op. cit., p. 166.

e. A better physical development in students (endurance, industriousness, strength, and activeness).①

2. China Youth Corps

The China Youth Corps (CYC) is an important political phenomenon which greatly affects education. The Corps was founded in Taiwan on October 31, 1952 under the leadership of General Ching-Kuo Chiang, eldest son of Chiang and Director General of the Political Department in "the Ministry of National Defense" at that time. Since its beginning, the Corps has remained closely related to the Political Department.

The aim of the Corps as stated in the *China Yearbook, 1962 – 1963* is to unite the youth for national restoration.② In its program "it seeks to assist the intellectual and physical development of youth in line with the national purpose, cultural values, and educational policies as well as to meet the needs of individuals."③

From the onset, the Corps has been criticized for making membership compulsory for all students in the senior sections of secondary schools and in colleges; however, because of the healthy and practical activities it offers, a large portion of students are being attracted to it and becoming active supporters.

The regular programs offered by the Corps can be roughly classified into three categories:
a. Educational
(1) Publication of books and periodicals for the benefit of young men and women through its affiliated Youth Book Company.
(2) Promotion of creative writing and art work through the Chinese Young Writers Association which has branches in many schools and is responsible for student publications. Other similar organizations have been established to promote activities in music, opera, drama, etc.
(3) Leadership training through participation in group activities, international youth conferences, and special seminars for student leaders.
(4) Summer and winter seminars for academic discussions and pursuits in various subjects such as politics, science, history, education, law, culture, etc.
(5) Substantial fellowship and scholarship programs.
(6) Scholastic and vocational assistance through services to students taking collegiate admission tests and classes in languages, accounting, typing, driving, sewing, etc.
b. Recreational
(1) Annual summer and winter camps which have expanded in scope and variety of programs since their founding in 1954. The activities include combat training, academic discussions and field research, and recreational functions.
(2) Sport activities are encouraged. The CYC is actively engaged in the training of athletes and the development of sport experts. Collegiate competitions are held at regular intervals with outstanding athletes being awarded medals.
c. Militaristic
(1) Combat training both in summer camps and as regular activities of the Chinese Youth Aviation Association and the Chinese Youth Navigation Association.
(2) Encouraging youth to enroll at military academies and providing active assistance for a large percentage of them, and inviting teachers and parents to visit military academies.
(3) Up until 1960, administration of military training in schools.④

The Corps is regarded by some critics as an organ for political indoctrination, but to the Nationalist authorities, it is an organ which supplements formal education by providing valuable

---

① *Ibid.*, pp. 169 – 70.
② *China Yearbook, 1962 – 1963*, *op. cit.*, p. 524.
③ *Ibid.*
④ *China Yearbook, 1961 – 1962*, *op. cit.*, pp. 517 – 19.

educational experiences necessary for individual enrichment and for national survival.

E. Educational Program in Taiwan for Overseas Chinese Students

As soon as the Chinese Communists seized power on the China mainland in 1949, they launched a "back home" movement among the young overseas Chinese in southeast Asia. The Communists called on them to join their efforts in "reconstruction of the mother land," but in practice trained them as fifth columnists. Most of the 34,000 students who returned to the mainland from 1949 to 1952 returned to their resident countries as expert subversives.

The Kuomintang administration in Taiwan initiated its own program for overseas students in 1951. It was made clear from the start that the program was designed (1) to provide overseas youth with a healthy education, and (2) to train useful citizens for Chinese communities abroad with a view toward helping build up the economic prosperity of the resident countries.① Throughout the years, these principles have been scrupulously observed.

The task has by no means been an easy one. Two major obstacles were encountered during the early period of the program. First, the government had to convince skeptical overseas Chinese of the advisability of sending their children to Taiwan for schooling. Second, the already inadequate funds for education had to be shared to expand facilities to accommodate the incoming students. In spite of these difficulties, the Kuomintang administration set out to do what seemed impossible. As expected, only 60 youths went to Taiwan for study in 1951, but word of their treatment spread quickly and dedicated work brought rich rewards as an increasing number of students went for study in the ensuing years. TABLE 21 shows the number of overseas students who went to Taiwan from 1951 to 1962.

The table shows that between 1951 – 1962 some 17,303 overseas Chinese students went to Taiwan for study. About 73.40 per cent of these were at the college level while 26.60 per cent were at the secondary level. The number of students graduating from colleges between 1951 – 1961 (1962's figures were not available) was 3,453. Most of these returned to their resident countries.

TABLE 21 OVERSEAS CHINESE STUDENTS STUDYING IN TAIWAN, 1951 – 1962②

Year	New Arrival	College	Secondary School	Total in School	No. Graduation from College
1951 – 52	60	60	0	60	0
1952 – 53	208	182	26	222	5
1953 – 54	427	329	98	502	46
1954 – 55	1,058	738	320	1,288	113
1955 – 56	1,831	1,321	510	2,662	186
1956 – 57	1,870	1,396	474	4,169	172
1957 – 58	3,178	2,064	1,114	6,363	454
1958 – 59	2,008	1,446	562	6,778	589
1959 – 60	2,427	1,813	614	8,404	642
1960 – 61	2,554	1,857	697	8,218	1,246
1961 – 62	1,682	1,495	187	7,836	—
Total	17,303	12,701	4,602		3,453

---

① Liang-cheng Chu, "Free China's Overseas Student Program," *Free China Review*, IX, No. 9 (September, 1959), p. 17.

② Data for the years between 1951 – 1961 were drawn from China Ministry of Education, Chiao Yü Kai Ku'ang, op. cit., pp. 154 – 55; data for 1961 – 1962 were drawn from *China Yearbook, 1962 – 1963*. op. cit., p. 527.

According to the report of "the Ministry of Education", as of June 30, 1961, there were 8,218 overseas students studying in Taiwan. Of these, 5,804 were college students attending 16 colleges and universities and the remaining 2,414 were enrolled in 73 secondary schools.[1] The geographical distribution of these students is shown in TABLE 22.

TABLE 22　PLACE OF FOREIGN SOJOURN OF OVERSEAS CHINESE STUDENTS IN TAIWAN IN THE ACADEMIC YEAR, 1960 – 1961[2]

Resident Country	College	Secondary School
Hongkong and Macao	2,078	—
Singapore	189	3
Malaya	1,133	62
North Borneo	228	41
Indonesia	861	899
Thailand	71	348
Cambodia	58	87
Vietnam	695	512
Laos	4	46
Burma	47	29
India	26	47
Philippines	175	34
Korea	189	225
Japan	20	11
South Africa	8	3
United States	4	2
Panama	1	—
Pakistan	1	—
Timor	9	18
Denmark	1	—
Peru	3	—
Tahiti	1	2
France	1	2
Australia	1	—
Malagasy	—	27
Reunion	—	1
Portugal	—	10
Canada	—	1

---

[1] China, "Ministry of Education", Chiao Yü Kai Ku'ang, *op. cit.*, p. 155.
[2] Data were drawn from China, "Ministry of Education", Chiao Yü Kai Ku'ang, *op. cit.*, pp. 156 – 58.

(Continuing)

Resident Country	College	Secondary School
Saudi Arabia	—	2
Italy	—	1
Cuba	—	1
Total	5,804	2,414

This breakdown of geographical representation shows that most of the students are from areas near the mainland. The fields of study as shown in a 1959 analysis are given in TABLE 23. The wide distribution gives a rough idea of the important part they will play in the communities they are to serve.

Fortunately, since 1954 the expenses for the educational programs for overseas Chinese students have been defrayed with U. S. aid. The money was used largely for physical expansion of the nation's educational institutions. The construction of new classrooms, laboratories, dormitories, libraries and recreational facilities has contributed to the general improvement of facilities and equipment in Taiwan schools.

TABLE 23 FIELDS OF STUDY OF OVERSEAS CHINESE STUDENTS IN INSTITUTIONS OF HIGHER LEARNING IN TAIWAN IN THE ACADEMIC YEAR, 1958 – 1959①

Field of Study	Percentage of Students
Engineering	30
Education	18
Liberal Arts	12
Law and Political Science	11
Medicine	8
Natural Science	7.5
Commerce	5
Agriculture	4
Marine Studies	0.5
College Preparatory Classes	4

Beyond the general areas of construction and equipment, specific attention has been given to the development of student guidance work. The government is keenly aware of the importance of a guidance program different from the traditional disciplinary measures performed by the dean of students which have too often been confused with guidance work. Since overseas students could be expected to have difficulty in adjusting to the language, customs and educational system, a guidance committee was established in each school where overseas students were enrolled. Guidance centers were also established at "the Ministry of Education" and the Overseas Chinese Affairs Commission. The "Ministry" is primarily responsible for the educational placement, instructional programming, and educational guidance of the overseas students. "The Overseas Chinese Affairs Commission" is responsible for the selection, transportation, and general care of

---

① U. S. Technical Cooperation Education Projects, *op. cit.*, p. 63.

the students during their stay in Taiwan.

F. Problems And Trends in Secondary Education

Attempts have been made to examine some notable progress made in secondary education including the improvement in curriculum and teaching methods; development of science education; adoption of unit-trade training in vocational industrial schools; promotion of craftsmanship training for out-of-school youth; and an educational program for overseas Chinese students. To conclude, some of the major trends and their concurrent problems will be pointed out. They are: (1) the change in attitude toward vocational training, (2) increasing demand for teachers in critical subject areas, (3) re-evaluation of the present type of examination-dominated education. Confined by the space of the study, only brief analysis is attempted.

1. Changing Attitude Toward Vocational Education

A healthy trend prevailing in Taiwan's education in recent years has been the increasing awareness on the part of both governmental authorities and teachers of the importance of vocational education. This awareness stems from the recognition that skilled manpower is vital to meet the needs of rapid industrialization and economic development. However, due to the fact that the traditional attitude of honoring literary education is so deep-rooted in Chinese society. A complete change in public attitude making it favorable to vocational education is still far from being an accomplished fact.

Foster, in his doctoral research on the relationship between education and economic development in Taiwan, has pointed out this traditional lag:

> Traditionally, in the Chinese culture, societal rewards are given to those with classical education. While the government may have placed emphasis on the skills which vocational education could provide, the people continue to think of education in traditional terms. This contradiction between educational goals of the government and the goals of the people has complicated the role which vocational education has played. [1]

In the past decade, rapid economic development has been the Kuomingtang administration's prime objective. This is attested by the adoption of a series of four-year economic development plans beginning in 1953. The most notable innovation was the incorporation into the Third Four-Year Economic Plan of a section on manpower planning which stipulated the future demand for and supply of trained manpower necessary to achieve the economic aims of the nation. In order to seek close coordination between educational planning and economic development and "to identify ways by which the educational system can contribute more effectively to the achievement of national economic goals—both short range and long range," [2] a team of experts from Stanford Research Institute was invited to Taiwan in 1962 by "the Ministry of Education" to undertake such study. The team, under the chairmanship of Dr. Henry F. McCusker, Jr., arrived in Taiwan in March, 1962 and stayed for five months. A report of their findings and recommendations entitled *Education and Development. The Role of Educational Planning in the Economic Development of the Taiwan* was made public later in that year. Among their recommendations for improving human resource development was a set of measures aimed at the improvement of the prestige and attractiveness of economically important occupations. These measures include expanded publicity programs to explain the national importance of these vital occupations, a change in Chinese terminology which does not distinguish skilled from unskilled labor, giving better rewards both in monetary and non-monetary ways for the achievements of technicians and skilled and semiskilled workers, increased scholarship opportunities for vocational school and technical institute students, closer cooperation between education and industry through work-study programs to upgrade employee skill levels, stressing vocational and educational guidance and counseling, and

---

[1] Foster, *op. cit.*, p. 140.
[2] Stanford Research Institute, *op. cit.*, p. 1.

improvement in the prestige of vocational schools and technical institutes by establishing minimum qualifications for young people entering the labor force in certain jobs.① All these measures are aimed at the installation of a positive influence on the prestige attached to vocational education and at the elimination of the traditional lag.

2. Increasing Demand for Qualified Teachers in Critical Subject Areas

Vast expansion of secondary education and increasing educational opportunities at the post-elementary level has in itself created a serious shortage of teachers. The problem is further complicated by the extraordinary demand for qualified teachers in critical subject areas which previously had received little emphasis. Shortages are mainly in the following areas: (a) the higher grades, (b) the science subjects, (c) the vocational subjects.

According to the 1962 Educational Survey, in the middle schools, only 27.92 per cent of the total number of 12,648 teachers surveyed had teachers' training at the college level. Another 56.41 per cent had college degrees but did not have teacher training and the remaining 15.67 per cent had only a high school education although about half had received teachers' certificates through a qualifying examination.② In vocational schools, only 15.32 per cent of the total number of 4,779 teachers surveyed had teachers' training at the college level, another 67.69 had college degrees but no teachers' training, and the remaining 16.99 had only a high school education. Again, about two-fifths of the last mentioned group received teachers' certificates through a qualifying examination.③

Regarding the teachers' field and the subject taught, the survey further revealed that on the main campuses of the senior middle schools, 71.54 per cent of the total number of 3,946 teachers are teaching subjects in their own fields and the remaining 28.46 per cent teach subjects in which they have not specialized.

The percentage of teachers specializing in the major subjects such as Chinese, English, mathematics, physics and chemistry is 68.05 per cent, a figure slightly lower than that when all subjects are considered. On the main campus of the junior middle schools, the situation is much worse. Only 54.54 per cent of the total number of 8,712 teachers are teaching in their own field and the remaining 45.46 teach those in which they have not specialized.④ In the branches, the situation is not any better than on the main campuses. The corresponding figures are seen in TABLE 24.

In TABLE 24 the same situation in the vocational schools is analyzed and can be seen to be slightly better than in the middle schools, especially as evidenced by the teachers' backgrounds in technical subjects—87.15 per cent who teach technical subjects are specialized in that field.

Among the steps taken in coping with the situation have been the expansion of the Provincial Teachers College into a full-fledged Normal University consisting of 3 colleges (Arts, Education, Science), 17 departments, 10 training divisions and 3 graduate research institutes; the establishment of a Department of Agricultural Education at the Provincial Chung Hsing University in 1955; and the reestablishment of National Chengchi University in 1954 which initially consisted of four graduate research institutes, one of which was education. The undergraduate division which also had a department of education was resumed in 1956. For other college and university graduates wishing to teach in secondary schools, short-term evening courses in education are offered by the Normal University. Detailed analysis of teacher education will be given in Chapter VIII.

---

① Stanford Research Institute, *op. cit.*, pp. 46, 57–58.
② Taiwan, Department of Education, *A Survey Report...*, op. cit., p. 52.
③ *Ibid.*, p. 73.
④ Stanford Research Institute, *op. cit.*, pp. 23–24.

TABLE 24   AN ANALYSIS OF THE FIELDS OF SPECIALIZATION AND SUBJECTS TAUGHT BY THE MIDDLE AND VOCATIONAL SCHOOL TEACHERS[①]

School	No. of Teachers Survey	Percentage Teaching Their Own Field	Percentage Not Specialized in the Subjects	Percentage Teaching the Major Subjects in Their Own Field[②]
Senior Middle (Main Campus)	3,946	71.54	28.46	68.05
Junior Middle (Main Campus)	8,712	54.54	45.46	54.72
Senior and Junior Middle (Branches)	715	52.30	47.70	49.00
Senior Vocational	3,250	72.60	27.40	
Junior Vocational	2,168	59.45	40.55	87.15

A major problem in the recruiting and retention of teachers has been that of very low salary. Merely having the traditional respect and social prestige no longer is incentive enough to motivate good teachers to stay in the profession or to inspire capable young people to enter the profession. The government's present policy of keeping teachers' salaries in line with the government employees has made it difficult to raise teachers' salaries without raising the others. With the financial difficulties the Kuomingtang administration faces, there is little possibility that any substantial raise could be given to all government employees.

3. Reappraisal of the Examination-dominated Educational System

Just as in elementary schools, also in middle schools students face the problem of "malign reviewing" with the only differences being in the degree of practice and the effects. There are entrance examinations for entering senior middle school, for college, for graduate school, for study abroad, and for civil service. Student life is just like a steeple chase from one examination to the next with a constant temptation to resort to techniques for "scraping through" which "though often effective" bears little resemblance to any legitimate goal of learning. The ill effects on secondary students of the over-loaded course of studies is to some extent less serious than the effects on elementary students since the former are more mature physically and mentally and thus better able to sustain some of the pressure. However, the consequences cannot be overlooked. The basic cause for concern is that the burden of too much intellectual work and the strain of prolonged study combined with anxiety over possible failure in the examinations has a deleterious effect on the physical and mental health of students.

Visitors from the West, especially those from the United States have been alarmed at the malpractice in the examination system and have made suggestions for improvement. The experts from Stanford Research Institute have presented their criticism thus:

> The system tends to dictate the curriculum and teaching methods at all levels. Some of its harmful effects are that it emphasizes the student's ability to recall memorized facts; it minimizes creative problem-solving, logical thinking, and practical knowledge; and it puts a severe strain on the physical and mental health of young people. [③]

They suggested the following recommendations aimed at developing a more equitable system of allocating students to fields of study in order to improve the quality of human resources available to sustain the economic and social development of the country:

---

① Based on the statistics given by the Taiwan, Department of Education, *A Survey Report...*, *op. cit.*, pp. 44–45, 70.
② The major subjects for middle schools are Chinese, English, mathematics, physics, and chemistry. For vocational schools they are the technical subjects.
③ Stanford Research Institute, *op. cit.*, p. 26.

a. Modifying the content and form of the entrance examinations and changing some of the procedural details which accompany these examinations.

b. Examining the feasibility of establishing an independent educational testing service.

c. Considering the formation of a National College Admissions Commission. ①

Their recommendations included changing the content of the present entrance examinations to test for understanding rather than for simple recall of facts. This would mean giving greater emphasis to logical thinking, problem-solving and imaginative analysis of complex problems. The changes in procedural details would mean encouraging applicants to choose their preferred field of study first and then choose an institution where they could carry out their plans for study, not vice versa. Also, the qualifications for admission to higher levels of schooling instead of being based solely on the scores from the entrance examination should also take into consideration the student's previous academic record and the results of aptitude or I. Q. tests. Since designing aptitude and I. Q. tests has become a specialized profession demanding the full-time attention of experts, it was also recommended that an independent educational testing service be established to take charge of the examination design, application, and evaluation. The third recommendation of the Stanford experts involved establishing a National College Admission Commission with a major function "to even out the distribution of student talent in the higher educational institutions." ②

Dissatisfied with the over-emphasis on the examination system, yet maintaining that the system is desirable if improvements can be made, the government has vigorously undertaken steps toward its modification. Changes are frequently being made to improve procedural details. Only recently middle schools with good academic standing are allowed a certain quota of top students to be admitted to colleges and universities without examination.

VII. The Development of Higher Education

In 1945, the last year of Japanese occupation in Taiwan, only four institutions of higher education remained: the Taihoku Imperial University, the Taihoku Technical College of Commerce, the Taichung Technical College of Agriculture, and the Tainan Technical College of Industry, All but the Imperial University were at the junior college level. Of the total enrollment of 1,814 at these four institutions, only 357 students were enrolled at the university and only 18 per cent or 331 of the 1,814 students were Taiwanese. ③ When Taiwan was restored to China, the Taihoku Imperial University was changed to the Taiwan University and in the next year, the technical colleges were elevated to the four-year college level. ④ The same year, to meet the urgent need for teachers, the Provincial Teachers College was established.

When the Kuomingtang administration moved to Taiwan in 1949, the large influx of students from the mainland exhausted the existing facilities for higher education. In order to accommodate these students, existing facilities were expanded and two two-year institutes, one in industry and one in public administration, were established. These were staffed with many of the great number of college teachers who followed the Kuomingtang administration in its withdrawal to Taiwan. The existing facilities were augmented with books and educational equipment that "the Ministry of Education" was able to salvage from the mainland. ⑤ From this modest start, higher education has developed as shown in TABLE 25.

The 30 institutions of higher learning fall into three categories: the five established directly by "the Ministry of Education"; the ten established by the Provincial Department of Education; and the fifteen privately established institutions. A complete list of these institutions can be found in the Appendix. In the one decade from 1953 to 1963, graduate research institutes also increased in

---

① *Ibid.*, p. 51.
② *Ibid.*, pp. 51 – 56.
③ Taiwan, "Bureau of Statistics", *op. cit.*, pp. 1214 – 18.
④ The Provincial College of Commerce merged with the Taiwan University in 1947.
⑤ Pei-lin Tien, "Kao Teng Chiao Yü" [Higher Education], <u>Chung Hua Min Kuo Chiao Yü Chih</u>, *op. cit.*, I, pp. 34 – 35.

number, from 3 to 40.

The necessity for rapid expansion was the main theme of a verbal report to the Sino-American Technical Cooperation Association in 1961 by Dr. Sze-liang Chien, President of Taiwan University. He cited the following factors as contributing to the urgent need for rapid expansion: (1) the population growth, (2) the increasing number of women entering college, (3) the raised living standards, (4) a more universal demand for college degrees, (5) better opportunities for well qualified youth, and (6) an increasing influx of overseas Chinese students.① A factor which was equally important, but not mentioned by Dr. Chien, was the rapid expansion of secondary education as a result of the universal elementary schooling begun in 1946.

Along with the quantitative expansion has also come qualitative improvement. Examination will be made of the efforts made in this area, to be preceded by a brief analysis of the legal foundations of higher education and to be followed by an exploration of some of the problems thus far encountered.

TABLE 25 INSTITUTIONS OF HIGHER EDUCATION AND STUDENT ENROLLMENT, 1945 – 1962②

Year	Univ.	College	Technical College③	Sub-Total	Male	Female	Sub-Total	Number of Graduates
1945 – 46	1	0	3	4	—	—	2,022	—
1946 – 47	1	3	0	4	2,929	54	2,983	154
1947 – 48	1	3	0	4	3,096	80	3,176	315
1948 – 49	1	3	1	5	3,838	274	4,112	263
1949 – 50	1	3	2	6	5,382	578	5,906	1,185
1950 – 51	1	3	3	7	5,939	726	6,665	1,537
1951 – 52	1	3	4	8	7,107	1,102	8,209	1,352
1952 – 53	1	3	4	8	8,688	1,349	10,037	2,071
1953 – 54	1	3	5	9	10,189	1,754	11,943	2,589
1954 – 55	2	5	7	14	11,535	2,135	13,670	2,872
1955 – 56	4	6	5	15	15,414	2,760	18,174	3,168
1956 – 57	6	5	6	17	18,710	3,896	22,606	3,350
1957 – 58	6	5	6	17	20,884	4,735	25,619	3,759
1958 – 59	7	7	7	21	22,235	5,703	27,938	5,773
1959 – 60	7	7	8	22	23,386	6,384	29,770	6,331
1960 – 61	7	8	12	27	26,856	8,204	35,060	7,472
1961 – 62	8	8	14	30④	29,421	8,982	38,403	6,755

---

① <u>Chung Yana Jih Pao</u> [Central Daily], December 20, 1961.

② 1945 – 1946 to 1960 – 1961 figures are adapted from China, <u>Chiao Yü Kai Ku'ang</u>, op. cit., pp. 62, 79; 1961 – 1962 figures are adapted from China, <u>Educational Statistics, 1962</u>, op. cit., pp. 42, 49, 53.

③ Including two-year junior colleges.

④ This is excluding the 10 military academies which are accredited as colleges and authorized to confer degrees. See *China Yearbook, 1962 – 1963*, op. cit., p. 516.

A. Basic Laws Governing Institutions of Higher Education

The two basic Laws governing institutions of higher education are the "University Law" (Ta Hsüeh Fa) and the "Technical Institute Law" (Chuan K'o Hsüeh Hsiao Fa), both of which were last revised in 1948.① The "University Law" is applicable to both the universities, which consist of at least three colleges, and the independent colleges. According to the law, both might offer courses of study at the graduate level. Undergraduate study at both is for four years in all subject fields except medicine which requires a fifth year. Medical students along with students from teachers' colleges are also required to complete one year of practical work before being awarded a Bachelor's degree. Upon approval by "the Ministry of Education", universities and colleges may also offer two-year courses in any subject field for those who can afford only a two-year college education; however, this does not lead to a degree.②

In technical institutes the course of study is two years for all subject fields except medicine which requires a third year. Just as in colleges and universities, medical students and students in teachers' training are required to have an additional year of practical experience.

The objectives of a university as stipulated in Article 1 of the University Law are "to pursue advanced study and research and to prepare professionally trained persons."③ These two objectives have been criticized as being too narrow in view of the actual role of a university in a changing society. Because of this criticism, "the Ministry of Education" has undertaken steps to revise the University Law. According to a recent editorial of the Chung Yang Jih Pao, a government-owned newspaper, "the Ministry of Education" is asking for comments from many eminent educators regarding the revision. The "Ministry" even made available an earlier law, the "University Regulations" promulgated by the Canton Military Government in 1924, for the purpose of comparison. The 1924 regulations are in a sense more broadly conceived than the one adopted in 1948,④ and give the following objectives for a university:

> The basic aims of a university rest primarily upon the dissemination and expansion of new theories and technological advances and striving for their practical utilization in meeting the needs of the country. These aims should also be supplemented with improvement in social morality and justice and with development of material resources.⑤

In his supplementary chapters to Dr. Sun's Three People's Principles, Chiang also pointed out the inadequacy of the university objectives as set up in the present law. He suggested in their place the following objectives:

1. It is the function of colleges and universities to train men and women for service in the various social strata and occupations, and not for the glorification of any particular privileged class.

2. In order to carry out the normal duties of instruction and research, colleges and universities should maintain effective liaison with the research bureaus of business and governmental organizations and set up research centers on a cooperative basis.

3. In order to furnish social, political and cultural leadership, colleges and universities should train all-round individuals who are at once capable of efficient service and administration as well as being inspired with a full sense of responsibility and being devoted to their duties.⑥

These three objectives are significant in that they promote democratization of higher education. They also seek to maintain equilibrium between specialization and general education, between professional preparation and preparation for life and citizenship.

Somewhat different from the objectives of the university, the objectives of technical institutes as specified in Article 1 of the Technical Institute Law are: "To teach applied science and to train

---

① China, Chiao Yü Fa Ling, op. cit., pp. 97 – 103.
② Ibid.
③ Ibid.
④ Chung Yang Jih Pao [Central Daily], April 24, 1964.
⑤ Ibid.
⑥ Chiang, Chapters..., op. cit., p. 61.

technicians."[1] It is unjustifiable, however, to judge the present technical institutes on the basis of these prescribed objectives. The current thinking of many Chinese educators in higher education, including educational authorities in the government, tends to favor a broader curriculum. In practice, many non-specialized courses which were designed to contribute to the student's general intellectual training have been offered by technical institutes.

B. The Qualitative Development of Higher Education

1. Improvement of Science Education and Scientific Research

A significant segment of the qualitative improvement of higher education has been the improvement of science education. Also, the "National Long-Range Program for the Development of Science" (NLRPDS), which was approved by the Kuomingtang administration in January, 1959, has placed great importance on improvement of scientific research in institutions of higher learning. In this project, effort has been exerted to make conditions more favorable for research through expansion of existing equipment and research facilities and through the procurement of a large number of research grants to stimulate scientific research. The NLRPDS program has sought to undertake the following measures:

   a. Raising funds for the development of science education over a five year periods.

   b. Setting up a joint organization with personnel drawn from the "Ministry of Education" and the Supervisory Council of the Academic Sinica to be responsible for the detailed planning5 administration and distribution of funds.

   c. Allocating funds for developing science in the following areas:

   (1) furnishing universities and graduate schools with modern research facilities;

   (2) establishing special academic chairs for local professors and visiting professors from other countries;

   (3) financing research projects of college teachers;

   (4) building more faculty residences; and

   (5) supporting journals and academic publications of universities and research institutes.

   d. Assuring that funds are to be used for the natural sciences, the basic medical sciences, and the humanities and social sciences with 80 per cent exclusively for use in improving research facilities, 10 per cent for improving the status of scholars as well as their working conditions, and 10 per cent for miscellaneous uses.

   e. Drafting detailed plans and raising sufficient funds for improving science education and increasing apparatus and equipment in middle schools and colleges.[2]

Implementation of this program is the chief purpose of the "National Council for the Long-Range Development of Science" (NCLRDS). The council was sub-divided into three committees, one each for the pure and physical sciences, the humanities, and the social sciences. Funds were drawn from (a) special yearly appropriations from the government, (b) the basic fund derived from a fixed percentage of the yearly profits of government-owned industries, (c) United States aid, and (d) foundation grants. TABLE 26 shows the amount of funds pooled since 1959.

In a recent interview in the *China Post*, an English daily in Taipei, K. P. Zi, Executive Secretary of the NCLRDS, reported that between 1959 and 1962 some NT $131 million out of a total NT $230 million had been granted by the council to various Chinese research institutes and universities in Taiwan for modernization of research facilities, while NT $90 million had been given to individual scholars and professors for approved research projects.[3]

As a means of counteracting the frustration of professors and research scientists, whose meager pay forces them to forego research, and also as a means of attracting competent Chinese

---

[1] China, Chiao Yü Fa Ling, *op. cit.*, p. 102.
[2] China, Chiao Yü Kai Ku'ang, *op. cit.*, pp. 145-46.
[3] *China News Service*, June 18, 1963.

scholars and scientists abroad to return to Taiwan, the council has set up thirty Research Professorships. These are awarded yearly and are renewable. Their monetary rewards are high when compared with normal salaries of university professors. Aside from these professorships, for the 1961 – 1962 academic year, the council awarded 25 fellowships for one year of research abroad for professors and for two years of advanced study abroad for scientists and technical specialists. In the same year it also awarded① individual grants to conduct research in projects approved by the council. ② Of these 533 grants, 366 have been reported in the *Handbook of Current Research Projects in the "Taiwan"* compiled by "National Central Library" in 1962. The projects fall into nineteen categories and are being carried out by scholars and scientists from organizations included in the following four groups:

TABLE 26   FUNDS OF THE LONG-RANGE PROGRAM FOR THE DEVELOPMENT OF SCIENCE, 1959 – 1961③

Year	Government Sources		U. S. Aid		Foundation Grants	
	Appropriations	Profits from Government Enterprise	In US $	In NT $	China Ed. Foundation	Asia Foundation
1959	2,500④		200	14,300		
1960	5,000		340	22,518		
1961	5,000	12,000	253	18,650	30	15
Total	12,500	12,000	793	55,468	30	15

a. Academies (Academia Sinica, Academia Historia).
b. Universities and the "National Central Library".
c. Research institutes including laboratories, experiment stations, government bureaus and others.
d. Industries.

The number of projects in nineteen categories undertaken by scholars in each of the four groups is given in TABLE 27.

From this table it can be seen that applied sciences have received top priority with agriculture heading the list with 139, or more than one-third of the total number of projects. Considering the number of projects under each group, universities provided 231, or more than two-thirds of the total number. This would indicate that there is a reserve of manpower in institutions of higher learning that could be called upon to undertake urgent projects when funds and equipment are available. It also indicates that the NLRPDS has stimulated scholars to do research projects of their own choice.

2. Strengthening the Teaching Staff And Research Facilities

Despite increasing difficulties in staffing institutions of higher education, "the Ministry of Education" has undertaken various measures to improve the quality of college teachers. When the Kuomingtang administration was still on the mainland, a scrutiny procedure was adopted which authorized the Academic Council, an affiliate body of the "Ministry of Education", to issue certificates for qualified college teachers. After the government moved to Taiwan, the Academic

---

① The article by Maureen Sly, "Improving Accessibility to Development Literature: Some Activities of the International Development Research Centre (IDRC)," pp. 117 – 122, in this issue presents information on the programs of the International Development Research Centre (IDRC) which has been particularly active and effective in this arena. Cf. , Thorpe, Peter. "Third World Agricultural Information," *Agricultural Information Development Bulletin*, III, 2 (June 1981), pp. 3 – 7.
② *China Yearbook, 1962 – 1963, op. cit.* , p. 522.
③ China, Chiao Yü Kai Ku'ang, *op. cit.* , p. 145.
④ Unit: NT $ thousands

Council was temporarily suspended. Until the Council resumed its activities in 1954, the responsibility for certifying college teachers was delegated to evaluation committees for the appointment and promotion of teachers established at each of the institutions of higher education. The Regulations Governing the Qualifications of College Teachers were revised and put into immediate effect in August, 1954. These regulations give detailed requirements in regard to the qualifications for college teachers at each of the four ranks—professor, associate professor, instructor, and assistant instructor. In 1953, minimum requirements for presidents of institutions of higher education were set forth in the Regulations Governing the Qualifications for College and University Presidents. ①

TABLE 27 RESEARCH PROJECTS CONDUCTED IN 1961 – 1962 UNDER NCLRDS GRANTS ②

Category	Academies	Universities and Libraries	Research Institutes	Industries	Sub-Total
1. Social Sciences, Humanities, etc.					
General Works	1	2			3
Philosophy		7			7
Political Science	1	11			12
Economics	1	9			10
Education		11			11
Sociology and Customs	3	9			12
Social Science Miscellanea		4			4
Philology and Literature	3	12			15
History	4	8			12
Historical Science					
Miscellanea	—	3			3
Sub-total	13	76			89
2. Natural Science					
Mathematics	1	3			4
Physics		16	5		21
Chemistry	3	24	2	3	32
Geology		12	4	4	20
Botany	4	5			9
Natural Science Miscellanea	—	1	2	1	4
Sub-total	8	61	13	8	90
3. Applied Science					
Medicine		25	7		32
Agriculture		59	44	36	139
Applied Science Miscellanea		10	3	3	16
Sub-total		94	54	39	187
Total	21	231	67	47	366

---

① China, <u>Chiao Yü Kai Ku'ang</u>, *op. cit.*, pp. 64 – 65.
② *China Yearbook, 1962 – 1963*, *op. cit.*, pp. 553 – 54.

Other measures taken in this regard include the 1955 enactment of Regulations Governing the Vacation and Leave of College Teachers, which (a) grants one-year sabbatical leave to teachers who have taught for seven successive years; (b) provides opportunities for research or study abroad either under government sponsorship or under the cooperative program between Taiwan universities and universities in the United States; and (c) awards special research grants to college teachers each year through the NCLRDS. Also, Chinese scholars abroad are invited to Taiwan to lecture at colleges and universities.

In the efforts to improve educational facilities, the educational authorities, the NCLRDS, the China Educational Foundation, the Asian Foundation, and the ICA Mission to China have joined forces to make the best use of available financial sources to improve facilities in colleges and universities. This program has included construction of libraries and laboratories and the purchase of Western books and periodicals.

3. International Cooperation at the University Level

Closely related to the improvement of higher education has been the cooperation between universities in the United States and in Taiwan. Through arrangements by the ICA Mission to China, a number of cooperative projects were adopted by the universities of the two countries. The cooperating institutions not only exchange educational information and professors, but the universities in Taiwan also obtain assistance in acquiring new equipment and facilities through funds provided by ICA. Brief accounts of some of the notable projects are given below.

a. <u>Educational Cooperation between Taiwan University (NTU) and the University of California (and later the University of Michigan) for the Improvement of Agricultural Education in Taiwan</u>. This project was initiated in 1953 in support of the government's Land Reform Program which called for improved agricultural education and research at the university level. The first contract was signed in 1954 between NTU and UC to make the college of agriculture at NTU a training center for agricultural teachers, personnel in the development of agricultural extension and research and agricultural specialists. The contract was successfully concluded in 1957. Another of a more extensive scope was signed in 1959 by the College of Agriculture of NTU and Taiwan Provincial Chung Hsing University and the University of Michigan to develop curricula, improve teaching materials and methods, improve agricultural research and extension, and procure educational facilities and equipment. ①

b. <u>Educational Cooperation between the Medical School of the Taiwan University and Duke University for Improvement of Medical Education in Taiwan</u>. Although no formal contract has been signed, cooperation has been in progress since 1953 when the Dean of the Medical School of Duke University went to Taiwan to act as consultant in the curriculum revision at NTU Medical School. In subsequent years other specialists were sent to assist in the improvement of the administration of the Affiliate University Hospital. Financial assistance to the Medical School also came from a score of other organizations such as the China Medical Board in the United States and the World Health Organization for the purpose of procuring medical equipment, books and journal, and construction of new buildings. Under grants made available through United States aid and the two forementioned organizations, between 1953 and 1961 some 107 faculty members of the medical school were sent abroad for study and research and 36 visiting professors were invited to teach in Taiwan. ②

c. <u>Educational Cooperation between Taiwan Provincial Normal University (TPNU) and Pennsylvania State University for Improvement of Industrial Vocational Education and Home Economics Education</u>. This project on industrial vocational education was also initiated in 1953 and was concluded in 1958. Under the contract signed by the two universities, a department of industrial education was established at TPNU, two industrial surveys were conducted and the new unit-trade curriculum was introduced into the industrial vocational schools. All of this was done

---

① *Ibid.*, p. 81.
② *Ibid.*, p. 82.

with the assistance of an advisory team of experts from Pennsylvania State University. The remarkable progress made in the development of industrial education in Taiwan has been regarded as a model for other such projects. As a result of this project, the government of Ryukyu requested the TPNU to render similar assistance through a one year contract which was extended twice. The exchange of professors between the TPNU and Ryukyu University proved to be of mutual benefit. ①

The cooperative project in home economics education originated in 1956 and was concluded in 1959. Under this contract the following were accomplished: (1) the curriculum of the Department of Home Economics of the University was expanded to include family living, (2) teaching facilities were strengthened, (3) in-service training for teachers of home economics was provided, (4) preparation was made for the establishment of a graduate institute in home economics, (5) melioration of the teaching staff, and (6) an exchange of educational information with home economics specialists in other countries. ②

d. Educational Cooperation between Taiwan Provincial Cheng Kung University (TPCKU) and Purdue University for Improvement of Engineering Education. Since this project was initiated as early as 1952, it was the first systematic and direct cooperative venture ever taken between the United States and Taiwan. The contract which was signed in 1953 aimed at upgrading the standards of engineering education in Taiwan in order to meet the needs of rapid industrialization. The original contract was for 30 months, but was extended three times and finally concluded in 1959.

The objectives of the project as stated in the *Comprehensive Report* written by Dr. R. Norris Shreve, Director of the Purdue-Taiwan Engineering Project are as follows:

> The objective of such a project was to help the industry of Taiwan both small and large through modernization and improvement of engineering education and by connecting Taiwan College of Engineering③ closely with the entire industry and economy of Taiwan. ④

The scope of the project can be illustrated by the following list of principal responsibilities under the contract:

(1) Maintain Purdue professors in residence in Taiwan as advisors to the principle engineering departments of the college.

(2) Bring short-time consultants in education to the college to observe and advise.

(3) Send teachers from the college for training at Purdue.

(4) Modernize the laboratories and introduce the best principles of teaching methods in connection therewith.

(5) Modernize the library and textbook facilities.

(6) Integrate the new facilities (equipment, visual aids and buildings) with modernized curricula in the engineering departments.

(7) Insure the modernization and strengthening of supporting courses in general studies, especially in physics and English.

(8) Insure cooperation between the college and industry for the benefit of both. ⑤

The project was satisfactorily carried out in all aspects. It was supported through United States aid which was matched with local funds. In a short period of 8 years, as stated by Deputy Commissioner of Education, Mr. Shun-sheng Lai, Cheng Kung University had become one of the best institutions of engineering in the Far East. ⑥

e. Educational Cooperation between National Chengchi University (NCU) and the University

---

① *Ibid.*, p. 84.

② *Ibid.*, pp. 83 – 84.

③ In 1956 the College of Engineering was designated a university by the "Ministry of Education" with the name of Taiwan Provincial Cheng Kung University.

④ R. Norris Shreve and Wilfred I. Freel, *The Cooperative Project Between Purdue University and Cheng Kung University to Aid Engineering Education in Taiwan*, *Comprehensive Report for Years 1952 – 1959*, Submitted to Taiwan Provincial Cheng Kung University and the International Cooperation Administration (Lafayette, Indiana: Purdue University, 1959), p. 3.

⑤ *Ibid.*, p. 5.

⑥ *Chung Yang Jih Pao* [Central Daily] February 5, 1964. Report of the Deputy Commissioner at the Provincial Assembly.

of Michigan for the Improvement of Education and Training in Public and Business Administration. This is the latest of the cooperative projects. On April 16, 1962 the contract for three years was signed agreeing that the University of Michigan would assist in establishing an Institute of Public and Business Administration at the NCU. The objectives of this institute as described by the University of Michigan's advisory team in the second semi-annual report are:

(1) to improve academic education and in-service training in public and business administration

(2) to stimulate research on Chinese administrative problems, and

(3) to serve as a national center for information and advice on improving administration. ①

At the time of the study, considerable progress had already been made in the improving of the curriculum, the training of teaching staff, the development of an organizational structure for the Institute the conducting of in-service training and extension work, and the building of a library collection of pertinent materials.

The above mentioned projects have been mainly between the United States and Taiwan; however, projects of similar nature have been undertaken between Taiwan and other nations or international organizations. The cooperation between the Research Institute of Tele-Communications and Electronics of National Chiaotung University and the International Tele-Communications Union to provide advanced training facilities and promote research and development in tele-communications and electronics is one such example entered upon in 1961 for a contract of 3 years. Another example is the establishment of an Agricultural Mechanic Training Center at the Taiwan Provincial Junior College of Agriculture, Pingtung in 1961 with the technical assistance of and with the facilities provided by the Trade and Trust Development Company of the Federal Republic of Germany.

4. Revision of Curriculum

The curriculum in higher education in Taiwan is prescribed by law. The first standards of curriculum for the seven faculties (arts, science, law, education, agriculture, engineering, and commerce) ②were adopted in 1938 and 1939. They include three types of courses, the "general courses" required for all faculties, the "basic courses" required for the various departments within each faculty, and the "basic courses", and "elective courses" for each department. These first standards were the result of the joint efforts of professors, subject specialists, curriculum experts and the staff of "the Ministry of Education". Guidelines in the formulation of these standards as announced by the government were:

a. Establishment of uniform standards closely in line with the national policies on culture and reconstruction and aimed at upgrading the academic level of existing colleges and universities

b. Emphasis upon basic training (the general courses) in order to provide students with a solid and broad foundation in their college education

c. Integration of the course of study by setting up a system of priorities and a sequence of study. ③

Using these guidelines, the following points of emphasis were decided upon as a basis for the formulation of the standards:

a. All basic courses and part of the elective courses are to be promulgated by law and made uniform throughout the country. Flexibility is permitted in the elective courses.

b. The freshman year is to be devoted to the general courses required for all faculties (colleges).

c. Chinese and one foreign language are to be regarded as the general instrumental courses students must master by the end of the freshman year. Those who fail to pass the examination given

---

① U. S. Agency for International Development, University of Michigan Contract, *Second Semi-annual Report on the Establishment of a Center for Education And Training in Public And Business Administration* (Mushan, Taiwan: National Cheng Chi University, 1962), p. 1.

② The standards of curriculum for medical schools were adopted in 1935.

③ China, "Ministry of Education", Department of Higher Education, Ta Hsüeh K'o Mu Piao Hui Pien [Tabulation of University Curriculum] (Taipei: Cheng Chung Shu Chü, 1961), pp. 187 – 88.

at that time must continue to take such courses and meet the requirements before graduation.

  d. The credit system is to be adopted.

  e. A comprehensive examination is required for graduation. It must contain major courses in no less than five subject areas. ①

Explanation is necessary at this point to differentiate the Chinese university from the American university. First, the institutions of higher learning in Free China do not have "liberal arts" courses. Students enter directly from secondary school into the professional faculty of their choice. The pre-professional programs of general studies (or the "general courses") are given in the first year of any professional or specialized studies.

Since the promulgation of the standards of curriculum for colleges and universities, there have been several revisions, the last of which began in 1953 and concerns only the required general and basic courses. The work on it progressed very slowly. The revised standards for required courses for education and engineering colleges were first announced in August, 1956, followed by those for agriculture and science in September, 1957 and again, for medicine, arts, law, and commerce at the end of 1958. The complete set of standards of curricula is published in the Ta Hsüeh K'o Mu Piao Hui Pien (Tabulation of University Curricula) complied by the Department of Higher Education of the "Ministry of Education" in 1961. ②

The revised standards were supplemented by an order issued by the "Ministry" on December 31, 1958 specifying the following requirements:

  a. The length of study for students in the colleges of arts, science, law, agriculture, engineering, commerce, and education is four years (one additional year for practical training is required for teachers' college students). The minimum number of credits required for graduation is 142, except for the medical college where the number is yet to be decided upon.

  b. Physical education for 2 hours per week throughout the four years of study is required. Although no credits are given for it, those who fail the course cannot graduate.

  c. A total of 120 hours of military training is required and is to be scheduled in the first two years. Although no credits are given for it, those who fail the course cannot graduate.

  d. A graduation thesis can either be required or be an elective according to the regulations of each department. Credits are to be given for it.

  e. The courses of study for those departments not provided for by the standards are to be specified by the school and to be submitted to the Ministry for approval. ③

The "general courses" required for all faculties as last revised in 1958 are listed below.

TABLE 28   REVISED "GENERAL COURSES" REQUIRED FOR ALL FACULTIES④

Subject	Credit	First Year		Second Year	
		1st	2nd	1st	2nd
Three People's Principles	4	2	2		
Chinese	8	4	4		
English (first foreign language)	8	4	4		
International Organizations and World Situation	2			2	
Modern Chinese History⑤	4–6 (2–3)⑥	2–3	2–3	(2–3)	
Military Training					

---

① *Ibid.*, pp. 188–89.
② *Ibid.*
③ *Ibid.*, pp. 1–2.
④ *Ibid.*, p. 4.
⑤ Those departments already having a course in Chinese History need not require students to take Modern Chinese History in the first year, instead, a course of 2–3 credits on Modern Chinese History is to be taught in the first semester of the second year.
⑥ Including the "History of Russian Aggression toward China."

(Continuing)

Subject	Credit	First Year		Second Year	
		1st	2nd	1st	2nd
Physical Education					
Thesis					
Total	—	—	—	—	
	26 – 28	12 – 13	12 – 13	2	

In the past few years, general criticism of the revised curriculum standards has been that there are too many required courses resulting in a lack of flexibility in the curriculum and that the required 142 credits for graduation are too many. Others feel that military training, although important, is somewhat overemphasized. In response to these criticisms, "the Ministry of Education" founded a Committee for University Curriculum Revision on September 18, 1963 to scrutinize the present standards and initiate necessary revisions. ① Latest information available shows that the committee has agreed to reduce the requirements of 142 credits to 134 and to offer alternatives for some of the "general courses" required for all faculties. ②

5. University Extension

Extension courses at the college level were first offered at the Taiwan University in September, 1955. No entrance examination was required and anyone having high school education or its equivalent could apply for admission. Upon successful completion of the course, a certificate was issued. The overwhelming interest as evidenced by the favorable response it received encouraged other institutions of higher education to follow suit. Some schools even promised to accept the credits if a student later passed the joint entrance examination and became a student. At the Taiwan University alone there were 4,300 applicants at the beginning. ③ Taiwan Normal University also established an evening school in 1956 to provide in-service training for teachers and for those who want to teach but lack professional training.

Beginning in 1960 "the Ministry of Education" initiated a new evening school program which converted the former evening classes from "extension education" into a regular "university program" or evening school which conferred degrees and required an entrance examination designated as the "Joint Entrance Examination", since it was the same examination required for day-school students. The privilege of being exempt from the military draft as long as in school was extended to students enrolled in such evening schools, This was done to extend the opportunity for higher education to those who fail the entrance examination for day schools and also to make maximum use of the existing facilities of colleges and universities, including the teaching staff.

Although this program has worked out well, it defeats the purpose of extension education. It curtails the opportunity for those who are not interested in a degree but are merely interested in self-advancement. Also, the new program emphasizes the degree rather than practical knowledge. In order to correct these shortcomings, "the Ministry of Education" drafted "Regulations for the Improvement of Evening Schools of Universities" in 1962 which were subsequently approved by the Executive Yuan and were implemented in the fall of 1963.

Evening schools under the new regulations will bear the following four characteristics:

a. They will admit both degree and non-degree students. Degree students must be secondary school graduates who pass the entrance examination administered by the evening school (not the

---

① Chiao YüYü Wen Hua [Education and Culture], No. 311 (October 15, 1963), 38.
② Chung Yang Jih Pao [Central Daily], December 29, 1963.
③ Wang, op. cit., p. 260.

joint entrance examination). Non-degree students need not meet the above requirement. ①

b. The expenses of the evening schools are to be under-written by tuition and fees. ②

c. Priority in the establishment of departments in evening schools is given to those areas where the practical needs exist. ③

d. The privilege of draft exemption is not applicable to evening school students regardless of whether or not the student is studying for a degree. ④ This is aimed at preventing adults from enrolling in order to dodge the draft. ⑤

C. Study Abroad

One peculiar phenomenon in Taiwan's higher education in recent years has been the large flow of college graduates going abroad for advanced study. The number of students applying each year is rising at an accelerated rate. In 1957 there were 1,399 college graduates taking part in the annual qualifying examination for students going abroad, of whom 839 passed. More recent statistics made available by "the Ministry of Education" show that the figures have jumped to 6,083 with 1,933 passing in 1962. ⑥ The latter figures do not include the large number of students who were exempt from the examination by having fulfilled one of the following qualifications as specified in the Revised Regulations Governing Students Going Abroad for Advanced Studies promulgated in July, 1961:

1. Possessing an assistantship appointment or full scholarship from a recognized foreign university.

2. Possessing a Master's degree.

3. Having been an assistant instructor at the college level for two years. ⑦

College professors, associate professors and instructors are automatically exempt from the qualifying examination.

The revised Regulations were an important step in liberalizing the rules governing the exit of students going abroad. In addition, the government has recognized that study abroad:

1. Provides more opportunities for advanced study since at present in Taiwan, facilities will accommodate only a meager number of graduate students.

2. Provides opportunities for rich experiences in Western learning and practical experiences in the scientific and technical knowledge which is much needed in China.

3. Facilitates cultural exchange and enhances international understanding.

4. Entails smaller governmental expenses since, with only a few exceptions, most of these students are financed through scholarships obtained from foreign universities or through their own private means.

A somewhat hidden advantage not mentioned in the government source is that it lessens, at least temporarily, the pressure of seeking placement for these graduates.

Despite all of these advantages, one grave problem remains. The great majority of those who study abroad remain there after completion of their studies. The reasons for this are clear enough: (1) the research facilities and environment, particularly in the United States, are far superior to those in Taiwan and (2) there are better opportunities for employment and better financial rewards. Students returning each year number less than 100, ⑧ a very small proportion of those who complete their studies.

---

① "Hsin Chih Yeh Chien Pu Ying Shen Shen T'ui Hsing" [The New Type of Evening Schools Must Be Implemented With Great Care] Editorial, <u>Chung Yang Jih Pao</u> [Central Daily] September 12, 1963.
② "P'ing Ta Hsüeh Yeh Chien Pu Chih Cheng" [Comments on the Arguments Concerning the University Evening Schools] Editorial, <u>Cheng Chih P'ing Lun</u> [The Political Review] IX, No. 1 (September 10, 1962), pp. 3-4.
③ *Ibid.*
④ *Ibid.*
⑤ *Ibid.*
⑥ <u>Chiao Yü Yü Wen Hua</u> [Education and Culture] No. 309 (August 15, 1963), 28.
⑦ *Ibid.*, p. 3.
⑧ *China Yearbook, 1959-60, op. cit.*, p. 475.

There seems to be some dilemma about the official policy on the matter of study abroad. Although the government is very concerned about the loss of the nation's intelligentsia, at the same time it is relaxing the restrictions placed upon those intending to study abroad. The government is convinced that the Chinese trained abroad constitute a rich reservoir of manpower necessary for future national reconstruction upon recovery of the mainland. The number of Chinese students studying abroad in 1961 was estimated at about 10,000, most of whom were pursuing their studies in the United States. ① A survey of those attending schools in the U. S. in 1961 – 1962, conducted by the Office of the Cultural Counselor attached to the Chinese Embassy in Washington, D. C., disclosed that there were 7,317 Chinese students studying in some 624 universities and colleges in the United States. Of these 7,317 students, 3,557 or 48.62 per cent were graduate students, 3,112 or 42.56 per cent were undergraduates, 78 or 1.07 per cent were special students, and 570 or 7.75 per cent were not disclosed. ② Classified in major fields of study 2,204 or 30.01 per cent of the students majored in engineering fields and 1,710 or 23.37 per cent of the students majored in physical and natural sciences. TABLE 29 gives a complete breakdown of this data.

Another survey conducted by the same Office of Cultural Counselor, but directed toward Chinese professionals and scientists who were currently teaching or doing research in American universities, disclosed that there were 1,571 Chinese scholars in the United States in 1962. Among these, 1,122 or 71 per cent held the doctorate, 270 had Masters' degrees and 67 had Bachelors' degrees. A breakdown of the subject fields they represented is seen in TABLE 30. A further breakdown of positions held showed that 47 of them were deans or heads of departments in colleges and universities 639 were professors, and 119 were researchers. There were 145 experts and 94 senior researchers. The others held positions as assistant researchers and assistant engineers, etc. ③

TABLE 29   NUMBER OF CHINESE STUDENTS IN THE U. S. AND THEIR SUBJECT FIELDS, 1961 – 1962④

Major Subject	Number of Students	Percentage
Agriculture	154	2.10
Business Administration	391	5.36
Education	179	2.45
Engineering	2,204	30.01
Humanities	1,084	14.81
Medicine	444	6.10
Physical and Natural Sciences	1,710	23.37
Social Science	709	9.69
Unclassified	442	6.11
Total	7,317	100.00

The government is fully aware of the importance of these manpower assets in reserve in the United States and realizes that if only the number of students returning to Taiwan after study abroad could be increased in the years ahead to fill the limited but vitally important positions open for teachers, doctors, scientists, engineers and administrators in order to accelerate the process of modernization and industrialization, it would not matter how many others chose to remain in the

---

① *China Yearbook*, *1961 – 1962*, *op. cit.*, p. 515. These students are not necessarily all from Nationalist China, many are overseas Chinese.
② *Chinese Student News Bulletin*, Nos. 59 – 60 (December, 1962), 11.
③ *China News Service*, August 14, 1962.
④ *Ibid.*, pp. 10 – 11.

United States. In an attempt to set up better liaison with Chinese students and scholars abroad, the government established in 1955 a Guidance Committee for Students Studying Abroad and created an office of cultural counselor attached to the Chinese embassies in countries such as the United States, Japan, and France where a large number of Chinese students are found. Special privileges including free transportation home, government placement service, and the facilitation of going abroad again, are awarded to returning students. ①

TABLE 30   FIELDS OF SPECIALIZATION OF CHINESE SCHOLARS IN THE U. S. IN 1962②

Field of Specialization	Number of Scholars
Physical and Natural Sciences	479
Engineering	402
Humanities	216
Social Science	170
Medical Science	167
Agriculture	67
Education	41
Industrial Management	13
Unclassified	14
Total	1,571

To meet the teachers' shortage in the pure and applied sciences, a number of distinguished Chinese scholars have been invited by the government to give lectures in Taiwan on a short-term basis. The arrangement has worked out quite well. Efforts also have been made to strengthen the research facilities of the universities and research institutes, and to improve the living conditions of college teachers as a means of attracting students to return.

Since most of the European countries do not allow Chinese students to remain after they have completed their studies, and since the opportunities for employment there are also limited, a large percentage of students who went to study in Europe have returned to Taiwan. Therefore, the government has made a great effort to encourage students to study in European countries rather than in the United States. A European Languages Center was established by "the Ministry of Education" to provide short-term language courses in German, French, Italian, and Spanish for those who intend to study in Europe. ③

D. Problems Confronting Higher Education

Improvements in education, especially in higher education, take a long time and require laborious effort. Seventeen years is too short a time to reveal any valid results. The government's policy in regard to the development of higher education has been to place emphasis on quality; however, the many factors mentioned earlier, such as the population growth, the increasing demand for higher education, the increasing number of overseas Chinese students returning for

---

① The recent regulation concerning returned students who apply to go abroad again is an attempt to eradicate the fear of some students that after returning home, any future departure would be difficult. The regulations make no restriction on future departures other than that returned students who receive free transportation or use the government placement service are required to stay one year. See Chi-lu Huang, "Chin Jih Ti Liu Hsüeh Cheng Ts'e [Today's Policy of Study Abroad] Chiao Yü Yü Wen Hua, No. 309 (August 15, 1963), 4.

② China News Service, August 14, 1962.

③ Ibid., pp. 2-5.

study, *etc.*, ① are forcing higher education to develop quantitatively also. Without question, difficulties have arisen. The notable ones are the shortage of teachers and the lack of a favorable atmosphere for research.

1. The Shortage of Teaching Staff

The teacher shortage is the most serious block to the development of higher education, both qualitatively and quantitatively. A survey on "Social Science Research in Taiwan" conducted by Eberhard indicates that "there are just not enough qualified teachers available for the positions which exist. Even now, some necessary courses in some departments cannot be given because no teacher can be found."② This shortage is the result of many factors, of which the two most important are:

a. <u>The Low Salary of Teachers</u>. Although the salary for college teachers compares favorably with the income of the grossly underpaid government employees of the upper-middle rank, it is still not enough to make the profession attractive. To earn more money, many teachers hold other teaching jobs. This is easily managed because the shortage of teachers makes it necessary for most schools to "borrow" instructors from other institutions for one or more courses. Although this helps teachers increase their salaries to the extent that they can maintain a fairly high standard of living, it is certainly at the expense of the quality of their work.

b. <u>The Lack of Provision for Teachers' Supply</u>. Although graduate programs have expanded rapidly, they are still small in number and limited in the fields of study. Due to this, many potential college teachers among college graduates have to look for opportunities for graduate study abroad. As noted before, very few return. As a result of the above situation, a vacuum has been created in the lower level of the university hierarchy. There is a serious shortage of qualified young college teachers to fill the junior positions in the teaching ranks.

In an address on "Solving Some of the Problems of Higher Education in Taiwan," made at the opening session of the mid-year conference of the U. S. Educational Foundation in China held in Taipei in February, 1961, Dr. Sze-liang Chien, president of Taiwan University, stressed the problem of teacher shortage as the major concern of higher education. In order to cope with this problem, Dr. Chien made the following recommendations:

a. Expand post-graduate schools of the leading colleges and universities to prepare more scholars to be teachers;

b. Continue and further promote the Chinese – U. S. educational exchange program;

c. Raise the pay scale for the teaching staff;

d. Stimulate the advancement of long-term science development projects. ③

These recommendations are certainly not new to educators and government authorities, but how effective they can be and how well they can be implemented are questions yet to be answered.

2. Lack of a Favorable Research Atmosphere

Closely related to the shortage of teachers is the lack of a favorable research atmosphere which has several contributing factors:

a. The shortage of funds to support basic research and lack of foreign exchange necessary to obtain an adequate supply of library acquisitions, purchase of science equipment, or carry out building plans.

b. The shortage of competent researchers. Those who have the ability are too busy to do research simply for the following two reasons: (1) the low salary compels college professors to undertake more than one job; (2) the shortage of qualified teachers makes the above condition

---

① *Supra*, p. 198.

② Wolfram Eberhard, "Social Science Research in 'Taiwan'", Typewritten Report to the Asia Foundation (Taipei, June 7, 1960), 29 pages. A portion of this report is appended in Foster, *op. cit.*, pp. 255 – 66.

③ *The Asian Students*, IX, No. 24 (March 4, 1961), 3.

necessary.

　　c. The heavy burden of earning a living allows little time or peace of mind for research and intellectual activity.

　　To tackle the first problem, the government has made available (under the National Long-Range Program for the Development of Science) a fixed amount of money each year to help the colleges and universities to modernize their research facilities and to stimulate research activities. Judging by actual need, however, the amount is far from adequate. In dealing with the second problem, educational authorities have taken steps to encourage colleges and universities of high academic standing to establish graduate programs. As a result of these efforts, forty graduate research institutes were affiliated to nine universities in 1962.① Two of these institutes (one at Chengchi University and another at Taiwan Normal University) even offer programs leading to a Ph. D. in political science and in Chinese literature. The admission standards for these institutes have been set high and many only accept five to ten students each year through elimination by the entrance examination. Monthly allowances of NT $600 are awarded to doctoral students and NT $400 to Master's degree students. These are the foundations being laid by the government in an effort to prepare more college teachers.

　　An article written presumably by a graduate student and entitled "Our University's Research Institute" clearly reflects the magnitude of the problem. It states that first, there are not enough books for research; second, there are not enough competent teachers to guide the research; third, although the allowance helps to pay room and board, it does not cover other living expenses. Thus, since there is not enough research going on in the institutes, many students find time to work either part time or full time while supposedly studying.②

　　Another contributing factor to the poor research atmosphere is the perpetuation of the lecture-and-note taking method of teaching, a practice which has been prolonged by the shortage and expense of texts and other learning materials. Even the libraries are grossly deficient in materials. TABLE 31 shows that only 6 out of the 32 colleges and universities have a collection of 70,000 or more volumes. Even among the largest collections, at National Taiwan University, an earlier survey disclosed that nearly one-third of the 720,000 volumes were outdated Japanese books. Current books of scholarly nature occupied only a minute proportion.

TABLE 31　UNIVERSITY LIBRARIES HAVING COLLECTIONS IN EXCESS OF 70,000 VOLUMES③

University	Number of Volumes
Taiwan University	720,000
Taiwan Provincial Normal University	170,872
Provincial Chung Hsing University	96,899
Provincial Cheng Kung University	94,251
Cheng Chi University	84,495
Tunghai University	79,137

　　The most difficult problem of all is perhaps the third factor mentioned above because until the salary of college teachers can be substantially raised and each teacher allowed to hold only one teaching position, it will be very difficult to revivify the research atmosphere. As long as this situation exists, the attempts to persuade students to return from abroad will be fruitless. Conscientious students continue to be afraid that they will soon become outdated in their respective

---

　　① *China Yearbook, 1962–1963, op. cit.*, p. 516.
　　② Mu-tzu Lee, "Wo Men Ti Ta Hsüeh Yen Chiu So" [Our University's Research Institute] Cheng Chi P'ing Lun [The Political Review] VIII, No. 3 (April 10, 1963), pp. 8–9.
　　③ *China Yearbook, 1962–1963, op–cit.*, p. 542.

fields because of the lack of a favorable research atmosphere in which to keep abreast of the growing world of knowledge. This is especially true in the pure and applied sciences.

VIII. The Development of Teacher Education

Throughout Chinese history, teaching has been, and still is, the most respected vocation in Chinese society. The esteem for teachers has penetrated into the Chinese family system where teachers are frequently looked upon as second parents to the students. This respected status of teachers, although not matched with appropriate financial rewards, has nevertheless succeeded as a stimulus to direct many able young people into a teaching career and to keep those who are already teaching satisfied despite heavy responsibilities and small material rewards.

In the training of teachers, however, it is interesting to note that not until the turn of the 20th century was there any formal system of teacher education. In the traditional society, scholars often had only two alternative paths—the officialdom or teaching. The supply of teachers was in a state of laissez-faire. No formal school for teacher training was in existence in a strict sense. The first provision for teacher education did not come until 1897 when, with the establishment of the Nanyang College in Shanghai, a normal department was added for the training of its teachers. ①

The actual inauguration of a systematic teacher education program came in 1903 with the introduction of the first modern school system in China. The school system since then has undergone several radical changes, with the present form of teacher education based largely on the 1929 revised school system with a few minor modifications. Generally speaking, education of elementary school teachers is provided at the so-called "normal schools" (of senior middle school level), or only recently at the "junior normal college." The education of secondary school teachers is provided at the Provincial Normal University (formerly the Provincial Teachers College). The "Normal School Law" and the "Regulations Governing the Normal Schools" were promulgated by the National Government in 1932 and 1933 respectively. These gave legal status to the independently established normal schools side by side with the senior sections of middle schools and vocational schools. The regulations were later revised in 1935 and 1947. The major points of the Law and the Regulations are as follows:

1. The provision of teacher education including the establishment of normal schools is the government's function. (Article 4 of the Law).

2. The department of education of each province shall take into consideration the local situation and divide the whole province into several normal school districts. Each district shall have one normal school and one girls' normal school. (Article 10 of the Regulations).

3. The normal schools will admit students who have completed junior middle school. The length of study is to be three years. (Article 78 of the Regulations).

4. Normal schools may offer special one-year courses for those who have graduated from senior middle or senior vocational schools. (Article 78 of the Regulations).

5. The normal school students are exempt from paying tuition and fees. Their room and board is to be paid by the local government either in full or in part, depending on local conditions. (Article 87 of the Regulations).

6. The graduates of normal schools are required to teach at least three years. (Article 92 of the Regulations). ②

The legal foundation for the establishment of a Normal University was a point of discussion at the Fourth Education Conference held at Taipei on February 12 – 17, 1962. In the case of Taiwan Provincial Normal University, there is no legal provision now in existence. The only existing laws which have anything to do with teacher education at the university level are the "University Law"

---

① J. P. Chu, "Normal School Education in China," *Chinese National Association for the Advancement of Education, Bulletin*, 11, II (1923), 1.

② China, Chiao Yü Fa Ling, *op. cit.*, pp. 170 – 79.

of 1948 and the "Regulations Governing the Teachers Colleges," adopted in 1942 and last revised in 1948. Both the Law and the Regulations are concerned mainly with the college of education within a university or an independently established teachers' college, with no provisions for a full-fledged normal university.

Article 4 of the "University Law" prescribed that "Teachers colleges shall be established separately by the National Government or as a college of a national university."① The "Regulations Governing Teachers Colleges" is actually a supplement to Article 4 of the "University Law" giving detailed elaboration in regard to the organization, curriculum, discipline, students, service, examination, and academic requirements of teachers' colleges. But neither the Law nor the Regulations are applicable to the Taiwan Provincial Normal University. First, the present TPNU is established by the Provincial Government, not by the government; second, it is a university, not a college. To correct these deficiencies a complete revision of existing laws or the drafting of a set of new laws is deemed necessary. The proposals concerning the draft of the "Normal University Law" or the "Laws on Teachers Education," submitted by TPNU at the "Fourth National Education Conference", are now being carefully studied by "the Ministry of Education".② In the remaining section of this chapter attempts are made to examine the existing provisions for teacher education for both the primary and secondary schools as well as the problems confronting teacher education.

A. Education of Primary School Teachers

1. The Development of Normal Schools in Recent Years

The training of elementary school teachers until recently had been the sole responsibility of the normal schools. Although the emphasis of normal schools has been placed on pre-service training, considerable attention is also being given to the in-service training of teachers within each of the normal school districts.

Immediately after the restoration of Taiwan, there were three normal schools and two branches: The Provincial Normal School of Taipei, The Provincial Normal School of Taichung, The Provincial Normal School of Tainan, The Hsinchu Branch of the Provincial Normal School of Taichung, and the Pingtung Branch of the Provincial Normal School of Tainan. The new provincial administration not only elevated the two branches to two independent normal schools, but also added a Girls' Normal School in Taipei. In 1948, two more new normal schools were established in the eastern part of Taiwan: The Provincial Normal School of Taitung and The Provincial Normal School of Hualien. Two others, one in Kaohsiung for girls and one in Chiayi, were added later, making a total of ten normal schools. The student enrollment jumped from 3,409 in 1945 to 7,572 in 1960 and the number of new graduates increased from 446 in 1945 to 3,280 in 1960.③ The supply of elementary teachers has thus far been able to meet the demands.

According to the Ministry's report to the 24th International Conference on Teacher Education, it was confirmed that:

> As there has been a planned supply of teachers, there has been no shortage of teachers at the elementary level even with a rapid increase in population.④

In the past seventeen years there has also been qualitative improvement in normal schools as well as quantitative progress. The notable improvements made in the quality of teacher education are examined below:

a. <u>Student Recruitment and Selection</u>. Both the social respect for teachers and the scholarship provisions for students in normal schools have attracted many promising youth to

---

① *Ibid.*, p. 97.
② Chung Yang Jih Pao [Central Daily] March 28, 1962.
③ China, Chiao Yü Kai Ku'ang, *op. cit.*, pp. 51-52.
④ China, Ministry of Education, *Report on Education Progress of "Taiwan", 1960-61*, Prepared for the 26th International Conference on Public Education (Taipei: 1961), p. 10.

teaching. Because the number of applicants to normal schools has been so high in recent years, the schools have been able to raise their admission standards and select the best students. The scholarship provisions for these normal school students are very attractive. The students are not only free from paying tuition and fees but are also provided with uniforms, books and stationery, room and board, laboratory fees, traveling expenses for the graduation trip and the fare from the school to the district where the student is assigned to teach.

In recent years there has been much discussion concerning whether or not the scholarship provision for students in normal schools or in the Taiwan Provincial Normal University should be continued. A number of provincial legislators have felt that the present scholarship program, which is estimated to amount to NT $ 69,000,000 in the 1962 – 1963 academic year, only serves to make the financing of education more difficult. In their opinion, the scholarship program should be replaced by one based solely on the needs and academic merits of each student. ① Many prominent educators, however, take a different view. They feel the present scholarship provision is one of the most important factors which attracts youth to the teaching profession. With the low salaries of present-day teachers, abolishment of the scholarship provision would make recruitment even more difficult. ②

b. <u>Adoption of Training Standards</u>. In line with the effort to improve elementary education and with the "Program of Upgrading the Quality of Elementary School Teachers" promulgated in 1955, "the Ministry of Education" had drawn up a "Standard for the Training of Normal School Students" which was enacted in July, 1958. The seven major objectives of the standard are as follows:

(1) training for physical fitness,
(2) formulating good morality and character,
(3) fostering national culture and promoting national spirit,
(4) imparting scientific knowledge and skill,
(5) instilling industrious and laboring habits,
(6) stimulating interest in the study of child education, and
(7) cultivating the desire for a lifetime teaching career.

Under these seven broad objectives there are a total of 423 guiding principles, giving detailed instruction as to the means of attaining these objectives. ③

c. <u>Improvement of Language Training</u>. The training of elementary school teachers in their ability to speak the Chinese language (Mandarin) correctly and precisely and to read and write Chinese appropriate to their educational level has been a major concern of the educational authorities. In order to assure the language proficiency of future teachers, extensive training in the national language has been enforced. Beginning in 1958, an annual joint language examination for normal school graduates was introduced by the Provincial Department of Education. Those who fail the examination may repeat it the next year, but anyone who fails the test three consecutive years is to be dismissed from school.

d. <u>Improving Educational Facilities</u>. Despite financial difficulty, the normal schools are always given priority by the educational authorities in allocation of special funds available for strengthening educational facilities. In 1959 a considerable amount of U. S. aid was allocated for normal schools to remodel their science laboratories and to procure scientific apparatus and equipment. In 1960, U. S. aid was again made available to normal schools to purchase teaching facilities. In order to set up a minimum standard for normal school facilities, the "Ministry of Education" is in the process of drawing up a "Standards for Normal School Facilities" which includes basic requirements regarding health care; audio-visual equipment; school plant; library; and laboratories or teaching facilities for the following subjects—biology, physics, chemistry, psychology, history, geography, workshop, fine arts, music, physical education, home

---

① <u>Chung Yang Jih Pao</u> [Central Daily] April 18, 1962.
② Pang-cheng Sun, "Tang Ch'ien Chiao Yü Shang Ti Chi Ko Wen T'i" [Contemporary Problems of Education] <u>Hsin Shih Tai</u> [New Age] IV, No. 1 (January 15, 1964), 12.
③ <u>Ibid.</u>, p. 53.

economics, etc.

e. Revision of Curriculum. One important aspect of the qualitative improvement of teacher education is the modernization of curriculum. The curriculum for normal schools, as for other schools, is prepared by "the Ministry of Education" and prescribed by curriculum standards. The first curriculum standard for normal schools was promulgated in 1925. Since then, it has undergone major revisions, the last one in 1952. Some adjustments in regard to course offerings and time allocations was made in 1955 which were in accord with the following principles:

(1) to reduce the course load of academic subjects in order to allow for more co-curricular activities,

(2) to increase the time for practical teaching,

(3) to add to the curriculum the following two subjects: Three People's Principles and military training.

Awareness of the importance of cultural education led to the addition of a course called "The fundamentals of Chinese Culture" which is required for all normal school students. For the three-year course of study, most normal schools offer the following five different programs of concentration: general education, fine arts, physical education, music, and kindergarten education.

The program in general education attracts the largest number of students. There is also a one-year special course intended for graduates of senior middle schools or senior vocational schools who desire to teach in elementary schools. In the past, in meeting the urgent need of teachers for lower grades and for schools in less accessible mountain areas, a number of normal schools were allowed to offer a four-year provisional course admitting elementary school graduates. This course has now been discontinued. The curriculum for students in "general education" as last revised in 1955, including both the required courses and elective courses, is given in TABLE 32.

In April, 1961, "the Ministry of Education" again decided to revise the curriculum of the normal schools. An "Outline for Revision of Curriculum Standards for Normal Schools," was formulated and a revision committee was appointed. According to *China Yearbook, 1962–1963*, a draft of curriculum standards for normal schools was completed in June, 1962. ①

2. The Conversion of Normal Schools to Junior Teachers' Colleges

The most unique renovation in teacher education in recent years has been the ascension of normal schools to junior teachers' colleges. It has long been felt that the graduates of normal schools were still immature both intellectually and physically and their education insufficiently broad. In an attempt to correct this situation and to upgrade the educational level of elementary school teachers, the educational authorities decided to convert all normal schools to junior normal colleges.② The process of change began in 1960 with the conversion of the Provincial Taichung Normal School, followed by Taipei Normal School and Tainan Normal School.

TABLE 32 CURRICULUM OF THE NORMAL SCHOOL (GENERAL EDUCATION)③

Subject	First Year		Second Year		Third Year	
	1st Sem.	2nd Sem.	1st Sem.	2nd Sem.	1st Sem.	2nd Sem.
Required Course						
Three People's Principles					2④	2

---

① *China Yearbook, 1962–1963*, op. cit., pp. 514–15.

② As early as 1955, the Taiwan Provincial Normal University had founded a Division of Elementary Education offering a two-year program of study. This Division was founded on an experimental basis in an attempt to upgrade the quality of elementary school teachers.

③ China, Chiao Yü Kai Ku'ang, op. cit., pp. 57–58.

④ Unit: Hour per week

(Continuing)

Subject	First Year		Second Year		Third Year	
	1st	2nd	1st	2nd	1st	2nd
Civics	2	2				
Chinese	6	6	6	6	6	6
Mathematics	2	2	2	2	2①	
History	3	3	2	2		
Geography	2	2	2	2		
Biology	4	4				
Chemistry			4	4		
Physics					4	4
Physical Education	2	2	2	2	1	1
Fine Arts	2	2	2	2		
Manual Work			2	2	2	2
Music	2	2	2	2		
Introduction to Education	2	2				
Educational Administration					2	2
Materials and Methods of Teaching			2	2	2	2
Educational Psychology	3	3				
Tests and Statistics			2	2		
History of Education						3
School Hygiene					1	
Military Training	3	3	3	3	3	1
Practical Teaching			2	2	8	10
Elective Course	0–3	0–3	3	3	3	3
Total	33–36	33–36	36	36	36	36
Elective Course②						
Group A						
Physical Education					3	
Music			3	3		
Singing and Games						3
Group B						
Fine Arts			3	3		

① One hour learning on the abacus, one hour reviewing
② Students may elect any one of the four groups.

(Continuing)

Subject	First Year		Second Year		Third Year	
	1st	2nd	1st	2nd	1st	2nd
Manual Work①					3	3
Group C						
Audio-Visual Aids			3	3		
Social Education					3	
Guidance						3
Group D						
English		3	3	3	3	3

The course of study was originally set for two years, admitting students who graduated from senior middle school or its equivalent. But in the past few years there has been considerable discussion of the new system, with many educators holding the opinion that two years of professional training is still inadequate and therefore recommending a five-year program of study to include the original three-year normal school education plus two years of professional training at the college level. The five-year program was adopted by the government and immediately put into effect in 1962–1963.

3. Consultation Service and In-Service Training

In addition to the primary function of turning out qualified teachers, the normal schools are also vested with the second but equally important function of providing consultation and guidance to elementary schools within their districts. At present the whole island of Taiwan is divided into ten normal school districts, one for each normal school. In order to fulfill the second function, each normal school set up a bureau of consultation and guidance to take charge of the planning, execution, and evaluation of the consultation service. The service is generally rendered in the following three forms:

a. Group consultation—conducted by a team of consulting personnel who visit one school at a time holding meetings with school teachers to discuss their findings and offering recommendations for improvement;

b. Subject consultation—conducted by subject specialists who provide consultation and guidance for the subject concerned;

c. Individual consultation—assistance is provided to any individual teacher who needs the consultation.

The most common methods employed in the process of consultation are: (a) teaching demonstrations, (b) correspondences, (c) discussions, (d) educational tests and measurements, (e) exhibits of teaching aids, (f) contests, (g) educational experimentations, and (h) booklets and publications.② This service, if implemented effectively, will help to accomplish the following objectives: (a) to set up close contact between normal schools and elementary schools, (b) to acquaint the normal schools with the actual needs of the elementary schools, and (c) to provide follow-up education to new graduates. To assure that it is effectively carried out, this service is emphasized by educational authorities as one of the major points in the annual grading of the performance of each normal school.

In addition to regular teacher education and the consultation service mentioned above, the

---

① Including agricultural and industrial arts and home economics.
② Hsüeh-ch'un Chu, <u>Tai-wan Shang Shih Fan Chiao Yü Chih Yen Chiu</u> [Study of Teacher Education in Taiwan] Research Report No. 901 (Taipei: Central Committee of the Kuomintang, 1962), pp. 14–16.

government has attached great importance to the continuing education of teachers. Beginning in 1950 almost all normal schools have conducted summer in-service training workshops for elementary teachers. In accordance with the "Program for Upgrading the Quality of Elementary School Teachers" adopted in 1955, two normal schools were selected on an experimental basis to offer six-month in-service training courses to elementary teachers who had no previous professional training.

A great step forward in upgrading the quality of elementary teachers has been the establishment in 1956 of a unique center of in-service training for elementary school teachers: the Taiwan Provincial Elementary School Teachers' In-service Training Center. As of 1962, 47 one-month in-service training classes have been conducted with a total of 5,500 elementary school teachers and administrators receiving their refresher courses. ①

B. Education of Secondary School Teachers

1. The Expansion of Taiwan Provincial Normal University

Taiwan Provincial Normal University, formerly Taiwan Provincial Teachers College, is the only institution in Taiwan devoted entirely to the training of secondary school teachers. The Teachers College was founded in 1946, only one year after Taiwan had been restored to China. At that time, the sweeping change in the educational system of the Island following the change in its sovereignty, created a vast and urgent need for well-trained teachers in schools of all levels. It was to meet a part of this imperative demand that the Provincial Government, setting apart and expanding the buildings of the former Taihoku Higher School, established the Teachers College and inaugurated it on June 5, 1946.

Since its inception, the teachers college has expanded rapidly to provide the much-needed teachers. During his term as president of the college between 1949 and 1957, Mr. Chen Liu introduced many fundamental improvements and strengthened the faculty by appointing to professorship a number of distinguished scholars. Between 1947 and 1955 the student enrollment had more than tripled, jumping from 588 to 1,983 in eight years. In showing the government's concern for and understanding of the important role the teachers' college played, and in anticipating the future demand for more and better trained secondary school teachers, the educational authorities decided to change the teachers' college into a full-fledged normal university in 1955 with substantial expansion both in its organization and its curriculum. In 1946, when the teachers' college came into existence, the institution had only nine departments and a number of two-year programs of study. In 1961 – 1962, Taiwan Normal University had three graduate research institutes (Education, Chinese, and English) and three colleges (Arts, Education, and Science) consisting of sixteen departments and ten two-year programs of study. ② The student enrollment reached 5,108 which is two and one-half times more than the 1955 figure and almost nine times more than the 1947 figure. ③

The graduate research institutes offer a two-year program leading to either a Master of Education degree or a Master of Arts degree. Beginning in 1956, after the regulations governing the examination of candidates for the Doctor's degree was promulgated by "the Ministry of Education", the Graduate Research Institute of Chinese was authorized to offer a program of study leading to a Doctor of Philosophy degree in Chinese literature. A minimum of two additional years of study beyond the Master's degree is required.

---

① *Supra*, Chapter V. p. 126.

② In the College of Education there are Departments of Education, Social Education, Industrial Education, Health Education, Physical Education, and Home Economics. In the College of Arts there are Departments of Chinese, English, History, Geography, Fine Arts, and Music. In the College of Science there are Departments of Mathematics, Physics, Chemistry, and Biology. See China, Ministry of Education, Department of Higher Education, Kung Szu Li Chuan K'o I Shang Hsüeh Hsiao I Lan Piao [Directory of Public and Private Institutions of Higher Education] (Taipei: 1962), p. 5.

③ China, *Educational Statistics, 1962, op. cit.*, p. 40.

The sixteen undergraduate departments offer five-year programs leading to one of the Bachelor degrees in education, arts, or science. The whole term of residence consists of four years of academic studies and one year of teaching practice. The minimum requirement of credits for a Bachelor's degree is 142. The ten two-year programs do not lead to a degree; however, students who have successfully fulfilled the specific requirements are awarded a diploma.

2. The Curriculum Standards and Their Revisions

a. <u>Objectives</u>. In addition to providing professional training in various specialized fields, the university also has the following four broad objectives:

(1) The attainment of health, both physical and mental;

(2) The cultivation of the Chinese national culture;

(3) The acquisition of an integrated knowledge of the problems of contemporary life and education;

(4) The development of the best of university scholarships, such as independent thought, informed judgment, intelligent interest in related fields of study, and the habit of impartial inquiry and research.①

b. <u>Curriculum</u>. Pursuant to the above objectives, the former curriculum standard promulgated by "the Ministry of Education" for the teachers' colleges was deemed inadequate. Therefore, in meeting the new functions of the university and the demands of the time, "the Ministry of Education" undertook to revise the former curriculum standard. After consultation with scholars and specialists, the "Ministry" adopted a new standard for the Normal University in August, 1956. The courses of study under the new standard are grouped in three categories: (1) basic or general courses, (2) special courses, and (3) materials and methods of teaching and practical training. The basic courses, along with materials and methods of teaching and practical training, are required for students in all departments within the university. They include the Three People's Principles, Chinese, English, Modern History of China, Introduction to Philosophy, Educational Psychology, Teaching Methods in General, Practical Training, International Organizations and World Situation, the Four Books of the Confucian Classics, Military Training, Chinese Phonetics Physical Education, etc. Each student is required to take 60 to 70 credits in this area. The special courses vary according to the subject concentration of each department. Generally, each department has both a number of required courses (prescribed by law) and elective courses (to be decided by each department) in its particular subject area. Students are required to take 70 to 100 credits in their specialized area.② Using the Department of Education as an illustration, the required special courses are given in TABLE 33.

TABLE 33 REQUIRED SPECIAL COURSES FOR THE DEPARTMENT OF EDUCATION③

Subject	1st Year	2nd Year	3rd Year	4th Year
Sociology	3④			
Physiology	3			
Psychology	6			
Educational Psychology		6		
Secondary Education		6		
Educational Statistics		4		
History of Western Education		4		

① Taiwan Provincial Normal University, *Bulletin of Information, 1956* (Taipei: 1956), pp. 1 – 2.
② China, Chiao Yü Kai Ku'ang. *op. cit*., pp. 50 – 51.
③ China, "Ministry of Education", <u>Ta Hsüeh K'o Mu</u>, *op. cit*., pp. 148 – 49.
④ Unit: Hour/Week

(Continuing)

Subject	1st Year	2nd Year	3rd Year	4th Year
Elementary Education		3		
Ethics			3	
Principles and Practice of Discipline and Guidance		3		
History of Chinese Education			4	
Principles of Teaching			3	
Educational and Mental Testing			4	
Educational Administration			3	
Materials and Methods of Teaching			6	
Philosophy of Education				4
Comparative Education	—	—	—	4
Total①	12	23	20	14

3. The Consultation And Supervisory Function of the Normal University

Besides the regular program of instruction, the Normal University is also vested with the responsibility to provide guidance and supervision for secondary education in Taiwan, to offer in-service training to teachers and school administrators, and to stimulate and guide educational workers into research fields offering practical and constructive considerations to educational theory and practice. ② These responsibilities are largely discharged through the Secondary Education Supervisory Committee and the various departments of the University.

a. The Secondary Education Supervisory Committee. The consultation and supervisory function of the Normal University is prescribed by law. Article 4 of the "Regulations Governing the Teachers' Colleges," last revised in December, 1948, has clearly indicated that:

... the teachers' colleges should seek close cooperation of the educational authorities in their assigned areas in providing guidance and supervision for secondary education and in conducting research and experiments on pertinent problems. ③

In pursuance of the Regulations, the Normal University (as early as 1948) established a Secondary Education Supervisory Committee to take charge of these important functions. In cooperation with local (city and hsien) educational authorities, the committee has established branches in eight cities and hsiens. The regular duties of the committee and its branches are: (1) conducting educational surveys, (2) initiating research on a given problem of local concern, (3) holding conferences on selected topics, (4) instituting correspondence services, (5) directing educational experiments, (6) exhibiting, (7) school visiting, (8) leading demonstrations, (9) publishing serials and periodicals on secondary education, (10) giving lectures and conducting discussions, (11) broadcasting, and (12) promoting work in the branches, etc. ④ The monthly publication, Chung Tang Chiao Yü (Secondary Education), published by the committee since November, 1948, has been maintaining a high quality of content, Taking into account the limited funds available and the inadequate number of personnel, the work the committee has done can be

---

① There are a total of 69 required credits (each credit is one hour per week per semester).
② Taiwan Provincial Normal University, op. cit., p. 10.
③ China, Chiao Yü Fa Ling, op. cit., p. 135.
④ Pen Lin, "Shih Fan Chiao Yü," [On Normal Education] Chung Hua Min Kuo Chiao Yü Chih, op. cit., I, p. 38.

regarded as satisfactory.

b. The Consultation Activities of the Department of Industrial Education. With the technical assistance of a Pennsylvania State University team, the Department of Industrial Education has also provided direct educational consultation for vocational schools all over Taiwan. The consultations were given through special training sessions for vocational school teachers and the preparation of books and reference materials for use in the vocational schools.

4. The In-Service Training of Teachers And Extension Education

The Normal University has been very active in providing in-service training for teachers through its six-week summer institutes. These institutes have been conducted each year since 1947 on a subject basis, with special programs for school administrators frequently being given since 1949, In 1959, with the assistance of the ICA Mission, a Secondary School Teacher In-service Training Center was established in conjunction with TPNU. The center is offering both short-term (four weeks) and long-term (seventeen weeks) classes to science teachers in secondary schools. Other subjects will be added later. ①

As already mentioned in an earlier chapter, evening classes have been offered by the University since the spring of 1957. In addition to providing in-service education to teachers, the evening classes are also open to middle school graduates and to those college graduates lacking the necessary professional training to qualify as teachers in secondary schools. ②

C. Problems Confronting Teacher Education

The remaining part of this chapter is intended to disclose some of the problems confronting teacher education and to discuss some of the measures thus far taken by the government.

1. Inadequate Financial Reward for Teachers

It seems to be a universal phenomenon that all teachers are underpaid. Taiwan is no exception. During his term as the Provincial Commissioner of Education, Mr. Chen Liu vigorously attempted to raise teachers' salaries. As he stated in the Conference of Local Educational Administrators held in Taichung:

> To raise the scholastic level of the students we must have devoted teachers, to have teachers devoted to teaching we must stabilize their livelihood. If it is the teachers' duty to raise the scholastic level of the students, it must be the government, s responsibility to stabilize the teachers' livelihood ... ③

Despite great financial difficulties he was able to introduce certain improvements in the pay scale resulting in a general increase of teachers' income. He recognized, however, that having merely a nominal increase in salary is far from sufficient for the betterment of the teachers' livelihood. Other measures, including an effective welfare system, were also needed. ④

To move in this direction, Mr. Liu proposed two practical approaches which subsequently evolved into two administration orders, namely, " the Austerity and Mutual Aid Measures Governing the Nuptial and Funeral Affairs of Provincial School Teachers and Staff Members" and " The Measures Governing the Collection and Custody of the Welfare Fund for the Public Secondary And Elementary School Teachers And Staff Members," both of which were put into effect in January, 1959.

The first set of measures are designed to lighten the financial burdens in cases of marriage and death. In cases of marriage, it encourages austerity by doing away with the traditional extravagant

---

① China, Chiao Yü Kai Ku'ang, op. cit., p. 33.
② **Supra**, Chapter VII, pp. 221 – 22.
③ Taiwan Public Elementary and Secondary School Teachers Welfare Fund Commission, Teachers Welfare Institution in Taiwan (Teachers Welfare Series; Taichung: 1961), p. 1.
④ Taiwan Public Elementary and Secondary School Teachers Welfare Fund Commission, Wei Kai Shan Chiao Shih Sheng Huo Erh Nu Li [Striving for the Improvement of Teachers Livelihood] (Teachers Welfare Series; Taichung: 1961), p. 105.

practices of giving expensive gifts and having large parties, both of which create financial hardship. In cases of death, it promotes a spirit of fraternity in extending mutual aid to the bereft among teachers. As one example, in the Provincial Department of Education when any staff member marries, each colleague presents the new couple with a mutual aid donation of a set amount, according to income. The Department conducts the wedding ceremony and gives a simple tea to celebrate. This not only saves money and trouble for the new couple, but also gives them a lump sum of money. At the same time, the modest donations do not put financial burdens on the staff. A similar principle is applied in cases of bereavement where money is collected and sent to the designated beneficiary. All of this is on a voluntary basis. Each school or group of schools may adopt these measures within their respective schools or districts. On these mutual aid programs, the Chung Yang Jih Pao comments:

> There is at present a very imperative need for such mutual aid programs of marriage and funeral. For the time being at least, it seems simply out of the question to bring about a fundamental adjustment of salary scales for government employees and teachers. Only through mutual aid can we see a most direct and economical solution, i. e., through the union of the limited strength of each to solve the urgent problems of one individual. ①

To implement the second set of measures, the Department of Education established the "Taiwan Public Secondary and Elementary School Teachers Welfare Fund Commission" to raise and administer funds. The major source of funds is from membership dues of the Parents' Associations of all public schools. One-fifth of the dues is allocated for this purpose. Funds are used for: loans and scholarships for the children of school teachers; subsidies for teachers' advanced studies or observation trips; emergency aid to teachers in case of accidental disablement, loss of property due to fire, or death of a member of the immediate family; retirement allowances; recreational activities; and house-building loans. ②

2. Inadequate Provision for the Training of College Teachers

The three sources from which new college teachers are drawn are (a) students returning from study abroad, (b) graduates of domestic graduate research institutes with Master's degrees, and (c) experienced secondary school teachers. There is no available data showing positively the proportion of each of these three groups among the new college teachers. However, the list of college teachers who received the Type 2 research grants③ from the National Council for the Long-Range Development of Science indicates that the majority of recipients belong to the second group④. In other words, it would seem that the majority of young teachers in colleges and universities have had only two years of graduate study. However, even assuming that two years of graduate study is sufficient for college teaching, the present number of graduates receiving Master's degrees each year is far short of the actual demand created by the rapid expansion of higher education. According to *Educational Statistics* of 1962 published by "the Ministry of Education", the number of college teachers had more than doubled between 1955 and 1961. (For figures, see TABLE 34). The average annual increase in the seven-year period is 322 teachers while the number of graduate students receiving Master's degrees in 1960 – 1961 (which had a larger number of graduates than any other year in the seven-year period) was only 269, a shortage of 53 teachers. This shortage does not take into account that many of these graduates probably went into business or government service instead of college teaching.

---

① *Ibid.*, p. 28.
② *Ibid.*, pp. 12 – 26.
③ Type 1 grants are for professors and associate professors; Type 2 grants are for instructors and assistant instructors.
④ Chung Yang Jih Pao [Central Daily] September 18, 1963.

TABLE 34 THE ANNUAL INCREASE OF COLLEGE TEACHERS AND THE NUMBER OF SECOND AND THIRD YEAR GRADUATE STUDENTS IN TAIWAN BETWEEN 1955 – 1962[①]

Year	Number of Teachers	Increase Over the Preceding Year	Number of 2nd and 3rd Year Graduate Students
1955 – 56	1,650		73
1956 – 57	1,910	260	107
1957 – 58	2,216	306	189
1958 – 59	2,520	304	214
1959 – 60	2,801	281	252
1960 – 61	3,149	348	269
1961 – 62	3,523	374	253

Based on the Stanford Report (previously cited in regard to secondary education), the inadequate supply of teachers in the years to come will be extremely difficult to overcome unless young Chinese scholars now teaching and studying abroad can be persuaded to return to Taiwan. The suggestion offered by Stanford experts to cope with this problem is that:

> Such incentives as higher salaries, better housing, improved research opportunities, and challenging academic environment are factors which should be reviewed closely, with the impending shortage in mind. [②]

3. The Need for Education Courses in Other Universities

The inability to supply a sufficient number of trained secondary school teachers constitutes another serious problem for the educational authorities. In recent years there have been a large number of university graduates going into teaching; however, although many are quite competent in their subject fields, they lack knowledge in the art and science of teaching. There is only one university other than TPNU offering educational courses, the Department of Education of the Chengchi University. Just as at its counterpart at TPNU, the primary function of this department is to prepare educational administrators for both the local education bureaus and secondary schools and teachers for the normal schools.

In order to provide teacher education to college students who wish to be qualified for teaching in secondary schools, Professor Pen Lin, College of Education, TPNU, recommended that basic elective courses should be offered at other universities so that a large number of students in these institutions might receive teacher training before graduation and thereafter be regarded as qualified teachers in their particular subject areas. [③] The evening school of TPNU presently offers courses for college graduates wishing to be qualified for secondary school teaching, but to meet future needs, it seems to be practical and certainly desirable to offer education courses in other universities. There is also a monetary advantage to this since the teachers trained in this manner are not totally financed by the Kuomingtang administration.

4. Training Teachers in Vocational And Special Education

At present, the training of vocational school teachers in agricultural, industrial, home economics, and fishery education is provided by the Department of Agricultural Education of the Provincial Chung Hsing University (formerly the Provincial Agricultural College of Taichung), the Departments of Industrial Education and Home Economics of TPNU, and the Provincial Maritime

---

① China, Educational Statistics, 1962, *op. cit.*, pp. 43, 52.
② Stanford Research Institute, *op. cit.*, p. 63.
③ Pen Lin, <u>Chiao Yü Szu Hsiang Yü Chiao Yü WenT'i</u> [Educational Thoughts And Educational Problems] (Taipei: Chung Hua Ts'ung Shu Wei Yuan Hui, 1958), pp. 428 – 49.

Junior College, respectively. All of these have substantial educational programs for the training of future teachers in their respective fields. The problem lies in the lack of provision for the training of teachers in commercial vocational schools and in special education schools such as the three schools for the blind and the dumb. It seems advisable that training programs in these two areas be provided at TPNU through establishment of Departments of Business Education and Special Education. The latter may be founded as one of the divisions of the Department of Social Education, since in Taiwan special education comes within the realm of social education.

IX. The Development of Social Education
A. The Meaning and Scope of Social Education

Social education has a broad meaning. According to Professor Pang-cheng Sun, "Any educational activity which is not a part of formal school education, which is for all people and which is aimed at a general upgrading of the cultural level of the people" is a part of social education. ① From this definition, it is explicit that social education

(1) is for all people, regardless of sex, age, wealthy intelligence, class, or vocation;

(2) is lifetime education including supplementary (make-up) education for those who did not attend elementary school, and the continuation education for those who have completed their formal school education;

(3) is made up of all phases of human activity including health education, language, general knowledge, education for livelihood, citizenship education, fine arts, and science education;

(4) is far-reaching and penetrating;

(5) is conducted in any appropriate place and implemented by any means necessary in order to adapt to the various needs of the people.

Since social education has such an immense scope and such a variety of functions, no single agency or organization can undertake complete responsibility. Yet there must be some system and coordination in such a huge enterprise if it is to be effective and efficient. At present, the responsibility for planning, implementation, supervision, and evaluation of social education at the national level is vested in the Department of Social Education of the "Ministry of Education"; at the provincial level, in the Social Education Section of the Taiwan Provincial Department of Education; and at the local level, in the Social Education Section under the Bureau of Education of the municipal or hsien governments. ②

The basic tasks of social education as prescribed in the "Social Education Law" promulgated by the Government in 1953 are as follow:

(1) to promote national spirit and the morality of Chinese,

(2) to disseminate scientific knowledge and information on national defense,

(3) to provide training for self-government and for the proper use of the "four powers" (election, recall, initiative, and referendum),

(4) to improve language ability and to wipe out illiteracy,

(5) to foster health habits and physique,

(6) to encourage a sense of aesthetics in arts, music, and folklore,

(7) to protect landscape and cultural and historical monuments and antiques,

(8) to improve popular readers and recreational facilities,

(9) to increase the productivity of people through training in basic skills. ③

In this chapter, an attempt is made to examine the present status of social education by studying its development in the two major areas of emphasis—supplementary education and continuation education. A third area—special education—which has been considered as a part of

---

① Pang-cheng Sun, Chiao Yü Kai Lun [Introduction to Education] (Taipei: Taiwan Commercial Press, 1956), p. 89.

② Chi-hung Liu, "She Hui Chiao Yü [Social Education] Chung Hua Min Kuo Chiao Yü Chih, op. cit., II, pp 1 – 3.

③ Hsin-chou Wang, "I Nien Lai She Hui Chiao Yü Kai Shu" [A Brief Sketch of the Year's Social Education] Chung Kuo Chiao Yü Hsien Ku'ang, op, cit. II, p. 437.

social education, is also to be briefly examined. Efforts are also made to identify some of the pressing problems obstructing the implementation of social education. Since modern library development in Taiwan in recent years constitutes a major force in the enhancement of the cultural level, a considerable portion of this chapter is devoted to the study of the development of library service in Taiwan and to the present trends in education for librarianship.

B. The Development of Social Education in Taiwan

1. Supplementary Education

Supplementary (or make-up) education is designed primarily to supplement formal education. The three main types at present are: (a) supplementary classes for complete illiterates, (b) vocational supplementary education for out-of-school adults offering vocational training, and (c) general supplementary education for those who are not able to attend a formal school, but are interested in receiving a general education or in studying particular academic subjects.

a. <u>Supplementary Classes</u>. The problem of illiteracy was very difficult to deal with in the post-war years when Taiwan was first restored. The consequences of the intensive campaign of the Japanese colonial officers to institute Japanese as the only language in Taiwan were indeed grave and profound. In addition to the illiterates themselves, there were also a considerable number of young people in the population who had to be trained because they were ignorant of the Chinese language. In an attempt to overcome this ignorance, the government utilized all available means in the teaching of the Chinese language to those unversed in it. A number of language specialists were recruited from the mainland. The Provincial Commission for the Improvement of the National Language was established in 1946, followed by the setting up of local commissions in each municipality and <u>hsien</u>. Radio broadcasting was employed. A Provincial Training Center was established to provide short-term in-service training in Chinese to civil servants and teachers. Mandarin texts were compiled for use in the supplementary evening classes which were conducted by most elementary schools and some public libraries. At the end of 1950, a total of 296,150 persons had received Mandarin training in 6,338 such classes with very satisfactory results.[1]

Beginning in 1951 the Kuomingtang administration resumed the normal functions of supplementary education, with elimination of illiteracy receiving top priority. According to regulations promulgated by "the Ministry of Education", supplementary classes are at two levels, primary and advanced. The former is from four to six months and the latter, six months to one year (two hours per day, twelve hours per week). All such classes are established in elementary schools and are staffed with qualified teachers. The cost is borne by the municipal or <u>hsien</u> governments. The subjects taught include Chinese, citizenship, general knowledge, music, and arithmetic, with reading and speaking of Chinese the area of emphasis.[2] According to the Constitution, attendance in these supplementary classes is compulsory.[3]

A survey conducted in Taiwan in 1951 showed that there were 1,413,569 illiterates, or 17.96 per cent of the total population.[4] To eliminate this illiteracy, the Provincial Department of Education drew up a Five-Year Plan to provide supplementary education to all adults lacking any previous formal education. This required all municipal and <u>hsien</u> governments to set up enough supplementary classes to accommodate the number of illiterates in their respective regions within the five-year period from 1951 to 1955. Because of financial difficulties, only provision of primary classes was required. The plan had limited success. A recent survey shows that the number of illiterates between the ages of 13 and 45 had been reduced to 904,852 in 1962 or a reduction of

---

[1] China, <u>Chiao Yü Kai Ku'ang</u>. op. cit., pp. 119 – 20, 126.
[2] <u>Ibid</u>., p. 119.
[3] <u>Supra</u>, Chapter IV, p. 77.
[4] China, <u>Chiao Yü Kai Ku' ang</u>, <u>op. cit</u>., p. 120.

the illiteracy rate to 8. 2 per cent of the total population. ①

b. <u>Vocational Supplementary Education</u>. The second type of supplementary education provides vocational training to adults. There are two kinds of vocational supplementary education in Taiwan. One is through "short-term vocational classes" ranging in length from three months to one year. These have been an outgrowth of the increasing need for skilled labor in various small industries. In an eleven-year period, the number of such classes increased twelve times (from 110 in 1950 to 1,278 in 1960). ② Recent developments include setting up "vocational skill training centers" in vocational schools and industrial and agricultural organizations. ③

Another kind of vocational supplementary education is given in "vocation supplementary schools" which are of three grades (primary, intermediate and higher) with courses of study for two years, three years, and three years, respectively. Training in these schools has far more substance than that given in the short-term classes. Upon passing the qualifying examination given by the local educational authorities, students are certified as having vocational training equivalent to that of regular vocational schools. The primary grade graduates are considered equivalent to elementary school graduates; the intermediate grade graduates, to junior vocational school graduates; and higher grade graduates, to senior vocational school graduates. This type of vocational supplementary school is also increasing in number, multiplying nearly three times between 1945 and 1960 (from 9 to 34) and with a rise in enrollment from 696 to 10,852. ④

c. <u>General Supplementary Education</u>. The third type of supplementary education provides general supplementary education to adults who wish to further their knowledge. The set up of these "general supplementary schools" is similar to that of the three graded "vocational supplementary schools" but the course of studies in each grade corresponds to the elementary schools and middle schools. Because the curriculum is so similar they have become substitutes for middle schools, and are attended by students who fail the entrance examination to enter junior or senior middle schools. Because of the severe shortage of secondary schools, many of these schools which had high academic standings were converted into formal middle schools. For this reason the number of such schools has decreased from 38 in 1948 to 16 in 1960 even though the enrollment has been increasing. ⑤

2. Continuation Education

Differing from supplementary education, the activities of continuation education are not confined to classrooms, but are carried out through use of a variety of educational media such as social education centers, libraries, museums, science halls, art galleries, motion pictures, athletic fields, parks, tea houses, theatres, the press, radio and television, etc. A select few of these media will be studied here.

a. <u>Social Education Centers</u>. In pursuance of the Social Education Law of 1953, four social education centers were instituted, one in each of the four strategic areas—Changhua City, Hsinchu City, Tainan City and Taitung hsien. The social education center is not new to China. Formerly, on the mainland, it was called a mass educational center. The social education centers in Taiwan are a multi-functional educational agency with activities generally centered around six areas: citizenship education, language education, health education, vocational education, science education and fine arts education. The administrative organization of the centers varies. As an example of organization, at Tainan there is one director and fourteen staff members, each of whom is assigned to one of the four departments: education and supervision, fine arts, research and

---

① <u>Chuna Yang Jih Pao</u> [Central Daily] September 5, 1962.
② China, <u>Chiao Yü Kai Ku'ang</u>, op. cit., pp. 124 – 25.
③ <u>Supra</u>, Chapter VI, pp. 177 – 78.
④ China, <u>Chiao Yü Kai Ku'ang</u>, op. cit., pp. 122 – 24.
⑤ Ibid., pp. 123 – 24.

guidance, or general affairs.①

b. <u>Other Social Education Agencies</u>. There are many agencies providing services to meet a wide range of needs in continuation education. The most prominent are the Historical Museum, the Taiwan Provincial Museum, the Taiwan Science Hall, and the 62 broadcasting stations.

(1) The Historical Museum. As a social education institution, the museum is unique in that it embraces all branches of human knowledge and serves as a center for the study of world problems. It has a rich collection of some 20,000 articles of artistic and historical value, among which are 6,250 antiques. In addition to the 20 museum galleries, the museum also has an art gallery. Besides regular displays, special exhibitions stressing important Chinese historical events and achievements in the arts are held in these galleries.

(2) Taiwan Provincial Museum. This museum also has a rich collection of 18,605 specimens and objects of historical value and general interest. Besides the regular historical, botanical, and zoological exhibits, there are many special exhibits.

(3) Taiwan Science Hall. The Science Hall has four units: a science museum, a planetarium, a micro projection room, and an auditorium which serves both as a movie hall and a lecture room. In addition to regular exhibits, there are also special exhibits. In 1961 – 1962, 139 scientific films were shown and eighteen lectures on science, technology, and topics of general interest were held in the auditorium.②

(4) Broadcasting Stations. In Taiwan, the most important mass communication medium is the radio. Some 707,000 radios were registered at the end of 1960. There were 41 stations in July of 1957 and by August, 1961 there were 62, including an educational station established in 1960 by the Educational Materials Center. An analysis of program content shows that 12.5 per cent of the time is allocated for news, 22.5 per cent for educational programs, 20 per cent for community service programs and 45 per cent for entertainment.③ The educational radio station broadcasts ten hours each day. Its programs include regular courses for all school grades. It also broadcasts courses in music, fine arts, home economics, industrial arts, accounting, infant care, etc.

In addition to these four, social educational agencies, there are a number of others also dedicated in some particular aspects to social education. They include the China Youth Corps, the Provincial Taiwan Symphony Orchestra, the Taiwan Arts Center, the Palace Museum (Taiwan) and the Central Museum, and the Educational Television Station.

The Educational Television Station is the newest among the social education agencies. It began broadcasts on February 14, 1962, operating on an experimental basis. A plan is under study to turn the station into a television extension school which will have courses for both young people and adults.④

c. "<u>School on the Air.</u>" In the past few years there has been much discussion on the feasibility of setting up a "school on the air." In an address entitled "An Educational Strategy Suitable Both in Time of War And in Time of Peace" delivered at the annual joint conference of ten educational organizations, Minister Huang strongly urged the utilization of modern mass communication media such as radio and television to provide education in the form of a "school on the air." He suggested that appropriate recognition should be extended to those registered in such a program and were able to pass the examination given by the educational authorities afterward. He saw the following advantages to such a "school on the air":

(1) it will release some of the pressure created by limited school facilities and the shortage of teachers;

(2) it can assure continuing of education in time of emergency;

(3) it can stimulate continuous self-education to those who are presently employed, thereby

---

① Chin-ch'eng Ts'ao, "Tai-wan Sheng She Hui Chiao Yü Chi Kou" [The Social Education Agencies in Taiwan] <u>Chung Kuo Chiao Yü Hsien Ku'ang</u>, *op. cit.*, IV, pp. 516 – 17.
② <u>China Yearbook, 1961 – 62</u>, *op. cit.*, pp. 545 – 54.
③ *Ibid.*, pp. 577 – 83.
④ *China Yearbook, 1962 – 1963*, *op. cit.*, p. 600.

upgrading the general cultural level of the people; and

(4) it can bring good teachers and vivid learning experiences to students especially through television. ①

According to the results of a public opinion poll taken by the Chinese Public Opinion Survey Association, 72.9 per cent of the 2,720 people polled thought that the "school on the air" program would be effective. This reflects the general desire for continuous self-education and the interest in an acceptance of the public of such a form of schooling. ②

3. Special Education

Somewhat arbitrarily, special education in Taiwan comes within the realm of social education. In 1961, there were three schools for the blind and the dumb in Taiwan, located respectively in Taipei, Fengyuan, and Tainan. All are provincial establishments. Each comprises three divisions: elementary, junior vocational, and senior vocational. The length of studies are for six years, three years, and three years, respectively. The enrollments of these schools, although rising from 82 in 1944 to 1,509 in 1961, constitutes a very small proportion of all blind and dumb children in the population. Emphasis in the curriculum is being given to vocational training. ③

C. Basic Problems Confronting the Implementation of Social Education

Although the importance of social education has long been recognized in China and considerable progress has been made in its implementation in recent years, two basic problems remain, namely, the lack of sufficient funds and the need for effective enforcement. These will be analyzed separately.

1. The Lack of Sufficient Funds

The lack of sufficient funds not only has prevented social education from having more far-reaching results but also has curtailed many of its worthwhile services. The expenditures used in social education at the various government levels have been very small in comparison with expenditures for other types of education. In the 1960–1961 school year, only 3.59 per cent of the total educational expenditures of government, 4.10 per cent of the total educational expenditures of the Provincial Government, and an average of 1.08 per cent of the municipal and hsien governments were used in social education. ④ These percentages are far too low for the gigantic tasks of social education. Through the efforts of the Chinese Association of Social Education, the Fourth National Educational Conference held between February 14 and 17, 1962 in Taipei, passed a motion that

> ... the expenditures for social education shall be, in respect to the government, not less than 10 per cent of the total educational budget; in respect to the Provincial Government, not less than 15 per cent of the total educational budget; and in respect to each municipality or hsien, not less than 20 per cent of the total educational budget. ⑤

Unfortunately, lack of funds forced the educational authorities to shelve the motion for the time being.

2. The Need for Effective Enforcement

In spite of the financial shortcomings, improvement still can be made in the implementation of social education. A general criticism of social education has been that it does not reach the masses. The most serious problem at present is that the roots of social education have been planted

---

① Huang, *op. cit.*, pp. 1–7.
② *China Today*, V, No. 5 (May, 1962), 29.
③ China, Chiao Yü Kai Ku'ang, *op. cit.*, pp. 32–33.
④ China, *Educational Statistics*, *1962*, *op. cit.*, pp. 71–73.
⑤ Ming-tung Cheng, "Tang Ch'ien She Hui Chiao Yü Lang Ko Chung Yao WenT'I [Two Major Problems Confronting Social Education] Chiao Yü Yü Wen Hua [Education and Culture] No. 308 (July 15, 1963), 5.

in only a few of the urban centers with none in the rural areas. This pattern vastly limits its influence. According to the "Social Education Law," in addition to the establishment of social education centers in large cities or populated areas by the Provincial Government, the municipal, hsien, village, and township governments also should establish social education centers within their respective regions, but so far this has not been done.

Consequently, the task falls to the elementary schools which, according to the "Citizen School Law," are vested with two major responsibilities—to provide fundamental education to children of school age and to provide supplementary education to adults who have not been properly educated as children.① Both of these types of education are compulsory according to the Chinese constitution.② To carry them out, the elementary school should be composed of two divisions, one for elementary education and one for adult education. In practice, however, many schools have neglected the second function.

It would seem that the most effective way of implementing social education would be through the public elementary schools, of which there were 1,877 located throughout Taiwan Province in 1961 – 1962. If these schools could be set up to discharge this function also, they could facilitate the implementation of social education without much difficulty. The problem is whether or not the educational authorities will enforce the existing laws and make them effective.

D. The Development of Modern Library Service

Since the modern library is undoubtedly one of the most dynamic agencies in the promotion of social education in the sense that it is described above, the remaining section of this chapter examines some of the major developments both in library service and in education for librarianship.

1. Historical Background

As the original home of paper and the art of printing, China has always been noted for her imperial and private libraries.③ However, the modern Chinese library cannot boast of such a long tradition. Before the first modern public library was established in China half a century ago, libraries in China were either imperial collections and palace archives, government agency libraries, monastic libraries, school libraries, or private collections. Thus, the traditional library was nothing more than a place where books and records were preserved for scholars.

The first attempt to establish a modern library can be traced back to the "Hundred-days Reform" in 1889. In a memorial submitted to the Manchu Court, Tuan-fen Li, then Secretary of Rites and an advocate of the Reform, suggested that Ts'ang-shu-lou (book-storing pavilions) be established for the enlightenment of the people. Before the word T'u-shu-Kuan④ (meaning library) was introduced to China, "book-storing pavilion" was the term used for libraries, which, according to Dr. Chiu "emphasized the function of libraries as depositories of valuable records of the past rather than as centers from which to distribute useful books to all classes of readers."⑤ Then a number of imperial edicts were issued. In 1905, Hunan Province established the first public library in China.⑥ Other provinces soon followed. In 1909 the first law about the establishment of public libraries was promulgated. It provided for the establishment of the Peking Library (Ching Shih T'u Shu Kuan) and a provincial library in the capital of each province. It

---

① China, Chiao Yü Fa Ling, op. cit., p. 207.
② Supra, Chapter VI, pp. 177 – 78.
③ T. F. Carter, *The Invention of Printing in China And the Spread Westward* (New York: Columbia University Press, 1925), 285 pp.
④ Fu-tsung Chiang, "Modern Chinese Libraries Under Sino-American Cooperation," *Chinese Culture*. IV, No. 1 (October, 1960), 141.
⑤ A Kaiming Chiu, "Modern Library Movement in China," *Libraries in China*, Library Association of China, Papers prepared on the occasion of the tenth anniversary (Peiping: Library Association of China, 1935), p. 2.
⑥ *Ibid.*, p. 3.

stipulated also the gradual establishment of public libraries in <u>hsiens</u> and municipalities. ① The purpose of the library, according to this law, is to preserve Chinese classics, to disseminate knowledge, to provide research facilities, and to collect materials for the free use of the public. ② After the Revolution of 1911, the new "Ministry of Education" was founded, consisting of three bureaus, one of which is known as the Bureau of Social Education which, among other functions, has charge of the promotion and supervision of public libraries. ③

During this period there emerged a great patron of the Chinese library movement in the person of the late Miss Mary-Elizabeth Wood (1862 – 1931), the founder of the Boone Library and the Boone Library School in Wuchang. Miss Wood, an American, went to China in 1899 after having graduated from Simmons College Library School. When she arrived in China, Miss Wood saw the need for modern libraries to facilitate the modernization of Chinese education and society. She borrowed an octagonal pavilion from the Wen-hua University in Wuchang to start a small public library. The pioneer work of Miss Wood marked the beginning of a new era in the development of modern library service in China. In a recent article entitled "Modern Chinese Libraries Under Sino-American Cooperation" written by Dr. Fu-tsung Chiang, Director of the Central Library for the past 30 years, Miss Wood's pioneer work is vividly depicted:

After ten years of such tireless efforts, she finally established the <u>Wen-hua-Kung-shu-lin</u> (The Public Book Collection of Wen-Hua) in 1910. Although this library was located on the campus of Wen-Hua, it was not the university library, consequently, it was called a "public book collection." This collection was heavily used as it offered free access to the public in general. A touring book collection was also started. Under this project, books were selected to be deposited with the several schools in the Wen-Hua area. Students of these schools were thus offered library service. ④

Miss Wood's contribution is not limited to the establishment of the modern public library in China. A significantly greater contribution was the establishment of the first library school at Wen-hua University in 1919. It later became an independent library school, the Boone Library School, or the Wen-hua Institute of Library Science (Wen-Hua T'u Shu Kuan Chuan K'o Hsüeh Hsiao) where a number of distinguished professional librarians were trained. ⑤ Apart from this, Miss Wood was also instrumental in obtaining the second part of the Boxer Indemnity Fund from the United States Government to be used to improve Chinese cultural educational institutions. As a result of her endeavors, in 1926 a program establishing one model library in each major city was adopted and the Metropolitan Library of Peiping was founded. In 1929, the Peking Library and the Metropolitan Library of Peiping were amalgamated to form the National Library of Peiping. ⑥

Between 1910 and 1937, the modern library movement in China flourished. A number of library schools were established and university libraries and public libraries began to grow in number. The Library Association of Peiping was founded in 1919. Other cities soon followed suit and library associations were established in Nanking, Shanghai and Wuhan. In 1925, as a result of the joint efforts of these associations, the Library Association of China was founded. It is worth mentioning, however, that previously, in 1922, a Committee on Library Education had been organized under the auspices of the Chinese National Association for the Advancement of Education to discuss cooperative buying, inter-library loan of books, union catalogues and other important topics. ⑦ The second national library, the National Central Library, was founded in Nanking in 1936.

---

① *Ibid.*
② Lincoln H. Cha, "Library Legislation in China," *Libraries in China*, op. cit., p. 67.
③ *Ibid.*, p. 4.
④ Fu-tsung Chiang, *op. cit.*, p. 142.
⑤ *Ibid.*
⑥ Fu-tsung Chiang, "National Libraries in China," *Libraries in China*, op. cit., p. 94.
⑦ T. C. Tai, "Library Movement in China," *Chinese National Association for the Advancement of Education*, Bulletin, II, No. 3 (1923), 19.

The National Library of Peiping was very active in promoting library service. Indexes were compiled, *The Quarterly Bulletin of Chinese Bibliography* began publication in 1934, and an arrangement was made with the Commercial Press to reprint a series of rare books in order to make them more available to the public. Another noteworthy contribution of the library was the printing and distribution of catalog cards for Chinese books, a service similar to that rendered by the Library of Congress. ①

It is quite unfortunate that all the progress made in the modernization of library service was disrupted by the Sino-Japanese War. Cultural centers, such as schools, universities, libraries, museums, and other institutions of learning, suffered irreparable damage. In spite of almost insurmountable obstacles, a number of libraries, including the National Central Library, were successfully evacuated inland during the war. This helped China to save a large portion of its rare books and manuscripts. ②

In Taiwan, the largest library founded during the period of Japanese occupation was the Government-General Library of Taiwan, established in August, 1915. Before the bombings near the end of the Second World War destroyed the buildings and one-fourth of the collection, the library consisted of 200,167 volumes, mostly in the Japanese and Chinese languages. After the war, the library was converted into the Provincial Taipei Library and was housed with the Taiwan Provincial Museum. In addition to the Government-General Library, there were 93 public, municipal, and "street-established" libraries in 1944 with the "street-established" libraries comprising the majority. ③

When the China mainland fell into the hands of the Communists, only the "National Central Library", the Library of the Institute of History and Philology of the Academia Sinica, the Library of the Palace Museum, and a few governmental bureau libraries were moved to Taiwan. According to Sing-wu Wang's report, Taiwan in 1961 had one "National library", two provincial libraries, seventeen municipal and hsien libraries, 405 reading rooms affiliated to the public service centers, fifteen college and university libraries, 249 school libraries, and 21 special libraries. ④ Jurisdiction over the "National Central Library" is exercised by "the Ministry of Education" and jurisdiction over the provincial, municipal and hsien libraries falls to the educational authorities at each respective government level.

2. Development of Modern Libraries in Taiwan

Since the major emphasis of the Japanese administration was to make the Taiwanese loyal Japanese subjects, great attention was given to elementary and adult education for the purpose of indoctrination. As public libraries were the most effective means toward this end, they were widely established and well equipped. Unfortunately, the bombings destroyed many and those which remained were almost entirely of Japanese books.

The general improvement in the economic, social, and educational fields gave impetus to the redevelopment of library service, both public and academic. Under the technical assistance program of the ICA Mission, a portion of United States aid has been used for library building construction, for purchase of Western books, and for advice from the many visiting American librarians. This program greatly expedited progress.

Following is a brief survey of recent significant developments in both public and academic libraries during this period.

    a. Public Libraries. There are four types of public libraries: the "National Central Library", provincial libraries, municipal and hsien libraries, and public reading rooms.

    (1) "National Central Library". This library, with one of the largest Chinese rare book

---

① Sing-wu Wang, "A Brief Sketch of the Development of Modern Libraries in China", *Chinese Culture*, III, No 4 (October, 1961), pp. 81 – 82.
② *Ibid.*, pp. 82 – 83
③ *Ibid.*, p. 121.
④ *Ibid.*, pp. 89 – 90.

collection, *was reactivated in Taipei in August*, 1954. By 1962, the collection reached 234,442 volumes. ① Of these, 121,376 are rare, ancient editions, 153 are hand-copied books from the Tun-huang caves, and 5,581 are stone rubbings. ② In addition to possessing one of the richest collections of Chinese rare books, the library also represents Taiwan in handling international exchange of publications, compiles and publishes "*The National Bibliography of Taiwan*", and, under the provisions of the National Publications Law, also is a depository library for all books published in Taiwan.

(2) Provincial Libraries. The two provincial libraries are the Provincial Taipei Library and the Provincial Taichung Library. Because the building which housed the former was destroyed during the war, it continued its services housed in the Taiwan Provincial Museum. The library is well known for its special collection on Southeast Asia, which contains some 34,139 volumes of books and 77,000 pamphlets. The total collection in 1962 reached 288,385 volumes. ③ In 1963, construction was begun on a new four-story building which will include the following rooms: children's room, young adult room, general reading room, general reference room, subject departments, study rooms, auditorium, art gallery, music room, and stack areas. The total seating capacity is to be 1,500 and the storage capacity, 900,000 volumes. The Taichung Provincial Library, although small in size (64,570 volumes in 1962) has been maintaining very effective service.

(3) Municipal and Hsien Libraries. A network of library service has been implemented through the seventeen municipal and hsien libraries which serve an estimated population of 3,164,264. Data relating to the size of the collection, the number of staff members, seating capacity, average number of readers and the number of loans per day are tabulated in TABLE 35.

An analysis④ made by Sing-wu Wang, Librarian of the Provincial Taipei Library, shows that the total expenditure for public libraries in Taiwan in the 1961–62 fiscal year was NT $ 2,633,822. The average expenditure per capita for the seventeen local libraries was only NT $.88. Their total book collections numbered 312,231 volumes. ⑤ From this analysis it can readily be seen that the expenditures are far from sufficient and the collections are too small to provide adequate service.

TABLE 35   THE MUNICIPAL AND HSIEN LIBRARIES IN TAIWAN, 1961⑥

Library	Total Volume	Seating Capacity	Book Budget⑦	Average Reader Per Day	Average Loan Per Day	Regular Staff⑧	Additional Staff
Taipei City	58,064	770	60.0	2,500	3,200	8	9
Tainan City	32,386	282	51.3	698	986	6	
Kaohsiung City	21,391	220	10.0	200	600	8	
Keelung City	10,329	84	48.0	258	252	4	1
Taipei Hsien	8,462	70	16.8	300	250	3	
Taoyuan Hsien	12,749	36	13.5	700	300	4	
Hsinchu Hsien	28,287	190	39.8	450	760	4	
Miaoli Hsien	6,004	40	13.7	200	110	2	

① *China News Service*, July 2, 1963.
② *China Yearbook, 1962–1963, op. cit.*, pp. 540–41.
③ *Ibid.*
④ Sing-wu Wang, "A Proposal for Development of Public Libraries in Taiwan," *China Today*. VI, No. 9 (September, 1963), 32.
⑤ Sing-wu Wang, "A Proposal...," *op. cit.*, p. 33.
⑥ "Survey of Municipal and Hsien Libraries," *Library Association of China, Bulletin*, No. 12, Conducted by Provincial Taipei Library, March, 1961 (July 25, 1961), pp. 31–32.
⑦ In NT $ 1,000.
⑧ Including professional and clerical workers.

(Continuing)

Library	Total Volume	Seating Capacity	Book Budget	Average Reader Per Day	Average Loan Per Day	Regular Staff	Additional Staff
Nantou Hsien	13,427	150	389	200	205	1	2
Chanahua Hsien	36,710	300	56.5	1,500	450	8	
Taichung Hsien	10,297	80	1.6	500	190	3	
Chiayi Hsien	13,279	60	16.0	200	60	3	
Kaohsiung Hsien	13,000	200	10.0	300	70	3	
Pintung Hsien	13,932	100	15.0	400	420	4	
Hualien Hsien	12,774	100	12.6	250	400	4	2
Ilang Hsien	10,138	120	14.4	350	350	2	3
Penghu Hsien	11,000	72	21.0	100	140	2	1
Total	312,231	2,874	439.1				
Mean	18,366.4	169	25.9				

The public libraries share the same fate as social education in general because of insufficient funds. In addition to the aforementioned problems, the public libraries face several others:

a. Of the 22 local administrative units, except Taichung where the provincial library is located, three units (Tainan hsien, Yulin hsien and Taitung hsien) still have no public library facilities.

b. The hsien libraries, with very few exceptions, are inadequately housed.

c. Because government regulations classify public libraries into class A, B, or C with fixed staffs of 8, 6, and 4 respectively, libraries have difficulty expanding service, since salaries for any additional staff would have to be obtained from sources other than the normal budget appropriations.

Despite these difficulties, libraries have been striving for improvement in their services. To reach rural areas, a number of public libraries are now providing traveling library service. The Provincial Taipei Library has a book-mobile unit, and public libraries in Hsinchu, Taoyuan, Taipei, and Penghu hsiens are utilizing circulating bookcases.① To help with the problem of inadequacy of book collections, inter-library loans and other programs of inter-library cooperation have been established. New educational media such as films, records, and radio broadcasting are also being used to better advantage. The two provincial libraries are equipped with film projectors and provide operators to show films to various civic groups. In 1956, the Provincial Taipei Library provided 250 showings to some 450,000 spectators.② Furthermore, public libraries contribute to the implementation of the extension courses by broadcasting on the radio. Besides regular record concerts, many public libraries also give or organize night classes, lectures, exhibits, and reading clubs.

(4) Public Reading Rooms. In accordance with the "Social Education Law" promulgated in 1953, the provincial government established a Social Education Center in Hsinchu, Changhua, Tainan, and Taitung, each with a public reading room. The largest of the four is in Taitung where the library has 14,792 volumes and 108 seating capacity. It serves an average of 103,000 readers annually. In addition to the centers, there are 405 reading rooms attached to Public Service Centers which provide newspapers and magazines and a few books.③

---

① Sing wu Wang, "A Brief Sketch...," op. cit., p. 92.
② Ibid., p. 93.
③ Ibid., p. 92.

b. <u>Academic Libraries</u>. This includes college and university libraries, school libraries and research libraries.

(1) College and University Libraries. Most college and university libraries are better off financially than public libraries, since a substantial amount of United States aid has been allocated for the construction of library buildings for colleges and universities and for the acquisition of foreign books and periodicals. The libraries of National Taiwan University and Taiwan Provincial Normal University are among the best. National Taiwan University has 720,000 volumes, the largest collection of any library in Taiwan. The Provincial Normal University collection is 170,872 volumes. ① There are college libraries having less than 50,000 volumes; however, many of these were established within the last ten years and are expected to build up their collections in the near future.

(2) School Libraries. In recent years, the changes in teaching method concurrent with the broadening of curriculum and course content has made it necessary for school libraries to play a more important role than they had in the past. Some elementary schools already have good library facilities, but others are still far from adequate. The educational survey of 1961 (conducted by the Department of Education) shows that among the 1,883 elementary school libraries surveyed, the average collection of the elementary school library is 713.1 volumes. ② In the secondary schools, the library facilities are considered much better than in the elementary schools; however, there is still room for improvement. Many secondary school libraries already have separate library buildings, but others have only reading rooms and stack areas adjacent to the classrooms. The educational survey of 1961 also shows that, based on the 275 middle schools surveyed, the average library collection is 6,128.89 volumes. ③ The average collection, based on all ten normal schools surveyed, is 12,551 volumes and the average collection, based on 111 vocational schools surveyed, is 6,770.5 volumes. ④ Thus, it would seem that the normal schools have better collections than the middle and vocational schools and that, strangely, vocational schools have better collections than the average middle schools. This is another indication that the rapid expansion of the middle schools has tended to lower the quality of middle school education.

(3) Research Libraries. There are a few outstanding research libraries in Taiwan, including the Library of the Institute of History and Philology of the Academia Sinica and the Library of the "National War College". The former has a collection of 200,000 volumes and the latter, more than 130,000 volumes. A score of other special libraries exist in governmental, industrial, and scientific organizations. ⑤

c. <u>The Library Association of China</u>. Ever since its inauguration in 1925, the Library Association of China has been very active in the modernization and upgrading of library service in China, but its activities were disrupted when the mainland was taken over by the Chinese Communists. The need for a professional organization in library service in Taiwan was increasingly felt as the number of libraries multiplied and the size of existing libraries increased. Therefore, after four years of interruption, the Association was reestablished in Taiwan in 1953.

The aim of the Association as stated in its constitution is to conduct research in library science and to promote library services. The major activities, also stipulated by the constitution, are as follows:

(1) studying the library systems and their administration;
(2) assisting members through in-service training in library science;
(3) issuing periodicals on library science;
(4) conducting book exhibits;
(5) compiling and editing library science series;

---

① *China Yearbook*, 1962 – 1963, op. cit., p. 542.
② Taiwan, Department of Education, *A Survey Report.*., op. cit., Appendix p. 23.
③ *Ibid.*, Appendix pp. 58 – 59.
④ *Ibid.*, Appendix p. 38.
⑤ *China Yearbook*, 1961 – 1962. op, cit., pp. 538 – 39.

(6) promoting international cooperation in library science;
(7) extending library education;
(8) advocating the establishment of a network of libraries;
(9) improving social education through library service.

The library association consists of a Council of 21 members and a seven-member Board of Trustees. The Executive Board consists of seven members elected from the Council. An executive secretary is appointed by the Executive Board to carry out its various activities. Within the association, there are seven committees—committees on the improvement of library service in Taiwan; on education for librarianship; on compilation and translation; on cataloging and classification; on publication of the Bulletin; on finance; and on public relations. The association holds an annual conference on library problems.

The notable activities of the association in recent years have been the conducting of summer in-service workshops since 1956, the publishing of professional papers and pamphlets, working on the draft of standards for public, school, and academic libraries and the standards for library facilities. Dr. Fitzgerald has rightfully appraised the association's work thus:

> No library association of which I have been a part has been more library-minded or more enthusiastic in behalf of library ideals. [1]

3. Education for Librarianship

Although libraries existed in China before the Christian era, throughout Chinese history there was no idea of formal library training as we understand it today.[2] The concept of a librarian as a highly specialized professional person was not fully recognized until recent years. In the past, the only qualification to be a librarian was that one must be a scholar or learned person who had thoroughly acquired a knowledge of books. In other words, he must be a "bookman". Today, this situation is still valid to a considerable extent. The "chief librarian" of the large libraries, public and academic, is usually a distinguished scholar or a senior professor. The rank-and-file workers as such have enjoyed little more than a clerical status of a very low category. This explains why there were no library schools or library programs at the university level on the China mainland before 1919, and in Taiwan, before 1955.

As mentioned earlier, the first library school in China, the Boone Library School, was established in 1919.[3] In the same year, a committee on library education was founded under the auspices of the Chinese National Association for the Advancement of Education. The committee adopted a number of resolutions in connection with libraries and training for librarianship. One was that no library training should be given without adequate library facilities. Another was the normal schools should, as far as possible, have a course in library science as a part of their curriculum.[4] In 1920, the first four-week summer course was inaugurated at the National Normal College of Peiping which, according to Tai, was a great success. A total of 78 men and women, most of whom were librarians from all parts of China, were sent to attend the summer school.[5] This summer course was followed by three others established in Nanking, Soochow and Tientsin, The one in Nanking was held under the auspices of the Library Association of China.[6]

In 1928, three years after the inauguration of the Library Association of China, the first national conference of librarians was held in Nanking. The section of the association on library training presented two important recommendations:

    a. that the national universities be requested to offer courses in librarianship; and
    b. that the "Ministry of Education" be requested to set up a standard as to what should

---

[1] William A. Fitzgerald, "Library Mission in Taiwan," *ALA Bulletin*, LIII (June, 1959), 492.
[2] Samuel T. Y. Seng, "Professional Training for Librarian-ship in China," *Libraries in China*, op. cit., p. 59.
[3] *Ibid.*, p. 6.
[4] *Ibid.*, p. 62.
[5] Tai, *op. cit.*, p. 17.
[6] Seng, *op. cit.*, p. 61.

constitute professional education for librarianship. ①

Soon after, several universities and colleges began to offer courses in library science. The most important ones were those given at the University of Nanking, Honan University, Great China University, and the Provincial Girls Normal College of Tientsin. ② In addition to the formal course offerings, a number of library training institutes were organized. Also a correspondence training school was established in Shanghai under the auspices of the Shanghai Library Association.

In the two decades between 1920 and 1940, the curriculum offered in the Boone Library School was the model for other library schools. The course of study was generally two years. The requirement for admission was at least two years of college although college graduation was much preferred. Upon successful completion of the two years of study, students were awarded diplomas. ③

During World War II, only the Boone Library School moved to Chungking, the war capital of China, and continued to train professional librarians. In 1941, the National College of Social Education in Soochow established a Department of Library Science and Museum Technology which offered a four-year undergraduate program, but this department did not survive very long. In the postwar years, efforts were made to revive education for librarianship at the recommendation of two visiting American librarians, Dr. Charles Harvey Brown, then chairman of the Committee on the Orient and Southwest Pacific of the American Library Association and Mr. Verner Clapp, Deputy Librarian of the Library of Congress. They suggested that at least five library schools be established in China, including the Boone Library School which was still in existence. As a result, at National Peiping University a library division was founded which was designated to provide professional training to interested students in any department of the university. In addition to the number of credits required in the student's own field of studies, a student who wished to receive a librarian's certificate along with a B. A. or B. S. degree was required to take up to 70 extra credits in library science. The program was unique because it was the first one in China to offer a course of study in library science at the postgraduate level. ④ It is unfortunate that before any judgment could be made of the results of the program, the mainland was taken over by the Chinese Communists.

In Taiwan during the Japanese occupation, the only available form of library education was the so-called Koshukais or short courses which were held on occasion by the Government-General assisted by the Japanese Library Association (Nippon Toshokan Kvokai). ⑤ After the Kuomingtang administration moved to Taiwan, the first formal library education at the college level was begun when the Department of Social Education, which contained a section of library science, was founded at Taiwan Normal University in 1955.

As do other departments of the Normal University, the section of library science of the Department of Social Education offers a four-year course of study with one year of practical training leading to the B. Ed. degree. The curriculum is divided into three areas: the general courses, the professional courses in library science, and the courses in social education. Generally speaking, the freshman year is entirely devoted to general education including the set of courses required for all college students. In the sophomore year, the three areas are equally presented in the curriculum, each receiving one-third of the time. In the junior year, only the professional courses and courses in social education are taught, each taking one-half of the time. In the senior year, professional courses are increased to include two-thirds of the curriculum while the courses in social education are reduced to only one-third of the time. ⑥

---

① *Ibid.*, pp. 62 – 63.
② *Ibid.*, p. 61.
③ *Ibid.*, p. 59.
④ Fu-tsung Chiang, "Chung Kuo T'u-Shu-Kuan Ti Chiao Yü Wen T'i" [Problems Concerning the Education for Librarianship in China] *Library Association of China, Bulletin.* No. 11 (December 10, 1960), 2.
⑤ Robert L. Gitler, "Japan", *Library Trends.* XII (October 1963), 280.
⑥ Pang-cheng Sun, "Shih Ta She Chiao Hsi T'u Shu Kuan Tsu Kai Ku'ang" [Sketch of the Section of Library Science, Department of Social Education, Taiwan Normal University] *Library Association of China, Bulletin.* No. 11 (December 10, 1960), pp. 16 – 18.

In professional courses, equal emphasis is placed on both theory and practice. In addition to the actual practice in the fifth year, students are also given practical training beginning in the sophomore year. The training takes place both in and out of school. The new library of Taiwan Normal University provides an ideal training ground within the university and other libraries in the Taipei area give additional experience in other types of libraries. The summer of the junior year is again taken up with practical training in a library arranged for by the section.

A set of courses designated for interested students in other departments is also offered. Any student wishing to receive a certificate in librarianship is required to take all the required courses plus a number of elective courses. Those courses offered are listed in TABLE 36.

TABLE 36   COURSES OF STUDY FOR INTERESTED STUDENTS IN OTHER DEPARTMENTS①

Course	Credit	Year
Required Course		
Introduction to Library Science	4	Sophomore
Cataloging and Classification	6	Junior
The School Library	2	Senior
Reference and Service	2	Senior
Sub-total	14	
Elective Course		
Chinese Bibliography	3	Junior
Rare Books	3	Junior
Materials for Children and Adolescents	4	Sophomore
Information Control	2	Senior
History of Libraries	3	Senior
Sub-total	15	
Total	29	

Since the demand for trained librarians is far greater than the number the Normal University can supply, rudimentary courses in library science for undergraduate students have also been offered at the National Taiwan University and Tunghai University. Beginning in 1956 an intensive summer in-service training program has been conducted each year by "the Ministry of Education" in cooperation with the Library Association of China. The curriculum for the summer program, although varying slightly each year, largely follows the following pattern offered in 1961:

Course of Study (6 weeks)②

A. Required Courses	Hours Per Week
①Introduction to library science	4
②Chinese reference materials	5
③Information control	4
④Cataloging and classification of materials in Chinese, or	8

---

① *Ibid.*
② "Chiao Yü Pu Wu Shih Nien T'u Shu Kuan Kung Tso Jen Yuan Yen Hsi Hui Ch'ou Pei Ching Kuo" [Report on the Preparation of the 1961 Library In-Service Training Institute Conducted by the "Ministry of Education"] *Library Association of China*, *Bulletin*, No. 12 (July 25, 1961), 5.

| （Cataloging and classification of materials in Western languages） | 8① |

B. Elective Courses
①History of libraries　　2
②University librarianship　　2
③School librarianship　　4
④Public librarianship　　2
⑤Reference materials in Western languages　　5

In addition to the regular courses, much time is allotted for such activities as special lectures, informal discussions, visits to libraries, etc.

In view of the need for specialists to handle the Chinese classics and rare books, the Graduate Research Institute of Chinese Literature at Taiwan Normal University has offered a number of elective courses in library techniques, including introduction to library science, cataloging and classification of Chinese materials, bibliography, rare books and classics, etc. In this program, the facilities for practical training are provided by the National Central Library. ②

With the active support of the ICA Mission, beginning in 1954, a large amount of U. S. aid was made available to schools, secondary and higher, to expand their physical facilities to accommodate the increasing number of overseas Chinese students going to Taiwan to study. Many new school libraries were constructed as a part of the school physical expansion program. In order to improve the library facilities and services, the position of special library consultant in the ICA Overseas Chinese Education Section was created and William A. Fitzgerald, Director of Peabody Library School, George Peabody College for Teachers, was invited to Taiwan in 1959 for two years. Among other responsibilities, Dr. Fitzgerald was assigned to assist in the formulation of a program in education for librarianship. ③

Recognizing the urgent need for professionally trained librarians to staff the growing libraries and to improve library standards, it was felt that the existing facilities for the training of modern librarians was inadequate to meet the rising demands. The increasing awareness of the importance of librarianship is not peculiar to Taiwan, but also exists in other developing countries. As stated by Dr. Harold Lancour in "Education for Librarianship Abroad in Selected Countries", the forces behind this awakening are:

　　a. The rapid expansion of knowledge and its records and the steady growth of literacy have greatly increased the library's role and functions throughout the world.

　　b. The librarian's duties and responsibilities have multiplied in number and degree.

　　c. This broadening and deepening calls for library personnel with a high degree of general and professional education. ④

In order to meet the changing needs of society and at the same time to enrich the substance of librarianship, a Department of Library Science was established in the College of Arts of Taiwan University in 1961. It offers a regular four-year undergraduate curriculum. In August, 1962, the American Library Association selected Dr. David Berninghausen, Director of the Library School of the University of Minnesota, to be visiting professor at NTU for a period of ten months.

In recent years, many visiting American librarians have made the suggestion that library education in Taiwan should be mainly at the graduate level. Professor Berninghausen also made the following comments:

　　For the future economic, educational, and cultural development of Taiwan, a graduate library school is essential. President Chien Ssu-ling and Dean Shen Kang-pei of Taiwan

---

① Students may select either one of the two cataloging and classification courses.
② Yung-hsiang Lai, "Chung Hua Min Kuo Hsüeh Hsiao T'u Shu Kuan" [School Libraries in "Taiwan"] *Library Association of China. Bulletin*, No. 8 (October 31, 1957), 16.
③ Fitzgerald, *op. cit.*, p. 49.
④ Harold Lancour, "Introduction," *Library Trends*. XII, (October, 1963), 121.

University have recognized the need for library education and through the aid of the Rockefeller Foundation and the American Library Association a library of library literature has been established to support a graduate library school. ①

It was Professor Berninghausen's recommendation that a graduate library school be established at Taiwan University with the faculty, equipment, library and budget necessary to prepare professional librarians for the public, academic, special and school libraries of Taiwan and Asia. ② His recommendation in library education includes the following:

Undergraduate Study

a. <u>General Education</u>, including study in all three major divisions of human knowledge: the humanities, the social sciences, the natural sciences.

b. <u>Foreign Languages</u>, two years study in English, as a minimum, and two years study in another foreign language, if possible.

c. <u>A Major Field of Inquiry</u>, studied thoroughly so that the student be prepared to continue in this field for graduate degrees.

Graduate Study

d. <u>Library Science</u>, at least one year of full-time study in librarianship, chiefly at the graduate level, though introductory courses may be at the undergraduate level.

e. <u>Post-graduate Study</u>, either in library science, or in any other field, in some cases, leading to additional Master's degrees or the Ph. D. ③

The idea of setting up a library school at the graduate level is also advocated by leading Chinese librarians. In an article written on December 10, 1960, Dr. Fu-tsung Chiang also urged the establishment of a graduate library school at National Taiwan University while maintaining the undergraduate program at the Normal University. ④

At present these moves are still premature because of the lack of competent teachers at the graduate level and the small amount of library literature in existence. However, in view of the rapid improvement during recent years, it is reasonable to predict that at least some of these recommendations will be realized in the near future.

The needs for graduate training in librarianship have been partially met by library schools in the United States which have been rendering a great service by extending the opportunity for graduate study to a considerable number of Chinese students seeking a career in library science. In the fall of 1960, there were 84 Chinese students enrolled in accredited American library schools. This figure represents nearly one-third of all foreign students enrolled. ⑤ Even though only a small portion of American-trained Chinese librarians have returned to Taiwan, those who have are currently holding very high positions in the libraries or are teaching in the Department of Library Science at Taiwan University.

If the number of returning librarians could be increased, the modernization of libraries and training for librarianship could be greatly hastened to supply the much needed teaching personnel at the undergraduate level at present and at the graduate level in the near future.

X. Summary and Conclusion

A. Summary

Historically, education in Taiwan underwent three periods of change corresponding to the changes of sovereignty. The traditional period (before 1895), the colonial period (1895 to

---

① David K. Berninghausen, "Library Education in Taiwan and Recommendations for Advanced Library Education", *China Today*. VII, No. 2 (February, 1963), 27.

② *Ibid.*, p. 28.

③ *Ibid.*

④ Fu-tsung Chiang, "Chung Kuo T'u-Shu-Kuan," *op. cit.*, p. 2.

⑤ Total foreign students enrolled in fall, 1960 were 274. Among them 84 or 30.65 per cent were Chinese students. See "Accredited Library School Enrollment Statistics: 1959 - 1960," *Journal of Education for Librarianship*. IV (Fall, 1960), 179.

1945), and the present Nationalist period (1945 to 1962). In the traditional period education was modeled after classical Chinese education in which the examination system was predominant. After the island was ceded to Japan, education was characteristically colonial with much discrimination. The stratified dual system offered only limited educational opportunities for Taiwanese. The present Nationalist educational system which was formulated on the mainland of China under the Kuomingtang administration was introduced on the island when Taiwan was restored to China. After a brief period of post-war turbulence and confusion, rehabilitation began. Within four years, the Japanese system, Japanese language, Japanese curricula and teaching staff had all been replaced. With the withdrawal of the Kuomingtang administration to Taiwan in 1949, profound transformation took place in the political, social, and economic lives of the people. The government first set about to regenerate itself through self-criticism and reform. Recognizing the importance and immediacy of implementing Dr. Sun Yat-sen's Three People's Principles as a means of competing against Communist ideology, the government wasted no time in introducing a land reform program, in initiating local self-government, in improving education, and in adopting various measures to accelerate economic growth and industrialization—all of which follow Dr. Sun's blueprints. Despite extreme difficulties and heavy financial burdens, improvements can be noted in all of these fields of endeavor.

In education, the number of schools and the enrollment at all levels have shown remarkable increase over the seventeen years under study. Between 1944 and 1962 the number of kindergartens increased more than 7.6 times while the enrollment increased nearly 9.6 times; the number of elementary schools increased 1.8 times over the 1944 figure while the enrollment jumped 2.3 times; the number of secondary schools (including middle, vocational, and normal schools) jumped 5.8 times over the 1944 figure while the enrollment jumped more than 10 times. Most notable has been the increment in higher education where the increase in number over the eighteen years multiplied 6.6 times and the enrollment, 21 times. The percentage of school-age children (six to twelve) attending school also increased, from 73.3 per cent, the highest ever attained in the colonial period, to 96.52 per cent in 1962 – 1963. These figures are impressive indications of the government's effort to provide more education to more people and of the general trend toward prolonged education for every individual who can profit from such education.

In qualitative development, critical assessments made throughout the study are the bases for the following generalizations. Although the student-teacher ratio remains high, the quality of elementary school teachers has been considerably upgraded. This has made possible a general improvement in teaching materials and methods in elementary schools. The traditional emphasis on textbook study has gradually given way to more emphasis on the life of the child. In the middle schools, the curriculum of the junior section has been measurably broadened, preparing the way for the extension of compulsory education. The curriculum for the senior section has also been modernized. The development of science education has received top priority in secondary education and higher education. Educational equipment, laboratories, and libraries have all been improved in order to adapt to the new needs.

In view of the national policy for rapid economic growth and industrialization, great stress has been given to the improvement of both vocational education and technical training. Innovations noted in the revision of traditional curriculum in various vocational schools include the adoption of "unit-trade" courses in the industrial vocational schools and the alteration of the traditional departmental course of study in the agricultural vocational schools. For out-of-school youth, "vocational skill training centers" have been established. In recent years, the government has been striving for better coordination between education and training and economic growth and industrial development. One evidence of this has been the incorporation of a section on manpower planning into the third four-year economic plan of the nation.

In higher education, improvement has been made in library resources and research facilities, more research grants have been made available through the National Long-Range Program for the Development of Science, revisions in curriculum are now in progress, technical assistance from foreign scholars and specialists has been obtained through international cooperation projects, and extension education at the college level is being offered and expanded. Teacher education, regarded as fundamental to the improvement of education at all levels, has received much stress. The government scholarship program has enabled schools to recruit the most able youth for teaching, thereby keeping a high standard for teachers. Professional education for elementary school teachers has been extended to five years.

In social education, rapid strides have been made toward the modernization of library service. United States' aid has been invaluable in the strengthening of school facilities and in the carrying out of exchange programs. A number of new projects, including use of audio-visual aids, experimentation with community — centered education, provision of an educational program for overseas Chinese, and the Long-Range Program for the Development of Science have all been financed with U. S. aid and given assistance by American experts.

Educational development has not been totally free of problems. Many obstacles have stood in the way of progress, chief among them being the population problem. Not only does Taiwan have a high population growth rate, but it also has a relatively large proportion of young people in its population, placing almost insurmountable pressure on educational facilities. An added difficulty is that of limited funds. National defense exhausts nearly 75 per cent of the total national budget with all other governmental activities, including education, competing for the remaining 25 per cent. Even though the constitution stipulates that no less than 15 per cent of the total national budget should be allocated for educational programs, scientific studies and cultural services, in recent years the average yearly expenditure for education at the national level has been less than 3 per cent.

A third major impediment to educational progress has been the difficulty encountered in the attempt to have the quality of instruction keep up with the ever-increasing school enrollment. This problem is further complicated by the increasing desire for more education and prolonged schooling for more people.

The advancement of education has been further thwarted by the shortage of teachers in the higher grades and the critical subjects. Most severe is the shortage of secondary teachers, a condition which will become even more critical if the length of compulsory education is extended. The lack of qualified college teachers is already curtailing the course offerings of many colleges and universities. Due to the shortage of teachers, many universities and colleges have to "borrow" instructors from each other. This situation makes it necessary for many college teachers to hold more than one job. Although this means more income for the teachers, it is usually at the expense of the quality of their teaching and research.

Another major hindrance can be attributed to unfavorable elements in the socio-political environment. People of any agrarian society tend to look with suspicion and reservation at the changes and innovations necessary for scientific and technical advances. They prefer to examine proposed changes in terms of customs and traditions rather than on the basis of functional advantages. In Taiwan, the traditional lack of respect for labor and manual work has proved to be a stumbling block of considerable magnitude.

Many of the obstacles summarized here are inherent difficulties common to most developing countries—difficulties almost unavoidable in the process of transition from the old to the new. In the case of Taiwan, however, it has added complexity because of the unsettled war condition existing across Straits and the determination of the Kuomingtang administration for national recovery.

B. Conclusion

The educational achievements in Taiwan are spectacular in view of the many difficulties encountered. To conclude this study some of the facts revealed will be presented in view of the bearing they have on the future progress of education.

1. Education in a Changing Society

This study has revealed that tremendous changes in education have taken place concurrent with political changes on the mainland before 1949 and the rapid social and technological development in the post-war period. Having important bearing on the educational developments and trends were the retrocession of Taiwan to China, the withdrawal of the Kuomingtang administration to Taiwan, the influx of "mainlanders" and the interaction between them and "Taiwanese," the subsequent social, economic, and political reforms, the improved standard of living, the rising aspirations of the people, the population growth, and the mounting store of knowledge. The persistent struggle of the Chinese people to transform their traditional social institutions into those consistent with the needs of the modern world has no doubt helped shape the course of educational development in the period under study.

2. Centralization Versus Decentralization

From the onset, the administrative structure of education in Taiwan has been centralized. A high degree of uniformity in school system, curriculum, and standards of requirements has been attained through detailed governmental regulations promulgated by "the Ministry of Education". According to the "principle of equilibrium" of Dr. Sun as it is incorporated into the constitution "power that should belong to a region should be vested in the local government as in the case of education..."[①] It was Dr. Sun's view that, except for the organization of education (which should be regulated on a national scale), all educational matters should be left completely to the local government. In this time of national emergency, there are some aspects of the educative enterprise in which uniform policies are desirable and necessary, but extreme caution need be exercised to safeguard the principle of equilibrium. "the Ministry of Education" has tried to follow this principle. In the experiments on community-centered schools, it allowed more flexibility and local initiative in the undertakings involved. Also, in prescribing a general course of study for the nation as a whole, certain adaptations to local needs were allowed. In maintaining the various levels and types of schools, the division of responsibility among national, provincial, and local governments has worked out well. The supervision and financing of higher education is largely the government's responsibility except for those institutions established by the Provincial Government. The Provincial Government is charged with the responsibility of supervising and financing provincial universities and colleges, teacher training institutes, senior middle schools, and vocational schools, while the local municipal and hsien governments regulate the junior middle and elementary schools.

3. Quantity Versus Quality

Historically, Chinese education has been of high quality, but rapid increases in school enrollment has caused degradation. The question is often asked as to whether the school should strive to provide more education for more people or to provide more education for the select few and a little education for the many. In view of the rapid industrialization and the desire for a genuine democracy, the best answer seems to be more education for more people in order to enlighten the masses. With limited financial resources and meager educational facilities, however, it is very difficult to meet the two-fold demand for quantity and quality. To cope with this problem, two important steps can be taken simultaneous with the general increase in the number of schools: (a) an effective policy to reduce the population growth rate can be put into effect; and (b) new sources of revenue to support education can be sought. It is unfortunate that although these steps have been discussed on various occasions, no positive measures have been adopted. At present, the general policy is to emphasize quantity in the elementary and, as far as possible, the junior middle schools while insuring certain minimum standards. At the senior middle school and college levels, the emphasis is on quality.

To meet the educational needs of the adult population, efforts have been made to improve

---

① *Supra*, Chapter IV, p. 96.

social education. Libraries, museums, and various social education agencies have been going through a process of expansion and modernization. A variety of opportunities for supplementary and continuation education have also been provided but, due to the lack of sufficient funds, progress has been moderate as compared with that of formal schooling.

4. General Education Versus Departmental Education

With the rapid transformation from an agrarian society to a more industrial one, the educational program in Taiwan has been considerably broadened. In the past, the path of specialization often began too early and was too narrow in its offering. Recent changes postpone specialization and broaden the traditional curriculum by adding activities necessary to prepare students to cope with the complexities of life. Attention has been given to activities in health, physical education and recreation, vocational and technical orientation, personal and social adjustment, appreciation and expression of the arts and humanities, and education for citizenship.

Although the senior middle schools are now divided into a department of science and a department of arts, students are being required to take a number of courses in the other field of concentration. At the college level, the problem of specialization remains as students are required to select a major before entering and then are offered very few courses in any other area of study. The result is a narrow professionalism.

5. Stress on Vocational and Technical Education

A healthy trend has been the due emphasis being given to vocational education and technical training. The traditional lack of respect for labor is still present, but is gradually being shaken. In the wake of rapid economic growth and industrial development, there has been a gradual decline of previously existing unfavorable factors such as the negative attitude of educated youth toward manual work, their desire to seek high-prestige positions in the already overcrowded sectors of administration, government, and public service and their inability as well as their unwillingness to pursue technical and professional occupations. The changes in outlook and attitude have come about not only through changes in the social and economic structure, but also through the improvements made in vocational and technical training. Out-dated courses in "handcrafts" have been replaced with courses in "industrial arts", modern shops with new machinery are being provided, vocational guidance is being accepted as one of the functions of middle schools, and curricula of various vocational schools have undergone drastic and profound revision. Besides vocational schools, many short-term vocational skill training centers have been instituted, most directly by industrial firms, experimental farms, or large commercial establishments.

Just as in many other developing countries, China faces two persistent manpower problems: the shortage of persons with critical skills and the surplus of unskilled labor and intelligentsia. The key to the solution of these two seemingly diverse, yet intimately related problems lies in education and training. Widespread education in Taiwan has made its labor force both intelligently and physically fit. What is now required is additional training to prepare for meeting the needs of accelerated economic development.

6. Emphasizing and Improving the Teaching of Science

No nation can afford to remain ignorant of the rapid advances in science and technology. For the Chinese people, the importance of modern science is not merely for the sake of material well-being, but also for the emergence of the scientific mind. Dr. Paul Monroe has said:

> The great need in the intellectual life of the Chinese is the introduction of the scientific mind to modify the philosophical, speculative and theoretical attitude towards the problems and activities of everyday life.[1]

---

[1] Paul Monroe, *A Report on Education in China for American Educational Authorities* (Institute of International Education Bulletin, Third Series, No. 4; New York: 1922), p. 23.

Although the traditional attitude toward science has retarded the process of modernization, in recent years the importance of science education has received new recognition.

The Kuomingtang administration's emphasis on upgrading the teaching of science at all school levels is manifest in the many measures it has taken. The "National Long-Range Program for the Development of Science" is one of the best examples. Under this multi-purpose program, a large sum of money is allocated yearly to strengthen science laboratories and equipment; to modernize course content and method of teaching; to provide financial assistance for scholars and scientists so that they may be freed from financial burdens and able to devote themselves fully to research; to provide living quarters for college teachers; and to publish and subsidize the findings of research. The program has proved to be timely and effective; however, these efforts by the educational authorities have been hampered by the continuing lack of competent science teachers at the secondary level and the shortage of qualified professors and research scientists in institutions of higher learning. The large number of college graduates seeking opportunities to study abroad each year and the reluctance of those already having completed their study to return from abroad for teaching and research is one of the major causes for the shortage of teachers. The best remedy is to improve the research environment by allocating more funds for scientific research, thereby attracting more Chinese scientists abroad to return home to serve in various capacities.

7. Education for Economic Growth

Education is critical for both social development and economic growth. The important role education plays in the process of social development has long been recognized. What education can do to accelerate the process of economic progress remains a question of concern for the government officials as well as for the populace and the educators. The experiences of economically advanced countries have shown that investment in education and training yield a high rate of return and that the investment in people, through education and training is considered the best growth promise of a country's capital.[1] Chinese educators are now seeking to closely coordinate education and economic growth and to adapt education and training to the manpower needs of the nation. This is manifested in the inclusion of manpower planning into the Third Four-Year Economic Plan of the nation in the first attempt in recent Chinese history to achieve greater accomplishments in the economic goal of the nation. Precautions are being taken not to subordinate educational development to economic exigencies so that education will serve to meet not only the economic needs but also continue to have the more significant humanistic and democratic ends as well.

APPENDIX
UNIVERSITIES AND COLLEGES IN TAIWAN[2]

Name	Location	Colleges, Departments, and Research Institutes
Public Institutions		
Taiwan University	Taipei	6 colleges (Arts, Law, Medicine, Science, Engineering, Agriculture), 40 departments, 1 night school, and 25 research institutes.
Chengchi University	Mushan, Taipei	3 colleges (Art, Law, and Commerce), 18 departments, 1 night school, and 5 research institutes
Chinghua University	Hsinchu	Research Institute of Nuclear Science
Chiaotung University	Hsinchu	Research Institute of Electronics
Chung Yang University	Miaoli	Research Institute of Geophysics

---

[1] See Frederick Harbison and Charles A. Myers, *Education, Manpower, and Economic Growth: Strategies of Human Resources Development* (New York: McGraw-Hill Book Company, 1964), pp. 229.
[2] *China Yearbook, 1963 – 1964, op. cit.*, pp. 502 – 04.

(Continuing)

Name	Location	Colleges, Departments, and Research Institutes
School of Arts and Crafts	Panchiao, Taipei	4 divisions
Taiwan Provincial Normal University	Taipei	3 colleges (Arts, Education, and Science), 17 departments, 10 training divisions, 1 night school and 3 research institutes
Taiwan Provincial Cheng Kung University	Tainan	3 colleges (Arts and Science, Law and Commerce, and Engineering), 19 departments, 1 night school, and 4 research institutes
Taiwan Provincial Chung Hsing University	Taichung and Taipei	3 colleges (Science and Engineering, Law and Commerce, and Agriculture), and 1 research institute
Taiwan Provincial Taipei Junior College of Technology	Taipei	5 divisions of 3-year course, 6 divisions of 5-year course, and 2 divisions of 2-year course
Taiwan Provincial Junior College of Agriculture	Pingtung	6 divisions of 3-year course
Taiwan Provincial Maritime Junior College	Keelung	1 division of 3-year course and 6 divisions of 4-year course
Taiwan Provincial Junior College of Nursing	Taipei	1 division each of 3-year and 5-year course
Taiwan Provincial Junior Taichung Normal College of Taichung	Taichung	1 division each of 3-year and 5-year course
Taiwan Provincial Junior Normal College of Taipei	Taipei	1 division each of 3-year and 5-year course
Taiwan Provincial Junior Normal College of Tainan	Tainan	1 division each of 3-year and 5-year course
Taiwan Provincial Junior College of Physical Education	Taichung	1 division each of 3-year and 5-year course
Private Institutions		
Tunghai University	Taichung	3 colleges (Arts, Science, and Engineering) and 12 departments
Soochow University Law School	Taipei	6 departments
Chung Yuan College of Science and Engineering	Chungli	7 departments
Kaohsiung Medical College	Kaohsiung	1 department each of 7, 6, 5, and 4 year course
Tamkang College of Arts and Science	Tamsui	6 departments, 3 divisions of 3-year course, and 1 division of 5-year course
China Medical (Chinese-Herb) College	Taichung	2 departments
Taipei Medical College	Taipei	3 departments
Fengchia College of Science and Engineering	Taichung	7 departments

(Continuing)

Name	Location	Colleges, Departments, and Research Institutes
Catholic Fujen University	Taipei	3 colleges (Arts, Law, and Science), 9 departments, and research institute
Shih Chien Girls College of Home Economics	Taipei	4 divisions of 3-year course
Ching Yi Girls English Junior College	Taichung	4 divisions of 3-year course
Tatung Institute of Technology	Taipei	3 divisions of 3-year course
Ming Chuan College Girls Junior of Commerce	Taipei	5 divisions of 3-year course
Chung Shan Medical College	Taichung	2 divisions of 4 year-course
World Junior College of Journalism	Mushan, Taipei	4 divisions of 3 year-course
China Culture College	Yangraing-shan	15 departments and 1 research institute

BIBLIOGRAPHY

A. Government Documents
(In Chinese)

China, Chiao Yü Fa Ling [Educational Laws and Regulations], edited by the "Ministry of Education", Taipei: Cheng Chung Shu Chü, 1953.

China, Executive Yuan, Council for U. S. Aid. Chung Mei Ho Tso Ching Yuan Kai Yao [Resume of the Sino-American Cooperation and Economic Assistance]. Taipei: 1960.

China, Executive Yuan, Secretariat. Chung Hua Min Kuo Tai-wan Sheng Chi Fu-chien Sheng Chih Chin-Ma Ti Ch'u Wen Chiao Kai Ku'ang [A General Survey of Education and Culture in Taiwan Province and in the Quemoy and Matsu Areas of the Fukien Province] Taipei: 1961.

China, "Ministry of Education". Chiao Yü Kai Ku'ang, Chung Hua Min Kuo San Shih Chiu Nien Chih Wu Shih Nien [General Survey of Education from 1950 to 1961]. Taipei: 1961.

────── . Chung Hua Min Kuo Chiao Yu T'ung Chi [Educational Statistics of Taiwan]. 4 vols. Taipei: 1958 – 1962.

────── . Chung Kuo Chiao Yü Nien Chien [Educational Yearbook of China]. 3rd ed. Taipei: Cheng Chung Shu Chu, 1957.

────── . K'o Hsüeh Chi Shu Chi Chuan Yeh JenTs'ai Chih P'ei Yang Chi Hua [The 12th Section of the Third Four-Year Economic Plan Dealing Specifically with the Training of Scientific, Technical, and Professional Manpower]. mi chien (Classified)

China, "Ministry of Education", Department of Higher Education. Kung Szu Li Chuan K'o I Shang Hsüeh Hsiao I Lan Plao [Directory of Public and Private Schools from Junior College Up] Taipei: 1962.

────── . Ta Hsüeh K'o Mu Piao Hui Pien [Tabulation of College and University Curricula]. Taipei: Cheng Chung Shu Chü, 1961.

China, "Ministry of Education", Department of Social Education, Tai-wan Sheng Pan Li Shih Hsüeh Min Chung Pu Hsi Chiao Yu Kung Tso Pao Kao [Report on the Work of the Supplementary Education for Adults in Taiwan]. Taichung: 1959.

China, "Ministry of Education", Office of Research of Education Materials. Chiao Yü Fang Chen Yü Chiao Yü Cheng Ts'e Tzu Liao [Materials on Educational Principles and Policies], rev. ed. Taipei: Chung Yang Wen Wu Kung Ying She, 1953.

China, National Educational Materials Center. Ch'i Nien Lai Ti Ch'ung Mei Chiao Yü Ho Tso [Seven Years' Sino-American Educational Cooperation]. Taipei: 1959.

Chung Yang Pan Yueh K'an. Yan-ming-shan Ti Erh Tz'u Hui T'an Chuan Chi [Special Issue on the 2nd Phase of the Yangmingshan Forum]

P'ingtung, Taiwan, Municipal Government. P'ing-tung Shih Chiao Yü Kai K'uang [General Survey of Education in the City of P'ingtung] P'ingtung: 1947.

Taiwan, Bureau of Statistics. Tai-wan Shena Wu Shih I Nien Lai T'ung Chi T'i Yao [Statistical Abstract of Taiwan for the Last 51 Years]. Taipei: 1946.

Taiwan, Department of Education. Chiao Yü Kai Ko Ts'an K'ao Tzu Liao [Reference Materials on Educational Reform]. Vol. I. Taipei: Tai-wan Shu Chü, 1952.

────── . Pen Sheng Chiao Yü She Shih Ta Wen [Questions and Answers on Education in Taiwan Province]. Taichung: 1961.

────── . Shih Nien Lai Ti Tai-wan Chiao Yü [Education in Taiwan in the Past Ten Years]. Taipei: Tai-wan Shu Chü, 1955.

────── . Tai-wan I Nien Lai Chih Chiao Yü [The Past Year's Education in Taiwan]. "Hsin Tai-wan Chien She Ts'ung Shu," No. 5. Taipei: 1946.

────── . Tai-wan Sheng Chiao Yü Fa Lina Hui Pien [A Compendium of Educational Laws of Taiwan Province]. Taipei: Tai-wan Shu Tien, 1958.

────── . Tai-wan Sheng Chiao Yü Kai Ku'ang [A Gcncral Survcy of Taiwan's Education]. Taipei: 1946.

────── . Tai-wan Sheng Chiao Yü Yao Lan [Brief View of Education in Taiwan

Province]. Taipei: 1947.

———. *Tai-wan Sheng Wu Shih Nien Kuo Min Chiao Yü Chi Chung Tend Chiao Yü Tiao Ch'a Pao Kao Shu* [Report of the 1961 Survey of Elementary and Secondary Education in Taiwan Province]. Taichung: 1962.

Taiwan, Public Elementary and Secondary School Teachers Welfare, Fund Commission. *Wei Kai Shan Chiao Shih Sheng Huo Erh Nu Li* [Striving for the Improvement of Teachers' Livelihood]. "Chiao Shih Fu Li Ts'ung Shu," No. 2. Taichung: 1961.

Yangmingshan Forum. *Yen T'ao Tang Ch'ien Chiao Yü Ts'o Shih Wen T'i Chieh Lun...* [Additional Comments on the Conclusions of the Discussion on the Practice and Problem of Present Education]. (2nd phase, August 25 – 31, 1961). Taipei: "Ministry of Education", 1961.

(**In English**)

China. Directorate General of Budgets, Accounts, and Statistics. *Statistical Abstract of Taiwan*. Taipei: 1959.

China. Executive Yuan, Council for U.S. Aid, Economic Research Center. *Taiwan Statistical Data Book, 1963*. Taipei: 1963.

China. Industrial Development and Investment Center. *Industrial Development in Taiwan*. Taipei: 1962.

China. "Ministry of Economic Affairs". *Taiwan's Third Four-Year Economic Development Plan*. Abridged ed. Taipei: 1961.

China. "Ministry of Education". *Education in Free China*. Taipei: 1952.

———. *Education in Taiwan During the Past Ten Years*, Taipei: Taiwan Book Company, 1955.

———. *Education in Taiwan*. Taipei: 1958.

———. *The Mandarin Movement in Formosa*. Taipei: Taiwan Book Company, 1948.

———. *Pre-school Education in Taiwan, 1961*. Taipei: 1961.

China. "Ministry of Education", Department of Elementary Education. *Elementary Education in Taiwan*. 1962. Taipei: 1962.

China. "Ministry of Education", Department of Secondary Education. *Secondary Education in Taiwan*. Taipei: 1960.

China. "National Educational Materials Center". *Report on U. S. Aid Education Projects, 1953 – 1957*. Taipei: 1957.

Taiwan. Bureau of Census. *A Summary Report on the 1956 Census Taken in Taiwan Province and Fukien Offshore Area of Taiwan*, Taipei: 1960.

Taiwan. Department of Education. *Education in Taiwan, Tai-wan Chiao Yü Kai Ku'ang*. Taichung: 1961. (Text in English and Chinese).

———. *Education in the Province of Taiwan; A Synopsis in Pictures*. Taichung: 1960. (Text in English and Chinese)

———. *A Survey Report on Taiwan Elementary and Secondary Education in 1961*. Taichung: 1961.

Taiwan. Department of Information. *Taiwan: Ten Years of Progress*. Taipei: 1956.

Taiwan. Government-General. *Annual Report on Education in Formosa, 1907 (6th)*. Tokyo: 1907.

———. *The Progress of Taiwan (Formosa) for Ten Years, 1895 – 1904*. Taihoku: 1905.

———. *Progressive Formosa*. Taihoku: 1926.

Taiwan. "Government-General", Department of Educational Affairs. *A Review of Educational Work in "Formosa"*. Tokyo: 1916.

Taiwan. Public Elementary and Secondary School Teachers Welfare Fund Commission. *Teachers Welfare Institution in Taiwan*. "Teachers Welfare Series," No. 1. Taichung: 1961.

Taiwan. A Unique Colonial Record. 1937 – 38 edition. Issued by Kokusai Nippon Kyokai.

Tokyo: 1938.

United Nations. Bureau of Social Affairs. *The Population of South East Asia (Including Ceylon and China: Taiwan) 1950 - 1980.* "U. N. Population Studies," No. 30. New York: 1958.

U. S. Mutual Security Mission to China. *Economic Progress of Free China*, 1951 - 1958. Taipei: 1958.

U. S. Office of Naval Operations. *Taiwan (Formpsa).* Civil Affairs Handbook, OPNAV 50E - 12. Washington: 1944.

―――――. *Japanese Administrative Organization in Taiwan (Formosa).* Civil Affairs Handbook, OPNAV 50E - 14. Washington: 1944.

U. S. Technical Cooperation Education Projects in Taiwan. *The Road to Tomorrow: A Progress Report 1952 - 1959.* Taipei: "National Educational Materials Center". 1959.

B. Books

(In Chinese and Japanese)

Chang, Chi-yun. Ching Shen Chiao Yü [Spiritual Education] Taipei: Cheng Chung Shu Chü, 1952.

―――――. Chung Hua Min Kuo Ta Hsüeh Chih [Universities in China]. 2 vols. "Hsien Tai Kuo Min Chi Pen Chih Shih T'sung Shu" Taipei: Chung Hua Wen Hua Ch'u Pan Shih Yeh Wei Yuan Hui, 1954 - 1956.

―――――. Hsin Chiao Yü Lun Chi [Essays on the New Education]. 4 vols. Taipei: Chung Kuo Hsin Wen Ch'u Pan Kung Szu, 1955 - 1957.

―――――. Ko Ming Chiao Yü [Revolutionary Education]. Vol. I. Taipei: Chung Kuo Hsin Wen Ch'u Pan Kung Szu, 1955.

―――――. San Min Chu I Mo Fan Sheng Chih Chien She [Building a Model Province Based on the Three People's Principle]. "Hsien Tai Kuo Min Chi Pen Chih Shih Ts' ung Shu," No. 4. Taipei: Chung Hua Wen Hua Ch'u Pan Shih Yeh Wei Yuan Hui, 1956.

Chang, Chih-chih. Chung Shan Hsien Sheng Chih Chiao Yü Szu Hsiang [The Educational Thought of Dr. Sun Yat-sen]. Chungking: Cheng Chung Shu Chü, 1940.

Chang, Chih-chih and Yao, Chiu-yi. Tsung Ts'ai Ti Chiao Yu Szu Hsiang [The Educational Thought of the Generalissimo]. Chungking: Kuo Min T'u Shu Ch'u Pan She, 1942.

Chen, Hung-tao. Ts'ung Shih Kuo Min Chiao Yü San Shih Nien Chih Nu Li Chi [Record of 30 Years of Service in Elementary Education]. Taipei: Yuan Tung, 1958.

Chen, Kuo-fu. Chung Kuo Chiao Yü K'i Ko Chih T'u Ching [The Road to Chinese Educational Reform]. Chungking: Cheng Chung Shu Chü, 1944.

Chen, Ping-ch' üan (ed.). Ta Hsüeh Chiao Yü [University Education]. 2 vols. "Hsien Tai Kuo Min Chi Pen Chih Shih Ts'ung Shu," Taipei: Chung Hua Wen Hua Ch'u Pan Shih Yeh Wei Yuan Hui, 1959.

Cheng, Hsiao-chieh. Min Tsu Ching Shen Yü Chiao Yü Hsin Li Chien K'ang [National Spirit and Mental Hygiene in Education]. Taipei: Chung Yang Wen Wu Kung Ying She, 1960.

Cheng, Yen-fen. Hua Ch'iao Wen Chiao Kung Tso Fang Chen Yü Jen Wu [Aims and Objectives of Cultural and Educational Work for Overseas Chinese]. Taipei: Hai Wei Ch'u Pan She, 1961.

Chiang, Kai-shek. Chiang Tsung T'ung Chiao Yü Yen Lun Lei Pien [Classified Collection of Statements and Essays on Education by Chiang] Edited by Ch'un-hui Yuan. Taipei: Chung Yang Wen Wu Kung Ying She, 1958.

―――――. Tsung T'ung Yu Kuan Ko Ming Chiao Yü Ti Hsun Shih [Addresses of Chiang Concerning Revolutionary Education]. Taipei: Kai Tsao Ch'u Pan She, 1956.

Chu, Hsüeh-ch'un. Tai-wan Sheng Shih Fan Chiao Yu Chih Yen Chiu [Study of Teacher Education in Taiwan] Research Report, No. 901. Taipei: Kuo-min-Tang, Chung Yang Wei Yuan Hui, She Chi K'ao Ho Wei Yuan Hui, 1962.

Chu, Tzu-shuang. Chung Kuo Kuo Min Tang Chiao Yü Cheng Ts'e [Educational Policy of the Kuomintang]. Chungking: Kuo Min T'u Shu Ch'u Pan She, 1941.

Chung Hua Min Kuo Chiao Yü Chih [Education in Taiwan]. 2 vols. "Hsien Tai Kuo Min Chi Pen Chih Shih Ts'ung Shu," No. 3. Taipei: Chung Hua Wen Hua Ch'u Pan Shih Yeh Wei Yuan Hui, 1955.

Chung Kuo Chiao Yü Hsien Ku'ang [The Present Status of Chinese Education]. 4 vols. "Hsien Tai Kuo Min Chi Pen Chih Shih Ts'ung Shu," No. 5. Taipei: Chung Hua Wen Hua Ch'u Pan Shih Yeh Wei Yuan Hui, 1958.

Chung Kuo Chiao Yü Hsüeh Shu Yü Wen Hua [Chinese Education, Scholarship and Culture]. Edited by Chiao Yü Yü Wen Hua She. Taipei: Chung Kuo Hsin Wen Ch'u Pan Kung Szu, 1955.

Ko Ming Shih Chien Yen Chiu Yuan (ed.). Wen Chiao Lei Ts'an K'ao Tzu Liao [Reference Materials on Education and Culture]. 2 vols. Yangmingshan: 1953.

Liang, Chung-quen. Chin-chu Hsin Shih Shih "Mien Shih Shena Hsüeh" Ti Ch'eng Kuo [Achievements and Accomplishments in the Implementation of the Plan of "Admission Without Examination" in Hsinchu Hsien]. "Hsien Tai Kuo Min Chi Pen Chih Shih Ts'ung Shu," No. 6. Taipei: Chung Hua Wen Hua Ch'u Pan Shih Yeh Wei Yuan Hui, 1960.

Lien, Heng. Tai-wan T'ung Shih [A General History of Taiwan]. 2 vols. New ed. Taipei: Chung Hua Ts'ung Shu Wei Yuan Hui, 1958.

Lin, Pen. Chiao Yü Szu Hsiang Yü Chiao Yü Wen T'i [Educational Thoughts and Educational Problems]. Taipei: Chung Hua Ts'ung Shu Wei Yuan Hui, 1958.

Liu, Chen. Chiao Yü Hsing Cheng [Educational Administration]. Chungking: Chung Hua Shu Chü, 1945.

————. Pen Sheng Chiao Yü Liang Yü Chih Ti Wen T'i Chih Chien T'ao [Appraisal of the Problem of Quantity and Quality in Taiwan's Education]. Taichung: Department of Education, 1960.

————. Tai-wan Chiao Yü Fa Chan Ti Fang Hsiang [The Direction of Educational Development in Taiwan]. Selected reports, addresses, essays, and letters of Mr. Chen Liu since the time he took charge of the educational administration of Taiwan Province, Taipei: Taiwan Chiao Yu Fü Tao Yueh K'an She, 1960.

Liu, Po-chi. Liu I T'ung Lun [Essays on the Six Art]. Taipei: Chung Hua Shu Chü, 1956.

Sato, Genji. Taiwan Kyoiku No Shinten [The Development of Education in Taiwan]. Taipei: 1943.

Sheng, Ko-yu. Ling Hsiu Ti Chiu Kuo Chiao Yü Szu Hsiang Chi Ch'i Fang Fa [The Generalissimo's Thought on Education for National Salvation and Its Application]. Chungking: Tu Li Ch'u Pan She, 1942.

Sun, Pang-cheng. Chiao Yü Kai Lun [Introduction to Education]. Taipei: Taiwan Commercial Press, 1956.

Teng, Tsui-ying et al, Shih Shih "Mien Shih Sheng Hsüeh" Fang An Ti Yen T'ao [Discussion on the Implementation of the "Mien Shih Sheng Hsüeh" Prograin]. Taipei: Chung Kuo Shu K'an Yi Ch'i She, 1958.

Ting, Chih-pin. Chung Kuo Chin Chi Shih Nien Lai Chiao Yü Chi Shih [Records of Educational Events in China Over the Past 70 Years]. Shanghai: Commercial Press, 1935.

Wang, Chih-ting. Tai-wan Chiao Yü Shih [The History of Taiwan's Education]. Taipei: Tai-wan Shu Tien, 1959.

Wang, Feng-chieh. Chung Kuo Chiao Yü Shih [History of Chinese Education]. rev. ed. Taipei: Chung Cheng Shu Chü, 1954.

Wang, Yun-wu. T'an Chiao Yü [Talks on Education]. Taipei: Hua Kuo Ch'u Pan She, 1951.

Wu, Chün-sheng et al. K'o Hsüeh Chiao Yü Yü K'o Hsüeh Fang Fa [Scientific Education and the Scientific Method]. "Hsien Tai Kuo Min Chi Pen Chih Shih Ts'ung Shu," No. 3. Taipei:

Chung Hua Wen Hua Ch'u Pan Shih Yeh Wei Yuan Hui, 1955.

Yanaihara, Tadao. <u>Jih-Pen Ti Kuo Chu I Hsia Chih Tai-wan</u> [Taiwan Under Japanese Imperialism]. Translated from Japanese by Hsien-wen Chon. "Bank of Taiwan; Office of Economic Research: Taiwan Yen Chiu Ts'ung K'an," No. 39. Taipei: Bank of Taiwan, 1956.

(**In English**)

Aguilar, J. V. *First Visits to Taiwan Community Schools*, Taipei: International Cooperation Administration, 1954.

Arnold, Julean H. *Education in "Formosa"*, U. S. Bureau of Education Bulletin 1908, No. 5. Washington, D. C.: Government Printing Office, 1908.

Barclay, George W. *Colonial Development and Population in Taiwan*, Princeton: Princeton University Press, 1954.

Brown, H. Emmett. *Public Education in "Formosa"*, Taipei: Chinese - American Corporation. 1952.

Carley, V. A., Yang, H., and Ko, T. *Community School Education in Taiwan*, Taipei: International Cooperation Administration, 1956.

Chang, Chi-yun. *Education in Free China*. Pamphlets on Chinese Affairs. Taipei: China Culture Publishing Foundation, 1954.

_____. *The Essence of Chinese Culture*, Taipei: China News Press, 1957.

Chen, Li-fu, *Chinese Education Durina the War: 1937 - 1942*. Chungking: "Ministry of Education", 1943.

Ch'eng, T'ien-fang. *Educational Developments and Reforms in Free China*. Taipei: "Ministry of Education", 1953.

_____. *Selected Speeches and Writings*. Taipei: "Ministry of Education", 1954.

Chiang, Kai-shek. *Chapters on the National Fecundity*, Social Welfare. Education, and Health and Happiness. Written as supplements to Dr. Sun Yat-sen's lectures on the Prinicple of People's Livelihood; rendered into English by Durham. S. F. Chen. Taipei: China Cultural Service, 1953.

Chiang, Monlin. *Tides From the West*. Taipei: China Publishing Foundation, 1957.

China Yearbook, 1937/43 - 1963/64. Taipei: China Publishing Company, 1943 - 1963. (Title varies: *China Handbook* 1937/43 - 1956/57)

Chinese National Association for the Advancement of Educatioru *Bulletin*, Vol. II (1923). Peking: 1923.

Chou, Ts'e-tsung. *The May Fourth Movement: Intellectual Revolution in Modern China*. Harvard East Asian Studies, No. 6. Cambridge, Massachusetts: Harvard University Press, 1960.

Davidson, James Wheeler. *The Island of "Formosa", Past and Present: History, People, Resources, and Commercial Prospects*. London: Macmillan, 1903.

Far East and South Asia ICA Regional Conference on Education, Manila, 1956. *Education in the Far East: A Summary Report of the ICA Regional Conference on Education*. Manila: 1956.

"Formosan" Education Association. *Modern Formosa, With Special Reference to Education*, Taihoku: 1923.

Freyn, Hubert. *Chinese Education in the War*. Council of International Affairs. Political and Economic Studies, No. 9. Shanghai: Kelly and Walsh, 1940.

Grajdanzev, Andrew Jonah. *Formosa Today: An Analysis of the Economic Development and Strategic Importance of Japan's Tropical Colony*. Institute of Pacific Relations. International Research Series. New York: 1942.

Han, Lih-wu. *Taiwan Today*. Taipei: Hwa Kuo Publishing Company, 1951.

Heath, Kathryn G. *"Ministries of Education: Their Functions and Organization*. U. S. Office of Education Bulletin 1961, No, 21. Washington, D. C.: Government Printing Office, 1962.

Hu, Chang-tu et al. *China: Its People, Its Society, Its Culture*. Survey of World Cultures. New Haven: HRAF Press, 1960.

Hu, Shih. *The Chinese Renaissance*. Chicago: University of Chicago, Press, 1933.

International Yearbook of Education, *10th - 23rd*, *1948 - 1961*. Geneva: UNESCO, International Bureau of Education, 1948 - 1961.

Kuo, Ping-wen. *The Chinese System of Public Education*. New York: Teachers College, Columbia University, 1915. (Also Ph. D. dissertation)

Library Association of China. *Libraries in China*. Papers prepared on the occasion of the tenth anniversary. Peiping: 1935.

Rhynshurger, Willert, *Area and Resources Survey: Taiwan*. Taipei: U. S. Mutual Security Mission to China, 1958.

Sassani, Abul Hassan K. *Education in Taiwan (Formosa)*. U. S. Office of Education Bulletin 1956, No. 3. Washington, D. C. : Government Printing Office, 1956.

Shreve, R. Norris. *Inspection Report to Taiwan Provincial Cheng Kuna University and International Cooperation Administration*. Lafayette, Indiana: Purdue University, Purdue-Taiwan Engineering Project, 1960.

Shreve, R. Norris, and Freely Wilfred I. *The Cooperative Project Between Purdue University and Cheng Kung University to Aid Engineering Education in Taiwan: Comprehensive Report for Years 1952 - 1959*. Submitted to Taiwan Provincial Cheng Kung University and the International Cooperation Administration. Lafayette, Indiana: Purdue University, 1959.

Stanford Research Institute. *Education and Development: The Role of Educational Planning in the Economic Development of the "Republic of China"*. Prepared for "Ministry of Education", Government of Taiwan, Taipei, Taiwan, by Henry F. McCusker, Jr. , and Harry J. Robinson. Vol. I Menlo Park, California: The SRI, 1962.

Stanford University. China Project. *Taiwan (Formosa)*. Sub-contractor's Monograph, HRAF -31. New Haven: Printed by HRAF, 1956.

Taiwan Provincial Normal University. *Bulletin of Information*. 1956, Taipei. 1956.

U. S. Agency for International Development, University of Michigan Contact. *Second Semi-annual Report on the Establishment of a Center for Education and Training in Public and Business Administration*. Mushan, Taiwan: National Chengchi University, 1962.

Wang, Yi-chu. *Foreign Educated Chinese*, *1872 - 1948*. Chicago: University of Chicago, 1957.

Wu, C. Y. *The Taiwan New Rural Extension Education Movement: With Thirty Good Examples*. Taipei: Taiwan Provincial Farmers Association, 1956.

Yang, C. T. *Economic and Social Development in the "Republic of China" During the Past Decade*. Taipei: Ministry of Economic Affairs, 1960.

Yuan, Tung-li (comp.) *A Guide to Doctoral Dissertations by Chinese Students in America*. *1905 - 1960*. Washington, 1961.

World Survey of Education. Vol. I - III. Paris: UNESCO, 1955 - 1961.

C. Periodicals and Newspapers
(In Chinese)

<u>Cheng Chih P'ing Lun</u> [The Political Review]. Vols. I-XT. Taipei, 1953 - 1963.

<u>Chiao Yü Yü Wen Hua</u> [Education and Culture]. Nos. 21 - 309. Taipei, 1954 - 1963. (Formerly <u>Chiao Yü T'ung Hsun</u>).

<u>Chung Kuo T'u Shu Kuan Hsüeh Hui Hui Pao</u> [Library Association of China Bulletin]. Nos. 1 - 12. Taipei, 1953 - 1961.

<u>Chung Teng Chiao Yü</u> [Secondary Education] Vols. I-XIH Taipei: Taiwan Provincial Normal University, Secondary Education Supervisory Committee, 1948 - 1962.

<u>Chung Yang Jih Pao</u> [Central Daily]. Taipei, 1961 - 1963.

<u>Hsin Shih Tai</u> [New Age]. Vols. I-IV. Taipei, 1961 - 1964.

<u>K'o Hsüeh Chiao Yü</u> [Science Education]. Vols. I-VIII. Taipei: Chinese Association for the Advancement of Natural Science, 1955 - 1962.

Min Chu P'ing Lun [Democratic Review]. Vols. I-XIII. Hong Kong, 1949 – 1962.

Shih Ta Hsüeh Pao [Taiwan Provincial Normal University Bulletin]. Nos. 1 – 5. Taipei, 1956 – 1960.

Tai-wan Chiao Yü [Education in Taiwan]. Nos. 25 – 130. Taipei: Taiwan Education Association, 1953 – 1961.

Tai-wan Sheng Li Shih Fan Ta Hsüeh Chiao Yü Yen Chiu So Chi K'an [Taiwan Provincial Normal University, Research Institute of Education Bulletin]. Nos. 1 – 3. Taipei, 1958 – 1960.

Tai-wan Chiao Yü Fu Tao Yueh K'an [Monthly Bulletin of the Educational Supervision in Taiwan]. Vols. I-XII. Taipei, 1950 – 1962.

Tai-wan Wen Hsien [Historical Documents of Taiwan]. Vols. I-XIII. Taipei: Taiwan Provincial Archival Commission, 1949 – 1962.

Tzu Yu Chung Kuo [Free China Fortnightly]. Vols. I-XXIII. Taipei, 1949 – 1960.

(**In English**)

China News Service (New York). 1957 – 1963.

China Today, Vols. I – VI. Taipei, 1958 – 1963.

Chinese Culture. Vols. I – VI. Taipei, 1958 – 1962.

Free China Review. Vols. I – XIII. Taipei, 1951 – 1963.

D. Unpublished Materials
(**In Chinese**)

Huang, Chi-lu. "Chiao Yü Ts'e Hua Yü Ching Chi Fa Chan" [The Strategy of Education and Economic Development]. Address delivered at the fiftieth anniversary conference of the Chinese Institute of Engineers, Taipei, Taiwan, November, 1961.

⎯⎯⎯⎯. "Chin Nien Lai Chiao Yü Wen Hua Ti Fa Chan Ho Chin Hou Nu Li Ti Fang Hsiang" [The Development o? Education and Culture in Recent Years and Its Future Direction]. Report of the Minister of Education on Education and Culture at the second phase of the Yangmingshan forum, Yangmingshan, Taipei, Taiwan, August 25 – 31, 1962.

⎯⎯⎯⎯. "I Ko Chin Hou Fa Chan K'o Hsüeh Chiao Yu Ti Lu Hsiang" [Present and Future Direction in the Development of Science Education]. Address delivered at the 116th birthday anniversary of Thomas Alva Edison to a group of top middle school students in science studies, Kaohsiung, Taiwan, February 11, 1963.

⎯⎯⎯⎯. "I Ko Ho Yü Chan Shih Yü P'ing Shih Ti Chiao Yü Ts'e Hua" [An Educational Strategy Suitable Both in War Time and in Time of Peace]. Address delivered at the annual joint conference of ten educational organizations, Taipei, Taiwan, January 6, 1963.

⎯⎯⎯⎯. "Tang Ch'ien Chiao Yü Wen T'i Chi Chin Hou ChihTs'e Hua" [Current Educational Problems and the Strategy to Be Used in Coping With Them]. Report of the Minister of Education at the fourth National Conference on Education, Taipei, Taiwan, February 14 – 17, 1962.

Taiwan. Department of Education. "Yeh Wu Pao Kao" [Administrative Report]. n. p., n. d. (Mimeographed)

(**In English**)

Arens, Richard, "The Impact of Communism on Education in China, 1949 – 1950." Unpublished Ph. D. dissertation, University of Chicago, 1952.

Atterbury, Marguerite. "A Study of Some Phases of Chinese-American Cooperation in Promoting China's Agricultural Extension." Unpublished Ph. D. dissertation, Columbia University, 1954.

Cheng, Lillian Li-ling. "The Educational Program of the Chinese 'Nationalist Government' in Formosa." Unpublished Master's thesis, American University, 1953.

Eberhard, Wolfram. "Social Science Research in Taiwan." Report to the Asia Foundation,

Taipei, 1960 (Typewritten)

Foster, Donald Murray. "Education as an Instrument of National Policy for Economic Development in Taiwan." Unpublished Ed. D. dissertation, Stanford University, 1962.

Leung, Florence Yu. "Application of Audio-Visual Aids to Secondary Education in Formosa: Problems and Possibilities." Unpublished Master's thesis, American University, 1953.

Nee, Nelson Ven-chung, "A Program of Vocational Industrial Education in Taiwan, Republic of China." Unpublished Master's thesis, University of Tennessee, 1958.

Rodd, William G. "A Cross-Cultural Study of Taiwan's Schools." Unpublished Ph. D. dissertation, Western Reserve University 1958.

Tzeng, Jenn. "Charting Educational Philosophy for Free China." Unpublished Master's thesis, De Paul University, 1956.